Retailing

Concepts, Strategy and Information

CAROL H. ANDERSON CRUMMER GRADUATE SCHOOL OF BUSINESS—ROLLINS COLLEGE

WEST PUBLISHING COMPANY

Minneapolis/Saint Paul   New York   Los Angeles   San Francisco

PRODUCTION CREDITS
Art by Patti Isaacs, Parrot Graphics
Cover images (clockwise from top left): (1) courtesy of Lands' End, Inc. (2) Superstock
(3) H. Armstrong Roberts (4) Doug Beasley
Copyediting by Cheryl Wilms
Text Design by David Farr, ImageSmythe Inc.
Composition and Lithography by Parkwood Composition
Production, Prepress, Printing and Binding by West Publishing Company

WEST'S COMMITMENT TO THE ENVIRONMENT

In 1906, West Publishing Company began recycling materials left over from the production of books. This began a tradition of efficient and responsible use of resources. Today, up to 95 percent of our legal books and 70 percent of our college texts are printed on recycled, acid-free stock. West also recycles nearly 22 million pounds of scrap paper annually—the equivalent of 181,717 trees. Since the 1960s, West has devised ways to capture and recycle waste inks, solvents, oils, and vapors created in the printing process. We also recycle plastics of all kinds, wood, glass, corrugated cardboard, and batteries, and have eliminated the use of styrofoam book packaging. We at West are proud of the longevity and the scope of our commitment to the environment.

COPYRIGHT © 1993   By WEST PUBLISHING COMPANY
610 Opperman Drive
P.O. Box 64833
St. Paul, MN 55164-0833

Library of Congress Cataloging-in-Publication Data

Anderson, Carol H.
  Retailing: concepts, strategy, and information / Carol H. Anderson
      p.   cm.
  Includes index.
    ISBN: 0-314-01137-4 (Annotated Instructors Edition)
    ISBN: 0-314-92052-8 (Student's Edition)
    1. Retail trade—Management. 2. Retail trade. I. Title
HF5429.A663 1992
658.8'7—dc20   91-29097
                                                                          CIP

dedicated to the memory of

DONALD T. ANDERSON

Brief Contents

CONTENTS

PART 1   STRATEGIES AND DECISIONS   30

CHAPTER TWO   STRATEGIC PLANNING AND RETAIL MANAGEMENT   32

CHAPTER FIVE   RETAILING OF SERVICES   168

PART II   EXTERNAL ENVIRONMENT   220

CHAPTER SIX   CONSUMER MARKETS AND BEHAVIOR   222

CHAPTER SEVEN   REGULATORY AND ETHICAL ENVIRONMENT 270

PART V ANALYSIS AND TECHNOLOGY 644

CHAPTER SIXTEEN   RETAILING DECISIONS: ANALYSIS AND EVALUATION 646

CHAPTER SEVENTEEN   TECHNOLOGY IN RETAILING 686

PART VI   INTERNATIONAL RETAILING   734

CHAPTER EIGHTEEN   GLOBAL ASPECTS OF RETAILING   736

PREFACE

Retailing is an exciting and dynamic part of everyday life. It is one of the few areas of business about which students are already fairly knowledgeable because of their personal experiences. Those experiences provide a good starting point for understanding the importance and complexity of the retail management decisions that make retail purchases possible.

Massive, fast-paced changes are taking place in society, creating new challenges for retailers. Traditional formats are giving way to innovative methods of reaching customers when and where they are ready to buy. The retail environment is fiercely competitive and often uncertain. Power retailers and "category killers" dominate the scene on one end of the spectrum, while specialty retailers, carving out their well-defined niche markets, prosper at the other end. Successful department store retailers are repositioning their operations to address the needs of today's consumers. All retailers are challenged to develop strategies that will give them a sustainable competitive advantage throughout the nineties and into the twenty-first century. Strategic positioning requires an understanding of environmental threats and opportunities and of the company's competitive strengths and weaknesses. Therefore, this book is written from a strategic planning and information processing perspective, two major factors in achieving competitive advantage.

When this project was conceived, a number of retailing texts were available. Several others have been written since that time. However, my rationale for writing *Retailing: Concepts, Strategy & Information* is as valid today as it was when I wrote the first words of this book. Nearly two decades of teaching retail management to college students, preceded by hands-on retail industry experience with several major retail firms, have convinced me that there is still a need for a pragmatic retailing text that integrates rather than isolates retail management concepts. The integrative approach makes possible a more in-depth analysis of retail situations. Further, this book addresses several broader management issues that not only have an impact on retailing, but on a wide variety of other businesses.

The Key Strengths of this Text:

1. The strategic planning process is emphasized early in the text, and intertwined with the subject matter in each chapter. A "Remarkable Retailer" scenario is highlighted in each chapter to illustrate retail strategy in actual practice.

2. External and internal environmental information needed by retail managers is presented within the context of an Integrated Retail Information Model (IRIM). Environmental information is interpreted within the context of the IRIM in relation to the major topics in each chapter.

3. Business ethics have become a major corporate and societal issue. Since retail practices are highly visible to the public, they are particularly susceptible to charges of unethical behavior. Thus, each chapter contains a "Responsible Retailer" scenario that illustrates ethical situations. Ethical concerns are also woven into general discussion throughout the book.

4. In addition to the integration of an analytical approach throughout the text, an entire chapter focuses on the analysis and evaluation of operating results—the outcome of the strategic planning process. Primary emphasis is on analysis at the functional level of operations, including the types of questions to be answered, key ratios and criteria to be used, and sources of data to be analyzed.

5. The global aspects of retailing are becoming increasingly important. Therefore, in addition to inclusion with other topics, an entire chapter is devoted to this dimension from the perspective of both international retail firms and international influence on merchandise assortments.

6. Technology is another important topic that is short-changed in many texts. Although technological applications are discussed with other chapter concepts, a separate chapter is included to give more attention to this critical aspect of retail operations. It is impossible to present a completely up-to-date picture of current technology in a textbook, but the chapter is a starting point in understanding the impact of high-tech tools on successful retail operations.

7. The retailing of services represents one of the fastest growing segments of the U.S. economy. Since many students will be employed in the services retailing industry, this is another important topic that is highlighted in a separate chapter.

8. Theory and practice are integrated throughout the text. Applied practical retail management principles are discussed within the framework of relevant marketing theories and empirical studies, thus providing a basis for decision making that transcends any one situation.

What this Textbook Offers the Student and the Instructor

The student is provided with a straightforward discussion of basic retailing principles and the challenges that confront retail managers. Numerous examples are used to illustrate the practical application of principles and theory. The approach taken in the text is intended to improve the student's analytical skills and problem-solving ability, and to challenge students to think. For those students who have not taken an introductory marketing course or who need a review, basic marketing concepts and definitions are discussed as they relate to retailers. Extensive information on retail careers is included in the appendix.

The instructor is provided with a text that is broad-based in its coverage, yet offers a basis for stimulating classroom discussion on a wide range of retailing topics. The ideas presented in the text are timely and provide insights into retail management issues in the 1990s and beyond. The strategic planning model and the decision making approach provide a foundation for innovative experiential learning and applied projects. Combined with features of the Instructor's Manual and the Student Project Manual, the text offers the opportunity for improved teaching effectiveness.

Chapter Pedagogical Features

Pedagogical features in each chapter are designed to support the learning process. Chapter scenarios include the "Remarkable Retailer" and "Responsible Retailer." The "Remarkable Retailer" highlights the outstanding operation, strategy, and performance of real-world retailers. In keeping with today's views on ethics, the "Responsible Retailer" highlights ethical, legal, and social responsibility issues related to retailing while emphasizing the importance of a retailer's integrity regarding customers, suppliers, advertising, and pricing. Other pedagogical features include learning objectives and an outline of major topics at the beginning of each chapter, margin definitions of key concepts, and end-of-chapter questions for review and comprehension.

Supplements to Accompany Text

A comprehensive **instructor's manual** prepared by Richard C. Leventhal, Metropolitan State College, and the text author, is available to facilitate the teaching process and thus enhance learning. Instructional aids include chapter teaching notes through an annotated outline, suggested readings, answers to end-of-chapter questions, case solutions, experiential exercises, suggested course syllabi and additional materials not included in the text. A Lotus 1-2-3 based disk of student and instructor files on retail merchandise mathematics and financial ratios is included, for the instructor to copy and use as needed.

A **test bank** by Randall E. Wade, Rogue Community College, contains over 1000 test questions which are designated as definition, comprehension, factual, or application and page-referenced to the text. The questions are multiple choice, true and false, and essay/application and are also available on WESTEST.

Transparency masters are available and include not only figures and tables from the text, but also materials not in the book.

A **student activity manual** prepared by the author and Sande Richards Stanley of Northwest Missouri State University, contains experiential activities and projects for students, as well as self-tests. Also included in the activity manual is **Lotus 1-2-3-based software,** along with documentation. This software package allows the student to learn about the finances of a small retail company by determining budgets, inventories and other financial aspects of the retailing process.

Extensive **videos** are available which bring a real-world perspective to the study of retailing and enable students to see how the concepts of retailing are applied. A video has been compiled from footage from J. C. Penney, Mary Kay Cosmetics, Home Shopping Network, Pathmark, Pep Boys, Von's Companies, United Parcel Service and others. Documentation consisting of suggested related text chapters, descriptions of each segment and questions for students is placed in the instructor's manual.

Acknowledgements

This book could not have been conceptualized and completed without the encouragement, help, and contributions of many individuals—my students, colleagues, West Publishing editors and reviewers, retailers, family, and others who have provided invaluable support.

Thank you, students . . .

Perhaps the greatest inspiration has come from my students. I believe they have taught me as much as I have taught them. The challenge has always been to choose the teaching materials and methodology that will maximize students' learning. As a result, most of the content of *Retailing: Concpets, Strategy & Information* has evolved through many semesters of teaching the introductory retailing course and trying to prepare students for life after graduation. They have responded with honest appraisal of my efforts and an abundance of suggestions that have been incorporated into the text. My reward has been the excitement of watching my students' personal and professional development in and out of the classroom. My challenge is to continue to develop better teaching materials and methods, and I continue to invite my students to make sure that I do so.

Thank you colleagues . . .

So many colleagues have contributed in one way or another to this project that some names will inadvertently be omitted. I apologize for any oversights. I owe a great debt of gratitude to my former colleagues at Southern Illinois University—Carbondale. In particular, I want to acknowledge Clif Andersen, Chair of the Department of Marketing at SIUC, for his support and encouragement from the beginning of this project. The final months of text preparation have been spent at the Crummer Graduate School of Business where deans Marty Schatz and Sam Certo have created a professional and technical environment that supports textbook writing. My faculty colleagues at Crummer have been generous in helping me through the last stages of this project.

The contributions of Karen Glynn, George Kirk, Glynn Mangold, Thomas Parker, Joy Peluchette, and Sande Richards Stanley have enriched the content of this text. I am deeply appreciative of their efforts. Kim Knight, Susan O'Rourke, and Crevolyn Wiley also provided assistance with development of materials for the retailing course while they were at SIUC.

I would also like to thank the following case contributors: John S. Berens, Indiana State University; Richard C. Leventhal, Metropolitan State College; Richard A. Engdahl, University of North Carolina—Wilmington; K. Douglas Hoffman, University of North Carolina—Wilmington; Sandra D. Skinner, Western Carolina University; Keith T. Stephens, Western Carolina University; Scott D. Alden, Whittier College; Sandra Loeb, University of South Dakota; Leonard J. Konopa, Kent State University; David M. Currie, Rollins College.

Thank you West Publishing editors and reviewers . . .

Arnis Burvikovs, Editor, and Susanna Smart, Developmental Editor at West have been particularly helpful in the development of this text. I am deeply grateful for their untiring efforts on my behalf. Others who have provided valuable suggestions for improving the content and presentation in this text include Amelia Jacobson in marketing at West Publishing and Debra Meyer in production. In addition I would like to acknowledge the role of Rich Wohl, my original editor, who convinced me to undertake this project and was a constant source of encouragement throughout the early stages.

The following reviewers drew on their wealth of retailing knowledge to enrich the content of the text through their many insightful and helpful suggestions:

Scott D. Alden
  Whittier College

Vicki Blakney
  University of Dayton

David J. Burns
  Youngstown State University

Joseph D. Chapman
  Ball State University

Anthony D. Cox
  Indiana University—Purdue

C. Richard Devey
  Brigham Young University

Letty C. Fisher
  Westchester Community College

Fliece Gates
  University of Arkansas

Linda K. Good
  Michigan State University

Larry G. Gresham
  Texas A&M University

Douglas F. Harris
  Bemidji State University

Joseph C. Hecht
  Montclair State College

K. Douglas Hoffman
  University of North Carolina

John Konarski, III
  Florida International University

Rosetta S. LaFleur
  University of Delaware

Marilyn A. Lavin
  University of Wisconsin—Whitewater

Richard C. Leventhal
  Metropolitan State College

Carole Lissy
  William Rainey Harper College

Calvin Lowe
  Utah State University

Eleanor Maliche
  West Virginia State University

Irving Mason
  Herkimer County Community College

Leo F. McMullin
  Lander College

Patricia A. Robinson
  University of Akron

Bernard H. Saperstein
  Passaic Community College

Irwin A. Shapiro
  University of Lowell

Ray Tewell
  American River College

Alicia Thompson
  James Madison University

Margaret A. Trossen
  Mount Vernon College

Randall E. Wade
  Rogue Community College

Edward T. White
  Danville Community College

Thank you retailers . . .

Many retailers and retailing-related businesses have contributed materials for use in the text and ancillary materials. I wish to thank all of the many corporations credited throughout the text.

In addition, I would like to acknowledge my former retail employers who provided me with practical experience and role models: Mercantile Stores, Neiman-Marcus, and Saks Fifth Avenue.

Thank you family . . .

My daughter, Wendy, and my sons Chris and Jeff are very much a part of everything I do—in spirit if not in deed. Their love, understanding, and encouragement through the good times and the bad times have been a constant source of strength. Wendy spent many hours in the library and on the computer to help with this project. I also want to thank my parents and brother for instilling in me deeply held lifelong values and the determination to see a project through to completion.

Thank you to other important people . . .

I am deeply grateful to Susan Crabill at the Crummer School and to Janice Fry and Sharon Harward at SIUC for their patient assistance with word processing, manuscript preparation, and other tasks through numerous drafts.

Carol H. Anderson, Ph.D.
Emerita, Southern Illinois University—Carbondale;
Roy E. Crummer Graduate School of Business, Rollins College
Winter Park, Florida

Retailing

CONCEPTS, STRATEGY AND INFORMATION

The Nature and Scope of Retailing

CHAPTER One

Learning Objectives

After studying this chapter, the student will be able to:

1. Explain the importance of retailing in the U.S. economy.
2. Explain the relationship between retailing, marketing, and the marketing concept.
3. Describe retailing as a distribution strategy, including the rationale for channel intermediaries, the determinants of channel structure, and the steps retailers take to provide a link between customers and suppliers.
4. Recognize retailing functions from both a distribution perspective and a societal perspective.
5. Provide an overview of the retailing strategy mix, and how the various retailing functions "fit" together.

NORDSTROM

Pentagon City, Virginia store

REMARKABLE RETAILER

On the one hand, everybody's talking about Nordstrom, considered a threat by some and an outstanding example of retailing success by many. The retailer's main claim to fame is exceptional customer service, with the Nordstrom culture held up as an example for retailers in the United States and abroad. However, Nordstrom management is reluctant to discuss this aspect of their business. As Bruce Nordstrom says, "We don't want to talk about our service. We are not as good as our reputation. It is a very fragile thing. You just have to do it

every time, every day." And when asked what Nordstrom does best, his response is "Ask the customer."

As one observer told the Fourth Asian Retailers Convention in Singapore in September, 1989:

"Superior customer service is absolutely critical for the success of department stores in the '90s . . . Customer delight is giving customers what they want, when they want it and sometimes even before they know they want it. One way Nordstrom's does that is to carry the broadest assortment of styles and sizes of any major U.S. retailer. It goes out on a limb to develop exclusive sources. You see styles, colors and items you just don't see anywhere else, plus the fact you see them in depth.

"But Nordstrom doesn't stop there. It has elevated customer service to an art form. Nordstrom understands that a sales transaction involves more than delivering a piece of merchandise."

Nordstrom's philosophy benefits both employees and customers. While customers are responding to superior customer service, the retailer's incentive compensation plan motivates employees to increase their own incomes while keeping the customers happy. Nordstrom accomplishes this by

continued

focusing on communication with sales-people, training programs, and goal setting and monitoring. Goals, which may be either quantitative or qualitative, are defined in daily, monthly, quarterly, and annual terms, as well as in departmental, storewide, and company terms. Salespeople can even keep track of their own performance by inspecting computer printouts available in back offices.

Nordstrom's service philosophy is summed up on the store directory: "Our sales staff is genuinely interested in seeing that all of your needs are met. They are professionals who will help you with everything from gift suggestions to wardrobe planning. They will even accompany you from department to department until you find exactly what you're looking for."

On the other hand, as noted earlier, "reputation . . . is a very fragile thing." Nordstrom's commission plan for compensating and motivating employees has been adopted by many other retailers in an effort to link pay to sales productivity and customer service. However, this has created a high pressure selling environment that some believe has taken its toll on employee morale and profits.

By early 1990, a group of discontented employees gained the attention of leading business publications who proclaimed that although service does come first at Nordstrom stores, it comes at a big price to the sales clerks. As a result,

the chain suffered from demands by employees for millions of dollars in back pay, charges of illegal employment practices by the Washington State Department of Labor and Industry, and claims by the National Labor Relations Board that Nordstrom violated federal labor laws. This is in addition to a 34 percent drop in profits in the previous year, which may have been a reflection of the economy rather than employee problems.

At the same time, the United Food and Commercial Workers Union was attempting to increase its influence in the Nordstrom chain. Company spokespersons believe this may have been related to reports of less-than-ideal working conditions by employees. For example, employees claimed that they were told to punch out on their time clock before performing any non-selling duties such as stock work, deliveries, and customer "thank you" letters. No matter how much friendly service they gave to customers, or how much they smiled at them, some salespeople reported that they lived in fear of losing their jobs if they missed sales quotas or had to be absent from work for legitimate reasons.

Management has a different perspective, reporting that union and nonunion employees make an average income in excess of $23,000 a year, compared to the national average of $12,000. In fact, one men's clothing department salesman and many other Nordstrom salespeople earned over $100,000 in 1990. The union's primary complaint was the amount of unpaid time the salespeople spent looking after their customers. However, the Nordstrom environment attracts and rewards a special type of employee who is willing to expend the necessary effort to generate a more lucra-

tive income based on what they produce.

While support can be found for both sides of the dilemma confronting this remarkable retailer, this scenario illustrates the all-encompassing and dynamic world of a successful retailer. It appears that the bottom line for retailers in the 1990s will not only be measured by the strength of their relationships with their customers, but also by the quality of their relationships with their employees. Perhaps Nordstrom's relationship with its employees is reflected in a vote of more than 2 to 1 against continued representation by the United Food and Commercial Workers in July, 1991.

Adapted from: Coletti, Jerome A. and Leland T. Murray, "Linking Retail Sales Commissions to Customer Service," *National Productivity Review* (Spring 1990), 157–168; Faludi, Susan C., "At Nordstrom Stores, Service Comes First—But at a Big Price," *The Wall Street Journal* (February 20, 1990), A1, A12; Ferguson, Tim W., "Sun shines (in Seattle!) on Nordstrom's Again," *The Wall Street Journal,* (July 30, 1991), A15; Miller, Cyndee, "Labor Strife Clouds Store's Service Policy," *Marketing News* (May 28, 1990), 1, 18; "Why Nordstrom Got There," *Stores* (January 1990), 75–76; Zimmerman, Nancy, "Motivation or Manipulation?" *Incentive* (June 1990), 82–85, and company sources.

Introduction: A Micro View of Retailing

Every day of your life you are affected by retailing—in the clothing you wear, the products you use, and the things you do. Take a look at what you are wearing right now. Think about all the products you use to keep yourself clean and comfortable, and socially acceptable. Think about all the food you eat—fast food, home-cooked food, snack food, sodas from the vending machine, and all the rest. On top of all that, there are the haircuts, drycleaning, repairs, insurance, bank deposits and withdrawals, and other services that you are likely to purchase from time to time.

Where do you get all these products and services? If you are like most consumers, you buy them from a retailer. There are many types of retail businesses. Some are large chains with hundreds of stores; others are single store "mom and pop" businesses. Some retailers operate without stores. For many purchases, you do not even need to leave home—or your car. To meet the needs of their target markets, retailers follow a wide spectrum of strategies.

Definition and Scope of Retailing

Retailing consists of all the activities involved in selling goods or services directly to final consumers for personal, family, or household nonbusiness use. A **retailer** or **retail store** is any business organization that derives more than half of its sales from retailing. This distinction is made because some types of retailers, such as auto parts, building supply, and hardware stores, sell both at wholesale prices to other businesses, and at retail prices to ultimate consumers.

Retailing sales activities can be performed by several types of business organizations, including manufacturers, wholesalers, or retailers. They can be performed in a store, where customers either serve themselves or are assisted by a salesperson. Customers can make purchases from nonstore retailers by mail, telephone, or computer. They also can make purchases from vending machines or street vendors.

Nature of Retail Transactions

Retail transactions tend to be numerous and small. Consumers make many repeat purchases of low cost items, and generally infrequent purchases of higher cost items. These small sales often require as much effort as the larger sales. Each transaction requires preparation on the part of the retailer. The store must be open for business at the right time and in the right place. The merchandise must be available in the right form and size, and at the right price. Personnel must be available to serve customers and take care of the store's inventory. In other words, the whole retail mix must be in place and functioning to serve the customers, regardless of the size of the sale.

Retailers serve a diverse group of customers. Successful retailers focus on identifying the characteristics, needs, and wants of specified customer groups, in order to offer products and services that will satisfy them. The

RETAILING
activities involved in selling goods and services to final consumers for personal and household use

RETAILER OR RETAIL STORE
business deriving more than half its sales from retailing

dynamic nature of the retailing industry is driven largely by the pressure to provide what customers want, where and when they want it, and at prices they are willing to pay—while returning a profit to the retailer. Thus, competitive strategies must be both effective and efficient in order to accomplish these objectives simultaneously.

IMPORTANCE OF RETAILING IN THE U.S. ECONOMY: A MACRO VIEW

The importance of the retailing industry in the U.S. economy can be assessed by a number of measures, such as dollars (sales, profits), people (employees, customers), stores (size, number), and inventory. The health of the U.S. economy is highly dependent upon the success of retail businesses in generating sales and profits. The retail sector alone was responsible for 9.6 percent of the gross national product (GNP) in 1988, while all of manufacturing contributed 19.5 percent. During the same year, retail payrolls exceeded 19 million employees, as shown in Exhibit 1–1 (excluding those who work part-time or are self-employed). Retailing contributed estimated sales of more than $1.8 trillion in 1990, a six percent increase over 1989 figures. (See Exhibit 1–2.) Department stores, eating and drinking places, and apparel and accessory stores generated $178, $179, and $93 billion of the total retail sales respectively. (See Exhibit 1–3.)

Exhibit 1–1
Retail Employment 1985–89
••••••••••••••••••••••••••

SOURCE: Adapted from *U.S. Industrial Outlook 1989—Retailing*, 54–1; *U.S. Industrial Outlook 1990—Retailing*, 41–1; *U.S. Industrial Outlook 1991—Retailing*, 40–1.

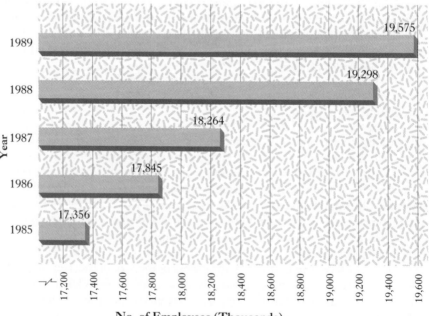

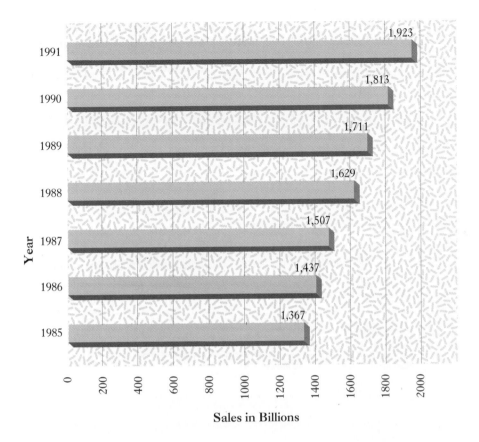

Exhibit 1–2
Retail Sales 1985–91
....

SOURCE Adapted from *U.S. Industrial Outlook 1989—Retailing,* 54–1; *U.S. Industrial Outlook 1990—Retailing,* 41–1; *U.S. Industrial Outlook 1991—Retailing,* 40–1.

Consumer demand for goods and services at the retail level also affects the economic output of many other types of businesses who depend upon derived demand. That is, manufacturers and wholesalers must provide the retailer with inventories. Manufacturers must obtain raw materials, parts, and other production needs from their suppliers. Transportation and storage companies, insurance and financial institutions, and other businesses are also involved in support activities related to retail inventories. Thus, the importance of retailing is felt in its effect on revenues and payrolls in many other industries.

Consumers and their spending patterns are another measure of interest to retail analysts. This includes personal income, consumer credit, and personal consumption expenditures. Exhibit 1–4 itemizes these figures for 1988 through 1990. Selected industry statistics are given for sales of durable and nondurable goods, apparel and shoes, and department stores. Disposable personal income reached nearly $4.0 trillion in 1990. Outstanding consumer credit averaged approximately $729 billion on a monthly basis in 1988. Contrary to expectations of lower levels of consumer spending due to higher levels of debt, in January 1989 consumers borrowed $4.4 billion more than they paid off, continuing the rise in the ratio of consumer installment debt to personal income. In the battle to attract consumer dollars, many department stores have been repositioning themselves with specialty stores. One example of the impact of specialty store competition is illustrated in Exhibit 1–4

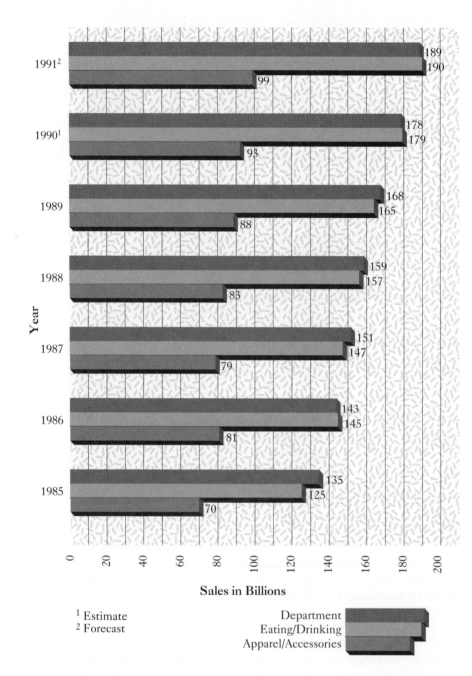

Exhibit 1–3
Comparison of Selected Retail
Areas 1985–91
• •

SOURCE: Adapted from *U.S. Industrial
Outlook 1989—Retailing*, 54–1; *U.S.
Industrial Outlook 1990—Retailing*, 41–1;
U.S. Industrial Outlook 1991—Retailing,
40–1.

by the sales generated by clothing and shoe stores (Statistical Abstract of the
U.S., 1990 and 1991; Survey of Current Business, 1990, 1991 and 1992; U.S.
Industrial Outlook, 1991 and 1992). When one considers the small dollar
amount involved in each sale, and the total number of retail transactions
needed to generate billions of dollars in revenues, the nature of competition
comes to life.

The top 50 retailers had sales increases of 7.6 percent and a 38 percent
increase in profits in 1991 over the previous year (The Service 500, 1992).
The largest gains were made by high-efficiency, no-frills operators like

Exhibit 1–4
Selected Retail Industry Statistics (in billions of dollars)

	1988	1989	1990	1991
Retail Sales	$1,629	$1,711	$1,813[2]	$1,888[2]
Disposable Personal Income	3,479.2	3,725.5	4,058.8	4,218.4
Consumer Credit Outstanding	731.5	778.0	n/a	n/a
Personal Consumption Expenditures	3,238.2	3,450.1	3,742.6	3,889.1
Durable Goods	418.2	428.0	465.9	445.2
Nondurable Goods	909.4	919.0	1,217.7	1,251.9
Clothing and Shoes	165.0	127.7	208.7	211.0
Food	462.2	462.9	595.8	619.3

[1] 1,982 billion retail sales forecasted for 1992, other statistics not available.
[2] Estimated Sales.

SOURCE: Adapted from *Statistical Abstract of the U.S., 1990*, Table 829: . 506; *Statistical Abstract of the U.S., 1991*, Tables 706–7,830:.436–8, 510; *Survey of Current Business*, Tables 2.1, 2.2: . 7, September 1990; *Survey of Current Business*, Tables 2.1, 2.2: . 11, February 1991; *Survey of Current Business*, Tables 2.1, 2.2:.9, March 1992; U.S. Industrial Outlook 1991—Retailing, 40–1; U.S. Industrial Outlook 1992—Retailing, 39–41.

Exhibit 1–5
Sears, Roebuck and Co.: Principal Business Group Contribution for Selected Years

	Percent of Total[1]							
	Revenues				Profit Before Taxes			
Business Group	1991	1990	1989	1985	1991	1990	1989	1985
Sears Merchandising Group	54.8	57.0	58.6	67.9	40.3	37.2	51.0	72.7
Allstate Insurance Group	33.8	32.6	31.2	23.3	26.8	25.3	30.8	21.0
Dean Witter Financial Services	8.6	8.0	7.5	5.6	27.7	33.8	13.3	(0.4)[2]
Coldwell Banker	2.8	2.4	2.7	3.2	5.2	3.7	4.9	6.7
Total	100.0	100.0	100.0	100.0	100.0	100.0	100.0	100.0

[1] Net of corporate and other and intergroup transactions not included in total.
[2] Numbers in parenthesis represent loss.

SOURCE: Adapted from Sears, Roebuck and Company, *Annual Report* (1989; 1990; 1992).

Home Depot with a 42 percent increase in earnings. Sears Roebuck maintained its number one position on the *Fortune* top retailer list, generating over $57 billion in sales for 1990. However, profits fell 40 percent from 1989 figures. However nearly half of Sears' revenues are derived from sales of real estate, insurance, and stocks rather than from retailing, as shown in Exhibit 1–5. The company's assets topped $106.4 billion, including real estate (e.g., shopping centers, stores) and an extensive management information system.

Wal-Mart Stores, the second largest service firm, bypassed Kmart in 1990 to become the world's largest merchant. In 1991, Wal-Mart had sales of $43.9 billion and profits of $1.6 billion, generated by assets valued over $15.4 billion. The company achieved its number one profit position by combining bargain prices, traditional values, and a sophisticated computer- and satellite-assisted distribution system. Wal-Mart moved from fifth place in 1987 to third in 1988, and many analysts believed then that the retailer was on its way to becoming number one. American Stores, operator of Alpha Beta supermarkets, became the top volume food retailer in 1989 after a hostile takeover of Lucky Stores (Standard & Poor's, April 1989), but Kroger reclaimed its number 4 position in 1991. J.C. Penney has consistently held its number 6 position for a number of years. Figures for these stores and the remainder of the top twenty retailers for 1991 are provided in Exhibit 1–6. Federated Department Stores (which emerged from Chapter 11 well ahead of schedule), Wal-Mart, and Price had the largest increases in sales; Sears and Wal-Mart had the largest increase in profits over 1990. American Stores had the largest decrease in sales and Woolworth had the largest decrease in profits. The most profitable of the top 50 retailers were Service Merchandise and Safeway with 72.9 and 26.6 percent return on common stockholders' equity respectively, and The Limited with 11.8 percent return on assets.

While impressive, the statistics used here to emphasize the importance of retailing cannot adequately describe the exciting and dynamic environment that "makes the numbers happen," making some retailers grow while others falter. Retail managers must make decisions that will lead to purchases by satisfied customers and, subsequently, profits for the company. As a final indicator of the highly competitive nature of this industry, the number of starts and failures for retailing and service businesses are summarized for a three-year period in Exhibit 1–7. Note that the failure rate for retail firms is 79 out of every 1,000, and for service businesses is 126 out of every 1,000 (Statistical Abstract of the U.S.: 1990).

Exhibit 1–6
Top 20 Retailers (1991)

Rank by Sales				Sales	Profits	Assets	Employees
1991	1990	1989	Company	(millions)	(millions)	(millions)	(numbers)
1	1	1	Sears Roebuck	57,242.4	1,278.9	106,434.8	450,000
2	2	3	Wal-Mart	43,886.9	1,608.5	15,443.4	364,000
3	3	2	K mart	34,969.0	859.0	15,999.0	348,000
4	5	5	Kroger	21,350.5	79.9	4,114.4	170,000
5	4	4	American Stores	20,100.0	199.4	6,950.0	148,000
6	6	6	J.C. Penney	17,295.0	80.0	12,520.0	185,000
7	8	8	Dayton Hudson	16,115.0	301.0	9,485.0	157,000
8	7	7	Safeway	15,119.2	54.9	5,181.2	110,064
9	9	10	Great Atlantic & Pacific Tea	11,390.9	151.0	3,307.5	99,300
10	10	9	May Department Stores	10,615.0	515.0	8,728.0	115,000
11	12	11	Winn-Dixie Stores	10,074.3	170.9	1,817.5	106,000
12	11	12	Woolworth	9,914.0	(166.0)	4,618.0	144,000
13	13	14	Melville	9,886.2	346.7	4,085.2	110,148
14	14	15	Albertson's	8,680.5	257.8	2,216.2	60,000
15	15	13	Southland	8,076.0	82.5	2,595.8	42,616
16	27	23	Federated Department Stores	6,932.3	836.4	7,501.1	73,900
17	16	16	R.H. Macy	6,761.6	(150.2)	4,811.6	69,500
18	23	22	Price	6,756.0	134.1	1,845.5	19,000
19	19	19	Walgreen	6,733.0	195.0	2,094.6	51,000
20	17	18	McDonald's	6,695.0	859.6	11,349.1	168,000

[1] Losses appear in parenthesis

SOURCE: Adapted from *Fortune,* "The 50 Largest Retailing Companies," June 3, 1991, 274–5, copyright © 1991 and *Fortune,* "The 50 Largest Retailing Companies," June 1, 1992, 188–9, copyright © 1992 The Time Inc. Magazine Company. All rights reserved.

Exhibit 1–7
Retailing and Services Businesses Starts and Failures

Year	1985	1986	1987	1988	Percent Change 1986–1987	Failure Rate (per 10,000 firms) 1988
Retail Trade						
Starts	72,578	72,509	65,381		-9.8[1]	
Failures	13,494	13,620	12,260	11,488	-10.1	79
Services[2]						
Starts	57,702	59,424	54,788		-10.8	
Failures	16,649	20,967	23,802	22,686	13.8	126

[1] (-) indicates decrease
[2] Services include: Hotels and other lodgings; personal services; business services; auto repair, services, and garages; motion pictures, amusement, and recreation; health services; legal services; educational services; social services; museums, art galleries, gardens; membership organizations.

SOURCE: Adapted from *Statistical Abstract of the United States: 1990*, Table No. 878, p. 531.

RETAILING AND THE MARKETING CONCEPT

The relationship between the overall field of marketing and the more narrowly defined field of retailing can be viewed within the context of the marketing concept. Retailing was defined earlier; now we will define marketing and describe the marketing concept.

Marketing

There are several acceptable definitions of marketing, including the following: **Marketing** consists of individual and organizational activities that facilitate and expedite satisfying exchange relationships in a dynamic environment through the creation, distribution, promotion, and pricing of goods, services, and ideas" (Pride and Ferrell, 1989, 8). In order for exchange activities to take place, four conditions must be present:

1. There must be two or more parties (retailer, customer),
2. Each party must have something of value that is wanted by the other (product, service, money),
3. Each party must be willing to give up its "something of value" to obtain that of the other (willingness to sell, agreement to pay),
4. There must be communication between the parties to facilitate the exchange (media, mail, phone, personal). This can be reduced to a very simple definition: "Find a need and fill it."

Marketing Concept

The **marketing concept** is based on a customer orientation. The underlying philosophy is that the ideal way to achieve sales and profit objectives is to determine the needs and wants of customers, and to provide the desired satisfactions more effectively and efficiently than competitors (Kotler, 1988).

MARKETING
activities that facilitate and expedite exchange relationships through the creation, distribution, promotion, and pricing of goods, services, ideas

MARKETING CONCEPT
achieve sales and profit objectives by determining the needs and wants of customers and satisfying those needs and wants more effectively and efficiently than competitors

ENVIRONMENTALISM: THE NEW CRUSADE

Environmentalism has been called the "New Crusade," one of the most important business issues for the nineties, the Earth Decade. Trend spotters believe that environmentalism will be a movement of worldwide force, and the cutting edge of social reform. What are retailers doing about it?

The responsible retailers—and the smart ones—are finding opportunities emerging from the public's concern with clean air and water, recycling, pollution, and other issues. McDonald's, which generates hundreds of millions of pounds of paper and plastic waste annually, has become a crusading proponent of recycling and plans to become one of the country's leading educators about environmental issues. The company also launched an innovative program in the fall of 1989, asking customers at 100 New England outlets to dispose of recyclable polystyrene packaging separately.

Wal-Mart is one of the first retailers to respond to environmental issues by actively supporting the "green revolution" in the United States. Wal-Mart challenges its suppliers by promising to highlight product improvements of marketers that try to "help prevent lasting environmental problems." It has encouraged manufacturers to provide the retailer and its customers with more merchandise and packaging that is better for the environment from three perspectives: manufacturing, use, and disposal—all geared to help prevent lasting environmental problems. For example, the stores display Tide detergent with a sign that congratulates "Proctor and Gamble for sharing in our environmental commitment. Tide . . . is packaged in 100% recycled paper." And the sign is printed on 100% recycled paper, too.

Wal-Mart's executive vice-president of merchandising sales summed up the company's position:

> We're all linked to our environment by the products we manufacture, sell, and consume. This program is a positive first step to improving our environment. . . . Our customers are concerned about the quality of our land, air, and water, and want the opportunity to do something positive. We believe it is our responsibility to step up to their challenge. . . . For Wal-Mart, environmentalism is a cause and not a marketing scheme.

Adapted from: Fisher, Christy and Judith Graham, "Wal-Mart throws 'green' gauntlet," *Advertising Age* (August 21, 1989), 1, 66; Kirkpatrick, David, "Environmentalism: The New Crusade," *Fortune* (February 12, 1990), 44–55.

Retailing and the Marketing Concept

The marketing concept can be applied to retailing exchange activities according to the following guidelines:

1. Customers are better served and satisfied by retailers who develop management, marketing, and merchandise plans based on an understanding of their customers' wants, needs, and desires.
2. Merchandise and services can be offered profitably when retailers base their selection on perceived customer wants, needs, and desires.
3. Goods and services should not be offered for sale until after the retailer has determined customers' wants, needs, and desires.
4. If a retailer is to survive, grow, and prosper, the firm must recognize changes in customers and in their needs. (Promotion Exchange, 1979).

The marketing concept also means that retailers must keep their long-term survival in view while simultaneously serving their customers. In order to follow these guidelines successfully, the retailer must maintain a continuous research program to gather customer information, by constantly monitoring changes in customers, competitors, and other environmental forces. At the same time, the retailer must remain fully aware of what suppliers have to offer and be able to negotiate effectively to make available the goods and services desired by their customers.

Retailing as a Distribution Strategy

The **marketing mix** consists of four components: products, prices, promotion, and distribution. Distribution refers to the various methods of moving products from the original producer or manufacturer to the final consumer. While product characteristics, pricing, and promotional strategies are essential factors in the marketing process, the focus here is on retailers as members of the **channels** of distribution. Channel members include manufacturers, wholesalers, and retailers, who work together to deliver the right quality and quantity of goods and services in the right form, to the right place, and at the right time. Each channel member plays an integral role in making goods and services available to retail customers.

Recall that according to the marketing concept, the consumer is the central focus of marketing mix (and retailing mix) decisions. These decisions must be made within a dynamic, constantly changing environment, where social, economic, competitive, technological, political, and regulatory forces have a major impact on company outcomes. Exhibit 1–8 shows the relationship between the marketing mix, distribution, and the external environment.

Rationale for Channel Intermediaries

Channel intermediaries are wholesalers, retailers, and other merchants or agents who serve both producers and buyers. These intermediaries exist

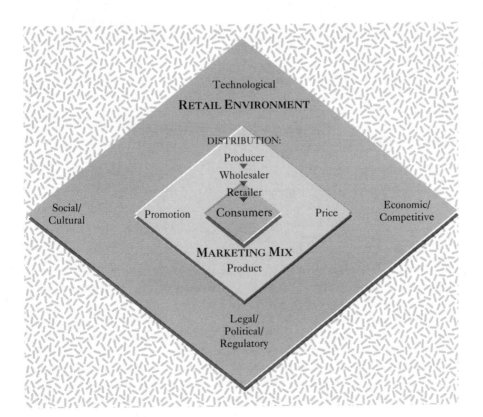

Exhibit 1–8
Retailing: An Integral Part of the Marketing Mix

MARKETING MIX

consists of products, prices, promotion, and distribution

CHANNELS OF DISTRIBUTION

means by which goods and services are delivered and made available to customers

because of the need to minimize the number of contacts required to move each product from the manufacturer to the consumer. The emergence and arrangement of the various distribution-oriented intermediary institutions can be explained in terms of four logically related steps in an economic process (Stern and El-Ansary, 1988, 5).

First, intermediaries arise in the exchange process because they make the process more efficient. The most basic form of exchange exists in primitive cultures where household needs are produced within the household. However, when production exceeds current household requirements, exchange activities with other households begin to take place to satisfy individual needs. Over time, as exchange activities become more numerous and more complex, efficiency may be increased by moving from a decentralized exchange, where transactions occur at each place of production, to a centralized exchange, where a network of intermediaries operates in centralized markets (see Exhibit 1–9).

Second, intermediaries arise to overcome the discrepancy between the assortment of goods and services generated by the producer and the assortment demanded by the consumer. Manufacturers generally produce a large quantity of a limited variety of goods, but the typical consumer wants only a small quantity of a wide variety of goods. To satisfy this need, intermediaries perform the following activities:

- **Sorting Out**—e.g., grading agricultural products into a homogeneous supply, such as grading meat as prime or choice
- **Accumulation**—gathering similar stocks from numerous sources to make one larger homogeneous supply
- **Allocation**—breaking a large homogeneous supply into smaller lots
- **Assorting**—building up the assortment of products for resale to customers

Wholesalers accumulate assortments from manufacturers for retailers, and retailers buy these goods and accumulate them for their customers. The wholesaler may buy in carloads, and sell in case lots to the retailer who, in turn, will sell single units to the end consumer. Each channel intermediary builds an assortment for the customer at the next level in the distribution process.

Third, marketing agencies work together in channel arrangements in order to routinize transactions. Each **transaction** involves ordering, placing a value on, and paying for goods and services. Without some form of standardization, each buying and selling situation would result in bargaining and inefficiency. Standardized procedures for payment, shipping, communication, and other aspects of the exchange process remove the need to start over with each purchase or sale. Automatic ordering via on-line computers to streamline the ordering process and shorten delivery time is one example of routinization that has benefited retailers.

Fourth, channels facilitate the search process at all levels. The search process works both ways. Manufacturers, wholesalers, and retailers are not certain what their customers want and need, and customers are not certain they will be able to find what they want. Therefore, channel structures have evolved to facilitate the search process. For example, retail and wholesale institutions are organized by industry groups (e.g., apparel, grocery, hardware, automotive

---

CHANNEL INTERMEDIARIES

wholesalers, retailers, and agents who serve both producers and buyers

SORTING OUT

grading agricultural products into a homogeneous supply

ACCUMULATION

gathering similar stock from numerous sources to make one larger homogeneous supply

ALLOCATION

breaking a large homogeneous supply into smaller lots

ASSORTING

building up the assortment of products for resale to customers

TRANSACTION

ordering, placing a value on, and paying for goods and services

parts). Drug, automotive, and other types of suppliers are located close to their customers to shorten the time between placement and delivery of orders. The same type of merchandise is available at many different locations to make the search process easier for consumers. (Just think of all the places that sell aspirin or other widely used products.)

Retailers purchase goods from manufacturers and wholesalers, and maintain inventories for resale to final consumers. At this level of the channel, retailers serve as intermediaries between the producer and user of a particular product. Exhibit 1–9 depicts the number of contacts that would need to be made to move goods from three manufacturers to ten retailers with, and without, wholesalers to act as intermediaries.

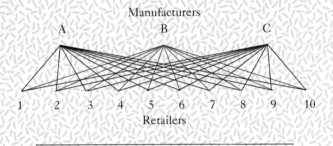

Direct Sales from 3 Manufacturers to 10 Retailers

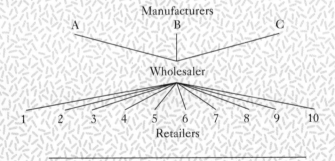

Effect of One Wholesaler Added to the Channel

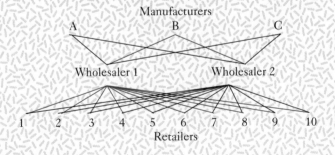

Effect of Two Wholesalers Added to the Channel

Exhibit 1–9
The Role of Channel Intermediaries
● ● ● ● ● ● ● ● ● ● ● ● ● ● ● ● ● ● ●

SOURCE: Adapted from Stern, Louis W. and Adel I. El-Ansary, *Marketing Channels*, 3d ed. Englewood Cliffs, N.J.: Prentice-Hall, (1988), 8.

Determinants of Channel Structure

Marketing channels consist of a network of interdependent institutions and agencies, adapting to some variation of the following:

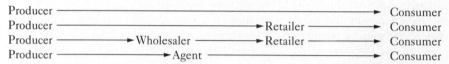

Producer ———————————————————————————→ Consumer
Producer ———————————————————————→ Retailer ———→ Consumer
Producer ———————→ Wholesaler ———→ Retailer ———→ Consumer
Producer ———————————→ Agent ———————————→ Consumer

     The form of the **channel structure** is determined by a number of factors, such as costs, technology, and consumer lifestyles. For example, busy customers may prefer to purchase by direct mail or home shopping networks from the manufacturer if that channel alternative is available, or from direct sales agents (e.g., Avon, Mary Kay), rather than shop in a store.

     Bucklin (1966) used the concept of service level outputs to explain how channel structures are determined. Because of the economic rules of specialization, the separation of production from consumption requires that various marketing functions or flows be performed to meet expressed demand for service outputs. (See Stern and El-Ansary, 1988.) In those channels with the highest level of service outputs, where more functions are performed for them, consumers will have less search, waiting time, storage, and other costs. Obviously, consumers prefer a marketing channel that offers a higher level of service outputs, as long as price, quality, and other considerations remain the same.

     The four service outputs described by Bucklin are spatial convenience, lot size, waiting or delivery time, and product variety. **Spatial convenience** refers to market decentralization, i.e., location of retail outlets to reduce customers' travel time and search costs. **Lot size** is related to the number of units that a customer can purchase at any one time. When customers can

CHANNEL STRUCTURE

a network through which goods and services travel from producer to consumer, determined by cost, technology, and consumer lifestyle

SPATIAL CONVENIENCE

decentralized markets at locations convenient to customers

LOT SIZE

number of units a customer can purchase at any one time

Ingram Video Inc. is one of the largest distributors of pre-recorded videos in the country, with over 14,000 titles.

COURTESY OF INGRAM DISTRIBUTION

PHOTO COURTESY OF ROUSE CO.

A large number and range of retailers provide spatial convenience, reduce waiting time by facilitating immediate purchase, and increase product variety for the consumer.

purchase in small lots, they can consume the goods faster, and will not need to store them for long periods of time. The smaller the lot size allowed by the channel, the higher the output of that channel and, usually, the higher the price to the consumer.

Waiting time is the time a customer must wait between ordering and receiving goods. Longer waiting times mean more inconvenience and the need for advance planning by the consumer. Longer waiting times usually mean lower prices. **Product variety** refers to the depth and breadth of assortments. Making a broad assortment of goods available to the customer requires the channel member to carry a high level of inventory, thus resulting in higher channel output and higher distribution costs.

In general, as more service outputs are demanded by consumers, more intermediaries will be required to provide the necessary marketing functions and flows. In this case, channel outputs will be higher, and prices paid by consumers will be higher. When customers are willing and able to provide more of the marketing functions for themselves (search, financing, delivery,

WAITING TIME
time a customer must wait between ordering and receiving goods

PRODUCT VARIETY
depth and breadth of assortments

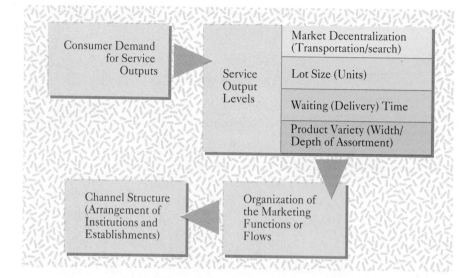

Exhibit 1–10
Channel Structure: A Result of
Consumer Demand for Service
Outputs
• •

SOURCE: Adapted from Stern, Louis W.
and Adel I. El-Ansary, *Marketing Channels*,
3d ed. Englewood Cliffs, N.J.: Prentice-
Hall, 1988, 19.

etc.), the channel outputs and consumer prices will be lower. (For further
discussion, see Stern and El-Ansary, 1988.) Exhibit 1–10 illustrates the role
that consumer demand for service outputs plays in determining channel
structure.

Retailers: The Link Between Customers and Suppliers

The retailer is the critical link between suppliers and customers, as illustrated in Exhibit 1–8. This means that what the retailer offers is dependent
upon a correct interpretation of the desires and expectations of its target market. It also means that the retailer must be able to identify and negotiate
with those suppliers who can provide the best assortments and services to
make the venture both satisfying for customers and profitable for the retailer.

The retailer is both buyer and seller—buyer of goods and services from
other channel members (manufacturers, wholesalers, financial institutions,
transportation companies, etc.), and seller to final users of their products and
services. (See Exhibit 1–11.) Retailers are the most visible of all marketers to
ultimate consumers. Thus, they are in a strategic position to obtain important feedback from their customers, which can then be used to provide
insights for producers and channel intermediaries.

**RETAILING FUNCTIONS FROM A DISTRIBUTION
PERSPECTIVE** Retail activities are focused on delivering goods and services for personal, family, or household use. In order to meet consumer
needs, retailers are responsible for moving products from manufacturers and
wholesalers to a location that is convenient for customers (place utility),
making products and services available when customers want them (time
utility), and assuming risk through ownership and financing of inventories
(possession utility).

Retailers are expected to perform a number of distributive functions:

1. Creating product and service assortments to satisfy the desires of an identified group of consumers,

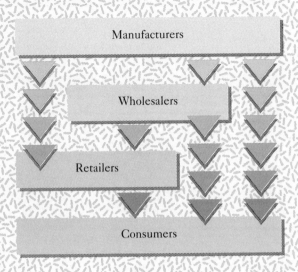

Exhibit 1–11
Retailers: Key Members of the
Channels of Distribution

2. Making products and services available in sizes and quantities suitable for personal or household use,

3. Facilitating consumer purchases by providing useful information for purchase decisions,

4. Offering quality products at competitive (or at least fair) prices,

5. Making it generally convenient for customers to shop (e.g., location, store hours, credit).

These functions are related to the concept of service output levels described earlier. The retailer's distributive functions are illustrated in Exhibit 1–12.

RETAILING FUNCTIONS FROM A SOCIETAL PERSPECTIVE

Since retailers are the most visible of all marketing firms within our society, it is appropriate to consider retailing activities from a societal perspective. Retailers contribute to an improved standard of living by offering goods and services to the buying public, providing jobs to a large segment of the workforce, and acting as an important source of income to suppliers and other channel intermediaries (including bankers, attorneys, architects, maintenance personnel, and many others). Retailing careers offer many opportunities for rapid advancement to bright young people with the skills and initiative to take on this responsibility. Many achieve success with major retail firms; others strike out on their own to become independent retailers. Joey Crugnale started assembling his 14-store restaurant chain, Bertucci's Inc., while he was still in his twenties (Mamis, 1989). The story of this young entrepreneur, who sold his first chain for $4.5 million at the age of 23, is told in Remarkable Retailer.

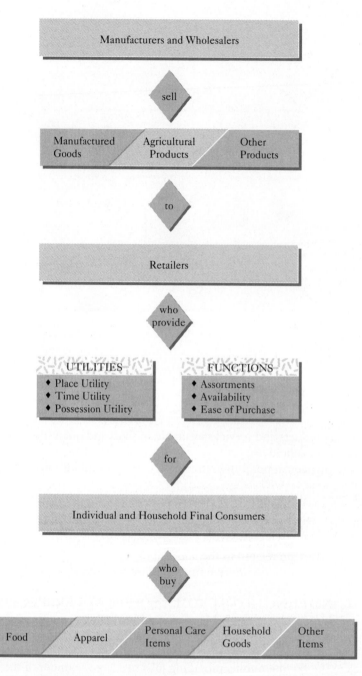

Exhibit 1–12
Retailing Functions: A
Distribution Perspective

Retailers offer alternatives to both customers and employees that support a wide variety of lifestyles—not only in the goods and services they sell, but also in the store environments and business formats that allow individuals to choose among times and places they might work or shop and the ways they might pay or be paid. Retail stores offer a social environment that provides an alternative form of entertainment for many people.

In their prominent position among other businesses and within the communities where they operate on a daily basis, retailers have a moral, social, and economic responsibility to each of their constituencies. This includes

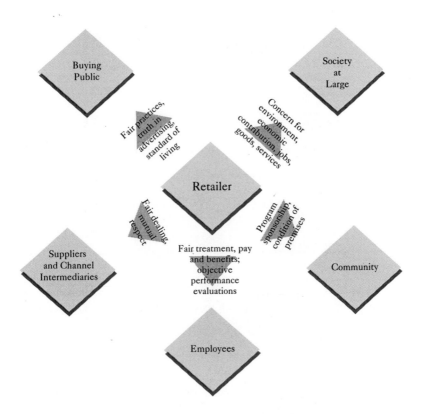

Exhibit 1–13
Retailing Functions: A Societal
Perspective

honest dealings with customers in the design and execution of pricing, promotion, and other strategies; fair treatment of employees; and ethical dealings with other channel members, intermediaries, and competitors. The
retailer is also expected to be a socially responsible force in the community.
Social responsibility may range from sponsoring a Little League team to providing surplus food for a local food bank or making wheelchairs available to
handicapped or elderly shoppers in stores. Selected aspects of the role of
retailing in society are illustrated in Exhibit 1–13.

The Retailing Strategy Mix and Philosophy of the Text

The Retail Mix

The **retail mix** is a subset of the familiar marketing mix, often referred to as
the "4 Ps" (product, place, promotion, and price), plus service. It is a blend of
strategic decisions made by managers concerning merchandising, pricing,
location and physical facilities, human resources and organizational structure,
promotion/communication, and service levels and types. By implication, performance standards are incorporated into the design and evaluation of the

RETAIL MIX
a subset of the marketing mix; the 4
Ps (product, price, promotion, place,
and service)

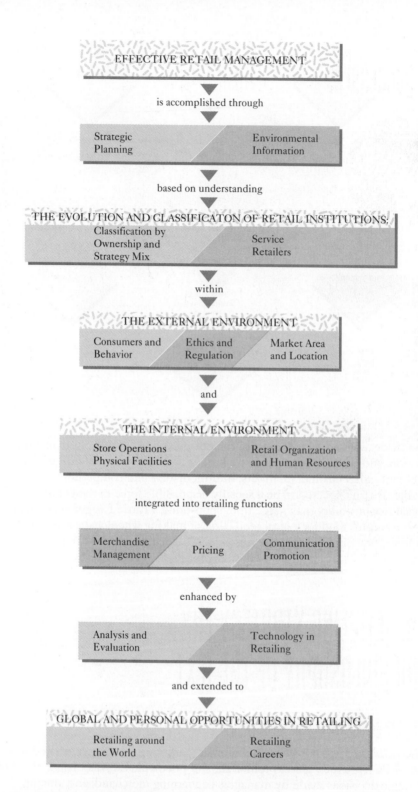

Exhibit 1–14
A Framework for Studying
Retailing Concepts and Strategy

retail mix. The objective is to combine all elements of the retail mix in a way that will achieve competitive advantage in the marketplace. This text explains the interaction between retailing strategies and the environments in which retailers must operate.

A Successful Young Entrepreneur

INC. magazine's top 500 businesses for 1989 included Bertucci's, Inc., a 14-store chain of gourmet pizza restaurants in New England. Joey Crugnale, Bertucci's founder, started the chain while still in his twenties.

A Bertucci's interior

That was after he sold his first chain, Joey's Ice Cream, for $4.5 million when he was 23. His strategy has been to ignore the fads, and take a familiar product, boost it to homemadelike quality, promote it with a lot of pizzazz, and then charge a high price for it. He uses a huge open oven ablaze with a real fire to distinguish his customized, all-fresh fare from the standardized fast food approach—an inspiration from a trip to visit his grandmother in Italy.

He views his employees as volunteers "since they can leave tomorrow" and treats them well so that, in turn, they will treat his customers well. Conversely, Crugnale also figures that "a well-treated customer makes for a well-treated employee." All of his stores are company owned and operated, and he has avoided franchising as being "last resort financing." He has a business plan, but is not afraid of leverage, preferring not to tie up cash in property while expanding rapidly to saturate the Greater Boston Market. One idea he has to make the units cost less is to find a regional dairy that he

Joey Crugnale of Bertucci's

can purchase to churn out mozzarella cheese for pizza toppings.

Joey Crugnale threatens, "When business isn't fun anymore, I'll quit." But based on his success and obvious enjoyment of his business, it doesn't seem that he will quit any time soon.

Adapted from Mamis, Robert A., "Upper Crust," *INC.*, (December 1989), 134.

What You Can Expect As You Read This Book

A managerial approach is taken in this text to familiarize the reader with basic retailing concepts, focusing on information for strategic decisions. An applied integrative retail information model provides a conceptual and structural outline for the book. The model is also used to describe the relationships between aspects of the retailer's internal and external environments, and the sources, uses, and flows of information used by retail managers in making decisions. Important concepts include bottom-line profitability, small business retailer applications, and ethics and social responsibility issues. A framework for studying retailing concepts and strategy, and for the organization of this textbook, is presented from the retailer's viewpoint in Exhibit 1–14.

In Part I, the strategic planning process and information needs for retailers are described beginning with the firm's mission statement, and continuing through establishment of performance objectives, execution, and evaluation

COURTESY OF LANDS' END

Lands' End manufactures its own products, which are sold through direct mail and outlet stores.

and control. The strategy includes initial decisions about type of ownership and store formats, as well as evolving formats in response to environmental changes. Strategic retail management decisions are made at different organizational levels, involve different levels of technology, and have a direct relationship to the firm's operating results.

An effective strategic plan is based on gathering, analyzing, and interpreting information about the firm's internal and external environments. The integrative retail information model is used as a structure for understanding the types of environmental information needed for retailing decisions. The external environment consists of consumer markets and behavior; competitors, suppliers, and intermediaries; ethical and regulatory forces; and physical location and trade area characteristics. The internal environment consists of the retailer's resources (financial, human, and physical) and the functions to be performed (personnel, store operations, merchandising, pricing, communicating with the store's customers, and control/accounting). Information is not only essential in making initial strategic decisions; information captured throughout the entire process is used to evaluate the results of executing the strategic plan. A typical formal retail information system (RIS) for gathering useful information is described, along with an overview of data sources and information uses.

Next, strategy mix decisions for both product and service retailers are addressed. The evolution and classification of retail institutions, along with theories of institutional change and the retail life cycle, are discussed. There are a number of ways to classify stores based on type of ownership and retailing mix strategies. Emerging retail formats offer new opportunities for creative retailers. Service retailing is discussed in terms of the nature of services, consumer behavior in the service encounter, service quality, strategies for services retailers, and evaluation of operating results. Retailing's external environment is discussed in Part II. This includes consumers, the legal and ethical environment, and store location. The consumer decision process, consumer decision types and influences, and methods of aggregating consumers into retail market segments, are described. Legislation regulating competition and growth, the impact of legislation on the marketing mix and on human resources, ethics, and social responsibility are addressed. The importance of retail location is related to the strategic planning process. Regional, market, trade area, and site analyses are defined, along with their characteristics, decision criteria, and organizational structure for location decisions. Emphasis in Part III shifts to the retailer's internal environment. Aspects of store operations and physical facilities are described, including the store's interior, exterior, physical distribution activities, and security and risk management. The retail organization and its human resources are discussed relative to the retail tasks to be performed, organizational structure for accomplishing those tasks, and staffing and human resource management. A comprehensive discussion of the history, rationale and impact of mergers and acquisitions in retailing over the past ten years is provided.

Part IV focuses on the coordination of the retailer's external and internal environments through functional decisions. Merchandise management concepts and price determinations are discussed from both an internal and an external perspective. Methods of financial control of merchandising operations also are described. Insights are provided into negotiations with suppliers and the effect of strategic decisions on operating results. Influences on pricing strategies also are viewed from both an internal and an external perspective. Methods of determining and calculating prices are presented. The various ways a retailer can communicate with customers are considered, including services offered, store image, advertising, sales promotion, publicity, and personal selling.

Part V returns to the broader perspective, integrating concepts from previous sections of the book in a discussion of information processing, financial analysis, and technology in retailing. Basic information for analyzing and evaluating retail management decisions is provided, including what to analyze, levels of analysis, how to analyze, and data sources and quality. Advances in technology have made it possible to have more timely data, better inventory management, and more innovative retail formats, benefiting both retail managers and customers. An appendix introduces an environmental perspective for analysis in terms of competitive advantage and market opportunity.

Part VI gives special attention to the international influence that is pervasive throughout the retailing industry. Global aspects of retailing are discussed relative to U.S. retailers abroad, foreign ownership of retailers in the U.S., transfer of retail strategies and know-how, and international retail market entry procedures and decisions. An appendix to the book concentrates on career information to provide insights about a future in the retail industry. Topics include reasons for pursuing a retailing career, potential career paths, tasks and job descriptions, and helpful information on job search, resumé writing, interviewing, and executive development programs. In addition, the reader is introduced to career opportunities in small business retailing.

Summary

Discussion in this chapter has been primarily from a macroperspective, describing the importance of retailing in the U.S. economy and its place in the total spectrum of marketing activities. Retailers play an important role in interpreting, serving, and satisfying consumers' wants, needs, and desires.

Retailers play a critical part in distribution, providing an economic and societal link between customers and suppliers. They exist because they make the exchange of goods and services more efficient for the producers at one end of the channel and customers at the other end. The structure of distribution channels is determined by the level of service outputs desired by customers. This basically involves the time and cost of search, amount to be purchased at one time, assortment desired, and the length of time the customer is willing to wait to complete a purchase. Generally, as customers' requirements increase in any of these categories, the channels of distribution become longer and more complex. As retailers perform their exchange activities, they are placed in a position of highly visible dual responsibility. They not only contribute to an improved standard of living and more fulfilling lifestyles by making goods and services available to customers; they also offer jobs and career opportunities for their employees and contribute to the communities where they operate.

Finally, the major concepts to be discussed in the remainder of the book have been introduced. Emphasis is on strategic planning and information needs at the functional level. Both the external and internal retail environments are considered relative to their impact on retail management decisions.

Questions for Review and Comprehension

1. Based on the definition of retailing given in this chapter, describe at least five different types of retail businesses in your community. Include those that sell to both retail and wholesale customers, and in-store as well as nonstore retailers. Determine the general characteristics, needs, and wants of the customer group(s) that each retailer serves.

2. In what ways does retailing contribute to the U.S. economy? Explain some ways in which the distribution of retail sales, employees, and numbers of various types of stores tend to shift or change over time.

3. Name the top 10 U.S. retailers. Have any major changes occurred in the positions of the top five retailers over the past several years? If so, cite some factors that may have contributed to these changes.

4. Explain the relationship between retailing and the marketing concept. Using a specific example, describe the four conditions that must be present for exchange activities to take place between a retailer and a customer.

5. Discuss the role that retailers play in the distribution of goods and services from producers to final customers. Describe several different types of distribution channel structures that involve retailers.

6. Describe and defend the role that intermediaries, other than retailers, play in moving goods from producers to consumers.

7. Name each of the four types of service level outputs described by Bucklin to explain how channel structures are determined. Show how each of these concepts is applied by (a) department store, (b) convenience store, (c) mail order catalog, and (d) fast-food restaurant. Each of your answers can be related to the distributive functions that retailers are expected to perform.

8. Explain the implications of the statement: "A retailer is both a buyer and a seller."

9. Find several examples of the performance of "retailing functions from a societal perspective" in your local newspaper or in national news media. What exactly does this mean, and just how important is it to the success of a retail business?

10. Describe the components of the retail mix. Give an example of each aspect of the retail mix within the context of your last shopping experience. Could any of these have been improved by the retailer that you were patronizing?

References

Bucklin, Louis P. (1966), *A Theory of Distribution Channel Structure*, Berkeley, Calif.: IBER Special Publications.

Kotler, Philip (1988), *Marketing Management: Analysis, Planning, Implementation, and Control*, Sixth Edition. Englewood Cliffs, N.J.: Prentice-Hall, Inc.

Mamis, Robert A. (1989), "Upper Crust," *INC., 500 Top Businesses*, (December), 134.

Pride, William M. and O. C. Ferrell (1991), *Marketing: Basic Concepts and Strategies*, Sixth Edition. Boston, Mass.: Houghton-Mifflin Company.

Promotion Exchange (1979), New York: National Retail Merchants Association (August), quoted in Pride, William M. and O. C. Ferrell (1987), *Marketing*, Fifth Edition. Boston, Mass.: Houghton-Mifflin Company, 337.

Sears, Roebuck and Co. (1990), *Annual Report*.

Standard & Poor's Industry Surveys: M-Z, no. 2, April 20, 1989, New York: Standard & Poor's Corporation, R-87.

Standard & Poor's Industry Surveys: M-Z, no. 2, July 1989, New York: Standard & Poor's Corporation, R-61–85.

Statistical Abstract of the United States:1990 (110th Edition), Washington, D.C.: U.S. Bureau of the Census (U.S. Department of Commerce).

Stern, Louis W. and Adel I. El-Ansary (1988), *Marketing Channels*. Englewood Cliffs, N.J.: Prentice-Hall, Inc.

"The Service 500," (1990) *Fortune*, (June 3), 274–275.

U.S. Industrial Outlook (1989), U.S. Department of Commerce, International Trade Administration (January), Retailing, 54-1–54-7.

U.S. Industrial Outlook (1990), U.S. Department of Commerce, International Trade Administration (January), Retailing 41-1.

1.0 HIGHAM LTD.: AN EXTENDED SPECIALTY STORE

"Jeff Jones, manager of the suit department of Higham Ltd, a men's wear store in an upscale mall, was thinking about what James Garcia had said to him the other day. Garcia, one of his salespeople, asked why the department wasn't taking suits directly to the businessmen in their offices. Garcia had noted that this was done occasionally when requested but this kind of business was not sought out aggressively. With executives "on the run," many had little time to spend shopping for clothes.

Garcia said that he had coffee with an acquaintance who was making in-office service his principal form of business. Charles Boreman, Garcia's acquaintance sold men's suits and shirts on a made-to-measure basis; when the merchandise was ready, he delivered it directly to the executive. He assured himself of the fit and often left with a cool $1,000 or more.

Boreman called his business Boreman Custom Tailors and brought a wide range of suit and shirt fabrics to the client. The executive didn't even have to leave his desk until a decision to buy was made. Charles Boreman took twelve measurements to fit a shirt and I don't know how many to fit a suit. He told Garcia that he has been kept busy for the last two weeks at the mall's office complex. Garcia said that Boreman had told him that he was averaging two sales a day. "And that business could have been our business," Garcia told Jeff. "After all, we have Armani and other designer labels that the custom tailor does not have. An Armani sale could be as high as $2,000. There is potential out there."

He asked Jeff, "Why can't we do something similar? We could contact executives who returned a favorable response to a mailing requesting the service. Then we could take three or four suits of the customer's size to the executive's office. We would always be sure that we had sizes larger and smaller than the customer's stated size just in case our suit sizes were too small or too large. We could also carry with us shirts and ties that might complement the customer's suit selection. In this way we could make related sales right on the spot. After we had sold these fashion items we could ask if the customer needed any of the basics such as underwear or hosiery. Further sales could result from this final sales ploy."

"When we completed a sale, we could enter sizes, color preference, suit mode, and other things into our P.C. Then when it came time for a second visit to an executive we would have lots of data to help us. When electronic mail really gets going we could use our computer to 'tickle' the customer about his need for another visit from Higham to keep his suit stock up-to-date."

Jeff Jones had listened carefully to Garcia and told him that he would think about Garcia's suggestion. Jeff, upon thinking about the proposal, found that it had serious drawbacks. How could Higham's Ltd. be sure that it was not just getting sales it would have gotten anyway were the executives not sold in the office? After all, it's just a five-minute walk from the Office Complex to the store. However, it would be a way of protecting the established market against operators such as Boreman Custom Tailors.

"But what about staffing?" thought Jones. "I can't have two salespersons at the office complex leaving one or two on the selling floor. To do Garcia's suggestion right, we would need additional staff.

"However, who says we have to concentrate exclusively on the mall's office complex. There were several others close to the mall and several dozen at some distance from the mall. It would be especially difficult for many of the potential customers in the distant offices to come to Higham with any frequency. Garcia's suggestion might get us some genuine plus business. If the customer can't come to Higham Ltd., Higham would take the business to the customer." As far as Jones knew, no other stores were pushing in-office selling, and the custom tailor operation couldn't be everywhere.

However, other problems had to be overcome. If the suits weren't of the customer's size, a second trip would be needed to make a sale, and a third would be necessary to deliver the final product (as altered). When a suit was a customer's size, the salesperson would have to measure for alterations. He/She would not have the store's experienced tailor along to make proper measurements for alterations. Sales people could make mistakes, some of which might not be correctable, which could result in markdowns.

Related sales of shirts, ties, underwear, and hosiery would not present special problems if the salesperson were a good estimator of size. Problems could result when estimates were not accurate or when the store was out of stock on some items.

Another problem related to transportation. Jeff wondered if the store would have to acquire a fleet of trucks to transport sales personnel to and from appointments? Or could salespeople be expected to furnish their own car? After all, they are on commission.

These and other thoughts left Jeff Jones in a state of "puzzlement." If in-office sales were to become a major way of reaching businessmen, Higham had to be a part of it. On the other hand, if Higham did start in-office sales and strong results were not forthcoming, the venture could dig deeply into profits. Jones would "sleep on it" and make his decision in the morning. There was no need to worry the general manager until he had thought it through.

Requirement: Advise Jeff Jones.

QUESTIONS:

1. Discuss the advantages and disadvantages of Garcia's suggestion.

This case was inspired by Bates, Albert D., "The Extended Specialty Store: A Strategic Opportunity for the 1990s." *Journal of Retailing* 65, no. 3. (Fall 1989), pp. 379–88. This case was prepared by John S. Berens, School of Business, Indiana State University, Terre Haute, IN 47809 as a basis for class discussion rather than to illustrate effective or ineffective handling of an administrative situation. All rights reserved to John S. Berens. Used with permission.

STRATEGY AND DECISION MAKING

Part 1

Strategic Planning and Retail Management

Chapter Two

Outline

Learning Objectives

*After studying this chapter, the
student will be able to:*

1. Define and provide a rationale for strategic planning.
2. Describe and understand
the stages in the retailing
strategic planning process.
3. Explain how the mission
statement guides the establishment of objectives and
determination of strategies.
4. Discuss the difference and
the relationship between
financial and marketing
objectives.
5. List requirements for a comprehensive situation analysis.
6. Describe the qualitative
dimensions of the retail environment.
7. List and discuss the importance of the factors included in
external and internal situation
analyses.
8. Describe the management
levels and focus where retail
decisions must be made.

A Powerful Strategy for a Small Retailer

Step Ahead Investments Inc., owned by Gary Cino, was rated number 79 in the 1989 *INC. 500* list of America's fastest growing small private companies, and in 1990 it was ranked number 101. Cino started his retail company with the intention of bringing "unprecedented efficiency and sophistication to discounting" (mission statement).

Performance objectives for the 14-store chain retailer included the achievement of projected revenues of $25 million by the end of 1990 and the achievement of targeted profit figures by controlling expenses. As a point of comparison, Step Ahead's 1984 revenues were $223,000 with profits of $17,000, generated by three employees.

Step Ahead's customers have been identified as hard-core bargain hunters who want to feel they are getting more than their dollar's worth. During the Christmas season, as many as 100,000 bargain hunters a week go through boxes of bargain merchandise that includes everything from hose nozzles to brewer's yeast. Cino says that his customers don't have to shop for bargains—they just love deals and like to feel that they are getting more than their dollar's worth. This aspect of the firm's situation analysis has identified a profitable opportunity among the retailer's identified target market. In addition, Cino also has carefully analyzed competitors and suppliers to identify his own strengths.

Step Ahead's strategic objectives and strategy definition are focused on discount retailing with a one price strategy—a 98 cent price cap for all items in the store. This is a penetration pricing strategy that determines decisions and activities in the implementation and execution stages. For example, in order for the business to be profitable with the built-in 98 cent price tag, Cino has to emphasize operating efficiency. His focus is on achieving profits at the time that merchandise is bought, rather than when it is sold. Cino believes that if merchandise is bought right, the selling will take care of itself. He sometimes buys merchandise that he can't sell just to be able to buy other products that he can sell. This merchandise is then marketed through a subsidiary wholesale division. Although he haggles with suppliers, he never begins negotiations by belittling merchandise just to get a better price. The retailer goes as far as he can with suppliers without "hitting their panic button," believing that although they might lose money, they still feel they have done a prudent thing.

In addition to negotiating profitable deals on everything he sells, Cino's efficiency and sophistication in discount merchandising extends to every economy that can be achieved in negotiating a lease, in designing a store, and in controlling labor costs. Step Ahead, based in West Sacramento, California, operates as a regional chain in northern California. Because most of the company's suppliers are located east of the Mississippi, freight costs must be controlled. One employee is solely responsible for holding freight costs to a maximum of 10 percent of the inbound cost of goods. To get better deals from truckers, Cino offers them pickups from locations where they are likely to have less-than-full trucks. Cino also keeps advertising costs down by haggling with newspapers and radio stations, frequently buying ads

Gary Cino

on a standby basis. Step Ahead negotiates on things that many believe are nonnegotiable, and finds that it works more often than most people would think.

An evaluation of the results of Step Ahead's operation in 1988 shows that the discounter earned $185,000, a profit of nearly 3 percent, on revenues of $6.5 million with 110 employees. The stores provide weekly "hot" and "cold" lists with rankings of the fastest- and slowest-selling items. Past experience is considered in future decisions, although Cino admits that instinct is a major factor in buying decisions. He says that "With one price it's really very simple: 'Will this sell for 98 cents or not?' . . . And one other thing: you never, ever buy anything at the normal price."

Adapted from: Hyatt, Joshua (1989), "Buy the Buy," *INC* (December), 127.

Introduction

Think back to the last time you bought a shirt at the local department store, or a hamburger at your favorite drive-through fast-food restaurant. Did you stop to consider the many decisions the retailer had to make so you could buy that shirt or hamburger? Though most consumers are not aware of the complexity of retail management decisions, managers generally arrive at the most successful long-range decisions through a strategic planning process. An understanding of this process and the types of decisions involved provides the basis for discussion throughout the chapters of this book.

Retailers operate in a dynamic, highly competitive environment. If a company is to survive and prosper, managers must not only operate profitably in the present, but must anticipate and plan for future events. They must have a sense of direction and a plan for achieving company goals, a process referred to as strategic planning. Strategic planning and successful retail management are related because a retail company is an integrated system of resources (financial, human, physical, etc.), functions (customer needs to be served), and activities (buying, selling, sorting, etc.). Each of these factors is interdependent. A decision made by a manager in one area affects other managers and their decisions, and ultimately affects the profitability of the company as a whole.

This chapter focuses on the strategic planning process. First, the various management levels within the organization and the types of decisions that must be made are described. The steps in the strategic planning process and factors involved in retail management decisions in each of these steps are discussed. An introduction to the effect of technology on strategic planning and to the relationship between strategic planning and operating results, is provided in this chapter and discussed further in later chapters.

Organizational Levels and Retail Management Decisions

Within a retail organization, managers at a number of levels are responsible for making a successive group of interrelated decisions. The types of decisions made by these managers may vary in financial and marketing dimensions and by functional areas or product lines within the retail business.

Each retail firm is organized according to the company's mission, functions, and activities that need to be performed, size and geographical distribution, business classifications, and other factors. For example, a retail organization may be "tall" with many layers of management reporting upward in a hierarchy, or "flat" with few layers of management. Regardless of the individual structure, however, there are four generally recognized levels of retail management: corporate, divisional, functional, and departmental. (See Exhibit 2–1).

Corporate Level

Corporate-level managers include CEOs, presidents, vice presidents, other top ranking executives, and the Board of Directors. These individuals have the greatest responsibility for the financial performance and social behavior of the entire company, and their decisions are made accordingly. Their planning horizon is concentrated on the long term. Primary concerns of corporate level managers include the company's overall policy decisions, major financial decisions, and defining the relationships among the various divisions or SBUs (strategic business units) that make up the company.

Division and Strategic Business Unit (SBU) Level

The terms *division*, *SBU*, and *profit center* have been used to identify individual businesses that are operated separately within a larger company. These may be mutually distinctive categories, or they may overlap. For purposes of discussion in this chapter, however, division and SBU are used as similar terms within the context of the strategic planning and management process. An SBU or division has its own separate and identifiable mission within the corporation, and also may be considered a profit center. It competes with its own set of external competitors and controls the development of its own strategies and performance of its own functions.

Many large retail organizations consist of a number of divisions or SBU's. Divisions of Sears, Roebuck and Co. that are operated as individual businesses include Sears Merchandise Group, Allstate Insurance Group, Dean Witter Financial Services Group, and Coldwell Banker Real Estate Group.

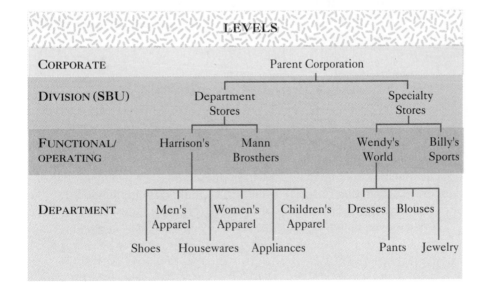

Exhibit 2–1
Organizational Levels for Decision Making

Likewise, Pizza Hut is a division of PepsiCo, Inc., and Lord & Taylor, Foley's, and Famous Barr are divisions of the May Company.

At the divisional level, decisions are focused on ways to compete in that particular retailing industry or geographical area. Competitive strategies might be determined by divisional managers based on consumer demands for service outputs, types of competitors, or margin-turnover classifications. Just as a major concern of corporate managers is defining relationships among divisions, a major concern of divisonal managers is defining relationships among the various functional areas within each division. Some of these concerns and functional relationships may be as follows for the divisional (SBU) managers:

External
1. Customer segment(s) to serve
2. Competitive environment (present and future)
3. Effect of division's selected strategy on environment

Internal
1. Allocation of resources to achieve strategic objectives (financial, personnel, physical, technology)
2. Coordination among functions within division(s) (merchandising, human resources, accounting/financial, operating, communication/promotion)
3. Goal setting (e.g., sales and profit growth, return on assets)
4. Evaluation of operations (e.g., productivity , goal achievement)

Functional (Operating) Level

In retail management at the functional level, the operating managers are confronted with the need to make both short- and long-term decisions. Their

concerns include the organization and interrelationships of the various departments required to carry out each function.

Functional areas within a retail firm include merchandising, human resources, store operations, promotion, and accounting and control. Strategic decisions must be made within each function. In addition, coordination of these decisions and cooperation among managers are needed to create the interfunctional relationships necessary to achieve corporate objectives. Successful retail strategies require the performance and coordination of many tasks and activities across many functional departments and work units in a division. Walker and Ruekert (1987) suggest that the performance of a business unit is affected by four factors. Each of these can be applied to the functional level within a retail firm:

1. Relative level of competence in carrying out specific functions, such as buyers' negotiating skills
2. Amount of resources allocated to functional areas relative to competitors, such as advertising budgets
3. Amount of participation and influence each functional area has in making decisions about policies regarding merchandising, cost control, etc.
4. Specific methods for coordinating activities across functional departments and resolving conflicts between departments

Department Level

At the departmental level, managers are generally responsible for making decisions within a given store relating to specific merchandise classifications, services, or operating functions. Strategic and tactical decisions at the departmental level must be coordinated with similar departments in other stores and with different departments in the same store.

Department managers typically are concerned with merchandise selection and presentation, salesforce supervision and motivation, and customer service within their areas. At this level, some very basic decisions are made within the broader merchandise classification in terms of SKUs (stock keeping units), in order to be prepared to meet customer needs on a daily basis.

As can be determined from the preceding discussion, retail organizations contain a hierarchy of objectives and strategies throughout their levels. Corporate level tactics become strategies at the divisional or SBU level. Divisional level tactics become strategies at the functional level, and functional tactics become strategies at the departmental level.

The Strategic Planning Process

The whole notion of planning means that the retailer is specifically prepared for expected events, while maintaining sufficient flexibility to respond to the unexpected. Thus, the retailer has greater control over the company's destiny, moving from day-to-day survival to long-range growth and prosperity.

and the right price. This is called inventory management. The amount of inventory on hand should be sufficient to offer customers a satisfactory selection, but not excessive enough to cause markdowns and loss of profits. Thus, the steps in the strategic planning process become critical in effective inventory control and other aspects of retail management. Before describing the steps in the strategic planning process, let us define the terms that are involved: planning, strategy, and strategic planning.

Whenever something needs to be accomplished—whether by a nation, a business, an organization, or an individual—a plan is required to make it happen. One approach is to allow events to take care of themselves; but this is a high-risk approach and may lead to unwanted results. A more satisfactory approach is to prepare a formal plan in advance, using available information and resources to map out a direction for the company. Planning is a routine function that human beings perform each day. We develop shopping lists to plan purchases at the grocery store or map out routes and develop timetables for vacation trips. The more extensive the task, the more attention we pay to the development of the plan.

While planning does not automatically guarantee success, it does have a number of advantages to a retailer. It contributes to more effective management, provides a benchmark to evaluate progress, and increases the probability of achieving desired financial and marketing objectives. **Planning** may be defined as "a process directed toward making today's decisions with tomorrow in mind and a means of preparing for future decisions so that they may be made rapidly, economically, and with as little disruption to the business as possible" (Warren, 1966, p. 5).

Strategy involves the company's basic objectives and reasons for being in business, its corporate policies, resource allocations, and customer markets and the competitive environment in which it has decided to operate. Strategy is needed because the retailer's resources generally are limited, resource commitments are difficult to reverse, competitive strengths and behavior often are unpredictable, decisions must be coordinated over time and across geographic locations, and managers must be assigned responsibility for initiating various activities. **Strategy** may be defined as a "game plan" that provides a unified sense of direction in both the long and short runs for retail managers at all organizational levels.

For example, assume that one of McDonald's corporate objectives was to increase profitability. Strategy at the corporate level was to increase the productivity of its operating restaurants. The corporate level tactic to accomplish this objective was the expansion of hours and menu items to include breakfast items. As an extension of the corporate tactic, the business level had a market focus strategy.

Business units (franchisees and corporate stores) focused on product and service expansion. One tactic that helped to implement the business unit strategy was the successful launching of the Egg McMuffin, which was followed later with a broader product line. The broader product line is viewed by McDonald's as getting a greater share of the overall food dollar. Competition is seen by the fast-food retailer as anyone who sells food. Therefore, McDonald's introduced McExtras in a Minneapolis, Minnesota restaurant in 1991. McExtras is a refrigerated case containing basic grocery items such as eggs, milk, and bread that are for sale at the counter or drive-through. Other new product tests have included McDonald's Pizza, McFish Fry, and subma-

PLANNING
preparation for future events and decisions

STRATEGY
planning that provides a unified direction for organizational action

At McDonald's, product and service expansion resulted in the breakfast menu, successfully launched with the Egg McMuffin.

rine sandwiches (Hume, 1991). Thus, the introduction of Egg McMuffin and other new products illustrates how a company can achieve its corporate financial objectives through market driven strategies and tactics, such as those related to Bucklin's (1966) customer demands for service outputs. A wider product assortment and increased productivity through better use of manpower and space contribute to an increased (or stabilized) market share. Longer hours of operation also increase cash flow. Each of these actions helps to achieve corporate profitability.

Strategy provides the retailer with a broadly stated plan of action for changing or adapting to its environments; the basic thrust is *what* to do. Identification of tactics, on the other hand, describes *how* the strategy will be carried out. Strategies and tactics themselves may not have time dimensions, but plans and the planning process do. *Planning* is the entire multi-level process, including strategy identification, implementation of tactics, and determination of when and where the strategy will be carried out. However, neither strategy nor planning can be effective by itself. **Strategic planning** combines the two to provide the key ingredient in the strategic retail management process.

The strategic planning process consists of seven basic steps (see Exhibit 2–2):

1. Mission statement
2. Performance objectives
3. Situation analysis
4. Strategic objectives and strategy definition
5. Implementation and tactics
6. Execution
7. Evaluation and control

In general, the evolution of strategy follows a certain pattern. For a small company, its "strategic purpose" simply may be cash flow or survival, and

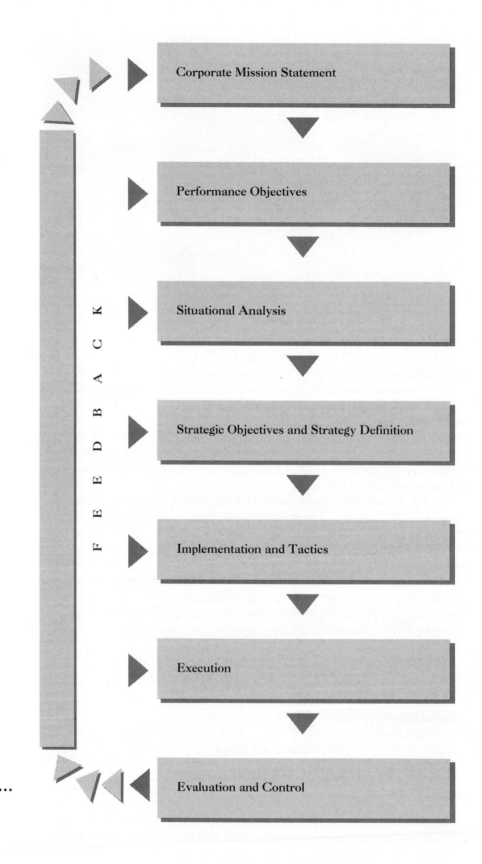

Corporate Mission Statement

Performance Objectives

Situational Analysis

Strategic Objectives and Strategy Definition

Implementation and Tactics

Execution

Evaluation and Control

FEEDBACK

Exhibit 2–2
Strategic Planning Process

decisions may be made on a day-to-day basis. As a company grows, the development of strategies becomes more complex, although it is not always clear at what point strategies become explicitly stated. Well-defined strategies are particularly important in larger companies so that they can be communicated to the managers and employees who will execute them, used for control and evaluation purposes, and to achieve a balance between marketing and financial objectives.

Note that strategic planning is an ongoing process, with the results of one decision providing inputs for the next. Because strategic planning is dynamic and continuous, our discussion could start from any point shown in Exhibit 2–2, However, for convenience and purposes of this text, we begin with the corporate mission. An illustration of each stage in the strategic planning process for a large retailer is provided in the Chapter 2 Retail Spotlight on J.C. Penney. A small retailer can benefit from a simpler strategy as is described in the Chapter 2 Retail Spotlight in the Perfumery on Park.

Mission Statement

The **mission statement** defines, or can redefine, the purpose of the business. Strategic retail management depends on a clear statement of the firm's identity in the present and on how it wants to be identified in the future. The mission statement is usually already in place in an established organization, but may be nonexistent in a newer or smaller firm. Some large firms do not have a clear statement of purpose. Although developing a mission statement is not as easy as it may sound, the manager who does not know what business his company is in, or what business it wants to be in, cannot make effective decisions. For example, a motel operator may believe he is in the business of offering efficient, friendly service to business professionals who want comfortable sleeping accommodations and good food at reasonable prices. In reality, his employees may be poorly trained, inefficient, and rude to guests who find their rooms uncomfortable and the food unpalatable. In this case, the motel operator is not fulfilling his mission.

The mission statement provides guidelines for development of the retailer's goals and objectives, and the policies and strategies to achieve the desired results. The direction and focus of the retailer's activities will be determined by specific answers to the questions:

1. "What business are we in?" (Who/where are our customers; what do they want? Which customers will we serve?)
2. "What business will we be in?" (What changes in the environment are likely, and how do we expect to deal with them? Which customer needs—or functions—will we serve? What methods or technologies will be used to satisfy these needs?)
3. "What business should we be in?" (Are there opportunities in new customer markets, or new products or services to satisfy new or existing markets? Are we still selling the right things to our customers?)

An effective mission statement is customer oriented, is feasible in terms of how broadly or narrowly the business is defined, motivates or inspires employees to be more productive, and is specific enough to provide the necessary guidelines for operating the retail business. (Digman, 1986)

MISSION STATEMENT
defines the purpose of a business

The *J.C.Penney Stores Positioning Statement* and *The Penney Idea* provide an easily understood statement of the company's mission, as illustrated in Exhibits 2–3 and 2–5 (J.C. Penney Co. managers' literature and personal interviews). Penney's positioning statement is one example of the relationship between a retailer's mission statement and the entire strategic planning process, as it applies throughout the levels and divisions of the firm. Even though its positioning statements may change over time to reflect changing markets, J.C. Penney's fundamental mission has remained the same since 1913. Fred Meyer's philosophy statement appears in Exhibit 2–4.

Exhibit 2–3
J.C. Penney Positioning Statement
(Revised January 1990 to reflect
repositioning strategy)

MESSAGE FROM THE CHAIRMAN

This positioning statement is a directional guide. It should serve as a framework to form our plans, programs, and actions. Using this framework will move us toward our goal of being a growth company.

Achieving and maintaining fashion credibility depends upon every associate action and every department decision being consistent with this positioning statement. All store associates, services and presentation, fixtures, and signs must be in harmony with our fashionable merchandise assortments. Qualiity standards, pricing, and advertising must work to support the total effort.

We have made tremendous progress in repositioning ourselves with consumers. Our challenge is to enhance our fashion credibility and to maintain consumers' confidence and our image of integrity, quality, and service.

Everything we do gives a signal to consumers about who we are, what we believe in, and what we want to be.

Warmest Regards,

TARGET CONSUMERS

Middle to middle-upper income consumers who shop the centers where JCPenney is located for ego-sensitive apparel, accessories, and home furnishings.

The focus is consumers who want fashionable lifestyle merchandise with recognizable value.

POSITIONING OBJECTIVE

To be perceived by target consumers as having timely and competitive selections of fashionable, quality merchandise with recognizable value. Consumers who shop for traditional and updated merchandise are the key to achieving future growth; therefore, the focus will be on the appropriate balance of updated, traditional, and conservative merchandise, with an emphasis on traditional.

Within this overall positioning framework, each business entity will begin with the customer's point of view in developing its quality standards, merchandise offerings, branding and pricing strategies, visual merchandising, and service levels.

. . . having timely and competitive selections of fashionable, quality merchandise with recognizable value.

Performance Objectives

Retail management describes what it expects to accomplish over a specified period of time by establishing **objectives** or goals. These generally are stated in quantitative terms of exactly "how much" and "how soon" (e.g., increase return on investment to 10 percent within two years).

Objectives are determined for both the long- and short-term, with the primary emphasis placed on expectations for the long term. Objectives should be arranged in a hierarchy from the most important to the least

OBJECTIVES
statement of a business's expected accomplishments

MERCHANDISE

arget consumers will be offered a balanced selection of merchandise in a variety of styles, colors, fabrics, and brands. Fashion merchandise must be timely, offering the newest colors and styles that are just beginning to gain target consumer acceptance. Only quality merchandise will be offered to each consumer lifestyle segment.

To create a sustainable competitive advantage, the emphasis in most lines will be on JCPenney private brands. Consistency and longevity in the private brand identification will build brand acceptance, encourage repeat purchases, and result in increased market share.

Where national brands are the clear choice of consumers, they will be offered to enhance JCPenney's competitive position as a national department store. In some entities, national brands may dominate.

Only quality merchandise will be offered to each consumer lifestyle segment.

VALUE

alue is the summation of how the consumer views the combination of quality, timeliness, fashion, style, the environment, and price. The value a consumer places on a specific item is reflected in that item's rate of sale.

The importance of price in the value equation varies with the ego intensity of the merchandise. In highly ego-sensitive merchandise, factors such as quality, fashion, and style are most important in the buying decision, while price is less important. Commodity merchandise, on the other hand, is more price-sensitive and must have a value edge, with a focus on quality and availability.

JCPenney private brand merchandise must be perceived by target consumers as having greater value than department store and specialty store competition. This value should be derived from a combination of quality, timeliness, fashion, style, environment, and price.

ENVIRONMENT

he total store environment will contribute to an enjoyable experience and build confidence that JCPenney has fashionable lifestyle merchandise.

Merchandise will, in most cases, be grouped and presented by consumer lifestyle to make shopping easier for the time-pressured consumer. The in-store environment will be in harmony and good taste and will enhance the merchandise statement of fashion and quality. Visual presentation, store decor, and design are critical to creating an ambiance that reinforces fashion credibility.

The in-store environment will be in harmony and good taste and will enhance the merchandise statement of fashion and quality.

continued

important. In order to be successful, performance objectives must be realistic and achievable, as well as measurable. For example, a retailer might have the following objective: 50 percent increase in sales, to be achieved within one year. While the performance results can be measured, the objective may not be realistic if available company resources, or customer base to generate this level of sales, does not exist. Therefore, an achievable objective must be realistic.

Objectives are then determined for each level of the organization and for each strategic business unit (SBU). If the retailer is to operate effectively, these individual goals must be compatible so that the various operating units

MARKETING

Communications to consumers will be achieved through an appropriate mix of advertising media, special events, and pub—licity. The look of the advertising should reinforce the quality message to target con-sumers. The character of the merchandise being advertised should reflect a com-petitive and a fashionable image.

Marketing activities will create top-of-the-mind awareness and will ensure JCPenney's position as a destination store for target consumers. While continuing to market to all potential customers, direct communications will be increasingly targeted to specific consumers.

The use of regular and off-price advertising should be con-sistent with Company objectives and be designed to achieve pric-ing integrity. Prices are never set just to off-price.

Marketing activities will create aware-ness and ensure our position as a destination store for target consumers.

CUSTOMER SERVICE

All associates will be sensitive to providing service that is superior to that of department store competition. All customer contacts will be conducted in a friendly, professional, and knowledgeable way that enhances the customer's confi-dence in JCPenney and fos-ters repeat business.

Store associates will present an appearance that supports the character of their departments and the merchandise they sell.

Consistently applying these stan-dards reconfirms JCPenney's com-mitment to customer service.

All customer contacts will be conducted in a friendly, professional, and knowl-edgeable way.

Used with permission of J.C. Penney

of the company, stores, divisions, departments, and so forth are not working against one another. When specific goals are established for each unit, those responsible for achieving the goals have a better idea of what is expected of them. They also have a guideline—or a benchmark—against which to measure their success in reaching the goals, and they can identify their personal contribution to the process.

Objectives at one level of the retail firm must support those at the next level, and in total must support the company's mission, thus forming a hierarchy of objectives: primary, secondary, and subobjectives. (Digman, 1986) As previously noted, an effective mission statement is customer oriented. In

PHILOSOPHY

"Always strive to offer customers the service, selection, quality, and price that satisfies them best, for by doing that we will serve our customers well and continue to prosper and grow."

FRED G. MEYER, FOUNDER (1886-1978)

AT FRED MEYER WE ARE GOVERNED BY THE BELIEFS THAT:

Customers are essential, for without them we would have no business. Customers shop most where they believe their wants and needs will be satisfied best.

Satisfactory profits are essential, for without profits our business can neither grow nor satisfy the wants and needs of our customers, employees, suppliers, shareholders, or the community.

Skilled, capable, dedicated employees are essential, for the overall success of our business is determined by the combined ideas, work, and effort of all Fred Meyer employees.

BASED ON THESE BELIEFS, WE ARE COMMITTED TO:

Serving customers so well that after shopping with us they are satisfied and want to shop with us again.

Operating our business efficiently and effectively so we earn a satisfactory profit today and in the future.

Providing an environment that encourages employees to develop their abilities, use their full potential, and share ideas that further the success of the business so they gain a sense of pride in their accomplishments and confidence in their capabilities.

We believe that by following this philosophy we will satisfy customers and earn their patronage, provide for the profitable growth of our company, and enrich the lives of Fred Meyer employees and their families.

Exhibit 2–4
Fred Meyer Philosophy Statement
. . . .

Although he died in 1978, Fred G. Meyer continues to guide the company he founded through a corporate philosophy based on the retail principles he followed. This philosophy serves as the company's mission statement and is the basis of the company's strategic plan.

Mr. Meyer's fundamental approach to retailing was simple—"think like a customer." From that basic principle emerged one innovation after another that molded his namesake company into a truly unique retail concept whose approach to one-stop shopping has not been matched.

FRED G. MEYER

reality, financial and marketing objectives are inseparable; it is the revenues from customer sales that determine achievement of financial objectives. Thus, a marketing orientation is assumed to influence each level of performance objectives. In general, the retailer's primary objectives are related to financial goals and profitability, while secondary objectives are related to marketing (or retailing) goals. Subobjectives provide support for the retailer's primary and secondary objectives.

PRIMARY OBJECTIVES: FINANCIAL   Within the context of strategic planning, a retailer's **primary objectives** typically are stated in terms of financial goals and profitability, broken down to specific targets for each operating unit (e.g., Sears' Merchandising Group) and division (e.g., Men's Division) of the firm. They focus on expectations of returns to the company resulting from the use of its resources.

Broad financial objectives include desired levels of sales, profits, and growth rate. They also include return on capital employed and return to shareholders. Financial objectives are established for each operating unit and division of the company, since achievement of individual goals at each level contributes to the retailer's overall long-term profitability. In turn, long-term profitability provides the resources necessary to achieve these objectives.

SECONDARY OBJECTIVES: MARKETING/RETAILING   **Secondary objectives** are additional targets to be attained by the company and its divisions, described in terms of marketing or retailing goals. Marketing objectives are related to desired results of the retailing operation, and are oriented toward the retailer's relationship with its customers and its competitors.

Objectives related to customers typically are expressed in terms of satisfaction of one or more market segments, accomplished with the appropriate blend of the retailing mix (products, price, promotion, services, and location). Focus may be on factors such as merchandise quality, selling methods, or positioning of the store against its competition in the minds of its intended customers.

Objectives related to competitors are expressed in terms of required market share, rate of market growth, and other factors that will give the retailer a competitive advantage. For example, a primary financial objective of 20 percent return on net assets may be supported by a secondary objective of achieving productivity increases of 30 percent in sales per square foot of selling space in all stores. Planning for effective achievement of these goals requires two-way communication up and down the corporate ladder. For example, a companywide target for return on assets may not be the same as that for an individual store, department, or product line, which are combined for overall corporate performance.

SUBOBJECTIVES   **Subobjectives** related to achieving desired return on assets could include selling higher margin merchandise in space previously allocated to lower margin merchandise. A related subobjective could be to decrease selling expenses by increased self-service and more productive salesforce scheduling. Likewise, subobjectives to achieve higher sales per square foot could include a more efficient store layout or more effective vertical display fixtures. Each of these subobjectives should be measurable and have a time dimension for accountability.

Exhibit 2–5
J.C. Penney Company: The Penney Idea
· ·
SOURCE: Used with permission of J.C. Penney Company, Inc.

The Penney Idea

1. To serve the public as nearly as we can to its complete satisfaction.
2. To expect for the service we render a fair remuneration, and not all the profit the traffic will bear.
3. To do all in our power to pack the customer's dollar full of value, quality and satisfaction.
4. To continue to train ourselves and our associates so that the service we give will be more and more intelligently performed.
5. To improve constantly the human factor in our business.
6. To reward the men and women in our organization through participation in what the business produces.
7. To test our every policy, method and act in this wise: "Does it square with what is right and just?"

–Adopted 1913

Environmental Situation Analysis

Because retailers operate in a particularly dynamic environment, they must monitor their external and internal environments constantly. In this way they can anticipate and respond to changes that may have an impact on the achievement of long- and short-term objectives. An ongoing analysis provides relevant data on the retailer's current situation, such as the market in which the firm operates, products being sold or desired by target markets, competition, and distribution. This information is used in forecasting for the future, assessing strengths and weaknesses, and identifying potential threats, opportunities, and constraints. An understanding of the company's environment influences company policies and objectives, and affects the allocation of resources and the implementation of retailing strategies.

Environmental analysis has three separate purposes in planning activities: (1) policy orientation, (2) integration with strategic planning, and (3) functional orientation. From a policy orientation perspective, the search for information is relatively unstructured in order to define the most relevant environmental factors. Once top management is aware of these factors, they can anticipate major emerging issues and plan accordingly.

Secondly, environmental analysis is integrated directly with strategic planning, usually at the corporate or divisional level. Macro (e.g., economic or legislative conditions) and micro (e.g., conditions within the firm) environmental analysis provides detailed information that can be used to prepare environmental forecasts and to create a link between corporate and business level plans.

Third, a function-oriented analysis concentrates on the environment of a particular retail function (or task) at either the corporate or business unit level. Functional areas include merchandise management, promotion, store operations, human resources, and accounting and control. Analysis is closely linked to the planning process in order to improve future performance in each of these functions (Engledow and Lenz, 1985).

The term **"strategic window"** means there is generally only a limited time period in which what the market needs "fits" with what the retailer has to offer (Abell, 1978). Analysis to identify strategic windows would apply to such decisions as building or acquiring more stores, innovative ways of selling to new and existing customers, adding new or unrelated merchandise lines, or even "getting out" of some aspect of the business at the right time. While many retailers have taken advantage of their strategic windows of opportunity, others have failed to do so. Many department stores have lost their strong customer loyalty and have been hurt by the evolution of specialty stores, discounters, and catalog retailers. Some have begun to restructure and reposition themselves successfully; others, such as Sears and Bloomingdale's, have not been as successful. Foreign investors entered into free-for-all merger and acquisition activities in response to what they perceived as a window of opportunity in U.S. retailing. However, many of these deals "went wrong." George Herscu, an Australian real estate tycoon, added B. Altman and Bonwit Teller, among others, to his retail empire. Because of over-expansion in the U.S. and high interest rates in Australia, he was unable to meet cash needs, and filed for bankruptcy in 1989. Canadian real estate developer, Robert Campeau, similarly misjudged his "strategic window" in a takeover of Allied Stores in 1987 and Federated Department Stores in 1988. In spite

PRIMARY OBJECTIVES
specific targets stated in terms of financial goals and profitability

SECONDARY OBJECTIVES
targets stated in terms of marketing or retailing goals

SUBOBJECTIVES
support a firm's primary and secondary objectives

STRATEGIC WINDOW
time period in which a retailer has an opportunity to meet market needs

of Campeau's sale of some of the premier Allied and Federated divisions, such as Brooks Brothers, Bullock's, Foley's and Filene's, Campeau was unable to generate the necessary cash to cover the overdue payments. Conversely, May Co. successfully acquired other department store chains such as Associated Dry Goods in 1986 and Foley's in 1989 (Standard & Poor's, January 1990).

As illustrated by the preceding examples, a comprehensive analysis requires the following elements:

1. A understanding of why environmental information is needed, i.e., identification of the types of decisions to be made and potential problems related to the environment, as well as how the information will be used by managers
2. An awareness of all critical environmental factors to be considered, both inside and outside of the company
3. Identifying and locating sources of data and information
4. Obtaining or gathering the information in the form of factual data or based on perceptions of environmental conditions
5. Analyzing, interpreting, and summarizing information so that it is useful for management decisions

While such an analysis should strive for "perfect" information that can be conveniently measured and quantified, in reality this is difficult. The retailer's environment contains a great deal of uncertainty. Therefore, many dimensions of the environment must be described and analyzed in qualitative (or subjective) terms. Qualitative dimensions may be classified in two broad categories: environmental scope and rate of change. Each of these is described briefly below. (For additional discussion, see Achrol, Reve, and Stern, (1983) and Jurkovich, (1974).)

ENVIRONMENTAL SCOPE   Scope issues include environmental capacity, complexity, concentration, and heterogeneity relative to an industry, geographical area, or market segment.

Environmental capacity is the balance between those resources (products, services) that the retailer can provide to the market(s) where it competes and those resources that the market(s) can provide to the retailer (customers, etc.). For example, Red Lobster will not move into a city with a population less than 50,000 because the market capacity (or demand) is viewed as too limited. The number of sources of supply available to the retailer represents another measure of environmental capacity.

Environmental concentration is related to environmental capacity. It is the degree of control over the resources flowing into and out of the retail firm by organizations, individuals, or locations. For example, a retailer may choose to concentrate purchases with only a few suppliers, although many suppliers may be available. Likewise, a large city may provide a large potential market in a general sense, but a store located in that city may choose to serve only one or two precisely defined segments within that market. In either case, the concentrated conditions may result in a more uncertain environment because, although retailers may have control, they are more dependent on forces that affect their particular concentration of suppliers or customer segments.

Environmental complexity is related to the degree of similarity or diversity within the environment and the complexity of decision making. As

ENVIRONMENTAL CAPACITY
balance between the resources a retailer provides to the market and what the market provides to the retailer

ENVIRONMENTAL CONCENTRATION
degree of control over resources flowing in and out of the retail firm

ENVIRONMENTAL COMPLEXITY
degree of similarity or diversity of elements within the environment

environmental elements become more numerous and diverse (heterogeneous), decision making becomes more complex. Decisions are made much simpler when they can be based on fewer information inputs, and those inputs are more similar or homogeneous in nature. For example, many retailers must make decisions in a highly complex legal and regulatory environment, where actions are influenced by government requirements, such as those mandated by OSHA (Occupational Safety and Health Administration) and EEO (Equal Employment Opportunity). In addition, regulations such as federal credit laws and local store ordinances, and many others, create an even more complex decision making environment.

Environmental heterogeneity is the degree of fit between the retailer and outside forces, i.e., how well the firm is suited to the customers, businesses, and others that affect its resources, and vice-versa. Heterogeneity refers to the number of different environmental influences impacting the retailer. For example, large metropolitan areas such as Los Angeles may provide larger absolute markets in terms of population, but these markets may be divided into many distinct or heterogeneous customer groups based on cultural and occupational differences. In contrast, a retailer in a rural agricultural community most likely would face a more homogeneous group of customers.

ENVIRONMENTAL RATE OF CHANGE   Rate of change issues include environmental stability and turbulence. In turn, planning horizon issues, i.e., how far out into the future the company can plan safely, are related to how fast the retailer's environment is changing and how erratic or uncertain those changes are.

Environmental stability is the degree to which the retailer's environment affects the rate of change and the complexity of decision making. Stable environments experience relatively slow change and decision making is simpler. As environmental elements become less stable, change occurs more rapidly, leading to more uncertainty and more complex decision making. For example, where there is little change in technology, less environmental fluctuation and a higher degree of certainty allow for longer planning horizons. Another illustration of environmental stability occurred in the late 1970s, which marked the beginning of a period of instability in financial markets. This affected the retailer's ability to determine the desirability of internal versus external credit offerings to customers. It also taxed the financial officers' abilities to balance between long- and short-term debt funding.

Environmental turbulence is the extent to which one environment is disturbed by its interconnectedness or degree of interrelationships to other environments. Turbulence cannot be separated completely from organizational size and scope, which in turn are related to demands from both customers and other constituencies that businesses behave responsibly. These factors increase the interconnectedness of environmental elements, and as they become increasingly interconnected, managers find it more difficult to predict the overall effects of environmental change. The precise cause-and-effect relationships among environmental factors and sales response become obscured.

For example, in a midwestern metropolitan area comprised of a few manufacturing companies, a number of financial institutions and some insurance companies, it becomes difficult to predict sales trends in the face of an

ENVIRONMENTAL HETEROGENEITY
degree of fit between the retailer and outside forces

ENVIRONMENTAL STABILITY
degree to which the retailer's environment affects the rate of change and complexity of decision making

ENVIRONMENTAL TURBULENCE
extent to which the environment is disturbed by interrelationships with other environments

agricultural drought. On the surface, the city would appear to be protected. In reality, large banks with subsidiaries or branches serving the rural markets may begin to experience high loan losses, which drain the availability of cash for consumer and commercial loans. Payouts for crop losses may represent a substantial cash drain for the insurance providers and cause them to cut back in some areas of personnel, thereby increasing unemployment. Furthermore, if the largest of the manufacturing firms is agriculturally related, additional employment cuts may occur in this sector. So, what will be the impact on the retailer's sales? Probably they will decrease . . . but by how much?

External Environment

A retailer's external environment can be viewed from both a macro- and a microenvironmental perspective. Macroenvironmental factors, such as economic, political, and social forces, are beyond the immediate control of the retailer—but must be dealt with in order to operate stores successfully. Microenvironmental factors, such as customer markets and other businesses, also are considered uncontrollable by the retailer; however, the company can have an impact on these through strategic management decisions. Specific external factors to be considered in a situation analysis are discussed briefly in the following sections. As shown in Exhibit 2–6, the retailer's suppliers and intermediaries, competitors, and customers (microenvironment) carry out their activities within the macroenvironment that affects them all. Execution of the retailer's strategy occurs in relationship to all aspects of the microenvironment. In turn, the environmental response to that strategy occurs within the economic, legal, social, and other dimensions of the macroenvironment.

MACROENVIRONMENT   The retail manager who does not know what is happening now and what is expected to happen in the future in the macroenvironment—economic, legal/political, sociocultural, demographic, physical, and the technological environment—is handicapped in developing successful strategies.

Economic conditions and trends are monitored to determine a population's ability to buy goods and services, and to assess how potential customers will respond to a particular retail mix. Indicators of economic conditions include inflation, recession, increases or decreases in corporate and personal debt and incomes (and disposable personal income), income distribution (geographic, social class), changing consumer expenditure patterns, and unemployment rate.

Legal/political and public policy developments affect retailing decisions, since they consist of laws to obey, government officials and agencies to be answered to, and political pressures that cannot be ignored by managers. Legislation regulating business has been enacted to (1) protect one business from another, (2) protect consumers from businesses, and (3) protect society in general from irresponsible actions by businesses. Retailers must be familiar with these laws and how they have been interpreted by the courts.

Deregulation in the retail banking industry has led to a variety of nontraditional competitors for financial services and products. Knowledge of the legal/political environment—what is permitted and what is not—is essential

MACRO ENVIRONMENT

Economy: Disposable Income, GNP, Unemployment, Interest Rates, Inflation

Legal/Political: Consumer Protection, Labeling, Equal Employment, Job Safety, Working Hours, Minimum Wage

MICRO ENVIRONMENT

Socio-cultural: Cultures, Sub-cultures, Social Classes, Reference Groups

Suppliers and Intermediaries
Channels, Availability, Number of Alternatives, Locations, Geographic Concentration, Volume Concentration

EXECUTION

ENVIRONMENTAL RESPONSE

Competitors
Number, Strategies, Potential New Entrants, Ease of Exit, Rivalry

Demography: Age, Sex, Geographic Location, Marital Status, Household Size, Education

Markets
Segments, Sizes, Behaviors, Trends, Locations, Service Demand

Physical: Air/Water Quality, Raw Material Availability, Visual Clutter, Noise Pollution

Technology: Product, Process, Production, Information, Management

Exhibit 2–6
External Business Environments
....
SOURCE: Parker and Anderson, 1988.

to developing new marketing approaches. For example, many banks have begun to focus more on individual consumers than corporate clients to generate future profitability. (*Banking + Retail*, RPA, 1987) Legal developments generally have a cost attached. The need for companies to comply with OSHA regulations for a safe working environment, and to provide access for handicapped employees and customers, requires attention to store design, construction, equipment, and fixtures.

An assessment of the *sociocultural* environment provides information about the beliefs and values of society. Social and cultural influences determine an acceptable retail mix for a potential customer market. Characteristics of a particular culture or subculture have a major influence on that group's buying behavior. For example, the market for McDonald's hamburgers may be limited in India because of its proportion of Hindus who have cultural-religious taboos regarding the consumption of beef.

Society determines to a large extent how people express themselves through purchases. Products and services that people buy are an indication of how they view themselves and the world around them, and how they relate

Social Responsibility in a Volatile Economic Environment

Somehow, it seems easier for a business to be socially responsible in a booming economy than in a poor economy. Perhaps the most difficult test of a company's performance relative to customers, employees, and society in general is during the "hard times." Palais Royal is one retailer that demonstrated that it could be both responsible and profitable during the volatile economic environment of the 1980s in Houston, Texas. Houston was suffering from a depressed economy with 1,600 business failures and a 12 percent unemployment rate in 1986 (not including those who moved or ran out of unemployment benefits). Based on the company's interpretation and response to economic information for the Houston market, Palais Royal set realistic, attainable goals to protect its market share, provide training and incentives for employees, increase collections from credit customers, improve merchandising, and increase profitability.

Strategies to protect market share in a fiercely competitive retailing environment were based on being innovative,

Palais Royal, Houston

courageous, and having integrity. The company's strategies for turning adversity into advantage included making a greater dollar commitment to advertising and direct mail, store refurbishing and expansion, introduction of new merchandise classifications, and

increased concentration on generating more profit, although this might result in achieving lower maintained markups.

Although difficult to give incentives to employees during "hard times," incentives were given on monthly per-

to other people and institutions in society. For example, a cultural emphasis on physical fitness has provided retail opportunities in health-related products and services. Health spas, leisure activities, apparel and food products have experienced increased sales by using environmental information to develop marketing strategies. Service providers, such as Pacific Bell, have acknowledged their diverse ethnic customer base by making it possible for Mexican-Americans, Asian-Americans, and others to speak with customer service representatives in their native languages.

The *demographic* environment is of interest because of trends in population growth and birthrate, population shifts according to geographic location, age distribution, household size, ethnic backgrounds, educational levels, and other developments. Aging "baby boomers" are being watched with interest

formance rather than on year end profits. Some subjective criteria were included to keep employees from being demoralized. Attention was given to training both newly hired salespeople and tenured associates, so the stores would have a more knowledgeable and motivated sales force. Newly hired salespeople were reviewed and counseled regularly; those not meeting company standards were terminated. Another motivational device was the implementation of a career path program that provided associates with a goal to strive for and recognition for their accomplishments. In addition, roundtable sessions were held throughout the company for two-way feedback so that associates could inform management about their concerns, and management could respond with what the company could do about those concerns.

Over seventy percent of Palais Royal's business came from its own credit card. Although the company was writing off $100,000 a month in bad debts due to bankruptcies, Palais Royal's credit records contained valuable information on its customer base. As a result, the retailer was able to develop creative programs to reward

extra-special qualified customers. Customers whose purchases reached at least $1,000 a year received special considerations that included free gift wrap, discounts on alterations, and check cashing. Palais Royal also responded to customer needs by creating "amnesty programs" for customers in temporary financial stress.

The firm increased profits by increasing productivity and decreasing expenses, without compromising customer benefits. They set high standards for service for sales associates, identified service areas that other

retailers were ignoring, and differentiated their stores on the basis of customer service. Attention to customer service included a "Never say no" policy, even for unreasonable customer requests—except at the store manager level. The phrase "Reason for return" was removed from the merchandise return forms, and customers' returns were accepted without question. Very few customers abused this privilege. Call buttons were installed in fitting rooms to indicate that a customer needed assistance, but sales associates tried to "beat the chime" in providing service to their customers. Performance standards were established for sales associates, such as greeting customers within 30 seconds, revisiting fitting rooms every five minutes, and writing at least two customer letters a day.

Palais Royal's strategy was summed up in this quote attributed to Henry Ford: "Business is never so healthy as when, like a chicken, it must scratch for what it gets."

Adapted from: Fuchs, Bernard (1987), "Surviving and Growing In Overstored Markets," Presentation, Survival and Growth in Volatile Economies, 1987 Special Topic Symposium, Sponsored by Center for Retailing Studies, Texas A&M University, Dallas Market Center, Dallas, Tex. (September 30).

to determine their impact on the retail industry—the types of products they buy, how they buy them, and how they use them. Other demographic trends such as the increasing number of nonfamily and single person households, a better-educated U.S. population, and a fast-growing Hispanic population are monitored by retailers as they develop strategies to meet the needs of these customers.

Related in many ways to the demographic environment, the status and trends in the *physical environment* have an effect on strategic management decisions. The situation analysis includes the impact of possible raw materials shortages, air and water quality, changing temperature and weather conditions, energy costs and availability, and intervention in environmental matters by government agencies and public pressure groups. Such occurrences may impact on decisions about what type of merchandise to sell, what prices to charge, where to locate stores, and other strategic choices.

The effects of *technology* on society, and the accelerated pace of technological change, have been emphasized over the past two decades (Naisbitt, 1982; Toffler, 1970, 1980). Technology is a powerful force within the retail environment. It affects the type of products and services that can be merchandised, and how they will be delivered to target markets. In many cases technology is related to planned obsolescence. New and improved products offer retailers and their customers an opportunity to have the latest technological innovations. Technology is an important determinant of the efficiency of retail information systems and store operations.

Each aspect of the macroenvironment can be analyzed from a worldwide or national perspective, as well as from a more narrowly defined geographic and/or demographic market perspective. The resulting information can be used to provide a direction for retail strategies.

MICROENVIRONMENT   The microenvironment, also referred to as the market environment or the operating or task environment, is the company's immediate external environment. Although the retail firm cannot control suppliers and intermediaries, facilitating agencies, competitors, or consumer markets, it can influence their behavior through strategic management practices.

An analysis of the characteristics and activities of **suppliers** and **intermediaries,** who control the flow of goods and services needed by the retailer, provides information about sources of supply and other assistance. It also provides an indication of the retailer's relative position with respect to bargaining power and control of distribution channels. Microenvironmental analysis also includes facilitating agencies such as financial institutions, research firms, and advertising agencies. Relationships with these other businesses provide the basis for long-term cooperative efforts.

The process of identifying and evaluating sources of supply for products and services provides retail managers with fundamental information such as availability of merchandise lines and specific items, terms of sale, reliability of the vendor, and transportation costs and methods.

Competitors are included in a situation analysis because retailers seek a competitive advantage in the markets where they operate. Retailers need to know what other retailers are doing now and plan to do in the future that may attract customers to them. Attention usually is focused on direct competitors who are selling the same goods and services in a similar manner. However, indirect competition also needs to be monitored. These competitors are retailers who are not in the same primary line of business but sell the same products or services in their stores (grocery store selling t-shirts), as well as nonstore retailers (catalog sales of shirts through direct mail), and retailers who use nontraditional formats (selling t-shirts via an interactive cable TV system).

The retailer evaluates the strengths and weaknesses of its retail mix against that of present and potential competitors, taking into consideration merchandise quality and assortment, pricing strategies, promotional methods, store location, services offered, image, stage of primary merchandise lines in the product life cycle, and so forth. This information is then used to determine the company's ability to gain competitive advantage and market share.

SUPPLIERS AND INTERMEDIARIES
businesses that move goods from the manufacturer to the retailer

COMPETITORS
other retailers selling similar products or services in the same market

CONSUMER MARKETS
group of customers defined by size, behavior, and specific characteristics

The situation analysis includes an assessment of the retailer's position of power in negotiations with suppliers and how other retailers will react to innovative or aggressive strategies. Competitors' locations, geographical concentration, and expansion plans also are analyzed.

An analysis of **consumer markets** provides information about market size, behavior, and trends. Data are obtained to determine the characteristics of present and potential customers, thus enabling the retailer to know the number of buyers in a market, their purchasing power, buying habits, and consumer needs and wants.

As described earlier, Bucklin's (1966, 1972) concepts regarding the level of consumer demand for service outputs provide a useful framework for analyzing consumer preferences, i.e., spatial convenience, lot size, delivery or waiting time, and product variety or assortment. Knowledge of consumer demands in each area can be instrumental in shaping retail strategy. For example, a market where the retail stores are decentralized and, therefore, closer to the consumer, (convenience stores, neighborhood supermarkets, or community shopping centers) provides spatial convenience by decreasing the time and expense associated with transportation and search. Consumer purchases made in larger quantities (lots) generally result in lower prices to the consumer and shorter distribution channels, while smaller lot sizes result in higher prices and longer channels. The amount and timing of inventories may be adjusted according to how long customers will wait for a product or service and the assortment they demand for selection.

The situation analysis provides information about the feasibility of pursuing a particular market segment. There are five criteria for segmentation. A segment must be (1) identifiable (measurable), (2) accessible (location, available promotional media and communication vehicles), and (3) substantial enough to be profitable. In addition, the segment must (4) exhibit behavioral response differences, and (5) its characteristics must remain stable over time. Furthermore, market segments are assessed as to their overall quality, present growth rate, and potential for future growth.

All five conditions are important because not every market needs to be divided into smaller segments. For example, we would likely find it easy to measure the number of customers in a given age group, such as 20 to 35 and 36 to 50. However, if these two groups are exposed to the same media, respond to the same marketing appeals, and show no differences in behavioral responses in regard to our products or stores, then they are really just one group.

Based on market analysis, J.C. Penney has identified five distinct consumer types for its Women's Division (Traditional, Updated, Conservative, Junior, and Young Junior), representing different lifestyles, fashion attitudes, and merchandise needs. Consumer types have become the focus of eight separate departments in Women's Sportswear and three sub-departments in Women's and Petites, with specific brands targeted toward each type, (*J.C. Penney TODAY*, September 1988).

Internal Environment

A situation analysis of a retailer's internal environment is a self-assessment of company resources, measured relative to resource strengths and competitive weaknesses. These resources may be classified as financial, physical, human,

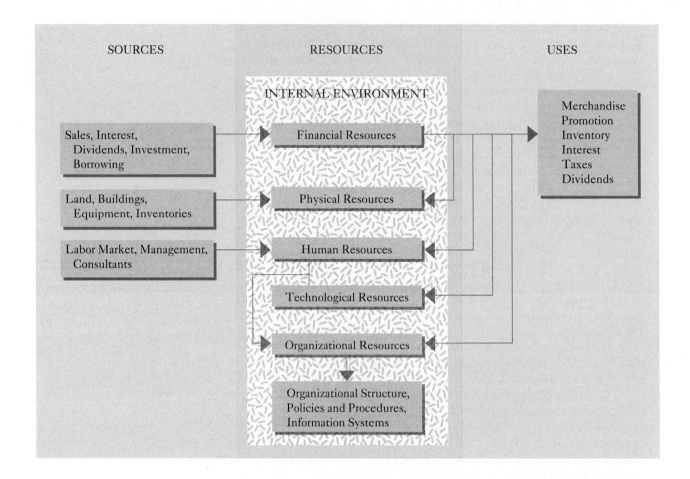

SOURCES   **RESOURCES**   **USES**

INTERNAL ENVIRONMENT

Sales, Interest, Dividends, Investment, Borrowing → Financial Resources

Land, Buildings, Equipment, Inventories → Physical Resources

Labor Market, Management, Consultants → Human Resources

Technological Resources

Organizational Resources

Organizational Structure, Policies and Procedures, Information Systems

Merchandise
Promotion
Inventory
Interest
Taxes
Dividends

Exhibit 2–7
Internal Retail Environment
••••••••••••••••••••••••••••
SOURCE: Parker and Anderson, 1988.

organizational, and technological (Hofer and Schendel, 1978). See Exhibit 2–7.

FINANCIAL RESOURCES   One of a retailer's most important resources is its current financial position. A healthy financial position makes it possible to operate the business on a day-to-day basis. Financial resources include cash and other liquid assets (i.e., those assets, such as marketable securities, that can be converted to cash in a short period of time), the ability to attract new investors and to borrow funds for current or long-term use, and the ability to handle more debt to finance the business. Financial resources are obtained from sales, interest income, dividends, investments, and borrowed money. This information is readily available from a retailer's annual report or income tax records.

PHYSICAL RESOURCES   A retailer's physical assets typically are reported on financial statements as property, plant, and equipment (PPE) and inventory. PPE refers to real estate, stores, warehouses, shopping centers, computers, and other tangible items. **Inventory** is the merchandise on hand in stores and warehouses available for sale to customers during current and future selling periods and is considered by many to be a retailer's most important investment.

HUMAN RESOURCES   A retailer's human resources are found in the talents and abilities of each of its employees. The company's human resource needs are analyzed and compared to the actual contributions made by its top executives and managers at all levels, store managers, merchandisers, buyers, salesforce, and other personnel. Human resources for the organization may be extended to include the expertise of outside specialists, such as management consultants and marketing research firms, as well as members of the board of directors, stockholders, and the like. An even broader interpretation of human resources might include the retailer's relationship with its external publics—loyal customers, cooperative suppliers, supportive government officials—that were included in other aspects of the situation analysis.

ORGANIZATIONAL RESOURCES   Organizational resources are related to the structure, systems, and procedures that make the company "work." Efficient and effective use of these resources often results in cost savings that give the company a low price capability.

Organizational structure involves the division and grouping of various business units, and the degree of centralization or decentralization of operations. For example, as part of its repositioning strategy, the J.C. Penney Company moved its corporate headquarters from New York to Dallas and elected regional presidents for each of the five geographical sections of the United States to maintain regional identities. Likewise, major chains such as K-Mart locate multiple stores in and around large cities to take advantage of the impact and synergy in promotion and distribution.

Systems encompass resources such as computerized information systems and decision-making models. Systems can be sophisticated, high-technology applications or simply a successful manual method of gathering, analyzing, and interpreting data for retail management decisions.

Procedures embody management techniques and operating policies—the rules and regulations for running the business efficiently. This includes job descriptions, work methods, personnel requirements, employee compensation and evaluation, and so forth. Other important resources, although intangible and difficult to measure, are the company's reputation and image and the goodwill it has earned from its customers.

TECHNOLOGY   A manufacturer's technological resources are centered on production equipment, patents, and processes. In contrast, a retailer's technology is more apt to involve information processing and store operations. Examples of these resources are computerized inventory systems, sophisticated cash registers, merchandise handling equipment, physical distribution systems, and accounting systems. A related resource is the ownership of copyrights and trademarks, particularly with the increased popularity of licensing arrangements with manufacturers and private labeling by retailers, to gain competitive advantage with an exclusive image.

In keeping with strategic management definitions, information systems are usually viewed as organizational resources. However, particular proprietary software, such as Sears' RIM System, could be viewed as a technological resource. Furthermore, franchise formats are, in a sense, technological resources because they are entire business formats, which are protected. Perhaps, then, a franchise format is to a business what a patent is to a product, or a copyright is to a computer software developer.

ORGANIZATIONAL STRUCTURE
division and grouping of various business units

SYSTEMS
method of gathering, analyzing, and interpreting data for decision making

PROCEDURES
management techniques and operating policies

Each of these resources can be analyzed to determine its contribution to improved short-term and long-term decisions, operating efficiencies, cost reductions, customer satisfaction, and other benefits. Because there is a price attached to each technological resource, it must deliver a particular advantage to the retailer.

Strategic Objectives and Strategy Definition

Strategic objectives are the retailer's long-range desires, generally stated as financial or marketing goals. Strategic objectives evolve from the company's mission statement and situation analysis. They enable managers to determine strategies for achieving those objectives. **Strategy definition** refers to the set of key decisions made by upper level management that provide the general thrust for the company's efforts in order to accomplish the strategic objectives.

Competitive advantage is based on clearly defining and competing on the basis of several key dimensions such as those identified by Porter (1980):

1. *Cost leadership:* resulting from a company's economies of scale and experience, which permits lower prices to customers
2. *Differentiation:* providing a unique product line or service or delivering it in an innovative manner
3. *Focus:* emphasizing a specific customer market, product or service line, and/or geographical region.

However, there is some concern that Porter measures execution rather than strategy (Parker, 1987). Another set of basic dimensions underlying strategy definition includes customer groups (markets and market segments), customer function (customer needs addressed by a product or product line), and technology (methods used to satisfy customer needs) (Abell and Hammond, 1979). Identification of these three dimensions provides support for management decisions concerning the extent and type of participation by the retailer within the market, product, and method dimensions, as illustrated in Exhibit 2–8. For example, a specialty catalog retailer might pursue a single product line–single market segment strategy of selling health products to 20- to 50- year olds. Another retailer might follow a product specialization strategy, such as selling personal computers and software to all customer segments, using methods such as in-store sales, direct mail, and television shopping networks. A department store retailer might choose to sell a broad range of products to an upscale customer segment.

Not surprisingly, competitive strategy is determined by the nature of the competitors and may be classified according to several typologies, based on a company's position within the industry (Kotler, 1988; Miles and Snow, 1978; Parker, 1987). Competitive strategies include objectives such as market leadership, challenging or following the market leader, defending present market share, or seeking market niches or broad new markets to penetrate.

Strategic objectives and strategy definition are necessarily integrated with the retailer's financial and marketing objectives. Although these were discussed earlier, financial and marketing objectives are examined here in regard to their direct relationship to strategic decisions.

Financial objectives are related to the company's strategic objectives in terms of desired levels of profitability, performance, and operating effi-

STRATEGIC OBJECTIVES
long-range desires of a retailer

STRATEGY DEFINITION
set of key decisions made by upper-level management to direct efforts to achieve objectives.

FINANCIAL OBJECTIVES
desired levels of profitability, performance, and operating efficiencies

MARKETING OBJECTIVES
desired levels of market share, customer satisfaction, recognition, and sales

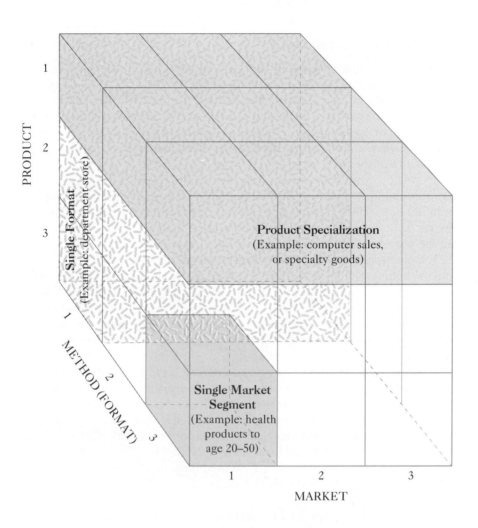

Exhibit 2–8
Strategic Decisions: Markets,
Products, and Methods

ciencies. For example, achieving a desired profitability level affects the quality and price of merchandise sold, the selling methods used, and the choice of location. A retailer's markup or profit margin can be combined with rate of inventory turnover for strategy definition. (See Stern and El-Ansary, 1982, 46–53.) For example, a higher markup is generally associated with higher quality goods sold at higher prices and in more prestigious locations. A high markup may be combined strategically with high inventory turnover (convenience stores) or low turnover goods (fine jewelry), but expenses also will be higher. A low markup may also generate high profits, but through volume sales and strict expense control (discount stores). The retailer's strategy must be defined so that all elements of the retail mix will work together to achieve the company's financial objectives.

Marketing objectives, such as market share, customer satisfaction, or sales, have an impact on strategy definition and the elements of the retail mix that will appeal to an identified target market. Strategic decisions are made about merchandise inventories, pricing, promotional efforts, store locations and interior/exterior store appearance, and service levels. Other strategic marketing objectives may encompass innovative retailing formats, the targeting of specific market segments, or market share growth rate.

Customer satisfaction was the focus of A & P's strategic marketing objective in their "Look at us now" campaign.

Implementation and Tactics

A broad definition of *implement* is "any thing or person used as a means to accomplish some end" or "to provide the means for the carrying out of some plan." At this stage, management answers the questions: Who does what; when, where, and how is it done; and for what specified end? Implementation is differentiated from execution in that implementation is the pencil and paper allocation of resources to the task, and execution is the actual physical performance of the task.

During the **implementation** phase, the retailer commits the required resources and makes them available to achieve strategic objectives. These commitments include the assignment of managers and other personnel to the task, the allocation of funds for salaries, supplies, and needed activities, and the provision of other necessities for carrying out the plan.

It is the strategies of top management that are implemented. Thus, implementation can be viewed as the subsequently more refined allocations of internal resources to plans of action which, when executed, will fulfill the strategic intent. These strategies generally move from long-range development plans (product-market, financial, organizational) to short-range operating (functional) plans to precise (tactical) action plans which guide resource utilization.

As previously described, strategies determine what is to be done. Tactical plans address how to do it. For each strategic decision there are a number of related tactical decisions to be made. **Tactics** are short-range operating or action plans that outline the steps necessary to achieve the long-range strategic plans for product-market, financial, or organizational development. Whereas strategies are planned for several years ahead—often five to ten years—tactical programs typically are planned for a shorter time period of six months to two years. Tactical activities are designed to be implemented at various checkpoints within the long-range strategic plan, in keeping with the retailer's overall objectives. Tactical decisions are primarily involved with specific aspects of the retailing mix: merchandise, location, promotion and advertising, pricing, services, and channels of distribution.

Execution

Execution is the physical performance of the task for which resources were allocated in the implementation phase. A plan without action is a useless fantasy; therefore, this is the phase where the required actions are performed. For example, merchandise is selected, priced, and placed on the selling floor. Store displays, media advertisements, and other promotional tools attract customers' attention. The salesforce is hired, trained, and actively making sales to the store's clientele. Inventory, sales, and credit activities are being performed by accounting personnel. Store operations personnel keep the physical store open and in good working order. Managers are carrying out their decision-making and supervisory responsibilities. These and other activities are expected to produce results in accordance with the strategic plan and objectives.

Evaluation and Control

Strategic objectives are established as a target for performance. Once the plan has been executed, or during the process of execution, performance results are measured against planned performance goals. At this point in the strategic planning and management process, the focus is at the tactical rather than the strategic level. Strategic **evaluation** of objective attainment usually occurs during the strategic situation analysis.

Benchmarks established in the tactical operating plans generally serve as the tests against which actual performance is judged. This logically follows a hierarchy of strategies and plans from the upper to the lower levels of the firm. For example, if a short-term sales goal is not met, operating managers will attempt to bring performance back into line with "fix-it" merchandising or marketing programs. At this point, reevaluating strategy is not necessary just because the retailer did not reach short term sales objectives.

Control mechanisms are devised in order to monitor and measure progress toward reaching these goals and to determine whether that which was implemented is the same as that which was intended. The retailer's information system serves as a method of collecting, storing, and analyzing performance data throughout the execution of the strategic plan. At any point in time managers have available accounting, financial, customer, vendor, and other data for analysis and decision making.

Finally, the strategic planning process would not be complete without feedback to managers for future decisions. The retailer is looking at long-range changes in areas such as retail formats and market behaviors, which may be difficult to predict in the short run. Social and cultural changes are long range, but can be anticipated and prepared for by the retailer. The Great Atlantic & Pacific Tea Company (A&P) has strategically repositioned itself as a leading supermarket chain after several decades of disappointing results. Feedback from previous operating results led to a change in top management, the purchase of strong regional chains to build dominant market share, and the decision to avoid the debt obligations of its highly leveraged competitors. A&P has gained a variety of store formats through its acquisitions and can choose the right one to fit a given market's characteristics, and information systems provide managers with important feedback on their operations (Saporito, 1990).

Types of Decisions

A wide range of decision areas have been described throughout this chapter as they relate to phases of the strategic planning process, particularly in regard to the situation analysis and strategic objectives. Examples of types of decisions to be made at the various management levels are presented within the two broad categories of financial and marketing decisions in Exhibit 2–9.

STRATEGIC PLANNING AND TECHNOLOGY

In retail, as in most areas of business, strategic planning and technology go hand-in-hand. Capon and Glazer (1987) define technology as "know how." Each of the stages in the strategic planning process, from development of a mission statement to evaluation and control of operating results, requires

IMPLEMENTATION
allocation of resources to a retailer's task

TACTICS
short-term operating plans outlining steps necessary to achieve long-term strategic plans

EXECUTION
physical performance of a retailer's task

EVALUATION
measurement of performance results against planned performance goals

Exhibit 2–9
Examples of Strategic Financial and Marketing Decisions in Retail Management

Financial Decisions

Return on Investment	Market Share	Employees	Information Technology
● What level of assets does the company require, and what form should they take (cash, real estate, etc.)?	● What share (percentage) of the existing market should belong to the retail firm in its defined market area(s)?	● What level of financial resources should be committed to personnel as a major operating expense?	● What resources should be committed to the purchase, use and maintenance of information processing systems?
● How much leverage can the company handle, i.e., how much debt can they assume without endangering the business?	● What type and amount of resources should/can be committed to attaining desired market share?	● What impact does this decision have on the ability to provide full service to customers versus self-service, and ultimately on sales and profits?	● What is the value of the quality and timeliness of information that can be provided by such technology?
● What should the targeted return on investment be (as a percenage of investment dollars), and how long should it take to achieve that level of return (hurdle rate)?			

Marketing/Retailing Decisions

Customer Segments	Customer Functions	Technologies
● What customers should the retailer serve? The customer segment determines everything else!	● What customer needs should be satisfied by the retailer? (For example, a shoe retailer must decide what needs for footwear to satisfy with product lines selected, such as athletic activities, work shoes, etc.)	● How will customer needs be satisfied?
● Is there a match between the retailer's offering and retail format and the target customer segment? (Requires customer analysis relative to retail mix decisions: product assortment, price, promotion, place, service, etc.)	● What benefits will the retailer's products and services provide to the customers?	● How will the products and services be created, communicated, and delivered to the customer?
● Which geographic, demographic, and behavioral profiles provide the most opportunity for sales and profits?		● What are the implications of customer demands for service outputs as described by Bucklin? (For example, direct mail and electronic shopping versus traditional in-store sales, ATMs at local banks, etc.)
● With what degree of intensity should an identified segment be pursued by the retailer?		

some form of "know-how." Within this context, technology refers to the stock of relevant knowledge that allows the retailer to develop new techniques for retail strategy and management.

The shift from an industrial society to an information society in the United States is described as one of the key directions for the future (Naisbitt, 1982). The strategic planning process is dependent upon accurate and timely information derived from a reliable data base. Computerized information systems (or well-managed file cabinets) can provide this type of technological assistance for decision making. Retailers operate in a world that is constantly changing, with many unknowns. The environmental uncertainty that is characteristic of retailing can be reduced through the management and interpretation of information obtained by means of technology, in developing successful retail strategies. Consider, for example, point-of-sale scanner technology and its effect on strategic and tactical plans (e.g., assortment decisions, pricing). A more elaborate discussion of this topic is provided later.

Relationship Between Strategic Decisions and Operating Results

From a strategic perspective, a retailer can gain competitive advantage by emphasizing the relationship between strategic decisions and various measures of profitability. A basic objective of management is to utilize the company's resources (financial, physical, human, etc.) as efficiently and effectively as possible to generate a high rate of return.

While profitability can be determined in a number of ways, several ratios are introduced here briefly to illustrate their relationship to strategic planning. Each of these ratios is discussed in greater detail in Chapter 16 within the context of evaluating operating results.

1. **Net profit margin = (Net profit ÷ Net sales):** The amount of change from each dollar of sales received from customers that the retailer can keep for himself (and taxes). In general, a higher markup (profit margin) strategy results in higher profits. The same increase in markup can be achieved in two ways: decreasing costs while holding sales constant or increasing sales while holding costs constant.

2. **Asset turnover ratio = (Net sales ÷ Total assets):** The number of dollars in sales produced by each dollar invested in the total assets of the firm (total value of inventory, land, property, fixtures, etc.). For example, a low cost, "no frills" location and store decor combined with large sales volume will yield higher dollar sales for each dollar invested.

3. **Return on assets = (Net profit ÷ Total assets):** The amount of net profit obtained on all funds invested in assets of the firm (by both creditors and owners). This ratio is a combination of the previous two, providing an evaluation of how well the company's assets are working to produce profits.

4. **Leverage ratio = (Total assets ÷ Net worth):** The relationship between all of the firm's assets and net worth (dollars invested by owners

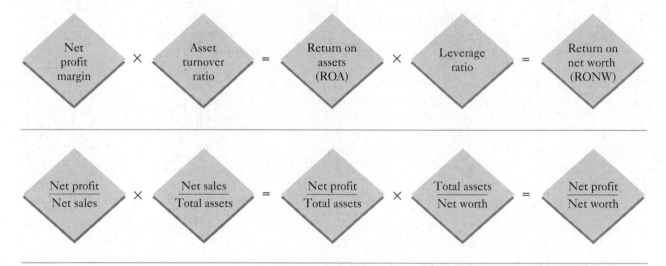

Exhibit 2–10
Strategic Profit Model

only; does not include debt). Expansion of the business through building new stores or acquiring other retailers, for example, generally involves a long-term debt commitment. A highly leveraged firm may be vulnerable to creditors or takeover attempts. The trade-off is the ability to generate sales and profits with assets that are financed by someone else without tying up owners' capital.

5. **Return on Net Worth = (Net profit ÷ Net worth):** The amount of net profit returned to the owners for each dollar of their own money they have invested in the firm. For example, expansion strategies may be limited to the extent of internal funding that is available, if management does not want to grow by incurring debt.

The measures of profitability presented above are combined to form a Strategic Profit Model, as illustrated in Exhibits 2–10 and 2–11. The relationship between retailing strategies and profitability will be explored further in Chapter 16.

SUMMARY

The strategic planning process involves managers at all levels of the organization. At the corporate level, managers are concerned with the financial performance and social behavior of the entire company, and concentrate on the long term. Division and SBU managers are concerned with their specific mission, which is identifiable and separate from other divisions of the corporation. They focus on strategies for competing in their particular industry, geographical area, and/or market segment (i.e., scope issues). Functional (operating) managers are concerned with the organization and interrelationships of the various departments required to carry out the work of each function.

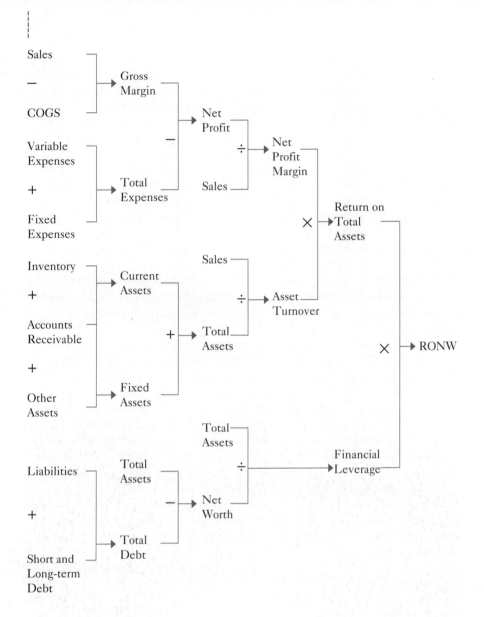

Exhibit 2-11
Model for Financial Ratio
Analysis

They focus on the store level. Department level managers are concerned with merchandise, sales force, services, and other factors to meet customer needs on a daily basis.

The strategic planning process provides retail managers with a clear direction for both long- and short-run efforts. Strategic planning begins with a definition of the retailer's identity in the present and the identity it seeks for the future, i.e., a mission statement. The mission **statement** provides guidelines for the retailer's goals and objectives and helps to determine policies and strategies to achieve the desired results. Performance objectives describe what the firm expects to accomplish over some period of time. Objectives must be realistic, achievable, and measurable. They are stated in terms of financial and marketing goals.

Strategic planning requires knowledge of both the present and the anticipated situation in the retailer's environment. The situation analysis includes an assessment of the firm's external environment, from both a macro- and microenvironmental perspective. The macroenvironment includes economic, legal/political, and social forces that must be dealt with, although they are beyond the immediate control of the retailer. The microenvironment includes those external forces closest to the firm: customer markets, suppliers, competitors, and other businesses. Although the retailer cannot control these forces, it can influence their behavior through strategic management factors. The situation analysis of the retailer's internal environment includes an assessment of company resources: financial, physical, human, organizational, and technology.

Determination of strategic objectives and strategy definition evolve from the company's mission statement and situation analysis. Strategic objectives are the retailer's long-range desires, expressed as financial or marketing goals. Strategy definition refers to upper level management decisions that provide the general thrust for the retailer's efforts in order to accomplish the strategic objectives.

The next stage in the strategic planning process concerns implementation and tactics. Implementation is the allocation of resources to the task, and tactics are short-range operating or action plans consisting of the steps necessary for achieving the long-range strategic plans. Execution is the next stage, differing from implementation in that it is the physical performance of the task for which resources were allocated during the implementation phase. The final stage is evaluation and control, which measures actual performance against intended performance. In addition, feedback from this analysis must be provided to managers as inputs for future decisions.

Finally, the strategic planning process is closely related to the use of technology or "know how" used in carrying out the company's mission. The effect of retailing strategies on performance can be demonstrated by several profitability measures, such as net profit margin, return on assets, and return on net worth.

Questions for Review and Comprehension

1. Briefly describe the organizational levels within larger retail organizations: corporate, divisional (SBU), functional, and departmental. How does the primary focus of decision makers change from one level to another?

2. Define *strategy*. Provide a rationale for strategic planning by retailers, and discuss each of the steps involved in the strategic planning process.

3. Assume that you are opening a new retail business. Write a mission statement that will drive your retail strategy, and explain how this statement can provide a basis for strategic decisions for your store.

4. Determine at least one financial and one marketing objective that are consistent with the mission statement developed in #3.

5. Discuss three purposes of conducting an environmental analysis in strategic planning activities.

6. Based on current events, identify a potential strategic window that has opened for a specialty (or other) retailer. Can you identify a strategic window that has closed, or may be closing, for an established retailer?

7. Discuss the requirements for a comprehensive environmental analysis and state why each should be included.

8. Since the retail environment contains a great deal of uncertainty, it is often necessary to describe the environment in qualitative (subjective) terms. Within this context, discuss the concepts of (a) environmental scope and (b) rate of change, and the issues involved in each dimension.

9. Within the present macroenvironment confronting retailers, give examples of (a) economic, (b) legal/political, (c) sociocultural, (d) demographic, and (e) technical environmental events that can affect retail strategies.

10. Explain why it is necessary for a retailer to analyze the company's internal environment within the strategic planning process. Give examples of the potential effects of (a) financial, (b) physical, (c) human, (d) organizational, and (e) technological resources on the development of retail strategies.

11. Porter identified three key dimensions for competitive advantage: cost leadership, differentiation, and focus. Describe how each of these dimensions (and combination of dimensions) is applied by a familiar retailer. Evaluate the success of these strategies.

12. Distinguish between financial objectives and marketing objectives. Do financial objectives ignore the consumer's interest? Why or why not?

13. Define the (a) implementation, (b) tactics, and (c) execution phases of the strategic planning process. How do tactics differ from strategies?

14. Discuss the importance of incorporating evaluation and control into the strategic planning process. When should the strategic plan be evaluated? Justify your answer.

15. Briefly describe three ratios that can be used to determine a retailer's profitability. How and when does each of these relate to the strategic plan?

References

Abell, Derek F. (1978), "Strategic Windows," *Journal of Marketing* 42, no. 3, 21–26.

Abell, Derek F. and J. S. Hammond (1979), *Strategic Market Planning: Problems and Analytical Approaches*. Englewood Cliffs, N.J.: Prentice-Hall, Inc.

Achrol, Ravi S., Torger Reve, and Louis W. Stern (1983), "The Environment of Marketing Channel Dyads: A Framework for Comparative Analysis." *Journal of Marketing* 47 (Fall), 55–67.

Bucklin, Louis P. (1966), *A Theory of Distribution Channel Structure*. Berkely, Calif.: IBER Special Publications.

Bucklin, Louis P. (1972), *Competition and Evolution in the Distributive Trades*. Englewood Cliffs, N.J.: Prentice-Hall, Inc.

Capon, Noel and Rashi Glazer (1987), "Marketing and Technology: A Strategic Coalignment," *Journal of Marketing* 51 (July), 1–14.

"Customer Focus Generates Sales," (1987), *Banking + Retail*. Columbus, Ohio: Retail Planning Associates, Inc., 1–2.

Digman, Lester A. (1986), *Strategic Management: Concepts, Decisions, Cases*. Plano, Tex.: Business Publications, Inc.

Engledow, Jack L. and R. T. Lenz (1985), "Whatever Happened to Environmental Analysis?" *Long Range Planning* (April) 93–107.

Fuchs, Bernard (1987), "Surviving and Growing In Overstored Markets," Presentation, Survival and Growth In Volatile Economies, 1987 Special Topic Symposium, Sponsored by Center for Retailing Studies, Texas A&M University, Dallas Market Center, Dallas, Tex.: (September 30).

Hofer, Charles W. and Dan Schendel (1978), *Strategy Formulation: Analytical Concepts*. St. Paul, Minn.: West Publishing Co. (Cited in Digman, Ch. 5).

Hume, Scott (1991), "McDonald's Takes Nip at Supermarkets," *Advertising Age* (March 11), 1, 38.

Hyatt, Joshua (1989), "Buy the Buy," *INC. 500* (December), 127.

Jain, Subhash C. (1990), *Marketing Planning and Strategy*, 3d ed. Cincinnati, Ohio: South-Western Publishing Co.

J. C. Penney Co., Annual Reports.

J. C. Penney Co., Company management literature, (Positioning Statement, The Penney Idea) 1988; *J. C. Penney TODAY*, September 1988.

Jurkovich, Ray (1974). "A Core Typology of Organizational Environments," *Administrative Science Quarterly*, 19, 380–394.

Kotler, Philip (1984), *Marketing Management: Analysis, Planning and Control*, 5th ed., Englewood Cliffs, N.J.: Prentice-Hall, Inc.

Kotler, Philip (1988), *Marketing Management: Analysis, Planning, Implementation, and Control*, 6th ed., Englewood Cliffs, N.J.: Prentice-Hall, Inc.

Miles, Raymond E. and Charles C. Snow (1978), *Organizational Strategy, Structure, and Process*. New York: McGraw-Hill Book Company.

Naisbitt, John (1982), *Megatrends*, New York: Warner Books, Inc.

Parker, Thomas H. (1987), *Toward Integrating Strategic Process and Strategy Content: Conceptual Foundations and Empirical Results from Commercial Banking*. Lincoln, Neb.: University of Nebraska–Lincoln, A Dissertation (UMI no. 8806149).

Porter, Michael E. (1980), *Competitive Strategy*. New York: The Free Press.

Porter, Michael E. (1979), "How Competitive Forces Shape Strategy," *Harvard Business Review* (March–April), 137–145.

Saporito, Bill (1990), "A&P: Grandma Turns a Killer," *Fortune* (April 23), 207, 210, 211, 214.

Standard & Poor's Industry Surveys (1989), "Retailing: Current Analysis," (January 11), R61–R64.

Stern, Louis W. and Adel El-Ansary (1982), *Marketing Channels*, 2d ed., Englewood Cliffs, N.J.: Prentice-Hall, Inc.

Toffler, Alvin (1970), *Future Shock*. New York: Bantam Books, Inc.

_____ (1980), *The Third Wave*. New York: Bantam Books, Inc.

Walker, Orville C., Jr. and Robert W. Ruekert (1987), "Marketing's Role in the Implementation of Business Strategies: A Critical Review and Conceptual Framework," *Journal of Marketing* 51 (July), 15–33.

Warren, Kirby E. (1966), *Long Range Planning: The Executive Viewpoint*. Englewood Cliffs, N.J.: Prentice-Hall, Inc., 6. Quoted in Jain, Subhash C. (1990), *Marketing Planning and Strategy*. 3d. ed., Cincinnati, Ohio: South-Western Publishing Co.

J. C. Penney: Strategic Planning and Repositioning

"J.C. Penney Takes Top Spot" in *STORES'* ranking of the exclusive Top 100 Department Store chains and companies. This recognition of excellence among national department stores is testimony to the success of Penney's ongoing repositioning strategy. Penney's achieved sales of nearly $14.5 billion in 1,328 stores and catalog operations in 1989, outdistancing *STORES'* number 2 department store chain by $10.6 billion.

> *. . . In claiming the top spot in STORES' 1990 Top 100 listing, J.C. Penney has completed a nearly decade-long transformation from mass merchandiser to a department store with an emphasis on fashion and tightly-edited non-apparel merchandise classifications. Penney has also greatly increased the amount of branded merchandise in its stores, to the extent that private label goods now account for less than half the volume in most departments.*
>
> *During its transformation, Penney moved its headquarters from midtown Manhattan to the plains of north Texas. Recently the company has been scouting retail locations in the New York City area including, reportedly, the former B. Altman flagship location on Fifth Avenue and 34th Street, and has just opened a unit in Queens Center, a part of New York City. Penney, in general, has been placing more of its stores in regional shopping centers in metropolitan markets while cutting back on the number of units in nonmetropolitan areas or in satellite locations within metropolitan areas.*
>
> *Penney's fashion awareness has included investing in small specialty retailers, such as the Alcott & Andrews specialty chain that was very hot for a few years before collapsing into bankruptcy last year. Penney has been more successful with its Units operation, with more than 200 stores selling knit separates for women. This chain has expanded to Canada, Mexico and the United Kingdom. Earlier this year, the Penney subsidiary entered into an agreement with the Miki Corporation to open a hundred Units stores in Japan. It is also experimenting with a new chain, Amanda Fielding, aimed at career women in their 30's and older. . . . Penney's overwhelming number of stores and volume—approximately 20 percent of the entire Top 100's aggregate sales—forced Mervyn's down to the second slot, even as the latter was staging a successful turnaround. (Schulz, 1990, pp. 9–11)*

(See Exhibit 2A–1 for a complete listing of *STORES'* Top 100 Department Stores and a description of the criteria for inclusion on this list.)

The ongoing repositioning strategy implemented by the J. C. Penney Company over the past decade provides an outstanding example of the dynamic and vital nature of strategic planning. While the strategic planning process can be quite complex and decisions at the various stages in this process tend to be interrelated, an attempt is made in the following sections to categorize repositioning decisions and actions into the various elements of the strategic planning process. Discussion is simplified for the sake of illustration, but the reader is challenged to think about the types of information, analysis, and activities that lie behind each illustration.

Exhibit 2A–1
The Top 100 Department Store
Divisions:
Ranking for 1989
••••••••••••••••••••••••••••••

Rank	Company/Division (Headquarters)	Affil.	Units	Sq.Ft. (000)	Volume (000,000)
1.	J. C. Penney (Dallas, Tex.)	(Ind)	1,325	112,800	$14,469
2.	Mervyn's (Hayward, Calif.)	(DH)	221	17,486	3,858
3.	Macy's Northeast (New York)[a]	(RHM)	46	14,937	3,350
4.	Dilllard's (Little Rock, Ark.)[b]	(Ind)	146	20,898	2,769
5.	Nordstrom (Seattle)	(Ind)	59	6,890	2,671.1
6.	Macy's South (Atlanta)[a]	(RHM)	48	10,138	1,875
7.	Dayton Hudson (Minneapolis)	(DH)	37	7,711	1,801
8.	Macy's California[a] (San Francisco)	(RHM)	25	5,846	1,545
9.	Bloomingdale's (New York)	(Cmp)	17	4,518	1,295
10.	Saks Fifth Avenue (New York)	(Bat)	45	N/A	1,244
11.	Neiman Marcus (Dallas)[a]	(NMG)	22	3,230	1,230
12.	The Broadway (Los Angeles)[a]	(CHH)	43	7,459	1,195
13.	Foley's (Houston)	(May)	35	7,735	1,121
14.	Marshall Field (Chicago)	(Bat)	25	7,392	1,090.7
15.	Lord & Taylor (New York)	(May)	47	6,244	1,034
16.	Lazarus (Cincinnati)	(Cmp)	43	8,265	975
17.	May Co. (Los Angeles)	(May)	35	6,470	954
18.	Rich's (Atlanta)	(Cmp)	26	6,216	920
19.	Woodward & Lothrop (Washington, D.C.)	(Ind.)	32	6,533	913
20.	Burdine's (Miami)	(Cmp)	30	5,254	905
21.	Hecht's (Washington, D.C.)	(May)	22	3,785	829
22.	Abraham & Straus (Brooklyn)	(Cmp)	15`	5,590	775
23.	Carson Pirie Scott (Chicago)	(Pab)	36	4,025	770
24.	Kaufmann's (Pittsburgh)	(May)	23	4,249	753
24	Robinson's (Los Angeles)	(May)	29	4,787	753
26.	Emporium-Capwell (San Francisco)[a]	(CHH)	22	5,260	750
27.	Kohl's (Menomonee Falls, Wis.)	(Ind)	70	4,450	750
28.	Jordan Marsh New England (Boston)	(Cmp)	26	5,054	730
29.	Stern's (Paramus, N.J.)	(Cmp)	27	5,028	710
30.	Maas Bros./Jordan Marsh (Tampa)	(Cmp)	38	5,895	660
31.	Hess's (Allentown, Pa.)	(CAC)	76	5,412	616.9
32.	The Bon (Seattle)	(Cmp)	39	4,581	605
33.	Strawbridge & Clothier (Philadelphia)	(Ind)	13	2,900	575
34.	Famous-Barr (St. Louis)	(May)	17	3,839	508
35.	Filene's (Boston)	(May)	18	2,309	484
36.	Maison Blanche (Baton Rouge)	(Ind)	22	2,316	468
37.	Boscov's (Reading, Pa.)	(Ind)	16	2,330	450
37.	P. A. Bergner (Milwaukee)	(Pab)	29	2,925	450
39.	I. Magnin (San Francisco)[a]	(RHM)	30	2,235	440
40.	May Co. (Cleveland)	(May)	16	3,105	436
41.	Alexander's (New York)[d]	(Ind)	11	2,899	426
41.	G. Fox (Hartford, Conn.)	(May)	11	2,016	426
43.	Thalhimer's (Richmond, Va.)[c]	(CHH)	26	2,865	415
44.	Elder-Beerman (Dayton)	(Ind)	44	3,980	414.6
45.	McAlpin (Cincinnati)	(MS)	9	1,575	395
46.	Jacobson's (Jackson, Mich.)	(Ind)	24	2,391	394.2
47.	McRae's (Jackson, Miss.)	(Ind)	28	2,371	386
48.	Gayfer's (Mobile, Ala.)	(MS)	12	1,825	380
49.	Liberty House (Honolulu)	(Ind)	9	866	360
50.	Higbee's (Cleveland)	(DDeB)	12	2,766	345
51.	L.S. Ayres (Indianapolis)	(May)	14	2,376	328
52.	Younkers (Des Moines)	(Eoff)	36	2,456	316.7
53.	Parisian (Birmingham)	(Ind)	20	1,502	316
54.	Ivey's (Charlotte, N.C.)	(Bat)	23	2,611	310.2
55.	May D & F (Denver)	(May)	13	2,009	297
56.	Castner-Knott (Nashville)	(MS)	11	1,395	280
56.	D. H. Holmes (New Orleans)	(Dill)	16	2,590	280
58.	Meier & Frank (Portland)	(May)	8	1,932	274
59.	Weinstock's (Sacramento)[c]	(CHH)	12	1,935	265

Rank	Company/Division (Headquarters)	Affil.	Units	Sq.Ft. (000)	Volume (000,000)
59.	Jones Store (Kansas City)	(MS)	8	1,790	265
61.	Joseph Horne (Pittsburgh)	(Ind)	16	2,270	263
62.	Prange's (Sheboygan, Wis.)	(Ind)	23	2,338	252
63.	Frederick & Nelson (Seattle)	(Ind)	17	2,450	250
64.	Joslin's (Denver)	(MS)	11	1,455	240
65.	Gottschalk's (Fresno, Calif.)	(Ind)	20	1,761	236.8
66.	The Broadway Southwest (Phoenix)[c]	(CHH)	11	1,744	235
67.	Steinbach's (White Plains, N.Y.)	(Amc)	30	1,210	210
68.	Gayfer's (Montgomery, Ala.)	(MS)	6	975	200
69.	Bacon's/Roots (Louisville)	(MS)	8	950	190
70.	ZCMI (Salt Lake City)	(Ind)	13	1,618	188.1
71.	Bergdorf Goodman (New York)[c]	(NMG)	1	250	185
72.	Beall's Florida (Bradenston)	(Ind)	49	N/A	175.2
73.	S. Grumbacher (York, Pa.)	(Ind)	25	N/A	170
74.	Bonwit Teller (New York)	(Hook)	16	1,196	168
75.	J.B. White (Augusta, Ga.)	(MS)	7	540	165
76.	G.R. Herberger (St. Cloud, Minn.)	(Ind)	30	N/A	150
77.	Peebles (Richmond, Va.)	(Ind)	48	1,203	149
78.	Adam Meldrum Anderson (Buffalo)	(Ind)	10	1,185	139.7
79.	Stone & Thomas (Wheeling, W.Va.)	(Ind)	20	1,170	127
80.	Lion (Toledo, Ohio)	(MS)	3	655	125
81.	Buffum's (Long Beach, Calif.)	(Ind)	16	1,108	120
82.	Dunlap (Fort Worth)	(Ind)	35	N/A	115
83.	Crowley-Milner (Detroit)	(Ind)	11	773	113.6
84.	Harris' (San Bernardino, Calif.)	(Ind)	6	534	103.0
85.	Ira Watson (Nashville, Tenn.)	(Ind)	26	N/A	100
86.	Steigers (Springfield, Mass.)	(Ind)	9	N/A	95
87.	Proffitt's (Alcoa, Tenn.)	(Ind)	11	689	94.8
88.	Sage-Allen (Hartford)	(Ind)	13	560	87.6
89.	Kline Brothers (Cleveland)	(Ind)	35	850	79.6
90.	Hennessey's (Billings, Mont.)	(MS)	5	660	75
90.	Spurgeon Mercantile (Chicago)	(Ind)	85	N/A	75
92.	McCurdy & Co. (Rochester)	(Ind)	7	720	70
93.	Uhlman's (Bowling Green, Ohio)	(Ind)	32	450	52.5
94.	Carlisle's (Ashtabula, Ohio)	(Ind)	10	385	49.2
95.	Boston Store (Carson, Calif.)	(Ind)	4	N/A	41
96.	Dey's (Syracuse)	(Ind)	4	446	40
97.	Swezey's (Patchogue, N.Y.)	(Ind)	3	120	38
98.	Watt & Shand (Lancaster, Pa.)	(Ind)	2	268	35
99.	The Globe (Scranton, Pa.)	(Ind)	1	140	26
100.	H. Leh & Co. (Allentown, Pa.)	(Ind)	4	290	23.7

STORES' Top 100 Department Store divisions and companies includes traditional department stores and multi-department soft goods stores (or specialized department stores) with a fashion orientation, full mark-up policy, carrying nationally branded merchandise and operating in stores large enough to be shopping center anchors. Excluded are general merchandise chains, catalog chains, discount stores, mass merchandisers and specialty stores.

Figures on the chart are either provided by the companies or are estimates based on *STORES'* research and consultation with retail industry and financial sources.

STORES has made every effort to exclude revenues other than from department store operations. Excluded are sales (or estimated sales) generated by discount, specialty or other operations. Leased department and direct marketing sales, however, are generally included.

[a]—For 52-week period ended January 27, 1990
[b]—Does not include D.H. Holmes, acquired May 9, 1989
[c]—For 53-week period ended February 3, 1990
[d]—For 52-week period ended February 10, 1990
N/A—Not available

Affiliate Code
Amc, Amcena, Bat, Batus Inc.; CAC, Crown American Corp.; CHH, Carter Hawley Hale; Cmp, Campeau Corp.; DDeB, Dillard and DeBartolo; DH, Dayton Hudson; Dill, Dillard; Eoff, Equitable of Iowa; Hook, L.J. Hooker; Ind, Independent, May, May Department Stores; MS, Mercantile Stores; NMG, Neiman Marcus Group; Pab, P.A. Bergner, RHM, R.H. Macy & Co

SOURCE: Reprinted from Schultz, David P. (1990), "J.C. Penney Takes Top Spot," *STORES* (July), 9–12.

MISSION STATEMENT

The mission statement defines the identity and purpose of the business for the present and in the future. It provides guidelines for development of goals and objectives, and for the policies and strategies to achieve objectives. Penney's mission statement is reflected in the J.C. Penney Positioning Statement and in The Penney Idea. See Exhibits 2–4 and 2–5 in the main chapter 2 text. The key elements of Penney's mission statement are:

- To serve the public as nearly as possible to its complete satisfaction, particularly in meeting target consumer expectations.
- To give the customer appealing selections of good quality, fashionable merchandise, with recognizable value.
- To instill confidence in consumers that in all of its actions, Penney's is competent, fair, and of the highest integrity.
- To live by the principle of the Golden Rule: "Does it square with what is right and just?"

While Penney's fundamental mission has not changed significantly since 1902, the company has successfully changed its strategic thrust in an attempt to meet the challenge of satisfying the changing consumer. A new positioning statement was created in January 1990 to reflect this new strategy. (See Exhibit 2–4 in the main Chapter 2 text). As one Penney executive expressed it:

> *After 86 years, Penney's has seen many changes. And, we know that the Penney store of today won't be the same as the Penney store of the year 2000. We look forward to the change. It's what makes retailing so exciting and rewarding. The challenge is to incorporate new ideas without giving up ongoing values.*
>
> *As we change and grow, we must keep in mind that we serve several groups of constituents: customers, stockholders, associates, and communities. So we must stick to the fundamental values that we have as a company. From the beginning, we have had the company golden rule and the concept of "doing what is right and just."*
>
> *Secret of success—personal and corporate:*
> - *Always go the second mile.*
> - *Do more than is expected of you.*   *(Miller, 1988)*

PERFORMANCE OBJECTIVES

Performance objectives indicate what is to be accomplished over a specified time period, both for the long term and for the short term. Financial objectives are stated in terms such as sales, profit, or return-on-investment. Marketing objectives are stated in terms such as market share or market growth. Objectives are established for each organizational level and each SBU (e.g., division, department). Individual goals must be compatible and objectives at one level must support those at the next level, and so forth.

Penney's corporate financial performance objectives are straightforward. Financial objectives are set forth within the framework of the company's mission and business objectives. The company aims

> *to be an attractive investment for our shareholders and creditors, and for this purpose:*
>
> *a. To achieve a return on equity in the top quartile of major competitors for the Company as a whole and for each operating division.*

At the present time, this will require us to achieve an after-tax return on equity of a minimum of 16 percent.
b. To achieve consistent growth in earnings at a rate required to meet or exceed the return on equity objective.
To achieve the minimum 16 percent ROE will require a consistent earnings growth rate of 11 percent.
c. To maintain consistency and growth in dividend payout through increased earnings.
At the current time our objective is a payout in the range of 35–40 percent of net income.
d. To maintain a capital structure that will assure continuing access to financial markets so that we can, at reasonable cost, provide for future resource needs and capitalize on attractive opportunities for growth.
Specifically, we will maintain a minimum of A1/A+ ratings (Moody's/Standard & Poor's) on senior long-term debt and the A1/P1 ratings on commercial paper.
e. To ensure that financing objectives governing the amount, composition, and cost of capital are consistent with and support other corporate objectives.
All performance objectives will be reviewed at least once a year and, if necessary, revised to reflect the results required to be in the top quartile of our major competitors.

Based on a statement to stockholders in the company's 1989 Annual Report, J. C. Penney "made significant progress in 1989 as measured by four key indicators of corporate performance: sales, income from operations, net income per share, and return on stockholders' equity." The actual results could be measured against predetermined target performance objectives for each of these criteria, stated in terms of specific dollars, percentages, or ratios. For example, *hypothetical* criteria stated in dollar amounts might have been:

	Target	**Actual (*1989 Annual Report*)**
Sales	$ 15 billion	$ 16.1 billion (including drugstore and nonstore catalog sales)
Net income	$750 million	$802 million
Earnings per share	$ 6.25	$ 6.31 (primary earnings per share)
Quarterly dividends	$ 2.20	$ 2.24 (per common share)

In a typical situation, objectives would be broken down into in-store sales, catalog sales, sales by store, by department, and other strategic business units (SBUs). Target market growth rate, market share dominance, profitability, and productivity ratios would also be established.

ENVIRONMENTAL SITUATION ANALYSIS

All retailers need to monitor their internal and external environments constantly in order to anticipate and respond to change. Environmental analysis is used to identify opportunities and threats in the external environment, as well as to identify internal resource strengths and weaknesses. The following statements made by J. C. Penney executives reflect the results of selected environmental analysis on the company's repositioning decision.

Consumer shopping behavior:

> *Our research reveals that 72 percent of all women's apparel and 68 percent of men's is purchased in [regional] malls. Conversely, regional malls account for only about 38 percent of home lines sales—and for categories like paint and hardware, it's less than 20 percent.*
>
> *As income rises, people buy more of their apparel in specialty and department stores. At the high end of the income scale, families spend 82 percent of their apparel dollars in specialty and department stores, and only 18 percent in price-oriented stores. But even low-income families spend 68 percent of their apparel dollars in specialty and department stores—so no matter what income group you're talking about, most of the apparel dollars are spent in mall environments. (Howell, 1989)*

Consumer shopping motives

Shopping motives include elements of value and the customer's ego-involvement.

> *Everyone is looking for value. But how do you define it? The definition of value depends on who you are and what you are buying.*
> • *People tend to shop for goods in the lowest cost environment acceptable for the type of goods they are buying.*
> • *But, depending what you are buying, you may have more or less* ego-involvement *in the purchase. The ego-involvement is not the same for all goods. The type of environment that is acceptable is influenced by the ego-portion of the purchase.*

For example, a customer may have a winter coat that provides sufficient warmth, but may want a new one to be more fashionable—and may want to make fashion purchases in a nice store with a good assortment to choose from. (Miller, 1988)

Considering the increasing influence of ego, the following factors are expected to influence a customer's choice of store: quality, price, selection, look of merchandise (fashionability), ambiance, merchandise mix, location, and customer service. The relative importance of these characteristics varies among demographic groups and with economic and social conditions. The relative importance also varies with the type of merchandise purchased. The value of a product is influenced by both intrinsic factors (objective quality/performance of merchandise) and extrinsic factors (designer labels, ambiance, etc., that satisfy the ego-side of the purchase). (Miller, 1988)

Consumer demand

Major influences on total consumer demand have been identified as (1) changes in the economy and (2) changing demographics, including household income. Some highlights of these two aspects of the situation analysis are listed below.

Changes in the economy   Major economic changes occurred during the 1970s and 1980s, including higher inflation and lower productivity due to pressure to create jobs for baby-boomers, the oil crisis, costly environmental clean-up efforts, and less governmental impact on business. The 1990s are expected to be a period of reasonable growth with moderate inflation, a more productive labor force, and increased consumer confidence and willingness to spend.

Growth in personal consumption expenditures, which make up about two-thirds of the economy, outpaced the overall growth of the economy. (Miller, 1988)

Changes in demographics From 1988 to 1998, the total population is expected to increase from 245 million to 265 million, or less than 1 percent a year. Children and older Americans are groups of approximately the same size and will maintain the same relative position in the population. The number of young adults between the ages of 15–34 will decline, resulting in fewer new households. By 1988 the 80 million baby boomers who make up 30 percent of the population will be in the 35–54 age group—a huge middle-aged working population.

The changing age composition of the population will affect growth in average household income. The median household income is expected to increase from $28,000 (1988) to $33,000 in 1998. The number of households earning under $20,000 will remain about the same, but the number of households earning over $20,000 will increase, with the greatest increases in those earning over $60,000. (Miller, 1988)

Effect of changes in economy and demographics on shopping behavior Factors resulting from the situation analysis to consider in developing strategy include working women (time constraints, customer service); housing starts (upgrading existing home rather than building a new home); increasing median age (economy less driven by needs of young families, children, and teenagers); and more disposable income due to growth of 35–54 year old group (discretionary income rises with age). (Miller, 1988)

Location and shopping environment:

> *We are located where the action is . . . as most of our prime real estate—nearly 100 million square feet—is already in regional malls. This is an enormous competitive advantage—an advantage that . . . is difficult if not impossible to replicate. (Howell, 1989)*
>
> *Over the past 20 years, total shopping center space per person has grown 225 percent. In 1965, we had 3 1/2 square feet of shopping center space per person; today, it stands at 12 square feet, giving today's consumer a tremendous array of shopping options. During the same period, J.C. Penney's space per person has grown 150 percent—to about 1/2 square foot for every American. . . . As a result of growth in retail space and disposable income— retailing (is) very competitive . . . with more emphasis on differentiation and specialization.*
>
> *. . . [T]here has been a shift from the general to the specific—and it is changing (traditional retailing). Those who [are] average are losing, while those with highly focused, dominant merchandise formats are winning . . . there are two main shopping environments: those with shopping carts and those without shopping carts. The grocery cart group . . . is composed of retailers like discount stores, warehouse stores, and hypermarkets . . . located primarily in strip shopping centers or free-standing stores, and sell mainly commodity [non-ego-satisfying] merchandise. It's a self-service, shopping cart environment—with large check out areas. The primary emphasis is on price. The second environment . . . is composed of specialty stores, specialty department stores, and*

department stores. These are located primarily in the large regional shopping malls, and generally provide a high level of customer service. With respect to merchandise, the emphasis is on ego-sensitive, fashionable apparel.

The gap is widening between these two formats—and retailers are being forced to choose which market they want to serve. While you would generally say that these two formats separate income groups, they really separate merchandise. Most apparel, in fact, is bought in regional comparison environments— department stores and specialty stores. . . . Department store-type merchandise (DSTM) . . . includes sales of general merchandise stores; apparel and accessory stores; furniture, home furnishings and equipment stores; and miscellaneous stores such as sporting goods, books and toys.

. . . [A]s household income rises, people buy more of their apparel in specialty and department stores. Even low income families buy only 32 percent of their clothing in discount stores, and 68 percent in specialty and department stores. At the high end of the income scale, the regional comparison environment is even more dominant. These people buy 82 percent of their apparel in specialty and department stores, and only 18 percent in discount stores. There's a great deal of ego-sensitivity in any *apparel.*

As a result of these trends, the traditional middle-of-the-road department stores with broad assortments of general merchandise are caught in the middle. Thirty years ago they dominated the retail scene when they matched up naturally with a strong middle income America. Today, however, it's very difficult for any one retail format to be broadly effective in all income groups—particularly in more ego-sensitive merchandise categories. The more affluent and more demanding consumers of today want something more from their stores.

. . . These realities have had a profound effect on J.C. Penney's strategies. Because J.C. Penney occupies primarily multi-level space in the regional malls, the low-cost shopping cart format is not an option for us. We must compete as a department store. (Miller, 1988)

Internal environmental analysis
(resource strengths and weaknesses):
Focus

To meet the needs and expectations of the American consumer, we made the following strategic changes:
• In 1983, we eliminated major appliances, paint & hardware, lawn & garden; automotive; and restaurants from our stores. Combined, these discontinued lines represented approximately 1 billion dollars in sales;
• In that same year, we also launched our store modernization program, with its focus on improving the shopping environment;
• And last year we discontinued home electronics, hard sporting goods, and photography. They represented over 500 million dollars in annual sales. [Timing (is) critical]. (Howell, 1989)

Change in floor space allocation 1982 vs. 1989
[Exhibit 2A–2 shows] . . . [T]he way a typical metro store looked prior to our line eliminations in 1983. Women's, men's, and children's were usually all on the same floor—and often shared space with the fabric shop. Home and

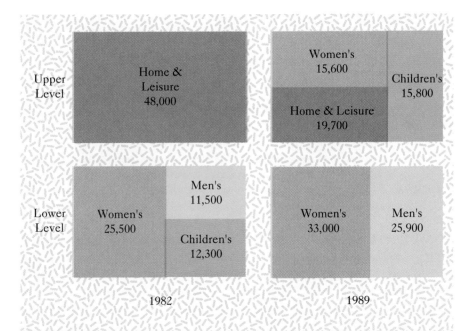

Exhibit 2A–2
Change in Floor Space
Allocation—Typical Metro Store

SOURCE: J.C. Penney Company
literature

leisure generally occupied a whole floor by itself—and included major appliances, paint & hardware, home electronics, furniture, photography, and housewares, as well as soft home furnishings. Many stores also had automotive centers and restaurants, and we were supporting a large product service organization. This wide array of businesses required an enormous amount of management time, energy, and training. . . . (Howell, 1989)

Competitive advantage in reaching catalog sales goal

Our strongest competitive advantage in reaching toward that goal (#1 in catalog sales) is our state-of-the-art infrastructure. Our systems and facilities are second to none in the industry. In fact, our catalog division today operates the largest privately held telecommunication network in the country. We are already clearly a leader from a volume growth standpoint and a service standpoint. We have tied together retail and catalog in such a way that the consumer thinks of them as one . . .

. . . Our real competitive advantage (in catalog sales) is in technology. We believe our on-line catalog reservation system is the best in the industry. Most of our customers are assured with one phone call that they will receive the item they want—and exactly when and where it can be picked up. (Howell, 1989)

STRATEGIC OBJECTIVES AND STRATEGY DEFINITION

Strategic objectives
Strategic objectives are long-range financial and marketing goals derived from the company mission statement and situation analysis.

J. C. Penney Catalog:

Today, we're #2 in sales in the 50 billion dollar catalog and direct mail indus-
try—but we've set our sights on becoming #1 sometime during the first half of
the '90s.

We planned [the 1989 Spring and Summer Catalog] . . . at a double-
digit increase over last year's book—and it's currently tracking over plan.
Every merchandise category is strong—and this momentum should continue
throughout the first half and into the Fall book. In addition to the big Spring
and Fall books, there's excellent growth potential in our specialty catalogs.

[The] . . . catalog has had 3 consecutive years of double-digit sales
increases—and our five-year projections call for that to continue. Clearly, J.C.
Penney Catalog continues to be an area of great strength. (Howell, 1989)

Overall objective:

. . . [W]e have the opportunity to concentrate our time and effort on what we
do best—make full use (of) our talents and skills as merchants, *which equates*
to achieving our key objective of improving our stores' sales per square foot.

One of our company's great strengths is that virtually all of our policy
makers are *merchants, and have devoted their professional careers to retail and*
catalog. Our goal is to capitalize on that strength—and out-merchandise the
other merchants across the street and down the mall. We're positioned to do
it . . . and we're confident that we can *do it. (Howell, 1989)*

Our objective for the J.C. Penney store is: to be perceived as the number
one choice in each community for apparel and home furnishings for middle to
middle-upper income America. This objective incorporates our target consumers
and what they want to buy in the malls. That's why we changed our merchan-
dise offering and are devoting more space to apparel. It will enable us to serve
our customer better. (Miller, 1988)

Strategy definition

The strategy definition consists of a set of key decisions made by upper level
management that provide the general thrust for the company's efforts to
reach its strategic objectives. Together the strategic objectives and strategy
definition are expected to provide a sustainable competitive advantage for
the firm.

Department store and fashion retailing positioning perspective:

We have made a full commitment to serving the fashion needs of middle and
middle/upper income consumers. We are their national department
store. . . . We have from a strategic point of view chosen to compete with depart-
ment stores!! (Howell, 1989)

. . . [W]e are also exploring other opportunities in the retail market
place. The growth in the middle-aged and upper-income groups mean there are
exceptional opportunities in apparel and home furnishings, compared to an
emphasis more on basics by younger less affluent households. These groups
should be more interested in specialty stores and good service; price will be less
dominant as the value they are seeking from merchants. Therefore, we have
formed two specialty retailing groups: apparel-related and home decorating
(Portfolio, MixIt, Tezio, In Detail, Kinder Harris, Units). (Miller, 1988)

(Note that a decision was made to close Tezio and In Detail and to open a new concept, Amanda Fielding, since 1988. Currently all specialty businesses report to one specialty retailing group head.)

Merchandise mix changes:

During the 1960s, when we first moved out of the cities and towns and into the suburbs, we tried to copy the typical middle-America merchandising format—to be a major one-stop shopping store carrying a full line of merchandise from apparel to appliances and automotive. As this format grew to over 50 percent of our business, our profit margins began to suffer. In the mid-70s we discovered what we just looked at—people were going more and more to low-cost environments for their hard goods. We saw that we had to re-focus our store on lines that require more ambiance. Internally, we also looked to the profitability of our individual lines. As a result, in 1983, we eliminated automotive, major appliances and other hard lines to allow us to concentrate more on Women's and Men's apparel. This year, we further streamlined our mix and eliminated home electronics, photography, and hard sporting goods. Our merchandise mix is continuing to evolve, with more concentration on apparel and soft home furnishings. (Miller, 1988)

Consumer focus:

As we changed and updated our merchandise mix and store format, we also found that it was necessary to have a much clearer picture of our target customer. We needed to know who we want to attract and what their needs are. Just as we focused our merchandise assortment, we needed to focus on our target customer. We are targeting the middle to middle/upper income households. . . . They account for 50 percent of all households, 60 percent of total personal income and 60 percent of total department-store-type merchandise expenditures . . . 40 percent of all households account for only 20 percent of total DSTM expenditures . . . if you believe in stratification of the market, you've got to decide who you're going to serve—and our sights are now set squarely on the middle to middle-upper income segment.

To be successful, you have to be the first choice—to be known as the best. Therefore, we have decided to be in fewer businesses and to be dominant in the ones in which we compete. (Miller, 1988)

We have clearly identified our target customer and focused our merchandise mix on what she wants. We have also re-designed our store to match the shopping preferences of our target customers. Today's customer is very specialty store oriented. Our strategy, therefore, is to turn the Penney store into a "mini mall" of "stores within the large store," each geared to the apparel and lifestyle needs of a target consumer segment. Our in-store shops are arranged by lifestyle more than by any other factor. We have specific branding strategies, visual merchandising, and advertising for each "shop." (Miller, 1988)

In a message to the stockholders in the company's 1987 annual report, Chairman W. R. Howell states:

Significant progress in the implementation of J.C. Penney's repositioning strategies was achieved in 1987. Our merchandise organization was restructured during the year, establishing four business groups with each focusing on a major merchandise category: women's, men's, children's and home furnishings. This new structure brings together the buying and marketing functions for each of these merchandise categories, and has as its goal improved coordination, team decision-making, and strengthened communication lines.

In a variety of other management speeches, additional points have been made that demonstrate Penney's focus on the consumer. After nearly two years of study and research, in 1988, the Women's Division identified five different consumer types to be targeted. These five consumer types are the Traditional, Updated, Conservative, Junior and Young Junior. Each type has a different lifestyle, a different fashion attitude, a different demographic profile, and different merchandise needs. Now, eight separate departments in Women's Sportswear and three sub-departments in Women's and Petites focus on these five distinct consumer types. In effect, each department forms a separate "store" within the larger J.C. Penney store. The new focus on target consumers has reshaped the Women's Sportswear department from the ground up. Its merchandising, branding and buying structures have all changed to keep in step with today's woman.

> *"Our new shopping environment is designed to help today's woman shop more quickly and conveniently," says David F. Miller, the then Vice Chairman and Chief Operating Officer of J.C. Penney Stores and Catalog. "She will be able to tell at a glance—through labels, the decor, the merchandise, and other elements—which department fits her lifestyle and features her type of merchandise. She will feel at home there because it will be 'her' store."*

Marshall Beere, co-director of Merchandise for the Women's Division, explains the concept of departmentalization. "Departmentalization represents a more consumer driven approach to the way we offer our merchandise. It involves the arrangement of merchandise in a way that recognizes lifestyle differences and provides consumers with a more organized, pleasurable, and exciting shopping experience."

In addition to departmentalization, buying responsibilities, subdivisions and entities have been restructured to align with departmentalization. Separate buyers are now buying for Updated and Traditional Sportswear, Casual Sportswear, Top Shop, Main Floor Sportswear, Juniors, Young Juniors, and Jeanswear. These buyers think and breathe that target consumer and her lifestyle. "Until now, a Top Buyer in Misses bought tops for all segments—Updated, Traditional, Casual, and Budget," says Marshall Beere. "The same was true in other areas. Buyers were constantly changing hats and mind sets. Now they can achieve a clear focus for each of the brands assigned to them."

Electronic shopping

J.C. Penney has been in the forefront of the experimentation taking place to test the long-term viability of in-home electronic shopping. J.C. Penney's two experiments have been *Telaction*, an interactive, customer-controlled cable television service, offering merchandise from a variety of merchants, including J.C. Penney, Marshall Field's, Dayton Hudson, Neiman Marcus, FootLocker, and Sears, and *J.C. Penney Shop Television*, a programming and marketing operation offering J.C. Penney merchandise exclusively, and delivered by the Catalog operation. While J.C. Penney ultimately decided to end its participation in both of these electronic shopping formats (Telaction was discontinued in 1989 and JCPTV in 1991), the company believes that in-home electronic shopping may be a viable and profitable shopping option at some future point in time, under a different set of conditions and focus.

IMPLEMENTATION AND TACTICS

Implementation is the commitment of resources for the task, i.e., the means to accomplish the end. It is the determination of who does what, when, where, and for what specified end. The tactical plan outlines how the task is to be done.

Change in floor space allocation 1982 vs 1989: (refer to Exhibit 2A–2)

After the line eliminations and the launching of our store modernization program in 1983, a marked change is seen. This floor plan is typical of a 1985 store. Home and leisure has been reduced by over 20 percent to 35,000 square feet. Our apparel lines—women's, men's, and children's—have all been expanded. Women's—at 39,000 square feet—is now the largest department.

Finally, here's a typical floor plan of today. Women's has increased to nearly 49,000 square feet—up over 20 percent from the 1985 plan. Usually, 1/3rd of our new women's space is on the second floor, occupying the home electronics square footage. Men's has gone from 20,000 to 26,000 square feet; children's has remained the same; and home and leisure has been reduced by nearly half to 20,000 square feet. In total we have realigned over 15 million square feet in our stores in the past 5 years.

So there's no mistaking the strategy we're following. All of the assets . . . the space . . . and the training needed to support our discontinued lines in the past are now being refocused on what the regional mall customer prefers—apparel . . . furnishings . . . accessories . . . and shoes for the career minded and the family oriented. (Howell, 1989)

Communication of new look:

You've seen these changes during your store visits—and you've asked us how we were going to communicate our new look. Well, we listened to you—and developed a new image-building ad campaign. Referring to two commercials introduced at Academy Awards, Howell says "I believe you'll agree they're on target for the consumer we want to attract."

. . . [N]o major changes for the retail store are planned for the foreseeable future. I firmly believe these changes have positioned us for future growth, and provide a firm foundation for enhanced shareholder value. (Howell, 1989)

Technical support for strategic changes

Penney's exclusive *Direct Broadcast System—DBS* represents a major operational change. This system is used to communicate between Penney's buyers and store merchandisers. In 1989, about 750 stores were equipped to receive the direct broadcast signals. One-way video is provided from Dallas to the stores; two-way audio makes it possible for questions and comments from the stores to be addressed during the broadcast. The typical format for the broadcasts starts with the buyers' overview of information such as trends, what is new, and what has changed. This is followed by presentation of individual merchandise samples. The store merchandise managers receive printed material on all of the items prior to viewing them on the DBS. They then select items from the entire merchandise assortment that will appeal to local consumer preferences on style, color, fabrication, and price points—so that their assortment can be tailored to their particular market.

> *The most obvious advantage to the system is that stores can tailor their merchandise purchases to local market preferences—something that's extremely important for a nationwide organization like J.C. Penney. There has to be fashion buying flexibility at the local market level. . . . (Howell, 1989)*
>
> *Howell stated that in 1989 the company started using DBS for consumer market research: "We've set up research centers at selected stores in 16 major markets across the country. A cross-section of consumers is invited into these stores to view a live satellite broadcast or videotape on a product or service—usually merchandise samples. Then, these consumers are asked to express their opinions or preferences about the product or service by answering questions on personal computers at each site. The responses from each store are electronically transmitted to the company's mainframe system in Dallas. There, the nationwide results are summarized in a market research report." (Howell, 1989)*

Direct broadcast technology provides flexibility and diversity for nearly 600 department stores without losing the J.C. Penney identity. (Miller, 1988)

EXECUTION
Execution of the strategic plan is the physical performance of the task for which resources were allocated in the implementation phase. The functional retail managers are responsible for activating the various elements of the retail mix.

J.C. Penney Catalog:

> *We look at catalog—in effect—as a huge 12-million-square-foot back-up store. It supplements our other stores with an enormous selection of sizes, colors, and styles that no retail store—by itself—can compete with. The average store, for example, might offer . . . St. John's Bay fleecewear in 8–10 colors in the most-asked-for-sizes. In catalog, you can get it in 19 colors and virtually every conceivable size.*
>
> *Draperies are another good example. Even our largest stores can only carry about 325 of the 5,600 sizes and colors we have available. But with catalog as a back-up, we can deliver the exact style, color, and size our customer wants in 2–3 days. That's the kind of service that makes us so dominant in this business. In fact, more than one out of every four drapes purchased in America is bought through a Penney store or J.C. Penney Catalog. . . . (Howell, 1989)*

Targeting the Hispanic market
J.C. Penney is one of just a few retailers specifically targeting the Hispanic market, and one of the very few who are attempting to communicate with Hispanics in their own language.

Hispanics comprise about 8 percent of the U.S. population today. By the year 2010, Hispanics will be the largest American minority group and will account for 12 percent of the U.S. population. "Research shows clearly that Hispanic consumers buy from companies that are sensitive to their language needs and become involved with Hispanic community events," says Patricia V. Asip, manager of corporate special segment marketing at J.C. Penney. "As a group, Hispanic consumers show more brand loyalty than the U.S. population as a whole."

J.C. Penney pioneered Hispanic marketing with publication of its first Spanish-language catalog in 1979, according to Asip. Penney now has Hispanic marketing teams operating in 14 markets—mostly in Southwestern markets, Miami, Chicago, Denver and New York/New Jersey. J.C. Penney runs about 20 Spanish-language television commercials each year as well as print ads and radio spots for events and holidays. The company also sponsors numerous promotional and special events (Fry, 1991; Linden, 1991; Ritzer, 1991).

Promoting fashion

In October 1989, Penney's launched an advertising campaign and promotion based on the theme, "The Spirit of the American Woman." The emphasis is on fashion rather than hard-sell price advertising, in keeping with the retailer's repositioning strategy (Fisher, 1989).

J.C. Penney launched a successful campaign, "Fashion Comes to Life," in 1990. Brands such as Stafford Executive, Jacqueline Ferrar, and Hunt Club were featured in advertisements, as shown in the pictures below.

J.C. Penney "Fashion Comes to Life" and Hunt Club promotions

PHOTOS COURTESY OF J.C. PENNEY

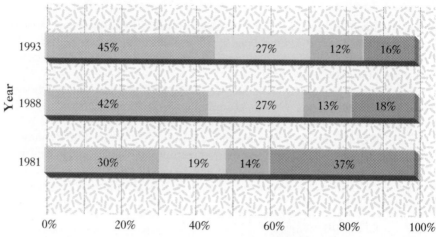

J.C. Penney Stores Merchandise Mix
Total Stores
Percent of Total Merchandise Sales

Exhibit 2A–3
Store Mix as a Percent of Total
Merchandise Sales
••••••••••••••••••••••••••
SOURCE: J.C. Penney Company
literature.

EVALUATION AND CONTROL

Strategic objectives are a target for performance. The actual performance results are measured against the planned performance (i.e., against the benchmarks established in tactical operating plans). An effective evaluation procedure requires control mechanisms. In particular, information systems are needed to collect, store, and analyze performance data.

Evaluation of merchandise mix:

> *Let's look at the progress we've made. Here's how our store mix has changed as a percent of our total merchandise sales. [See Exhibit 2A–3.]*

1981 figures reflect the percentage of total merchandise sales allocated to home, children's, men's, and women's lines before the first major changes were made in Penney's merchandise mix in 1983. Note that home lines (37 percent) were larger than women's (30 percent).

> *By the end of 1988, a trend line developed. Women's apparel, furnishings, and accessories sales had increased to 42 percent of our volume, and home lines had dropped back to 18 percent. That trend is continuing, and the third column shows how our store mix should look by 1993. Combined, women's and men's will represent 72 percent of our total merchandise sales. (Howell, 1989)*

Other observations from an evaluation of operating results:
- Recent success in children's lines, expected to continue due to addition of important national brands, such as OshKosh and Health-Tex.
- Success with branding strategy in men's.
- In spite of drop from 37 percent in 1981 to 18 percent in 1988 for all home lines share of merchandise mix, Penney's has improved market share in fashion soft home lines, plus a marked improvement in gross margins.

Effect of Direct Broadcast System (DBS)
Penney's Direct Broadcast System (DBS) has had an important impact on the retailer's inventory management.

Prior to DBS, we had a two-tier inventory system. The buyers would commit in the wholesale market for what they thought the stores would want. The store, in turn, would order from the buyer what they thought they could sell. When these two independent decisions didn't match, a wholesale problem occurred. This resulted in unwanted merchandise which had to be sold in our stores, creating markdowns. Today, the buyer shows the assortment over DBS—and stores determine what and how much they plan to sell. Buyers then make the wholesale commitments based on store orders. . . . (Howell, 1989)

[In market research,] the primary benefit of the (DBS) system is speed, although it has also proved to be both accurate and cost-effective. For example, consumer data can be collected, analyzed, and reported in 2-to-3 days, instead of the usual 30-to-60 days required by focus groups or mall interviews. . . . Let me give you a concrete example of how we put the research to work. The sportswear buyers from our men's division returned to Dallas with merchandise samples the week of March 28th after their major buying trip to the Far East for next spring. Within a week of their return, a live broadcast was aired to the 16 markets. Consumer preferences for the merchandise were researched all in one evening, and the results delivered to the merchandise manager in time for the line review on April 5—prior to merchandise commitments with suppliers, and well ahead of the direct broadcast to store merchandisers. Used in this way to determine consumer merchandise preferences in advance, satellite research becomes a part of the merchandise selection process—part of the way we do business. (Howell, 1989)

J.C. Penney Business Services

J.C. Penney is offering its extensive marketing and technological know-how to other retailers, thereby increasing the company's profits and using its in-house resources more cost effectively. The company can offer a variety of "products" to retailers and other business clients by merging the networking, credit services, and Direct Marketing Group with J.C. Penney Business Services (Neal, 1990).

Evaluation of catalog sales

The big Fall/Winter (1988–1989) catalog generated 860 million dollars in demand, up 18.5 percent from a year ago. Many of the pages in the book produced enormous amounts of business. . . . Sales figures for some of the leading 1989 sellers were:

- *Silk dress—$1.4 million*
- *Denim for kids—$1.7 million*
- *Stafford International suits—$1.9 million*
- *Elizabeth Gray bedroom coordinates—$2.3 million*

In 1988, two leading sellers were:

- *TV and VCR (on back cover of catalog)—$9.6 million*
- *Nintendo and Atari–$39.5 million*

Today, our "Big and Tall Men's Specialty Catalog" is one of the most profitable books in the industry—and we see similar opportunities in other areas. These are highly focused books directed at targeted consumers, so the return per book is greater than the larger general catalogs. Our specialty catalogs have contributed to the increase in profits we've experienced in catalog— and since we've just scratched the surface, we see good sales and profit potential for these books in the years ahead. (Howell, 1989)

Summary of actions/results:

. . . I'd like to take a moment to review the programs we have implemented over the past 5 years to enhance shareholder value. They've happened one-by-one, but taken collectively they represent a significant achievement.

- *We closed 270 stores that were not meeting our hurdle rate—and did not have the potential of achieving a satisfactory return on equity;*
- *We bought back 1.1 billion dollars of high cost debt, replacing it with less expensive debt that is providing an annual interest savings of about 50 million dollars;*
- *We initiated a stock buy-back program of up to 35 million shares. To date, 28 million shares have been acquired at a purchase price of 1.3 billion dollars.*
- *We sold our interest in Sarma, our unprofitable Belgian retail operation.*
- *We relocated to Dallas, which should result in a permanent reduction of 40 to 50 million dollars a year in operating costs.*
- *We organized our merchandising, marketing, and regional operations.*
- *We established a LESOP, thereby increasing our cash flow and return on equity.*
- *We financed approximately 250 million dollars of customer receivables from our credit operation—thus providing for the liquidity of a major corporate asset.*
- *We sold our former New York office, resulting in an after-tax profit of 139 million dollars.*
- *We are in the process of disposing of our casualty insurance business;*
- *And we have raised our dividend over the past 3 years from $1.24 to $2.24.*

During this time, we have still returned an average annual rate of return to our stockholders of 25 percent. *As a result of these actions, our R.O.E. has increased from the 10-to-12 percent level a few years ago to the 16 percent level today—with an outlook that indicates that R.O.E. will continue to rise. (Howell, 1989)*

Overall assessment of operating results

The following is a 5-year profile of pre-tax earnings for J.C. Penney Stores and Catalog (in millions) (Miller, 1988):

1983	$ 666
1984	743
1985	740
1986	1,053
1987	1,125

We've come a long way since we announced our first line eliminations and store modernization program in 1983. The elements are in place to carry us forward. We are a new J.C. Penney Company . . . and we know the best is yet to come. (Howell, 1989)

SOURCE: Adapted from *Annual Report* (1989), J.C. Penney Company, Inc.; Fisher, Christy (1989), "Refashioned Penney's Struggles to Sway Shoppers," *Advertising Age* 60, no. 31, (July 17), R2; Fry, Susan L. (1991), "Reaching Hispanic Publics With Special Events," *Public Relations Journal* (February), 12–13, 30; Howell, William R. (1989), *Presentation: New York Analysts Group Meeting* (April 19); Linden, Shira (1991), "Usted Habla Espanol?" *Catalog Age* 8, no. 1 (January), 65–68; Miller, D.F. (1988), *Presentation: Brigham Young University* (November 17); Neal, Mollie (1990), "Retail: A Penny Earned," *Direct Marketing* 53, no. 4, (August), 70–72; *Positioning Statement* (1990), J. C. Penney Stores (January); Ritzer, Julie (1986), "Chains Reach Out to Hispanic Consumers," *Chain Store Age Executive* 62, no. 10, (October), 52–56; Schultz, David P. (1990), "J. C. Penney Takes Top Spot," *Stores* (July), 9–12; *The Penney Idea* (1913), J. C. Penney Company, Inc., and other company sources.

Strategic Planning Process
for a Small Business Retailer:
The Perfumery on Park

The strategic planning process for a small business retailer is generally not as formal as it is for a large retailer. The small business owner starts with a concept, often developing a niche strategy based on his or her understanding of the firm's strengths and weaknesses within the context of its operating environment.

The Perfumery on Park, Inc. is a successful small retail perfumery located in Winter Park, an affluent community adjacent to Orlando in Central Florida. The owners, Anna and David Currie, continue to evaluate the strategic options that become available as the business grows. A review of the initial business plan and history of The Perfumery on Park suggests the manner in which its strategic planning process has evolved since the store's opening in May 1984. Some examples of the Curries' analysis and decisions are provided in this appendix to give the reader insights into this process.

MISSION STATEMENT

The **mission statement** represents the purpose of the business. For The Perfumery on Park, Inc., no formalized written mission statement existed. However, the first sentence of the Curries' business plan outlined the retail purpose: "The business will be a quality perfume shop, selling only upper-middle-priced and high-priced items." The store's key customers are also identified in the business plan: "The target market consists of natives and tourists of medium- to upper-income levels."

PERFORMANCE OBJECTIVES

Performance objectives articulate what management expects to accomplish over a specified time period. For The Perfumery's first year of operation, the owners established sales objectives at $200,000 based on their assessment of market potential. They estimated a gross profit objective of 40 percent of sales, the industry standard.

ENVIRONMENTAL SITUATIONAL ANALYSIS

Environmental situational analysis monitors internal and external environments for strengths/weaknesses and opportunities/threats. In their analysis the Curries determined several key factors from their assessment of The Perfumery's external environment:

1. The local economy and sociocultural structure was capable of supporting their business.
2. Area demographics were conducive to success for their chosen niche, although business was expected to be seasonal.
3. Their shop on Park Avenue was in a prime location for customer traffic.
4. Department stores were a potential threat because of their wide assortments of popular fragrances and relationships with manufacturers, but a major trend in the perfume business in Florida was the formation of boutiques.

5. No other perfume shops existed in Winter Park, although a similar successful operation had been converted to another line of business by its owner during the previous decade.

Highlights from an internal environmental analysis revealed the following strengths and weaknesses:

1. The owners started their business with sufficient capital from a local bank and personal resources.
2. Although neither Anna nor David had experience with a retail perfume shop, they brought managerial and financial expertise to their new venture.
3. In addition to Anna and David, store personnel included retired family members who wanted to work and remain active, but did not want to earn a wage due to tax considerations.
4. An efficient internal control system had been developed for inventory management and ordering.

STRATEGIC OBJECTIVES AND STRATEGY DEFINITION

Strategic objectives are based on the retailer's long-range desires, generally stated as financial or marketing goals. In this case, even though research suggested that a typical specialty shop realized sales of $350,000 per year, the Curries did not expect The Perfumery to realize that level in the first year. Therefore, the Curries established a more conservative initial objective of $200,000. Their estimate was based on the results of industry studies, which show that the average sale is $40 to $50 per customer per visit. At this rate, it would require 5,000 purchases to achieve the $200,000 sales objective which the owners felt was reasonable given their location and tourist traffic. Market share objectives were not stated explicitly, but The Perfumery on Park expected to obtain a large share of the local market for fragrances.

Strategy definition, on the other hand, is a set of key parameters that provide the general thrust for the retailer's efforts in order to accomplish the strategic objectives. The Perfumery's target market was defined as natives and tourists of medium- to upper-income levels. The product was defined as quality perfume in assorted sizes. Product lines would be

Personal attention plays a significant role in customer satisfaction and word-of-mouth referrals at The Perfumery.

COURTESY OF THE PERFUMERY ON PARK

focused on those traditional and hard-to-find fragrances that have a strong brand loyalty, but are not typically found among the more fashionable fragrances carried by department stores and other specialty shops. Pricing was not a major consideration for this type of product or market, since there is little price competition in the perfume industry. Personal service and knowledgeable personnel would be emphasized as a competitive advantage to a perfume boutique.

IMPLEMENTATION AND TACTICS

Implementation requires the commitment of necessary resources to achieve strategic objectives. The strategic plan was implemented by obtaining a lease on a prime retail location, purchasing an adequate assortment of fragrances that would appeal to the target market, staffing the shop with capable personnel, budgeting funds for promotion, and other considerations.

To achieve the long-range strategic plans, retailers use **tactics**, which are short-range operating or action plans. The Perfumery on Park's advertising plans provide an example of tactical activities. Fragrance manufacturers have generally used traditional national media such as television and magazines, while newspapers have been emphasized in local campaigns. Initially, The Perfumery's sales had depended on reputation, word-of-mouth, and walk-by traffic. A marketing campaign was planned to increase the shop's sales potential. This included newspaper ads, magazines prior to special occasions, scent strips in special mailings, video terminals in local hotels, and product samples and gifts.

EXECUTION

Execution, the physical performance of the task for which resources are allocated in the implementation stage, occurs when required actions are performed to achieve strategic objectives. Examples of execution of the strategic plan include all of the activities outlined in the tactical plan, such as product availability; effective sales personnel; use of the shop's management control system to track sales and inventory, actually running the ads in magazines like *Florida Symphony,* and *Central Florida Magazine,* and direct mailings to selected Winter Park residents.

EVALUATION AND CONTROL

Evaluation and control are the activities in which actual performance is judged against the tactical operating plan and objectives, and progress toward achieving goals is monitored and measured. Anna and David felt encouraged by the results of the first six months of operation (nearly $56,000 in sales), given national and local economic trends during the Christmas retail season and major retailers' introduction of Giorgio, a fragrance that quickly gained a large market share. Other aspects of the operation were also evaluated, such as a roster of names and fragrances that was maintained so gifts could be purchased for a specific customer, and the feasibility of expanding to another location at the request of several shopping mall representatives.

SOURCE: Adapted from Currie, David M. (1988), "Perfumery on Park, Inc." Case in *Strategic Management: Text and Cases, 4th ed.,* James M. Higgins and Julian W. Vincze, eds., Chicago: The Dryden Press, pp. 358–377. (For additional details and an update, see the case, *Perfumery on Park, 1991* following Chapter 16.)

AN INTEGRATIVE RETAIL INFORMATION MODEL

Learning Objectives

*After studying this chapter, the
student will be able to:*

1. Recognize the need for
information in the retail environment.
2. Understand the complexity
of the relationships between
the retail firm and its external
and internal environments, as
depicted in the Integrative
Retail Information Model.
3. Describe the impact of
forces within the external and
internal environments on management decisions and the
effect of decisions on the environment.
4. Provide a rationale for gathering and using information in
retailing decisions.
5. Identify sources of information within the external and
internal environments.
6. Identify uses of information
in short-term and long-term
planning.

INFORMATION SYSTEMS IN ACTION

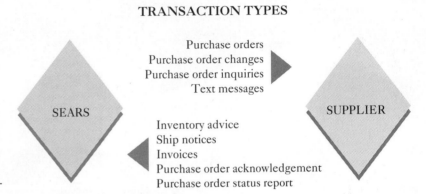

Sears, Roebuck and Company has one of the most sophisticated information systems to be found in business anywhere. Although Sears' advanced equipment and sophisticated systems encompass all of the company's business segments, the focus in this text is on the Sears Merchandise Group where data processing is part of the company's strategic business planning.

Sears, Roebuck and Company is comprised of four major companies. . . the Sears Merchandise Group, the Allstate Insurance Group, the Dean Witter Financial Services Group and the Coldwell Banker Real Estate Group. The Sears Merchandise Group includes 850 full line retail stores, the Sears Catalog, the Sears Charge, the 14,000 Sears service trucks, Sears Canada, Sears Mexico and over 1,000 specialty stores such as Sears Paint and Hardware, Eye Care Centers of America, Pinstripe Petites and Western Auto.

The Sears Merchandise Group took an active and early leadership role in the introduction of retail technology. And today it has one of the best, if not the best, technology platforms in the retail industry. It allows for the capture and sharing of information throughout the many Sears locations and those of its business partners.

The Sears Merchandise Group was one of the first retailers to recognize the advantage of computer-to-computer communications with its many suppliers. It began transmitting purchase orders and receiving invoices electronically over twenty years ago. Back then it used its own proprietary formats. Now it has established a leadership role in using the standard Electronic Data Interchange (EDI) formats. It believes EDI and the integration of internal systems is required for the quick response and quality of service its customers deserve and want.

The Sears Point of Sale Reservation System, for example, is used for merchandise that is delivered to a customer's home direct from a Sears Distribution Center. The system checks to see if the desired item is available, then reserves the item and schedules the delivery date for the customer. All of these activities take place immediately on-line and at the point-of-sale. For furniture items, the system actually reserves merchandise against the manu-

facturer's inventory that, in many cases, is not yet produced.

Quality is improved due to fewer manual hand-offs. With fewer opportunities for things to be communicated or handled incorrectly, fewer errors and exceptions occur. Customer service is improved by providing more immediate and accurate information to the customer and by providing more timely delivery of merchandise.

The company also believes that in order for it to stay competitive in the quickly changing business environments in which it operates, information generated outside of the company must be merged and analyzed against company

continued

generated information. For instance, census and current sales and credit information help the company plan advertising coverage and decide where new stores should be located. Customer information is used to hone direct marketing efforts, and information about the competition is used to validate and revise its business strategies.

Information technology is totally interwoven in how the Sears Merchandise Group is run today. It touches every job and activity. . . from the CEO to the receiving docks in the stores. The company believes effective use of information technology is a critical success factor for the future of the company. For the Sears Merchandise Group, it means having the right information, both internal and external, available at the right time in the right format for whoever requires it.

Courtesy of Margaret L. Edidin, National Manager of Development Support and Strategic Planning, Sears, Roebuck and Co., June 21, 1991.

The Electronic Data Interchange (EDI) system enables the many Sears locations to share information generated inside and outside the company.

Introduction

Each of us is accustomed to using an information systems model, readily available within our own memory, that collects, stores, recalls, integrates, and analyzes a variety of information needed for personal decisions. Some of these decisions are made frequently; some are made infrequently. The routine problems usually require quick solutions based on mentally processing information that is already known. If all the details are not memorized, we still know how to access needed information to add to the model.

For example, we memorize frequently called telephone numbers such as those of our best friends, or we know how to access numbers quickly from directory assistance, a telephone directory, or personal "black book" of telephone numbers. We then use the appropriate number to access or relay information to others, to make plans, to complete transactions, or to obtain more information prior to making a decision. Thus, various internal and external sources of information are integrated, analyzed, and interpreted to fulfill a variety of needs.

However, even for the most routine decisions, conditions may change within our external or internal environments. Phone numbers may be outdated, friends or businesses may change, personal resources may improve or decline, and needs may be redefined. Any modification of the original situation may lead to a new problem-solving scenario, but the basic decision model remains in place. Once the necessary information is added and analyzed appropriately, new decisions can be made systematically and effectively.

While the preceding example may oversimplify use of an information systems approach to personal decision making, it should not cause us to underestimate the value of the acquisition, analysis, and use of information. Retailing is a dynamic process, operating in an environment that is constantly changing. Numerous problems, of varying degrees of importance and duration, must be solved. The successful retailer monitors and controls information as it flows into, within, and out of the company, and uses that information in making effective and efficient decisions.

An Integrated Retail Information Model

Environmental and economic uncertainties, rapidly changing technology, accelerating competitive, better-educated consumers and employees, a fast-paced society with changing lifestyles, and more sophisticated communication networks have resulted in an information explosion. All of these factors must be taken into account throughout the strategic planning process, as well as in the implementation, evaluation and control of the strategic plan, and analysis of results as shown in Exhibit 3–1.

The complexity of gathering, storing, processing, and using information has led to the increased use of well-defined and well-managed information

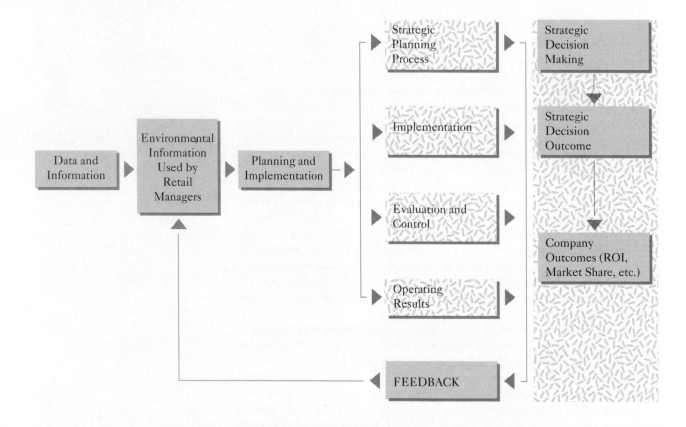

Exhibit 3–1
Information Needs and the
Strategic Planning Process
•••••••••••••••••••••••••••••

systems by retailers. Within this context, an integrative retail information
model is presented to illustrate the relationships among retail management
concepts and to highlight the importance of the uses of data and flows of
information in the retail environment.

The **Integrative Retail Information Model (IRIM),** shown in Exhibit 3–2, is a simple presentation of an extremely complex set of relationships
and information flows. It is essentially a decision support model that places
the formal retail information system in perspective as only one part of the
entire retail scene. IRIM is based on three major components: the retailer's
external environment; the **internal environment** within the organization;
and **data and information processing** for use by management in planning,
executing, and evaluating strategic decisions. The model will be used to
establish a logical path through the upcoming chapters. Each model component is discussed further below in terms of specific information needs.

Environmental Information Components

EXTERNAL RETAIL ENVIRONMENT   All groups and forces beyond
the direct control of the retailer, even to the extent of weather and climate
conditions, might be considered as factors in the **external retail environment.** Within the context of strategic planning in Chapter 2, environmental
factors were subdivided into macro and micro categories. The microenvironment, which the retailer is most apt to affect and be affected by, consists of

INTEGRATIVE RETAIL INFORMATION MODEL

IRIM: decision support model
which places the retail information
system within the external and
internal environments and the data
and information processing context

EXTERNAL RETAIL ENVIRONMENT

factors—groups and forces—beyond
the retailer's control

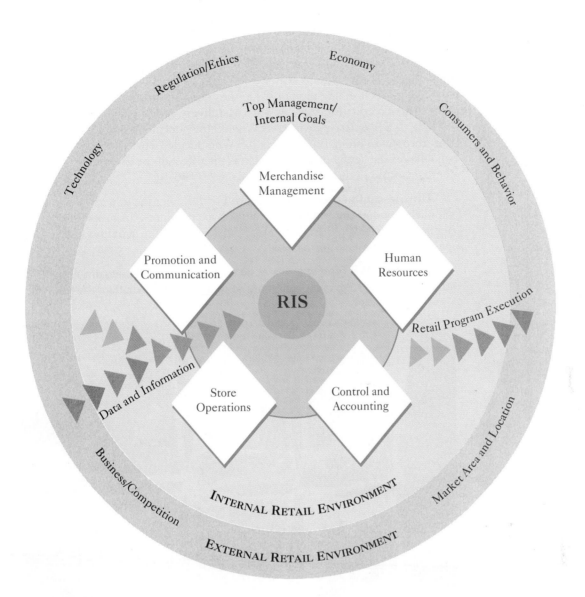

Exhibit 3-2
Integrative Retail Information
Model
••••••••••••••••••••••••••••••
SOURCE: Anderson and Parker, 1988.

the firm's customers and their buying patterns as well as other businesses
(suppliers, intermediaries, competitors). The macroenvironment includes
economic, legal/political, technological, and market (physical, demographic,
sociocultural) factors. However, discussion here is organized within the broad
areas of consumers and their shopping behavior, other businesses, legal and
political factors, the economy, characteristics of a retail market area and location, and technology.

Consumers and **consumer shopping behavior** refer to both present
and potential customers in the retail market. Retailers need information
about the following for strategic planning and evaluation of merchandising
and operating results:

1. *Who are consumers?* What are their characteristics? What are the demographics, psychographics, or lifestyles of selected target markets?

CONSUMERS
present and potential customers in
the retail market

CONSUMER SHOPPING BEHAVIOR
characteristics and actions of
customers

2. *Where are consumers?* Where are they located geopraphically? Are there barriers to access? How long have they been there? Are populations shifting?

3. *How and where do consumers buy?* How do they think? How do they decide to purchase? What are their attitudes? Where do they buy? Are they responsive to high-tech selling methods? Do they shop at home? Do they purchase with cash or credit? Are services, such as delivery, required or expected?

4. *What or who influences purchases?* Why do they decide to purchase? How do they respond to promotional methods? Who decides what to purchase, and who makes the actual purchase? What is the effect of the economy? Are there unserved or dissatisfied markets?

   Business influences in the external environment include competitors, suppliers/vendors, intermediaries, and service providers. The retailer does not operate in isolation and, therefore must consider the activities and strategies of other relevant businesses.

1. *Competitors:* Who and where are the competitors? What are competitive strategies in regard to each aspect of the retailing mix? What are the innova-

A non-profit, educational organization, Hispanic Designers, Inc., teams up yearly with retailer J.C. Penney to sponsor the "Hispanic Designer's Model Search." The contest is open to male and female nonprofessional models of Hispanic descent between the ages of 16 and 22. Prizes include scholarships and modeling opportunities, or wardrobes courtesy of J.C. Penney.

tive new formats being introduced in the market? What activities are taking place, or are imminent, regarding mergers, acquisitions, or divestitures?

2. *Suppliers and intermediaries:* What vendors are available? What are the advantages and disadvantages of dealing with each? Who has channel control?

3. *Service providers:* What services are provided directly to customers (credit, delivery, etc.) by the retailer or outside providers? What services are provided to the retailer by outside providers (computer services, financial services, etc.)? What are the trade-offs involved in each case?

Legal and political factors include governmental activities and the effects of legislation and public policy. Note that laws may vary from state to state and county to county.

1. *Legislation:* What are the existing federal, state, local, and international laws and regulations, and what is their effect on retail strategies and operations? What legislative activities are anticipated in the future? What is the effect on after-tax income?

2. *Public Policy:* What is the position of the retailer and society regarding ethical behavior and social responsibility? What are the expectations of the public that go beyond the letter of the law? What actions are special interest groups taking that may affect the retailer?

Economic factors include present and forecasted economic conditions and their relationships to consumer spending patterns and strategic considerations.

1. *Economic status:* What is the present status of the economy? Are the economic forecasts favorable or unfavorable, and how dependable are they?

2. *Consumer purchasing:* What is the effect of the economy on consumer buying power? How do economic trends affect shopping behavior?

COURTESY OF DUTY FREE INTL.

Duty Free International, Inc. provides duty free, tax free merchandise to world travelers through its Border, Airport, and Diplomatic/Wholesale Divisions. Pictured here is the Gourmet Food and Confectionery Shop at JFK International Airport.

BUSINESS

competitors, suppliers/vendors, intermediaries, and service providers in the external environment

LEGAL AND POLITICAL

factors of the external environment involving governmental activities and the effects of legislation and public policy

3. *Retail strategy:* What is the effect of the economy on the retailer's sources of supply? Are adjustments needed in the firm's short-range and long-range plans?

Market area and location factors and characteristics of a specific site need to be evaluated for an existing store, as well as for a new location or an expansion. As with other external environmental factors, the retailer has varying degrees of control over the location decision. The firm has the most opportunity to exercise control when deciding where to open a new store, i.e., a go/no go decision. Once the site is selected and the store is opened, the retailer has little control over all that occurs in that retail area. This aspect of the environment is subject to change during the lifetime of a retail store, and information should be available to monitor it constantly. Thus, the decision variable with an existing store is whether to keep a store open, modify the retail mix, or close it down. Information is needed to make decisions and answer questions similar to the following:

1. *Market area:* Where is the best geographical area to locate a store? Which region of the country and which local market within that region is best? What are the characteristics of the market in terms of consumer and work-force demographics, economy, climate, and so forth?
2. *Trade area:* Within the market area selected, where are the preferred shopping areas? Are they in free-standing locations? Or in a shopping center or mall? What are the characteristics of customers and other businesses in the area? For example, is it a downtown office center? Or a neighborhood shopping center? What is the drawing power of other businesses or attractions in the trade area?
3. *Specific site:* Within the trade area, which site has the most profit potential? Are other businesses in the proximity of the site compatible with the retailer's image and objectives? What is the condition of the site? Does it require new construction or remodeling of an existing building? Has the value of this site changed over time, in which direction, and how rapidly? What are the costs versus the benefits of locating on this site? What is the expected return on investment and payback period at this location?

Technology is depicted in the Integrative Retail Information Model as an external environment factor. In reality, its influence is pervasive throughout both the external and internal environments of a retail firm. Some questions to be answered about technology are suggested here.

1. *External technology:* What technology is available from outside sources to enhance performance in each of the functional areas (e.g., physical distribution systems, POS data capturing capability, accounting software, security devices, etc.)?
2. *Internal technology (present):* How does present technology used by the firm affect the operation of the business? How does it affect selling methods? How does it affect information gathering, retrieval, and analysis? How does it affect customer relations (e.g., POS, promotions, credit)?
3. *Internal technology (future):* What technology is needed that is not presently in use? What is the expected payoff from adding this new technology (e.g., increased sales, ROI, better use of assets)? Are the resources available to acquire and implement the technology (e.g., financial, human, physical)?

ECONOMIC
factors of the external environment that include present and forecasted conditions of the economy

MARKET AREA AND LOCATION
factors concerning the geographic area, market characteristics, and site conditions

TECHNOLOGY
factors influencing the operations of a retail firm, such as data entry and interpretation, security equipment, accounting, inventory control, and distribution systems

INTERNAL RETAIL ENVIRONMENT
resources and events in each of the store's functional areas

Technology plays a vital role in Walgreen's prescription services, and computer systems are constantly evaluated to increase service and productivity. Toward this end, the new SIMS inventory system will continue to expand throughout the 90's.

A retailer must consider many other aspects of technology. One of the most important uses of technology is the Retail Information System, which is discussed later in this chapter. Other uses are discussed in later chapters.

Just as retailers need to be informed about and deal with the external environment, they also must be knowledgeable about the internal aspects of the company.

INTERNAL RETAIL ENVIRONMENT   The **internal retail environment** includes resources and events in each of the store's functional areas: human resources, store operations and physical facilities, merchandise management (and pricing), promotion and communication with customers, and control and accounting. Retail managers at all levels of the organization need information to solve problems and plan for the short-term and long-term operation of the company. The retail organization's internal needs for information are introduced below for each functional area.

*A typical J.C. Penney departmental
floor plan facilitates the arrangement
of merchandise to provide an
organized and pleasant shopping
environment for consumers with
different lifestyles.*

Human resources information is required in order to determine tasks
to be performed, organizational structure, staffing of the store, and personnel
management and evaluation. Emphasis is on the importance of employees
and an understanding of the organizational structure in which they work.

1. *Retail tasks:* What are the various tasks to be accomplished within the
company at all levels and for all functions? What are the job descriptions for
each of these tasks? How are the tasks to be prioritized for budgeting and
use of company resources?
2. *Organizational structure:* What is the relationship between the various tasks
to be performed? What are the lines of authority and communication? How
many tiers of management are needed? Does the organizational structure
allow for expansion? What are the opportunities for advancement? Is there
an "informal" organization, and how is it described?
3. *Staffing and human resource management:* What qualifications are needed by
personnel to perform required tasks? What is the best source of personnel?
What is the policy toward hiring, training, and promoting employees? How
should employees be compensated? How well do employees perform? What
is their attendance?

Store operations and physical facilities include all factors involved in
keeping the store open for business and in good working order and the logistics involved in moving inventory and supplies from one place to another, as
well as store security and risk management.

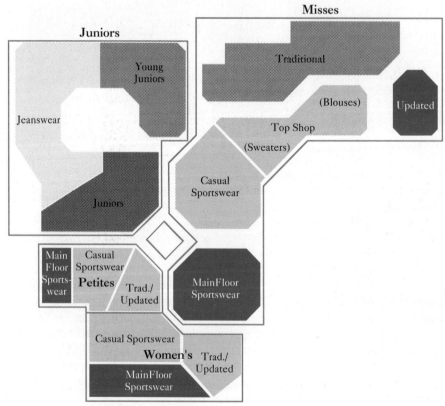

SOURCE: Used with permission of J.C. Penney

1. *Layout:* What is the most efficient and effective physical layout for the selling and nonselling areas of the store? How can the proportion of non-selling space be reduced? Is there enough space? What is the productivity of the space and fixtures used? Is there a "prototype" layout that can be used in more than one store successfully? Which layout will yield the highest profit per square foot of selling space? How much space should be allocated to offices, stairways, elevators, service areas, and where should they be placed relative to the selling areas?

2. *Inventory and merchandise handling:* How will merchandise be transported from vendors to the stores? How and where will inventory be stored until it is sold? How much storage space should be available in a distribution center, or on or near the selling floor? What equipment (including electronic equipment) is needed to mark, move, and care for inventory?

3. *Security and risk management:* What equipment and procedures are needed to prevent loss and inventory shrinkage? How can the percentage of stock shrinkage to sales be reduced? What resources and policies are needed to prevent injury to customers and employees? What kinds of risk (such as fire, theft, etc.) does the company need to be protected against? And at what levels?

Merchandise management information is necessary in order for managers to make decisions regarding channel strategies, merchandise assortments, and inventory management. A related area of concern includes information for determining pricing strategies.

Albertson's fully integrated distribution system meets increased demand and improves efficiency.

COURTESY OF ALBERTSON'S

1. *Channel strategies:* How should merchandise be purchased? Where and from whom should it be purchased? What is the relative strength and bargaining position of each of the channel participants?
2. *Merchandise assortments:* What merchandise should be purchased? And in what quantity and proportions?
3. *Inventory management:* When should merchandise be purchased? Where should it be stored? How often should the stock be turned over? How long should inventory be kept?
4. *Pricing strategies:* What level of operating expenses and profits must be covered by the price in order to meet the company's financial objectives? What price lines have the highest consumer acceptance? What pricing strategy should be pursued relative to competition? How do other channel members influence retail prices? How do legislation and government regulations affect the prices that can be charged?

Promotion and communication tools, such as advertising, personal selling, sales promotion, publicity and public relations, customer services, and store image, are among the primary methods used to attract, influence, and maintain customers. Information is needed to plan, execute, and evaluate all promotional efforts, in order to resolve questions such as the following:

1. *Advertising:* What type of advertising would be most effective? What size budget is required? What media should be used? What should the message be? How frequently should the advertising appear? Who is the target audience? What is the cost versus the benefit of advertising?
2. *Personal selling:* Would the merchandise be sold more advantageously by a salesperson or by self-service or direct mail? What type of salespeople are needed? How should they be trained and compensated? How and by whom are they supervised and evaluated? What is the cost versus the benefit of employing a sales force?
3. *Sales promotion, publicity, and public relations:* How will these tools support and supplement the advertising and personal selling strategies used by the retailer? Are they compatible? What is the cost versus the benefit of using sales promotion? What types of sales promotion will elicit the desired response from customers? For publicity and public relations, who are the major contacts and the primary intended audiences? What are their expectations?
4. *Customer services:* What services do customers expect? Which services can feasibly be provided? At what level should the services be performed? Do customers need to "qualify for services?
5. *Store image:* How do customers and employees perceive the store? Which factors contribute to the store's and the company's images? Are the images favorable or unfavorable? If unfavorable, what can be done about them? If favorable, how can they be capitalized upon? How is the retailer managing store image? Has the image changed significantly in one direction or the other?

Control and accounting information enables managers to answer the basic question, "Are customers buying what we are selling, and at what level of profit (or return on investment)?" Accounting and financial data can provide answers to this question as well as the following:

1. *Accounting system:* What sales and profit levels have been achieved in the past? What levels of sales and profits are desired and projected for the

PROMOTION AND COMMUNICATION
functional area concerned with advertising, personal selling, sales promotion, publicity and public relations, customer service, and store image

CONTROL AND ACCOUNTING
functional area concerned with costs and revenue, financing the business and analyzing performance compared with strategic objectives

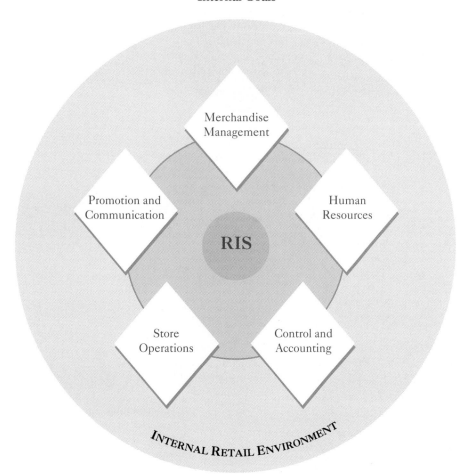

**Top Retail Management
Internal Goals**

Merchandise Management

Promotion and Communication

Human Resources

RIS

Store Operations

Control and Accounting

INTERNAL RETAIL ENVIRONMENT

Exhibit 3-3
Management Decision Areas by
Retail Function
....
SOURCE: Anderson and Parker, 1988.

future? Are operating costs being controlled properly? What is the break-down of sales, costs, and profits by selling unit? Are payments to vendors taking advantage of discounts for early payment? How should balance sheet items be valued (including inventory valuation method)? What are the company's cash flow projections? Is short-term financing needed?

2. *Financial analysis:* What are the company's growth plans? Are they feasible? Is creative financing needed? Is the company a takeover target? What are its financial strengths and weaknesses? How do operating results compare to projections for strategic plans? Are important profitability ratios in line with the rest of the industry?

Each decision and each event in the functional management areas create a "ripple effect" throughout the company. For example, a corporate mission statement issued by top management at one extreme, or a seemingly insignificant purchase of an inexpensive item by a customer, at the other extreme, each have a wide-reaching effect. In the first case, the corporate mission statement provides direction for management decisions that affect each of the functional areas of the store, as illustrated in Exhibit 3–3.

"Ripple Effect" of Corporate Decisions on Functional Management Areas in Retailing

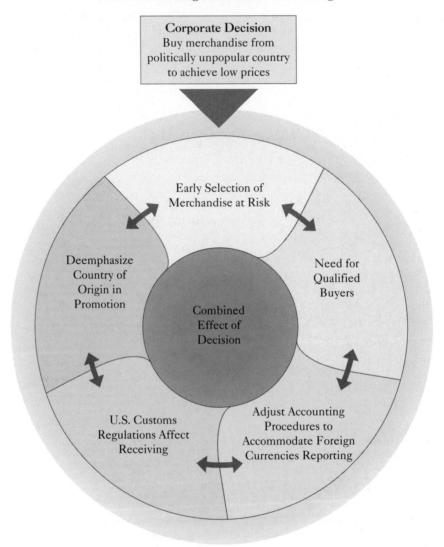

Corporate Decision
Buy merchandise from politically unpopular country to achieve low prices

Early Selection of Merchandise at Risk

Deemphasize Country of Origin in Promotion

Combined Effect of Decision

Need for Qualified Buyers

U.S. Customs Regulations Affect Receiving

Adjust Accounting Procedures to Accommodate Foreign Currencies Reporting

Exhibit 3–4
"Ripple Effect" of Corporate Decisions on Functional Management Areas in Retailing

An example of the "ripple effect" is the decision to purchase merchandise from a politically unpopular foreign country to fulfill a corporate mission of providing customers with the lowest prices in town. This decision affects each of the five functional areas as follows: merchandise managers and buyers need to make selections early, but may not receive what they ordered; human resources are required for overseas buying, either separate specialized buyers, outside buying services, or extension of present buyers' responsibilities; country of origin may be deemphasized in promotional messages; store operations may be affected by the need to receive foreign goods accord-

ing to U.S. Customs regulations; and accounting procedures may have to be adjusted to process invoices billed in foreign currencies. (See Exhibit 3–4.)

On the other hand, the seemingly insignificant purchase also has a far-reaching impact, affecting inventory and accounting records, future buying decisions, customer relations, and profitability. The sale is recorded electronically or manually; the item is removed from inventory, leaving a merchandise gap to be filled; the cash or credit transaction is added to the company's assets; and a portion of each transaction is used to pay vendors, employees, and overhead costs, as well as to provide a profit (or loss) to the company. The quality of the shopping experience also may determine the customer's attitude toward future purchases in the store.

While each of the functional areas has defined requirements and responsibilities, their decisions and actions are interdependent, requiring the coordination and integration of information for achieving corporate objectives. A simple operating decision to keep the store open later in the evening is an illustration of this interdependence and need for cooperation. Buyers may need to stock more merchandise, or different merchandise for a different target market. Depending upon the target market attracted, advertising in a morning paper may be more effective than in an evening paper. The later hours will require additional supervisory and sales personnel. Credit and other office workers, as well as maintenance and security people, must be on the job. Transactions and personnel records become the responsibility of the accounting department and a part of the retail information system.

Retail Information System

The formal **Retail Information System (RIS)** is an integrated and interactive network of people, equipment, events, data, and procedures, organized to collect, store, analyze, and distribute information to managers for planning, control, and evaluation. Within the context of the Integrative Retail Information Model, emphasis is placed on users of the information system rather than processors of information, of foresight rather than hindsight, and on proactive rather than reactive decision making.

The RIS consists of the gathering of data inputs from various sources, data storage and processing, and the uses of information outputs. In other words, it represents all data, facts, and information in various stages as it flows into, through, and out of the organization.

In order to identify opportunities and solve problems in a timely manner, retailers need to visualize at least a simple model of these information flows. The most basic model is not necessarily dependent upon sophisticated technology or computers, but it does show managers how to deal with the mass of data, facts, people, and environmental influences with which they are confronted daily. Even though some retailers may tend to use such a model primarily for accounting and financial control, the model's capabilities are critical to effective planning and evaluation activities.

Like other information systems, such as management information systems, merchandise information systems, and retail decision support systems, the RIS is primarily concerned with computerized (or sometimes manual) data management.

RETAIL INFORMATION SYSTEM (RIS)
integrated and interactive network of people, equipment, events, data, and procedures, organized to collect, store, analyze, and distribute information to managers for planning, control, and evaluation

Using Information To Make a Difference in the Environment

RESPONSIBLE RETAILER

"Walgreens . . . Your neighborhood drugstore" is the slogan that introduces the reader to the company's 1989 annual report. Walgreen Company enjoys a reputation as the largest and most technologically-advanced retail drugstore in the United States. The company has nearly 1,500 drugstores located in over 650 communities in 28 states and Puerto Rico. These stores are operated by 47,000 employees who serve more than 1.7 million customers daily. Sales of $5.38 billion were achieved in 1989.

In spite of Walgreens' dedication to aggressive growth and the resource commitment required to meet that objective, the drugstore chain has also made a commitment to being a responsible member of the community. An understanding of the environments in which its stores operate has not only led to corporate success, but has also identified areas where the company can give something back to its communities. The following excerpts from their 1989 annual report highlight the human side of one of America's largest corporations:

"Forty people—many of them children—died in Memphis fires last year," explains Patty Wong, pharmacy manager. "I thought, 'Hey, we're a family drugstore—we should be able to help out here.'" She contacted Captain Jack Bacon of the Memphis Fire Department, and soon Walgreen stores throughout the market were distributing fire prevention literature and applications for free smoke detectors. So far, firefighters have installed 2,000 detectors in our customers' homes. Last summer Pattie organized a fire safety slogan contest for kids. . .

Bronx assistant manager Elba Serrano discovered $280 in cash and a fistful of credit cards when she opened the purse lying on the floor in her store. "I knew the owner would be frantic," says Elba, who first worked for Walgreens in Puerto Rico. "I found an identification and reached the lady that night." The next day, the customer appeared at the store with a huge bouquet of flowers, just to say "thanks for caring, Elba."

In Tucson, store managers developed a program where students from the Arizona School for the Deaf and Blind could work at Walgreens a few hours a week. This year, a former student asked Walgreens for a full-time job. He was attending a special school in New York, but he missed Tucson and Walgreens. Today he rotates through three Walgreen stores as an inventory/pricing clerk.

Walgreen store managers volunteer many hours to their communities. Bob Beyer, a Walgreen store manager in Pekin, Illinois (population 35,000) felt that Walgreens was getting a lot *from* the community, but not giving much back. As chairman of the United Way Board of Directors, Beyer organized a "Battle of the Stars" charity day which raised more than $4,000. Walgreen employees' goal was to beat K mart in tug-of-wars, swimming events and raft races—but "this day, the *real* winner was Pekin." Beyer is also on the Chamber of Commerce board, helps out at the senior citizens' home and the United Way, in addition to his kids' sports.

"For nearly twenty-five years, we've offered programs for

HOW RIS WORKS   An information system is designed to provide a variety of users with a basis for making the best decisions possible. First, the retailer must identify potential problems and questions that need to be answered. The problems then are evaluated in terms of their relative importance, frequency of occurrence, and degree of risk, so that the retailer can prioritize them and evaluate the cost versus the benefit of obtaining information.

Second, relevant sources of information are identified, both inside and outside the company. Data is then gathered from these sources, added to the

seventh through twelfth graders on the Near West Side," says Chicago's Midtown Center Executive Director Art Thelen. "We're successful—in an area with a 50 percent dropout rate; 95 percent of our kids graduate from high school, and more than 60 percent go on to college. But until this fall, we weren't reaching younger students." Through a four-year, $190,000 grant from Walgreens, Midtown is now offering a "One on One" tutoring program for fourth through sixth graders. "If you put excellence in front of kids, they'll probably reach for it," adds Thelen. "Thanks to Walgreens, more kids will get that chance."

As these examples show, a retailer's responsibility extends far beyond the traditional "4 Ps" of the marketing mix: products, prices, promotion, and place. An important fifth "P" is the "people" in the retail environment—customers and employees of the store, citizens of the community, and business partners—that is ultimately where a retail business obtains its long-term profits.

Adapted from: *Walgreen Co., 1989 Annual Report*, Deerfield, Ill.

On the steps of Chicago's Midtown Center, fourth through sixth graders proudly wear sweatshirts from Walgreens "One on One" learning program.

information system as meaningful inputs, and stored for later use. Third, the necessary information is integrated and analyzed, either manually or electronically, providing output for retail management decisions.

Finally, the manager interprets the results provided by the information system and makes a decision. By implication, the manager's quantitative and qualitative skills are a part of this process and are integrated into the information system.

ADVANTAGES OF A FORMAL RIS   Information, tailored to the retailer's needs, can be stored so it is readily available for use in decision making, thus saving valuable time. The type of information needed, sources, and data collection methods are determined in advance. Data collection is a coordinated and continuous effort. Operating results can be compared with past and/or planned performance. Scenarios can be generated to determine costs versus benefits of proposed projects or strategies.

DISADVANTAGES OF A FORMAL RIS   The greatest deterrent to establishing a formal RIS is the initial effort necessary to develop the system. Development requires qualified personnel, time, and financial resources. Discrimination must be used in gathering the correct information. Design of a formal RIS is dependent upon correct identification of the necessary uses and sources of information, and upon understanding the complexity of many retail decisions.

RELATIONSHIP TO THE PROBLEM SOLVING PROCESS   The problem-solving process involves a sequence of stages: awareness of some stimulus or cue; recognition of a problem; search for information; evaluation of alternative solutions; choice of a solution or action; evaluation of the decision; and feedback for the next decision. (See Exhibit 3–5.) An information system can provide inputs and facilitate decisions at any stage of the problem-solving process, as illustrated in the following scenario.

The manager of a high-priced specialty clothing store (Store A) learned that a major competitor (Store B) had decided to change from a high-priced strategy to that of a discount operation (stimulus). The two stores would carry a similar merchandise selection. After Store B had been following the discount strategy for a few weeks, a problem was recognized when Store A's sales records indicated that revenues were seriously lower than anticipated for that period. Manager A consulted store records, industry information from publications, and vendors, customers, and others to obtain information and identify possible solutions (information search).

Available data was then used to evaluate the estimated costs versus benefits of each alternative, such as maintaining the status quo with changes in promotional strategy or services offered, competing by matching the discounter's prices, or by maintaining regular prices with more frequent special sales (evaluation of alternatives). The information system provided the needed data to choose the best alternative. The operating results of that decision were put into the system for evaluation purposes and to provide feedback for future decisions.

As shown in this scenario, each stage of the problem-solving process is also closely interwoven with the three major components of the integrative retail model: external environment, internal organization, and information processing.

Data Sources and Information Uses

An important component of the Integrative Retail Information Model is the information itself, including the source of the data and how the information is used by retail managers. Therefore, the model indicates the sources of

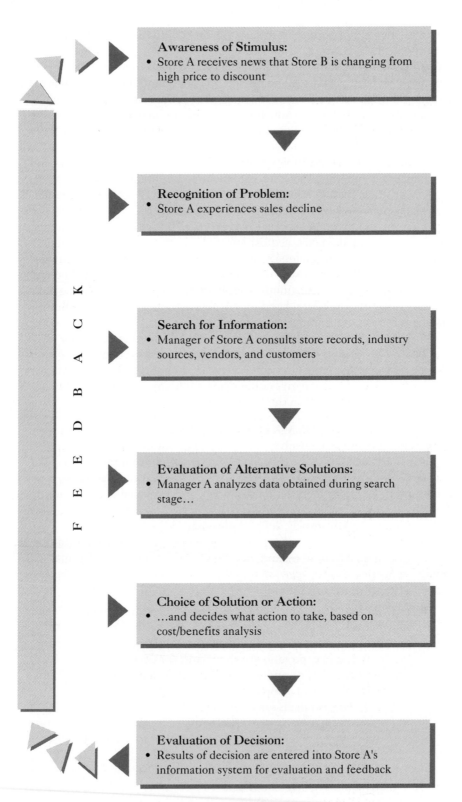

Awareness of Stimulus:
- Store A receives news that Store B is changing from high price to discount

Recognition of Problem:
- Store A experiences sales decline

Search for Information:
- Manager of Store A consults store records, industry sources, vendors, and customers

Evaluation of Alternative Solutions:
- Manager A analyzes data obtained during search stage...

Choice of Solution or Action:
- ...and decides what action to take, based on cost/benefits analysis

Evaluation of Decision:
- Results of decision are entered into Store A's information system for evaluation and feedback

F E E D B A C K

Exhibit 3–5
The Problem-Solving Process
and Information Systems

data and information inputs, as well as the use of information in planning, execution, and evaluation.

A data base of useful information can be compiled from many personal and published sources inside and outside the company. Once the data is collected, put into a usable format, and analyzed (perhaps in a statistical or mathematical model), the results provide a basis for management decisions. The decisions may have either internal or external implications (or a combination of the two).

Internal uses include applications such as determination of policies and procedures for operating the store, establishment of budgets, evaluation of expansion strategies and retailing formats, calculation of profitability ratios, and assessment of potential acquisitions or mergers.

Examples of external uses include reports to stockholders, location decisions, filing of income taxes, acquisition of short- or long-term financing, selection of distribution channels, and possible actions to thwart takeovers. In general, information is used to influence external constituencies such as intended markets, political groups, special interest groups (advertising, consumer advocates), or those related to business activities, such as the Better Business Bureau or Chamber of Commerce.

An essential element of the Integrative Retail Information Model is feedback. The results of previous decisions can be fed back into the system to provide valuable inputs for future decisions. Feedback allows comparison of results with strategic and operating plans, updating of records, and may be presented to management in the form of summary reports.

WHAT KIND OF INFORMATION IS NEEDED?   In order for a retail information system to be useful, the nature of the problems to be solved and the decisions to be made must be clearly understood. An information system, after all, is only as good as the quality of data it captures and how that data is used. Knowing the location and types of data available is also helpful. Some information can be generalized to a variety of similar situations; other information serves a narrowly defined purpose.

While managers rely on their own experience, judgment, and intuition to a considerable extent in making decisions, they also must be familiar with related concepts, such as *information system*, *information*, *facts*, *data*, and *intelligence*. Each of these terms is described below.

- *Information system:* The coordination of data and facts obtained from the external and internal environments; the systematic processing and analysis of data using mathematical, statistical, or qualitative methods; the interpretation of the results for decision making; feedback on the company and its environment as a part of the system; information generally stored in and retrieved from a computer, although the system also may be manual
  - Retail Information System (RIS): A total broad management information system tailored to the retail setting; two example subsets are MIS and RDSS
  - Merchandise Information System (MIS): subset of RIS; focused on merchandise management data
  - Retail Decision Support System (RDSS): also a subset of RIS; analytical support packages and statistical models to facilitate decision making

- *Information:* Something communicated; news; intelligence; knowledge, generally acquired from interpretation of data; facts that are considered to be true; often represented by data, but data must be analyzed and interpreted before it becomes information; quantitative or qualitative
- *Fact:* Something that has actually happened, or is supposed to be true; reality; basic information about a situation; quantitative or qualitative
- *Data:* Things known or assumed; facts or figures (considered to be true) from which conclusions can be drawn; numerical or quantitative
- *Intelligence:* News, information; sometimes implies the covert gathering of proprietary information; quantitative or qualitative

All levels, divisions, and functional areas of the retail organization require timely and accurate information. The scope of retail management responsibilities requires the application of a wide range of information to specific decision needs. However, decisions can be only as effective as the quality, timeliness, and appropriateness of information and data analysis used in making them. Assumptions and interpretation play an important role in data collection and analysis. In effect, interpretations are based on managers' assumptions. Such assumptions might include cause and effect relationships, which may or may not exist, or a proposition about a future condition that will affect the retail operation.

Information can be categorized in a number of acceptable ways. However, the classifications discussed here are simplified to include its characteristics (a micro vs. a macro scope; quantitative vs. qualitative), and data location (external vs. internal) and types (secondary vs. primary). An understanding of how information is classified provides a basis for choosing the appropriate data and method of analysis and in interpreting the results for decision making.

INFORMATION CHARACTERISTICS   Information used by retailers can be described according to whether it is predominantly micro versus macro or quantitative versus qualitative, although most information contains elements of both. Exhibit 3–6 illustrates this relationship between the micro versus macro and the quantitative versus qualitative aspects of information.

In order to make effective decisions, retailers must recognize the relationship between quantitative and qualitative information. They need to understand that qualitative information may have quantitative consequences. For example, a qualitative description of customers' status-seeking motives may explain their preference for patronizing a small exclusive retailer, thereby affecting the retailer's pricing strategy and revenues. Likewise, quantitative information may have qualitative consequences. In this case, a retailer's quantitative decision to increase inventory turnover through mass displays and low prices may lead to consumers' qualitative perceptions of undesirable merchandise.

Financial, economic, and accounting data are necessarily quantitative to determine sales forecasts, employee compensation, capital investments, budgets, inventory levels, and store productivity. Both internal and external data are analyzed in order to keep a particular store's operations in perspective.

Qualitative information often is gathered to assist the retailer in understanding behavioral and psychological phenomena, as well as social, legal,

Exhibit 3–6
Information Characteristics and Relationships

	Quantitative (Financial, Economic, and Physical)	*Qualitative (Behavioral and Psychological)*
Macro (Environment)	U.S., and world economic trends	Workforce characteristics
	Demographics	Aggregate consumer trends, attitudes
	Scarcity of resources	Psychographics
	Inflation, interest rates	Consumerism
		Environmentalism (protect, conserve)
Micro (Individuals and Firm)	Retailer's annual report information, operating results	Individual employee: interviews, evaluations
	Inventory, in units and dollars	Company employees (as a group): interviews, evaluations
	Employee schedules and compensation	Company customers: focus group discussions

and political concerns. Because mere numbers are inadequate in describing and explaining human behavior, retailers also must be concerned with why people think and act as they do and why situations exist. Behavioral and psychological information would include a description of why customers follow certain traffic patterns through a store in response to a store layout, or the explanation of a link between high employee absenteeism and unpleasant working conditions. Social, legal, and political information can provide an understanding of how other forces in the retailer's environment "behave" and "feel."

Exhibit 3–7 includes examples of decisions typically made by retail managers within each of the store's five functional areas, based on the use of quantitative or qualitative information. An example illustrating the use of information in changing retail strategies appears in Exhibit 3–8.

LOCATION AND TYPES OF DATA   Retailers obtain information from data that can be conveniently classified according to location and type of data. The **location of data** can be categorized broadly as either external or internal to the firm. The **type of data** used is either secondary or primary. **Secondary data** is already available, having been gathered for some purpose other than the present problem; **primary data** is gathered to answer specific research questions.

These two classifications overlap to define four separate types of data: (1) external secondary, (2) internal secondary, (3) external primary, and (4) internal primary. Examples of each type are provided in Exhibit 3–9.

Since secondary data has already been captured, it can be evaluated once its source has been identified. Internal secondary data frequently exists within the retailer's computerized accounting subsystem (inventory records, sales reports, personnel files, etc.), but may need further utilization in order

LOCATION OF DATA
information from internal or external sources

TYPE OF DATA
categorized as secondary or primary data

SECONDARY DATA
data already available; gathered for some purpose other than the present problem

PRIMARY DATA
gathered to answer specific research questions

Exhibit 3-7
Uses of Qualitative Versus Quantitative Information by Functional Management Areas

	Information Characteristics	
Information Uses	*Quantitative*	*Qualitative*
Merchandise Management	Data for sales forecasts	Customer awareness survey
	Actual inventory levels; planned inventory levels; open-to-buy	Price/quality perceptions
	Pricing information (price, points, price lines, markups)	Psychological response to sales presentations
Store Operations	Productivity of store space	Customer image of physical store attributes
	Evaluation of equipment and technology	Perceptions of in-store shopping convenience
	Store location analysis	
Human Resource Management	Compensation, pay scale	Hiring, training, evaluation of personnel
	Effectiveness measures of employee training programs	Employee attitudes
	Labor force data	Exit interviews
	Records of management contribution to profits	Customer addresses
Promotion and Communication	Promotional budgets	Advertising messages
	Media effectiveness measures	Verbal description of target market response to advertising
	Image of advertising (measured on numerical scale)	Observed avoidance of sales personnel
Control and Accounting	Financial objectives and goals	Subjective adjustment of forecasts, trends based on managers' judgment
	Annual reports: income statements and balance sheets	"Value added" pricing strategy
	Operating results and financial ratios	Use of judgment in preparing financial reports

to enhance its value. It may also be stored in a file cabinet or in a manager's head. External secondary data is already acquired and available, but exist outside the retail organization from such sources as census data, professional journals, trade publications, or corporate annual reports of competitors. The basic advantage of secondary data is that it is less expensive and more expedient than primary data.

Forms of secondary data include commercial shopping service reports about competitors' pricing strategies, reference to previous consumer surveys at another mall, real estate broker descriptions and photographs of a

Characteristics and Uses of Information
by Retail Drugstore Managers in Decision to Sell Condoms

Functional Decision Areas

Merchandise Management	Promotion & Communication	Human Resources	Store Operations	Control & Accounting

Quantitative Information

Increasing Number of AIDS Cases	Sales Forecasts	Employee Scheduling & Pay	Amount of Space Devoted to Product	Processing Orders & Recording Sales

Qualitative Information

Public Attitude Toward "Safe Sex"	Attitudes Toward Promoting Use of Condoms	Personal & Psychological Characteristics	Impulse Purchase Positioning	Product Classification

Decision

Increase Sale of Condoms	More Obvious Point-of-Purchase Display	Druggist Will Give Advice	Store Layout Change	Inventory & Purchase Records

Exhibit 3–8
Characteristics and Uses of Information By Retail Drugstore Managers in Decision to Sell Condoms
· ·

potential location, and a computerized inventory status printout. Secondary data often provide a starting point for decision making and problem solving; if suitable information is available, it may not be necessary to expend the resources necessary to collect more data.

When a retailer is confronted with a particular problem or decision, but existing data are inadequate, inaccurate, or nonexistent, collecting data specifically for that purpose, although costly and time consuming, may be necessary. Primary data may be generated in one or a combination of four ways: (1) observation, e.g., traffic patterns, (2) survey, e.g., mail, telephone, or personal interview, (3) experiments, e.g., sales or advertising tests, and (4) simulation, e.g., synthetic data based on a model of observed behavior.

Comparison shopping in competitors' stores to determine their pricing strategies, shopping mall intercept surveys to determine customer preferences, on-site store location analysis to determine the condition of an existing building, and taking physical inventory in order to identify stock shortages are all examples of primary data.

Exhibit 3–9
Location and Type of Data Used in Retail Decisions

	Location of Data	
Type of Data	*Internal*	*External*
Primary	Employee surveys	Market surveys
	Incentive tests	Promotional tests
	Time and motion studies	License plates by county to assess trading area (in locations where this can be ascertained)
	Customer addresses on personal checks written in store	
Secondary	Accounting and financial records	Census data
	Inventory records	Other government publications
	Personnel files	Trade publications
		Professional journals

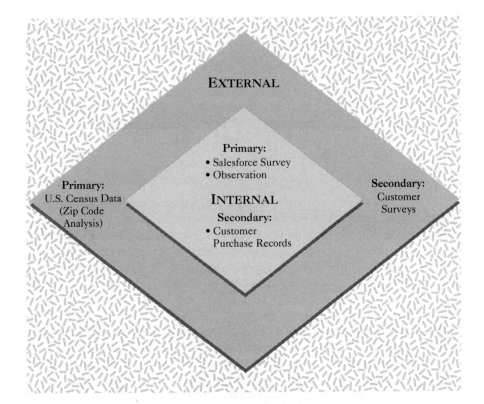

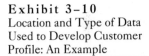
Exhibit 3–10
Location and Type of Data
Used to Develop Customer
Profile: An Example

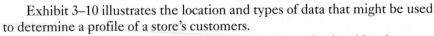

Exhibit 3–10 illustrates the location and types of data that might be used to determine a profile of a store's customers.

Company personnel, in various positions and organizational levels, may gather **external information** about environmental conditions and trends, as well as **internal information** about store operations. An obvious example of this is a formal market research department within the organization. A less obvious example is the buyer who combines knowledge derived from store records and sales personnel with that from trade publications and conversations with vendors and other buyers to develop a seasonal buying plan.

Similarly, retailers may hire outside providers of information to accomplish the same thing. They may subscribe to a research service or contract with a variety of professionals and consultants to keep them abreast of competitive intelligence, market trends, promotional response, legal and political activity, and other external information. Likewise, external parties may be hired to conduct research within the company regarding all aspects of the retail operation and to provide information in other areas such as accounting, finance, and the training and evaluation of personnel.

Why Is Information Needed?

Well-informed managers make better decisions. Retailers are confronted with a wide range of problems to solve and decisions to make in order to achieve company goals. They must anticipate the future, while considering both the realities of the present and the lessons of the past. The dynamic and competitive nature of the world of retailing dictates the need for an abundance of high quality and timely information. This information must be sorted out from the numerous facts and suppositions with which a retailer is continually bombarded.

As a result, retailers must be able to access and use information to identify and evaluate internal strengths and weaknesses and external opportunities and threats, facilitate the exchange of goods, financial resources, and ideas with external and internal groups, as well as to communicate with each of their constituencies. The one common denominator in the need for information is the desire to improve profitability.

STRENGTHS/WEAKNESSES AND OPPORTUNITIES/THREATS EVALUATION   This is often referred to as SWOT analysis, in which a retailing firm first looks inward to assess its own strengths and weaknesses and then looks outward to identify new business opportunities or potential dangers for the company. Strengths and weaknesses are internally based and are evaluated within the context of competition. This requires a clear understanding of the retailer's corporate mission, competitive advantages, resource availability for present and future operating periods, and areas of potential vulnerability.

Each aspect of the retailing mix (merchandise assortment, location, promotion, pricing, service) should be examined to determine strengths and weaknesses relative to competitors. Strengths generally evolve from positive external responses to internal management decisions about the use of company resources. Conversely, possible weaknesses are indicated by negative external responses. Collecting and analyzing information about each decision allows the retailer to know why a particular action succeeded or failed.

A common example of a retailer's strengths and weaknesses relates to choice of store location. Large retailers use sophisticated procedures to evaluate both new and existing locations; small retailers generally do not. For

EXTERNAL INFORMATION
data about environmental conditions and trends

INTERNAL INFORMATION
data about store operations

this scenario we will consider the plight of a small restaurant owner, Mike Allen, who did not have sufficient experience or information to evaluate the location of the restaurant he just purchased. The restaurant is in a college town and has menu items and prices that appeal to students. However, the location is farther away from campus than most dormitory residents care to walk, and many students do not have cars.

Feedback from a survey administered by a university marketing research class identified the restaurant's main strengths as quality and price of food, and the main weakness as its distance from campus. Mike's solution was to offer free delivery to campus customers with a minimum $5.00 purchase and to provide "family style dorm packs" to serve 10 or more on Sundays when the dining halls were closed. Student response was positive, and sales increased by 25 percent within two months. In this case, external response to an internal management decision was favorable, placing Mike's restaurant in a stronger market position.

Some areas of strength common to retailers are presented in Exhibit 3–11.

Once the retailer has assessed its internal strengths and weaknesses, it can scan the company's external environment to identify possible opportunities and threats. These opportunities and threats occur because of changes in

Exhibit 3–11
Retailer Strengths

Strength:	Example:
Merchandise Assortment	High quality at low prices Distinctive or exclusive goods Wide selection
Pricing Strategy	Everyday low prices, high efficiency Services included in fair prices Exclusivity at high prices, "value added"
Promotional Strategy	Effective media coverage to target market Professional sales force Customer service, personal relationships
Location	Easily accessed by target market Growth area with new businesses Resident customer base increasing
Channel Position	Vertically integrated Dominant buying power, leadership Strong, positive vendor relations
Reputation	Loyal customer base Positive image for quality, price Ethical, socially responsible company
Political Strength	Local Chamber of Commerce "clout" State legislature representation National representation in consumer affairs
Balance Sheet	Successful asset management, R.O.I. Available capital, cash flow Healthy debt to equity ratio
Organizational Structure	Advantages of large corporation, or Advantages of small retailer Effective human resources utilization

external environmental factors. Analysis requires both the knowledge of the present situation and an investigation of environmental trends or developments that could affect future strategies. All facts must be obtained, then filtered out, analyzed and evaluated. Once this is accomplished, each opportunity can be ranked according to its attractiveness, and each threat can be ranked according to its potential danger. Some possible scenarios that might indicate either a threat or an opportunity for a retailer include the following:

1. Changes in the retailer's or competitor's corporate structure, such as mergers and acquisitions
2. Favorable or unfavorable economic changes
3. Price wars and shortages of goods
4. Low unemployment rate.
5. Demographics, including an aging population and population shifts
6. Social problems, such as a poorly educated labor market
7. Store location changes for retailer or competitor; changes in the designs of major streets or highways

For example, Campeau's acquisition of the Allied and Federated Department Store chains opened up new ownership opportunities for other retailers, such as the May Company. Economic downturns have devastated some retailers; for others, it has spawned lower-priced hypermarkets and wholesale clubs. The threat of a dwindling population of young workers has caused fast-food operators to tap previously underutilized labor sources, such as McDonald's hiring of the elderly. Thus, it can be seen that what is a threat to one retailer can be an opportunity for another.

EXCHANGE FACILITATION   The factors that facilitate the exchange process include convenient locations, effective transportation, acceptable prices, and desirable services. Information enables the retailer to determine the most appropriate exchange partners and the most advantageous strategy for a satisfactory exchange to take place.

The information system contains facts obtained from order forms, inventory records, sales and markdowns, freight bills of lading, traffic counts, credit records, and countless other sources. These facts can be analyzed and interpreted to make the exchange process more profitable for all concerned.

COMMUNICATION   Without information, a retailer's efforts to communicate with its internal and external constituencies would be ineffective or nonexistent. Since customers do not always have sufficient knowledge to make informed choices, retailers must provide them with the appropriate information about their store and its merchandise and services. In addition, an information system would be incomplete without feedback from internal and external constituencies. The expected result is satisfaction for all concerned and profits for the retailer.

PROFITABILITY IMPROVEMENT   The need for information in evaluating environmental opportunities and threats, in facilitating the exchange process, and in communicating with others can be summarized as the need for information in improving the company's profit position. The increased

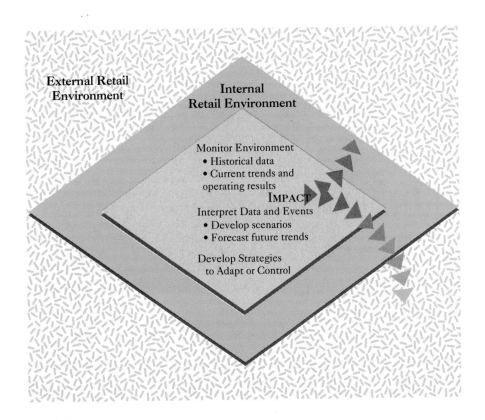

External Retail Environment

Internal Retail Environment

Monitor Environment
• Historical data
• Current trends and operating results

IMPACT

Interpret Data and Events
• Develop scenarios
• Forecast future trends

Develop Strategies to Adapt or Control

Exhibit 3–12
Retailer's Effect on Environment

pressure on profit margins has focused management's attention toward the "bottom line."

In order to develop strategies to increase profits, retail managers must constantly gather information that will allow them to monitor and evaluate results of their actions. Analysis and interpretation of this data provides insights into how to increase sales, decrease costs, and control inventory. It also provides a basis for more effective human resource management, store space utilization, sales forecasting, and planning in other areas.

In summary, a well-designed comprehensive information system allows the retailer to monitor the environment, interpret events, and use this information in developing strategies that will enable the firm to adapt to or control the environment; retail managers who take a proactive, rather than a reactive, approach to decision making can make a serious impact on their environments as shown in Exhibit 3–12. A knowledge of historical data, current operating results, and anticipated trends for the future can be combined to develop scenarios that predict the effect of various decisions.

Although it has been said that information is power, the question of just how much information is enough remains. Too much can result in an information overload if it is not categorized and prioritized, weeding out nonessential data. Logical relationships between management problems and data are needed to arrive at solutions to those problems. Therefore, retailers must decide what information is needed to accomplish the retailer's goals and tasks at hand, where that information is located, and how to access, store, analyze, and interpret data for retailing decisions.

Summary

Retailing is a dynamic process, operating in a constantly changing environment. Therefore, retail managers need the right information on a timely basis to operate their stores effectively. They must be aware of, and able to evaluate, what is happening both outside and inside the company. An Integrative Retail Information Model (IRIM) is presented to describe a complex set of relationships and information flows.

External environmental information desired by retailers focuses on consumer markets and shopping behavior, business influences, legal and political factors, the economy, and market and trading area characteristics.

Internal environmental information includes personnel, resources, and events in each of the store's five functional areas: human resources, store operations and physical facilities, merchandise management and pricing, promotion and communication with customers and other constituencies, and control and accounting.

Information about events in the external and internal environments is processed as data within a Retail Information System (RIS). While this process is usually a computerized system for a large retailer, it can also be a manual system for a small retailer. The RIS represents all data, facts, and information in various stages as they flow into, through, and out of the organization. The RIS is only as valuable as the quality and appropriateness of data inputs and analysis and the ability of managers to use it effectively in decision making. The major advantage of RIS is the availability of useful data on a timely basis. The major disadvantages are the initial effort and resources required to start and maintain the system. RIS can be used at all stages of the problem-solving process: recognition that a problem exists, search for information, evaluation of alternatives, choice of solution, evaluation of the resulting decision, and feedback for the next decision.

Retailers need to be able to access and use information in order to identify and evaluate strengths and weaknesses, opportunities and threats; facilitate exchange of goods, financial resources, and ideas with external and internal groups; communicate with each of their constituencies; and improve profitability.

The information required ranges from micro to macro in scope. Microenvironmental information is concerned with events, resources, and people within the individual firm, and macroenvironmental with those outside the firm. Information can also be in the form of quantitative data or qualitative verbal descriptions. Its location can be either external or internal to the firm. Data types include secondary data captured for some other purpose or primary data gathered to answer the retailer's specific question. The location and types of data combine to form four data categories: external secondary, external primary, internal secondary, and internal primary.

Questions for Review and Comprehension

1. Describe the important forces in the external environment that are beyond the direct control of the retailer, yet can have a significant effect on retail operations.

2. A video store owner has been losing sales to a new competitor. Recommend the types of information that he should obtain about his target market and competitors. Suggest some ways in which this information could be used in developing strategy.

3. Since retailers do not operate in isolation from other businesses, what are some questions that should be answered relative to suppliers and intermediaries, service providers, and technological advances?

4. Consult local legislation to determine the current regulatory environment for retailers in your community. Describe any retail activities that may be influenced by public policy or public interest groups.

5. Downturns in the economy present retailers with both opportunities and problems. Given the present economic situation in the United States, what types of retailers are in a position to capitalize on current trends? What types may have difficulty maintaining profitable operations?

6. A regional hardware store chain is considering geographic expansion. Discuss pertinent market and trade area factors and site characteristics that should be considered by the owners. Explain how locational considerations might be related to other macroenvironmental factors.

7. Discuss the important internal environmental factors that should be analyzed for each functional area of the store in order to determine a retail firm's strengths and weaknesses relative to competition.

8. Describe the three basic types of information that should be gathered and analyzed about the human resource aspect of a retail firm. Should retail tasks, organizational structure, and staffing/human resource management be viewed as separate issues, or should the retailer also consider how these factors might interact with one another? Defend your answer.

9. Outline a set of questions about store operations and physical facilities that a supermarket retailer should attempt to answer. Explain whether (and how) this list might differ for a new store versus an existing store.

10. What types of merchandise management information should be analyzed by an appliance retailer in order to determine the most efficient channels of distribution, merchandise assortments, inventory management, and pricing strategies?

11. Determine the most important questions that should be asked in planning, executing, and evaluating a retailer's promotional efforts. Evaluate the promotional efforts of one or more retailers with whom you are familiar, and explain whether you believe they did/did not consider the answers to these questions in designing their promotional strategy.

12. Discuss the relevance of the statement to managers who are responsible for designing systems for accounting and control: "Are customers buying what we are selling, and at what level of profit (or return on investment)?"

13. Explain the purpose of a retail information system (RIS), and describe the general procedures followed in order to provide managers with useful information. Discuss the advantages and disadvantages of a RIS for both a small retailer and a large retailer.

14. Give examples of data sources that might be consulted by an entrepreneur who is considering a new retail venture, as well as several critical uses of this information. Discussion should include specific types of data that might be needed to evaluate internal strengths and weaknesses and external opportunities and threats (i.e., SWOT analysis).

Retail Information Systems: A Supplier Perspective

The Ingram Distribution Group Inc., a division of Ingram Industries Inc. (Nashville, Tennessee), is the world's largest distributor of trade books and periodicals and microcomputer hardware, software, and accessories. It is the second largest video distributor in the United States. The Ingram Distribution Group serves nearly 100,000 accounts from 40 distribution centers around the world. The company is organized into three operating groups: the Book Group, the Entertainment Group, and the Microcomputer Group. Each group and its subsidiaries provide good examples of information systems support that is provided by a wholesaler to improve the operations of its retail customers.

The Ingram Book Company, one division of the Book Group, serves more than 25,000 retail outlets and represents more than 1,200 publishers, creating a crucial link between retailers and their suppliers. The company maintains a broad selection of over 95,000 book titles in inventory, and ships over 90 million books each year to customers around the world—providing delivery within two days to 90 percent of the United States population. How does Ingram Book Company manage this massive inventory and avoid stockouts for its retail customers? Systems technology includes alphabetically-arranged weekly inventory updates published on microfiche or CDROM-based systems. Inventory is managed through a microcomputer-based Title Review System networked with the company's mainframe computer. Retailers are also offered other innovative services such as electronic ordering, instant confirmation of product availability, 24-hour order fulfillment, opening store inventory assistance, and a variety of marketing support programs.

Ingram Micro Inc., a division of the Microcomputer Group, is the largest distributor of microcomputer products in the world with affiliates in Canada, United Kingdom, Belgium and Luxembourg, France, Netherlands, and Italy. These organizations, plus Ingram Laboratories, make up Ingram's Microcomputer Group. The company markets and distributes more than 8,000 microcomputer hardware, software, peripheral equipment, boards, and accessory products from over 500 suppliers to more than 64,000 computer retail specialty stores, value-added resellers, and other computer resellers. With the broadest product selection and largest inventory in the industry, Ingram Micro is the leader in product availability, delivery and competitive pricing. Ingram Micro provides extensive marketing support to retailers, including special merchandising programs, product information, and the creation of a wide variety of catalogs. This extensive support helps retailers compete successfully in a world that is becoming increasingly automated.

Ingram Entertainment Inc., a division of the Entertainment Group, is one of the two largest distributors of prerecorded video cassettes in the United States. Ingram Entertainment maintains an inventory of 14,000 video titles, representing all of the major studios and video suppliers, and a broad range of video releases. The company offers distribution and marketing support services to help its retail customers remain leaders in their local markets. Ingram Entertainment networks all its branches by using a sophisticated computer system to provide the highest fulfillment rate in the industry. Video products can be ordered and shipped from twelve fully-stocked warehouses and three "will-call" centers—giving Ingram the ability to provide the closeness and market knowledge of a small regional distributor. At the same time customers are given the systems and inventory support that only a large national distributor can provide. This division of the company also provides weekly microfiche updates and catalogs featuring new and upcoming titles for its customers.

Ingram Entertainment plc is one of the largest video cassette wholesalers in the United Kingdom (U.K.), serving more than 4,000 customers in the U.K. and other parts of Europe.

Another Ingram division, Ingram Merchandising Services Inc., offers complete merchandising and rack jobbing services for mass merchants, department stores, grocery stores, drug stores, video stores, and computer stores. Ingram Merchandising will take full responsibility for the inventory it places in a retail store—including stocking and restocking, processing merchandise returns, complete inventory accounting, and merchandising support and point-of-sale displays.

The Ingram Distribution Group divisions and their services described here are only part of a much larger enterprise. Ingram Book Company, Ingram Micro Inc., Ingram Entertainment Inc., and Ingram Merchandising Services Inc. are examples of service innovations that require information technology. Microcomputer products, books and video cassettes are popular consumer or small business purchases. However, they represent relatively small dollar transactions per customer and a monumental challenge for inventory management. These companies could not manage such an enormous number of titles, stockkeeping units (SKUs), and customers in such fast-moving industries without superior information systems. By managing information so effectively, Ingram's services help make their retail customers' operations more profitable.

Note: Ingram Industries Inc. is a large, privately held American company whose diverse business activities include in addition to those of the Ingram Distribution Group: inland marine transportation; aggregate supply; coal sales; manufacture of oil and gas wellhead equipment; oil exploration and production; and insurance.

SOURCE: Adapted from Ingram Industries, Inc. and Ingram Distribution Group company literature, courtesy of Philip M. Pfeffer, Chairman of the Board, Ingram Distribution Group Inc. (October, 1991).

EVOLUTION AND CLASSIFICATION OF RETAIL INSTITUTIONS

Outline

Learning Objectives

*After studying this chapter, the
student will be able to:*

1. Explain the retail life cycle,
wheel of retailing, retail accordion, dialectic process, adaptive behavior, and scrambled
merchandising theories.
2. Describe the different
types of retailers based on
ownership and control.
3. Discuss both margin-
turnover merchandise-type
classifications of retailers.
4. Discuss classification
schemes for general merchandise and food-based retailers.
5. Explain the implications of
intratype and intertype
competition.
6. Describe emerging non-
store retailing formats.

WHAT CUSTOMERS REALLY WANT: SERVICE, SERVICE, SERVICE

● ●

REMARKABLE RETAILER

Customers want low prices, but they also want service—personal service. The problem facing retailing executives is how to provide such personal service in the face of a shrinking and poorly trained labor market.

Super Valu's CEO, Michael Wright, one of the most successful service company managers, observed "We're used to competing for customers, but now we'll be faced with a growing need to compete for our work force." In response to this problem, companies like Super Valu are revamping their hiring and pay practices, searching for employees in some unusual places and compensating them on the basis of how well they have served their customers. Managers at Super Valu Stores' Cub Food markets in Denver must teach employees how to smile and walk erectly. They must even instruct some of them to dress for work with their shoes tied and shirts ironed.

The service ethic has a reciprocal effect. When employees are contented, they serve their customers better, and there is increasing evidence that improvements in customer satisfaction lead directly to higher retention of employees. Labor turnover is an important issue, both because employees are increasingly difficult to replace and because of the lost recruiting and training costs. It also affects customer service.

Full-service bank at Cub Foods . . .

Super Valu CEO, Mike Wright, says: "You always put the interests of the customers first. You provide the services they want, then you find a way to manage the business to do it efficiently." The company's Cub Food Stores are self-service, warehouse-style retail stores. Wright considers the service question broader than 'how do you interface with the customer at the deli counter.' He looks at variety as another service that should be offered to customers—because shoppers say that one of the most important things to them is choice. They have in-house pharmacies, fax centers, and full-service banks. They carry gourmet foods and some offer floral delivery and sell gasoline in the parking lot. At the same time, Cub's prices are 10 to 15 percent below the competition.

Super Valu has developed a strategy for meeting customers' demands for service, while running the lowest-cost food-based warehouse operation possible. Thus, it is not surprising that Super Valu was rated Number 3 on *Fortune's* list of the largest diversified service companies.

SOURCE: Sellers, Patricia (1990), "What Customers Really Want," *Fortune.* (June 4), 58–62, 66, 68.

Introduction

A colorful history characterizes the evolution of the retailing industry and the changing forms of its participants. Discussion of the evolution and classification of retail institutions in this chapter focuses on product retailers, but is also related to the retailing of services, i.e., intangible products. Service retailers are discussed extensively in the next chapter.

Present and Evolving Retail Formats and Strategic Planning

The form of operation chosen by most retail firms is an integral and intentional part of the company's strategic plan, as shown in Exhibit 4–1. As such, the operating format must support and complement all aspects of the retail strategy. To illustrate, consider the type of store that might evolve from a strategic plan for The Fix-It Center, a local independently owned hardware retailer. The owners want to provide their customers with a wide selection of home repair products at reasonable prices. This is the company's mission and the basis for its identity. Performance objectives include annual sales of $1 million with a seven percent return on assets. A situation analysis of the store's external and internal environments indicates that the trade area has a 10 percent annual growth rate in new households, but that these households primarily are occupied by low to middle income, young families with school age children.

The Fix-It Center's strategic objectives are to penetrate this market and to become the leading area retailer for this type of goods. To accomplish this, a discount pricing policy is established, accompanied by heavy promotion through advertising in newspaper inserts and sponsorship of special weekend events. Store personnel are knowledgeable about the merchandise in their departments and prepared to answer customers' questions. To illustrate, Joe, who works in plumbing, can give advice to the inexperienced customer who wants to repair his or her own stopped-up sink. In order to provide this type of service, and achieve the desired objectives, the retailer must use all assets as efficiently as possible within a low-cost, no-frills environment. The resulting format is an independently owned discount hardware store that competes on the basis of both price and service. The owners realize, however, that they need to continue to monitor their environment—particularly customers and competitors—to be sure that their format and retailing mix remain viable. For example, the population of the trade area might shift to older couples, and more residents might choose to rent rather than own their homes, or there might be other factors that would suggest a need for change.

Retail Formats and Environmental Influences

In selecting the most appropriate format for a particular retail business, managers must investigate and evaluate important factors in both the external and internal environments, as shown in Chapter 3 in the Integrative Retail

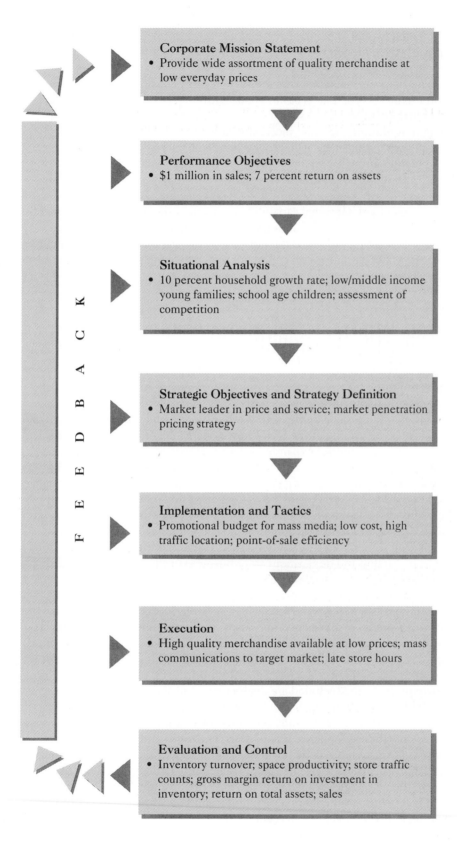

Corporate Mission Statement
- Provide wide assortment of quality merchandise at low everyday prices

Performance Objectives
- $1 million in sales; 7 percent return on assets

Situational Analysis
- 10 percent household growth rate; low/middle income young families; school age children; assessment of competition

Strategic Objectives and Strategy Definition
- Market leader in price and service; market penetration pricing strategy

Implementation and Tactics
- Promotional budget for mass media; low cost, high traffic location; point-of-sale efficiency

Execution
- High quality merchandise available at low prices; mass communications to target market; late store hours

Evaluation and Control
- Inventory turnover; space productivity; store traffic counts; gross margin return on investment in inventory; return on total assets; sales

FEEDBACK

Exhibit 4–1
Retail Formats and Strategic
Planning: An Illustration

Information Model. The managers can use this information to design the business, based on determination of external opportunities and threats and internal strengths and weaknesses.

The first external factor that the retailer must consider is the consumer market to be served. The types of goods and services desired by customers, and how they want to shop for those goods and services, will play a major role in determining the most successful format for a retail business. Likewise, the type of business will depend on the characteristics of competitors in the market and what strategies they are pursuing, availability of the "right" suppliers, possible legal constraints, and ability to obtain profitable locations.

The company's internal capabilities also affect the form of operation chosen by the retailer. In addition to the necessary financial resources, other internal factors that influence the design and success of retail formats include management preferences and expertise, merchandising ability, pricing structure, and competitive strategies. (See Exhibit 4–2.)

Retail Strategies and Structural Changes

Throughout the history of the retailing industry, managers have made strategic decisions about the best ways to meet the needs of their customers. In 1886, Richard Sears decided to sell watches directly to customers through the mail, the beginning of the well-known Sears mail order catalog. Sears observed that as America expanded westward, each town had its own train station and post office, a necessary combination for his new business. His watches-by-mail business soon developed into a general merchandise catalog operation. In 1925, Sears opened the company's first retail store, followed by the addition of Allstate Insurance in 1931. Following World War II, Sears led the way in suburban mall development, placing retail stores closer to customers who were moving out of the cities in large numbers. Sears grew from a full-line catalog and department store business to a comprehensive business that includes financial services (Dean Witter Financial Services), real estate (Coldwell Banker), and a credit card business (Discover Card), in addition to Allstate. Sears' Financial Network produced 41 percent of the company's profits in 1989, covering losses from its merchandising operations. The company strives to change with the times by upgrading stores, lowering everyday prices, and modernizing merchandise lines. It is dividing each of its 850 large stores into over a dozen specialty businesses, each responsible for its own profitability. Included are distinctive retail shops for men's, women's and children's clothing, paint and hardware, home furnishings, Brand Central appliances and electronic goods, and automotive supplies. The company's service operations (appliance repair, delivery, credit) and unprofitable catalog business are also stand-alone businesses. The hoped-for turnaround in Sears merchandising business has been slow in coming, but company executives believe their strategies will work in the long run (Weiner 1990a).

The evolution of individual retailing firms such as Sears, and of the retailing industry in general, has been explained by various theories of institutional change. The theories are important because they help retailers

Exhibit 4–2
Retail Formats and The IRIM

SOURCE: Anderson and Parker 1988

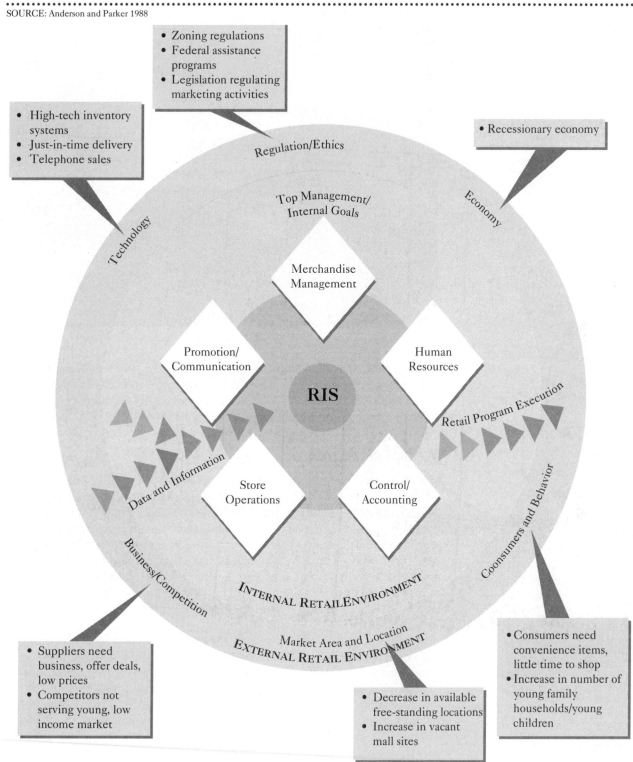

- Zoning regulations
- Federal assistance programs
- Legislation regulating marketing activities

- High-tech inventory systems
- Just-in-time delivery
- Telephone sales

- Recessionary economy

Regulation/Ethics

Technology

Economy

Top Management/
Internal Goals

Merchandise
Management

Promotion/
Communication

Human
Resources

RIS

Retail Program Execution

Data and Information

Store
Operations

Control/
Accounting

Consumers and Behavior

Business/Competition

INTERNAL RETAIL ENVIRONMENT

Market Area and Location
EXTERNAL RETAIL ENVIRONMENT

- Suppliers need business, offer deals, low prices
- Competitors not serving young, low income market

- Decrease in available free-standing locations
- Increase in vacant mall sites

- Consumers need convenience items, little time to shop
- Increase in number of young family households/young children

COURTESY OF SEARS

The Sears Laboratory on Chicago's West Side opened in 1911 to provide quality control for the catalog operation.

develop proactive and adaptive strategies for change. These theories include the retail life cycle concept, wheel of retailing, retail accordion, dialectic process, natural selection or adaptive behavior, and scrambled merchandising. Each of these is described below.

Retail Life Cycle

The **retail life cycle concept** provides a framework for understanding how the strategy and structure of retail institutions change over time. The theory suggests that, like products, retail institutions evolve through four major identifiable stages: innovation, accelerated development, maturity, and decline. Although no one can say for certain just how long each stage will last, the life cycle framework provides a tool for managers to use in evaluating present strategies and anticipating future changes. The general characteristics of each stage of the retail life cycle, from the inception to the demise of a business, are shown in Exhibit 4–3.

INNOVATION   The first stage in the retail life cycle is **innovation** or introduction, representing a drastic departure from the existing norms in retail practice. The difference may be due to a low-cost advantage achieved by today's discounters and off-price merchants, or an unusual or distinctive product assortment such as that of the Sharper Image, or unique features or operating methods such as videodisc kiosks (free-standing interactive computer terminals) where customers can view and order merchandise outside of the traditional store setting. Approximate dates of important retail innovations include the downtown department store in 1860, variety store in 1910,

RETAIL LIFE CYCLE CONCEPT
retail institutions evolve through four stages: innovation, accelerated development, maturity, and decline

INNOVATION
first stage in the retail life cycle; a drastic departure from existing norms in retail practice

Exhibit 4–3
Retail Life Cycle

| Area or subject of concern | Stage of Life Cycle Development | | | |
	Innovation	Accelerated development	Maturity	Decline
Market Characteristics				
Number of competitors	Very few	Moderate	Many direct competitors Moderate indirect competition	Moderate direct competition. Many indirect competitors
Rate of sales growth	Very rapid	Rapid	Moderate to slow	Slow or negative
Level of Profitability	Low to moderate	High	Moderate	Very low
Duration of new innovations	3 to 5 years	5 to 6 years	Indefinite	Indefinite
Appropriate Retailer Actions				
Investment/growth/risk decisions	Investment minimization, high risks accepted	High levels of investment to sustain growth	Tightly controlled growth in untapped markets	Minimal capital expenditures only when essential
Central management concerns	Concept refinement through adjustment and experimentation	Establishing a preemptive market position	Excess capacity and "overstoring" Prolonging maturity and revising the retail concept	Engaging in a "runout" strategy
Use of management control techniques	Minimal	Moderate	Extensive	Moderate
Most successful management style	Entrepreneurial	Centralized	Professional	Caretaker
Appropriate Supplier Actions				
Channel strategy	Develop a preemptive market position	Hold market position	Maintain profitable sales	Avoid excessive costs
Channel problems	Possible antagonism of other accounts	Possible antagonism of other accounts	Dealing with more scientific retailers	Servicing accounts at a profit
Channel research	Identification of key innovations	Identification of other retailers adopting the innovation	Initial screening of new innovation opportunities	Active search for new innovation opportunities
Trade incentives	Direct financial support	Price concessions	New price incentives	None

supermarket in 1930, discount department store in 1950 and home improvement center in 1965 (Davidson, Bates, and Bass, 1976).

Successful innovators tend to be creative entrepreneurs with a high tolerance for risk. Since there are few or no competitors during this stage, the
retailer can expect rapid growth in sales, although the uniqueness of this
offering must be promoted to potential customers.

ACCELERATED DEVELOPMENT   During the **accelerated develop-
ment** stage of the retail life cycle, sales and profits escalate rapidly. This, in
turn, attracts new competitors, and the innovator attempts to defend market
share with strategies such as pursuit of new market segments, or expansion
of product lines or geographic coverage. However, these measures tend to
increase operating costs and have an adverse effect on profits. If a retailer
attempts to expand too rapidly during this stage, management may not be
able to manage the larger organization. Some fast-growing Mexican restaurant chains and others have suffered because of this.

On the other hand, retailers such as The Limited have been successful
during this stage while simultaneously developing strategies to remain viable
as they move into the mature phase of the retail life cycle. The Limited,
considered by many to be the nation's most successful specialty store merchant, has amassed seven specialty-apparel store divisions, including The
Limited, Lerner, Limited Express, Victoria's Secret, Lane Bryant, Henri
Bendel, and Abercrombie & Fitch. These stores have different styles and

*A typical A&P of the 1880's (left)
featured a long line of gaslights
across the facade. A model of A&P's
"Futurestore" (right) has wide aisles
and an uncluttered glass facade.*

price ranges, having the impact of a department store in many shopping malls. The Limited's chairman, Leslie H. Wexner, projects sales of $10 billion by the mid-1990s (Phillips and Duncan, 1989).

MATURITY   The **maturity** stage is characterized by intense competition in a relatively saturated market. This tends to have a stabilizing effect on market share. Increased competition results in lower consumer prices, accompanied by higher promotional expenses to gain customer loyalty. At this point, other innovators can be expected to enter the market. The challenge to "mature" retail institutions is to extend this life cycle stage to achieve long-term stability, particularly if they have made a considerable investment in development and expansion. This requires creative solutions. For example, as mass merchandisers have been faced with increased competition, and continually lower prices have threatened profit margins, Wal-Mart has protected its position by opening Sam's Wholesale Clubs and hypermarkets. As noted previously, Sears' repositioning strategy has included the division of stores into specialty businesses, as well as lower everyday prices.

The progression of the traditional department store into the mature phase of the retail life cycle has occurred for several reasons. They have been replaced in part by specialty retailers who have responded to the increasing fragmentation of shoppers by providing dominant assortments and an entrepreneurial approach to meeting customer needs in emerging or underdeveloped market niches. In addition, the mall has replaced the department store as a primary shopping destination; overstoring has led department stores to engage in heavy off-price promotions; and individual store identities have become blurred by the sameness of their assortments that are dictated to a large extent by suppliers. Department stores are forced to develop strategies to remain viable. Such strategies include more attention to customer service, more efficient buying organizations that are more sensitive to customer needs, specialty chain spinoffs such as Bloomingdale's Express airport shops and Carson's Corporate Level, and direct marketing businesses such as Saks Fifth Avenue's Folio and Bloomingdale's By Mail (Levy, 1987).

DECLINE   For some retailers, **decline** is inevitable as customers are attracted to newer, more exciting shopping opportunities and as sales and profits fall below the level of survival. Other retailers are able to postpone or avoid this final stage in the retail life cycle by modifying, repositioning, or adapting their strategies—perhaps leading to another retailing innovation, starting the cycle all over again. The variety store illustrates a retail establishment in the decline phase. W.T. Grant, for example, was not able to reposition itself in order to survive and subsequently closed its doors.

A common dilemma faced by retailers is changing customers. Most shoppers are so conditioned to sales and bargains that they never expect to pay full price. Mergers and buyouts have also accelerated the process of losing touch with customers. Retailers have failed to grasp the implications of merchandising to an older U.S. population, with a notable increase in the 35–44 age group and decrease in the 14–25 age group. A case in point is the disastrous reintroduction of the miniskirt in 1987. Customers who were old

ACCELERATED DEVELOPMENT
second stage of retail life cycle; sales and profits escalate rapidly

MATURITY
third stage of the retail life cycle; characterized by intense competition in a relatively saturated market

DECLINE
final stage of the retail life cycle; sales and profits fall below survival level

enough to wear miniskirts two decades earlier "just said no" at an older age (Caminti, 1989).

Wheel of Retailing

The **wheel of retailing** hypothesis was developed by Professor Malcom McNair, a retailing authority at Harvard University, over 30 years ago. This popular theory explains the evolution of retail institutions in terms of a cyclical or wheel-like progression. Although the wheel of retailing does not provide an adequate explanation for the evolution of all retail institutions, it does help in understanding the upward spiral of retail innovators who enter the marketplace as low-margin, low-priced, low status operators. In the beginning, these retailers appeal to price-conscious consumers by controlling costs through a no-frills store atmosphere, little or no customer service, and lower quality of merchandise. Over time, competitive pressures result in upgrading of physical facilities, addition of customer services, and higher quality merchandise. In the quest for expanding market share, the retailer has moved away from the original low-cost structure. As a result, the original price-conscious, nonloyal customer base is attracted to a new low-cost innovator. Eventually, the new low-end retailers will succumb to the same "wheel" effect as they seek competitive advantage. (See Exhibit 4–4.)

The wheel of retailing theory does help managers realize that changes that move a retailer to a higher cost, and thus more upscale, position on the wheel may be very gradual and not easily observed in short-term decisions. The theory may not be valid for all retailing because not every firm enters the system with a low-price strategy. However, it does provide insights about how to slow down this upward spiral—or even to take advantage of it. (See Hollander, 1960.)

The wheel of retailing hypothesis is based on four generally accepted premises:

1. New retail institutions enter the system as highly aggressive, cost-conscious entrepreneurs. They appeal to price-sensitive shoppers who are willing to sacrifice convenience and service for lower prices.
2. The retailer achieves the low-price strategy through low operating costs resulting from less expensive locations and store decor, volume buying, and few or no customer services.
3. Once the retailer has become established, it begins to increase the quality and price lines of its merchandise, refurbish stores, and generally appeal to a higher-end market, essentially changing its target market focus.
4. The original price-conscious customers are attracted by price, not store loyalty. Thus, a new low cost innovator enters the market to satisfy these customers, filling the place on the "wheel" vacated by its predecessor.

To illustrate the wheel of retailing theory, the department store originally appealed to a mass market with a broad range of merchandise at moderate prices. Over time department stores increased their focus on customer service, fashion merchandise, and more attractive stores to appeal to a more upscale market. This created a void that was soon filled by the discount store, which attracted the price-conscious customer with a relatively wide assortment of goods at low prices. Once again, the "wheel turned" as the discounters became more upscale—leaving the nonloyal price-conscious cus-

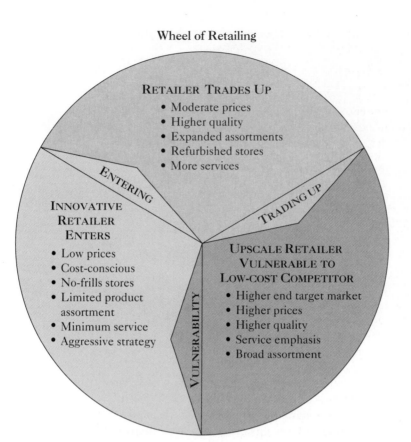

Wheel of Retailing

RETAILER TRADES UP
- Moderate prices
- Higher quality
- Expanded assortments
- Refurbished stores
- More services

ENTERING

TRADING UP

INNOVATIVE RETAILER ENTERS
- Low prices
- Cost-conscious
- No-frills stores
- Limited product assortment
- Minimum service
- Aggressive strategy

VULNERABILITY

UPSCALE RETAILER VULNERABLE TO LOW-COST COMPETITOR
- Higher end target market
- Higher prices
- Higher quality
- Service emphasis
- Broad assortment

Exhibit 4–4
Wheel of Retailing

tomers to the new low-price innovators, such as the catalog showrooms and off-price chains.

Retail Accordion

The **retail accordion concept** is an alternative explanation of changes in retail structure. Its name is derived from a general–specific–general pattern that emerges from the expansion and contraction of merchandise lines. Early American settlers made their purchases from the covered wagons of itinerant peddlers, or shopped in general stores that carried a broad assortment of unrelated merchandise—farm implements, fabric, food products, clothing items, and cure-all elixers. The general store is still needed in sparsely populated rural areas today. In many cases, the general–specific–general evolution has been gradual. For example, the department stores became a more specialized form of the general store to meet the needs of a growing population. In some cases, segmentation strategies have controlled the development of new types of retailers.

As customers became more concentrated geographically, department store lines became more and more specialized to meet the needs of those customers. Eventually, specialized stores that carried narrower lines of goods became more prevalent. Some focused on a few related lines of merchandise and others, like Singer Sewing Machine Co., on a single product line. However, little by little, these same retailers who had focused on specific product

WHEEL OF RETAILING
explanation of the evolution of retail institution as a wheel-like progression

RETAIL ACCORDION CONCEPT
general-specific-general pattern that emerges from expansion and contraction of merchandise lines

COURTESY OF TOYS 'R' US

While Toy's "R" Us has expanded its merchandise assortment, it remains specialized in that it targets the youth market.

lines now began to add other, unrelated lines, once again moving toward broad assortments of unrelated goods.

Supermarkets started in the 1930s, which became popular in the 1950s by concentrating on basic groceries, now carry many other nonbasic and specialty foods, clothing, appliances, and other general merchandise. Some food-based retailers have gone the other direction and limited their lines to gourmet foods, delicatessans, and so forth. Drug stores have experienced a similar type of evolution, moving from a simple pharmacy to a broad merchandise mix of cosmetics, magazines, food products, small appliances, and many other unrelated items. Some have returned to a narrower line, focusing on pharmaceutical needs and health-related items. (See Exhibit 4–5.)

Since the early 1980s, retailers have evolved in two different directions. One trend has been a continued movement toward highly specialized merchandise lines. Examples include Waldenbooks for Kids, Docktor's Pet Centers, Benetton and Toys "R" Us. Even the broader-based department stores

Exhibit 4–5
Retail Accordion

General ⟶	*Specific*	⟶ *General*	
General Store	*Department Store*	*Single-line; Specialty Store*	*Superstore*
Wide assortment	More specialized than general store	One or a few merchandise lines	Wide assortment
One-stop shopping			One-stop shopping
	Urban-dense populations	Drug stores, bookstores	
Rural/sparse populations			Serve large populations

have adopted specialty formats for many merchandise lines in order to compete with specialty retailers.

The other trend has been toward a general merchandise mix, with broad assortments represented in large retail establishments such as hypermarkets. While the specialty store is a predominant retail institution today, a broad assortment of specialty merchandise is available to customers in one-stop locations such as a shopping mall or superstores.

Dialectic Process

As old and new, or substantially different competitive forms of retail institutions adapt to each other, distinctly different forms often emerge. This continual transformation can be explained by a **dialectic process** consisting of thesis–antithesis–synthesis. Thesis represents the original operating method, antithesis the opposite operating method, and synthesis some new creative combination of the two. This blending process also has been referred to as the melting pot theory. (See Exhibit 4–6.)

As Maronick and Walker (1975) state:

> *In terms of retail institutions, the dialectic model implies that retailers mutually adapt in the face of competition from "opposites." Thus, when challenged by a competitor with a differential advantage, an established institution will adopt strategies and tactics in the direction of that advantage, thereby negating some of the innovator's attraction. The innovator, meanwhile, does not remain unchanged. Rather, as McNair noted, the innovator over time tends to upgrade or otherwise modify products and facilities. In doing so, he moves toward the negated institution. As a result of these mutual adaptations, the two retailers gradually move together in terms of offerings, facilities, supplementary services, and prices. They thus become indistinguishable or at least quite similar and constitute a new retail institution, termed the synthesis. This new institution is then vulnerable to "negation" by new competitors as the dialectic process begins anew (pp. 147–151).*

The dialectic process can be illustrated by the early full-service department stores, high-margin, high-price operations in downtown locations (thesis). Next, discount stores opened in suburban locations with lower margins and

Exhibit 4–6
Dialectic Process
•••••••••••••••••••••••••••••

SOURCE; *Proceedings:* Southern Marketing Association, "The Dialectic Evolution of Retailing," B. Greenberg, ed.

prices, higher inventory turnover, and self-service (antithesis), are followed by a combined format—discount department stores such as Fred Meyer, Target, or K mart (synthesis). On a smaller scale, the dialectic process can be illustrated with the example of the old-fashioned gas station, followed by the convenience store, and today's combined format that often makes one industry indistinguishable from the other.

Adaptive Behavior

The **adaptive behavior theory** of institutional changes in retailing is based on Darwin's theory of natural selection—the survival of the fittest—as described by Dreesman (1968). Those retailers that have survived and prospered have found ways to adapt to their changing environments, particularly in regard to consumer buying habits, competition, technology, and legal aspects. Changes in consumer buying habits include less store loyalty than in the past, more heterogeneous lifestyles, and large numbers of working women who place increased value on their time. Major changes in the competitive environment include an overstored economy where the only way for retailers to grow is to take business away from someone else, increased num-

Exhibit 4–7
Adaptive Behavior
· ·

SOURCE: Adapted from G. Brockway, Gary R. and P. Niffenegger (1988), "Retailing Evolution in the 1980s: Survival Through Adaptive Behavior," *Journal of Midwest Marketing*, 3:2, p. 13.

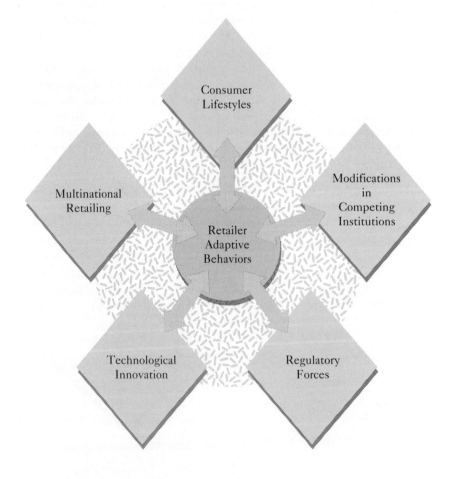

Exhibit 4–8
Adaptive Behaviors Practiced by Retail Institutions During the 1980s

Behavior	Form	Example
Experimentation	Trying out the innovation in the retail mix on a small scale	Kroger's testing of self-service checkout scanners
Copycatism	Rapidly duplicating the successful innovation of another institution	Many newly emerging home shopping programs
Joint Retailing	Combining two normally separate institutions under a single roof	7-Eleven outlets selling Kentucky Fried Chicken
Vertical Integration	Taking over an added function performed either higher or lower in the channel	Benetton building U.S. factories; Sharper Image opening retail stores
Horizontal Integration	Acquiring control over similar retail institutions	Dillard's of Little Rock acquires Cain Sloan of Nashville
Physical Premises Mutation	Changing the normal locations or combinations of the institution	Off-price stores cluster in strips and malls
Focused or Micro-merchandising	Identifying a demographic/lifestyle segment, then creating a store for it	Waldenkids books; Gap Kids clothing

SOURCE: Adapted from G. Brockway, Gary R. and P. Niffenegger (1988), "Retailing Evolution in the 1980s: Survival Through Adaptive Behavior," *Journal of Midwest Marketing*, 3, no. 2 (Fall), 1–16.

ber of multinational retailers entering the market (e.g., Swatch, IKEA, Conran's), and the entry of upscale apparel manufacturers and designers who are marketing their products through their own stores. Retailers also have been greatly affected by technology-driven innovations, such as computers and optical scanning and satellite technology. In the legal environment, retailers have been impacted by the demise of fair trade laws and more liberal banking laws (Brockway and Niffenegger, 1988). The interaction between the environment and retailers' adaptive behavior is illustrated in Exhibit 4–7.

In some ways the adaptive behavior of retail institutions can be related to the retail life cycle. Those firms in the innovation and growth stages have adapted to changing conditions by starting new business forms, or restructuring old businesses. Retailers in the mature stage are surviving in the midst of severe competition. From here, they have two alternatives: extending the life cycle by adapting to change with one or more elements of the retailing mix; or heading for extinction in the decline stage. Examples of adaptive behavior are given in Exhibit 4–8.

Scrambled Merchandising

Adding product lines or services that are unrelated to a retailer's business is referred to as **scrambled merchandising.** Retailers use this strategy primarily to increase sales and profits, generally through higher margin items that sell quickly—often impulse purchases. For example, grocery stores have

DIALECTIC PROCESS

continual transformation of retail institutions; thesis-antithesis-synthesis pattern

ADAPTIVE BEHAVIOR THEORY

retailers survive and prosper because they can adapt to changing environments

SCRAMBLED MERCHANDISING

adding unrelated product lines or services to existing business

added selected hardware and auto supplies to their traditional grocery offerings. Not only does this offer the consumer one-stop shopping, but the markup is usually higher, leading to a higher gross margin for the company. This retailing action may result in reactions by hardware and auto supply competitors who are losing sales to the grocer. They may respond by selling convenience foods and snacks or cleaning supplies to recoup some of their losses.

Examples of scrambled merchandising, include the gasoline service station that sells soda and sunglasses and the drugstore that sells milk and eggs. Many traditional retailers have added unrelated service lines to their mix, such as banking services at K mart and financial services and insurance at Sears. A customer can buy long-distance telephone service, and products ranging from barbecue grills to exercise bicycles from the AT&T Callers' Club direct marketing catalog. At Carson, Pirie Scott's Corporate Level, a woman can buy designer outfits and accessories, have her shoes repaired and her hair styled, and make a bank deposit, all in one stop.

CLASSIFYING RETAILERS BASED ON OWNERSHIP AND CONTROL

A commonly used classification of retail institutions is based on the form of ownership. The diversity of U.S. retailers can be described and analyzed in terms of the following ownership types: independent or single-store; chain; and leased departments. Retail firms can also be classified acording to the structure of the channel systems in which they operate, a combination of both ownership and control. Here the designation is usually in terms of vertical marketing systems, coordinated systems of producers, wholesalers, and retailers. The primary types of vertical marketing systems are corporate, administered, and contractual, which includes the rapidly growing franchise segment. Retail institutions also may be owned by consumers (cooperatives),

The operation of Akron, Ohio's independently-owned West Point Market, known for its specialty and gourmet foods, has been studied by food industry executives from as far away as Japan.

COURTESY OF WEST POINT MARKET

federal and state government, farmers, and public utilities. Each of these is described below.

Independent or Single-Store

The **independent ownership** classification is defined as a one-store operation. The legal form of ownership may be a sole proprietorship, partnership, or corporation. Many are family-owned small businesses. Comparisons of ownership types show that the independent owner with only one store remains the single most important retail institution. Independents account for 79 percent of all retail establishments, and slightly over 50 percent of all retail sales. (See Exhibit 4–9.) Although not included in these figures, service retailing represents major economic growth opportunities for small independents.

The advantages of independent ownership versus the larger chain store organization include easy entry into the business, lower capital requirements, lower operating costs, fewer legal restrictions, and more opportunities for specialization or for developing a unique identity or customer niche. Managers are closer to the customers and have a better understanding of their needs. They have more flexibility in running the business and can make

INDEPENDENT OWNERSHIP
a one-store operation

Exhibit 4–9
Individual Proprietorships and Partnerships: 1987 Summary Statistics

Kind of Business	Number	Sales (thousands of dollars)	Individual Proprietor- ships	Partnerships
All retail trade	2,419,641	1,540,263,330	1,242,788	144,943
Building materials and garden supplies	106,744	83,454,152	45,113	5,915
General merchandise	56,868	181,970,504	24,777	2,651
Food stores	290,245	309,460,345	152,937	19,706
Automotive dealers	194,315	342,895,775	103,803	8,303
Gasoline service stations	137,180	104,769,093	65,960	7,586
Apparel and accessories	197,411	79,322,241	65,589	11,277
Furniture and home furnishings	180,012	78,071,676	8,983	109,653
Eating and drinking places	490,383	153,461,612	209,000	39,541
Miscellaneous retail stores	710,498	152,715,991	472,259	39,212

SOURCE: *1987 Census of Retail Trade.* U.S. Department of Commerce, Bureau of the Census, Washington, D.C.: U.S. Government Printing Office.

decisions quickly without consulting higher level managers. On the negative side, independent businesses have experienced a high failure rate. They lack the economies of scale that are common to multiple store operators, and their limited buying power places them at a disadvantage in negotiations with suppliers. Independent store management tends to be less professional than the better trained chain store executives, and there is an overreliance on the manager/owner who finds it difficult to set aside time for planning.

Chain

Chain store organizations involve common ownership of more than one store, typically selling similar merchandise in similar-appearing stores that are operated in a similar manner. **Chains** include the small two-store "mom and pop" grocery chain, as well as the Southland Corporation with more than 13,000 units throughout the world, or other large chains, such as Sears, J.C. Penney, and American Stores. The product or service mix has a broad appeal, which facilitates a high degree of centralized management and buying.

The forerunners of the American chain store were A&P and F.W. Woolworth, established in the mid-1800s as a sole proprietorship and corporation respectively. Supermarket and variety store chains expanded rapidly during the 1920s and 1930s. The leading chains in the United States today are Sears, K mart, Wal-Mart, American Stores, and Kroger, as noted in Chapter 1. Exhibit 4–10 provides an overview of the sales and profitability of selected chains in six categories in 1989, underscoring the importance of this ownership type to the U.S. economy.

A *Forbes* article referred to 1989 as the "year of the fire sale—not only for merchandise, but also for the stores themselves." Major retail chains were in turmoil as owners who were deeply in debt, or fighting possible takeovers, tried to sell off units in a time of great uncertainty. Offered for sale were Bloomingdale's by Campeau Corp., Saks Fifth Avenue and Marshall Field's by B.A.T. Industries, and Bonwit Teller and Sakowitz by Hooker Corp. (Weiner, 1990b).

Chain store ownership has a number of advantages. Economies of scale can be realized because fixed costs can be shared by more stores. The multi-store firm can lower costs through standardization of store designs, fixtures, and operating procedures and the ability of the firm to perform more of its own functions, such as wholesaling, warehousing, and shipping. In addition, management expertise can be transferred, and the company has bargaining power in dealing with suppliers and intermediaries. A chain also has a competitive advantage in attracting customers and resources, and has been media access.

Disadvantages of chain versus independent ownership include high capital investment, higher overhead, more government regulation, and the difficulty of controlling a widely dispersed company. Managers do not have the flexibility to make autonomous decisions if the organization is highly centralized, which may make it difficult to adapt to local needs.

Leased Department

A **leased department** is usually operated under the retailer's (lessor's) name by an outside company (lessee) that owns the merchandise and has expertise

CHAIN

ownership of more than one store; typically look similar and operate in a similar manner

LEASED DEPARTMENT

operated under the retailer's name by an outside company that owns the merchandise

Exhibit 4–10
Sales and Profitability of Selected Chains (1989)

Retailer	Sales	Sales Growth			Net Income
	Latest 12 mos. ($mil)	10-year avg. (%)	5-year avg (%)	Latest 12 mos. (%)	Latest 12 mos. ($mil)
Department Stores					
Dillard's	2,715	24.2	23.2	13.9	121
Mercantile	2,249	9.6	7.2	2.7	141
May Dept.	10,415	11.0	7.3	-1.6	491
Sears	53,181	8.4	6.7	8.4	1,024
Industry medians		9.5	7.3	6.1	
Apparel					
Limited	4,421	38.4	32.2	18.7	314
Gap	1,465	16.1	22.6	23.2	96
Nordstrom	2,579	23.9	24.4	19.2	131
Brown Group	1,782	3.6	2.4	5.8	10
Industry medians		14.1	12.6	12.7	
Drug & Discount					
Wal-Mart	24,335	37.4	34.7	26.6	973
Walgreen	5,380	15.4	15.7	10.2	154
Dollar Gen'l	613	16.3	10.3	2.0	11
Industry medians		15.0	14.6	11.7	
Speciality					
Price Co.	4,901	54.4	43.6	20.9	117
Circuit City	1,877	35.0	37.3	22.0	71
Tandy	4,230	13.8	8.6	8.7	321
Toys 'R' Us	4,349	27.0	24.2	18.9	276
Industry medians		14.8	18.5	12.5	
Supermarkets					
Food Lion	4,449	28.4	26.6	26.3	127
Giant Food	3,110	10.1	8.8	9.6	104
Winn-Dixie	9,292	7.2	5.5	2.8	139
Bruno's	2,198	18.8	23.8	11.1	50
Industry medians		10.8	10.7	12.2	
Restaurant Chains					
McDonald's	5,967	12.8	12.9	11.7	707
Morrison	849	11.4	10.0	19.2	32
Wendy's	1,052	19.3	6.6	-0.2	25
TGI Friday's	387	22.8	11.6	-3.0	14
Industry medians		14.5	11.5	8.6	

SOURCE: Excerpted by permission of *Forbes* magazine, January 8, 1990. © Forbes Inc., 1990.

in a particular line of goods. The lessee generally assumes responsibility for the department (fixtures, personnel, etc.), and pays the retailer a percentage of sales. Merchandise lines, such as shoes, millinery, jewelry, and cosmetics, and services such as watch and shoe repair, beauty salons, and photographic studios, are typically sold in leased departments. The lessee is required to adhere to store policies and procedures. This is because a negative store image could result if the department is not operated in a manner that is consistent with the rest of the store. When customers have problems they may blame the retailer rather than the lessee.

A leased department operator can benefit from an association with an existing store that is well-known and has a positive image. The leased department can take advantage of the traffic generated by other departments in the store, shared operating expenses, and economies of scale. On the negative side, the lessee must adhere to the retailer's hours and other requirements. The retailer also may impose certain restrictions on merchandise lines and services that can be offered, and may not give the leased department an ideal location in the store. The lessor can benefit (or suffer) from the image of the lessee and additional traffic and revenues, with minimum use of the retailer's resources other than space.

Vertical Marketing System

In a conventional marketing channel the producer, wholesaler, and retailer are operated as independent firms. No one channel member controls the others; each exists as a separate business attempting to maximize its own profits. In contrast, a **vertical marketing system (VMS),** coordinates any number of producers, wholesalers, and retailers. A VMS exists when a single firm owns two or more stages of production and/or distribution. A VMS also exists when one channel member franchises others, or can exert enough power to gain their cooperation. A vertical marketing system can be controlled by a producer, wholesaler, or retailer. If the channel is totally integrated, all three stages are under one ownership. However, partial integration is most common where only two stages are integrated (e.g., producer-wholesaler, producer-retailer, wholesaler-retailer).

VERTICAL MARKETING SYSTEM (VMS)
system that coordinates producers, wholesalers, and retailers

Giant Foods Bakery is only one of many Giant manufacturing facilities which allow for direct control of quality.

COURTESY OF GIANT FOODS

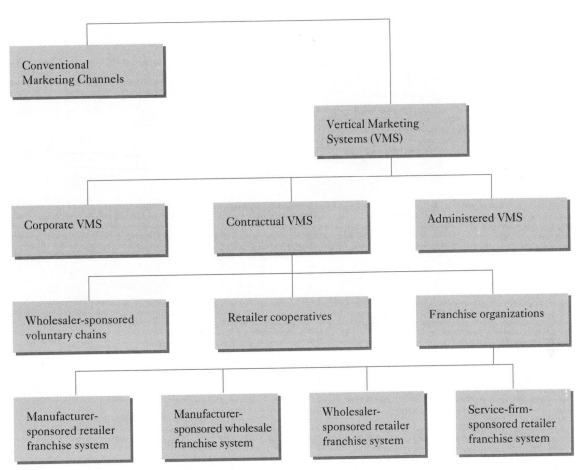

Vertical Marketing Systems

Conventional Marketing Channels

Vertical Marketing Systems (VMS)

Corporate VMS

Contractual VMS

Administered VMS

Wholesaler-sponsored voluntary chains

Retailer cooperatives

Franchise organizations

Manufacturer-sponsored retailer franchise system

Manufacturer-sponsored wholesale franchise system

Wholesaler-sponsored retailer franchise system

Service-firm-sponsored retailer franchise system

Exhibit 4–11
Vertical Marketing Systems

VMSs have emerged to fill the need for more cost-effective and profitable distribution alternatives and to eliminate interfirm conflict that exists in conventional channels. A VMS benefits from economies of scale, better bargaining power in negotiations, and guaranteed supply. They also have the opportunity to implement new retail formats, innovative products, and unique merchandising approaches. Because of these and other advantages, vertical marketing systems have become a major factor in distribution and are expected to account for nearly 90 percent of total retail sales in the 1990s (Jain, 1990, p. 539).

Vertical marketing systems take three major forms: corporate VMS, administered VMS, and contractual VMS, as illustrated in Exhibit 4–11. (See Jain, 1990; Kotler, 1991; Stern and El-Ansary, 1988). Each of these will be described briefly.

CORPORATE VMS Companies may integrate backward or forward to combine successive stages of production and distribution under single ownership. Corporate backward integration occurs when retailers own wholesalers or producers who precede them in the channels of distribution. For

Part

In addition to their bakery and this ice cream plant, Giant Foods also owns its own dairy, a plastic milk-container factory, and beverage and ice cube plants.

example, many retail food chains, such as Giant Food, Safeway, and Kroger, have integrated their wholesaling functions and many have company-owned processing facilities. Southland Corporation has ownership in Citgo Petroleum Corporation and sells Citgo gasoline through its 7-Eleven stores. Sears has a financial interest in many of its suppliers. Although Sears is a minority stockholder in most cases, channel power generally is based on the retailer's sales and buying power.

Corporate forward integration exists when a manufacturer owns its own retail or wholesale outlets, or distribution centers. Sherwin-Williams manufactures paint and performs wholesaling functions for its 2,000 retail stores. This is an example of total vertical integration. Other corporate VMSs owned and operated by manufacturers include Goodyear, Singer, Radio Shack (Tandy), International Harvester, and Hart, Shaffner & Marx (Hartmarx). Hartmarx manufactures clothing, which it sells through its own retail stores as well as to other retailers, representing a dual distribution system. Liz Claiborne, Gucci, Ralph Lauren, Esprit, and other designers and manufacturers of fashion apparel have begun to follow the same strategy in order to gain more control over the distribution of their fashions. Wholesalers also may own and operate a corporate VMS. For example, W.W. Grainger, an electrical distributor, has seven manufacturing facilities.

ADMINISTERED VMS   An administered VMS resembles a conventional marketing channel in many ways. Each channel member remains independently owned and autonomous, but collaborates informally with the others in performing marketing functions. Coordination of an administered VMS occurs through the size and power of one channel member, rather than through common ownership. Fleming Companies and Wetterau are two grocery wholesalers who provide a wide range of services to independent retailers to assist them in their operations. Powerful retailers, such as Sears, Penney's, and Safeway are able to obtain this type of integration with their producers and wholesalers. Likewise, Procter & Gamble, Kraft, Lever Brothers, General Foods, Frito Lay, and General Electric exert considerable influence over the retail outlets that sell their products. Many travel agencies operate in a VMS administered by American Airlines because of their Sabre system, a computerized system for flight information, reservations, and other services.

CONTRACTUAL VMS   Independently owned firms at different levels of production and distribution integrate their programs on a contractual basis to achieve economies and increased market impact. The marketing roles to be assumed by all partners are clearly specified in a legal contract. Contractual VMSs have become increasingly important in recent years, as firms seek economical and effective expansion strategies. There are three major forms of contractual vertical integration: wholesaler-sponsored voluntary groups, retailer-sponsored cooperative groups, and franchise systems.

Wholesaler-sponsored voluntary chains have been formed as a strategy to compete with large retail chains. In this form of VMS, wholesalers take the initiative to organize independent retailers into voluntary groups. The arrangement is attractive to small retailers who benefit from buying economies through group purchases and from following similar merchandising programs developed by the wholesaler. Wholesaler-sponsored voluntary groups, such as Independent Grocers Alliance (IGA) and Super Valu, are particularly prominent in the food industry. Other examples include Sentry in the hardware industry and Western Auto in automobile accessories.

Retailer-sponsored cooperative groups are also voluntary, but in this case, it is the retailers who provide the impetus for organizing. The retailers create and operate their own wholesale company to perform the middleman functions for member retailers. As a group, the retailers can receive rebates or discounts based on the ability to purchase in greater quantities. Retailer-sponsored cooperatives are an important marketing channel in the hardware industry, as shown by the strength of groups such as Cotter & Company and Ace Hardware. Examples in other lines include Associated Grocers and Topco Associates in the food industry, and ValueRite in the drugstore industry.

A **franchise** is a contractual arrangement between a sponsoring organization, which may be a manufacturer, producer, or wholesaler (franchisor), and an independent owner or group of owners (franchisee). The franchisor authorizes or licenses the franchisees to market a product or service under the franchisor's trade name according to specified terms and within a specified geographic area. Franchising is discussed further in the next section.

Franchise

Franchise systems were responsible for $639.6 billion in sales of goods and services in 1988, generated by about one-half million businesses involved in franchise arrangements (*Franchising in the Economy*, 1988). Franchising is expected to account for half of retail sales by the year 2000 (Jain, 1990 p. 539).

WHOLESALER-SPONSORED
VOLUNTARY CHAINS
wholesalers organize retailers into voluntary groups

RETAILER-SPONSORED COOPERATIVES
retailer formed and owned wholesalers that sell only to members of the co-op

FRANCHISE
contractual arrangement between a sponsoring organization and an independent owner

A franchise agreement takes advantage of many of the benefits of both independent and chain ownership formats, while keeping the disadvantages at a minimum. Under most franchise arrangements, the franchisee pays an initial fee plus a percentage of gross sales to the franchisor. In return, the franchisee is permitted to operate a business under an established name, using established procedures. Other benefits to the franchisee may include protected sales territory for that franchise, training, assistance with store location decisions, accounting, promotion, and other aspects of retail management. Benefits to the franchisor include improved cash flow, opportunity for rapid expansion, standardization of a multi-unit operation, and dedication of franchisees who have their own funds invested in the business.

There are four major types of franchise systems: manufacturer-sponsored retailer franchise, manufacturer-sponsored wholesaler franchise, wholesaler-sponsored retailer, and service-firm-sponsored retailer franchise. Perhaps the most evident franchises are found in the fast-food industry. Examples of less traditional franchises include child care centers, beauty shops, lawn care, accountants, and funeral homes. As long as the business can be taught to someone else satisfactorily, it can be franchised. An example of a franchise information package for The Box Shoppe, "the one-stop headquarters for every packaging need," is included on page 165.

Manufacturer-retailer franchises are prominent in automobile dealerships and gasoline service stations. For example, independent dealers are licensed by Ford and General Motors to sell their cars, with the provision that they will observe the manufacturer's conditions for sales and service. Shell, Gulf, and Exxon are examples of manufacturer-retailer franchise systems in the oil industry.

Manufacturer-wholesaler franchises are illustrated by the contractual relationships in the beverage industries, by companies such as Pepsi-Cola, Coca-Cola, and Seven-Up. The wholesalers, in this case, bottle and distribute soft drinks to retailers.

Wholesaler-retailer franchises are exemplified by Rexall Drugs in drug-store retailing and True Value in hardware retailing. Wholesalers organize the retailers as distributors for their products.

Service-firm sponsored retailer franchise systems are particularly evident in the fast food industry with restaurants such as McDonald's, Burger King, and Kentucky Fried Chicken. Other examples of service-firm sponsored retailers include Holiday Inn in the hospitality industry, Kelly Services in temporary office employment, and Midas Mufflers in the auto repair business.

The *1991 Directory of Franchise Organizations* lists 36 major categories of franchising opportunities, as shown in Exhibit 4–12. A full disclosure regulation required by the Federal Trade Commission and a checklist for evaluating franchise opportunities are included in Exhibits 4–13 and 4–14.

Other Forms of Ownership or Control

Retail institutions also can be owned by consumers (consumer cooperatives), the government, farmers, and public utilities.

CONSUMER-OWNED COOPERATIVE Consumers can band together in a **consumer cooperative** and operate their own retail business. Generally

Exhibit 4–12
Selected Franchising Opportunities

Retail Category	Company Name	Initial Investment
Automotive Products and Service	AAMCO Transmissions, Inc.	$ 48,000
	Firestone Tire & Rubber Co.	85,000
	Jiffy Lube International, Inc.	130,000
	Midas International Corporation	175,000, plus working capital
Automobile Rentals	Dollar Rent-A-Car Systems, Inc.	50,000–500,000
	Rent-A-Wreck	25,000
Beauty Salons, Services and Cosmetics	Hair Performers	25,000–50,000
	Fantastic Sam's	25,000–120,000
Candy Shops	Frontier Fruit & Nut Company	40,000 and up
	Karmelkorn Shoppes, Inc.	70,000–93,000
Donut Shops	Dunkin' Donuts Inc.	50,000–60,000
Food: Drive-In, Carry-out Restaurants	Arby's	525,000 and up
	Benihana of Tokyo, Inc.	1,200,000
	Domino's Pizza, Inc.	84,700–150,000
	McDonald's	300,000 and up
Retail Food Stores	Convenient Food Mart	40,000 and up
	Hickory Farms	160,000–220,000
	Swiss Colony Stores, Inc.	50,000–150,000
Ice Cream Stores	Baskin-Robbins	75,000–95,000
	TCBY—The Country's Best Yogurt	98,000 and up

Note: This is only a small representation of available franchising opportunities.

SOURCE: *1991 Directory of Franchising Organizations.* Babylon, N.Y.: Pilot Industries, Inc.

a fee is charged to each consumer member, which allows the operation of a store location managed by a hired employee. Participants enjoy competitive prices and may qualify for annual dividends calculated on the total amount they purchased during the year. Co-ops have grown up in a number of consumer sectors, with the most related to grocery purchases. However, co-ops also exist in financial services (credit unions) and in some utility companies. This form of ownership has not enjoyed rapid growth, primarily due to the need for personal involvement of time and effort on the part of the consumer-owners.

GOVERNMENT-OWNED   There are two primary types of **government-owned** and operated retail establishments. One reason for government ownership is to provide benefits for an identified group of citizens. The military exchanges and commissaries are the best known example of this type of retail institution. The U.S. Army/Air Force, Navy, and Marine Corps Exchanges and Commissaries account for billions of dollars in yearly sales. This ranks the Department of Defense as one of the largest retailers in the U.S. To illustrate, in 1989, the U.S. Army/Air Force Exchange Service (AAFES) alone generated $6 billion in retail sales.

CONSUMER COOPERATIVE
consumers organize and operate their own retail business

GOVERNMENT-OWNED RETAIL ESTABLISHMENTS
government ownership provides benefits to identified groups of citizens

Exhibit 4–13
Federal Trade Commission Full Disclosure Regulation
••

The Federal Trade Commission requires a franchising company to provide a full disclosure statement at least ten days before the contract is executed or before any money is paid; whichever comes first. The Regulation forbids the franchisor to make any statements about profits and sales unless they are backed up by a detailed written statement. The franchisor's statement must be valid for the most current fiscal year and must also include:

- The business background and record of the franchisor and key management personnel
- Involvement in any past or present litigation or bankruptcy proceedings
- Number of franchises including company-owned outlets and rate of termination
- Details of the franchise agreement dealing with renewal and termination terms as well as the number of franchises terminated within the past year and reasons for termination
- Description of available training programs
- Rules regarding personal participation and absentee management
- Initial and recurring costs to be paid by the franchisee as well as restrictions on the operation of the business, including types of products that can be sold, site selection and approval, financial assistance available from the franchisor, and rules regarding celebrity involvement
- An explanation of royalties or fees paid to the parent company as a result of the franchisee's purchases from third party suppliers and a list of suppliers that a franchisee is required or advised to patronize.

There is a $10,000 fine for every violation of this procedure.

Earning claims must contain a notice stating that supporting evidence is available on request. The percentage of units achieving the claimed results, and their location should also be included. This information must be presented either during the first meeting or ten days prior to contract or payment. Any other information which is not required by the FTC or state law, would not appear on the financial disclosure document.

SOURCE: *1989 Directory of Franchising Organizations.* Babylon, N.Y.: Pilot Industries, Inc.

Another reason for government ownership is to achieve some good for society, such as decreasing the distribution of alcoholic beverages through state-owned liquor stores that sell liquor for consumption off the premises. (However, some would contend that the real reason is a profit motive by the government.)

FARMER OWNED   **Farmers markets** are becoming increasingly popular in most communities. They typically are made up as independent small retailers, or perhaps a variation of a cooperative. Growers set up their fruits and vegetables for sale to final consumers in open-air or partially covered areas, often operating off the back of a truck or a makeshift table. In many smaller communities, the farmers market is a weekend gathering place, perhaps replacing the cracker-barrel of colonial times. Both customers and farmers benefit: customers can buy fresh produce directly from the farmer, usually at lower prices than in the supermarkets, and the farmer can obtain ready cash for products sold at a higher margin than to grocery stores.

PUBLIC UTILITY-OWNED   Many utility companies have been engaged in selling appliances and other products related to their service cate-

FARMERS MARKET
independent small retailers who gather in a common area to sell (usually fresh produce) to consumers

Exhibit 4–14
Franchise Checklist
....

To evaluate a franchise opportunity check the following:

- Does the company comply with state and federal full disclosure laws?
- Check the company's reputation and credit rating. Draw a report.
- What are the true costs for entering the franchise?
- Check case histories.
- How long has this product or service been on the market? Is there much competition?
- Is it a staple or luxury item?
- What territory is being offered? Is it clearly defined? Will you get continuous help from the parent company?
- Will you be able to buy, at reasonable prices, merchandise from the franchisor? Will you be furnished with promotional help? At what cost?
- Can you sell, trade or convert your franchise? Is the franchise renewable and for how long? Has the franchisor the right to sell the franchise?
- Always have a good attorney review the contract.

There are other considerations that you should check most carefully. Is the initial equipment fairly priced? Are the franchise fees justified? Are there unusually high income claims in the ads? Is the franchisor employing high pressure tactics to secure a down payment? Are royalties out of line with the potential profits and sales? Some companies always advertise for franchisees. Is this their major business?

There should be no rush to take an option on a franchise. Be wary of salespeople who pressure you into an immediate contract and closing on the basis that others are being likewise considered.

SOURCE: *1991 Directory of Franchising Organizations.* Babylon, N.Y.: Pilot Industries, Inc.

gory. For example, telephone companies have retail outlets to sell telephones and other equipment; natural gas and electric utility companies sell yard lights, barbecue grills, large and small appliances, and other items directly to consumers through direct marketing or retail outlets. With increased attention to energy conservation, sales frequently are positioned as "energy-savers."

Classifying Retailers Based on Strategic Positioning

Although retailers may be classified as primarily product or service retailers, the focus in this section is on product retailers. From a strategic perspective, retailers may be classified according to generic merchandise categories, retail strategy mix, and strategic groups. The two major generic classifications based on type of merchandise are food-oriented and general merchandise retailers.

Each retailer decides how to combine the traditional elements of the marketing mix (place, product, price, promotion) and an array of services into an overall retail strategy mix. The resulting combinations tend to form

COURTESY OF ALBERTSON'S

strategic subgroups within the broader food-based and general merchandise classifications. To illustrate, a neighborhood retailer who sells nationally advertised, frequently purchased, convenience items at premium prices (to pay for customers' savings in time and effort) may be classified as a food-based convenience store.

The high profit margin and high inventory turnover experienced by this retailer illustrate another classification scheme: the margin-turnover classification. Another way to classify retailers is according to strategic groups. While the other classification schemes are helpful in understanding many aspects of retailing operations, they fail to dramatize the significance of different types of retailers who sell the same type of merchandise. By examining the elements that these retailers have in common, strategic groups can be identified to form another classification system based on similar retailing strategies and target markets.

These classifications must be considered simultaneously when analyzing intratype and intertype competition. **Intratype competition** is the traditional form of retail competition, when retailers within the same classification compete with one another for the same consumer dollars. For example, McDonald's competes with Burger King, Sears with Penney's, and Safeway with Kroger. **Intertype competition** is more difficult to identify and assess due to the increased amount of scrambled merchandising, but is exemplified by a supermarket carrying pots and pans in competition with the local department store and hardware store.

Margin-Turnover Classification

The **margin-turnover classification** is a framework for analyzing all types of retail organizations, based on a strategic combination of two dimensions: gross margin and rate of inventory turnover. **Margin** is equivalent to average

INTRATYPE COMPETITION
retailers within the same classification compete for the same consumer dollars

INTERTYPE COMPETITION
retailers of different classifications compete, often through scrambled merchandising

MARGIN-TURNOVER CLASSIFICATION
framework based on gross margin and turnover rates within which to analyze retail organizations

MARGIN
average markup percentage; difference between price retailers are charged and the price they charge customers for the goods

TURNOVER
number of times the average amount of inventory is sold during the year

Grocery store video rental departments, such as this one at Albertson's (left) face stores like Blockbuster Video (right) in intertype competition.

markup percentage, or the difference between the retail price charged to customers and the amount paid to suppliers for the goods that were sold. **Turnover** refers to the number of times that the average amount of inventory on hand is sold during a year. Retail stores can be classified into one of four categories, as shown in Exhibit 4–15. The width and depth of merchandise assortment carried by a store, and the level of services provided to customers suggest another classification scheme. However, this is combined with the margin-turnover classification for discussion.

High margin-low turnover goods are characterized by wide assortments of higher priced goods, such as jewelry or furniture or original works of art. The markups tend to be higher because the stores are in more expensive locations and customers receive more personal services. Inventory turnover is necessarily lower in order to offer customers an adequate selection.

Convenience stores are an example of retailers with a high margin–high turnover strategy. Customers are willing to pay higher prices for the convenience of buying where and when they need the items. The markups are above average, but because of the frequent purchases and inventory replenishment, the inventory turnover also is high.

The lower prices offered by low margin-high turnover retailers entice customers to buy a higher volume of goods. Therefore, the merchandise is usually in the store for only a short time before it is sold and replaced with new merchandise. Discount stores like Target, Mervyn's, Home Depot, and Silo follow this strategy. *Category killers* like Toys "R" Us and IKEA are specialty stores who carry very large selections of specialty merchandise at such low prices that they are able to take sales from department stores, mass merchandisers, and other more traditional retailers who sell the same category of goods.

A retailer who is in the low margin–low turnover quadrant is probably in trouble, perhaps about to go out of business. The firm may be in the decline stage of the retail life cycle, or the retailer's strategies are not effective in generating sales.

Some applications and effects of margin-turnover strategies include the following:

● One of the fastest growing retail segments is the warehouse clubs that offer high quality merchandise at low prices in multiacre megastores. Sales were estimated at $20 billion in 1987 for this group. Sam's Wholesale Club (Wal-Mart), Price Club (San Diego-based), Costco Wholesale (Kirkland, Washington), PACE Membership Warehouse (Aurora, Colorado), and Wholesale Club (Indianapolis, Indiana) are leading warehouse club retailers (Kupfer, 1989).

Exhibit 4–15
Margin-Turnover Classification

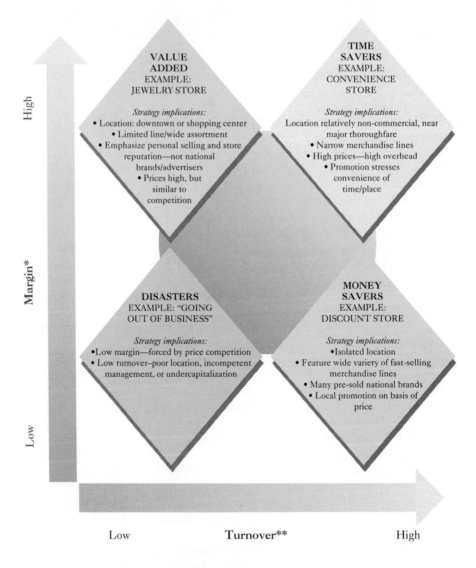

* Margin is the percentage of markup at which store inventory is sold.
** Turnover is the number os times average inventory on hand is sold in a year.

- Discounters have squeezed small retailers out of business. Increased operating costs and the proliferation of discount stores have made it difficult for an independent to survive (VandeWater, 1990).
- Retailers are offering cheaper goods and stressing service in order to keep menswear customers. Hartmax decided to place greater emphasis on its lowest priced merchandise, e.g., the $275 suit and $120 dress shoe versus $400-500 and $180 respectively (Agins, 1989).
- Low prices alone no longer give off-price clothing chains a competitive edge. Now, in addition to promoting low prices, retailers like National Brands Outlet (NBO) emphasize customer service and TJ Maxx emphasizes specific products in its ads (Agins, 1990).
- Sears adopted an "everyday low prices" strategy to compete with the low margin–high turnover mass merchandisers, although this action has been met with limited success.
- A number of high margin retailers have opened their own discount stores. Retailers such as Neiman-Marcus Group, Inc., Woodward & Lothrop, and John Wanamaker have opened separate stores to sell marked-down merchandise from their regular stores (Agins, 1989).

Product and Service Strategy

Most retailers offer their customers some combination of products and services. It would be virtually impossible for a retailer not to be involved in services to some extent. Firms whose primary business is selling products can be classified into two major groups. One group offers services to its customers as separate business lines. Some examples include Sears Allstate Insurance, Montgomery Ward's Law Store, and repair services at a car dealership. The second group offers facilitating services only. Examples include bagging groceries, delivery, and giftwrap. These are provided to the customer to help sell the retailer's merchandise. Sometimes the services are free; sometimes the customers are charged for them. A more extensive discussion of customer services is provided in a later chapter.

Type of Merchandise Carried: General Merchandise

Three broad terms can be used to describe retailers according to the extent of product lines carried for customer selection: general, variety, and specialty. The specialty store has become increasingly dominant and its definition is relatively clear. Although the general and variety store classifications continue to be used to describe stores, these institutions have undergone drastic changes, primarily due to competition from other types of stores. In the past, the general merchandise classification applied primarily to department stores. However, generalization has become more of a strategy than a distinctive classification as modern retailing operations diversify their traditional lines of generically related products into a broader range of unrelated lines. Variety chains have had difficulty competing with supermarkets, drugstore chains, and other retailers who sell traditional variety store merchandise items. After the bankruptcy of W.T. Grant in 1975, F.W. Woolworth is the last national variety store chain in U.S. retailing (Stern and El-Ansary, 1988).

For the sake of discussion, the term general merchandise will be used to describe all nonfood based retailers. These retailers can be classified as specialty, variety, and department stores. Other general merchandisers, most

Community Disasters: Opportunity for Responsible Retailer Actions

It was Tuesday afternoon, October 17, 1989—the day of the California earthquake that saw a one mile stretch of highway collapse, power outages, fires and the closing of the San Francisco Bay Bridge, among other calamities. Everything was chaos, hundreds were feared dead—and those who survived needed basic supplies to sustain them in the earthquake's aftermath.

Frank Crivello, manager of the Safeway Store in Aptos, California, stood in the midst of the canned fruits and vegetables when the earthquake struck—and watched the devastation in his store. As it became dark, worried customers came to Safeway in search of water, batteries, flashlights and other staples that would help them to survive for the next few days. However, the fire department had ordered Crivello to keep people out of his store—but he felt he could not just sit by and do nothing. "We think of ourselves as part of the community," he said. "It was an emergency. We couldn't sell anything, so we dug out batteries, bottled water, whatever we could find, and we stood there and gave the essentials away until they were gone."

This is a story of how one company kept its priorities straight in a crisis situation, rather than a tale of heroics. Safeway's managers, store clerks, truck drivers, and even customers joined in a determined cooperative effort to keep vital services—water, food, and other essentials—flowing to a panicky population. They had the system back up and running within 48 hours, confirming that experience and a strong sense of community are better guides in a crisis than any rule book.

After the earthquake struck, the most pressing need was for water for area residents. Within minutes, phone calls had been made to the chain's area warehouses where trucks were loaded with one-gallon bottles of Safeway-brand water and then dispatched. Where the power was out, refrigerated cars were sent in to be used for storing frozen foods. Orders also went out to supply the Salvation Army, the Red Cross and other relief agencies with food.

Safeway is a $13.6 billion a year chain with over 900 stores, and deep roots in the San Francisco Bay Area. The company was hard hit by the quake, with about 140 of their 240 Northern California stores damaged and 30 forced to close. Yet, "when other stores might close their doors to clean up and restock, Safeway's overriding goal was to get the stores open, get customers what they wanted, and worry about the cost later."

Adapted from Hector, Gary (1989), "How Safeway Coped with the Quake," *Fortune.* (November 20), 101–102, 104.

---

of whom offer a price advantage, can be classified as full-line discount stores, retail catalog showrooms, off-price chains, factory outlets, buying clubs, and flea markets and resale shops. The characteristics of each type are described next.

SPECIALTY STORE   There are different levels of specialization, ranging from one to a limited number of merchandise lines. In either case, the typical **specialty store** sells a limited assortment of products or services. However, the consumer is generally offered a wide choice within the single or limited number of lines carried by the retailer. Most specialty stores are small and medium-sized establishments or boutiques carrying very few lines. However, some are large departmentalized stores, such as Filene's and I. Magnin. Almost every type of product or service has potential for specialty retailing. Examples include retailers that concentrate on apparel and accessories, gourmet foods, books, electronics, greeting cards, hair care, physical fitness, drycleaning, and automotive repair.

VARIETY STORE   **Variety stores** offer a wide assortment of low-priced goods. Assortments may include items such as notions and needlework, school supplies, stationary, toys and games, housewares, and health and beauty aids. The variety store as an institution is in the decline phase of the retail life cycle, and virtually obsolete as originally structured. As noted, Woolworth is the last survivor of the traditional national variety store chains. Woolworth has adapted its operations to the evolving retail environment by diversifying into specialty chains, which now provide the majority of the company's revenues. K mart, one of today's leading full-line discount stores, evolved from the S.S. Kresge Company in the 1960s. Kresge was a leading variety store chain that reorganized its operating format to that of a discount department store, offering few services and low prices.

DEPARTMENT STORE   **Department stores** are large retail institutions that range in size from a strategic business unit within a larger conglomerate to national and regional chains, and even to local independents. They carry an extensive assortment of noncompeting lines of goods that are organized into separate departments. The departmentalized organizational structure results in more specialized buying and promotion, more efficient accounting and financial control, and improved customer service.

According to the U.S. Bureau of the Census, a retail business can be classified as a department store if it employs at least 25 people and carries a merchandise assortment that includes some items in family wearing apparel, furniture, home furnishings, dry goods and household items, appliances, and TVs. If the retailer's annual sales are less than $10 million annually, sales from any one of these lines cannot exceed 80 percent. However, there is no limitation on the percentage of sales that can come from any one line if the department store's sales are $10 million or more, and the total sales from the two smallest lines are at least $1 million. The traditional department store and the full-line discount store are the only two retailers that meet these criteria.

FULL-LINE DISCOUNT STORE   Although there are many types of discount stores, some specializing in one or a few lines of merchandise, the most comprehensive is the **full-line discount store** that carries a wide assortment of merchandise. The major difference between full-line discount stores and department stores is based on prices charged to customers. The discounter's lower prices are related to other strategic differences: lower profit margins, high inventory turnover, self-service, limited customer services, inexpensive store design and fixtures, and lower cost locations.

One form of the full-line discount store is the discount department store, generally located in the suburbs. In these stores, the prices tend to be average when compared to discount and department stores. They have average inventory turnover and offer limited service to their customers.

CATALOG SHOWROOM   **Catalog showrooms** are low-overhead, low-cost warehouse stores where customers make selections from catalogs. The catalogs show both the list prices and the discounted prices for each item, to emphasize their low-cost advantage. The merchandise mix consists mainly of housewares, jewelry, watches, electronics, and gifts. Most also carry a variety of other popular items, such as sporting goods, photography equipment,

SPECIALTY STORE
sells a limited assortment of products or services

VARIETY STORE
offers a wide assortment of low-priced goods

DEPARTMENT STORE
large retail institution that carries an extensive assortment of noncompeting goods organized into departments

FULL-LINE DISCOUNT STORE
carries wide assortment of moderately to low-priced merchandise

CATALOG SHOWROOM
Warehouse that stores merchandise consumers may select from a catalog

tools, luggage, and toys. In many of the stores, samples of the merchandise are displayed for inspection, but customers do not have access to the inventory stored in an adjacent warehouse. The general procedure followed by a customer when making a purchase starts with selection of an item from a catalog or from a showroom display. The customer then places an order with the cashier, using the stock number displayed on the sample or in the catalog. The consumer pays for the order, and is given the merchandise at a pick-up desk.

OFF-PRICE RETAILER   **Off-price retailers** may be either factory outlet stores or independent stores that promote national brands at exceptionally low prices. Although the concept of off-price retailing has been in existence since Filene's basement opened in Boston in the early 1900s, it is only in recent years that it has gained widespread popularity. There are two major types of off-price retailers: manufacturer-owned factory outlets and off-price chains or independents. An expanded form of the off-price retailer is the outlet mall, a group of factory outlets that operate from one location to share costs and take advantage of one another's customer traffic.

The leading **off-price chains** include T.J. Maxx (Zayre), Marshall's (Melville), and Loehmann's. These retailers buy in large quantities from manufacturers at prices lower than those paid by discounters. Purchases include factory overruns, end of season and last season's styles, close-outs, irregulars, and samples.

Factory outlets or direct manufacturers' outlets sell their own seconds, overruns, closeouts, and canceled orders. Burlington Coat Factory, Levi Strauss, Bass Shoes, Palm Beach, Hartmarx and other manufacturers have a vertically integrated organization to sell these products through their own retail stores.

FLEA MARKET AND RESALE SHOP   Flea markets and resale shops are an organized and expanded form of the garage sales and yard sales that crop up in every community. **Flea markets** rent space to individual vendors for a given period of time. The flea market may be operated outside or inside, and usually is in a low-cost, out-of-the-way location with plenty of parking spaces.

Flea markets attract a large number of bargain hunters who buy antiques, bric-a-brac, and a wide variety of used clothing, household items, tools, and other goods. Some flea market retailers sell new merchandise that they have bought in odd lots at close-out prices. These retailers will negotiate prices with their customers, who are attracted by the bargain prices.

Resale shops have grown in popularity as consumers seek ways to convert goods that are usable, but for which they no longer have a use, to cash. These stores operate more like a traditional retailer, arranging attractive displays of the merchandise, and being selective in taking items to sell. They use a limited amount of personal selling. A large number of these retailers focus their merchandise assortments on apparel (predominantly women's and children's) and bric-a-brac items. Others sell furniture, appliances, and other items. Many resale shops take customers' goods to sell on consignment, keeping a large percentage of the selling price for themselves. Customers' goods that are not sold within an agreed upon period of time are returned to

OFF-PRICE RETAILER
promotes national brands at exceptionally low prices

OFF-PRICE CHAIN
offers goods purchased from manufacturers at prices lower than those paid by discounters

FACTORY OUTLET
sells manufacturers' seconds, overruns, closeouts and canceled orders

FLEA MARKET
individual vendors rent space for a specified amount of time; expanded form of the garage sale

RESALE SHOP
retail outlet that sells others' used goods that are still usable

the customer or may be given to a charitable organization. Other resale shops may rent shelf or floor space to individuals for their own used merchandise or handicraft items that they have made. The shop has personnel available to handle customer transactions and to maintain the store, so the individual who owns the merchandise does not have to be present.

Type of Merchandise Carried: Food-Based Retailers

Food retailers can be categorized according to strategic combinations of width and depth of merchandise assortment, and price and service levels. Most food stores can be broadly classified as supermarkets. Supermarkets, the first of the large food store retailers, are departmentalized, full-line, self-service food stores that carry groceries, meat and produce, and have annual sales of at least $2 million. In this section we will describe the major types of supermarkets: conventional supermarket, combination store, superstore, limited assortment (box) store, and warehouse store. The convenience store, another form of food-based retailer, also is described, as well as the hypermarket.

CONVENTIONAL SUPERMARKET   Conventional supermarkets are conveniently located and offer relatively low prices. The low prices, in turn, result in higher sales volume and more frequent stock turnover. **Conventional supermarkets** carry a full line of groceries, meat and produce, along with a limited assortment of general merchandise. Although the stores are self-service, they do offer their customers some services, such as bagging groceries and check cashing. Conventional supermarkets are finding it difficult to compete with other food retailers who offer lower prices, larger selections, or more convenience, such as Safeway, Kroger, American Stores, A&P, and Winn-Dixie.

COMBINATION STORE   A **combination store** is primarily a food-based retailer, but is combined with a general merchandise store or a drugstore. The combined merchandise groups generally are operated under one management and under one roof, with a common checkout area. Several leading combination stores are Jewel, Biggs, and Albertson's.

SUPERSTORE   The **superstore** is larger than the conventional supermarket. Store sizes range upward of 30,000 square feet, and annual sales top $8 million. They offer many nonfood items, and specialty foods such as baked goods, deli items and seafood.

BOX (LIMITED ASSORTMENT) STORE   A **box store** carries a limited selection of goods (typically less than 1,000 items), which they sell at low prices. They concentrate their offerings on low-priced private labels and generic brands, and generally do not carry perishable foods. Merchandise usually is sold directly from cut cases or shipping cartons—hence, the name "Box" store. Little service is provided; in fact, customers generally bag their own groceries. Aldi is as well-known box store.

WAREHOUSE STORE   **Warehouse stores** offer a limited number of brands, but carry a wider assortment of products than box stores, concentrating

CONVENTIONAL SUPERMARKET
carries full-line of groceries, produce, and meats, plus a limited assortment of general merchandise

COMBINATION STORE
primarily food-based combined with general merchandise or a drugstore

SUPERSTORE
larger than a conventional supermarket, and offers many nonfood items and specialty foods

BOX STORE
carries limited selection of goods sold at low prices

WAREHOUSE STORE
offers wide assortment of products, but limited number of brands

on dry goods with few perishables. These retailers—such as Cub Foods—use an aggressive, low-price strategy, made possible by opportunistic buying of special deals from suppliers (items and brands available today may not be tomorrow), no-frills store decor, and efficient operating procedures. Super-warehouse stores are a combination of the superstore and warehouse store. These large high-volume, low-price stores carry a full line of products, including perishables.

CONVENIENCE STORE   **Convenience stores** provide shopping convenience for their customers by locating in high traffic areas near their customers and staying open long hours. Most of the stores are small, neighborhood retailers who offer a moderate amount of service. They carry limited lines of frequently purchased, quickly consumed staple items (milk, bread, personal care items, etc.), snacks and some fast foods, which they sell at higher than average markups. Many also sell gasoline. Examples of convenience stores include 7-Eleven and Convenient Food Mart.

HYPERMARKET   **Hypermarkets** usually range in size from 100,000 to 300,000 square feet, and combine both the supermarket and the full-line discount general merchandise store under one roof, with a central checkout. Customers benefit from one-stop shopping, along with substantial cost savings made possible through economies of scale and self-service to keep overhead low.

The hypermarket format was created by French merchants (e.g., Carrefour, Euromarchè) to fill a need for efficient distribution after World War II. In the mid 1980s, a partnership called Hyper Shoppes (Super Valu, French real estate developers, and Euromarchè) opened Bigg's in Cincinnati. Carrefour, which has 115 stores in Europe and South America, opened a hypermarket in Philadelphia in 1988 (Saporito, 1988).

In 1987, Hypermart USA was opened in Garland, Texas. The store is a joint venture between Wal-Mart Stores Inc. and Cullum Cos. Inc., containing 35 general merchandise departments and a full-line supermarket, including apparel and accessories, auto center, lawn and garden, electronics and major appliances, bakery, delicatessen, hair salon, and many others. Store officials estimated that 40,000 customers were in the store on opening day (*Dallas Times Herald*, 1987; Fine, 1988).

Fred Meyer, a leading retailer in the Pacific Northwest, opened a one-stop megastore in the Hollywood West neighborhood of Portland, Oregon. The 187,000 square foot prototype is designed and merchandised to provide customers with a dramatic and entertaining shopping experience. Special lighting, a creative layout and interior decor all add to the sense of theater for the 29 specialty shops that together make up 11 main store departments ("Fred Meyer Megastore Goes Hollywood," 1990).

In spite of their optimistic beginnings, hypermarkets have not been as successful as expected. After opening its fourth hypermarket in Kansas City in early 1990, Wal-Mart announced that it would concentrate instead on its SuperCenters, combinations of its discount department stores and grocery stores that total about 150,000 square feet. Carrefour has not built the five hypermarkets originally planned, confining itself only to its Philadelphia store. Likewise, K mart's hypermarket in Atlanta has not met expectations (Kelly and Dunkin, 1990).

CONVENIENCE STORE
carries limited lines of frequently purchased staple items; located in high traffic areas and has higher markups

HYPERMARKET
combines supermarket and full-line general merchandise store under one roof for one-stop shopping

NONSTORE RETAILER
uses direct marketing or direct selling strategies

Intratype and Intertype Competition

As retailers place more reliance on scrambled merchandising in an attempt to increase sales and profits through sales of items unrelated to their basic business, intratype competition becomes a more serious threat. The consumer electronics market has been in the midst of a shake-out, eliminating rivals such as Crazy Eddie Inc., but also attracting powerful mass merchandisers such as Montgomery Ward and Sears. The increased competition has led Tandy Corp. (Radio Shack) to sell its computers through American Express and at military post exchanges (Zipser, 1990). Conventional department stores face competitive attacks from high-fashion specialty retailers (Lord & Taylor, Neiman-Marcus, Saks Fifth Avenue), national general merchandisers (J.C. Penney, Sears), price/value retailers (K mart, Marshalls, Price Club, Wal-Mart) and market niche and product specialist retailers (Benetton, Land's End, The Limited, Sharper Image) (Berry, 1987).

Intratype competition exists in all retail industries. The broadly defined fast-food industry provides an example of the battle for market share among the same type of retailers. If broken down into subcategories, however, a case could be made that these retailers actually face intertype competition (e.g., hamburger versus pizza versus chicken restaurants). McDonald's has test-marketing pizza, to which PepsiCo's Pizza Hut has responded with commercial spots that caution customers not to be "McFooled." They added that Pizza Hut's product is not "McFrozen" (Gibson, 1989). Although McDonald's major rivals are Burger King, Wendy's and Kentucky Fried Chicken, their fastest growing competition comes from supermarkets, convenience stores, mom-and-pop delicatessens, gas stations, and other places that sell reheatable packaged food, rather than from the national chains (Henkoff, 1990).

Emerging Retail Formats

Beyond the traditional retail formats, several other types include **nonstore retailers** who use direct marketing or direct selling strategies. They sell directly to customers by mail or telephone, in person at a location other than a store (home, office), by vending machines, or by electronic and computerized retailing. Some retailers, such as Sears, Talbots, and Sharper Image, use both instore and nonstore formats to serve their customers. These formats are discussed only briefly here since they are covered in greater detail in later chapters within the contexts of promotion and technology.

Direct selling involves contact between the retailer and the customer in person or by telephone. Tupperware, Avon products, magazines, and encyclopedias are sold in this manner. Direct marketing media include catalogs and other direct mail, as well as ads in print and electronic media. Mail order sales are growing 10 to 12 percent a year, double the sales of all general merchandise stores. J.C. Penney's catalog sales have risen to 20 percent of its sales of $15 billion. Penney expects this figure to double in the next decade (Dunkin, 1990). Computerized data bases have improved the quality and appropriateness of mailing lists, and improved customer responses to retailers' offerings.

Vending machines are not a new retailing device, but they continue to be an important form of nonstore selling. Coins or cards are used to buy snacks, soft drinks, and other food products in convenient locations near where people work, go to school, travel, and so forth. In addition to food and beverages, customers can buy a wide variety of other goods, such as newspapers, cigarettes, and cosmetics from vending machines.

Technological advances have revolutionized retailing in many ways. One of these is in the selling function. Customers can shop via the various home shopping networks to make purchases of items displayed on their television sets. Generally, the actual purchase transaction is completed by calling an 800 telephone number. Customers can also shop via computer shopping services, such as CompuServe's Electronic Mall. By subscribing to a computer service, individuals can have access to a broad range of products that they can purchase by using the computer to transmit the order and billing information.

Summary

The operating format chosen by a retail firm should be an integral part of its strategic plan, developed with an understanding of its internal and external environments. There are several theories to explain the evolution of retailing institutions: retail life cycle; wheel of retailing; retail accordion; dialectic process; adaptive behavior; and scrambled merchandising.

Retailers can be classified on a number of dimensions. Based on type of ownership and control, retailers can be categorized as an independent or single-store, a chain, leased department, or vertical marketing system (VMS). Vertical marketing systems may be divided further into corporate VMS, administered VMS, and contractual VMS. Contractual VMSs include franchises, an increasingly important form of retail ownership. Other forms of ownership and control include consumer-owned cooperatives, and establishments that are owned by the government, farmers, or public utilities.

Retailers can be classified according to their strategic positioning. This may take the form of margin-turnover classification (including merchandise assortment and service strategy), general merchandise retailers, food-based retailers, and intertype or intratype competition.

Emerging retail formats are focused primarily on nonstore retailing. This includes direct marketing and direct selling, vending machines, and the use of technology associated with a television set or personal computer.

Questions for Review and Comprehension

1. Explain the relationship between the elements of the strategic planning process and a decision by management to change an existing retail format. Specify changes in the retail environment that might make this necessary.

2. Discuss the evolution of food retailing within the context of the retail life cycle concept. Identify at least one type of food retailer in each of the life cycle stages.

3. Describe the four premises that underly the wheel of retailing hypothesis. Use this concept to illustrate the evolution of discount retailers such as K mart.

4. Illustrate ways in which an understanding of the retail accordion concept and the dialectic process might be useful to managers of department stores who want to maintain growth in sales and profits.

5. Give examples of retail strategies that have been implemented to adapt to environmental changes (e.g., relative to customers, competitors, suppliers), and discuss their relationship, if any, to stage(s) in the retail life cycle.

6. Define scrambled merchandising. How many examples of scrambled merchandising can you identify in local retail stores? In mail order catalogs?

7. Discuss the advantages and disadvantages of the various types of store ownership: independent, chain, and leased departments. Identify a successful/unsuccessful retailer in each category.

8. Explain what is meant by a vertical marketing system (VMS). Describe the different types of VMS operations and the rationale for each type.

9. Discuss the growth of franchising in the United States, and several franchising opportunities that might be attractive to a new college graduate. A great deal of information can be obtained by contacting the franchisor for details and by talking with present franchisees to learn more about their operations.

10. What are the reasons for the emergence of consumer-owned cooperatives, farmers markets, and government and public utility owned retail businesses?

11. Describe the benefits of using the margin-turnover classification as a framework for designing a successful retail strategy. Include a definition and an example of the type of retailer that can be classified in each of the four quadrants. Can a retailer shift from one quadrant to another? Why or why not?

12. General merchandise retailers can be classified according to several major categories. State the nature of each of these classifications, and identify successful/unsuccessful retailers in each one. Explain why some retailers extend their businesses into other categories.

13. Discuss the various classification schemes used to describe food-based retailers. Can institutional growth in this industry be explained in terms of any of the theories of retail evolution presented in the chapter?

14. Explain what is meant by intratype and intertype competition. Why must retail managers be aware of both sources of competition. How should they monitor and respond to each type of competitor?

15. Consult recent business publications and report on trends in emerging retail formats. These might include a variety of direct selling strategies and involve new age technology.

References

Agins, Teri (1989a) "Trying to Patch Up Menswear Sales," *Wall Street Journal* (November 24), B1.

Agins, Teri (1989b), "Upscale Retailers Head to Enemy Turf," *Wall Street Journal* (August 25), B1.

Agins, Teri (1990), "Discount Clothing Stores, Facing Squeeze, Aim to Fashion a More Rounded Image," *Wall Street Journal* (March 15), B1, B6.

Berry, Leonard L. (1987), "Editor's Corner," in *Retailing Issues Newsletter*. College Station, Tex. Arthur Andersen & Co. and Texas A&M University, 1, 1, 1–4.

Brockway, Gary and Phillip Niffenegger (1988), "Retailing Evolution in the 1980s: Survival Through Adaptive Behavior," *Journal of Midwest Marketing*, 3, 2, 1–16.

Caminiti, Susan (1989), "What Ails Retailing?" *Fortune* (January 30), 61–62.

Census of Retail Trade: 1987. U.S. Department of Commerce, Bureau of the Census. Washington, D.C.: U.S. Government Printing Office.

Dallas Times Herald (1987), "Hypermarket Comes to Dallas," (Special Advertising Supplement), (December 27).

Davidson, William R., Albert D. Bates, and Stephen J. Bass (1976), "The Retail Life Cycle," *Harvard Business Review* (November-December), 92.

Directory of Franchising Organizations: 1989. Babylon, N.Y.: Pilot Industries.

Directory of Franchising Organizations: 1991. Babylon, N.Y.: Pilot Industries.

Dunkin, Amy (1990), "It's A Lot Tougher to Mind the Store," *Business Week* (January 8), 85.

Fine, Jennifer (1988), "Hypermart Generates Hyper-crowd," *Dallas Times Herald* (January 5), C-1, C-2.

Franchising in the Economy: 1986–88. U.S. Department of Commerce, Washington, D.C.: U.S. Government Printing Office (February 1988).

"Fred Meyer Megastore Goes Hollywood" (1990), *Chain Store Age Executive*, 66, 3, (March), 76–78.

Gibson, Richard (1989), "Two Giants Give Each Other the Works as They Fight to Slice Up Pizza Market," *Wall Street Journal* (September 15), B1, B5.

Henkoff, Ronald (1990), "Big Mac Attacks with Pizza," *Fortune* (February 26), 87–89.

Hollander, Stanley (1960), "The Wheel of Retailing," *Journal of Marketing* 25, (July), 37–42.

Jain, Subhash (1990), *Marketing Planning and Strategy*, 3d ed. Cincinnati, Ohio: South-Western Publishing Co.

Kelly, Kevin and Amy Dunkin (1990), "Wal-Mart Gets Lost In the Vegetable Aisle," *Business Week* (May 28), 48.

Kotler, Philip (1991), *Marketing Management: Analysis, Planning Implementation and Control*, 7th ed. Englewood Cliffs, N.J.: Prentice-Hall.

Kupfer, Andrew (1989), "The Final Word in No-frills Shopping," *Fortune* (March 13), 30.

Levy, Walter K. (1987), "Department Stores—The Next Generation: Form and Rationale,"in *Retailing Issues Newsletter*. College Station, Tex.: Arthur Andersen & Co. and Texas A&M University, 1, 1, 1–4.

Maronic, Thomas J. and Bruce J. Walker (1975), "The Dialectic Evolution of Retailing," in Barnett Greenberg, ed., *Proceedings: Southern Marketing Association*. Atlanta, Ga.: Georgia State University, 147–151.

McNair, Malcolm P. (1958), "Significant Trends and Developments in the Postwar Period," in A. B. Smith, ed., *Competitive Distribution in a Free High Level Economy and Its Implications for the University*. Pittsburg, Pa.: University of Pittsburg Press, 17–18.

Phillips, Stephen and Amy Dunkin (1989), "Is There No Limit To The Limited's Growth?" *Business Week* (November 6), 192, 196, 199.

Saporito, Bill (1988), "Retailers Fly Into Hyperspace," *Fortune* (October 24), 148, 149, 152.

Stern, Louis W. and Adel El-Ansary (1988), *Marketing Channels*, 3d ed. Englewood Cliffs, N.J.: Prentice-Hall.

VandeWater, Judith (1990), "Discounters Squeeze Out Small Retailers," *St. Louis Post-Dispatch* (April 22), 1, 8.

Weiner, Steve (1990a), "It's Not Over Until It's Over," *Forbes* (May 28), 58, 60, 64.

Weiner, Steve (1990), "Retailing," *Forbes* (January 8), 192, 194, 196, 198.

Zipster, Andy (1990b), "Tandy Corp. Loses Luster in Glitzy Lines," *Wall Street Journal* (January 23), A12.

Franchise Agreement: The Box Shoppe

The Box Shoppe is a one-stop headquarters for every packaging need. At the Box Shoppe, you can buy many kinds of boxes and supplies for moving and storage, gifts, home or office, packing and shipping, and for any special need. The retailer also provides custom services and will wrap, pack, and ship items for its customers.

Included here are selected items from the complete packet of information that is sent to a prospective franchisee: letter of introduction, company brochure, and a media article. Media articles, such as the following editorial from *Paperboard Packaging*, accompany these materials.

THE BOX SHOPPE
America's Professional Boxing Team

Castle Point Business Center
7165 East 87th Street
Indianapolis, IN 46256
(317) 842-4120   FAX (317) 845-1957

Dear Potential Franchise Owner,

Thank you for your interest in a Box Shoppe franchise. We always appreciate the opportunity to share with people the exciting concept that we introduced nearly seven years ago.

For the small business owner, The Box Shoppe offers a convenient way to obtain needed supplies in an efficient, effective, and economical manner. For the general public we offer an array of items needed to ship a package, wrap a gift, or simply store something away.

Through centralized purchasing, warehousing, and distribution of goods we can help you establish a profitable business with ease. [T] our knowledge we are the only company in the business that provide[s] floor to floor delivery of inventory needed to make the business successful. Most franchisors will set you up in business and the[n] give you a list of suppliers where inventory can be obtained at [a] discount.

We maintain extensive warehousing of goods and our own fleet of trucks to insure that you get what you need, when you need it, [at] a price that will enable you to compete in the marketplace. Ou[r] method allows us to purchase in huge quantities and pass the s[avings] onto our franchise owners. Our system also allows us to priva[te] label nearly every item that we sell, providing you with stro[ng] market identification. And finally, our system allows us to [make] strong commitments for the introduction of new products and [the] growth as demonstrated by our expansion from 33 items in 84 [to] 3,900 items today.

The value of a franchise is determined by the level of sup[port] provided by the franchisor and by the success of its franc[hise] owners. We challenge anyone in the business to match our [success] on either....we know that our success is mirrored by your[s].

Please look over the enclosed materials and decide wheth[er this is] the kind of business for which you have an interest. I[f so,] complete the enclosed Preliminary License Application, [and we will] then forward additional information about our franchise[. Let us set] a convenient time for you to visit with us.

Sincerely,
THE BOX SHOPPE, Inc.

Duke Smith
Duke Smith
President

- Moving Boxes
- Gift Boxes
- Storage Boxes
- Specialty Boxes
- Bags
- Roll Dispensers
- Gift Wrapping
- Ribbon & Bows
- Floral Tissue
- Package Shipping
- Expert Packing Service
- Mailing Tubes
- Tape
- Loose Packing Material
- Shipping Envelopes & Containers

8

Questions most frequently asked about

THE BOX SHOPPE®
America's Professional Boxing Team

SOURCE: The Box Shoppe, Indianapolis, Indiana

*HURRAY FOR THE BROWN BOX!**

Color! Value-added graphics! Preprint! This industry has been reading and hearing about the color boom for quite a few years now. Consultants like Glen Buckner (direct printing) and Eli Kwartler (laminating) have been quite busy, telling converters how to take advantage of the new color opportunities.

Brown is beautiful

One would think that that's all there is. The old brown box is dead, right? Not quite. Take a look at what Margie and Duke Smith are doing with Box Shoppe Inc. They started the company three years ago in Castleton, Ind. It has grown into a franchise that will reach 90 stores in the Midwest and Florida by the end of this year. In fact, it's America's seventh-fastest-growing franchise, according to Venture magazine. After 20 years in the Army, Mr. Smith managed a U-Haul dealership and was constantly confronted with a shortage of boxes. His wife worked in a gift shop and experienced the same problem.

"There wasn't a place you could go to buy a box, so we decided to start Box Shoppe," says Mr. Smith. "No one else was doing it. We had no market knowledge. If I knew how the (corrugated) industry worked I wouldn't have thought it possible. But we determined that there was a niche: the small businessperson who didn't want large quantities."

Seventy percent of the company's inventory is corrugated, and 98% of that is brown boxes. The other two percent is in white boxes and individual diecuts for mailings. Mr. Smith says that on the opposite end of the spectrum he is working on a multicolored toy chest with a lacquer finish.

Spreading the sources

The Box Shoppe purchases its corrugated boxes (there are close to 4000 items in stock) from three sources. The majority is acquired from a nearby corrugator with the rest coming from either sheet plants or brokers. According to Mr. Smith, most of the company's income comes from retail businesses and small industrial firms. Print shops are also big customers. The Box Shoppe serves as their warehouse, no matter how small their orders might be.

When asked about the most challenging aspect of starting up Box Shoppe Inc., Mr. Smith didn't cite traditional small business problems or financing but industry attitudes.

"This industry is very traditional. Its whole marketing scheme is based on concepts that are 50 years old. Eighty percent of the market is catered to what we do but we've had to educate manufacturers to this new market. It has been profitable for those who have been convinced. But there are still a lot who aren't."

What improvements would the Smiths like to see in corrugated boxes?

"They're pretty much serving our needs but I still think that the box can be made lighter, stronger and less expensively. Also, I was told that with all the sheet plants out there you couldn't ship corrugated (to other parts of the country) but you can."

Complacency is a deadly trait in the business world. The Box Shoppe is an excellent example of filling a need that many people in this industry figured was nonexistent or nonprofitable.

* "Comment" by Mark Arzoumanian from *Paperboard Packaging* (August 1987), p. 6. Reprinted by permission of *Paperboard Packaging*.

Franchisee's initial investment

Item	Amount	Method	When Due	To Whom Paid
Initial Franchise	$13,500	$500 Lump sum	Upon signing reservation agreement	The Shoppe
		$13,000 Lump sum	Upon signing franchise agreement (before commencing initial training)	The Shoppe
Opening Inventory	$10,000–12,500	Lump sum	Upon delivery to to store	The Shoppe
Window Graphics	$ 600	Lump sum	Prior to opening	The Shoppe
Retail Merchants Certificate	$ 50	Lump sum	Prior to opening	City or State
Advertising	$ 500	As incurred	As incurred	Third Parties, for direct mail, etc.
Utilities Deposits	$100–500	Lump sum	Prior to opening	Third Parties
Building Deposit	$500–1,500	Lump sum	Upon signing lease	Lessor
Insurance (see below)	$200–400	Lump sum	Prior to opening	Insurance Co.
Exterior signage	$1,500–2,500	Lump sum	As incurred	Sign company
Fixtures, Displays, Accessories	$3,000–3,450	As incurred	As incurred	Third Parties
Legal	$ 500	As incurred	As incurred	Lawyers
Accounting	$ 250	As incurred	As incurred	Accountants

TOTAL ESTIMATED START-UP COSTS: $30,700–$36,250
WORKING CAPITAL NEEDED: $10,000

RETAILING OF SERVICES

CHAPTER Five

Learning Objectives

After studying this chapter, the student will be able to:

1. Differentiate between the retailing of products and the retailing of services.
2. Describe the types of service retailers and their strategic planning process.
3. Discuss the effect of the risk associated with services on the consumer purchase decision process.
4. Discuss how service attributes are evaluated in the consumer's purchase decision.
5. Explain customer loyalty to service providers and brands.
6. Discuss some of the problems involved in gaining wide acceptance of innovations in the marketplace.
7. Explain why problems with perceptions of quality arise and what causes them.
8. Describe the services marketing mix, including distribution channels, pricing, and promotion strategies.

AMERICAN EXPRESS

● ●

REMARKABLE RETAILER

To many people, American Express is the successful charge card company with the "Do you know me" and "Membership has its privileges" ad campaigns. However, as the result of its acquisition strategies of the 1980s, the company has bought up Shearson Loeb Rhodes, Investors Diversified Services, and First Data Resources, making 1986 the first year it made more than $1 billion. And the money keeps coming in. Since the early 1980s, American Express has generated an average shareholders' rate of return of better than 15 percent a year. In the first three quarters of 1989 alone, profits were up by 11 percent.

Although it has evolved from credit card company to corporate mega-giant, service is still the name of the game at American Express. As Amexco chairman, chief executive officer, and chief quality officer, James D. Robinson III, explains, "You have to manage for delivery of quality rather than quality itself." It doesn't matter how well the company runs on the inside if that efficiency doesn't translate into better service for the customer. American Express now has the Quality University in Phoenix, where employees and managers take courses like, "How to Treat the Customer 101." The company also highlights great service moments, such as "The Boston Minuteman (actually a woman) who arose in the dead of the

night to deliver a card to a stranded customer at Logan Airport," in a series of "Great Performers" booklets that are distributed to all American Express employees. The Great Performers program rewards employees for providing outstanding customer service.

While some VISA and Master Card issuing banks offer lower annual fees, American Express nonetheless holds its own against these competitors with a 10.1 percent share of the card market. But, as Robinson says, "Our chief competitor is not VISA or MasterCard. It's cash." The company relentlessly surveys it customers and is constantly marketing new ideas to determine the "enhancements" that customers want. American Express currently provides card holders with services like automatic car rental insurance and 24-hour assistance phone lines, which cost very little to provide, but really make a difference for customers. Likewise, it has merged its card services with its travel agency operations to provide discount air travel to customers.

Amexco has extended its commitment to service from its established card business to new acquisitions like Investors Diversified Services (IDS). IDS's sales force of over 6,500 people markets annuities, life insurance, and mutual funds to middle America. Unlike other companies that use their sales reps to peddle their products, IDS reps are trained as financial planners, who will understand all aspects of their clients' fiscal situation. As a result, customers get to know their agents better, and they buy more products. Michael Frinquelli of Salomon Brothers has called the acquisition and subsequent handling of IDS a "Masterstroke, not only for the

PAUL DANCE/TSW

obvious reason that it has grown nicely, but IDS gets Amexco's toe, if not their entire foot, into the middle income market." As a result, in 1990 IDS made $207 million.

The company's service philosophy may best be summed up by Jonathan S. Linen, formerly head of direct marketing for American Express, who says, "The more places we can touch and enrich these people's lives, the better our relationship with them becomes. We keep them as card members longer, and we make more money."

Adapted from "American Express: Service That Sells," *Fortune,* (November 20, 1989), 89–94, and company sources.

INTRODUCTION

The focus of this chapter is on the retailing of services rather than the retailing of products. The services sector of the U.S economy deserves special attention since individuals spend more than 50 percent of all personal consumption dollars on services (U.S. Department of Commerce, 1988). (See Exhibit 5–1.)

Hairdressers, automobile mechanics, car rental agencies, retail banks, credit card companies, travel agencies, and appliance repair companies are all in business to sell their services to the final consumer. Other retailers offer both products and services to the customer. McDonald's for example, sells both food and fast, convenient service. In addition, many retailers who concentrate primarily on the sale of products offer related services as well. Department stores offer alteration, gift wrapping, and credit services to their customers. Appliance and furniture stores deliver products to the customer's home; retailers such as Sears offer automobile repair services. Exhibit 5–2 illustrates some ways a retailer might be involved in selling services. However, customer services offered by predominantly product retailers are discussed elsewhere.

Retailing of Services and Strategic Planning

The strategic planning process for service retailers is similar to that for product retailers, starting with the business philosophy or mission, which provides the basis for the company's objectives and the other elements of the strategic plan. (See Exhibit 5–3.) For example, ServiceMaster provides cleaning services for homes, schools, hospitals, factories, and other businesses and institutions. The company has four official goals: pursuit of excellence, pursuit of prosperity, executive commitment to help people develop, and commitment to honor God in all that they do. (In fact, the company name is a shortened version of "Service to the Master.") The goal of pursuing prosperity was quantified as $2 billion in revenues by 1990. The goal of pursuing excellence has been implemented by precise attention to detail. Tasks are standardized in three-inch thick manuals, and ServiceMaster makes or designs its own chemicals and equipment. As illustrations, a worker uses a special floor finish with a prescribed drying time when polishing a floor, and vacuum cleaners are battery operated so time will not be wasted in moving an electrical cord.

Exhibit 5–1
Consumer Expenditures for Selected Services ($ in billions)

	1984	1985	1986	1987
Personal Household Services	16	17	17	18
Apparel Services	119	131	127	137
Medical Services	41	45	44	43
Entertainment	28	29	29	30
Personal Care	26	28	29	31

SOURCE: Consumer Expenditure Survey, 1987, June 1990.

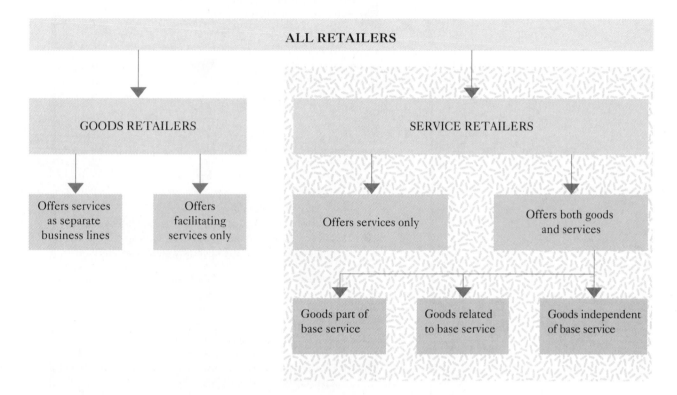

Forms of Retailer Involvement in Services

ALL RETAILERS

GOODS RETAILERS

Offers services as separate business lines

Offers facilitating services only

SERVICE RETAILERS

Offers services only

Offers both goods and services

Goods part of base service

Goods related to base service

Goods independent of base service

A situation analysis revealed a decrease in growth of profits and earnings in 1986 associated with tighter operating budgets at hospitals, the fastest growing market for the company's services. The cutbacks were primarily due to government-imposed cost controls. ServiceMaster's analysis of external opportunities and internal operating results led to a strategy of diversifying through the acquisition of Terminix (pest control services) and American Food Management (food service management for colleges and universities) (Oneal, 1987).

Exhibit 5–2
Forms of Retailer Involvement in Services
. . . .
Adapted from Dr. Leonard Berry (1987).

Retailing of Services and the IRIM

Both new and existing service retailers need to gather and analyze environmental information. An understanding of consumer demographics and lifestyles is necessary in order to identify business opportunities and assess competition. An older, more affluent population presents a sizable market for travel and leisure activities, health care, and personal services. An increased number of working women has resulted in opportunities for outside businesses that provide the services that women previously performed themselves (cleaning, food preparation, child care).

Concerns about polluting the environment have created numerous opportunities for service businesses. Examples include recycling firms and the return of diaper services that launder and deliver cloth baby diapers to diminish the problems caused by nonbiodegradable disposables in landfills.

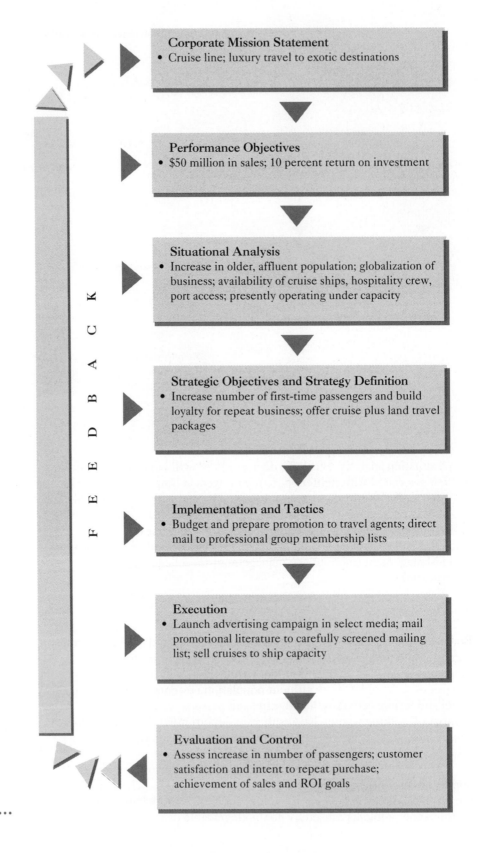

Corporate Mission Statement
• Cruise line; luxury travel to exotic destinations

Performance Objectives
• $50 million in sales; 10 percent return on investment

Situational Analysis
• Increase in older, affluent population; globalization of business; availability of cruise ships, hospitality crew, port access; presently operating under capacity

Strategic Objectives and Strategy Definition
• Increase number of first-time passengers and build loyalty for repeat business; offer cruise plus land travel packages

Implementation and Tactics
• Budget and prepare promotion to travel agents; direct mail to professional group membership lists

Execution
• Launch advertising campaign in select media; mail promotional literature to carefully screened mailing list; sell cruises to ship capacity

Evaluation and Control
• Assess increase in number of passengers; customer satisfaction and intent to repeat purchase; achievement of sales and ROI goals

F E E D B A C K

Exhibit 5–3
Retailing of Services and Strategic Planning: An Illustration

Other services are geared toward the children of the busy baby boom generation. To illustrate, pediatric centers that deliver immediate after-hours medical care have been opened in cities such as Gaithersburg, Maryland, and Salt Lake City, Utah (James, 1989).

Since many service retailers are small business operations, they can serve only a limited trade area. Therefore, they must locate a critical mass of customers for their services. Many services are subject to legal regulations and ethical concerns, particularly if they are performed on a person (e.g., cosmetology, dentistry, optometry, weight loss clinics). Others affected by some degree of regulation include utilities, pest control (chemicals), real estate, financial services, and some aspects of transportation services. Many service retailers, such as cleaning services, yard maintenance, interior decorators, and rental businesses, serve other businesses, as well as final consumers. However, more than half of a service firm's revenues must come from retail trade in order for it to be classified as a retailer.

Service retailers need to analyze their own internal strengths and weaknesses relative to the opportunities and threats that exist in the external environment. Service retailing generally is not as capital intensive as product retailing. Inventory consists primarily of supplies needed to perform the service. Expensive locations are not as important for those services that can be performed off-premises at the customer's home or in a setting less elaborate than a retail store.

Human resource capability is critical to the success of most service businesses. Service providers must have the necessary training and technical and interpersonal skills to perform successfully. The retailer's expertise and positioning strategy, together with level of customer demand, play a major role in determining pricing and promotional strategies. Analysis of the firm's operation is needed to estimate expenses and profits at different levels of demand. Managers can use internal data for preparing budgets for capital expenditures, determining promotion, or guiding the hiring and compensating of personnel. (See Exhibit 5–4.)

The Nature of Services

Many marketing principles apply to the marketing of both goods and services. For example, segmentation strategies and an emphasis on customers' needs are important for success in both areas. Elements of the marketing mix are also similar for both product and services retailing. Some ways that services differ from products are described next, along with a classification scheme developed to provide insights into the types of services that are available.

Characteristics of Service Retailing

Four characteristics of services that distinguish them from products must be taken into account in planning retail strategies: intangibility, inseparability, perishability, and variability.

Exhibit 5-4
Retailing of Services and the IRIM
....
SOURCE: Anderson and Parker, 1988.

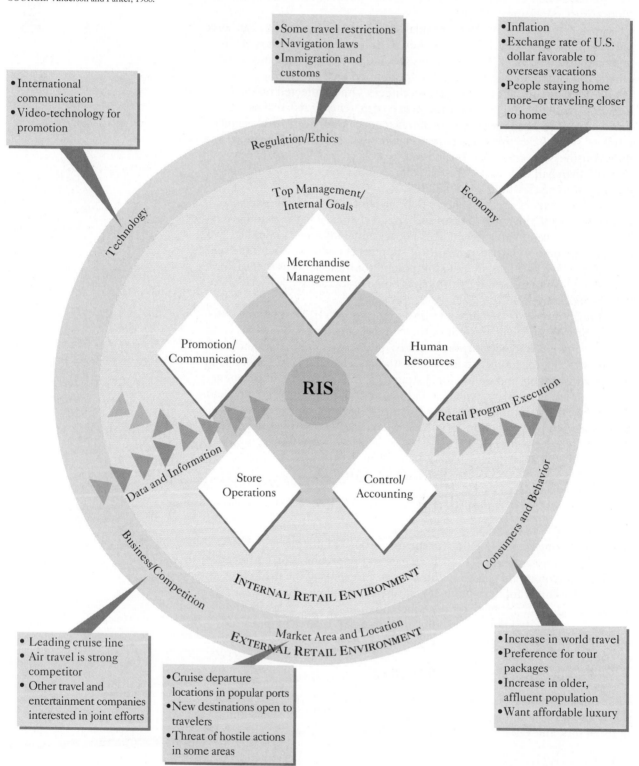

- International communication
- Video-technology for promotion

- Some travel restrictions
- Navigation laws
- Immigration and customs

- Inflation
- Exchange rate of U.S. dollar favorable to overseas vacations
- People staying home more–or traveling closer to home

Regulation/Ethics

Technology

Economy

Top Management/
Internal Goals

Merchandise
Management

Promotion/
Communication

Human
Resources

RIS

Retail Program Execution

Data and Information

Store
Operations

Control/
Accounting

INTERNAL RETAIL ENVIRONMENT

Business/Competition

Consumers and Behavior

Market Area and Location
EXTERNAL RETAIL ENVIRONMENT

- Leading cruise line
- Air travel is strong competitor
- Other travel and entertainment companies interested in joint efforts

- Cruise departure locations in popular ports
- New destinations open to travelers
- Threat of hostile actions in some areas

- Increase in world travel
- Preference for tour packages
- Increase in older, affluent population
- Want affordable luxury

INTANGIBILITY   The first difference between products and services is the **intangible** nature of services—they cannot be seen or touched. For example, when a travel agent buys an airline ticket for a customer, the only tangible manifestations of the service are pieces of paper that give the customer the right to fly on an airplane. That is, services can be consumed but not possessed.

The intangibility of services has several implications for the retailer. The actual services cannot be protected by patents, nor displayed in the retail window or on the showroom floor, and it is difficult to provide guarantees. The intangible nature of services also makes communication difficult and influences consumers' purchase behavior. Services must be **tangibilized** to the extent possible by using all tools in the marketing mix. Location, promotional efforts, pricing strategies, personnel, and equipment lead to inferences about service quality.

INSEPARABILITY   **Inseparability** of services from their source leads to less standardization and uniformity, making quality control more difficult for the service provider. For example, a barber produces a haircut at the same time the purchaser consumes it. If the barber is distracted and accidentally cuts a cluster of hair too short, the problem cannot be corrected until the hair has time to grow back. However, inseparability does enable the service provider to customize his service to the needs of an individual customer. The hairdresser, for example, may use his or her professional skills to tailor a hair style to the customer's needs or unique facial characteristics. Due to inseparability, in many service establishments other consumers are involved in the production process (e.g., other patrons in a restaurant or movie theater) and can influence service evaluation.

Since services are inseparable from their sources, managers of retail operations often must be both production managers and marketing managers. Although machinery can sometimes be substituted for human service providers, service retailing is usually labor intensive with little opportunity for centralized production. As the producer of the service, the retailer has all the responsibilities associated with manufacturing, such as research and development, acquiring raw materials, scheduling production, monitoring quality, and maintaining consistency in quality and services across branches. As the manufacturer of the service, the retailer also may have legal liability for defects in the service, much as a product manufacturer may have liability for defective products. All things considered, the inseparability dimension illustrates the importance of selecting and training customer contact personnel.

PERISHABILITY   The production and consumption of services are simultaneous. Thus, they are **perishable** and cannot be inventoried. The inability to carry inventories means that services cannot be mass produced for sale at a later time. Therefore, it is often difficult to balance supply and demand, by meeting demand in peak periods and attracting customers in slow periods. People who buy their clothes during busy sale times, for example, often have to wait a long time to have those clothes altered. During slower periods, alteration personnel may not have enough work to keep them busy. Strategies for overcoming these problems include differential pricing, increasing demand during slow sales periods, and hiring more part-time employees during peak periods.

Merry Maids, the nation's largest residential cleaning service, has 550 franchises, including several in Canada and Japan.

INTANGIBILITY
services cannot be seen or touched

TANGIBILIZE
create an association between the service and a visual image

INSEPARABILITY
services cannot be separated from their source

PERISHABILITY
services are produced and consumed simultaneously and cannot be inventoried

Enormous consumer response has made electronic retailing, such as Home Shopping Network's, shop-at-home services, the fastest growing segment of the direct marketing arena.

When an airplane leaves the terminal with an empty seat, that potential sale is lost forever. That seat on that flight can never be sold again. The perishability of services also results in cost structures different than products' cost structures. The incremental cost of selling an additional ticket is very small as long as the airplane is not filled to capacity. Consequently, airlines may offer very low fares to customers when they anticipate excess capacity on the airplane.

Because services are produced and consumed simultaneously and cannot be inventoried, a smaller capital investment is often required to open and operate a service retailing business. The lower capital requirements minimize barriers to entry and often attract entrepreneurs who have limited resources but want to be in business for themselves. The inability to inventory services also prohibits them from being bought and resold by traditional wholesalers and distributors, resulting in shorter channels of distribution.

VARIABILITY Service retailers are confronted with a problem of **variability,** or inability to standardize the end result purchased by the customer, because services are performed by different human beings at different times under different circumstances. Even though there may be a detailed instruction manual for employees to follow, the service will be performed differently from one time to another. Variability can be decreased by controlling service quality through better personnel hiring and training practices and setting up a formal system for obtaining feedback on customer satisfaction.

Classifications of Service Retailers

Consumer products traditionally have been classified as convenience, shopping, specialty, and unsought goods. Classification schemes also have been

VARIABILITY
services cannot be standardized because they are performed by different people at specific times and places

proposed for services, so that they can be grouped according to relevant marketing characteristics as a basis for marketing strategies. One classification system (shown in Exhibit 5–5) includes:

1. People-based vs. equipment-based
2. Customer presence
3. Personal vs. business
4. Service provider's motives
5. Degree of customer contact

PEOPLE-BASED VERSUS EQUIPMENT-BASED   Services can be classified according to whether the service delivery is people-based or equipment-based (Kotler, 1991), even though most services involve both elements

Exhibit 5–5
Classifications of Service
Retailers

Polarities in Classifications of Service Retailers

Day care centers   Automatic car wash
Dentist   Self-service dry cleaner

PROVIDER BASIS

People   Equipment

Barber   Dry cleaning
Exercise facility   Auto repair

CUSTOMER PRESENCE

High requirement   Low requirement

Residential maid service   Office cleaning

SERVICE CUSTOMER

Personal   Business

Disneyworld   Park service

SERVICE PROVIDER'S MOTIVE

Profit   Not-for-profit

Cosmetologist   Stockbroker   Credit card provider

CUSTOMER CONTACT

Personal   Indirect   Remote

A daycare center's services are people based, personal and require the customer's presence.

The services provided by an automated car wash, such as this one at a Fina station, are equipment based requiring minimal customer contact.

to some degree. For example, the services of a dentist or a day care center are people-based. All those who are involved in providing the service must be adequately trained and evaluated. On the other hand, the service of an automatic car wash is equipment-based. The equipment should function properly at all times. However, in the absence of car wash personnel, customers should be able to understand operating instructions and to obtain assistance if needed. While the services of an airline are primarily equipment-based (i.e., airplanes, terminals), they also require travel agents, pilots, flight attendants, mechanics, and other people to perform the service.

CUSTOMER'S PRESENCE   The extent to which the customer's presence is necessary provides another basis for classifying services (Kotler, 1991). The customer's physical presence is necessary for barbers' services, exercise clinics, surgery, or funeral services. The customer's mental presence is necessary for education or broadcasting services. Conversely, the customer need not be present for lawn care or drycleaning services, or automobile repair, although there may be brief contact with the service provider. A customer may need to be physically present in a movie theater, but does not require contact with the service provider to enjoy the movie. The management implication is that where the customer must be physically present, the service is performed in a "service factory," where customer satisfaction is influenced by service personnel, facilities, and other customers.

PERSONAL VERSUS BUSINESS   Services can be classified as to whether they are personal or business services (Kotler, 1988). Some service providers cater to both types of clients. An attorney may supply both personal services such as divorces, wills, and estate planning, and business services such as contracts and product liability litigation. Likewise, a professional cleaning service may clean both private homes and office buildings. The two sets of customers may be seeking different benefits, and may have different criteria for evaluating service quality.

Some service providers choose to serve only one clientele. A delivery service might find business-to-business delivery more profitable than business-to-consumer. A bus line may choose to serve only individual travelers and community residents, rather than accept a contract with a business.

SERVICE PROVIDER'S MOTIVES   The service provider's motives provide another basis for classification (i.e., public versus private and for-profit versus not-for-profit) (Kotler 1988). For example, Humana hospitals are privately owned for-profit hospitals in the Midwest, whereas Veterans' Administration hospitals are publicly owned, not-for-profit institutions. Tourists can enjoy the services of Disneyworld, a for-profit theme park, or hike the trails of Yellowstone, a not-for-profit national park. The marketing strategy, and perhaps the customer base, will vary for the two types of service providers.

DEGREE OF CUSTOMER CONTACT   Finally, service providers can be classified on the basis of degree of customer contact (Berry, 1981; Shostack, 1985). Note that customers can have personal contact with the service provider without being physically present. A **remote encounter** involves no human interaction. For example, credit card services require no human interaction except when billing problems arise or when the customer inquires about an account. Even these infrequent human contacts require well-trained, service-oriented personnel in order to maximize customer satisfaction.

Indirect personal encounters involve verbal interaction but no face-to-face contact between the customer and the service provider. Discount stock brokers and telephone operators maintain contact with their customers primarily by telephone. A **direct personal encounter** takes place when the customer interacts with the service provider on a face-to-face basis. Cosmetologists maintain a high degree of customer contact and personal interaction with their customers. In this case, it is difficult to separate the service provider from the service itself, and the evaluation of service quality becomes more complex.

REMOTE ENCOUNTER
a service is provided with no human interaction

INDIRECT PERSONAL ENCOUNTER
customer and service provider interact verbally without face-to-face contact

DIRECT PERSONAL ENCOUNTER
customer and service provider interact face to face

Consumer Behavior in the Service Encounter

The differences between products and services are reflected in consumers' purchase behaviors. These differences are manifested in consumers' perceptions of risk, evaluation of service attributes, loyalty to specific service providers and service brands, and the diffusion of innovations. A possible contrast in consumer perceptions in buying a car versus insurance for that car is illustrated in Exhibit 5–6.

Perceived Risk

Exhibit 5–6
Purchase of a Car and Car
Insurance: Relative Differences

The degree of perceived risk associated with service purchases is generally higher than the risk associated with product purchases due to several factors: lack of purchase information, customer involvement, no returns or exchanges, and lack of standardization (Zeithaml, 1981). (See Exhibit 5–7).

Purchase of a Car and Car Insurance: Relative Differences

CAR **INSURANCE**

Relative perceived risk

Low High

Evaluation of attributes

Easy Difficult

Retailer/brand loyalty

High Low

Diffusion of innovations

Rapid Slow

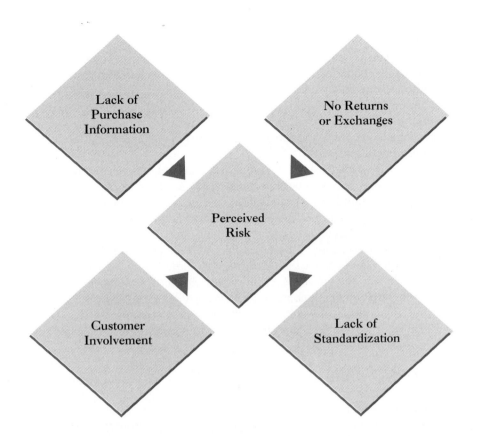

Exhibit 5–7
Perceived Risk Associated with
Service Purchases

LACK OF PURCHASE INFORMATION   Services are characterized by
a lack of evaluative criteria and a lack of purchase information (George,
Weinberger, and Kelly, 1985). The inability to evaluate many service
attributes before purchase or even after purchase leads to increased risk perceptions by the consumer.

CUSTOMER INVOLVEMENT   Perceived risk is increased significantly
by the personal nature of many services, the high degree of customer
involvement in the production process, and the simultaneous production and
consumption of many services. For example, people often experience feelings of anxiety about going to the dentist. This anxiety is usually associated
with a fear of pain; thus, measures should be taken to minimize personal discomfort. This high level of personal involvement often leads to differences
in consumer purchase behavior, as discussed later in the chapter.

Customer involvement in restaurant services has resulted in concerns
about the cleanliness of restaurant food. Rax and Burger King decided to cut
back on salad bars because of the potential for contamination, and McDon-
alds decided to offer only prepackaged salads (Pae, 1989). Customer involvement also is evident in the travel industry. To lessen perceived risk for traveling families (i.e., children will prevent parents from having a good time),
hotels and resorts have added elaborate day care and activities programs. For
example, Club Med began to reshape itself into a leader in the family-
vacation market by catering to kids (Wells, 1988).

NO RETURNS OR EXCHANGES   Since many services, such as dental services, are consumed as they are produced, a dissatisfied customer cannot return or exchange defective work in the same way that he can return a toaster or other product. Guarantees and service warranties may be difficult to issue because of the limitations imposed by simultaneous production and consumption (George, 1985; Zeithaml, 1981). However, more service retailers (e.g., Sears) are providing service warranties and guaranteeing their work to differentiate their firms.

Rental services have some degree of risk attached to them, but it tends to be less of a problem than with personal services. Although a customer may miss an appointment because of a malfunctioning rental car, or be embarrassed when a tuxedo arrives too late for the wedding, some restitution can be made. It may be argued that there is some personal damage, but it is not of the same magnitude as having a healthy tooth pulled by mistake or having all your hair fall out because the hairdresser used the wrong permanent wave chemicals. In fact, the option of renting rather than buying removes considerable risk. Take, for example, rent-a-dress shops like One Night Stand in New York. The shop has a stock of about 700 special occasion dresses, including designer gowns that retail for $4,000 and rent for fees from $30 to $350 (*Business Bulletin*, 1988).

LACK OF STANDARDIZATION (VARIABILITY)   The degree of perceived risk is increased even more by the fact that services are more variable and less standardized than products (Zeithaml, 1981). Since services cannot be separated from their source, and human service providers are not machines that can be calibrated to close engineering tolerances, their output usually is not as consistent as that of manufactured products. On the other hand, variability can be an advantage where the service can be customized to the needs of the individual purchaser.

Evaluation of Service Attributes

Consumers' purchase behavior is also influenced by the degree to which services lend themselves to evaluation, based on the following attributes:

1. Search Properties—attributes of the service that the consumer can discern prior to purchase such as price or smell
2. Experience Properties—attributes that can be discerned only during or after purchase such as taste or purchase satisfaction
3. Credence Properties—attributes that cannot be determined even after purchase of the service such as the quality of a surgical procedure or car repair (Zeithaml 1981)

These properties can be arrayed along a continuum ranging from easy-to-evaluate to difficult-to-evaluate. Most goods are high in search qualities and, therefore, relatively easy to evaluate. Most services are high in credence qualities and, therefore, relatively difficult to evaluate. Restaurant meals, haircuts, and recreational services are high in experience qualities, and so more difficult to evaluate than those high in search qualities. As an illustration of how consumers evaluate service attributes, let us consider the typical case of an individual seeking a dentist's services. (See Exhibit 5–8). **Search**

SEARCH PROPERTIES
attributes of a service the consumer can discern prior to purchase

EXPERIENCE PROPERTIES
attributes discernible only during or after purchase

CREDENCE PROPERTIES
attributes that cannot be determined even after purchase

properties will be limited to such attributes as location, office hours, and appearance of physical facilities and personnel. **Experience properties** will pertain to the degree of pain experienced and the patient's evaluation of the dentist's care and concern. The technical quality of the dentist's work often falls into the category of **credence qualities,** since patients do not usually have the training to evaluate their dentist's work even after purchase.

A number of strategies have been used to assist patients in evaluating dental services. Some dentists locate in malls or nearby string locations, and are associated to some extent with the other retailers at that location. In addition, many offer free dental examinations and estimates, provide educational programs, and show videotapes of their dentists performing the service.

Consumers' Evaluation of Service Attributes

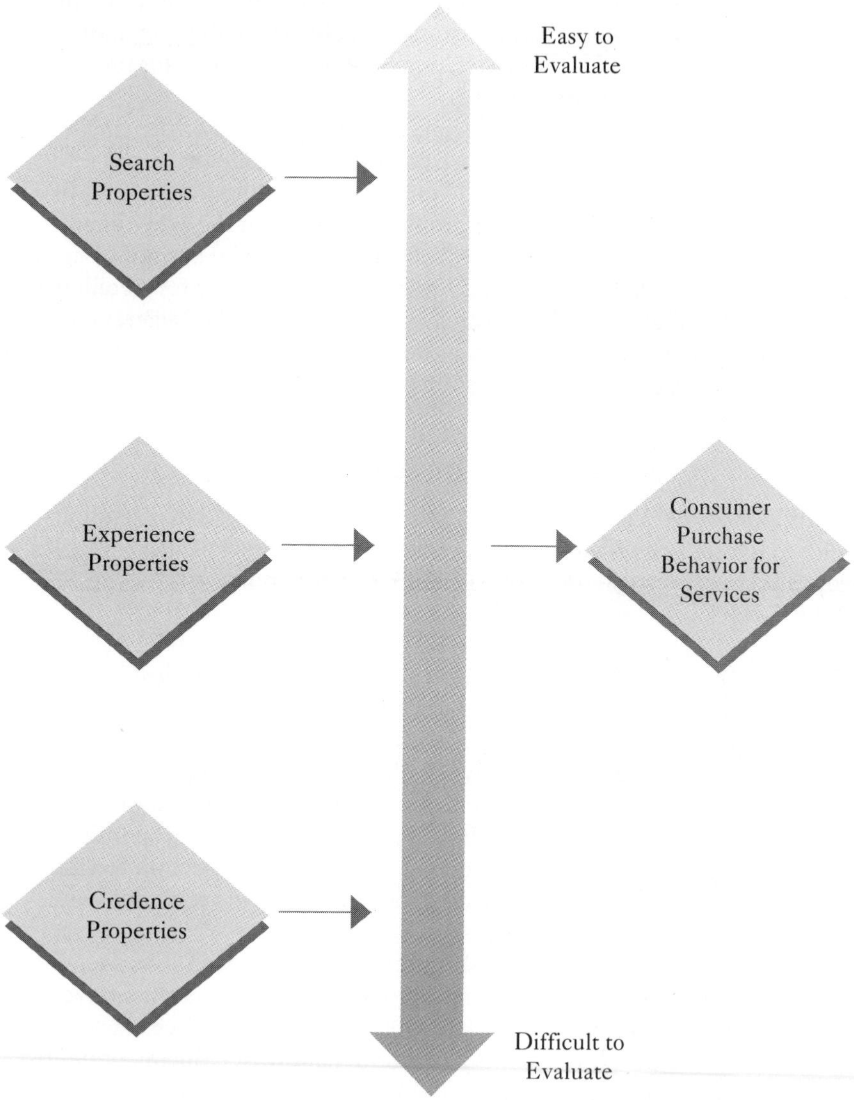

Exhibit 5–8
Consumers' Evaluation of
Service Attributes

Easy to
Evaluate

Search
Properties

Experience
Properties

Consumer
Purchase
Behavior for
Services

Credence
Properties

Difficult to
Evaluate

IMPLICATIONS FOR SERVICE RETAILERS   As the dental service example illustrates, services often are dominated by experience and credence qualities, rather than the more tangible search qualities, which implies several implications for service retailers. First, purchasers of services tend to rely more heavily on personal sources, or word-of-mouth, information x(Zeithaml, 1981). This reliance is a risk-reduction technique since personal sources are considered to be more trustworthy than nonpersonal sources, and provide a partial substitute for the absence of search properties.

The dominance of experience and credence properties influences the degree to which mass media is used to market retail services (Zeithaml, 1981). Mass media can convey information about search properties very effectively. However, since it is the experience and credence properties that have the greatest influence on service purchase decisions, the usefulness of the mass media as a promotional tool for retail services is diminished.

Because retail services are characterized by an absence of search properties, relatively little information is available to the consumer before the purchase is made. Consequently, the consumer's set of acceptable purchase alternatives is often smaller for service purchase decisions than for product purchase decisions (Zeithaml, 1981).

The smaller set of alternatives for a given service is due to the smaller number of service retailers and because each service retailer normally offers only one brand of service. This lack of alternatives requires a high level of trust on the part of the consumer. In product retailing, on the other hand, similar products usually are offered by several retailers, who each offer multiple brands of the same basic product. For example, relatively few retailers in a given city offer drapery cleaning services. Of those who do, each retailer offers only one brand. On the product side, however, multiple brands of draperies are offered by a variety of stores (Zeithaml, 1981).

Brand and Service Provider Loyalty

The differences between products and services are reflected in consumers' loyalty to the service provider and the service brand due to (1) psychological involvement (2) personal interaction and (3) fewer impulse purchases. (See Exhibit 5–9)

PSYCHOLOGICAL INVOLVEMENT   A customer's physical involvement in the production of the service can add a deeper level of **psychological involvement** (Kelly and George, 1982). This involvement, combined with a relatively high level of perceived risk and a lack of prepurchase information about substitute services, increases the psychological cost of changing service brands or service providers. Perceived risk extends to economic costs (fees for new x-rays when changing doctors, or a new membership fee for changing health clubs), and time costs associated with switching from one service brand or provider to another.

The increased psychological cost, in turn, brings about a higher degree of consumer loyalty for services than for products. Consumers who move from one city to another have been known to drive long distances back to their homes to use the services of their favorite hairdresser, doctor, or dentist. Likewise, consumers who patronized the Fantastic Sam's chain of hair salons

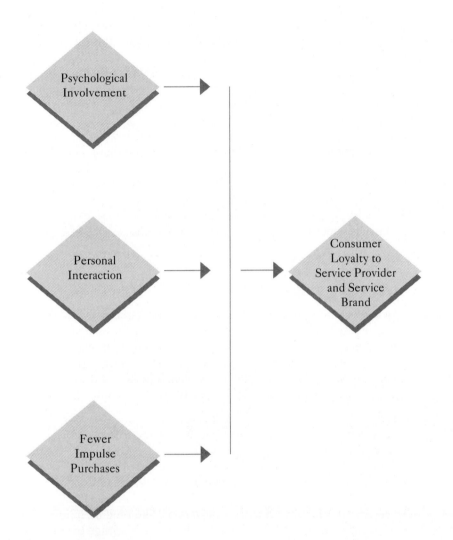

Exhibit 5–9
Brand and Service Provider
Loyalty

in their home towns may look for another Fantastic Sam's near their new homes.

PERSONAL INTERACTION   The **personal interaction** that occurs between the customer and the service provider—inseparability—tends to result in a relationship that is based on mutual trust (Zeithaml, 1981), increasing consumer loyalty to services brands and providers. This trust is reinforced by the retailer's ability to provide a better quality service as he or she gains more knowledge of the customer's needs. A hairdresser who knows his or her customer's tastes, preferences, and hair texture is likely to generate a higher level of loyalty from the customer than a hairdresser who does not have those insights. Likewise, as the customer gains more experience with a given service or service provider, a higher level of loyalty can be expected.

PSYCHOLOGICAL INVOLVEMENT
an association with the production of the service

PERSONAL INTERACTION
contact between the customer and the service provider

The U.S. airline industry has responded to the needs of traveling families in a number of ways. One of these is a push by the airlines to have the FAA require that all children under the age of two be strapped into safety seats during flights. Although this would increase the cost of travel for some families, many deaths and injuries would be prevented (McGinley, 1990).

FEWER IMPULSE PURCHASES   A third factor contributing to the higher level of consumer loyalty is that **impulse purchases** are more likely to occur for products than for services (Kelly and George, 1982). Products are sometimes purchased with little need recognition, prior planning, or evaluation. On the other hand, first-time service purchases normally come about only after a need for the service is recognized. The recognition of a need is followed by a search for information and evaluation of service alternatives. This process may be extensive or abbreviated, or even nonexistent if the consumer has purchased the service before and has developed a loyalty to the service provider or brand. Because need recognition is an integral part of the service purchase decision, impulse purchasing for most service categories is minimized.

Diffusion of Innovations

Service innovations tend to be diffused into the market—generally accepted by consumers—at at slower rate than product innovations. Often it is difficult to implement change because of customers' resistance to trying a different, unproven way of performing or delivering the service. There generally is more reluctance to be the first to try the innovation. The rate of diffusion depends on five characteristics (See Exhibit 5–10):

1. Relative advantage over existing alternatives
2. Degree to which the innovation can be communicated to consumers
3. Complexity of the innovation
4. Compatibility with consumers' past experience and existing values
5. Degree to which a service can be sampled or tested (Zeithaml, 1981)

RELATIVE ADVANTAGE   Service innovations, like product innovations, may have either a high or low degree of **relative advantage** over existing offerings. When consumers believe a service innovation has a significant relative advantage, they are quicker to accept it. However, when the degree of relative advantage is low, consumers are less motivated to change and the rate of innovation diffusion is slowed.

Automated teller machines (ATMs) have been in use for two decades and have become commonplace for many bank customers. Some banks are achieving relative advantage by spicing up their ATM menus with noncash transactions. These include rail passes, gift certificates, postage stamps, and grocery coupons (Chipello, 1989).

EASE OF COMMUNICATION   Service innovations are more difficult than product innovations to communicate to the potential purchaser because services cannot be displayed in retail stores or presented in print media and point-of-purchase displays in the same manner as products. Services are

IMPULSE PURCHASE
product bought with little need recognition, prior planning, or evaluation

RELATIVE ADVANTAGE
perceived benefits of one service over another

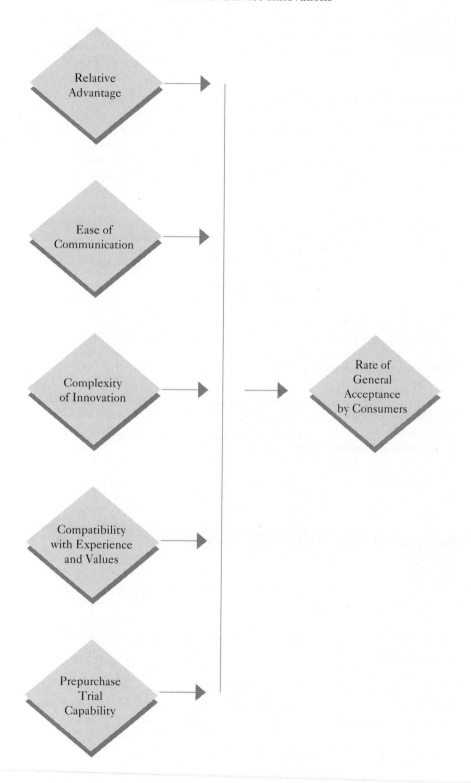

Exhibit 5–10
Diffusion of Service Innovations

often tailored to the needs of the individual buyer, and so are not easily compared to other services. However, consumers do perceive similarities or differences as they compare one retailer's services with those of another. This contributes to the difficulty of communicating service innovations and slows their rate of acceptance. When a service can be related to a product (e.g., use of Airfone in-flight telephone service, the communication task is easier. The service can be shown "in use."

COMPLEXITY   The communication problems that characterize service innovations often are magnified by the fact that many services consist of various attributes, some of which may be very complex and not applicable to the needs of every buyer. For example, companies that specialize in painting and refinishing automobiles, such as MAACO, offer the purchaser a range of service options at various price levels. Most consumers know very little about the refinishing process. Therefore, the complexity of the purchase decision is increased. When complexity makes the service difficult to understand or use, acceptance of the innovation will be slower.

For many consumers, the vast array of services offered by banks and other financial institutions are extremely complex. As a result, many financial institutions have focused on shifting considerable attention to satisfying the needs of private banking customers. Citicorp, for example, launched a private banking team in Japan in 1986, concentrating on tax consulting, acquiring fine art, and financing for second homes in places like New York and Hawaii for wealthy Japanese clients (Borrus and Miller, 1988).

COMPATIBILITY   The rate at which service innovations are diffused into the marketplace is also influenced by the degree of compatibility between that service and consumers' past experience and existing values. **Compatibility** is related to self-provision, a major difference between products and services. While self-provision is not usually an option for the purchaser of a product, it is often a realistic option for the purchaser of a service. The idea of purchasing the service from someone else may or may not be compatible with the consumer's experience and values. Bionic Broom, a company offering maid services, may find that customers who have not previously used a maid service feel guilty for not doing the work themselves. Such a lack of compatibility can be expected to slow the popular acceptance of an innovation.

On the other hand, Personics Corp. in Menlo Park, California, developed a system that will let a customer create a cassette "album" with up to 25 songs in less than five minutes in a local music store ("Mix Mozart . . .," 1988). This innovative system can be related to past experience and, therefore, should be accepted more readily.

PREPURCHASE TRIAL   The degree to which a service can be sampled or tested also influences the rate at which innovations are diffused. In product retailing, consumers can taste a new cola beverage or test drive a new automobile. If they do not like the product, the cost has been minimal. However, services are often difficult or impossible to sample. The customer has to purchase an entire haircut, have an entire tooth pulled, or have an entire car painted before he can assess whether or not he likes the service. In other

COMPATIBILITY
a positive association between a service and the consumers' past experience and existing values

words, the haircut, or tooth extraction, or paint job cannot be divided into smaller "pieces" for sampling or testing. This lack of divisibility also can be expected to slow the diffusion of innovations.

SERVICE QUALITY

Representing the epitome in luxury services, hotel chains such as Westin and Hyatt have launched enormous "fantasy hotels." Room rates range up to $1,500 a night, and the hotels are staffed with thousands of employees (Dolan, 1988). Customers evaluate service quality, whether they are purchasing fantasy hotel services or driving through the local car wash.

Most consumers have relatively clear definitions of product quality. If the shirt is comfortable, its buttons and seams remain intact, and continues to look good for a reasonable period of time after purchase, the consumer is likely to consider the shirt to be of high quality. Manufacturers can improve the level of quality perceived by the consumer by incorporating these features into their garments, but service quality is not as easy to define, because of intangibility. This is particularly true for services that possess a large number of credence properties. For example, the average customer has no way to determine the quality of a dentist's filling.

Consumers do judge service quality in spite of retailers' difficulty in defining the concept. Studies have shown that products perceived as high in quality are at least twice as profitable as those that are perceived as low in

COURTESY OF WEST EDMONTON MALL

The West Edmonton Mall's Fantasyland Hotel and Resort includes 125 theme rooms such as the Roman, Victorian Coach, Arabian, and Hollywood Rooms, and the Polynesian Room pictured here.

COURTESY OF THE WESTIN KAUAI

Westin Kauai Resort personnel strive to close service quality gaps and meet guests' expectations through a "management by values" philosophy. Pictured here is the Colonnade Pool.

quality. This conclusion gives no reason to believe that quality is less important for services (Buzzell and Gale, 1987; Townsend and Gebhardt, 1988). Only recently has the importance of service quality led researchers to seriously examine its nature and determinants.

Perceived Service Quality

The importance of customers' perceptions of service quality cannot be overestimated. The performance of services has a high potential for causing problems and for tarnishing or destroying a retailer's image. It is, therefore, an area that must be handled with great care. The service delivery process has been conceptualized as a series of five gaps, shown in Exhibit 5–11.

1. Expected service–perceived service gap
2. Consumer expectation–management perception gap
3. Management perception–service quality specifications gap
4. Service quality specifications–service delivery gap
5. Service delivery–external communications gap (Parasuraman, Zeithaml, and Berry, 1985)

Exhibit 5–11
Service Quality Gaps

Before	After
Expected Service	Perceived Service
Consumer Expectation	Management Perception
Management Perception	Service Quality Specifications
Service Quality	Service Delivery Specifications
Service Delivery	External Communications Gap

Other variables impacting on service quality perceptions include technical and functional quality dimensions and image.

EXPECTED SERVICE–PERCEIVED SERVICE GAP   The expected service–perceived service gap represents the difference between customers' expectations for the service and their perceptions of the service actually delivered. If the perceived quality of service delivered meets or exceeds expectations, service quality will be perceived as high. On the other hand, if the service delivered did not meet expectations, overall service quality will be considered low. In effect, this gap implies that service quality is defined according to customers' perceptions. In other words, a service retailer should not let customers' expectations exceed possible realization. Conceptually, the expected service–perceived service gap is a function of the remaining four gaps, which are described next.

CONSUMER EXPECTATION–MANAGEMENT PERCEPTION GAP   The consumer expectation–management perception gap represents the difference between consumers' service expectations and management's perceptions of those expectations. For example, a customer having his car repaired may be most concerned with quality of workmanship and prompt service, regardless of the friendliness of the employees. However, the manager may believe that if the customer is treated in a friendly and personal manner, he will be willing to wait for his car or bring it back for any needed adjustment. Likewise, the airline that believes it is in the transportation business, when its real business is providing service, can expect to have passengers who are dissatisfied with in-flight meals, baggage handling, and other services even if they reach their destination on time.

MANAGEMENT PERCEPTION–SERVICE QUALITY SPECIFICATION GAP   The management perception–service quality specification gap represents the difference between management's perceptions of consumers' expectations and how those perceptions are translated into service quality specifications. Continuing with the car repair scenario, management may perceive that the customer wants fast repair service. As a result, shortcuts may be specified to speed up the repair process, resulting in mistakes that need to be corrected later.

The Marriott's employees must follow a rigid 54-step procedure in making up a hotel room. The firm's CEO, Bill Marriot, Jr., sometimes drops by a hotel kitchen unannounced to check up on the cleanliness and flow of food ("Rooms At The Inn," 1989), thus narrowing this service quality gap. United Parcel Service (UPS) has not been as successful in identifying and fulfilling customers' service needs. As a result, Federal Express gained the advantage by offering overnight service, the ability to track packages en route, and volume discounts—services the customer wanted (Vogel and Hawkins, 1990).

SERVICE QUALITY SPECIFICATIONS–SERVICE DELIVERY GAP   The service quality specifications–service delivery gap represents the discrepancy between the service delivery specifications set by management and the service delivered by the actual service provider. In other words, the manager of the car repair service may outline specifications for service quality that are in accord with the customer's expectations. However, the mechanic performing or delivering the service may not follow those specifications. Or a retailer may advertise fast speedy checkout service, but customers who shop there may be delayed and frustrated by long waiting lines.

SERVICE DELIVERY–EXTERNAL COMMUNICATIONS GAP

The service delivery–external communications gap consists of the discrepancy between the service delivered to the customer and the organization's external communications or promotional efforts about the service. If customers are promised a higher quality of service than can be delivered, their expectations probably will not be met, and their perceptions of service quality will be low. On the other hand, external communications can be used to raise perceptions by informing customers about aspects of the service that are deliverable, but not readily apparent.

TECHNICAL QUALITY AND FUNCTIONAL QUALITY

DIMENSIONS   Within the expected service–perceived service framework, service quality can be defined along two other dimensions: technical quality and functional quality (Gronroos, 1984). **Technical quality** is related to the outcome of the service encounter and can be defined as "what the customer gets." For example, if the customer's hair is cut to the right length, in the right style, and looks good, the haircut will be considered to be of high technical quality. **Functional quality** is related to the process by which the service is received and can be defined as "how the customer gets it." If the customer is uncomfortable with the barbershop's cleanliness or if the barber has body odor or pulls the customer's hair, the functional quality of the haircut will be deficient.

IMAGE   Image impacts service quality perceptions by performing a filtering function in the customer's evaluation processes (Gronroos, 1984). Service must be consistent with the image the retailer wants to project. If the customer has a positive image of the service provider, minor shortcomings are likely to be overlooked. However, if there are too many minor shortcomings, the positive image will deteriorate. If the customer has a negative image of the service provider, mistakes and minor shortcomings will be magnified in his or her mind, offsetting the positive aspects of the service encounter.

Service Quality Research

Consumer research across four categories of service providers (bank, credit card company, repair and maintenance company, and long distance telephone) has identified five dimensions as reliable determinants of service quality, known as the SERVQUAL scale (Parasuraman, Zeithaml, and Berry, 1986):

1. Tangibles—physical facilities, equipment, and appearance of personnel
2. Reliability—ability to perform the promised service dependably and accurately
3. Responsiveness—willingness to help customers and provide prompt service

TECHNICAL QUALITY

outcome of the service encounter; "what the customer gets"

FUNCTIONAL QUALITY

process by which the service is received; "how the customer gets it"

The shift from a product-driven economy to a services economy will continue to accelerate worldwide through the 1990s. While exact figures may differ, analysts predict that the U.S. economy will become dominated by service, with an increase from 55 percent of the gross national product in 1991 to over 70 percent by the twenty-first century. Opportunities and challenges abound for retailers who specialize in selling services directly to consumers, as over one-half of every personal consumption dollar is spent on services, a figure expected to increase during the next decade. In addition, retailers of products are providing more product-related services in order to compete. When customers can buy similar products at similar prices from a variety of retailers, the delivery of high-quality customer services can make the sale. A retailer's survival depends on learning to compete successfully in a service economy.

Busy people increase the demand for "instant" products and services. Time is of the essence– whether it's drinking a quick cup of coffee from the local 7-Eleven on the way to work, or picking up a bucket of Kentucky Fried Chicken for the family dinner on the way home.

As more parents work outside the home to provide a better standard of living for their families, responsible child care centers have become a necessity. KinderCare has responded to this need with its chain of day care centers.

Nearly everyone needs banking services, but not everyone has "banker's hours" for making deposits or cash withdrawals. The technology of automatic teller machines (ATMs) allows customers to have access to their accounts at any hour of the day or night.

Images of fast-paced lives are captured by automatic cameras, and the film is developed in hours or even minutes for customers who are in a hurry.

Transportation services include everything from Amtrak trains to city buses (below), international airlines to local taxis for a highly mobile society.

Business people on the go can discuss business as they travel. Car phones (right) abound, and air phones are now available for frequent flyers.

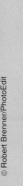

An interior decorator helps a customer choose wallpaper from a number of alternatives. Other home-oriented services are available, such as house-cleaning, chimney sweeping, and many others.

Financial constraints faced by consumers of the 1990s, along with increasing product complexity, have contributed to the growth of numerous renovation, repair and maintenance services.

Here an exterminator gets rid of unwelcome visitors...

Automotive retailers cover a broad spectrum from car dealers to auto parts and mechanical services. In the economy of the 1990s, many drivers will keep their cars longer than in the past-requiring repair services and replacement parts to keep the vehicles on the road.

This quick oil-change shop (right) is one example of a retail service that meets the needs of time conscious consumers.

Product retailers add special services to their venues to attract customers. Drug stores offer home delivery of prescriptions, department stores employ interior decorators and wardrobe consultants. Some services offered are at no cost to the customer because they are so critical to the retailer's success. The Vons Company's Tianguis stores tailor their product offerings to Los Angeles' Hispanic population; in addition, most employees are bilingual and store signs are printed in Spanish and English.

Two service providers team up though this McDonald's restaurant located in Mercy Hospital, Springfield, Mass.

Health conscious Americans are flocking to fitness centers (right) to keep their bodies in shape with aerobics, weight training, swimming, and other physical exercise. Services extend to many aspects of wellness, including counseling for stress management, nutritional guidance, or marriage and family relationships.

© Tom McCarthy/The Picture Cube

© David Young-Wolff/PhotoEdit

Physical appearance (left) can be enhanced by service retailers such as hair stylists, manicurists, color analysts and others.

Preventive medicine is receiving more attention than ever before. This patient (below, left) is having her eyes checked during a routine office visit. In addition to traditional doctors' and dentists' offices, many health care providers are conveniently located in malls where busy patients can drop in without an appointment.

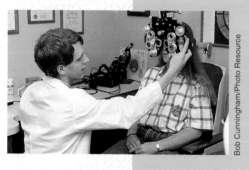

Bob Cunningham/Photo Resource

Courtesy of The Westin Kauai

The general aging of the U.S. and Canadian population along with their higher level of discretionary income, and a growing trend for busy families to spend leisure time together have increased opportunities for service retailers in the leisure, travel, entertainment, and hospitality sectors.

The hospitality industry has become extremely service-oriented. Some are economy-priced for business and vacation travelers. Others are high-priced, luxurious accommodations. In either case, customers expect to receive a range of quality services. Many provide activities for children so that both parents and children can share and enjoy their vacation to the fullest.

Courtesy of West Edmonton Mall

Courtesy of Hilton Hotels

Courtesy of Hilton Hotels

Vacationers such as these on a Carnival Cruise Lines "fun ship" enjoy a relaxing cruise where service is the key word.

Retailers have benefitted from customers' interest in other recreational pursuits, such as the challenge of games in an arcade, video rentals, cable television, movies, or bowling. Others may be attracted to a game of pool.

4. Assurance—employees' knowledge and courtesy and their ability to convey trust and confidence

5. Empathy—caring, individualized attention provided by the firm for its customers

Responsiveness, assurance, and empathy are determinants of functional quality because they are related to the service delivery process. The reliability dimension is outcome related and, therefore, is a determinant of technical quality. The tangibles dimension is image-related. For many consumers, the tangible aspects of the service delivery process can be expected to influence the image of the service retailer and provide a clue to overall service quality.

Causes of Service Quality Problems

Various factors have been blamed for poor service quality, including some of the same characteristics that distinguish services retailing from product retailing. As shown in Exhibit 5–12, service quality problems can be caused by inseparability, inadequate organizational structure, inadequate organizational systems, failure to communicate, service proliferation and complexity, customers viewed as statistics, short-run view of the business, and consumer as a major competitor.

INSEPARABILITY   Inseparability is a major contributor to service quality problems (Berry, Zeithaml, and Parasuraman, 1988), If the service provider is in a bad mood, dressed inappropriately, or makes controversial political statements, the purchaser of the service may have a negative view of the shopping situation.

INADEQUATE ORGANIZATIONAL STRUCTURE   An inadequate organizational structure also can create service quality problems. For example, the loan officer at the branch bank needs to be able to give rapid loan approval and prompt responses to customers' banking problems. If the bank's organizational structure prohibits prompt response, negative perceptions of service quality should be expected.

INADEQUATE ORGANIZATIONAL SYSTEMS   Inadequate organizational systems, or the mechanisms that enable service employees to do their jobs, can contribute to service quality problems (Langevin, 1988). Service businesses need a system to ensure that customer complaints are channeled to the individuals who are responsible for and can correct the problem. The correct forms and procedures must be adequately defined and the proper tools and equipment provided if the organization's systems are to be effective.

FAILURE TO COMMUNICATE   Failure to communicate with the customer and other members of the service retailing organization may create service quality problems (Langevin 1988). Deadlines may be missed if the service provider is not told when service delivery is promised to the customer. Dissatisfaction can also be expected when the service provider is not informed about the customer's unique needs.

Exhibit 5-12
Causes of Service Quality
Problems
....

SERVICE PROLIFERATION AND COMPLEXITY   Service proliferation and complexity are also responsible for service quality deficiencies (Berry, Zeithaml, and Parasuraman, 1988). Many service organizations respond to technological and competitive changes by offering new services or by enhancing existing services. When these changes come about, various organizational adaptations are required.

New service delivery systems are sometimes added, and old systems are adapted to the changes in the service offering. Employees have to be given additional training, and customers have to be informed about the availability of the new or improved service offering. Therefore, while changes to the service offering can provide additional market opportunity, they also provide

Causes of Service Quality Problems

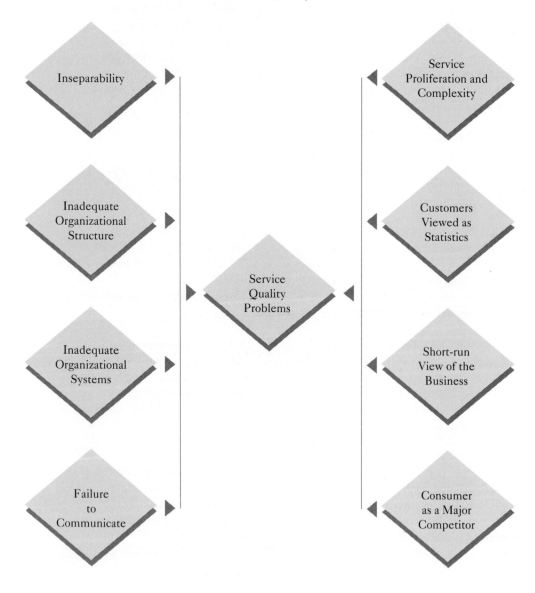

additional opportunities for things to go wrong. The benefits of such changes must be carefully weighed against the costs before changes are made. The organizational details surrounding the change must be thoroughly planned, and adequate time must be devoted to smooth transitions.

CUSTOMERS VIEWED AS STATISTICS   Many service providers view customers as statistics, contributing to low levels of service quality (Berry, Zeithaml, and Parasuraman, 1988). Although customers interact with a relatively small set of service retailers, the retailer interacts with a large number of customers. Consequently, the service retailer may see customers as numbers rather than individuals. Since impersonal treatment generally leads to customer dissatisfaction, care must be taken to see that each customer is treated as a special, unique individual.

SHORT-RUN VIEW   A short-run view of the business is a pitfall that affects many service retailers (Berry, Zeithaml, and Parasuraman, 1988). Just making decisions from day to day and reacting to situations without planning ahead may lead to problems. When service retailers focus on the short-run, they risk sacrificing long-run goals for short-run results. For example, reducing the number of employees may decrease the costs in the short-run, and could enhance long-run profits if there truly were too many employees. On the other hand, if reducing the number of employees results in longer waiting times, customers may decide to do business with competitors. Other customers may complain about the wait and blame employees for poor service. Management may blame the employees rather than assume responsibility for their own decisions. Such a situation usually results in rapid employee turnover, increased training costs, job dissatisfaction, low levels of motivation, and decreased profits.

CONSUMER IS A MAJOR COMPETITOR   Low levels of service quality may be related to the fact that the consumer (i.e., the do-it-yourselfer) is sometimes the service retailer's major competitor (Zeithaml, 1981). When the customer knows how to perform the service and has performed the service before, he or she may have more exacting standards by which to judge service quality. This can be particularly troublesome when the service retailer does not know what those standards are, and the customer finds it difficult to articulate those standards. Consequently, the service retailer may have to provide more individualized attention to compensate for the customers' more exacting standards for a service that they could have provided for themselves.

Strategies for the Retailing of Services

In order to achieve high levels of service quality, the retailer must incorporate a number of factors into the firm's overall strategy. These factors include a quality-oriented corporate philosophy, quality-oriented training and organi-

1. • Commit to maximizing customer satisfaction
   • Avoid mistakes and defects
   • Do not confuse the marketing department with the marketing function
   • Take a long-run view of the business

2. • Market the performance of employees
   • Provide for training that stresses customer interaction techniques and consistency in providing services
   • Reward employees for producing quality services

3. • Educate the customer about the service and the nature of the problem

• Communicate policies, procedures, and qualifications of service provider
• Match service provider and customer
• Help customer establish evaluative criteria

4. • Provide evidence of service quality in the service delivery process
   • Choose optimal distribution channel(s)
   • Determine optimal pricing strategy (cost vs. demand, standard price ranges, discounts)
   • Use promotional mix to tangibilize service and convey service quality (word-of-mouth communication, mini-encounters, visual presentations)

Exhibit 5–13
Strategies for Service Retailing
• •

zational support for employees, a focus on the customer, and development of a service marketing mix that results in high levels of customer satisfaction. (See Exhibit 5–13.)

Corporate Philosophy

CORPORATE PHILOSOPHY
values and basis upon which a business operates

Customer satisfaction is the key to success in service marketing. Maximization of customer satisfaction requires total employee commitment and the development of a "quality culture" (Berry, Zeithaml, and Parasuraman,

1988). Several factors must work together to achieve a "quality culture" in a service retailing environment.

MISTAKES AND DEFECTS CAN BE AVOIDED   Service retailers must be willing to settle for nothing less than zero defects (Gummesson, 1988). Product manufacturers traditionally have accepted a certain percentage of defective products under the assumption that 100 percent perfection is too costly, and that it is cheaper to discard a few defective products or listen to customer complaints when the defects are not caught.

Acceptance of defects as a part of doing business cannot work in a service environment, because defective services cannot be retrieved once they are consumed. The personal nature of the service delivery process makes it more serious to have a defective service than a defective product. A defective toaster can be exchanged for a new one with relatively little effort. A defective hair style, on the other hand, may be personally embarrassing to the customer and may not be correctable until weeks or months have passed and the hair has had time to grow back.

A serious weakness is built into the corporate philosophy when a service retailer decides that mistakes and defects cannot be avoided. In effect, the retailer who is willing to accept errors as a natural part of business puts a seal of approval on imperfection. The expense of lost sales and the administrative problems of dealing with dissatisfied customers can be far more expensive than the extra investment required to do the job right the first time.

DON'T CONFUSE THE MARKETING DEPARTMENT WITH THE MARKETING FUNCTION   If a quality culture is to be achieved, service retailers must be careful not to confuse the marketing department with the marketing function (Berry, 1986). Even though the marketing department may be assigned certain market-related responsibilities, everyone in the organization must be responsible and accountable for customer satisfaction because the marketing and production of services cannot be separated. Thus, the successful service retailing organization must recognize the service employee as the key to success. Service employees often have the authority to commit the retailer to production deadlines, customize the service to the unique needs of the customer, make decisions relating to the handling of customer problems, and counsel customers about the best ways to utilize the service.

Consequently, all employees who provide services to their customers are "managers." Some managers have supervisory responsibility and some do not, but they all make decisions directly relating to delivery of the service and customer satisfaction. In smaller businesses, the owner-manager who performs most of the services also has the responsibility for marketing. As the firm grows larger, top caliber employees must be hired and trained to assume the perspective of a manager as they make decisions about the best ways to perform services for their customers.

Employees who are responsible for an outcome should have the authority to see that the correct outcome is achieved (Townsend and Gebhardt, 1988). For example, employees of a print shop who commit the organization to production deadlines and are responsible for meeting the deadline should have input into scheduling the work. Otherwise, production deadlines will be missed and service quality will be deficient.

TAKE A LONG-RUN VIEW OF THE BUSINESS   A third element of corporate philosophy that is critical for success in service retailing is a long-run view of the business (Berry, Zeithaml, and Parasuraman, 1988). Short-run cost reductions are suitable tactics if they do not damage long-run profitability. Likewise, the service retailer must be careful not to outgrow short-run capabilities in efforts to maximize sales and profitability. Adding new services and expanding existing services may be a good short-run competitive move, but can result in long-run customer dissatisfaction and lost sales if quality cannot be maintained in the face of rapid change.

Training and Organizational Support

Service employees often have direct contact with the customer and are critical to the service delivery process. Therefore, service retailers are really marketing the performance of their employees, leading to the success or failure of the organization. This suggests that employees be treated as the retailer's internal customers (Townsend and Gebhardt, 1988). Their needs and wants should be researched and given a high priority in an effort to minimize employee turnover and increase productivity.

Because it is necessary to attain consistency in the production process, employees must be trained to produce very similar products using similar production methods. Policies and procedures should be thorough and easy to understand, and tight organizational controls should ensure adherence to company guidelines (Upah, 1980). However, service retailers should be careful not to apply organizational controls in a manner that denies employees the freedom and flexibility to tailor the service to the customer's needs—an advantage that service retailers have over product retailers (Berry, 1986).

Training programs should teach employees how to interact with customers as well as how to provide the service (Shostack, 1985). Customer needs and preferences as they relate to the retailer's services should also be addressed, perhaps through simulated customer contact situations. The costs of training may seem substantial, but must be weighed against the cost of lost sales, lost profits, and image problems that may result from lack of training.

Finally, employees should be genuinely rewarded for producing quality services (Townsend and Gebhardt, 1988). Rewards may include monetary incentives, formal recognition of outstanding performance, or simple acknowledgment of a job well done. An important motivator for service employees is the satisfaction of having ultimate control over the quality of the services they produce, and being told that the quality is good.

Focus on the Customer

Given the customer's higher levels of perceived risk, lack of adequate information on which to base a purchase decision, and poorly defined service quality criteria, the service retailer can do several things to improve customers' perceptions of service quality.

EDUCATE CUSTOMERS ABOUT THE SERVICE   First, the service retailer can educate customers about the service, i.e., which services are best for them as well as when and how to use the service (Berry, 1984). For example, a pest control company can explain the different pesticides they use, the different options they offer for controlling pests, possible harmful effects of the pesticides, and how often the treatment is needed. Such an explanation will enable customers to make better decisions and reduce their level of perceived risk. Some retailers may even find it advantageous to teach customers when they should perform the service for themselves and when they should hire an expert. Often, when a retailer does the extra, unexpected things over and above the customer's expectations, the customer considers the retailer's service to be superior.

EDUCATE CUSTOMERS ABOUT THE NATURE OF THE PROBLEM

The service retailer may educate customers about the nature of the problem that the service is intended to solve (George, Weinberger and Kelly, 1985). Dry cleaners, for example, may use visual aids to describe different types of stains or fabrics, and the chances that a given stain can be removed without damaging the fabric. Medical professional may use brochures, diagrams of the human body, and videotaped presentations to explain problems to patients.

COMMUNICATE POLICIES, PROCEDURES, AND QUALIFICATIONS

Customers' perceptions of service quality can be improved by explaining store policies and procedures and informing customers about the service providers' professional qualifications. Informing customers about store policies regarding warranties, guarantees, and money-back refunds will reduce risk perceptions. Some store policies may not make sense to the customer and may even be a source of irritation. Explaining the reason for these policies can make them more palatable and increase overall satisfaction. The display of professional certificates, diplomas, and commendations for providing excellent service will inform customers about the service providers' credentials as well as reinforce positive service quality perceptions.

MATCH SERVICE PROVIDER AND CUSTOMER

Consumers tend to develop loyalty and a sense of confidence in service providers they associate with the service (George, Weinberger, and Kelly, 1985). Therefore, perceived risk can be reduced by assigning the same service provider to a given customer whenever possible. This strategy will enable the service provider to establish a personal relationship with the customer, learn the customer's needs and wants, and tailor the service to the individual purchaser.

HELP THE CUSTOMER ESTABLISH EVALUATIVE CRITERIA

The service retailer can help the customer establish the criteria by which services are to be evaluated (George, Weinberger, and Kelly, 1985). For example, a hairdresser may suggest to a customer that the ideal hair style complements facial features and requires little time and attention. Once these criteria are agreed upon, misunderstandings about what constitutes good service should not occur. Also, the service retailer will know the criteria on which his services are to be evaluated and can feel reasonably assured that satisfaction will result if he or she does the job properly.

The Service Marketing Mix

The service marketing mix consists of the management of four variables:

1. The service delivery process
2. The channels of distribution
3. Pricing
4. Promotion.

These four variables can be coordinated to maximize service quality and customer satisfaction (see Exhibit 5–14).

THE SERVICE DELIVERY PROCESS   The **service delivery process** is the primary determinant of perceived service quality. Service retailers can influence customers' service quality perceptions in a positive way by providing evidence of service quality and by managing supply so that services are provided promptly and efficiently.

Exhibit 5–14
The Service Marketing Mix

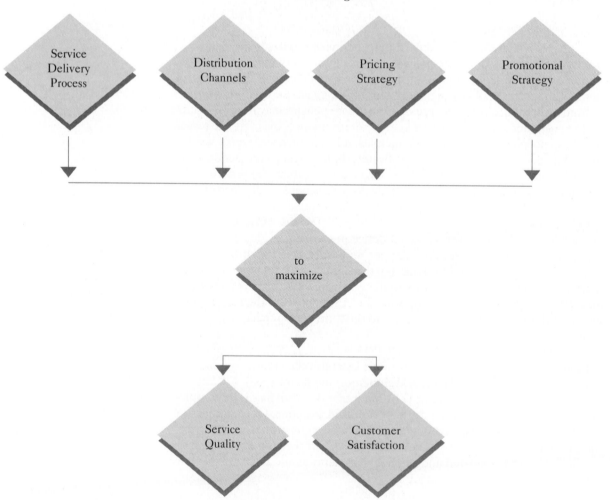

The Service Marketing Mix

The delivery of a pizza involves all variables of the service marketing mix: service delivery, distribution channel, pricing and promotion.

Because the intangibility of services makes it difficult to evaluate quality, service encounters are defined largely by sensory input (Shostack, 1985). In other words, customers usually do not have enough information to make objective assessments about service quality, so service quality assessments are made on the basis of available evidence. Since the customer's impression of a service business is often heavily influenced by things that can be comprehended with the five senses, it is important that the service be "tangibilized" (Berry, 1981). In other words, nonabstract manifestations that can be seen, heard, and otherwise sensed should be established for the intangible service.

Sight is the most dominant sense, and visual aspects of the service delivery provide strong clues to the quality of the service (Berry, 1984; Shostack, 1985). Visual clues, such as office decor, attractive uniforms worn by service providers, company stationery and signs, and advertising should be coordinated to portray a consistent image and achieve the maximum effect.

The sense of hearing is the second most dominant sense (Shostack, 1985). Therefore, it is important that telephone workers have appealing voice qualities and use correct diction and grammar. Background music should be appropriate for the customers served.

The store layout also affects service quality assessments (Wener, 1985). In a product retailing environment, layout refers to variables such as merchandise arrangement on the sales floor, cash register locations, and traffic patterns through the store. In a service retailing environment, layout refers to getting the customer to the correct office, department, or service area with a minimum amount of confusion and disorientation. Store layouts should be easily understood. Landmarks such as plants, statues, and paintings can help customers find their way around the service facility. Movement around the

SERVICE DELIVERY PROCESS
maintaining service quality and managing supply so that services are provided promptly and efficiently

facility is also easier if the setting is similar to others with which the customer is familiar. In some cases, service retailers can provide maps before the customer enters the retail setting. In other cases, retailers can minimize customers' frustration by warning them in advance that finding their way around the facility may be confusing.

Company names can act as "brands" and thereby tangibilize the service in much the same way as visual images (Berry, 1986). The company brand should set the company apart from competition, communicate the company's reason for being, possess a tangible quality, and link the most important services to specific brands, to each other, and to the overall company brand. For example, the ServiceMaster Company and VISA names meet most of these criteria.

Other details of the service encounter that provide evidence of service quality include service employees' ability to answer questions, account statements that are easy to read, and services that are delivered at the designated time. Temperature, lighting, noise, design of furniture and facilities, seating arrangements, and interpersonal distances also influence customers' service quality assessments (Zeithaml, 1981; Wener, 1985).

In addition to tangibilizing the service, customers' service quality perceptions are strongly influenced by the retailer's ability to supply its services promptly and efficiently. The ability to provide quality services often entails reshaping supply to account for fluctuations in demand. Of course, the service provider must consider the target market's needs and preferences when deciding how to manager supply. For many retail services, supply can be reshaped by hiring part-time employees during periods of peak demand and by cross-training existing employees (Berry, 1981). For example, the movie theater may be able to hire part-time employees to work in the concession stand and ticket booth. Likewise, flight attendants can be cross-trained to work at the registration counter and to provide in-flight customer service.

In some cases, supply can be reshaped by substituting equipment for human labor (Berry, 1981). For example, automatic car washes require less labor than manual car washes and automatic bank tellers reduce the personnel time required for routine transactions. The personal nature of services, however, dictates that service automation be used with caution (Berry, 1986). Retailers must know what part of the service can be performed with high-tech machines and what should be performed with "high-touch" employees. The answer to the question depends on the service, the retailer, and the customer. An understanding of all three is necessary before the decision can be made.

CHANNELS OF DISTRIBUTION   Production of a service usually occurs at the point of consumption. Consequently, service businesses are often unable to provide convenience to the customer while achieving the economies of scale inherent in centralized production facilities. Some retailers are able to overcome these limitations by combining centralized production with multisite distribution (Upah, 1980). Dry cleaners, for example, often produce the service at a centralized production facility and distribute the cleaned clothes at various retail locations across town. Sometimes, additional economies of scale can be achieved through the sharing of production facilities (Upah, 1980). For example, multiple dry cleaning companies may share the same cleaning equipment, or airlines may share the same airport terminals and baggage claim areas. The service retailer can also compensate for the inability to achieve economies of scale through centralized production by combining complementary services into one production facility (Upah, 1980). For example, optometrists often share office space with optical dispensaries.

Sometimes, economies of scale can be achieved by encouraging customers to travel longer distances, thereby minimizing the need for decentralized production and distribution facilities (Upah, 1980). For example, coupons and other price discount offers can be extended to distant customers. Service retailers can also achieve economies of scale by reducing the range of needs satisfied by the service offering (Upah, 1980). An automobile repair service, for example, may specialize in tune-ups or transmission work.

Some banks have taken a novel approach to distributing services away from a centralized facility. First National Bank of Jackson, Tennessee, has converted an armored car into a mobile bank to take into areas often ignored by banks such as nursing homes, factory sites, and public housing projects. First Citizen's Bank & Trust of Raleigh, North Carolina, has a mobile ATM, embedded in the side of a van, which travels to fairs and other big gatherings to dispense cash to ATM customers (Christie, 1990).

PRICING   Pricing may be one of the most challenging tasks for service retailers. Service pricing strategies tend to be based on the cost of providing the service more than on the demand for the service, or the prices charged by competition (Zeithaml, 1985). However, the unique characteristics of services make it difficult to determine the cost of providing them (Kelly and George, 1982).

Because production costs are difficult to determine, service retailers often use standard prices based on overall costs and projected demand levels. In this way if a given service delivery costs more than anticipated, the loss will be offset by another, more profitable, service delivery. When costs are difficult to estimate, prices may be quoted in a range (Kelly and George, 1982). The final price will be determined after the service has been delivered and costs can be estimated more accurately.

Pricing strategies can be used to reshape fluctuations in demand (Berry, 1981). For example, movie theaters level out demand by offering afternoon matinees at reduced prices, and resorts offer lower rates in off-seasons. Pricing strategies designed to level fluctuations in demand are often combined with special promotions, such as professional sports teams offering reduced prices and free t-shirts to encourage attendance at middle-of-the-week games.

The use of price discounts to smooth out fluctuations in demand should be used with caution, however. Because services are characterized by experience and credence properties, the purchaser has little information available during the search stage of the decision-making process. Therefore, in the absence of better information, lower prices may signal the customer that the service is in some way inferior to the higher priced services offered by competitors (Berry, 1981).

One aspect of pricing that is less obvious to customers, although it does increase the retailer's expenses, is found in retail banking. BankAmerica offers free checking accounts, gives $5.00 to any customer who waits in line more than five minutes, and provides a 24-hour loan-by-phone dial-a-banker banking (McCoy, 1989).

PROMOTION   Because services are low in search properties, the first-time purchaser of services has little information on which to base a decision, and is likely to use price and the tangible aspects of the service as clues to service quality (Zeithaml, 1981). Service retailers can "tangibilize" the service through visual representations as the Rock of Gibraltar (Prudential Insurance), umbrellas (Travelers' Insurance), and "good hands" (Allstate) (Berry 1981). In-store signs also may be used to increase the degree of tangibility and inform customers about the service.

Service purchasers rely heavily on word-of-mouth communication for information about the service's search properties. These interpersonal communications are the single most important promotional tool available to the service marketer. Therefore, favorable word-of-mouth communication should be stimulated to the greatest extent possible (Zeithaml, 1981). This may be accomplished through the use of advertisements that contain testimonials or are high in conversational value (Zeithaml, 1981; Berry, 1981), writing thank-you letters to satisfied customers and other sources of favorable communication, and marketing aggressively to opinion leaders. Brochures, business cards, and information pieces (e.g., magazines containing articles about community health issues distributed by hospitals) can stimulate interpersonal communication. Satisfied customers can be encouraged to tell a friend and pass along these materials.

Word-of-mouth communication and the quality of the face-to-face encounter can be stimulated through mini-encounters (Blackman 1985). **Mini-encounters** are a series of communications that build awareness of the service retailer, create a feeling of trust on the part of the customer, and increase the customer's knowledge about the nature of the service and how the service transaction can be expected to occur. Each mini-encounter should reinforce every other mini-encounter and send similar messages and images to the potential purchaser. Examples of mini-encounters include radio commercials, letters, brochures relating to the service, birthday and Christmas cards, informative newsletters, signage, and uniforms.

The service provider may wish to make the mini-encounter increasingly personal in nature. For example, radio commercials may be used initially to make the potential customer aware that the service is available, followed by direct mail to inform the customer about the nature and availability of the service and, finally, a telephone call to the potential customer. This approach might be used by an exterminator who would like to check your home for pests, or a heating company that would like to check your heating system before the beginning of the winter season.

These mini-encounters increase the customer's awareness of the service retailer, and make him feel more knowledgeable about the retailer's services, even though he has never purchased them. This perceived familiarity can compensate for the absence of search properties and for a lack of word-of-mouth communications. The benefits of mini-encounters include:

1. Creating a proper continuing series of mini-encounters that serves to educate potential users and positively reinforce previous users

MINI-ENCOUNTER
one of a series of communications that build customer awareness and knowledge of the service retailer and the nature of the service

2. Providing concrete stimuli through mini-encounters to prepare users for the actual service, giving them visual, procedural, and psychological clues to define a reasonable set of expectations for the service process
3. Giving many service businesses a way to maintain customer contact over long periods between service use incidents (Blackman, 1985)

Because consumers often find it difficult to evaluate the quality of services and are less confident in their consistent quality, promotional efforts should emphasize the quality factors of the service and build on the service retailer's image (Kelly and George, 1982; Berry, 1981). Promotional messages can be used to suggest preferred criteria for evaluating services. Because the purchase of services involves uncertainty, personal selling should be a dominant promotional tool for many service retailers (Kelly and George, 1982). Service salespeople should be able to reduce perceived risk by providing the customer a sense of assurance. This risk reduction should occur both before and after the service is provided to reduce the dissonance associated with the purchase. Successful service salespeople need to display a natural interest in people and their needs (Kelly and George, 1982). (See Exhibit 5–15.) In addition, customized services usually require higher levels of skill.

Exhibit 5–15
A Key to Service Salespeople's Success
....

SOURCE: Reprinted by permission of NEA, Inc.

Sales promotions, such as coupons and free visits, may be used as short-run price decreases to stimulate trial use, build sales, counter competitive activity, and smooth fluctuations, in demand (Berry, 1981). Since consumers often equate price with service quality, care should be taken not to dilute the service retailer's quality image (Kelly and George, 1982).

Finally, some service retailers are able to achieve economies of a scale in promotion when the outlets are identified as members of a larger group and when the services are consistent across providers (Upah, 1980). McDonald's, for example, advertises on a national basis and takes advantage of the rate structures available to national advertisers.

Evaluation of Operating Results

Three measures of operating results exist for service businesses:

1. The customers' perceptions of service quality
2. The service providers' perceptions of service quality
3. The financial performance of the retail service operation

Customers' Perceptions of Service Quality

Customers' perceptions of service quality can be determined through survey research. The SERVQUAL scale, previously discussed, was developed to measure customers' assessments of service quality (Parasuraman, Zeithaml and Berry, 1986). Its reliability and validity have been examined in four service categories: banking, credit card services, repair and maintenance, and long distance telephone, and it can be modified for use in other service businesses.

Service Providers' Perceptions of Service Quality

Customers' evaluations should not be considered the final word on service quality. The customer does not see many elements of the service delivery process (Shostack, 1985). In a bank, for example, checks and loan applications are processed, loan applications are analyzed and approved, records are maintained and audited, and community relations work is performed. Even though these aspects of the service delivery process are not visible to the service retailer's customers, they are visible to the employees.

Survey research can be used to examine employees' perceptions of service quality in the same way that customers' perceptions were assessed and to provide a second measure of operating performance. The SERVQUAL scale can be modified to assess employees' perceptions of service quality as well as those of customers. Use of the same scale for both customers and employees will enable the service retailer to acquire an additional dimension of information by comparing responses between the two groups.

Financial Performance

The financial performance of the organization is a final measure of operating results. However, many of the standard measures of financial performance

Alamo Car Rental

Over the past seventeen years, Alamo Rent A Car has established itself as the big price cutter in the car rental industry, with advertised rental rates 20 percent lower than those of its major competitors with no extra charge for mileage. If you are in Los Angeles and rent a Chevy Beretta with no extras between Wednesday and Friday, Alamo will charge you $38 per day with free mileage. Hertz, on the other hand, will charge you $51.93 per day for the same car, and, if you do not reserve the car at least three days in advance, will tack on an additional $0.32 a mile for every mile you drive over 100 miles.

As the result of its low rental prices, Alamo's revenues have risen to more than $500 million per year, controlling 8 percent of the airline rental car market. In fact, it now ranks fifth behind "The Big Four" (Hertz, Avis, National, and Budget) in terms of the overall rental car market. Alamo's profit margins, claims company president, Charles Platt, range between 3 percent and 5 percent, a return second only to Avis. Charles Finnie, of Alex Brown & Sons, responds to Alamo's image as "one of the most profitable players" in the rental car business by explaining that "Alamo has one of the smartest, most aggressive managements in the industry."

One of the reasons Alamo chairman, Michael Egan, is able to lower costs is that he is very careful about the way he picks his rental locations. While Hertz rents 300,000 cars at 5,400 locations in the United States and United Kingdom, Alamo rents only 75,000 cars at 90 of the most highly trafficked locations. In addition, most of Alamo's rental counters are not in airport terminals, where the retail space is the most expensive, but in nearby cheaper locations.

However, Alamo has needed more than low overhead and cheap cars to put itself ahead of the industry's giants, and this is where it has drawn much criticism. The company was known for pushing its agents to talk to customers into trading up for more expensive cars than those advertised. Alamo also prodded its customers into signing up for what were the most expensive collision insurance rates in the industry, at $11.99 per day for a mid-size car. As the company tacked on these additional expenses, the customer who listened to his agent discovered that the "savings" had vanished.

Recently, the Federal Trade Commission and the National Association of Attorneys General charged that, concealing a variety of charges that would boost the final bill, Alamo was misleading customers. In response, the company agreed to change its advertising. Likewise, when a July 1989 *Consumer Reports* listed Alamo last among 11 rental companies in terms of customer satisfaction, it started its "Best Friends" program, which retrained the company's 4,000 employees to be more friendly and courteous. To assure the service is improved, Platt sends "Phantom Shoppers" out to monitor the program. The result—Alamo's complaints decreased by more than one half, while reservations increased by 30 percent.

In the early 1980s, Egan realized that lower fares brought on by airline regulation would allow more people to fly on their vacations, and, consequently, would cause them to need rental cars once they reached their destinations. Alamo's early decision to concentrate on vacationers has turned into a boon for the company, as the leisure rental car market has grown between 10 percent and 15 percent per year, as opposed to the commercial market, which has grown 5 percent. In response to this success, other companies are going after Alamo's travel customers. This has led the flexible Alamo to work to stake out a new territory—the budget-minded business traveler. This change in strategy has resulted in the company tailoring 31 of its locations for these customers, a market that now accounts for nearly 30 percent of Alamo's total revenues.

Adapted from "Born to Hustle," *Forbes*, (May 28, 1990), 190–194.

must be used with caution when evaluating service retailers. Services cannot be inventoried and do not move through warehouses and pricing rooms as products do. For the same reasons, the service retailers' capital requirements are different (Kelly and George, 1982). Therefore, traditional measures of product retailers' performance, such as return on investment and sales per square foot, may not be comparable to service retailers' figures. Likewise, measures such as stock turnover and open-to-buy are not applicable to the service retailing operation because of the intangibility of services. Markups and markdowns cannot be applied to service retailing operations in the same way they are applied by product retailers. Market share figures are difficult to obtain since services do not physically move through warehouses and across retail shelves. Comparisons of labor costs between products and services areas of the retail store should also be used with caution since services are much more labor intensive than products.

The establishment of each service area as its own profit center appears to be the best way to measure financial performance in a service environment. The gauge of worth would then be the level of profit generated after labor costs (Kelly & George, 1982). Even these figures should be used with caution, however. Many services in the retail environment (e.g., customer cafeteria, repair services) are required to support the sale of products. Compensation to the service department is in the form of revenue transfers between departments, which in many retail environments does not reflect the market value of the services. For example, the repair department in an appliance store produces revenue from repairing appliances, but also supports the retail floor selling function. When warranty work is done, the repair department's compensation may be less than the amount that would be charged to outside customers. If managers of service departments are evaluated on the basis of revenue generated, they may be unduly penalized for performing warranty work in support of the retail selling function (Kelly & George, 1982).

SUMMARY

Services differ from products in several ways: intangibility, inseparability from their source, variability in outcomes, and simultaneous production and consumption. Consequently, products and services are normally classified on different bases. A classification scheme for services includes: people-based or equipment-based, the extent to which the customer's presence is necessary; personal or business services; the service provider's motives; and degree of customer contact.

Consumer purchase behavior differs between products and services on several dimensions. When purchasing services, consumers perceive a higher degree of risk and are more apt to base first-time service purchase decisions on experience properties rather than the search properties that characterize first-time product purchases. Service purchasers tend to have a smaller set of alternatives to consider, and word-of-mouth communication is often used as a substitute for search properties. Consumers tend to be more brand loyal to services, and the diffusion of service innovations is often slower.

Consumers' service quality perceptions are a function of their expectations about service delivery and their perceptions of the quality of service actually provided. Within this framework, service quality can be defined on the dimensions of technical and functional quality. Image, a third variable relating to service quality, performs a filtering function.

Maintaining high service quality is difficult for several reasons: inseparability of production and consumption, inadequate organizational structure and systems, failure to communicate with the customer and other members of the service retailing organization, service proliferation and complexity, tendency of many service providers to view customers as statistics, short-run view of the business, and the possibility that the consumer may be able to perform the service him- or herself and therefore be a major competitor.

Achievement of high levels of service quality depends on: development of a quality-oriented corporate philosophy, quality-oriented training and organizational support for service employees, customer orientation and focus by the entire service retailing organization; and development of a services marketing mix that results in high levels of customer satisfaction.

The service marketing mix consists of a service delivery process, channels of distribution, price and promotion. A prompt and efficient service delivery process must provide evidence of service quality and enable the service retailer to manage supply. The distribution limitations that often prevent the service retailer from achieving economies of scale through centralized production, may be overcome by combining centralized production with multisite distribution, combining complementary services into one production facility, encouraging customers to travel longer distances, and economies in promotional strategies.

The difficulty in determining costs creates pricing problems for service retailers. Thus, they often quote a range of prices, or set standard prices based on overall costs and projected demand levels. Differential pricing can be used to smooth fluctuations in demand for services.

Service purchasers have little information on which to base initial purchase decisions. Therefore, the most important promotional tool is word-of-mouth communication, which can be stimulated by testimonial advertisements, "thank you" letters to sources of favorable communication, and mini-encounters. Mini-encounters can compensate for a lack of interpersonal communication and for the absence of search properties.

Promotional efforts should emphasize service quality factors, build on the service retailer's image, and suggest criteria for evaluating the service. Personal selling is the the dominant promotional tool, with sales promotions used to effect short-run price decreases.

Service businesses can measure their operating results in several ways: perceptions of service quality by both customers and service providers and the retailer's financial performance. Financial performance measures must be used with caution, however, because capital requirements and labor costs are different for service businesses. Traditional measures such as stock turnover and open-to-buy do not apply to the service environment, and the intangibility of services makes it difficult to determine market share. One way to measure financial performance is to establish each service area as its own profit center. When services are performed to support the sale of products, measures should not penalize managers for performing required support work.

Questions for Review and Comprehension

1. Describe and give examples of the strategic planning process for a service retailer. Information can be obtained from personal interviews with service company managers, annual reports, and media articles about firms in a variety of service industries, such as banking, airlines, entertainment, and others.

2. Discuss the important aspects of the firm's macroenvironment and microenvironment that should be analyzed by (a) a dry cleaning business, (b) airline, and (c) movie theater owner.

3. For the retailers discussed in Question 2, what factors within the firm's internal environment should be assessed to determine the retailer's strengths and weaknesses relative to competition?

4. Explain the key distinctions between the retailing of products versus the retailing of services based on the concepts of intangibility, inseparability, perishability, and variability.

5. Classify the services of (a) a hairdresser, (b) an exterminator, (c) an automatic car wash, (d) a car rental agency, and (e) a day care center according to one or more of the classification schemes presented in the chapter. Justify your choices and explain how these classifications can be helpful in strategic planning.

6. Bart has just moved to a new city to start his first job after graduating from college. He must find new service providers to replace those that are now too far away to patronize. Specifically, he needs to open a new bank account, find a mechanic to service his aging car, and arrange for utilities and cable TV hook-up. Based on your understanding of consumer behavior in the service encounter, how will each of these purchase decisions be affected by (a) perceived risk, (b) evaluation of service alternatives, (c) loyalty to specific service providers and service brands, and (d) the rate of diffusion of innovations related to the services?

7. Outline some strategies that each of the service providers discussed in Question 5 might use to increase the probability that you will choose them as your service provider.

8. Discuss the difficulty in evaluating service attributes that confront buyers of services. What are the implications of the attributes of search properties, experience properties, and credence properties as they differ in the evaluation of products versus services? Which is easier to "manage" with the marketing mix?

9. Explain several ways that consumer loyalty to service providers and service brands differs from loyalty to product retailers and product brands, and suggest strategies for dealing with each of these differences.

10. Discuss the major reasons why service innovations are diffused into the marketplace at a slower rate than product innovations. What are some ways that service retailers can "speed up" customers' general acceptance of service innovations (for example, the ability to insert a credit card into the gas pump at a service station)?

11. Perceptions of service quality can create a number of problems between customers, employees, and managers. Using your favorite restaurant or recreation facility as an example, explain how they do/do not minimize or overcome the five service quality gaps based on differences between what is expected and what is delivered. Now compare this to another service business in the same category that you would never patronize again.

12. Illustrate several ways that a telephone company or local power utility might apply an understanding of the five dimensions of service quality (tangibles, reliability, responsiveness, assurance, empathy) in order to deal successfully with its customers.

13. Name the seven major causes of service quality problems, and discuss

some ways that a moderately priced motel chain might avoid or minimize these problems.

14. Justify the necessity to incorporate a quality-oriented corporate philosophy, quality-oriented training and organizational support for employees, and a focus on the customer into a service retailer's strategic plan.

15. What aspects of each element of the service marketing mix are most apt to maximize service quality and contribute to high levels of customer satisfaction for the clientele of a physical fitness center? Include the service delivery process, channel(s) of distribution, pricing, and promotion in your discussion.

16. Briefly describe three methods that can be used to measure the results of a service retailing operation, including both customers' and service providers' perceptions of service quality and financial performance. Do service retailers evaluate their operating results in the same way as product retailers? Why or why not?

References

Berry, Leonard (1986), "Big Ideas in Services Marketing," *Journal of Consumer Marketing*, 3, no. 2 (Spring), 47–51.

Berry, Leonard L. (1981), "Perspectives on the Retailing of Service" in *Theory in Retailing: Traditional and Nontraditional Sources*, Ronald W. Stampfl and Elizabeth C. Hirschman, eds., Chicago: American Marketing Association, 9–20.

Berry Leonard L., Valarie A. Zeithaml, and A. Parasuraman (1988), "Quality Counts in Services, Too," in *Managing Services: Marketing, Operations, and Human Resources*, Christopher H. Lovelock, ed., Englewood Cliffs, N.J.: Prentice-Hall, Inc., 216–225.

Berry, Leonard L. (1984), "Services Marketing Is Different," in *Services Marketing*, Christopher H. Lovelock, ed., Englewood Cliffs, N.J.: Prentice-Hall, Inc., 29–37.

Blackman, Barry A. (1985), "Making a Service More Tangible Can Make It More Manageable," in *The Service Encounter: Managing Employee/Customer Interaction in Service Businesses*, John A. Czepiel, Michael R. Solomon, and Carol G. Surprenant, eds., Lexington, Mass.: D.C. Heath and Co., 291–302.

Borrus, Amy and Frederic A. Miller (1988), "In Japan, Banks Get Personal to Get Rich," *Business Week* (November 28), 166.

"Business Bulletin" (1988), *Wall Street Journal* (May 26), 1.

Buzzell, Robert D. and Bradley T. Gale (1987), *The PIMS Principles: Linking Strategy to Performance*, New York: The Free Press.

Christie, Rick (1990), "Banks Take to the Road In Search of Customers," *Wall Street Journal* (May 11), B1.

Chipello, Christopher J. (1989), "Banks Start Spicing Up Their ATM Menus," *Wall Street Journal* (October 5) B1, B12.

Dolan, Carrie (1988), "As If Hawaii Weren't Fantastic Itself, Hotels Are Spinning Fantasies," *Wall Street Journal* (June 30), 1, 12.

George, William R., Marc G. Weinberger, and J. Patrick Kelly (1985), "Consumer Risk Perceptions: Managerial Tool for the Service Encounter," in *The Service Encounter: Managing Employee/Customer Interaction in Service Businesses*, John A. Czepiel, Michael R. Solomon, and Carol F. Surprenant, eds., Lexington, Mass.: D.C. Heath and Co.

Gronroos, Christian (1984), "A Service Quality Model and Its Marketing Implications," *European Journal of Marketing*, 18, no. 4, 36–44.

Gummesson, Evert (1988), "Service Quality and Product Quality Combined," *Review of Business*, 9, no. 3, (Winter), 14–19.

James, Frank E. (1989), "Pediatric Centers Spring Up to Provide Off-Hour Care," *Wall Street Journal* (February 13), B1.

Kelly, J. Patrick and William R. George (1982), "Strategic Management Issues for the Retailing of Services," *Journal of Retailing*, 58, no. 2 (Summer), 26–43.

Kotler, Philip (1991), *Marketing Management: Analysis, Planning, Implementation, and Control*, 7th ed., Englewood Cliffs, N.J.: Prentice Hall.

Langevin, Roger G. (1988), "Service Quality: Essential Ingredients," *Review of Business*, 9, no. 3 (Winter), 3–5.

Mangold, W. Glynn (1989), "Retailing of Services: A Conceptualization," Research in process (Unpublished working paper), Louisville, Ky.: University of Louisville. (Conceptual contribution to chapter.)

McCoy, Charles (1989), "A Slashing Pursuit of Retail Trade Brings Bank American Back," *Wall Street Journal* (October 2), A1, A4.

McGinley, Laurie (1990), "Airlines Now Push Baby Safety Seats," *Wall Street Journal* (February 22), B1, B2.

"Mix Mozart With Motown—In Minutes" (1988), *Business Week* (October 31), 153.

Oneal, Michael (1987), "ServiceMaster: Looking for New Worlds to Clean," *Business Week* (January 19), 60–61.

Pae, Peter (1989), "Salad Bar Is Poised to Make Fast Exit from Fast Food," *Wall Street Journal* (March 24), B1.

Parasuraman, A., Valerie A. Zeithaml, and Leonard L. Berry (1985), "A Conceptual Model of Service Quality and Its Implications for Future Research," *Journal of Marketing*, 49 (Fall), 41–50.

Parasuraman, A., Valerie A. Zeithaml, and Leonard L Berry (1988), "SERVQUAL: A Multiple-Item Scale for Measuring Consumer Perceptions of Service Quality," *Journal of Retailing* 64:1 (Spring), 12–40.

"Rooms at the Inn" (1989), *Business Week* (January 2), 62.

Shostack, G. Lynn (1985), "Planning the Service Encounter," in *The Service Encounter: Managing Employee/Customer Interaction in Service Businesses*, John A. Czepiel, Michael R. Solomon, and Carol F. Surprenant, eds., Lexington, Mass.: D.C. Heath and Co., 243–253.

Townsend, Patrick L. and Joan E. Gebhardt (1988), "Quality: 20th Century Snake-Oil," *Review of Business*, 9, no. 3 (Winter), 6–9.

Upah, Gregory D. (1980), "Mass Marketing in Service Retailing: A Review and Synthesis of Major Methods," *Journal of Retailing*, 56, no. 3 (Fall), 59–76.

U.S. Department of Commerce (1988), *Survey of Current Business*, 68, no. 2 (February), S-1.

Vogel, Todd and Chuck Hawkins (1990), "Can UPS Deliver the Goods in a New World?" *Business Week* (June 4), 80–82.

Wells, Ken (1988), "Hotels and Resorts Are Catering to Kids," *Wall Street Journal* (August 11), 25.

Wener, Richard E. (1985), "The Environmental Psychology of Service Encounters," in *The Service Encounter: Managing Employee/Customer Interaction in Service Businesses*, John A. Czepiel, Michael R. Solomon, and Carol F. Surprenant, eds., Lexington, Mass.: D.C. Heath and Co., 101–112.

Zeithaml, Valarie A. (1981), "How Consumer Evaluation Processes Differ Between Goods and Services" in *Marketing of Services*, James H. Donnelly and William R. George, eds., Chicago: American Marketing Association, 186–190.

1.1 WHAT SHOULD WE DO ABOUT A FALTERING DEPARTMENT STORE?

● *continued* ● ● ●

CASE

For more than one hundred and forty years, Stuart Brothers had been one of the enduring names in American retailing. For more than half that time its gray, hulking structure on Chicago's famous Michigan Avenue has been its best public face. But when one of the store's brass nameplates was whipped off by a famous Lake Michigan gust of wind recently and never replaced, it may have been the beginning of the end for the venerable retailer.

In January 1989, X.Y.Z. Industries, the British company that has owned Stuart Brothers since 1974, said it would divest itself of the 36-store Stuart Brothers chain in Chicago, Milwaukee, Indianapolis, and Pittsburgh, as well as three other store divisions. X.Y.Z. said Stuart Brothers lacked the "organic growth potential" that it preferred—which people in the industry took as a euphemism for the actuality that Stuart Brothers was losing so much money, X.Y.Z. would waste any further cash it invested.

Stuart Brother's fall from grace was long and bumpy. For decades it was the prototype of America's middle-class, middle-price store, a strong competitor of Marshall Fields, its neighbor on Michigan Avenue, which sold similar merchandise. But in the early 1970s, Stuart Brothers seemed to lose its direction. Within a few years, just as the revived Marshall Fields started to boom, Stuart Brothers began to falter.

In effect, it failed to cope with demographic changes, such as population growth among the young, free-spending professionals, and the shift by consumers to a less formal and more home-oriented way of life.

Worse, it could not seem to capture a market. It was pressured in the higher-priced end by the upgrading efforts of Marshall Fields and Saks Fifth Avenue, which catered to more affluent consumers buying contemporary clothes, sophisticated electronics, and expensive home furnishings. But it was also squeezed on the lower end of the scale by such discounters as Caldor, Bradlees, and promotional retailers, such as Zayre's, Alexanders, and J. W. Mays. Chicago shoppers—perhaps amongst the toughest and most cynical of all—seemed to know that Stuart Brothers had lost its touch.

Upgrading to better, more fashionable goods, an option Stuart Brothers had, would have required a large outlay of funds, which X.Y.Z. refused to commit. In a way, Stuart Brothers had always been X.Y.Z.'s black sheep, reportedly acquired so X.Y.Z. could buy Saks Fifth Avenue, which the Stuart family was selling in a package deal. (Saks is not up for sale at this time). X.Y.Z. held on to Stuart Brothers, which was already sputtering when it was acquired, for a dozen years, hoping Stuart Brothers could turn itself around with little investment. The strategy clearly did not work. Under several managements in the last decade, Stuart Brothers concentrated on price cutting, but the tactic did not create loyal customers; instead, Stuart Brothers drew bargain-hungry shoppers who were interested only in the lowest price and would flock to whichever store offered it.

According to people close to X.Y.Z., the British company had hoped it could prop up Stuart Brother's profits by maintaining a drive for the low- and middle-income customers. And unlike its competitors, it did not invest heavily in improving the store's physical appearance or merchandising mainly to woo more affluent customers.

In 1983, the ten Chicago stores were merged with the ten Milwaukee stores that had been somewhat more profitable. The merger, however, did not seem to produce the desired results. Then, about a year ago, X.Y.Z. started putting out feelers for a buyer of the Chicago and Milwaukee division. Now everything is on the market.

X.Y.Z.'s decision to sell may have been spurred by a near-disastrous 1985, when so-called Stuart Brothers Midwest—the Chicago and Milwaukee divisions—reportedly lost more than $10 million on static sales of more than $450 million. Its flagship store on Michigan Avenue simply wallowed in the big swells created by the reinvigorated Marshall Field's. Its new store in Evanston never drew the customer base it had wanted, partly because of its location in a mixed residential and commercial area, but also because shoppers in Evanston were more attracted to the new Bloomingdale's on Michigan Avenue in downtown Chicago.

In the Chicago suburbs, Stuart Brothers had held its own, particularly with stores in strong regional shopping malls that have other vibrant anchor stores, such as in Skokie. The more profitable suburban stores are now far more important to the

continued

213

chain than its faded flagship on Michigan Avenue, which has been losing money for years.

In Pittsburgh, Stuart Brothers attempted to attract younger customers through a fashion-cum-price strategy. Unfortunately last year the nine stores reportedly lost $2 million on sales of $140 million. Only in Milwaukee, where management seems to have plotted a clearer strategy and had less competition, were the Stuart Brothers stores consistently profitable and the market leaders.

Although its is probably too early to say what will happen to Stuart Brothers, the initial reaction from potential buyers, such as Associated Dry Goods and The May Company, was that they were not interested in Stuart Brothers as a whole, but would consider looking at some of the more profitable branch stores. The profitable Milwaukee group, by contrast, appears to be a more likely candidate to be taken over in one piece, with May Department Stores and Dayton-Hudson considered possible buyers.

Can Stuart Brothers be saved as a retailer in Chicago, Indianapolis, and Pittsburgh—or be salvaged only in a real estate deal? "I don't think that it has a future," said one top Chicago merchant. "The stores have to be modernized and merchandising radically changed. But it would take so much money that it would be a very tough thing to do." Others think such a view is unduly grim.

QUESTIONS

1. Are Stuart Brothers giving customers a real reason to shop at its stores?
2. From a strategic standpoint, how can Stuart Brothers survive in the 1990s?
3. Why should Stuart Brothers reduce the number of storewide promotions it holds?
4. If you were running Stuart Brothers, what would you do to attract customers?
5. What should be done to the flagship store on Michigan Avenue? Would you recommend closing it or perhaps remodeling the facility?

This case was prepared by Richard C. Leventhal, Metropolitan State College, Denver, Colorado.

1.2 World Airlines: A Customer Service Air Disaster

During a recent trip to Germany, Dr. Cheshire and his wife boarded a World Airlines flight that turned into a service disaster. Upon returning home, Dr. Cheshire immediately sent the following letter to the Customer Relations Manager of World Airlines:

Monday, July 23, 1990

Dear Customer Service Manager:

Through the Carolina Motor Club my wife and I booked round-trip first-class and clipper-class seats on the following World Airlines flights on the dates indicated:

1	July	World Airlines	3072 Charlotte to Kennedy
1	July	World Airlines	86 Kennedy to Munich
21	July	World Airlines	87 Munich to Kennedy
21	July	World Airlines	3073 Kennedy to Charlotte

We additionally booked connecting flights to and from Wilmington and Charlotte on Trans Air flights 263 (on 1 July) and 2208 (on 21 July).

The outbound flights 3072 and 86 seemed pleasant enough, especially since World Airlines had upgraded our clipper class seats on flight 86 to first class. However, mid-flight on 86 we discovered that we had been food poisoned on flight 3072, apparently by the seafood salad that was served in first class that day (it seemed warm to us and we hesitated to eat it but unfortunately did so anyway). My wife was so ill that, trying to get to the restroom to throw up, she passed out cold hitting her head and, we discovered during the next few days, apparently damaging her back (she will go for x-rays tomorrow). The flight attendants were very concerned and immediately tried to help her but there was nothing they could do except help her clean herself up and get the food off her from the food trays she hit. In addition to the nausea and

diarrhea, she had a large knot on her head and headaches for several days. Her lower back (possibly tailbone) has been in constant pain ever since. I too, was very ill for several days. A nice start for a vacation! But it gets worse.

During the long layover between flights at Kennedy there was a tremendous rainstorm and our baggage apparently was left out in it; a situation that we discovered when we arrived at our first night's lodging and discovered ALL of our clothing was literally wringing wet. In addition, four art prints we were bringing as gifts for friends were ruined.

The return flights were better only in that we did not get poisoned; instead we did not get fed! Flight 87 out of Munich was apparently short-handed and due to our seating location, the flight attendant who had to do double duty always got to us last. We had to ask for drinks; there were no hot towels left for us; the meals ran out and we were given no choice but an overdone piece of grey meat with tomato sauce on it—we tasted it but it was odd tasting and given our experience on flight 3072, we were afraid to eat it.

We cleared our baggage through customs adjacent to baggage carousel #5 at Kennedy and rechecked them through to Wilmington immediately. They were dry and undamaged at that point. We went into the unair-conditioned first class waiting lounge where we sat and sweated for several hours until fight 87 boarding time neared. Has World Airlines ever considered providing some ventilation or air conditioning for their Kennedy terminal?

Flight 87 was delayed in boarding due to slowness in cleaning the aircraft (according to the announcement made) and also due to the late arrival of the crew. In addition, the flight was further delayed due to a heavy rainstorm, which backed up traffic for takeoff. However, had the flight boarded on time it would have not lost its takeoff priority and could likely have taken off two hours sooner than it did. We might have been able to make our connection in Charlotte. On board the flight the plane was the dirtiest and in the most disrepair of any aircraft I have ever flown on—pealing wall coverings, litter on floors, overhead bins taped shut with duct tape, etc. As first class passengers I asked for some cold beer while we were waiting for the rest of the passengers to board; it was warm. We were quite hungry having not eaten much in the past 12 hours and asked for some bags of peanuts, there were none; the plane had not been stocked. I asked for a pillow and blanket for my wife; there were none. What a great first class section! There were only three flight attendants for the whole plane and I felt sorry for the pregnant one who had to do

continued

215

double duty in both first class and the rear cabin. She was very sympathetic to the poor conditions; I don't see how you keep employees when they are treated like that.

Due to the excessive delay at Kennedy, flight 87 was very late and we could not make our connection from Charlotte to Wilmington. As it turned out, we would have barely been able to make it if the flight had been on time because World Airlines had changed not only the flight numbers but also the flight times on the Kennedy-Charlotte leg of our journey— AND WE WERE NEVER NOTIFIED OF THIS CHANGE UNTIL WE ARRIVED AT THE AIRPORT! I deplaned in Raleigh to try to alert the people meeting us in Wilmington that we would not be in that night; however, it was too late and they had already gone to the airport. The gate attendant at Raleigh assured me that World Airlines would put us up for the night in Charlotte so I returned to the plane (I had considered a taxi, 2 hours, from Raleigh to Wilmington). However, when we arrived in Charlotte, the World Airlines representative, Mr. Mason Jar, refused to take care of us stating that, since we had not booked the Wilmington-Charlotte portion of our trip through World Airlines, "it is not our problem." Yet he proceeded to arrange for rooms and meals for two other passengers from the same flight. I called World Airlines customer service via the 800 number and discussed the problem with a Mr. Howard Cunningham in Miami. Mr. Cunningham was most sympathetic in trying to get some rational thinking back into the situation, but his supervisor finally said it was up to the local manager in Charlotte to decide. The local manager (I did not get his name, no name tag) tried to wash his hands of it saying we had an "illegal connection" due to times between flights and that he wouldn't provide lodging or meals. After I pointed out to him at least three times that the connection was not illegal when booked and World Airlines changed its flight times without notifying us, and further made it clear that not only was I not going to go away, but that there was going to be a lot more said about this matter, he finally capitulated and gave us a voucher.

After traveling for 24 hours, receiving lousy service, poor food, no amenities, it is a real pleasure to run into an argumentative SOB like your agent in Charlotte. He should be fired!!! As first class passengers we have been treated like cattle! But, it does not end here.

Upon arriving in Wilmington the next morning only two of our four bags arrived with us. We had to initiate a baggage trace action. Our missing two bags were finally delivered to our house around 3:00 PM on 23 July. And SURPRISE, they were left in the rain at Kennedy again and EVERYTHING was so wet that water poured out of the pockets. I poured water out of the hairdryer. ALL of our paper purchases, maps, guide books, photos, souvenir brochures, etc. are ruined. I don't yet know if the dryer, radio, electric toothbrush, voltage converters, etc., will work—they are drying out as this is being written. In addition, my brand new bag now has a hole in the bottom on a corner where it is obvious that World Airlines baggage handlers dragged it on the tarmac (obviously a *water logged* duffle bag size piece of luggage is too heavy to lift).

As near as I can figure we have lost at least a roll of color prints (irreplaceable); approximately $100.00 in travel guides and tour books, many souvenir booklets, brochures, menus, etc.; $100.00 in art prints; $50.00 in damage to luggage; unknown amount in electronics that may not work; a lot of enjoyment due to pain and suffering resulting from illness and injury (bill for x-rays enclosed; Attention Mr. Kelly); and all sense of humor and patience for such inexcusable treatment by an airline.

If there is to be any compensation for what we have suffered it should be in monetary form. There is no recapturing the lost time and pleasure on the vacation. The art, books, etc., (except for photos), can be replaced. . . . assuming we make such a trip again. But if we do, you can be assured we would not choose World Airlines . In closing, I am particularly angry and adamant about this whole fiasco as we wanted this vacation to be special and treated ourselves to the luxury of first class treatment . . . which we got everywhere except on World Airlines . . . it is almost unbelievable how poorly we were treated by your airline, almost a perfect negative case study in customer service. I have purposely tried to mention every little nit-picky thing I can recall because I want you to realize just how totally bad this whole experience has been!

In disgust,
Dr. R. A. Cheshire
Cheshire Place
6048 Wrightsville Avenue
Wilmington, NC 28403

QUESTIONS

1. How do the service characteristics of intangibility, inseparability, perishability, and variability pertain to the airline industry?

2. Classify the airline industry based on the five retail service classification schemes presented in the text.

3. Based on gap analysis, where did service quality fall through the gaps? Explain your answer.

4. According to the determinants of service quality, where did World Airlines appear to fail? Explain your answer.

5. Based on the causes of service quality problems presented in the text, which of the problems seem to apply to this case?

6. Services can be characterized as having search, experience, and/or credence properties. What type(s) of properties pertain to the airline industry?

7. The airline's responses to Dr. Cheshire's problems are presented in Case Exhibit 1 and Case Exhibit 2. Do you feel that this was an appropriate response? Explain your answer.

This case was prepared by Richard A. Engdahl, Assistant Professor of Management, and Dr. K. Douglas Hoffman, Assistant Professor of Marketing, University of North Carolina at Wilmington, Wilmington, North Carolina.

September 25, 1990

Case Exhibit 1

Dear Dr. & Mrs. Cheshire:

This letter confirms the settlement agreed upon during our phone conversation just concluded.

Accordingly, we have prepared and enclosed (in duplicate) a General Release for $2,000.00. Both you and your wife should sign in the presence of a Notary Public, have your signatures notarized, and return the Original to this office, keeping the copy for your records.

As soon as we receive the notarized Release, we will forward our draft for $2000.00.

Again, our sincerest apologies to Mrs. Cheshire. It will be most helpful for our Customer Relations staff if you include with the Release, copies of all available travel documents.

Very truly yours,

U. B. Green
Manager-Claims

continued

Case Exhibit 2

Dear Dr. Cheshire:

Let me begin by apologizing for this delayed response and all of the unfortunate incidents that you described in your letter. Although we try to make our flights as enjoyable as possible, we obviously failed on this occasion.

Mr. Green informs me that you have worked out a potential settlement for the matter regarding food poisoning. We regret you were not able to enjoy the food service on the other flights on your itinerary because of it. I assure you that such incidents are a rare occurrence and that much time and effort is expended to ensure that our catering is of the finest quality.

Fewer things can be more irritating than faulty baggage handling. Only in an ideal world could we say that baggage will never again be damaged. Still, we are striving to ensure baggage is handled in such a way that if damage should occur, it will be minimal.

Flight disruptions caused by weather conditions can be particularly frustrating since, despite advanced technology, accurate forecasts for resumption of full operations cannot always be obtained as rapidly as one would wish. These disruptions are, of course, beyond the airline's control. Safety is paramount in such situations and we sincerely regret the inconvenience caused.

We make every reasonable effort to lessen the inconvenience to passengers who are affected by schedule changes. Our practice is, in fact, to advise passengers of such changes when we have a local contact for them and time permits. We also try to obtain satisfactory alternate reservations. We are reviewing our schedule change requirements with all personnel concerned and will take whatever corrective measures are necessary to ensure that a similar problem does not arise in the future.

You made clear in your letter that the interior of our aircraft was not attractive. We know that aircraft appearance is a reflection of our professionalism. We regret that our airplane did not measure up to our standards since we place great emphasis on cabin maintenance and cleanliness. Please be assured that this particular matter is being investigated by the responsible management and corrective action will be taken.

As tangible evidence of our concern over your unpleasant trip, I have enclosed two travel vouchers, which may be exchanged for 2 first class tickets anywhere that World Airlines flies. Once again, please accept our humble apology. We hope for the opportunity to restore your faith in World Airlines by providing you with completely carefree travel.

Sincerely,

Iwancha Togoaway
Customer Relations

1.3 THE CONVENIENCE STORE: THE TREND IS NOW MORE UPSCALE

For convenience stores, these should be the golden years. First, supermarkets all but killed off corner groceries. Then supermarkets consolidated into sprawling, remote megastores. The convenience store chains, with the field wide open, eagerly expanded across the nation.

Yet today, all the chains have to show for thousands of new stores are sharply reduced profits. And they face formidable opponents in the big oil companies, which have responded to lowered sales and higher labor costs by switching to self-service pumps and adding stores.

The convenience chains are trying desperately to woo their customers back. Chains like 7-Eleven and Stop&Go boast not only gas pumps, but also car washes, deli counters, video rentals, automated teller machines, and fast foods. In their rush to regain an edge, convenience stores now risk sacrificing convenience. The new stores are challenging the industry's creed that parking out front and having everything within reach matter more than price and selection. "They are walking a fine and dangerous line here," states a retail industry expert. "If the urge to satisfy everyone's needs means much bigger stores, it may wind up killing the convenient shopping that these stores are supposed to offer."

Traditional stores have to take the chance. A food retailing analyst has stated that "The gas stations simply have nicer stores at nicer locations. The only traditional convenience stores that are going to do well are those with special product or geographic niches."

The gas stations' prime corner locations and sleek new markets easily persuade customers to pass by the traditional convenience store. *Convenience Store News* reports that since 1986, the number of convenience stores attached to gas stations has almost doubled from 16,000 to 30,000. Already, 7 of the 20 largest convenience store owners are oil companies.

The gas stations are everywhere. The Atlantic Richfield Company, jumping into the business early, now operates 750 AM/PM Mini Marts. Exxon, which did not open its first store until 1984, has 500 shops at its gas stations and operates half of the shops itself. Shell Oil, stalled at about 300 Food Marts for three years, came up with a gleaming new store name, "Silverado," gleaming decor for some older stores, and plans to resume building new ones. Texaco Inc. is so pleased with the profits from its 950 stores, also called Food Marts, that it started experimenting with stand alone convenience stores that do not even sell gas!

The new oil-company stores bear no resemblance to the tiny cigarette-and-soda kiosks that gas stations have sported for years. Chevron, Shell, Ashland Oil, and many others are putting up spacious, brightly lighted stores larger than the old, thousand-square foot standard. Canopies shield pumps, stores, and customers from the weather. Smoothly contoured buildings, slick signs, tile floors, and brick or enameled aluminum exteriors welcome customers to stores where grime has been permanently banished.

While the gas station stores multiplied, the convenience chains lapsed into complacency. Convenience stores had all the appeal of overgrown vending machines. Cramped coolers and shelves offered beer, tobacco, soft drinks and, too often, dusty packages of peanuts and cookies. Displays were as rough-hewn as the clientele. New stores tended to be clones of the old ones, no matter what neighborhood or region.

Several trends compounded the industry's problems. The growth in convenience stores finally became a glut. By the end of 1988 there were more than 69,000 such stores, 1,700 more than the year before, with sales in excess of $61 billion. Labor and capital costs have been rising, including the expense of complying with new Environmental Protection Agency rules on gasoline storage tanks and underground lines. The population of young male blue-collar workers, the stores' most loyal customers, has been shrinking.

So even as the industry's expansion increases sales, profits have been falling—pre-tax profits peaked in 1986 at $1.4 billion, falling 6.3 percent to $1.31 billion in 1987 and another 11.5 percent to $1.16 billion in 1988. Although these profit figures include the oil companies' stores, the convenience store chains are clearly suffering the most. At convenience stores, average gas sales rose forty-two cents to $7.62. The average gas sale at a combination gas station and convenience store was $7.80—a sign that customers are dropping by more often and making more impulse buys. Convenience stores are struggling to invigorate their marketing and broaden their appeal.

QUESTIONS

1. As a marketing strategist hired by a convenience store chain, what recommendations would you make to increase customer usage of the convenience store corporation that has hired you?

2. Is there a risk for the oil companies in converting their service stations to convenience stores in terms of customer satisfaction?

This case was prepared by Richard C. Leventhal, Metropolitan State College, Denver, Colorado.

EXTERNAL ENVIRONMENT

Part II

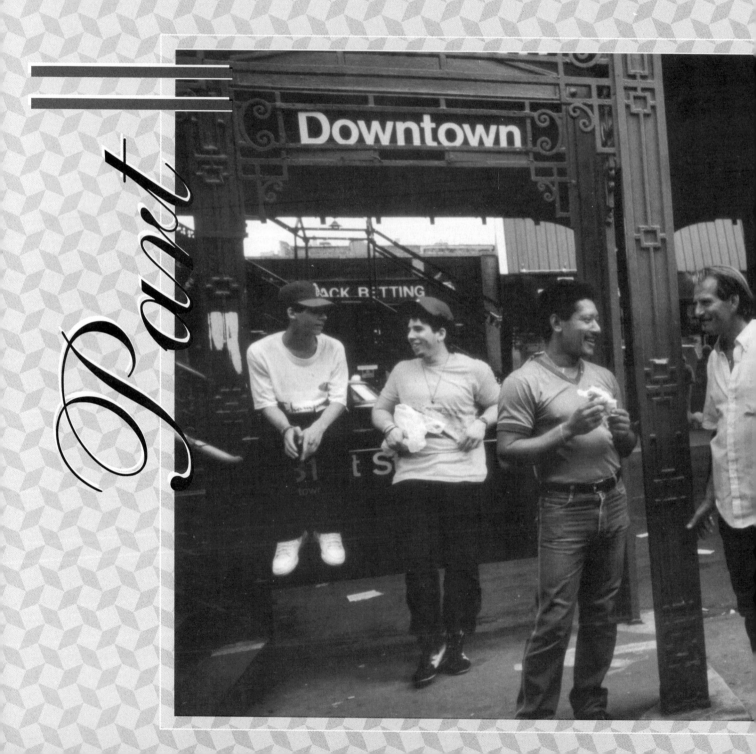

CONSUMER MARKETS AND BEHAVIOR

CHAPTER Six

Outline

Introduction

The Consumer Decision Process

Influences on the Consumer Decision Process

Aggregating Consumers

Summary

Learning Objectives

After studying this chapter, the student will be able to:

1. Define consumer behavior and its importance to strategic planning.
2. Describe briefly the major types of consumer decisions.
3. Discuss the steps in the consumer decision process.
4. Explain the factors influencing problem recognition states.
5. Understand the factors associated with search behavior and evaluative criteria.
6. Describe possible consumer activities in the choice stage of the purchase decision.
7. Describe post-purchase evaluation.
8. Discuss the situational, psychological, and social influences on consumer decisions.
9. Recognize the basis for retail market segmentation.

CATERING TO THE RICH

The main floor of Tiffany and Co.'s flagship store on Fifth Avenue in New York

REMARKABLE RETAILER

As a response to stagnant retail sales and the number of people who made their fortunes during the "affluent eighties," many retailers have focused their attention on the super rich. These are people who routinely shop at Chanel, Gucci, Cartier, Brooks Brothers, and Tiffany's, and would find something purchased off the rack at Bloomingdale's or Neiman-Marcus to be unacceptable. They don't concern themselves with words like "sales" and "discount"; they are interested in quality—at any price.

Today's members of the monied class want the items that represent peak quality. They are shopping for state-of-the-art designs, for the ultimate in taste, for classics that will not go out of style. Adam Stagliano of the Doyle Graf Mabley ad agency that handles Steuben Glass, Taittinger Champaigne, and Morgan Bank explains, "The top people today want fewer and better objects. In the sociology of affluence, it's not a prestigious name but craftsmanship and design that's important. Old money or new money, we have to make it active money."

These consumers do not come to shop; they come to buy. They are informed and sophisticated and do not want to be bullied by high-pressure salespeople. They expect special treatment when they enter the door. Salespeople must be understanding, patient, and polite. Retailers in this market have no competition, because their customers are searching for the finest one-of-a-kind products. Money is no object.

In order to meet the special needs of such clients, several "private banks," which require a minimum of $1 million to establish an account, have opened. In a building next to the Waldorf-Astoria, customers of the Commercial Bank of New York "lounge on antique furniture, while bank officers pour coffee and offer to arrange theater tickets or travel reservations." U.S. Trust pays bills and makes nursery school referrals, while Citibank offers the services of its art advisory unit to assist clients in making art investments. Chase Manhattan gives wealthy clients the opportunity to invest in "unusual, potentially high-profit ventures such as backing new tanker ships."

Like many of us, the rich hate taxes, are occasionally late paying bills, and like to swap information about the latest "in" restaurants or plays. But an abundance of money may create unique needs and worries. As Neil Gluckin of Doyle Graf Mabley explains, "There is a romantic vision that wealth is the answer to every problem, but it also causes anxiety. Money is a psychological thing."

Adapted from "When Money Is No Object" (1989), *TWA Ambassador* (March), 44–47, 82, 89–90.

INTRODUCTION

"Nothing moves until something is sold." This old adage underlines the importance of understanding consumers and how they shop. If customers do not make purchases, the entire channel of distribution is affected. Revenues and profits suffer. Retailers, wholesalers, and manufacturers are left holding expensive inventories, typing up capital that could be used for more saleable goods. Therefore, retailers need to correctly judge customer wants and needs, as well as how customers like to make their purchases, in order to offer a desirable assortment of merchandise and services in a preferred shopping environment. The retail format and strategic objectives chosen by any type of product or service retailer are dictated to a large extent by knowledge of target market characteristics.

In this chapter, customers and their decisions to make retail purchases are examined from three perspectives:

1. The purchase decision process and types of decisions made by consumers
2. Psychological, social, and situational influences on the consumer decision process
3. The use of demographic and psychographic information to aggregate consumers into an identifiable target market that can be served with a specific merchandising mix.

We will first define consumer behavior, then briefly discuss consumer markets within the context of the strategic planning process and the Integrative Retail Information Model (IRIM).

Consumer Behavior Defined

"**Consumer behavior** is the study of the decision-making units and processes involved in acquiring, consuming, and disposing of goods, services, experiences, and ideas" (Mowen, 1987, 3–4). Note that this definition is in keeping with the information-processing and decision-making focus of this text. That is, the consumer, like the manager, is viewed as a decision maker. The term "units" is used because many consumer decisions are made by household members or groups. Note also that the definition includes the acquisition, consumption, and disposition of goods, services, experiences, and ideas. Until recently the focus of consumer behavior has been primarily on the acquisition of goods, because much of the discipline was developed for managerial purposes. However, recent trends have shifted toward understanding the consumption process and the final disposition of goods. The reasons for this are clear. The consumption environment often plays a large role in the kinds of products or brands that will be purchased. For instance, if you are giving a dinner party you may want to purchase an expensive cut of meat and an imported wine, items you would not normally purchase for your everyday menus.

Studying the disposition of goods is also of interest to retailers. Flea markets and yard sales are burgeoning around the United States, indicating that the goods some people no longer need or want do have economic value and

CONSUMER BEHAVIOR
study of decision-making units and processes involved in acquiring, consuming, and disposing of goods, services, experiences, and ideas

are sought by others who still consider them to be useful. Further, as a society, we are becoming more aware of environmental concerns, which may lead to different means of disposing of things we no longer use. For instance, we may want to recycle cans and bottles or use biodegradeable plastic bags to help reduce the problems of solid waste. Concerns of this type have an impact on merchandising decisions. Studying and understanding these aspects of the consumer decision process may lead to new business opportunities. In fact, retailers may begin to play larger roles in this "reverse flow" of the distribution channel. They can promote socially responsible consumption and environmental concerns to position themselves favorably with consumers. However, this type of activity requires the use of resources, including an inventory of "desirable" products, space, personnel to handle recycling, and so forth.

Consumers and the Strategic Planning Process

The relationship between the strategic planning process and consumer behavior is illustrated in Exhibit 6–1. All aspects of the strategic plan are directed toward some group of consumers, tailored to finding a "fit" between the company and an identified market, as discussed in Chapter 2. Some consumer-related issues to be considered include:

1. *Corporate mission:* What groups of customers will the company serve? What benefits do those customers expect from transactions with this company (i.e., how will their wants and needs be satisfied)? And how are answers to these questions integrated into the mission statement?

2. *Performance objectives:* Will the retailer's customer base support the sales, return on investment, market share, or other performance levels required by the retailer? That is, are there enough of the right customers, and will they spend in the way predicted to accomplish these goals?

3. *Situation analysis:* What is the relationship between the attitudes and behavior of consumers and the company's external and internal environments? For instance, consider consumer interaction with the legal-political process, economic concerns, employee relations, and other issues. What changes are taking place, and what opportunities or threats do they present to retail managers?

4. *Strategic objectives and strategy definition:* How are customers expected to respond to different aspects of the retail mix, such as pricing strategies, merchandise assortments, store type and location, and promotional methods?

5. *Implementation:* Are the financial, human, and physical resources available to support the strategy to reach the right customers? And are those customers actually reachable?

6. *Execution:* At the operational level of the stores, is the strategy carried out according to plan? Do merchandise displays appeal to customers? Are the salespeople well-trained and attentive to customer needs? Are customers inconvenienced by out-of-stock conditions or long waits at the check-out counters?

7. *Strategic and operating control:* Are strategic objectives being met? Why or why not? What products or services do customers want that they are not getting? Is it feasible to provide them? What adjustments need to be made, if any?

Lack of attention to who customers are, and how they feel and act, can adversely affect any stage of the strategic planning process. As a result, a brilliantly conceived plan can become ineffective.

Consumers and the Integrative Retail Information Model

The importance of obtaining and processing information about the retailer's external and internal environments is stressed again relative to consumers. Remember that customers also may be stockholders, employees, suppliers, and voters. The attitudes and behavior of these people affect, and are affected by, environmental forces. Therefore, retailers who want to attract customers to their stores must view them within the context of a total environmental perspective, as illustrated in Exhibit 6–2.

EXTERNAL ENVIRONMENT A retailer's customers are an integral part of the legal and political process. For example, they may, or may not, favor "blue laws" that keep stores closed on Sundays, bottle bills that require containers to be returned to the grocery store for recycling, zoning ordinances that restrict store locations, or state legislation that raises the drinking age to 21. The state of the economy affects not only the amount of consumer spending, but also the types of goods and services purchased.

Customers may interact with—or be employed by—competitors, suppliers, and other businesses. Knowing how customers respond to other retailers' strategies and how they are treated as business partners is important. This

Home buying, the ultimate example of the consumer decision making process, is characterized as an extended type of decision, as it is highly involved and elaborate.

COURTESY OF COLDWELL BANKER

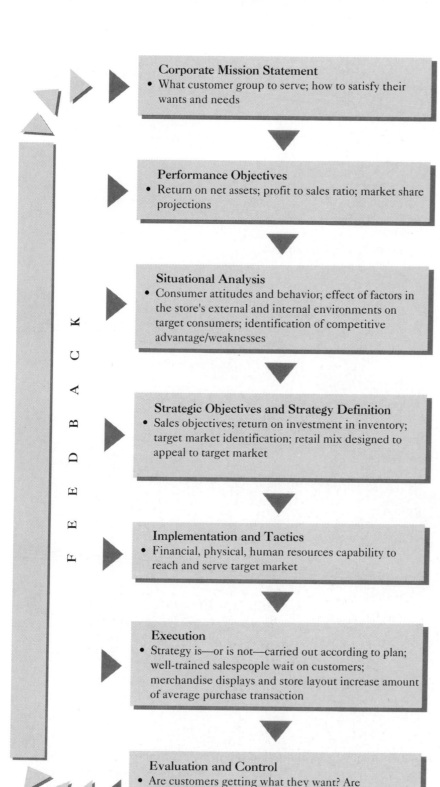

Corporate Mission Statement
• What customer group to serve; how to satisfy their wants and needs

Performance Objectives
• Return on net assets; profit to sales ratio; market share projections

Situational Analysis
• Consumer attitudes and behavior; effect of factors in the store's external and internal environments on target consumers; identification of competitive advantage/weaknesses

Strategic Objectives and Strategy Definition
• Sales objectives; return on investment in inventory; target market identification; retail mix designed to appeal to target market

Implementation and Tactics
• Financial, physical, human resources capability to reach and serve target market

Execution
• Strategy is—or is not—carried out according to plan; well-trained salespeople wait on customers; merchandise displays and store layout increase amount of average purchase transaction

Evaluation and Control
• Are customers getting what they want? Are adjustments needed? If so, what are they? Monitor customer satisfaction, repeat purchases. Evaluate productivity of salespeople and store space.

FEEDBACK

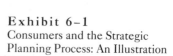

Exhibit 6–1
Consumers and the Strategic Planning Process: An Illustration

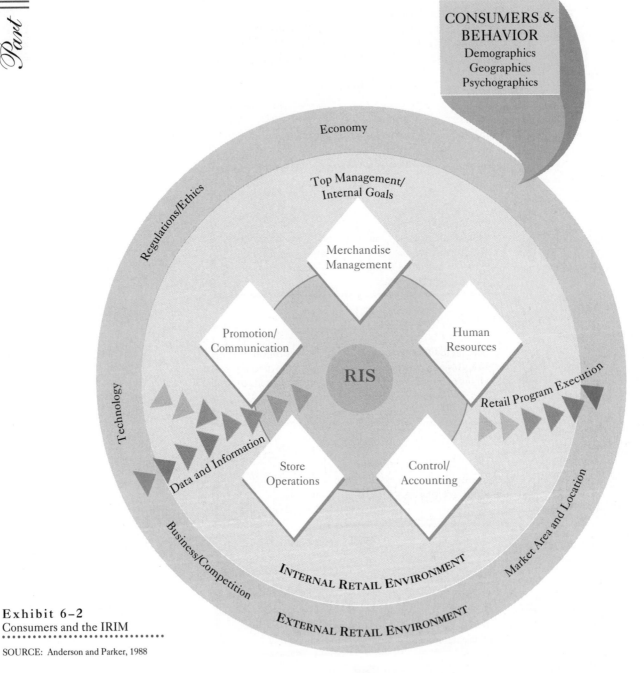

CONSUMERS & BEHAVIOR
Demographics
Geographics
Psychographics

Economy

Regulations/Ethics

Top Management/
Internal Goals

Merchandise
Management

Promotion/
Communication

Human
Resources

RIS

Technology

Retail Program Execution

Data and Information

Store
Operations

Control/
Accounting

Market Area and Location

Business/Competition

INTERNAL RETAIL ENVIRONMENT

EXTERNAL RETAIL ENVIRONMENT

Exhibit 6–2
Consumers and the IRIM
. . . .
SOURCE: Anderson and Parker, 1988

information generally is communicated in some form to other potential customers. Finally, retailers must make a very careful assessment of their consumer markets and consumer buying behavior, the focus of this chapter.

INTERNAL ENVIRONMENT   Customers interact with the internal retail environment in a number of ways. Of course, employees also are customers and can influence many other customers to shop in a store, based on their own experiences. More importantly, all functional aspects of a store's internal environment should be designed to make a major impact on customers. Customer preferences are the key to effective merchandising and promotional strategies. The interaction of customers and store personnel should be a positive experience, whether the situation involves a sale, a problem related to a previous purchase, or simply providing information for a future purchase. Accounting and credit personnel make an impact on customers in the way they handle billing and collections. Store operations personnel affect customers' willingness to shop by a store's physical appearance, overall convenience, and atmospherics for which they are responsible. These are just a few of the reasons why it is important to understand the relationship between retail environments and the consumer purchase decision process.

THE CONSUMER DECISION PROCESS

Consumer behavior is not one act, but a series of related activities. Some believe the apex of these activities may very well be the purchase; others believe it may be the consumption act itself. In any event, current theories of consumer behavior assume that consumers engage in processes: the **purchase process;** the **consumption process;** and the **disposition process.** Taking a process approach to consumer behavior allows us to break down the behavior into identifiable steps, investigate the consumer's behavior in each step, study and speculate on the influences on the consumer during each step, and relate one step to the next.

The Engel, Kollet, and Blackwell (EKB) model is used as a basis for discussion in this chapter. This consumer decision model involves five basic steps: (1) problem recognition; (2) search; (3) evaluation of alternatives; (4) choice; and (5) postpurchase evaluation (Engel, Blackwell, and Miniard, 1989, pp. 23;500). However, the amount of effort expended by consumers is affected by the type of purchase being made. Therefore, before examining the steps in the decision-making process, we will take a brief look at the types of decisions made by consumers.

Types of Consumer Decision Making

Traditionally, consumer decision making is categorized as habitual, limited, or extended, based on the amount of effort expended (Hawkins, Best, and Coney, 1989). (See Exhibit 6–3.) These categories are dependent upon the level of involvement the consumer has for a particular purchase. Involvement is defined as. ". . . the level of concern for, or interest in, the purchase process triggered by the need to consider a particular purchase" (Hawkins, Best, and Coney, 1989, pp. 532–533). Cost is another determining factor in the amount of time and effort devoted to consumer decisions, with effort generally increasing as the purchase price increases.

HABITUAL DECISION MAKING In **habitual decision making,** the consumer generally has very low involvement with the purchase process and

HABITUAL DECISION MAKING
low involvement with the purchase process because problem has frequently been dealt with in the past

LIMITED DECISION MAKING
somewhat more involved than habitual decision making

EXTENDED DECISION MAKING
high involvement, characterized by elaboration of one or more of the decision-making steps

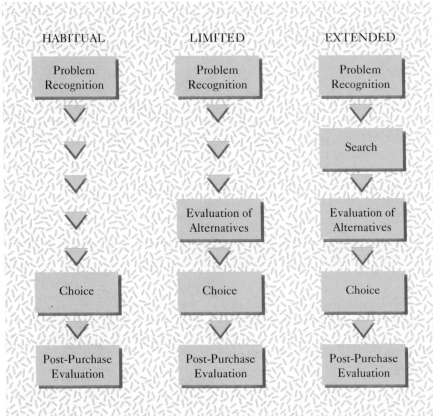

Exhibit 6-3
Types of Consumer Decision
Making

has dealt with the problem frequently in the past. That is, a problem is recognized, memory yields up a preferred brand, and the purchase is made. A student may develop a hunger for soup on a cold day, prefer the Campbell's brand, and purchase Campbell's chicken noodle soup. Interestingly, a conscious evaluation will be made only if the brand fails to perform as expected (i.e., bad flavor, not enough noodles).

LIMITED DECISION MAKING   Although **limited decision making** is similar to habitual decision making, it is somewhat more involved. Limited decision making is characterized by a departure from the ordinary, routinized process typical of habitual decision making (Mellot, 1983). The student in the previous example may want to purchase a new pair of jogging shoes. He knows that he can purchase Reeboks in one of several stores and has a general style preference. Once he gets to the store, he must consider several styles of Reeboks, and perhaps some other brands as well before making his final decision. The purchase is familiar, somewhat routine, but may involve new styles or brands not previously experienced.

EXTENDED DECISION MAKING   **Extended decision making** is highly involved and characterized by elaboration of one or more of the decision-making steps. In habitual and limited decision making, a consumer may skip or just briefly consider some of the steps in the decision-making process. However, in extended decision making each step is considered in sequence, and some steps may be pondered for quite some time. For example, a recent college graduate would be expected to expend a great deal of effort in purchasing her first new car, starting with problem recognition, search, evaluation of alternatives, choice, and post-purchase evaluation. Extended decision making generally is reserved for product categories with a high degree of perceived financial or social risk, such as the purchase of an automobile or a home.

COMMENTS ON TYPES OF DECISION MAKING   Consumer behavior, especially the purchase process part of that behavior, is only a subset of other human behaviors. Consequently, consumers develop strategies to reduce the complexity of the buying process. The attempt to reduce the complexity of the buying process, through brand preference choices or other routinized behaviors, is called the psychology of simplification. The student who bought the Campbell's soup may buy tomato juice for the first time. Rather than reading nutritional information on the labels of the three brands carried by the store, he selects the familiar Campbell's brand. The graduate buying the car may choose a Ford, because her family has always had Fords. In other words, people develop what might be referred to as habits, patterns, styles, heuristics, or "rules of thumb," in order to make decisions easier.

Paradoxically, the routine-decision making process can become very boring. When this occurs, the consumer may actually take steps to complicate the process. This phenomenon is called the psychology of complication. The soup and juice purchaser may consider similar products in a health food store, and the automobile purchaser may test drive other manufacturers' brands, or go to dealers in other cities. The purchase process itself, the brands sought, and possibly the stores patronized, may all be subject to this continuous cycle of simplification and complication (Howard and Sheth, 1981). More research is needed in this area to determine the extent of the phenomenon, and to assist retailers and manufacturers in developing strategies to adjust to the phenomenon. One thing is clear: retailers must recognize the importance of fresh, new, and even exciting atmospherics and store appearance. On the other hand, continuous renovation or adjustments in the retailing mix may cause confusion.

Steps In the Consumer Decision Process

The general framework for the decision process experienced by a consumer in making a purchase is illustrated in Exhibit 6–4, following the steps previously outlined. Discussion is generally from the perspective of a product or a brand but the same concepts apply to the selection of a store. Many retail purchase decisions may start with selection of a store or mall rather than a specific product.

Some sort of environmental (social, physical, psychological, etc.) cue or stimulus usually starts the process. Hunger may prompt the decision to purchase a pizza. An advertised sale may lead to the purchase of videotapes. Or a scheduled job interview may make a college senior aware of the need for a new suit. This type of stimulus is highly related to the problem recognition stage, described next.

Exhibit 6–4
Steps in the Consumer Decision Process

Problem Recognition

Search

Evaluation of Alternatives

Choice

Post-Purchase Evaluation

STEP 1: PROBLEM RECOGNITION   "Problem recognition is a perceived difference between the ideal state of affairs and the actual situation sufficient to arouse and activate the decision process" (Engel and Blackwell, 1982, p. 309). **Problem recognition** is a process: the process of becoming aware of a discrepancy between the real and the ideal ("desired") states and evaluating whether that discrepancy is large enough or important enough to take action. (See Exhibit 6–5.)

As consumers go through the problem recognition stage, or process, many factors influence their perceptions of the actual, the desired, or both states. Knowing and understanding these factors helps retail managers develop a retail mix and place their marketing efforts more efficiently and effectively.

Exhibit 6–5
The Problem Recognition Process
• •

Adapted from Bruner, Gordon C. II (1990), "Problem Recognition Style: Is It Need Specific or a Generalized Personality Trait?" *Journal of Consumer Studies and Home Economics* (14), 29–40. Reprinted by permission of Blackwell Scientific Publications Limited, Osney Mead, Oxford OX2 OEL.

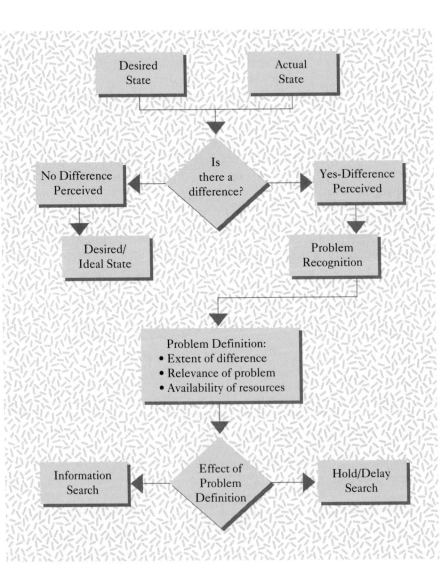

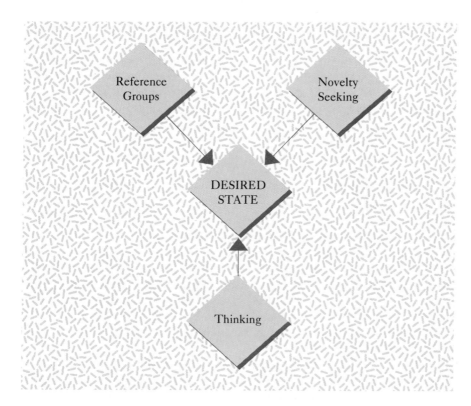

Reference Groups

Novelty Seeking

DESIRED STATE

Thinking

Exhibit 6–6
Problem Recognition:
Influences on the Desired State

FACTORS INFLUENCING THE DESIRED (IDEAL) STATE   At
least three factors are generally considered to influence the desired state: reference groups, novelty seeking, and thinking (Bruner and Pomazal, 1988).
(See Exhibit 6–6.)

Reference groups consist of others to whom an individual looks for
guidance. They are an important aspect of purchase behavior, because they
provide a consumer with information about standards accepted by the group,
offering explicit or implicit suggestions about what he or she should be
doing, influencing an individual's socialization and identification process.

Reference groups serve two functions: normative and comparative
(Stafford and Coconougher, 1971; Bruner and Pomazal, 1988). The normative
function sets and enforces standards or norms for the individual. For example, students tend to "hang out" in places that are acceptable to their friends
or to people they would like to be accepted by. The comparative function
allows the referent to serve as the point of comparison so the person can evaluate both him/herself and others. For example, students preparing for a job
interview tend to compare their appearance to that of the recruiter.

The composition of a reference group will change over time. Also, a reference group that is important today may be exchanged in the future for
another that seems more relevant, as in the transition from high school bud-
dies to college friends to business associates. Further, an individual may
change his or her position in comparison to reference others, thus increasing
or decreasing their influence on decisions (child dependent upon parents for
guidance, to independent young adult capable of making his or her own
decisions). Any of these changes can produce variations in the desired state

PROBLEM RECOGNITION
process of gaining awareness of a
discrepancy between the real and
ideal states

REFERENCE GROUP
others to whom an individual looks
for guidance

as retail customers seek new ways to maintain or advance their status relative to referents or to those whose opinion is considered important.

Many consumers constantly seek new experiences in making their purchases. **Novelty seeking** and its role in problem recognition can be viewed in two ways. First, substantial evidence shows that people change brands simply for the novelty value of trying something new (Faison, 1977). For example, a person might switch from Michelob to Beck's to Lowenbrau beer to experience the different brands and tastes. Second, people may become bored with routinized decision making and periodically complicate the process (Howard and Sheth, 1981, p. 219). Perhaps a person is accustomed to habitually buying the same brand of computer disks from an office supply store, then decides to look at other retail stores and direct mail catalogs to learn about the availability of other brands, prices, or delivery methods. No matter which "rut" the customer is trying to escape, a product/brand rut or a procedural rut, novelty seeking affects the desired state. Retailers of clothes, music, and movies, for example, plan their offerings to satisfy this need. New store or restaurant formats, for example, are more attractive to an innovator, so retailers must always provide pleasing, exciting store atmospheres. Of course, the novelty motivation is particularly obvious, but retailers should be aware that as any kind of purchase motives change, consumers' desired states can change along with them.

Through a cognitive process, human beings can study, consider, and reflect on any topic of interest, including retail purchases. A special gift, termed "autistic thinking," allows us to think about, plan for, and anticipate desired outcomes (Engel and Blackwell, 1982). This type of **anticipatory thinking** is unrelated to the current situation, but gives definition to the desired state (Bruner and Pomazal, 1988). Of course, this may depend upon what the person anticipates. If he anticipates running out of milk, he relates it to his actual state. His actual state, i.e. "having a supply of milk," has not changed. In other words, consumers can envision future purchase requirements and outcomes, thus facilitating the purchase decision process.

FACTORS INFLUENCING THE ACTUAL STATE   The factors generally considered to affect the actual state are assortment deficiency, arousal of needs, and post-purchase evaluation (Bruner and Pomazal, 1988).

Assortment deficiency is perhaps the most common reason for problem recognition to occur, since it simply refers to running out of a normal supply of goods. For example, Ann wants to tape a new album but discovers that she has used her last blank cassette, or Scott wants to make spaghetti but finds that he does not have enough spaghetti noodles. The retailer who can remove this deficiency, with the least effort on the part of the consumer, has the competitive advantage.

When the consumer is put in a state of physical or emotional disequilibrium or discomfort, that consumer experiences an **arousal of needs.** That is, something happens which triggers a physical or emotional need state, leading to the recognition of a purchase problem. Changes in the physical environment can trigger an arousal of need. For instance, present or anticipated changes in the weather can make a consumer aware of the need for a warm coat, an umbrella, or a new bathing suit. Likewise, events or information can trigger an arousal of need. A prerecruiting reception given on a college campus by a major employer may arouse a need for a haircut or new

NOVELTY SEEKING

looking for new experiences in making purchases

THINKING

cognitive process through which to study, consider, and reflect on any topic of interest, such as retail purchases

ASSORTMENT DEFICIENCY

running out of a normal supply of goods

AROUSAL OF NEEDS

state that leads to recognition of a purchase problem

POST-PURCHASE EVALUATION

deciding whether a purchase has lived up to expectations

clothes, or news of a forthcoming exam may cause a headache and arouse a need for aspirin. Each of these situations presents an opportunity for the retailer.

When a product does not live up to a customer's expectations, then dissatisfaction results (Engel and Blackwell, 1982). Subsequently, this dissatisfaction defines the discrepancy between the actual state and the desired state. For example, Sally may purchase a new brand of shampoo, expecting it to give body and shine to her hair. Instead, she is disappointed that her hair is droopy and dull after using the shampoo.

The purchase that is evaluated poorly and causes dissatisfaction was originally purchased in recognition of a problem. Thus, the negative **post-purchase evaluation** leaves the consumer problem unresolved. The consumer's experience with the unsatisfactory purchase becomes part of memory and provides an input for the search process in later stages of the decision-making process. The challenge to retailers is to be particularly good at resolving their customers' problems.

FACTORS INFLUENCING EITHER THE DESIRED OR ACTUAL STATE
Seven factors are considered to affect either the desired or the actual state, or both, depending on the situation: financial considerations, previous decisions, family characteristics, culture and social class, individual development, current situation, and marketing efforts (Bruner and Pomazal, 1988).

The first factor is financial considerations. A change in the financial state of a consumer often causes changes in the desired state. Consider how an increase or a reduction in income will influence what we purchase, how much we purchase, and where we purchase. Further, an anticipated change in financial position will affect consumers' perceptions of their actual and desired states. For instance, vacations or major home purchases may be accelerated or deferred simply because consumers anticipate an increase or decrease in their financial status, or a student who is about to graduate and start a new job may buy a new state-of-the-art stereo system.

A negative post purchase evaluation can have this result . . .

. . . while numerous factors such as financial considerations, individual development, and marketing efforts can create a desired state—owning a new car.

Physically handicapped consumers face numerous problems which have been brought to the attention of retailers. Needs for close parking, wider aisles, lower counters, ramps and other amenities to make shopping easier for wheelchair bound customers are being addressed.

The second factor is previous decisions. When a decision is made to purchase one product or service, this decision often triggers other purchases of supplementary and complementary goods. In other words, we have no purchase motivation in one category *until* we make a purchase in another related category. For instance, the decision to take a summer vacation may lead to the purchase of supplementary goods such as bathing suits, sports equipment, or plane or train tickets. In a similar vein, some products are complements for each other and are often bought together: peanut butter and jelly, pizza and soda, washers and dryers, or personal computers and printers. Retailers should consider supplementary and complementary goods in planning merchandise assortments and services that they will offer to their customers.

Family characteristics are the third factor. Family characteristics, particularly the consumer's stage in the family life cycle, affect either the desired or the actual state. As the composition of the family changes, so do the desired and actual states. Requirements for food, shelter, and clothing are different for families than for single-person households. Further, families with young children have different purchase desires and requirements than families with older children. Package sizes, product specifications, time available for shopping and other considerations are important in designing a retail strategy mix based on family characteristics.

Culture and social class make up the fourth factor. Culture and social class position indicate what we should desire and what kinds of products we ought to consume. Both culture and social class are discussed later within the context of social influences that affect the entire purchase decision process. In particular, social class serves as a point of reference and comparison affecting our perceptions of the actual state of affairs and helps us shape our view of the actual state (Bruner and Pomazal, 1988). Social class tends to dictate choice of stores, leisure activities, food preferences, automobile models, and other purchases. The consumer who is attempting to move upward from one social class to the next will purchase according to perceptions of what is considered "right" by members of that class.

The fifth factor is individual development. The individual's physical and psychological development also affect the actual and desired states. As a person grows in size and strength and achieves a higher level of intellectual and social development, different purchase needs arise. For instance, youngsters may desire games and other diversions for recreation; adolescents and young adults may desire sports equipment; and older adults may desire books and more sedentary hobbies or leisure activities.

The current situation is the sixth factor. The current situation often affects the desired and the actual states; they include time constraints, weather conditions, spatial (distance) perceptions, and the nature of the purchase, i.e., whether it is intended for everyday use or for special occasions or gifts. Time constraints may lead consumers to seek fast service and convenience items. Weather conditions often influence the desire for climate control products such as air conditioners or space heaters. Spatial perceptions (generally related to travel distance and effort required to shop) often affect a consumer's store choices or how much time the consumer is willing to spend on the shopping process (Mowen, 1987). The type of purchase has a major impact on the kinds of products purchased and where they are purchased. For instance, gifts and products for special occasions often require more expensive purchases and perhaps are purchased in more upscale stores.

The final factor is the marketing efforts. Marketing efforts often affect the desired and actual states. Advertising, for example, may make the consumer aware of new products or new uses for old products, thus encouraging a change in the desired state. Influencing the consumer's actual state is somewhat more difficult than influencing the consumer's perceptions of the actual state. To illustrate, a consumer may think that she does not need a new refrigerator, until she learns that some older models have a tendency to leak freon and harm the ozone layer. Thus, her perceived actual state changed due to the information; however, her desired state did not. Likewise, marketing efforts, such as the introduction of new models of automobiles each year, may increase the discrepancy between the actual state (old clunker, "low status" car) and desired state (new "high status" car).

STEP 2: SEARCH   Once the consumer has recognized a problem, he or she may or may not begin to search for a solution. (See Step Two in Exhibit 6–7).

Exhibit 6–7
The Internal Search Process
. . . .

Some material adapted from unpublished work by Gordon C. Bruner II, 1989.

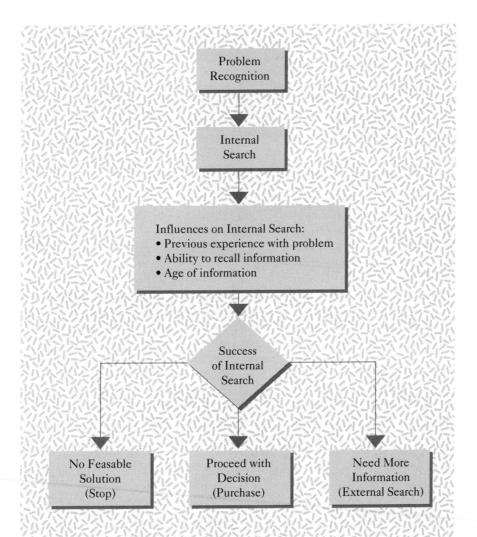

Exhibit 6–8
A Framework for Consumer Information Search

Determinants	Prepurchase Search	Ongoing Search
	• Involvement in the purchase • Market environment • Situational factors	• Involvement with the product • Market environment • Situational factors
Motives	• To make better purchase decisions	• Build a bank of information for future use • Experience fun and pleasure
Outcomes	• Increased product and market knowledge • Better purchase decisions • Increased satisfaction with the purchase outcome	• Increased product and market knowledge leading to future buying efficiencies and personal influence • Increased impulse buying • Increased satisfaction from search and other outcomes

SOURCE: Bloch, Peter H., Daniel L. Sherrell, and Nancy M. Ridgway (1986), "Consumer Search: An Extended Framework," *Journal of Consumer Research* 13 (June), 119–126.

If the consumer is not motivated to solve the purchase problem immediately, an active search for information is likely to be delayed. However, if search is engaged in at all, it will always involve an internal search of the consumer's memory—even though this might not yield a satisfactory solution. Internal search consists of an attempt by the consumer to remember anything that is directly or indirectly related to the present purchase problem. (See Exhibit 6–7.) External search is sometimes engaged in, and can be one of two basic types: prepurchase search and ongoing search (Bloch, Sherrell, and Ridgeway, 1986). **Prepurchase search** has been defined as ". . . information seeking and processing activities which one engages in to facilitate decision making regarding some goal objective in the marketplace" (Kelly, 1968, p. 273). In other words, the consumer has recognized a purchase problem and is directing search efforts toward solving that problem.

Ongoing search involves activities that are ". . . independent of specific purchase needs or decisions." The consumer who continually "window shops" clothing stores, reads weekly grocery ads, or talks with friends about their new purchases, without any specific purchase need in mind is engaging in ongoing search. This type of search provides information that may be used for the same or similar type of purchase at some future time.

The distinction is made between the two types of searches because they have different purposes. That is, prepurchase search has the purpose of gathering information to solve a specific consumer problem, whereas ongoing search may be used to simply increase the consumer's store of knowledge or to provide the consumer with new experiences. To the outside observer, both types of search may employ the same mechanics, i.e., visiting several stores, reading advertisements, asking friends' opinions, or reading *Consumer Reports*. However, the distinction is made here because the determinants, motives, and outcomes of each type of search are different. Further, while retailers are obviously interested in prepurchase search, ongoing search may be of equal importance since "window shopping" and browsing in the retail environment are a major aspect of ongoing search. These activities lead to

PREPURCHASE SEARCH
efforts in solving a recognized purchase problem

ONGOING SEARCH
activities independent of specific purchase needs or decisions

changes in the desired state, trigger problem recognition, and result in an immediate purchase.

Notice in Exhibit 6–8 that the determinants of prepurchase and ongoing search are similar: involvement with the purchase, market environment, and situational factors. However, ongoing search is determined by involvement with the product or product category rather than with the purchase itself.

The motivation for prepurchase search is the desire to seek information to make better decisions. The motivations for ongoing search are to build a store of consumer information for future use and perhaps simply to attain pleasure from the search process without a sense of immediacy. Window shopping is fun to some people!

The outcomes of prepurchase search should be increased product and market knowledge, better purchase decisions, and increased satisfaction with the planned purchase. Ongoing search results in increased product and market knowledge, but this knowledge will support future purchases by making internal search more likely to yield satisfactory solutions to perceived problems. Also, this knowledge may be used to advise friends on their purchases, thus enhancing the consumer's status with an important reference group or individual. The final outcome of ongoing search is essentially hedonistic.

Another outcome of ongoing search is an increase in impulse purchases, as shown in Exhibit 6–9. Since ongoing search involves browsing and "window shopping," people tend to increase their buying simply because they are in the buying environment more often and exposed to retail stimuli, which influences the desired state. This "impulse purchase" factor is important in determining the availability and placement of merchandise in retail stores

Exhibit 6–9
The Impulse Shopper

SOURCE: Reprinted with permission of Hallmark Cards, Inc.

SOURCES OF INFORMATION   When consumers recognize a problem, they will first scan their memory for the answer, searching for previous experiences with the same or a related problem. Most of the time a purchase problem can be solved with an **internal search,** which is the basis of routine or habitual purchase behavior (Hawkins, Best, and Coney, 1989). When memory yields insufficient information to solve the problem, the consumer initiates an **external search.** "External search . . . represents a motivated and completely voluntary decision to seek new information" (Engel and Blackwell, 1982, p. 323). For both types of search, retailers can play an important role in making information readily available on a continuous basis, so that customers are familiar with retail stores and their products. The challenge to retailers is to reduce search costs for consumers, but without overloading them with information.

Retail catalogs have become an increasingly important influence on customers' information search. Sears is one of many retailers who have recognized the need to improve catalog operations in order to benefit from changing customer shopping patterns and decreased shopping time. This includes better management of catalog mailing lists, so that merchandise information is provided to those customers who are most interested. Sears and other retailers have expanded customer intercept opportunities by selling on television home-shopping programs and other nonstore modes of aiding the search process ("Bozic Reveals Plans . . .," 1987).

FACTORS INCREASING THE EXTENT OF THE SEARCH PROCESS   Search for information increases when we have experience with a store or a brand or product category, but perceive that our experience is out of date (Robertson, Zielinski, and Ward, 1984). For example, Joe has owned three cars, but bought the last one five years ago. Substantial changes have occurred in technology and desired performance criteria since that time, rendering previous information inadequate.

Search also increases when various types of risk are perceived to be high. For example, before purchasing higher priced or more socially visible products, the consumer is more likely to engage in an extensive external search to avoid financial or social risk. Finally, external search will increase if substantial differences are perceived between the purchase options. For example, when competing brands, and the perceived benefits from those brands, are thought to be different from each other, consumers will weigh the differences more carefully (Claxton, Fry, and Portis, 1974).

COSTS OF INFORMATION SEARCH   External information search is not without its costs. The costs associated with search are in the expenditure of time and money and in psychological costs or opportunity costs. To mount an extensive and exhaustive search may require many trips to different stores. This can be expensive in transportation and/or parking costs, as well as in the time spent to visit several stores. Sometimes the consumer cannot "afford" to put off a decision in order to do an adequate search.

Researchers suggest that an extensive search involves psychological costs. For instance, the consumer may become tension-ridden fighting traffic jams and store traffic and trying to resolve conflicting or contradictory information (Robertson, Zielinski, and Ward, 1984). Other researchers have studied the costs to consumers of imperfect information. This includes not only

INTERNAL **S**EARCH
scanning memory for information to solve purchase problems

EXTERNAL **S**EARCH
solving purchase problems with efforts towards gaining new information

the costs of search, but also opportunity losses due to not choosing the "best" brand (Ratchford and Gupta, 1986).

Finally, extensive information search may result in information overload. Information overload occurs when the consumer is presented with too much information on a subject and reacts by either blocking additional information inputs or by becoming confused. In either case, the consumer who has experienced information overload is more likely to make poor decisions (Hawkins, Best, and Coney, 1989). This problem has important implications for the retailer. For example, it presents an unusual opportunity for the trusted merchant who can help the consumer identify the most important information and simplify the purchase decision.

STEP 3: EVALUATION OF ALTERNATIVES   Once the consumer has recognized a purchase problem and gathered information through internal or external search in order to make that purchase, the next step in the decision process is the evaluation of available alternatives, as shown in Exhibit 6–10.

EVALUATIVE CRITERIA   A consumer judges a product according to some specified set of criteria and the amount of importance attached to each criterion. "Evaluative criteria are the particular features that consumers seek in choosing among brands within a product category to achieve the benefits they desire" (Dommermuth, 1984, p. 100). Evaluative criteria may be based on objective features of the product or service, such as price, fit, warranty, or some measure of performance. Consumers also may be subjective in their evaluations, considering the more symbolic aspects of the product, such as anticipated status, social acceptance, pleasure, or other benefits.

Quality and style have become important criteria for consumer purchases. Some of the most successful contemporary designs are a blend of form and function, quality and style, art and engineering. Design must combine objective features (stylish, pleasing to look at) and subjective, substantive features (reliable, easy and economical to operate and service). This approach has been successful for products ranging from automobiles to baby bottles, computers, and tools (Nussbaum et al., 1988). To illustrate status as a criterion for purchase, inner city youth are the fashion trend setters for pricey sneakers. They buy them by the dozens, often for $100 or more. Status extends to wearing the right brand and style at the right time, and even to wearing the right brand on the right street to avoid conflict where brands control neighborhood turf (Pereira, 1988). In other cases, criteria may shift over time for the same basic product. Classical music that is acceptable in popular movies (e.g., Puccini aria in *The Witches of Eastwick*) will not be purchased as a traditional "stuffy" classical record by many music lovers. To adapt to this evaluative criterion, successful albums, such as "The Movies Go to the Opera," include classical music used in *Raging Bull*, *Fatal Attraction*, and other films (Rothman, 1988).

The importance the consumer attaches to the various criteria differs from one consumer and buying situation to another. In spite of the many criteria that may be considered before making a purchase, in the final analysis many experts estimate that six or fewer (usually only two or three) criteria are salient in the decision to buy.

The consumer has evaluative criteria for choosing stores as well as for products. These tend to be related to factors that contribute to a store's atmo-

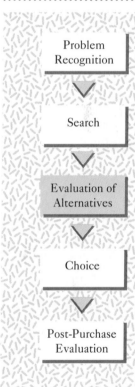

Exhibit 6–10
Step 3: Evaluation of Alternatives

Problem Recognition

Search

Evaluation of Alternatives

Choice

Post-Purchase Evaluation

sphere and image. Again, criteria used to judge a store may be either objective or subjective, including the type and amount of merchandise available, pricing strategies, store location, type and quality of services offered, store personnel, and even the characteristics of other shoppers in the store.

BRAND CRITERIA RATINGS AND BRAND PREFERENCE LEVELS   When the consumer is in the decision-making mode, he or she assigns importance weights and otherwise categorizes the evaluative criteria into a hierarchy, whether it is for brands, products, or stores. Exhibit 6–11 describes customer's mental picture or memory of a particular automobile, competing automobiles, and relationships among them and dealerships. According to Howard (1983), the product hierarchy is a taxonomy of products, where product categories are related to one another by inclusion in a product class such as: (1) vehicle, (2) car, (3) subcompact, and (4) Toyota Corolla. The hierarchy includes all of the customer's mental associations with these products, such as how to identify, how good, and how available each one is. Thus, it is easier to compare products and brands, rating them on the relevant criteria (Dommermuth, 1984). Different brands within a product category are ranked based upon the brand criteria ratings or "beliefs" to determine brand preference levels. Consumers tend to somehow aggregate their beliefs and develop attitudes toward brands that they actually would consider buying.

STEP 4: CHOICE   After the consumer has gathered sufficient information and evaluated the available alternatives according to important criteria, he or she is ready to make a choice, the next step in the purchase decision process. (See Exhibit 6–12.) While our discussion focuses primarily on products or

Exhibit 6–11
A Hierarchy of Evaluative Criteria
....

SOURCE: Howard, John A. (1983), "Marketing Theory of the Firm," *Journal of Marketing* 47 (Fall), 90–100.

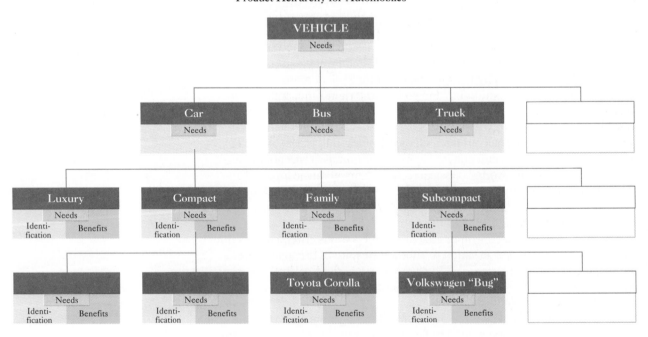

Product Heirarchy for Automobiles

brands throughout each stage of the consumer decision process, consumers make decisions about the stores they will patronize in a similar fashion. In fact, store choice is commonly made prior to, or in place of, product choice.

Alternative evaluation results in placing brands in one of three categories: the evoked set, the inert set, or the inept set. (See Narayana and Markin, 1975.) Briefly, the **evoked set** contains the group of brands from which the final selection will be made. The **inert set** contains the group of brands for which the consumer holds neither strongly positive nor strongly negative attitudes. The **inept set** contains all those brands the consumer would never consider purchasing. Other brands of which the consumer is unaware makes up the unaware set. To illustrate, Stacy will purchase a soda from among the CocaCola, PepsiCola, and 7-Up brands (evoked set). She is indifferent towards the Crush and Mello-Yellow brands (inert set), absolutely would not buy A&W Root Beer (inept set), and is not aware that the Nehi brand exists (unaware set). Remember that the same logic can be applied to store choice, an interesting challenge for retailers to keep their stores among the consumers' evoked set.

The actual choice is the result of a complex process of "mapping attitudes into motivations" (Nicosia, 1966). During this process the consumer narrows down the number of acceptable brand offerings, generally by establishing brand criteria ratings. At the same time, the consumer's motivational drive for those brands is increased. Exhibit 6–13 shows a graphic description of this process (Glynn, 1990).

STEP 5: POST-PURCHASE EVALUATION   The purchase decision process does not end when the customer buys the chosen product. After the purchase, consumers tend to make evaluations of the purchase. These evaluations then feed back into the consumer's memory and are stored to orient the consumer when faced with the next instance of problem recognition.

Generally, the result of an evaluation is satisfaction or dissatisfaction with the product when actual performance is compared to expected performance, as shown in Exhibit 6–14. Some would argue that nonsatisfaction also may occur. Satisfaction will occur if the customer has high expectations and those expectations are met. For example, when buying a new car, he expects outstanding performance from the sales and service personnel at the dealership and from the car he buys. When both exceed his expectations, satisfaction occurs. Likewise, dissatisfaction will occur when the customer has high expectations, and they are not met. This is particularly true in the case of more expensive items, such as a car, because a higher degree of risk is involved. A third outcome, nonsatisfaction, can be said to occur if the customer has low expectations and evaluation after the purchase confirms that what the customer expected is what actually happened. Nonsatisfaction is most apt to occur in the situation where the customer really does not have a good alternative from which to choose. (Perhaps the car customer could only buy an inexpensive used car, and the only used car dealer in the area had a questionable reputation.) Although a retail shopping experience may result in varying degrees of satisfaction or dissatisfaction, consumers usually are satisfied with their purchases (Hawkins, Best, and Coney, 1989).

Retail management decisions can contribute to satisfactory outcomes. For instance, warranties and guarantees that can be satisfied by the retailer,

Exhibit 6-12
Step 4: Choice

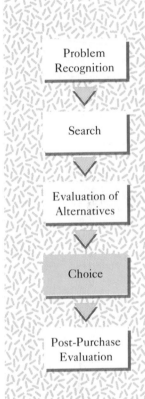

EVOKED SET

group of brands from which a consumer's final selection will be made

INERT SET

group of brands about which a consumer has neither strongly positive or negative attitudes

INEPT SET

group of brands a consumer would never consider purchasing

. . . .

At any time, the consumer is aware of a number of possible brands within a product category, and holds differing perceptions of these various brands. The total set of available products is the complete area described by the axes. The aware set is that area under the curve described by vector *s*. The unaware set is that area above the curve described by vector *s*. The evoked set is that area of specific brands and a high positive driving force. The inept set is that area of specific brands and a high negative driving force. The inert set is that area of specific brands with low positive or negative driving force, i.e., those brands toward which the consumer is somewhat neutral.

In order to get the information needed to produce such a graph, the retailer must conduct market research. However, once the information has been gathered and analyzed, the graphic display suggests many possible actions for managers. For instance, if the brand is in the unaware set, then more advertising is required to help with awareness levels. If the brand is in the inert or inept set, then more research is required to determine if it is inept or inert due to a failure in the product, its price, its method of distribution or promotion, or in the basic positioning. Since it is more difficult to move customers to products (or stores) in the inept set, the costs and benefits of research must be evaluated.

A brand determined to be in the evoked set suggests point-of-purchase promotions, packaging designs, shelf positioning, and other cues at the point of decision making. It is important for the retail manager to know these things so that s/he can seek the best possible support from the manufacturer or wholesaler, and design the most effective retailing mix. The graph also can be applied to development of strategies related to store choice decisions.

. . . .

SOURCE: Glynn, Karen A. (1990), "A Model for Teaching the Relationship Between Attitudes, Motivations and Evoked Sets," *Making Marketing Magic*. Proceedings of the Twelfth Annual A.M.A. Conference. R. Viswanathan, ed., New Orleans, La.: American Marketing Association (March).

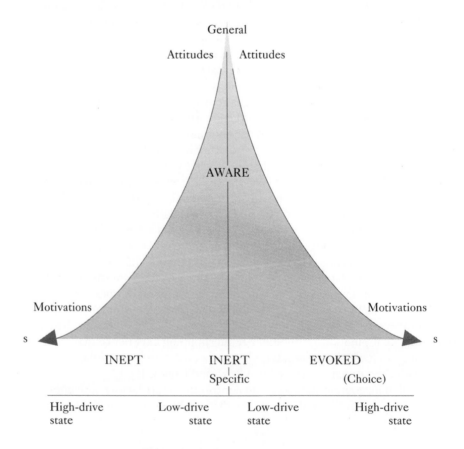

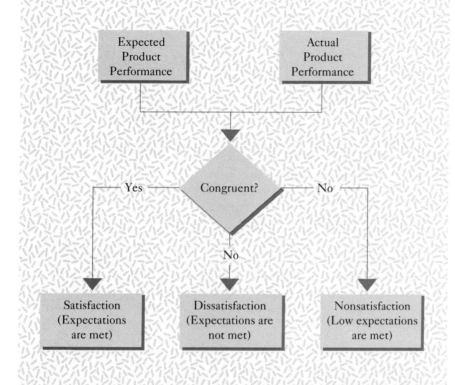

liberal merchandise return policies, repair and maintenance agreements, and other tactics can aid the consumer in making a positive post-purchase judgment. Some researchers have noted that resolving consumer complaints can diffuse dissatisfaction and actually can encourage satisfaction (Hawkins, Best, and Coney, 1989, p. 678). Converting dissatisfied customers into satisfied loyal customers is less expensive than converting noncustomers into loyal customers. Therefore, a great deal of effort is justified in dealing with customer dissatisfaction.

Exhibit 6–14
Post-Purchase Outcomes
. . . .
Some material adapted from unpublished work by Gordon C. Bruner II, 1989.

INFLUENCES ON THE CONSUMER DECISION PROCESS

The influences on the consumer and on the consumer's decision making processes are numerous and varied. In this chapter, we will look at the psychological, social, and environmental influences that affect shopping behavior.

Psychological Influences

Psychological influences include learning and memory, attitude formation and motivations for purchase, and theories of self-concept. Each of these has relevance for retail management decisions.

PSYCHOLOGICAL INFLUENCES
include learning and memory, attitude formation and motivations for purchase, and theories of self-concept

WHAT DO CONSUMERS REALLY WANT?

If companies are out to give the people what they want, it may pay for them to first find out what their customers are looking for.

When Constantine Pavsidis of San Mateo, California, rents a car from Hertz, he is not looking for extras like wet bars and cellular phones. Instead, he is interested in how the rental will earn him extra miles on his frequent-flier program. So, Mr. Pavsidis was understandably upset when Hertz did away with its frequent-flier program because of cost concerns, while adding an additional 700 car phones to its fleet.

His response to this change was to take his business elsewhere, commenting, "These guys never seem to know what I want."

Unfortunately, today many companies are either unaware of or unwilling to find out what their customers really want. They are discovering that rather than prescribing to the idea that more is better, today's consumers are eschewing frills in favor of good old-fashioned basic services. A *Wall Street Journal* survey, for example, indicates that many airline passengers are not only uninterested in gimmicks like on-flight movies and stereo entertainment, but find other perks like airplane telephones to be offensive. As one traveler asks, "Have you ever sat next to someone gabbing on one of those things?" Instead, people seem to be interested in basic conveniences like frequent-flier bonus mileage, wider seats, and better airline food.

Likewise, hotel chains are discovering that guests find the service of having newspapers delivered to their rooms more important than the luxury of in-house health clubs. In this case, paying attention to its customers would also help the hotel save money, with newspaper delivery costing 10 cents per room and health clubs costing as much as $50,000 to build.

Of course, it's not always easy to give the people what they want. When it comes to services, people have different needs. What may not be popular or deemed as necessary to the bulk of travelers, may be crucial to others. Car phones, for example, may not be universally popular, but Hertz says they are still widely used. Companies must also cope with logistical problems like trying to improve the quality of airline food in low humidity cabins that dry up meat. As Pat O'Brien, vice president of Food Service for United Airlines explains, "Food wasn't necessarily designed to fly."

In spite of some companies' efforts to define their customers needs, many critics nonetheless say that the members of the travel industry are not doing enough consumer research. "A lot of travel companies just put their heads in the sand," says Chekitan Dev of Cornell University's School of Hotel Administration. "They don't ask the right questions or listen to the answers."

Adapted from "Giving People What They Want" (1989), *The Wall Street Journal* (November 30) B1, B3.

LEARNING AND MEMORY "Learning is any change in the content or organization of long-term memory" (Mitchell, 1983, as quoted in Hawkins, Best, and Coney, 1989, p. 317). There are two general theories of learning: cognitive and associative. Cognitive theories of learning and memory are based on mental activity or reasoning. **Cognitive theory** focuses on determining how people receive and evaluate a stimulus, store the information, and retrieve it from memory. For example, your hairdresser tells you that a certain hairstyle makes you look like a famous movie star. If you like the movie star, and the hairstyle makes you look like him or her, then you are likely to reason that this is the way your hair should look.

Associative learning "involves making a new association or connection between two events in the environment"(Engel and Blackwell, 1982, p. 237). Associative learning often is discussed within the context of operant conditioning, where the promise of a reward elicits a certain response. For example, learning may take place when a customer is influenced to buy a new brand of trash bags because he receives a 40 cents-off coupon in the mail. A 25 cents-off coupon enclosed in the package, along with suggestions for other uses of trash bags, may elicit a second response. At a later date, a newspaper ad for the same brand may trigger another purchase of these trash bags.

ATTITUDE FORMATION AND MOTIVATION   Other psychological influences of interest to the retailer are theories of attitude formation and motivation. **Attitudes** are generalized predispositions toward, or away from, an object or class of objects. Attitudes have three components: cognitive, affective, and behavioral.

The cognitive component is what is known or believed about the object (Mercedes is a well-made luxury car). The affective component is the feelings toward or against the object (I like the design of the Mercedes sports car). The behavioral component is the tendency to take some action toward the object (I will buy the Mercedes sports car).

People seek internal consistency among the cognitive, affective, and behavioral components of attitudes. Retailers can use methods to change attitudes related to each of the three components; the specific situation might determine which is most appropriate. For instance, if consumers believe a retail store charges high prices for quality merchandise, then they may avoid that store if they prefer to shop for the same merchandise in a lower-priced environment. Notice that there need not be any objective truth attached to attitudinal components. The attitude is a composite of the perceptions of the individual. The retailer's strategy mix and communications with the customer will have a major impact on store perceptions.

Motivations are forceful drive states toward or away from a specific object. Often attitude formation precedes motivations, but not in every instance (Nicosia, 1966). For example, impulse purchases and brand switching behavior would seem to preclude the attitude-motivation link for all cases. As the consumer goes through the decision-making process, part of the process involves a mapping of attitudes into motivations. Generally, attitudes and motivations will be consistent (Festinger, 1957). That is, people at least will feel dissonance if attitudes and behaviors are inconsistent. Further, inconsistency in these factors makes them easier to change. The consumer who believes that sugar-coated cereals are not healthful or nutritious will not be inclined to buy or eat them. The student who feels that "hanging out" at the student center is a great way to meet new people, will spend considerable time there. Body Shop International PLC is a retail specialty store in England that has experienced success because consumers' attitudes regarding natural ingredients and reasonable prices are consistent with purchases of cosmetics and personal care products at Body Shop (Maremont, 1988).

When the consumer is faced with an inconsistency between his or her attitudes and behaviors, **dissonance** occurs. Dissonance involves a sense of discomfort or uneasiness which may be attributed to purchases that fail to meet customer expectations. People attempt to reduce dissonance in one or some combination of four ways (Festinger, 1957). First, the person may minimize the importance of the decision or choice, thereby rationalizing away the inconsistency. Second, the person may seek outside information to support the decision or choice. Third, the person may rationalize that he or she

COGNITIVE THEORY

focuses on determining how people receive and evaluate a stimulus, store the information, and retrieve it from memory

ASSOCIATIVE LEARNING

involves making a connection between two events in the environment

ATTITUDES

predisposition toward or away from objects; includes cognitive, affective, and behavioral components

MOTIVATIONS

drive states toward or away from objects

DISSONANCE

inconsistency between a consumer's expectations and post-purchase outcomes

really had no control over the situation, and therefore is not responsible for the outcome. Fourth, the person may change his or her behavior. The latter alternative is probably the least likely event. People will change their attitudes to meet their behaviors. Rarely will they change their behaviors to meet their attitudes. The retailer's role is to remove as many causes of dissonance as possible, including reassuring customers that they have made the best decision possible.

SELF-CONCEPT   "The self-concept represents the 'totality of the individual's thoughts and feelings having reference to himself as an object'" (Mowen, 1987, p. 105). Most conceptualizations of **self-concept** identify the actual and ideal self-concepts. The actual self-concept is how a person really perceives himself, while the ideal self-concept is how a person would like to perceive himself. (See Exhibit 6–15.)

Self-concept is important because people purchase products to "communicate symbolically various aspects of their self-concepts to others" (Mowen, 1987, p. 106). Retailers can provide goods and services to help consumers remove the inconsistency in their perceived ideal and actual self-concepts. Further, self-concept is intimately a part of a person's personality, so behavior should be consistent with self-concept (Mowen, 1987, p. 105). (See also Sirgy, 1982.) Because shopping at a certain store may be more consistent with some self-concepts than others, a retailer needs to project an image that appeals to the ideal self-concepts of those in its target market.

Social Influences

A number of **social influences** have a major impact on shopping behavior, on the products people buy, and where and how they buy them. A person's culture and subculture may have the greatest effect on the consumer decision process. Cultural values and norms, the "correct" ways to think and behave, are passed down from one generation to another through the socialization process. Reference groups, social class, and the family are the key socialization agents that help consumers adapt to the norms of their own social environments. Each of these is discussed briefly next.

CULTURE AND SUBCULTURE   "**Culture** consists in patterned ways of thinking, feeling and reacting, acquired and transmitted mainly by symbols, constituting the distinctive achievements of human groups . . . the essential core of culture consists of traditional (i.e., historically derived and selected) ideas and especially their attached values" (Kluckhohn, 1951, p. 86). A diversity of cultures is represented in the U.S. population. Cultural influence is all-pervasive and present in our lives. As a result of this constant presence we are rarely aware of the influence of culture. Mowen (1987) notes that only when we encounter another culture do we become aware of our own.

While any organized group can be said to have a "culture," the term is used here in the broader sense to refer to societies. "Societies merit special consideration in the study of cultures because they are the most complete human groups that exist" (Hofstede, 1980, p. 26). That is, a society is the highest level and most self-sufficient social system within a given environment.

SELF-CONCEPT
how people perceive or would like to perceive themselves

SOCIAL INFLUENCES
include culture, subculture, and the socialization process

CULTURE
patterned behavior within a group of people, pertaining to traditional ideas and their attached values

Cultural norms are based on deeply held values (e.g., work ethic, gender roles), beliefs (e.g., religious orientation), and customs (e.g., marriage ceremonies). Societies set up institutions to maintain, promote, and transmit their societal norms from one generation to the next. These recognized institutions reinforce the societal norms and the ecological conditions that led to them (Hofstede, 1980, p. 26). According to McNeal (1987), the societal institutions are family, education, government, media, and business. The ecological factors are those that affect the physical environment and include technology, demographics, the economy, urbanization, and others. Norms rarely change by the adoption of new values; rather, they change because the ecological condition slowly shifts and changes. These changes become relevant to the learning of new behavior patterns (Hofstede, 1980, p. 27).

THE SOCIALIZATION PROCESS   **Socialization** is ". . . the process by which individuals acquire knowledge, skills, and dispositions that enable them to participate as more or less effective members of groups and the society" (Brim, 1966, as quoted in Goslin, 1969, p. 2). The socialization process continues throughout a person's life. The societal institutions, which serve to transmit cultural values and norms, consist of two types of socializaton agents: proximal and distal (Davies, 1977). **Proximal agents** are those with whom the person comes in direct contact, such as family, peers, and school. **Distal agents** are those who never have direct contact with the person being socialized, such as government, business, and media. The effects of the distal agents are said to be filtered or colored by the influence of the proximal agents (Davies, 1977). For instance, a T.V. ad (distal agent) may urge the purchase of a particular brand of shoe and the consumer will be receptive to the ad. However, where the shoe will be purchased or even the style of shoe to be purchased may be influenced more by peers (proximal agent). Retailers must take this information into account when communicating with customers.

Socialization occurs as a result of the interaction of the consumer with the socialization agent(s). The basic model of consumer socialization includes four components: (1) the learner, described by his/her demographic makeup, (2) the agents: family, peers, school, government, business, and the media, (3) the agent-learner relationship described as modeling, reinforcement, or some combination of the two, and (4) the learned outcomes (Moschis and Churchill, 1978, pp. 600–601).

Retail managers who are aware of their position as socializing agents can obtain a competitive advantage. For instance, one of the socializing mechanisms is learning through imitation. Within this context, a retail salesperson in a women's dress shop would appropriately dress in clothes from the shop or in comparable outfits. Likewise the retailer can encourage customers to make initial and repeat visits to the store by using premium offers, discounts or a personalized follow-up after the purchase. This is **reinforcement,** the process of learning through conditioning.

REFERENCE GROUPS   People tend to consider the outlook of others, called reference groups, as a frame of reference in developing their own attitudes and behavior. An individual usually has a number of reference groups, which may be categorized as automatic, membership, aspiration, and negative. Consumers imitate and adopt the values of these groups and make retail

SOCIALIZATION
transmission of cultural values and norms to its participating members

PROXIMAL AGENTS
socialization agents with whom a person has direct contact

DISTAL AGENTS
socialization agents with whom a person does not have direct contact

REINFORCEMENT
process of learning through conditioning

purchases based on their perceived norms. Reference group influence is most noticeable when a customer is purchasing an item that is highly visible and can be readily recognized as conforming to the desired group's norms.

Each of us automatically belongs to certain groups based on demographic descriptors such as age, sex, education or marital status, or socioeconomic factors such as income or occupation. Membership groups include those that a person joins and "belongs to." Some membership groups involve face-to-face contact (proximal groups such as a church, work group, sports team), while membership in others is primarily nonpersonal (distal, such as the American Automobile Association or Book-of-the-Month Club).

An individual can aspire to membership in other groups. Although a person does not yet belong to a particular group, he or she still adopts its attitudes and behavior. A teenager may dress and have a haircut like a favorite rock star, or a college senior may buy a new car or new clothes that resemble those of colleagues at a future workplace. Finally, attitudes and behaviors are influenced by negative reference groups. These are groups that an individual does not belong to, does not intend to belong to, and does not want to be associated with in any way. Negative reference groups provide a model of what is "wrong" to think or do, such as an honest stockbroker who does not want to be associated with insider trading, or a college student who intensely dislikes the "Preppie" lifestyle and will not buy any clothing that conveys that image.

The residents of neighborhoods often serve as a reference group for individuals during the socialization process. The effects of socialization then play important roles in consumer behavior.

SOCIAL CLASS Although the social class structure in the United States seems to be less clearly defined than that in other societies, the shopping behavior of American consumers is influenced by the degree of prestige or esteem attributed to their particular social class by others in society. In the

COURTESY OF WALGREEN CO.

United States, a person may change social class with changes in education or occupation; in fact, many retail purchases are driven by the social class an individual aspires to, as well as the one he or she does belong to. Social class is usually a better indicator of shopping behavior than income alone, for example, because people in different social classes may earn the same income (e.g., truck driver, teacher, salesman), but spend their money differently to support entirely different lifestyles. General characteristics of U.S. social classes and approximate percentages of the population are described in Exhibit 6–15.

Low-income shoppers have been largely ignored by many retailers. The gap between rich and poor Americans appears to be widening, and barriers to upward mobility appear to be increasing. As a result, by the year 2000 the

Exhibit 6–15
U.S. Population by Social Class

Social Class	Characteristics
Upper upper class: (less than 1 percent)*	Social elite with inherited wealth, old wealthy families, socially prominent. Buy exclusive luxury goods and are an important market for jewelry, antiques, travel, vacation homes.
Lower upper class: (about 2 percent)*	New wealth through earnings in the professions or business, socially prominent, involved in community affairs. Usually move up from the middle class. Products and services purchased tend to be status symbols in hopes of being accepted by upper uppers.
Upper middle class: (12 percent)*	Successful business owners or managers and professionals. Characterized by career orientation rather than family status or abundant wealth. Civic-minded and concerned with quality of life. Good market for goods and services for gracious living, cultural events, and education.
Middle class: (31 percent)*	White- and blue-collar workers who earn medium level incomes. Concerned with better living, nice neighborhoods, doing the right thing. Many purchases are focused on their children, whom they encourage to obtain a college education. Buy products that reflect the popular trends, want better brands.
Working class: (38 percent)*	Blue-collar workers who earn average pay, and lead working class lifestyle in spite of income, education, or job. Family members are main source of all types of support and assistance. Sex role stereotypes. Stay closer to home and favor American-made products.
Upper lower class: (9 percent)*	Live just above poverty level, although employed—usually in lower-paying unskilled, blue-collar jobs. Usually poorly educated, but attempt to appear self-disciplined. Striving toward higher standard of living. High reliance on marketing sources for information.
Lower lower class: (7 percent)*	Poverty level, depend on welfare or charity for income. Out of work or have most menial, unskilled, nonrespectable jobs. Have poorly kept homes and possessions, but need to buy necessities and products focused on enjoying the present.

* all percentages are estimates

number of households with incomes of $15,000 or less (in 1984 dollars) is expected to reach about 36 percent of the U.S. population, or about 40 million families. Retailers are beginning to recognize that this market is too large to ignore. American Express Company has launched a national campaign to market money-wiring services to low income individuals. The Limited is targeting lower-paid working women with its Lerner/New York chain. Lerner's strategy included renovations to create elegant shops that offer low prices but make customers feel better about themselves and more inclined to spend money in the stores (Bremner, 1990). Even upscale stores like Bergdorf Goodman and Bloomingdale's are devoting more space to costume jewelry, scarves, and other lower-priced items, hoping to attract dollar-conscious shoppers.

FAMILY   Family is the primary, and most influential, reference group that determines shopping behavior. Family influence can be partitioned into (1) family of orientation and (2) family of procreation. The **family of orientation** is the family a person is born into and shapes attitudes and behavior in regard to religion, politics, use of money, and self-concept. The influence of the family of orientation is felt, perhaps subconsciously, even when amount of interaction between consumer and parents lessens.

The **family of procreation** consists of a person's spouse and children. Retailers should be aware of the different roles played by husbands, wives, and children in family purchases and how these roles are changing to reflect emerging lifestyle trends. While many decisions are made individually (although the "decider" may not actually be the buyer), husbands and wives tend to make joint decisions for more expensive purchases.

Retailers must be aware of the roles played by family members in purchase decisions, and how these roles can change to reflect emerging lifestyle trends.

COURTESY OF HOME DEPOT

FAMILY OF ORIENTATION

family that one is born into and that shapes one's attitudes and behavior

FAMILY OF PROCREATION

family formed by individual choice generally consisting of one's spouse and children

SITUATIONAL INFLUENCE

includes consumer situations of the physical surroundings, the social situation, the task definition, the effects of time pressures, and the consumer's internal mood states

Family size has an effect on the shopping behavior of individual family members, e.g., buying "large, economy size" food products and cars, rather than smaller, more expensive items. Stage in the family life cycle also has a major impact on shopping behavior. For example, lifestyles—and products purchased to support those lifestyles—vary as one moves from the status of a young single adult who does not live at home (fashion, recreation), to that of a newly married couple without children (cars, appliances). As children are added to the family, they become the focus of many purchases (homes, baby items followed by lessons, larger packages). Parents' consumption patterns change as the children grow up and move toward independence from their parents (more durables, luxury items, gifts). The final stages in the family life cycle occur with retirement (health care, medical supplies) and solitary survivor (attention, security). As can be seen from these brief examples, different types of goods and services are required by single versus married individuals, those with and without children based on ages of the children and whether they still live at home, and young versus elderly people who live alone.

Situational Influences

Another major group of influences on the consumer decision process is related to specific situations. **Situational influences** include five types of consumer situations: the physical surroundings, the social situation, the task definition, the effects of time pressures, and the consumer's internal mood states, as illustrated in Exhibit 6–16 (Mowen, 1987).

Consumer situations are characterized as being relatively short-term events, affecting people differently at different stages in the consumption process (Mowen, 1987). For instance, gift giving is an example of a task definition situational event. Certainly the purchase of a gift is quite different from the routine purchase of an ordinary household product. Further, a gift for a very close friend is a different type of purchase from a gift for a business or professional associate.

Situational influences should not be overlooked by the retail manager. The store's layout, crowded or spacious appearance, and the noise level may

Exhibit 6–16
Situational Influences on Consumer Decisions

Five Types of Consumer Situations

1. *Physical surroundings:* the concrete physical and spatial aspects of the environment encompassing a consumer activity

2. *Social surroundings:* the effects of other people on a consumer in a consumer activity

3. *Task definition:* the reasons that occasion the need for consumers to buy or consume a product or service

4. *Time:* the effects of the presence or absence of time on consumer activities

5. *Antecedent states:* the temporary physiological states and moods that a consumer brings to a consumption activity

SOURCE: Mowen, John C. (1987), *Consumer Behavior*. New York: MacMillan and Co., 307.

all affect the shopper's mood state. Further, situational factors can be used to position products or segment a market, i.e., occasion segmentation. Finally, people may be exposed to specific advertising or promotional messages, dependent upon the specific situation. For example, people who commute to work by way of trains or buses may be influenced more by transit advertising than radio or TV.

The design of effective retail strategies requires an analysis of the purchase decision process and of influences on consumer decisions, as described above. In the next section, consumers are viewed from another perspective, that is, how they can be grouped into target markets that will buy the retailer's goods and services.

Aggregating Consumers

An understanding of who consumers are, how they live, and how they make purchase decisions allows the retailer to aggregate individual consumers into viable market segments. Effective segmentation strategies lead to increased customer satisfaction and improved retail performance. There are several basic ways to describe large groups of consumers: demographic, psychological, and psychographic descriptors. Behavioral descriptors also are used to define market segments. Each of these is discussed briefly. Then, examples are given to illustrate how a retailer might use these descriptors in profiling a target market.

Demographic Descriptors

Demographics might be called the mass descriptors of a population. In general, they can be used to identify and count groups of people. Demographic characteristics may be either primary or secondary. Primary demographics include attributes such as age, sex, and race. Secondary demographics include attributes such as social class descriptors and geographic dispersion.

Exhibit 6–17
Demographic and Socioeconomic Descriptors

Dimension	Variable	Example
Demographic		
	Age	19–34; 35–49 years
	Sex	male, female
	Religion	Protestant, Jewish
	Family Size	1, 2–3; 4–5
	Life Cycle Stage	young married, one child under 6
Social Class		
	Income	under $10,000; $10–14,999; $15–19,000
	Education	grade school or less; some high school; high school grad
	Occupation	unemployed; professional; farmer; manager
Ethnic		
	Race	Caucasian, Black, Hispanic, Asian
	Nationality	American, Korean, British, German

A retailer can design a merchandising strategy to attract a meaningful combination of demographic subgroups, such as those illustrated in Exhibit 6–17.

Primary demographics are those characteristics that cannot be influenced by the individuals within the demographic groups. That is, one cannot change one's age, sex, or race. The primary descriptors often involve physical distinctions that demand different products. For instance, people of different races may have distinct cosmetic requirements, due to skin color, hair texture, or other racial characteristics.

In the United States, where social class is not as rigid as in other societies, **secondary demographic** descriptors are subject to change. For instance, a person's social class usually is measured by income, education, and/or occupation, although income may not be as important an indicator today due to the growth of dual career couples. Type and location of housing also may be used as a determinant of social class. An individual may attain a higher level of education, become employed in a more prestigious occupation, and earn a higher salary, and thereby improve his or her social class status.

Gender has become a less distinct way of categorizing consumer market segments as contemporary men and women continue to assume additional aspects of the traditional roles and responsibilities of the opposite sex. For example, retailers (and magazines) are discovering the "stylish male," an often-ignored species. New York's Bergdorf Goodman Men is a posh $20-million colonnaded, two-story Fifth Avenue shop that avidly pursues fashion-conscious males. Men are making more of their own purchases and seem to be favoring a more stylish look. J.C. Penney Company estimates that 70 percent of men's apparel purchases will be made by men by 1993, compared to 55 percent in 1990. Therefore, the company increased advertising targeted to men and spent $20 million to build sportswear boutiques in 500 of its stores. This strategy is supported by demographic trends. According to the Census Bureau, the number of men between the ages of 30 and 49 (i.e., aging baby-boomers) will grow to 41 million by 1995, a 51 percent increase over 1980. New fashions are designed to reflect new attitudes and lifestyles—not just the traditional male look (Landler, 1990).

Psychological Descriptors

Although more elusive in terms of ability to identify specific individuals, **psychological descriptors** provide another method for aggregating potential retail customers. Two psychological factors of interest to retailers are personality types and buyers' motives, as shown in Exhibit 6–18. Consumers may be described in terms of their innovativeness, extroversion, compulsiveness,

Exhibit 6–18
Psychological Descriptors

Dimension	Variable	Example
Personality Types		
	Innovativeness	innovator, follower
	Ambitiousness	high achiever, low achiever
	Gregariousness	introvert, extrovert
Buyers' Motives		
	Economic	thrifty, status seeker
	Patronage	degree of brand loyalty

DEMOGRAPHICS
characteristics of a specific population

PRIMARY DEMOGRAPHICS
characteristics that cannot be changed by individuals in a demographic group

SECONDARY DEMOGRAPHICS
characteristics of a demographic group that are subject to change

PSYCHOLOGICAL DESCRIPTORS
personality types and buyers' motives, as well as personality traits

or a variety of other personality traits. Buyers' motives are related to choice of a product, brand, service, or store. Motives of interest to retailers include a consumer's need to be an economical shopper or to patronize loyally the same store for certain goods or services.

Psychographic Descriptors

Psychographics are the ways in which researchers try to measure or quantify consumer's lifestyles, essentially a combination of demographic and psychological characteristics. **Psychographic descriptors** include lifestyle analysis and a delineation of consumers' activities, interests, and opinions (AIO). Market segmentation on this basis assumes that people with similar lifestyles, activities, interests, and opinions will tend to behave in similar ways. A number of retail strategies have incorporated these variables into lifestyle merchandising, so that customers can find related products and services tailored to their needs and preferences in one central location. In this way, retailers can develop more effective strategies to reach their target markets if they have a clear understanding of the kinds of activities that their customers are involved in (e.g., work, entertainment/hobbies, memberships), their interests (e.g., community, family, home, goal achievement), and the opinions they hold about themselves and society. As noted, lifestyle descriptors are combined with demographic descriptors to develop strategies. For example, a university might target a summer educational travel program focused on environmental concerns toward 45- to 60-year-old alumni, who are business executives and professionals. Further, this target market would have demonstrated attitudes, interests and opinions that follow the theme of "save the earth," either through club memberships, speeches and media articles, or political activities.

A number of psychographic segmentation methods are used. One example of these methods is the VALS (Value and Lifestyle Segments) system, developed by SRI International. The original VALS questionnaire and typology identified nine psychographic segments that could be grouped into four major ways that consumers live, based on a hierarchy of needs ranging from Survivors to Integrators.

1. *Need Driven*—Survivor, Sustainer
2. *Outer-Directed*—Belonger, Emulator, Achiever
3. *Inner-Directed*—I-am-me, Experiential, Societally Conscious
4. *Combined Outer- and Inner-Directed*—Integrated Lifestyle

However, these segments were characteristic of the population of the late 1970s, dominated by people in their 20s and 30s, making it difficult for today's managers to use VALS to predict buying behavior or target customers. As a result, SRI introduced VALS 2 in 1989 to overcome these problems.

VALS 2 dropped values and lifestyles as the basis for its psychographic segmentation scheme, because the link between values and lifestyles and purchasing choices did not seem as strong as it had been. The change was attributed to aging baby boomers, an increasingly diverse population, a rising global economy, and declining consumer expectations for the future—combined with the increasing diversity of products, distribution, and media. The new questionnaire reflects unchanging psychological stances, instead of

PSYCHOGRAPHIC DESCRIPTORS

include lifestyle analysis, such as consumers' activities, interests, and opinions

shifting values and lifestyles. The psychographic groups in VALS 2 are grouped according to their resources (minimal to abundant) and their self-orientation (principle, status, or action oriented). The VALS and VALS 2 hierarchies are presented in Exhibit 6–19, and used to profile a radio station audience.

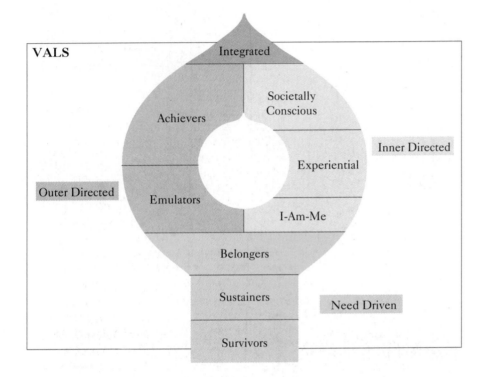

Exhibit 6–19
Value and Lifestyle Segments (VALS and VALS 2)

Reprinted with permission © *American Demographics*, July 1989.

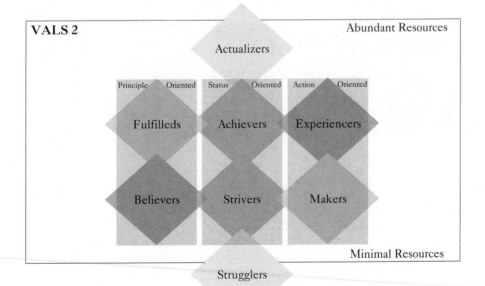

continued

Exhibit 6–19
(continued)
••••••••••••••••••••••••

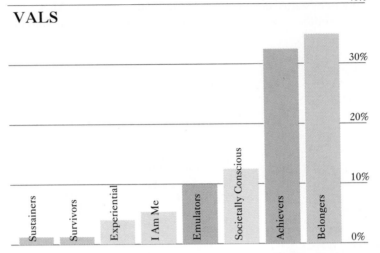

(1988 audience profile of WISH-TV, Indianapolis, based on original VALS segmentation system)

VALS

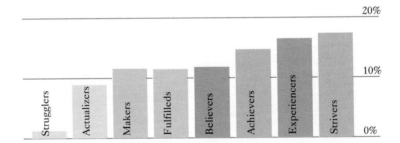

(1989 audience profile of WISH-TV, Indianapolis, based on VALS 2 segmentation system)

VALS 2

Behavioral Response Descriptors

Retailers are interested in how consumers respond to all aspects of the retail mix. Responses may be measured subjectively or objectively, as shown in Exhibit 6–20. Subjective measures include behavioral responses to the retailer's product, price, and promotion decisions. Responses are mainly in the form of preferences and perceptions. Responses to the retailer's product, price, promotion, and distribution strategies can be measured objectively in terms such as usage rates, sensitivity to advertising and deals, or loyalty.

Exhibit 6-20
Behavioral Descriptors
••

SUBJECTIVE RESPONSE MEASURES

Dimension	Variable	Example
Product		
	Preference	fresh, frozen, or canned vegetables
	Perceived Benefits	nutrition, safety
	Perceived Product Substitution	fresh oranges, vitamin C tablets, fruit juice
Promotion		
	Perception of Brand	high quality, low quality
	Advertising	motivating, offensive
	Packaging	convenient, environmentally safe
	Sales Message	informal, hard-sell
Price		
	Perceptions	economical, extravagant

OBJECTIVE RESPONSE MEASURES

Dimension	Variable	Example
Product`	Usage	heavy, light user
		degree of brand loyalty
Promotion	Sensitivity	deal proneness
		media exposure
Price	Elasticity	price sensitive/insensitive
Distribution	Store loyalty	number of store visits
		size of salescheck

Consumer Characteristics and Market Segmentation

The overriding purpose of demographic and psychographic research is to identify viable target markets. **Market segmentation** is the process of dividing a population of consumers into smaller groups in order to select one or more clearly defined segments as the target of focused marketing efforts. In order for a market segment to be viable and worth pursuing, the customers within the segment must be similar or homogeneous on important dimensions; the identified segment should be sufficiently different or heterogeneous from other segments; it must be large enough to be profitable; and it must be reachable through available channels of communication.

A segmentation strategy allows the retail manager to utilize resources more efficiently and effectively in serving a store's customers. Potential retail market segments can be defined according to demographic and psychographic characteristics and geographic dispersion. That is, people in the same demographic groups and with similar lifestyles, tend to consume similar products and in similar ways. Further, people from different parts of the country have different tastes and preferences, i.e., snowmobiles in the northern and mountain regions versus water skis and boats on the Gulf Coast.

MARKET SEGMENTATION

process of dividing a population into viable target markets

Exhibit 6–21
Aging Baby Boomers:
Vital Statistics on the generation
born between
1946 and 1964[1]
• • • • • • • • • • • • • • • • • • • •

**...Boomers are Swelling
Middle-Aged Ranks...**

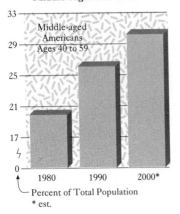

Percent of Total Population
* est.

**...Are Better
Educated...**

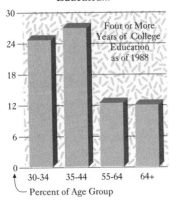

Percent of Age Group

continued

[1] DATA: U.S. Census Bureau: *The
Economic Future of American Families* by
Frank Levy and Richard C. Michel.
SOURCE: Susan Garland, Laura
Zinn, Christopher Power, Maria Shao,
and Julia Flynn Siler (1991), "Those
Aging Boomers," *Business Week* (May
20), 106–112.

Several examples of the many possible segmentation strategies for retail markets follow.

Retail Market Segments: An Illustration

The Hispanic population in the United States, aging baby boomers, economic trends and economizing consumers, and combined personal and situational characteristics provide four diverse methods of aggregating groups of consumers.

HISPANIC POPULATION   By 2015, an estimated 40 million Hispanics will live in this country (excluding illegal immigrants), making this ethnic group the nation's largest minority and a viable segment for retail goods and services. Although this market tends to have meager to modest incomes, their overall purchasing power in 1989 was $140 billion a year. Hispanic supermarkets, such as Tianguis, a three-store California chain opened by Vons Cos. in Southern California, have flourished in the western and southwestern United States. Other supermarkets catering to the Hispanic population are Fiesta Marts, Inc. (fourth largest grocer in Houston), Danal's Food Stores, Inc. (Dallas), Viva stores (Los Angeles), and Winn-Dixie and Publix (South Florida), as well as numerous mom-and-pop grocers.

Most of the Hispanics shopping in these stores are recent immigrants who seek a familiar environment. They want products that are not easy to find in typical supermarkets and expect services such as gold-and-silver exchanges and Western Union booths where they can wire money home to Mexico. They want to speak Spanish and shop leisurely in a fiesta atmosphere. Tianguis spent two years and $2.5 million researching the market from both the customer and retailer perspectives in the Untied States and Mexico before opening its stores. As a result, their customers are attracted by the outdoor patios for dining on Mexican foods, festive colors and designs, mariachi music, and employees who speak their language and understand their special needs (Corchado, 1989; Wallace, 1989).

BABY BOOMERS AND AN AGING POPULATION   Shifting demographic patterns, such as the aging of the U.S. population and of the baby boomer generation in particular, have created a challenge for retailers. Baby boomers are moving out of the prime spending years for many products, ages 25 to 40, and there are fewer young buyers to replace them. By 1995, the 25 to 34 age group is expected to decline by 6.6 percent, and the 35 to 44 age group and 45 to 54 age group will increase by 19 and 29 percent respectively. Top-level managers and strategic planners at major retail chains, such as Marshall Field's in Chicago, have recognized the magnitude of the problem. A fierce battle is ensuing for market share where the maturing baby boomer rejects the more youthful fashions and other goods and services formerly purchased. Lerner stores increased sales by shifting emphasis from young adult women to older customers, while sales fell off for other chains who did not pay attention to the demographics. Pier 1 Imports Inc. has carved out a profitable niche by selling moderately priced home decorative items, and other value-driven stores like Toys "R" Us and Wal-Mart are expected to succeed in this changing market (Dunkin, 1989).

Some industries and product classes will decline (e.g., dairy), while others may boom (e.g., travel, entertainment). For example, retailers in the home furnishings industry have positioned themselves to cash in on the demographics of aging baby boomers and growing home ownership, as spending shifts from apparel to the home. Macy's, for instance, has opened free-standing home-furnishing stores, while others have expanded their assortments of tabletop goods, linens, and other home furnishings ("Home Furnishings Become . . . ," 1988).

Baby boomers have been known as "big spenders," and older workers generally earn more than young ones. Thus, baby boomers are expected to make a major contribution to the economy as they continue above-average spending patterns (Wessel, 1989). In order to attract customers from the baby boomer generation, however, retailers must recognize that their spending patterns and preferences will not mirror those of their parents. Boomers are showing a tendency to think and act young while grappling with the new realities of midlife, including family stress and career changes. They are good customers for time-saving services and products as they try to balance work and family. They still want the fashionable jeans of their youth—now probably cut for a fuller figure. Married boomers with children are spending millions for educational toys, videos, books, and tutoring services. They have outgrown their tiny sports cars and now are buying roomier family cars. Travel marketers are appealing to boomers with child-oriented approaches to vacations. Boomers also are prime customers for catalog sales, home delivery restaurant food and ready-to-eat deli foods. Vital statistics on the baby boomer generation are illustrated in Exhibit 6–21.

Economic Trends and Economizing Consumers

The basic nature of some consumers drive them to find the best "deal" possible whenever they shop. Others respond to economic necessity. Interest rates, unemployment, rising consumer debt, and other factors affect consumer spending patterns. For example, in the cooling economy of mid-1989, *Fortune* magazine suggested that the ideal conglomerate would sell food, drugs, conservative clothes, psychiatric care, and life insurance (Hutton and Prewitt, 1989). In an economic downturn, big-ticket items like cars and appliances are most affected by declining sales and profits. Women are less inclined to reckless buying and frivolous purchases, opting instead for classic fashions that are expected to last two to three seasons.

In spite of a slowing economy, consumers are buying more health and convenience foods, diet foods, and microwaveable products. New Product introductions, along with the "graying" of America, have caused increases in drug and health care purchases, although the government is emphasizing generic drugs in the programs it funds. Consumers do, however, resist the purchase of some retail services. Higher airfares have caused many would-be airline passengers to stay home or seek other methods of travel. Financial services have felt the effect of the increased attractiveness of life insurance to an aging U.S. population, because it is one of the few remaining legal tax shelters.

The grocery industry has been faced with the need to satisfy customers who have made relatively permanent changes in their shopping behavior,

continued

...Are Marrying Less and Divorcing More...

Marital Status of Americans
Ages 35 to 44

	1960	1989
Married	87.5%	75.9%
Divorced	2.9	12.7
Widowed	1.9	1.3
Never Married	7.7	10.1

...Are Having Fewer Children...

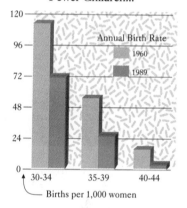

Annual Birth Rate
1960
1989

Births per 1,000 women

...And May Never Catch Up With Their Parents ...

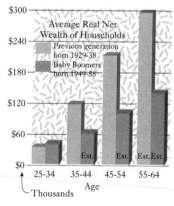

Average Real Net Wealth of Households
Previous generation born 1929-38
Baby Boomers born 1949-58

Thousands
Age

due to an economic recession. Many of these individuals have found it necessary to change their lifestyles in order to cope with their economic problems. Grocers such as Safeway Stores Inc. benefit from a recessionary economy, because in a slump, eating at home replaces going out. Customers do not seem to stop buying soft drinks and snack foods, they are just more inclined to buy them at the grocery store.

Results of a research study conducted by Olsen and Granzin (1986) suggest an economizing sub-market exists that is made up of two segments. One is made up of highly involved shoppers who actively compare prices, buy items on sale, purchase generics, and use coupons, engaging in considerable search effort. The other segment appears to have a fixed criterion of buying the cheapest alternative that is readily available without engaging in extensive search behavior. Retailers can serve these markets with desirable information, product lines, store layout, pricing, promotion, and other aspects of the retail mix.

Person-Situation Segmentation

Finally, consumer descriptors can be combined with characteristics of the situation in which a purchase will be used. Dickson (1982) has outlined a procedure for segmenting a market on this basis, as shown in Exhibit 6–22. Person-situation segmentation strategies require an understanding of how and where consumers use a product and how they perceive product benefits.

Economizing consumers will be more likely to eat at home during adverse economic times, and are more likely to shop for bargains.

COURTESY OF GIANT FOODS

Exhibit 6–22
Person-Situation Segmentation

Part A   *Person-Situation Segmentation Procedure*

Step 1   Use observational studies, focus group discussions and secondary data to discover whether different usage situations exist and whether they are determinant, in the sense that they appear to affect the importance of various product characteristics.

Step 2   If step 1 produces promising results, undertake a benefit, product perception and reported market behavior segmentation survey of consumers. Measure benefits and perceptions by usage situation as well as by individual difference characteristics. Assess situation usage frequency by recall estimates or usage situation diaries (Belk, 1979).

Step 3   Construct a person-situation segmentation matrix. The rows are the major usage situations and the columns are groups of users identified by a single characteristic or combination of characteristics.

Step 4   Rank the cells in the matrix in terms of their submarket sales volume. The situation-person combi-

nation that results in the greatest consumption of the generic product would be ranked first.

Step 5   State the major benefits sought, important product dimensions and unique market behavior for each nonempty cell of the matrix (some person types will never consume the product in certain usage situations).

Step 6   Position your competitors' offerings within the matrix. The person-situation segments they currently serve can be determined by the product feature they promote and other marketing strategy.

Step 7   Position your offering within the matrix on the same criteria.

Step 8   Assess how well your current offering and marketing strategy meet the needs of the submarkets compared to the competition.

Step 9   Identify market opportunities based on submarket size, needs and competitive advantage.

Part B   *Speculative Person-Situation Segmentation Matrix for Suntan Lotion*

Persons: *Situations*	*Young Children*		*Teenagers*		*Adult Women*		*Adult Men*		*Situation Benefits/Features*
	Fair Skin	*Dark Skin*	*Fair Skin*	*Dark Skin*	*Fair Skin*	*Dark Skin*	*Fair Skin*	*Dark Skin*	
beach/boat suntanning	combined insect repellant				summer perfume				a. windburn protection b. formula and container can stand heat c. container floats and is distinctive (not easily lost)
home-poolside sunbathing					combined moisturizer				a. large pump dispenser b. won't stain wood concrete or furnishings
sunlamp bathing					combined moisturizer and massage oil				a. designed specifically for type of lamp b. artificial tanning ingredient
snow skiing					winter perfume				a. special protection from special light rays and weather b. antifreeze formula
person/benefit features	special protection a. protection critical b. nonpoi-sonous		special protection a. fit in jean pocket b. used by opinion leaders		special protection female perfume female		special protection male perfume male		

SOURCE: Dickson, Peter R. (1982), "Person-Situation: Segmentation's Missing Link," *Journal of Marketing* 46 (Fall), 56–64. Reprinted by permission of the American Marketing Association.

A retail strategy that stresses the purchase of American-made products appeals to a large segment of American consumers who prefer products made in the U.S.A.

Retail managers can apply this segmentation approach to designing merchandising strategies for a variety of products and services. Exhibit 6–22 represents a possible person-situation segmentation matrix for suntan lotion, information that would be useful to a retailer in determining merchandise assortments and promotional messages.

SUMMARY

Understanding consumer behavior is essential for the retail manager because the individual purchases goods and services within the retail setting. All aspects of a retailer's strategic plan are directed toward a specified group of consumers, starting with the corporate mission statement. Consumers are an integral part of both the internal and external environments as they affect, and are affected by, the retailer.

Consumer decision making may be habitual, limited, or extended, depending upon the level of involvement in the purchase, or other factors such as available information and perceived risk. Steps in the consumer decision process start with problem recognition, followed by search, evaluation of alternatives, choice, and post-purchase evaluation.

Problem recognition is based on the difference between the actual and desired states. The desired state is influenced by reference groups, novelty seeking, and thinking. The actual state is influenced by assortment deficiency, arousal of needs, and post-purchase evaluation. Other factors affect both states similarly.

Search may be prepurchase or ongoing. Prepurchase search is directed toward solving an immediate consumer problem. Ongoing search is conducted without any specific purchase need in mind, providing information for future purchases. Information may be obtained from internal search (memory) or external search. The search process is extended when experience is outdated, risk is perceived to be high, and products or brands are highly differentiated. Both financial and psychological costs are associated with information search.

Alternative purchase opportunities are evaluated on features, or criteria, that are considered important by the consumer. Criteria may be either objective or subjective. Consumers tend to weigh the importance of evaluation criteria and categorize them into a hierarchy.

Choice is the next step in the purchase decision process. The consumer will make a selection from the evoked set of brands, but will be indifferent toward the inert set, and will not consider the inept set. A complex process of "mapping attitudes into motivations" results in a narrowing down of the number of acceptable alternatives from the aware set.

Post-purchase evaluation measures the satisfaction or dissatisfaction resulting from the purchase which then becomes feedback for the next decision.

The consumer decision process is influenced by psychological, social, and environmental factors. Psychological influences include learning and memory, attitude formation and motivation, and self-concept. Social influences include culture and subculture, social class, reference groups, family, and other sources. Physical surroundings, the social situation, task definition, time pressures, and consumers' moods are considered to be situational influences.

Given the numbers of people who are being served in our markets today, businesses must seek ways to aggregate consumers for the purposes of production, promotion, and distribution. Consumers can be aggregated into viable market segments on the basis of demographic, psychographic, and behavioral descriptors. Demographic characteristics may be primary or secondary. Psychographic descriptors focus on consumers' lifestyles and on their attitudes, interests, and opinions. By understanding both consumer behavior and the methods of targeting markets, the retail manager is best able to develop the most appropriate retail mix and to promote the store's goods, services, and the overall image effectively.

Questions for Review and Comprehension

1. Recall the last time that you shopped at the grocery store, and relate this to the definition of consumer behavior provided in this chapter.
2. Explain how an understanding of a retailer's consumer markets and their shopping behavior is an important component of the strategic planning process.
3. Describe several ways in which current international affairs can affect consumers' purchase behavior—the products or services they buy, and how and where they buy them.

4. Define each of the stages that may be involved in the purchase decision process for a typical consumer.

5. Discuss how the amount of effort expended by a customer may differ for the purchase of (a) a personal computer for the first time, (b) clothes for school or work, and (c) a loaf of bread. Include each of the steps involved for each purchase.

6. Consider the many sources of information that are available to a customer who is about to purchase a new car. Identify each of the major categories that might be consulted, and locate at least one example of each source.

7. For the college student who is purchasing a new outfit to wear to a party on Saturday night, what are the reasons he or she might seek more information. What is the trade-off between the costs and benefits of search if the student's school and part-time work schedule do not leave much time for shopping?

8. Define the following terms, and state how each might be used in making a purchase decision: brand criteria ratings, brand preference levels, and hierarchy of criteria.

9. Give examples of evaluative criteria that are important to you when you are purchasing (a) an education, (b) a fast-food meal, (c) a gift for someone special, (d) laundry detergent, and (e) automobile repairs.

10. Define and explain the significance of an evoked set, inert set, inept set, aware set and unaware set of products/brands/stores to a customer who is in the choice stage of the purchase decision process and is ready to buy. Should the retailer be concerned about how customers categorize products and brands on this continuum? Why or why not? How can a retailer shift product/brand/store to the customer's preference set?

11. Talk to some of your friends or family members, and assess their satisfaction or dissatisfaction with recent purchases. What factors have contributed to either state? And how can retailers prevent or overcome these problems?

12. Explain several ways that psychological influences can affect consumer behavior. Describe a retail strategy that demonstrates an understanding of these influences in attracting and keeping customers.

13. Describe the socialization process, and discuss the effect of several major social influences on buying behavior. In particular, discuss the role of culture and subculture, family, reference groups, and social class.

14. Briefly explain and illustrate several ways that situational influences can affect purchase behavior. Give an example of a strategy that a retailer might use in each case to make it easier for a customer to meet their personal needs in a given situation.

15. Define market segmentation, typical bases for segmentation, and the conditions that should be present for a segment to be worthwhile. Give specific examples of market segments and products and/or services, as well as store formats, that have been targeted to their needs.

References

Bloch, Peter H., Daniel L. Sherrell, and Nancy M. Ridgeway (1986), "Consumer Search: An Extended Framework," *Journal of Consumer Research* 13 (June), 119–126.

"Bozic Reveals Plans for Sears" (1987), *Chain Store Age: General Merchandise Trends* (January, 13–15.

Bremner, Brian (1990), "Looking Downscale—Without Looking Down," *Business Week* (October 8), 62, 66–67.

Brim, O.G., Jr. (1966), "Socialization Through the Life Cycle," in O.G. Brim, Jr. and S. Wheeler, *Socialization After Childhood*. New York, NY: Wiley (as quoted in Goslin, 1969, p. 2).

Bruner, Gordon C. II and Richard J. Pomazal (1988), "Problem Recognition: The Crucial First Stage of the Consumer Decision Process," *Journal of Consumer Marketing* 5, no. 1, (Winter), 53–63.

Claxton, John D., Joseph N. Frye, and Bernard Portis (1974), "A Taxonomy of Prepurchase Information Gathering Patterns," *Journal of Consumer Research* 1 (December), 35–42.

Corchado, Alfredo (1989), "Hispanic Supermarkets Are Blossoming," *The Wall Street Journal* (January 23), B1.

Davies, James C. (1977). *Human Nature and Politics*. Westport, Conn.: Greenwood Press.

Dickson, Peter R. (1982), "Person-Situation: Segmentation's Missing Link," *Journal of Marketing* 46 (Fall), 56–64.

Dommermuth, William P. (1984). *Promotion: Analysis, Creativity, and Strategy*. Boston, Mass.: Kent Publishing Company.

Dunkin, Amy (1989), "A Storekeeper's Caveat: Let the Seller Beware," *Business Week* (January 9), 84.

Engel, James F. and Roger D. Blackwell (1982), *Consumer Behavior*. 4th ed., Hinsdale, Ill.: The Dryden Press.

Engel, James F., Roger D. Blackwell and Paul Miniard (1989), *Consumer Behavior*, 6th ed., Chicago, Ill.: The Dryden Press.

Faison, Edmund W. J. (1977), "The Neglected Variety Drive: A Useful Concept for Consumer Behavior," *Journal of Consumer Research* 4, 172–175.

Festinger, Leon A. (1957), *A Theory of Cognitive Dissonance*. Stanford, Calif.: Stanford University Press.

Garland, Susan, Laura Zinn, Christopher Power, Maria Shao, and Julia Finn Siler (1991), "Those Aging Boomers," *Business Week* (May 20), 106–112.

Glynn, Karen A. (1990), "A Model for Teaching the Relationship Between Attitudes, Motivations and Evoked Sets," in *Making Marketing Magic*, Proceedings of the Twelfth Annual American Marketing Association Collegiate Conference. R. Viswanathan, ed., New Orleans, La.: American Marketing Association (March).

Goslin, David A. (1969), *Handbook of Socialization Theory and Research*. Chicago, Ill.: Rand McNally and Co., p. 2.

Hawkins, Del T., Roger J. Best, and Kenneth A. Coney (1989), *Consumer Behavior*. Homewood, Ill.: BPI-Irwin.

Hofstede, Geert (1980), *Culture's Consequences*. Beverly Hills, Calif.: Sage Publications.

"Home Furnishings Become A Bright Spot On the Retailer's Horizon" (1988), *The Wall Street Journal* (November 17), 1.

Howard, John A. (1983), " Marketing Theory of the Firm," *Journal of Marketing* 47 (Fall), 90–100.

Howard, John A. and Jagdish N. Sheth (1981), "A Theory of Buyer Behavior," in *Great Writings in Marketing*, 2d ed., Howard A. Thompson, ed., Tulsa Ok.: Penwell Books, 215–239.

Hutton, Cynthia and Edward Prewitt (1989), "Who Will Do Well?" *Fortune* (July 17), 67–70.

Kelly, Robert F. (1968), "The Search Component of the Consumer Decision Process: A Theoretical Examination," in *Marketing and the New Science of Planning*, Robert King, ed., Chicago, Ill.: American Marketing Association, 271–274.

Kluckhohn, Clyde (1951), "The Study of Culture," in *The Policy Sciences: Recent Developments in Scope and Method*. D. Lerner, ed., Stanford University Press.

Landler, Mark (1990), "Suddenly, The Stylish Male Gets Discovered," *Business Week* (October 1), 72, 76.

Maremont, Mark (1988), "A Cosmetics Company With a Conscience," *Business Week* (May 23), 136.

McNeal, James U. (1982), *Consumer Behavior: An Integrative Approach.* Boston, Mass.: Little Brown & Company.

Mellot, Douglas W., Jr. (1983), *Fundamentals of Consumer Behavior.* Tulsa, Ok.: Pennwell Books.

Moschis, George P. and Gilbert A. Churchill (1978), "Consumer Socialization: A Theoretical and Empirical Analysis," *Journal of Marketing Research.* 15 (November), pp. 599–609.

Mowen, John C. (1987), *Consumer Behavior.* New York: Macmillan Publishing Co.

Narayama, Chem L. and Rom J. Markin (1975), "Consumer Behavior and Product Performance: An Alternative Conceptualization," *Journal of Marketing* 25 (October), 1–10.

Nicosia, Francesco M. (1966), *Consumer Decision Processes: Marketing and Advertising Implications.* Englewood Cliffs, N.J.: Prentice Hall.

Nussbaum, Bruce, Otis Port, Rich Brandt, Teresa Carson, Karen Wolman, and Jonathan Kapstein (1988), "Smart Design: Quality Is the New Style," *Business Week* (April 11), 102–117.

Olsen, Janeen E. and Kent L. Granzin (1986), "The Economizing Sub-market of the Grocery Industry: An Explanatory Theory and Empirical Investigation," Proceedings of the American Marketing Association Annual Conference. (August), 184–189.

Pereira, Joseph (1988), "Pricey Sneakers Worn in Inner City Help Set Nation's Fashion Trend," *The Wall Street Journal* (December 1), 1, A6.

Ratchford, Brian and Pola Gupta (1986), "On Measuring the Informational Efficiency of Consumer Markets," Unpublished working paper. Amherst, N.Y.: State University of New York at Buffalo.

Riche, Martha Farnsworth (1989), "Psychographics for the 1990s," *American Demographics* (July), 25–26, 30–31, 53–54.

Robertson, Thomas S., Joan Zielinski, and Scott Ward (1984), *Consumer Behavior* Glenview, Ill.: Scott, Foresman & Co.

Rothman, Andrea (1988), "Classical Records Take on a New Look," *The Wall Street Journal* (November 30), B3.

Sirgy, M. Joseph (1982), "Self-Concept in Consumer Behavior: A Critical Review" *Journal of Consumer Research* 9, (December), 287–300.

Stafford, J.E. and A. B. Cocanougher (1981), "Reference Group Theory," in *Perspectives in Consumer Behavior, 3d ed.*, Harold H. Kassarjian and Thomas S. Robertson, eds., Glenview, Ill.: Scott, Foresman & Co., 329–343.

Wallace, David (1989), "Marketing to Hispanics: How to Sell Yuccas to YUCAS," *Advertising Age* (February 13), S6.

Wessel, David (1989), "One Sure Fact: Baby Boomers Are Aging," *The Wall Street Journal* (January 3), B1.

REGULATORY AND ETHICAL ENVIRONMENT

CHAPTER Seven

Learning Objectives

After studying this chapter, the student will be able to:

1. Recognize the constraints placed on retail strategy by the regulatory and ethical environment.
2. Discuss the effects of regulation on decisions and actions related to the marketing mix.
3. Describe the effects of regulations on discrimination and working conditions.
4. Describe the role of ethics and social responsibility in relation to legal requirements faced by retailers.
5. Explain how ethics and social responsibility issues might arise in relation to elements of the marketing mix.
6. Suggest ways that public attitudes toward the ethics of businesses can be changed.
7. Discuss whether a lawfully operating retail business should have an ethical code for managers and employees.

"When You Care Enough to Send the Very Best"

Hallmark Cards, Inc. was rated among the top 100 companies to work for in the U.S. in 1987. Eighteen-year-old Joyce Hall started the company in 1910, with two shoeboxes of postcards stored under his bed in a Kansas City YMCA. From that time on, Hall built his company on value for his customers and concern for his employees—two legal, ethical, socially responsible objectives.

Hallmark has no record of antitrust activities or deceptive advertising. In other words, the company that makes $2 billion a year and controls 45 percent market share in the "social expression" industry has enjoyed a reputation as a model supplier, retailer, and employer.

Hallmark is ranked at the top for benefits, ambiance, job security, and opportunity for promotion, although only average in pay. The company employs 19,000 full-time and 8,500 part-time employees who receive some unusual benefits. Some perks are adoption benefits, employee profit-sharing and ownership plan (Hallmark is privately held), 100 percent tuition reimbursement, loans up to $8,000 for a child attending college, interest-free loans up to $1,000 for employees with an unexpected emergency, free indoor parking in the Kansas City headquarters, free physical-fitness facility, and some free medical services. They also reward employees handsomely for good ideas passed along to management.

Hallmark remains the industry leader because a unique work force believes in the underlying importance of our corporate mission. Without these people—our employees and our various retailers—Hallmark could not protect and preserve the trust we believe we have earned. For these reasons, our people always have been and always will be the most distinguishing attribute of Hallmark Cards.

—Irvine O. Hockaday, Jr., president and CEO

A reputation for legal and ethical behavior can be fragile, however, no matter how "good" a company has been, or for how long. Recently, Hallmark came under fire for allegations of questionable actions regarding employees, possible plagarism, and restraint of trade. A fired executive claimed that several hundred people, mostly managers, in their forties, fifties, and sixties, left Hallmark abruptly within a two-year period. He was given no reason for his discharge, and made to sign an agreement that he would not sue the company for age discrimination. Hallmark faced other problems as owners of the Crown Center Plaza Hotel in Kansas City, Missouri, when a catwalk fell and several people were injured as a result of the disaster.

Several makers of alternative cards (non-occasion, humorous, or offbeat as opposed to traditional) filed multi-million dollar lawsuits against Hallmark for copying their products. Hallmark responded that they had been making this type of card since they introduced their contemporary cards in the 1950s, and that they had sold non-occasion cards since the earliest days of the company. Hallmark now sells its alternative-style designs under the names Personal Touch and Shoebox Greetings.

A former Hallmark salesman told an ABC-TV 20/20 program audience about a "buyback" policy, whereby the company paid stores to get rid of competitors' cards. Some retailers said they were told if they stocked non-Hallmark cards, they would get no Hallmark cards. Others view Hallmark's retailer incentive programs as a smart business strategy for regaining market share.

President Hockaday stated: "Pressuring them [independent retailers] does not make good business sense and would violate our policies".

Adapted from: "What It's Like to Work for Hallmark," Moss, Phil *Business Week Careers,* (1987), (Fall), 84–87; Wang, Penelope (1986), "A Not-So-Nice Greeting," *Newsweek,* (November 3).

INTRODUCTION

Retail firms must compete within an environment controlled largely by other forces—competitors, customers, economic conditions, and legal and social constraints. In this chapter, the focus is on the retailer's need to operate within legal and social boundaries, ranging from explicit legal statements to implicit ethical standards of conduct dictated by social norms and expectations. For convenience in discussion, **regulation** includes the broad spectrum of legislation, ordinances, rules, or codes that can be enforced to some extent by a government body, industry association, or other party. **Ethics** is used to describe behavior that goes beyond the law, socially sanctioned but not legally enforceable, and often subject to interpretation (i.e., ethical and moral behavior, social responsibility).

The legal/political environment was described earlier within the contexts of the strategic planning process (Chapter 2) and the Integrative Retail Information Model (IRIM) (Chapter 3). Each is examined briefly here, to emphasize the importance of regulation and socially responsible behavior in planning and executing retail strategies.

Strategic Planning and the Regulatory Environment

The effect of the regulatory environment on the strategic planning process is illustrated in Exhibit 7–1. At each stage laws must be obeyed, government agencies must be satisfied, and social-political pressures cannot be ignored. Some legal and ethical implications to be considered by retail managers are as follows:

1. Corporate mission: Does the mission statement indicate corporate responsibility to society? How does it affect customers, employees, suppliers, and others?
2. Performance objectives: Are market share, profitability, and other objectives within antitrust guidelines? Will they lead to unfair competition or labor practices? Will customers suffer loss or discomfort? Will society suffer loss or discomfort?
3. Situation analysis: Are legislation, ordinances, business codes, and social and political trends monitored closely? What is right or wrong according to the value system of the public?
4. Strategic objectives and strategy definition: What are the legal and ethical aspects of the marketing mix? Is anything such as unfair pricing, deceptive advertising, illegal location, defective products, or black market involved? Is the retailer selling "legal" products, and to legitimate customers?
5. Implementation: Is it fair to employees, managers, customers, and vendors? Are funds used and accounted for appropriately?
6. Execution: Do management and employees act to avoid deceptive or dishonest practices?
7. Strategic and operating control: Are checks on managers, salespeople, credit employees, and others made and used to evaluate operating methods and form and use of records of results?

REGULATION
legislation, ordinances, rules, or codes used to legally guide business behavior

ETHICS
socially sanctioned, moral behavior that goes beyond the law and is not legally enforceable

Corporate Mission Statement
- Dedication to operating in a socially responsible and ethical manner

Performance Objectives
- Fairness to competitors, customers, employees, and other constituencies

Situational Analysis
- Awareness of social and political trends, societal values, legislation

Strategic Objectives and Strategy Definition
- Attention to legal and ethical aspects of marketing mix, such as pricing practices, promotion, product safety, etc.

Implementation and Tactics
- Appropriate use and control of resources; fairness to all constituencies–including vendors and intermediaries

Execution
- Avoidance of dishonest and deceptive practices (advertising, personal selling, pricing, merchandise availability, etc.)

Evaluation and Control
- Checks on managers and all personnel; honest analysis and reporting of results

F E E D B A C K

Exhibit 7–1
Strategic Planning Process and the Regulatory Environment: An Illustration

SOURCE: Anderson and Parker, 1988

Note that an illegal or unethical decision or action at any stage places the entire strategic plan in jeopardy if it "backfires."

Integrative Retail Information Model (IRIM) Perspective

Although most environmental influences are beyond the control of the retailer, they can be monitored through the retail information system. Retail firms must operate within the legal system with its explicit rules and regulations for conducting a business. Violation of legal requirements can result in serious loss. Therefore, knowledge of the details of specific legislation—what is allowed and what is not allowed, and how it might be interpreted in the retailer's favor—is absolutely necessary. The intent and enforcement of laws, ordinances, and codes are explicitly stated for clear interpretation. However, retailers are also regulated by a more elusive, implicit set of guidelines demanded by society—honesty, ethics, and socially responsible behavior. A business must "keep a finger on the pulse" to know what the public expects beyond that which is mandated by law.

Relationships between the regulatory environment and other external and internal environmental factors are illustrated in Exhibit 7–2. Note that retailers can make informed choices and develop competitive strategies within the same legal and social boundaries that constrain their competitors. Successful retailers have been doing just that for years.

Next, we will consider some regulations that affect company growth and competition, the marketing mix, and human resources. This is followed by a discussion of the impact of ethics and social responsibility on retailing decisions.

LAWS REGULATING COMPETITION AND GROWTH

Retailers are affected by legislation that has been passed for several basic purposes, such as protecting businesses from each other and from consumers; and protecting consumers and employees from businesses. The major focus is on regulating growth, competition, or any action that could be construed as restraint of trade.

A retail business is a legal entity. As such, it must meet certain legal requirements. The form and size of a retail organization are subject to regulation. Legal forms of ownership (sole proprietor, partnership, corporation) were discussed in Chapter 4. Growth strategies through mergers and acquisitions are discussed in a later chapter.

Essentially, there are limits to how large a company can grow. A retailer who successfully maximizes profits and shareholder wealth through increased sales and effective cost controls may be in a position to experience phenomenal growth through expansion of the present business, or acquisition of other businesses. However, if this success makes the business so large that it becomes a monopoly, it may be in violation of federal antitrust laws.

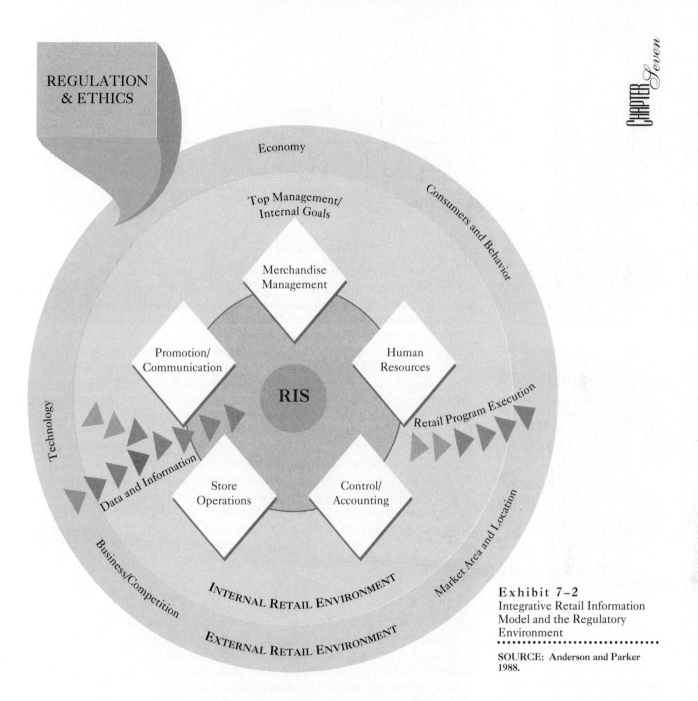

REGULATION
& ETHICS

Economy

Consumers and Behavior

Top Management/
Internal Goals

Merchandise
Management

Promotion/
Communication

Human
Resources

RIS

Technology

Retail Program Execution

Data and Information

Store
Operations

Control/
Accounting

Business/Competition

Market Area and Location

INTERNAL RETAIL ENVIRONMENT

EXTERNAL RETAIL ENVIRONMENT

Exhibit 7–2
Integrative Retail Information
Model and the Regulatory
Environment
....
SOURCE: Anderson and Parker
1988.

Federal legislation designed to regulate competition (i.e., protect one retailer
from another) includes the Sherman Antitrust Act, Clayton Act, Federal
Trade Commission Act, and the Wheeler-Lea Act, as discussed briefly in the
following sections. (See Corley and Reed, 1987; Holley and Jennings, 1983.)
The Robinson Patman act is discussed within the context of price-related
regulations. Exhibit 7–3 presents a time line for the major laws affecting
retailers.

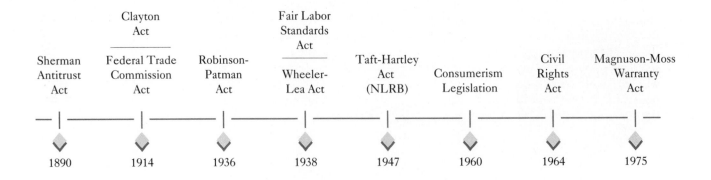

Sherman Antitrust Act	Clayton Act Federal Trade Commission Act	Robinson-Patman Act	Fair Labor Standards Act Wheeler-Lea Act	Taft-Hartley Act (NLRB)	Consumerism Legislation	Civil Rights Act	Magnuson-Moss Warranty Act
1890	1914	1936	1938	1947	1960	1964	1975

Exhibit 7–3
Major Laws Affecting Retailers:
A Time Line (1890–1975)
....

Sherman Antitrust Act

The **Sherman Antitrust Act,** passed in 1890, is the grandfather of all laws regulating competition. The act was designed to prohibit businesses from becoming too large and forming monopolies. Sections 1 and 2 contain the major provisions of the Sherman Act, making every contract, combination, conspiracy, monopoly, or attempt to monopolize illegal. At the time it was written, the law was considered comprehensive in setting forth regulations against restraint of trade. However, unscrupulous businesses soon found ways around the law, based upon the *rule of reason.* According to this rule, before any legal action can be taken, it must first be proven that a company is acting with the intent of an *unreasonable* restraint of trade.

The retailing of services, as well as products, comes under the jurisdiction of the Sherman Act. In 1987, for example, the U.S. Justice Department brought an antitrust suit against the State Board of CPAs of Louisiana. The suit alleged that the Board's promulgation, interpretation, and enforcement of its advertising and solicitation rules restrained trade and diminished competition, by preventing consumers from obtaining truthful and useful information about the availability, quality, and price of CPA services. However, the antitrust suit was dismissed because, as a state regulatory agency, the Board was immune from antitrust liability ("Louisiana State Board . . ." 1987).

Clayton Act

The **Clayton Act** was passed in 1914 as an amendment to the Sherman Antitrust Act. It was designed to close the loopholes associated with the Sherman Act. The primary feature of the law was the prohibition of specific actions that might lead to a restraint of trade. These actions are concerned with various aspects of the retail mix, such as price discrimination or illegal distribution practices. The Clayton Act prohibits tying arrangements where purchase of one item is contingent upon purchase of another and exclusive dealing that may substantially lessen competition or create a monopoly. The act also prohibits the existence of interlocking directorates—an individual sits on the board of directors of competing firms—that substantially reduce commercial competition.

Mergers are regulated by Section 7 of the Clayton Act, amended by the Celler-Kefauver Act. (Mergers and acquisitions are discussed in Appendix 11–A.) A merger occurs when one company acquires the assets of another

company. According to the law, mergers are illegal if they reduce competition. For example, one growth strategy for a retailer is backward integration (buying a manufacturer or supplier) to reduce costs and to secure a steady source of supply. If this gives the retailer an unfair advantage, the purchase will not be allowed. Likewise, horizontal integration, a merger between competitors, is subject to regulatory action if it will lead to a monopolistic situation and give the firm an unfair competitive advantage.

Federal Trade Commission Act

In 1914, the **Federal Trade Commission Act** (FTC), was passed. This law was designed to prohibit practices harmful to competition or competitors, with primary focus on advertising and sales practices. The Federal Trade Commission (FTC), established by this act, is a particularly important regulatory agency for retailers. The FTC has primary responsibility for enforcing the provisions of the Clayton Act. Enforcement procedures include formal court action, voluntary compliance, and consent orders.

Wheeler-Lea Act

The **Wheeler-Lea Act** was passed in 1938 as an amendment to the FTC Act. This law banned deceptive practices regardless of their effect on competition. The general intent was to protect consumers from business.

Regulation not only has a direct effect on competitive activities, it also has a profound impact on marketing mix decisions, which in turn have an effect on consumers and/or competitors. Some of the legal restrictions concerning the retailer's products, promotional activities, pricing strategies, and distribution practices are described in the next section.

IMPACT OF REGULATION ON THE MARKETING MIX

Federal, state, and local laws, combined with social and political influences such as the 1960s consumerism movement, have led to more precise guidelines for responsible retailers to follow in dealing with customers and vendors. This is evident in regulations related to products, promotion, pricing, and distribution, as described in the following sections. (See Exhibit 7–4.)

Product-Related Regulations

Although retailers may not be the manufacturers of the products they sell, they are affected by certain product-related legal requirements. Most of these regulations concern product warranties, product liability, and trademarks and copyrights.

PRODUCT WARRANTIES   A **warranty** is a promise made by a manufacturer or retailer about the quality or performance of a specific product. Prior to 1975, a consumer who bought a product that did not function as

SHERMAN ANTITRUST ACT
legislation passed in 1890 to regulate competition, particularly with regard to monopolies

CLAYTON ACT
legislation passed in 1914 to close the loopholes of the Sherman Act

FEDERAL TRADE COMMISSION ACT
legislation passed in 1914 to prohibit practices harmful to competition

WHEELER-LEA ACT
legislation passed in 1938 to protect consumers by banning deceptive practices

WARRANTY
promise regarding the quality or performance of a product

Exhibit 7–4
Impact of Regulation on the
Marketing Mix
....

promised could hold only the seller responsible under traditional common
law. In 1975, the **Magnuson-Moss Warranty Act** was passed to ensure that
warranty information would be made available to customers. It also gave
aggrieved consumers rights against the manufacturers of faulty products, as
distinct from sellers.

Disputes over "lemon" automobiles provide one example of the application of this law. Although there is some problem in defining what constitutes
a "lemon," and the process can be somewhat frustrating for the consumer,
automobile manufacturers can be held responsible for malfunctioning cars
under the federal warranty act. This act is further supported by 44 state laws
(Fanning, 1988).

Warranties are becoming more and more important in today's marketplace. They may be classified as either express or implied. An **express warranty** is a written or oral statement that specifies aspects of the product or its
performance. A typical statement might be, "This motor is guaranteed to be
free of defects for 90 days from purchase." Express warranties are covered by
section 2-133 of the Uniform Commercial Code (UCC). An express warranty
places an obligation on the seller and/or manufacturer to guarantee that the
product lives up to the standards set forth by the warranty.

Express warranties can be stated as either limited or full warranties.
Under a full warranty the defective product must be repaired or replaced at
no charge to the consumer during the duration of the warranty. A limited
warranty places conditions on the guarantee, or only covers certain aspects of
the product. Statements or promises made by the seller to the buyer before

the sale may be considered express warranties, because they may become an element of the bargain between the store and the customer.

Consumers also are entitled to an **implied warranty** under section 2-314 of the UC when they purchase a product. This guarantees their rights to a product fit for normal use and purpose (i.e., warranty of merchantability) and the right of title to the product.

Providing a product that is *fit for normal use and purpose* has major implications for retailers. This means that products sold by the retailer must perform as expected under normal conditions. For example, if a retailer sells a bathing suit that shrinks when wet, the product is not fit for its intended purpose, leaving the retailer in violation of the implied warranty. To reduce the risk of this violation, a number of retailers have taken on the responsibility of testing products within their own organizations.

Retailers are obligated under the law to honor product warranties. They are required to give full disclosure of warranty information in language that is easy to read and understand. That is, the type of warranty (full or limited) and specific terms must be clearly defined. In addition, retailers are required to establish a policy for dealing with complaints, such as a prescribed return policy for products that are under warranty.

The need to stand behind product warranties has added another dimension to retailers' responsibilities and overhead costs, as described above. However, innovative retailers and manufacturers have seized this as an opportunity to increase sales. They have found a competitive edge in reassuring consumers that products are reliable, and assuring satisfaction with their use. Several companies that have used this approach successfully include American Express, Lufthansa German Airlines, General Electric Co., and Whirlpool Corp. In effect, many retailers conduct their own testing of merchandise, and other store guarantees in addition to the manufacturers' warranties.

American Express offered its credit card customers the opportunity to extend manufacturers' warranties for as long as one year on some products they bought. Response was extremely positive. Lufthansa increased passenger loads and minimized claims by introducing a guarantee program for first and business class passengers promising passengers $200 for missed connecting flights or late baggage, if the airline was at fault. GE and Whirlpool experienced sales increases by guaranteeing that new appliances would be replaced (within a specified time) if customers were not satisfied with their purchases. Toll-free 800-numbers are associated with quality products and companies who have nothing to hide, according to one study. Companies can increase consumer loyalty by 10 percent just by getting people to complain about their product or service problems, and increase it to 80 to 90 percent if the complaints are addressed (Singer, 1987).

PRODUCT LIABILITY   Retailers have an obligation to monitor the quality and safety of products they sell and to provide adequate information to their customers about product use. For example, a retailer can be held for **product liability** if a customer who purchases a product is injured by it, and the retailer has failed to explain the dangers associated with its use.

Product liability lawsuits have become increasingly prevalent, with settlements reaching millions of dollars. Therefore, product safety issues and possible product recalls have become a major source of concern for retailers

MAGNUSON-MOSS WARRANTY ACT
legislation passed in 1975 to ensure warranty information would be made available to customers

EXPRESS WARRANTY
written or oral statement that specifies aspects of the product or its performance

IMPLIED WARRANTY
guarantee that a product will perform as expected under normal conditions

PRODUCT LIABILITY
obligation to insure quality and safety of products

and manufacturers alike. In fact, some claim a fifth *P* for plaintiff has been added to the original "4 Ps" (product, price, place, promotion), due to increased legal activity against businesses.

To illustrate the potential magnitude of this problem, consider a $2.25 million settlement by Fisher-Price Toys in 1987, one of the largest individual settlements ever by a toy manufacturer. The suit was filed in 1973 in Canada by the parents of a child who suffered physical and mental handicaps after choking on a figurine that was included with a toy schoolbus. Plastic pigtails protruding from the wooden figurine acted like a fishhook, lodging it in the child's throat, and causing him to go into a coma. The parents believed the toy was safe for their one-year-old child because it was marked "safe" and "non-toxic," although the box also stated that the toy was for children between the ages of 2 and 6. New Fisher-Price toy packages containing redesigned figurines warn that, regardless of age, the product is not intended for children who still put objects in their mouths (Collins, 1987). The retailer apparently was not named in this suit, but still has responsibility for the safety of all products he sells.

Product liability cases increased 758 percent between 1977 and 1988. According to legal experts such as F. Lee Bailey, and managers of leading corporations, fear of liability litigation can have a stifling effect on product innovation, leading manufacturers to make only mediocre or "safe" improvements in proven designs or formulas. A large percentage of the firms have responded by involving lawyers in product development, manufacturing, and marketing activities to minimize lawsuits. The result is increased insurance and legal costs, which are passed along to retailers and consumers ("Civil Justice . . . ," 1990; Cortes-Comerer, 1988; "Fear of Lawsuits . . . ," 1988; Huber, 1989).

Food retailers must monitor the safety of their products within Food and Drug Administration guidelines, although the manufacturers also are held responsible. In 1990, proposals for pesticide control under the Environmental Protection Agency (EPA) had a potential impact on grocers. The question centers on whether allowable pesticide levels for farm products should be set according to what is safe for children or for adults (Bennett, 1990). In any event, pesticide legislation will affect food merchandising.

Promotion-Related Regulations

The promotional aspect of the marketing mix is subject to many regulations which must be observed by retailers. Since the retailer has direct control over promotional decisions, and these decisions are highly visible to the public, the implications are far-reaching. Federal legislation concerned with promotional activities includes the Federal Trade Commission (FTC) Act and the Wheeler-Lea Amendment.

A number of practices are considered deceptive, according to the FTC. Several of the more common violations involve bait and switch practices, price-off promotions, and merchandise availability. Sellers also are required to have prior substantiation of all claims made in their advertising.

BAIT AND SWITCH   **Bait and switch** refers to the deceptive practice of advertising a product at a very low price, with no intention of actually selling that particular product. The promotion is used as bait to lure customers into

BAIT AND SWITCH
advertising a product at a very low price in order to attract to a store customers who are then encouraged to buy higher priced merchandise

the store, where they are encouraged, even pressured, to buy higher priced merchandise.

For example, suppose that two retail stereo outlets, Joe's Stereo and PW Sound have been offered a deal to purchase good quality stereo equipment at a very low price. Both retailers have decided to purchase the product and advertise the low price to consumers. Joe's buys one of the stereo outfits, in order to claim in a newspaper advertisement that he has Brand X components at a very low price. While it is true that he does have the merchandise (but only one) in stock, he has no intention of selling it. He only wishes to draw customers into the store, where he will attempt to sell them other, more expensive lines. PW, on the other hand, advertises that the store has a very limited amount of the equipment on hand at the advertised low price. The company also indicates that no rain checks will be issued, and that it is first come, first served to be able to buy the equipment at the advertised price. The PW manager also intends to try to sell his customers another brand of merchandise. However, unlike Joe, his methods are legal. Bait and switch does not outlaw salesmanship. It outlaws the deceptive practice of advertising merchandise a retailer has no intention of selling. Bait and switch may also include disparaging remarks made by a salesperson about the merchandise, or lack of availability of credit for selected items.

PRICE-OFF PROMOTIONS   It is illegal for a retailer to advertise a false price reduction. If a price is advertised as a 20 percent reduction from the original, it must actually have been 20 percent higher for an extended period of time. Otherwise, the retailer is making a false claim. The same logic holds true for coupon offers. It is illegal to offer a coupon on merchandise, and then raise the price of the merchandise to cover the cost of the coupon. For example, the local burger restaurant down the street normally sells hamburgers for $1.09. They offer a coupon for 25 cents off, but raise the price of the burgers to $1.34. The consumers are being misled into believing that they are receiving a price reduction while, in reality, they are covering the cost of the coupon when they pay the discounted price. Some questionable price promotion tactics have caused legal action against the use of the word *sale*. Further, some suppliers have applied pressure to establish a set price.

MERCHANDISE AVAILABILITY   The FTC requires that quantity limitations be stated in advertising for low stock products. Some stores advertise the numbers of sale items that are available at each outlet (e.g., "at least 20 per store" under a picture of item) in order to combat the problem of customers feeling they have been cheated. Rain checks can reduce the risk of violation of this law, and result in a higher level of customer satisfaction.

DECEPTIVE ADVERTISING   Each of the promotion-related violations described above involves an attempt to deceive customers. A number of examples follow to emphasize the far-reaching effects of advertising regulation on product and service retailers.

The U.S. Justice Department ordered the regional Bell telephone companies to suspend potentially misleading advertising. The telephone credit card system was said to discriminate in favor of AT&T, since long distance calls made on either AT&T or regional credit cards were routed over AT&T,

even if the consumer had chosen another long distance company. The regional companies were told to advise customers of this fact (Davis, 1987).

An increasing amount of responsibility for the regulation of national advertising is moving from the federal to the state level. In 1988, the National Association of Attorneys General (NAAG) tested their guidelines on airfare advertising against U.S. Department of Transportation orders, regarding whether international fares should comply with state or federal law. The NAAG action is an example of states working together to establish national standards, which would in effect make them a national regulatory force that supercedes federal authority (Lawrence, 1988).

In another case, the National Association of State Attorneys General approved a plan to set standards for car-rental practices. The standards call for car-rental companies to advertise the charges consumers actually pay, including fueling, collision damage waivers, and other costs often hidden in the advertised rates (Roberts, 1988).

Nongovernment groups, such as Consumers Union (publisher of *Consumer Reports*), can file deceptive advertising lawsuits. Consumers Union charged that Alta-Dena, the largest U.S. dairy, was misleading customers about the health benefits of raw milk in promoting it as safe, wholesome, and healthy, while ignoring a potential risk from bacteria in unpasteurized milk (Lowry, 1985). Many other food products have come under fire for misleading advertising, particularly those making (or implying) medical claims. Kellogg Co.'s All-Bran cereal ads that link fiber and cancer prevention were accused of being misleading and objectionable by the California Cancer Advisory Council, under the auspices of the state's Department of Health Services and the U.S. Food and Drug Administration (Colford, 1984).

ADVERTISING SUBSTANTIATION   While the enforcement of advertising substantiation claims falls under the jurisdiction of the FTC, competitors and industry groups often perform this role. For example, two competitors challenged Sterling Drugs regarding their Stri-Dex Triple Action pads and their Clearasil Deep Pore Cleanser. They charged that Sterling could not produce published clinical studies to support product superiority claims ("Acne Treatment . . . ," 1986). The case was brought before the National Advertising Division (NAD) of the Better Business Bureau and the National Advertising Review Board (NARB). Decisions by industry regulatory groups generally result in either withdrawing or changing the ad, rather than legal action in the courts.

Price-Related Regulations

The laws regulating price have a dual purpose. They are designed both to protect and to constrain the retailer. On the protection side, the small retailer is protected from pricing practices used by larger retailers that may drive the smaller firm out of business. On the constraint side, legislation has a major impact on retail strategy in terms of pricing decisions.

PROTECTION   The retailer is protected from unfair pricing practices by suppliers under the **Robinson-Patman Act,** a 1936 amendment to the Clayton Act. The act's primary area of protection is price discrimination. Dis-

crimination occurs when more attractive prices are extended to only one or a few buyers, but not to others. The Robinson-Patman Act does not restrict price differentials completely, but it does establish ground rules which must be followed.

Price differentials are allowed if:

1. The transaction results in lower costs for the manufacturer. For example, if a retailer orders 100,000 units, making it possible for the manufacturer to take advantage of economies of scale, the resulting lower costs can be passed along to the retailer.
2. Changing conditions also can be justification for charging lower costs to certain retailers. For example, if a food retailer is purchasing perishable items with a limited shelf life, the supplier can reduce the price to move the merchandise.
3. Meeting of competition in good faith.

This protective pricing legislation has particular implications for retailers. First, quantity discounts and allowances are not illegal under the Robinson-Patman Act. However, a supplier that offers quantity discounts is required to offer these discounts to all buyers on proportionate terms. Second, the same rationale applies to special services and allowances given by vendors. If they are offered at all, they must be made available to all on proportionate terms.

The FTC accused six of the nation's largest book publishers of engaging in illegal discriminatory pricing practices, in violation of the Robinson-Patman Act. The publishers were charged with selling books at lower prices to major bookstore chains and at higher prices to independent bookstores. The FTC also alleged that the publishers provided services or facilities for promotion, display and inventory control to the chains, but did not make them available to all customers on the same terms. As a result of these practices, independent bookstores had a limited ability to compete with the chains (Langley, 1988).

The Robinson-Patman Act is one of the most important pieces of legislation that affects retailers. However, according to a 1990 *Progressive Grocer* survey, issues dealing with this act are dwarfed by other major concerns, as shown in Exhibit 7–5. Those of most concern to retailers were solid waste, food safety, local marketing, green products, pesticides, and slotting allowances. Robinson-Patman was at the bottom of their list, with 21 percent believing the act's provisions should be strengthened, 60 percent left as they are, and 19 percent that they should be eased (*Progressive Grocer*: 57th Annual Report, 1990).

RESALE PRICE MAINTENANCE   **Resale price maintenance** violations occur when a supplier sets the retail price on a product, and controls the price paid by consumers in all retail outlets. Although legal at one time, this practice is now illegal, and retailers have control over the price charged to their customers.

OTHER RETAIL PRICING VIOLATIONS   Two other pricing strategies that place retailers in violation of the law include predatory pricing and price-fixing. Of these, **predatory pricing** tends to be the most prevalent

ROBINSON-PATMAN ACT

legislation passed in 1936 to protect retailers from unfair pricing practices by suppliers

RESALE PRICE MAINTENANCE

supplier sets and controls prices charged to consumers by retailers

PREDATORY PRICING

retailer prices below cost to drive out competition

offense. This occurs when a retailer prices a product below cost, with the intent of driving other retailers out of business. The key to determining whether this practice is a violation lies in the reason for selecting the price. It is not illegal for retailers to lower prices below cost under some circumstances. For example, a men's clothing store owner may have a large inventory of out-of-date styles on hand from the previous season. These items may be sold below cost to place the retailer in a position to purchase current, more saleable styles. This tactic is also used as loss leader pricing to draw customers into the store for other retail purchases.

Price-fixing is another illegal practice pursued by some retailers. Price-fixing occurs when firms, otherwise independent of one another, have a mutual agreement that they will set prices at some coordinated level, allowing all who are involved to achieve a desired profit margin. However, it also tends to limit competition by creating a type of monopoly.

Exhibit 7–5   Robinson-Patman Act: An Industry Viewpoint

Food safety/environmental concerns climb. . .

Concern Index	Wholesalers	Concern index	Chain executives	Concern index	Manufacturers
Solid waste	88.3*	Solid waste	93.7*	Solid waste	88.8*
Food safety	85.4	Food safety	92.8	Slotting allowances	88.4
Slotting allowances	79.9	Local marketing	84.9	Food safety	83.0
National deals/pricing	79.0	Green products	83.3	Green products	83.0
Green products	75.0	Pesticides	79.7	Failure fees	81.1
Failure fees	72.5	Slotting allowances	79.5	Category management	77.7
Pesticides	70.7	Category management	76.4	Local marketing	77.0
Category management	69.6	Failure fees	73.4	Contract buying	73.9
Contract buying	68.4	National deals/pricing	72.1	National deals/pricing	70.9
Local marketing	62.7	Street money	69.6	Pesticides	69.9
Street money	60.5	Contract buying	65.5	Street money	63.6
Robinson-Patman	52.9	Robinson-Patman	47.3	Robinson-Patman	55.9
Wholesalers		Chain executives		Manufacturers	

While Robinson-Patman fears lessen
Do you believe the provisions of the Robinson-Patman Act should be strengthened, eased or left as they are?

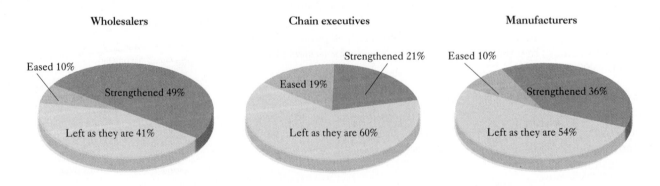

Wholesalers — Eased 10% — Strengthened 49% — Left as they are 41%

Chain executives — Strengthened 21% — Eased 19% — Left as they are 60%

Manufacturers — Eased 10% — Strengthened 36% — Left as they are 54%

* Responses were converted to a 0-100 scale with 50 indicating no change.

Numbers higher than 50 indicate increasing concern, lower numbers, a decreasing concern.

SOURCE: *Progressive Grocer: 57th Annual Report.* (1990), "1989: A Solid, Yet Unspectacular Year," (Mid-April), pg. 23.

Regulations concerning retail pricing and advertising practices are closely related. Regulatory agencies look closely at low-price guarantees, price-matching policies, and sale ads. Many retailers have come under fire for deceptive, misleading, or unclear price ads. As a result, the Council of Better Business Bureaus has held meetings with Sears, Roebuck & Co., Montgomery Ward & Co., Zayre Corp., May Department Stores Co. and other major retailers to establish ground rules for comparative price advertising. For example, in switching to its new everyday low price strategy, Sears, Roebuck & Co. has been confronted with decisions about how to implement and advertise its new pricing policy within legal boundaries (Fitzgerald, 1988).

**EFFECT OF NONPRICE RELATED LEGISLATION:
AN EXAMPLE** A number of laws are not specifically directed toward pricing practices, but do have an indirect effect on the amount charged by retailers. A case in point is a bill introduced in Congress in 1989 to abolish the penny. The bill calls for rounding selling prices down to the nearest nickel if the price ends in 1, 2, 6 or 7 cents, and rounding up if the sum ends in 3, 4, 8 or 9 cents (Warren, 1990). There are arguments for both sides of the issue, and the controversy is not a new one. However, if the bill is passed, it will have a major impact on the use of the penny in retail prices.

Distribution-Related Regulations

The retailer is also subject to regulations that affect distribution policies. The purposes of these laws are to protect retailers, suppliers, and consumers from one another. Several examples of these regulations are reciprocal dealings, tying contracts, and exclusive dealings.

RECIPROCAL DEALINGS A **reciprocal deal** may occur when suppliers and retailers are customers of each other. For example, company A produces dry cleaning supplies, which it sells to company B, a dry cleaner. Company B is a member of a large retail chain that represents a major sales account for Company A. Company B will buy from Company A only if A's uniforms are drycleaned at B's shop. If this arrangement is put into contract form or if B uses force, then the arrangement is illegal and B could be charged for enforcing a reciprocal dealing. It is not illegal, however, for A and B to trade with each other out of goodwill. It is only illegal if force is used.

TYING CONTRACTS Violations in the form of **tying contracts** occur when suppliers force retailers to purchase unwanted products in order to obtain a desired product. A common form of tying contract is *full-line forcing*. Continuing the dry cleaning example, assume that Company B must buy all cleaning supplies from A to get a prespotter solution. If B has a licensing agreement with A then the full-line forcing is legal. However, if B does not have such an arrangement with A, then the situation would be illegal.

EXCLUSIVE DEALINGS **Exclusive dealings** are allowed only if they do not restrain trade. This type of deal exists when a company has the legal rights to be the sole retailer of a specified product (or products) from a given manufacturer within a prescribed area. This has been a popular practice for

PRICE-FIXING
independent firms mutually agree to set prices at some coordinated level

RECIPROCAL DEALING
situations where suppliers and retailers are customers of each other; illegal if force is used

TYING CONTRACTS
suppliers illegally force retailers to purchase unwanted products in order to obtain a desired product

EXCLUSIVE DEALING
retailer has legal rights to be only retailer of a product from a manufacturer in a specific area; illegal if trade is restrained

franchised products, and an accepted practice in certain fashion goods, although the importance of exclusive dealings seems to have diminished over time.

DISTRIBUTION VERSUS RETRIBUTION   Many distribution irregularities exist within loosely structured business arrangements that leave the injured party in a vulnerable position. Bennetton S.p.A. is a trendy, modern retail apparel chain of about 6,300 stores throughout the world. The Italian company has experienced rapid growth since its start as a sweater maker in 1965, basing its growth on small business investors who open Benetton stores. Benetton believes that the "right spirit" to work in a Benetton shop is more important than prior business experience.

Stores are required to sell only Benetton merchandise, and operate according to the Benetton marketing plan. This arrangement has most of the characteristics of a franchise, but there is no formal contract—just a handshake and verbal agreement. Therefore, the owners are not protected under the U.S. franchise laws. Luciano Benetton claims that retail pacts involving lawyers and contracts are not necessary because the company possesses unique ties with its store owners, based on rapport and faith.

Even though many satisfied store owners are operating profitable businesses, others are disenchanted with the arrangement. Benetton and its company representatives—who receive a commission on merchandise sold to stores—have been accused of using high pressure tactics to place unwanted, unsuitable, or excessive apparel in the stores, and of enforcing pricing schedules under its right to cease supplying merchandise and to terminate store owners for any reason. At least four civil lawsuits have alleged fraud, extortion, and various financial misrepresentations. They have charged that since Benetton is actually run as a franchise operation, the company has violated laws that protect small businesses from abuses by franchisers. However, Benetton has not met the FTC registration and disclosure requirements for franchises, so no official recourse through the FTC is available. To further complicate the issue, Benetton sent store owners an "authorization" to sign, stating that any disputes between store owners and Benetton are to be settled in Italian courts (Agins, 1988).

The Benetton controversy may be due to unscrupulous corporate practices or inexperienced store owners. Regardless of the cause, the situation cannot be ignored because of the effect on the company, the stores, and their customers. This scenario illustrates the difficulty in resolving many of the legal and ethical problems facing retailers, and the rationale for operating within clearly defined legal boundaries.

IMPACT ON HUMAN RESOURCES

Retailers are also subject to laws regarding discriminatory practices and working conditions. Under the law, employees are protected from discrimination in being hired or discharged by the company and are assured of satisfactory working conditions. Each of these areas of regulation is discussed briefly. (See Exhibit 7–6.)

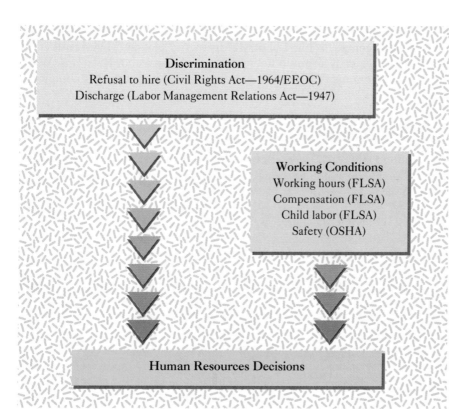

Discrimination
Refusal to hire (Civil Rights Act—1964/EEOC)
Discharge (Labor Management Relations Act—1947)

Working Conditions
Working hours (FLSA)
Compensation (FLSA)
Child labor (FLSA)
Safety (OSHA)

Human Resources Decisions

Exhibit 7–6
Laws Regarding Human
Resources

Discrimination

The primary emphasis in human resources regulation is on avoidance of **discrimination.** It is illegal to discriminate on the basis of sex, race, color, religion, or national origin according to Title VII of the Civil Rights Act of 1964. The law, which is administered by the Equal Employment Opportunity Commission (EEOC), specifically covers refusal to hire, discharge, compensation, and terms of employment.

REFUSAL TO HIRE In order to be in compliance with the law, retailers must ensure that employment decisions are uniform, and that their personnel policies are supportable. Failure to observe these two requirements can result in lawsuits and charges against the retailer. Good intentions do not avoid problems with this law, which is based upon effect. Therefore, retailers need to establish appropriate standards and policies for dealing with employment decisions. In particular, measures must be taken to remove any indication of race, sex, age, color, or religion. Unless this information has a direct effect upon the performance of the job, it must be excluded from the hiring process.

DISCHARGE Decisions to discharge an employee and the reasons for the discharge should be documented. The retailer must be careful to have available proof concerning the discharge of other employees for committing similar acts.

DISCRIMINATION
basing decisions or actions on a person's sex, race, color, religion, or national origin

Procedures for terminating an employee may also fall under the jurisdiction of union contracts. The Labor Management Relations (Taft-Hartley) Act of 1947, which is an amendment to the National Labor Relations (Wagner) Act, is the primary legislation to be considered in dealing with employees in unionized firms.

Working Conditions

In addition to the Civil Rights Act, retailers are also subject to laws regulating working hours, minimum wage, child labor, and worker safety and protection.

WORKING HOURS   The **Fair Labor Standards Act** (FLSA) of 1938 set forth guidelines establishing the 40-hour work week. Under this law, any employee working more than 40 hours in one week is entitled to overtime pay.

COMPENSATION   Most retailers are subject to federal minimum wage laws in compensating hourly employees, according to the Fair Labor Standards Act of 1938. The law also requires that employers must pay overtime to all employees who work more than 40 hours a week. However, certain employees (managers, technical workers, professionals) are exempt from this requirement. The act also does not apply to some small businesses. The recent increase in the minimum wage has significantly increased personnel expenses for many retailers, calling attention to the need for more effective hiring practices and increased employee productivity.

Some state laws also require compensation in the form of disability and accident insurance or unemployment compensation. Wages for union employees are determined according to a contractual arrangement between the retailer and the union for various job categories. The legal and regulatory aspects of compensation are discussed further in Chapter 11.

CHILD LABOR   The FLSA regulates the usage of child labor. Guidelines have been established to dictate the age at which a child can work, the type

Exhibit 7–7
Common Legal Questions Facing Retailers: Some Examples

Question	Related Legislation
What if a customer/employee falls on a slick floor that is still wet after mopping?	Liability laws
What if a child or adult gets caught in the escalator?	Public safety regulations
What is the retailer's responsibility, if any, when a manufacturer fails to honor a product warranty to a customer's satisfaction?	Product warranty laws Product liability laws
What if merchandise inventory on hand for an advertised special is insufficient to satisfy consumer demand for the item?	Bait and switch Merchandise availability
How much can prices be reduced to counter a competitor's aggressive pricing tactics without being in violation of the law?	Pricing legislation

of job a child can hold, the hours a child can work, and whether the amount paid to a child can deviate from that paid to others for doing the same job. In spite of this legal protection, stories about "sweatshops" that hire children to work at low wages appear in the nation's newspapers and television programs. While retailers may not be as apt to hire children, they may be buying and selling goods that were produced by children, possibly implying an ethical responsibility.

SAFETY   Worker safety is regulated under the Organizational Safety and Health Act. This legislation established the **Organizational Safety and Health Administration (OSHA).** The Act requires that employers provide a hazard-free work environment, and provides guidelines for this purpose. Penalties of up to $1,000 per day for each serious violation, plus additional optional penalties, may be assessed against employers.

Local Laws

In addition to federal and state laws, retailers are subject to a number of local laws and ordinances. These regulations include zoning, building standards, hours of operation, product line limitations, and other factors.

Local zoning ordinances are of particular concern to retailers, since they restrict the usage of property. For example, a retailer may have identified a perfect retail location, but will not be able to open a store on that property if it is not zoned for commercial use. A car dealership on the fringe of a residential neighborhood may want to expand its service area, but local zoning ordinances will not permit this expansion (even if the property is for sale). These examples illustrate the importance of knowing the restrictions imposed by zoning ordinances before proceeding with any plans for new locations or expansion of existing facilities.

Some communities have blue laws, statutes that prohibit or restrict various activities on Sunday. Entertainment, work, and selling activities are regulated under blue laws, which originated in colonial New England for religious reasons. However, the constitutionality of blue laws has been challenged in many communities because of the needs and desires of a diverse population.

In the absence of considerable federal regulation of retail practices from 1976 to 1986, many state, county, and local governments established formal guidelines for a variety of retailing practices. Examples of everyday legal issues and concerns that confront retailers are listed in Exhibit 7–7. Corresponding legislation related to each issue is included.

Controlling the Regulatory Environment

Most aspects of the regulatory environment are beyond the direct control of a retail firm. However, political influence can be exerted by industry or other

Fair Labor Standards Act
legislation passed in 1938 setting guidelines for overtime pay and the 40-hour week

Organizational Safety and Health Administration (OSHA)
monitors and enforces regulations of the Organization Safety and Health Act

The Paradox of Social Responsibility

Retailers have close ties to their communities. Retailers may follow the "letter of the law," believing they are being responsible and ethical. However, the public may take a different view, as illustrated in the following scenarios.

Fast-food chains are a major force in inner-city ghettos, providing affordable food and jobs for low-income residents. In some cases, they are even a surrogate for a home life, or even status (i.e., having enough money to eat at McDonald's before the welfare check comes). The heavy consumption of fast-food fare that is high in fat, sodium, and sugar by low-income, undereducated Americans has been criticized as a significant factor in poor nutrition and health problems. (Freedman, 1990)

Save the earth—a timely theme for retailers. Target, a division of Dayton-Hudson Corp., introduced the nation to "Kids for Saving Earth" on Earth Day in April 1990. This is a nonprofit organization that educates children about the environment and helps them take action. Target's international sponsorship of the group is but one aspect of its involvement in environmental programs. ("Save the Earth . . .," 1990)

Cloth diapers have been applauded by environmentalists because disposables are piling up in landfills. However, Kinder-Care Learning Centers and other child care facilities continue to favor disposable diapers because they can be dealt with more sanitarily. This position is supported by the American Academy of Pediatrics and the American Public Health Association. (Paul, 1990)

The U. S. Justice Department and the Consumer Product Safety Commission sued seven major toy distributors (and their chief executives) for selling imported toys the government considered hazardous. Most of the product labels recommended the toys for children over three but their design seemed intended for young children, a violation of federal health and safety standards. Several retailers voluntarily recalled certain products, even though Toys'R'Us and others said the suit was without merit. ("Seven Distributors Sued . . .," 1990)

The Dayton Hudson Foundation stopped its 22-year support of Planned Parenthood in response to complaints by anti-abortionists. Pro-choice supporters responded by boycotting Dayton's stores. The company subsequently reversed the decision. The controversy continues as a major retailer has unwittingly become involved in the national abortion rights debate. (Kelly, 1990)

Southland Corporation, parent of 7-Eleven Convenience Stores, decided to ban the sale of *Playboy, Penthouse,* and *Forum* magazines. The company felt it would be better positioned to serve the neighborhoods where it does business. (Winkleman, 1987)

Freedman, Alix M. (1990), "Fast-Food Chains Play Central Role in Diet of the Inner-City Poor," *The Wall Street Journal* (December 19), A1, A6.

Kelly, Kevin (1990), "Dayton Hudson Finds There's No Graceful Way to Flip-Flop," *Business Week* (September 24), 50.

Paul, Bill (1990), "Day Care Centers Environment: Stick with Disposables," *The Wall Street Journal* (May 17), B1.

"Save the Earth: Retailing and the Environment" (1990), *Retail Register,* Illinois Retail Merchants Association, no. 82, (May 14), 1.

"Seven Distributors Sued for Selling Toys U.S. Considers Unsafe: (1990), *The Wall Street Journal* (August 21), B4.

Winkleman, Michael (1987), "Not Just Skin Deep," *Public Relations Journal* 43 no. 1 (January), 18–21.

groups to have an indirect effect on the legislative process. Two of these influences are Political Action Committees (PACs) and lobbying efforts.

Political Action Committees (PACs)

Trade associations and retail firms may organize **political action committees**. They are supported by funds from various organizations and individuals to help elect (or defeat) political candidates and to exert whatever pressure possible to encourage the passage or defeat of legislation.

Action taken by loggers in Washington state against Burger King demonstrates the strength of even a loosely organized coalition of consumers. The loggers staged an angry boycott of Burger King because the fast-food chain was serving salad dressing made by actor Paul Newman's company. The loggers objected to a controversial television documentary, "Ancient Rain Forests: Rage Over Trees," produced by the National Audobon Society to chronicle the disappearance of the old-growth forests of the Northwest. The loggers felt that the documentary made it look like the loggers did not care about the earth and objected to Newman's environmentalist position.

Environmentalists have also used boycotts. For instance, they boycotted fast-food chains for using styrofoam containers and serving beef raised in areas where tropical rain forests have been cleared. Actions such as these present dilemmas for retailers. In the case of Burger King's use of Newman's dressing, all the profits from his company go to charity—a boycott could harm programs assisting those in need ("Loggers Making Beef . . . ," 1990).

Lobbying Efforts

Many retail firms and industries engage in lobbying efforts in Washington in an attempt to control legislation that is either favorable or unfavorable to retailers. In the late 1970s, the FTC ruled that the soft drink industry violated antitrust laws by granting exclusive sales territories to distributors. This practice constrained the retailer's options in choosing a distributor for a particular brand of soft drink. The soft drink industry launched a well-financed lobbying effort at proposed legislation that would excuse the industry from engaging in competition between producers of the same brand of soft drink. The campaign was conducted by professional lobbyists and bottling company executives, and directed toward members of the Senate and the House. Over a million dollars was collected and spent for receptions, fees for expert testimony, and support of certain political candidates (Zuckerman, 1981).

Ethics and Social Responsibility

Ethical Standards and Business Conduct

"Business Ethics: An Oxymoron?" is the thought-provoking title of a *New York Times* News Service press release (Fowler, 1987). An oxymoron is a figure of speech that combines contradictory ideas and, in the minds of many, business and ethics are not compatible terms. Part of the debate also centers on whether a business can have an "ethic," or whether we are really dealing with personal ethics. Whatever the definition, public attention to ethics in business is growing. Since retailers are the most visible link between a vast array of businesses and the final consumer, at this point it seems appropriate to discuss a more subtle type of regulation that goes beyond the letter of the law.

Ethical Attitudes of Store Managers

A 1986 study indicated that the ethical attitudes of today's store managers are more consumer-oriented in their perceptions of what constitutes an ethical

POLITICAL ACTION COMMITTEE
groups organized to influence the outcome of pending legislation and the election of public officials

practice than those of a decade ago (Gifford and Norris, 1987). These attitudes are expected to result in ethical actions, with the changes likely attributed to the regulatory environment and the profit motive. The profit motive is served by loyal customers who make repeat purchases and are satisfied in all aspects of their dealings with the retailer.

A related study compared retail store managers' and retail students' perceptions of ethical retail practices (Norris and Gifford, 1988). A significant increase was found in the ethics of store managers, as noted above. However, student perceptions of what they considered to be ethical behavior changed very little over a 10-year period, widening the ethical gap between the two groups. Since these students represent the managers of the future, this finding may have serious implications.

Ethical Behavior of Employees

While the focus of ethics in business is generally on managers' behavior toward employees and customers, the responsibility works both ways. Retail employees at all levels are expected to behave in an ethical manner. Some examples include honest dealings between sales associates and customers, not falsifying time records or excuses given for absences, or stealing from an employer. Supervisors should be fair and accurate in evaluation of their staff, and in representations of their own efforts to upper management. Such ethical considerations as company loyalty and nonacceptance of gifts have particular importance for buyers. The acceptance of inexpensive gifts, free meals, or theater tickets may cause buyers to make unwise purchase decisions because they feel a subconscious obligation to manufacturers or other suppliers.

Framework for Understanding Ethical Decisions

Retail managers are responsible for making many decisions that have ethical implications. Although there are no "black and white" guidelines for choosing alternatives in these situations, managers may be held accountable for the consequences. Several oversimplified maxims for ethical behavior range from the golden rule (act in the way you would expect others to act toward you), to the TV test (Would I feel comfortable explaining to a national TV audience why I took this action?). A more complete explanation of ethical decisions is found in several theoretical frameworks (Laczniak, 1983). (See Exhibit 7–8.) Although an extensive discussion of these frameworks is beyond the scope of this book, they are introduced briefly within a retailing context:

1. The **Prima Facie Duties** Framework—self-evident moral obligations, what people *ought to do*, including:
   a. Duties of fidelity—keeping promises, honoring contracts, telling the truth, etc. (honoring warranties, refraining from deceptive advertising)
   b. Duties of gratitude—special obligations between friends, relatives, partners, customers and business, etc. (special consideration for a valued supplier or customer who is experiencing temporary difficulty)
   c. Duties of justice—distribution of rewards based on merit (not discriminating against all customers in a ghetto store because of a few shoplifters or troublemakers)

Exhibit 7–8
Framework for Understanding Ethical Decisions
....

1. Prima Facie Duties Framework
- Duties of fidelity
- Duties of gratitude
- Duties of justice
- Duties of beneficence
- Duties of self-improvement
- Duties of nonmaleficence

2. Proportionality Framework
- Intentions
- Means
- Ends

3. Social Justice Framework
- Liberty principle
- Difference principle
- Duties of self-improvement
- Duties of nonmaleficence

d. Duties of beneficence—take actions that improve the intelligence, happiness, or virtue of others (support human rights through business decisions)

e. Duties of self improvement—take actions that improve your own intelligence, happiness, or virtue (improve your unit's financial performance since it may lead to pay increases and promotion)

f. Duties of nonmaleficence (noninjury)—take actions not to injure others (ensure product safety, consumer information)

2. The **Proportionality** Framework—ethical decisions that focus on the actions themselves, rather than the consequences of the actions. In other words, the ends should not justify the means. For example, high profits should not be achieved by deceiving customers or taking advantage of employees. These ethical decisions consist of the following components:

a. Intentions—motivation behind one's actions

b. Means—method used to carry out one's intentions

c. Ends—outcomes, results, or consequences of one's actions

3. The **Social Justice** Framework—assumes no knowledge of social status, education, abilities, etc., in advance, resulting in an ideal system of justice. There are two principles of justice:

a. **Liberty** principle—everyone has the right to determine his or her own destiny and to always be treated equitably by others, including equal opportunity employment and consumer rights

b. **Difference** principle—emphasis on not exploiting one group for the benefit of others or not taking advantage of social and economic inequalities, by such methods as "dumping" unsafe products in less developed countries, underpaying illegal aliens, overcharging ghetto customers

Applied Ethics and the Marketing Mix: Some Examples

In this section, a few ethical situations are presented in which managers have had to make decisions that go beyond strict legal interpretation. (See

PRIMA FACIE DUTIES
framework based on self-evident moral obligations

PROPORTIONALITY
framework based on ethical decisions that focus on intentions, means, and ends

SOCIAL JUSTICE
framework based on ideal system of justice that assumes no knowledge of social status, education, abilities, etc.

While retailers are working to change it, the image of the "sleazy" salesperson remains in the memories of many consumers.

Exhibit 7–9.) Often, these decisions add to the retailer's expenses and may hurt short-term profits. Look for the trade-offs in the following examples.

ETHICS AND PRICING   Pricing decisions are responsible for many ethical quandaries. Some of the ethical issues related to retail pricing are:

1. Setting a price that meets the company's profit objectives, while being fair to consumers
2. Changing the quality or quantity of merchandise without changing price
3. Using psychological pricing (intending the consumer will perceive $3.99 as $3.00)
4. Taking excessive markups on products that are given as premiums
5. Engaging in price fixing
6. Suppliers giving less competitive prices or terms of sale to retail buyers who use the firm as their only source of supply
7. Retailers or suppliers using their size or economic power to gain unfair advantage in price negotiations
8. Using special price codes so customers cannot tell the real price
9. Not putting the price on the product or at the point of purchase, as with UPCs
10. Retailers' failure to pass on to consumers discounts to which they are entitled (adapted from Kehoe, 1985).

Exhibit 7–9
Ethics and the Marketing Mix

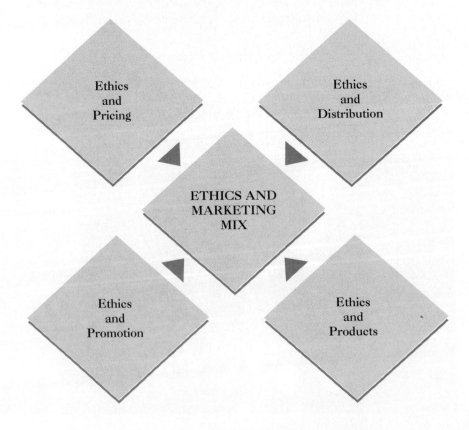

Sometimes the regulatory process backfires, as in the case of Kroger Company's shift from a high-priced "quality" chain to an aggressive price leader in 1972. It targeted its lowest price competitors in major markets and established internal surveys to monitor compliance within its stores. The strategy was successful, profits rose sharply, and Kroger moved past A&P to the number two food chain, behind Safeway. Customers were given considerable price savings.

The problem arose when the FTC took exception to the company's highly promoted advertising campaign called "price patrol." Local checkers made weekly comparisons of about 150 brandname products sold by major competitors, so that Kroger could maintain its low-cost leadership. The FTC took exception because the price comparisons did not include private label goods, meats, fresh fruits and vegetables, which accounted for about half of Kroger's sales. Who was right in this situation? Kroger was highly competitive in its prices, the price patrol made an honest effort to make comparisons, price comparisons were posted in stores for public viewing (even for items where Kroger "lost"), and customers benefited. The FTC argued that Kroger did not have a "reasonable basis" for its advertising claim, although the FTC staff itself was unable to devise a workable random sample for food price comparisons because of quality differences (Samuelson, 1979).

A number of studies of ghetto shopping conditions suggest that the phrase, "the poor pay more," is a reality. This is partly due to the number of mom-and-pop stores in disadvantaged neighborhoods. These retailers do not have the economies of scale of the larger chains, nor the management expertise. Therefore, their customers pay higher prices for lower quality merchandise, often in substandard stores. Other problems arise from high pressure and unethical merchants who take advantage of ghetto shoppers, using deceptive credit arrangements, bait and switch advertising, and other unscrupulous methods. Higher prices in these neighborhoods are often defended on the basis of a higher cost of operating the business, because of high crime rates and insurance rates.

Hertz Corp. admitted overcharging customers and insurers $13 million for repairs, in spite of the company's ethics code, which employees agree to uphold. An internal audit identified the national accidents control manager as the probable culprit. This manager and 18 other employees were fired, and control was centralized. About 80 percent of the $13 million resulted from charging the retail cost (rather than the actual discounted cost) of fixing cars from 1978 to 1985, a practice approved by senior management. The company now charges the actual repair costs ("Hertz Is Doing . . . ," 1988).

ETHICS AND PROMOTION Many of the legal aspects of promotion discussed earlier in the chapter have ethical implications, as well. Deception is difficult to define and to prove, since it is based to a large extent on the percentage of the audience that is deceived.

The travel industry has engaged in many promotional schemes, which have escalated since deregulation of the airlines industry. Frequent flyer programs have experienced abuses by companies and customers alike. One of the latest ethical issues concerns travel agents who compete for prizes by booking clients with a contest's sponsor. Contest prizes include $125,000 in a National Car Rental sweepstakes, Cracker Jack boxes with gold jewelry from

Alamo Rent A Car Inc., free maid service from Hertz Corp., and European vacations from Avis Inc. The more clients that are booked, the better the chances of winning the prize. These contests were a great marketing success. Over 16 weeks, Hertz alone had over one million entries in its sweepstakes.

Air carriers, cruise lines, and limousine services have launched similar contests. The question is, are these promotions in the best interests of travelers? Promotional expenses are eventually borne by the traveler, and the agent may be tempted to steer customers in the wrong direction. On the other hand, professional travel agents are trained to work for the best interests of their customers, which might be the option that leads to a bonus or prize. Some feel that agents should disclose their commissions and incentives (Rose, 1988).

Promotional tie-ins between retailers or credit card companies and charities also have raised some concerns. For example, the message might read, "If you charge a purchase on your account between May 1 and July 1, 1992, 1 percent of your total will be donated to the National Society for. . . ." The question arises as to who really benefits from this type of promotion.

Misleading the customer has become a prevalent practice in the electronics industry. Verbal games are being played with so many electronics products that the industry is in danger of losing credibility with its customers. Examples include the following:

- The stereo compatible television that is actually a monaural television and needs a decoder at an additional price if it is to be converted to a stereo television.
- Advertisements for the stereo video cassette recorder without built-in MTS or hi-fi sound.
- The 100-watt stereo rack system, which (in fine print) delivers 50 watts per channel, using perverse mathematics to call itself a 100-watt system.

A large part of this problem is attributed to deep discounting and drastic price competition in the industry.

An exception is Dayton Hudson's Target discount division, which uses an everyday low price strategy, and does not mark merchandise down again for sales other than bonafide clearances. This policy has given Target price credibility among customers and helped the company avoid questionable promotional practices followed by other retailers (Gallagher, 1986).

ETHICS AND PRODUCTS   Many ethical issues arise in decisions about merchandise assortments. Some of the most difficult decisions are related to legal products sold under legal conditions, but perhaps not in the best interest of the retailer's target market. One of the most familiar examples to college students is serving alcohol to underage drinkers. The retailer makes more sales, profits are higher, customers are happy, and the exception is breaking a local or state law, which "everyone" does anyway, the conditions seem favorable for this decision. Right? Wrong?

A similar controversy arose over Chelsea, a soft drink beverage that was promoted as an adult alternative to alcoholic beverages. Chelsea contained about one-half of one percent of naturally fermented alcohol. Alcohol control

UPI/BETTMANN

A bookstore manager is interviewed by New York City police after receiving bomb threats for selling the controversial book The Satanic Verses, *by Salman Rushdie.*

boards and the FDA ruled that the product fit the definitions of a soft drink. Anheuser-Busch packaged and promoted the product to reinforce its "Cadillac" image of a natural, adult product. Socially concerned individuals and organizations condemned Chelsea as a contributor to alcohol abuse, and pressured stores to remove it from their shelves. The problem was that, as a soft drink, Chelsea could be purchased by children although it was targeted to adults. Critics argued that children did not need a socially acceptable substitute for alcohol.

Anheuser-Busch realized that action had to be taken, and demonstrated that it valued social responsibility more than profits. Five weeks after starting the test market, it stopped all manufacture and promotion of Chelsea, and began a social screening process. The first task was to identify the social issue: the social conditioning of young children toward alcohol consumption. Consumers were involved in the discussion and decision in order to make changes that would meet with public approval. This was a win-win situation. Chelsea critics were able to influence the marketing practices of a major corporation in their favor. Anheuser-Busch ended up with a product more suited to consumer needs than the original product. Consumers benefitted from democracy in the marketplace—without government intervention (Jones, 1981).

The largest bookselling chains in the U.S. pulled Salman Rushdie's book, *Satanic Verses*, from their shelves after the Iranian government called for the execution of the author and publishers, following claims that the book was blasphemous ("Satanic Times . . . , 1989). Do consumers have a right to buy this book? Likewise, a Florida retailer was arrested for selling CDs of rap records with questionable offensive lyrics—even though the CDs were on the market legally.

Consumer Reports labeled Suzuki Motor Co.'s Samurai as unacceptable because the off-road vehicle tended to tip over in driving tests. Safety rules for cars and light trucks do not apply to off-road vehicles, pickups, and vans, because they are not intended for use as passenger cars. However, common safety standards for cars and any vehicles used as cars are expected soon (Treece, 1988). Should retailers stock and sell the Samurai?

Entrepreneurs are offering products and services that give customers a false sense of security about AIDS. These include membership cards, good for discounts at local stores, for members of Peace of Mind who test negative for the disease. This Michigan social club charges $349 a year for such membership privileges. Other products range from Sani-Phone protective mouthpieces for telephones to a proliferation of books on AIDS to home diagnostic kits (Yandel, 1987). Are these businesses taking advantage of the public's fear of a dreaded disease?

"Thunderchicken" is the name given to Ernest & Julio Gallo's Thunderbird wine by street alcoholics who can buy the dollar-a-pint wine made with cheap ingredients, fortified with 18 to 21 percent alcohol in certain liquor stores across the country. Cheap, fortified wines of this type are not sold in many liquor stores other than those in low-income neighborhoods. However, the major producers of these wines see their customers differently—some as lower middle class and low-income blue-collar workers, or retired and older folks (Freedman, 1988). If the market is street alcoholics and down-and-out poor and homeless, the retailer may be facing an ethical decision. The sale of Everclear, the 200 proof alcohol, to teenagers and college students poses another ethical dilemma, because its use could result in death.

On a lighter note, but still a serious ethical dilemma, a rumor was started that McDonald's Corporation was putting ground-up red earthworms in its hamburger meat. At first, this was somewhat amusing to managers, but headquarters was asked to take action when it began to hurt business in 40 to 50 McDonald's in the Atlanta area. The rumor was spreading to other hamburger outlets as well, so the notion of a smear campaign started by competition could be rejected. Although the rumor was thought to have started in Chattanooga in May 1978, it was November when most of the inquiries were received by people who said, erroneously, they had seen a report on "60 Minutes" or "20/20." The source of the rumor was never determined, and McDonald's launched an ad campaign featuring former network newscaster, Frank Blair, who gave a testimony to the fact that McDonald's hamburgers were 100 percent beef—without mentioning the rumor ("Rumors of Worms . . . , 1978).

Social Responsibility

The American public has taken on a watchdog role in pressuring business managers to be more socially responsible. Many businesses have taken on this role voluntarily through active involvement in education programs, assistance to the disadvantaged, and going well beyond what is absolutely required by law in fair treatment of customers, employees, and others.

Social initiatives cost money, perhaps diminishing financial resources needed for operating expenses. Retailers have found over time, however, that also being a responsible member of society pays off in improved corporate image and profitability. There are many examples of responsible retailers and their suppliers; a few are described here to illustrate the broad spectrum of activities that might be considered.

The May Company provides space for the San Diego Children's Museum as a public service in its LaJolla, California shopping center. Wal-Mart, Fred Meyer, and others make special shopping carts available for handicapped customers. The local pizza restaurant sponsors a Little League baseball team. A retailer provides restructured credit arrangements to customers who are behind in their payments in a troubled economy. Food stores contribute safe but unsaleable food products to local food banks.

True, these decisions have promotional value, but an important segment of the population benefits from the retailer's generosity. Environmentalism and other social responsibility issues also offer merchandising opportunities to retailers. To illustrate, a June 1990 Retail Merchants Association newsletter advised retailers to "find out how local communities are going to handle yard waste disposal programs to determine which products might quickly become in greater demand." This was in response to a new law banning the landfilling of landscape waste (grass and tree clippings) that previously had been discarded along with other household trash. The Department of Energy and Natural Resources had reported that communities were showing a preference for degradable bags, as opposed to rigid containers, for collecting materials ("Lawn Waste Ban . . . , 1990). This may be interpreted as responsible or opportunistic. Either way, the customer, community, and retailer all benefit.

Giant Foods, Inc., has enjoyed excellent community relations, even during the heydays of the consumerism movement of the 1960s. During the 1968 Poor People's March on Washington, Giant Foods and others fed the

In one year over 40 people—many of them children—died in fires in Memphis. This prompted Walgreens to distribute fire prevention literature, offer applications to residents for free smoke detectors, and to initiate a fire safety slogan contest for children.

COURTESY OF WALGREEN CO.

3,000 demonstrators camping on the capitol mall in "Resurrection City." Later, Giant Foods was spared the fate of many retailers during the riots that followed the assassination of Dr. Martin Luther King, Jr. The company was also excluded from a 14-city boycott to protest minority hiring practices during the Operation Bread Basket movement.

As further evidence of its committment to the consuming public, Giant Foods hired Esther Peterson, former White House Special Assistant for Consumer Affairs, as vice president of consumer affairs for the grocery chain. She later developed Giant's version of Kennedy's (1962) Consumer Bill of Rights: the right to safety; the right to be informed; the right to be heard; the right to choose; and the right to redress. Implementation of the program included better point-of-purchase information, educational advertising, nutritional labeling, quick and individualized responses to customer complaints, and unconditional money-back guarantees on all products. These extras reduced Giant's return on equity, but improved the company's image and customer loyalty (Burke and Berry, 1974–1975); "Joseph B. Danzansky . . . , 1974). Again, the trade-offs are there.

Or consider Smart Start, an educational program for four-year-olds, sponsored by the U.S. government and supported by CEOs of major corporations. Business leaders, from firms such as Stride Rite, Goodyear Tire & Rubber, Pittway, Time Inc., and General Electric, have decided that investing in the nation's children is a sound business practice. Over a five-year period, Smart Start would offer $4 billion in federal matching funds to states that provide comprehensive preschool programs, including federally funded Head Start centers. One of the executives observed that his company and the country could not maintain a leadership position with a workforce with an education that limits them to mopping floors (Lieblich, 1989). This is a long term strategy for these companies and for the retailers who sell their products. Is the cost worth it in the short run? All else being equal, should retail buyers place orders with suppliers who demonstrate social responsibility versus those who do not?

A 1987 New Year's Eve celebration at the Dupont Plaza Hotel in San Juan, Puerto Rico ended in tragedy when a fire killed 96 people and injured more than 100 employees and guests. The fire was caused by arson, resulting from intense and hostile labor negotiations between the local Teamsters union and hotel management. Lawsuits against the hotel and its owners contain allegations of negligence. The charges were made because the hotel had received threats of a fire on that date related to the labor dispute, permitted the highly agitated Teamsters to meet in the hotel ballroom (where the fire started), locked doors to the casino and at different floor levels in an effort to maintain security (apparently without realizing that they were creating a death trap), permitted storage of highly flammable furniture wrapped in a volatile plastic material without adequate safeguards for fire protection, and other actions that were considered irresponsible (Tarnoff, 1987). Could this disaster have been prevented, and at what cost?

Giant Foods has awarded over 30,000 free computers and related equipment to schools in their "Apples for the Students" program.

Public Concerns and Corporate Cultures

In a 1989 *Business Week*–Harris Poll, Americans reported that they still have deep misgivings about business ethics ("The Public Is Willing . . . ," 1989).

Many believe that companies would sacrifice the environment, safety, or health for the sake of bigger profits. Sixty-two percent believe business would engage in price gouging. Many also would take action to stop companies from doing something they did not agree with, ranging from a boycott of the company's products (76 percent) to sabotaging its operations (2 percent). Proving that action speaks louder than words, over one-third of the public has already engaged in some type of protest over a company's actions. They plan to continue to do so, based on the belief that public activism by ordinary people can change corporate behavior. Those responding to the poll also agreed that American business deserved most of the credit for the prosperity of the 1980s, but that it had gained too much power over too many aspects of American life and had benefited more than consumers from government deregulation.

How can retailers prosper in an environment where consumers are predisposed to have negative attitudes toward business? Some believe that the answer lies in a company's corporate culture, and in moral and ethical behavior which starts with top executives. Retailers may, or may not, be aware of their "corporate culture," but however it is defined, it can represent ethical and socially responsible behavior that begins at the top. Some successful examples are found in Wal-Mart's friendly clerks and cashiers, Nordstrom's attitude toward keeping customers happy and no questions asked, Dayton Hudson Corporation's management book, *Management Prospectives,* which clearly communicates its culture to employees, and major changes in Montgomery Ward's corporate culture made by Bernard Brennan when he took over as chairman in 1985 (Bivens, 1989).

Most business executives believe that the rhetoric of business ethics exceeds the reality for most companies and that business ethics are either the same or lower than ten years ago. They also believe that, in general, good ethics is good business ("Ethics Are Good Business . . . , 1987). Conversely, a damaged corporate image can have far-reaching repercussions. An example is found in Benetton's attempt to sell around $150 million in company stock on the New York Stock Exchange. In spite of the company's financial successes, its corporate image has been sullied by legal actions and an FTC investigation in the United States, and the defection of many senior managers in Italy (Rossant and Dunkin, 1989). This has created an uphill battle in obtaining investor confidence, and attracting funds to the company.

Often the issues are not clear cut, and retail managers must make decisions within an uncertain environment. For example, furriers have been besieged by animal activists who protest the slaughter of animals to be used for clothing items. Fur manufacturers and retailers have been picketed and their customers have been attacked and cans of paint have been dumped on their coats. Likewise, McDonald's has been the brunt of environmentalists who have protested the use of styrofoam packaging by the fast-food chain. McDonald's has begun to take measures to encourage recycling and encourage the public to protect the environment, and recently switched from foam to paper packaging in U.S. restaurants. Pictured on the following page is an "environmental" placemat used by McDonald's.

Tom Haggai, president and CEO of IGA (fourth largest U.S. supermarket chain), expects the supermarkets' employees to use common sense and behave morally. Thus, he has rejected the idea of drafting a formal code of ethics, because it implies you have a reason to question a person's behavior.

AP/WIDE WORLD

Public pressure is applied to manufacturers and retailers alike through boycotting and protests, such as the Animal Rights Activitsts' stance against the slaughter of animals for fur.

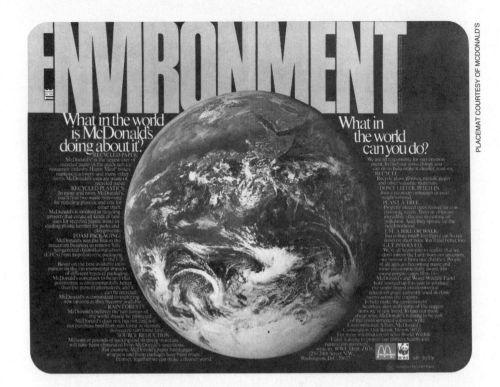

McDonald's placemats not only emphasize their own role in environmental responsibility, but also offer suggestions to the consuming public.

This executive believes that ethical behavior is giving the most quality possible in every situation, that quality is a sense of integrity, and that a sense of worth goes beyond merely doing what is legal. Haggai's philosophy is further manifested in his belief that retailers within an industry can decide together how to best serve the public without turning to the government for help (Weinstein, 1988). Thus, individuals and companies can make a difference.

Summary

Retailers operate in a regulated environment, where legal and social influences place constraints on management decisions and operating methods. Regulatory and ethical considerations are an integral part of the strategic planning process, and interact with other external and internal environmental factors to affect retailing results.

Federal, state, and local laws affect company growth and competition, the marketing mix, and human resources. Federal laws regulating company growth and competition include the Sherman Antitrust Act, Clayton Act, Federal Trade Commission Act, and Wheeler-Lea Act.

Regulatory constraints affect all aspects of the marketing mix. Product-related regulations concern product warranties and product liability. Promotion-related regulations concern bait and switch advertising, price-off promotions, merchandise availability, deceptive advertising, and advertising substantiation. Price-related regulations involve both protection and constraints in addition to resale price maintenance and other pricing violations.

Distribution-related regulations include reciprocal dealings, tying contracts, exclusive dealings, and others.

Human resource management is affected by regulation aimed at prevention of discrimination in hiring and discharging employees and at safe working conditions. Local laws and ordinances include zoning, building standards, hours of operation, product line limitations, and other factors.

The regulatory environment has been controlled to some extent by Political Action Committees (PACs) and lobbying efforts by individuals, groups, and industries.

Retail managers are also held accountable for decisions that go beyond the letter of the law, such as ethical behavior and social responsibility. Ethical behavior of business managers has gained importance to the American public, creating a need for retail managers to be aware of the far-reaching effects of this sometimes nebulous influence. Each aspect of the marketing mix is subject to criticism on the grounds of unethical practices. On the other hand, companies have increased customer loyalty and profitability by establishing ethical standards for business conduct, and making socially responsible decisions.

The Coca-Cola Company uses recycled plastic bottles in response to environmental concerns over the disposal of plastic, a trend which many retail consumers appreciate.

Questions for Review and Comprehension

1. Discuss the relationship between regulatory constraints and the strategic planning process. How might the retailer's strategic plan be affected by ethical considerations?

2. Name the key federal legislation passed for the purpose of regulating competition and growth. How has each of these regulations affected one or more components of the retail mix?

3. Describe local laws, ordinances or codes that affect retailing activities in the town or city where you live. What is their purpose, and who are they intended to protect? Are they enforced, and if so, how?

4. If you were really upset about present or impeding legislation that would affect your retail business, how could you influence its outcome and exert more control over the regulatory environment?

5. Name at least one current ethical or social responsibility issue and explain how it might affect marketing strategy decisions relative to each aspect of the retail mix: merchandise assortments, pricing, promotion, store location or nonstore selling, and customer service.

6. Consult personal or published sources to determine whether a particular retail firm has a written ethical code for its managers and employees, whether it is enforced, and how it is enforced. Obtain a copy of the ethical code, if possible, and critique it.

7. Discuss the argument that if a manufacturer provides a product warranty or guarantee, then the retailer does not have to worry about customer complaints or problems with that product.

8. Based on a review of recent business media, determine specific cases of discriminatory practices and poor working conditions that can have an impact on retail personnel. Suggest some ways that these problems might be overcome without requiring additional legislation or court actions.

References

"Acne Treatment Dispute Goes to NARB" (1986), *Advertising Age* (January 20), 12.

Agins, Teri (1988), "Handshake Deals: Benetton Is Accused of Dubious Tactics By Some Store Owners," *The Wall Street Journal* (October 24), 1, A4.

Bennett, Stephen (1990), "The View From the Hill," *Progressive Grocer* (February), 110.

Bivens, Jackie (1989), "Corporate Cultures" *Stores* (February), 9–15.

Burke, Marion C. and Leonard L. Berry (1975), "Do Social Actions of a Corporation Influence Store Image and Profits?" *Journal of Retailing* (Winter 1974–1975), 63.

"Civil Justice: F. Lee Bailey vs. Bill Bailey" (1990), *Insurance Review* 51, no. 1, (January), 20–23.

Colford, Steven W. (1984), "M.D.s Move to Halt Kellogg Health Ads," *Advertising Age* (November 1), 1, 58.

Collins, Linda J. (1987), "Toy Maker Settles Suit for $2.25 Million", *Business Insurance*, (June 15), 1, 42.

Corley, R. N. and O. C. Reed (1987), *The Legal Environment of Business*, 7th ed., New York: McGraw-Hill Book Company.

Cortes-Comrer, Nhora (1988), "Defensive Designing: On Guard Against the Bizarre," *Mechanical Engineering* 110, no. 8 (August), 40–42.

Davis, Bob (1987), "U.S. Orders Bell Companies to Suspend Advertising of Telephone Credit Cards," *The Wall Street Journal* (June 10), 40.

"Ethics Are Good Business, But Not Always Practiced" (1987), *New York Times News Service* (August 24).

Fanning, Deirdre (1988), "What Makes A Lemon," *Forbes* (January 25), 86.

"Fear of Lawsuits Stymies U.S. Innovation, Execs Say," (1988), *Automotive News* (January 15), 58.

Fitzgerald, Kate (1988), "Sears Low-Price Strategy Runs into Hot Ad Issue," *Advertising Age* (November 21), 58.

Fowler, Elizabeth M. (1987), "Business Ethics: An Oxymoron?" *New York Times News Service* (August 17).

Freedman, Alix M. (1988), "Winos and Thunderbird Are a Subject Gallo Doesn't Like to Discuss," *The Wall Street Journal* (February 25), 1, 9.

Gallagher, Rick (1986), "Misleading the Customer," *Chain Store Age* (April), 24.

Gifford, John H. and Donald G. Norris (1987), "Research Note: Ethical Attitudes of Retail Store Managers: A Longitudinal Analysis," *Journal of Retailing* 63, no. 3 (Fall), 298–311.

"Hertz Is Doing Some Body Work—On Itself," (1988), *Business Week* (February 15), 57.

Holley, W. H. and K. M. Jennings (1983), *Personnel Management Functions and Issues*. Chicago, Ill.: The Dryden Press.

Huber, Peter (1989), "Litigation Thwarts Innovation in the U.S.," *Scientific American* (March), 120.

Jones, Keith M. (1981), "Chelsea, The Adult Soft Drink: A Case Study of Corporate Social Responsibility," in Roy D. Adler, Larry M. Robinson and Jan E. Carlson, eds., *Marketing and Society: Cases and Commentaries*. Englewood Cliffs, N.J.: Prentice-Hall, Inc.

"Joseph B. Danzansky of Giant Foods: Consumerism as a Competitive Tool," (1974), *Nation's Business* (October), 53.

Kehoe, William J. (1985), "Ethics, Price Fixing, and the Management of Price Strategy," in *Marketing Ethics: Guidelines for Managers*. Laczniak, Gene R. and Patrick E. Murphy, eds.,Lexington, Mass.: Lexington Books.

Laczniak, Gene R. (1983), "Framework for Analyzing Marketing Ethics," *Journal of Macromarketing* 3 (Spring), 7–18.

Langley, Monica (1988), "FTC Accuses Six Large Book Publishers of Bias Against Independent Stores," *Wall Street Journal* (December 23), B4.

"Lawn Waste Ban Effective July 1st," (1990), *Retail Register*, Illinois Retail Merchants Association, no. 83 (June 1), 1–2.

Lawrence, Jennifer (1988), "State Ad Rules Face Showdown," *Advertising Age* (November 28), 4, 66.

Lieblich, Julia (1989), "CEOs for 4-Year-Olds." *Fortune* (March 13), 28.

"Loggers Making Beef About Burger King's Salad Dressing," (1990), *The Southern Illinoisan* (June 10), 15.

"Louisiana State Board Wins on Advertising," *Journal of Accountancy* (July, 1987), 18.

Lowry, Brian (1985), "Alta-Dena Plans to Fight False Ad Charge," *Advertising Age* (September 16), 12.

Moss, Phil (1987), "What It's Like to Work for Hallmark," *Business Week Careers*, 84–85, 87.

Norris, Donald G. and John B. Gifford (1988), "Retail Store Managers' and Students' Perceptions of Ethical Retail Practices: A Comparative and Longitudinal Analysis (1976–1986)," *Journal of Business Ethics* 7, no. 7 (July), 515–524.

Progressive Grocer: 57th Annual Report (1990), "1989: A Solid, Yet Unspectacular Year," (Mid-April), 6–41.

Roberts, Johnnie (1988), "States Seek a Crackdown on Deceptive Car-Rental Ads," *Wall Street Journal* (December 8), B1.

Rose, Robert L. (1988), "Travel Agents Games Raise Ethics Issue," *The Wall Street Journal* (November 16), B1.

"Rumors of Worms in Hamburgers Hurt McDonald's Business" (1978), *The Wall Street Journal* (November 23), 21.

Rossant, John and Amy Dunkin (1989), "Benetton Targets A New Customer—Wall Street," *Business Week* (May 29), 32–33.

Samuelson, Robert J. (1979), "The Kroger Case: Regulation AMOK," *The National Journal* (reprinted in *The Washington Post*, July 10, 1979, D-6).

"Satanic Times for Stores and Statesmen" (1989), *The Wall Street Journal* (February 22), B1.

Singer, Karen (1987), "Marketing's New Watchword: Satisfaction Guaranteed," *Advertising Week* (November 2), 59–61.

Tarnoff, Stephen (1987), "DuPont Plaza Fire Suits Seek $158 Million," *Business Insurance* (January 19), 3, 34.

"The Public Is Willing to Take Business on" (1989), (*Business Week*–Harris Poll), *Business Week* (May 29), 29.

Treece, Jim (1988) "If It Has Wheels and Carries People, Shouldn't It Be Safe?" *Business Week* (June 20), 48.

Warren, Wendy (1990), "Is the Penny Worth Keeping?" *The Southern Illinoisan* (June 10), 21.

Weinstein, Steve (1988), "A Conversation With Tom Haggai," *Progressive Grocer* (May), 91.

Yandel, Gerry (1987), "Businesses Try to Capitalize on Fear of Aids," *Atlanta Constitution* (April 9), 1-B, 1-C.

Zuckerman, Ed (1981), "Soft-Drink Lobby Claims Its Due," in Adler, Roy D., Larry M. Robinson, and Jan E. Carlson, eds., *Marketing and Society: Cases and Commentaries*. Englewood Cliffs, N.J.: Prentice Hall.

REGIONAL, MARKET, AND TRADE AREA ANALYSIS

CHAPTER Eight

Outline

Introduction

Overview of the Site
Selection Process

Regional Analysis

Market Area Analysis

Trade Area Analysis

Summary

Learning Objectives

After studying this chapter, the student will be able to:

1. Relate the store location decision to the strategic planning process.
2. Describe the hierarchy of location decisions.
3. Define regional markets and discuss the data sources used to delineate regions.
4. Discuss the characteristics of regional markets and selection criteria.
5. Define a market area and discuss its characteristics.
6. Name the types of decision criteria that are used in selecting a market.
7. Define a trade area and discuss its characteristics.
8. Name the types of decision criteria that are used in selecting a trade area.

LOCATION STRATEGY FOR CUSTOMERS ON THE GO

For Duty Free International, Inc. (DFI), headquartered in Ridgefield, Connecticut, trade area analysis can take an interesting twist. Location decisions have been a major factor in achieving an outstanding growth record since DFI's formation in 1983, making it one of the largest chains of duty free stores in the world with over $100 million in revenues and 750 employees. *Business Week* ranked DFI number *sixty-five* among the best small growth companies in the United States and number *thirty-five* among the leading discount and fashion retailers in 1990 based on growth in sales, growth in earnings, and return on invested capital. In 1991, *Business Week* ranked Duty Free International number 915 among the *one thousand* most valuable companies in the United States.

Duty Free International's location strategy differs from that of most retailers in that the company looks for trading areas that attract international travelers—people on the go from one country to another. DFI operates in several distinct markets of the United States duty free industry through its three divisions: Border Division, Airport Division, and Diplomatic/Wholesale Division. With

Harrod's first "Signature Shop" in North America, at Toronto International Airport.

ninety shops, the company is the leading operator of duty free stores along the U.S./Canadian border and one of the leading operators of duty free and retail stores in United States international airports. In addition DFI is the largest supplier of duty free merchandise to foreign diplomats in the United States, and to ships engaged in international travel and trade in the northeastern United States.

The duty free industry is highly specialized and characterized by sales of merchandise such as liquor, tobacco products, perfume, and luxury items to international travelers, foreign diplomats, cruise and merchant ships, and international airlines. Duty Free International offers savings of 20 to 60 percent off retail prices of high-quality, brand-name merchandise in the countries of its customers' destinations. No duties, sales or excise taxes are paid on retail purchases.

The Airport Division operates sixteen duty free shops and fourteen retail gift shops at seven international airports, and has a 49 percent equity interest in a company that operates duty free and retail concessions at four Florida international airports. It also has a 15 percent equity interest in thirty-one natural snack and nut concessions at twelve airports.

Duty Free International has launched new retailing concepts such as the Harrods Signature Shops and America-To-Go shops to capitalize on increased international travel to the United States. DFI has entered into

continued

an exclusive license agreement with Harrods Limited to operate its Signature Shops in North American airports. Harrods makes approximately 40 percent of its sales to overseas customers, but has royal warrants to supply provisions and household goods to Her Majesty the Queen and to other members of England's royal family. DFI's strategic intent is to bring "a taste of Harrod's to those people who cannot visit the London store. Each store site is evaluated separately, and each store design is unique to its particular airport location, incorporating important architectural features from the London store. The layout is adapted to the high-intensity use that is characteristic of airport retailing operations. The first Signature Shop, consisting of three thousand square feet, was opened early in 1991 in the Toronto International Airport.

The America-To-Go concept is a unique, total store concept for airports. Merchandise assortments will consist of a broad selection of American-made products including seven distinct themes: The American West, America's Toyland, The American Scene, Team Sports U.S.A., America's Kitchen, American Jewelry/Collectibles, and The American Mind. The shops place a high premium on customer service. Customers can have their purchases shipped to any destination in the United States and, whenever possible, to other countries.

Corporate growth strategies are keyed to location decisions. The Border Division plans continued store expansion and improvements to accommodate a higher volume of cross-border shopping, pursuit of acquisition opportunities, and expansion of convenience and gift stores adjacent to duty free store locations. The Airport Division plans to bid for or acquire additional duty free and retail locations in airports, as well as launching its new retailing concepts and increasing the size of existing stores.

The Diplomatic and Wholesale Division plans to capture a larger share of the increasing cruise ship activity in the Northeast, and possible expansion to other ports in the United States. The market analysis that is required to evaluate each of these location decisions should be both interesting and challenging.

SOURCE: Adapted from Duty Free International, Inc. Annual Report, year ended January 1991; "The Best Small Growth Companies" *Business Week.* (May 21, 1990), 117; *The 1991 Business Week 1,000* (May, 1991), 161; and Duty Free International company literature.

INTRODUCTION

The typical retailer seeks growth. Growth can happen in one of two ways: by increasing sales from existing stores or by adding more stores. Adding more stores requires a location strategy for planning physical expansion into existing or new markets. The strategy must consider a retailer's growth objectives in adapting its strengths to new market opportunities. This decision process is very exciting and dynamic, but involves a high degree of risk.

The store location decision begins with the analysis and selection of the broad geographical region in which the retailer wants to compete. This decision is an important aspect of strategic planning, both as a competitive strategy and as a development strategy. The locational characteristics, decision criteria, and information needs for analysis at the regional, market, and trade area levels are discussed in this chapter. Once the trade area has been selected, the retailer must decide upon a specific store location. The criteria for selecting a retail site are discussed in the next chapter.

Store Location and the Strategic Planning Process

Store location decisions incorporate aspects of each stage in the strategic planning process. In the decision process, the mission statement must be considered because it implicitly prescribes the type of location that is needed to support a new store. As discussed in Chapter 2, the retailer's mission statement represents the reasons for the firm's existence. It generally provides either an explicit or implicit description of the target market, merchandising strategies, and other variables related to the retailing mix. A well-chosen store location, based on an environmental situation analysis, can be instrumental in achieving performance objectives. Location is also related to the establishment and achievement of strategic objectives, the selection of retail strategy mix, and the implementation, execution, and evaluation of the strategic plan. (See Exhibit 8–1.) Store location is a critical element in a retailer's competitive and developmental strategies as discussed next.

LOCATION AS A COMPETITIVE STRATEGY
Every retailer has a competitive strategy, whether explicit or implicit. Explicit competitive strategies evolve from the objectives and policies determined during the corporate planning process. Implicit competitive strategies evolve from the retailer's functional activities and programs, such as store operations, merchandising, and cost controls. As more attention is given to formal strategic planning, location decisions require answers to questions, such as:

1. What (or who) is driving competition in my industry? Will it be population, products, other channel members, profits, or market share?
2. What actions will my competitors take? How will I react to new market entries, new formats, increased promotion, and discounted prices? Action/reaction patterns have become a major consideration.
3. How will my industry evolve? What changes will there be in existing and nearby markets, foreign investors, and indirect forms of competition? These are difficult but increasingly important questions to address.

Exhibit 8–1
Strategic Planning and Store Location: An Illustration

Strategic Planning Process	*Relationship to Store Location*
Mission Statement: Sell high quality, high fashion goods to upscale professionals	Trading area and location must conform to identified target market
Objectives: Achieve 15 percent return on net assets (RONA) within 2 years	Price of land, building, lease, etc. and asset value of equipment investment must allow target RONA at estimated sales and profit levels
Situation analysis: Locate near similar competitors to achieve synergy	Identify markets where competitors are successful, and analyze according to important criteria
Strategic objectives/strategy definition: Obtain 25 percent share of the market within one year with strong promotional thrust	Analyze media availability to determine whether TV and newspapers are available that will reach the target market effectively and efficiently
Implementation and execution:	Analyze ability of location to draw desired customers
Evaluation and control:	Reassess location and effectiveness of strategic plan, monitor customer movement, competitive actions, etc. Store may be drawing customers from outlying areas, which may constitute a potential market for a future store location.

4. What is the best positioning for my business in the long run? How will I obtain key locations as foundations for future expansion and find out how customers feel about convenience, merchandise assortments, prices, store environment, and services?

Location as a competitive strategy can be interpreted as relating a store to its environment, particularly in respect to its own retail industry. The structure of a retail industry may set the tone for competition and strategies relative to pricing policies, advertising, national brands versus private labels, profit margins, and such. Competitive advantage may be gained in the retailer's ability to deal with forces outside the industry. These forces might include energy costs, wage levels, local and state taxes, population characteristics, distribution costs, and available advertising methods.

The importance of locational strategy as a competitive advantage depends on the overall economic structure of the retail industry, as well as present and potential competitors, suppliers, consumers, and substitute shopping places and products. These factors combine to determine the profit potential that exists for the industry as a whole, and in particular markets. Strategic store locations can be selected so that the retailer can either defend itself against other retailers or develop strategies to influence existing conditions in its favor. For example, competitive advantage might be obtained by utilizing a location that is more convenient, more attractive, and generally better suited to customer lifestyles. Many retailers expand on this premise (adapted from Grossman, 1984).

The retailer can choose where and when to compete in various markets. In determining the scope of the market to serve, the retailer may choose to serve the entire market or to concentrate on one or more key customer segments—called **niches.** Similarly, the retailer may choose to define the market in which it competes according to geographical boundaries, ranging from a neighborhood in a small east coast community to San Francisco to the European market.

Strategic location decisions are related to the timing of market entry. Those who are first in the market enjoy certain competitive advantages by taking the lead with a new product line or concept, such as that experienced by Kinder-Care Learning Centers. Kinder-Care is a chain of child care centers operated according to a standardized format. The first entrants often have an advantage in acquiring locations. However, they also may face possible risk from a strong contender or unsuccessful idea. An early entry strategy closely following the first retailer into the market can be successful if the second firm has sufficient strength and superiority. Other retailers may choose to compete in a particular market with a late market entry strategy. While the late entrants may be imitators, creativity and initiative may make them strong competitors (Jain, 1985).

In addition to an assessment of the present marketing environment, successful competitive retail location strategies need to anticipate possible changes in competitive and economic environments. A variety of future scenarios can be developed to help retailers formulate a strategic location plan in a changing and dynamic environment. Using a competitive equilibrium framework, Ghosh and Craig (1983) developed a model to aid this type of formulation. The model allows simultaneous evaluation of a retailer's location decision relative to possible competitive actions, while considering geographic shifts in consumer demand.

LOCATION AS A DEVELOPMENT STRATEGY   Retail growth requires the strategic development of new and existing sites. The development plan is formulated through several stages: (1) determine where the retailer is at present; (2) determine where the retailer wants to go; and (3) determine how the retailer is going to get there. A fourth stage in this process is a continuous update of the development plan, including an assessment of the desired level of commitment to a given market. We will use Danny's Discount Drugstore, a fictitious retailer, to illustrate each stage.

In stage one, the status of existing development plans needs to be reviewed before considering further expansion. This review includes taking an inventory of physical assets and evaluating both the good and bad locations currently operated by the retailer. An analysis of the retailer's strengths and weaknesses includes the company's overall concept (i.e., retail mix and image), human resources, and facilities for warehousing and distribution.

Development strategies require an assessment of the retailer's present financial resources and available alternatives. Danger can come from expanding when undercapitalized. Sources of funds for expansion that should be identified and considered include outside investors, stock offerings, loans, and mergers or acquisitions.

In stage one, Danny's analysis reveals that three of the five stores operated by the company are operating below projected sales. The stores are old

NICHES
narrowly defined key customer segments

and need remodeling. Further, Danny's has experienced a problem in keeping good managers, and these stores are located at the greatest distance from the distributor.

In stage two, the retailer determines a direction for the future. Among the areas of concern here are the identification of both overall and specific objectives, preparation and adoption of a "development philosophy," and a time frame for implementing development plans.

Overall objectives to be achieved by the development plan include desired annual sales or number of stores to be added each year. More specific business performance or improvement objectives may include return on investment, after-tax profits, shareholders' equity, market share or leadership, and growth rate. A "development philosophy" may be expressed according to store size and dimensions (perhaps a prototype), geographic locations, and number of store openings per year in each geographical area. Developmental time frames basically state how soon the retailer plans to be in the new locations, perhaps in one, three, five, or ten years.

In stage two, Danny's sets objectives for modernizing the stores' image and increasing sales by 25 percent over the next two years. Plans include relocation of two of the underachieving stores.

A specific direction for future development is planned in stage three for both the long term and short term. Development strategies involve decisions about whether to buy, build, or lease property, trade some of the company's real estate for more desirable property, or acquire other retail firms. The establishment of clearly understood policies and standards is also a necessary part of a successful development strategy, which includes definition of desired trading area and site characteristics, target market profiles, and other important variables.

In stage three, Danny's investigates available real estate options and determines a timetable for remodeling and construction.

The dynamic and often volatile retail environment requires constant monitoring and updating of development plans. The Retail Information System provides a source of data required for this analysis, which typically is conducted at least annually. Some of the reasons for updating development plans include changes in economic climate, number or type of competitiors, company resources, and new market opportunities (Sack, 1984).

Shoppers at a Wal-Mart Hypermart USA find improved merchandise assortment and greater convenience. The Hypermart contains store-size grocery, drug, soft goods, automotive supply, garden center, and accessories sections with 40 to 50 checkouts, all under one roof in approximately 222,000 square feet.

COURTESY OF WAL-MART

Market expansion is one aspect of a retailer's development strategy. Location decisions for expanding an existing retail market consist of eight major steps:

1. Identify major geographic target areas
2. Screen target areas' demographics
3. Select potential areas for initial entry
4. Plot competitive and shopping activity data
5. Reevaluate potential areas and prioritize target sites
6. Conduct field inspection and real estate screening
7. Determine final evaluation and ranking
8. Begin real estate acquisition (Gay 1984)

Trends in Store Location Methods, Practices, and Strategies

Many large retailers are "downsizing." For example, Sears has opened smaller stores in smaller cities to capture new markets. Wards has reduced the amount of selling area in many of its stores, leasing part of its original selling area to other retailers such as Toys "R" Us and other specialty stores. Wal-Mart has moved in the other direction, opening stores in larger communities, as well as larger stores in the format of wholesale clubs and hypermarkets. The rapid growth of specialty stores, particularly in apparel lines, has led to a market entry strategy of multiple locations within overnight distance of a distribution center. This strategy maximizes the efficient use of company resources.

Shopping patterns and the structure of retailing have undergone revolutionary changes in the last two decades. Relatively affluent, highly mobile, and innovative American consumers have played an important role in these changes. At the same time, technological developments, changes in economic conditions, and the effect of inflation on retail cost structures have been even more influential in bringing about changes in retail structure. Each of these changes has an effect on store location strategies (Davies and Rogers, 1984, p. 11–14).

Structural changes are driven by two major forces to which the retailer must pay attention, with the ultimate motive of increasing profits: (1) response

COURTESY OF WEST POINT MARKET

In Akron, Ohio, urban consumers who want top-shelf quality, convenience, and service can shop at West Point Market, a one-store specialty grocery retailer.

to changing consumer preferences and needs through new products, services, greater convenience, and improved merchandise assortment and presentation; and (2) need to control or reduce operating expenses and achieve economies of scale for competitive advantage. Major changes that have impacted on location strategies include the growth of shopping centers, specialty retailing, larger retail chains, increased "scrambled" merchandising, and the emergence of non-store retailing (Davies and Rogers, 1984).

Because of the complexity of location decisions, and in order to reduce the risk associated with a bad location, more sophisticated analytical methods for evaluating markets and sites have evolved. Even though the judgment of the real estate executive is still important, reliance on statistical models for forecasting the degree of success that can be expected at alternate locations has increased.

OVERVIEW OF THE SITE SELECTION PROCESS

The retail site selection process follows a hierarchy from macro-analysis at the regional and market levels, to areal or trade area analysis, and finally micro-analysis related to a particular site. (See Exhibit 8–2.) A region consists of diverse geographic markets. Each geographic market consists of trading areas, generally encompassing metropolitan regions, cities, or towns. Each trade area contains a number of potential sites. Depending upon the retailer's objectives and strategy mix, the site may be a free-standing location, an unplanned business district (central business district, secondary business district, neighborhood business district, string), or a planned shopping center (regional, community, neighborhood, specialty).

The ultimate responsibility for site selection rests with one or several top retail executives, although the total process depends on the combined efforts of many individuals. Large retailers tend to assign this important task to seasoned real estate professionals who have been trained to carry out all aspects of location analysis and negotiation. Regardless of the size of the firm, however, informed location choice decisions depend upon the quality of supporting research as well as the ability of the retail manager to interpret that information in selecting a site. In 1964, some forty years after systematic store location research came into being, Applebaum reported that few retail chains conducted long-range store location strategy studies, and only a minority made follow-up studies. Today, these techniques have developed into sophisticated statistical methods designed to decrease the risk in site selection. Statistical models are only as good as the data they use. Eisenpreis (1965) noted that store location research must be guided by, and measured against, each individual retail firm's own market plan. Locational strategy is an integral part of the retailer's total strategic plan.

An introduction to regional analysis is provided in the next section, followed by a discussion of locational characteristics and criteria for selection of a market area and trade area.

Exhibit 8–2
Location Decision Hierarchy

Regional Analysis

Market Analysis

Trade Area Analysis

Site Analysis

REGIONAL ANALYSIS

Definition of Regional Markets

A **regional market** is a subset of a national market. Business and nonbusiness organizations find it useful to divide the United States into relatively homogeneous regional markets, classified according to one of several schemes, for effective marketing and resource management. Of course, the retailer should recognize that a number of differences do exist within each of these regional markets. Their primary value is in providing a scheme for gathering, storing, analyzing, and reporting population data. The U.S. Census Bureau has defined nine regions as shown in the map included in Exhibit 8–3: Pacific States Mountain States, West North Central States, West South Central States, East North Central States, East South Central States, South Atlantic States, Mid-Atlantic States, and New England.

The Census Bureau classification is used as a framework for reporting statistics by a number of data sources, including the *Survey of Buying Power*,

REGIONAL MARKET

relatively homogeneous division of a national market

Exhibit 8–3
Regions and Census Divisions of the United States

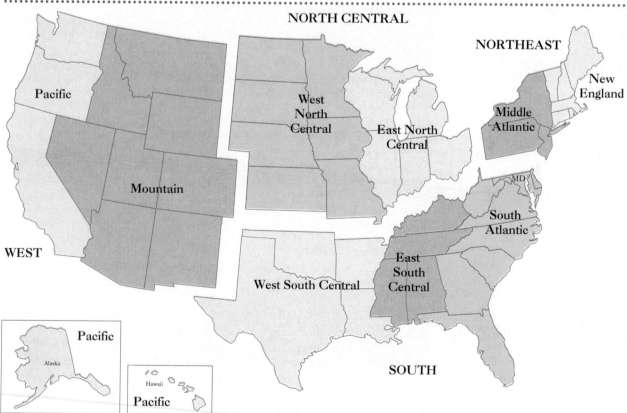

MAP SOURCE: U.S. Department Commerce, Bureau of the Census (1990).

Exhibit 8–4
Standard Units of Geography for the Reporting of U.S. Census Data

• *United States of America*—50 states and District of Columbia

• *State*—major U.S. political unit; District of Columbia treated as a State

• *Regions*—large groups of states that form first-order subdivisions of U.S. for Census purposes. The four largest groups are: Northeast; Midwest; South; West.

• *Metropolitan Statistical Area (MSA) (formerly SMSA)*—qualifies if city has at least 50,000 inhabitants, or is a Census Bureau defined urbanized area of at least 50,000 with a total metropolitan population of at least 100,000 (75,000 in New England).

• *Consolidated Metropolitan Statistical Area (CMSA)*—area with more than one million population and certain other specified requirements.

• *Central City*—new standards for identifying central cities adopt two commuting measures as a basis for designating cities of central character. Many new central cities are older, larger communities, many with significant minority populations.

• *County*—primary political and administrative subdivision of a State.

• *Place (Incorporated Places)*—concentration of population with or without legally prescribed limits, powers, or functions (but do not cross state boundaries). Most of the 23,000 places recorded in the 1980 census are incorporated as cities, towns, villages, or boroughs.

• *Minor Civil Division (MCD)*—primary political and administrative subdivision of a county, generally called townships. Used for census data in 29 states.

• *Census County Division (CCD)*—statistical subdivision of a county, somewhat comparable to a MCD.

• *Census Tract*—small statistical sudivision of a county, with fairly stable boundaries. Designed to be relatively homogeneous regarding population characteristics, economic status, and living conditions.

• *Enumeration District (ED)*—area used in 1980 census for data collection and tabulation where blocks are not present. EDs do not cross boundaries of legal or statistical areas; therefore, they vary in population size. Generally do not exceed population of 1,000.

• *Block Group (BG)*—combination of numbered census blocks that is a subdivision of a census tract or block numbering area (BNA). Defined in all areas for which block statistics are prepared.

• *Block*—usually a rectangular piece of land, bounded by four streets. Or may be irregular shape, or bounded by other features, such as streams, railroad tracks, etc. Does not cross county, census tract, or BNA boundaries.

• *Area of Dominant Influence (ADI)*—geographic definition of each television market, exclusive of all others, based on measurable viewing pattern. Most consist of one or more entire counties, may cross state lines, etc. Each ADI is named after the major city/ies within its boundary.

• *Zip Codes*—U.S. Postal Service areas designated by 5 (or 9) digit codes.

published annually by *Sales and Marketing Management.* Media data sources, such as *Standard Rate and Data Service,* also find this classification useful in describing homogeneous markets to improve communication with viewers, readers, or listeners on behalf of retailers, manufacturers, and other clients.

Census Bureau data are reported for standard units of geography, ranging from aggregate data for the entire United States to city blocks and zip codes. See Exhibit 8–4 for a listing of Census Bureau classifications. Exhibits 8–5 and 8–6 illustrate the types of Census data included in the *Survey of Buying Power* and *Standard Rate and Data Service* reports, respectively.

Other regional market classification schemes include the Bureau of Economic Analysis' division of the United States into 183 economic areas for more meaningful economic analysis, and Management Horizon's 15 consumer products regions, an aggregation of economic areas with homogeneous characteristics (Davidson, Sweeney, and Stampfl, 1988). Regional segmentation by retailers is generally dictated by corporate structure and managerial concerns. Many large national chains have divided the United States into regions that facilitate their operations. For example, J.C. Penney has divided the country into five geographical sections to enable each region, and its districts and stores, to respond effectively to local competition, customer needs, climate and lifestyle differences, and other conditions (J.C. Penney, 1987). The regional headquarters are in Buena Park, California (Western), Chicago, Illinois (North Central), Dallas, Texas (South Central), Pittsburgh, Pennsylvania (Northeast) and Atlanta, Georgia (Southeast).

Garreau (1981), on the other hand, conceptualized the regions of the United States as the Nine Nations of North America, based on cultural and anthropological, rather than political, boundaries. (See Exhibit 8–7.) Of interest is the extension of these regions throughout North America and the Caribbean, beyond the traditional U.S. borders. Consumer values are differentiated among regions described as: New England, Quebec, The Foundry,

Exhibit 8–5
Survey of Buying Power Census Data Example

Florida, Population—12/31/89

Metro Area County City	Total Population (Thousands)	% of U.S.	Median Age of Pop.	% of Population by Age Group				Households (Thousands)
				18–24 Years	25–34 Years	35–49 Years	50 & Over	
Bradenton	192.1	.0769	45.7	7.0	12.5	15.9	46.1	83.5
Manatee	192.1	.0769	45.7	7.0	12.5	15.9	46.1	83.5
• Bradenton	41.0	.0164	43.9	7.7	13.3	14.8	44.7	17.5
Suburban Total	151.1	.0605	46.3	6.8	12.3	16.3	46.5	66.0
Daytona Beach	359.6	.1439	42.2	9.3	13.2	17.0	41.7	153.9
Volusia	359.5	.1439	42.2	9.3	13.2	17.0	41.7	153.9
• Daytona Beach	64.6	.0259	38.0	14.2	13.8	14.6	38.4	28.6
Suburban Total	294.9	.1180	43.0	8.3	13.1	17.4	42.4	125.3

Metro Area County City	Total Retail Sales ($000)	Food ($000)	Eating & Drinking Places ($000)	General Mdse. ($000)	Furniture Furnish/ Appliance ($000)	Automotive ($000)	Drug ($000)
Bradenton	1,387,724	318,870	137,277	158,961	63,263	330,356	52,234
Manatee	1,387,724	318,870	137,277	158,961	63,263	330,356	52,234
• Bradenton	575,811	154,588	46,929	42,269	22,662	170,670	21,241
Suburban Total	811,913	164,282	90,348	116,692	40,601	159,686	30,993
Daytona Beach	2,661,267	652,732	291,015	321,356	131,115	543,638	114,714
Volusia	2,661,267	652,732	291,015	321,356	131,115	543,638	114,714
• Daytona Beach	1,013,584	113,489	111,393	164,552	34,077	323,651	36,536
Suburban Total	1,647,683	539,243	179,622	156,804	97,038	219,987	78,178

NOTE: figures are estimated

SOURCE: *Sales & Marketing Management*, August 13, 1990.

Exhibit 8–6
Standard Rate and Data Service: Census Data Example
••

State, County, City, Metro Area Data

This list shows counties in which cities are located. Cities are first, counties next.

Estimates for: STATE COUNTY—Map Loc. City Metropolitan Area	Population 4/1/90 (000)	Households 4/1/90 (000)	Gross Household Income—1989					
			($000)	Per Household ($)	00000 to 14999	15000 to 34999	35000 to 49999	50000 and over
VERMONT STATE								
TOTALS	572.9	219.09	7,652,669	34,929	23.1	36.8	18.7	21.4
ADDISON	33.5	11.59	416,760	35,959	20.3	37.5	19.7	22.5
BENNINGTON	36.8	14.65	502,394	34,293	22.3	40.7	18.7	18.3
CALEDONIA	28.3	10.89	311,357	28,591	29.2	42.0	17.5	11.3
CHITTENDEN	133.5	49.89	2,113,310	42,359	16.9	29.5	19.7	33.9
Burlington	37.2	14.33	490,132	34,203	...	...	...	...
Burlington Metro Area (Official MSA)	132.9	49.81	2,094,970	42,059	17.0	29.7	19.9	33.3
Burlington Metro Area (county basis)	139.1	51.90	2,191,420	42,224	16.9	29.7	19.8	33.6
ESSEX	7.0	2.46	67,692	27,517	29.8	44.8	16.2	9.3
FRANKLIN	39.5	14.31	457,282	31,955	26.7	37.8	18.8	16.7
GRAND ISLE	5.6	2.01	78,115	38,863	17.7	33.7	21.7	26.9
LAMOILLE	19.6	7.46	237,066	31,778	25.5	40.0	17.8	16.7
ORANGE	25.9	9.71	303,005	31,205	24.2	42.3	17.7	15.8
ORLEANS	24.8	8.86	253,156	28,573	30.4	42.7	15.3	11.6
RUTLAND	63.4	24.42	829,238	33,957	23.4	37.0	19.8	19.8
WASHINGTON	56.4	22.59	733,450	32,468	24.5	38.8	18.6	18.2
WINDHAM	41.9	17.57	560,886	31,923	26.1	39.7	17.5	16.7
WINDSOR	56.7	22.68	788,958	34,787	22.1	38.0	20.0	19.8

SOURCE: *Srds Newspaper Standard Rates and Data*, Vol. 73 (5), (May 12, 1991), Wilmette, IL: Standard Rate and Data Service, pp SM-118, SM-119.

Dixie, The Islands, Empty Quarter, Breadbasket, MexAmerica, and Ecotopia. These distinctions may be a useful basis for market segmentation, although problems that arise in applying the Nine Nations theory suggest that the U.S. Census Bureau's nine regions are more useful in practice (Kahle, 1986).

Regional Market Characteristics

Retailing opportunities vary from one regional market to another. Large national retailers can fine tune their strategies to meet the needs of a regional market, based on consumer characteristics and geography. Many retailers choose to confine operations to one or more regions. Chains that are predominantly regional include Winn-Dixie (Southeast) and Lucky Stores (West Coast). While big cafeteria chains have flourished in the South, they have had a negative image in the North. However, chains such as Piccadilly Cafeterias, Inc., Luby's Cafeterias, Inc., Pancho's Mexican Buffet Inc., and Furr's/Bishop's Cafeterias L.P. have overcome the negative image and found

Exhibit 8–6
(continued)

—Total HH Expend.—.		Household Expenditures—1989 By Selected Store Types							Pas-senger Cars 4/1/90 (000)	Black Pop. 4/1/90 (000)	Spanish Pop. 4/1/90 (000)
($000)	Per Household ($)	Food ($000)	Drug ($000)	General Mdse. ($000)	Apparel ($000)	Home Furn. ($000)	Auto-motive ($000)	Service Station (000)			
3,692,428	16,853	788,675	120,770	520,332	178,713	197,819	628,780	324,797	337.56	1.8	4.06
199,805	17,239	42,438	6,445	27,849	9,727	10,865	34,068	17,538	19.25	.1	.21
245,162	16,735	52,456	8,053	34,666	11,844	13,073	41,732	21,580	22.46	.3	.18
172,587	15,848	37,450	5,866	25,075	8,215	8,851	29,284	15,273	16.19	…	.12
897,627	17,992	188,692	28,216	122,588	44,160	50,137	153,403	78,482	76.14	.5	1.25
234,342	16,353	50,432	7,807	33,510	11,253	12,300	39,838	20,673	17.09	.2	.38
895,164	17,972	188,225	28,158	122,318	44,026	49,965	152,973	78, 275	75.63	.5	1.23
932,929	17,976	196,156	29,342	127,464	45,886	52,080	159,429	81,576	79.62	.5	1.26
38,225	15,539	8,340	1,316	5,612	1,809	1,929	6,478	3,390	3.60	…	.03
232,611	16,255	50,137	7,779	33,362	11,152	12,157	39,530	20,532	21.71	.1	.10
35,303	17,564	7,464	1,126	4,877	1,727	1,943	6,025	3,093	3.47	…	.02
121,765	16,322	26,219	4,062	17,430	5,844	6,381	20,697	10,744	11.60	.1	.12
158,048	16,277	34,055	5,281	22,654	7,579	8,267	26,860	13,949	16.24	…	.14
137,818	15,555	30,051	4,739	20,211	6,526	6,969	23,358	12,219	13.26	…	.08
411,406	16,847	87,884	13,460	57,989	19,909	22,033	70,056	36,190	37.71	.2	.36
372,997	16,512	80,081	12,355	53,092	17,956	19,705	63,443	32,875	33.03	.1	.92
285,355	16,241	61,526	9,550	40,953	13,675	14,899	48,489	25,191	26.59	.2	.33
383,719	16,919	81,882	12,522	53,974	18,590	20,610	65,357	33,741	36.31	.2	.20

growth opportunities in the northern states. Wal-Mart initially had a South Central U.S. regional focus, but later launched an expansion strategy to other regions of the country (Charlier, 1988). Dillard's Department Stores is another southern chain that has expanded to the North. Each of these chains has found a way of combining states, counties, municipalities, or other contiguous areas into groups that are meaningful for their particular type of retailing operation.

Regional markets, like their submarkets and trade areas, may be analyzed according to physical and geographical, customer, economic, and competitive characteristics. Physical characteristics include travel ease, climate, proximity to the retailer's headquarters, distribution center(s), and other store locations. Customer analysis focuses on demographic and psychographic population characteristics, growth trends, and buying behavior. Economic analysis requires attention to source of employment, income, industrial base, unemployment rate, and other indicators of economic health. Competitive analysis includes an evaluation of the nature and proximity of trade areas and competitors from a regional market perspective.

Exhibit 8–7
The Nine Nations of North America

The finishing touches are placed on the Mall exterior as construction is completed.

Pictured here is one of the four anchors, Macy's, several weeks before the grand opening of Mall of America in August of 1992.

"It's like the difference between a space station and a bus station."
The New York Times

"A city within a city...they're building a tourist attraction as well as a mall."
Joan Lunden, *"Good Morning America"*

The nation's largest, fully-enclosed combination retail and family entertainment complex, the Mall of America opened in August of 1992 with 4.2 milllion square feet of enclosed space on 78 acres of land—a retail extravaganza in Bloomington, Minnesota. Four hundred specialty shops join Bloomingdale's, Macy's, Nordstrom, and Sears, four major department store anchors located under the same roof for the first time, to make up a center four times the size of a regional shopping mall.

At the center of the Mall is the country's largest indoor theme park, Camp Snoopy, a seven-acre amusement park with 28 rides and attractions, operated by Knott's Berry Farm. In addition, the Mall includes the LEGO Imagination Center, Golf Mountain, 14 movie theaters, over 30 restaurants and eating establishments, comedy clubs, and nightclubs. It also offers extensive guest services.

The Mall of America Company (a joint venture of Indianapolis-based Melvin Simon & Associates and Edmonton–based Triple Five Corporation, Ltd.) had the vision and expertise to design, build, and manage the project. Simon is one of the two largest U. S. shopping center developer's and managers, owning or managing more than 140 developments in 30 states. Triple Five—a leading developer in Canada, the States, continental Europe and England—developed and manages the 800–store West Edmonton Mall in Alberta, the world's largest enclosed mall. Some factors that affected the choice of location of the Mall of America follow.

The Making of a Megamall

Center of a broad regional market, the Minneapolis/St. Paul (Twin Cities) metropolitan area is large enough to support such a project as the Mall of America, nicknamed "megamall" by Minnesotans. Studies of the Twin Cities retail market consistently indicate that the area is "underretailed." In addition to the 2.5 million Twin Citians, another 4.8 million people live within a 15–mile radius. Twenty-seven million people live within a 400–mile radius, a day's drive for shoppers from 11 states. The Mall is located five minutes from an international airport, and main traffic arteries and access to freeways have been redesigned to accommodate increased traffic. Two seven-level decks and four surface lots provide 12,750 parking spaces.

Design and Construction
Instead of different firms operating from several locations using separate sets of drawings to handle different areas of construction (resulting in communication delays), a new concept of "fast tracking" has been used in creating the Mall. Fast-Trak construction means that all planning takes place on one floor near the construction site itself. Electrical, mechanical, and structural engineers sit side by side, working on the same computer-aided design (CAD) system. Nearby, on the same floor, are the architects, tenant coordinators, marketing staff, leasing agents, and city engineers. Changes made in one area are updated immediately and made available to other members of the team.

Economy
A highly visible tourism magnet, the Mall of America will attract visitors from throughout North America and the world, visitors whose revenues will boost the local economy. The project will generate $40 million in state taxes and $16.5 million in local real estate taxes annually. The Twin Cities area supplied a qualified labor pool for the nearly 3,000 construction workers required to build the Mall, and to fill more than 10,000 permanent jobs in retail sales, management, operations, support services, and hospitality positions after opening. Potential profits have attracted preferred retail tenants.

The Mall Tenants
Many Mall tenants have strong track records and have had previous profitable experiences with the developer. One of the strongest small store retailers nationwide, The Limited was among the first to sign on with Mall of America and required space for several stores including Victoria's Secret and Abercrombie & Fitch. Other tenants include 9 West,

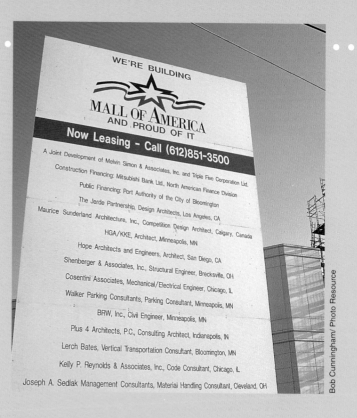

WE'RE BUILDING

MALL OF AMERICA
AND PROUD OF IT

Now Leasing - Call (612)851-3500

A Joint Development of Melvin Simon & Associates, Inc. and Triple Five Corporation Ltd.
Construction Financing: Mitsubishi Bank Ltd., North American Finance Division
Public Financing: Port Authority of the City of Bloomington
The Jerde Partnership, Design Architects, Los Angeles, CA
Maurice Sunderland Architecture, Inc., Competition Design Architect, Calgary, Canada
HGA/KKE, Architect, Minneapolis, MN
Hope Architects and Engineers, Architect, San Diego, CA
Shenberger & Associates, Inc., Structural Engineer, Brecksville, OH
Cosentini Associates, Mechanical/Electrical Engineer, Chicago, IL
Walker Parking Consultants, Parking Consultant, Minneapolis, MN
BRW, Inc., Civil Engineer, Minneapolis, MN
Plus 4 Architects, P.C., Consulting Architect, Indianapolis, IN
Lerch Bates, Vertical Transportation Consultant, Bloomington, MN
Kelly P. Reynolds & Associates, Inc., Code Consultant, Chicago, IL
Joseph A. Sedlak Management Consultants, Material Handling Consultant, Cleveland, OH

Built on 78 acres, the Mall's stores, restaurants and nightclubs fill over 50 football fields and, as a place unparalleled anywhere else in the nation, is predicted to attract 40 million visitors a year.

Ann Taylor, Toys "R" Us, Kids "R" Us, Lerner, J. Riggings, Top Kapi, Spectrum, Camelot Records, FAO Schwartz, Service Merchandise, along with specialty stores such as bath shops, book stores, luggage shops, sporting goods stores, etc. Service retailers such as travel agencies and optometry facilities are also located in this megamall.

Competition
Dayton's department stores will be strong competitors for Mall of America's anchors. The Minneapolis-based Dayton-Hudson Corporation, the fourth largest retailer in the nation, operates Target, Mervyn's, Marshall Field's, Hudson's and Dayton's. In 1987, hometown Dayton's rejected Simon's offer to sign on as a Mall of America anchor. Both parties have been preparing for a battle ever since. Dayton's started preparing its defenses four years in advance by redesigning and adding retail space, adjusting its merchandise mix, improving customer service, and applying cost-cutting measures. An estimated 50 percent of the $2.3 billion in general merchandise sold in the Twin Cities metro area each year is purchased by Target and Dayton's customers, and industry research has shown that Dayton's customers are extremely loyal.

Courtesy of Mall of America

Knott's Camp Snoopy, developed and managed by Knott's Berry Farm, is a complete family entertainment park in the center of the Mall. It features a north woods atmosphere and has 26 rides and attractions, as well as shows, food, merchandise and educational venues.

The interior of the Mall in front of Macy's takes shape, as the myriad of details are integrated through a system of construction called "fast tracking." (bottom)

Each of the four anchors has a court at its interior entrance, designed in a style coinciding with that of its adjacent corridor. (right)

Under construction (above) is the West Market corridor, with the traditional look of a European railway station, combining richly painted metal and wood, and ample, tile, chorme and brass.

Between Sears and Bloomingdale's is East Broadway, an upbeat, contemporary boulevard designed to create a lively atmosphere of fun and entertainment, with plenty of high-tech lighting, metal and glass.

The completed West Market is shown in this model.

South Avenue is a cosmopolitan promenade centered between Bloomingdale's and Macy's. On its third level, overlooking LEGO Imagination Center, is one of the two major good courts in the Mall, and on the fourth level is the theater district with its multi-screen theater complex.

North Garden is a lushly landscaped "street," situated in a park-like setting between Nordstrom and Sears. The outdoor ambience is completed with large skylights and abundant trees, flowers and shrubbery.

The Eddie Bauer Home Collection store has a place in West Market. In late spring of 1992, construction here was well under way.

These stores appear ready for display racks and merchandise.

Displaying the shipboard theme, Cruise Holidays, a travel agency listed among the many service retailers at Mall of America, nears completion.

The Malls We Know

A majority of U.S. consumers are most familiar with shopping malls much smaller than a mega-mall. Regional malls—about one-fourth the size of as Mall of America—and community malls play important roles in the areas they serve. They provide a wide variety of retail and specialty shops and entertainment centers. Often, community events such as pageants and competitions, musical performances, and art and antique shows take place in such locales, and special events with guest performers and speakers also are offered.

While regional and community malls often have retailers in common nationwide, the design theme of malls frequently take advantage of unique aspects of the surrounding community or region. Some are revitalized urban centers and others are newly constructed; a few are pictured here. Malls of all types—from community to megamall—have developed rapidly across the country and the world since J. C. Nichols developed the first shopping center, Country Club Plaza, in Kansas City in 1923. Yet the precursor to this notable achievement, the country store, has existed since the early 1700s and, until about 20 years ago, every small town had one; it continues to thrive in many rural areas.

Courtesy Of The Gallery

At The Gallery (above), near Harbor Place in Baltimore, musical entertainment is provided for shoppers and diners; The Gallery provides local businesses with easily accessible restaurants and shops in this downtown location.

The Pomona General Store (left), in Pomona, Illinois, is a rustic bit of Americana which boasts a working pot-bellied stove, glass jars of candy, and an old-fashioned soda-fountain, and its motto is: "No shirt, no shoes...no problem!" The store has been in continuous operation since the turn of the century.

Courtesy of Pomona General Store

Courtesy of Pottery Place

Red Wing Pottery Place, in Red Wing, Minnesota, is a former pottery facility now converted into a factory outlet mall. It is also filled with specialty shops and restaurants, and the top floor houses numerous antique vendors, many selling the famous Red Wing pottery.

In keeping with the surrounding architecture, the Galleria shopping mall (below) in Milan, Italy, reflects a traditional European style, and the avenues are replete with shops and outdoor cafes.

Courtesy of Harbor Place

© Alena Vikova/TSW

Harbor Place Mall in Baltimore shows off the wharf site on which it is situated. The customers in the open cafes can take advantage of the harbor scene, with its many sailboats.

This nighttime photograph of the River Falls Mall, in Clarksville, Indiana, displays the lighted carousel in the center of the mall. The second level of this regional mall, which also serves the Louisville, Kentucky, area, contains the River Fair Family Fun Park, with a miniature golf course, bumper cars, food courts and theaters.

Water Tower Place, on Michigan Avenue in Chicago, is brightly lit and decorated during the Christmas holidays, as the festive decor is reflected in the abundant brass and glass of the architectural design.

In Bridgewater, New Jersey, 50 miles southwest of New York City, Bridgewater Commons mall (below) is anchored by Lord & Taylor, Macy's and Stern's three of the mall's 160 stores. The mall's three levels appeal to different lifestyles; the Campus level, pictured here, is targeted toward the junior/trendy crowd with its specialty stores, 16-merchant food court and seven-screen cinema.

The new food court in Clearwater Mall (above), Clearwater, Florida, mirrors the relaxed atmosphere of oceanside living. "Chocolate Fantasy," One of many community events at the mall, offers shoppers samples of chocolate fare for a small donation to the National Kidney Foundation.

Decision Criteria

Decision criteria evolve from those characteristics considered to be the most important for retail success. In general, a region is selected on the basis of its ability to support the retail enterprise which includes accessibility by both the customers and the retailer, a favorable economy, population growth trends, and a competitive environment that will make it possible for the retailer to achieve both short-term and long-term goals. For example, a region that exhibits high growth in number of residents, comprising the retailer's target market profile, presents an opportunity worthy of further exploration. If this premise is not followed, however, an area can become over-saturated with retailers.

MARKET AREA ANALYSIS

Definition of Market Area

Just as a nation consists of regions, a region consists of diverse geographic markets. Location decisions involve an extensive analysis of the geographic market for the retailer's products and services. Market potential can be determined for a metropolitan region, city, or town, in addition to the regional level described above. Market definition is followed by an analysis of one or more trade areas within the identified market and of specific sites within a selected trade area.

A market can be defined in a number of ways. As a basis for the present discussion, **a market** is composed of customers (and their buying power), distance, and time. Travel time and distance to destination stores or market centers—known as spatial convenience—places limitations on market size. Central place theory provides a long-standing explanation of the hierarchical interdependence of market centers, explained by the concepts of threshold and range. **Threshold** refers to the smallest market size needed to support a certain type of store or shopping center. **Range** is the maximum distance that customers are willing to travel to a shopping destination (Davies and Rogers, 1984). Central place theory is discussed further in relation to trade area analysis.

Companies such as the Zale Corp. have focused on market-driven strategies for planning new jewelry store locations. At the height of the suburbanization of the United States, sales distribution strategies within defined corridors of suburban growth dominated location decisions. Today the suburban movement has slowed down, and consumer preferences are more highly differentiated. Thus, a market-driven approach to store location decisions can increase performance. This approach involves clearly identifying the store's unique target customer segment, knowing where they live and shop, and designing a marketing program to reach them (Cina, 1984).

Market analysis is a constant ongoing process, because the boundaries of market areas may shift over time. Therefore, the retailer must remain aware at all times. Changes may be due to the entry of new competitors, customer locations or characteristics, addition or modification of major traffic arteries, and other factors (Huff and Rust, 1984).

MARKET
composed of customers, their buying power, distance, and time

THRESHOLD
smallest market size needed to support a specific type of store

RANGE
maximum distance customers are willing to travel to a shopping destination

Market Area Characteristics

From a macro viewpoint, the spatial structure of a market includes intraurban shopping areas, and the relative strengths of trading areas within the market. A market can be described in terms of its physical attributes, competitive concentration, population characteristics, and economy.

PHYSICAL ATTRIBUTES   Physical attributes of a market area include its geography, urbanization, proximity of towns, and retail concentration.

Geographical characteristics of a market extend beyond merely those shown on a map, although the overall geographic placement of a market is an important factor to the retailer. Proximity to other retail markets is analyzed, along with the nature of those markets and their ability to draw customers away from the market being considered. Ease of access to a market area and barriers to access may determine a retailer's success. Major highways or transportation lines, such as bus routes, may provide easy access for desired customers to shop in that market. The absence of good roads or public transportation going to the right place, inconvenient schedules, or other problems may make a market area inaccessible.

Geography, urbanization, competitive concentration, population, income and economic conditions affect the marketing and location strategies of retailers.

COURTESY OF CITY OF SAINT PAUL

Geography also includes the market's climate, which may affect the type of merchandise and services that can be sold. In addition, climate may be related to customer demographics and lifestyles. For example, a Sunbelt state like Florida attracts the elderly, retired segment of the population.

Urbanization or the size of cities and towns in an area, is an indicator of potential retail markets. The total population, as well as its distribution, is of interest. The retailer should, for example, be aware of the percentage of residents living in urban and in nonurban areas.

Market analysis involves an assessment of the *proximity of towns and cities.* Their closeness and relative size is of particular concern because of their relative attractiveness and possible outshopping by consumers.

Market analysis includes identification of major concentrations of retail establishments. *Retail concentration* may occur within a city or town or in areas outside their geographical boundaries. The types of stores, merchandise lines, and other aspects of the retailing mix within these areas are useful in identifying potential opportunities and problems.

COMPETITIVE CONCENTRATION   The characteristics and locations of competitors will have a major impact on the selection of a market. A market with few, widely dispersed competitors presents a different retail opportunity than a market with many competitors concentrated in one or more trade areas within the market. Typically, market concentration is viewed within a radius of 30 to 75 miles, an acceptable distance for many customers to drive to a shopping center.

POPULATION   Population characteristics investigated in market analysis include density, growth trends, median income, and buying power index.

Measures of population *density* include the number of people residing in a county, within a square mile, a city block, or other geographic boundary. Heavily populated areas can then be identified throughout the entire market to assist in the next step in the location decision, identification of desirable trade areas.

Knowledge of the size and location of a market's population at any given time is necessary, but insufficient. Retailers also need to identify significant changes or *growth trends* in that population, such as demographic shifts that may occur in targeted age groups, family or household sizes, or income levels. Likewise, the population of the market or an important market segment may be experiencing growth or decline.

Median family income is included in virtually all site selection models as an important predictor of potential sales. For many retailers, a measure of household income is more important than individual income. This distinction is particularly true for those selling durable household goods, such as appliances and furniture. *Sales and Marketing Management's* "Survey of Buying Power" also provides useful geographic market information, which is updated annually.

The *Buying Power Index* (BPI) is reported for different metropolitan areas, cities, states, and television viewing areas (ADIs). The BPI rates the overall retail sales potential for an area, stated as a percentage of the total U.S. retail sales potential. Based on a weighted average of population,

DENSITY
population within a specific geographical area

income, and total retail sales for the previous year, the index is a quantitative measure of the relative purchasing power or demand in an area, calculated as follows (Ghosh and McLafferty, 1987):

$$BPI = 0.5 \text{ (percentage of U.S. effective buying income)}$$
$$+ 0.3 \text{ (percentage of U.S. retail sales)}$$
$$+ 0.2 \text{ (percentage of U.S. population)}$$

ECONOMY   Economic analysis is basically concerned with the market's potential for producing sales and profits. Thus, evaluation includes factors such as source of income, economic stability, tax base, and financial support from local institutions. Two frequently used indicators of these factors are the markets' employment base and unemployment rate. A market is judged according to the source(s) of income for the population or *employment base*. The nature of employment includes industry type and economic stability, and whether the business is seasonal or cyclical. The percentage of a market's population that is employed is a general indicator of economic health. A high *unemployment rate* may signal problems in a retailer's ability to achieve sales objectives or to collect payment on credit sales.

Decision Criteria

Criteria for selection of a market area are related to the retailer's growth and expansion strategies. These generally involve the ability to achieve market share objectives and an estimated potential for market growth. The retailer may seek to enter new markets or market niches or to expand existing markets. In each case, the potential of the market is the ultimate criterion for profitability of individual stores. The market characteristics described above must include an economic base of sufficient population and income, an existing level of competition that provides market share and growth opportunities, and a customer base with desirable demographic and socioeconomic characteristics. Retailers must constantly monitor present and proposed trade areas because their strength and attractiveness tend to change over time.

Market selection includes an assessment of the net trade flows into and out of retail trade centers within the market, with the net trade flow index calculated as Area Retail Sales/Area Effective Buying Power. The interactive nature of population shifts, income changes, intermarket transportation construction, and the development of new competitive retail structure make it necessary to understand the competitive attraction of contiguous retail trade centers. The net trade flow index is one criteria for determining the share of retail buying power for each trade area within the market (Stanton, Reese, and Miller, 1981).

TRADE AREA ANALYSIS

Definition of Trade Area

Trade areas are geographic subsets of markets, containing target market populations from which a store draws its customers. A trade area contains

destination stores and intercept stores that can be reached by customers in a certain length of time. Destination stores tend to create their own trade areas through their ability to attract customers. Large department stores, discount stores, or supermarkets are examples of major destinations for shoppers. Intercept stores depend on other traffic generators, such as shopping centers, downtown business districts, or recreational centers, to bring customers to their doors. For example, convenience stores often locate in interceptor locations between residential areas and grocery stores.

Trade area boundaries are determined by the point at which competitive advantage is lost to an alternative shopping destination. Since trade areas typically offer alternative shopping opportunities, customer movement within each area must be evaluated. This evaluation includes points of origin, such as residential or employment areas, preferred shopping destinations, and the nature of stores that might be bypassed by consumers on their way to these destinations.

As noted by Ghosh and McLafferty (1987), the broad geographic scope of market analysis generally does not reveal the spatial variations in market potential within a city or metropolitan region. Significant intracity differences in the attractiveness of markets exist, due to spatial variations in land use and residential patterns. The evaluation of a local area's demographic characteristics, land use patterns, and level and quality of competition is referred to as **areal analysis.**

Trade Area Characteristics

The characteristics of a trade area may be described in terms of geography, population, demographics, competition, and regional economy and government. Each of these characteristics is discussed only briefly, whereas a comprehensive analysis of a trade area can be quite complex.

GEOGRAPHY   A trade area is more easily and conveniently comprehended when it is delineated as a circle from which the retailer will derive most of its business. Population density, demographics, and competition within the circle can be assessed with considerable accuracy for developing sales forecasts. In general, the amount of business coming from beyond the circle is determined by the population density within the circle. That is, the greater the population within the circle, the smaller the percentage of business that comes from beyond it.

Concentric zone theory can be used to explain the development of a city's internal structure. A city develops as a series of five concentric zones: (1) central business district, (2) zone of transition, (3) zones of independent workers' homes, (4) zone of better residences, and (5) commuters' zones.

The **central business district** is the economic and social hub of a city, containing several economically related districts, such as retail and office. The **zone of transition** represents an area that is changing from residential to nonresidential use, where factories or other industrial uses and slum areas are replacing the earlier residences—an undesirable location for most retailers. The **zone of independent workers' homes** consists of low- to middle-income groups, often in ethnic groupings, who take pride in their neighborhoods. The **zone of better residences** consists of middle-class, white-collar workers who provide incentive for shopping mall

TRADE AREA

geographic subset of a market containing target market populations

AREAL ANALYSIS

evaluation of an area's demographic patterns, land use patterns, and competition levels

CENTRAL BUSINESS DISTRICT

economic and social hub of a city

ZONE OF TRANSITION

area changing from residential to nonresidential use

ZONE OF INDEPENDENT WORKERS' HOMES

area of low- to middle-income neighborhood groups

ZONE OF BETTER RESIDENCES

area of middle-class white collar workers' neighborhoods

COMMUTERS' ZONE

"bedroom communities"—towns and small cities—for people who work in the central business district

© 1992 ROBERT BRENNER/PHOTO EDIT

Bloomingdale's is an example of a destination store that creates its own trade area through its ability to attract customers. It is surrounded by numerous intercept stores.

development. The **commuters' zone** consists of a number of small towns and cities that serve as "bedroom communities" for many middle- and higher-income people who work in the central business district. Retailers tend to locate along major traffic arteries.

However, many trade areas are not truly concentric. They are actually amoeba-shaped, making sales estimates more difficult to calculate. Experienced analysts have been known to delineate trade areas covering different areas with different shapes rather than using fixed circles (Thompson, 1982). Determinants of the size and shape of a non-circular trade area include alternative shopping choices, barriers and pockets, and in-bound bias. Considerable importance is given to the location and strength of major malls, central business districts, and secondary shopping areas that provide alternative shopping opportunities.

Geographical constraints may exist in the form of natural and manmade barriers. Natural barriers, such as unbridged rivers or mountain ranges, or manmade barriers, such as railroads or lack of highway access can restrict a trade area. On the other hand, trade areas may be favorably affected by such barriers. For example, geographical constraints may form pockets where people in a trade area have no easy alternative shopping choices, making them a somewhat captive market (Thompson, 1982).

Delineating a trade area for an existing store is considerably easier than doing so for a new store. Company records, customer surveys, and other sources of data provide a profile of the store's present market. In spite of the use of statistics and sophisticated mathematical models, projections for a new store involve a certain amount of guesswork.

POPULATION AND DEMOGRAPHICS Once the trade area has been defined for a proposed retail store, the next step is to estimate and forecast the area's population. Population estimates are a critical factor in site location decisions. Incorrect estimates may have serious consequences.

The primary data source for this calculation is the U.S. Census, supplemented by local area data (usually cities or counties). Knowledge of a trade area's population size in numbers is important, but insufficient for comparing the desirability of one trade area against another. The size and density, distribution, and vital statistics of that population, such as its demographics, must also be assessed.

Two types of demographic characteristics that generally appear in some form in site location models are median family income and average family size. Statistics of this type tend to be quite stable and can provide a useful index of trends. Median family income can be updated with the government's Consumer Price Index, and family size data can be updated with special censuses conducted by cities and counties. Obviously, the more recent the data, the more reliable the forecast is expected to be.

Demographics are important to all retailers, but various aspects are of more concern to some retailers than to others. For example, toy store retailers and fast-food restaurants are interested in family size and ages of family members. A grocery supermarket may not be as concerned about family demographics, but may evaluate trade areas based on a population's median household income if it is important to their price structure and merchandising philosophy.

In addition to customer demographics, knowledge of customer lifestyles is becoming increasingly important in trade area analysis. A method of pinpointing potential markets, called Neighborhood Selector, profiles the lifestyles and leisure interests of more than 90 percent of U.S. residential neighborhoods. The data base consists of demographic and psychographic information about 23 million U.S. consumers. Using this system, for example, a national department store chain can target women, ages 25 to 54, with incomes of $30,000 plus, and who live in neighborhoods indicating high interest in fashion clothing, arts and culture, foreign travel, wine drinking, and gourmet foods ("System Profiles Neighborhood Lifestyles . . . ," 1986).

COMPETITION   Competition can be assessed from both a visual and statistical perspective. Analysis may begin with a map delineating trade areas and sub-areas containing the retailer's estimated target population. All competitors can then be located on the map. Large direct competitors are the easiest to identify and locate accurately. However, it also may be important to locate indirect competitors. As Thompson (1982) illustrates, areal analysis for a home improvement center chain may concentrate on direct competitors—other home improvement centers—and eliminate from consideration smaller hardware stores, lumberyards, or paint and wallpaper stores. However, the combined impact of these smaller indirect competitors may be a source of strong competition and cannot be ignored.

Knowing who and where the competitors are is just the beginning. The level of competition in an area must be assessed in terms of number and sizes of stores and the strengths and weaknesses of each competitor. Total competition should be analyzed relative to the level of total demand. Ratios of retail saturation can be developed using a combination of population estimates and data on the number of retail stores per capita, retail sales per capita, average sales per establishment, and average sales per square foot. The **index of retail saturation (IRS)** is a frequently used measure of a market's attractiveness, calculated as shown below.

$$IRS_{ij} = \frac{POP_{ij} \times EXP_{ij}}{RSS_{ij}} = \frac{\text{Demand}}{\text{Square feet of selling space}}$$

where

IRS_{ij} = index of retail saturation in area i for product j
POP_{ij} = population in area i who are likely to buy product j
EXP_{ij} = per capita retail expenditure in area i on product j
RSS_{ij} = retail selling space (in total square feet) in area i selling product j

The IRS formula measures the level of demand relative to supply for a particular product, as illustrated in Exhibit 8–8. Therefore, the higher the value of the index, the more attractive the trade area would be for opening a new store carrying a given product line. A lower index value would indicate that the area is saturated with similar competing stores and products. A market area may be overstored, understored, or saturated, depending on the competitive environment. An **overstored market** exists when retail capacity exceeds demand capacity. In an **understored market,** demand capacity exceeds retail capacity; and in a **saturated market** the retail capacity equals the capacity to consume. Note that an area can be overstored for one product, but not necessarily for another.

An increase in competition in a trade area may fuel the entry of other retailers. The rapid growth of shopping centers in Chicago's suburbs has resulted in strong leasing activity by national chains like Marshall's, TJ Maxx, Phar-Mor, Highland, Child World, Toys "R" Us, and Builders Square, in addition to escalating competition in the grocery business involving Cub Foods, Jewel, and Dominick's (Bossey and George, 1988). Target and Mervyn's and others have found opportunities in understored areas such as Detroit. Although the city has had a negative image, it still ranks fifth in retail sales (Shostak, 1987; Wolz, 1987). Other cities, such as Charlotte, N.C. and Des Moines, IA, have enjoyed a steady growth in retail development, attracting a wide mix of retail tenants.

INDEX OF RETAIL SATURATION (IRS)
measure of a market's attractiveness based on an area's population, per capita, expenditures, and competing retail space

OVERSTORED MARKET
retail capacity exceeds demand capacity

UNDERSTORED MARKET
demand capacity exceeds retail capacity

SATURATED MARKET
retail capacity equals capacity to consume

Exhibit 8–8
Index of Retail Saturation: A Comparison for Three Market Areas

	Market Area		
	A	B	C
Population (POP)[1]	40,000	25,000	10,000
Annual per capita expenditure for shoes (EXP)	$250.00	$200.00	$400.00
Retail Selling Space (RSS)[2]	20,000	15,000	10,000
Index of Retail Saturation (IRS)[3]	$500.00	$333.37	$400.00

[1] Number of customers in this market who buy shoes.
[2] Including the proposed shoe store.
[3] Assuming that the shoe retailer requires annual sales of $450.00 per square foot of selling space, Area A offers the most potential since it exceeds the retailer's sales criteria by $50 per square foot.

WHERE DID ALL THE SHOPPERS GO? . . . KEEPING CUSTOMERS DOWNTOWN

As new shopping malls continue to open on the outskirts of U.S. cities, the "downtown" merchants echo a familiar theme: "How will we compete with the mall to keep our customers downtown?"

Retailers in Shelby, North Carolina, were forced to come up with a new action plan when the 350,000 square foot Cleveland Mall opened five miles east of the city on the Asheville-to-Charlotte Highway in 1982. Shelby is a 143-year-old city with a population of 17,000, serving a trading area of 70,000 people. Two of the malls anchors, Belk's and Penney's, moved to the mall—abandoning their original downtown locations.

"Downtown Shelby" became "Uptown Shelby" after competing local family department store executives Hill Hudson and Stough Wray combined their promotional thinking to suggest that "Uptown" is a more upbeat and challenging word. In fact the Uptown Shelby Association initials—USA—have a patriotic ring and are easily remembered.

Nearly 130 Uptown Shelby merchants have a "spirited rivalry" with about 60 merchants in the Cleveland Mall. A few feet off mall property, within sight of the mall's massive entrance sign, is another sign: "Uptown Shelby . . . An Exciting Tradition." The merchants' association's efforts have paid off. In the three years following the Belk and Penney

pullout, retail sales in Uptown Shelby increased 12 percent from $29 million to $32.5 million. Many stores have been renovated and expanded, new businesses have opened, and new full- and part-time jobs have been created.

A resource team of experts, sponsored by the state of North Carolina, made the following recommendations about Shelby. These can serve as a guide for any group of in-city retailers that want to protect its turf against outside competition and is willing to make the necessary effort and spend the necessary money to do so.

Possible Plan

1. Engage a full-time coordinator.
2. Set up an assisting board with small committees for each association activity.
3. Encourage financial institutions to create a low-interest loan pool to assist businesses and property owners in making physical improvements.
4. Draft a five-year agenda for improvements in the Uptown Civic and private sectors.
5. Conduct a survey of historic sites in the Uptown area with the objective of

tax-abating inclusion in the National Register of Historic Places. (Shelby had several historic sites that qualified for inclusion.)
6. Trace ownership of vacant lots in the Uptown area and their approach lanes. Contact owners and induce them to develop their property for desirable businesses or medium-to-high-income housing, or to sell to others who will do so.
7. Correlate civic and merchant promotional advertising and staging of events.
8. Establish parking zones with varied fees, including validation of fees by merchants and designated employee parking areas in secondary locations.
9. Offer professional design advice and financial assistance to merchants for updating storefronts, interiors, and signing—preferably encouraging an overall harmonious framework.
10. Recruit timely and sensitive assistance to present desirable businesses with ways to forestall their closing or moving out.
11. Provide Uptown business owners with frequent updates on association activities through news releases, newsletters, and personal contacts.
12. Emulate the ingenuity of successful shopping centers in staging events that will draw a crowd, because people will go where the excitement is—and retailers will want to rent space where the people are.

Adapted from Spalding, Lewis A. (1985), "How the Opening of Cleveland Mall Forced a New Action Plan for Uptown Shelby, N.C.," *Stores Magazine* (September), 70–73.

REGIONAL ECONOMY AND GOVERNMENT Those responsible for retail location decisions are concerned with growth and stability of a trade area's economy. Important factors to be assessed include present and potential retail sales volume, industrial base, availability and quality of local advertising media, and a competent and affordable workforce. Economic conditions should be conducive to consumer spending and payment of consumer debt.

Government-related factors that may determine a preference for one trade area over another include expense items such as property taxes and energy costs, which can have a major impact on profit margins. Legislation also affects a retailer's ability to operate successfully and profitably. Building codes and zoning laws are two examples of governmental actions that may determine the suitability of a given trade area.

Retail business land use trends indicate the direction of growth within a trade area. Analysis will reveal shifts in dominant retail locations, such as a move from downtown stores to suburban malls and shopping centers. Additionally, it will provide insights into land use according to various types of stores.

The trade area characteristics described in this section are all important variables in the success of a retail store. However, they are also the product of the response and behavior of the consumers in that area who are attracted to some shopping areas and resist others. Shoppers may be attracted by merchandise availability, price advantage, convenience, or service. Resistance is generally the result of a deficiency in one or more of these retail mix variables.

Decision Criteria

Each of the characteristics described in the previous section must meet the retailer's specifications for a profitable operation. Selection of a trade area depends largely upon the sales levels that can be achieved, market growth potential, and anticipated market share. Pro forma financial statements can provide sales estimates for alternative areas, in order to determine which is most desirable and will achieve the retailer's objectives. The area must be able to support the additional retail space generated by a new store, based on the difference between total demand and the amount of retail space already in existence that is attributable to that type of store.

The area's population must be a "match" with a store's required target market characteristics. For example, criteria for a typical fast food restaurant includes 7,000 households within an acceptable radius of the proposed business, 20,000 people within 10 minutes drive, 10,000 to 20,000 within one mile, 20,000 to 40,000 within two miles or a major termination point, such as a large regional mall. The fast-food retailer also specifies a medium average household/family size of 3.5 people (1.5 children), ages ranging from 18 to 49 years (average age 29 to 34), and a median family income of $15,000 to $18,000.

At the level of areal analysis, each type of store (discount, department, specialty clothing, supermarket, drugstore, etc.) will have its own specific criteria for making the trade area decision, based on geography and physical characteristics, population and demographics, competition, and the economic and political makeup of an area. Retailers must be aware of the environmental trends of a trade area or city and the direction and quality of growth. A number of specific criteria related to these factors are discussed further in Chapter 9, which covers analysis of retail sales.

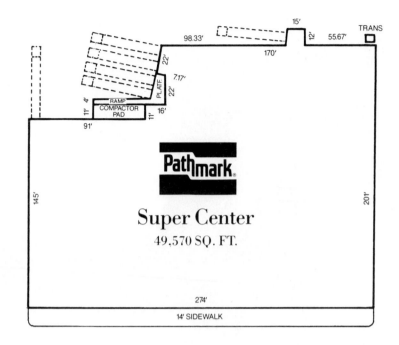

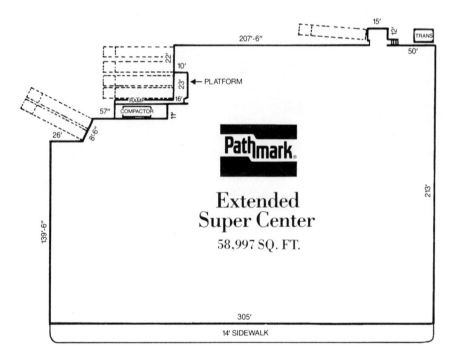

Exhibit 8-9
General Cite Requirements for
Pathmark Division,
Supermarkets General Corp.
Used with permission.

Land
A minimum of 5 acres is normally required, however, this number can increase where stringent
landscaping and/or non-useable
set back requirements exist. It is
possible to somewhat reduce the
acreage requirements when the
topography lends to incorporating basement parking into the
project.

Building Size
(See attached footprints)
Super Centers are 49,000 square
feet (274 feet wide and 201 feet
deep irregular). The Expanded
Super Center is 59,000 square
feet (305 feet wide and 213 feet
deep irregular).

Parking
6 cars per 1,000 square feet of
building area is preferred for
free standing units, however,
this number can be somewhat
reduced in larger centers.

SUMMARY

In this chapter, we have examined the location decision from the macroperspective of the larger regions and market areas compatible with the retailer's
strategic plan for future growth. We then narrowed our focus to trade area analysis.

Apple South's priority is to reach maximum market penetration in its targeted market areas for Applebee's restaurant.

Incorporating aspects of each stage in the strategic planning process, store location decisions become a critical element in a retailer's competitive and developmental strategies. As a competitive strategy, location can be interpreted as relating a store to its environment—particularly in respect to its own retail industry. As a development strategy, location involves determining (1) where the retailer is at present, (2) where the retailer wants to go, and (3) how the retailer is going to get there, as well as a constant updating of the development plan.

Store location trends include downsizing of stores by larger retail chains, opening of stores in either larger (Wal-Mart) or smaller (Sears) communities in contrast to earlier strategies, and multiple locations of high-growth specialty stores within overnight distance of a distribution center. Structural changes have become necessary due to changes in the demographics and shopping patterns of American consumers, technological developments, and changes in economic conditions.

The site selection process follows a hierarchy from regional and market analysis, to trade area analysis, and then to selection of a particular site. A

region is a subset of a national market and can be defined according to classifications such as those provided by the U.S. Census Bureau or *The Survey of Buying Power*. Characteristics of regional markets, like their submarkets and trade areas, include physical and geographical, customer, economic, and competitive factors. In general, regions and markets are selected on the basis of their ability to support the retail enterprise.

A market is composed of customers and their buying power, distance, and time. Markets are evaluated in terms of physical attributes, competitive concentration, population characteristics, and economy. Trade areas are geographic subsets of markets, containing target market populations from which a store draws its customers. Geography is analyzed in terms of both physical structure and growth patterns. Population estimates, demographic characteristics such as median family income and average family size, and customer lifestyle profiles are useful in predicting trends and forecasting sales. Location analysis requires an assessment of who and where the competitors are, as well as their strengths and weaknesses.

A market's attractiveness can be measured by the index of retail saturation, which incorporates population, per capita retail expenditures, and retail selling space for a given product in a given area into its calculation. At this level of analysis each type of store will have its own specific criteria for making the trade area decision. In the next chapter, we will take a micro-view of the selection of a specific site within a selected trade area.

Questions for Review and Comprehension

1. Explain how a store location decision can be an integral part of a retailer's (a) competitive strategy and/or (b) development strategy. Illustrate with examples of each type of strategy.

2. Describe the location decision process following a hierarchy of analysis and decisions from the macro-level (region) to the micro-level (store site). Does this entire process apply to a small local retailer who only wants to operate a store in his or her own home town? What aspects do apply? Why?

3. Give a definition of a regional market, and discuss how boundaries of a region might be determined.

4. Assuming you wanted to expand a regional chain of supermarkets from the northeastern United States to the southeastern United States, what regional characteristics would be most important to the success of your stores? Describe the criteria that you would use to determine the feasibility of expanding to this region.

5. Define market area and discuss how the major market characteristics (physical attributes, competitive concentration, population, and economy) might be of interest to a children's apparel retailer. Would these characteristics have the same degree of importance if the retailer decided to sell through mail order rather than in stores? Why or why not?

6. Discuss the basic decision criteria used to determine the "best" market area.

7. How does a trade area differ from a market area? Discuss the trade area characteristics and selection criteria that would be considered by an expanding fast-food restaurant chain. Would these characteristics and criteria be different for an elegant sit-down restaurant? Why or why not?

References

Bossey, David P. and Michael D. George (1988), "Wal-Mart Targets Chicagoland for Rapid Expansion," *Midwest Real Estate News* (July), 42–43.

Charlier, Marj (1988), "Southern Cafeteria Chains Plot Expansion into North," *The Wall Street Journal* (June 17), 17.

Cina, Craig E. (1984), "Selecting Store Locations: A Market-driven Approach," *Marketing News* (September 14), 41.

Davidson, William R., Daniel J. Sweeney, and Ronald W. Stampfl (1988), *Retailing Management*, 6th ed., New York: John Wiley & Sons.

Davies, R. L. and D. S. Rogers (1984), *Store Location and Store Assessment Research*. New York: John Wiley & Sons.

Eisenpreis, Alfred (1965), "An Evaluation of Current Store Location Research," *New Directions in Marketing*. American Marketing Association, 243–250.

Garreau, Joel (1981), *The Nine Nations of North America*. New York: Avon Books.

Gay, Thomas R. (executive vice president and general manager, Marketing Information Systems, and executive vice president, National Decision Systems, Encinitas, Calif.) (1984), "The Science of Gathering Market Research and Demographic Data," presentation at NACORE Institute for Corporate Real Estate, Inc., Retail Site Selection Seminar, Cambridge, Mass. (May 2–4).

Ghosh, Avijit and C. Samuel Craig (1983), "Formulating Retail Location Strategy in a Changing Environment," *Journal of Marketing* 47 (Summer), 56–68.

Ghosh, Avijit and Sara McLafferty (1987), *Location Strategies for Retail and Service Firms*. Lexington, Mass.: D. C. Heath and Company.

Grossman, Howard (president, The Howard Grossman Company, Inc., Nashua, N.H.) (1984), "Competitive Strategy," presentation at NACORE Institute for Corporate Real Estate, Inc., Retail Site Selection Seminar, Cambridge, Mass. (May 2–4).

Huff, David L. and Roland T. Rust (1984), "Measuring the Congruence of Market Areas," *Journal of Marketing* 48 (Winter), 68–74.

Jain, Subhash (1985), *Marketing Planning and Strategy*, 2d ed., Cincinnati, Ohio: South-Western Publishing Co., 596, 605–606.

Kahle, Lynn R. (1986), "The Nine Nations of North America and the Value Basis of Geographic Segmentation," *Journal of Marketing* (April), 37–46.

Penney, J. C., Inc. (1987) Annual Report.

Sack, Burton M. (president, Exeter Hospitality Group, Boston, Mass.) (1984), "Development Strategy," presentation at NACORE Institute for Corporate Real Estate, Inc., Retail Site Selection Seminar, Cambridge, Mass. (May 2–4).

Shostack, Robert I. (1987), "New Retailers Enter Market, Others Expanding Presence," *Midwest Real Estate News* (November), 46.

Stanton, Wilbur W., Richard M. Reese, and Stephen J. Miller (1981), "Structural Determinants of Retail Trade Flows," in *Progress in Marketing Theory and Practice*, proceedings of the Southern Marketing Association (November), 55–58.

"System Profiles Neighborhood Lifestyles to Target New Markets" (1986), *Marketing News* (April 11), 21.

Thompson, John S. (1982), *Site Selection*. New York: Chain Store Publishing Corp.

Wolz, John L. (1987), "Negative Image Leaves Detroit with Retail Opportunities," *Real Estate Times* (October 1), 15.

RETAIL SITE ANALYSIS

CHAPTER Nine

Learning Objectives

*After studying this chapter, the
student will be able to:*

1. Explain the importance of
store location within a retailer's
external environment.
2. Describe how each of the
internal retail functional areas
relates to a store's location.
3. Understand the definition of
a retail site.
4. List some myths and pitfalls
of site selection and tell how to
prevent them.
5. Discuss characteristics of
isolated or free-standing locations.
6. Discuss characteristics of an
unplanned business district.
7. Discuss the characteristics of
planned shopping centers.
8. Describe the decision criteria
used in evaluating a store site.
9. Understand both subjec-
tive/intuitive and statistical/
mathematical methods of
location analysis.
10. Give a brief overview of
how a retail firm is organized
for retail location decisions.

Abandoned Gas Station: Eyesore or Opportunity?

● ●

The current trend toward larger gas stations, with 20 or more pumps under one canopy, has left companies like Sohio with numerous sites that are too small for the superstations, although they are in good locations. These old stations can offer potential for a small business or office building.

Creative usage of old Sohio stations include a gutter business, Rain King Industries, and Mario's International Hotel and Spa. Rain King's location gives high visibility to its innovative gutter design, emphasized by the design of a 5,000 square foot addition. Another service station was transformed into a two-story Victorian office building. The station was located in front of the existing, exclusive Mario's International Hotel and Spa. The spa owners purchased the station. Their renovation included a cascading rock fountain in what was originally a gully behind the station.

Other gas stations have been converted into businesses such as a respiratory equipment supplier, florist shop, and pizza restaurant. Now the Kokoroki Bonsai shop, the building pictured at the top of the page was constructed as a gas station in 1945. In the early 1970s the gas station closed, and since then it has

The Kokoroki Bonsai, Waukegan, Illinois

The Grand Produce Market, Waukegan, Illinois

served as a real estate office, a pager sales and repair shop, a second-hand store, a driving school and a sporting goods store. The Grand Produce Market was a gas station until around 1980. The service bay doors to the left of the front door were replaced with windows, and the bay doors on the right side were walled in.

Adapted from Harding Megan (1989), "Auto Service Stations: After 'Service' Life Use Limited Only by Imagination," *Acquisition* (September), 16.

INTRODUCTION

Once the trade area for a new store has been defined, the next step is to identify the general type of location desired and evaluate the characteristics of available sites. In this chapter, the characteristics of different types of store locations, as well as the criteria and methods of analysis used in location decisions are described. First, we will discuss the store location decision from an environmental perspective.

Importance of Store Location for a Retailer

Good store locations are essential elements in a retailer's competitive and developmental strategies. Of all the strategic decisions that must be made, the most critical—and the most binding—is that of store location. Location decisions typically involve a major investment and a long-term commitment. Making a change in this aspect of the retailing mix is difficult and costly, compared to changes in merchandising, pricing, or promotional strategies.

Mistakes due to the selection of bad locations have a high cost attached to them, with conservative estimates ranging from hundreds of thousands to millions of dollars. These costs may be related to lost sales, higher advertising expenses, breaking a lease, moving and remodeling a new location, and other factors. Spending more money on a bad location usually does not provide a satisfactory cure for the problems associated with it. A bad location invites competitors to enter the market and undermines confidence in the company's strategic plan. It negatively affects the company's profits, return on investment, short-term programs, and long-term strategic plans, as well as the lives and careers of key employees. Small retailers, in particular, have experienced failure because of poor locations.

Conversely, the benefits of selecting good sites are numerous. A good location maximizes the retailer's sales, profits, and return on investment. Such positive results encourage the company to make further capital outlays for additional growth and profits. The selection of optimum sites can discourage the entry of competitors, particularly in a high interest rate economy, and highlight the inferiority of second and third rate sites previously chosen by competitors. Within this context, emphasis should be placed on a good location as an asset rather than an expense, as illustrated by the fact that over 26 percent of all corporate assets are in real estate (Grossman, 1984).

LOCATION AND THE INTEGRATIVE RETAIL INFORMATION MODEL

The Integrative Retail Information Model (IRIM) provides a useful framework for viewing the relationship between store location decisions and the components of the retailer's operating environment. It also highlights the interrelationship between location and the functional management areas within a store.

Relationship Between Location and the Retail Environment

Opportunities and threats within the retail environment need to be continually evaluated in order to optimize store location decisions and allow the store to remain competitive. Location dictates the retailer's ability to communicate effectively with customers and to facilitate the exchange process, which in turn affects the retailer's ability to operate profitably. In addition to trade area characteristics discussed in the previous chapter, this ability requires knowledge of consumer markets and their behavior; activities of competitors, suppliers, and intermediaries; and legal and political forces. (See Exhibit 9–1.)

Exhibit 9–1
Store Location and the External Environment

SOURCE: Anderson and Parker, 1988.

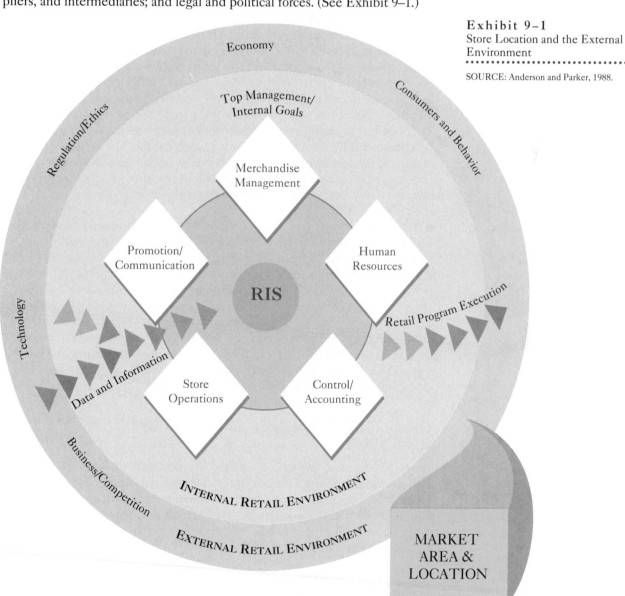

CONSUMER MARKETS AND BEHAVIOR A retail store must be accessible to its customers. Location decisions are market oriented so that a desired group of customers will find visiting the store and purchasing its goods and services easy to do. Therefore, retailers need to know who the potential customers are, where they are located, and how and where they currently buy.

A retail location is a specific and unique site, geared toward an identified consumer market. It may be a tract of land for a shopping center, a store area in a building, or a counter space in an airport terminal. Any one of these places where consumers appear in person to buy goods or services is subject to the type of in-depth analysis that estimates expected sales volume. (Nelson, 1958, p. 44)

BUSINESS Business influences include competitors, suppliers, vendors, intermediaries, and service providers. Of these, competition, both present and future, is the most significant variable to be considered by those who make store location decisions. When examining a specific site, a retailer must know who and where the competitors are now, as well as where they plan to be in the future, what their strengths and weaknesses are, and any innovative methods they may be using to reach consumers.

Proximity to suppliers and wholesale markets is an important consideration because of high costs of travel and transportation. The level and quality of outside services available to retailers may vary from one location to another. For example, cooperation of local financial institutions in new retail ventures may make the difference in whether a new store is opened.

REGULATORY AND ECONOMIC Some serious mistakes have been made by retailers who have not researched local legislation and political trends sufficiently. A supermarket that depends on beer and wine sales to enhance profits, for instance, cannot overlook whether a community is "dry" or "wet." Some communities also have laws against Sunday openings. Likewise, the effect of present or pending legislation on after-tax revenues must be calculated.

Economic trends also need to be assessed to determine growth potential, level of anticipated consumer buying power, unemployment rate, and so forth. Each of these factors can be related to a specific trading area and location in identifying the best site for a new store.

Relationship Between Location and Functional Retail Areas

A retailer must not only understand the external retail environment in a location decision, but must also look at how location decisions relate to the merchandising, personnel, promotion, store operations, and accounting and control functions within the company. (See Exhibit 9–2.) This understanding helps identify internal strengths and weaknesses that may affect the profitability of a new store at a given location.

MERCHANDISE MANAGEMENT Merchandise assortments must be tailored to those customers who are attracted to a particular location. Product

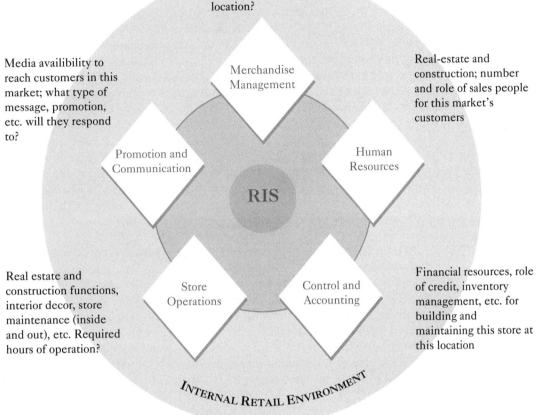

Top Retail Management Internal Goals

What type of merchandise for this location?

Media availibility to reach customers in this market; what type of message, promotion, etc. will they respond to?

Real-estate and construction; number and role of sales people for this market's customers

Merchandise Management

Promotion and Communication

Human Resources

RIS

Real estate and construction functions, interior decor, store maintenance (inside and out), etc. Required hours of operation?

Store Operations

Control and Accounting

Financial resources, role of credit, inventory management, etc. for building and maintaining this store at this location

INTERNAL RETAIL ENVIRONMENT

quality, variety, and assortments are also selected to reflect the needs and preferences of the target market within the store's trading area. Retailers attempt to charge prices that will appeal to customers and result in planned sales volumes.

In addition, inventory levels may depend on storage areas in or near the store. If all merchandise must be displayed on the selling floor due to lack of stockroom space, then smaller orders will need to be placed with vendors at more frequent intervals to assure satisfactory assortments for customers.

HUMAN RESOURCES   New locations require new managers, supervisors, and entry-level employees. These individuals must be recruited, hired or promoted, and trained in accordance with the needs of the new location. Labor market constraints, such as the presence and strength of unions, availability of a suitable quality workforce, and so forth, may affect this process. More salespersons and other personnel may be required to cover longer store hours and Sunday openings to conform to the hours of operations in malls and shopping centers.

Exhibit 9–2
Store Location and Functional Management Areas
SOURCE: Anderson and Parker, 1988.

The structure of the organization may also change as new locations are added or as old locations are closed. Such changes may result in centralization or decentralization of responsibilities, as well as changing positions and job descriptions.

PROMOTION   One of the most important variables considered by professional retail site selectors is media access. Stores depend upon promotional strategies to reach and influence customers. Major retailers have been known to turn down otherwise good locations for lack of media support in the area. Therefore, location decisions are likely to be tied closely to the specific type of media available and its ability to reach a particular target audience efficiently and effectively. That is, the retailer should be able to avoid expensive and/or excessive coverage of areas outside the company's intended market.

Customer services are another facet of a retailer's promotional strategy to be considered. Customers who will shop in a certain location generally have a preconceived notion about those services that make it more desirable for them to shop in one store than another. If area customers demand a high level of services (credit, delivery, etc.) but are unwilling to pay for them, then the retailer's cost of doing business will increase accordingly.

STORE OPERATIONS AND PHYSICAL FACILITIES   The actual physical appearance of the store usually needs to conform to prescribed guidelines for a community, shopping center, or business area. Meeting these "guidelines" may involve architectural specifications, store size (including floor space at ground level, heights, etc.), parking lots, energy systems, inventory delivery methods, and other requirements.

Store operations may also differ from location to location because of variables, such as store hours, need for security and risk protection, and provision for special needs of the store's customers—such as the need to make shop-

A retailer's location decisions not only address the needs of the community and the retailer, but also consider the physical aspects of the site.

COURTESY OF SMITH'S STORES

ping easier for the elderly and handicapped with physical devices, including wheelchair access, special shopping carts, or wider aisles.

CONTROL AND ACCOUNTING   Assessment of present locations and evaluation of potential locations depend upon accurate financial and accounting records. Sales and profit figures for existing locations are analyzed to determine whether expectations are being met. Data can be broken down from total company figures to individual stores, departments, and merchandise lines to reveal strengths and weaknesses at each location.

Pro forma income statements and balance sheets provide an important basis for weighing the value of one site against another, or of a proposed site against an existing store. Accounting and financial data are determined for each location, in order to calculate the bottom-line profitability at each site and to identify the most profitable site.

DEFINITION OF RETAIL SITE

Selection of a retail site, the specific physical store location where a retailer operates its business, is the final stage of the locational analysis process. According to Nelson (1958, p. 44), a retail store is any place that a consumer may visit in person to purchase goods or services, and a location is any fixed place, a specific and unique site, where people may visit. Therefore, a **retail site** is a specific physical location where a retailer operates a store, and where customers may come to make purchases.

The suitability of a retail site is determined in part by its location relative to the existing retail structure in the area, and commercial, recreational, and residential areas. Of course, the location should be consistent with the retail-

RETAIL SITE
specific physical location where a retailer operates a store

The Jacksonville Landing is a marketplace consisting of sixty shops, 50 percent of which are restaurants and 50 percent small retailers.

COURTESY OF JACKSONVILLE LANDING, THE ROUSE CO.

er's mission and strategy. As noted by Ghosh and McLafferty (1987, p. 50), the spatial organization of retail outlets in a metropolitan region may form a hierarchical structure. Each level of the hierarchy contains different numbers and types of retail outlets. Regional shopping malls and central business districts (CBD) are at the highest level in the hierarchy, because they have the greatest retail concentration in both numbers and types of stores. Community shopping centers and smaller malls are the next step downward in the hierarchy, and neighborhood centers and freestanding sites are at the lowest level.

MYTHS AND PITFALLS OF RETAIL SITE SELECTION

Before discussing the retail location decision in detail, let's look at some of the myths and pitfalls of retail site selection that have been identified by real estate professionals. See if you can identify the fallacies in these site selection myths:

1. We're magic! We're so good that we can go anywhere and be successful.
2. We need this location (whether it's a good one or not) to meet our new store opening goals, and it's very important that we meet our goals.
3. If we don't make this deal, our competition will get it, so we'd better take it.
4. A good friend of mine (my dentist) says this is a great site for my new store.
5. I'm not sure just how well we'll do here, but we should at least break even.
6. This is a beautiful building and shopping center. We're sure to do well here.
7. I'm proud of the fact that I don't waste any of the company's money on those fancy market research projects or computer analysis.
8. It's not my problem to figure out how to service this new site (distribution, supervision, advertising), which is 100 miles away from our nearest store.
9. Since real estate is a "risk business," I will just take a chance on this site.
10. This location meets most of our site requirements—EXCEPT parking, visibility, size, and access. In fact, there's hardly any competition *now*, and the demographics are outstanding.

Here are some ways that real estate professionals prevent the myths from becoming pitfalls:

1. Understand the basic deal variables and their relationships to each other: population and demographics; competition; building dimensions, size, and placement; visibility; access; parking; company strengths (advertising, supervision and distribution); and the economics and/or terms of the deal (if cost is too high, profits may be too low).
2. Accept that retail site selection is both a science and an art, where risks can be determined for the most part. Decisions cannot be left to chance and luck.

3. Be aware that retail site selection personnel are professionals who need constant training, interaction with other company executives, and assistance from other professionals.

4. Base location decisions on facts and predetermined standards, rather than opinions, rumors, or emotions.

5. Remember that retailers are in business to make a profit, not just to break even. Two or three profitable stores may be needed to make up for one unprofitable location, in addition to the added strain on management and supervisory personnel.

6. Consider goals as estimates, not absolutes. If, for example, the goal is to add 10 new locations, but only 9 good ones are available, then 9 is the best number.

7. Observe budgets, but allow additional expenditures if needed to reduce risks or to increase opportunities for sales and profits.

8. Let the competition take a bad site. In fact, it may slow them down. (Adapted from Ferron, 1984.)

Retail Site Characteristics

Throughout the regional, market, and areal analysis, the retailer is guided by a general location description. Before specific alternative sites can be analyzed, the retailer must make a choice among the broader categories of an isolated (freestanding) location, or an unplanned or planned shopping center. A related decision is whether to locate in a downtown business district, a suburban shopping center, or somewhere between the two. The choice of basic type of location will depend largely on the type of retail store and the retailer's objectives and strategy mix.

COURTESY OF 7-ELEVEN

High visibility and the absence of competition are only two of the advantages of a free standing location, a typical choice for convenience stores such as 7-Eleven.

Isolated or Freestanding Location

Isolated store sites are **freestanding.** They are separated from other retail stores, although other types of nonretail businesses or activities may be nearby. They are usually located along a highway or side street. Although generally not thought of as a freestanding location, the sidewalk newsstand on the street corners of Manhattan that sells sunglasses, t-shirts, snack foods, and newspapers, also falls into this classification (McCain, 1987).

A discount store, such as K mart or Wal-Mart, or a convenience store, such as 7-Eleven, finds advantages in locating in a freestanding location. Of course, those retailers who are most successful in an isolated location are well-known and have a large clientele. Advantages include lower rental costs, more space, absence of competition, flexibility of operations (e.g., no control by shopping center management), and higher visibility. On the negative side, customers must be attracted to the site, and they may prefer to visit more than one store during a shopping trip. Additionally, there are no shared costs for advertising, parking lots, and other expenses.

This type of location is the simplest site to evaluate, but is becoming more difficult to find. The two major factors to be assessed include whether enough land is available to allow for adequate parking and for future expansion. For example, parking for a supermarket should range between five and eight spaces for each thousand square feet of building area (Davies and Rogers, 1984, p. 225).

Unplanned Business District

Unplanned business districts evolve over time in areas with little or no zoning control. Two or more stores are opened near one another, with no preconceived plan for store placement or retail mix strategies. More stores may be added to the area, continuing a haphazard growth pattern.

Although unplanned business districts take many forms, there are four basic types: central business districts, secondary business districts, neighborhood business districts, and strings or strips, as described below. While many of the larger retailers (e.g., department stores, supermarkets) are located in unplanned business districts, many small retailers tend to locate in these shopping areas.

CENTRAL BUSINESS DISTRICT (CBD)   A **central business district** is commonly known as "downtown." It is the area of a city where the majority of office buildings and retail stores are located and where major changes have taken place. With population shifts to the suburbs, the CBD lost its position as a major shopping area. In most cases, as retailers vacated downtown areas, they were replaced by a greater concentration of offices, entertainment facilities, and hotels. However, many CBDs have been revitalized through urban renewal projects and the commitment of city officials and businesses, resulting in residential and retail developments. St. Louis' Union Station, developed by the Rouse Corporation from an old train station, and St. Louis Center have brought customers downtown to shop. Other examples of CBD renewal and development efforts include Faneuil Hall in Boston, Ghirardelli Square in San Francisco, the Gallery in Philadelphia, and the Nicollet Mall in downtown Minneapolis. The Grand Avenue is a four-

Many central business district areas have been revitalized through urban renewal. Faneuil Hall in Boston is pictured here.

FREESTANDING
isolated stores, separate from other retail stores

UNPLANNED BUSINESS DISTRICTS
business area that evolves over time and has little or no zoning control

CENTRAL BUSINESS DISTRICT (CBD)
economic and social hub of a city

PHOTOS COURTESY OF GRAND AVENUE MALL AND ROUSE CO.

Another downtown shopping center is Grand Avenue in Milwaukee. The Grand Avenue is a four block revitalization which is attracting suburban shoppers back to the city.

block revitalization of downtown Milwaukee's shopping district, which is attracting suburban shoppers back to the city. This shopping center links two department stores and skillfully blends five historic buildings with dramatic shopping concourses and glass skyways over downtown streets (see photos). In many cases, federal and state agencies have provided grants or subsidies to encourage the redevelopment of downtown areas and to overcome the lack of funds for such projects.

Major concerns to be addressed regarding CBD sites include the availability of sufficient land for parking and expansion, congestion and traffic, and position of a new development with respect to the existing focal point of the CBD (Davies and Rogers, 1984, p. 230). The turnover rate, particularly for independent retailers, tends to be quite high in a central business district. Another drawback may be a lack of cooperation by other businesses, municipalities, and politicians.

SECONDARY BUSINESS D0PISTRICT (SBD)   The **secondary business district** is usually located at the intersection of two major streets. Most larger cities have several SBDs, which may have been the original downtown areas of other cities or neighborhood shopping areas in earlier stages of the city's growth. The SBD has many of the same characteristics as the CBD, but has smaller stores, more limited assortments, more convenience goods, lack of parking space, and serves a smaller trading area.

NEIGHBORHOOD BUSINESS DISTRICT (NBD)   The **neighborhood business district** evolves to serve the convenience goods needs of nearby residential areas. The NBD usually consists of several small stores, including a food store and perhaps a variety store, drug store, and service retailers such as drycleaners, beauty shops, or neighborhood bars. The NBD is located on the major street of a neighborhood, often on the four corners of an intersection. Most customers make a large share of their purchases in NBD stores because of their convenient location.

STRING OR STRIP   A group of retail stores located along a major thoroughfare is known as a **string or strip shopping center.** A string may begin when a single retailer is successful and attracts competitors or retailers who carry compatible lines. Car dealerships, fast-food restaurants, gasoline service stations, full-line automotive service centers, and furniture outlets often choose this type of location. Typically, strings are not as conducive as other locations to the sale of impulse goods.

Strip shopping centers are of two types: straight and L-shaped. Each configuration may be subject to high or low traffic conditions. Either end of a strip center is more desirable than a center location for a high-traffic convenience goods retailer because of accessibility and opportunity for future expansion. Just as with other types of shopping centers, the existing complementarity and appropriateness of the present or proposed tenant mix must be assessed. The more successful strip centers tend to have one or more anchor stores, such as drug, variety, or grocery stores.

Upscale strip centers, such as the 280 Metro Center in a San Francisco suburb, attract specialty retailers like Pier 1, Herman's Sporting Goods Emporium, and Federated Electronics. However, the firm that designed and manages the center gets away from the strip center image, by referring to it as a "linear visual statement." This format is characteristic of a new breed of shopping areas, called "power centers" (Totty, 1988).

Planned Shopping Centers

A **planned shopping center** contains a group of stores whose merchandise and service offerings complement one another. The shopping center is planned, developed, owned, and managed as a unit. The mix of stores is

---

SECONDARY BUSINESS DISTRICT (SBD)

usually located at the intersection of two major streets

NEIGHBORHOOD BUSINESS DISTRICT (NBD)

evolves to serve the convenience goods needs of nearby residential areas

STRING OR STRIP SHOPPING CENTER

group of retail stores located along a major thoroughfare

PLANNED SHOPPING CENTER

contains a group of stores whose merchandise and services complement each other based on balanced tenancy, which means that the number and types of stores in the center, as well as their merchandise assortments, are specified in advance in order to meet the needs of area consumers. It is not uncommon to leave a store space vacant for a period of time while waiting for the "right" tenant, rather than upset the balance of retailers in the center.

The planned shopping center has one or more anchors, such as major department stores, and various types of smaller stores. Typically, the anchor stores generate traffic for the smaller stores. In combination, they provide the customer with comparison shopping in a one-stop location.

The shakeout among large retailers has left mall owners with decreasing occupancy rates. As a result, mall developers have been wooing smaller retailers and offering them assistance. In Irving, Texas, Melvin Simon & Associates, Inc., the nation's second largest mall developer, leased space to the New Products Showcase, a retail store for inventors. The entrepreneurial retailer developed the concept where inventors of cutting-edge products such as disposable grass catchers for lawn mowers, fog-free shaving mirrors, and blinking jogger wear with batteries included can be sold to innovative customers. Simon believes the shop has potential for expansion to some of the 70 other Simon properties. However, the retailer has recognized the need to make some changes in the store's appearance and merchandising tactics. Melvin Simon offers its expertise and support to promising entrepreneurs like New Products Showcase and has been able to expand some of these shops to multiple mall locations (Helliker, 1991). Other shopping center developers are offering workshops on retailing techniques and, in some cases, hiring consultants to help individual stores. The landlords' objective is to help stem rent concessions in their malls as many retailers falter. Developers have come to realize that it is in their best interest to lend assistance to increase tenant sales, rather than waiting for the retailer to fail. In May 1991, vacancy rates at U.S. shopping centers had risen to an average 9 percent from 7 percent in 1990. As many as 20 percent of the tenants were receiving some form of rent relief. The Rouse Company has experienced success with its counseling program in malls such as Denver's Tabor Center where a large number of the 65 tenants received help. Some tenant-assistance programs have not been as successful. A seminar program for retailers at the Sherman Oaks Galleria near Los Angeles was discontinued because sales increases did not meet expectations. However, DeBartolo, owner of the mall, planned to continue using a consultant to assist in areas such as customer service and ability to make a sale. Other mall developers focus on the overall objective of attracting more shoppers to their malls (Greenberg, 1991).

Today's shopping centers represent more than just a collection of stores and merchandise. Across the nation, they have become places to "hang out" as well as hubs of commerce. In many communities, the mall is a social and cultural center. For example, the Rouse Company's Art in the Marketplace program integrates the arts into daily life in its malls in cooperation with the public and private sector and matching programs of the National Endowment for the Arts and other agencies. Some of these activities are pictured here to provide a broader understanding of total ambience of a shopping center location.

The three major types of planned shopping centers are regional, community, and neighborhood. In addition, some specialty centers and convenience centers are planned shopping centers. (For a comprehensive example of the planning, location, and development of a shopping center, see Applebaum, 1970.)

REGIONAL SHOPPING CENTER   Planned **regional shopping centers** serve widely dispersed groups of customers, each with a mix of 50 to 150 stores. The largest of the planned shopping centers, they range in size from 400,000 to 2,000,000 square feet of gross leasable area (GLA) and serve an average of over 100,000 people who live within 30 minutes of driving time from the center. As indicated by these statistics (and probably by your latest trip "to the mall"), many consumers do a large portion of their shopping in regional centers.

The largest of all regional centers is the **super regional shopping center,** which is anchored by three or four major department stores compared to one or two for the typical regional shopping center. The West Edmonton Mall is a five million square foot super regional megamall in Alberta, Canada, in a community of 700,000 people. West Edmonton combines amusements and hundreds of retailers under one roof to attract nine million customers a year. The merchandise mix in regional centers is focused on shopping goods, although specialty goods and some convenience goods are also available. Typically, the major structure in this retail center contains various shopping goods and specialty stores, service retailers, entertainment (theaters, videogames, etc.), and restaurants.

The anchor department stores are important traffic generators for the smaller chain and independent retailers. The anchor store decision is usually

REGIONAL SHOPPING CENTER
largest of planned shopping centers, with 400,000 to 2 million square feet of gross leasable area

SUPER REGIONAL SHOPPING CENTER
largest of all regional centers, anchored by three or four major department stores

The Rouse Company's "Art in the Marketplace" program is one attraction provided by many malls. In addition to the ballet pictured here, musical events, art shows and other presentations integrate the arts through cooperation with the public and private sectors throughout the community or region.

COURTESY OF ROUSE CO.

In addition to shopping at the West Edmonton Regional Mall, numerous forms of entertainment are available under one roof. Some of these include the Deep Sea Adventure, Pebble Beach Miniature Golf Course, Fantasyland Amusement Park and the World Water Park.

made before a new mall is developed. This agreement should be finalized before an independent retailer ever signs a lease. An interesting variation to the two retailer anchor concept is for one retailer to occupy two anchor positions in the same mall. Dillard's, based in Little Rock, Arkansas, has used this two-store strategy at a number of locations and will gain a dominant twin-anchor presence in the Florida Mall in Orlando, Florida, through implementation of a similar plan. Each store will have more than 100,000 square feet of retail space with merchandise lines divided between the two. The mall also has four other major department store anchors (Suris, 1991). The outer perimeter of the center may contain retailers of services or convenience goods, financial institutions, restaurants, offices, and perhaps even a strip center and residential units. The combined shopping center and outer perimeter facilities form areas referred to as mixed-use developments.

Retailers must expect constant change in the competitive environment of shopping centers. For example, Marshall Field's has dominated the Chicago-area shopping scene for many years. Under the ownership of Dayton-Hudson Corporation, Field's launched a major renovation program, including its store in Oak Brook, Illinois, and the retailer's policy of frequent sales draws large crowds of customers. However, Nordstrom Inc., a strong West Coast-based retailer, has opened in the Oak Brook mall—a formidable competitor. The question is whether the strength of an established, respectable retailer like Marshall Field's that frequently offers sale prices for its customers, can compete with a relative newcomer to the region, when

COURTESY OF HAHN CO.

The Horton Plaza in San Diego is a regional shopping center known for its unique architecture. It contains seven city blocks of shopping, dining and entertainment amid three designs—historic San Diego, European marketplace, and an amusement park—which combine to give it its unique flavor.

COMMUNITY SHOPPING CENTER
planned center ranging in size from 100,000–400,000 square feet and serving neighborhoods within a twenty-minute drive

NEIGHBORHOOD SHOPPING CENTER
usually a strip location at an intersection site along a major thoroughfare

that newcomer is Nordstrom, a full-priced prestigious retailer with a reputation for offering high quality and pampering its customers (Schwadel, 1991).

Within the regional center, each retailer must evaluate individual store sites according to its own needs. Although the mall itself might be well-located, not every location within the mall is a good location. Some of the concerns to be addressed by a small specialty retailer, for example, would include whether the store is located in a high traffic area or close to a mall entrance, its accessibility and visibility, and if anchor tenants attract customers similar to those of the proposed store. Drug stores, restaurants, and card shops might prefer to be near a mall entrance. Apparel and specialty shops need high-traffic locations, preferably between the anchor stores. Accessibility and visibility are generally determined by location near main entrances relative to road patterns, various levels of a multi-level center, and anchor store locations within the mall (Davies and Rogers, 1984, p. 228).

The regional shopping center can take a number of shapes and forms, with an increasing number developed as covered malls. They have become an important aspect of social life in suburban communities. Senior citizens meet for early morning walks, teenagers congregate after school and on weekends, and charitable organizations set up booths to educate the population. Outside merchants may sponsor automobile shows, set up temporary kiosks to sell handicrafts, and initiate a variety of other activities.

Waldenbooks is an example of a national retailer who seeks regional mall locations across the nation. In a new concept targeting children and their baby-boomer parents, the chain's expansion strategy has included locating Waldenkids, Brentano's, and Waldenbooks stores in regional malls that attract an upscale, well-educated population ("Waldenbooks Launches . . . ," 1987).

COMMUNITY SHOPPING CENTER   A planned **community shopping center** serves all neighborhoods within a 20-minute drive time, with a mix of

15 to 25 stores. They range in size from 100,000 to 400,000 square feet of GLA, and serve 20,000 to 100,000 people. The community shopping center typically has a junior department store, supermarket, or variety store as the major tenant, with a focus on shopping goods and convenience goods. The tenant mix is similar to that found in the neighborhood center, although it is usually more diverse.

Major concerns, as with other types of centers, include location of the proposed site within the center and availability of adequate nearby parking. Since this type of location appeals to a time-conscious shopper, parking spaces close to the store are important. Exhibit 9–3 outlines the new parking standards for community, regional, and neighborhood shopping centers.

New retail growth in suburbs is not always welcomed by the local stores that claim the entry of pricey national chains has pushed rents up too high for their survival, in spite of the extra shoppers they attract. Benetton, Laura Ashley, Ralph Lauren, Banana Republic, The Limited, and other chains have run out of upscale mall locations and have found new opportunities in affluent suburbs (DePalma, 1987).

NEIGHBORHOOD SHOPPING CENTER A planned **neighborhood shopping center** is usually a strip location, along a major thoroughfare. Many are placed at intersection sites to take maximum advantages of vehicular traffic patterns. Each center serves customers from one or more neighborhoods in the vicinity—5 to 15 minutes of driving time—selling mostly convenience items. Neighborhood shopping centers range in size from 30,000 to 100,000 square feet of GLA, and contain 5 to 15 stores. The predominant store is generally a supermarket or drugstore, or both. The retail mix may include a dry cleaner, beauty shop, gas station, and goods and services that people will purchase close to home.

Exhibit 9–3
Parking Standards for Shopping Centers

New Parking Standards

Size of Center	No. of Spaces Per 1000' GLA
250,000–400,000	4
400,000–600,000	4 to 5
600,000	5

Current Parking Availability

Type of Center	% of Spaces per 1000' GLA
Regional	5.7
Community	5.6
Neighborhood*	5.5

*Some older centers have as much as 11 spaces per 1000' GLA (gross leasable area) SOURCE: *Dollars & Cents of Shopping Centers*. 1984. Urban Land Institute, Washington, D.C.

COURTESY OF STRUCTURES UNLIMITED

Sawgrass Mills Mall, Sunrise, Florida, is the world's largest outlet mall, with 2.2 million square feet of space, and a unique logo. Their alligator mascot appears in area parades and other functions, and two animated alligators and a toucan put on a show in a mall pool.

Harborplace in Baltimore is a converted downtown warf area of 135,000 square feet, containing fourteen restaurants overlooking Chesapeake Bay, as well as many specialty retail shops.

COURTESY OF HARBORPLACE

SPECIALTY SHOPPING CENTER The secret of **specialty centers** is found in their name: special. Each tends to be unique in its interesting architecture and decor, although much of the merchandise mix may be available in local malls. Examples of urban specialty centers include Faneuil Hall Marketplace (Boston), The Gallery at Market Street East (Philadelphia), Harborplace (Baltimore), Santa Monica Place, The Grand Avenue (Milwaukee), South Street Seaport (New York City), Yerba Buena Center (San Francisco), and St. Louis Station.

Because of the importance of shopping centers in retail site selection decisions, Exhibit 9–4 is provided as an overview of the past, present, and future of shopping centers in the United States.

In summary, a major department store or shoe store chain may prefer a location in a planned shopping center. Other retailers, large or small, may be successful in an unplanned shopping center. The choice of whether to seek an isolated location or locate in an unplanned or planned shopping center should be consistent with the retailer's mission, objectives, and resources. Once a decision has been made among these three alternatives, specific sites can be analyzed. If, for example, a general merchandise discounter seeks an isolated location, the search can begin for possible freestanding sites away from shopping centers and other stores.

Decision Criteria

Checklists of important factors that affect retail sales and costs have been developed for site evaluation. Available sites are analyzed on these dimensions in order to determine their relative attractiveness. The checklist, one of the first systematic procedures for evaluating a site, continues to be a useful tool in the evaluation process. Exhibit 9–5 illustrates a list of site characteristics that might be evaluated in finding a "100 percent location," that is, a site

SPECIALTY SHOPPING CENTER
group of specialty retail stores located together

that has all the features a retailer desires for a successful store—assuming, of course, that such a site is available for lease or purchase.

Nelson (1958) proposed eight principles to observe when applying selection criteria to each specific site. Although developed more than three decades ago, the principles described below continue to be valid.

1. *Adequacy of Present Trading Area Potential:* If the retailer could obtain all the business available in this trading area, how much would it amount to? And how much of this total business can this particular store capture?

2. *Accessibility of Site to Trading Area:* The object is to secure the maximum accessibility in order to have available as much of the business potential as possible. The sources of business may be produced by the store itself through promotional efforts or competitive advantage or generated by neighboring businesses or people whose main purpose in being near the store is other than buying (such as a newsstand in an airport). In a broader sense,

Exhibit 9–4
A History of Shopping Center Development

Chronological History in the United States

Early 1700s	Midwest towns develop around a central square.
Early 1800s	First department stores appear, begin to replace the country store.
1870s	Start of the chain store.
Late 1800s	Creation of first "streetcar" suburbs. Beginning of specialized downtowns.
Early 1900s	Start of mail-order retailing.
1907	First free parking pioneered by Edward H. Bouton at Roland Park Shopping District, Baltimore.
1923	First shopping center, Country Club Plaza, Kansas City: J. C. Nichols—developer.
1929	First inward-facing shopping center—Highland Park Village, Dallas. Developed by Hugh Prather, Sr. Still a charming, highly successful center.
1930s	Self-service retailing begins (supermarkets).
1947	One of the first regional centers—Crenshaw Center, Los Angeles.
1950s	FHA and VA programs spur rapid suburbanization. Shopping center construction boom begins. First enclosed mall, Framingham, MA.
*1950	First enclosed regional mall anchored by a full-service department store—Northgate Center, Seattle, WA. Developed by James B. Douglas, Allied Stores. Pioneered truck service tunnels.
1957	International Council of Shopping Centers founded.
1958	First year in which more retail sales occurred in suburbs than in central business district.
1960s	Self-service retailing expands to department stores. Variety stores start disappearing. Decade of the open mall. Founding of big retail development firms. Development of large regional centers. First use of boutique layout, Henri Bendel, New York, N.Y.
1967	First food/drug combination, Pathmark, New Jersey.
1970s	Enclosed malls proliferate. Superregional centers emerge. Off-price clothing stores start in New England.
1972	Peak year for construction of regional malls.
1980s	Decade of retail market segmentation. Development of more specialized retail product. Increase in rehabilitation activity. Start of "in-fill" development, increased attention to rural markets. Renewed interest in CBD. Rapid growth of gas/convenience market.

SOURCE: *Development Magazine*, NAIOP, (June 1986), p. 21.

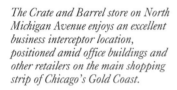

The Crate and Barrel store on North Michigan Avenue enjoys an excellent business interceptor location, positioned amid office buildings and other retailers on the main shopping strip of Chicago's Gold Coast.

accessibility refers to the ease of entering and exiting a store site, from both a physical and psychological perspective. Accessibility is not always easy to quantify, since it is relative to the expectations of customers and the attractiveness of competitors. Barriers to accessibility may be natural (rivers, lakes, hills, etc.), psychological (socioeconomic, ethnic neighborhood characteristics, etc.), or manmade (railroads, bridges, highway cloverleafs, etc.). The effect of these barriers on shopping behavior may not be readily evident to the site analyst, due to their often subjective nature.

3. *Growth Potential:* In a time of declining profit ratios, total business volume must be increased to maintain or increase profits. Therefore, the site should be in a trading area that is experiencing population and income growth.

4. *Business Interception:* In adhering to this principle, a site would be selected between the market (people in the trading area) and the marketplace (traditional source of the same goods). Thus, customers would be intercepted on their way to previous destination stores to buy the same products. They may also be intercepted on their way to other destinations, such as residences, offices, or industrial plants. The best downtown interceptor locations tend to be positioned on the easiest and most normal route between office buildings and other stores selling similar merchandise. For instance, a card shop located a block from the office building in the direction of a concentration of retail stores where customers might also buy cards will generally attract more customers than a comparable card shop located a half-block away in the opposite direction. The key to a successful interception is location at a well-known and reputable address, on a logical well-traveled route, composed of the "right" working population.

5. *Cumulative Attraction:* Two types of cumulative attraction represent shared business. One is based on similar types of retailers who can draw more business together than they can individually. For example, a group of car dealers may locate near or adjacent to one another to attract more customers. Some sources have predicted that the downturn in domestic car sales may lead to auto malls where customers can shop back and forth from one automobile make and model to another. The other type of cumulative attraction is based on complementary units. These are compatible retailers with a high degree of customer interchange, such as a group of apparel and accessory stores, or a supermarket and a drugstore. In the automotive market, auto parts dealers, tire retailers, and automotive repair services find that a synergy comes from locating near one another.

6. *Compatibility:* This principle is closely related to the principle of cumulative attraction. However, the principle of compatibility requires uninterrupted shopper traffic and maximum customer interchange between stores in order to obtain maximum business potential at a given location. Stores located close together with complementary and compatible merchandise lines should experience an increase in sales volume directly proportionate to the degree of customer interchange, i.e., customers going back and forth between two or more stores. Cross-shopping is most apt to occur when compatibility includes all aspects of the retail mix such as pricing strategy, merchandise quality, service level, and store atmosphere, for related merchandise categories.

7. *Minimizing of Competitive Hazard:* Site selection and business volume projections should consider the location, size, and type of existing competitors and the possible business losses to them, which also include minimizing the hazard of vacant properties that could be occupied by competitors in the future. Davies and Rogers (1984, pp. 177–179) point out that retailers need to know the number and square footage of retail units that are being added to, or deleted from, the market area, as well as the quality of these retail units relative to remodeling, deterioration, etc. They cite the following examples. An opportunity for expansion of gasoline outlets by Mobil, Texaco, and ARCO occurred in upstate New York when Shell, Cities Service, and British Petroleum (BP) withdrew from the area. In the supermarket industry, independent and regional chains were able to expand their market share by acquiring stores from A&P when the company closed its smaller rural locations throughout its entire operating territory. Further examples are found in the fast-food outlets and in shopping malls, where the presence of more of the same type of competition actually increases the opportunity for each individual company.

8. *Site Economics:* Cost of the site is analyzed relative to its productivity. This assessment includes site efficiency, size, shape, topography, adjacent amenities, utilities, condition of street and sidewalk, and off-site factors that might affect cost or desirability. A number of obstacles and difficulties must be considered relative to laws and regulations (zoning, permits, environmental impact, etc.), difficult building sites (steep slopes, wetlands, etc.), land preparation costs, and other factors (Freedman, 1984).

Inherent in each of the criteria described above is the ability of the site to meet the retailer's predetermined financial and marketing objectives. Suitability of each site is determined through sales forecasting and pro forma statements, return-on-investment or return-on-net-assets analysis, calculation of capital project costs, breakeven analysis, and assessment of the expected hurdle rate and internal rate of return. Site selection criteria also include market share requirements and growth potential.

In the next section, we will focus our attention on some of the analytical methods retailers use to make store location decisions.

METHODS OF ANALYSIS USED IN LOCATION DECISIONS

The analytical tools used to evaluate store locations range from simple pencil-and-paper checklists to complex computerized statistical models. While the simpler methods are more subjective or intuitive in nature, the more complex methods require quantitative data inputs and mathematical formulas as a basis for decision making. Most site selection decisions are based on a combination of these methods. A brief description of each type of analysis is included in this section.

Subjective or Intuitive Methods

Subjective or intuitive methods are used to evaluate opportunities in regional or area markets, as well as individual sites. A checklist of important factors to be considered, real estate professionals' experience, judgment, and intuition may play roles in this type of decision.

CHECKLIST OF IMPORTANT FACTORS The checklist of important locational factors presented in Exhibit 9–5 could be described in more detail to provide the real estate executive with a list of desirable site characteristics. A retail location checklist, suggested by Nelson (1958, pp. 328–352) is summarized below:

  I. Trading Area Potential
      A. Public utility connections (residential)
      B. Residential building permits issued (number of dwelling units)
      C. School enrollment
      D. New bank accounts opened
      E. Advertising linage in local newspapers
      F. Retail sales volume
      G. Sales tax receipts
      H. Employment—specific (local key business firms and plants)
      I. Employment—general (from state employment service office)
 II. Accessibility
      A. Public transportation (serving site)
      B. Private transportation (serving site)
      C. Parking facilities

D. Long-range trends (transportation facilities)
III. Growth Potential
   A. Zoning pattern
   B. Zoning changes
   C. Zoning potential (proposed changes)
   D. Utilities trend
   E. Vacant land market (land zoned for residential use)
   F. Land use pattern (in areas zoned for other than residential)
   G. Retail-business land use trend
   H. Retail-building trend (permits issued for new retail construction)
   I. Retail-improvement trend (permits issued for remodeling, expansion, etc., in existing retail business properties)
   J. Retail-location trend (changes in occupancy of retail business locations)
   K. Income trend for average family unit
   L. Plant and equipment expenditure trend
   M. Payroll trend
IV. Business Interception
   A. Location pattern—competitive businesses between site and trade area (miles from site)
   B. Location pattern—competitive businesses between site and trade area (served by and sharing one or more traffic arteries with site)
V. Cumulative Attraction Potential (neighboring business survey)
VI. Compatibility (determined by characteristics of neighboring and nearby businesses)
VII. Competitive Hazard Survey (competitive pattern)
   A. Competitors within 1 mile of site (nonintercepting)
   B. Potential competitive sites (vacant lots, presently unoccupied buildings, available for competitive units)
VII. Site Economics
   A. Cost and return analysis
   B. Site efficiency
   C. Natural description
   D. Adjacent amenities (for both vacant land and existing building sites)

For an example of comprehensive competitive checklists for a supermarket and a department store, see Nelson (1958, pp. 353–356).

JUDGMENT OR INTUITION   Site selection is both an art and a science. Data bases and modeling techniques provide a systematic way of controlling subjectivity and reducing risk in site analysis. Real estate executives carefully weigh the results of quantitative analysis and detailed reports, using the resulting models to give a better sense of the opportunities and threats associated with a location. However, practical application of the data in making the final decision often requires the executive's judgment or intuition to adjust for factors that cannot be quantified or for which no definitive statistical research is available. For example, people in San Francisco tend to shop downhill, not uphill, and people buy convenience items where they are, not necessarily where they live. Thus, managers must rely on their own expertise and judgment as well as data in developing retail strategies.

Exhibit 9–5
Checklist of Important Factors for Site Evaluation
••••••••••••••••••••••••••••••
Demographics
....
Local area population base
Local area income potential
Local area growth trends
Employment/unemployment

Traffic Patterns
....
Number, type, and flow of vehicles (and average speed)
Number, type, and flow of pedestrians
Access to public transportation
Access to main thoroughfares
Traffic generators (destinations)

Competition and Retail Structure
....
Number and location of competitors in area
Number and types of stores in area
Affinity of neighboring stores
Proximity to commercial areas

Physical Site Characteristics
....
Lot size and shape
Condition of existing building, or suitability of site for new building
Grade of land, topography, soil conditions
Parking area size, distance, condition
Ease of access
Visibility, signage
Present and proposed land use patterns
Availability of utilities
Ambience

Legal and Cost Factors
....
Taxes
Zoning
Lease (terms of occupancy, cost, restrictions, etc.)
Voluntary regulations by local merchants
Costs of operations and maintenance
Land and development costs for new structure
Utilities
....
For additional information, see Applebaum (1966), Ghosh and McLafferty (1987), Nelson (1958), and others.

Benetton, a national specialty store chain, relies heavily on "a gut feeling" when choosing new suburban locations (DePalma, 1987). Ray Kroc, the founder of McDonald's, acknowledged the need for computers for analysis, but cautioned that they would never replace "gut feel." Likewise, top management at PepsiCo, Inc. relies on gut feelings and quick reflexes in decision making for their business units, including the Taco Bell and Pizza Hut chains (Dunkin, 1986). "Gut feel" is simply when you believe something is "right," a way of making adjustments to reflect special circumstances that are beyond the capability of the computer (Segal, 1987). Even with the use of high-tech, computerized, mathematical models, an analyst must interpret the data and apply it to the retailer's particular situation. The analyst cannot be taken out of analysis; in the end, a person, not a computer, draws the conclusions (Zbytniewski, 1980).

Statistical or Mathematical Models

Statistical and mathematical methods of analysis include regression and discriminant analysis, analogs, gravity models, and sophisticated multi-location models for making multiple decisions simultaneously. Regional and trade data can provide inputs for these models, whose primary function in location decisions is sales forecasting. Of course, forecasting is not as precise at the regional macro level as at the more narrowly defined trade area or site analysis level.

REGRESSION   A **regression model,** as it is applied in location decisions, is a mathematical equation that relates sales outcomes (the dependent variable) to one or more factors (independent variables) that are positively or negatively related to sales. Weights are given to population, economic, income, and other factors, according to their importance in predicting the sales potential of a region. Thompson (1982) describes the steps used in regression analysis in site selection.

1. Pose an initial question or idea of real world factors that may be related to a store's sales volume.
2. Translate the idea into measurable variables.
3. Test the relationship statistically.
4. Retranslate the results to the language of the original question.
5. Come to a conclusion as to whether the original idea can be supported by the "hard" numbers.

The results can be compared to existing similar stores for future development; the larger the data base of stores, the more reliable is the analysis (Green, 1986).

Regression is preferred by many real estate executives and consultants. Although Volume Shoe Corporation does not rely completely on regression analysis, the company does use four types of multiple regression models to predict new store sales based on quantitative information from existing stores. The four separate site selection models, which allow evaluation of each proposed site based on a sample of comparable stores, are: white neighborhood stores, and low, medium, and high density stores (Wood, 1986). The models contain demographic data from the new store location, such as popu-

REGRESSION MODEL
mathematical equation that predicts sales outcomes based on one or more sales-related factors

Getting into That First Mall Location: A Dilemma for Many Retailers

Many small independent and chain retailers express frustration over mall versus street location decisions. Mall locations typically are more expensive and place more restrictions on the tenant. On the other hand, mall tenants—particularly the smaller retailers—benefit from customer traffic generated by other stores and from mall promotional efforts.

Most small retailers seek a lower cost location where they can maintain autonomy in store hours, decor, promotion, and other aspects of the retail mix. All too often, unless these merchants have a creative strategy or an innovative concept, they may watch "their" customers drive by on their way "to the mall."

Those smaller retailers who do decide to move or expand to a shopping mall location may meet resistance in obtaining a lease—even though they are willing to spend three times as much rent as in a non-mall location. New or unknown retailers often face a struggle in getting into malls. One retailer claims that malls are like an exclusive club—where, if you are not a member, you cannot join.

Innovation and perseverance have paid off for many smaller retailers in getting their first mall locations. (After the first, others are easier to obtain if the store has a successful track record.) Shopping center developers seek fresh retailing concepts to overcome the "cookie-cutter" look-alike image of malls. Conversely, they get nervous when a hot new idea comes from a small company without a track record in mall selling. Several retailers have overcome resistance from mall developers and have expanded to numerous other mall locations: Mothers Work, a chain of maternity wear stores targeted toward professional working women; Westminster Lace, whose stores sell apparel and furniture that use lace; and Boxer Bay, an upscale men's underwear store.

The Rouse Company, of Columbia, Maryland, operates shopping centers throughout the United States. According to a Rouse executive, the search for new merchandise from small companies is at the heart of their business, rather than just an interesting sideline. For over a decade, Rouse has nurtured cash-poor entrepreneurs by allowing them to sell merchandise from mobile carts or stalls in mall locations. Those who establish a good sales history can graduate to leased store space. For example, Kristine Brewer started selling handmade sweaters from Latin America on a cart in Rouse's South Street Seaport in New York City and on a street cart outside Filene's department store in Boston. Her $500 investment led to annual gross sales of over $1 million. Six years later she grew to full-fledged stores called Accents in Rouse markets in Boston and Baltimore and had stores in New York and New Orleans. Rouse's approach enabled Ms. Brewer to test her market with only a small investment. (She also had to learn to operate without glass doors and telephones.)

Adapted from Eugene Carlson (1990), "New Retailers Face Struggle Getting in Malls," *The Wall Street Journal* (July 24), B1, B2. Used with permission.

lation per square mile, median household income, percentage of low to middle income households (under $25,000), percentage of children, percentage of population age 55 and over, median age, percent of total nonwhite population, and occupation (Wood, 1986).

Regression also has been used to identify location variables related to store sales performance in state-operated liquor stores in North Carolina. For a location in Charlotte, the model contained annual sales volume for each existing liquor store. Independent predictor variables included population within 1.5 miles of the store site, mean household income, distance from subject store to next nearest liquor store, daily traffic volume on street where store was located, and amount of employment within 1.5 miles of the store (Lord and Lynds, 1981). As another example, Hartfield-Zodys used a computer-generated model to rank the sales potential of counties throughout a number of states when it was ready to expand beyond southern California. Data consisted of each county's population, demographics, and number of existing discount stores. Variables that explained sales performance in the chain's existing 44 discount stores included competition, demographics, and traffic patterns. This analysis permitted ranking of the counties in order of their desirability ("Regression Modeling," 1981).

DISCRIMINANT ANALYSIS   **Discriminant analysis** is a statistical modeling technique closely related to regression analysis. The major difference is that, where regression models have one dependent variable, discriminant models indicate the probability of a potential site belonging to high, middle, or low performance groups of existing stores, for example. Prediction is based on an evaluation of predictor or independent variables.

The procedure consists of selecting a sample of "good," "poor," and "average" stores. A trade area is then defined for each store with customer addresses obtained in each store. Marketing factors associated with each trade area are evaluated in detail. These marketing factors might include geographic distance from the store to trade area boundaries, levels of competition, accessibility, income levels, population, and others. Data for each of these factors is obtained from on-site evaluation, the U.S. Census, and other published records. After the data are collected, discriminant analysis is used to "discriminate" between "good," "poor," and "average" stores in a chain. As a result of this analysis, the retailer can determine (1) which marketing factors are responsible for store performance, (2) a ranking of their importance, (3) a classification of all stores in a chain as to how they *should* perform, regardless of *actual* performance, and (4) the level of performance expected at a proposed location (Klocke, 1985).

ANALOGS   An **analog** is a picture of a store's performance at a given point in time. A series of analogs provides a historical record to be used as a basis for sales forecasts. The analog method of sales forecasting was pioneered by William Applebaum in 1932 for the Kroger Company. This method was the first effort to quantify the performance characteristics of existing stores as an aid to forecast sales at new sites. With some modifications, it is still used successfully by retailers and consultants in location decisions (Rogers and Green, 1979). Applebaum stated that analog forecasting depended on quantified experience and subjective judgment. Quantified experience refers to what is known about the relationship of existing store sales and market penetration performances with known market factors, such as trade area demographics, customer shopping patterns, store characteristics, and competition. Although the analyst must be as objective as possible, subjective judgment is used to some extent when comparing a prospective site and an analog, since no two situations are exactly alike.

The analog system focuses on the degree of market penetration, based on per-unit store sales in dollars or market share. A proposed new location is expected to achieve market penetration performances similar to those achieved at similar units, after adjustments have been made for differences between the proposed store and the analog store. The success of the analog system is dependent on high-quality data collection efforts, based primarily

DISCRIMINANT ANALYSIS
statistical modeling technique that indicates the probability of a potential site belonging to high, middle, or low performance groups of existing stores

ANALOG
analysis of an existing store's performance at a given point in time used to forecast sales at new sites

on customer spotting surveys. It is also dependent on choosing the right existing stores to be used as analogs.

The **spotting survey** is an in-store intercept interview of an existing store's customers (Applebaum, 1966). The typical spotting survey includes questions concerning customers' (1) address, (2) socioeconomic characteristics, (3) patronage of competition, (4) shopping behavior, and (5) media habits. From the data, a retailer can identify the demographic composition, shopping behavior, and media usage habits of the customers of existing stores. Obviously, the design of the questionnaire is critical in obtaining accurate information.

In addition to the customer spotting surveys, other data is required for building the analog data base. This includes demographic and socioeconomic information for a trade area and subareas and current and projected population per household, which is largely obtainable from census reports. A quantitative (distance, square footage, etc.) and qualitative (store appearance, service level, merchandise quality, etc.) evaluation of competitors is also included in the data base. Store and location data are collected and updated for the existing store analogs. Again, the data are both quantitative (sales, profits, square footage, etc.) and qualitative (subjective rating of site characteristics, such as accessibility, visibility, parking, etc.) (Davies and Rogers, 1984, pp. 281–298).

Once the analog data base has been collected and analyzed, store level forecasts can be developed for proposed sites within a defined trade area and its subareas. Forecasts of subareas are aggregated to provide a more accurate sales estimate for the total trade area. Merely using an average forecast does not allow the retailer to determine differences in market potential and shopping behavior for each subarea. (For further discussion of the theory and application of the analog system, see Thompson, 1982, pp. 113–125.)

GRAVITY MODELS   The **gravity model** was developed to determine the relative pulling power of two competing cities on customers in an intervening area. This method of trade area analysis was first introduced in 1925 by William Reilly, who referred to it as "The Law of Retail Gravitation." Reilly's law is often expressed in terms of a "breaking point" formula (Ghosh and McLafferty, 1987, p. 69):

$$\text{distance from breaking point to city B} = \frac{\text{distance between cities A and B}}{1 + \sqrt{\dfrac{P(\text{A})}{P(\text{B})}}}$$

where $P(\text{A})$ = *population of city A*
$P(\text{B})$ = *population of city B*

The breaking point or point of indifference, is where the relative attractiveness of two cities are equal, as illustrated below. The consumer on either side of the breaking point will tend to patronize retailers in the community on their respective side.

SPOTTING SURVEY
in-store intercept interview of an existing store's customers

GRAVITY MODEL
method of trade area analysis that determines the relative pulling power of two competing cities on customers in an intervening area

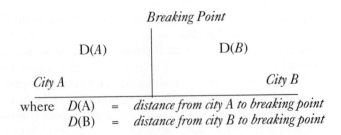

where   D(A) = *distance from city A to breaking point*
        D(B) = *distance from city B to breaking point*

For example, if the distance from city A to city B is 30 miles, and the population of city A is 50,000 and city B is 20,000 the trade area boundary or breaking point would be:

$$\text{distance from breaking point to city B} \quad = \quad \frac{30}{1 + \sqrt{\dfrac{50,000}{20,000}}} = 11.6 \text{ miles}$$

City A	18.4 miles		11.6 miles	City B
Population		*Breaking*		*Population*
50,000		*point*		*20,000*

Although Reilly's law is based on a relatively simple model, it has been used widely to estimate the trade areas of towns and cities, particularly where sizable population differences are involved. The model's predictive ability is limited to assumptions based on population and distance. It does not consider other factors that may attract or discourage shoppers, such as personal safety, general ambience of a shopping area, traffic patterns, or "psychological" distance, for example.

More sophisticated, probabilistic models on an intra-urban scale were developed by David Huff from his pioneering work with shopping center development during the late 1950s and early 1960s. Huff's adaptation of the gravity model made it possible to determine the trading area of competing shopping centers for any given product class. The premise of the Huff model is that a store's trade area depends on its attraction to customers relative to other stores in the area. In the late 1960s, Huff was retained by Super Value, which gave him an opportunity to test his retail gravity model against real world data. The model has proven particularly useful for forecasting sales at new sites. Super Valu's follow-up work on Huff's model provides the basis for all gravity simulation systems now referred to as spatial interaction models in use today (Huff, 1963; Thompson, 1982, pp. 152–160). Others have also extended the basic Huff model of consumer store choice, such as the use of maximum likelihood to estimate central-city food trading areas (Haines, Simon, and Alexis, 1972).

The process of developing a gravity model data base is similar to that for analogs. The gravity model is designed for simultaneous analysis of the effect of distance and competitive effectiveness. Gravity simulation systems consist of three parts: (1) distance (a surrogate measure for location convenience); (2) store size (a surrogate measure for merchandise selection and depth); and (3) image (calibrated for each retailer or retail group). Gravity models lend themselves best to forecasting for convenience goods retailers because of their simple underlying assumptions. Accuracy of prediction is highly dependent upon the ability of the analyst and additional evaluation of consumer patronage and past performance data of existing stores, if available.

Although store size and distance are basic factors in both the Reilly and Huff models, Huff argued that customer attraction is greater for larger and closer stores than for smaller and distant stores. The same principles can be applied to the relative attractiveness of shopping centers within the same trade area. The attraction of larger stores or shopping centers can offset the negative influence of distance. A simplified representation of the model is:

| *Probability of consumer visiting store A* | = | *attraction of store A* | ÷ | *cumulative attraction of all stores in the area* |

where the attraction of store A is a function of the size of store A, the distance or travel time between the customer and store A, and the degree of the customer sensitivity to store size and distance.

An illustration of the gravity method is provided by Price Chopper Supermarkets, based in Schenectady, N.Y. The retailer undertook an in-depth analysis to determine the present and future impact of competitive action to turn two ordinary food stores into cost-slashing warehouse markets in Price Chopper's biggest trade areas. Gravity models were used to examine a nearly 400 square mile area with a population of nearly 500,000, spanning Albany, Schenectady, and Troy, in upstate New York. Thus, the 54-store Price Chopper was able to measure in advance the effect of the warehouse units. Although the competitor dropped its conversion plans, Price Chopper still uses the model to test potential sites and develop strategies ("Gravity Method," 1981).

MULTIPLE LOCATIONS IN ONE TRADE AREA Optimizing individual location decisions may not result in optimum corporate performance for a multi-store company operating in a highly competitive retailing environment. MULTILOC is a decision model developed to determine the optimum network of multiple store locations within the same market area, with the number of stores specified in advance (Achabal, Gorr, and Mahajan, 1982). The strength of this approach lies in the realization that store locations interact strongly with other strategic elements, such as advertising and distribution, allowing the retailer to achieve greater impact on customers in a market.

This method of location analysis is best suited to retailers with a wide choice of available locations, relatively small unit size, broad market appeal, and many freestanding units. Therefore, it is most appropriate for supermarkets, service stations, convenience store chains, fast-food outlets, and financial institutions.

Analysis Summary

Retail location decisions are based on a combination of statistical analysis and the experience and ability of the real estate expert. The quality of data collection and analysis is critical for accurate sales forecasts. Primary consumer

The entrance to the Bridgewater Commons shopping center in Bridgewater, New Jersey, includes a greenbelt with bicycle paths and walkways.

research and secondary demographic data, such as information available from census reports, provide inputs for market analysis. Market characteristics that have been found to predict a retailer's success can also be entered into mathematical equations to develop predictive models.

Evaluation of Location Decisions: An Ongoing Process

As an important element of a retailer's strategic plan, locations must continue to be evaluated beyond the initial new store site decision. Customers move in and out of neighborhoods, stores age, and changes occur in the store's competitive, legal, and physical environment. Over time, a once "perfect" location may become a problem location. Therefore, customer and market analysis should be an ongoing process as a location is reevaluated. Perhaps the original checklist of important factors or the variables in statistical models will require adjustment to new conditions. The result may be a need for creative competitive strategies or a move to a new site.

Distinct advantages of certain locations are directly associated with increased sales and performance levels. Ongoing analysis is instrumental in identifying success factors related to a particular site. Once these factors are known, they can be used as criteria in evaluating future sites, as well as existing locations.

Summary

One of the most challenging decisions facing retail managers is related to store location. The location of the store will be a major determinant of its success. Once the location decision is made, it is very difficult—or perhaps impossible—to change.

In Chapter 8 we considered the broader geographical areas that must be analyzed and evaluated against the retailers' criteria for store locations. In this chapter, the actual store site was the focus of discussion.

The retailer may choose a freestanding location or unplanned business district (central business district, secondary business district, neighborhood business district, and string). Many retailers choose to locate in planned shopping centers, which may be classified as regional, community, neighborhood, or specialty shopping centers.

Subjective decision criteria used to evaluate retail sites include checklists of important factors and the real estate professionals' experience and judgment. However, statistical or mathematical models provide the most important inputs for the location decision. The methods described in this chapter include regression analysis, discriminant analysis, analogs, and gravity models. Analytical models also have been developed to assess the optimum network of multiple locations within the same market area.

Successful retail location decisions require an organizational structure with assigned responsibilities and training for those involved in the analysis from the beginning of the process to the final "Go/No go" decision.

Questions for Review and Comprehension

1. Explain why store location is considered by many to be the most important element of success in a retail strategy.
2. A retailer's store location decision affects, and is affected by, all functional management areas of the store: merchandising, human resources, promotion, store operations and physical facilities, and control and accounting. Discuss this two-way relationship in regard to a drug store that does a large prescription business.
3. Describe the four types of unplanned business districts: central business district (CBD), secondary business district (SBD), neighborhood business district (NBD), and string or strip. Give examples of (a) retailers who would be expected to succeed and (b) retailers who would be expected to fail, in each type of location. Include reasons for including each example in the particular category.
4. Discuss the four types of planned shopping centers: regional, community, neighborhood, and specialty. Describe and evaluate the tenant mix in a shopping center near you. Include an assessment of the shopping center's strengths and weaknesses in serving its target market and your recommendations for improvement.
5. Compare and contrast the general characteristics of freestanding stores, planned shopping centers, and unplanned business districts. Evaluate each type of shopping area for (a) a mass merchandise discount store and (b) a small specialty discount store.
6. Give an overview of the decision criteria used to evaluate a store site. Explain how these might be applied for a (a) bank, (b) supermarket, (c) video store, (d) family restaurant, and (e) dentist's office.
7. Describe two methods of subjective or intuitive methods that are used to evaluate retail sites. Evaluate the wisdom of using only these methods without also considering the results of quantitative analysis.

8. Briefly describe the statistical methods used most often to evaluate retail sites. State the purpose and underlying principles of each method. Discuss whether these methods are foolproof without the benefit of executive judgment or intuition. Defend your answer.

References

Achabal, Dale, Wilpen L. Gorr, and Vijay Mahajan (1982), "MULTILOC: A Multiple Store Location Decision Model," *Journal of Retailing* 58, no. 2, (Summer), 5–25.

Applebaum, William (1964), "Store Location Research—A Survey by Retail Chains," *Journal of Retailing* (Summer), 53–56.

Applebaum, William (1966), "Methods for Determining Store Trade Areas, Market Penetration, and Potential Sales," *Journal of Marketing Research* vol. III (May), 127–141.

Applebaum, William (1970), *Shopping Center Strategy*. New York: International Council of Shopping Centers.

Davies, R. L. and D. S. Rogers (1984), *Store Location and Store Assessment Research*. New York: John Wiley & Sons.

DePalma, Anthony (1987), "The Malling of Main Street," *The New York Times* (April 19), 4.

Dunkin, Amy (1986), "Pepsi's Marketing Magic: Why Nobody Does It Better," *Business Week* (February 10), 52–53, 56–57.

Ferron, David (vice-president of Properties, Consumer Value Stores, Woonsocket, R.I.) (1984), "Biggest Myths and Pitfalls," presentation at NACORE Institute for Corporate Real Estate, Inc., Retail Site Selection Seminar, Cambridge, Mass. (May 2–4).

Freedman, Maurice (principal and director of Engineering and Environmental Services, Sasaki Associates, Inc., Watertown, Maine) (1984), "Evaluation of the Physical Site Characteristics," presentation at NACORE Institute for Corporate Real Estate, Inc., Retail Site Selection Seminar, Cambridge, Mass. (May 2–4).

Ghosh, Avijit and Sara McLafferty (1987), *Location Strategies for Retail and Service Firms*. Lexington, Mass.: D. C. Heath and Company.

"Gravity Method" (1981), *Chain Store Age Executive* (March), 47–48.

Green, Howard (1986), "The Art and Science of Retail Site Selection," National Association of Corporate Real Estate Executives Annual Symposium, San Antonio, Tex. (April 14).

Greenberg, Larry M. (1991), "Developers of Big Shopping Malls Tutor Faltering Tenants in Retail Techniques," *The Wall Street Journal* (April 24), B1.

Grossman, Howard (president, The Howard Grossman Company, Inc., Nashua, N.H.) (1984), "Competitive Strategy," presentation at NACORE Institute for Corporate Real Estate, Inc., Retail Site Selection Seminar, Cambridge, Mass. (May 2–4).

Haines, George H. Jr., Leonard S. Simon, and Marcus Alexis (1972), "Maximum Likelihood Estimation of Central-City Food Trading Areas," *Journal of Marketing Research* vol. IX (May), 154–159.

Helliker, Kevin (1991), "Showcase for Inventions Prospers at Mall Following Shakeout Among Big Retailers," *The Wall Street Journal* (January 28), B1, B2.

Huff, David L. (1963), "A Probabilistic Analysis of Shopping Center Trade Areas," *Land Economics* 39, 81–90.

Klocke, William J. (1985), "What Makes a Store Good?" *WriteUps* vol. VI, no. 2 (Autumn), 1–2.

Lord, J. Dennis and Charles D. Lynds (1981), "The Use of Regression Analysis in Store Location Research: A Review and Case Study," *Akron Business and Economic Review* (Summer), 13–19.

McCain, Mark (1987), "Retailers Resent Their Bargain-Rent Competition," *The New York Times* (May 10), 2.

Nelson, Richard L. (1958), *The Selection of Retail Locations.* New York: F. W. Dodge Corp.

"Regression Modeling" (1981), *Chain Store Age Executive* (March), 46–47.

Rogers, David S. and Howard L. Green (1979), "A New Perspective on Forecasting Store Sales: Applying Statistical Models and Techniques in the Analog Approach," *The Geography Review* (October), 449–458.

Schwadel, Francine (1991), "Nordstrom Aim: Midwest Success Amid Recession," *The Wall Street Journal* (April 4), B1, B8.

Segal, David (vice president, Corporate Real Estate, Dunkin' Donuts of America, Inc.) (1987), "Retail Site Selection," in *Corporate Real Estate Handbook.* Robert A. Silverman, ed. New York: McGraw-Hill, Inc., chapter 13.

Suris, Oscar (1991), "Retailer Plans Two-Store Project at Florida Mall," *The Orlando Sentinel* (February 15), C 1,6.

Thompson, John S. (1982), *Site Selection.* New York: Chain Store Publishing Corp.

Totty, Michael (1988), "'Power Centers' Lure Shoppers by Mixing Elements from Big Malls and Small Plazas," *The Wall Street Journal* (December 27).

"Waldenbooks Launches 12–15 Stores for Kids in Malls Nationwide" (1987), *Real Estate Times* (March 31), 4.

Wood, R. Victor, Jr. (sr. vice president/director of Real Estate and Construction, Volume Shoe Corporation) (1986), "Restaurant/Retail Site Selection—Is It an Art or a Science?" Panel presentation, National Association of Corporate Real Estate Executives Annual Symposium, San Antonio, Tex. (April 14).

Zbytniewski, Jo-Ann (1980), "Beyond Site Selection: Programming Answers to Planning Problems," *Progressive Grocer* (May), 113–116.

2.1 Betty Campbell: Confronted with a Consumer Protest

CASE

It was the day after Thanksgiving, typically the biggest selling day of the year for Hatties' Department Store. Betty Campbell was excited. This was her first Christmas season with Hatties' as the buyer for ladies coats. Last spring she had bought for the fall season and her selections had brought much success for Hatties'. In October she made a special trip to market to buy for the holiday season and had gotten an excellent buy on a line of fur coats.

Although Hatties' had always had a small fur salon as part of the coat department, it had never received much recognition. Betty felt that the great buy on furs was a perfect opportunity for her to boost her success as buyer and promote Hatties' as a fashion leader by offering a luxury item to her customers at a price they could afford.

Betty knew she needed to sell the furs early in the Christmas season, otherwise there would be major markdowns. She was confident, however, that with the additional advertising dollars and window display space allotted to her department for the Christmas season, she would have no trouble selling the majority of the furs at full price. With a full page ad in the previous Sunday's paper and three window displays on Main Street promoting the furs, Betty was sure that this first day of the Christmas selling season was going to be her most successful selling day of the year.

Soon after the store opened at 10:00 a.m. a sizable group of consumers gathered outside the store's main entrance protesting Hatties' selling of furs. Slogans on posters such as 'Fur is Dead,' 'Get a Feel for a Fur Coat; Slam a Door on Your Hand,' 'Buy a Fur and Slip into Something Dead,' 'Fur: The Look that Kills,' and 'It Takes up to 40 Dumb Animals to Make a Fur Coat; But Only One to Wear It' decorated the street in front of the main entrance into Hatties.' Protesters distributed leaflets informing passersby of the gruesome story behind the making of fur coats. One protester, dressed in a fox costume, read the leaflet over a megaphone.

The leaflet was entitled "The Fur Industry: An Ugly Business." It stated that millions of animals killed for fur garments each year in the United States were caught in traps, including the steel-jaw leghold trap, which more than 70 countries had banned because of its extreme cruelty. Animals caught in the trap could suffer for hours or days before trappers returned. The intense pain and terror caused many animals to escape by chewing off their limbs. Animals who remained trapped faced freezing, starving, and predator attack, unless the trapper arrived first to kill them by clubbing, stomping or drowning. Traps also maimed and killed millions of what trappers called "trash" animals each year, including birds and companion dogs and cats.

The pamphlet also condemned fur "ranches." It stated that ranched furbearers suffered from crowding and confinement, which induced contagious diseases, as well as self-mutilation and even cannibalism. Selective breeding techniques produced painful genetic defects. The open sheds in which the animals were raised were usually not heated or cooled. Killing methods on fur farms included poisoning with strychnine or hot, unfiltered automobile or lawnmower exhaust; neck-snapping; gassing; decompression; and anal electrocution.

Across the street in front of Nobel's Book Store, a video was being shown from a mobile unit. The video depicted animals suffering in steel jaw leg-hold traps, and 'ranched' animals living in tiny, cramped, dirty cages. It showed the animals being killed by inhumane methods that would not damage the furs. At the end of the video celebrities disapproving of furs were interviewed. Protesters at the mobile unit passed out flyers promoting a "Rock Against Fur" concert scheduled for Saturday night and urging consumers to boycott Hatties.'

By midday the media had arrived to cover the event. Reporters had interviewed the protesters and were beginning to seek out the store manager for statements. The store manager, Mr. Cohen, was seeking out Betty. By this time both Mr. Cohen and Betty were quite upset over the negative publicity the store was getting. Mr. Cohen approached Betty asking "What were you thinking about when you made the decision to do an all out promotion on furs, especially since it is such a sensitive issue with the public? Two other department stores in the area have recently closed their fur salon."

Betty responded heatedly, "What is wrong with furs? Man has worn fur since time began. Besides it is a luxury item that is now affordable to the average woman. It is a status symbol; it represents success. These people are just being emotional. I like furs; they feel great."

She showed Mr. Cohen a booklet on furs she had been given by one of the fur sales reps entitled "Fur the Renewable Resource." The booklet stated that the majority of furs came from ranches where the furbearing animals were raised for their fur. Ranched animals, such as mink and fox, were scientifically bred to obtain superior quality and more colors. These animals were humanely raised in spacious settings and fed excellent diets—how else could the furs look so good.

In regards to the trapping of animals, the booklet said it was a well-regulated activity and was necessary to prevent starvation and diseases, such as rabies, in wild animal populations. The booklet pointed out that everyone involved in conservation, including the fur industry, agreed the present traps were not perfect, but they were the best available. The money from trapping licenses went toward conservation to maintain an ecological balance of nature. The booklet also mentioned that the fur industry promoted wildlife conservation and supported the protection of endangered species in every way.

"Obviously," Betty told Mr. Cohen, "the public is just misinformed."

"Certainly someone is misinformed," replied Mr. Cohen. "We need to straighten this situation out or Hatties' sales for the holidays is going to suffer. You got Hatties' into this dilemma. By tomorrow morning I want you to come up with a plan to get us out of it."

Questions

1. What are the main issues that Betty needs to address?
2. Offer several suggestions that Hatties' could undertake to remedy this situation.
3. If you were Betty, what would be your proposed plan to Mr. Cohen?

This case was prepared by Sandra D. Skinner, Western Carolina University, Cullowhee, North Carolina.

2.2 BORDER-TO-BORDER STORES: A STORE LOCATION PROBLEM

Border-to-Border Stores, Inc. is a subsidiary of the merchandising arm of a large financial organization. In return for a franchise fee, the company offers franchisees a "turn-key" operation. Thus, the company conducts analyses of markets and their potential; selects a store size and location which they feel will help the franchisee to meet his/her goals; and additionally, because the franchisee often lacks retail experience, the company assists in ordering (like many franchise organizations, the company is vertically integrated and also acts as a wholesaler), promotions and advertising, bookkeeping, accounting, taxes, store layout, and so on. This assistance may be particularly necessary because the merchandise mix of a Border-to-Border store is "scrambled"; the typical outlet stocks recreational equipment (e.g., small pools, bicycles, basketballs), housewares (e.g., dishes, vases, placemats), small appliances (including stereo systems), toys, and gift items in addition to more traditional hardware lines.

Border-to-Border Stores consists of over 1,160 stores primarily located in small, semi-rural towns in the midwestern United States. Aside from the fact that the "total hardware" approach of Border-to-Border stores may be best suited to small towns, many franchisees are drawn by the attractiveness of living and working in semi-rural areas.

By 1976, Border-to-Border Stores had began to expand to areas outside the Midwest. Their goals, as the organization's name implies, is to franchise stores across the nation. In 1977, Mr. Coslyn, a store location specialist, was hired to conduct an analysis of the market for a store in the city of Visalia, a community in the agriculture-rich San Joaquin Valley of central California. In addition to assessing the general Visalia market for a Border-to-Border store, Mr. Coslyn was asked to analyze the attractiveness of an available store site located in the northeastern section of town.

AN ECONOMIC OUTLOOK FOR HARDWARE AND RELATED LINES

Mr. Coslyn began his analysis by compiling various data pertaining to hardware sales and related products at the state and local level. He knew these data would provide a useful indication of the probable economic climate in Visalia for the lines of merchandise typically carried by a Border-to-Border franchise.

Case Exhibit 1 shows hardware sales and sales of various hardlines items for the years 1966 to 1976 for the state of California. These are lines typically carried by an 8,000-square foot Border-to-Border store. This is the most typical size of a Border-to-Border store and the size of the available site in Visalia. As shown in the note to Case Exhibit 1, this size of store carries a variety of hardware and other hardline items. Average annual growth in sales volume for hardware and hardline items was 10.8 and 8.9 percent for the period, respectively.

Case Exhibit 2 shows similar data for Tulare County (in which Visalia is located). The figures in Case Exhibits 1 and 2 can be compared to an approximate average national growth rate of 10 percent.

Since sales data reported by city is not disaggregate enough to allow for a separate examination of hardware and other related items, Mr. Coslyn examined total retail sales data for all stores in Visalia. He felt this would help him develop a clearer idea of the market opportunity for a store in Visalia. Case Exhibit 3 displays this information.

For comparison purposes, Mr. Coslyn noted that the average annual growth in volume for all retail stores in Tulare County for the same period (1968–1976) was 13.3 percent; however, the average volume per store was lower than that of retail stores in Visalia. In 1976, the average volume per store in Tulare County was $240,450. The average annual growth in volume for retail stores in the state of California during the same period was 10.4 percent; the average volume per store in 1976 was close to $296,000.

A PROFILE OF THE TARGET MARKET

Demographics are measurable statistics about populations. Often demographics—such as age, income and education, for example—are reasonably good indicators of purchase behavior. Additionally, Mr. Coslyn knew that with data available from secondary sources, he could develop a demographic market profile of the heavy user of hardware and related lines. This data could then be compared to a demographic breakdown of the trading area.

By carefully checking library sources, Mr. Coslyn discovered a study that had been published in 1976 by *Hardware Age* magazine. The study had been conducted by Chilton Research Service (a division of the company that publishes the magazine) using a national probability sample of telephone households. Interviews had been conducted with 753 men and 254 women.

The data in the study included the purchase of sporting goods, toys, building materials, and automotive supplies, as well as the more "standard" hardware and hardline categories.

Case Exhibit 4 shows product purchase by store type. Case Exhibit 5 shows purchase behavior broken down by the demographics collected in the study.

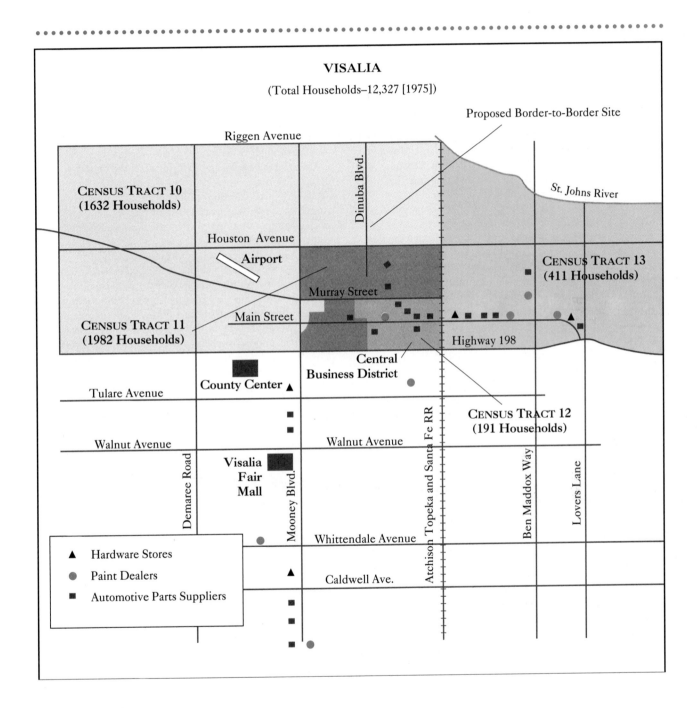

VISALIA

(Total Households–12,327 [1975])

Riggen Avenue

Proposed Border-to-Border Site

St. Johns River

CENSUS TRACT 10
(1632 Households)

Dinuba Blvd.

Houston Avenue

Airport

CENSUS TRACT 13
(411 Households)

Murray Street

Main Street

CENSUS TRACT 11
(1982 Households)

Highway 198

Central Business District

Tulare Avenue

County Center ▲

CENSUS TRACT 12
(191 Households)

Walnut Avenue

Walnut Avenue

Atchison Topeka and Santa Fe RR

Demaree Road

Visalia Fair Mall

Mooney Blvd.

Ben Maddox Way

Lovers Lane

Whittendale Avenue

▲ Hardware Stores

● Paint Dealers

■ Automotive Parts Suppliers

▲ Caldwell Ave.

A DEMOGRAPHIC VIEW OF THE POPULATION RESIDING IN THE RETAIL TRADING AREA

The Visalia Retailing Areas

Mr. Coslyn determined that three areas within the Visalia community provided almost all of the regional retail uses. The downtown area (the Central Business District), the Mooney Boulevard strip (which includes the Visalia Fair Shopping Center), and the County Center shopping area were the primary retail areas (see map of Visalia).

In 1975, regional retail expansion had been proposed to be located at the intersections of Ben Maddox Way and Highway 198, and Lovers Lane and Highway 198. Mr. Coslyn thought these retail developments (when built) would likely have good visibility and accessibility via Highway 198 and Lovers Lane (both major county arterials). An interview with a planner for the city of Visalia indicated that due to southward growth trends, the city had felt it was in danger of filling in the corridor between Visalia and the city of Tulare and, in response, had begun planning activities designed to draw the city's population toward the east.

The Central Business District, or downtown Visalia, as described in a document published by the City of Visalia in 1976, is "an economically viable area for retail, financial, and other types of commercial businesses and services. The character of the Central Business District—is slowly changing to one of a business center rather than dominantly retail sales."

Mooney Boulevard is where a large amount of the retail and service businesses exist in Visalia. Retail activity is strong from Highway 198 south to Caldwell Avenue. This is the area where the Visalia Fair shopping mall is located.

County Center, located at County Center Drive and Mineral King Highway (Highway 198), has a Montgomery Ward and a K mart, as well as a grocery and smaller retail stores.

The N. Dinuba Boulevard Location

A retail store has a definite trading area surrounding it from which the majority of its sales are gained. Mr. Coslyn knew that studies of shoppers have shown that a retail store's trading area is limited by the factor of driving time. These studies show that smaller centers or stores without a wide variety of goods are more dependent upon patrons who reside close to the center; i.e., larger shopping centers (those with a wide variety of stores or products) are often able to draw patrons from a further distance than are smaller centers or stores. Additionally, Mr. Coslyn knew that consumers are likely to travel farther to purchase highly visible items of relatively high unit costs and with important status connotations.

From experience, Mr. Coslyn had found that natural or man-made obstructions also tend to influence the boundaries of a trading area. The location and design of main traffic arteries and other streets influence the direction and intensity of traffic through an area. Additionally, obstructions such as bridges, railroad tracks, and so forth, affect the drawing power of a retail store.

Mr. Coslyn also needed to identify competitors and the extent of their trading areas. He knew that where the trading zones of competing stores overlap, the draw of any single store would be reduced.

Mr. Coslyn identified the boundaries of the primary area (simply the area from which the store is likely to secure a considerable part of the purchases made by consumers) and the secondary and tertiary area, which would represent weaker and less substantial markets for a Border-to-Border retailer. (A tertiary trading area can be drawn from only in rare instances. Sometimes, price advertising or unique merchandise may draw a few of the potential customers who reside in this area to a particular store location. Thus, beyond the secondary area, patronage at the store is generally considered to be relatively insignificant.)

Mr. Coslyn determined that the N. Dinuba location (N. Dinuba Boulevard at Prospect Avenue) is nearly at the northern boundary of Visalia (which is Riggen Avenue) in a small shopping center comprised of a grocery store, a dry cleaner, an automotive parts store, and a pizza restaurant. Visalia is the type of small town where the city limits clearly separate population from other land uses. Since the area north of the city limits is predominantly used for agriculture, Mr. Coslyn deemed the northern boundary of both the primary and secondary trading areas to be Riggen Avenue (see map of Visalia).

Mr. Coslyn felt that the western boundary of the primary and secondary trading areas was Mooney Boulevard, because the area west of Mooney Boulevard is primarily industrial.

Mr. Coslyn considered the southern boundary of the primary trading area to be Houston Avenue. He felt that the area between Houston Avenue and Murray Street is an overlapping trading area for the N. Dinuba location and the downtown stores and thus, represents a secondary trading area. He reasoned that consumers living in this area would likely be indifferent as to which direction to travel to a hardware store, although the "point of indifference" might vary by product class. Mr. Coslyn decided it would be highly unlikely that a consumer living south of Murray Street would ever bypass the Central Business District with its large offering of hardware and other items in order to visit the proposed Border-to-Border store and, thus, considered this area to be a part of the tertiary trading area.

The eastern boundary of the primary trading area is shown as the railroad tracks. Because the area east of the tracks is predominantly industrial and the arterial system from those areas that are inhabited leads toward the downtown area, Mr. Coslyn figured the area east to Ben Maddox Way should be considered part of the secondary trading area. Due to driving time and the drawing power of the agglomeration of stores in the Central Business District, Mr. Coslyn considered the area east of Ben Maddox Way to Lover's Lane a tertiary trading zone.

Case Exhibits 6 through 8 exhibit demographic information for the analysis of the trading area. Specifically, Case Exhibit 6 examines population and households for the primary trading area in both 1970 and 1975. The data is displayed by statistical blocks, which are small areas within a census tract. This breakdown was necessary because Mr. Coslyn had designated the primary trading area for the Border-to-Border store to be smaller than the census tract it was located in (tract 10). Case Exhibit 7 displays data for the tracts within which the primary, secondary, and tertiary markets exist (see map of Visalia). For comparative purposes, Case Exhibit 8 displays available characteristics of the population in the state of California.

COMPETITION

Mr. Coslyn examined competition by producing a map of the location of hardware stores, paint stores, and automotive parts and suppliers. He obtained the names and addresses of these stores from the yellow pages of the telephone directory. Additionally, he noted the location of the two major shopping centers and the CBD. This information is shown on the map of Visalia.

QUESTIONS

1. What should Mr. Coslyn recommend? Is the N. Dinuba Blvd. location a good one for a Border-to-Border store? Why?
2. Is there a more preferable retail area for a hardware store in Visalia? Why?
3. Critique Mr. Coslyn's method of determining the attractiveness of the proposed store location. If you were the consultant, would you have done anything differently?

This case was developed by Scott D. Alden, Whittier College, Whittier, California.

Case Exhibit 1

Sales of Hardware and Various Hardline Items* for the State of California (1966–1976)

Hardware

Year	Number of Permits	Volume (000's)	% of Change in Volume	Volume Per Store (000's)
1966	1885	$283,053	—	$150.16
1967	1842	286,653	1.3	155.62
1968	1787	317,261	10.7	177.54
1969	1770	346,929	9.4	196.01
1970	1773	368,300	6.2	207.73
1971	1741	419,707	14.0	241.07
1972	1764	482,167	14.9	273.34
1973	1794	543,978	12.8	303.22
1974	1856	623,889	14.7	336.15
1975	1865	685,681	9.9	367.66
1976	1888	780,166	13.8	413.22

Average Annual Growth in Volume: 10.8%

Hardline Items

Year	Number of Permits	Volume (000's)	% of Change in Volume	Volume Per Store (000's)
1966	23,479	$2,366,231	—	$100.78
1967	23,488	2,347,397	–0.8	99.94
1968	23,922	2,593,940	10.5	108.43
1969	24,559	2,764,344	6.6	112.56
1970	25,257	2,835,404	2.6	112.26
1971	26,235	3,140,264	10.8	119.70
1972	27,519	3,531,739	12.5	128.34
1973	29,125	3,987,670	12.9	136.92
1974	30,886	4,357,424	9.3	141.08
1975	32,474	4,675,593	7.3	143.98
1976	34,792	5,467,252	16.9	157.14

Average Annual Growth in Volume: 8.9%

* Includes plumbing and electrical supplies; paint, glass, and wallpaper; automotive supplies and parts; farm and garden supplies; household appliances; household and home furnishings; sporting goods; gifts, art goods, and novelties.

SOURCE: Compiled from State Board of Equalization, *Taxable Sales in California.*

Case Exhibit 2
Sales of Hardware and Various Items for Tulare County (1966–1976)

Hardware

Number of Permits Store (000's)	Volume	% of Change (000's)	Volume Per in Volume
26	$3,176	—	$122.15
27	2,948	7.2	109.19
27	2,921	0.9	108.19
27	3,335	14.2	123.52
28	3,547	6.4	126.68
26	3,751	5.8	144.27
28	5,152	37.4	184.00
27	5,616	9.0	208.00
28	6,486	15.5	231.64
27	6,909	6.5	255.89
27	7,765	12.4	287.59

Average Annual Growth in Volume: 9.9%

Hardline Items

Number of Permits	Volume (000's)	% of Change in Volume	Volume Per Store (000's)
311	$20,803	—	$ 66.89
311	20,260	–2.6	65.14
324	22,521	11.2	69.51
326	24,779	10.0	76.01
335	24,686	–0.4	73.69
333	26,947	9.2	80.92
353	32,100	19.1	90.93
364	37,121	15.6	101.98
394	45,681	23.1	115.94
439	50,695	11.0	115.48
457	60,124	18.6	131.56

Average Annual Growth in Volume: 11.5%

Case Exhibit 3
Total Sales for Retail Stores: Visalia (1968–1976)*

Year	Number of Permits	Volume (000's)	% of Change in Volume	Volume Per Store (000's)
1968	426	88,603	—	$207.99
1969	443	98,059	10.7	221.35
1970	458	102,501	4.5	223.80
1971	468	117,745	14.9	251.59
1972	485	137,386	16.7	283.27
1973	505	150,926	9.9	298.86
1974	515	177,390	17.5	344.45
1975	538	197,248	11.2	366.63
1976	555	234,948	19.1	423.33

Average Annual Growth in Volume: 13.1%

* City data was not reported by the state of California for the years 1966 and 1967.
Compiled from State Board of Equalization, *Taxable Sales in California.*

Case Exhibit 4
Purchases of Hardline Items by Type of Store

	Hardware Stores	Mass Merchant
Hand Tools	43.3%	48.7%
Power Tools	38.1	50.9
Hardware	68.2	25.8
Plumbing/Electrical	56.5	24.1
Building Materials	40.9	15.5
Lawn and Garden	31.1	44.6
Paint and Decorating	37.3	38.5
Housewares/ Small Appliances	16.0	75.7

Case Exhibit 5
Product Categories Purchased in Three-Month Period by All Consumers*

	Age				Sex		Education			Income			Marital Status		Residence			Dwelling	
	Under 25	*25–44*	*45–64*	*65 and over*	*Male*	*Female*	*Some high school*	*H.S. graduate/some college*	*College graduate*	*Under $10,000*	*$10,000–$20,000*	*Over $20,000*	*Married*	*Not married*	*Home*	*Apartment*	*Other*	*Own*	*Rent*
Hand and Power Tools	18.1	21.7	22.8	16.5	29.5	14.6	18.3	22.6	19.8	14.1	22.4	26.7	24.1	14.1	23.5	13.3	20.5	23.4	16.4
Hardware	55.4	67.1	58.3	42.8	64.9	57.5	57.8	61.7	60.9	50.9	65.1	64.5	63.7	53.8	62.6	53.4	63.7	63.1	55.7
Building Materials	29.2	38.8	34.0	18.5	40.6	29.5	29.1	38.3	30.7	23.9	40.3	34.8	38.3	24.7	38.7	20.8	28.7	39.1	23.8
Housewares and Appliances	35.7	44.2	50.5	41.6	44.8	45.7	40.1	46.1	46.0	41.6	43.0	58.6	46.6	41.5	44.9	46.6	45.0	46.1	43.3
Lawn and Garden Supplies	26.2	27.5	28.8	17.7	26.0	28.0	20.8	29.2	25.1	21.7	27.1	37.9	29.7	20.1	29.2	17.3	32.2	30.4	19.1
Paint and Decorating Products	54.6	46.4	41.4	34.5	46.9	42.9	37.1	46.8	43.9	37.2	46.4	50.1	46.2	40.7	46.8	38.2	39.2	46.0	41.4
Plumbing and Electrical Supplies	39.8	38.7	40.2	29.6	45.3	33.1	42.6	36.9	40.9	32.8	40.4	41.2	41.4	31.7	40.1	31.5	45.0	41.6	31.7
Sporting Goods/Toys	53.5	57.5	38.5	11.1	49.0	45.3	34.8	47.8	52.8	38.5	41.6	48.5	50.0	39.0	47.3	45.1	49.7	45.7	49.9
Automotive Supplies	58.8	65.1	51.3	30.0	63.1	52.0	44.8	58.2	61.9	45.3	65.4	58.0	62.1	43.4	58.3	50.9	61.4	56.3	58.8
Average Amount Purchased**	45.9	82.1	154.7	45.8	91.2	107.7	64.8	109.3	184.0	43.4	188.9	97.3	110.6	72.0	107.8	57.6	150.2	116.4	—

* *Figures represent percentage of consumers of various types who purchased product category*
**Compared to national average of $427.06 per household*

Case Exhibit 6
A Comparison of Population and Households for the Primary Trading Area (1970 and 1975)

Tract 10 Block Number	Population 1970	Population 1975	Households* 1970	Households* 1975		Tract 10 Block Number	Population 1970	Population 1975	Households* 1970	Households* 1975
101	112	112	30	35		210	78	40	18	13
102	213	272	65	79		211	75	57	23	19
120	3	14	2	4		212	88	47	26	14
121	180	7	45	3		213	64	47	18	16
122	388	196	97	49		214	59	53	19	19
123	114	49	30	9		215	49	38	18	16
124	116	52	27	15		216	57	62	20	18
125	71	89	21	23		217	99	62	32	17
126	104	65	29	20		218	64	66	17	19
127	266	197	61	55		219	85	67	21	17
128	71	18	15	6		Totals	3064	2167	829	649
129	78	44	17	15						
130	29	25	9	6		103	43	N	11	N
131	27	4	8	3	C	104	69	O	19	O
138	5	5	2	2		105	106	T	26	T
139	21	18	9	9	O	106	56		17	
140	33	27	8	9		107	160	A	44	A
141	44	38	13	12	U	108	129	V	35	V
142	46	34	16	13		109	52	A	15	A
143	84	49	15	13	N	110	81	I	18	I
201	32	30	10	10		111	66	L	21	L
202	31	51	6	14	T	112	45	A	12	A
203	15	15	4	4		113	52	B	14	B
204	74	35	22	13	Y	114	72	L	19	L
205	67	52	19	18		115	206	E	65	E
206	6	40	3	13		Total County	1137	1137	316	316
207	39	24	12	7		Total Trading Area	4201	3304	1145	965
208	35	27	9	9						
209	42	39	13	13						

* Excludes vacant units
Compiled from U.S. Bureau of the Census, *Block Statistics for Selected Areas in California—1970* and *City of Visalia Special Census, 1975.*

Case Exhibit 7
Tract Summary Information for Tracts 10, 11, 12, and 13 and City of Visalia (1975)

	Tract 10	Tract 11	Tract 12	Tract 13	Total Visalia
Total Population	5100	5041	418	1467	35050
Households (excludes vacant units)	1632	1982	191	411	12327
Population per Household	3.03	2.52	2.08	3.28	2.84
Industry Employing Head of Household:					
No Response	17.1	15.2	31.3	26.6	15.0
Agriculture, Forestry, Fishing, Mining	7.6	5.4	1.6	7.1	5.1
Construction and Manufacturing	8.8	11.9	6.3	9.5	10.6
Transportation, Communication, Public Utilities		3.7	3.1	5.4	5.0
Wholesale and Retail Trade	5.6	7.3	6.3	9.5	9.7
Finance, Insurance, Real Estate	1.7	1.8	1.1	1.2	2.9
Services	14.3	11.4	14.1	11.2	12.0
Professional and Related Services	8.3	7.2	5.8	2.4	10.7
Public Administration	1.8	2.4	1.1	1.5	3.2
Retired, Unemployed, Not Working Labor Force	30.8	33.7	29.3	25.6	25.8
Length of Time Residing in Visalia:					
No Response	16.9	15.5	28.3	33.0	15.6
Less than 1 Year	8.8	8.2	6.3	5.4	10.1
1–3 Years	12.6	9.1	5.8	5.8	12.1
3–5 Years	5.3	5.3	4.2	3.7	7.0
5–10 Years	7.2	7.2	3.7	7.1	9.5
10 Years or More	49.2	54.7	50.8	45.0	45.7
Location Where Majority of Shopping Done:					
No Response	21.0	19.4	31.9	39.4	21.5
Downtown	16.5	19.4	28.3	9.3	12.7

	Tract 10	Tract 11	Tract 12	Tract 13	Total Visalia
Location Where Majority of Shopping Done: cont'd.					
Mooney Blvd. Strip	7.8	12.7	6.3	2.9	9.9
Visalia Fair	7.6	34.7	28.3	31.4	43.8
County Center	12.4	7.9	2.6	10.7	7.2
Outside of Visalia	1.7	1.1	1.6	0.7	1.8
Other	3.0	4.8	0.5	5.6	3.1
Level of Education of Head of Household:					
No Response	24.7	18.4	31.9	35.5	19.0
High School or Less	54.8	64.2	51.3	52.8	53.2
Two Years of College	7.9	9.1	6.3	6.1	11.6
Bachelor Degree	6.9	6.2	3.7	2.4	9.2
Graduate Degree	5.7	2.1	5.8	1.5	7.0
Racial Ethnicity of Head of Household:					
No Response	15.1	12.1	22.5	18.8	14.6
Caucasian	50.7	67.1	62.3	57.4	73.7
Mexican-American	29.4	16.7	11.5	20.4	10.4
Other	4.8	4.1	3.2	3.4	3.2
Average Yearly Household Income:					
No Response	32.2	25.3	43.9	49.4	29.4
Less than $10,000	45.4	56.0	45.1	32.9	36.9
$10,000–$15,000	9.4	12.1	6.8	10.7	17.1
$15,000–$20,000	5.3	4.3	2.6	5.1	9.2
$20,000–$25,000	2.9	1.1	1.6	1.0	3.9
Over $25,000	4.8	1.2	0.0	0.9	3.5
Age (Male/Female):					
Less than 20 years	19.0/19.0	16.9/17.1	10.4/11.0	21.1/18.3	
20–29	8.2/ 7.8	11.0/11.5	16.3/10.9	6.4/ 7.9	
30–39	5.9/ 5.7	4.5/ 4.6	3.7/ 4.7	6.2/ 7.3	
40–49	5.0/ 5.6	3.1/ 4.3	4.6/ 3.9	4.8/ 4.6	
50–59	4.9/ 5.2	4.6/ 4.8	3.4/ 4.6	3.0/ 2.3	
60 and above	6.4/ 7.1	7.0/10.3	10.9/15.5	6.1/11.0	

Compiled from City of Visalia Special Census, 1975.

Case Exhibit 8
Characteristics of the Population—State of California

	1970	1975
California Population		
(civilian)	19,963,503	20,909,000
Tulare County Population	188,322 (4-1-70)	209,400 (7-1-75)
Fresno County Population	413,329 (4-1-70)	447,900 (7-1-75)
Households	6,574,000	7,437,000 (1974)
Population Per Household	3.04	2.81

Wage and Salary Workers by Major Industry
Mining (does not include Agriculture)	0.4
Construction and Manufacturing	24.0
Transportation and Public Utilities	6.0
Wholesale and Retail Trade	22.7
Finance, Insurance, Real Estate	5.7
Services	20.1
Public Administration	21.1

Adjusted Personal Gross Income
Less than $10,000	18.4
$10,000–$15,000	17.9
$15,000–$20,000	17.6
$20,000–$25,000	14.2
Over $25,000	31.9

*Population by Age**
Less than 20 Years	35.8
18–20	5.9
21–44	34.0
45–64	20.5
65 and above	9.7
Under 18	30.0

*The 1970 population was comprised of 49.2% males and 50.8% females.
Compiled from U.S. Bureau of the Census, *Statistical Abstract of the U.S. Census*, 1976; State of California, *California Statistical Abstract*, 1970, 1976; State Board of Equalization, *Annual Report*, 1976.

Internal Environment

Part III

CHAPTER OUTLINE

Chapter 10
Store Operations and
Physical Facilities

Chapter 11
Retail Organization and
Human Resources

Store Operations and Physical Facilities

CHAPTER Ten

Outline

Introduction

Store Interior

Store Exterior

Physical Distribution

Security and Risk
  Management

Summary

Learning Objectives

*After studying this chapter, the
student will be able to:*

1. Explain the relationship
between store operations and
the retailer's strategic plan.
2. Explain the relationship
between store operations and
the retailer's internal and
external environments.
3. Describe the basic considerations in design and maintenance of a store interior.
4. Discuss how interior decor
and climate control affect store
atmosphere.
5. Describe the basic considerations in designing the exterior
of a store.
6. Discuss the physical distribution activities performed by
store operations personnel.
7. Discuss loss prevention
problems associated with
employee theft, shoplifting.
8. List the types of operating
risks that must be covered by
retailers.

STORE DESIGN: THEMES THAT MAKE A DIFFERENCE

Customers can purchase the same goods and services from a wide variety of retail establishments. What makes the difference in where they shop? In many cases it is the ambiance—the store decor and atmosphere—that attracts them. Two of the many creative approaches that abound in store design are described as examples of themes used to achieve a unique retail identity.

British Passage: Luxury Liner Nautical Theme

British Passage is a Houston-based retailer that specializes in women's traditional sportswear. The company has 16 stores that generated sales of $9.5 million in 1989. The stores are located in upscale, enclosed malls in Texas, Georgia, Florida and Maryland. The average store size is 1,100 square feet, and generates sales of about $500 per square foot.

James Metz, the owner, began the process of giving the store a new image by changing its name from British Khaki to British Passage in 1986. Along with the name change, the merchandise

selection was expanded and a store prototype was designed with a nautical theme. The resulting decor conveys an ambience with an air of adventure and romance that is in keeping with the British Passage name and the "sportswear with a flair" carried by the stores.

Metz, inspired by the luxury transAtlantic ocean liners of the 1920s, with

their elegant staterooms and grand ballrooms, decided to recreate the glory days of ocean travel in his stores. Metz searches for authentic nautical memorabilia in ship salvage yards, which carries out the cruise theme throughout the store. One of the first stores to feature

continued

PHOTO COURTESY OF BRITISH PASSAGE

A boat obtained from a salvage yard is refurbished and displayed as the store's signature piece.

385

Owner James Metz searches salvage yards for the memorabilia used in British Passage stores.

the new prototype was in Bethesda, Maryland. Here the dressing rooms are designed to resemble state rooms, and are marked by mirrored portholes; teak deck-plates are featured in the display window and large photo reproductions of life on board the Queen Mary and other luxury liners of the 1920s and 1930s are placed strategically throughout the store. An authentic 4,000-lb. lifeboat, with the store's name on the bow, hangs from the ceiling as a dramatic focal point. To entice the shopper to walk through the store and up the stairs to the balcony area, merchandise displays were arranged to flow with the customer as

she moves up the staircase and to the far end of the balcony.

Posh Showrooms for Japanese Cars

Japanese luxury-car makers have attempted to set strict design standards for their dealerships. Dealership design specifications are provided by Toyota Motor Corp.'s Lexus division, but only two-thirds of the dealers are constructing new buildings according to Lexus recommendations. However, some have

developed their own novel designs, including a second-floor showroom in Louisville, Kentucky.

Nissan Motor Co.'s Infiniti division would like every dealer to construct and furnish a building in a Japanese style. Specifications call for a tile bridge spanning a stream that flows into the building from outside, a polished bronze sculpture at the center of each showroom, and other details that even include the ashtrays. In some cases, franchises have been turned down because the buildings are too expensive. Infiniti attempts to overcome this by offering cash bonuses and low-interest construction loans to dealers.

SOURCE: Wilson, Marianne (1989), "British Passage Recalls Era of Luxury Liners," *Chain Store Age Executive* (July), 86–87; Pierson, John (1989), "Japanese Firms Push Posh Car Showrooms," *The Wall Street Journal* (October 18), B1.

INTRODUCTION

Store operations managers are responsible for the appearance, safety, convenience, and comfort of the retail environment. Tasks performed by store operations personnel include development and maintenance of all interior and exterior physical facilities, preparation and movement of merchandise inventories within and among facilities, and a variety of service activities such as delivery, gift wrap, alterations, and repair. Store security and risk management also come under the jurisdiction of store operations.

Store Operations and Strategic Planning

Store operations both reflect and support the retailer's strategic plan. The size, style, and general appearance of the store are dictated by the *corporate mission statement and performance objectives*. (See Exhibit 10–1). For example, the mission of a retail firm might be to provide value and convenience to its customers with high-quality goods at low prices and shopping ease. From an operations standpoint, this might be interpreted as a no-frills store with functional layouts and an emphasis on "streamlining" or automating tasks.

Information obtained through external and internal environmental **situation analysis** is used for decisions ranging from climate control systems to the color of carpet, from customer demand for services to prevention of shoplifting, and from high-tech communication systems to supplies such as shopping bags, and other aspects of keeping the store open for business.

Financial and marketing objectives have a major effect on store operations. The use of tangible assets is directly related to achieving financial objectives. Typically, operations managers are held responsible for the purchase, use, and maintenance of equipment, floor space, and other capital expenditures.

Implementation and tactics are the wherewithal to do the job. Does the store have adequate and suitable space for a new line of merchandise, satellite or other communication system for instant reordering, telephone lines for phone orders, or even delivery vehicles?

Execution of the strategic plan cannot be accomplished without physical facilities, equipment, and supplies, whether the retailer is a multi-unit major chain or a small business operated by a sole proprieter. Product retailers must have a retail store for customers to visit, or a distribution center for a direct marketing operation. Facilities may run the gamut from Wal-Mart's enormous Hypermarket in Garland, Texas, to the elegant Water Tower Place in Chicago to the local neighborhood ice cream truck.

Service retailers must have a facility for customers to visit if the service is performed on their premises. If the service is performed off-premises at the customer's home or other location, physical facilities must be provided for nonselling purposes. These needs may be office space, storage buildings, processing plants, or work areas.

An *evaluation of operating results* focuses considerable attention on the use of physical facilities, loss through shrinkage, and the cost of materials and supplies for daily operations. Rising costs of goods from suppliers and customer resistance to high prices make adequate profit margins difficult for

SITUATION ANALYSIS
assessing aspects of the internal and external environment to be used for decision making

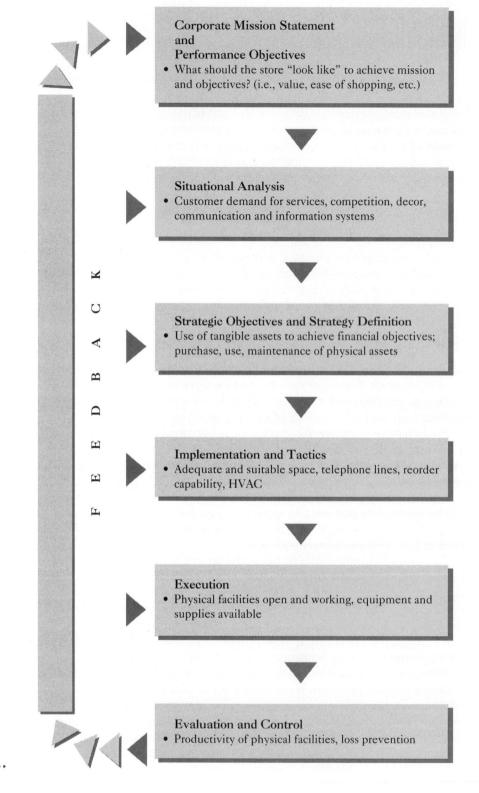

**Corporate Mission Statement
and
Performance Objectives**
• What should the store "look like" to achieve mission
and objectives? (i.e., value, ease of shopping, etc.)

Situational Analysis
• Customer demand for services, competition, decor,
communication and information systems

Strategic Objectives and Strategy Definition
• Use of tangible assets to achieve financial objectives;
purchase, use, maintenance of physical assets

Implementation and Tactics
• Adequate and suitable space, telephone lines, reorder
capability, HVAC

Execution
• Physical facilities open and working, equipment and
supplies available

Evaluation and Control
• Productivity of physical facilities, loss prevention

F E E D B A C K

Exhibit 10–1
Store Operations and Strategic
Planning: An Illustration

retailers to maintain. As a result, emphasis in many firms has shifted from the merchandising function to the operating division to improve margins by controlling expenses.

Store Operations and the Integrative Retail Information Model (IRIM)

The store operations function affects, and is affected by, factors in the store's internal and external environments. Exhibit 10–2 illustrates some of these relationships.

Exhibit 10–2
Store Operations and the Integrative Retail Information Model
. . . .
SOURCE: Anderson and Parker, 1988

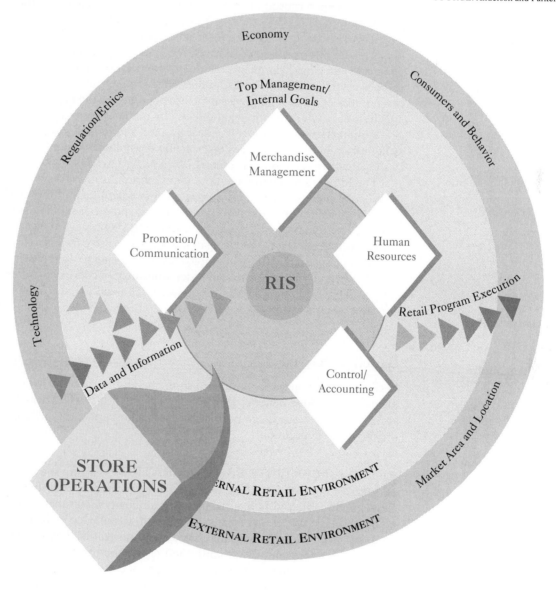

Store operations decisions and activities must be coordinated with other aspects of the **internal environment.** Without this function, merchandise could not be prepared for sale, moved through the store, displayed on the selling floor, wrapped, or delivered to customers. Store personnel could not perform their jobs efficiently or effectively without needed equipment, technology, or space. Promotional activities, such as advertising, display, and telemarketing, could not be accomplished without the appropriate materials and equipment. Accounting and control personnel might be faced with inadequate or unreliable technology for performing their activities. The company's retail information system collects data about customers, vendors, employees, and others, which is used in evaluating operating performance. In turn, this information provides direction for future operating efficiencies.

As with other retailing functions, store operations has little control over the **external environment.** However, the store's appearance, shopping convenience, and general ambiance or image can influence positive or negative responses form customers and suppliers. The retailer can affect the economy in a number of ways. The physical facility provides a wide range of jobs to area residents, who are employed directly by the retailer, or indirectly by outside suppliers or service providers. Local, state, and federal governments benefit from property and sales taxes, made possible because of a retail facility that serves the needs of customers.

The retailer's regulatory environment determines many decisions about store operations, as described in Chapter 7. For example, building codes, fire prevention, restroom facilities for handicapped, and other standards that will guarantee acceptable conditions for working and shopping, are prescribed by numerous federal, state, and local laws. Regulation also extends to less obvious matters, such as bonding of employees or licensing of delivery truck drivers. Beyond the law, ethical considerations may become even more difficult to resolve when managers are faced with the need to cut costs to improve operating profits.

Benefits Desired

Because of the resources invested in store operations, these activities are planned to produce benefits for the company and for its customers. Both groups have a set of expectations of acceptable and unacceptable aspects of the physical environment.

INTERNAL ENVIRONMENT
financial, physical, human, organizational, and technological resources that influence the operation of a business

EXTERNAL ENVIRONMENT
economic, political, and social factors, as well as competitors and customers, that influence the operation of a business

RETAILER BENEFITS FROM OPERATIONS   From the retailer's perspective, physical assets are expected to carry out the retail function efficiently and profitably. The initial planning and daily maintenance of the interior and exterior areas of the store will help to enhance its image and ability to attract customers and to maximize sales and profits. The retailer also requires carefully planned nonselling and sales-support areas. Retailers who offer many supporting services for customers, or carry high levels of inventory, will have a higher proportion of nonselling space. Service retailers, such as bakeries and drycleaners, require only a small percentage of their total space for sales.

CUSTOMER BENEFITS FROM OPERATIONS   Many benefits desired by customers as part of the total shopping experience become a reality due to the efforts of store operations managers. Customers want shopping convenience. That is, they want to be able to get in, around, and out of a store with as little effort as possible. They expect the appearance of the store to be clean and appealing. Regardless of how much time, money, or tolerance customers have for shopping, the amount of their purchases is largely affected by the perceived functional and psychological aspects of the store atmosphere. Operations managers control a major influence on customer perceptions through their treatment of the physical store environment.

Planning for New and Existing Stores

Operating managers are concerned with establishing new stores, maintaining the status quo condition in existing stores, and remodeling or reformatting older stores. Whether the retailer is modernizing or building, a detailed plan should be developed and followed. Retailers often hire outside store planners, architects, or other professionals for this purpose. An evaluation of store design, layout, available technology, and other factors, is an ongoing process in order to attain the retailer's sales volume goals and maintain a desired image. The projected image should be attractive to the store's target market.

Lack of attention to store design may result in lost opportunities and can spell disaster for some retailers. Consider, for example, a favorite restaurant that neglects its interior appearance. It may become less appealing to customers as it loses its original attraction or as newer and more inviting restaurants are opened. Many companies have found that they have to update their formats on a fairly regular basis to retain their customer base. Ground Round, for example, started with an English pub atmosphere for its restaurants, then converted their decor to a greenhouse theme with protruding greenhouse-style windows and hanging baskets filled with live plants. They have found that a concept change is needed about every five years to remain a viable business. In fact, the product life cycle concept can be applied to the timing of layout changes.

J.C. Penney, Sears, K mart, Kroger, and other major retail chains update and reformat their facilities periodically to keep the appearance of stores in line with their strategic thrust. The hotel industry experienced a major infusion of top-notch new competition in recent years, making it necessary for existing hotels to upgrade to meet the higher standards. For example, ten years ago, it was acceptable to use vinyl wallcovering in a hotel lobby. Today, people expect marble or wood paneling. Hyatt Hotels Corp. budgeted nearly $400 million for a three-year redecoration plan, a 150 percent increase from the three previous years. Whereas hotels formerly were redecorated every eight years, they are now being redone every four to six years—at considerable expense ("Hotel Face-lifts . . .," 1989).

Given the need for retail managers to focus on the firm's physical facilities, discussion now turns to specific dimensions of the interior and exterior of a store. This is followed by a brief introduction to two other responsibilities of operations managers: physical distribution and security and risk management.

STORE INTERIOR

A store's interior can be described from a number of perspectives. The first is in terms of overall size and physical characteristics that comprise a general appearance. Second, the allocation and productivity of space are a major concern to retailers, both for selling and non-selling areas. Third, a related aspect is the actual layout and visible treatment of selling areas. Fourth, the concept of store atmosphere encompasses a combined impression of the store's general appearance, space allocation, and layout.

General Appearance

The most global measures of a store's general appearance are the overall store type (i.e., supermarket, apparel specialty store, etc.) and size. Large chains have developed prototypes of successful existing stores, and have incorporated these dimensions when designing new stores or redesigning outdated formats. The number of floors or levels in the building is another contributor to appearance. A different cost structure and set of operating decisions exist for a single level versus a multi- or split-level building design.

Store Size and Type

Store planners and designers must work within the constraints of capital expenditures budgets to create a physical store environment and image that will maximize sales. Exhibit 10–3 compares the average size of six major types of stores for those in existence in mid-1988 versus the previous year, and those opened in 1987–1988 ("Store Sizes Reflect . . .," 1988).

Several types of stores are becoming larger, primarily because of added space for new merchandise: drug stores, supermarkets, and home centers.

The large size of Target Greatland stores requires visible, easy to read signs to facilitate shopping, as in this prototype store.

COURTESY OF TARGET

Exhibit 10–3
Trends in Average Store Size by Type of Store

	Average Store Size (square feet)		
	All Existing Stores		*New Stores Opened*
Type of Store	*July 1987*	*July 1988*	*1987—1988*
Apparel Specialty	21,200	23,700	25,900
Department	148,300	136,300	110,200
Discount	88,700	61,800	67,700
Drug	14,300	24,600	20,600
Home Center	28,300	32,400	31,800
Supermarket	48,800	35,900	52,000

SOURCE: Adapted from "Store Sizes Reflect Broader Mixes," (1988) *Chain Store Age Executive* (July), 62–63; "Annual Decision-Makers' Digest," (1987), *Chain Store Age Executive* (July), 36–37. Copyright © Lebhar-Friedman, Inc., 425 Park Ave., New York, NY 10022. Used with permission.

The average size of existing drug stores increased from 14,300 to 24,600 square feet within one year, reflecting the rapid growth of deep discount drug stores that tend to be much larger than the more traditional units. Average supermarket size increased from 35,900 for existing stores to 52,000 square feet for those opened during the previous year. The size of existing home centers increased from 28,300 to 32,400 square feet, due primarily to format changes.

On the other hand, the size of department stores and apparel specialty stores has remained relatively unchanged. The average size of existing department stores in 1988 was 136,300 square feet compared to 148,300 for 1987. A continued decrease in square footage is indicated by an average size of 110,200 square feet for those opened in 1987–1988. The typical apparel retail store had a slight increase in size, up from 21,200 to 23,700 square feet. The upward trend continues, however, with stores opened during 1987–1988 averaging 25,900 square feet. Discount stores are the only group experiencing a significant decline in store size, with the average decreasing from 88,700 to 61,800 square feet. However, the size of new stores opened in the previous year increased to 67,700 square feet.

PROTOTYPES   In an effort to increase the productivity of space and fixtures, many retailers have developed a basic store design model, referred to as a **prototype.** The trend in using prototypes by chain stores is evident to anyone who shops in the same retailer's stores in a number of cities. Prototype stores use relatively standardized building construction, storefronts, interior design and layout, and operating specifications for all units. This uniformity results in a consistent image from one location to another. The retailer also obtains cost savings from quantity purchases of materials and fixtures that can be moved from one store to another.

The driving force behind the decision to use prototypes is maximizing productivity of all available retail space. Professional store planners use all dimensions of space the landlord rents to retailers like Collar Bar and Field's Hosiery. Their designs include maximum use of walls and ceilings, in addition to floors. Walls can be used for display, storage of merchandise, and/or graphics or photos. An example is the design of the 1,500 square foot Collar Bar where, with the exception of some free-standing fixtures and glass dis-

PROTOTYPE
a basic store design model used by retailers

play counters, nearly all merchandise is displayed on hangrods or on shelves built into the walls. The prototype store is only 15 feet wide, but appears larger through the use of lighting, a vaulted ceiling, and a mirrored rear wall. The prototype utilized by Field's Hosiery is similar to that designed for the Collar Bar. This approach has allowed Field's, a 50-unit chain, to reduce the average size of its stores from 2,000 to 1,000 square feet without sacrificing merchandise flexibility (Klokis, 1986).

Radio Shack, a retail division of Tandy Corp., developed a new proto-type after deciding that their stores "looked like a circus, with parts and junk all over the place." The company launched an $80 million remodeling pro-gram for its 4,405 consumer stores in 1986. Although practical materials were chosen, the cleaner, more fashionable design has a high-tech look for the name, appearance, floors, and walls. Merchandise is arranged on walls and free standing display units according to planograms, detailed layouts for product placement. The more orderly series of departments acquired the name, The Technology Store, which is further emphasized with compatible fixturing and product packaging. In spite of the high-tech image, Radio Shack's new design was developed to be less intimidating to nontechnical customers, and to attract more women shoppers ("Radio Shack . . .," 1987).

The new design of Tandy Corporation's Radio Shack stores is orderly and departmentalized, and is less intimidating to non-technical customers than their previous arrangement.

COURTESY OF TANDY CORP.

Some caution should be exercised in the decision to use prototypes, however, since they are not always successful. A more conservative approach is to test a new design before rolling it out to all stores, since cleverness and creativity do not necessarily ensure that customers will buy. For example, when The Limited's Lerner Shops hired an outside design firm to create a new look for Lerner's, the customers did not like shopping in the new environment. The company started over with a successful new design based on research about customer lifestyles, including the cars they drive and TV shows they watch.

A design expert cites several reasons for having to abandon one prototype in favor of a better one:

1. Poorly developed criteria for a prototype
2. Inadequate and unrealistic budgets
3. Insufficient research on customer demographics
4. Failure to test new prototype designs

Further, the designs should have durability and flexibility built in, with an eye to the future, rather than just copying competition. General Nutrition Centers has accomplished the need for flexibility by developing and testing individual prototypes for sections of the store, rather than the entire store. For example, special marketing schemes have been developed for certain categories, such as vitamins. St. Louis-based Edison Brothers has used a similar approach for stores like Fast and Fun, a women's athletic shoe store, in trying to attract mall shoppers ("Prototype: What If . . .," 1988).

ONE LEVEL VERSUS MULTI-LEVEL   The general appearance of a store's interior includes the number of levels, or floors, in the building. Stores may consist of ten or more floors, or only one floor at ground level. The levels may be positioned directly above one another, requiring vertical customer transportation in the form of elevators, escalators, and stairways. The store may be built in a split-level configuration, particularly in a hilly terrain, where the floors are not directly above one another, but still require vertical transportation. Some stores also have a mezzanine or balcony-type addition that is generally visible from other floors and houses special merchandise assortments.

The factors described in this section (store appearance, use of prototypes, and general configuration of the facility) are related to another major decision about store space. The total space must be divided among selling and nonselling areas. Within each of these areas, space is further allocated among individual selling departments and retailing support activities, as discussed next.

Space Allocation and Productivity

Whether a store is large or small, operations managers are faced with difficult decisions about the allocation of space among competing needs. This valuable asset must be divided among essential selling and nonselling activities and evaluated in light of its ability to yield the highest possible return. Because of rising building and rental costs, the profitable use of space is receiving increased emphasis. The result is a trend toward downsizing some stores and attempting to sell more merchandise in proportionately less space.

Professional store planners are concerned with maximizing the use of cubic footage, as well as square footage, of retail space (Klokis 1986). This means using all the space that is being paid for by the retailer, that is, the walls and ceilings as well as floor space. Costs of stores' space go beyond the monthly rent or mortgage payment to include expenses for heating, cooling, and lighting. However, the space maximization concept can be executed with design and merchandising techniques that require less selling and storage space for the same amount of merchandise.

SELLING SPACE ALLOCATION   **Selling space** which customers can visit to make their purchases from merchandise displays, occupies the majority of a store's total area. Ideally, the amount of selling space required for an entire store is determined by combining space needs for individual departments, taking into consideration the nature of the merchandise sold in those departments. However, the "ideal" amount of selling space may be modified by a limited availability of square footage, and/or budgetary constraints.

The type of store and level of service have an impact on space utilization. The typical allocation of selling space, as a percentage of total square footage, is presented in Exhibit 10–4 for different types of stores. Selling space for all stores in a category as of mid-1988 is compared to new stores built during the preceding year. Although the total size of some stores increased and others decreased, selling area as a percentage of the total remained relatively unchanged. The percentage ranged from a low of 72.4 percent in the older stores to over 83 percent in newer apparel specialty and department stores.

Sales forecasts contained in the retailer's merchandise plan provide a basis for allocating space among departments. Sales per square foot and gross margin per square foot are two important criteria used in determining and evaluating the use of retail space. Sales volume estimates and square footage of selling space to achieve those sales should be in agreement. (Average fig-

Exhibit 10–4
Space Allocation: Selling versus Non-Selling by Type of Store

Store Type	Total Store		Average Space Allocation (square feet)[1] Selling Area		Non-selling Area	
	Existing[2]	New[3]	Existing	New	Existing	New
Apparel Specialty	23,700	25,900	19,648	21,548	4,052	4,352
Department	136,300	110,200	111,085	92,127	25,215	18,073
Discount	61,800	67,700	50,368	53,763	11,432	13,937
Drug	24,600	20,600	19,477	16,026	5,123	4,574
Home Center	32,400	31,800	25,045 (77.3%)	24,104 (75.8%)	7,355 (22.7%)	7,696 (24.2%)
Supermarket	35,900	52,000	25,991 (72.4%)	38,376 (73.8%)	9,909 (27.6%)	13,624 (26.2%)

[1] Average square footage based on annual physical supports census, conducted by *Chain Store Age Executive*, July 1988.
[2] All stores in this category in existence as of July 1988.
[3] Only for those stores opened in 1987–1988.
SOURCE: Adapted from "Store Sizes Reflect Broader Mixes" (1988), *Chain Store Age Executive* (July), 62–63. Copyright © Lebhar-Friedman, Inc., 425 Park Ave., New York, NY 10022. Used with permission.

SELLING SPACE
part of a store customers visit to make their purchases

*The Home Depot utilizes large
overhead signs to show where specific
item areas can be found. Related
products are grouped in close
proximity to each other.*

ures for similar stores are published annually by the National Retail Merchants Association and other retail industry trade groups.)

Some locations within a store are more valuable for sales than others,
because they receive more customer traffic. In a multistory store, the most
valuable space is on the main floor. In turn, the most valuable space on the
main floor is between an entrance and an escalator or elevator. Customer traffic diminishes, causing decreasing space values, with each succeedingly higher floor. Department stores, for example, generally place items like cosmetics, shirts and neckwear, handbags and accessories on the first floor. Furniture and floor coverings, the restaurant and beauty salon are usually found on
higher floors, with apparel and other departments in between.

Basement floors originally had a budget image and received little
through traffic. However, more recently this space has become a prime location for upscale or specialty goods, such as Macy's Cellar (Gillespie, Hecht
and Lebowitz, 1983). Carson, Pirie Scott's Corporate Level is another example of an upscale, high fashion use of basement space.

In an existing store, the size and location of departments is constrained
to a large extent by the amount and configuration of available space. Merchandise classified as "traffic generators" (frequently purchased, high
demand products such as milk or bread in a grocery store) can be situated so
that customers are exposed to other products as they walk through the store.
Impulse goods are placed in high traffic locations and high visibility areas
such as near the cash register. The right-hand conditioned reflex of most customers may also be considered. Departments with related merchandise lines
can be placed near one another for multiple sales to the same customer, for
example, charcoal grills and lawn equipment in a hardware store and shoes
and hosiery in a department store. This logical relationship of departments is
an important element of customer convenience. Based on a study conducted

by DuPont, nine department stores, including Jordan Marsh in Boston and Hudson's in Detroit, reorganized and simplified their dress departments. Dresses were regrouped from areas determined by styles, sizes, or prices to subgroups labeled "Career," "Casual," and "Social Occasion." Fashion consultants and fitting room assistants also were available to help customers. Customers responded to this convenience with 9 to 52 percent increases in dress sales in the first year (Gillespie, Hecht, and Lebowitz, 1983).

Within departments, space is assigned to various merchandise classifications. Merchandise that "gets results," such as high profit margin items or those that encourage impulse shopping, will be given the best locations. Here, too, sales forecasts provide a guide for space allocation in placing impulse versus demand goods. Generally customers will travel a considerable distance through a store to obtain demand goods such as milk or prescriptions. Impulse goods usually are placed strategically along the "pathway" from the store entrance to the location of the demand goods.

Each department within a department store, specialty store, or specialty shop can be divided into as many as five areas: fashion forward area, test area, shops, basics, and key items (Bell, 1988). The fashion forward area consists of merchandise that is an accepted current fashion trend, purchased in large quantities. Display techniques are used for maximum impact. The test

The arrangement of space and fixtures in this Merry-Go-Round store provides maximum impact of displays of demand and impulse goods.

COURTESY OF MERRY-GO-ROUND

area is used for the latest trendy items, purchased in small quantities. Small fixtures are used, and consumer response to the items is watched closely in order to determine future inventory investment. Shops are areas where related products are merchandised together, highlighted perhaps by custom-made fixtures and props. Basics contains the majority of the department's stock. The basic items are continuously available although they may be modified slightly. Key items are included in the Fashion Forward, Shops, or Basics areas. Key items are proven sellers, often under a private label identified with the retailer, and purchased in depth.

The arrangement of space and fixtures within a department has become so important that a new trend is developing in apparel retailing. Liz Claiborne and other apparel manufacturers have assumed responsibility for selling space devoted to their inventory in department stores, similar to familiar practices in the cosmetic industry. Liz Claiborne hired an architect to design the selling space to their specifications at Jordan Marsh and Marshall Field's. They believe they have a better understanding of how to present and sell their merchandise to the customer. Apparel makers who have followed this strategy report sales increases of 20 to 40 percent. The increased volume has offset the added expense without the need to raise prices (Hagedorn, 1988).

Sportswear firms such as Espirit, Generra, UNIONBAY, Levi Strauss, and others have become more involved in developing selling floor layouts for their collections. They believe that they can design more successful fixturing, for example, to enable customers to mix and match coordinated items. Besides fixturing and signage, manufacturers are training the retailers' visual merchandising staffs and providing other assistance (Prinzing 1988).

NONSELLING SPACE ALLOCATION   In addition to selling space allocation, some areas of the store are devoted to sales support functions, rather than revenue generation. **Nonselling areas,** such as offices and customer credit departments, typically are located in the least valuable space such as the top floor. Merchandise receiving, marking, and ticketing areas are generally located in the basement near the receiving docks if possible.

Refer to Exhibit 10–4 for the average square footage and percentage of retail space assigned to nonselling activities. Again, note that there is little more than two percent change in either direction for any type of store. As a percentage of the total, nonselling space ranges from a low of 16.4 percent for newer department stores to a high of 27.6 percent for existing supermarkets.

The rationale in keeping a low ratio of nonselling to selling space lies in the need to use the maximum amount of space to generate revenues. The average building cost per square foot ranges from $22.90 for discount stores to $38.20 for department stores just for the basic structure. Based on typical store size, total costs of the building shell range from nearly $600,000 for a drug store to $4.2 million for a department store.

In the nonselling areas of the store, space is needed for customer service, management and staff offices and workrooms, merchandise storage and servicing, and vertical transportation. Each of these is discussed briefly.

- Customer service activities are essential to completing most sales and can give one retailer a competitive advantage over another. Therefore, store operations managers must allocate and furnish the space

NONSELLING SPACE
part of a store devoted to sales support functions

required to provide important services. Areas may include customer credit offices, dressing rooms in apparel departments, alterations workrooms, food preparation areas, repair shops, giftwrap, restrooms, adjustments, telephone and mail order departments, bridal registry, and other desired services.

● Office space is needed for managers at all levels, from the executive suite to the department manager's desk in the back of the stockroom. Accounting personnel require office space and equipment, which may include computers and telecommunications systems. Merchandising, promotional, personnel, security, and other functional managers and staff also need office and work space.

● The retailer's inventory policies will determine to a large extent the amount of space required for storing and servicing merchandise. Space for this purpose may be allocated within the store, or in a warehouse or distribution center. This includes the necessary equipment for maintaining the inventory and a place to keep it.

● While it may not be as obvious, valuable space is given to elevators, escalators, and stairs. A significant amount of merchandise could be stacked or suspended in the space that it takes for a stairway.

Layout

The physical **layout** of a store is another aspect of the operations function. Walls, aisles, and fixtures are arranged to obtain the desired traffic flow throughout a selling area. For example, most customers have a tendency to turn to the right as they enter a store, so traffic patterns can be designed to take advantage of this movement. Merchandise such as shopping goods that requires more leisurely selection is placed in more remote areas, such as against outer walls or on higher floors, rather than in main traffic aisles of the store.

Common store layout designs are described next. Decisions about layout also include the use of display fixtures and shelf space, as well as the need for flexibility to accommodate shifting emphasis on merchandise assortments.

TYPES OF LAYOUT   Retailers have a number of alternatives in designing stores that will accomplish their objectives within the framework of a predetermined merchandise plan and desired image. Four of the most common types of store layout are the grid or gridiron, free-flow or open, racetrack or loop, and boutique. Although each design serves a particular purpose, advantages and disadvantages are associated with its use.

The grid layout is commonly used in supermarkets, drug stores, and discount stores. The **grid** is a formalized, rectangular design with one or more primary aisles, similar in width, running the length of the store. A number of secondary aisles are placed at right angles to the major aisles. (See Exhibit 10–5.) The wider aisles may contain tables, gondolas, or other display units.

The grid is particularly suitable for displaying merchandise that is inexpensive and purchased frequently, such as grocery, hardware, or stationary items. Space and fixtures are used economically in this type of arrangement for several reasons: there is little or no unused space; support beams and

LAYOUT
arrangement of walls, aisles, and fixtures within a store

GRID
rectangular design with aisles running the length of the store

FREE-FLOW
open design that allows customers to shop leisurely through store

other structural elements can be incorporated into the design; and fixtures can be standardized. High traffic locations, such as corners or ends of aisles, can be used advantageously for displaying new merchandise or impulse goods that will create extra sales. In addition, the openness of this layout makes it possible to use surveillance methods to deter shoplifting. Although customers can shop quickly and efficiently, movement through the store is a function of aisle layout, rather than merchandise desired by the customers. The grid layout is not conducive to designing innovative and creative displays, which can be a disadvantage at point-of-purchase. Exhibit 10–5a shows a specific store's grid layout.

The **free-flow** layout is an open design that allows customers to shop leisurely through departments or entire stores, as shown in Exhibit 10–5. It is well-suited to higher priced apparel and other types of specialty stores. Merchandise is grouped into areas of various shapes, where customers can follow a logical pattern from one display fixture of related items to another. This layout provides flexibility for changing the amount of space devoted to classifications or departments with changes in seasons or demand. Imaginative displays, low fixtures, wall and floor treatments, and other design elements are used to separate merchandise categories. Shopping in this atmosphere is unhurried and pleasant, encouraging the customer to stay longer and browse. The visibility and ease of movement in the open layout increases the number of unplanned purchases.

A free-flow plan can be used to minimize a store's structural flaws. For example, a narrow and deep store can be made to look wider, and provide visibility from the entrance. Space is not used as efficiently in the free-flow design, making it less economical. Additionally, creative, custom-designed

Exhibit 10–5
4 Types of Store Layouts
....

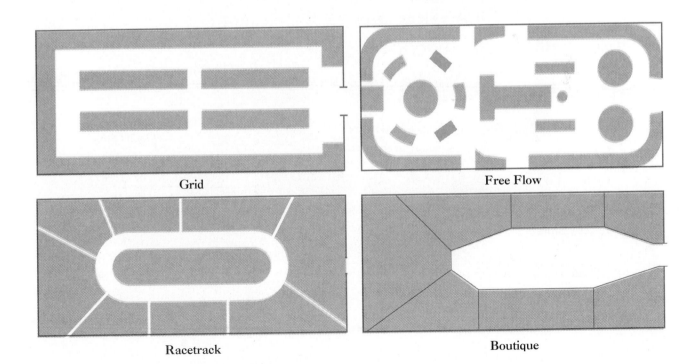

Grid

Free Flow

Racetrack

Boutique

displays are more expensive than the spartan fixtures used in the grid. This layout may result in frustration for customers who cannot find wanted merchandise. It also adds to security problems because it is more difficult to control shoplifting.

The **racetrack** layout consists of one major aisle in the shape of a loop, circling the selling area, such as the main floor of a junior department store. (See Exhibit 10–5.) Departments and merchandise groupings open onto the aisle, or can be accessed from secondary aisles. Lower fixtures and higher or suspended displays permit visibility of a wide array of items. Like the free-form layout, the racetrack design results in wasted space. However, it does provide flexibility, particularly in expanding and contracting the space allocation for various departments or merchandise lines as customer demand shifts.

Boutiques take on the character of specialty or "concept" shops within a store, generally following an open, free-flowing design, as shown in Exhibit 10–5. They may occupy a small percentage of the available selling space, or they may occupy the entire store.

Boutiques are stocked with related merchandise assortments combined along nontraditional lines, such as customer lifestyles or special themes. For

Exhibit 10–5a
Store Layout Grid Design as used in Fred Meyer Store

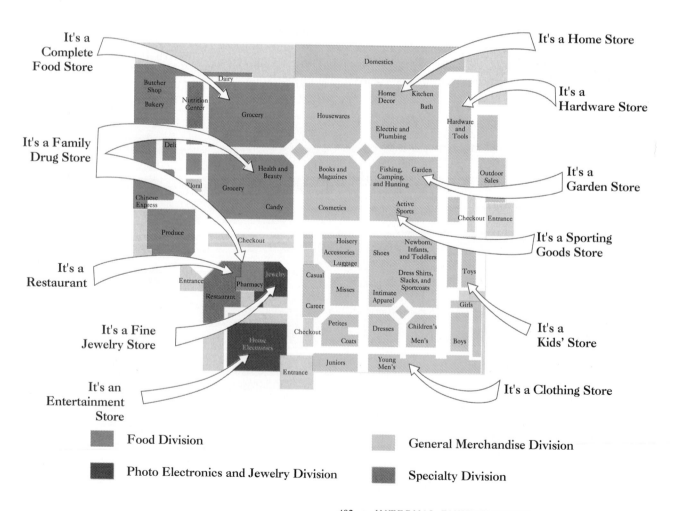

example, a "Teen Scene" boutique might carry junior apparel, jewelry, shoes, cosmetics, cassette tapes, books, and stuffed animals geared toward high school girls. Boutiques may follow a variety of themes, such as gourmet cooking, weekend handyman, healthy living, bridal, or international, or be devoted to a particular fashion designer or to a special holiday or season. The boutique design offers customers convenience in coordinating purchases for a total "look" or purpose.

Retailers often combine some or all of the traditional layout designs according to merchandise lines, shopping behavior, and floors of multi-level stores. Two or more designs also may be combined within one department. One departure from traditional grocery design uses a layout geared to "the efficient shopper." Lucky Stores Inc. implemented a new concept in its Advantage store in San Diego that considers it more important to offer quick, convenient shopping to suit customer lifestyles than to force a customer to walk through an entire store ("New Grocery Store . . .," 1988). Most of the staple goods are clustered and located near the checkout. Customers may shop only in the specific areas that fulfill their needs.

DISPLAY FIXTURES   There are many types of **display fixtures,** created to serve a variety of purposes. Some fixtures sit on the countertop or floor; others hang from the wall. In order to be used to its best advantage, a fixture should relate to both the merchandise requirements and the overall store image. Fixturing can be used to enhance merchandise presentation, store reserve stock at point-of-sale, and act as a silent salesman. Fixtures may be standard or custom designs purchased from suppliers, or they may be supplied by vendors. Others may be furniture (curio cabinets, armoires) used as merchandise fixtures.

Countertop fixtures increase the productivity of counter selling areas through additional displays of the same or related merchandise. Floor fixtures include round, rectangular, or box (four-way) racks, t-stands, bins, gondolas, tables, and cubes. Wall fixtures include brackets and shelves, rods, pegboard, slotwall, and high-tech looking metal grids. Sign holders are a complementary type of fixture used to identify and promote merchandise (Cahan and Robinson, 1984).

Since fixture designs and materials can run the gamut from the classic elegance of mahogany to the contemporary look of perforated metals, their selection requires the answer to certain questions. First, what type of merchandise is to be displayed? Second, what display techniques (hanging, folded, etc.) will be used? Third, will the fixture be moveable or stationary? Fourth, what textures and colors are used in the surrounding floorcovering, wallcoverings, architecture, etc.? Fifth, what kind of lighting is used? Finally, what is the fixture's projected and expected lifespan? (Camilletti, 1988.)

Antilla, a Finland-based general merchandise retailer, uses fixtures to define the chain's image, integrating a flexible metal fixturing system into the store design ("Antilla's Fixtures . . ., 1987). Use of appropriate fixtures provides better utilization of wall, ceiling, and floor space, with a resultant increase in sales and profits. Fixtures should be selected with an eye to their flexibility for a number of purposes and seasons. In other words, they should be treated as another valuable resource.

Most of the discussion in this section is focused on fixtures at point-of-purchase. Dividers and signs are also important features of a store interior.

CHAPTER Ten

RACETRACK

design with one major loop-shaped aisle circling the selling area

BOUTIQUE

specialty area within a store usually using a free-flow design

DISPLAY FIXTURE

rack, stand, table, shelf, or other way of physically presenting merchandise

Electronic equipment requires specific types of displays to promote consumer interest with both visual and audio appeal.

Shelf space at the ends of grocery aisles draws attention to special sale items.

Point-of-purchase displays have become increasingly important for a number of reasons. Product manufacturers have found that it is important to reach potential buyers at the time and place that the buying decision is made, particularly for impulse purchases and convenience items. In addition, the need to reduce sales force expenses increases the importance of display in achieving sales levels. In an attempt to evaluate the effectiveness of floor displays on retail sales, researchers studied sales data for an antibiotic ointment sold from floor stands in three different merchandise sections in pharmacies and grocery stores. In comparing the average number of units sold from store shelves with those sold from the floor displays in all stores studied, it was found that floor displays increased average sales by 388 percent in grocery stores and 107 percent in drug stores (Gagnon and Osterhaus, 1985).

In order to assure that their products get to the consumer, many manufacturers are concentrating on the retailer's needs for display fixtures and increasing profitability through space allocation and inventory control in a fixed store environment. By increasing the volume of product in a given space, costs can be decreased. Further, the design of the fixture can increase efficiencies related to housekeeping, reordering, and stocking. L'eggs and Cover Girl products have experienced success in grocery and drug chains by using fixtures that are easier to stock, with more products in less space and more facings of products. Further, computer software is available to plan and evaluate the effectiveness of layout and fixtures ("Building Profitability . . . ," 1988).

Eckerd's remodeled 250 of its drug stores, focusing on upgrading the stylings of its display fixtures. The design, color, and height of fixtures are now geared to showcasing particular merchandise categories, with the aim of achieving more of a boutique look in the stores ("Fixtures Enhance Product Identity . . . ," 1988). Exhibit 10–6 gives an example of the lifespan, cost per square foot, and types of fixtures used in various types of stores.

A variety of methods are used to divide one merchandise classification or department from another. Permanent walls and columns do not offer the necessary flexibility for changing emphasis on merchandise assortments. Therefore, more creative methods are used as **dividers.** These may include wall colors, flooring materials, hanging plexiglass dividers, and temporary walls.

G.I. Joe's, a West Coast discount chain, wanted a layout that would give each department its own identity and make it easier for customers to shop without help from the sales force. The result was seven color-coded "worlds" of merchandise, developed as a prototype for the 1990s. From a basic racetrack layout with hardgoods on the outside and softgoods in the center, color-coded floor tile, perimeter stripes on the walls, and lighting are used to designate athletic, sporting goods, home electronics, automotives, hardware, housewares, and softgoods (clothing, etc.) departments. This strategy has been successful in attracting and maintaining customers in a stagnant economy ("G.I. Joe's Prepares for 1990 . . . ," 1988).

Signage and graphics are important elements of interior store design and layout. They are used to identify departments, product groupings, "shops within shops," and to direct customers throughout the store. Retailers use **signs** primarily as promotional tools; however, some signs are more functional (gift wrap, credit department) or required by law (exit, fire escape).

Chains such as Ups & Downs, a junior women's apparel store, have used signage to project a more consistent image throughout the chain. The company integrated graphics into the total store environment and other promotional devices, including repetition of the graphics on shopping bags. The designer given the responsibility for this program at Ups & Downs breaks

POINT-OF-PURCHASE DISPLAY
products displayed to reach consumer at time and place the buying decision is made

DIVIDER
flexible "wall" used in merchandise display

SIGN
graphics or words used to identify or promote various aspects of the store

Exhibit 10–6
Internal Store Expense

	Total	Discount	Drug	Super-market	Depart-ment	Home Center	Apparel Specialty
Fixtures							
Lifespan (yrs.)	11.0	12.4	12.9	12.3	8.7	11.9	7.9
Cost (sq. ft)	$8.06	$7.95	$6.68	$14.97	$8.39	$5.72	$4.51
Internal Signage							
Lifespan (yrs.)	6.6	7.4	8.5	9.2	3.5	5.5	4.3
Cost (sq.ft.)	$0.43	$0.39	$0.30	$0.88	$0.43	$0.36	$0.29
Internal Lighting							
Lifespan (yrs.)	12.4	14.4	11.1	13.6	13.1	14.2	7.9
Cost (sq.ft.)	$1.06	$0.98	$0.70	$1.17	$1.47	$0.63	$1.43
Flooring							
Lifespan (yrs.)	10.2	11.7	10.8	11.4	7.4	13.6	6.8
Cost (sq.ft.)	$1.91	$1.12	$1.25	$1.50	$3.03	$1.25	$3.26

SOURCES: "Ups & Downs: Image Via Signage and Graphics," *Chain Store Age Executive*, July, 64, 68. "Lighting On the Bottom Line," *Chain Store Age Executive*, July, 68, 72. "Fixtures Enhance Product Identity At Eckerd," *Chain Store Age Executive*, July, 74, 77. "If It Looks Like Marble, Take a Closer Look," *Chain Store Age Executive*, July, 80, 82, 84–85. Copyright © Lebhar-Friedman, Inc., 425 Park Ave., New York, NY 10022. Reprinted with permission.

visual imagery into three categories: implicit communication, explicit communication, and promotions.

1. The implicit message is related to lifestyle (i.e., how fashions are worn by customers).
2. The explicit message may be a sign indicating that there is a sale.
3. The promotional message tells customers that something special is going on in the store for a limited length of time ("Ups & Downs . . . ," 1988).

The typical lifespan and cost per square foot for interior signage for different types of retailers are shown in Exhibit 10–6.

SHELF SPACE   The allocation and positioning of shelf space are a major concern, particularly to retailers such as grocery and drug stores, where most merchandise is displayed on shelves. In these stores, every square foot of a limited amount of shelving must produce the maximum revenues and profits. Not only specific products, but different size packages or containers, should be arranged on shelves to provide exposure for the highest margin and/or most frequently purchased items.

NEED FOR FLEXIBILITY   Store layout strategies must allow flexibility for expanding or contracting areas devoted to departments or merchandise categories in order to emphasize best-selling lines, seasonal items, or special events.

F&R Lazarus, a division of Federated Stores based in Columbus, Ohio, has incorporated a versatile layout design into its junior department stores ("Lazarus: Embarking on . . .," 1987). A junior department store is a scaled-down version of a department store, with more of a specialty store image.

Using a basic racetrack design, neutral colors, and moderately priced materials and fixturing, Lazarus has created an upscale impression where the merchandise itself provides color and excitement. No aisles separate departments. Moveable, mock pillars made of slatwall tiles, along with clip-on metal grid arches and other forms are used to denote different departments. Lighting is used to enhance the focal areas, displays, and feature merchandise. The store is divided into five *zones* of men's, women's, and children's apparel in different price categories. The size of the zones can be changed easily to meet sales objectives, a design strategy that would work in many smaller stores.

Contribution to Store Atmosphere

Many retailers carry the same national brands, use similar pricing strategies, and sell from convenient locations. However, retailers can gain competitive advantage by differentiating on the basis of **store atmosphere,** the objective and subjective dimensions of the physical retail environment that contribute to the store's overall image or ambiance. Operations managers are responsible for many of the physical and psychological attributes of the store's interior decor, such as lighting, flooring, colors, sounds, and scents. Climate control and the general comfort of customers and employees also are within the domain of store operations.

Store atmosphere is important to all types of retailers, from upscale specialty fashion chains and discount stores to independent grocers. One foods wholesaler claims that he would hire a movie producer to suggest ideas for layout, decor and merchandising strategy in supermarkets, in order to "set the stage" for sales. Independent grocers, in particular, have difficulty in competing on the basis of price alone and must depend on image to develop a unique market niche (Sullivan, 1988).

While store atmosphere can be accomplished with expensive design features, an exciting environment can be created within a limited budget. Two specialty retailers who have accomplished this are Ricciani, an Italian designer boutique on San Francisco's elite Union Street, and Janovic/Plaza, a home decorating shop on the first floor of a 20 story apartment building in New York City, as illustrated in photos.

Ricciani's store designer was faced with the challenge of creating a concept that would make the small shop stand out from the fashionable boutiques, upscale eateries, and Victorian architecture that characterize Union Street. The result was a theatrical motif, with the interior of the shop divided into a "front" and "back" stage. Dressing rooms are located behind wing walls, and display cases and a sales counter that give the illusion of movement are located in front of the wing walls. Merchandise kiosks are suspended from the ceiling via unusual "umbilical cords." Alcoves contain shelves and hanging merchandise. The design incorporates plexiglass fixtures, imitation marble, and halogen lighting for an elegant and dramatic look. The small store's exterior attracts customers with its sleek black awnings with the Ricciani logo and an elegant gold leaf door (Friel, 1987a).

Janovic/Plaza designed a distinctive 7,000 square foot New York store at minimal expense. The retailer carries custom paint, home decorating items (wallpaper, flooring, fabric, window treatments, bathwares), and do-it-

STORE ATMOSPHERE
physical and psychological attributes of the store's interior that contribute to its image

yourself tools. Merchandise falls into two categories, *quick sale*—stock paint, paint brushes—and *pensive purchase*—decorator items requiring more time and thought. Thus, two environments had to be created in the same store, complicated by 15-foot ceilings with pipes and valves that had to be accessible for maintenance. Quick sale items were placed at the front in an unfinished space. Expensive purchases were placed further back under lowered canopies with special lighting, more conducive to leisurely shopping. Problematical structural columns were integrated into point-of-purchase displays. The store has been successful in attracting both professional decorators and aspiring neighborhood do-it-yourself novices, perhaps because of its own creative budget and decorating solutions (Friel, 1987b).

INTERIOR DECOR   All physical aspects of a store's structural interior, that is, the wall, ceiling, and flooring surfaces, lighting, aisle placement and width, and other dimensions of decor, contribute to store image. Store designers create new and exciting selling environments in existing as well as new stores. A leading international British design firm, Fitch & Company Design Consultants plc, has transformed a number of older British retailers into modern, sophisticated establishments based on the premise that "retail is detail." The focus is on making shopping enjoyable and offering solutions to problems and generating business, rather than amusing customers to the extent that they lose sight of buying (Krienke, 1988).

Lighting can dramatize displays, create exotic effects, or merely illuminate merchandise selections. Interior lighting is a necessary retailing tool, but

At Dillard's in Fashion Square, Scottsdale, Arizona, the dramatic effect of lighting and ceiling design enhances a classic image and promotes leisurely shopping of expensive items.

COURTESY OF DILLARD'S

© RUSSELL ABRAHAM, SAN FRANCISCO

The flooring, ceiling, lighting and overall store design and decor can combine to provide a total atmosphere that the consumer finds appealing. Pictured here is Ricciani's, at Janovic Plaza in San Francisco.

it is also an operating expense, representing 60 percent of total electricity costs. Poor lighting can result in lost sales if merchandise cannot be seen easily and advantageously by customers—no matter how much has been spent on advertising to get them into the stores. Newer lighting systems offer cost savings if they are positioned to highlight the merchandise effectively. The proper placement of lighting has become increasingly important, considering that the cost of electricity has escalated 300 to 400 percent from 4 cents a kilowatt hour to an average of 12 cents a kilowatt hour since the early days of retailing ("Lighting On . . .," 1988). See Exhibit 10–6 for average cost per square foot and lifespan for interior lighting for different types of retailers.

The cost, appearance, and maintenance of flooring materials also contribute to store image. Upgrading of stores often includes carpeting, luxurious wood and marble, or synthetic look-alikes. Colored and patterned tiles offer versatility, generally at a more reasonable price than real wood or marble. Companies like General Nutrition Centers prefer the vinyl composition tile, rather than hard ceramic or quarry tile, because of the problem of breakage of bottles containing their products on the harder surface ("If it Looks Like Marble . . .," 1988). Exhibit 10–6 provides a summary of the average cost per square foot, lifespan, and types of flooring used by various retailers.

Flooring is an important aspect of store image for upscale food retailers like Dick's Supermarket chain in Wisconsin. Dull floors are not consistent with the clean and inviting atmosphere Dick's wants for its customers. Therefore, shiny floor tiles were chosen to convey to customers that Dick's prides itself on a crisp environment, meticulous maintenance crews, and customer service. After laying tiles in a new store, a conventional stripper was not successful in removing the manufacturer's protective mill coating. This made it impossible for the retailer to maintain a satisfactory wax finish. The company contacted Johnson Wax, who developed a solution to the problem that was shared by about 12 retailers, including Wal-Mart. Tile manufacturers are also revising their coating composition. All of this adds to higher maintenance costs, but Dick's believes the added cost is worth it because their customers deserve an atmosphere that is clean and conducive to shopping ("Supermarket Strips . . . ," 1988).

Ceilings are receiving greater emphasis in store design, commanding as much as three to four percent of total building costs for new construction. Camelot Music, a 215-store music chain, uses a 3,000 square foot open-cell ceiling in their 10,000 foot prototype stores to draw customer traffic into the center of the store. A spacious mood is created by the center ceiling which is three feet higher than the perimeter ceiling, creating a noticeable contrast. Supermarkets are varying ceiling heights as a way of differentiating departments. The ceiling, as other interior features, must be consistent with the total store design and image ("Ceiling Design . . . ," 1988). Types, costs, and expected lifespan of ceilings are presented in Exhibit 10–6.

Colors, sounds, and scents also contribute to store atmosphere. Color has been discussed in terms of differentiating departments and merchandise lines. Strategic use of color has a psychological effect on consumers and affects their shopping behavior, as illustrated in Exhibit 10–7.

Background sounds may include music or sound effects, designed to soothe, excite, or suggest benefits to customers. Seasonal music may put shoppers in a holiday (and buying) mood. Music may be used in different departments according to the tastes of target customers. For example, rock music may be played in a teen shop and easy listening in specialty goods departments for older clientele. If music is used, it should not be annoying or distracting. Other uses of sound include customer announcements. K mart's periodic *blue-light specials* are advertised over public address systems.

Perfume sprayed in a cosmetic department, food cooking in a restaurant or bakery, and other positive scents may encourage customers to make purchases. Other smells may have a negative connotation and turn customers away. For example, Wellpet, a chain of pet nutrition centers based in California, is competing with supermarkets and independent pet food and supply stores on the basis of store design, service, and cleanliness. The stores are maintained spotlessly clean, unlike many dark, smelly, poorly merchandised pet stores ("Wellpet: Felix and Fido . . . ," 1986).

COMFORT   Operations managers are responsible for providing a comfortable environment for customers and employees through the store's heating, ventilating, and air conditioning (HVAC) systems. Geographical climate characteristics must be taken into consideration. For example, more air-conditioning is required in Florida and more heating in Maine. In addition to

Exhibit 10–7
The Use of Color in Retailing
• •

Signing, Lighting, Fixtures

• Target Stores' newest 169,000 square-foot shopping concept, Target Greatland (Minneapolis, Minnesota), uses color-coded signing for easier identification of its seven major store areas as part of its high impact merchandising strategy. (Jacober, 1990)
• Popmedia introduced Popnet, a Point-of-Purchase Network system of light-emitting diode (LED) animated signs at the 1988 Food Marketing Institute supermarket industry convention. Popnet catches and holds customers' attention through the combined use of color, light and motion, resulting in substantial sales increases. (Bowman, 1988)

Interior Decor and Merchandise Arrangement

• Irondequoit Mall (Rochester, New York area) uses a coordinated external and internal color scheme for its contemporary mall design. The exterior blue-glazed tile trim has been carried through to a blue and teal color scheme on the building's interior. ("Striking Designs . . . ," 1989)
• White Hen Pantry changed its convenience store color schemes to a softened look with burgundy-rust, gold and beige replacing higher contrast colors. (Foussianes, 1989)

Catalogs and Advertising

• Honeybee By Mail Inc. received a 1990 American Catalog Silver Award for the way that merchandise of the same color was grouped in its holiday catalog. ("Dress to the Nines . . . ," 1990)
• Crate and Barrel won a 1990 American Catalog Gold Award for its artistry in arranging merchandise in its ads according to color and form, helping to make affordable products look expensive. (Crate and Barrel . . . ," 1990)

their initial costs, HVAC systems represent a major operating and maintenance expense for the retailer. Considerable technological advances have included sophisticated computerized thermostat controls. However, often these are not cost effective for the smaller square footage retailers like Waldenbooks. Humidity also can be a problem. It can curl the pages and covers of paperback books in a bookstore and melt candy in a candy store, making it necessary to install expensive dehumidification systems. Customers expect to be comfortable in a store; otherwise, they will not stay there to shop ("HVAC Systems . . .," 1988).

Devices called air destratifiers are used to control and "homogenize" air, that is, create more even temperatures vertically from ceiling to floor, and horizontally from one department or area of the store to another ("Retailers Warm . . .," 1988). This type of system is used, for instance, to keep dressing rooms at the back of an apparel store from being stuffy and uncomfortable, and frozen food aisles in a grocery store from being too cold.

STORE EXTERIOR

A store's exterior appearance contributes to customers' first impressions. There is a trade-off between uniformity and uniqueness in exterior store design. The uniformity of exterior design features for McDonald's and other retailers gives each location an easily recognized identity. Others choose to

The striking architectural design and features of this Safeway Store do not depict the traditional style of a grocery store.

have more individual identities for each store. In fact, McDonald's has changed its total "Cookie Cutter" approach by using an upscale decor in a Wall Street restaurant and an "olde time" decor in others. Features of the store exterior include building characteristics and appearance, architectural features such as storefronts, windows, and entrances, location aspects in a shopping mall, visibility and signs, the parking lot, and overall convenience.

Building Characteristics and Appearance

The architectural design and building materials used in constructing the exterior of a store convey an image to customers. This image may be related to customer perceptions of merchandise price and quality. Maintenance of the building and its surrounding areas also makes a statement about the retailer, and may affect a customer's willingness to shop in a particular store.

Exterior walls may be constructed of wood, concrete, brick, stone, or synthetic materials. Each has related perceptions about the quality and style of a store. Even roofing materials are an important exterior design and maintenance consideration. For example, Bloomingdale's in New York City had a leaky roof that presented many repair problems, because of the need to dig through many layers of built up roofing (BUR) material, and the multi-level store design that resulted in different heights for roofing. Bloomingdale's invested over $1 million to replace the BUR roof with Fiberglas, a material designed to minimize two conditions that lead to deterioration of a roof: ultraviolet rays and oxidation ("Bloomingdale's Solves . . .," 1988).

Storefronts, Windows, and Entrances

Architectural design features, such as storefronts, windows, and entrances create a positive or negative first impression for the customer. A freestanding discount store, with its name boldly displayed across the front, will create an entirely different image than the small electronics store with a small sign over its door in a neighborhood shopping center. In a mall, the storefront may

ABERCROMBIE & FITCH

Estab. 1892

This Abercrombie & Fitch storefront, rich with wood and displaying its crest, emanates an aura of exclusivity and masculinity. The company, now owned by The Limited, Inc., was established in 1892 as a "Purveyor of Fine Sportswear" and boasted of "Clothing Tailored in an Authentically English Manner."

consist only of display windows, where the merchandise itself is used to make the initial impression.

In addition, landscaping, lighting, and sidewalks contribute to this image. Well-maintained landscaping creates a finished look for the store's exterior. Lighting and sidewalks make a visual impact, and provide safety and security measures for customers.

Location Aspects in Mall

Many shopping centers suffer from boring or aging exteriors that are in need of revitalization. Growth in sales per square foot has slowed in maturing shopping centers, because customers often find them too big, too disorganized, and too bland. Remodeling can result in as much as a 20 percent increase in sales, but if the stores stay the same, within a year the shoppers will go elsewhere. Meret, an Ohio-based design firm, views malls as one enormous store that should be stocked according to one master plan that is based on what customers want. This may mean eliminating current tenants, including major anchor stores, and adding a mix of specialty retailers to meet consumer needs (Weiner, 1987). All of this must be done within an inviting exterior.

Visibility and Signs

The physical positioning of stores and signs announcing their location should be easily seen by prospective customers. Even those retailers with the most elegant architectural designs must be visible to consumers in order to draw them into the stores. For a fast food retailer, this means the passing motorist must be aware of the restaurant in time to turn into its parking lot or drive-through. Even highly sought after specialty goods and shopping goods stores must be easily identified and found by customers. Thus, visibility of the store itself and related signs are an important aspect of the store's physical exterior. Exterior store signs are an important aspect of store image. Further, many shopping centers and communities have stringent rules that govern the size and design of store signs.

Parking Facilities

A feature of the store's exterior that is sometimes overlooked is the parking area. The condition of a parking lot (or parking garage), ease of access to and from streets, traffic flow patterns, proximity to store entrances, and the availability of sufficient and safe parking facilities can affect a customer's desire to shop in a particular store. Consumers' perceptions of shopping accessibility are influenced by the way they view the parking area. In this regard, the visibility of available parking may have a greater effect on perceptions than the actual number of nonvisual spaces available.

In many communities, building codes specify a ratio of parking spaces per square footage of retail space. There are also community guidelines for public parking facilities. Some of these may be shared with other traffic generators, such as office buildings, hotels, or places of amusement. (Parking requirements for shopping centers were described in Chapter 9.)

Some retailers charge a fee for parking; others do not. Some who do charge will validate parking tickets, making it free for customers who make purchases. Decisions must also be made about hours of parking availability.

Construction of a parking facility involves many costs beyond purchase or lease of the real estate. The parking lot must be surfaced with pavement or other materials and driving lanes and parking spaces must be marked. Driveways and boundary protection must be constructed, and landscaping provided where appropriate. Allowances must be made for surface water drainage and snow removal where necessary. Multi-story parking is more expensive than a single level, and includes the building of ramps. Underground parking construction may also require ventilation and fire protection, adding to its cost.

Convenience

Shopping convenience, related to a store's exterior, is in many ways a perceived composite of all of the external physical features just described. Customers want to be able to enter and leave a store easily and safely. They want to move freely from one store to another in a shopping center location or cluster of stores. The visibility of the store and signs indicating the store's name, promotional events, and other information also make it easier for customers to shop. Finally, parking is a problem for many shoppers and, therefore, should be made as convenient as possible.

Retailers who have included convenience features in their exterior plan include Macy's and I. Magnin. A New York City branch of Macy's built a circular store with a parking area around the retail hub to offer its customers suburban shopping comfort in a big city. The Beverly Hills I. Magnin store made both the front and back entrances into main entrances (Gillespie, Hecht, and Lebowitz, 1983, p. 138).

Physical Distribution

The logistics involved in inventory handling are the responsibility of store operations managers. This may involve receiving, checking, marking, storing, and moving merchandise in the stores only, or in distribution centers and warehouses as well. Physical distribution requirements affect the allocation of selling and nonselling space, particularly if this function is entirely carried out in the store. The type of store also has an effect on the allocation of nonselling space for merchandise storing and handling. For instance, discount stores and warehouse stores incorporate reserve stock supplies into the selling floor, decreasing the need for nonselling space for inventory storage.

Physical Distribution Functions and Activities

Once the merchandise has been shipped by vendors and received by retailers, the physical handling of goods becomes the responsibility of store operations managers. This function may be performed in the store itself or in a distribution center or warehouse, or both. Activities involved may include the following: a system for handling incoming merchandise; centralized receiving and distribution for a number of stores from one distribution center; receiving, checking, marking, and otherwise preparing merchandise for sale; transferring unsold merchandise to vendors or other stores, or delivering goods to customers. Technological advances have increased the efficiency of the physical distribution function, as discussed in Chapter 17.

Handling Incoming Merchandise

After the retailer and vendor have determined the shipping method and negotiated the freight charges, goods are assigned to a freight carrier for delivery to one or more stores or warehouses. At this point, the retailer must have a system for accepting goods into the store. This may range from a simple back door approached from an alley behind the store to a sophisticated facility that will allow a delivery truck to back into a warehouse dock area, where it essentially can be "sealed off" for removal of cartons, hanging goods on racks, or enclosed containers.

Adequate space and equipment are required for an efficient receiving area. For a small retailer, receiving may be limited to a table in the backroom of the store. In larger firms, equipment for unpacking and sorting generally includes tables, bins, shelves, baskets, hanging racks, conveyor belts, and overhead trolleys. Technology, combined with established work procedures, has streamlined the receiving and checking process.

Some deliveries involve consolidated shipments of goods from two or more vendors that have been assembled at a central consolidation point for delivery to one or more retailers. Other shipments may contain a carload lot for one retailer. Some retailers own or lease their own trucks for these shipments; others use commercial carriers or a combination of the two. A common practice in either case is "backhauling." Companies who have their own trucks can haul goods for other companies on return trips, thus generating revenues to offset transportation costs.

CENTRALIZED RECEIVING AND DISTRIBUTION   Many retailers have centralized warehouse facilities, often within an overnight drive of the company's stores for quick replenishment of stock. This also reduces the need for distribution centers and storage areas for each individual store. In fact, many new store location decisions are made on the basis of proximity to a retailer's central distribution center.

Cost savings are realized by the retailer because vendors can ship to one destination for multiple stores. In addition, fewer purchase orders and accounts payable are required, thus reducing order costs.

PREPARING MERCHANDISE FOR SALE   Once goods have been received in the store, the contents of shipments are unpacked and inspected. Invoices are checked against purchase orders, and the shipment is logged into the retailer's receiving records. Verification is necessary to determine whether the correct items were shipped in the right quantity and at the right price, whether substitutions have been made, and whether the merchandise is in saleable condition. Incorrect or damaged shipments are returned to the vendor according to an agreed upon arrangement. Goods received later than the delivery date designated on the purchase order may be refused and returned if the retailer cannot use them. Some merchandise may need minor care before being taken to the selling floor. For example, apparel may need to be ironed and put on hangers, jewelry and furniture polished, and so forth.

Some vendors mark prices on merchandise prior to delivery to stores, saving time and money for retailers. Other merchandise is marked on individual items in the store or distribution center. Prices may be stamped on the product or attached with stick-on labels or hang tags. Vendor marking in food stores is accomplished primarily with Universal Product Code (UPC) symbols, which can be scanned easily at computerized point-of-sale registers. Products may not be marked individually, with prices marked on the shelves to inform customers about package and unit pricing. Merchandise often needs to be remarked to a lower price for markdowns and sale items or marked up to reflect increasing vendor prices.

TRANSFERRING AND DELIVERING GOODS   The operating division is responsible for moving and storing inventory from the time it arrives on the retailer's premises until it is delivered to the customer. If shipments contain incorrect merchandise or damaged goods, the operating division follows a prescribed procedure for return to vendors. When merchandise is delivered to a distribution center or warehouse rather than directly to a store, the shipment is broken down into smaller assortments as needed for reserve stock areas and the selling floor. Within a multi-unit chain, merchandise that is not meeting sales goals at one store may be transferred to another store where it is in higher demand. Merchandise purchased by the customer is delivered to the customer at point-of-sale, customer pick-up areas, or to the customer's home.

SECURITY AND RISK MANAGEMENT

Store security and risk management are important areas of concern for operations managers and, therefore, are discussed in this chapter. The primary responsibility of security personnel is to minimize stock shortages due to theft by employees and customers. (Other shortages may occur due to clerical errors, broken or damaged goods, or carelessness. While these are important in minimizing losses, they are not discussed in this chapter.) Risk management involves insuring against various types of disasters that may be harmful to customers, employees, or the store itself.

Security

Both internal theft by employees and shoplifting by customers are serious problems for retailers, as discussed below. These factors account for the majority of stock shortages, which in turn diminish profit margins.

INTERNAL EMPLOYEE THEFT   It is not the thief with the .38 calibre gun who holds up a cashier to obtain the contents of the cash register who is the greatest threat to retail security. Rather, it is dishonest retail employees, those who should be loyal to the source of their paychecks. Dishonest retail employees may steal merchandise and supplies, cash or negotiable instruments, or fail to charge friends or relatives any or all of the total amount for purchases. According to one source, businesses experienced a $40 billion loss due to the employee theft problem in 1985. This figure has grown drastically since 1955 when the Insurance Underwriters organization reported losses of $300,000,000. Internal theft accounted for $4 billion in 1965 and $14 billion in 1975 (Walls, 1988). (These loss figures refer to physical goods or property only.) Another study indicated that U.S. businesses lost an additional $161 billion in 1985 due to employees "stealing" periods of their work time (Carter, 1987). This is certainly the kind of growth that managers of retail stores and shopping centers want to discourage!

A U.S. Justice Department study estimated that retailers experienced a loss of $11.77 billion due to all types of crime. Almost 70 percent of this was due to employee theft (Solomon, 1987). Other studies indicated that three of every four retail employees know at least one other employee who is stealing from the company. Most of the thefts (39 percent) occur at point-of-sale, followed by the sales floor (17 percent), stock area (16 percent), receiving area and warehouse (10 percent each), trash (5 percent), and other (3 percent) (Carter, 1987).

One problem in identifying employee theft lies in the fact that it often appears legitimate. It is sometimes difficult to distinguish between acceptable fringe benefits and repeated acts of minor theft. In fact, most employees who steal do not see themselves as criminals because the practice is so widespread in the workplace. Examples of minor transgressions include use of the company telephone for long distance calls or piecemeal theft of office materials for personal use. One-time acts of theft of this type may not be significant. However, the cumulative effect can be damaging to company profits. Many conventional deterrents for these situations are oppressive for employee morale and ineffective in stopping theft of this nature (Carter, 1987).

Specialists attribute the major causes of employee theft to drug use and weakening morality, a younger workforce with less commitment to the retail trade, and smaller staffs with less supervision (Solomon, 1987). Others suggest several social-psychological explanations centered on the individual.

1. Some individuals are more inclined to steal than others.
2. Persons with certain problems are more likely to commit acts of theft.
3. Some use it as a negative response to unpleasant job situations, such as inequity and job dissatisfaction.

Thus, retailers must not only understand what motivates the individual, but also understand the work environment in which theft occurs (Barr and Balsmeier 1988).

SHOPLIFTING   **Shoplifting** refers to the theft of goods from a retail store by a person who otherwise appears to be a legitimate customer. Shoplifters use the stolen merchandise themselves, give it to friends or family members, sell it to another party, or return it to the store for exchange or refund. Some shoplifters are professionals who steal to provide themselves with an income. Others are amateurs who steal because of psychological disorders, the need to be "in" with some social group, or some other personal reason.

Shoplifters use a number of techniques to take merchandise from a store. They may use specifically designed coats, pants, boots, or other loosely fitting clothing that is equipped with large sewn-in pockets, bags, or hooks. They also may conceal merchandise in handbags, "fake" boxes, and packages, newspapers, and various types of bags.

Dishonesty by customers includes the actual theft of merchandise, switching price tags or package contents, fraudulent use of credit cards, bad checks and counterfeit money, and fraudulent refunding. Merchandise theft may range from an expensive diamond ring in a jewelry store to a couple of cookies taken from a package on the grocery shelf. (The latter theft is called "grazing.")

Customers may take a price tag or sticker from an expensive item, and replace it with one from a less expensive item, or actually change the price on the tag (like a markdown) so they pay less for the goods. Contents may be switched from a package containing an expensive product to one that is inexpensive. For example, butter might be put in a less expensive margarine package so the grocery store checker rings up the lower price.

Although retailers have safeguards against the misuse of credit cards, losses from this source continue to be a problem. Efficient systems are set up

SHOPLIFTING
theft of goods from a store by a person who appears to be a customer

BIG BROTHER: SECURITY AT THE MALL

Store owners and shopping center managers are plagued with problems related to shoplifting and crimes committed on their premises. Both customer safety and company profits are in jeopardy as retailers lose up to $35 million a day to dishonest customers and employees. According to FBI statistics, shoplifting is America's fastest growing crime, up 33 percent in four years. In 1987, companies spent $200 million to try to stop it—using high-tech electronic surveillance devices that are reminiscent of Big Brother.

Meet Anne Droid, a high-tech Mata Hari, who can catch shoplifters in the act. Is Anne a highly trained security officer? No, she is a mannequin that is being sold to department stores as an efficient and unobtrusive security device. Anne Droid has a camera in her eye and a microphone up her nose. She can catch shoplifters in the act on videotape. The system can be installed in any figurine for $1,150—as long as the mannequin has eyeballs. (See illustration.)

AP/WIDE WORLD

Inventor F. Jerry Gutierrez and one of his surveillance mannequins, Anne Droid, monitor a photographer as he takes their picture. Gutierrez has designed mannequins with surveillance cameras to detect shoplifters.

Other devices include closed-circuit surveillance systems that allow store managers to watch cashiers on one side of a split screen, while viewing cash-register receipts on the other. Marshall Field's in Chicago can station store detectives in "Trojan Horses," hollow eight-foot columns with two-way mirrors. Other retailers use the store's audio system to broadcast barely audible subliminal messages, ranging from police sirens and clanging jail-cell doors to muffled statements such as "Stealing is dishonest."

High-tech is not the only effective way to thwart shoplifting. For example, Marshall Field removed plastic tags from 70 percent of its merchandise and at the same time set up a comprehensive program to train its employees how to spot shoplifters. It also started holding managers accountable for losses, and offered $500 rewards for tips leading to pilfering employees. The result was a 33 percent drop in stealing. As Marshall Field's vice president for loss prevention, Lewis Shealy, said, "You can't solve the retail-theft problem by putting people in jail . . . but you can prevent theft by making employees aware of the problem and holding them accountable." Because a watchful salesperson may be the best security device of all.

SOURCE: Adapted from Tsiantar, Dody (1989), "Big Brother at the Mall," *Newsweek* (July 3), 44. Used with permission.

to approve charge purchases, assuming the rightful holder of the card. However, it is difficult and time consuming to verify that the person using the credit card is entitled to do so. Bad checks and counterfeit money are often passed by customers, particularly in a busy store situation when clerks and cashiers may be too rushed to exercise caution in accepting either of these.

Fraudulent refunding of stolen goods has increased steadily, accounting for a large portion of retail shrinkage. Shoplifters have discovered that they do not have to settle for selling stolen goods for a fraction of their value, when they can return them to the store for full value. For example, a shoplifter steals a $20.00 watch. After a short period of time, she returns to the store and asks for a refund, saying that her husband bought the same item without her knowledge and she can't use two of them. She also claims that she paid cash, but has lost the receipt. Most retailers will give customers the benefit of the doubt, so the shoplifter receives $20.00 plus tax in cash.

The retailer also has lost the cost of the watch plus any profit he would have made and the amount of the sales tax. A Boston shoplifter is reported to make so much money with the refunding scam that he takes a cab from one retailer to another, so he is never traced through his car license number (Clifford, 1988).

ROBBERY AND BURGLARY   Robbery and burglarly occur less frequently than employee theft and shoplifting. However, they are a serious and dangerous threat to retailers. Robbery generally implies the use of force to obtain money or goods from a retail employee, while burglary implies illegal entry to the retailer's property for dishonest purposes. These crimes are most apt to be a problem in poorly protected buildings, store interiors and exteriors that are dimly lit or have poor visibility, or where large amounts of cash are kept on hand.

The problem can be partially overcome with the use of more secure store construction features, burglar alarms and locks, and better lighting and visibility. Retailers, particularly service stations, liquor or convenience stores, that stay open during late hours, also can discourage robbery by keeping minimal amounts of cash on hand.

SECURITY ISSUES FOR STORES AND SHOPPING CENTERS
Shopping center managers and security directors are faced with an increase in the number of legal suits, as well as the size of awards to those accused of retail theft. The courts are holding shopping center managers and owners to stricter interpretations of security standards.

Security issues vital to shopping centers include the cost of security systems and personnel, parking lot security, and teenage loitering and rowdiness. Security costs include built-in systems (closed-circuit television, alarms, and communication systems), security personnel salaries, and legal expenses. According to a survey conducted by the International Council of Shopping Centers (ICSC) at 50 U.S. shopping centers of more than 300,000 square feet, annual security costs ranged from 10 to 77 cents per square foot of gross leasable area. Highest security costs were found in the Eastern and Western regions of the United States and in central city locations.

More than one-third of the shopping center executives in the ICSC study said their one greatest security problem involves vehicles. Car thefts, break-ins, and vandalism have made parking lots, lighting, and closed-circuit television important issues for security personnel. The next problem listed most frequently was the disturbance caused by teenagers in shopping centers and parking areas. It is difficult to manage this situation without alienating teenage customers and their parents. A landmark California case, Prune Yard, has made managers reluctant to ask people to leave. Prune Yard protects First Amendment constitutional or civil rights by giving freer access to malls in that state. Therefore, security staff members need to be well informed about the legal issues involved (Hunter, 1988).

STRATEGIES FOR REDUCING LOSSES   Loss prevention experts have developed a number of effective methods for reducing losses from employee theft and shoplifting. Security efforts may be focused on employees, customers, or both. Some successful strategies implemented by retailers are discussed next.

The biggest deterrent to employee theft is to hire honest people to start with. Research results from over 3 million test subjects at the Stanton Corporation led to a definition of three levels of risk related to dishonest employees: Low Risk; Marginal Risk; and High Risk. Low Risk individuals would return your wallet intact with all contents if they found it. Marginal Risks would keep the cash, discard the wallet and credit cards and go on their way. High Risks would keep the cash, sell the credit cards, clean up the wallet and give it to you for a present. The study further found that 49 percent of high risk job applicants admitted to merchandise theft on previous jobs, 23 percent said they would steal from a new employer, and 29 percent said they gave unauthorized discounts ($50 sweater for $20) to friends and others on their present job and would continue to do so. It was further found that 25 percent of applicants with a college degree were classified as high risk, and that high risk employees made up 41 percent of applicants for catalog showroom retail positions, 31 percent for supermarkets, 38 percent for specialty stores, and 32 percent for department stores. By screening for honest employees before hiring them, one department store was able to achieve a 44 percent reduction in employee turnover, 32 percent less termination for dishonesty, and a $300,000 increase in profits (Walls, 1988). Paper and pencil honesty tests, such as the Reed test, are useful for this purpose.

A number of retailers have reduced employee theft by offering rewards to employees who report dishonest co-workers. In New York, Bloomingdale's awards it employees $2,500 and Alexander's, a discount department store chain, gives "whistleblowers" $1,000 plus a year of chances in the New York state lottery game. Alexander's employees have received the award for tips ranging from stealing a slice of pie from the cafeteria to $2,000 worth of electronic equipment (Solomon, 1987).

Other deterrents to employee theft include regular and unscheduled audits, tighter controls over inventory and cash, and employee training. Security guidelines should be established, communicated, and enforced. Employees should be able to work in an environment where they are treated fairly and encouraged to be loyal to the company. However, dishonest employees should be apprehended and prosecuted, because inaction implies consent. Finally, honesty has to start at the top of the company. Top management must set an ethical example for others to follow.

There are a number of strategies for reducing losses from shoplifting and other dishonest acts by customers. To begin with, store layout, interior decor, and display fixtures can be designed to increase visibility of merchandise areas by store personnel and otherwise discourage customers from stealing. Retail employees can be trained to be alert to suspicious shoppers.

Fraudulent refunding can be reduced by requiring receipts for all returns. The retailer can take a tougher stand on returning "used" merchandise (such as the party dress that clearly has been worn, although the customer denies it). Cashiers can be trained to watch more closely for switched price tickets or merchandise, and bad checks or misuse of credit cards. They can also be warned of the penalties for entering into collusion with customers for extra merchandise, credit, or cash refunds.

Talbots, a women's specialty retail chain and catalog operation, has developed an effective loss prevention program. In addition to standard security devices and practices, key elements in Talbots' program include: ongoing employee training and education on how shortages can occur and how they affect the company's profits; company standard policies and procedures formalized in a manual; enforcement of procedures through an internal audit program; and customer service. Talbots believes that good customer service equals good loss prevention. For instance, employees greet customers as they enter the store, and give extensive customer service in the fitting rooms (Murphy, 1988).

Many retailers are emphasizing shoplifting deterrence over apprehension, although deterrence is not a cure for reducing security losses. Accordingly, a Broadway store in southern California employed a unique combination of anti-shoplifting devices, resulting in the lowering of shoplifting incidences as well as the recovery of high-ticket stolen merchandise. Closed circuit television, loop alarm cables, and videotaping capability were combined so that store personnel could observe and tape a theft in progress. A programmable camera that can scan 360 degrees in the fur department is continuously broadcast to a central security area ("The Broadway's System . . . ," 1986).

Anti-theft aspects should be built into store design for high theft areas such as fitting rooms and high ticket merchandise areas. For example, fitting rooms should be designed to give honest customers sufficient privacy to feel comfortable, but not enough privacy to encourage a shoplifter to steal. Doors should be as high as possible off the floor, and only go up as high as the average person's neck. Mirrors should be caulked so that merchandise tags cannot be hidden behind them ("Store Design . . . ," 1986).

More subtle approaches to loss prevention include the use of subliminal messages and high-tech mannequins. Subliminal messages are noticed by the subconscious, rather than the conscious, mind. Those used by retailers are audio messages played through the store's sound system. The customers are only aware of piped-in music, but a message linked to shoplifting prevention is also played at a frequency below conscious perception. Although this method has been successful for some retailers, it has no impact on the professional shoplifter or kleptomaniac. It is more inclined to be effective with the

Security measures at Alco include electronic surveillance equipment and employee loss prevention education.

COURTESY OF ALCO

occasional shoplifter ("Subliminal Messages . . . ," 1986). A sophisticated new electronic surveillance technique is disguised as a mannequin with a video camera in her eye and a microphone in her nose. The mannequin, Anne Droid, can videotape shoplifters in the act, and in most cases people cannot tell they are being watched (Tsiantar, 1989).

Alco Stores Inc., a discount chain headquartered in Abilene, Kansas, is an example of a retailer with a standardized loss prevention program that combines efforts to reduce dishonesty by corporate executives, store employees, and customers. When employees are hired at Alco, they automatically become part of the loss prevention team. In addition, security mechanisms oversee their actions. Before they are hired, new employees learn that the company policy is to arrest and prosecute shoplifters, and that employee theft is stealing, with the same penalties as shoplifting. Both customers and employees are monitored with surveillance equipment, employees are rewarded for information about theft by other employees, and all loss prevention measures are well publicized to employees (Russell, 1988).

Protection/Risk Management

The retailer's customers, employees, and property must be protected against fire, accidents, and potential hazards. Protection also is needed against natural disasters such as high water and floods, hurricanes and tornadoes, as well as human acts of violence. Precautionary measures can be taken to reduce or prevent many of these losses. Those that cannot be prevented must be insured against for replacement of property and protection against lawsuits brought against the retailer by the injured party. Insurance carried by retailers typically covers various types of liability, property, and workers' compensation needs.

Fire prevention starts with store construction and design, installation of alarm and sprinkler systems, availability of fire extinguishers, fire exits, and other measures. Safety procedures for building maintenance and inventory handling also should be developed to minimize fire loss.

Both employees and customers can experience accidents on the retailer's premises. They may fall, or be injured by sharp or falling objects, equipment or hazardous materials. Building designs can incorporate safety features to minimize accidents, employees can be instructed in the safe use of materials and equipment, and customers can be informed about potential hazards.

SUMMARY

The appearance, safety, convenience, and comfort of the physical store environment are the responsibility of retail operations managers. Store operations both reflect and support the retailer's strategic plan in establishing new stores, maintaining the status quo in existing stores, or remodeling or reformatting older stores. The store operations function interacts with internal and external environmental factors.

The interior of a store can be described in terms of its general appearance, the allocation and productivity of space, the layout and visible treatment of selling areas, and store atmosphere. The general appearance of a store can be measured on the basis of overall store type, size, and architectural design. Basic store design models, called prototypes, have become increasingly popular because of their ability to increase the productivity of space and fixtures.

Retail space must be allocated among essential selling and nonselling activities to maximize every square foot and cubic foot of available space. Selling space must be divided among departments, according to the merchandise plan and sales forecasts. Two space allocation criteria are sales per square foot and gross margin per square foot. Space also must be allocated to different merchandise lines within each department, with the best locations given to high sales or high profit margin items. Space allocation has become so important that vendors such as Liz Claiborne and Levi Strauss are designing their own retail floor layouts to merchandise their collections. While the proportion of nonselling space to selling space should be as low as possible, space must be allocated for sales support functions such as customer credit, merchandise receiving and marking, and offices.

There are four basic types of store layout: grid, free-flow, racetrack, and boutique. The grid, used in supermarkets and drug stores, is a formalized rectangular design with main aisles running the length of the store. The free-flow layout is an open design that is conducive to leisurely shopping and browsing, and is particularly suited to high priced apparel and specialty stores. The racetrack layout consists of one major aisle in the shape of a loop, circling the selling area. Departments and merchandise groupings open onto the aisle, or are accessed from secondary aisles. Boutiques are specialty or "concept" shops, with related merchandise for customer convenience, within a store.

Display fixtures are an integral part of the store's interior, and should reflect the merchandise requirements and overall store image. Display techniques also include dividers and signs, used to identify and separate departments and merchandise classifications. Store layouts must permit flexibility to expand or contract departments as needed.

Store atmosphere contains both objective and subjective dimensions. Aspects of interior decor such as lighting, flooring, colors, sounds, scents, and climate control make an important contribution to store image.

Customers receive their first impression of a store from its exterior appearance. This includes the building characteristics and appearance, architectural features, location in a mall, visibility and signs, parking, and overall convenience.

Store operations managers are responsible for the company's physical distribution functions and activities, the logistics of moving merchandise into, through, and out of the store. Space and facilities are made available for receiving, checking, and marking incoming merchandise. Some retailers centralize receiving and distribution into one distribution center.

Another major concern of operations managers is security and risk management. Employee theft is the greatest threat to retail security, accounting for most of the loss experienced in a store. Shoplifting by customers is another security problem. Some shoplifters are professional; others are amateur or occasional thieves. Dishonest employees and customers may not be apprehended and prosecuted because of an increased number of legal suits and size of awards. Major security issues include the cost of security systems and personnel, parking lot security, and teenage loitering and rowdiness.

Besides mechanical security devices, employee theft may be reduced by hiring honest employees, offering rewards to employees who report dishonest co-workers, regular and unscheduled audits, tighter inventory and cash control, and employee training. Shoplifting and other consumer dishonesty can be reduced by designing stores with security problems in mind, employee training, and anti-shoplifting devices.

Finally, operations managers are responsible for protecting customers, employees, and property against risks from fire, accidents, and potential hazards, as well as natural disasters through prevention and safety procedures and risk insurance.

Questions for Review and Comprehension

1. Give an example of the relationship between a retailer's strategic plan and the duties and responsibilities of a store operations manager. How might this relationship change with a redefinition of the company's mission statement or corporate objectives?

2. Assume that you are a store operations manager for a large department store chain. Discuss some specific ways that you would have to deal with both the internal store environment and the external environment—perhaps at the same time.

3. You have been given the responsibility for designing the interior of an auto parts store. Discuss the major factors that you must consider in not only designing an appealing decor, but also factors that must be considered for efficient maintenance over the long term. In addition, determine and justify the allocation of space between selling and nonselling areas of the store.

4. Discuss the most appropriate type of store layout for each of the following types of stores: convenience food store, junior girls' apparel, sporting goods, small department store (on one floor), and large bookstore. If possible, find and critique each type of layout in a store in your community.

5. Explain how display fixtures contribute to store design, image and flexibility. Debate the emphasis on fixtures for an upscale fashion merchandiser versus a hardware store. Is one more or less dependent upon good fixturing for success?

6. Describe and give an example of each of the major elements of store atmosphere.

7. Explain how the exterior design of a store contributes to store image and why congruence between the interior and exterior design of a store is important.

8. Assume that an order of merchandise is on its way from the manufacturer to your store. Describe the activities that store operations personnel will perform to move the goods from the receiving area of the store through the store and, ultimately, to the customer.

9. Discuss the problems of security and risk management that face retailers, and describe strategies that retailers are using to minimize or prevent loss from various sources.

References

"Antilla's Fixtures Define Chain's Image (1987), *Chain Store Age Executive* (July), 39–41.

Barr, Peter B. and Phillip W. Balsmeier (1988), "Losing Dough in Bakeries," *Security Management* (March), 86, 88–89.

Bell, J. A. (1988), *Silent Selling: The Complete Guide to Fashion Merchandising*. Cincinnati, Ohio: ST Publications, 33–40.

"Bloomingdale's Solves Multi-Level Problems" (1988), *Chain Store Age Executive* 64, no. 7, (July), 90, 92.

"Building Profitability Via Space Allocation" (1988), *Stores* 70, no. 7, (July), 50–51.

Cahan, L. and J. Robinson (1984), *A Practical Guide to Visual Merchandising*. Somerset, N.J.: John Wiley & Sons, Inc., 131–161.

Camilletti, Tony (1988), "The Finishing Touch," *Visual Merchandising and Store Design* (October), 66–69.

Carter, Roy (1987), "Employee Theft Often Appears Legitimate," *Accountancy* (July), 75–77.

"Ceiling Design Options Define Chains' Image" (1988), *Chain Store Age Executive* 64, no. 7, (July), 86.

Clifford, John T. (1988), "Something For Nothing," *Security Management* (February), 57.

"Fixtures Enhance Product Identity At Eckerd" (1988), *Chain Store Age Executive* 64, no. 7, (July), 74, 77.

Friel, Kathleen (1987a), "All the Store's A Stage," *Visual Merchandising and Store Design* (March), 82–84.

Friel, Kathleen (1987b), "Designing for the Do-It-Yourselfer," *Visual Merchandising and Store Design* (June), 126–127.

Gagnon, Jean Paul and Jane T. Osterhaus (1985), "Research Note: Effectiveness of Floor Displays on the Sales of Retail Products," *Journal of Retailing* 61, no. 1, (Spring), 104–116.

"G.I. Joe's Prepares for 1990" (April 1988), *Discount Merchandiser*. (16–19).

Gillespie, K., J. Hecht, and C. Lebowitz (1983), *Retail Business Management*. New York: McGraw Hill, 136–148.

Hagedorn, Ann (1988), "Apparel Makers Play Bigger Part on Sales Floor," *The Wall Street Journal* (March 2), 1.

"Hotel Face-lifts Become More Common as Competition Stiffens" (1989), *The Wall Street Journal* (Business Bulletin) (January 26), 1.

Hunter, Margaret (1988), "Who's Minding the Mall?" *Security Management* (February), 54–56, 58–60.

"HVAC Systems: Suitability Is the Key" (1988), *Chain Store Age Executive* 64, no. 7 (July), 88.

"If It Looks Like Marble, Take A Closer Look" (1988), *Chain Store Age Executive* 64, no. 7, (July), 80, 82.

Klokis, Holly (1986), "Space Exploration," *Chain Store Age Executive* 62, no. 3, (March), 13–14, 16.

Krienke, Mary (1988), "Fitch: Design Leader," *Stores* (June), 70–71, 75.

"Lazarus: Embarking On A Small Store Strategy" (1987), *Chain Store Age Executive* (March), 98–99.

"Lighting on the Bottom Line" (1988), *Chain Store Age Executive* 64, no. 7, (July), 68, 72.

Murphy, Joan H. (1988), "A Tailor-made Loss Prevention Program," *Security Management* (August), 116–120.

"New Grocery Store Design Gets Shoppers In and Out Quickly" (1988), *Marketing News* (June 6), 24.

Prinzing, Debra (1988), "Partners In Presentation: Vendors and Retailers Unite," *Visual Merchandising and Store Design* (October), 56–64.

"Prototype: What If It Doesn't Work?" (1988), *Chain Store Age Executive* 64, no. 6, (September), 15–16.

"Radio Shack Tunes up Its Image" (1987), *Chain Store Age Executive* (June), 70–71.

"Retailers Warm to Idea of Air Destratifiers" (1988), *Chain Store Age Executive* 64, no. 6, (June), 77.

Russell, Rebecca D. (1988), "Increase Profits by Reducing Losses," *Security* (May), 36, 38–39.

Solomon, David J. (1987), "Hotlines and Hefty Rewards: Retailers Step Up Efforts to Curb Employee Theft," *The Wall Street Journal* (September 17), 37.

"Store Design Needs a Secure Foundation" (1986), *Chain Store Age Executive* 62, no. 10, (October), 89–90.

"Store Sizes Reflect Broader Mixes" (1988), *Chain Store Age Executive* 64, no. 7, (July), 62–63.

"Subliminal Messages: Subtle Crime Stoppers" (1986), *Chain Store Age Executive* 62, no. 7, (July), 85, 88.

Sullivan, Erin (1988), "All the Store's a Stage," *Progressive Grocer* (May), 225–226, 228, 230.

"Supermarket Strips Away Dull Problems" (1988), *Chain Store Age Executive* 64, no. 7, (July), 82, 84–85.

"The Broadway's System: Deter and Protect" (1986), *Chain Store Age Executive* 62, no. 8, (August), 86–87.

"Ups & Downs: Image Via Signage & Graphics" (1988), *Chain Store Age Executive* 64, no. 7, (July), 64, 68.

Walls, James D. (1988), "The Workplace: America's Hot Bed of Crime," *Vital Speeches of the Day* (April), 381–384.

Weiner, Steven B. (1987), "Off With Their Heads," *Forbes Magazine* (February 9), 34–35.

"Wellpet: Felix and Fido Create Its Niche" (1986), *Chain Store Age Executive* (September), 74, 76–77.

Retail Organization and Human Resources

Learning Objectives

*After studying this chapter, the
student will be able to:*

1. Explain the importance
of the human element in
strategic planning.
2. Compare advantages/
disadvantages of centralized,
decentralized and combined
retail organizations.
3. Describe the major retail
organization structures.
4. Explain how organiza-
tional design can be applied
to the small retail store.
5. Discuss the retail tasks
performed in each of the
functional areas, and their
coordination.
6. Describe the tasks
involved in human resource
management and the regulations that affect HRM
decisions.
7. Outline several human
resource trends that have
evolved in response to labor
market needs.

WAL-MART: PEOPLE AND QUALITY

● ●

David Glass, CEO of Wal-Mart Stores, was selected as one of the top leaders of the most admired corporations in *Fortune's* 1990 annual survey. Wal-Mart was rated second only to Philip Morris for quality of management, the factor that the judges deemed most important in shaping a company's reputation.

Glass is a quiet, intense Missourian who relies on participation from the company's employees. He believes there are no superstars at Wal-Mart, just average people operating in an environment that encourages every one of them to perform way above average. To stay in close touch with "associates," top management relies on a communications network "worthy of the Pentagon" that includes everything from a six-channel satellite system to a private fleet of eleven planes. This is based on the belief that the best ideas come from people "on the firing line," rather than

COURTESY OF WAL-MART

from corporate headquarters in Bentonville, Arkansas.

The Wal-Mart CEO gives associates plenty of responsibility, and expects managers for each of the 34 departments within a typical Wal-Mart store to run their departments as if they were operating their own business. The idea is that there are 250,000 entrepreneurs, each running his or her part of the business, rather than one entrepreneur who founded the business (Sam Walton).

Wal-Mart continues to remain in the top ten most admired corporations—but this would not be possible without top quality management and dedicated associates.

SOURCE: Smith, Sarah (1990), "Leaders of the Most Admired," *Fortune* (January 29), 46.

INTRODUCTION

In this chapter, we are concerned with the structure of the retail organization and with the human resources needed to perform the necessary retail tasks. Organizational structure and personnel combine to achieve the company's objectives. Retailing is a "people business." Each time we walk into a store we experience the result of plans made by people and carried out by people. People assist us in finding merchandise, and check us out when we make a purchase. People decide what merchandise to stock, what price to sell it for, and how to sell it. Many physical products sold by retailers are identical, but the retail managers who plan the strategy for selling the products make the difference. In other words, our decision to buy a product from one store rather than from another is the result of human decisions—the price, the location of the store, the ad that attracted our attention, the service level of the store, and so forth. Therefore, an important retail management goal is to select the right people at all levels of the organization, and to create a working environment that allows them to operate successfully.

Importance of the Human Component of Strategic Planning

Strategic plans could not be made nor strategies executed without people. The strategic plan combines the efforts of top executives, mid-managers, financial experts, and staff analysts. Each contributes his or her intellectual and analytical abilities, as well as judgment, to the strategic decision making process, as shown in Exhibit 11–1.

Once the retailers's strategic thrust is determined, and specific objectives have been defined, it is the people in the organization who must implement and execute the plan. In the early 1980s many companies fell into the SPOTS trap (strategic plans on top shelf) (Ulrich and Yeung, 1989). Business strategies for these companies consisted of financial, marketing, and technological projections of future activities, with little regard for organizational capability. Strategies were thus formulated, but not implemented, because the human resources of the company were unable or unwilling to carry out the strategic plan to accomplish the firm's objectives.

For further proof of the importance of the human element in development of successful strategies, consider the dynamic leadership of some of the top retailing CEOs. Names like Stanley Marcus, former head of Neiman-Marcus, are legend among retailing success stories. Directories of the chief executives of the most valuable publicly held companies include the names of well known retailers (The *Business Week* CEO 1000, 1987). A brief description of a few top retailing chief executive officers provides some insights into the effect of leadership style.

Charles Lazarus, founder of Toys "R" Us, has developed a loyal group of capable managers who have helped in the expansion of his supermarket-style toy stores. Leslie Wexner, who is described as an exuberant leader who can whip a crowd into a frenzy, has made deft acquisitions, rapid turn-

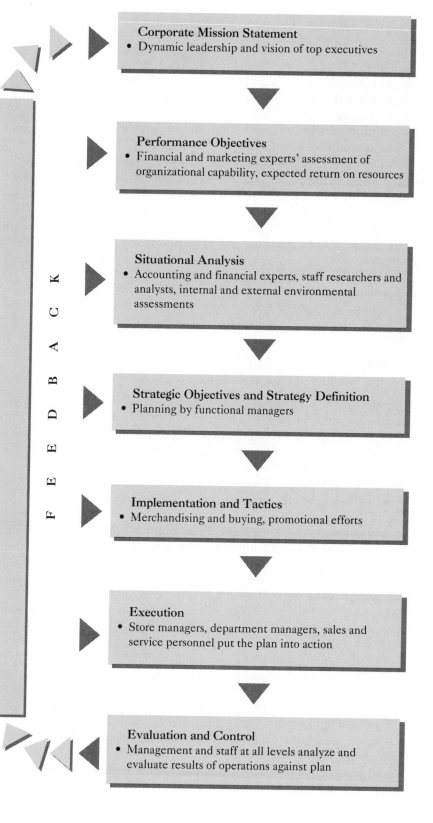

Corporate Mission Statement
• Dynamic leadership and vision of top executives

Performance Objectives
• Financial and marketing experts' assessment of organizational capability, expected return on resources

Situational Analysis
• Accounting and financial experts, staff researchers and analysts, internal and external environmental assessments

Strategic Objectives and Strategy Definition
• Planning by functional managers

Implementation and Tactics
• Merchandising and buying, promotional efforts

Execution
• Store managers, department managers, sales and service personnel put the plan into action

Evaluation and Control
• Management and staff at all levels analyze and evaluate results of operations against plan

F E E D B A C K

Exhibit 11–1
Human Resources and the
Strategic Planning Process: An
Illustration

arounds, rapid knockoffs of expensive styles, and a solid distribution network to make The Limited one of the most successful specialty retailers. John W. Marriott, Jr., a leading Mormon and "whirlwind" worker, aggressively expanded the Marriott family's lodging and food service company. Dillard's Department Stores has prospered due to William T. Dillard's instincts and attention to detail, which have given him the ability to buy poorly performing retailers and turn them around. Warren McCain nearly quadrupled Albertson's supermarket sales in a decade by stressing very large stores that were kept surgically clean and very price competitive. Lyle Everingham, Kroger's CEO, has kept the grocery chain at the top by streamlining operations and being a tough labor negotiator and tireless experimenter. David Farrell is described as an atypical retailer, one who runs the May Department Stores successfully with more of an iron hand than a glad hand. McDonald's Michael Quinlan is gregarious, earnest, communicates with employees, pays well, bangs the promotional drum, and plays "Dunk the CEO" at company meetings.

The insights and abilities of each of these executives have provided strategic direction to affect the future of their companies. They have also demonstrated the ability to adapt to environmental changes. Many other retailers have attempted to imitate their success formulas.

Personnel: The Organizational-Environmental Interface (IRIM)

The human resources element coordinates the retailer's resources and offerings with environmental needs and constraints. (See Exhibit 11–2.) Talented managers are able to assess the external environment and translate an understanding of environmental forces into appropriate organizational actions. The exchange process between the retailer and the environment is merely mechanical without people. First, this concept is true from the perspective of the firm looking at the effect the environment has on it. For example, an interactive marketing decision support system can be used routinely to collect data about markets, competitors, the economy, and legal forces. However, it takes astute managers and capable technical personnel to interpret the data for strategic and operating decisions and to act on that information.

Second, the organizational-environmental interface can be viewed from the perspective of the retail firm's effect on the environment. Store location, merchandising methods, inventory assortments, promotional campaigns, and other efforts do not accomplish the retailer's mission on their own. Competent site selectors and astute real estate negotiators make it possible for customers to shop in convenient locations. Qualified managers and strategic planners determine the best merchandising strategy for reaching a specified target market, whether the best method is through a traditional store setting, warehouse store, direct mail catalog, home shopping network, or other type of outlet. Effective buyers and merchandise managers obtain and merchandise the most saleable inventories. Likewise, human competencies are required to develop pricing strategies and a successful promotional mix. Finally, the store needs the right kind of people to meet the customer on a one-to-one basis and to be well-informed in answering questions, helpful during the selection process, and courteous and efficient in completing the sale.

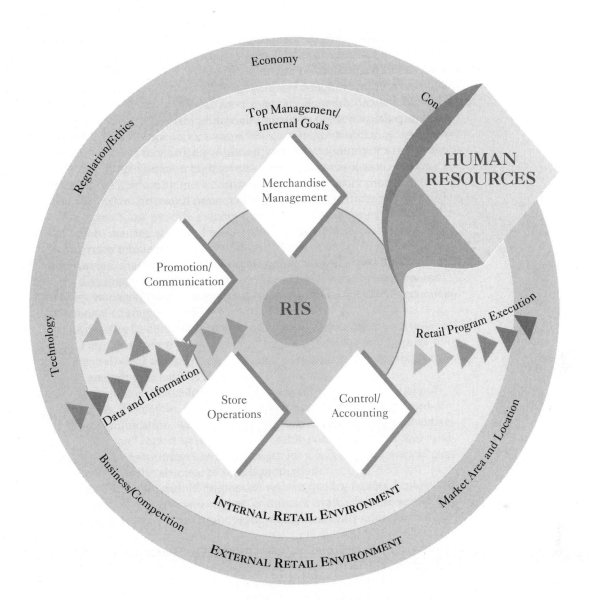

Within the diagram:

Economy

Con

Regulation/Ethics

HUMAN RESOURCES

Top Management/
Internal Goals

Merchandise
Management

Promotion/
Communication

RIS

Technology

Retail Program Execution

Data and Information

Store
Operations

Control/
Accounting

Business/Competition

Market Area and Location

INTERNAL RETAIL ENVIRONMENT

EXTERNAL RETAIL ENVIRONMENT

HUMAN RESOURCES AS A COMPETITIVE ADVANTAGE

There are three reasons why human resources are expected to be important
factors in creating and sustaining competitive advantage in the 1990s (Ulrich
and Yeung, 1989). First, no retailer's strategy, whether focused on growth,
quality, or market share, for instance, can happen without working through
people. A rather extreme example of the impact of human resources is seen
in the effect of employee stock ownership of their companies through leveraged buyouts. A leveraged buyout may occur when a retailer, such as Macy's,
wants to protect itself from being a takeover target by another firm. Macy's
managers invested their own funds to become part owners of the company.
As a result, they had more incentive to work long hours and to cut expenses
(Dunkin and Davis, 1987).

Exhibit 11–2
Personnel: The
Organizational–Environmental
Interface
· ·
SOURCE: Anderson and Parker 1988

Second, human resources focuses individual attention on a common mindset for shared organizational values, where the same set of values is shared vertically and horizontally throughout the company. (The common mindset of employees was a key element in the success of Japanese firms in building market share in the 1980s.) Retail firms like Wal-Mart have instilled shared corporate values in their employees. As a customer enters the store, the Wal-Mart "greeter" represents the retailer's value system. Disney World requires all new employees to undergo an extensive orientation program that communicates a set of values, based on the theme park's history and philosophy. These human resources practices build competitive advantage because they affect information and employee behavior to create a shared mindset both within and outside the company.

Third, individual capacity for long- and short-term change is affected by human resources practices. Retailers operate in a highly competitive environment that constantly faces restructuring through mergers and acquisitions. Personnel often have difficulty adapting to the resulting changes if the human resources department has not developed personnel practices to assist in this transition. The tools of communication, development, and organizational design can be used to help employees think about the future and build competitive advantage through their short- and long-term ability to adapt to change.

ORGANIZATIONAL STRUCTURE

The structure of a retail firm is an organized and coordinated network of activities and personnel, designed to accomplish the company's strategic, business, and functional objectives. Strategic, business, and functional (operating) levels of management are integrated into the structural design for an organization. The strategic-level mission and objectives, the business-level administration of organizational goals and resource allocation, and the functional-level execution and evaluation of strategic plans must be coordinated to achieve desired performance results.

An effective organizational structure reflects the corporate mission and strategy statement in both the vertical and horizontal relationships represented in the company's organization chart. It takes into consideration the type, quality, and assortment of merchandise carried by the retailer, type and level of services provided to customers, personnel requirements, store locations, and profit margin objectives.

Introduction to Organization Charts

An **organization chart** is a formal, written representation of the divisions of labor, hierarchy of authority, and channels of communication needed to carry out retail functions. It illustrates the vertical and horizontal relationships between areas of responsibility, as shown later in the chapter. Each position represents specific tasks to be performed and provides a basis for recruiting, hiring, training, and evaluating individuals who carry out those tasks. Similar activities are grouped together for management and supervision purposes.

ORGANIZATION CHART
formal, written presentation of division of labor, hierarchy of authority, and channels of communication that carry out retail functions

SPECIALIZATION
narrow and specific responsibility for performance

Because of the dynamic nature of retailing, organization charts must be flexible. Changes may occur for a number of reasons. Response to competitive activities and other environmental forces may result in adjustments in merchandising or operating approaches. Restructuring may be required over time to accommodate growth, increased use of automation, and other developments.

Organizational Principles

Several management principles are integrated into the design of an efficient and effective retail organization: specialization, departmentalization, unity of command, span of control, and delegated lines of responsibility and authority. Application of these principles is dictated by the size and number of stores, number of employees, geographical distribution, financial resources, number of product lines carried, and other factors.

SPECIALIZATION   Regardless of firm size, an individual's area of responsibility should be as narrow and specific as possible for higher performance and accountability. Responsibility, or **specialization** may be focused on functions, products, or even geographical territories.

Functional specialization may include operations, merchandising, promotion, personnel, and accounting and control. Tasks are grouped according to the type of work to be performed. Department managers must report to all functional executives. Tasks are clearly defined and easier to explain to employees. On the other hand, specialization may result in too narrow a focus, more complex communication, and coordination difficulties. An expanded functional organization for Zayre Corporation is shown in Exhibit 11–3.

Exhibit 11–3
Organization Chart: Functional Specialization
• • • • • • • • • • • • • • • • • •
SOURCE: Adapted from Quinn, James B., Henry Mintzberg, and Robert M. James (1988), *The Strategy Process.* Englewood Cliffs, N.J.: Prentice-Hall. Used with permission.

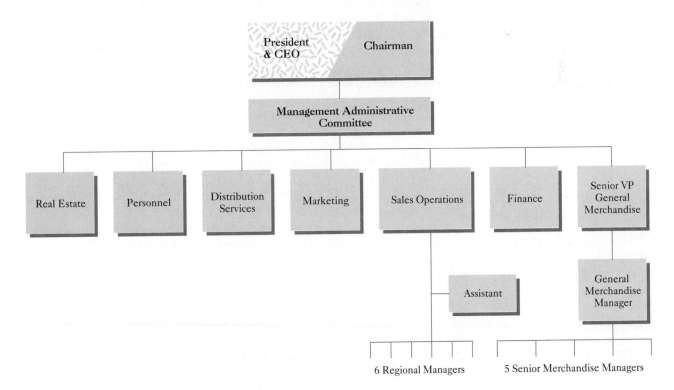

```
                        ┌─────────────────┐
                        │  Store Manager  │
                        └────────┬────────┘
                    ┌────────────┴────────────┐
         ┌──────────────────┐      ┌──────────────────┐
         │    Assistant     │      │    Assistant     │
         │  Store Manager   │      │  Store Manager   │
         │    Hardlines     │      │    Softlines     │
         └─────────┬────────┘      └─────────┬────────┘
          ┌────────┴────────┐        ┌───────┴─────────┐
    ┌──────────┐    ┌──────────┐  ┌──────────┐  ┌──────────┐
    │ Manager  │    │ Manager  │  │ Manager  │  │ Manager  │
    │Electronics│   │Appliances│  │ Women's  │  │  Men's   │
    └──────────┘    └──────────┘  │ Apparel  │  │ Apparel  │
                                  └──────────┘  └──────────┘
    ┌──────────┐    ┌──────────┐  ┌──────────┐  ┌──────────┐
    │ Manager  │    │ Manager  │  │ Manager  │  │ Manager  │
    │Furniture │    │Housewares│  │  Junior  │  │Young Men's│
    └──────────┘    └──────────┘  │ Apparel  │  │ Apparel  │
                                  └──────────┘  └──────────┘
```

Exhibit 11–4
Organization Chart: Product
Specialization

A product specialization structure gives area managers more control over daily operations. (See Exhibit 11–4.) For example, a hardware store may be divided into plumbing, electric, gardening, paint, tools, and other major departments. Advantages of product specialization include adaptability and flexibility, quicker decision making, and narrower focus on specialized merchandise. Disadvantages include duplication of effort, subordination of organizational interests to departmental interests, and conflict or lack of coordination between divisions.

The functional and product structures can be combined. Each specialized product area has its own functional divisions, for additional specialization. (See Exhibit 11–5.) However, personnel requirements are more expensive, and the principle of unity of command is jeopardized.

DEPARTMENTALIZATION
division of merchandise according to specific characteristics

UNITY OF COMMAND
consistent authority and direction for performance

SPAN OF CONTROL
number of employees managed by one supervisor

DEPARTMENTALIZATION Tasks and personnel can be **departmentalized** by products (produce, meat, and delicatessen in a grocery store), activities (accounting, credit, display, or security), location (budget/basement), or customer characteristics (leisure wear, gourmet foods, do-it-yourself, or "queen sizes"). Customers can locate merchandise more easily, and be served by more knowledgeable salespeople. The management structure is less complicated, and personnel are more accountable for specific tasks. Inventory management is improved through more precise tracking of sales. However, overlapping product categories may create problems between competing department managers, and customers may find it inconvenient to buy related items from many departments.

UNITY OF COMMAND   Each employee should answer to only one supervisor at a time for a given task. Problems and confusion result from a lack of **unity of command,** when an employee must please two or more supervisors while performing the same task. This is even more frustrating when supervisors do not agree about how the job should be done.

SPAN OF CONTROL   The number of employees managed by one supervisor is determined largely by firm size and tasks to be performed. A *tall* organization has a narrower **span of control,** that is many levels of authority with fewer individuals at any level. Tall organizations are more adaptable to change, but more costly to operate. A *flat* organization has fewer levels of authority, with a broader span of control. Each manager supervises more employees. Shorter communication lines allow prompt feedback and quick decisions. Flat organizations may be more cost effective and provide more job satisfaction.

DELEGATION OF RESPONSIBILITY AND AUTHORITY   These principles should go hand-in-hand. Employees find it ineffective and frustrating to be given responsibility for a task, without authority to see that it is done. The organization chart specifies established lines of authority to be observed by managers and employees.

Centralized versus Decentralized Organizational Structures

The forms of retail organization that have been described can be combined with either a centralized or decentralized structure, or a combination of the

Exhibit 11–5
Organization Chart: Combination Functional and Product

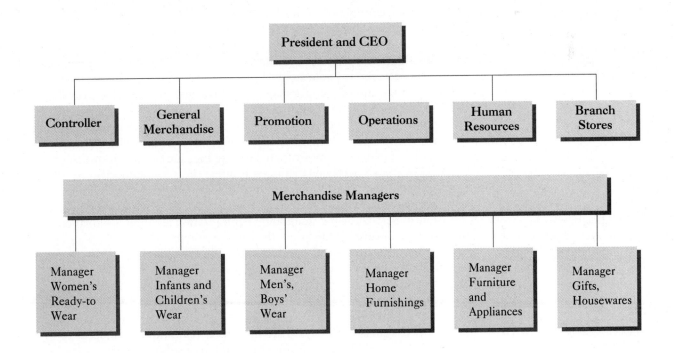

two. The locus of control in a retail firm may be centralized in a headquarters location, where authority and decision making for a group of stores rest with a few top managers. On the other hand, the primary responsibility for decisions may be given to individual store managers. The key to success is in determining the structure that is most profitable for the company as a whole.

CENTRALIZED STRUCTURE   Retail organizations with **centralized structures** have basic similarities. They are primarily concerned with standardization of facilities, merchandise assortments, operating procedures, and promotional mix. The physical appearance of stores differs little from one location to another. Basic architectural designs and layouts make one set of decisions possible for a number of stores, based on the most productive arrangements. Merchandise selections are made centrally for all stores to ensure similarity of assortments at all locations. Local managers may be permitted to make minor adjustments in their selections and assortments for local conditions, and to make some purchases locally.

Advertising campaigns and other promotional efforts are developed at headquarters for all stores, a task made easier by the standardized merchandise assortments. Centralized retailers often use planograms for floor displays. Diagrams or photos of displays are provided for merchandise assortment, placement, and quantity for shelf and hanging stock. The entire retailing mix is geared toward presenting a consistent company image for all stores. Centralized retailers such as McDonald's, K mart, Wal-Mart, and The Limited make major decisions and operate their stores from a headquarters location.

Advantages of centralization include the opportunity to have a more skilled and specialized management team at headquarters. Centralization generally results in more uniform decision making and a consistent image throughout the company. The firm may need fewer overall types of managers than a decentralized organization might need.

Central buyers can be highly specialized in procuring the right merchandise, leaving store managers free to focus their energies on the daily operations of selling and servicing customers. Economies of scale result from placing larger orders for multiple stores. Information systems capability allows sales, inventory, and other information to be available in one place to analyze performance for an individual store or an entire company.

Disadvantages of centralization include the situation in which local managers experience difficulty in adapting to local needs. This difficulty may decrease store managers' motivation, because they are not given sufficient autonomy to make decisions that directly affect their own performance. Further, centralization requires many mid-level managers to ensure coordination between headquarters and the stores.

From a merchandising standpoint, centralization assumes a similar customer base. However, if this is not the case, the same strategy and tactics may not be successful for all stores. Some retailers become so highly centralized that they are not as effective as they should be at the local level. Sears, for example, had to reconsider its organizational structure when they encountered this problem.

DECENTRALIZED STRUCTURE   **Decentralization** may occur at the level of the individual store, or a small group of stores operating some-

CENTRALIZED STRUCTURE
organization concerned with standardization of facilities, purpose, and procedures, with decision making from a central authority

DECENTRALIZATION
authority to make operating and merchandising decisions given to store managers

what like a local chain. Store managers are given considerable responsibility for merchandising and operating decisions. Some stores have separate managers for hardlines and softlines. However, buying may be centralized, with store managers making merchandise selections within corporate approved procedures. Because store managers in a decentralized firm have more authority to make decisions, they can adapt to the needs of local customers and market conditions, and take appropriate competitive actions.

A retail firm also may be decentralized acording to geographic divisions. Typically, divisional vice-presidents oversee decentralized functional groups in cooperation with headquarters. Retailers such as J. C. Penney and Kroger are able to obtain greater market share in regional markets through a geographically decentralized structure.

The primary advantage of decentralized organizational structure is the ability of those closest to day-to-day problems to make decisions. Managers can make decisions faster, and be more flexible in catering to local needs. This type of organization is more appropriate than a centralized organization where regional and local markets have sizable differences in customers and/or competitors.

Disadvantages of a decentralized structure include a possible lack of uniformity among stores, which may result in customer dissatisfaction or operating inefficiencies. Decentralization not only requires more branch executives, but it is essential that these store-level executives have the ability, experience, and training to make the right decisions. The retailer may also experience loss of quantity discounts and increases in transportation and billing costs. Finally, a successfully decentralized retailer is highly dependent upon an effective information system that can provide up-to-the-minute data on sales, inventory, and customers.

COMBINATION: CENTRALIZED AND DECENTRALIZED   A broad spectrum of organizational structures exists between completely centralized and decentralized organizations. For example, store managers may have limited authority to determine certain merchandise needs, promotional events, or other relatively minor decisions. The balance of authority may shift from time to time, between headquarters, region, and store-level. This may be due to management philosophy, need for operating efficiencies, mergers and acquisitions, or other factors.

According to the vice-chairman of the May Department Stores Co., senior management in that firm has an "autocratic partnership" with the stores. The stores are not told what to buy or from whom, although strong control is exerted (such as the requirement to carry Liz Claiborne in all stores). The "autocratic partnership" involves spending a tremendous amount of time and energy in discussing merchandising ideas, trends, suppliers, and how to take advantage of new developments. Both groups participate in identifying emerging themes and directions (Honig, 1988).

Traditional Department Store Organization

The traditional department store is the most common combination of centralized and decentralized organizations. The evolution of this structure was primarily due to the expansion of many local, family-owned businesses. Many of these retailers developed branch stores and/or were later acquired

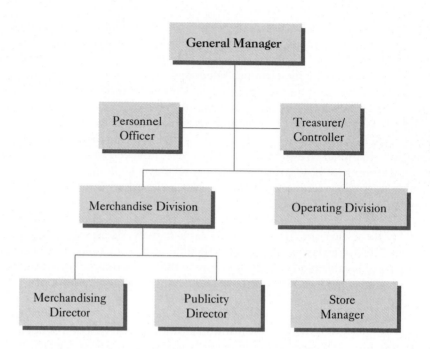

by larger retail organizations. Then dealing with different types of locations (downtown, suburban shopping malls, etc.), different store sizes and architectural designs and physical layouts, differences in competition and promotional capability, and larger numbers of employees and managers became necessary. Throughout this process, individual stores retained a high degree of local control while generally operating within specified guidelines determined by headquarters managers.

Department store organizational structure is affected by the size of the firm. Smaller department stores may define two major areas of responsibility: merchandising and store operations. (See Exhibit 11–6.) Merchandising includes all buying and selling activities. Store operations includes design and maintenance of the physical facility. Other retailing functions, such as personnel and accounting, are treated as staff functions.

The most widely applied organizational form for medium or large department stores had its beginnings in 1927, with a four-functional plan developed by Paul Mazur (Mazur, 1927). The Mazur Plan is described next, along with modifications to the original four-function structure.

THE MAZUR (FOUR-FUNCTION) PLAN   The **Mazur Plan** is the foundation of most department store organizations. The structure is based on the assignment of responsibilities according to functional areas. The four functional areas typically represented are merchandising, finance, promotion, and operations, as illustrated in Exhibit 11–7.

The merchandising division includes management of all buying and selling activities, such as planning, purchasing, and controlling stock assortments. This area of responsibility is particularly important, since merchandise provides the chief interface between the retail firm and its customers. It

MAZUR PLAN

structure based on assignment of responsibilities to four functional areas: merchandising, finance, promotion, and operations

Exhibit 11–7
Mazur Four-Function Plan
. . . .

is essential that merchandise managers integrate their activities with those of all other functional areas.

The finance division has primary responsibility for asset control, availability of working capital, accounting systems and other data bases, credit and collection, inventory control, and merchandising and operating budgets. This division also prepares and distributes financial reports.

The promotion (or publicity) function includes all methods used by the retailer to communicate with customers. Promotions managers are responsible for advertising, sales promotion (such as special events, etc.), visual merchandising (interior and exterior displays), publicity, and public relations. In many cases, this division also handles customer research activities.

The operating division has the responsibility for development and maintenance of the retailer's physical facilities. This includes the daily task of keeping the store clean and safe for customers and employees, warehouse maintenance, merchandise handling (receiving, checking, marking, stocking), customer credit and other services, and security and risk management. In some firms, operations managers are also responsible for personnel matters.

Since the Mazur Plan is based on functional divisions, modifications to meet the needs of individual retailers often are made in terms of functional combinations or extensions. As previously noted, the smaller retail firm may divide lines of authority and responsibility between two major functions: merchandising/promotion and store operations. Larger firms may separate the buying and selling functions, or they may add separate divisions for personnel, distribution, real estate and construction, or nonstore selling operations such as catalog sales.

Public relations at Fred Meyer stores includes Fred Bear, the company's ambassador of goodwill, who never speaks a word, but communicates volumes.

Reasons given for separating the buying and selling functions include the following:

1. Differences exist in personnel requirements.
2. Buyers may not be able to give enough attention to managing sales activities.
3. Information systems can provide feedback on sales to the buyer without distracting him or her from buying responsibilities.
4. Greater specialization can occur for both groups.

On the other hand, convincing arguments can be made for combining responsibility for buying and selling. Buyers who supervise the selling function have a better understanding of their customers' needs and wants and of how customers respond to merchandise offerings. Buyers are more careful in making merchandise selections, if they are held directly accountable for selling that merchandise in the stores. Likewise, performance evaluation can be more consistent if responsibility for buying and selling are combined.

As a retail firm expands geographically, the basic Mazur organizational plan may be changed to adapt to management needs at the store, district, or regional level. The three best known modifications of the Mazur Plan are the main store, separate store, and equal store approaches.

The **main store** approach also is referred to as the "mother hen with branch store chickens." Control over branch stores is centralized in the main store, where all merchandising functions are performed and major decisions are made. Focus in the branch stores is on the selling function and on the management of sales and sales support personnel. The main store approach is most effective where the parent store and branches are located relatively close to one another, customer needs and wants are similar for all stores, and where the number of branch stores does not exceed main store managers' ability to supervise all necessary activities.

As branch stores increase in number and size, they cover a large geographical area, and/or customers are very different from one location to another, retailers often use the **separate store** organizational structure. In the separate store approach, both merchandising and operating decisions are made at store level. Although they follow general policy guidelines established at the corporate level, separate store managers have a great deal of autonomy and the flexibility to adapt to local conditions. On the negative side, economies of scale are not realized from centralized buying, inconsistencies in company image may occur from one store to another, interstore coordination of stock, promotion, and other factors may be a problem, and an increase in the number of managers increases operating expenses.

The **equal store** approach combines the features of centralized and decentralized management structures. In particular, it separates the buying and selling functions. All buying activities are centralized. This includes inventory planning, buying, and merchandising. Promotional decisions also may be centralized. All stores, main store and branches, are treated equally, with each store managing its own selling, merchandise presentation, customer relations, and operating functions. The equal store organization offers a higher degree of specialization in buying (assuming an efficient, timely information system) without the distraction of supervising sales in the stores.

Chain Store Organization

Most consumers shop in many different types of chain stores for everything from apparel to groceries, hamburgers to hardware, auto parts to office supplies, and numerous other items. The variations in merchandise carried, as well as differences in size, number, and geographic distribution of stores, types and level of services provided to customers, and management preferences result in each chain having a unique structure, tailored to its own requirements. However, in spite of these differences most chain store organizations share some common characteristics in order to maintain a consistent company image. (See Exhibit 11–8.)

1. The majority of authority and responsibility is centralized in a headquarters (or home office) location for increased efficiency and effectiveness. The exception is the decentralization of responsibility for sales to local store managers. Some chains are increasing flexibility at the local level with limited decentralization of authority to regional, divisional, or local managers.

MAIN STORE

performs merchandising function and makes major decisions for branch stores

SEPARATE STORE

follows general corporate policy, but allows separate store managers flexibility to adapt to local conditions

EQUAL STORE

centralized buying activities, with each store responsible for selling activities

Exhibit 11–8
Chain Store Organization

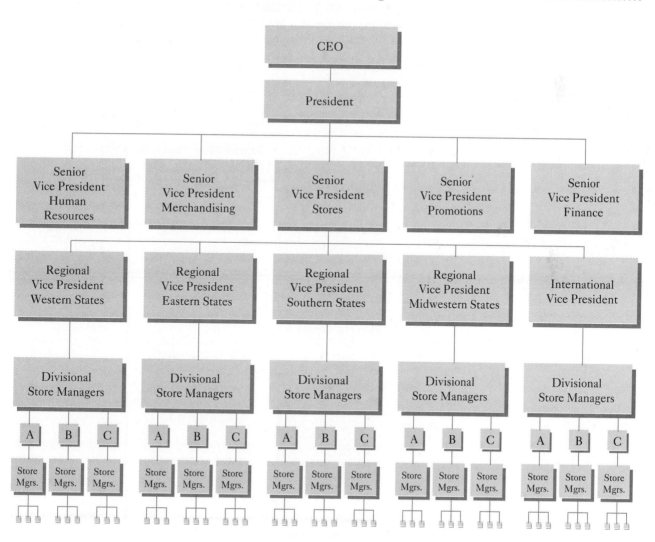

Part

2. Chains tend to include more functions than department stores in their organization charts. In addition to Mazur's basic four functions of merchandising, promotions, finance/accounting, and operations, one or more additional functions might be added. These include personnel, warehousing and distribution, real estate and construction, and others. The additional functions result in a higher degree of specialization and more skilled management.

3. To maintain consistency, chain organizations develop highly standardized procedures. Increased levels of supervision and efficient control systems ensure similarities in physical store characteristics, merchandise assortments and presentation, and personnel practices. This results in cost reductions and more effective operations.

Organization in the Small Independent Retail Firm

Many small, independent retail firms start with one owner-manager who assumes responsibility for the entire business. A limited number of personnel are added as required by growth in sales and tasks to be performed. Gen-

Exhibit 11–9
Small Independent Store Organization Chart: Three Employees

Owner/Manager

- Strategic Planning
- Financial Analysis and Control
- Supervision of Accounting Function (Outside Supplier)

Employee #1

- In charge when owner is absent
- Okays credit purchases
- Receives and checks merchandise (with Employee #2)
- Helps with inventory control (with Employee #3)
- Sells and provides customer service with (Employees #2 and #3)

Employee #2

- Writes advertising copy
- Arranges point-of-purchase and window displays
- Receives and checks merchandise (with Employee #1)
- Sets up sale racks (with Employee #3)
- Sells and provides customer service (with Employees #1 and #3)

Employee #3

- In charge of stockroom
- Places price tags on new merchandise
- In charge of markdowns (ticketing and recording)
- Helps with inventory control (with Employee #1)
- Sets up sale racks (with Employee #2)
- Sells and provides customer service (with Employees #1 and #2)

erally, there are no more than two organizational levels, as shown in Exhibit 11–9. Merchandising and operations are the basic functional divisions of responsibility. The organizational structure is simpler than its larger counterparts because of fewer merchandise lines and promotional activities, less specialization, and fewer services. However, the small number of employees means that each must perform a variety of tasks.

Conglomerchants: A Major Trend in Retail Organization

The size and diversity of large retailers and their markets have led to decentralized management structures. In addition, the large number of acquisitions and mergers of retail firms in recent years has resulted in complex organizational structures. Many of these firms deal only in diversified retail businesses. Others blend retail and nonretail businesses into one huge portfolio. For example, B.A.T.U.S. (British American Tobacco, U.S.) previously combined a tobacco empire with ownership of retail stores such as Marshall Field. These large, complex organizations are referred to as conglomerates or conglomerchants. The complexity of a conglomerate is shown in Exhibit 11–10. As the acquisition and divestiture process continues, the organizational structure must change to ensure that both corporate and business unit objectives are achieved.

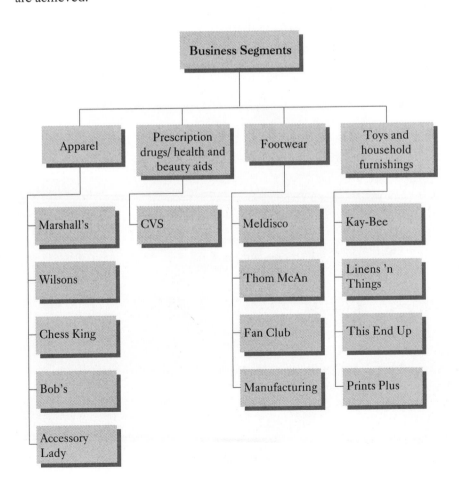

Exhibit 11–10
Conglomerate: Melville
Corporation*

* This chart is not intended to represent Melville Corporation's functional organizational structure. It is a summary of the strategic business units within each business segment.

SOURCE: Adapted by the author from Melville Corporation annual reports.

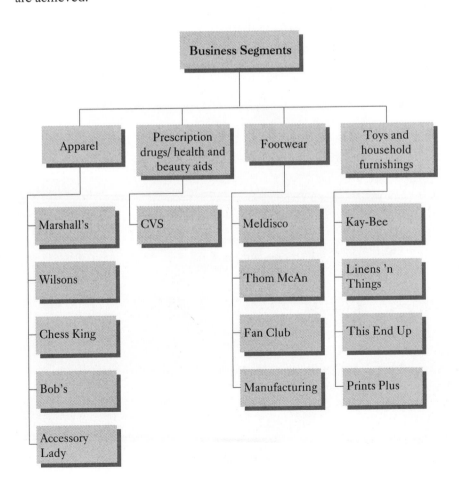

The dynamic nature of the conglomerchant structure requires flexibility to adapt to the need for capital to cover leveraged buyouts, or divestiture of units that do not contribute satisfactory revenues or profits to the corporate "bottom line." The predominant motivation for organizational design is profitability and return to stockholders. The focus is on operating efficiencies. In general, human resources efficiency is increased by trimming management and other personnel from the payroll.

Retail Tasks

All necessary retail tasks must be identified and described before designing an organizational structure and staffing each position. This requires an analysis of the type of work required for the five functional areas: merchandising, store operations, promotion, human resources, and accounting and financial. A job description is written for each task and used as a guide in hiring, training, and evaluating employees. Job analysis and job descriptions are affected by factors such as full-service versus self-service retailing, degree of specialization and administrative needs for each task, and high technology versus routine sales situations.

An analysis of all jobs to be performed serves several purposes:

1. It describes the work to be done.
2. It provides a profile of the type of employee needed to perform each job.

The Tandy Corporation employs its own service specialists for repair of Tandy products.

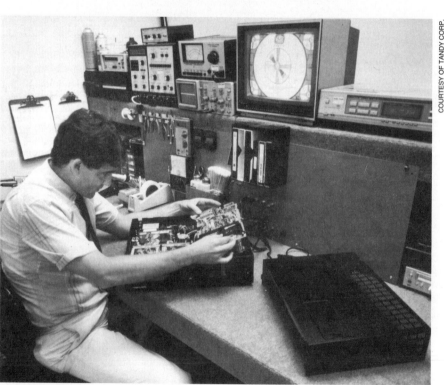

COURTESY OF TANDY CORP.

3. Related tasks can be grouped for supervision purposes.

Job analysis is also useful for determining training and equipment needed to perform a task.

In examining the company's needs relative to human resource availability and cost, management may find that having some functions performed by individuals outside the company is a more advantageous option. For example, customers bag their own groceries at checkout in many discount supermarkets or make unassisted selections in a variety of self-service stores. Vendors may pre-ticket merchandise or hold merchandise in a warehouse until it is sold to a customer. Outside specialists may be hired for accounting, computer applications, or employee training. Other tasks, such as delivery to customers, alterations, and product assembly or repair, may also be performed by outside providers.

A **job description** should be written for each identified retail task. This includes the job title (vice president, buyer, store manager, salesperson, accountant, security guard, etc.),. where the work will be performed (headquarters, specific store and department, etc.), how the work will be performed (description of all responsibilities and procedures), employee attributes (education, experience, skills, personal characteristics), and clearly defined position in the company relative to supervisors and subordinates.

The typical types of tasks to be performed within each functional area are described next. Emphasis is on the actual tasks and the human resources required to accomplish the retailer's objectives. Since a complete list of necessary tasks may differ from one retailer to another, those tasks common to most retailers are highlighted.

Merchandising

The **merchandising** function includes the planning and supervision involved in marketing particular goods or services at the places, times, and prices, and in quantities which will best accomplish the retailer's marketing objectives (Alexander, 1960). Planning encompasses decisions about inventory requirements, timing, and placement. Buyers and merchandise managers decide what to purchase, how much, when, and where to purchase. They also determine merchandise prices within profit margin guidelines, and plan special sales events. At the store level, department managers monitor inventory assortments, arrange merchandise displays, and supervise the salespeople.

Store Operations

The **store operations** function is responsible for maintaining and operating all physical facilities and for physical distribution activities. In many firms operations personnel are responsible for the design, construction, and remodeling of buildings. Tasks include opening and closing the store, cleaning the interior and exterior, and maintaining the building and fixtures. Operations personnel are involved in determining transportation methods, receiving, checking, marking, and moving merchandise through the store, security and risk management, and some customer services.

JOB DESCRIPTION
identifies job responsibilities for a specific position

MERCHANDISING
planning and supervising the marketing of specific goods

STORE OPERATIONS
maintaining and operating the store's physical facilities and physical distribution activities

Store management has increased in importance because of several industry trends ("Store Managers Assuming . . .," 1986). First, many retailers believe that future profits will come from increased profitability of existing operations, rather than new stores. Thus, greater emphasis is placed on recruiting, training, and developing strong store managers who can continue to improve performance in their stores. Second, today most department and specialty chains rotate their high potential people through all key functions, with greater cross-pollination between merchandising and store management. Third, the streamlining of executive staffs has resulted in fewer buyers, who cannot possibly visit all of the stores they service. Therefore, store managers provide important feedback on what is happening at store level. Most store managers are charged with overall responsibility for market share and for ensuring that the store is profitable. This includes sales, shortages, promotion, and customer service, and supervision of many diverse departments. Compared to a decade ago, more store managers are women. In terms of a career path, most store managers had been assistant general managers for merchandising, with previous experience as buyers. Successful store managers may be moved to bigger stores or promoted to regional vice president for stores, senior vice president, or back to the central organization as divisional or general merchandise manager.

Promotion and Communication

The **promotion function** includes all methods used by the retailer to communicate with customers, both in and out of the store. The primary tasks are advertising, personal selling, sales promotion, and publicity. Consumer and marketing research are often the responsibility of these functional managers. In order to attract customers to the store and persuade them to purchase the merchandise that the store has made available to them, many forms of communication are used. Personnel responsible for these tasks place paid advertisements in newspapers and magazines or air them on the radio or TV. They may design and schedule the ads and buy the media space or time. Other personnel plan and prepare displays, signs, and graphics for windows and selling areas, or obtain publicity by placing newsworthy stories about the company in the media. Managers in this area plan many types of sales promotion and special events, such as coordinated themes (e.g., International, holiday), fashion or bridal shows, bonus "give-aways" with purchases, contests, and other activities. In larger firms, these tasks can be quite specialized. In smaller firms, one person will be responsible for several areas.

Human Resources

The **human resources function** incorporates all tasks involved in designing and staffing the retail organization. Organizational design evolves from an identification of all tasks to be performed, vertical and horizontal relationships among the tasks, and the management hierarchy required for supervision, as discussed within the context of organizational structure. Human resources managers are responsible for recruiting, hiring, training, motivating, evaluating, compensating, and retaining personnel in a wide spectrum of positions. In addition, they may be involved in preparation of personnel budgets and schedules, and maintaining employee records. Human resources tasks related to recruiting, selecting, training, compensating, and evaluating employees are discussed in more detail later in the chapter.

Accounting and Financial

Tasks required to accomplish the **accounting and financial function** start with budgeting, and the location and allocation of resources. Personnel in this area are responsible for keeping accurate records of inventory, vendor and customer transactions, accounts receivable and payable, payroll and time records for employees, and generally maintaining financial control. They prepare financial statements for internal and external reporting, tax returns, and annual reports for shareholders. Financial executives develop budgets for all aspects of the operation, with the cooperation of functional managers. They monitor actual versus planned budget items, such as operating expenses, and analyze operating results. Responsibilities may also include managing the company's own customer credit plan, or working with outside credit companies.

Coordination of Functions

The tasks described for each functional area cannot be performed in isolation. If the work is to be performed effectively, all functions must be coordinated and work together in harmony. For example, one aspect of the merchandising function is to buy merchandise for resale to customers (such as shoes for a special sales event). The amount that can be purchased is a function of the budget allocated by accounting and finance managers. The sale of the merchandise is largely dependent upon the ability of the retailer to communicate its availability and desirability to customers through promotion (newspaper ads and point-of-purchase displays for the shoes). If customers are to make their purchases in the store, store operations personnel must have it open for business, with an attractive, clean, and safe shopping environment. Once customers are in the store, sales personnel and/or cashiers must be available to assist them. Availability of qualified sales personnel is dependent upon the personnel department, who must hire and train a sufficient number of salespeople and the managers to supervise them. Accounting personnel record receipts from sales for each department, pay vendors, and process payrolls. If any functional area is ineffective in its performance, the others will suffer.

STAFFING AND HUMAN RESOURCE MANAGEMENT

The quality of personnel at all levels in a retail firm can make the difference between success and failure. Maintaining a qualified and productive staff of selling and nonselling retail employees is a major challenge for human resource managers. While this is true at all levels of the company, perhaps the greatest challenge is in the lower, entry-level positions where turnover is particularly high. The magnitude of retail employment in the United States is illustrated in Exhibit 11–11.

PROMOTION FUNCTION
methods used by the retailer to communicate with customers

HUMAN RESOURCE FUNCTION
tasks involved in designing, staffing, and supervising a retail organization

ACCOUNTING AND FINANCIAL FUNCTION
budgeting and the location and allocation of resources

Exhibit 11–11

Retail Sales and Employment in The United States* *(in billions of dollars except as noted)*

Type of Retailer	1989	1990	1991[1]	1992[2]
Total Retail Sales	1,733	1,813	1,888	1,982
Dept. Stores	168	178	184	193
Eating and Drinking Places	174	179	191	202
Apparel and Accessory Stores	91	93	98	103
Employment, all retailing (000)	19,575	n/a	n/a	n/a
Average hourly earnings	$6.54	n/a	n/a	n/a

[1] Estimate
[2] Forecast
n/a = Not available

		Percent Change		
	Compound Annual		Annual	
	1981–86	1989–90	1990–91	1991–92
Total Retail Sales	6.7	3.7	5.0	5.0
Dept. Stores	4.1	4.2	5.1	4.9
Eating and Drinking Places	8.1	4.6	5.0	5.8
Apparel and Accessory Stores	8.8	3.3	4.3	5.1
Employment, all retailing (000)	n/a	1.1	n/a	n/a
Average hourly earnings	n/a	3.7	n/a	n/a

*Trends and Forecast: Total Retail and Selected Retail Establishments (SICs 52-59, 5812, 5813)
SOURCE: U.S. Department of Commerce: Bureau of the Census, and International Trade Administration (ITA). Estimates and Forecasts by ITA. As reported in *U.S. Industrial Outlook 1989*—Retailing, 54–1; *U.S. Industrial Outlook 1990*—Retailing, 41–1; *U.S. Industrial Outlook 1991*—Retailing 40–1; *U.S. Industrial Outlook 1992*—Retailing 39–1.

Retail positions must be filled within the company's forecasted personnel needs and policy guidelines. The number and type of employees needed varies according to the store size, level of customer service and specialization, store hours, and other factors.

Staffing and maintaining these positions involve a series of activities:

1. Recruiting potential applicants
2. Screening applicants to determine whether their skills match the job requirements
3. Training employees for initial and subsequent jobs
4. Determining compensation plans and benefits for each employee and evaluating employees against job criteria.

In some retail firms, human resource managers must consider the effect of labor unions and new trends in the workplace that affect day-to-day dealings with personnel.

Recruiting

Applicants for retail positions are recruited from internal and external sources. Both the method and source of **recruitment** will vary with the type

RECRUITMENT
methods of seeking and hiring store personnel

of personnel sought. That is, the search is more formalized at the mid-management and executive levels and less formalized for entry-level sales positions.

Mid-managers and executives are recruited from internal and external sources. Internal candidates are selected from present employees who are high performers and ready for promotion or from referrals from present personnel. External sources include professional and collegiate placement services, former employees, outside business associates, and competitors. Potential candidates can be reached through media ads, direct mail, personal contact, and other methods.

The recruitment of entry-level employees is a major problem facing retail managers. It is expected that nearly 1.7 million new jobs will be created by retail companies between 1984 and 1995. However, an acute shortfall in the labor supply has been anticipated, particularly for part-time sales help ("Incentive Programs Turn . . .," 1988). In 1981, 16- to 24-year-olds accounted for 32.1 percent of all sales workers, the largest group in the industry. By 1990, it was estimated there were only 515,000 of these workers to fill 645,000 jobs. Thus, the recruiting, hiring, and retaining of qualified employees has become a serious issue.

The shifting demographics of U.S. workers are evident in the composition of the labor force as of 1985 and anticipated new entrants from 1985 to 2000. Formerly, U.S. born, white males dominated the job market. Now employers are turning to women, minorities, and the elderly.

SOURCES OF APPLICANTS   Walk-ins are the main source of applicants for entry-level retail positions. Potential employees may be recommended by present or past employees, other business managers, friends, customers, or high school and college teachers and counselors. Previous employees with the right qualifications are often rehired. Other applicants may respond to newspaper ads, help-wanted signs in the store, or referrals from public and private employment agencies.

Retailers should keep a file of qualified applicants to consult when a position is open, which may include those who applied when a position was not available, former part-timers, and students who worked with the store in an internship, cooperative education program, or school project. Attracting applicants has become highly competitive in some areas, and requires a proactive approach to developing reliable sources for reaching potential employees.

RECRUITING METHODS   Promotional devices for recruiting employees include paid advertisements in newspapers and on the radio and TV. Posters and signs in departments and store windows are used to advertise openings. Publicity and public relations efforts in the local community keep potential applicants aware of the company. Contact may be made with identified individuals by phone, mail, or in person. Retailers can reach many students through college placement offices and campus career days. Recruiting requires a constant effort to attract qualified people through all means available. McDonald's used a placemat to invite customers to apply for jobs. Hardees used table tents and flyers on trays to attract applicants.

Exhibit 11–12
Hiring Legislation Summary

Employers should have at least a working knowledge of the federal antidiscrimination statutes to avoid inadvertent violations. Here is a handy summary of the major rules.

Act or Law	Prohibited Practices	Applicable To
Title VII of the Civil Rights Act of 1964 (as amended by the Equal Employment Opportunity Act of 1972)	Discrimination based on color, race, creed, national origin	Most employers of 15 or more employees, public and private employment agencies, labor unions with 15 or more members, and joint labor-management training programs. (Exemptions: Indian tribes and religious institutions with respect to religious activities)
Age Discrimination in Employment Act	Child labor, i.e., hiring a minor under 16 years of age without a permit	All public employers, private employers of 20 or more employees, employment agencies serving covered employers, and labor unions with more than 25 members
Executive Order 11246	Improper representation of minorities in companies participating in government contracts of $10,000 or more	All facilities of federal contractors or subcontractors and state and local agencies participating in government contracts
Equal Pay Act of 1963 (Amendment of Fair Labor Standards Act)	Misuse of payment under minimum wage requirements	All employers covered by the Fair Labor Standards Act
Rehabilitation Act	Discrimination against rehabilitated employees who meet job requirements	Federal contractors and subcontractors whose contracts are in excess of $2,500
Pregnancy Discrimination Act	Discriminatory hiring practices against pregnant women who meet job requirements	All Title VII employers
Vietnam Era Veterans Readjustment Assistance Act of 1974	Discrimination against Vietnam veterans because of their veteran status by companies participating in government contracts of $10,000 or more	Government contractors and subcontractors

Many questions commonly asked job applicants can be considered irrelevant and improper, and could lead to adverse consequences for the employer. Some of the questions are relevant only for limited purposes and only if properly phrased. Here are some of the consequences of frequently asked job interview questions.

Question	Relevance	Possible Adverse Impact	Preferred Phrasing
Name	Relevant	Demanding prior names might be discrimination against married or divorced persons who have dependents.	None
Address (Current and Previous)	Relevant	Might be deemed national-origin discrimination if inquiry made as to previous foreign addresses	None
Sex	Not relevant	Might be deemed sex discrimination if not a bona fide occupational qualification	None

continued

Exhibit 11–12 *(continued)*

Question	Relevance	Possible Adverse Impact	Preferred Phrasing
Citizenship	Relevant for determining that applicant is not an illegal alien	Might be deemed national-origin discrimination	"Do you have the right to live and work in the U.S.?"
Education	Relevant for determining job qualifications	Might be deemed age discrimination if inquiry made as to dates attended. Might also be racial discrimination where improper educational requirements are imposed. See the Supreme Court decision in *Griggs v. Duke Power*	None
Date of Birth	Relevant for determining proper age for job	Might be deemed age discrimination	"Are you less than 70 years of age?"
Arrest	Relevant only if necessary for bonding or security clearance	None	None
Physical Defects	Relevant for determining the existence of physical defects that might hamper job performance	Rehabilitation Act	"Do you have any physical impediments which might prevent or hinder you from performing this job?" "Do you need specific accommodations for fulfilling the job satisfactorily?"
Emergency Contacts	Relevant in the event employee is injured or ill on the job	Might be deemed discriminatory as to marital status, dependents, etc.	"Whom can we contact (name, address, telephone number) in case of an emergency?" (Should be asked *after* the employment selection is made.)
Honors, Awards, Organizations, Associations	Relevant for determining achievement, abilities, personality etc.	Might be deemed discrimination against religious, ethnic or racial groups by disclosing religious, ethnic, or racial affiliations	"List only clubs that do not disclose religious, ethnic, or racial background."

SOURCE: Reprinted with permission from "Managing Your Practice," in *The Practical Accountant*, Vol. 16, No. 12, copyright © 1983, Warren, Gorham & Lamont, Inc., 210 South Street, Boston, MA 02111. All rights reserved.

Selecting and Hiring

The next step is to select and hire the most qualified applicants. Established criteria should be used to match jobs and applicants. The appropriate interviewing and screening techniques are important aspects of the selection process, which can significantly decrease employee turnover and increase rate of retention. In addition, employers must be familiar with federal legislation on hiring and employment, as shown in Exhibit 11–12.

CRITERIA   The criteria for hiring new employees stem from the job analysis and job description. For example, a cashier in a grocery store would be expected to have basic math skills, ability to make change for customers, cash register experience or an aptitude for training, a pleasant personality, and neat appearance. The person hired as a cashier should match this description.

In general, criteria involve some level of education and the ability to communicate verbally and in writing. Experience working with people (in organizations, other jobs, or elsewhere) is usually important. Some positions require specific skills (e.g., typing, data processing, meat cutting, truck driving, alterations), and the applicant must have the necessary knowledge or experience to do the job. Most retailers want employees who are energetic and highly motivated, with good attitudes, attractive appearance, and pleasant personalities. These latter criteria are far more subjective and more difficult to determine in the screening and interviewing process.

New employees should "fit" the organization in line with the company's image and objectives. That is, employee characteristics should be compatible with the store's merchandise mix and with the store's clientele and other employees and managers.

INTERVIEWING AND SCREENING   Interviewing and screening potential new employees consists of three stages: pre-interview, interview, and evaluation. In the pre-interview stage, a profile of the ideal candidate is prepared from the job description. During the interview stage, information is provided to the applicant, and obtained about his or her qualifications for the job. In the final stage, the applicant's credentials are compared to the required profile characteristics, and the decision to hire, or not to hire, the applicant is made.

The personal interview is combined with other tools to screen applicants. These tools may include an application blank, testing, resumé and reference checks. The interview process and screening tools are discussed briefly.

For many retailers, particularly in smaller firms, the personal interview is the major (or perhaps only) basis used for hiring. The quality of the interview depends on the interviewer's ability to extract the right information from the applicant, and to diagnose his or her motivation and capacity for performing the job.

The interview process is affected by both legal and company constraints. Interviewers must be particularly sensitive to federal legislation on hiring practices, as summarized in Exhibit 11–12. There are acceptable ways of obtaining some of this information, without violating an applicant's civil rights or equal opportunity requirements. From the company perspective, personnel budgets may dictate the number, type, and ability of available interviewers, and the level of sophistication of any screening tools.

A completed application form gives the retailer more control over obtaining desired information than merely letting a prospective employee tell the interviewer about himself or herself. The information requested is subject to the same legal requirements as the interview. The intent of the government regulations for hiring practices is to discourage the use of invalid and marginal selection criteria. Therefore, these regulations can actually serve as a basis for designing an application blank that is an effective selection tool (Spivey, Munson, and Locander, 1979). Predictors of success include demographic, personal and social life history, personality, and job context factors (job position, etc.). An evaluation of this type of information helps the interviewer determine whether the applicant and the job requirements "fit" together. If so, one or more personal interviews follow.

In addition to physical exams, some retailers screen applicants with testing instruments such as aptitude, interest, personality, achievement (proficiency), or honesty tests. For example, interest inventories such as the Strong Vocational Interest Blank may be used to test sales ability. Other tests may assess intelligence, numerical ability, personality traits, or other personal characteristics.

One important form of testing is designed to reduce poor job performance or security risk due to theft, drug-related problems, or alcoholism. For example, a job-applicant honesty test (the Reid Report) helped Kay-Bee Toy and Hobby Shops reduce its inventory shrinkage 28 percent ("Prehire Tests Cut . . .," 1983). If given the chance, 40 percent of job applicants would steal from their employer, according to the Reid test results. Controversy surrounds the use of drug testing and the polygraph, or lie detector. Since millions of Americans are regular users of illegal drugs, employers are concerned about the relationship between drug use and theft and low productivity. If drug tests are used, they should be designed to avoid legal pitfalls. Federal law barred private companies from using the polygraph test to screen most job applicants after December 1988. However, Sears, Roebuck & Co. and other retailers were already questioning the validity of polygraph results. Others, such as Marshall Field's, object to the restrictions, but have switched to more credit checks and drug tests ("Polygraph Restraints . . .," 1989).

Applicants' resumés provide valuable information, but may not be as objective as the retailer-controlled application blank. The retailer may or may not check on the accuracy of previous employment or the cause of termination. Applicants generally provide references, but often they are not checked carefully. Because of an increased tendency to embellish previous jobs, salaries, and education, many firms now check applicants' backgrounds more carefully (Yu, 1985). Reference letters also may be suspect, because they can give a good indication of past performance, but generally avoid negative information (Von der Embse and Wyse, 1985). Privacy laws protecting criminals in many states make it difficult to check histories of applicants, creating a potential security problem for retailers.

A final interview may follow the initial interview and screening procedures giving both the interviewer and the prospective employee an opportunity to clarify answers. At this point, or soon thereafter, the applicant may be offered the job. Unfortunately, many applicants are treated poorly or left uninformed if an offer is not being made. This can result in a poor public relations image and have a negative effect on future recruiting efforts.

Training and Development

All selling and nonselling employees require some training. It may only consist of informal on-the-job instruction in procedures such as handwriting a sales check or using a noncomputerized cash register and an introduction to the type and location of merchandise being sold. On the other hand, training

Employees who experience job satisfaction tend to stay long with a company. John Chang, a chemist in Research and Development at Walgreen's, has been with the company for 18 years and feels that Walgreen's respect for its employees is an important factor. Here, his son, a Walgreen National Merit Scholarship winner, graduates as high school valedictorian.

Many retail tasks require the ability to communicate with customers.

may involve formal classroom instruction in techniques related to each job (sales, receiving area, etc.), orientation to the company history and philosophy, and other aspects of employment.

Periodic reorientation programs should be conducted for all employees, extending beyond the new-hire orientation (Martin and Peluchette, 1989). For many retailers, training is an ongoing process for developing productive, efficient, motivated, high-performing employees who make fewer mistakes, require less supervision, and stay with the company longer.

In a smaller firm, new personnel usually are trained by the owner, manager or another employee. In larger retail firms, personnel departments or training specialists generally assume responsibility for training and developing personnel at all levels. Training methods may include classroom lectures, case studies, movies, closed-circuit TV, conferences, role playing, demonstrations, and other methods. Training courses and instructional materials usually are developed in a centralized personnel or training department, although the actual instruction may take place at a headquarters location or in the store. Emphasis extends beyond initial training to the maintenance and improvement of an employee's current level of performance.

The impact of employee training is illustrated by F. W. Woolworth's drive for excellence in Britain. In 1982, the company suffered from a poor image that its acquiring firm, its suppliers, and the British public held. Among other problems, over 30,000 demotivated staff had the reputation for giving poor service. In 1986, new management launched new programs to turn around the declining business. This included a significant reorganization and culture change through a specially-designed, expensive staff training and development program. This training resulted in greater customer satisfaction and fewer customer complaints. The staff was more available, polite, and helpful, and customers perceived a higher service level. A better trained, more highly motivated staff helped Woolworth's achieve greater profits and sales (Rose, 1989).

Compensation

Retail employees are paid in a number of ways for the work that they perform. Compensation represents an area that requires careful analysis, because employee payrolls represent the greatest expense for most retailers. The wide variety of employees and tasks they perform complicate the issue further. The perceived adequacy and fairness of compensation plans also have a major impact on employee satisfaction. Fringe benefits are another form of compensation for employees at all levels.

Executives and mid-managers often work on a salary and bonus arrangement. The bonus is based on performance criteria, such as contribution to profits, for a particular area of responsibility. Employee stock option plans that make employees part owners of the company have become increasingly popular.

The required federal minimum wage must be paid to the majority of hourly retail employees. In 1938, the Fair Labor Standards Act was passed. This legislation included the first federally mandated minimum wage of 25 cents an hour, increasing to $3.35 an hour in 1981. Controversial legislation was proposed in 1988 to increase the minimum to $4.65 over a three year period. The National Retail Merchants Association predicts that increased labor costs will result in cutbacks in retail jobs. In fact, the layoff of nearly 5,000 variety store workers by F. W. Woolworth from 1978 to 1981 is attributed to increases in the minimum wage during that time (while sales increased by 17 percent). On the other hand, some retail unions support the increase on the premise that the 4.7 million workers currently paid at minimum wage have not had a raise since 1981, while the purchasing power of their earnings has dropped 30 percent due to inflation (Gallagher, 1988b).

Companies and the Three Rs

Reading, writing, and retailing . . . ? What are businesses doing to reverse the erosion of basic skills in the American educational system? They are finding innovative ways to help schools produce a new generation of workers who can read, write, compute, and think. Here is what some product and service retailers are doing to help:

- American Express combined classroom experience and on-the-job training in an innovative Academy of Finance for urban juniors and seniors at John Dewey High School in Brooklyn in 1982. Now several corporations support 35 finance academies throughout the country, where over 2,000 students participate in these career-based programs.
- Burger King established the Burger King Academy program for high school students in 1989. This is in partnership with the Justice Department and a national dropout prevention organization (Cities in Schools). Each of the six academies works with as many as 125 students, encouraging them to graduate. Burger King's academies are designed to prepare young people for careers in the restaurant industry that are more challenging than simply cooking and serving hamburgers.
- PepsiCo, parent of Pizza Hut and Taco Bell, sponsors a million-dollar Pepsi School Challenge program. Underprivileged children in inner-city schools are encouraged not to

As a service to students in the community, a Walgreen's pharmacist provides after-school education on drug abuse to a group of scouts.

drop out, through a variety of tactics ranging from financial incentives to mentor groups. Students who maintain a C average, attend school regularly, and stay drug-free are eligible for membership on the Challenge team, earning tuition credits and personal support.

- Pizza Hut has over half of U.S. elementary schools participating in the chain's Book It! reading incentive program. Students in grades one through six who reach their individual monthly goals (established by their teachers) get an individual pan pizza at their local Pizza Hut. If a class meets its goals in four out of the five months of the program, it can have a pizza party at the restaurant or in their classroom.
- Sears' major local initiative is the Academic Olympics, a competition that recognizes and rewards the achievements of "average" students in Chicago public schools. In addition, Sears has supported "Mister Rogers' Neighborhood" on public television for 20 years, and the Allstate subsidiary works closely with the American Association of School Administrators.
- Tandy Corporation, through its Tandy Technology Scholars program, gives financial rewards to recognize excellence in science and math. The company awarded $350,000 in cash and scholarships to 200 students and teachers in 1990.

SOURCES: Dumaine, Brian (1990), "Making Education Work," *Fortune* (Education 1990), 12+; Kuhn, Susan E. (1990), "How Business Helps Schools," *Fortune* (Education 1990), 91+; Sprout, Alison L. (1990), "Learning to Read the Word 'Pizza'," *Fortune* (Education 1990), 108.

In addition to legal requirements, compensation is based on other factors, such as supply of eligible workers, local economy, and union agreements. While many retailers anticipate a hike in labor expenses with the

$4.25 minimum wage, others such as Von's Grocery Co. (California-based supermarkets) do not expect much change. The unionized chain has no employees receiving less than $4.25.

With the declining birth rate and shrinking pool of low wage retail workers, the free market rather than Congress or labor unions may control wages (Gallagher, 1988). This is the case in many fast-food outlets where the traditional 16- to 20-year-old employees are not only fewer in number, but choosier about their jobs and demanding higher pay. Boston and other New England areas have a low unemployment rate, and few employable workers. A restaurant in Cape Cod could not open because it could not find help—in a market where unsophisticated salespersons were earning $6 to $7 an hour at the cash register. Some were earning $8 to $10 an hour and getting $2,000 toward their college expenses if they worked the entire summer (Abend, 1987). Retailers are challenged to develop a more creative approach to compensation and improved performance. Traditional compensation plans for sales personnel include straight salary, straight commission, salary plus commission, and salary plus bonus.

STRAIGHT SALARY   Under the popular straight salary plan, employees are paid a specified amount on an hourly, daily, weekly, monthly, or annual basis. There is no additional pay beyond this amount. Employees have the security of a known income, and straight salary is easier for employers to administer. Since compensation is not tied directly to sales levels, nonselling duties (stocking, customer service) can be assigned to employees. Disadvantages include inability to adjust compensation to sales levels in economic downturns, and possible lack of motivation for higher employee productivity.

STRAIGHT COMMISSION   A straight commission plan makes compensation a function of employee performance. The amount of commission is based on a percentage of net sales, which may be adjusted according to merchandise lines (big ticket, high or low margin, etc.) and other factors. This compensation plan has been used widely for those who sell cars, furniture, jewelry, and other high-priced items, and is gaining increasing popularity at department stores. For example, sales associates at Burdine's were placed on straight commission, encouraging them to maintain detailed clientele books to know their customers better (Zimmerman, 1989). Marshall Field's shifted from straight salaries to more incentive pay plans, giving higher commissions starting with Christmas 1988. Bloomingdale's switched to commissions in April 1989, continuing a three-year program on the assumption that better sales personnel are attracted and customers are given better service. (A successful sales associate at Bloomingdale's may earn $60,000 a year.) Neiman-Marcus contends it rarely loses sales associates to other stores because of its commission structure. On the other hand, Filene's Basement prefers straight salaries, on the assumption that their customers come for bargains, not service ("Commission Selling . . .," 1989).

Under this plan, employees are motivated to sell but may become too high-pressured in approaching customers. Such tactics may lead to customer dissatisfaction and a high rate of merchandise returns. Straight commission does not offer employees the security of a known income. However, the plan's flexibility gives retailers more control over payroll expenses.

SALARY PLUS COMMISSION The salary plus commission plan combines features of different types of compensation. Employees have the security of a known minimum income for a pay period, plus the incentive to build up their commission by achieving higher sales results. Most retailers establish a sales quota that the employee is expected to reach. Commission may be paid on only the amount above quota, or a smaller commission below and a larger commission above quota. This plan entails more bookkeeping and more effort for management, but tends to motivate employees to perform well.

While the trend toward increasing salesforce productivity through compensation plans that are weighted heavily in favor of commission appeals to retail managers, not all employees are happy with the results. For example, Sears slashed previously guaranteed base salaries for salespeople who sell big-ticket appliances and electronic goods, and changed its commission system on these items when it installed their Brand Central departments. Company executives believe the results have been positive and that employees are motivated and excited. However, many employees disagreed, stating that their earnings actually dropped under the new plan, with some advocating unionization to protect their base pay. Seattle-based Nordstrom, Inc. encountered similar employee resistance to its compensation plan. In spite of an outstanding reputation for service, some employees have accused the chain of failing to pay them for the time they spend in providing their customers with these extra services (e.g., phoning other Nordstrom stores to locate merchandise for customers, picking up and delivering goods to customers) (Schwadel, 1990).

BENEFITS The fringe benefits offered by a retailer are an important factor in attracting and retaining employees. Given the increasing costs of medical care and other cost of living expenses, workers seek employment in a firm that will provide adequate insurance (life, medical, accident, and disability). They also expect the benefits of paid holidays and vacations, sick leave, pension plans, employee discounts on purchases made in the store, and profit sharing plans. Each of these benefits is an expense for the retailer, resulting in lack of coverage for many employees—particularly part-time hourly workers and those working for small retailers.

OTHER FORMS OF COMPENSATION Retail salespeople have additional opportunities to increase their income by means such as extra dollar amounts or percentages of sales that are used to boost sales of slow selling items. These are called PMs (Prize Money, Push Money, Premium Money, or Pin Money). Employees can win prizes in sales contests, participate in profit-sharing plans, obtain cash awards for suggestions to management, or bonuses based on department performance or length of tenure with the company.

Performance Evaluation

Evaluation of an employee's performance serves a number of purposes. The main purpose is to increase overall employee productivity. At the outset, employees should be made aware of performance expectations, acceptable and unacceptable behavior, and the exact basis for evaluation. Then both employers and employees can make an objective assessment of whether the standards required for the job are being met. If not, additional training, reassignment, or possible termination may be indicated. If the standards are being met, or exceeded, the employee may be a candidate for a wage increase, promotion, or transfer.

Performance evaluation provides a basis for salary adjustments and job design (or redesign) to increase productivity through improved work methods. It can also reduce employee turnover and improve intraorganizational communication and recruiting efforts. Training and employee development programs can be based on performance evaluations, with particular attention to the areas with low scores. The review process can provide a system for two-way communication between supervisors and subordinates, assuming that it is objective, fair, and documented. The criteria for assessing retail employee performance stem from the job description. Some evaluation methods are described in the next section.

EVALUATION METHODS   There are a number of ways to evaluate employees. They vary in degrees of formality, timing between reviews, and standardization. Smaller retailers tend to use a relatively informal process, although a standardized rating form or checklist may be used. Larger retailers generally follow a formal procedure, assessing employees at regular intervals such as annually or semi-annually, and informally on a continuous basis. An effective rating form must reflect the specific job being evaluated. It may be based on a management by objectives system (MBO), whereby employees and managers work together to establish performance standards.

Employee productivity can be quantified and measured objectively. Records typically contain total dollar sales for a salesperson, number of transactions, number and amount of merchandise returns, and attendance data. Efficiency indexes can be calculated, such as sales volume per hour worked (VPH) or average transaction amount.

Professional shopping services are used to "shop" employees to observe their performance in a normal store situation. Shoppers play the role of an average customer, sometimes making a purchase without incident, and other times making it difficult for the salesperson. An evaluation of the shopping situation is then provided to management.

Supervisor appraisal of an employee may be informal and subjective. Therefore, it is wise to have more than one person make this type of evaluation. Supervisors also use formal and objective methods of appraisal, including standardized forms that should be designed to reflect the performance standards established in the job description. Accurate appraisals of employees are an important key to effective management.

A great deal of time and effort can go into evaluation of employees. However, if this process is to be successful, several things should occur. Employees should know from the beginning what is expected of them on the job. They should be given frequent feedback as to where they are performing well and where they need improvement. They also should have a clear idea of how and when they will be evaluated, to avoid uncertainty and frustration. A personal interview should follow the evaluation, with discussion of the results and an opportunity for the employee to explain or appeal. The ultimate goal of evaluation is to develop more productive, better satisfied employees.

Human Resources Regulations and Restraints

Many human resources decisions are affected by legislation, unionization, and social issues. Some federal and state legislation dealing with employment issues was discussed in Chapter 7. The major legislation governing unions is the Labor Management Relations Act of 1947 (Taft-Hartley Act), an amendment to the earlier National Labor Relations Act (Wagner Act). The National Labor Relations Board (NLRB) is the federal agency charged with the responsibility for dealing with unfair labor practices. Affirmative action and other employee rights lawsuits have been brought by the Equal Employment Opportunity Commission (EEOC) to ensure antidiscrimination and fair treatment in the workplace.

Although union membership is not widespread in the retail trade, about one out of nine retail wage and salary workers was a union member in 1978, excluding storeowners and their families (Job, 1980). Unions are more apt to be active in large cities, and in certain retail industries such as supermarkets. Human resource managers need to be aware of labor practices that lead to employee dissatisfaction and frustration, to avoid unionization in their stores.

Where labor unions do exist, everything possible should be done to develop a good working relationship between union and management, in order to have satisfied employees and a profitable company. Labor unions have made wage concessions to Kroger Co. and other retailers so stores could stay open and remain competitive in their markets, and so employees could retain their jobs. Tough union organizers, like the president of the 1.3 million member United Food and Commercial Workers, have cooperated with company management in certain situations for the common good ("William H. Wynn . . .," 1988). This union has been fighting to save jobs threatened by new owners selling off stores obtained in takeovers in the supermarket industry (Bennett, 1988). Stores may be closed completely or taken over by nonunion owners, affecting thousands of workers.

Three troublesome social issues that affect human resources managers and employees are sexual harassment, age discrimination, and affirmative action (Bradshaw, 1987; Cabot, 1987; O'Meara, 1987). Each of these is addressed by legislation, but still presents many problems. For instance, sexual harassment often is difficult to define or to deal with effectively. Amendments to the Age Discrimination in Employment Act (ADEA) eliminate mandatory retirement for most workers over age 70. As of 1987, those over 40 cannot be discriminated against in terms of pay, benefits, or continued employment. Add to this the affirmative action rulings that prohibit discrimination on the basis of race, sex, or other reasons, counterbalanced by the antagonism of some judges toward affirmative action quotas.

Trends

The changing composition of the workforce has resulted in an increasing percentage of working mothers, dual career couples, and other employees with special needs. Employers have responded with a variety of programs to accommodate them, such as flex-time, child care, job sharing, transfer policies, employee counseling and assistance programs, and quality circles.

FLEX-TIME   **Flex-time** refers to variable scheduling, which enables employees to work at times that are compatible with other demands on their lives (such as children coming home from school). Retailers can enrich their pool of productive employees by making scheduling concessions to attract high quality personnel who would otherwise not be able to work.

CHILD CARE PROGRAMS   Due to the increased number of working mothers and single parents, many businesses are beginning to offer assistance with child care for preschool children. As the labor pool of young workers decreases, more women will be hired to fill available jobs. Women with children under the age of 6 are the fastest growing segment of the workforce, and 73 percent of all working women are of childbearing age. In 1970, 39 percent of all school-age children had working mothers, compared to 60 percent in 1988 (Ehrlich and Garland, 1988).

A related problem is that about 40 percent of employees over 40 provide care to aging parents, sometimes finding it necessary to quit their jobs to do so. Programs to assist in child care and elder care are proving to be less costly than the loss in productivity from absences, tardiness, and stress on the job (Ehrlich and Garland, 1988).

An investment in this type of program must have a payoff to be cost effective. To illustrate, the Union Bank in Los Angeles opened a day-care facility for children. Managers consider this venture a "profit" center, since it saves up to $232,000 a year in decreased expenses related to employee turnover, absenteeism, and so forth. Media coverage of the center added an estimated $40,000 bonus in free publicity (Solomon, 1988).

JOB SHARING   While employees have needs for flexible scheduling, retailers need to have sales positions and other jobs filled during specified hours. One response has been **job sharing** programs, where two employees divide what was originally a full-time job into two part-time jobs. This is another method that may be used to attract and retain qualified employees who prefer to work part-time.

TRANSFER POLICIES   Moving to a new position in a new community presents a number of problems for employees. Transfer often means selling one house and buying another, an area where some companies are giving assistance to enable the employee to make the move. In addition, many employees are now part of a dual career couple. When one spouse moves, companies are helping the other spouse find satisfactory employment.

COUNSELING AND ASSISTANCE PROGRAMS   Many companies face problems due to employee use of alcohol and drugs, and provide professional counseling in these areas. Employee assistance programs may include physical and mental health care, financial planning, legal advice, preretirement counseling, and interpersonal-relationship counseling for problems with spouses, children, or supervisors. The objective is to improve employees' overall well-being and overall competence (Nollen, 1989).

Others provide educational assistance for employees and their families. For example, a Detroit Burger King owner spent $10,000 for employees'

FLEX-TIME
variable work schedules available to employees

JOB SHARING
one full-time position divided into two part-time positions, shared by two people

tuition and expenses at a community college in 1987–1988. However, the fast-food restaurant saved much more from reduced turnover, which had cost the store $62,000 in training and expenses the previous year. In addition to a lower turnover rate, absenteeism and tardiness decreased, productivity rose three percent, and the district manager's rating of the store rose nearly 10 percent ("Prepaid Education Pays Off . . .," 1989).

QUALITY CIRCLES   **Quality circles** are a communications forum, where all levels and types of employees have an opportunity to provide input for company decisions. Many valuable suggestions for improving operations have evolved from this process. Employees experience satisfaction from knowing that management is interested in their ideas and that their ideas can make a difference.

"NEW AGE" HUMAN RESOURCES TRENDS   In general, businesses are faced with the need to retain qualified, productive personnel at all levels—from the hourly worker to the CEO. One response, although somewhat controversial, is the "Mommy Track" for female managers and professionals who are also working mothers. The "Mommy Track" allows women to retain their positions on a part-time basis until they are ready to resume full-time responsibilities and continue their climb up the corporate ladder. A retired female executive of Federated Stores was given the opportunity to work 3 days a week in the early 1960s as a part-time executive while her son was young. Although her career was on a plateau for a few years, she received three significant promotions in the ten years following her return to full-time employment (Ehrlich, 1989b.)

Another novel approach at the management level is the temporary chief executive, i.e., a rent-a-boss service. Companies hire temporary executives to assist in financial crises, or to fill in for managers who become ill or die without someone to take over the business. Small companies, in particular, have been taking advantage of this service (Feinstein, 1989).

Although all retailers are affected by the growing shortage of workers, companies hit the hardest are those in the service industries and small businesses. Average weekly earnings in retail stores amount to $185, compared to $425 for manufacturing production workers, and $340 for nonsupervisory financial firm employees (Brownstein, 1989). Small businesses employ two-thirds of all entry-level workers (both retail and nonretail), and tend to pay less, offer fewer benefits, and provide fewer chances for advancement than larger companies. The 16- to 24-year-old first-time employees are decreasing in number, presenting serious problems for the small retailer ("A Shrinking Labor Pool . . .," 1989). Add to this the increased attention to comparative worth, that is employees should receive equal pay for an equal amount of effort regardless of the type of job performed.

Managers are providing more benefits and better training for low-wage workers, rather than treating them like a commodity and firing them when they are no longer productive. Radisson Hotels International uses a detailed interviewing process to find candidates who meet the company's high service standards. The MMI Hotel Group bases pay raises on performance and gives many employees their first jet ride and hotel stay to demonstrate the level of

QUALITY CIRCLE

communication forum in which employees participate and provide input for company decisions

service they are expected to provide. Boston-area Pizza Huts are attempting to reduce employee turnover with a tuition reimbursement plan. Employees working 200 hours in a quarter earn credits, which increase with length of employment, toward tuition for themselves, their children, or grandchildren (Solomon, 1989). The message is clear: retailers must adapt to the needs of their employees.

Summary

The structure of a retail firm, as reflected in the organization chart, must support the company's mission and strategic objectives. However, retailing is a "people business," and it is the human element that makes strategies work and allows the retailer to interact with its external environment.

An organization chart is a formal, written representation of tasks, divisions of labor, and hierarchy of authority needed to carry out retail functions. Vertical and horizontal relationships between areas of responsibility are illustrated. Organizational design considers the principles of specialization, departmentalization, unity of command, span of control, and delegation of responsibility and authority.

Retail organizations may be either centralized or decentralized. In centralized firms, major decisions are made in a headquarters location, and highly standardized operations create a more uniform image and economies of scale. However, local managers may experience difficulty in adapting to local conditions. In a decentralized structure, local or regional managers are given considerable responsibility for merchandising and operating decisions, although buying may remain centralized. These managers can adapt to local conditions quickly, but the retailer may suffer from a confused image across stores and from operating inefficiencies. Many firms have a combined centralized and decentralized structure for more effective operations.

The traditional department store organization follows the Mazur Plan, with four functional areas of responsibility: merchandising, finance, promotion, and operations. Modifications to this plan are the main store (mother hen with branch store chickens), separate store, and equal store approaches. Chain store organizations generally are centralized, include more functions than department stores in their organization charts, and follow highly standardized procedures. Even the small independent retailer can design a formal organization, with responsibilities clearly defined and assigned to a few employees. At the other extreme, the largest, most complex organization is the conglomerate or conglomerchant with a wide variety of separate businesses under one corporate umbrella.

Retail tasks can be classified within functional areas: merchandising, store operations, promotions, human resources, and the financial function. All functions must be coordinated with one another.

Human resources managers are faced with developing job descriptions, recruiting, screening and hiring, training, compensating, and evaluating employees. Sources of recruits must be identified and developed. The interview and other selection tools are used to match the applicant and the job prior to hiring. Training may be formal or informal, performed on-the-job or in a classroom, and extended from the time of initial employment throughout an employee's tenure with the firm. Compensation plans may be straight salary, commission, or a combination of the two. Incentive plans and bonuses also may be offered. Performance evaluation may be formal or informal, objective or subjective, and on a regular or irregular basis. Methods include productivity analysis, shopping reports, and supervisor appraisal.

Personnel decisions are affected by legislation, unionization, and social issues. In addition, the changing demographics of the workforce at all levels have made it necessary to develop creative programs to attract and retain employees. These programs include flex-time, child care (and elder care) programs, job sharing, transfer policies, employee counseling and assistance programs, quality circles, and other innovations.

Questions for Review and Comprehension

1. Explain the statement: The human element in the strategic planning process can provide a retailer with a distinct competitive advantage.

2. Sketch an organization chart for a five-store junior department store chain (soft lines only) that is located around the perimeter of a large city. Determine whether a functional, product, geographic, or combination organizational structure would be most effective.

3. In the context of the organization chart that you designed in #2 above, explain how the principles of specialization, departmentalization, unity of command, span of control, and delegation of authority and responsibility are represented. Will this change, and how, if the company grows to ten stores? if it acquires three stores in another city?

4. Compare and contrast centralized versus decentralized retail organizational structures for large chain department store operations. Discuss whether the same arguments do or do not hold for a small office supply chain.

5. Discuss and evaluate the Mazur four-function department store organizational structure, as well as three modifications to this structure. State the conditions under which the modifications to the original plan would be advisable.

6. You have just opened a new restaurant, and can only afford three full-time and five part-time employees. Design an organization chart for your business that will ensure that all important tasks are performed, and that will assign these tasks to specific employees. Should the part-time employees be included in the organization chart? Why or why not?

7. Give two examples of conglomerchants, and one example of a mission statement that might provide direction for the company's strategies at each organizational level.

8. Discuss several retail tasks that must be performed in each of the store's functional areas. Include examples of how these tasks can be coordinated among functions.

9. Assume that you are the human resources manager for a new independent computer store. Describe the complete procedure that you would follow in recruiting, selecting and hiring, training/developing, compensating, and evaluating personnel. Would your approach be different for a large computer store chain such as ComputerLand? Explain.

10. The human resource function is particularly sensitive to regulations and/or restraints, and labor market trends. Explain how each of these has impacted on human resource management decisions and ability to staff a store with efficient and effective personnel.

11. Read the Chapter 11 Retail Spotlight. Summarize the major retail acquisitions/mergers that occurred during the 1980s, including general reasons for their escalation. Debate the pros and cons of merger/acquisition/divestiture activities in terms of impact on managers and employees.

References

"A Shrinking Labor Pool Is Really Cramping Small Fry" (1989), *Business Week* (April 3), 82.

Abend, Jules (1987), "Taking Care of Your Own," *Stores* (November), 95–98, 100, 103.

Alexander, Ralph S. (1960), *Marketing Definitions: A Glossary of Marketing Terms.* Chicago, Ill.: American Marketing Association, 66.

Bennett, Stephen (1988), "Trying Times for Labor Organizers," *Progressive Grocer* (May), 83–84.

Bradshaw, Davis S. (1987), "Sexual Harrassment: Confronting the Troublesome Issues," *Personnel Administrator* (January), 51–53.

Brownstein, Vivian (1989), "A Growing Shortage of Workers Is Raising Inflation Risks," *Fortune* (April 10), 33–34.

Cabot, Stephen J. (1987), "Living with the New Amendments to the Age Discrimination in Employment Act," *Personnel Administrator* (January), 53–54.

"Commission Selling Spreads at Department Stores" (1989), *The Wall Street Journal* (Labor Letter), (March 21), 1.

Dunkin, Amy and Jo Ellen Davis (1987), "The Year's Best Sale at Macy's: Itself," *Business Week* (January 12), 136–137.

Ehrlich, Elizabeth (1989a), "The Mommy Track," *Business Week* (March 20), 126–134.

Ehrlich, Elizabeth (1989b), "Is the Mommy Track a Blessing—Or a Betrayal?" *Business Week* (May 15), 98–99.

Ehrlich, Elizabeth and Susan B. Garland (1988), "For American Business, A New World of Workers," *Business Week* (September 19), 112–120.

Feinstein, Selwyn (1989), "More Small Firms Get Help from Rent-a-Boss Services," *The Wall Street Journal* (January 25), B1–B2.

Gallagher, Rick (1988b), "Minimum Wage Hikes Threaten Retail," *Chain Store Age Executive* (June), 22, 24–25.

Honing, Lawrence E. (1988), "The 'Autocratic Partnership' at May Stores," *Business Week* (Readers Report), (January 25), 10.

"Incentive Programs Turn to New Channels" (1988), *Chain Store Age Executive* (June), 19–20.

Job, Barbara Cottman (1980), "Employment and Pay Trends in the Retail Trade Industry," *Monthly Labor Review* (March), 40–43.

Martin, Thomas N. and Joy Van Eck Peluchette (1989), "Employee Orientation," *Personnel Administrator* (March), 60, 63–64.

Mazur, Paul M. (1927), *Principles of Organization Applied to Modern Retailing.* New York: Harper & Row.

Nollen, Stanley (1989), "The Work-Family Dilemma: How HR Managers Can Help," *Personnel* (May), 25–30.

O'Meara, John C. (1987), "Whither Affirmative Action?" *Personnel Administrator* (January), 54–55.

"Polygraph Restraints Are Greeted with Yawns at Many Companies" (1989), *The Wall Street Journal* (January 10), 1.

"Prehire Tests Cut Chain's Theft By 28%" (1983), *Chain Store Age Executive* (June), 25.

"Prepaid Education Pays Off for a Detroit Burger King" (1989), *The Wall Street Journal* (January 31), 1.

Rose, Don (1989), "Woolworth's Drive for Excellence," *Long Range Planning* 22, no. 1, 28–31.

Schwadel, Francine (1990), "At Sears, Unpopular Pay Policy Reflects Fuss in Retail Industry," *The Wall Street Journal* (January 31), B1, B2.

Solomon, Jolie (1988), "Companies Try Measuring Cost Savings From New Types of Corporate Benefits," *The Wall Street Journal* (December 29), B1.

Solomon, Jolie (1989), "Managers Focus On Low-Wage Workers," *The Wall Street Journal* (May 9), B1.

Spivey, Austin, J. Michael Munson, and William B. Locander (1979), "Meeting Staffing Needs Via Improved Selection," 55, no. 4, 3–19.

"Store Managers Assuming Major Roles in Retail Businesses," (1986), *Marketing News* 20, (June 6), 27.

"The *Business Week* CEO 1000" (1987), *Business Week* (October 23), 99+.

Ulrich, David and Arthur Yeung (1989), "A Shared Mindset," *Personnel Administrator* (March), 38–45.

Von der Embse, Thomas J. and Rodney E. Wyse (1985), "Those Reference Letters: How Useful Are They?" *Personnel* (January), 42–46.

"William H. Wynn: The Food Workers' Master Organizer" (1988), *Business Month* (September), 23.

Yu, Winifred (1985), "Firms Tighten Resume Checks of Applicants," *The Wall Street Journal* (August 20), 27.

Zimmerman, Robert (Burdine's–Florida) (1989), "Executive Recruitment: What the Retailers Are Looking For," presentation at American Collegiate Retailing Association, Annual Conference, Boston, MA, (April 1).

Mergers and Acquisitions

Mergers. Acquisitions. Divestitures. These are common terms that represent popular means for strategic redirection and growth.

A **merger,** or consolidation, is a business combination where the buyer and the seller have equal power in the transaction. The resulting structure combines characteristics of both parties. An example is the merger of Dayton Corporation and J. L. Hudson to form Dayton Hudson Corporation. An **acquisition** is a business combination where the buyer absorbs the assets and liabilities of the seller, and the seller ceases to exist. An example is the Jewel Companies acquisition by American Stores (Kerin and Varaiya, 1985).

The above forms of restructuring both involve "adding to" the original organization; whereas, a **divestiture** requires the sale of "pieces" of the organization that no longer fit the firm's strategy or structure (Kanter and Seggerman, 1986). For example, Campeau entered U.S. retailing with its purchase of Allied Stores, and subsequently divested itself of numerous divisions (Bivens, 1988; Gallagher, 1988a). U.S. Shoe Corp. sold most of its footwear division in order to concentrate on its eyeglasses and women's apparel businesses (Phillips, 1989).

Since 1981, retail trade has ranked among the top ten U.S. industry groups (by both number and dollar value) using such forms of restructuring. The percentage of foreign acquisitions of domestic retail firms exceeded the average of all other industry groups combined from 1981 to 1983 (*Mergers and Acquisitions Almanac 1982–1984,* cited in Kerin and Varaiya, 1985). More recent data indicate these trends are unlikely to diminish (*Mergers and Acquisitions Almanac,* 1986; 1989).

Despite their popularity, these activities have not been without problems. Retail firms have been party to some of the worst mergers in the last decade, causing such activity to come under the scrutiny of the Federal Trade Commission ("FTC Seeks . . . ," 1982; "The Decade's Worst Mergers," 1984). In addition, such efforts have not always been profitable for retailers ("Best Products . . . ," 1984; "Marshall Field's . . . ," 1982).

REASONS WHY MERGERS AND ACQUISITIONS OCCUR

A variety of economic, political, technical, and financial factors make it more advantageous for organizations to grow through external means than through internal development. Eighty-one percent of the CEOs and senior managers described their latest deal as either "very successful" or "successful" in a 1987 survey ("Improved Acquisition Score," 1987). Next, the motives behind such transactions are considered from both sides of the deal.

Why Should the Seller Sell?

Depending upon the size of the retailer, reasons to sell could be any one or combination of the following:

1. Decrease in consumer spending
2. Rise in competition
3. Expansion of major chains
4. Decrease in sales among independents

5. Competition from off-price retailers
6. Surplus cash generation from large retail companies
7. Slowdown in construction of new shopping centers
8. Increase in markdowns
9. Sale of private or family-owned public retail interests for personal reasons

Many of these factors put greater pressure on small retailers to sell (Harrison, 1983).

Why Should the Buyer Buy?

Reasons why the buyer is interested in acquiring or merging with another firm include the following:

1. Real estate value of not having to build
2. Good cash position or willingness to use capital stock
3. Value increases and higher price earnings from stock market recognition

The significance of these factors tends to differ from one organization to another (Harrison, 1983).

In a 1986 survey of 101 CEOs and senior executives, "very important" or "somewhat important" ratings were given to increasing profitability (92 percent), opening of new markets (81 percent), and increasing market share (66 percent). The importance of market share is illustrated by the fact that 81 percent stated that they would pay a higher price for a company that would "improve growth in market share" ("Improved Acquisition Score," 1987).

Evaluative criteria have been developed to assess acquisition candidates (Harrison, 1983). The buyer should compare candidates in terms of (1) market share, (2) market penetration and growth potential, (3) balance sheet items (return on sales, return on assets, return on equity, inventory turnover, liquidity, price/earnings, performance consistency, and cost position, and (4) residual values of seller's leases. Other methods of determining the value of a candidate are "going concern" and "value of assets," but above all, the buyer must have the cash to afford the deal.

IMPACT OF MERGERS AND ACQUISITIONS ON RETAIL PERSONNEL

In the intense analysis of financial and strategic factors, acquiring firms seem to give little attention to the human and organizational aspects of the transaction. Evidence of this problem is found in the results of a 1982 survey of 50 CEOs, who ranked 26 factors that were given serious consideration during the pre-merger evaluation of the acquired company. Only three of the top 12 ranked items dealt with personnel or organizational issues. When asked what the CEOs would investigate if given a second chance at the same acquisitions, seven of the twelve items were personnel and organizational issues (Marks, 1982).

These figures indicate the lack of consideration for "organizational fit," or personnel-related factors. The combination of two businesses can be very difficult for employees who have been recruited, hired, socialized, trained, managed, rewarded, and reinforced by the culture of their "home" organization (Peluchette, 1989). Retail organizations would appear to be particularly vulnerable to such problems due to their heavy concentration of personnel, wide geographic dispersion, and intensive customer/employee interface (Pritchett, 1988).

While mergers and acquisitions can be perceived by employees, customers and clients as having a positive impact on a firm's image, the internal functioning of the organization and the quality of worklife are not seen in such a positive light. The problems associated with such a process can be viewed as either organizational or personal concerns.

Organizational Concerns

Several aspects of an organization present difficulties in integrating two firms: structure, policies, procedures, formal reporting relationships, and management styles. Often, two firms must mesh organizational structures—causing an increase in size. This tends to have a ripple effect throughout the entire organization by increasing bureaucratization, and impacting employee motivation, communication, and decision making (Marks, 1982).

Seniority lists and compensation systems become very difficult to integrate and often require adjustment. Authority and reporting relationships can be unclear and frustrating. Management styles may be incompatible in regard to philosophies, attitudes toward risk taking, and delegation of responsibility. The greater the degree of integration between the two firms, the more compatibility becomes an issue.

Personal Concerns

Decisions made at the organizational level not only have an impact on the functioning of the "new organization," but also on the individual working with it. Mergers can cause a loss of organizational identity, which can affect an employee's motivation, morale, and feeling of organizational pride (Marks, 1982).

Most of the problems with individual behavior in a merger or acquisition situation stem from feelings of uncertainty and insecurity. These, in turn, cause feelings of vulnerability, loss of control, tension, distrust, and denial of the whole transaction. Many individuals fear changes in their careers, such as terminations, transfers, new working relationships, or forced early retirements. As many as 60 percent of key personnel may leave within five years after the deal is finalized. The CEO of the acquired company often is one of those most affected. He/she may be placed in a lower level of management and have great difficulty adjusting. This is the primary reason for the high turnover of top executives.

Impact on Retail Management Career Opportunities

Mergers and acquisitions appear to have made retail managers more pessimistic about their career opportunities. For example, a 1987 survey of retail managers found major changes compared to 1983 and 1984 surveys (Gallagher, 1987). Although these individuals tended to be well-paid and well-liked, they felt that the frequency of mergers and acquisitions has negatively affected their career opportunities. The higher retail ranks were most negative about the outlook for promotion. CEOs were most negative, followed by general merchandise managers (gmms), buyers, and store managers. They generally agreed that one must switch companies in order to move up.

In addition, decisions tend to be more focused on bottom-line profits, with fewer rewards for such achievement. These changes seem to be impacting the gmm and buyer positions in particular, which have seen little change in their compensation package over the past five years.

Avoiding Personnel Problems

A number of recommendations have been posed by executives in an effort to reduce the personnel problems associated with mergers/acquisitions (Gall, 1986):

1. Planning for human resource management issues should occur before, during, and after the merger process. Top management (representing both organizations) should provide direction as to the needs and goals of the "new organization."
2. A thorough assessment of both parties' corporate cultures needs to be made, as well as the skill and competencies of key personnel. External consultants may be most objective.
3. Efficient, consistent, and structured communication by key executives is necessary to avoid mistrust and rumors, particularly if decisions will adversely affect personnel (i.e., cutbacks, layoffs).
4. A transition plan needs to be developed so that the change process is outlined and understood, thus helping human resource managers address important questions and determine the design of the "new organization."
5. After the merger, efforts must be made to help individuals deal with the change in order to reduce stress and fear. Managers must be trained to deal compassionately with their subordinates.

The dramatic effect of merging two companies is illustrated by the possible loss of most of the 1,700 jobs, including up to 400 buyers and managers in the merchandise group, at Marshall Field's corporate headquarters following the company's 1990 acquisition by Dayton Hudson. The layoffs are the result of consolidation of Chicago-based Field's administrative and buying operations in Minneapolis, home of Dayton Hudson's corporate headquarters ("Marshall Field Executives . . .," 1990).

FAILURE OF MERGERS AND ACQUISITIONS

According to a survey of business executives, failures of mergers and acquisitions are most commonly associated with people problems, such as clashes of corporate cultures or human relations breakdowns; lack of understanding the target organization; lack of clear purpose of plan; inadequate financial analysis; and lack of synergy ("Improved Acquisition Score," 1987). Most of these executives felt that people have a greater impact than financial matters on the results of the merger, and considered corporate clashes to be a major postmerger problem. They would spend more time assessing the target company's management, as opposed to assets and liabilities, if given a second chance at previous mergers.

Another study compared successful and unsuccessful acquisitions (Jennings, 1985). The unsuccessful parent company tends to have a poorly defined strategy and places a greater emphasis on financial analysis. In unsuccessful deals, the integration process in not well-defined beyond financial or accounting concerns and often involves later changes. The profile of unsuccessful acquisitions includes a size of less than two percent of the parent's sales, a minor market share, a business unrelated to the parent firm, and a dissimilar corporate culture from the parent.

The successful parent company tends to have a well-defined strategy and a comprehensive analysis of the other firm's market, technology, union, and corporate culture. Successful acquisitions tend to have a comprehensive plan, clearly defined reporting relationships, and a minimum number of unplanned changes.

RECENT MERGERS AND ACQUISITIONS IN RETAILING

Major department store deals from 1984 to 1988 are shown in Exhibit 11A–1. Some of the recent mergers/acquisitions have been by both American and foreign firms desiring expansion, boosted by junk bonds and deflated stock prices (Henkoff, 1989). Following his acquisition of Allied

Exhibit 11A–1
Divestitures and Acquisitions (1984–1988)

Year completed	Divesting company	Unit	Acquiring company
1984	Associated Dry Goods	Powers Dry Goods	Allied Stores
1984	Associated Dry Goods	Stix, Baer & Fuller	Dillard Dept. Stores
1984	Dayton Hudson	John A. Brown	Dillard Dept. Stores
1984	Dayton Hudson	Diamond's	Dillard Dept. Stores
1984	Federated Dept. Stores	Bullock's North	Various retailers
1985	Federated Dept. Stores	Boston Store	Bergner
1986	Alexander's	Alexander's (42%)	Interstate Properties, Bass Groups
1986	Allied Stores	Total company	Campeau Corp.
1986	Associated Dry Goods	Total company	May Dept. Stores
1986	B. Altman	Total company	Private investor group
1986	BATUS	Gimbels, Frederick & Nelson and The Crescent	Allied Stores (Campeau Corp.)
1986	Carter Hawley Hale	John Wanamaker	Woodward & Lothrop
1986	R. H. Macy	Midwest division	Dillard Dept. Stores
1986	May Dept. Stores	Joseph Horne Co.	Maverick Fund I
1987	Allied Stores (Campeau Corp.)	Blocks, Inc.	Federated Dept. Stores
1987	Allied Stores (Campeau Corp.)	Cain-Sloan	Dillard Dept. Stores
1987	Allied Stores (Campeau Corp.)	Donaldson's	Carson Pirie Scott
1987	Allied Stores (Campeau Corp.)	Joske's	Dillard Dept. Stores
1988	Federated Dept. Stores	Total company	Campeau Corp.
1988	Federated Dept. Stores (Campeau Corp.)	Bullock's, Bullock's Wilshire and I. Magnin	R. H. Macy
1988	Federated Dept. Stores (Campeau Corp.)	Foley's and Filene's	May Dept. Stores
1988	Higbee's	Total company	Dillard Dept. Stores, Edward J. DeBartolo
1988 (pending)	Maverick Fund I	Joseph Horne Co.	Dillard Dept. Stores, Edward J. DeBartolo

SOURCE: Reprinted by permission from *Chain Store Age Executive* (August 1988). Copyright © Lebhar-Friedman, Inc., 425 Park Ave., New York, NY 10022.

Stores, Canadian developer Robert Campeau acquired Federated Department Stores, but divested large chunks of it to May Department Stores and R. H. Macy to cover his debt. However, debt continued to plague Campeau and the corporation went into Chapter 11 bankruptcy proceedings in January 1990 (Loomis, 1990; Trachtenberg, 1990). Exhibit 11-A2 shows the new structure of Federated stores after bankruptcy.

Many of the transactions in 1989 were hostile offers. Kroger warded off a hostile offer by Kohlberg Karvis Roberts (KKR) and the Haft family by making a special dividend payment and debenture to common stockholders. Similarly, Safeway eluded a takeover attempt by Dart Group Corp. and settled for a successful leveraged buyout by KKR (Hof, 1989). Other major retail deals included Montgomery Ward Holding Co.'s acquisition of Montgomery Ward from Mobil Corp., SSC Holdings' acquisition of Stop & Shop, and American Stores' acquisition of Lucky Stores (Henkoff, 1989). It may be too soon to determine whether the results of recent mergers and acquisitions will be successful. However, *Business Week* rates May Department Stores acquisition of Associated Dry Goods among the best deals of the 1980s, and the acquisition of Federated Department Stores by Campeau and National Airlines by Pan Am among the worst (Farrell et al., 1990). During the 1980s, General Mills divested businesses valued at nearly $3 billion, including Talbots and Eddie Bauer, and a dozen weak restaurant chains. The latter have been replaced with the company's successful Red Lobster and Olive Garden restaurant chains (Sellers, 1990). A summary of recent mergers and acquisitions is provided in Exhibit 11A–3.

Major corporate retail deals have continued into the 1990s. Among the most noteworthy were BAT Industries' sale of Marshall Field & Co. for $1.04 billion to Dayton Hudson, and Saks Fifth Avenue for $1.5 billion to Investcorp, which also owns 50 percent of Gucci (Berss, 1990; Jacob, 1990; "Marshall Field Sold . . .," 1990). In 1990, Hardee's acquired the Roy Rogers chain from Marriott (Hardee's Gobbles Up . . .," 1990).

FUTURE TRENDS IN MERGERS AND ACQUISITIONS

Growth through external expansion is a dynamic process. There is a constant search for companies that can add new vitality to the acquiring firm. Several trends are industry market share dominance, the move to specialty retailing by traditional department stores and mass merchandisers, and legislation regarding unwanted takeover attempts.

Market Share Dominance

"Bigger is better" seems to be the theme of many firms seeking expansion through mergers and acquisitions. The convenience store industry provides a good example. Convenience store customers will not go far to shop, so the retailer's success depends on controlling a large number of top locations. One of the most aggressive, fastest growing players in this industry was Circle K. In 1988, the company had tripled the number of stores to 4,600 over five years, with tremendous increases in sales and profits. Acquisitions included 473 7-Eleven stores purchased when rival Southland Corp. was scrambling to raise cash to pay off debt from its own LBO. National Convenience Stores also snapped up 270 of Southland's 7–Elevens to achieve better locations for its Stop-N-Go Stores. However, Southland still

Exhibit 11A–2
Federated corporate structure, post-bankruptcy, as of 1/92

• •

*Federated Department Stores, Inc.**

Abraham & Straus
Bloomingdale's
The Bon Marché
Burdines
Jordan Marsh
Lazarus
Rich's/Goldsmith's
Stern's

* Includes Federated Credit Holdings Allied Credit Holdings and Federated and Allied Real Estate Subsidiaries

Exhibit 11A–3
Selected Mergers and Acquisitions

Acquiring Firm	Acquired Firm
Jordache Enterprises Inc.	Hallwood Industries Inc. (discount retail division)
Private Investor(s) (increased common stock holding)	Neiman-Marcus Group Inc. (Neiman-Marcus, Contempo Casuals, Bergdorf Goodman)
Servistar Corp.	Coast to Coast Stores Inc.
DWG Corp.	Horn & Hardart Co. (Arby's Restaurants)
Private Investor(s)	Horn & Hardart Co. (Bojangles Chicken 'N Biscuits restaurants)
State of Wisconsin Investment Board (acquired interest)	TCBY Enterprises, Inc.
Melville Corp.	Circus World Toy Stores Inc. People's Drug Stores Inc.; K & K Toys
Dayton Hudson Corp.	Marshall Field & Company
Valassis Enterprises (acquired major interest)	Warehouse Club Inc.
Red Apple Cos.	Busy Bee Food Stores Inc.
Deb Shops Inc.	Syracuse Tops 'n Bottoms Inc.
Computerland Corp.	Computer Shoppe Inc.
Long John Silver's Holdings Inc.	Jerrico Inc.
Box & Ship Inc.	Bekins Boxstore Inc.
Perry Drug Stores Inc. (acquired unit—16 stores)	Revco Drug Stores Inc.
Reliable Holdings Corp. (acquired unit—221 stores)	Revco Drug Stores Inc.
Kmart	OfficeMax, Inc.
Woolworth	San Francisco Music Box Co.

SOURCE: "U.S. Mergers & Acquisitions" (1990), *Mergers & Acquisitions* 25, no. 2 (September/October), 146–149; "U.S. Mergers & Acquisitions" (1991), *Mergers & Acquisitions* 25, no. 4 (January/February), 132–135. See also *Mergers & Acquisitions* (March/April, 1992).

remains the largest chain with about 7,500 U.S. locations. Gasoline marketers are a prime target for convenience store retailers, because of their high traffic corner locations (Carson and Vogel, 1988).

The volatility of this type of activity has left some major retailers, like Circle K and Southland Corp. in an extremely vulnerable position. In May, 1990, Circle K filed for Chapter 11 bankruptcy, unable to restructure their $1.1 billion in debt. Both firms were forced to sell assets, restructure, and sacrifice their independence in order to obtain new funds from outside investors.

Move to Specialty Retailing by Department Stores

The traditional department store has suffered lost revenues to a wide variety of specialty retailers. In response, there is a growing trend toward the acquisition of specialty chains by department store organizations. For example, Sears has branched into specialty retailing with the purchase of a Texas-based chain of optical shops and a small closely held chain of women's apparel stores. Perhaps Sears' most important acquisition is Western Auto Supply Co. Western Auto, one of the largest U.S. auto parts retailers, owns 278 stores, and is a wholesale supplier for another 1,570 independently owned stores that use the Western Auto logo. Sears operates nearly 800 of its own auto supply stores as adjuncts of its larger retail outlets. While this may create some overlap between the stores, Western Auto stores are usually in roadside strip shopping centers and Sears' auto parts stores are usually in larger shopping malls (Richards, 1988). Many other mass merchandisers, such as K mart have expanded their businesses to include specialty chains in apparel, housewares, cafeterias, and other lines.

Unwanted Takeover Legislation

Hostile takeover attempts have prompted legislation in many states to protect the unwilling target. Minnesota passed a state law in 1987 to help prevent unwelcome acquisition attempts by outsiders, after the Dart Company tried to acquire the Dayton Hudson Corporation. Key provisions of the law include: no sales of assets for five years after purchase without company directors' approval; raiders must have definitive financing agreement, made public before offer; broader fiduciary responsibility by directors to consider interests of all involved over short- and long-term; requirements for special meetings; no "greenmail"; no "golden parachutes"; and eligibility expanded to any Minnesota-based company with at least 10 percent of its shareholders living in the state ("Minnesota to Raiders . . .," 1987).

To protect communities, employees and others from suffering caused by corporate restructuring, both business management and labor are pushing similar legislation in states such as New York, Texas, and Illinois. More than 30 states have adopted statutes to repel raiders. The U.S. Supreme Court upheld Indiana's antitakeover law in 1987, giving more clout to these laws (Smart et al., 1989). While there has been an interest in passing legislation at the federal level, the states have made the most impact.

SUMMARY

Retailers can be expected to continue to expand and contract as they find ways to restructure their organizations through acquisitions, mergers, and divestitures. Merely focusing on bottom line profitability will not ensure success; it is people that make the new organization "work." Restructuring can take many forms as two or more businesses are combined into one. Human resources managers must deal with personnel concerns as they strive for an "organizational fit" within the new company.

REFERENCES

Berss, Marcia (1990), "Coming Home," *Forbes* (May 14), 44.

"Best Products: Too Much Too Soon at the No. 1 Catalog Showroom" (1984), *Business Week* (July 23), 136–138.

Bivens, Jacquelyn (1988), "Campeau In Control At Federated," *Chain Store Age Executive* 64, no. 5, (May), 39–40, 42.

Carson, Teresa and Todd Vogel (1988), "Karl Eller's Big Thirst for Convenience Stores," *Business Week* (June 13), 86, 88.

Farrell, Christopher, Zachary Schiller, Wendy Zellner, Robert Hof, and Michael Schroeder (1990), "The Best and Worst Deals of the '80s," *Business Week* (January 15), 52–59, 62.

"FTC Seeking Trust Violations, Surveys Major Retailers on Mergers in the Past Two Years" (1982), *The Wall Street Journal* (April 6), 8.

Gall, Adrienne (1986), "What Is the Role of HRD in a Merger?" *Training and Development Journal* (April), 18–23.

Gallagher, Rick (1987), "Are Retail Management Careers At A Standstill?" *Chain Store Age General Merchandise Trends* (August), 19–25.

Gallagher, Rick (1988a), "Changes Set for Federated, Allied," *Chain Store Age Executive* (May), 44, 46, 48.

"Hardee's Gobbles up Roy Rogers" (1990), *Business Week* (February 12), 40.

Harrison, Gilbert W. (1983), "Retail Mergers," *Mergers & Acquisitions* 17, no. 4, (Winter), 40–50.

Henkoff, Ronald (1989), "Deals of the Year," *Fortune* (January 30), 162–170.

Hof, Robert D. (1989), "Safeway: It's Confounding Critics," *Business Week* (April 24), 141.

"Improved Acquisition Score" (1987), *Mergers & Acquisitions* 21, no. 5 (March/April), 19–20.

Jacob, Rahul (1990), "Retailers: 'They're Quick—or Dead'," *Fortune* (May 21), 13, 16.

Jennings, Olin R. (1985), "Preventing Acquisition Failures," *Management Review* (September), 37–39.

Kanter, Rosabeth Moss and Tobias K. Seggerman (1986), "Managing Mergers, Acquisitions, and Divestitures," *Management Review*, vol. 75, no. 10, 16–17.

Kerin, Roger and Nikhil Varaiya (1985), "Mergers and Acquisitions in Retailing: A Review and Critical Analysis," *Journal of Retailing*, 61, no. 1, 9–34.

Loomis, Carol J. (1990), "The Biggest Looniest Deal Ever," *Fortune* (June 18), 48–51, 54, 58, 62, 66, 68, 70, 72.

Marks, Mitchell Lee (1982), "Merging Human Resources," *Mergers & Acquisitions* 17, no. 2 (Summer), 38–44.

"Marshall Field Executives Announce Resignations" (1990), *Southern Illinoisan* (April 27), 11.

"Marshall Field Sold to Dayton-Hudson" (1990), *Southern Illinoisan* (April 20), 11.

"Marshall Field's Too Successful Strategy" (1982), *Fortune* (March 22), 81–84.

Mergers and Acquisitions Almanac, 1986, Philadelphia, Pa.: MLR Enterprises.

Mergers and Acquisitions Almanac, 1989, Philadelphia, Pa.: MLR Enterprises.

"Minnesota to Raiders: Keep Your Hands Off" (1987), *Management Review* 76, no. 11 (November), 7–8.

Peluchette, Joy Van Eck (1989), "Corporate Culture Integration: Role of the Human Factor in Acquirers' Assessment of Target Firms and Resulting Integration Decision," unpublished working paper, Carbondale, Ill.: Southern Illinois University.

Phillips, Stephen (1989), "If the Shoe Fits, Sell It," *Business Week* (March 13), 42, 44.

Pritchett, Price (1988), "Managing the Human Factor in Mergers and Restructurings," *Retailing Issues Letter*. College Station, TX: Arthur Andersen & Co. and the Center for Retailing Studies, Texas A&M University, 1, no. 5, (August), 1–4.

Richards, Bill (1988), "Sears Seeks to Buy Western Auto Supply as Part of Push into Specialty Retailing," *The Wall Street Journal*. (March 17), 11.

Sellers, Patricia (1990), "General Mills A Go-Go," *Fortune* (June 5, 1989), 173.

Smart, Tim, Teresa McGuire, Bill Smith, and Richard Anderson (1989), "More States Are Telling Raiders: Not Here, You Don't," *Business Week* (February 13), 28.

"The Decade's Worst Mergers" (1984), *Fortune* (April 30), 262–270.

Trachtenberg, Jeffrey A. (1990), "Lessons for Campeau: It's Not Easy Being a Chapter 11 Retailer," *The Wall Street Journal* (January 30), 1, A14.

3.1 MERCHANDISE LAYOUT FOR SHARP DEPARTMENT STORE

CASE

At a time when many well-known retailers are losing money, the use of marketing skills can be the key to strengthening retail sales for a store. Based on this theory, Alan Sharp gave instructions to the promotion manager of Sharp Department Store that all advertising, sales promotion, merchandising layout, contact with customers, store displays, and store design be coordinated and related to the store's position in the marketplace, which targets middle to slightly higher income groups.

A scheduled building renovation had the promotion manager especially worried about store design and merchandising layout, so she had an artist draw the layout of the store that best depicted customer behavior.

The merchandising layout was designed as a series of boutiques within the store. Coming in the main entrance, the men's apparel would be on the right and women's apparel on the left. Junior and young adult clothing would be next to the adult apparel. Shoes would be next to young adults, with infants wear at the end. Cosmetics and accessories would be in the center of the store. Primary and secondary arteries would lead from one boutique to another.

In addition to layout, lighting would be a crucial focus. The ladies and Jr. Miss would have carpeting and the walls would be a neutral color so the customer's attention would not be distracted from the merchandise. The noncarpeted floors would be hardwood. Since merchandise layout plays an integral part in projecting the image of a retail store, all merchandise and displays would be in good taste.

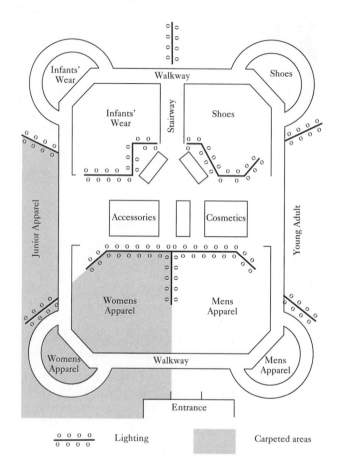

QUESTIONS

1. How does the above described layout facilitate customer buying behavior?
2. A superior store layout is one way to gain a competitive advantage in the marketplace. Discuss the importance of color, convenience, and lighting on merchandise layout.

This case was prepared by Keith T. Stephens, Western Carolina University, Cullowhee, North Carolina.

3.2 MIKE YOUNG: THE DYNAMICS OF INDEPENDENT RETAILING

Mike Young felt fortunate that during his last semester in college, Jane Weiss, a friend who had known him for years, asked him to enter into a joint venture in opening Joffree's, a privately owned apparel store. Throughout college, Mike had been employed by a men's specialty store and over a four-year period had worked his way up to assistant manager. In addition, he had done the store's displays each week and assisted in buying merchandise.

As part of their agreement, Jane Weiss, an accountant for the past 20 years, would provide the financial backing for the business venture and would handle its financial operation. Mike's major responsibilities would include buying, merchandising the store, and promotions. Mike would also oversee the renovation of the store site. They both agreed to co-manage the business and to split the profits 60/40 (Jane and Mike, respectively). The business was legally formed as a sole proprietorship, although informally it would function as a partnership.

Jane and Mike selected the name, Joffree's, because it had an upscale image, befitting the merchandise to be carried. The store would carry both men's and women's better-quality, fashion-forward merchandise and would cater to the middle to upper-middle income customer. Mike spent untold hours his last semester in school planning the selection of vendors and merchandise for both the men's and women's division. When it was time to go to market to make actual selections, Jane went with Mike. They had chosen the nearby Atlanta apparel market feeling they could find the selection there that would meet the needs of their target market. Since Jane was actually funding the venture and she had the accounting background, she felt she should be there to oversee the spending. Also, Jane wanted to gain an understanding of what "shopping the lines" entailed.

Mike informed Jane he preferred to shop the market by spending the first day or two looking over the vendor lines to feel out what was being offered in terms of style, quality, and price. During this process he took notes and picked up any written information vendors had available on their lines. In the evenings he analyzed each vendor's line and decided specifically what he would purchase. He followed this procedure to avoid impulse buying, to avoid buying duplicates, to insure he purchased a model stock, and to have better control over how much he was spending.

When they arrived at market, Jane was impressed with the professional manner in which Mike handled the purchasing procedure. At first she just observed and listened. However, by the second day Jane was ready to buy and began making some impulse purchases against Mike's wishes. That evening Mike tried to work her purchases into the overall plan he had for merchandising the store. On the third day, Jane was still committing to goods not in the plan.

By the end of the fourth day at market, they had bought significantly more than they had budgeted. Mike feared that this would affect the money allotted to him for the purchase of the men's wear lines. When he confronted Jane regarding these concerns, she told him there was still enough money available to stock the men's department and not to worry. After four very long days at market, they drove home excited about their purchases and turned their thoughts to what needed to be done to renovate the chosen store site.

Since Mike also had a strong background in merchandise display and a good eye for design and layout, Jane left the preparation of the store up to him. Mike was provided a budget to undertake basic renovations including painting, carpet, wall decor, lighting, store facade, signage, fixtures, mannequins, and props. He was excited to be given the

continued

freedom and flexibility to design the store and took on the project with much enthusiasm.

When the time came to return to market for the purchase of the men's wear lines, Mike went alone since Jane did not have an interest in its selection. Mike was somewhat intimidated to be going to market totally on his own because he knew his purchase decisions would affect the initial success of the store. However, he was relieved Jane would not be there making impulse decisions and confusing his merchandising plans. Although Mike worked the market as systematically as he had before, previewing the lines before making actual purchases, he missed Jane being there to support him in his decisions. He found himself working late into the evenings on his purchase plans until he was sure of his decisions.

Upon returning home he met with Jane to inform her of how the market had gone and gave her copies of the purchase orders. Then he turned his efforts to renovating the store interior and planning the store's grand opening. He hadn't heard from Jane in over a week, so he decided to give her a call. When she answered, she told him she had been analyzing the expenditures for the men's wear lines and was concerned that Mike had overspent. He reminded her that he had stayed within the agreed budget and that the overspending was in the purchase of women's wear.

Jane responded that she felt they needed to lower initial overhead because they were spreading themselves too thin. She told Mike to cancel the men's wear orders and just go with women's wear for the first six months or so, until they saw how things went. Mike was disappointed. Not only had he put many hours into the planning of the men's wear

merchandise, it was the area of the store he was to manage. When he expressed his concerns to Jane, she said there would be plenty for the both of them to do managing the women's apparel. Although it would take some rethinking and rearranging of the store interior, Mike knew they had ample merchandise to stock the store because of their overbuying in the women's lines. The next day he called the men's wear vendors and cancelled his orders.

Soon the women's wear purchases were arriving at the store and Mike's excitement returned. He stayed at the store round the clock, receiving the merchandise, pressing it, tagging and pricing it, and arranging it on the racks. He prepared ads for the newspaper and radio, and planned for the store's grand opening. Besides some special events at the store, a grand opening fashion show and dinner was being sponsored by the local Professional Women's Association. Each person attending would get a gift certificate that could be applied to any purchase at Joffree's.

The store opened June 1 and the customer traffic was exceptional. All of Mike's promotional activities and public relations efforts were paying off. Soon after, the fashion editor of the local newspaper sought them out and did a two-page spread on fashion trends for fall, using their merchandise and giving the store credits. Business boomed through August, then sales began to slow down. At first neither Mike nor Jane thought much about the decline in sales because September is typically a slow month in retailing. In fact when Mike went to market in October, Jane relented and allowed him to pursue a line of men's wear. But, October and November remained slow.

To combat the slow days, Jane would, on the spur of the moment, have half-off sales. This bothered Mike because there was no promotion of the sales and regular customers were becoming wary of buying at full price. He felt Jane's half-off sales caused business to suffer even more as regular customers would come in, try on merchandise, and then ask about the next sale. In addition, Jane didn't carry her weight in the store. She came in late, left early or did not come in at all. Mike had to cover her hours, and work his own. In fact, Mike came in early to clean and straighten the store, worked the store 10:00 a.m. to 6 p.m., closed the store, and worked on his merchandise plans in the evening.

As the end of November drew near and Christmas merchandise was arriving Mike felt the store needed strong promotions to get it back on its feet. He knew December should be the biggest selling month and he wanted to do what he could to turn around the downward spiral in sales. His efforts seemed to work. December was an excellent month for sales and, for the first time in months, Mike was able to draw a full week's salary at the end of December.

January brought mixed news for Mike. H.B. Men's Wear, one of the men's wear manufacturers he had pursued in October, agreed to accept Joffree's as a customer provided the store committed to the required $10,000 minimum order. To make this feasible for Joffree's, H.B. Men's Wear offered lenient payment terms, 2/10, net 90. The merchandise would arrive in February. Jane consented to the vendor terms and Mike began revamping the store to add the new line.

One afternoon, late January, while Mike was managing the store alone, one of his better customers, Eva Hanley, came into the store. As they were chatting Eva told him she had a business proposal she wanted to discuss with him. She said she had been observing the store's operations for some time and although she felt the store was teetering between success and failure, she felt Mike was exceptionally qualified to operate a retail business, if given the right backing.

She was interested in opening a combined men's and women's upscale apparel store in a nearby city and would like for him to be her partner. Like Jane's initial offering, Mike would be in charge of buying and merchandising, while Eva, who had been a corporate accountant for the past five years,

would provide the financial backing and oversee the financial operation. Both would co-manage the store. The proposed store site was three times the size of Joffree's and would necessitate an assistant buyer, a promotions manager, and a sales staff, and would legally incorporate. Mike would be paid an agreed-upon guaranteed salary, written into a contractual agreement.

Mike told Eva he would need to think about her offer and would get back to her within two weeks. When she left, Mike began to wonder if this was the break he needed. The idea of a steady income sounded great after the salary losses he had experienced over the past retail quarter. He would also have a staff to assist with the store's operation. Eva was nearly 20 years younger than Jane and was very interested in maintaining an active role in the business. The store was a much bigger undertaking, yet he felt he had acquired invaluable experience in opening Joffree's.

Mike decided to make a list of the pros and cons of staying with Joffree's or accepting the proposed offer. That Jane would be left with a $10,000 order from H.B. Men's Wear for which he was responsible weighed on his mind.

QUESTIONS

1. What would be the advantages/disadvantages of staying at Joffree's? Of accepting Eva Hanley's proposed offer?
2. If you were Mike, what would you do and why?

This case was prepared by Sandra D. Skinner, Western Carolina University, Cullowhee, North Carolina.

MERCHANDISING, PRICING AND COM

Part IV

MUNICATION

PLANNING AND BUDGETING

Learning Objectives

After studying this chapter, the student will be able to:

1. Explain the relationship between the merchandising function and other functional management areas in a retail environment.
2. Understand the use of data found in the income statement and balance sheet in forecasting sales and inventory needs.
3. Explain the role of the merchandise budget in inventory planning and the basis for planning each of its components.
4. Calculate planned purchases through the basic stock, percentage variation, weeks supply, and stock-sales ratio methods.
5. Discuss the perpetual book inventory and periodic physical inventory systems for both dollar and unit control.

CHAPTER Twelve

Back to Basics: The Gap's Strategy for Growth

Many retailers entered the 1990s laden with debt and suffering from a recessionary economy. Some resorted to bargain basement tactics with extensive discounts and promotional gimmicks to generate short-term cash flow.

Gap Inc. was not among the retailers who were threatened by the economy. Instead, the retail industry's bad times presented an opportunity to the Gap. The 21-year-old apparel chain continued to move ahead with an ambitious, albeit risky, five-year expansion plan in the face of a recession. Gap sales are projected to reach $4 billion by 1995.

Expansion plans in 1991 included the addition of as many as 165 new stores to its roster of 1,100 Gap, Gap Kids, and Banana Republic outlets. Most of the $220 million to accomplish this was to be financed from the company's cash flow.

The Gap's present strategy is based on the recognition that consumers, discarding their 1980s excesses, are turning back to the "basics" of an earlier, simpler life in America. The Gap, along with discounters Wal-Mart Stores Inc. and the Target unit of Dayton Hudson Corp., has been targeting department stores customers who might be trading down. In a recession, Gap's basic clothes are expected to retain their appeal. Gap stores are kept looking fresher than most competitors' by changing the colors of their stock every two months or so. Slow selling items' prices are slashed by one-third to move them out quickly.

The Gap offers quality and value, things that customers prize in tight times. One example is Gap's pocket T-shirt, positioned as a stylish but inexpensive fashion statement available in a dozen colors. By the end of 1990, nearly a million of the shirts had been sold at a low $10.50 price. As Millard "Mickey" Drexler, Gap's president, says: "Good taste doesn't have to be more expensive."

The Gap has become one of the top selling labels in the U.S., along with Levi Strauss and Liz Claiborne sportswear. Drexler discarded a dozen clothing labels previously carried by the stores, retaining only Levi's and the Gap brand that he intended to build. Gap's private label jeans are priced a few dollars below Levi's, but generate more profits.

Gap has made some mistakes: sticking with styles like shaker-knit sweaters and buffalo plaid shirts too long; failure in successfully launching Hemisphere, an upscale clothing chain; and over-extension of the safari look in the mid-1980s, which resulted in losses at its Banana Republic chain. However, the Gap's successes—many of them such as Gap Kids, which have been launched on the basis of Mr. Drexler's gut instincts, have continued to keep the chain profitable and growing rapidly.

The Gap has capitalized on the handing down of tradition, by adding Gap Kids and babyGap clothing lines. Most middle-class members of the baby boomer generation grew up with some relationship with the Gap. Now they can buy stylish, but sturdy and comfortable clothing for their children at Gap Kids and for their newborns to 2-year olds at babyGap. Other retailers who have turned to kids' clothes lines to capitalize on this $19 billion market opportunity are Toys "R" Us (Kids "R" Us), Limited Inc. (Limited Too), Benetton (Benetton 012), and Woolworth Corp. (Kids Mart, Little Talk Shop). Spiegel Inc. and Crayola have teamed up to create and sell a line of Crayola Kids clothing, accessories, and gifts. Large chains like Sears, J.C. Penney, and Montgomery Ward have increased attention to childrens' wear departments. Catalogers like Lands' End Inc. and Talbots have launched children's catalogs.

There seems to be a general recognition that no matter how sophisticated customers become, the retailer who offers quality, style, and good values will come out a winner.

Adapted from "Gap's New Line of Clothing for Infants Is Growing Up Fast" (1990), *Orlando Sentinel* (November 18), D1, D2; Schwadel, Francine (1990a), "Gap Inc. Is Prospering Even as It Disdains Usual Holiday Hype," *The Wall Street Journal* (December 19), A1, A6; "Schwadel, Francine (1990b), "Spiegel Crayola Plan Kids' Clothes Line," *The Wall Street Journal* (October 3), B1.

REMARKABLE RETAILER

INTRODUCTION

The selection and management of merchandise inventories involves some of the most critical decisions to be made by retail managers. These decisions require simultaneous attention to information about the retailer's internal company factors (philosophy, resources, future plans, policies) and external environmental factors (suppliers, intermediaries, legal restrictions, economy, product availability, etc.). Discussion in this chapter is presented from the perspective of budgeting and planning for inventories. Chapter 13 focuses on merchandise management and buying.

Merchandise Planning and the Environment

Merchandise assortment and inventory management decisions are not made in isolation from other aspects of the retail business. They must be made within the context of other functional management areas within the store's internal environment. Data inputs from each of the functional areas provide useful information to merchandise managers and buyers. The Retail Information System containing these inputs also provides financial data for evaluating operating results. Recall that an information system is generally associated with computerization and electronic data processing, but that on occasion, it may reside in a small retailer's file cabinet, or even in his or her mind. A written record is recommended, however, and should be maintained regardless of the size of the establishment. The right information in the right form must be accessible and used by retail management in critical merchandising decisions.

Information about the internal retail organization starts with an understanding of the company's mission, specific internal goals, and operating policies as shown in Exhibit 12–1. Simply stated, the buying and selling of merchandise must be congruent with what the company "stands for," the expected financial rate of return on inventory investment, and the way in which the company conducts its business.

Successful merchandise management requires coordination with human resources, promotion and communication, store operations, and accounting and financial managers. The merchandising function is dependent upon human resources personnel for staffing the buying office with buyers and for providing sales and support staff members. Information regarding job descriptions, employee qualifications, and resource allocation (hours, compensation, etc.) is communicated between merchandising and human resources managers.

Merchandise managers also share information with those responsible for the store promotion and communication function. Knowledge about promotional budgets, target markets, and merchandise specifications is essential in order to maximize the impact of customer communications efforts. Decisions about advertising, personal selling, sales promotion, publicity and direct mail campaigns, and point-of-purchase displays, as well as feedback on the effectiveness of each of these promotional tools require a shared information base. Store image, as it relates to merchandise, can be affected by the level of understanding and agreement achieved by these two groups.

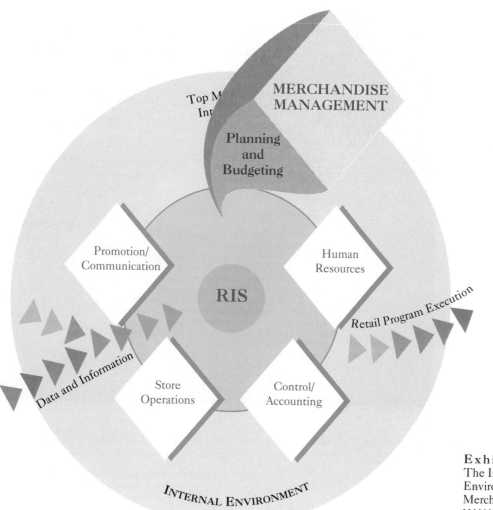

Top M...
Int...

**MERCHANDISE
MANAGEMENT**

Planning
and
Budgeting

Promotion/
Communication

Human
Resources

RIS

Retail Program Execution

Data and Information

Store
Operations

Control/
Accounting

INTERNAL ENVIRONMENT

Exhibit 12–1
The Internal Retailing
Environment: Information for
Merchandise Management
••••••••••••••••••••••••••••
SOURCE: Anderson and Parker 1988

Knowledge of store operations policies and procedures also is essential to effective merchandise management. Store operating personnel are responsible for receiving, marking, and delivering inventory, as well as for many aspects of customer service. They maintain the buildings and fixtures that "showcase" the merchandise, manage retail space assignments, and take measures to prevent theft and pilferage of the merchandise.

One of the most obvious functional areas for the availability and exchange of information for buying and merchandising decisions is in control and accounting. Up-to-date and accurate records provide data regarding sales, merchandise costs, inventory levels, profits, and performance results and evaluation. An understanding of the type of information required and how it is used is important to both merchandising and accounting managers in accomplishing their tasks.

A Retail Information System is used to acquire, store, and process the data required for the coordination of the merchandising function with each of the other four functional areas, as described in Chapter 3. It also provides a

Part IV

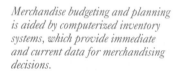

Merchandise budgeting and planning is aided by computerized inventory systems, which provide immediate and current data for merchandising decisions.

Merchandise Information data base, which focuses on buying and inventory management. The information provided may be in the form of inventory reports, merchandise on order, sales forecasts, vendor and/or product line data, or financial ratios (such as gross margin return on inventory investment, or sales productivity per square foot). (See Exhibit 12–2.)

The preceding discussion highlights the relationships between merchandising and other internal retail management areas. It also emphasizes the need for the availability and exchange of information in order to maximize individual and corporate efforts. The basic concepts apply to both large and small retailers. Large retailers have the advantage of a sophisticated computerized information system available for use in decision making. However, the successful small retailer can keep accurate and complete records that can be used for this same purpose on a more modest scale. This process is facilitated by increased usage of microcomputers and applied software by smaller firms.

Merchandise Budgeting and Planning: Strategic Implications

Internal factors that are considered in the strategic planning process include the retailer's merchandising philosophy and overall strategy, market position, budget requirements, historical and planned sales and inventory data, and merchandise assortment preferences based on experience and market information. Once these variables have been analyzed, the perspective becomes more external as described in the next chapter. Finally, the results of mer-

Company Goals
Policies
Philosophy
Resources
Etc.

Merchandise Information System
Inventory Reports
Buying Records
Vendor Analysis
Etc.

Promotion Information
Direct Mail Response
Customer surveys
Advertising Budgets
Etc.

Human Resources Information
Personnel Records
Schedules
Productivity
Compensation
Etc.

RIS

Operating Information
Receiving, Checking, and Marking
Risk Management
Warehouse
Etc.

Accounting and Financial Information
Status Reports
Budgets
Purchase, Open-to-buys
Inventory Reports
Sales, Costs
Financial
Returns

Data and Information

Retail Program Execution

Exhibit 12–2
The Retail Information System (RIS) and Merchandise Management

chandise management decisions are evaluated to determine their effectiveness and profitability, as shown in Exhibit 12–3.

Merchandising is the planning and activities involved in marketing the right merchandise and/or services at the right place at the right time in the right quantities at the right price, in order to satisfy customers and achieve company objectives. The merchandising function requires an understanding of desired store and merchandise image, its positioning relative to competition, the wants and needs of its customers, and the life cycle stages of the retail format and product lines carried.

MERCHANDISING

planning and supervising activities involved in marketing specific goods

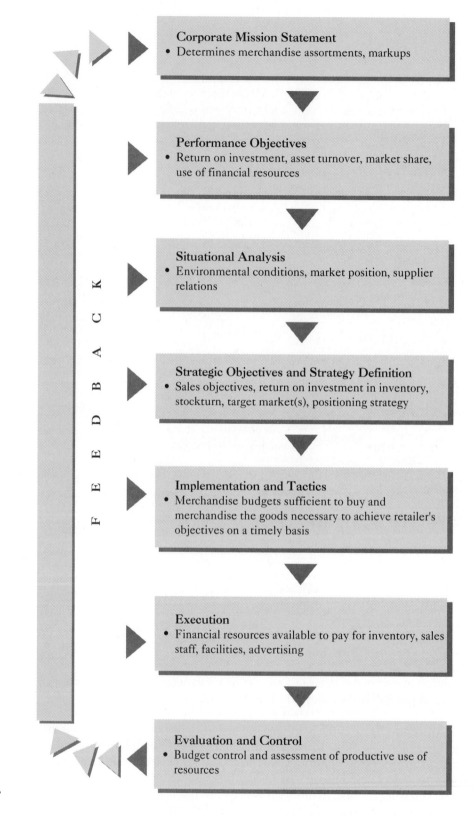

Corporate Mission Statement
- Determines merchandise assortments, markups

Performance Objectives
- Return on investment, asset turnover, market share, use of financial resources

Situational Analysis
- Environmental conditions, market position, supplier relations

Strategic Objectives and Strategy Definition
- Sales objectives, return on investment in inventory, stockturn, target market(s), positioning strategy

Implementation and Tactics
- Merchandise budgets sufficient to buy and merchandise the goods necessary to achieve retailer's objectives on a timely basis

Execution
- Financial resources available to pay for inventory, sales staff, facilities, advertising

Evaluation and Control
- Budget control and assessment of productive use of resources

FEEDBACK

Exhibit 12–3
Merchandise Management and
Strategic Planning: An
Illustration

THE MERCHANDISE BUDGET

Planning and controlling merchandise inventories to meet the retailers objectives have both financial and marketing implications. The merchandise plan is based on the use of merchandise budgets and merchandise lists. The merchandise budget is used to plan inventory levels in dollars; the merchandise lists are used to plan inventory assortments in units. The **merchandise budget** provides the retailer with a formal tool that can be used in planning, controlling, and evaluating merchandise inventories. Since inventories are a major investment—in the multimillion dollar range for many retailers—the budgeting process is critical. A successful merchandise budget requires the cooperation of many buyers and executives, both in planning and in carrying out its specifications. If budgeted inventories are forecasted too low, the retailer will suffer lost sales due to stockouts or inadequate assortment. If forecasts are too high, the retailer will have a problem with excess inventories and high markdowns. Further, the budget is a guide for buyers when they are placing orders. It tells them how much they can spend and when they can spend it. The budget also is a control mechanism to prevent overspending.

The merchandise budget is planned in advance by the buyers and other store executives for a particular selling period that can be estimated reliably. It should contain all required information, yet be simple enough for effective implementation and flexible enough to allow the retailer to make any necessary adjustments. In the following sections, the merchandise budget is discussed in terms of its financial information sources and components.

The Merchandise Budget: Financial Information Sources

Data for the merchandise budget are derived from two basic financial statements: the company's income statement and balance sheet. Before proceeding with further discussion of the merchandise budget and related calculations, the basic components of these two important sources of merchandising data are reviewed.

INCOME STATEMENT   The **income statement** (Exhibit 12–4) is a scoresheet that summarizes a firm's revenues (income) and expenses (outflows of cash) for a specified time period. Essentially, it captures a flow of performance over time, showing the effectiveness of management's decisions. The income statement begins with the total income for the firm for the time period. Total income is also referred to as gross income. This is the total dollar sales made by the retailer for the period, without subtracting customers returns or cash allowances.

This figure can be derived from many different sources. In this case it was taken from Exhibit 12–5, the firm's monthly sales totals. Monthly sales totals are calculated as (number of units sold) × (unit selling price) = (10,000 units) × ($30 per unit).

MERCHANDISE BUDGET
plan for inventory levels in dollars

INCOME STATEMENT
summary of a firm's revenue and expenses for a specified time period

INCOME STATEMENT FOR THE YEAR ENDING 12/31/19X1

Sales (1)		$300,000
Less returns and allowances		30,000
		$270,000
Net Sales		
Less cost of goods sold		
Beginning inventory (2)	$50,000	
Net purchases (3)	300,000	
Merchandise available	350,000	
Ending inventory	200,000	
Cost of goods sold		150,000
Gross profit		$120,000
Less operating expenses		
Advertising	30,000	
Rent	12,000	
Salaries	30,000	
Freight in	1,000	
Utilities	12,000	
Total operating expenses		85,000
Net Profit		$35,000

Exhibit 12–4

The **gross sales** from Exhibit 12–4 are:

Sales   *$300,000*

The next entry on the income statement is **reductions.** A reduction is any item that reduces the value of the inventory sold. Retailers record all reductions as they occur, with summaries typically available on a monthly basis. Examples include customer returns, employee discounts, and special merchandise markdowns within this context. Reductions only decrease the retail value of the inventory. Inventory value at cost is not affected.

Sales	*$300,000*
Less Reductions	**30,000**

Net sales is the next entry on the income statement. Net sales are the result of the gross sales minus the reductions.

Sales	*$300,000*
Less Reductions	*30,000*
Net Sales	*$270,000*

The preceeding entries conclude the income statement's revenue section. The next entries relate to expenses incurred to generate the sales.

Exhibit 12–5
Monthly Sales

Month	Sales
January	$40,000
February	30,000
March	30,000
April	20,000
May	17,000
June	16,000
July	12,000
August	18,000
September	22,000
October	25,000
November	30,000
December	40,000
Total	$300,000

The first entry on the cost part of the income statement is the **cost of goods sold (COGS)** section. The first part of the cost of goods sold section is the beginning inventory. This is taken from the firm's balance sheet which is displayed in Exhibit 12–6. The beginning inventory refers to the cost value of the merchandise the retailer has on hand at the start of the period for which the income statement was calculated.

The purchases refer to the total cost value of the merchandise bought for resale during the time period of the income statement. When added to the beginning inventory, this creates the total merchandise that the retailer has available for resale.

The final item in the COGS section is the ending inventory. This refers to the cost value of the merchandise which the retailer has left at the end of the time period covered by the income statement. (Note that the ending

Exhibit 12–6

BALANCE SHEET
1/1/19X1

Assets		
Current Assets		
Cash	$ 10,000	
Accounts receivable	15,000	
Inventory	50,000	
Marketable securities	5,000	
Total Current Assets		$ 80,000
Long-term Assets		
Property	$400,000	
Fixtures	150,000	
Total Long-term Assets		$550,000
Total Assets		$630,000
Liabilities and Owners Equity		
Current Liabilities		
Notes payable	$ 50,000	
Accounts payable	65,000	
Salaries payable	5,000	
Taxes payable	4,500	
Total Current Liabilities		$124,500
Longterm Liabilities		
Longterm debt	$300,000	
Total Liabilities		$424,500
Owner's Equity 12/31/19XO		$205,000
Net income for the year	$ 30,000	
Owner withdrawals	29,500	
Increases in Owner's Equity		500
Owners Equity		$205,500
Total Liabilities and Owner's Equity		$630,000

GROSS SALES

total dollar value of inventory sold

REDUCTION

item reducing the value of the inventory sold

NET SALES

gross sales minus reductions

COST OF GOODS SOLD (COGS)

cost of beginning inventory plus purchases, minus ending inventory

BALANCE SHEET
12/31/19X1

Assets

Current Assets
Cash	$ 6,000	
Accounts receivable	18,000	
Inventory	200,000	
Marketable securities	4,000	
Total Current Assets		$228,000

Long-term Assets
Property	$350,000	
Fixtures	135,000	
Total Long-term Assets		$485,000

Total Assets		$713,000

Liabilities and Owner's Equity

Current Liabilities
Notes payable	$ 60,000	
Accounts payable	70,000	
Salaries payable	5,500	
Taxes payable	5.000	
Total Current Liabilities		$140,500

Long-term Liabilities
Long-term Debt	$332,000	

Total Liabilities		$472,500

Owners Equity 12/31/19XX	205,000	
Net income for the year	35,000	
Owner withdrawals	0	
Increases in Owner's Equity		35,000
Owner's Equity		$240,500

Total Liabilities and Owner's Equity		$713,000

Exhibit 12–7

inventory for one period is the same as the beginning inventory for the following period). *The cost of goods sold is beginning inventory plus purchases minus ending inventory,* as shown in the following example:

Sales		*$300,000*
Less Reductions		*30,000*
Net Sales		*270,000*
*Less **Cost of Goods Sold***		
Beginning Inventory	*$ 50,000*	
Purchases	*300,000*	
Merchandise Available	*350,000*	
Ending Inventory	*200,000*	
Cost of Goods Sold	***150,000***	

To determine the gross profit for a selling period, cost of goods sold is subtracted from net sales. **Gross profit** is revenue in excess of variable and direct costs—revenue left to cover operating expenses and provide a profit.

Sales	*$300,000*
Less Reductions	*30,000*
Net Sales	*270,000*
Less Cost of Goods Sold	
Beginning Inventory	*$ 50,000*
Purchases	*300,000*
Merchandise Available	*350,000*
Ending Inventory	*200,000*
Cost of Goods Sold	*150,000*
Gross Profit	**$120,000**

Net profit is equal to gross margin (gross profit) minus total operating expenses. **Net profit** is the amount left for the retailer after all merchandise and expenses have been paid. **Operating expenses** are indirect expenses not attributable to any particular product or product grouping. From Exhibit 12–4, the operating expenses are advertising, rent, salaries, freight in and utilities. The following example represents a net profit. However, if the retailer's sales are not sufficient to cover cost of goods sold and operating expenses, the resulting figure will be a net loss.

Sales	*$300,000*
Less Reductions	*30,000*
Net Sales	*270,000*
Less Cost of Goods Sold	
Beginning Inventory	*$ 50,000*
Purchases	*300,000*
Merchandise Available	*350,000*
Ending Inventory	*200,000*
Cost of Goods Sold	*150,000*
Gross Profit	**$120,000**
Less Operating Expenses	
Advertising	*30,000*
Rent	*12,000*
Salaries	*30,000*
Freight In	*1,000*
Utilities	*12,000*
Total Operating Expenses	**85,000**
Net Profit (before taxes)	**$ 35,000**

BALANCE SHEET   Exhibits 12–6 and 12–7 represent the firm's balance sheet at the beginning and end of a calendar year. A **balance sheet** is a sum-

GROSS PROFIT

revenue less variable and direct costs

NET PROFIT

gross profit minus operating expenses

OPERATING EXPENSES

general expenses not associated with any particular product or group

BALANCE SHEET

summary of a firm's assets and liabilities at a given point in time

mary of a company's assets and liabilities at a given point in time. An **asset** is any item that increases the value of the firm. Assets can be divided into two categories, current and long-term. Current assets are items that can be quickly converted to cash and are said to be liquid. Current assets include inventory, cash, accounts receivable, and marketable securities. Merchandise inventory represents the primary asset for most retailers and the least liquid of all current assets. Thus, merchandise planning activities have a major impact on the results reported in financial statements. In fact, managing inventories and cost of goods sold is the primary mechanism a retailer can use to exert control over profitability, once the location and store design decisions have been implemented. Long-term assets are assets that cannot be quickly converted to cash.

A **liability** is any item that tends to reduce the value of the firm. Liabilities can also be subdivided into current and long-term. Current liabilities are debts that must be paid within one year's time, such as accounts payable, notes payable, salaries, and taxes. Long-term liabilities are debts for which payment extends beyond one year's time. Typically, capital expenditures for real estate, new store construction, information systems, and other major purchases are paid for over a number of years.

The final selection of the balance sheet is the **owner's equity** accounts. This section details how much money the storeowner, or the stockholders, have in the business. It represents the difference between all of the assets held by the retailer and those that the firm actually owns outright. Therefore, owner's equity plus total liabilities are equivalent to total assets.

The Merchandise Budget: Components

The merchandise budget is a summary of the dollar investment in inventory required to support a planned sales level at a required level of profitability for a specific time period (Exhibit 12–8). The total company merchandise budget represents the aggregate figures for each department or unit, consisting of planned sales, planned stock levels, planned reductions, planned purchases, and planned profit margins by season and by month.

Merchandise Budget: Planned Sales

The first step in planning inventory levels is to estimate sales for a future time period, usually for a year or a six-month selling season. An accurate sales forecast is the most critical component of the merchandise budget. Errors in the sales forecast will affect calculations for planned inventory levels, reductions, purchases, and profit margins.

FORECASTING SALES   Past sales provide a starting point for preparing sales estimates. For the existing stores, information can be obtained from internal accounting and financial records. For new stores, industry data and the results of similar operations can provide guidelines for a sales estimate. Some forecasting methods are based on sales trends over several years, rather than just the previous year's sales. For example, if annual sales had increased an average 6 percent over the past four years, the retailer might forecast sales for the coming year at 6 percent more than the previous year.

ASSET
item that increases the value of the firm

LIABILITY
item that reduces the value of the firm

OWNER'S EQUITY
value the owner or stockholders have in the firm

Forecasts based on past sales data must also take into account economic trends (e.g., unemployment rate, inflation, recession, new industry in area), competitive activities (direct and indirect competition in specific lines, opening new stores, closing stores), and estimated consumer demand. Anticipated changes that can cause adjustments in forecasts include planned store expansions or downsizing, and shifts in merchandise emphasis or customer charac-

Exhibit 12–8
Sample Merchandise Budget Form

Dept. # _____   Dept. Name_____   Seasonal (6-month) plan

Profit: Goal _____   Operating Expenses: Goal _____
         Actual _____   Actual _____

Spring 19X1	Season Total	Months					
		Jan	Feb	Mar	Apr	May	June
Sales							
Last Year							
Planned							
Actual							
Stock							
Last Year							
Planned							
Actual							
Reductions							
Last Year							
Planned							
Actual							
Markups							
Last Year							
Planned							
Actual							
Profit							
Last Year							
Planned							
Actual							
Expenses							
Last Year							
Planned							
Actual							
Purchases							
Last Year							
Planned							
Actual							
Comments:							

Merchandise Manager_____   Buyer _____   Controller _____

teristics. Both quantitative and qualitative information from internal and external sources may be used to adjust estimates. For example, the 1990s are referred to as the "Earth Decade." Increased attention to environmental problems have caused many consumers to change their consumption habits, which affects retail purchases. Once all of these factors have been analyzed, planned sales can be calculated on an annual, monthly, and seasonal basis.

PLANNED MONTHLY SALES   The **sales indexing** technique can be used to calculate planned sales on a monthly basis. Individual monthly forecasts can be combined into seasonal forecasts. Data from Exhibit 12–5 are used to illustrate the sales index method, following these steps. (See Exhibit 12–9.)

1. *Calculate monthly sales for a past time period.*
   January = $40,000; February = $30,000; March = $30,000; etc.
2. *Determine the average monthly sales, by dividing total sales for the period by the number of months included.*
   ($40,000 + $30,000 + $30,000 + $20,000, etc.)/12 months
3. *Divide actual sales for each month by the average monthly sales.*
   For June: $16,000/$25,000 = .64
   .64 × 100 = an index of 64 or 64% of the average monthly sales

This will produce a relationship between each month's sales and the average. A number equal to 100 indicates that the month is an average month. A number greater than 100 indicates that the month is above average, while a number less than 100 indicates a below average month. From Exhibit 12–9, October is an average month; January, February, March, November and December are above average months. The remaining months are below average. The general rule of thumb is, the larger the sales index, the higher the sales the retailer expects for that month.

Exhibit 12–9
Monthly Sales

Month	Sales	Sales Index*
January	$ 40,000	160.00%
February	30,000	120.00
March	30,000	120.00
April	20,000	80.00
May	17,000	68.00
June	16,000	64.00
July	12,000	48.00
August	18,000	72.00
September	22,000	88.00
October	25,000	100.00
November	30,000	120.00
December	40,000	160.00
Total	$300,000	
Average monthly sales	$ 25,000	
Average monthly stock	$ 29,167	

*Monthly Sales Index = $\left(\dfrac{\text{Planned monthly sales}}{\text{Average monthly sales}}\right) \times 100$

SALES INDEXING
method of calculating monthly sales

Merchandise Budget: Planned Stock

The second step in planning inventory levels is to determine the amount of inventory that should be on hand at the beginning of each month to meet monthly sales projections. Based on past inventory records, sales forecasts, market trends and the retailer's policy toward acceptable inventory levels, the amount of stock needed to achieve planned sales levels is calculated for each month and for the total planning period.

Retailers sometimes find it necessary to change forecasts used in their initial planning. For example, if a merchandise item or classification becomes a "hot seller," retailers can adjust the forecast upward to allow additional purchases to take advantage of increased sales. If a high-fashion look does not do as well as expected, maintaining previously planned high inventory levels would be foolish; or if a major employer in the community lays off thousands of workers, adjusting sales forecasts downward may be needed to avoid markdowns from holding too much inventory for out-of-work customers.

Although retailers need to calculate annual and seasonal inventory requirements as part of their merchandise plan, calculating specific inventory needs is most commonly done on a monthly basis. Although determined months in advance, purchase requirements and open-to-buy figures can be calculated with some degree of certainty for one month at a time and serve as an important guideline for buyers and merchandise managers.

BJ's Wholesale Club, and other volume retailers, carefully track inventory levels.

There are four basic techniques for developing the monthly inventory stock levels: basic stock method, percentage variation method, weeks supply method, and stock to sales ratio. An explanation of each method follows.

BASIC STOCK METHOD   The basic stock approach is preferred when the retailer has a stockturn of six or less, i.e., a fairly staple, basic stock with little fluctuation in sales. Stockturn, which is discussed further in Chapter 13, is calculated as (Net Sales/Average Inventory). A stockturn of six means that the retailer is replacing his average inventory six times a year—or every two months. In order to calculate the basic stock model, these steps are followed:

1. Calculate average monthly sales *(from Exhibit 12–5: $25,000)*.
2. Calculate average monthly stock by dividing merchandise available on the income statement by the number of months which the income statement covers *(Exhibit 12–4: $350,000/12 = 29,167)*.
3. Subtract average monthly stock from average monthly sales to determine the basic stock level *($29,167 - $25,000 = $4,167)*.
4. Add this figure to the forecasted planned monthly sales to determine the required inventory for each month *(Example for January: $40,000 + $4,167 = $44,167)*.

The basic stock level is actually a safety stock to be held by the retailer as a buffer against possible stockout conditions.

PERCENTAGE VARIATION METHOD   The percentage variation method is preferred when the stock turnover level is greater than six, which is characteristic of high turnover merchandise like fashion goods and perishables. For example, a stockturn of 12 would mean the retailer replenishes the

COURTESY OF BJ'S WHOLESALE CLUB

store's inventory an average of once a month. This method requires the following calculations:

1. Forecast a new average monthly sales figure *(Example for January: $25,000)*.
2. Apply the sales index to determine forecasted monthly sales *($25,000 × 1.6 = $40,000)*.
3. Determine planned average monthly stock *(Exhibit 12–9: $29,167)*.
4. "Plug" all figures from the first three steps into this formula:

> *(Planned average monthly stock)*
> *× {.5 × [1 + (forecasted monthly sales/forecasted average monthly sales)]}*
> *= ($29,167 × {.5 × [1 + ($40,000/$25,000)]}*
> *= $37,917.*

Inventory level calculations based on the basic stock method and percentage variation method are compared in Exhibit 12–10.

WEEKS SUPPLY METHOD The weeks supply method assumes that the inventory should be planned on a weekly basis. It is directly related to the retailer's desired turnover rate. The lower the turnover rate, the higher the amount of inventory that will need to be on hand for a given number of weeks. In order to use the weeks supply method, these steps are followed:

1. Determine average weekly sales *(average monthly sales/4 = $25,000/4 = $6,250)*.
2. Multiply average weekly sales by the number of weeks for which stock is needed *(Example for 8 weeks: 8 × $6,250 = $50,000)*.

STOCK-TO-SALES RATIO Of the four methods used to calculate monthly inventory requirements, the stock-to-sales ratio is the simplest. This method is based on the assumption that planned inventory levels should be based on some multiple of planned sales. This approach requires two steps:

1. Determine forecasted monthly sales. *(Exhibit 12–5: $25,000)*.
2. Multiply the forecasted monthly sales by the stock ratio *(Example 2:1 ratio = $25,000 × 2 = $50,000)*.

E x h i b i t   1 2 – 1 0
Planned Inventory Levels

	Basic Stock Method	Percentage Variation Method
January	$ 44,167	$ 37,917
February	34,167	32,083
March	34,167	32,083
April	24,167	26,250
May	21,167	24,500
June	20,167	23,917
July	16,167	21,583
August	22,167	25,083
September	26.167	27,417
October	29,167	29,167
November	34,167	32,083
December	44,167	37,917
Merchandise Available	$350,000	$350,000

In this example, the retailer requires twice as much inventory in retail dollars to provide customers an assortment of merchandise that will achieve planned sales levels. The stock ratio is a multiplier that also provides for safety stock. Stock-to-sales ratios, based on industry averages, are available from a variety of sources such as Dun and Bradstreet or National Retail Merchants Association publications.

COMPARING THE APPROACHES TO CALCULATING MONTHLY INVENTORY   The last two methods described, the weeks supply method and the stock-to-sales ratio are simple multipliers of an anticipated sales level. However, the other two methods can produce very different levels of planned inventory. Graphs in Exhibits 12–11 and 12–12 provide a comparison of inventory levels calculated according to the basic stock method (BSM) and the percentage variation method (PVM) relative to actual sales. As Exhibit 12–11 indicates, the BSM provides a consistent buffer against sales, while the PVM (Exhibit 12–12) maintains an above average inventory during slow periods, and a below average inventory during peak periods.

Merchandise Budget: Planned Reductions

The value of a store's inventory may be reduced by several factors other than sales. These include markdowns from the original retail selling price, employee discounts, and other shortages from shoplifting or internal theft. Planned reductions include any dollar amount that is subtracted from the original retail value and the actual final sales value of the merchandise.

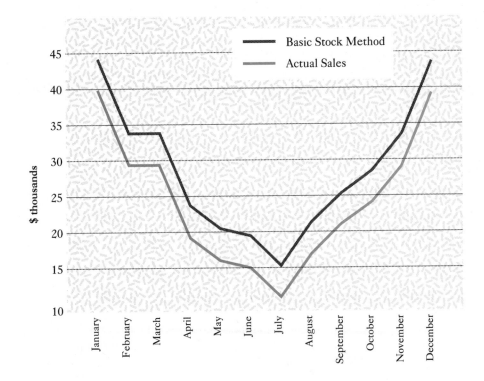

Exhibit 12–11
Basic Stock Method versus
Actual Sales

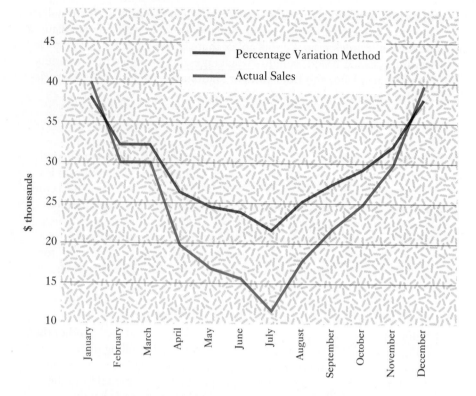

Exhibit 12–12
Percentage Variation Method
● ●

Reductions must be planned, since they decrease the total retail dollar value of the inventory available for sale to customers. In other words, the retailer has to take a higher markup in the beginning and/or sell more goods to make up for expected reductions. The amount of planned reductions can be estimated based on published industry averages or on a company's past experience. For example, Exhibit 12–4 itemizes reductions of $30,000 with gross sales of $300,000. This suggests that the retailer might expect to have reductions equal to 10 percent of the original retail value represented as gross sales ($300,000/$30,000).

Merchandise Budget: Planned Purchases

PLANNED PURCHASES   Once figures have been estimated for sales, required inventory levels, and anticipated reductions from dollar inventory, the amount of planned purchases can be calculated for each month. This figure is adjusted by subtracting the amount of inventory scheduled to be on hand at the beginning of a certain month, and by adding the amount of inventory scheduled to be on hand at the end of that month. In addition to calculating a planned amount for making inventory purchases, an amount is calculated for the amount of that purchase that remains "open-to-buy" after other orders have been placed, the amount that the buyer actually has to spend.

The formula used to calculate planned purchases calculates total inventory needs for a specified time period and subtracts the level of inventory on hand. The steps in applying the formula are as follows:

1. Determine planned sales using one of the previously described methods for calculating monthly inventory (basic stock method, percentage variation method, weeks supply, or stock-to-sales ratio).
2. Determine planned reductions.
3. Determine planned ending inventory.
4. Calculate current beginning inventory.

Using calculations 1 through 4 above, the formula for computing planned purchases is:

Planned purchases = Planned sales + Planned reductions
+ Planned ending inventory – Beginning inventory

Let's say a retailer has $20,000 worth of merchandise on hand, and plans to sell $50,000. In addition, the retailer plans reductions of 10 percent of sales and desires an ending inventory of $30,000. Then the planned purchases are:

Planned sales (what the retailer will use)	$50,000
+ *Planned reduction (what the retailer will lose)*	5,000
+ *Planned ending inventory (what the retailer has left)*	30,000
	85,000
– *Beginning inventory (what the retailer already has)*	20,000
= *Planned purchases*	65,000

The above model can be summarized as: A retailer begins by deciding what he plans to use, plus what he plans to lose, plus what he wants to have left, minus what he already has.

OPEN-TO-BUY   The **open-to-buy (OTB)** concept is an extension of planned purchases. It is simply planned purchases minus purchase commitments. A purchase commitment refers to any merchandise the retailer has agreed to purchase. For example, let us assume that you have planned purchases of $15,000, and you have already placed an order for $5,000 worth of merchandise during this period. The remaining amount budgeted for you to purchase is $10,000.

The open-to-buy calculation is important because it can keep purchases within budgeted levels for a specified period. It is most useful, particularly for a large store, when broken down by departments and by merchandise lines. The buyer considers planned purchases and open-to-buy in both dollars and units.

Merchandise Budget: Planned Profit Margin

Planned profit margin is probably the most important aspect of the merchandise budget to the retailer. Profit levels are planned to meet preestablished company financial criteria. There are a number of different ways of viewing profitability in relationship to the merchandise budget. One of these is in terms of gross margin, i.e., the difference between the selling price and cost of goods sold that is left to cover operating expenses and profit. Another is in terms of gross margin return-on-investment, which relates profitability directly to company assets that exist in the form of inventory.

OPEN-TO-BUY (OTB)
planned purchases minus purchase commitments

As shown in the six-month merchandise budget summary for the merchandise classification illustrated in Exhibit 12–8, dollar estimates are made for planned sales, beginning of the month stock levels, reductions from inventory purchases, and profit margin. In addition to estimated figures for these variables, the budget includes figures for the previous year as a benchmark and allows for any necessary adjustments should conditions change from the original assumptions. Finally, actual results are recorded at the end of each month and for the season. Thus, the merchandise budget provides buyers and managers a summary report of dollar results for the budgeted period. Results can be compared to last year's figures and this year's plan to assist in continued planning and evaluation.

Merchandise Budget: Dollar and Unit Control

Dollar and unit control methods provide a basis for maintaining a balanced stock to sales relationship. This results in higher sales and fewer markdowns or stockouts. Information is made available regarding what to buy, how much to buy, and when to buy it. The retailer's return on inventory investment is optimized, and merchandise assortments are consistent with customer wants.

DOLLAR CONTROL   **Dollar control** inventory systems focus on dollar investment in inventory at either retail or cost values. Dollar control may be applied to one or more departments, classifications, or price lines. The data obtained become an integral part of the retailer's merchandise information system. There are two types of dollar control systems: perpetual book inventory system and periodic physical inventory system.

The retailer using a perpetual book inventory system will have a continuous count of the amount of merchandise that should be on hand at any given time. The count of ending stock on hand is obtained from written or computerized accounting record entries, which include the dollar value of merchandise at the beginning of the selling period, plus merchandise received from vendors during the period (less vendor returns, interstore transfers, markdowns, and goods marked out of stock), less net sales (sales minus returns) to customers, as follows:

$$
\begin{aligned}
& \textit{Beginning inventory} \\
+\ & \underline{\textit{Merchandise received}} \\
=\ & \textit{Total inventory handled} \\
-\ & \textit{Sales} \\
+\ & \underline{\textit{Markdowns}} \\
=\ & \textit{Ending inventory}
\end{aligned}
$$

A dollar control perpetual book inventory system can give the retailer a "reading" at any time as to the value of inventory on hand, but the figures will only be reliable if entries are current and accurate and shortages from shoplifting or internal theft have been determined. In addition, considerable expense is involved in setting up such a system due to the need for continuous data inputs. The added cost may be a problem for small retailers. Most retailers verify the perpetual book inventory figures with a physical count at least once or twice a year and adjust their records accordingly.

DOLLAR CONTROL

system for measuring dollar
investment in inventory

Stanley Marcus: Retail Merchandising Starts with the Customers

The Neiman Marcus store in Dallas, Texas, at the turn of the century.

"Whenever, I hear involved explanations of the retail business and of merchandising, I throw my gears into reverse and think back on the principles of the store business that I learned from my father at the tender age of nine.

"Our family dinner table conversation was invariably devoted to a discussion of the day's events—what happened to my brothers and me at school, followed by a blow-by-blow description of the occurrences at Neiman Marcus, or the 'store,' as it was commonly referred to by family members. Frequently, Aunt Carrie Neiman, my father's sister and business partner, was a dinner guest, so the conversation gravitated to the triumphs and failures on the selling floor and the daily news from lower Madison Avenue, then the center of New York's garment industry.

"Mrs. Neiman's domain was the better-apparel selling floor, so she reported on what customers had come to buy that day and what she and her sales staff had sold them. 'Mrs. Waggoner came in around noon. We ordered sandwiches up for lunch in her fitting room, but my stock was so poor in size 18's that I was able to sell her only about 10 pieces. She's always good for at least 20, but order deliveries on 18's have been terribly slow.'

"That's great, my father replied admiringly, chiding her at the same time. 'It's your own fault. You buy everything in 12's and 14's and think of the 18's at the last minute. You should increase the number of 18's you order and then pressure the manufacturers to deliver them on time." Unabashed, my aunt continued her tale, with excitement: "But wait—

you've got to hear what we did with Mrs. Easterwood of San Angelo, who brought her youngest daughter who's going to make her debut in San Antonio this fall. She was so pleased with the way the Hattie Carnegie suit was made, which I insisted she buy last spring, that she bought four more Carnegies for herself and two for her daughter. We rang up a $12,000 sale. Remember how unhappy she was with the Mano Sano suit because of the fit? I took it back even though she had worn it. I wouldn't sell her the Bellar coat, for I thought it made her look too large, but I'll find one for her when she comes back next month to see our debutante gowns."

"My father complimented her on the size of the sale and also on her refusal to sell something that she believed to be unbecoming to the customer. And, the discussion would go on endlessly into the night, much to

the discomfiture of the young adolescents at the dining table, who failed to understand the high drama that was enacting itself.

"That's where I learned the fundamentals of retail merchandising, which served me in good stead for my subsequent career as a merchant.

"Two basic principles are illustrated in this dialogue: (1) The customer came back because of the satisfactory quality experience she had with the Carnegie suit. (2) It's good business to take something back that hasn't given the customer satisfaction—even after it has been worn. Those tenets became the basis of my own retail philosophy.

"I believe that retail merchandising is actually very simple: it consists of two factors, customers and goods. If you take good care in the buying of

continued

the product, it doesn't come back. If you take good care of your customers, they do come back. It's just that simple, and just that difficult. This is obviously an oversimplification of the problems of retailing. It's not quite that easy, but almost."

Where Modern Merchandising Fails
Mr. Marcus goes on to express concern that while customers want attractive stores, polite and knowledgeable service, and satisfaction from the merchandise they purchase, they are constantly confronted with a boring sameness from one store to another. Today many customers are buying for wants and not needs. They want excitement and merchandise that is unusual and different. Many retailers make bottom-line profit their chief objective, failing to realize that profits are the result of having produced goods or services that are so satisfactory that customers are willing to pay the retailer a bonus (i.e., profit) over and above the distributor's cost. 'The retail business is about serving customers and serving them well. That's where modern merchandising fails.'

"Before we can improve merchandising in America's stores, we have to improve the merchants and the merchandise. We have to establish a premium on individuality; we have to provide an accolade for creativity and ingenuity. There's no award given to those characteristics other than the

most important one—and that, of course, is the cash-register recognition. The customers eventually reward the store that gives satisfaction, that is more fun to shop in, that doesn't play it safe all the time, that makes it possible for you to find an out-of-the-ordinary dress or tie that your friends will notice and ask where you bought it. Better merchandising must begin with better goods—products with the integrity that has been eyeballed by the merchant, not second-quality products that get showcase preference because of vendor money.

"Better merchandising must begin with merchants who have been educated to have an understanding of the goods they stock and the customers to whom they are sold. It will require

merchants who understand the value of computers, but who recognize them as tools to facilitate customer satisfaction; merchants who will encourage buyers to lend support to smaller suppliers with the willingness to provide goods that fulfill localized demand; merchants who understand that risk-taking is part of successful retailing, and that stores need to be attractive, exciting and fun."

Professor Leonard Berry has summarized some of the retailing lessons that can be learned from Stanley Marcus' retailing philosophy:

1. "You build a great company on value, not price."
2. "The best specialty retailers specialize in customers, not just merchandise."
3. "Stores need sellers, not just merchants."
4. "The excellent retailers lead rather than follow."
5. "Retailing will always be a 'people' business."

Stanley Marcus' devotion to value and providing customers satisfaction has given him a well-deserved reputation as one of the most responsible retailers of this century.

SOURCE: Adapted from Marcus, Stanley (1990), "Merchandising for the 1990's," and Berry, Leonard (1990), "Editor's Corner," *Arthur Andersen Retailing Issues Letter*, Vol. 2, No. 7 (Center for Retailing Studies, Texas A&M University, July 1990).

The retailer using this system will have a periodic physical count of merchandise, usually on a monthly, quarterly or semiannual basis. Calculations start with the dollar amount of inventory on hand at the beginning of the period (equal to the amount on hand at the end of the preceding period), plus merchandise received from vendors during the period. At the end of the selling period, a physical count is taken of the inventory on hand to determine its dollar value, then (along with markdowns) is subtracted from the total value of goods available during the period to determine a sales figure:

$$
\begin{array}{rl}
 & \textit{Beginning inventory} \\
+ & \textit{Merchandise received} \\
\hline
= & \textit{Total inventory handled} \\
- & \textit{Ending inventory} \\
- & \textit{Markdowns} \\
\hline
= & \textit{Sales}
\end{array}
$$

A periodic system is simpler to maintain than a perpetual system, but the information is less timely. However, it is useful for certain merchandise categories and subcategories, such as basic items or goods in high theft areas.

UNIT CONTROL   **Unit control** inventory systems (keeping track of stock item by item) provide more detailed guidelines for inventory assortments. Unit control is a valuable buying and selling tool. It gives buyers information about individual merchandise items that are needed—styles, sizes, prices, colors, and so forth—it can help salespeople increase sales by having current information about product availability. Like dollar control, unit control may be kept on a perpetual book or periodic physical basis.

A perpetual book unit control system provides a continuous total count of the number of units of a specific stock item on hand. Sales and other reductions, such as damaged items or returns to vendor, are subtracted. New shipments and other inventory additions and customer returns are added to the total. A continuous inventory count is maintained manually, or with a computerized system. In a manual system, data from invoices, register receipts and other sources are recorded "by hand" to reflect the amount of inventory on hand after accounting for all incoming and outgoing merchandise. Computerized systems may involve manual input, but are more likely today to use scanner data. A physical inventory is taken at least once a year to determine if any corrections must be made to the book figures.

The amount of merchandise on hand for a particular classification or for any given stock number can be determined periodically by taking a physical count of inventory. It is also possible to visually scan shelves and stockrooms to determine when it is necessary to place orders to avoid stockouts or where measures should be taken to move slow sellers. This inventory control system is easy to apply for low cost staple items. For both types of unit control systems, inventory figures can be compared to sales figures to determine stock needs.

Regardless of the type of inventory control method used, both dollar and unit control, either perpetual or periodic, are management tools—not substitutes for judgment. This is true whether the retailer is dealing with fashion or staple merchandise. As with any aspect of the retailer's information system, the types of inputs and procedures should be reassessed periodically.

Overview of Retail Budgets

While buyers and merchandise managers are most concerned with the merchandise budget, it is but one of four types of budgets used by retailers. The

UNIT CONTROL

system for measuring inventory by number of items

other three are the operations budget, cash budget and capital budget. The **operations budget** is the "revenues and expenses" budget, which helps answer the question, "Are sales meeting projected goals?" It includes forecasts of expected sales and costs for a specified time period. Merchants must study daily flash reports, sales analysis, inventory turnover, exception reports, etc.

The **cash budget** is an estimate of cash receipts and cash disbursements for a specified time period. It defines cash requirements for future periods, and helps answer the question, "Do we need a short-term loan for the forthcoming selling period?" Length of time may depend on size of store.

The **capital budget** represents investment plans for assets of more than one year's duration, including future investment projects (such as adding new stores, remodeling existing stores, etc.) and justification for them. The capital budget answers questions about resources available for growth and provides a basis for calculating expected return on assets for each project.

SUMMARY

Merchandise assortment and inventory management decisions are influenced by many aspects of the internal and external environments. This chapter has focused on the merchandise budgeting and planning process.

The merchandising function must be coordinated with the other functional areas of the store (human resources, promotion and communication, store operations, and control and accounting) and be made operational to achieve the company's internal goals. Data for the merchandise budget are derived from two basic financial statements: the retailer's income statement and balance sheet.

The merchandise budget, a basis for planning and controlling merchandise inventories, consists of planned levels of sales, stock, reductions, purchases, and profits for a given period of time. Inventory and purchase planning involve forecasting sales, using techniques such as sales indexing; determining monthly inventory stock levels, using methods such as basic stock, percentage variation, weeks supply, or stock-to-sales; planning reductions from the original retail value; planning purchases and open-to-buy figures; and determining target profit levels. The merchandise budget provides both dollar control (total dollar inventory investment) and unit control (individual stock item) information. Unit control of stock on hand may be kept on a perpetual (continuous total) or periodic (physical count) basis.

Questions for Review and Comprehension

1. Describe the relationship between the definition of merchandising and the merchandise budgeting process.
2. Provide an outline of a merchandise budget for a sporting goods store. For *each* budget component, state the specific source(s) of financial information that can be obtained from the income statement and/or balance sheet.
3. Given the following planned monthly sales figures, calculate average monthly sales and the monthly sales index for each month.

OPERATIONS BUDGET

forecast of expected sales and costs for a specified time period

CASH BUDGET

estimate of cash disbursements and cash receipts for a specified time period

CAPITAL BUDGET

long-term investment plans for assets

January	$60,000	May	$25,000	September	$30,000
February	46,000	June	19,000	October	37,000
March	47,000	July	23,000	November	48,000
April	30,000	August	33,000	December	62,000

4. Using the basic stock method for planning inventory levels, calculate the dollar amount of inventory that should be on hand each month based on planned monthly sales in Question 3. Assume that the average amount of inventory on hand each month is $55,000.

5. Now use the percentage variation method to calculate planned inventory levels, given the planned monthly sales figures given in Question #3 and continuing with average inventory on hand in the amount of $55,000.

6. Explain when it is appropriate to use the basic stock method and the percentage variation method to plan inventory levels. Provide a rationale for the tendency of these two methods to produce different results.

7. A small hardware retailer wants to know how much inventory he should have on hand (in dollars) if he has average monthly sales of $3,000 and forecasts sales for 8 weeks. Use the weeks supply method to calculate the amount of inventory that he will need to have on hand for this period.

8. The same retailer is considering alternative approaches to planning his inventory levels. If he plans to sell $1,200 in light bulbs during March, and desires a 3:1 ratio of inventory to sales, use the stock-to-sales method to calculate the amount of inventory he should plan to have on hand in March.

9. Provide a rationale for the statement: "Reductions from the retail value of an inventory must be planned." Would your answer be any different for an apparel retailer than it would be for a grocery retailer? Why or why not? How does a retailer estimate reductions in advance of a selling period?

10. For the month of June, the Bermuda Shorts and Tops Shop plans retail sales of $70,000. The manager plans reductions in the amount of $5,000 and ending inventory of $40,000. His beginning retail inventory is valued at $22,000. Calculate the retailer's planned purchases for June.

11. Given the amount of planned purchases determined in Question#10, determine the Bermuda Shorts and Tops Shop's open-to-buy for June if the store's buyer has already placed $8,000 in orders for that month.

12. Define and describe the following: dollar control, unit control, perpetual book inventory system, and periodic physical inventory system. How and when is each inventory system used?

References

"Gap's New Line Of Clothing For Infants Is Growing Up Fast" (1990), *Orlando Sentinel* (November 19), D1, D2.

Marcus, Stanley and Berry Leonard, (1990), "Merchandising For The 1990's, "Editor's Corner", *Retailing Issues Letter*, publishing by Arthur Andersen & Co. and The Center for Retailing Studies, Texas A&M University, 2, no. 7 (July), 1–4.

Schwadel, Francine (1990a), "Gap Inc. Is Prospering Even as It Disdains Usual Holiday Hype," *The Wall Street Journal* (December 19), A1, A6.

Schwadel, Francine (1990b), "Spiegel Crayola Plan Kids' Clothes Line," *The Wall Street Journal* (October 3), B1.

Inventory Management and Buying

Learning Objectives

After studying this chapter, the student will be able to:

1. Recognize the impact of external environmental influences on the merchandise management process.
2. Discuss the relationship between corporate and merchandising philosophies.
3. Define and describe merchandise mix and assortment concepts and strategies.
4. Discuss distribution strategy decisions on how and what to buy.
5. Discuss the relationships between vendors and buyers in successful merchandising.
6. Calculate the value of merchandise inventories using the cost and the retail methods.
7. Describe the use of breakeven analysis, inventory turnover, and gross margin return on investment as control tools in evaluating results of merchandising decisions.

Chapter Thirteen

OVER 500 MILLION BARBIES — BUT NO IDENTITY CRISIS!

A very fashionable foot-tall platinum blonde revolutionized toy retailing when she first met the public in 1959. In 30 years, children have bought and dressed over 500 million Barbie dolls from Mattel. The company estimates that 90 percent of girls between the ages of 3 and 11 own at least one Barbie.

Barbie was later joined by her friend Ken and other companions, pets, and cars. She has had a number of career changes, including a teen-age fashion model, ballerina, nurse, flight attendant, astronaut, doctor, TV newscaster, and rock star—each requiring a new wardrobe. Mattel sells 20 million new outfits each year at prices ranging from $1 to $8. In spite of children's ability to change Barbie's look, this product has never suffered an identity crisis. It continues to be a bestseller among the proliferation of competing toys each year.

In 1990, Mattel decided that Barbie is not just a doll anymore, but Barbie, the "lifestyle." At the American International Toy Fair in New York early in 1990, Mattel unveiled new products designed for Barbie's target audience of 3 to 11 year old girls. Barbie "lifestyle" products include girl-sized costumes, real-life bedsheets, accessories, and other items with the Barbie theme. Thus, a single product has evolved into an expanded product line by a company that believes

COURTESY OF TOYS "R" US

the Barbie franchise has been under-marketed. Focus groups provided the inspiration for the Barbie Style product line, because Mattel found that older girls still liked the doll, but were sensitive to playing dress-up or admitting they still play with Barbies. Mattel also researched hot trends to determine that products such as trading cards could be tied to Barbie, with some to be produced under strict licensing agreements.

Toy retailers depend on the Christmas holiday season to meet annual sales figures, but they have to take a chance early in the year that they have identified and bought enough of the hottest toys. Some toys, like Barbie, have endured season after season. Others are blockbusters one year but fizzle the next. Others (like Trump the Game) are disappointing from the start.

The top three sellers in 1986 were Pound Puppies, G.I. Joe, and Barbie. Other long time favorites in the top ten were Transformers (5) and Cabbage Patch Kids (8). Top sellers in 1987

included Cabbage Patch Kids, Transformers, Masters of the Universe, Trivial Pursuit, and Pound Puppies (8).

In 1989 retailers placed their bets on Nintendo's high-tech Game Boy and Tyco's low-tech plain-Jane baby doll, Oopsie Daisy. Toys "R" Us, which has nearly 25 percent of the U.S. $13 billion toy market, stocked these toys among 18,000 items in its warehouse stores. Among the other top sellers in 1989 were Teen-Age Mutant Ninja Turtles, G.I. Joe, Batman, Barbie, Ghostbusters, and Cabbage Patch dolls. What should toy buyers buy for next Christmas?

SOURCE: "A New Babe Arrives In Toyland" (1989), *The Wall Street Journal* (August 12), B1; Hagedorn, Ann (1986), "Toy Firms Search for Next Blockbuster," *The Wall Street Journal* (September 12), B1; Hammonds, Keith (1987), "Toymakers Could Wake Up to Coal-filled Stockings," *Business Week* (October 12), 131; Pereira, Joseph (1989), "Christmas Toy Lineup Has Stars, but Few Bright Ones," *The Wall Street Journal* (November 21), B1, B6; Rice, Faye (1989), "Superelf Plans for Xma$," *Fortune* (September 11), 151; Yoshihashi, Pauline (1990), "Mattel Shapes A New Future for Barbie," *The Wall Street Journal* (February 12), B1, B6.

INTRODUCTION

In Chapter 12, merchandise management was discussed from the perspective of budgeting and planning. In this chapter, emphasis is on inventory management and buying. Environmental forces must be taken into consideration in planning and executing merchandise mix and assortment decisions, distribution channel strategies, the buying function, negotiations with suppliers, and vendor relationships.

Merchandise Management and the Environment

Starting at the macroenvironmental level, merchandising strategies are formulated within the context of the store's customer base and location, competition and other businesses (including suppliers), and economic, legal, and political realities as shown in Exhibit 13–1. The successful selection and presentation of merchandise depends upon a thorough understanding of customer markets and market behavior. This includes knowledge of the shopping attitudes and behavior of both present and potential customers and up-to-date location analysis to identify possible changes in growth patterns, population shifts, and the physical environment in which the store operates. The Retail Information System should contain data representing trends and attitudes of the general public that can affect the types of merchandise that consumers will buy, and how they will buy it. For example, as a result of the AIDS epidemic and increased awareness of sexually transmitted diseases, women buy 30 to 40 percent of all condoms—resulting in the product being displayed in the feminine hygiene section of stores ("Condom Makers Aim . . . ," 1988).

Other businesses operating in the retailer's environment also have an impact on merchandising decisions. Timely and accurate information about competitors, vendors, and other channel intermediaries, as well as the retailer's relative position or relationship to each of these business entities is also critical in formulating merchandising policies. The availability and use of information about service providers (such as financial institutions) and technological advances that can facilitate the acquisition and sale of goods can also give the merchandise manager an advantage.

Legal, political, and economic environmental factors can affect merchandising decisions and, therefore, must be monitored by the retailer. Knowledge of legislation at the federal, state, and local levels, which may affect whether and how certain products are sold, can prevent some costly mistakes or, perhaps, offer some merchandising opportunities.

Economic trends must be considered in preparing sales forecasts and merchandise budgets. In fact, inventory levels and economic indicators tend to be closely related. Attitudes and activities of politicians, special interest groups, and of the retailer's constituency groups also must be tracked due to their potential impact on merchandising decisions.

Merchandise Management and Strategic Planning

An accurate and up-to-date understanding of actions, attitudes, and trends in the external environment is necessary in order to develop merchandising

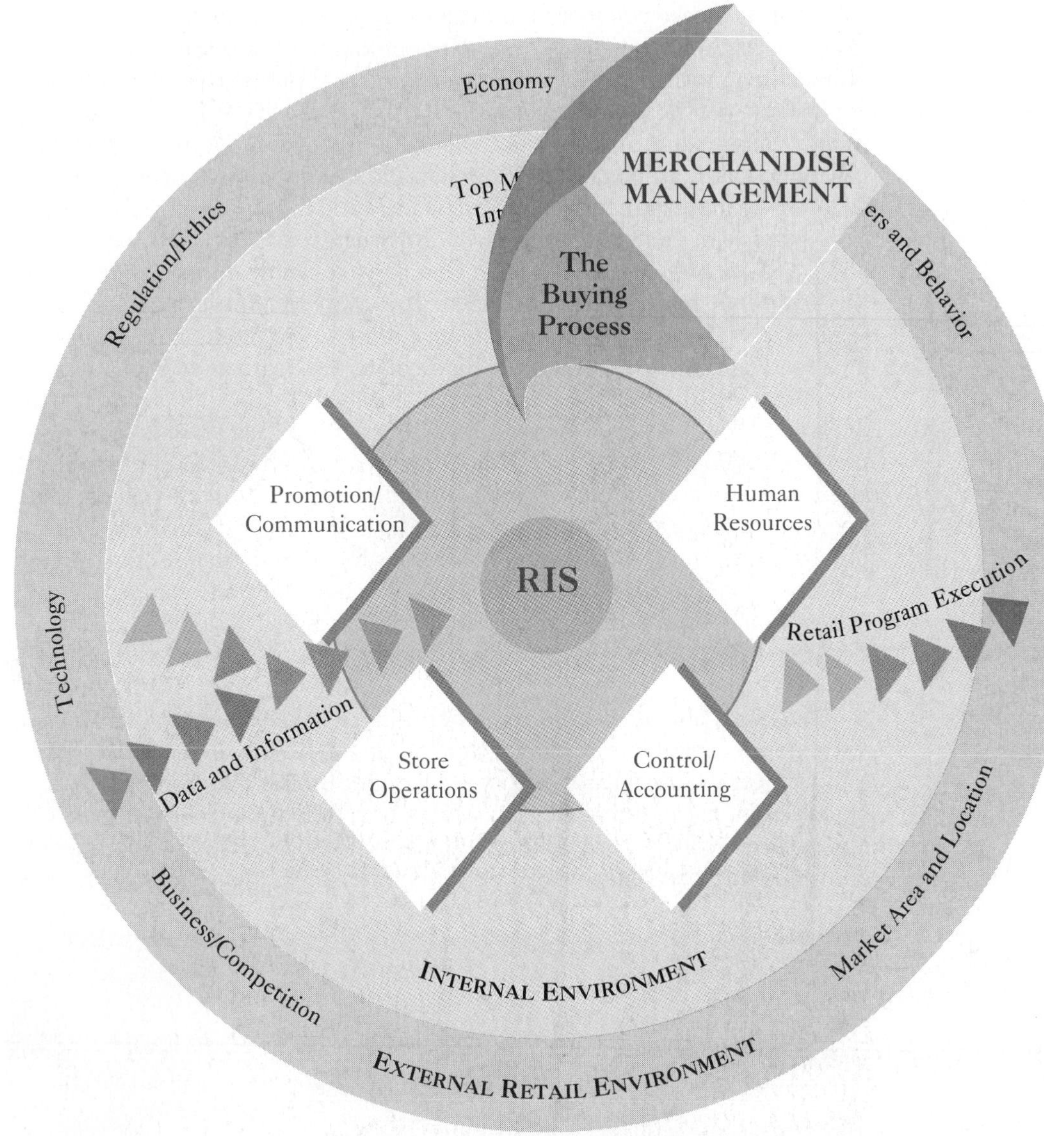
Economy
MERCHANDISE MANAGEMENT
The Buying Process
Regulation/Ethics
Promotion/ Communication
Human Resources
RIS
Technology
Retail Program Execution
Data and Information
Store Operations
Control/ Accounting
Market Area and Location
Business/Competition
INTERNAL ENVIRONMENT
EXTERNAL RETAIL ENVIRONMENT

Exhibit 13–1
Merchandise Management and the Environment

SOURCE: Anderson and Parker 1988

strategies. The strategic planning process requires the coordination of both external and internal data to determine the optimum merchandise mix and presentation for the retailer's target market. (See Exhibit 13–2.) With this information, merchandise managers can identify the optimal product and service assortment decisions and distribution channel strategies. Knowledgeable buyers and merchandise managers can execute the buying function more efficiently and effectively, based on their ability to build mutually profitable relationships with suppliers and to negotiate intelligently for the most desirable terms of sale.

MERCHANDISING STRATEGY IN A DYNAMIC ENVIRONMENT

Successful merchandising includes planning for change in a dynamic retailing environment. In October, 1987, the editors of *Business Week* published a list of America's most competitive companies, based on their ability to use capital and labor to conduct their business more efficiently than the competition over the preceding five years. Labor productivity was measured in terms of operating income, as well as company sales and profits per employee, in comparison to other companies in the *BW* 1000 industry groups. Environmental changes during that period included a recession, sharp swings in inflation and the value of the U.S. dollar, and a large number of corporate acquisitions and restructuring. Retailers included in the top tier of performers according to these performance criteria were Toys "R" Us, Circuit City, and The Limited ("America's Most Competitive Companies," 1987). During this same time period, retail customers were more price conscious and seeking better values in quality and fashion, adding to the pressure on profit margins for retailers. Charles Lazarus, chairman of the board and CEO of Toys "R" Us, has responded to a changing environment by developing successful strategies. Toys "R" Us evolved from a juvenile furniture store in Washington, D.C., where Lazarus added playthings to the furniture line in response to customers who wanted one-stop shopping for their children's needs. Toys became the major focus of the store, but Toys "R" Us customers can still purchase furniture, clothing, and accessories for children in one store. A new concept in retailing, the toy supermarket, was born from the company's recognition of trends and anticipation of responses in developing merchandising strategies in keeping with the company's basic philosophy (Toys "R" Us, 1988).

Wal-Mart, also a recognized top performer, has developed merchandising strategies to capitalize on change. Congruent with the retailer's motto, "We Sell for Less—Guaranteed Quality at Discount Prices," the company has extended its successful strategies through new formats and acquisitions. Sam's Wholesale Clubs operate warehouse type stores, selling to both retail and wholesale customers who obtain a membership. Growth of this division

Toys "R" Us responded to a changing environment by successfully evolving from a juvenile furniture store to the largest toy store chain in the country.

COURTESY OF TOYS "R" US

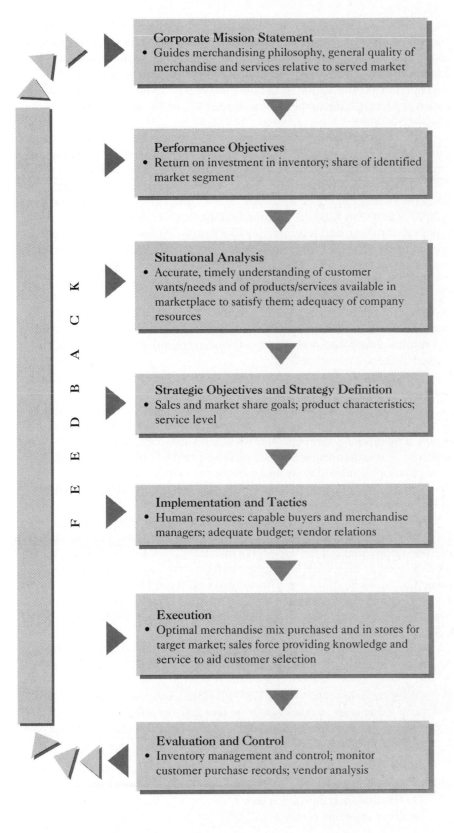

Corporate Mission Statement
• Guides merchandising philosophy, general quality of merchandise and services relative to served market

Performance Objectives
• Return on investment in inventory; share of identified market segment

Situational Analysis
• Accurate, timely understanding of customer wants/needs and of products/services available in marketplace to satisfy them; adequacy of company resources

Strategic Objectives and Strategy Definition
• Sales and market share goals; product characteristics; service level

Implementation and Tactics
• Human resources: capable buyers and merchandise managers; adequate budget; vendor relations

Execution
• Optimal merchandise mix purchased and in stores for target market; sales force providing knowledge and service to aid customer selection

Evaluation and Control
• Inventory management and control; monitor customer purchase records; vendor analysis

F E E D B A C K

Exhibit 13–2
Merchandise Management and Strategic Planning: An Illustration

was accelerated through the acquisition of 17 Super Saver Warehouse Club, Inc. stores in 1987. Hypermart* USA (an adaptation of the French *hyper-marche*) opened in Garland, Texas, in December 1987 and in Topeka, Kansas, in January, 1988. At the time of its opening, Hypermart was described as a combination of the best features of a Wal-Mart store, a combination supermarket/general merchandise store, and a Sam's Wholesale Club (Wal-Mart, 1988).

Other retailers have developed successful strategies in a changing environment. B. Dalton Booksellers, a division of Dayton Hudson, added more emphasis to computer software in its bookstores. ("B. Dalton Punches . . . ," 1984) The company recently altered its distribution strategy in buying from small publishers. By not dealing directly with publishers with whom Dalton's volume is less than $100,000, Dalton benefits from savings on the costs of ordering, shipping, and returning books, thereby improving profit margins eroded by freight costs. The small publishers sell to Dalton through larger publishers' distribution or through wholesalers (Crossen, 1988).

A successful merchandising operation depends on having the right types of personnel, who can work effectively within the organizational structure designed for this purpose, who are given the financial resources through the budgeting process to carry out their jobs, and who are held accountable for the results of their decisions through financial control. Each of these is discussed in the following sections.

Merchandising Philosophy

A company's business philosophy describes its mission and reason for existence. It guides long-term commitments and short-term decisions and behavior. A merchandising philosophy is an extension of the retailer's business philosophy, related to its merchandise and service offering.

A retailer's annual report usually reflects both the firm's business philosophy and its merchandising philosophy. For example, Wal-Mart's 1988 Annual Report makes some positive statements that are indicative of the philosophy that drives the company's buying and selling decisions. The merchandising philosophy that guides Wal-Mart's inventory assortments and how they are delivered to customers is simply stated on store signs: "Wal-Mart Discount City—We Sell for Less. Guaranteed Quality at Discount Prices." and on promotional materials throughout the stores, "Low Prices Every Day. Wal-Mart. Everybody Says It. *We Stand By It*" (Wal-Mart, 1988). (See Exhibit 13–3.)

Another leading retailer, Toys "R" Us, also describes its merchandising philosophy in the company's 1987 Annual Report (Toys "R" Us, 1987):

> *When consumers think of toys, Toys "R" Us instantly comes to mind. We are very proud of the customer loyalty we have achieved over three decades. Throughout that time, we have built a year-round market for toys through offering to customers in each of our toy supermarkets:*
>
> - *An extraordinary selection of first quality, brand name, nationally advertised merchandise.*
> - *True low prices 365 days a year.*
> - *Large quantities of stock.*

Exhibit 13-3
The Wal-Mart Merchandising Philosophy

TO OUR SHAREHOLDERS: "What's Important Is You! You . . . our customers, associates, vendors, and shareholders

OUR CUSTOMERS: "There is only one boss, and whether a person shines shoes for a living or heads up the biggest corporation in the world, the boss remains the same. It's the customer! The customer is the one who pays everyone's salary and who decides whether a business is going to succeed or fail. In fact, the customer can fire anybody in the company from the chairman on down, and he can do it simply by spending his money somewhere else." (Sam Walton)

OUR ASSOCIATES: "Why has Wal-Mart been so successful over the years? The answer is so simple, yet very few people really understand it—Our People Make the Difference."

OUR VENDORS: "We are committed to the purchase of quality branded products from vendors who produce for sales to the mass market. Our Wal-Mart company has always concentrated on building good, solid, long-term relationships. However, as we continue to grow, growth itself creates many interesting challenges for both Wal-Mart and its vendors." (Al Johnson) "To assure the potential of our long-term growth, we must be supportive of our vendors' concerns and mindful of their profitability."

- *A liberal, money-back, no questions asked return policy.*
- *Convenient locations and ample parking.*
- *46,000 square feet of building space designed for easy shopping.*

For over 35 years, catering to the needs of children has been our only business. We believe that our strength and expertise in the toy and children's market will sustain our continued growth of market share and customer loyalty.

Like Wal-Mart, Toys "R" Us recognizes its responsibility to its associates, suppliers, and customers in the same annual report. Of course, annual reports do serve as important public relations tools. Neither of these companies has a complicated merchandising philosophy. It is easily understood and applied by their employees, customers, suppliers, and shareholders.

ORGANIZING THE BUYING FUNCTION

Before merchandising activities can take place in a retail firm, someone must be charged with that responsibility. Organizational structure as it relates to merchandising and buying was described briefly in Chapter 11, including concepts such as specialization, departmentalization, and centralization versus decentralization. Steps in the buying process are described in this chapter, and specific job descriptions are provided later in the book within the context of retailing careers. In this section, the focus is on organizational design as it relates to buyers and merchandise managers.

In a small retail firm, often the owner or manager does the buying for the store—either by placing orders at major or regional market centers or purchasing from catalogs or manufacturers' sales representatives in the store.

The owner/manager is a generalist, buying many different types of merchandise. As the firm becomes larger, the buying function tends to become more specialized and more formal, and personnel requirements become more precise. The organizational structure must be consistent with the retailer's merchandising needs, allowing all tasks to be accomplished efficiently and effectively.

Merchandising Personnel

The key merchandising personnel include buyers, merchandise managers and department managers, as well as their support staffs. (See Exhibit 13–4.) **Buyers** are responsible for selecting merchandise that is consistent with target market needs, negotiating terms of sale with vendors, and following up to see that orders are shipped as specified. They work with merchandise managers to forecast sales and determine merchandise budgets, based on their knowledge of customers and suppliers. This involves the estimation of dollar figures by departments and product categories, as well as the specification of merchandise units represented by those dollars. Buyers are aided in their responsibilities by assistant buyers.

There are two levels of **merchandise managers:** general merchandise managers (GMM) and divisional merchandise managers (DMM), who report to the GMMs. Large retail firms typically have high ranking executives, usu-

Exhibit 13–4
Key Merchandising Personnel
• •

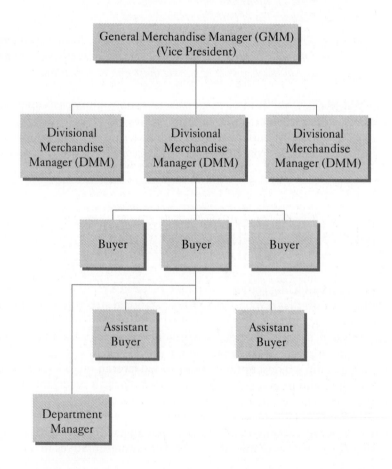

BUYERS
select merchandise, negotiate the terms of the sale, and follow up on shipment of orders

MERCHANDISE MANAGERS
forecast sales, determine merchandise budgets, and participate in strategic decisions

DEPARTMENT MANAGERS
oversee daily retail operations of one or more selling departments

ally at the vice-president level, designated as general merchandise managers. These executives are more involved in strategic decisions at the business level of the firm, than at the operations or functional level. They are accountable for the "big" picture, including merchandise planning, budgeting, and control activities, and may oversee a number of divisions.

Divisional merchandise managers are responsible for one or more lines of merchandise, such as men's or women's apparel, housewares, or electronics. They develop sales forecasts and budgets, determine dollar inventory levels, supervise and work closely with buyers, and evaluate the outcomes of merchandising decisions.

Department managers oversee the daily operations of one or more departments on the selling floor. They are directly responsible for aspects of the selling function: sales personnel, inventory management, appearance of the department, and customer service. Because of their daily interaction with customers and the salesforce, they can provide valuable feedback to buyers about customer likes and dislikes.

Support for merchandise managers, buyers, and department managers is available from either inside or outside the company. This includes assistance such as consumer and market research, accounting and financial services, and personnel evaluation and training. Buyers also may receive assistance from resident buying offices. These may be owned by the retailer, or by an outside company, and usually are located close to suppliers in major markets. Resident buyers can provide both small and large retailers with product and market information, the opportunity for special deals from vendors, and other merchandising expertise.

Organizational Structure for Merchandising

The three major factors to consider in designing an organizational structure for merchandising activities are the optimal degree of formality, centralization, and specialization. A buying organization may be formal or informal.

COURTESY OF J.C. PENNEY

Buyers must understand that the consumer marketplace changes along with lifestyle trends, in order to better serve the customer of the 90s.

Large retailers usually have formal buying organizations, with responsibilities clearly defined and separated along department or merchandise lines. These organizations are less flexible and more costly to operate. Smaller retailers usually have informal buying organizations, with buying responsibilities overlapping other aspects of managing the business. The informal organization is associated with greater flexibility and lower costs.

A buying organization for a multi-unit retail chain may be centralized or decentralized. In a centralized structure, all or most of the buying is done through headquarters where buyers place orders for all stores. The emphasis is on consistency of assortments and merchandise presentation. Centralized buyers have the ability to place large orders. This gives the firm a certain amount of clout in negotiating with vendors. A centralized buying staff tends to be more specialized and more knowledgeable about the merchandise lines they buy.

However, a centralized buying staff is not as close to the needs of individual stores and their customers, and does not have the flexibility to respond to local needs. Merchandising personnel in a decentralized buying organization have the flexibility to respond quickly to local customer needs, competitive actions, and economic conditions. On the negative side, though, merchandise assortments and presentations may be inconsistent from one store to another, and merchandise costs may be higher due to smaller orders. In both cases, performance has been improved through the use of sophisticated information systems that allow rapid transmittal of information between stores and headquarters to assist the buying staff.

Degree of specialization is the third factor to be considered by retailers in designing a buying organization. Buyers may be highly specialized, with responsibility for only one or a few lines of merchandise in which they have expertise and market knowledge. Specialized buying is an advantage for the retailer who carries many diverse merchandise lines. Generally, larger retailers have the financial resources necessary to have a buying organization staffed by specialists. Conversely, a buying organization may be more generalized, with one buyer responsible for many merchandise lines or departments. This type of buying organization may be used by retailers who have fewer, more similar lines of merchandise, or by smaller firms. Less expense is involved in this type of organization, but generalists may not be as knowledgeable about specific types of merchandise.

A retailer may pay a buying organization outside the company as an alternative—or a supplement—to an inside buying organization. Small and medium-sized retailers may use this option. Outside buyers are used by all types of retailers who are at considerable distance from their vendors. For example, a major chain may hire an overseas buying office that is staffed with local personnel. Two popular types of outside buying organizations are resident buying offices and cooperative buying groups. Resident buying offices usually are located in major market centers such as New York and Dallas. Because of their proximity to manufacturers and wholesalers, they can provide the retailer with up-to-date information and serve as a liaison with the market. Cooperative buying has become increasingly important for smaller retailers in their attempts to compete with larger firms. A group of retailers pool their orders to gain the advantage of volume buying and reduce costs. Cooperatives may be formed due to the efforts of retailers, wholesalers, or manufacturers.

Merchandise Mix and Assortment Decisions

While merchandise mix and assortment decisions are made internally within company guidelines and constraints, the successful execution of these decisions largely depends on their impact outside the company. A product strategy must consider all factors associated with a particular product or service by the manufacturer/producer, customer, and retailer.

Consumers seek both tangible and intangible benefits when they make a purchase. Thus, a single product becomes a complex concept. Likewise, within a store environment, a single product is not viewed in isolation. It is part of a total mix of related, and perhaps unrelated, merchandise, and may even include the store environment (salespeople, ambiance, layout, decor). Ideally, retail customers will be encouraged to make multiple purchases in one shopping trip. Thus, the merchandise mix includes decisions about the variety, assortment, width, and depth of products and product lines.

Product Concepts

The retailer's merchandise mix decisions start with the development of a product mix that is compatible with its customer preferences and merchandising philosophy. A **product mix** consists of individual products and product lines.

The typical product mix contains a combination of established products and new products. Manufacturers and retailers are taking fewer risks with new products than in the past due to the high cost of failures of new market entries. Packaged goods companies like Campbell Soup Co. and RJR Nabisco Inc. have been monitoring new products more closely and are focusing more on developing existing brands than taking risks with an unknown. Consumers do not always perceive the product in the same way its producers do. For example, Campbell believed its L'Orient line of frozen Chinese dinners would be a hit, with entrees like Firecracker Chicken and Rock Sugar Glazed Pork. However, shoppers shunned the product when it was introduced nationally, and it was eventually pulled off the market (Swasy, 1989). Retail buyers can spend their money only once for a given inventory. If the product or product line is not what the customer wants, mistakes can be costly.

PRODUCT   The **product** itself embodies more than just a physical object. It can be defined broadly to encompass a functional product, service, or idea, as well as the intangible or aesthetic aspects of each. When consumers consider the purchase of a particular product, they are influenced by many factors that have little or no relationship to the product's physical or technical features. They have expectations about social, economic, physical, and psychological benefits that will result from ownership of the product. They also are influenced by anticipated levels of service and support after the sale (e.g., money-back guarantees, warranties, repair service).

Watches and shoes are two familiar examples of the product concept. One of the most popular watches in recent years has been the trendy, colorful Swatch watch. In 1985, a *Chain Store Age* headline asked, "Is there life

PRODUCT MIX

combination of merchandise within a retail establishment

PRODUCT

a physical object; includes the functional product plus associated aesthetic and intangible aspects

after Swatch?" In the peak selling season of 1984, it was not uncommon for Saks Fifth Avenue or Bloomingdale's to sell over 300 Swatch watches a day. Over one million Swatches were sold that year. The bonus for retailers was that Swatches helped build overall watch sales by putting a whole new focus on the industry, creating additional business that did not detract from traditional lines like Timex or Lorus ("Watches . . . ," 1985). Five years later a *Wall Street Journal* headline announced that "Swatch says it's time to reach older crowd," although the watch had been the favorite of trendy teens for eight years in the United States. Sales peaked at five million units in 1986 and totaled four million in 1989. However, many customers over the age of 16 considered the watches simply cheap and plastic. In 1990, Swatch rolled out new models to change that perception and attract more adults—based on the knowledge that they are not a trend anymore, so they have to be a brand. Upscale products were added to respond to new demands of the market, including a $45 scuba watch and $75 chronograph watch at twice the price of a classic Swatch (Deveny, 1990).

In the shoe market, Hush Puppies has been a strong brand name for more than thirty years. However, Wolverine World Wide, Inc. has found that young customers think Hush Puppies are for somebody else. The Hush Puppies brand of casual shoes was slow to respond to competition from imports and from the athletic shoe market. After closing plants and retail chains, the company has attempted to change the brand's image to appeal to younger customers who buy more shoes than their older relatives. On the other hand, popular athletic shoes from companies such as Reebok are perceived as designer sneakers, a product concept that has captured a market for over one-third of all shoes sold by retailers (Helm, 1987; Zellner, 1987).

PRODUCT LINES Retailers combine groups of single products into **product lines** to be offered for sale to their customers. Product lines can be combined in a number of ways. Some of these are according to customer type (men, women, business executives, senior citizens), manufacturer (Liz

This Guerlain boutique, pictured here at Sax, illustrates a product line combined from the products of a specific manufacturer.

DOUG BEASLEY PHOTOGRAPHY, INC.

PRODUCT LINES
combinations of related products

Claiborne, Coca Cola, Foster Grant), customer need (dietary foods, medical supplies, entertainment), product use (recreation, do-it-yourself supplies), or related or coordinated use (bedroom or patio furniture, special occasion ready-to-wear, stereo systems). Merchandise managers and buyers must select product lines that will maximize sales and profits. The emphasis here is on selecting product lines to carry in a store. However, a related decision is discontinuing product lines that are no longer appealing to customers or do not contribute to achieving the retailer's objectives.

A product line can be expanded into less distinct categories or subdivided into more clearly defined groupings, based on the retailer's or manufacturer's preferences. For example, L. L. Bean sells a wide array of products in its line of outdoor clothing and sports equipment. The product line concept is strengthened by the company's practice of having its salespeople use the products and experience the outdoors. They get training in activities such as kayaking, backpacking, and snowshoeing, so they can talk intelligently to customers about L. L. Bean's product line. The company has built a $230-million-a-year business on customer perceptions of a product line that makes people feel rustic and look sporty and outdoorsy, even though they have never been in the woods of Maine. According to one observer, the appeal of the L. L. Bean product line has been that it represents the possibility of wilderness, the scent of pine, and the rush of bright water (Horrigan, 1985; Layfield, 1987).

The beverage industry offers another example of product line proliferation. In addition to the traditional beer brands and products, retailers can stock many new products from numerous brewers, such as dry beers, draft beers, light beers, red beers, seasonal beers and pale ales, and even nonalcoholic drinks. Along with packaged goods companies, Coors, Anheuser-Busch, and other brewers have come to realize that a brand can be hot for only so long before customers get bored with it (Charlier 1989). This phenomenon offers a continuous challenge to retailers to have the right product lines to sell to their customers.

The automobile industry offers examples of both expansion and subdivisions of product lines in an intensely competitive market. Clearly defined product groupings can be found in luxury car and pickup truck lines. Car dealers have found a profitable market niche for luxury cars like Toyota's Lexus, Honda's Acura, and Nissan's Infiniti that have been positioned to compete head-on with BMW, Mercedes-Benz, and Cadillac. As a Lexus executive observed, the college students of the 1970s who bought Corollas and trucks are good prospects for the luxury market (Zellner, 1989). Truck product lines have become trendy, appealing to city folks, women, and many customers who never owned a truck before. In the 1980s, sales of light trucks (pickups, vans, sport/utility vehicles) increased by 65 percent while car sales increased by only 10 percent (Treece, 1987). These well-defined product lines are geared to distinct retail markets.

PRODUCT MIX   A product mix consists of all product lines offered by the store, and the individual product items within each of the product lines. (See Exhibit 13–5.) In developing a product mix with a competitive advantage, the retailer is challenged to find the best combination of products and product lines consistent with its target market needs and its philosophy.

Product:	Product Line:	Product Mix:
Tide Liquid Laundry Detergent	Liquid Laundry Detergent	Specific Brands of Laundry Detergent (and Number)
(Including Physical Product, Chemical Formula, Smell, "Cleaning Power")	Powdered Laundry Detergent Laundry Bar Soap	Specific Items Within Each Brand (and Number)

Exhibit 13–5
Product, Product Line, and Product Mix

Merchandise Variety and Assortment

VARIETY   The **variety** of merchandise offered by a retailer refers to the number of different types of merchandise classifications carried within a store or merchandising unit. These classifications may be related (such as tennis shoes, dress shoes, and boots) or unrelated (shoes, cosmetics, kitchen appliances). The variety of merchandise carried by specialty stores tends to be related, but subdivided into more narrowly defined departments and classifications for selling and inventory management purposes. The greatest variety of merchandise is geared toward one-stop shopping in warehouse or discount stores, for example, where many unrelated items are carried.

There is a trade-off between variety and focus. To illustrate, fashion retailers may focus on a single look, but some have been burned by placing emphasis on styles that many customers will not wear. The disaster of the miniskirt in 1987 is a case in point, when top retailers like Macy's, The Limited, and The Gap focused on rising hemlines. Customers resisted, and the retailers lost money. The reaction was to emphasize variety the following year, letting customers choose what they really wanted from a selection of fashionable, but less trendy, clothing (Dunkin and Phillips, 1988).

ASSORTMENT   A merchandise **assortment** refers to the number of choices that a customer has available within a certain classification in a product line. Assortment refers to sizes, colors, styles, and brands. For example, the coat classification may include a number of brands and price lines of unlined raincoats, coats with zip-out linings, leather jackets, and wool coats, all available in a full range of sizes. (See Exhibit 13–6.) Merchandise assortments are measured in terms of stock keeping units or SKUs. Each SKU is the lowest common denominator in a merchandise group (e.g., Hanes white short-sleeved, V-neck t-shirt, in a medium size).

Supermarkets offer a familiar example of merchandise assortments in all classifications, including snack foods and canned goods. A less obvious example is found in the produce department which has become a major consideration of supermarkets around the country. Fruits and vegetables account for 21 percent of pretax profit at conventional supermarkets and 27 percent at larger stores. Having the right assortment to satisfy customer tastes means eliminating seasonality by purchasing from growers throughout the world and stocking more brand name fruits and veggies ("Business Bulletin," 1989). The meat department also has had to adjust its assortments to

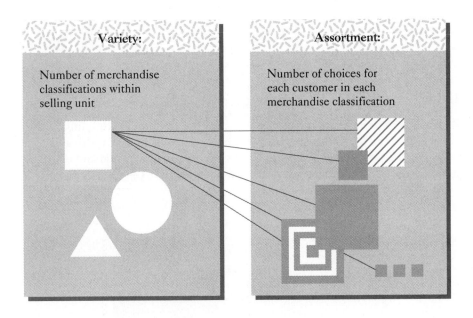

Variety:

Number of merchandise
classifications within
selling unit

Assortment:

Number of choices for
each customer in each
merchandise classification

Exhibit 13–6
Merchandise Variety and
Assortment
....

changing customer tastes. One such addition by some grocers is the "meat of
the 80s," buffalo meat (Atchison, 1987).

Width and Depth of Merchandise Assortments

Balanced merchandise assortments involve decisions about the width and
depth of stock available to customers.

WIDTH   **Width** of merchandise assortment refers to the number of different product lines carried by the retailer. Department stores and supermarkets
typically carry wide assortments, offering their customers many product categories from which to choose. A t-shirt shop or a Baskin-Robbins outlet carries
a narrow assortment, limiting its selection to only a few product lines.

DEPTH   The **depth** of an assortment describes the amount of stock that is
in inventory to support a planned sales level, and includes merchandise characteristics such as number of brands, styles, colors, prices, or sizes carried
within a single line. The assortment of unlined raincoats described above
might be considered relatively deep if it is stocked in two brands, three
styles in each brand, three colors in each style, and a range of sizes for each
style and color.

Each of these dimensions is quantified according to anticipated sales so
that inventory can be purchased in accordance with customer needs. However, assortment plans may require adjustments in order to adapt to internal
and external requirements. While the ideal assortment may consist of two
brands of raincoats, with three styles in each, along with a full range of sizes
and colors, such an assortment may not be financially feasible for the retailer.
Thus, the assortment plan may need to be modified to remain within budgeted amounts for purchases. Likewise, changes in customer preferences,
availability of the product from vendors, and other circumstances may

VARIETY

number of different types of
merchandise classifications within a
store or merchandising unit

ASSORTMENT

number of choices of merchandise
available within a certain
classification

WIDTH

number of different product lines
carried by a retailer

DEPTH

amount of stock in inventory to
support a planned sales level

require adjustments in the assortment plan. Exhibit 13–7 illustrates the relationship between product concepts, variety and assortment, and width and depth in making merchandising decisions.

Developing A Product Strategy

The retailer's product strategy forms a framework for merchandise mix decisions. There are four basic strategies, based on the concepts of width and depth. Assortments may be classified as: wide and shallow; wide and deep; narrow and shallow; and narrow and deep. (See Exhibit 13–8.)

This is only a small part of the product mix at Spiegel and Eddie Bauer; Spiegel also offers many other fashion and home items.

COURTESY OF SPIEGEL

Exhibit 13–7
Relationship Between Product and Merchandising Decisions

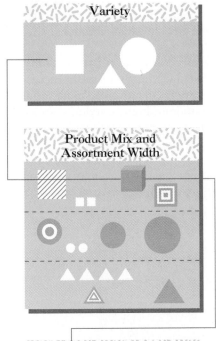

Variety

Definition:
Number of different types of merchandise classifications carried within a store or merchandising unit

Supermarket Example:
Household soaps/cleaners
Grocery products
Produce
Meat
Dairy
etc.

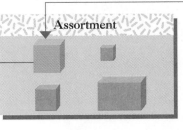

Product Mix and Assortment Width

Product Mix: All product lines and their individual product items offered by the store

Assortment Width: Number of different product lines carried

Cleaners: A, B, C, D
Groceries: E, F, G, H
Produce: K, L, M
Meat: N, O, P
Dairy: Q, R, S
etc.

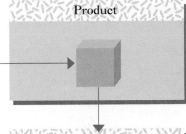

Assortment

Number of choices available within each product line within each classification (brands, sizes, colors, etc.—usually referred to as SKUs or Stock Keeping Units)

Cleaners: A_1, A_2, A_3, B_1, B_2, B_3, C_1, C_2, C_3, C_4, D_1, D_2, D_3, etc.

Product

Single product item

Cleaner A_1:
(Tide Liquid Detergent)

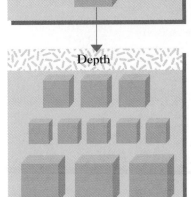

Depth

Amount of stock in inventory to support planned sales levels (number of units to have on hand for each SKU)

Cleaner A_1:
(Tide Liquid Detergent)
Size: 64 oz., 32 oz.,16 oz.

Package: Non-reusable plastic, reusable plastic

Note: Some categories overlap

WIDE AND SHALLOW   A "Mom and Pop" general store usually offers a wide range of unrelated merchandise, but has a shallow assortment (i.e., limited inventory support) within any one product category. A hardware store generally carries a wide, but shallow, assortment of merchandise (e.g., many types of nails, bolts, screws, etc.—but few of any one stock number or size).

WIDE AND DEEP   Department stores carry assortments that are both wide and deep. A broad array of merchandise, including apparel and accessories for the entire family, cosmetics, housewares, electronics, home furnishings, toys, and stationery is supported by numerous brands, styles, sizes and colors. The advertisement shown in Exhibit 13–9 represents a wide and deep assortment for Sears' Brand Central electronics and appliances.

NARROW AND SHALLOW   The traditional fast-food burger restaurant offers a narrow and shallow menu, perhaps just hamburgers, fries, and bever-

Exhibit 13–8
Width and Depth of
Merchandise Assortment

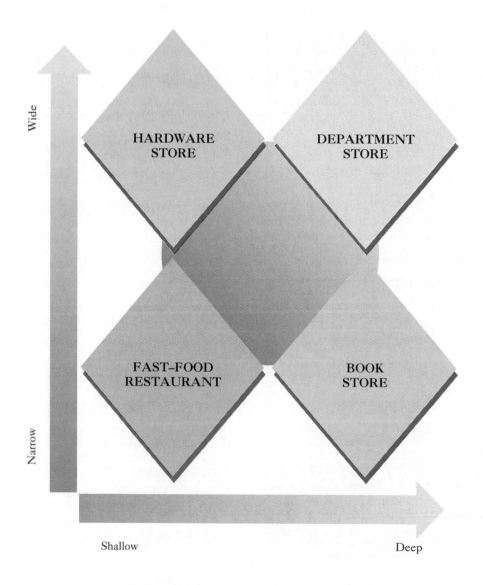

age. (However, most have expanded their menu items over time in response to consumer demand and the need to make more efficient use of their facilities.) Some specialty stores fall into this category. Perhaps they only offer one or two styles of t-shirts or neckties, for example. Fierce competition among an increasing number of video stores has resulted in some interesting product strategies. Originally, assortments in these retail outlets that opened in the video boom of the late 1970s could be classified as narrow and deep, with assortments limited to little other than videos, but deep inventory support within each category. "Batman" can be found in nearly every video store, but some stores like Video Vault in Alexandria, Virginia have found a way to attract attention in the maturing and overcrowded retail video industry where the overall growth rate has slowed, and major chains dominate with a "cookie cutter" approach to merchandise assortments. Video Vault's slogan is: "Guaranteed Worst Movies in Town," where the assortment consists of cult movie classics (Carlson, 1990).

Exhibit 13–9
Product Assortment Strategy:
Sears' Brand Central

SOURCE: Sears Brand Central; Sears, Roebuck and Company, Chicago.

NARROW AND DEEP   Baskin-Robbins has a narrow product selection, limiting its offering to ice cream products. At the same time, they carry a deep assortment of 31 flavors. Book stores also carry a narrow merchandise assortment, but considerable depth in each category of books.

Retail managers must constantly monitor their merchandise mix to determine whether products or product lines need to be added or deleted. On the one hand, there is a trend toward specialization, which involves narrower assortments. On the other hand, many retailers have resorted to scrambled merchandising tactics and broader product lines to remain competitive in today's environment. Balanced assortments that meet the needs of target customers are the key to successful merchandising.

Distribution Channel Strategies

How and where to buy merchandise is influenced by the retailer's buying organization and by the structure of available distribution channels. Some of the factors underlying these important decisions are discussed next.

How to Buy

The "how to buy" decision is a function of three factors—time, distance, and money—as they relate to the customer, retailer, and supplier. Ideally, these factors can be combined to provide the greatest consumer satisfaction and the lowest prices for all parties. For purchases that are made in a hurry, (e.g., prescription medicine, late night snacks), the merchandise must be closer to the customer. When suppliers offer a relatively short leadtime, and/or they are located near the retailer, buyers generally place orders more frequently and in small quantities, while maintaining a basic stock level to avoid stockouts. With long lead times and distances, larger orders may be placed to ensure an adequate supply for customers. However, in both cases there is a tradeoff between convenience and cost. If frequent, small orders are more costly to the retailer (and subsequently to the customer), then the retailer will hold a larger inventory.

Some trends in the operation of distribution channels that affect how retailers buy include the following:

- The balance of power between retailers and manufacturers is shifting in favor of retailers, giving them more clout in the buying process due to factors such as vertical integration, private labeling and increased size of firms through mergers and acquisitions.
- Competition for retail space has increased, with many retailers demanding a premium to stock manufacturers' goods.
- Manufacturers are providing more in-store assistance to retailers to improve layout, sales presentations, and other aspects of selling their products.
- The level of technology available to retailers and/or suppliers (e.g., satellite communications, on-line computerized ordering systems,

factory robotics) have resulted in improved production and order processing efficiencies.

● Service has become more important at all levels of the channel: suppliers to retailers and retailers to consumers.

Various strategies are used by retail buyers to maximize their clout with suppliers. Some of the following suggestions are from a survey of key electronics and appliance retailers:

● Work with suppliers on longer-term programs, promising a specified dollar volume upfront for a specified time period, then negotiating price and terms that are expected to remain stable. For example, a buyer for a regional chain in Denver usually locks up terms for three to six months. However, this may reduce the retailer's flexibility because it requires planning further ahead and may take longer to get out of an oversupply situation.

● Deal with fewer sources, in order to be more important to a supplier by carrying as much of their line as possible. (Of course, this is a two-way street, and buyers must also live up to their end of the commitments they make).

● Use computers for watching sales on a daily basis, allowing the buyer to react faster to changes on the selling floor. One buyer found the computer useful in tracking a rapid increase in refrigerator sales resulting from hot weather. Successful buyers also use computers to help determine the quantity of future buys. Merely looking at last year's figures may not be enough, because things change.

● Understand the importance of communication between the buyer and the sales force. The buyer can keep the sales force informed

COURTESY OF HOME SHOPPING NETWORK

The Home Shopping Network has an expansive telecommunications system available not only for selling, but also for the buying function. HSN buys in volume and can offer many items at prices much lower than consumers can find in discount stores or mail-order catalogs.

about product knowledge, and salespeople can keep the buyer informed about possible bad merchandise buys and serve as a source of product evaluation.

● Know the customer base, and understand the company's image in the market (e.g., a high-end or low-end image). Once buyers know who the customers are, they can find key suppliers.

● Good buying means knowing when to push and when to hold back. This includes keeping the information exchanged between buyer and supplier confidential as an element of trust, and remembering that the person on the other end of the buy has "both feelings and a boss to go home to," in order to maintain a relationship of mutual support (Sabin, 1987).

Where to Buy

Selection of where to buy may be determined by the type of distribution channel used by that market or individual vendors. Channel structures may take several forms for retailers, starting with the producer or primary manufacturer of finished goods. The most direct channel is from the producer to the retailer, next producer to wholesaler to retailer (limited channel), and the most indirect channel involves other functional intermediaries between the producer and wholesaler (extended channel). When the dimension of purchasing imported goods is added, the channel strategies become even more complex.

Retail buyers can make purchases without ever leaving the store. They can buy from manufacturers' representatives who bring various lines to the store. They can place mail or phone orders from catalogs and stocklists, or they can visit vendors' showrooms in market centers. Major market centers for many lines of merchandise are in New York, Chicago, Dallas, Atlanta, Los Angeles, and San Francisco. Many manufacturers and wholesalers maintain permanent showrooms in these centers; others are only there for industry trade shows. Retailers also can view merchandise and place orders at regional markets in other cities, where a group of manufacturers and/or wholesalers with related lines will sponsor a trade show. In other cases, one or more vendors may set up and show their lines in a local hotel or convention center for the convenience of nearby retailers.

When to Buy

The timing of purchase orders is affected by many factors. A few are discussed here as an introduction: merchandise type, seasonality, distribution factors, and reorder time, levels, and quantity.

MERCHANDISE TYPE   Merchandise can be broadly classified as either staple or fashion goods. Staple goods do not have wide fluctuations in sales during a year. Sales of nails in a hardware store, bread in a grocery store, or athletic socks in an apparel store remain reasonably steady regardless of season of the year, style of merchandise or other influences. The timing of orders for this type of goods is generally determined by a basic stock list.

The **basic stock list** is an itemized account of the amount of inventory needed on hand for each individual item in order to support expected sales levels. The basic stock list provides for a minimum level of stock, at which point reorders are routine.

On the other hand, fashion goods (e.g., apparel, home fashions, cars) experience greater variation in sales levels and are influenced by factors such as seasonality, current trends, and availability of new models. Timing of purchases is planned to maximize the availability of the newest and best styles in the retailer's inventory when customers are most interested in buying. Rather than the basic stock list used for staple goods, a **model stock plan** is used for fashion goods. The model stock plan consists of recommended dollar amounts in a particular line of goods by price lines, sizes, or other meaningful classification schemes, since last year's "hot" styles would not be a good barometer for this year.

SEASONAL FACTORS   Seasonal factors affect both staple and fashion goods, but to a different extent. Staple goods that are seasonal in nature include items such as charcoal for outdoor grills, beach towels, kerosene for heaters, soup, thermal underwear, and tree lights for the Christmas season. However, a basic stock list can be maintained for this type of merchandise for a defined seasonal period. The seasonality of fashion merchandise, particularly in apparel lines, is more obvious. Differences in activities, climate, and temperature conditions require different kinds of attire, resulting in purchases that conform to seasonal requirements.

DISTRIBUTION FACTORS   Distribution factors also affect the timing of order placement. New car models typically appear on the market once a year, and initial orders are placed accordingly. Giftware markets and holiday merchandise are presented and ordered well ahead of the selling season, with purchases concentrated in a short time period. Other distribution factors, such as the availability of quantity discounts for large orders, lead time for an order to be processed and shipped, and packaging units (i.e., must buy a case of 12), also affect the times when purchases are made.

REORDER TIME, LEVELS, AND QUANTITY   The above discussion is merely a brief introduction to some of the influences that determine when a buyer will actually place orders. Two other concepts related to the timing of orders (primarily for basic stock) are also introduced here: reorder point and economic order quantity.

 Reorder point is the stock level at which new orders must be placed. The actual reorder point depends on order lead time, usage rate, and desired safety stock. **Order lead time** is the total time from the date the order is placed with the vendor until the item is in the store ready to sell to a customer. The **usage rate** refers to the average number of units of an item sold each day or each week. **Safety stock** is the extra inventory kept on hand to decrease the possibility of out-of-stock conditions, which may result from increased demand, delivery delays by vendors, and such. There is no magic safety stock level. It depends on how much the retailer wants to risk running out of merchandise, the amount of each item needed to satisfy consumer

BASIC STOCK LIST
itemized account of amount of inventory needed to support expected sales level

MODEL STOCK PLAN
recommended dollar amounts in a particular line of goods and its subclassifications

REORDER POINT
stock level at which new orders must be placed

ORDER LEAD TIME
total time from order placement until merchandise is ready for sale

USAGE RATE
average number of units of an item sold every day or every week

SAFETY STOCK
extra inventory kept on hand to avoid out-of-stock conditions

demand, and to allow for delivery lead time. The reorder point is calculated as follows:

Reorder point without safety stock = Usage rate × Lead time.

If a drugstore sells 10 bottles of 100-count aspirin a day, and order lead time is 5 days, a reorder should be placed when the inventory reaches 50 bottles:

Reorder point without safety stock = (10 bottles × 5 days)
= 50 bottles.

If the drugstore wants to keep a safety stock of 15 bottles to accommodate fluctuations in demand:

Reorder point with safety stock = (Usage rate ×Lead time) + Safety stock
Reorder point with safety stock = 10 bottles × 5 days + 15 bottles
= 65 bottles.

The **economic order quantity (EOQ)** is based on a model that assumes that demand is predictable, constant, and continuous. The economic order quantity is the amount that minimizes all order processing costs, taking into consideration both the costs of ordering and of holding inventory. The basic formula is:

$$EOQ = \sqrt{\frac{2DS}{IC}}$$

where

EOQ	= order quantity in units
D	= annual demand in units
S	= costs to place an order
I	= percent of annual carrying cost to unit cost
C	= unit cost of an item

Example: Sales estimate	= 100 desk lamps a year
Cost	= *$20.00 each*
Breakage, insurance, capital invested, pilferage, etc.	= *10% of the costs*
Order Costs	= *$5.00 per order*

Therefore, EOQ = $\sqrt{\dfrac{2\,(100)(\$5)}{(0.10)(\$20)}} = \sqrt{\dfrac{\$1,000}{\$2.00}} = \sqrt{500}$ mugs = *22.36*

As can be seen in this example, the economic order quantity of 22.36 lamps may have to be modified to conform to packing requirements (i.e., 6 lamps to a box), or for changes in demand, variable holding and order costs, and quantity discounts. Common sense still prevails. The economic order quantity is taken into consideration when deciding how often to order inventory. The trade-off is between order costs and inventory carrying costs.

ECONOMIC ORDER QUANTITY (EOQ)
amount that minimizes all order processing costs, including ordering costs and inventory costs

Just-in-Time Delivery

An important aspect of inventory management for today's retailers is to minimize inventory investment without endangering sales. One response to this problem has been a cooperative effort between retailers and suppliers, called "just-in-time delivery" or JIT. Its overriding goal is to keep inventory levels as close to zero as possible and merchandise quality at the highest level possible. Ideally, retailers receive an item just at the time that a customer wants to purchase it. This involves close relationships and synchronization throughout the channel, with retailers placing orders more frequently and in smaller quantities. It also requires a close arrangement with fewer vendors who, in turn, often make the same type of arrangement with their suppliers. The process is facilitated by good telecommunication systems, closer locations, stable production schedules, and strict quality control to avoid customer dissatisfaction and returns due to faulty merchandise. The result is lower inventory costs and more efficient use of assets.

JIT partnerships are changing the way wholesalers do business, which has a major impact on deliveries to retailers. Manufacturers are counting on fewer wholesalers, and customers are switching to just-in-time delivery systems. To satisfy the need for reduction in lead times and delivery times, distributors must always be fully stocked, and there is less tolerance for delivery and billing mistakes. However, there is some danger if a close JIT partnership results in overreliance on a single supplier (Weber, 1990).

Knowing the location of merchandise in a JIT inventory environment is crucial. One company has developed a satellite technology for locating trucks and providing digital information between them and their home base. For example, the system would allow a carrier to tell Sears where a load of garments, purchased for a special sale, is located at any given moment and when it will arrive at the store. Further back in the channels, such information can help avoid a production line slowdown in a manufacturing plant ("Tracking Where Goods Are . . . ," 1987).

Steps in the Buying Process

There are those who believe that no single individual has a greater influence upon a retailer's profitability than the buyer—the individual who actually purchases the inventory to be sold to the store's customers. The buyer has significant influence on the following factors that contribute to net profit:

- *Sales volume*—the buyer is responsible for ordering the right goods in the right quantity at the right time and at the right place.
- *Gross margins*—the buyer is responsible for determining the cost price that can be paid for goods, and generally for the markup and retail price, as well.
- *Markdowns*—the buyer influences markdowns by what is purchased and when, and in what quantity and at what price.
- *Stock levels*—buyers and merchandise managers have considerable control over stock levels in their attempt to generate the highest level of sales with the lowest investment in inventory.

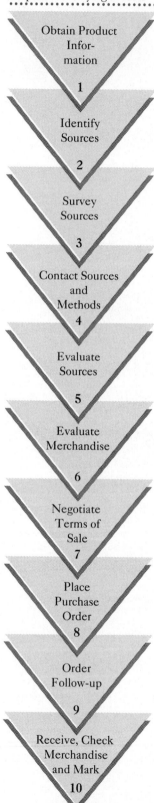

Exhibit 13–10
Steps in the Buying Process

Obtain Product Information

1

Identify Sources

2

Survey Sources

3

Contact Sources and Methods

4

Evaluate Sources

5

Evaluate Merchandise

6

Negotiate Terms of Sale

7

Place Purchase Order

8

Order Follow-up

9

Receive, Check Merchandise and Mark

10

Because of the importance of the buying function, buyers need to be adequately trained in each of these areas to improve their performance (Forrester, 1987). Buyers also must face a variety of issues related to ethics and social responsibility. Many buying and selling activities are regulated by federal, state, or local legislation. However, buyers are faced with many decisions that go beyond the letter of the law, but may be harmful or offensive to others. For example, a buyer's ethics may be in question when dealing with vendors who are involved in trade in South Africa, stocking merchandise that may be socially unacceptable to some customer group, or accepting inexpensive gifts from a vendor.

These concerns need to be addressed during the steps of the merchandise buying process. The buyer needs accurate and up-to-date information about products, sources of supply, the type and quality of merchandise carried by each supplier, and how to negotiate advantageously. Each of these steps is described briefly below, and illustrated in Exhibit 13–10.

Need for Product Information

Many of the internal and external sources of information previously described can provide the buyer with a wealth of information before any orders are placed. Internally, the store's accounting records include past sales histories by product line and vendor, customer returns, and the retailer's returns of undesirable merchandise to vendors. Salespersons' lists of items wanted by customers but not carried by the store or market research projects also may be valuable information sources. Externally, trade shows, publications, comparison shopping reports, vendors, other buyers, and professional research and reporting services have an abundance of information available to help make buying decisions.

Identifying, Contacting, and Evaluating Sources

To aid in the decision process of where and how to buy, the buyer must identify the most likely sources for the desired product lines, make contact with them, and evaluate their merchandise offerings. Sources of supply will be determined to a large extent by store policies and distribution strategies. Not all sources of supply are conveniently available or desirable to all retailers.

The information sources used by the buyer will provide a listing of potential vendors. Possible vendors may be identified from industry directories, lists of permanent market center tenants or trade show participants, telephone book Yellow Pages, and other sources. Buyers also can obtain vendor names from noncompeting buyers for other companies, other suppliers, by shopping brands carried by other retailers, and even from customer requests.

Contact between buyers and suppliers can be initiated by either party, and may be in person, by mail, or by telephone. Business may be transacted in a buying office, store, vendor's showroom or place of business, or central market. In addition to the suitability of the merchandise lines carried by the vendor, time, distance, and relationship between the two parties are weighed in the purchase decision. Many buyers prefer to concentrate purchases with a few key vendors because of the advantages in economies of scale in areas such as ordering and shipping costs. A "standard" in retailing is that 80 percent of the sales come from 20 percent of the inventory ("80-20 rule"); therefore, the vendors of that 20 percent of inventory become important to the success of the retailer.

Suppliers and their merchandise offerings can be evaluated in a number of ways. Some of these involve computerized simulations or analysis. Other ways are by using criteria such as the ability to fill reorders, adequate markup, customer demand, seasonal updates, and advertising and other types of support (e.g., salesforce training). In addition to the product offerings, the success of working with a particular vendor is related to pricing and delivery policies and to the level and quality of service provided to the retailer.

Negotiate and Buy

Once the merchandise lines and vendors have been selected, the terms of the purchase are negotiated. The key negotiation point is the price charged by the vendor. In addition to the price of the item itself, the cost of the merchandise can be adjusted in a number of ways, primarily through discounts and special allowances, as described in the next section. Following the conclusion of the negotiation process, the buyer places the order.

NEGOTIATIONS WITH SUPPLIERS

Negotiating with suppliers for the best cost price available is the most obvious way to reduce the cost of goods sold. However, buyers can minimize merchandise costs and subsequently increase profits in other ways. Two buyers, offered the same list prices, may be able to negotiate different terms of sale for their orders, resulting in one buyer actually getting a "better deal" than the other. Such arrangements include discounts, datings, shipping points and transportation methods, consignment, and other assistance (such as return privileges and private labeling). The relative size of retailer and vendor affects the negotiation process, with larger companies generally having an advantage. However, smaller retailers can develop strategies for taking advantage of many of these same terms of sale. For example, a number of small firms have successfully pursued a strategy of cooperative buying, enabling them to benefit from lower merchandise and shipping costs.

Discounts

A **discount** may be given in exchange for some cost advantage offered to the vendor by the retailer. Such advantages include reduced order processing costs for large quantities purchased (quantity discount), channel functions performed by the retailer (trade discount), use of plant capacity during the vendor's slow selling period through orders placed in advance of a season (seasonal discount), promotion of the vendor's goods at the local level by the retailer (promotional or advertising discount), and early recovery of cash due to retailer's prompt payment of invoices (cash discount). A brief explanation of each type of discount follows.

DISCOUNT
reduced cost advantage offered by a vendor

QUANTITY DISCOUNT   The cost of items is reduced when a larger quantity is purchased. The vendor can justify this lower cost because of decreased selling, production, packaging, and transportation expenses associated with large orders. In order to prevent price discrimination, the FTC expects vendors to be able to provide this justification.

Quantity discounts may be either noncumulative or cumulative, and expressed in dollars or in units. Noncumulative discounts are based on total dollars or quantity purchased on a single order. Cumulative discounts, which are not as apt to encourage overbuying, are based on total dollars or quantity of two or more orders. For example, if a total of 100 units is purchased, the retailer may receive a 5 percent discount. Sometimes the quantity discount is provided in the form of free merchandise (such as "buy one dozen, get the thirteenth free").

TRADE DISCOUNT   The most common type of discount is the **trade** (or functional) **discount**, so named because it is given in return for functions the seller would have to perform if the buyer did not. This type of discount may be given in addition to, or instead of, other discounts.

Trade discounts are expressed as a series of percentages of the list price (suggested retail) offered by the vendor to channel members. For example, a small appliance manufacturer sells to retailers through wholesalers. One item is a toaster with a list price of $12.00, with trade discounts of "less 30 percent and less 20 percent." To calculate the cost of the toasters to retailer and wholesaler:

Retailer pays ($12.00 × (1 − .30)) or ($12.00 − ($12.00 × .30)) = $8.40.
Wholesaler pays ($8.40 × (1−20)) or ($8.40 − ($8.40 × .20)) = $6.72.

Alternatively, the wholesaler's cost can be calculated as:

(100% × (1 − 30%)) = 70%; (70% × (1 − 20%)) = 56%;
(56% × $12.00) = $6.72

SEASONAL DISCOUNT   Vendors encourage retailers to purchase seasonal inventory ahead of the normal buying period. A **seasonal discount** can be given because of decreased production and selling costs, which tend to be higher during the peak of a season. However, the savings gained through early purchases must be greater than the costs incurred by the retailer.

CASH DISCOUNT   A **cash discount** may be given for early cash payment. The terms of sale include a given discount percentage, length of time the retailer has to take the discount, and the date the full payment is due if a discount is not taken. For example, a cash discount may be expressed as "3/10, net 30." The retailer can deduct 3 percent of the invoice amount (after trade, quantity, or other discounts are taken) if it is paid within 10 days, and the full amount is due in 30 days. The effective annual interest rate for the money saved in this illustration is 360/20 days × 3%, or 54%.

QUANTITY DISCOUNT
reduced cost when larger quantities are purchased

TRADE DISCOUNT
discount given for functions performed by buyer

SEASONAL DISCOUNT
discount given for merchandise purchased ahead of normal buying period

CASH DISCOUNT
discount given for early cash payment

Datings

Dating refers to the time when an invoice has to be paid in order for the retailer to take agreed upon discounts, as well as to the due date for full payment. Datings are generally stated in cash or future terms. Cash datings require immediate payment without discounts, such as cash on delivery (C.O.D.) and cash with order (C.W.O.).

Focus here is on future datings, which constitute a form of delayed payment or credit for the retailer. Types of future dating terms include end of month (E.O.M.), date of invoice (D.O.I.), receipt of goods (R.O.G.), advance, extra, and anticipation.

END OF MONTH (E.O.M.)   With an end of month dating the discount period begins on the first of the following month. For example, if an invoice is dated August 18, with terms of 3/10 EOM, the retailer can take a 3 percent discount if payment is made within 10 days of the end of the month, that is by September 10.

DATE OF INVOICE (D.O.I.)   Date of invoice terms are essentially the same as regular or ordinary dating. No statement is made on the invoice as to when a discount period begins; it is assumed that the time period in which a discount may be taken is counted from the invoice date (even if the merchandise has not yet been received by the retailer). In the example above, if the invoice was dated August 18, with terms stated simply as 3/10, the retailer would need to pay by August 28 (or 10 days from August 18) in order to take the 3 percent discount.

RECEIPT OF GOODS (R.O.G.)   Receipt of goods dating refers to the date on which the retailer received shipment of the merchandise. Discount periods would be counted from that date. When retailers and their vendors are located at a great distance from one another, or shipment may be slow, R.O.G. terms offer the retailer an advantage.

ADVANCE (OR POST) DATING AND EXTRA DATING   Both of these terms postpone the discount period until a later date, so that the retailer has more time to make payment and take discounts. For example, advance dating terms might be stated on a May 15 invoice "as of August 1," meaning that full payment is due 30 days later on September 1.

Extra dating allows the retailer extra time to take cash discounts. An invoice with the terms "3/10, 60 ✕" allows a 3 percent discount to be taken within 10 days plus 60 days (a total of 70 days) from the invoice date for payment in full.

ANTICIPATION   This is an agreement between the vendor and retailer that a discount in addition to the cash discount may be taken if the invoice is paid before the end of the discount period. In effect, the vendor is paying the retailer interest, say at an annual rate of 6 percent, for early retrieval of cash. Anticipation is an advantage to retailers who are in a good cash position to pay bills before they are due, particularly if they also have negotiated for advance or extra dating.

DATING
due date of a discount period or of total invoice

Shipping Points and Transportation Methods

Shipping costs, shipping points, and transportation methods are important negotiation points between retailers and vendors because of the high costs involved in moving merchandise. Shipping terms are negotiated to specify who pays transportation costs and at what point ownership of the goods is legally transferred.

Shipping costs are generally stated relative to where the retailer takes title to the shipment, with the retailer paying transportation costs and assuming risk for the merchandise from that point. The expression F.O.B. (freight on board, or free on board) is followed by this particular location. F.O.B. factory and F.O.B. store are frequently used. In the first case, the retailer takes title to the shipment at the factory, paying freight charges between the factory and store. F.O.B. store means that the retailer does not take title until the goods are in the store, and the vendor pays freight charges. Other shipping terms that might be arranged include: F.O.B. origin (vendor delivers goods to carrier, retailer takes title and pays freight from that point); F.O.B. shipping point (vendor pays to local shipping point, and retailer from that point to store); F.O.B. destination or F.O.B. (some city) (title is not transferred to retailer until shipment reaches this point, thus eliminating or reducing freight charges to retailer). Obviously, it is to the retailer's advantage to delay taking title to a shipment until it is in the store or as close to it as possible.

Promotional Allowances

This allowance is given to the retailer for assuming responsibility for promoting the manufacturer's goods at the local level. For example, a **promotional allowance** of 25 cents a toaster might be given in addition to the trade discount illustrated above. If a retailer bought 100 toasters, he would receive $25.00 for advertising or other promotion. Promotional allowances also may include window or interior display assistance.

Consignment

Consignment is an arrangement between the retailer and a vendor, whereby the vendor agrees to take back any merchandise that does not sell. Since the retailer does not take title to the goods until it is sold, under this agreement, little risk is involved (assuming the goods are suitable for the store), and inventory dollars are available for other merchandise.

Memorandum buying is a form of consignment buying. Under this arrangement, the retailer takes title to the merchandise upon receipt, but can return unsold merchandise to the vendor. The retailer does not have to pay for the merchandise until after it is sold.

Return Privileges and Other Assistance

A few additional ways in which buyers can negotiate for other assistance are suggested here. Mutually agreeable return policies are important, because misunderstandings may arise about routine procedures for returning goods to a vendor. Returns are never welcome, but there should be an established

PROMOTIONAL ALLOWANCE
funds given to retailer for assuming responsibility for promoting goods

CONSIGNMENT
arrangement in which vendor takes back any goods the retailer does not sell

procedure to follow so they will not become a source of irritation between the two parties.

Buyers may be able to make arrangements with vendors for the privilege of returning slow-selling (or nonselling) items. This allows the vendor to ship to another store that may be more successful selling the goods at the original price, and avoids a costly markdown for the retailer. Likewise, a markdown allowance may be obtained from the vendor to help absorb part of the retailer's loss.

Private Label Agreements

Another form of negotiation may center on **private labeling** agreements. The vendor manufactures goods to the retailer's specifications for sale under the store's own brand. The manufacturer is guaranteed a flow of orders and the retailer a source of supply, with more competitive retail prices generally resulting.

Evidence of agreements between retailers and private label suppliers is found in the supermarket industry, where retailers have increased their emphasis on private label lines and have upgraded many of their own brands. For example Pathmark, a grocery chain, makes and markets the Gourmet Bar, an ice-cream bar that bears the message, "If you like Haägen-Dazs, you'll love me." The product is positioned to compete with other rivals of Pillsbury's Haägen-Dazs brand, such as Dove, Frusën Gladje, or Ben & Jerry's. Along with a more upscale image for their private labels, many retailers are developing innovative products to compete with national brands. Jewel Cos. introduced the first squeezable ketchup bottle in Chicago; Kroger

PRIVATE LABELING
vendor manufactures goods under retailer's brand name

Lands' End needs no private label agreement, as they manufacture and sell their own products.

The Rite Aid merchandise mix is one of the largest selection of private label products in the drug store industry. The selection extends across all major drug, health and beauty aid product lines to include nearly 1,200 items, offered at a savings of 30–50 percent off comparable brand prices.

COURTESY OF LANDS' END

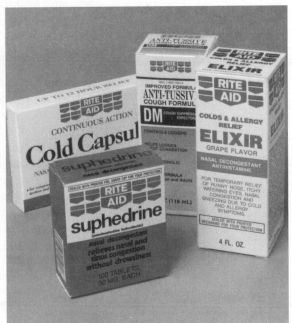

COURTESY OF RITE AID

Co. introduced the first low-calorie yogurt with Nutrasweet in the nation; and Supermarkets General Corp.'s Pathmark chain developed its own no-salt cracker product to compete with low-salt Ritz Bits crackers. Retailers believe that shoppers' confidence in private label goods is growing, and consumers pay 10 to 20 percent less for store brands than for national brands. Of course, the retailers' profits are typically 10 to 15 percent higher, offering further incentive to pursue this strategy (Freedman 1988).

Sears leads all other retail names in a survey of the "most powerful" corporate or consumer brands in the United States, ranking tenth out of 300 corporate or consumer brands. Penney's brands ranked number 60, Montgomery Ward 86, K mart 118, Saks Fifth Avenue 199, Neiman's 202, Macy's 221, and Wal-Mart 238. (Coca-Cola ranked first.) Private labeling agreements are generally initiated by the retailer, based on economics. It is most appealing to the manufacturer with a marginal business that needs all the orders it can process (Feinberg, 1989).

Licensing Agreements

What do Batman, Coca-Cola, Teenage Mutant Ninja Turtles, Crayola, Mickey Mouse, Budweiser, Garfield, designer clothings, Masters of the Universe and the Dallas Cowboys have in common? They are all popular names that are licensed for use with products sold by retailers. **Licensed products** are marketed through a contractual agreement between a licensee (manufacturer, retailer) and the owner of a particular name or trademark, character, or logo, for example. The agreement permits the licensee to make and sell products with the sponsor's identification, in return for paying royalties to the licensor. Licensed products have increased in popularity because of their association with famous names of real or fictional characters, companies, and organizations. Some prominent retailers who have been involved in direct licensing include Sears agreement with McDonald's to market McKids children's wear and Cheryl Tiegs fashion lines, and K mart's licensing agreement with Jaclyn Smith for fashion apparel. However, Sears announced in the fist quarter of 1991 that it would discontinue its 47 free-standing McKids specialty stores but would still sell the McKids brands through its department stores and catalogs because of growing competition in this market ("Sears, Roebuck & Co. . . . ," (1991).

One form of licensing is corporate licensing, which can be divided into two categories: brand awareness and brand extension. Under brand awareness, a corporation allows a marketer to sell a product emblazoned with its registered trademark, logo, or slogan. For example, Seven-Up licensed its name to a company that used imitation 7UP cans to package everything from handkerchiefs to nightshirts. Brand extension licensing occurs when a licensed product takes a brand into product categories that the trademark-owning company does not directly produce (e.g., Coca-Cola and Murjani International apparel). In addition to corporate licensing of trademarks and brand names, other forms of licensing include cartoon characters, sports, art, celebrities, designers, theatrical feature films, TV programs, publishing, and music (Norris, 1985). No matter how popular the licensed name, the product will not be successful if it is not well designed and of good quality.

LICENSING
contractual agreement for use between manufacturer or retailer and owner of trademark, character, or logo

Other Types of Negotiations

Buyers may negotiate for many other types of conditions to reduce costs or improve their operations. Some include use of the retailer's purchase order form (tailored to company specifications), exclusive goods, price guarantees for future deliveries, or pre-ticketing of goods by the vendor.

Vendor Relationships

The working relationship between retailers and suppliers is important to the success of both. The relationship does not just happen, however. It builds over time as two companies and their representatives work together, and is based not only on mutual success and profitability from the arrangement, but also on trust, consideration of one another's position, and fair treatment. A good relationship does not mean that each should not try to have the most advantageous position in the negotiation process. But it does mean that conditions should remain favorable for future orders and future negotiations.

Warnaco, a $650 million-a-year apparel company that sells Christian Dior, Hathaway, and Olga brands, is paying closer attention to what retailers want and giving them more assistance in selling its labels. The company's CEO believes that it is not enough just to teach department store salespeople to give good customer service, because the workforce is so transient. Rather, they decided to add more salespeople/merchandisers to go into key stores every day and make sure everything is in order on the selling floor (i.e., straightening stock, checking merchandise availability). In other words, the company is treating retailers as its selling partners. Warnaco believes the relationship includes determining what retailers want and making it happen. At the same time, it believes that retailers owe their suppliers prompt payment ("Treating the Retailers . . . ," 1989).

Retailers, manufacturers, and distributors feel the pressure to find new ways to improve their operations and cost effectiveness. One promising solution is "supply-chain management," which integrates management of the product, cash, and information flows through supply channels. Just-in-time (JIT) delivery systems, described previously, are one innovation being used to improve supply-chain management. Electronic Data Interchange (EDI) is another important tool, an electronic replacement of paper by direct computer-to-computer data transmission to facilitate internal and external partnerships. EDI applications can extend to anything that moves within or between companies, such as products, parts, purchase orders, shipping containers, invoices, and payments. The main advantage of EDI is its ability to promote long-term strategic alliances between supply-chain partners (Tyndall, 1988).

Follow-Up, Receiving, Checking, Marking

Placing the purchase order does not finalize the purchase process. Orders need to be followed up to be sure delivery schedules are being met, and once the merchandise is shipped, the store must process it through its receiving department, check shipments against invoices for discrepancies, mark the items, and place them on the selling floor or reserve stock areas. The receiving, checking, and marking process was described in Chapter 10.

Inventory Valuation: Cost and Retail Methods

An essential aspect of inventory management and control is determining the value of inventory on hand for a given selling period. There are two basic ways to value inventory, in cost dollars and in retail dollars.

Cost Method of Inventory Valuation

The cost method values inventory at merchandise cost plus inbound freight. In order to use the cost method of accounting, detailed inventory records must be maintained, and a physical inventory may be required to generate an income statement. The retailer's cost for each item is coded on a price tag or somewhere on the merchandise. For example, the numbers 0 1 2 3 4 5 6 7 8 9 might be represented by the word REPUBLICAN, where R=0, E=1 and so forth. The cost of each item is multiplied by the number on hand to determine the value of individual items, then totals for individual items are aggregated to determine the total value of the inventory at cost. The cost of goods figure of $150,000 shown in Exhibit 13–11 represents the recorded cost (or book value) of the merchandise that was sold during that period.

The primary advantage of the cost method is that it provides a simple basis for calculation for smaller retailers. With this method, they do not have to convert all figures to retail in order to value their inventory. Some accountants prefer the cost method, believing that it is a more realistic representation of the value of a retailer's merchandise on hand. Likewise, retailers who are willing to negotiate prices with customers (i.e., do not have a one-price policy for all) can use the cost codes on the tickets in bargaining with customers. This is based on the assumption that merchandise is "worth what you can get for it." For example, less desirable goods are marked down, reflecting a lower value. Goods in high demand and/or short supply are marked up, reflecting a higher value.

The cost method has several disadvantages, most related to changes in cost prices, market value, or customer demand. The cost method does not require a book inventory, which is a disadvantage in identifying shortages. It also requires a physical count of all goods, including the need to decipher cost codes.

Inventory may be valued one of two basic ways when using the cost method: Last In First Out or First In First Out. Each method has specific advantages and disadvantages as discussed below.

Last In First Out (LIFO) assumes that the inventory will be valued at the cost of the last units purchased. This method is not concerned with

Last In First Out (LIFO)
inventory is valued at cost of last units purchased

Customers are trying out this self-service scanner-equipped checkout unit in an A&P store. This future-oriented application is designed to improve customer convenience and satisfaction, while increasing the store's operational efficiency.

Shopping appeal for customers is enhanced by many aspects of the retail environment. Successful in-store retailers emphasize store design, inventory assortments, and technological advances to create attractive, efficient, effective, and satisfying shopping environments.

Features such as store exterior, interior decor and design, merchandise assortments, and promotional efforts are highly visible to the customer. Others, such as the technology that supports efficient retail operations, are not as evident. Inside the building, store layout and interior design set the stage for merchandise assortment. The merchandise, in turn, not only provides shopping opportunities for customers but also adds a design element to the store decor. Photos in this section represent some examples of the many types of store exteriors, interiors, merchandise assortments, and technology that are incorporated into retail strategies.

Often, customers form their first impression of a store from its exterior. The architectural design, entrance, use of signs, parking lot, landscaping, lighting, and other features affect a potential customer's attitude toward shopping in a particular store. Less obvious aspects of the store's exterior are related to locational characteristics and the appearance and reputation of surrounding stores.

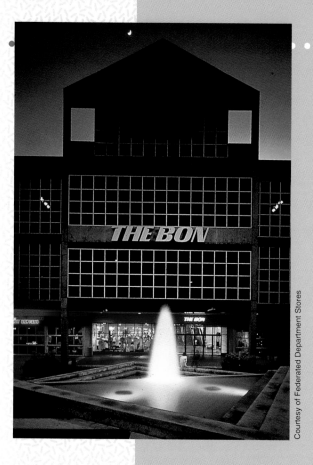

The initial store design is just the beginning; retailers also must change aspects of the store to meet the needs of their customers. Fred Meyer completed the most comprehensive store redesign program in its history in 1989. A store prototype for the 90s was designed with input from experts from all areas of the company. The design is based on the premise that shopping should be an entertaining activity within an easy-to-shop and friendly environment. The store is designed as a "stage," the fixtures as the "sets," and the merchandise and employees as the "stars." An example of Fred Meyer's redesign program is pictured below for the company's Stadium store, named for the nearby Civic Stadium and emphasizes a Roman coliseum theme.

The Bon, a division of Federated Department Stores, has integrated a lighted fountain into its exterior landscaping and decor. This creates an appealing contrast to the grid design on the front of the store. While it may or may not have been intentional, the forward tilt of the letters used in the store name gives a forward-looking, progressive impression.

As discussed within the context of site selection, retailers place considerable emphasis on target market characteristics when choosing store locations.

The exteriors of many stores are within the interiors of enclosed shopping centers or malls, such as this Cignal storefront shown above. Note that the window displays are integrated with the merchandise displays on the selling floor behind them. The total effect must be inviting to prospective customers, while meeting shopping center requirements. Specialty stores, such as Cignal, are often in high traffic mall locations where they have an opportunity to expose a large number of shoppers to their fashions through effective use of exterior window areas.

Once the customer enters the shopping environment, he or she will be influenced to buy not only because of the merchandise assortment, but also because of the attractiveness of its presentation and the ease of moving through the store to find desired items.

The interior design of this Merry Go Round store conveys a simple, contemporary look to complement the fashion-forward look of the apparel sold by the store. Note also that the customer demographics and lifestyles are reflected in mannequins, props, and apparel throughout the store.

Display fixtures are used effectively and efficiently in these Hartmarx stores, using all available space to display and store apparel inventory. The use of wall fixtures allows merchandise to be presented at multiple levels (below), with the highest at the back or along the side of the store where it can be seen easily from other areas of the store. Toward the center of a selling area (right), the lower display units give maximum visibility. The natural wood finish on the display units presents a masculine, tailored look that is consistent with most of the store's merchandise.

Sherwin Williams offers a large inventory of paint, stains, and related materials.

The produce section of food stores presents challenges to managers who want attractive displays of fruits and vegetables — products which often have natural shapes that can make such displays difficult. There is also a need to replenish the produce sections frequently to maintain their appeal to customers.

In an automobile-based economy, the variety of choices — styles, brands, models, and accompanying extras — add to the excitement of buying a new car.

Emphasis on healthy living, no preservatives, and buying in desired quantities has led many food retailers to sell foods in bulk, as shown here. The aisle is lined with barrels and other containers which give an impression of a wide selection that is more "natural" than the canned and packaged alternatives. The barrels serve as effective silent salesmen for customers who do not want prepackaged foods.

Bathroom fixtures such as wall or floor shelf units, hampers, and waste baskets are incorporated into this color-coordinated merchandise display for linens and bathroom accessories. This type of display often encourages impulse shopping as customers decide to buy related items shown together in a typical setting.

Fashionable housewares are displayed in shipping crate type fixtures to convey an impression of value at reasonable prices to Crate and Barrel customers. Others are shown in "natural settings" with related furniture and accessory items for suggestive selling. The arrangement of the items makes it easy for shoppers to coordinate a variety of goods and make multiple purchases in one transaction. Also note the vertical use of space for effective displays.

Retailers who carry narrow and deep merchandise assortments must find elements of contrast within similar shapes and designs for visual presentation on the selling floor. This shoe display uses color and geometric shapes to dramatize the merchandise in a relatively small display area.

J.C. Penney designed this children's wear department to appeal to its target customers. Small shoppers are greeted by the Cookie Monster who welcomes them to a colorful, fun environment with familiar objects such as the A-B-C building blocks.

Technological advances have affected all aspects of retailing such as inventory management, store design, and in-store promotion. The photos in this section represent but a few of the areas of retail management that have become more efficint and effective through the use of technology.

High-tech devices such as hand-held computers have made a major contribution to more efficient inventory management. In this photo (right), the shelf inventory status of English muffins is being recorded electronically. The captured information can be entered into the store's (or vendor's) computer to record sales, inventory on hand, and perhaps to place a new order.

Courtesy of Tandy Corp.

Courtesy of Catalina Marketing Corp.

Retailers and consumer goods manufacturers have benefitted from POS technology such as this checkout coupon machine that tailors promotional efforts to individual customers. Food companies previously used a shotgun approach to distributing coupons. With new technology, they can determine customers' purchase habits before they give them coupons — making this a highly targeted promotional effort that increases the likelihood of redemption. Coupons are automatically dispensed when a customer checks out. Sometimes the objective is to encourage the customer to buy more of the brand just purchased; other times, the intent is to encourage purchase of competing or complementary goods.

Courtesy of Catalina Marketing Corp.

Courtesy of US Order

Shopping at home has become easier. The Scanfone (left) is a combination bar-code scanner and telephone that enables customers to shop and pay bills via electronic home shopping. The customer uses a light pen that scans bar codes to order items from special bar-coded catalogs. After the grocery or catalog order is entered via Scanfone, it is registered immediately on a store's computer. The order is then pulled from the retailer's shelves, and delivered to the customer at a specified time. Payment can be made by running a credit card through the magnetic reader.

Computer technology has become a valuable promotional tool for retailers who sell interior design services and products. Here, a decorator experiments with a variety of upholstery fabric designs and colors using a computer assisted design (CAD) software program. Many combinations can be tried with a minimum effort and maximum customer satisfaction; as the customer can see immediately how the final product will appear.

Courtesy of Walter E. Smith Furniture, Chicago

Courtesy of Fingerhut Corp.

Computer technology has found many applications in retailing. In addition to the accounting, financial, inventory, and other important data base systems, computer software has been used to enhance the store design process, create store layouts, develop promotional materials, and many other applications. Here (left), desktop publishing is used to create direct mail catalogs: The consolidation of design, layout and typesetting functions represent a significant cost savings.

The technology behind the Vons Club card allows the consumer to take advantage of "cashless" electronic check-writing. The card (above) works in the same manner as a credit card or ATM card, but the Von's charges clear the customer's bank in two days.

Television shopping networks, combined with telecommunications technology, have satisfied the needs of many retail customers who do not have time to shop in stores, or who would rather shop at home. In this photo, the customer is calling in an order for an item shown on television shopping program.

Income Statement
For the Year Ending 12/31/19X1

Sales (1)		$300,000
Less returns and allowances		30,000
		$270,000
Net Sales		
Less cost of goods sold		
Beginning inventory (2)	$ 50,000	
Net purchases (3)	300,000	
Merchandise available	350,000	
Ending inventory	200,000	
Cost of goods sold		150,000
Gross profit		$120,000
Less operating expenses		
Advertising	30,000	
Rent	12,000	
Salaries	30,000	
Freight in	1,000	
Utilities	12,000	
Total operating expenses		85,000
Net Profit		$ 35,000

Exhibit 13–11

whether the first or last merchandise received is sold first. Since the prices of merchandise are usually increasing, this method will result in a higher cost of goods sold. A higher cost of goods sold will reduce the gross margin and subsequently the net profit, which will reduce the amount of taxes that the retailer will have to pay.

First In First Out (FIFO) assumes that the inventory will be valued at the cost of the first units sold. That is, the first merchandise received will be the first merchandise to be sold. This generally will result in a lower cost of goods sold, which will have the opposite effect of the LIFO method. That is, it will increase the gross margin and net profit figures, causing the retailer to pay higher taxes.

Exhibit 13–12 demonstrates how the LIFO and FIFO methods are used. As the exhibit illustrates, the valuation method used to calculate cost of goods sold can have a major impact on the bottom line (net profit) of the income statement. In a period of rising wholesale prices, LIFO results in a higher cost of goods sold and a lower gross margin. This, in turn, results in a lower tax liability. However, the choice of the LIFO versus the FIFO method is a complex decision that should consider the rate of inflation and inventory carrying costs.

FIRST IN FIRST OUT (FIFO)
inventory is valued at cost of first units sold

Product Liability and Package Tampering: A Merchandising Dilemma

Millions of dollars are spent every year on lawsuits against retailers and those who manufacture and distribute products that are involved in injury-producing accidents.

Product Liability

The Rand Corporation estimates that only 40 percent of the total expenditures in product liability cases finds its way to the injured person. The other 60 percent is spent on determining whether the accident could have been prevented by an alternate design or a properly manufactured product. At the manufacturer level, the improvement of product design is discouraged by the procedural rules that permit evidence of product improvements to be used to prove the defectiveness of a product.

A number of retailers have been involved in product liability cases. Jewel Food Stores, a subsidiary of American Stores Company, was the target of litigation by 13,000 class-action plaintiffs who sought $34 million to $100 million in punitive damages. The case was triggered by a 1985 salmonella epidemic arising from the sale of tainted milk in the company's supermarkets.

Although American Stores Company was found innocent of willful and wanton misconduct in connection with this incident, the company did agree to pay damages to some plaintiffs. In addition, American Stores and its insurers had paid over $16 million in defense and indemnity costs by early 1987.

Packaging Tampering

Food and drug retailers have been confronted with an increasing number of package tampering cases. In addition to lost sales and customer concerns, retailers may be involved in product liability litigation as well. In 1986 alone, there were 1,698 complaints about product tampering and over $1 billion worth of products were destroyed because of tampering-related emergencies. The average shopper was unaware of most of these incidents because a conspiracy of silence by manufacturers and retailers attempted to eliminate copycat tampering and avoid unduly alarming consumers.

While retailers want to offer their customers safe packaging, the procedures used to make a package tamper-resistant cause additional problems. The added protection causes problems for the elderly and arthritic when opening packages. More packaging adds to the solid waste disposal problem, and so on.

The food industry has shown a growing trend toward bulk sales of items such as baked goods and nuts. It is very difficult to provide protection for these items. The Food and Drug Administration decided to deal with food product tampering through statements on labels, consumer education, and emphasis on product tampering penalties.

Manufacturers are trying to correlate protection with current packaging procedures to minimize additional costs. Retailers may be able to improve control over tampering with increased store security such as electronic surveillance.

An example of the expense involved in actual and threatened product tampering is illustrated by Pepsi-Cola's 1986 threat of tampering with its Slice soft drink. The company removed the product from store shelves and gave refunds for returned products at a cost of $500,000. Additional costs were incurred for lost revenues to Pepsi-Cola and the retailers, as well as for additional advertising to recapture lost market share.

At the very least, product liability and package tampering incidents are disruptive to merchandising operations. More importantly, they have an impact on merchandise costs and level of consumer confidence in the products being sold by a retailer. What role should the retailer play in reducing or eliminating these problems?

Adapted from Fletcher, Meg (1987), "Jewel's Parent Not Liable for Punitive Damages: Jury," *Business Insurance* 51, no. 4, (January 26), 2, 74; "Food Packages Need Cues from Pharmaceutical Field to Thwart Product Tampering" (1987), *Marketing News* 21, no. 4, (February 13), 1, 24; Kanazawa, Sidney K. (1990), "Product Liability," *Agency Sales Magazine* 20, no. 7, (July), 54–59; "Tamper-Evidence in Perspective," *Packaging* 34, no. 7, (May), 34–36; Sloan, Pat (1986), "Marketers Seek Cure for Tampering Fears," *Advertising Age* 57, no. 45, (August 25), 3, 24–25; Stern, Walter (1989), "A Common-Sense View," *Packaging* 34, no. 7, (May), 37–39.

Retail Method of Inventory Valuation

The retail method calculates a dollar amount for inventory equal to the merchandise's retail value (i.e., the amount that can be charged to customers), plus any additional markups or markdowns that the store plans to add. The

Exhibit 13–12
LIFO and FIFO Calculations

. . . .

Sales Sept. 10, in units	1,000
Purchase Jan. 1	600 units @ $50/unit
Purchases Aug. 1	600 units @ $70/unit
Selling Price	$95

LIFO COGS: 600 units @ $70 + 400 units @ $50 = $62,000
FIFO COGS: 600 units @ $50 + 400 units @ $70 = $58,000

. . . .

	LIFO Income Statement	FIFO Income Statement
Sales	$ 95,000	$ 95,000
Less COGS	62,000	58,000
Gross Margin	$ 33,000	$ 37,000

. . . .

Exhibit 13–13
Retail Method of Inventory Valuation

. . . .

	Cost	Retail
Beginning inventory	$ 50,000	$ 83,333
+ Net purchases	300,000	500,000
+ Add markons	—	2,000
+ Freight-In	1,000	—
= Total merchandise available	$351,000	$585,333

Steps
1. Calculate cost complement.

$$\frac{\text{Cost}}{\text{Retail}} = \frac{\$351,000}{\$585,333} = .5997 = .60$$

2. Determine retail deductions and reductions.

Sales	$270,000
+ Discounts	8,000
+ Markdowns	20,000
+ Estimated shortages	2,000
Total	$300,000

3. Determine ending inventory value at retail and cost.

Total merchandise available	$585,333
– Deductions	300,000
= Ending inventory at retail	$285,333

Ending inventory at cost = Ending inventory at retail × cost complement
= 285, 333 × .60
= $171,200

Total merchandise available at cost	$351,000
– Ending inventory at cost	171,200
= Cost of Goods Sold (COGS)	$179,800

Sales	$270,000
– COGS	179,800
Gross Margin	$ 90,200

. . . .

steps in calculating the value of inventories when using the retail method are illustrated in Exhibit 13–13. All other factors held equal, the retail method will produce a higher value for the inventory.

Procedure for Using the Retail Method

In order to create an income statement, the retail value of the inventory must be converted to the cost value. Thus, the first step is to calculate the cost complement. The **cost complement** is the historical relationship between the cost value and the retail value of the inventory. Exhibit 13–14 shows each of the steps in the retail method.

First, the **cost value** of the inventory is calculated by adding the value of the beginning inventory (at cost) to net purchases (at cost) and freight in.

Then the **retail value** is determined by applying the store's customary markup (gross margin) to the cost values of the beginning inventory and net purchases. For example, let's assume that the retailer normally uses a 40 percent markup (at retail). The calculations are as follows:

$$\text{Retail selling price} = \frac{\text{Cost \$}}{(1-\text{markup \%})}$$

$$\text{Beginning inventory at retail} = \frac{\$500,000}{(1-.40)} = \$83,333$$

$$\text{Purchases at retail} = \frac{\$300,000}{(1-.40)} = \$500,000.$$

Next, additional markups are added in. Note that markups apply only to the retail figure.

The cost value is then divided by the retail value to find the cost complement. The net sales figure is multiplied by the cost complement (percentage) to determine the cost of goods sold.

A major disadvantage of using the retail method is that discrepancies may occur. Using figures from the income statement in Exhibit 13–11, the cost of goods sold (COGS) would be $179,800 using the retail method, as compared to the actual $150,000 based on the cost method and a physical inventory count. This difference could be interpreted to mean that the com-

COST COMPLEMENT

historical relationship between the cost value and the retail value of the inventory

COST VALUE

cost of beginning inventory plus net purchases and freight in

RETAIL VALUE

cost values of beginning inventory and net purchases plus store's customary markup

Exhibit 13–14
Cost Complement Calculation

	At Cost	At Retail
Beginning inventory	$ 50,000	$ 83,333
Net purchases	300,000	500,000
Additional markups	NA	2,000
Freight in	1,000	NA
Total	$351,000	$585,333

Cost complement: *

$$*\text{Cost complement} = \frac{\text{Total cost valuation}}{\text{Total retail valuation}} = \frac{\$351,000}{\$585,333} = .5996 = .60$$

pany has less ending inventory than they had expected. This phenomenon is called a "stock shortage," and will necessitate adjusting book entries by subtracting the amount of the shortage to reflect the actual inventory on hand. In the case of a stock overage, then the discrepancy will have to be added to the book value to reflect the actual physical inventory.

The following figures illustrate the differences in the value of ending inventory using the retail and cost methods with income statement data from Exhibit 13–11.

	Cost Method	Retail Method
Merchandise available for sale at cost	$350,000	$351,000
– Cost of goods sold	150,000	179,800
= Ending inventory at cost	$200,000	$171,200

The primary advantage of the retail method over the cost method of inventory valuation is ease of frequent calculation for income statement data. However, the method is based on average markups, and is dependent upon a detailed accounting or bookkeeping system to provide complete and accurate data. It also requires the extra step of converting ending retail value of inventory to cost to calculate gross profit.

Control of Merchandising Operations

Financial Control

The final, and perhaps most important, phase of the inventory management process is financial control. In this phase, the chief concern is with monitoring the inventory purchases. The basic tools to accomplish this purpose include breakeven point (BEP), inventory turnover, and gross margin return-on-investment (GMROI).

BREAKEVEN POINT The **breakeven point** is a financial measure that indicates the amount of sales required to cover fixed investments. It can be used to help determine what types of products should be sold. The basic requirements to calculate breakeven are fixed costs, unit variable costs and selling price.

Fixed costs refer to the capital that must be invested in order to stock a particular merchandise line. Fixed costs do not vary with activity and will be the same whether the retailer sells one unit or one hundred units. Examples of fixed costs include merchandise displays, rent or lease payments, taxes, insurance, and initial setup costs.

Variable costs are expenses that increase or decrease as volume goes up or down. The primary example of variable costs is the unit merchandise cost and personal selling costs that vary with sales volume.

Selling price is calculated according to the retailer's markup criteria. Pricing calculations will be discussed extensively in the next chapter.

BREAKEVEN POINT
amount of sales required to cover fixed investments

FIXED COSTS
capital that must be invested in order to stock a particular merchandise line

VARIABLE COSTS
expenses that increase or decrease as volume goes up or down

SELLING PRICE
amount charged to customer that is calculated according to retailer's markup criteria

INVENTORY TURNOVER
number of times per year that average amount invested in inventory is depleted to "zero"

Basically, the breakeven point lets the retailer know how many units will have to be sold to recover the fixed expenses, i.e., the point where expenses equal revenues. Let us say, for example, we are evaluating two retail lines, one of which will be added to our stock. The information on the two product lines is as follows:

	Product A	Product B
Fixed costs	$10,000	$15,000
Variable costs	50	60
Selling price	100	120

$$BEP = \frac{Fixed\ Costs}{Selling\ Price - Variable\ Costs}$$

$$BEP\ Product\ A = \frac{\$10,000}{\$100 - \$50} = 200\ Units$$

$$BEP\ Product\ B = \frac{\$15,000}{\$120 - \$60} = 250\ Units$$

As the example illustrates, Product A will break even with fewer sales than will Product B. All other factors held equal, Product A would be the best one to stock.

The breakeven model also can be used to determine the level of sales that will be required to achieve a desired profit level. This can be done by adding the desired profit level to the fixed costs. Using the above example, let us assume that the retailer wants to earn $25,000 profit from the new product line. The new breakeven points are:

$$BEP = \frac{Fixed\ Costs + Profit\ Level}{Selling\ Price - Variable\ Costs}$$

$$BEP\ Product\ A = \frac{\$10,000 + \$25,000}{100 - 50} = 700\ Units$$

$$BEP\ Product\ B = \frac{\$15,000 + 25,000}{120 - 60} = 667\ Units.$$

Now, with the profit figure included in the model, Product B becomes more attractive because the per unit contribution margin (selling price – variable costs) is higher.

INVENTORY TURNOVER   Another useful tool for evaluating the performance of inventory is **inventory turnover,** which tells a retailer how many times during the year the amount invested in inventory has turned over, or depleted to zero. This formula can be calculated by dividing total sales by average inventory on hand. All figures must either be in cost dollars, or in retail dollars, or in units; they may not be combined. There are three basic calculations to arrive at the turnover ratio. To determine the turnover in dollars, one can divide the net yearly sales by the average dollar value of inventory on hand. Either retail or cost values for merchandise sold and for inventory may be used. However, the formula requires that both sales and inventory be stated in like terms, i.e., either both at cost or both at retail:

$$\text{Inventory turnover (at retail)} = \frac{\textit{Total annual retail sales}}{\textit{Average inventory on hand at retail}}$$

$$\text{Inventory turnover (at cost)} = \frac{\textit{Cost of goods sold for the year}}{\textit{Average inventory on hand at cost}}.$$

Inventory turnover also can be calculated by dividing the number of units sold during the year by the average inventory (units) on hand. This will give the turnover in units:

$$\text{Inventory turnover (in units)} = \frac{\text{Total units sold during year}}{\text{Average units on hand}}.$$

Stockturn rate will be the same, regardless of whether it is calculated at cost or at retail or in units, as illustrated in the following example. Assume that each unit costs $6.00 and retails for $10.00. Annual sales total 100 units, and average inventory on hand is 10 units.

$$\text{Inventory turnover (at retail)} = \frac{(\$10 \times 100 \text{ units})}{(\$10 \times 10 \text{ units})} = \frac{\$1,000}{\$100} = 10 \text{ times}$$

$$\text{Inventory turnover (at cost)} = \frac{(\$6 \times 100 \text{ units})}{(\$6 \times 10 \text{ units})} = \frac{\$600}{\$60} = 10 \text{ times}$$

$$\text{Inventory turnover (in units)} = \frac{100 \text{ units}}{10 \text{ units}} = 10 \text{ times}$$

Using the retail figures provided for yearly net sales ($270,000) in Exhibit 13–11 and average monthly stock ($29,167) calculated in Exhibit 12–9, page 498, it can be seen that the inventory turnover for this retailer is 9.25 times (i.e., $270,000/$29,167). This indicates that the inventory on hand was reduced to zero nine times during the year ("on paper"), or that each dollar invested in inventory worked 9.25 times during the year.

Turnover ratios, such as that calculated above can be used to compare the efficiency of one retailer's operation with that of another. It can tell managers how they are doing relative to the competition, when compared to published industry data. There are distinct advantages to having a healthy stock turnover ratio: lower capital requirements on the average to stock the store (and therefore, higher cash flow); lower inventory holding costs; and fresher, more appealing merchandise. A grocery store, for example, would expect to turn produce, meat and dairy product inventories frequently. However, there are disadvantages to a high turnover rate, as well. The retailer may not have an adequate selection for customers, or have stockouts on important items. In addition, ordering goods in smaller quantities can result in higher merchandise costs and lower profits. Some retailers, such as jewelry and furniture stores, have relatively low turnover ratios because they must keep a broad selection of relatively expensive merchandise on hand.

GROSS MARGIN RETURN ON INVESTMENT (GMROI)   A third tool in evaluating inventory purchases is the **gross margin return on**

investment (GMROI). The GMROI combines the inventory turnover discussed above with a gross margin ratio to show the relationship between operating profits and inventory investment. Gross margin return on investment is an important strategic planning and control tool because it captures the trade-offs between high markup and high stock turnover. Gross margin (net sales – cost of goods sold) is actually a retailer's average markup when expressed as a percent of sales. Retailers with high markups usually do not depend on high volume turnover ratios to generate profits. Similarly, those who depend on high sales volume generally cannot achieve this at prices based on high markup percentages.

In the following formula, gross margin (net sales minus cost of goods sold) divided by net sales is a measure of profitability that takes into consideration only those costs that are related to the merchandise itself. Net sales divided by average inventory at cost is an asset turnover ratio, where merchandise is the only asset considered.

$$\text{Gross margin return on investment} =$$

$$\frac{\textit{Gross margin in dollars}}{\textit{Net sales}} \times \frac{\textit{Net sales}}{\textit{Average inventory at cost}}$$

$$= \frac{\textit{Gross margin in dollars}}{\textit{Average inventory at cost}}$$

For example, GMROI can be calculated using the net sales and gross margin figures included in Exhibit 13–11 and the average monthly inventory figure from Exhibit 12–9:

$$\text{Gross margin return on inventory} = \frac{120{,}000}{270{,}000} \times \frac{270{,}000}{29{,}167} = \frac{120{,}000}{29{,}167} = 4.11$$

In other words, the retailer generates a gross margin of $4.11 for each dollar that is invested in inventory on the average. The resulting GMROI can be compared with published data to determine how the retailer is performing relative to large competitors. Such data is available from sources such as National Retail Merchants Association (NRMA) and Dun & Bradstreet. Small retailers may find it difficult to make direct comparisons to other businesses of the same size. However, performance data and recommended ratios may be available from trade associations in the supermarket, hardware, and other retail industries. Examples of actual performance ratios for selected retail industries are provided in Exhibit 13–15.

SUMMARY

A retailer's merchandising philosophy is an extension of the company's business philosophy. It guides long-term commitments and short-term decisions within the context of a dynamic operating environment, where it is necessary to monitor trends and anticipate changes.

GROSS MARGIN RETURN ON INVESTMENT (GMROI)
inventory turnover combined with gross margin ratio; shows relationship between operating profits and inventory investment

Exhibit 13-15

Selected Industry Performance Ratios: Gross Margin Return on Inventory Investment (GMROI) and Stock Turnover

	Gross Margin Return per $ of Inventory at Cost		Stock Turnover (at retail)	
	Typical	Middle Range	Typical	Middle Range
Department Stores				
Sales under $100 million	2.22	1.94–2.53	2.47	2.35–2.63
Sales over $100 million	2.08	1.90–2.25	2.55	2.42–3.15
Sales $100–$500 million	2.18	2.01–2.27	2.55	2.33–2.98
All department stores	2.09		2.55	
Specialty Stores				
Sales under $20 million	2.34	1.69–3.10	2.72	1.88–3.78
Sales over $20 million	2.22	1.78–2.93	2.47	2.01–2.98
Sales $20–$100 million	2.00	1.55–2.79	2.60	2.10–2.88
Sales over $100 million	2.22	1.98–3.02	2.33	2.12–3.04
All specialty stores	2.22		2.47	

Inventory Productivity for Female Apparel: Department Stores Versus Specialty Stores

	Gross Margin $ Return per $ Average Cost Inventory		Stock Turn (times) at Retail	
	Median	Superior	Median	Superior
Department Stores				
Sales over $2 million	2.8	3.2	3.2	3.5
Sales $2–10 million	2.4	2.7	2.7	3.1
Sales $10–50 million	2.9	3.9	3.1	3.6
Sales $50–100 million	3.0	3.8	3.3	3.6
Sales over $100 million	3.0	3.2	3.4	3.7
Specialty Stores				
Sales over $1 million	2.3	3.1	3.1	3.4
Sales $1–10 million	2.2	2.7	3.1	3.8
Sales over $10 million	2.9	2.9	3.1	3.4
All chain specialty stores (20 or more stores)	3.8	4.1	3.9	4.1

SOURCE OF DATA: *Financial & Operating Results of Department & Specialty Stores in 1989*, 1990 Edition. New York, N.Y.: National Retail Federation; *Merchandising and Operating Results of Department & Specialty Stores in 1987*, 63rd Edition (1988), New York, N.Y.: Financial Executives Division, National Retail Merchants Association.

The buying function requires both an organizational structure and qualified personnel. The structure may be formal or informal, centalized or decentralized, and may vary in degree of specialization and departmentalization. Key merchandising personnel include merchandise managers, buyers, department managers, and support staffs.

Merchandise mix and assortment decisions must be made with a clear understanding of customer needs, competitive activities, and other environmental concerns. Product concepts extend beyond the physical product to include both tangible and intangible benefits to the buyer. Merchandising strategies involve decisions about the variety and assortment of products that will be made available to customers, and the width (number of noncompeting lines) and depth (level of support for each line) of these assortments. These concepts are combined to develop an overall product strategy.

Channel strategies are concerned with how and where the retailer buys goods and services. The buying process begins with obtaining product information and then identifying, contacting, and evaluating sources of supply. An important aspect of the buying process is the retailer's ability to negotiate with vendors for the best terms of sale possible. Once the terms of sale have been agreed upon, purchase orders are placed. It may be necessary to follow up on orders, prior to the time they are received into the store, checked, marked, and prepared for the selling floor. The success of channel strategies is largely dependent upon the nature and strength of the relationships between buyers and their vendors.

The value of inventory on hand can be computed by either the cost method or the retail method. The cost method uses the recorded cost (book value) of goods sold during a given period, all of which may be valued at the cost of the last units (LIFO) or first units (FIFO) purchased. The retail method values inventory according to the cost complement (a historical relationship between the cost and retail values), making calculations easier, but often producing higher inventory values.

Several basic tools are used to maintain financial control over merchandising operations: breakeven point, where expenses equal revenues; inventory turnover ratio, the number of times each dollar of inventory investment is used during the year; and gross margin return on investment (GMROI), which relates profits to inventory investment.

Questions for Review and Comprehension

1. Discuss some ways that merchandise assortments carried by All Wrapped Up, a coat and suit retailer, might be affected by macroenvironmental factors.

2. Give examples of merchandising strategies that have been used by leading retailers to capitalize on—or overcome—environmental influences.

3. Describe the relationship between a retailer's mission statement (generally found in the company's annual report or recruiting literature), merchandising philosophy, and merchandise assortment decisions.

4. Compare and contrast the organizational structure for the buying function in a large versus a small retail firm. Include the following in your discussion:
   a. a general job description of the various merchandising personnel who are involved in this process
   b. the major factors to consider in designing an organizational structure for merchandising activities (degree of formality, centralization and specialization)

5. Outline a potential product mix for (a) a grocery store, (b) a fast-food restaurant, (c) an electronics superstore, and (d) an auto parts store. For each type of retailer, identify a specific (1) *product* and (2) *product line* within the broader product mix, and discuss several perceptions that consumers might have in each case.

6. Discuss the merchandise variety and assortment within the context of (a) a major mass merchandiser such as Target and (b) a small independent general merchandise store. What is the trade-off between variety and focus?

7. Explain what is meant by width and depth of merchandise assortments. Give examples of retailers who are most apt to represent the following merchandise assortment strategies: (a) wide and deep, (b) narrow and deep, (c) wide and shallow, and (d) narrow and shallow.

8. Name some of the major trends in the operation of distribution channels that have affected how retailers buy merchandise. Include the role of channel power, competition for retail space, supplier assistance to retailers, technology and service in determining buying practices, and various strategies used by retail buyers to maximize their clout with suppliers.

9. A small business retailer has just opened the Gift Horse, a jewelry and gift store. Advise him as to the various sources of goods that are available to him, i.e., who can he buy from?

10. The Gift Horse store owner in Question #9 has identified several reliable sources of supply. Now he needs your help in determining the timing of his purchase orders. Provide him with a list of major factors to consider in making the when-to-buy decision, along with an explanation of why each is important.

11. The Green Goddess Nursery wishes to maintain an adequate supply of bagged fertilizer for its customers at all times throughout a six month selling season. During this time, Green Goddess sells an average of 25 bags of fertilizer a day, and has an order lead time of 10 days from its supplier.

    a. Given the figures above, calculate the appropriate reorder point (without safety stock).

    b. Assuming the manager desires a safety stock of 20 bags of fertilizer, given the same sales and lead time, what is the recommended reorder point with safety stock?

12. The Green Goddess Nursery estimates that it will sell 120 bird houses during a year, each bird house costs $12.00 and the cost of each order is $4.00. The manager estimates that breakage, insurance, invested capital, and pilferage will amount to 10 percent of the cost. Calculate the economic order quantity based on these estimates. Explain why the resulting quantity may need to be adjusted.

13. Explain what is meant by just-in-time delivery (JIT) and why it has become an increasingly important factor in merchandise management.

14. Name the factors that contribute to a retailer's net profit, and describe how a buyer can affect the contribution made by each factor.

15. Describe and give a specific example of each of the steps in the buying process. Is any one step more important than the others? Why or why not?

16. Briefly discuss the negotiation process between retail buyers and vendors in terms of each of the following: (a) discounts (quantity, trade, seasonal, cash), (b) datings (EOM, DOI, ROG, advance and extra dating, anticipation), (c) shipping points and transportation methods, (d) promotional allowances, (e) consignment, (f) return privileges and other assistance, and (g) private label and licensing agreements.

17. Debate the benefits of the cost method versus the retail method of inventory valuation. Include the basic premises, advantages, and disadvantages of each method.

18. Outline the steps involved in using the retail method of inventory valuation. Given the figures below, calculate the following (show all work):

    a. total goods available for sale (at cost and at retail)

    b. cost complement

    c. retail deductions and reductions

    d. ending inventory value at retail

    e. ending inventory value at cost

    f. gross margin

The retailer's beginning inventory was $120,000 at retail and $72,000 at cost. Purchases valued at $60,000 at retail and $36,000 at cost were received during the period. Returns to vendor totaled $6,000 at retail. Freight charges for incoming merchandise totaled $2,000. Markdowns totaled $5,000 at retail. Net sales were $90,000 after customer returns and employee discounts amounted to $4,000. A physical inventory taken at the end of the period indicated a stock shortage of $3,000.

19. State why it is useful to calculate a breakeven point as one aspect of financial control in the inventory management process. An appliance retailer is determining which of two brands of washing machines he should carry—the Sudso-Matic or the Laundry Lady which have the following costs and selling prices:

	Sudso-Matic	Laundry Lady
Fixed costs	$12,000	$14,000
Variable costs	75	90
Selling price	400	475

    a. Calculate the breakeven point for each brand based on the above data.

    b. Calculate the breakeven point if the appliance retailer desires a profit level of $30,000 from the chosen line of washing machines.

20. If a record store has total annual sales of $120,000, and monthly inventory on hand for January through December is $200,000, $150,000, $100,000, $120,000, $130,000, $100,000, $110,000, $120,000, $100,000, $180,000, $140,000 and $150,000, calculate the retailer's annual inventory turnover rate. Interpret the result. Discuss several ways that inventory turnover ratios indicate the efficiency of a retail operation as a determinant of profitability. Is a high inventory ratio always beneficial? Why or why not?

21. Provide a rationale for using gross margin return on investment (GMROI) as a tool for evaluating inventory purchases. For the record store retailer described in Question #20 above, calculate the GMROI if the retailer's gross margin is $40,000. Interpret the resulting ratio.

References

"America's Most Competitive Companies" (1987), *Business Week* (October 5) 86–87.

Atchison, Sandra D. (1987), "Cashing in on the Lean, Mean Buffalo," *Business Week* (June 8), 126–127.

"B. Dalton Punches into Software Business" (1984), *Chain Store Age Executive* (May), 14.

"Business Bulletin" (1989), *The Wall Street Journal* (January 26), 1.

Carlson, Eugene (1990), "Video Stores Try Sharper Focus in Market Glut," *The Wall Street Journal* (July 2), B1, B2.

Charlier, Marj (1989), "New Kinds of Beer to Tap a Flat Market," *The Wall Street Journal* (April 20), B1.

"Condom Makers Aim at Women Buyers" (1988), *The Wall Street Journal* (June 21), 33.

Crossen, Cynthia (1988), "B. Dalton Plans to Shut Out Small Publishers," *The Wall Street Journal* (April 22), 19.

Deveny, Kathleen (1990), "Marketing: Swatch Says It's Time to Reach Older Crowd," *The Wall Street Journal* (July 2), B1.

Dunkin, Amy and Stephen Phillips (1988), "This Season, Fashion Is Anything That Sells," *Business Week* (October 31), 157, 159.

Feinberg, Samuel (1989), "The Relevance of Brand Names: How They Rate," *Women's Wear Daily* (February 10), 9.

Forrester, R. A. (1987), "Buying for Profitability," *Retail & Distribution Management* (May/June), 25–26.

Freedman, Alix (1988), "Supermarkets Push Private-Label Lines," *The Wall Street Journal* (November 15), B1.

Helm, Leslie (1987), "Reebok's Recent Blisters Seem to Be Healing," *Business Week* (August 3), 62.

Horrigan, Kevin (1985), "L. L. Bean Built Empire Around Illusion, Mainly," *St. Louis Post Dispatch* 1D.

Layfield, Denise (1987), "They Practice What They Sell," *Southern Illinoisan* (October 13), 17.

Norris, Eileen (1986), "Companies Bring Logos and Profits Full Circle," Special Report: Corporate Licensing, *Advertising Age* (June 9), S-1, S-15.

Sabin, Rob (1987), "Heavyweight Strategies for Today's Buyer," *MART* (September), 7–9.

"Sears, Roebuck & Co. Plans to Discontinue McKids in 1st Quarter" (1991), *The Wall Street Journal* (January 11), B4.

Swasy, Alecia (1989), "Firms Grow More Cautious About New-Product Plans," *The Wall Street Journal* (March 9), B1, B8.

Toys "R" Us, Annual Report, Year Ended February 1, 1987.

Toys "R" Us, Career Brochure, 1988.

"Tracking Where the Goods Are in a JIT Environment" (1987), *Stores* (May), 45.

"Treating the Retailers as Partners" (1989), *Fortune* (December 18), 80.

Treece, James B. (1987), "Why All Those City Folks Are Buying Pickups," *Business Week* (July 13), 102–103.

Tyndall, Gene R. (1988), "Supply-Chain Management Innovations Spur Long-Term Strategic Retail Alliances," *Marketing News* (December 19), 10.

Wal-Mart, 1988 Annual Report.

"Watches: Is There Life After Swatch?" (1985), *Chain Store Age* (May), 61.

Weber, Joseph (1990), "Getting Cozy With Their Customers," *Business Week* (January 8), 86.

Zellner, Wendy (1987), "Why Hush Puppies Need Some Fancy Footwork," *Business Week* (August 3), 64.

Zellner, Wendy (1989), "The Coming Traffic Jam in the Luxury Lane," *Business Week* (January 30), 78.

CHAPTER *Thirteen*

PRICING STRATEGIES

CHAPTER Fourteen

Outline

Pricing and the Retailing Environment: An Overview

Internal Factors Affecting Price

Pricing Strategies

External Factors Affecting Price

Summary

Learning Objectives

After studying this chapter, the student will be able to:

1. Understand the relationships between a retailer's pricing policies, financial objectives, and pricing strategies.
2. Describe the impact of external environmental influences on pricing decisions.
3. Discuss the relationship between pricing decisions and other retail mix decisions regarding product assortments, store location and setting, promotion, and services.
4. Explain the major types of financial objectives associated with pricing policies.
5. Differentiate between a cost-oriented and a demand-oriented approach to determining retail prices.
6. Understand the potential impact of other channel members on retailers and pricing decisions.

VYING FOR "SHARE-OF-STOMACH": FAST-FOOD DISCOUNTS

● ●

REMARKABLE RETAILER

Some of the best bargains in town can be found in fast-food restaurants. McDonald's, Wendy's, Kentucky Fried Chicken, Taco Bell, and Hardee's are among those stepping up discounting efforts in the $60 billion fast-food industry. Although McDonald's has a $1 billion marketing budget—about twice that of No. 2 Burger King Corp.—the company is vulnerable in some sluggish markets, where it has been forced to compete on the basis of price discounts, such as Quarter Pounders at 99 cents (regularly $1.90).

McDonald's continuously fights for market share in an industry where sales growth slowed to 6 percent in 1989, down from double-digit growth in the late 1970s. However, the chain is concerned about the potential negative effect of too much price slashing on its products in the eyes of consumers. McDonald's is image conscious, and does not believe that discounting prices on a Whopper or Big Mac is the answer in the long term. Competition does not come from other fast-food chains alone. Supermarket delis, convenience stores, gas stations, home delivery, and products that can be prepared in the microwave all compete for the same customer dollars. Another source of competition is the trend toward eating at home,

leading to home delivery by chains such as Kentucky Fried Chicken.

McDonald's has turned to new products (e.g., pizza, low-fat milkshakes) and new markets (e.g., hospitals, museums, airports) in an effort to compete on a nonprice basis. On the average, McDonald's invests about $1.4 million in each new company-owned startup. When this capital outlay is combined with rising labor costs, and customers who are increasingly finicky about what they will eat and how much they will pay, the company that wants to gain sales and market share will have to let profit margins slip a bit, while making up for this through increasing sales volume. In this environment, pricing strategies are a double-edged sword—they must be low enough to appeal to customers, and high enough to recover costs and return a profit to the company.

In spite of their desire to avoid price discounting, McDonald's and many other fast food chains are caught between two major forces. On one side super-discounters such as Mexican chains and no-frills, drive-through-only hamburger outlets attract bargain hungry fast-food customers who are not brand loyal. On the other side, aging baby-boomers are losing their appetites for burgers and fries on the run, and are switching to casual restaurants that offer a healthier menu, table service, and a more relaxed atmosphere at prices that are relatively competitive with McDonald's. Although fast-food restaurants, such as McDonald's in Chicago's Northwestern food court, have extended their menu choices to include healthier fare (e.g., yogurt, salads, soups), discount burger menus are still needed to keep and win back customers. Late in 1990, McDonald's adopted a "value pricing"

A McDonald's restaurant in Miami

COURTESY OF MEDCENTERS

strategy to remain competitive with Taco Bell and Wendy's, among others. Each of the chains marked down several menu items to well below $1. However, high margin items such as soft drinks, french fries, salads, and entree sandwiches have not been discounted much, if at all, in an effort to maintain profitability.

Adapted from Bremner, Brian and Gail DeGeorge (1989), "McDonald's Stoops to Conquer," *Business Week* (October 30), 120, 124; Gibson, Richard (1990), "Discount Menu is Coming to McDonald's as Chain Tries to Win Back Customers," *The Wall Street Journal* (November 30), B1, B6. Gibson, Richard (1990), "Super-Cheap and Midpriced Eateries Bite Fast-Food Chains from Both Sides," *The Wall Street Journal* (June 22), B1, B5; Rigdon, Joan (1990), "Fast-Food Chains in Hungrier Times, Concoct Menus to Lure Penny-Pinchers," *The Wall Street Journal* (November 7), B1, B6.

PRICING AND THE RETAILING ENVIRONMENT: AN OVERVIEW

The concepts of price and product are closely related in the minds of consumers and in the development of merchandising strategies. Therefore, many of the relationships between the Integrative Retail Information Model (IRIM) components and merchandise management described in the previous chapter also apply to pricing merchandise. Exhibit 14–1 illustrates the

Exhibit 14–1
Pricing and the Environment
• •
SOURCE: Anderson and Parker 1988

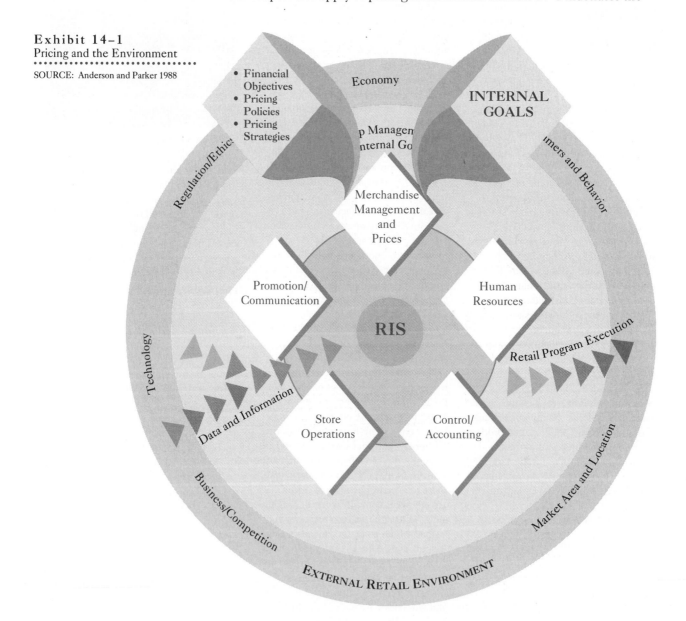

relationship between pricing and the environment. Again, data inputs are needed from both the external and internal environments to enable the Retail Information System to provide useful information to managers who must make pricing decisions.

External Environment: Influences on Pricing Policies

A retailer's pricing policies and strategies are affected by factors in its external environment: consumers and market behavior, competitors and suppliers, legal and political actions, and economic realities. Further, these forces tend to interact with the others to magnify their collective effect on the prices customers pay at the cash register. External influences are introduced briefly in this section and discussed in more detail later in the chapter.

Consumer markets play a major role in the pricing process. When customers exhibit a high level of demand for a store's products, particularly when supplies are limited, prices are driven upward. Conversely, situations of low demand and plentiful supply drive prices downward. The retailer's decision to adopt a particular pricing strategy or profit margin also must consider the cost and profitability associated with serving an identified market.

Pricing strategies are influenced by customer lifestyles and demographics, psychological responses, and shopping habits. Retail price points and price ranges must be acceptable to the store's targeted consumers and compatible with their shopping behavior. Consumer responses to prices are affected by factors such as their attitudes toward high versus low prices, sensitivity to "deals," willingness to pay for convenience or services, store loyalty, lifestyle, socioeconomic level, and disposable income.

Ongoing *location and trading area analysis* provides additional information about the store's customers that may help in identifying the best pricing strategy. For example, neighborhoods may change and populations may shift, bringing new residents who respond differently to the store's prices. The amount that a retailer can charge for an item is affected by the image associated with physical aspects of a store, such as its condition and location.

Business influences on retail prices come from a number of directions. Actions and reactions by competitors, vendors and suppliers, channel intermediaries, and service providers are taken in a constantly changing and sometimes volatile environment. Therefore, they must be monitored carefully, allowing the retailer to forecast possible effects on retail prices under different sets of assumptions. To illustrate, the pressure on retail prices and profit margins comes from two major sources: (1) lower prices by competitors, leading to customer expectations of lower prices in other stores and (2) increased merchandise costs and operating expenses.

Retailers are constantly seeking competitive advantage over one another, perhaps with new operating formats, reduced prices (perhaps even price wars), increased services, or promotional efforts. Vendors may exercise considerable control over retail prices, particularly if they are large enough and their products are important enough. Other channel members may make decisions that affect retail prices, such as the increased gasoline prices resulting from the Arab oil embargo in 1973.

Service providers may be confronted with situations that increase prices, such as labor strikes in transportation companies. Suppliers' prices may require adjustment due to conditions beyond their control. The summer drought of 1988 reduced the crop yield from midwestern U.S. farmlands, increasing prices of grains and other crops. The drought also reduced water transportation on the Mississippi River and other waterways, requiring shipments to be offloaded from boats and barges to more expensive trucks and railcars, passing on increased prices to retailers and consumers.

Legal and political influences on pricing decisions generally are in the form of rules and restraints. Regulatory constraints on the amount that can be charged for a product (at all channel levels) have been legislated by federal, state, and local governments. These regulations help ensure fair prices to consumers and prevent unfair business activities (particularly where either the buyer or seller has more "clout" than the other). Government regulation of interest rates and the money supply has an indirect effect on prices.

Macro- and micro-economic conditions also influence retail prices. Macro-environmental conditions are more global, pertaining to the industry, the nation, or the world. Micro-environmental conditions pertain to the individual firm. In both cases, economic forecasts provide information for estimating sales levels, merchandise costs, and industry trends. Economic influences have been evident in areas such as fluctuating retail sales, inventory levels, and end-of-year profits. Economic downturns may result in reduced consumer spending, leading to lower prices to move inventories and lower profit margins.

Internal Environment: Influences on Pricing Policies

All corporate levels, functions, and operating divisions within the retail firm have an impact on pricing strategies. Major influences within the internal environment include first the retailer's mission and business philosophy, internal goals (i.e., financial and marketing objectives), and company policies, all of which are interdependent. Financial objectives are expressed as desired levels of sales, profits, return-on-investment, and other internal goals, and are discussed in greater detail later in the chapter. Pricing policies are related to the financial objectives, providing a basis for pricing strategies that will allow sufficient sales volume and markup to achieve the retailer's goals.

RELATIONSHIP BETWEEN PRICE AND FINANCIAL STATEMENTS   The markups used by retailers have a major impact upon the financial statements. Price affects demand levels, gross margin, profit, and other elements in the income statement.

Exhibit 14–2 demonstrates how different markups affect the financial performance of a retailer. The first effect shown is the influence of price on demand. At a low retail price of $100, consumers will be willing to purchase 1,000 units. This quantity will allow the retailer to take advantage of a price break from the manufacturer, which lowers the cost of goods sold. Also, at a lower rate, the retailer may be able to decrease expenses for promotions and sales force.

Notice, however, that the low price is not always best. The retailer will be able to make the most profit (gross margin) at a retail price of $150, although both the cost of goods sold and operating expenses are higher.

Exhibit 14–2
Relationship Between Pricing and Financial Statement Items

Retail Price (Unit)	Cost (Unit)	Retail Markup %	Demand (Units)	Inventory Units
$100	$ 67	33%	1,000	1,100
150	75	50	800	880
200	90	55	500	550
225	93	59	300	330
250	100	60	200	220

Retail Price	Gross Margin ($)	Promotion Expenses	Sales Force Expenses	Dollar Profit
$100	$33,000	$10,000	$5,000	$18,000
150	60,000	12,000	6,000	42,000
200	55,000	10,000	5,000	40,000
225	39,600	6,750	3,375	29,475
250	30,000	5,000	2,500	22,500

Analysis of the *effect* of each pricing strategy allows the retailer to determine retail prices that will maximize number of units demanded, gross margin in dollars, dollar profit or other objective.

The key implications of understanding the relationship between price and financial statements are threefold. One, know the target market, and the degree of price elasticity associated with particular products. Two, study the cost structure of the merchandise. Three, create pro forma income statements to find the "optimal" price level.

RELATIONSHIP BETWEEN PRICE AND THE RETAILING MIX

The relationship of price to the other major components of the retailing mix (product, promotion, and place) can be expressed in terms of the influence of each of the store's functional areas: product (merchandise management); promotion and services (promotion/communication and human resources); place/location (store operations); and indirectly, control and accounting. All factors in the retailing mix interact with one another to create a synergistic effect on pricing strategies, as discussed next. (See Exhibit 14–3.)

Merchandise managers and buyers plan *product assortment*s in accordance with store policies and image. Pricing strategies are affected by product characteristics such as the type of goods offered (specialty, shopping, or convenience goods), stage in the product life cycle, quality of product, services and other intangibles available with the product, exclusivity, and innovativeness. Company policies regarding the sale of imported versus domestic goods, and national versus generic or private labels also have an impact on pricing. Imported goods require pricing strategies compatible with the quality and image of the products; some are low-priced, high-turnover items, while others are more prestigious, high-priced items.

National brands command higher prices than generic or private labels (although they may have a lower profit margin). Additionally, prices are set to allow for estimated reductions from the original retail price due to discounts, markdowns, and shrinkage, and to cover the costs of transporting, handling, and selling the merchandise. The negotiation process between retail buyers and vendors is a primary determinant of retail prices, since a lower cost of

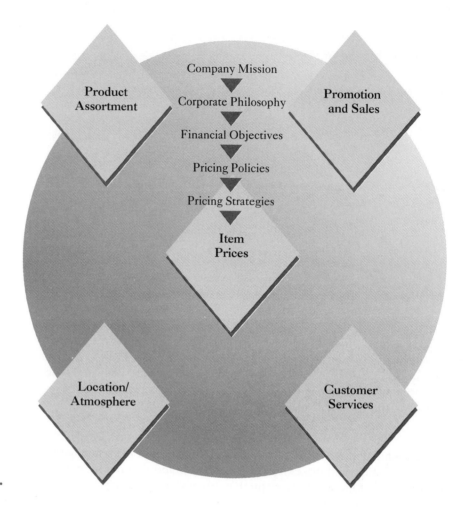

Company Mission

Corporate Philosophy

Financial Objectives

Pricing Policies

Pricing Strategies

Product Assortment

Promotion and Sales

Item Prices

Location/ Atmosphere

Customer Services

Exhibit 14–3
Interaction of Price and Retail Mix

goods sold allows the retailer more freedom in establishing prices charged to customers.

The *place* where merchandise is sold, i.e., the location and store setting project an image that is closely related to prices that customers are willing to pay. A new, upscale, fashionably decorated store can command higher prices than a dingy, out-of-date, poorly decorated store selling the same merchandise. The store's accessibility and shopping convenience also have an impact on prices. Customers often will pay higher prices for savings of shopping time and effort.

The *promotion* aspect of the retail mix affects prices in two ways. First, advertising, personal selling, and other promotional tools are used to provide product and price information to customers, encouraging them to accept the store's pricing strategies—whether high or low, regular or sale prices. The image projected by promotional efforts should be consistent with the prices charged. Second, promotional efforts have a price-tag attached. A retail salesforce, media advertising, direct mail, special events, visual merchandising, and other methods of communicating with customers add to operating expenses. Prices must be high enough to cover these expenses and allow for a reasonable profit; or promotion must generate enough sales volume to offset the additional expenses.

Services offered by retailers are an implicit part of the retail mix. Consumers have come to expect the value added to their purchases by services, but do not always want to pay for them. Prices may include services such as delivery, giftwrap, alterations, and so forth; retailers may offer these services for an additional charge, allowing customers the option of saving money by performing the services themselves.

Retail Information System

The Retail Information System (RIS) makes data available for managers to use in setting optimum retail prices. Such information is critical in achieving desired profit levels. The RIS provides an interface between what is known about the external and internal store environments, allowing managers to combine the two sources of data to prepare forecasts and pro forma financial statements and to simulate the effect of different pricing scenarios, for example.

Store records provide internal information about customer shopping patterns, merchandise inventories, fast- and slow-moving items, response to promotional efforts, salesforce effectiveness, space productivity, gross margins for product lines and merchandising units, and other insights for setting prices. Examples of information that should be contained within the RIS from the external environment as input for pricing decisions include historical data about vendors (performance, reliability, relative importance of suppliers, price concessions in the form of allowances, discounts, rebates, etc.),

COURTESY OF A&P

The retail information system provides information on income and outgo from both internal and external environmental perspectives. Such information is needed to determine pricing strategy.

competitors' sales of similar merchandise, anticipated economic growth or decline, and such. (See Exhibit 14–4.)

In the next section, internal factors affecting pricing decisions are discussed in terms of financial objectives and pricing policies.

Exhibit 14–4
Pricing Decision Inputs for the
Retail Information System

Internal Factors Affecting Price

Financial Objectives

Financial objectives are an important component of the planning and controlling process. Planning involves setting goals and objectives and developing strategies for reaching those goals. A **goal** is something the retailer would like to accomplish within a specified time period. Plans do not guarantee that objectives will be reached; therefore, it is also necessary to incorporate control, which are ways to assure that plans are carried out and goals reached by comparing actual and planned results and correcting serious discrepancies.

Financial, marketing, and retailing objectives were discussed in Chapter 2 as part of the strategic planning process. (See Exhibit 14–5.) Pricing is of particular importance to the retailer because of its role in achieving overall store objectives related to sales, return-on-investment, profit, and early recovery of cash. Since high prices do not always result in high profits, determination of financial objectives is driven by the need to cover all merchandise inventory costs, operating expenses, and profits for the retailer.

Financial objectives are quantified and stated in measurable terms, to be attained within a certain time. Some flexibility is needed for adjusting these objectives if conditions change, since their existence is important in order to evaluate performance; reaching these objectives can be critical to the survival of the firm. Some are focused on the short term (generally one to two years maximum), and some on longer periods of time. Short- and long-term objectives may be combined; for example, the retailer may have a five year return-on-investment target rate and a one year profit goal.

TYPES OF OBJECTIVES   The three major types of financial objectives include the retailer's desired sales volume, return-on-investment, and dollar profit. Cash flow objectives also may be established as a way to provide short-term financing without borrowing. (See Exhibit 14–6).

Sales objectives provide a framework for marketing objectives which, as discussed in Chapter 2, incorporate market share and market growth goals. Sales objectives may be stated in total dollar revenues or in number of units to be sold. Breakeven analysis (described in Chapter 13) is used to determine the sales level required to cover merchandise costs and operating expenses. Sales objectives go beyond the breakeven point to include a desired level of profit.

Sales objectives are established for short and long periods of time, generally adjusted according to factors such as seasonality in the short run, and economic forecasts and anticipated growth in the long run. In some economic or competitive environments, an important sales objective may be just to

Goal
specific point a retailer would like to reach within a given time period

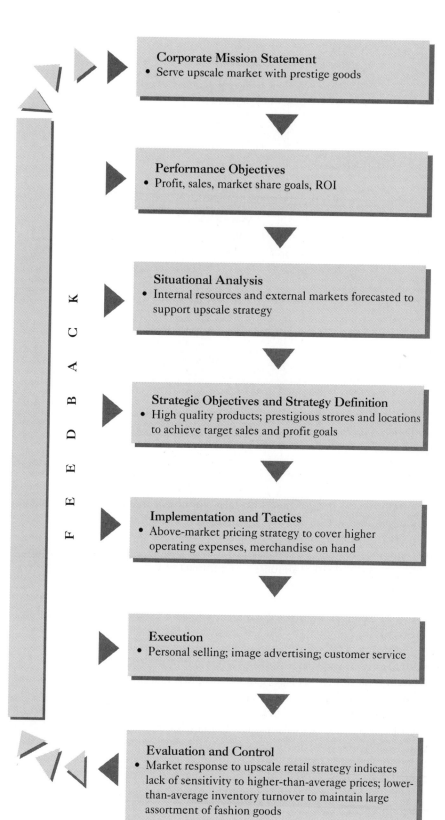

Corporate Mission Statement
- Serve upscale market with prestige goods

Performance Objectives
- Profit, sales, market share goals, ROI

Situational Analysis
- Internal resources and external markets forecasted to support upscale strategy

Strategic Objectives and Strategy Definition
- High quality products; prestigious strores and locations to achieve target sales and profit goals

Implementation and Tactics
- Above-market pricing strategy to cover higher operating expenses, merchandise on hand

Execution
- Personal selling; image advertising; customer service

Evaluation and Control
- Market response to upscale retail strategy indicates lack of sensitivity to higher-than-average prices; lower-than-average inventory turnover to maintain large assortment of fashion goods

F E E D B A C K

Exhibit 14–5
Pricing and the Strategic
Planning Process: An Illustration

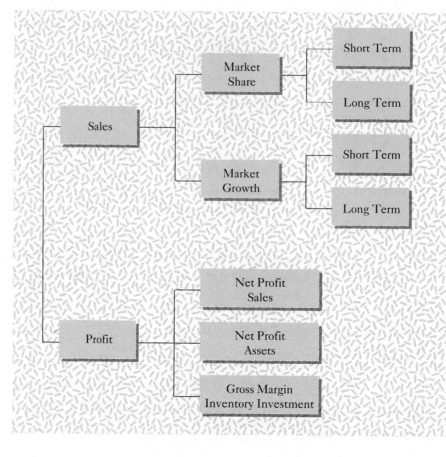

Exhibit 14–6
Types of Pricing Objectives

maintain the status quo and not lose sales volume or market share—perhaps by attracting business from a competitor in a declining market.

In order for pricing strategies to be successful in reaching sales goals, a number of factors must be considered. Realistic sales objectives take into account estimated market potential, the impact of various price levels on total demand, and actions by competitors relative to the merchandise being priced.

Return-on-investment as a financial objective establishes a relationship between profits achieved by the company and the amount the retailer has invested in assets in order to operate the business. Profit or return may be identified several ways: net profit as a percent of net sales; net profit as a percent of total assets, or of net assets; and gross margin or operating profit as a percent of investment in inventory.

Likewise, assets may be defined in several ways: total assets (all cash, property and equipment, inventories, etc.) including both those that are fully paid for, and those for which monies are still owed; net assets (those which are paid for and the company owns); and merchandise inventories. One of the retailer's greatest assets is the amount invested in merchandise inventories. Therefore, a financial objective may relate profits directly to inventory investment. Prices must be established to allow sufficient difference between total revenues and cost of goods sold to achieve a required gross margin, i.e., the amount needed to cover operating expenses and profit. This is referred to as gross margin return-on-investment (GMROI) as discussed in Chapter 13 and illustrated below.

An important financial objective is concerned with net profit, i.e., that portion of total net sales available to stockholders for dividends or for reinvestment in the company after all operating expenses have been paid. The use of dollar profit as a financial objective can be applied to the amount of profit expected from one unit or one line of merchandise, a merchandise classification, selling unit, department, store, or total company. Pricing policies and strategies are designed to achieve the maximum profit possible.

Role of Price in Achieving Profit Goals

GROSS MARGIN RETURN-ON-INVESTMENT (GMROI)   The effects of different pricing policies can be demonstrated in terms of their effects on a firm's GMROI. Recall that gross margin return on investment (GMROI) is calculated by the formula:

$$\text{GMROI} = \frac{\text{Gross Margin \$}}{\text{Net Sales}} \times \frac{\text{Net Sales}}{\text{Average Inventory at Cost}}$$

$$= \frac{\text{Gross Margin \$}}{\text{Average Inventory at Cost}}$$

The impact of a $2.00 price increase on a company's bottom line profitability can be used as an example, based on the assumption that the retailer is dealing with a product that has little or no price elasticity of demand. That is, if the price goes up, demand does not fall off. Assume that average inventory at cost is $1,000.

Sales before price increase:

Sales	1,000 units at $10.00 each	$10,000
Cost of Goods Sold	1,000 units at $ 6.00 each	$ 6,000
Gross Margin		$ 4,000

GMROI = GM$/Average Inventory at Cost = $4,000/$1,000 = 4.00 = 400%

Sales after price increase:

Sales	1,000 units at $12.00 each	$12,000
Cost of Goods Sold	1,000 units at $ 6.00 each	$ 6,000
Gross Margin		$ 6,000

GMROI = GM$/Average Inventory at Cost = $6,000/$1,000 = 6.00 = 600%

As this example illustrates, price has a definite impact upon a firm's financial performance.

STRATEGIC PROFIT MODEL   The Strategic Profit Model (SPM) was introduced in Chapter 2 within the context of strategic planning. As a reminder, the SPM is calculated by the formula:

$$\frac{\text{Net Profit}}{\text{Net Sales}} \times \frac{\text{Net Sales}}{\text{Total Assets}} = \frac{\text{Net Profit}}{\text{Total Assets}} \times \frac{\text{Total Assets}}{\text{Net Worth}} = \frac{\text{Net Profit}}{\text{Net Worth}}$$

$$\underset{\text{Margin}}{\text{Profit}} \times \underset{\text{Turnover}}{\text{Asset}} = \underset{\text{Total Assets}}{\text{Return On}} \times \underset{\text{Leverage}}{\text{Financial}} = \underset{\text{Net Worth}}{\text{Return On}}$$

EFFECT OF DIFFERENT PRICING OBJECTIVES   The effect of the three financial objectives described above can be demonstrated by referring to the Strategic Profit Model. A sales objective might lead to a market penetration strategy with a lower price, and thus a smaller profit margin relative to sales and assets. However, this could be offset by volume sales and decreased assets, i.e., "no frill" stores and high inventory turnover.

An objective stressing return-on-investment or dollar profit would concentrate on increasing profit relative to sales, inventory, total assets, and/or net worth. This might be accomplished through higher markups and/or reduced assets. Profit goals and other financial objectives are related to the retailer's pricing policies, as discussed next.

Pricing Policies

Broadly stated pricing policies are designed to govern specific pricing strategies selected by the retailer, taking into account all of the environmental influences described previously. At the same time, prices are governed by the retailer's financial objectives, because of the importance of price in achieving profit goals.

Pricing policies and strategies often are discussed in interchangeable terms. In this chapter, pricing policies are given a more global definition, and pricing strategies are related to determining specific prices. The concepts presented as pricing policies provide a general guideline for merchandisers to follow in the strategic pricing of individual items.

COMPETITIVE PRICING POLICY   One of the first decisions to be made is how the retailer's prices should be positioned relative to the prices of competitors selling similar merchandise lines. While price information is easily obtained from other stores, the competitive pricing policy is also based on consumer perceptions of "average" prices and is, therefore, somewhat judgmental. Basically three price levels can be selected: pricing with the market, above the market, or below the market. Competitive pricing policies are summarized in Exhibit 14–7.

A quick look around the stores in your community will confirm that most retailers who compete directly with one another charge similar prices. Since they do not compete on the basis of price, they rely on other aspects of the retail mix to attract customers away from competing retailers: increased promotion, better location, product selection, more services, or perhaps just making it more entertaining to shop in their stores.

Retailers who are most apt to price with the market include mass merchandisers and department stores, such as Foley's, Penney's, and Sears, and supermarkets, such as Kroger and Safeway. In the 1990s, middle-of-the-road retailers and brands are competing with numerous new competitors that strike from both sides—above and below. Upscale stores such as Neiman-Marcus and budget outlets such as Wal-Mart Stores have prospered while Sears, a longtime mainstream retailer, has floundered. Likewise, mid-priced brands, such as Kraft General Foods Corporation's Sealtest, have faced stiff

The retail price can be lower when consumers provide their own service.

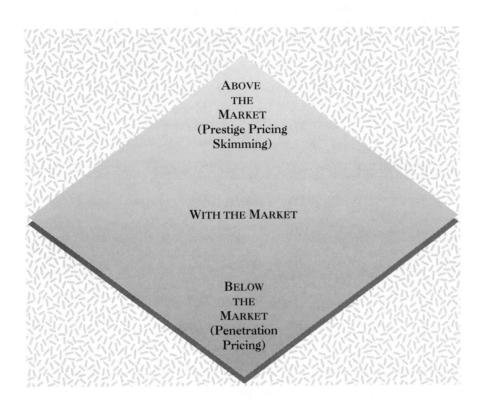

ABOVE
THE
MARKET
(Prestige Pricing
Skimming)

WITH THE MARKET

BELOW
THE
MARKET
(Penetration
Pricing)

Exhibit 14–7
Competitive Pricing Policies

competition from higher priced super-premium Haägen Dazs and Ben & Jerry's ice creams and grocers' own lower priced private labels (Deveny, 1990).

Most hardware stores and drugstores tend to use conventional industry markups, resulting in a with-the-market pricing strategy. Notice the price of gas at competing service stations in the same area, and you will see little variation in price from one station to another for the same type of gas. Regulated industries, such as telephone and electric utilities, (and airlines before deregulation) do not have an option in setting prices. They must price with the market.

The retailer who prices above the market (similar to a skimming strategy) must have a unique differential advantage over competitors. Some retailer characteristics that permit charging higher prices are a location that is prestigious, or offers time and place convenience; an unusual decor, compelling store atmosphere, or status image; an outstanding sales staff that offers exceptional personalized customer assistance; high quality, high fashion, exclusive, and/or wide assortments of merchandise; or services typically not offered by middle-of-the-road retailers. A power retailer who can command above market prices tends to have a number of these qualities operating at the same time.

Examples of retailers who price above the market are exclusive specialty stores like Neiman-Marcus, Saks Fifth Avenue, and F.A.O. Schwartz; gourmet restaurants with unusual or hard-to-get menu items; premium class

Unit pricing is clearly marked, and the difference in price between private label and brand name products is easy for the consumer to see.

hotels and resorts with a status image; or even the local hairdresser who is an outstanding stylist. The higher price must be justified by offering customers those advantages they perceive as important when they make a purchase.

Discounters and other low-end retailers price below the usual market price charged by middle of the road retailers in order to increase sales volume and inventory turnover. Below the market pricing is essentially a penetration strategy to expand market share. Lower prices are achieved by a no-frills approach to merchandising. The retailer deemphasizes customer services, store decor, and other expense-incurring extras, while emphasizing efficiency and volume selling. This is a low profit margin–high inventory turnover approach followed by retailers such as discounters (Wal-Mart, K mart), off-price retailers (Sam's Wholesale Club, Cub Foods), and warehouse retailers (furniture and appliances), for example. The merchandise assortment carried by off-price retailers may not be broad, or completely predictable, since low prices may depend on special purchases, buying odd lots of discontinued merchandise, factory overruns, and so forth.

The challenge of underselling competition tests the pricing skills of a retail manager. For example, a Woolworth manager visits a nearby K mart to check the store's prices, as well as his competitor's merchandise assortment and presentation. Then he checks toy prices at Toys "R" Us, and adjusts prices of Woolworth merchandise to meet or beat competition. Executives at Woolworth's national headquarters in Manhattan establish national prices for the chain. However they expect store managers to adjust prices, up or down, on hundreds of key items—to keep their stores locally competitive and profitable (Schwadel, 1989).

Retailers may follow more than one of the competitive pricing policies simultaneously by operating multiple formats. Some examples were described earlier, such as Wal-Mart with Sam's Wholesale Club, K mart with its Designer Depot and Accents chains, and the May Company with its

Exhibit 14–8
Competitive Pricing Policies

	Pricing Below Competition	Pricing Above Competition	Pricing With Competition
Retailer Example	Discount Store: Wal-Mart K mart Toys "R" Us	Specialty Store: Neiman-Marcus Haägen-Dazs Tiffany's	Department Store: Sears, Roebuck & Company J. C. Penney Dillard's

Exhibit 14–9
Pricing Policies

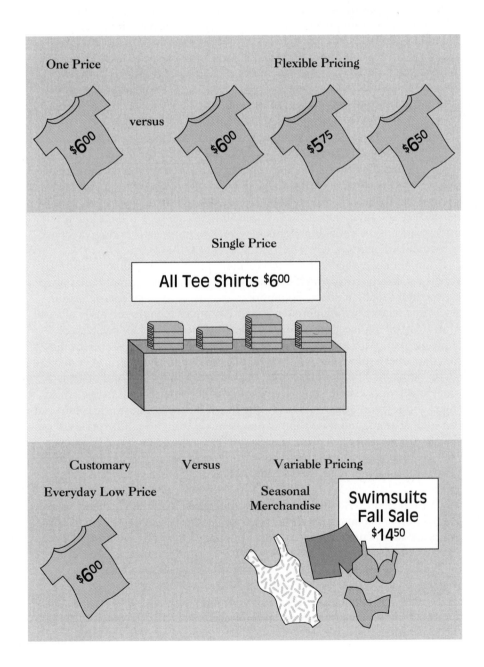

ONE-PRICE

policy where all customers pay same price for the same item at the same time

FLEXIBLE PRICING

policy that allows customers to bargain for a better price

SINGLE-PRICE

policy where same price is charged for every item in the store

ODD PRICING

policy that sets prices below even dollar amounts

Famous-Barr and Volume Shoe Corp. The hotel and motel industry has also moved in this direction with common ownership of luxury, standard, and budget class lodging operated under different names. Exhibit 14–8 provides examples of retailers according to the competitive pricing policy each pursues.

ONE-PRICE POLICY VERSUS FLEXIBLE PRICING   Most consumer goods are sold by retailers who follow a **one-price policy.** That is, all customers pay the same price for the same item at the same time. They cannot negotiate for a lower price with each transaction. However, the retailer may change the price from time to time for everyone, such as markdowns for a sale, or markups to reflect increased merchandise costs from vendors.

Flexible pricing policies allow the customer to bargain for a better price. Flexible prices are more apt to be used for higher priced "big ticket" merchandise, such as automobiles, boats, or large appliances. Lower prices may be negotiated for these items where the retailer has a trade-in policy, which allows customers to receive credit for used goods, as in the auto industry. This implies that a well-trained sales staff must be available to negotiate with customers so the transaction will be satisfying to both parties.

Occasionally, the one-price policy is actually a **single-price policy,** where the same price is charged for every item in the store. Low priced specialty shops might follow this policy to simplify buying and selling and attract customers into the store. Some types of merchandise sold this way include apparel (all T-shirts $6.00), jewelry (all earrings $3.00), neckwear (all men's ties $5.00), and other accessories. While all items are sold at the same retail price, markups on individual items may vary, requiring attention to average or maintained markup.

Another policy decision related to a one-price policy is that of customary versus variable pricing, which describes the length of time a particular price is expected to stay in effect. Some prices remain fairly constant, or customary, over a relatively long period of time. Examples include the price of a call from a pay telephone, subscription to the local newspaper, or package of chewing gum. With a variable pricing policy, on the other hand, prices may fluctuate over a relatively short period of time due to changes in cost or consumer demand. The changing price of gold causes increases and decreases in retail jewelry prices to enable jewelers to maintain margins. Resorts, cruise ships, airlines, and other retailers in the travel business adjust prices lower in the "off" seasons, and raise them when demand is highest. The prices of produce at the local supermarket change with seasons and availability. In each case, customers buying the same item at the same time will pay the same price. It is not negotiable. (See Exhibit 14–9.)

ODD PRICING   Retailers following an **odd pricing** policy will set prices below even dollar amounts. Although this practice is becoming less popular, prices are set to end in an odd number of cents, such as $1.98 instead of $2.00, particularly for less expensive items. Higher priced items might have the price expressed in an odd dollar amount, such as $2,995 rather than $3,000 for a fur jacket.

The difference of a few cents or dollars resulting from this pricing policy does not have a major impact on markups, but evolved for two reasons. Odd prices were first established to encourage sales people and cashiers to be honest. Even prices often resulted in the cash being pocketed without recording the sale. If sales people had to give change to a customer, even two cents, the sale had to be rung up on the cash register.

A more important rationale for an odd pricing policy is that consumers not only have become accustomed to it, but it has a psychological advantage. It is generally believed that customers perceive greater cost saving s for most merchandise when odd numbers are used, since they tend to round the price down to the lower dollar amount. (See Exhibit 14–10.)

LEADER PRICING   Another pricing policy decision is whether to use **price leaders,** i.e., items sold at retail prices below those normally expected. Merchandise that lends itself best to successful leader pricing is familiar to customers, frequently purchased, often nationally branded, and one with which bargain prices are easily identified. Food stores have adopted this policy extensively with weekly advertised specials, such as eggs for 39 cents a dozen, two loaves of bread for $1.00, or bargain meat prices. Price leaders are intended to increase store traffic, bringing in customers who will buy other items at regular or higher markups while they are in the store.

A form of leader pricing pursued by some retailers is **loss-leader pricing.** Loss-leaders are sold at or below the retailer's cost, requiring a high level of sales of higher markup goods to offset this loss. This practice has met with considerable criticism, and is prohibited in many states through unfair trade practice acts, as noted below in the discussion of regulatory constraints on pricing. (See Exhibit 14–11.)

PRICE LINING   A **price lining** policy involves two concepts: price ranges and price points. A price line is a series of prices associated with a merchandise classification, which is limited to specific price points, within a

Exhibit 14–11
Leader Pricing Policy

PRICE LEADERS
items sold at retail prices below those normally expected

LOSS-LEADER PRICING
products sold at or below retailer's cost to increase consumer traffic

PRICE LINING
series of prices in a predetermined range, associated with a merchandise classification

predetermined range of prices. The range of prices, from lowest to highest, is related to the competitive position of the retailer. For example, a regional junior department store chain might choose a middle to high end pricing policy if located in a regional mall with Sears who would have a low to middle price range. The price line for shirts at the junior department store might range from $25.00 to $50.00, with price points at $25.00, $30.00, $38.00, and $50.00. Sears' price range might be from $10.00 to $25.00, with price points at $10.00, $18.00, $22.00, and $25.00. (See Exhibit 14–12.)

A price lining policy provides a guideline for buyers and merchandisers in purchasing products compatible with the selected price line and price points. Additionally, price lining makes it more convenient for customers to shop and for salespeople to sell. Imagine how confusing it would be if you were trying to buy a shirt for about $10.00, and the price points of the ones you liked were $9.82, $10.41, and $10.16. Price lining also makes it easier to compare merchandise at the various price points. However, a price increase or decrease in one line affects the price of other merchandise lines. This is a particular problem in a time of increasing wholesale costs which, in turn, lead to increasing retail prices. The retailer must develop customer acceptance of higher prices for the same quality merchandise lines at the original price points.

MULTIPLE-UNIT PRICING   When more than one item is offered for sale at a single price, the retailer is using a **multiple-unit pricing** policy as a sort of quantity discount. Thus, customers are encouraged to buy a larger quantity than they might if each item was priced individually. Familiar multiple-unit pricing examples include athletic socks in units of three or six

Exhibit 14–12
Price Lining Policy

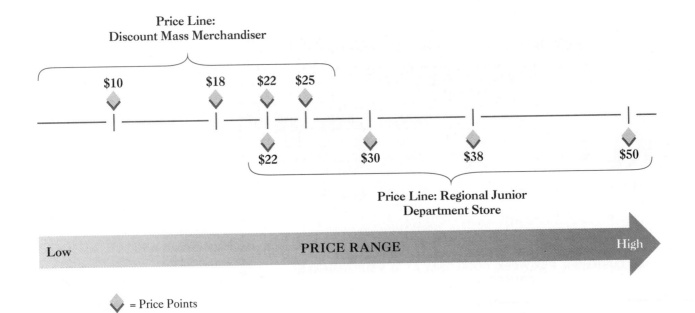

pairs, canned peaches at 2 cans for 98 cents, soft drinks and beer in 6-packs, or 3 bars of soap for $1.00.

Customers expect to save money when buying multiple units at a single price. Sometimes the saving is substantial (i.e., bread regularly $1.09 a loaf, now 2 for $1.59); sometimes it is misleading in that the saving may be very slight or none at all (i.e., bread regularly 59 cents a loaf, now 2 for $1.19). (See Exhibit 14–13.)

UNIT PRICING   Products that come in numerous sizes and shapes of packages make it difficult for customers to compare prices. The answer to this problem is a **unit pricing** policy, which has been adopted willingly by many retailers, and is legally required in some places as discussed later in the chapter. To enable consumers to calculate which product or package size is the best buy, prices are provided on a per-unit basis with the price per ounce, pound, quart, or other unit (along with the total price of the product) clearly marked—usually on the shelf above or below the item.

Unit pricing has been adopted by many large food retailers, and is particularly suitable to grocery and health and beauty aid products. Consumers have had to be educated to the advantages of using unit pricing information in making purchases, but have realized price savings through its use. It has become an important promotional tool for retailers who publicize their concern for customers. Unit pricing does not necessarily imply that individual products will not be marked. In response to customers who are not happy with the removal of prices from the products, some retailers mark items with total prices as well as placing unit pricing information on store shelves. The cost and effort required to accomplish this becomes a policy decision.

Pricing policies can be diverse, as described in this section. A retailer may choose how to position prices relative to competitors, whether to charge one price for all rather than flexible pricing, odd or even pricing, leader pricing, price lines (and the range of prices), multiple-unit pricing, and unit pricing.

Exhibit 14–13
Multiple-Unit Pricing

·····························

Golden Yellow Sweet
**Corn
5/99¢**
EARS

PRICING STRATEGIES

A retailers' pricing strategies are also affected by "stakeholders," those groups that the retailer cannot control, but who can have a major impact on the operation of the business. A retailer's stakeholders include consumers, government agencies, channel members, competition, and others. In general, pricing strategies must accomplish three tasks: return a profit to the retailer; provide satisfaction to customers; and adapt to environmental constraints.

There are two basic approaches to determining retail prices: cost oriented and demand oriented. A cost orientation to pricing relies on a basic formula that sets the retail price as a specific increase over the wholesale cost, usually expressed as a percentage of either cost or retail. A demand orientation to pricing also considers cost, but sets prices according to anticipated customer responses, choosing price points that will result in the highest vol-

MULTIPLE-UNIT PRICING
more than one item offered for sale at a single price

UNIT PRICING
price given is also broken down into a per-unit basis to facilitate price comparison

ume and/or profit. In reality, most retailers incorporate both cost- and demand-oriented pricing strategies. A combined cost-demand strategy takes cost and profit objectives into consideration first, then makes adjustments relative to the store's target market.

Cost-Oriented Pricing

OVERVIEW   The simplest pricing method is to add a standard markup to the cost of the product, high enough to cover cost of merchandise sold, operating expenses, and profit. Different products, product lines, merchandise classifications, and departments within the same store may have different markups. Markups often follow industry norms or averages, particularly for retailers who price their goods at the same level as their competitors. Markup percentages also may conform to retail (list) prices recommended by manufacturers, or they may be adjusted for the level of service provided to customers by the retailer.

Cost-oriented pricing is favored by many retailers for several reasons.

1. It is easier to determine the cost than the demand for an item. However, calculating the true cost of merchandise is not always as simple as it might seem. In addition to the merchandise cost, there may be charges for transportation and in-store labor charges to prepare goods for the selling floor. Cost may be reduced by the amount of any discounts or allowances paid to the retailer.
2. Price adjustments are not needed as frequently because of changes in consumer demand. The standard markup over cost remains fairly constant under the assumption the price will generate the desired sales volume.
3. Price competition is minimized where similar retailers take a standard markup on cost. Essentially, all retailers concerned will have comparable prices.

PRICING CALCULATIONS   As defined previously, a markup refers to the amount above the cost of an item that a retailer adds to the cost to recover operating expenses and make a profit. A markup can be expressed in two ways: at cost and at retail.

The cost method bases the percentage of markup on the cost of an item. The formula for calculating a markup at cost is:

$$\text{Markup at cost} = \frac{\text{Selling Price} - \text{Merchandise Cost}}{\text{Merchandise Cost}}.$$

Let us assume that we are planning to add a new line of sport coats, which we will buy at a cost of $97 each. We will sell the coats for $150 each. Based upon the above formula, we will be receiving a 54.64 percent markup:

$$\frac{\$150 - \$97}{\$97} \quad \text{or} \quad \frac{\$53}{\$97} = 54.64\%$$

This means that on each coat we sell, we will have $53 (54.64% × $97) of the cost to recover expenses and make a profit.

COST-ORIENTED PRICING
method that adds a standard markup to a product's cost

Now let us assume that we have purchased another line of sport coats for $80 each, and we need to know the selling price for each coat based upon a 54.64% markup at cost. By manipulating the formula, we can solve for the selling price:

$$\text{Merchandise Cost} \times (1 + \text{Markup \%}) = \text{Selling price}$$
$$\text{Therefore: } \$80 \times (1.5464) = \$123.71$$

The retail price would probably be rounded off to the next price line, such as $125 for each coat.

Additionally, if we know the selling price and the markup percent at cost, we can determine the merchandise cost. For example, we want to purchase a coat that will sell for $175 each, based upon a 54.64 percent markup at cost. To determine the merchandise cost, we would use the following formula:

$$\text{Merchandise Cost} = \frac{\text{Selling Price}}{(1 + \text{Markup \%})} \text{ or } \frac{\$175}{1.5464} = \$113.17$$

This means that we can pay $113.17 for each coat in order to make our desired markup on cost.

Markups can also be expressed as a percentage of the retail price:

$$\text{Markup At Retail} = \frac{\text{Selling Price} - \text{Merchandise Cost}}{\text{Selling Price}}$$

Using the past example, the markup at retail for the $150.00 sport coat is:

$$\text{Markup at Retail} = \frac{\$150 - \$97}{\$150} = 35.33\%$$

Notice how a fixed dollar markup will appear to be less if it is expressed as a percentage of the retail price. Relating this to the transactional dimension of price, we can advertise a lower markup percent to increase sales. (Note: The reason why a fixed markup on retail is less than a markup on cost, given the same basic figures, is due to basic mathematics. The selling price is usually greater than the cost, so we are dividing by a larger number.)

We can also manipulate the above formula to find the selling price or the merchandise cost, given the markup percent on retail. To find the selling price *(SP)*, given the merchandise cost *(C)* and markup percent on retail (MUR):

$$SP = C/(1 - MUR\%)$$

Therefore, if we buy an item for $140 and want to sell it at a 35.33% markup, the selling price is:

$$SP = C/(1 - MUR\%) = \$140/(1 - .3533) = \$140/.6467 - \$216.48$$

(which would be rounded off to the next price point).

We can also solve for the merchandise cost based upon the selling price and markup percent on retail. Given that we will sell a sport coat for $200 and have a 35.53 percent markup on retail, the merchandise cost is:

$$C = SP \times (1 - MUR\%) = \$200 \times .6467 = \$129.34.$$

Therefore, the cost of each sport coat is $129.34.

The retail approach is preferred over the cost method for the following reasons: (1) cost data may not always be available, and retail prices are readily known; and (2) the percent markup on a fixed dollar retail price is lower when calculated as a percent of retail, which can be a promotional advantage to the retailer. However, there are also advantages to the cost method, with the primary one being accuracy. Retail prices may change in terms of markdowns and markups. However, the initial cost of an item always remains the same.

The initial markup *(IMU)* formula is used to determine the markup that should be applied to merchandise in order to recover operating expenses and make a profit. The formula is:

$$IMU = \frac{\text{Planned Operating Expenses} + \text{Planned Profit} + \text{Planned Retail Reductions}}{\text{Planned Net Sales} + \text{Planned Reductions}}.$$

Using the data presented in Exhibit 14–4 on this page, initial markup would be calculated as follows.

$$IMU = \frac{\$21,0000 + \$6,000 + \$5,000}{\$100,000 + \$5,000} = \frac{\$32,000}{\$105,000} = 30.5\%.$$

This means that the retailer will have to mark up the merchandise by 30.5 percent in order to recover planned operating expenses and make the desired profit level.

The maintained markup *(MMU)* is an after-the-fact evaluation tool. It can be used by a retailer to determine how well the firm has met its established markup objectives. The formula is:

$$MMU = \frac{\text{Actual Operating Expenses} + \text{Actual Profits}}{\text{Actual Net Sales}},$$

or

$$MMU = \frac{\text{Average Selling Price} - \text{Merchandise Cost}}{\text{Average Selling Price}}.$$

So, in the above example, the maintained markup for 19XX would be:

$$\frac{\$21,000 + \$6,000}{\$100,000} = \frac{\$27,000}{\$100,000} = 27.0\%.$$

The above example indicates that initial markup will need to be about 3.5 percent (30.5 – 27.0) higher than the maintained or average markup.

Exhibit 14–14

Data for initial and maintained markup calculations

Net Sales.........................$100,000
Reductions 5,000
Operating Expense............21,000
Profit 6,000

Demand-Oriented Pricing

OVERVIEW   Although there are many arguments for using the cost orientation to pricing, the method does not allow adjustments for level of consumer demand or competitor's pricing strategies. The most successful prices for many products and target markets may be above or below a standard markup for some items, based on what consumers are willing to pay, or what they perceive is of value.

Rather than the standard markup percentage over cost applied in cost-oriented pricing, **demand-oriented pricing** may result in a variety of markup percentages within the same selling unit. For example, perhaps a grocer prices bread and milk at a low 6 percent markup in order to meet competition and increase store traffic, but prices a gourmet coffee that is popular with his customers at a 50 percent markup. In both cases, the price is related to anticipated demand and the amount customers are willing to pay for the items; however, there are some exceptions to demand-oriented pricing, such as in the sale of prescription drugs. Although the demand may be very high, the price is not determined by what the market will bear, a concept sometimes referred to as "gentleman's pricing."

Demand-oriented pricing considers the psychological aspects of consumer behavior, such as perceptions of the relationship between price and quality, or of the prestige of certain prices and products. The impact of consumer characteristics on pricing strategies is discussed further with other external environmental factors below.

PRICE ADJUSTMENTS AND CALCULATIONS   In the course of business, a retailer will find it necessary to adjust prices either downward (markdown) or upward (additional markup). For this reason, it is necessary to be able to calculate markdowns and additional markups. These concepts are discussed here relative to demand pricing strategies, but they also may be related to changes in merchandise costs from suppliers, or customer classifications (e.g., discounts to schools or churches).

An additional markup occurs when a retailer increases the price of a product. This can be brought about as a result of many factors. Examples might include:

1. Product sales are better than expected, indicating high demand.
2. Supply is limited, therefore the retailer wants to make as much profit as possible on a limited resource.
3. Competitors leave the market, decreasing supply of retail goods.

The formulas for additional markups are:

$$\frac{(New\ price - Old\ price)}{Old\ price,} \qquad or \qquad \frac{Total\ dollar\ additional\ markup}{Dollar\ net\ sales.}$$

For example, let's assume that a retailer has been selling sport coats for $150 each and decides to increase the price to $175 each. The price increase will not alter the cost of the coats, which will remain at $100 each.

DEMAND-ORIENTED PRICING
price markup based on what consumers are willing to pay

The additional markup at retail is: ($175 –$150)/$150 = 16.67%.
The new overall markup is 42.86%: ($175 – $100)/$175.

Assuming that the retailer had 1,000 of these coats, 50 percent of which were sold for $150 and 50 percent were sold for $175, the maintained markup is:

$$\frac{\text{Average Selling Price} - \text{Cost}}{\text{Average Selling Price}} = \frac{((\$150 \times .5) + (\$175 \times .5)) - \$100}{(\$150 \times .5) + (\$175 \times .5)} = \frac{\$162.50 - \$100}{\$162.50}$$

Adjusting retail prices upward can improve profit margins because of the higher markup. However, higher prices can hurt sales, as Circle K convenience stores found out in 1989. After a six-year, $853 million acquisition binge that quadrupled its outlets to 4,685, Circle K was deeply in debt and plagued with declining sales and earnings. In the face of fierce competition, the retailer raised overall prices substantially. Although this was an effort to overcome widespread discounting of high-volume items such as soft drinks in the past, sales dropped off significantly. Circle K tried to lure customers back into the stores by launching its "Price Busters" program, giving periodic deep discounts on milk, beer, and other popular items. This erratic pricing strategy was confusing to customers (Kerwin, 1989).

By the same token, there may be times when the retailer will be forced to lower the price of an item in the normal course of business. Examples include:

1. New retail competitors enter the market, increasing the supply of retail goods.
2. Demand drops off due to seasonal merchandise, end of a fashion cycle, or similar situation.

Markdowns can be calculated as a percentage of either the reduced selling price or of the original selling price.

The formula for calculating markdown as a percent of the reduced price is:

$$\text{Markdown Percent} = \frac{\text{Original price} - \text{Reduced price}}{\text{Reduced price}}$$

Continuing with the examples above, if the retailer has to mark the $150 coat down to $125, the markdown as a percent of the new price would be:

$$\text{Markdown Percent} = \frac{\$150 - \$125}{\$125} = .20 = 20\%$$

The formula for calculating markdown as a percent of the original price on a per-unit basis is:

$$\text{Markdown Percent} = \frac{\text{Original price} - \text{Reduced price}}{\text{Original price}}$$

Continuing with the coat example, the markdown in this case would be:

$$\text{Markdown Price} = \frac{\$150 - \$125}{\$150} = .167 = 16.7\%$$

Thus, the retailer's markup, based on the original price, will be 16.7 percent lower than the original markup for each coat sold.

© 1991 ROBERT BREMMEL/PHOTO EDIT

The markdown strategies of retailers may not be a routine consideration of most consumers, but shoppers are always willing to benefit from a sale.

Total markdown percentages can be calculated as:

$$\text{Markdown Percent} = \frac{\text{Total dollar markdown}}{\text{Dollar net sales}}$$

Assuming that the retailer has 1,000 coats with half sold at the old price, and half expected to sell at the new price, the maintained markup is:

$$\frac{((\$150 \times .5) + (\$125 \times .5)) - \$100}{(\$150 \times .5) + (\$125 \times .5)} = \frac{\$137.50 - \$100}{\$137.50} = 27.7\%$$

A retailer's pricing policy generally dictates when markdowns will be taken. Some retailers take markdowns early based on a period of declining sales, and of selling season, or the length of time the merchandise has been in stock. Two benefits can accrue from early markdowns: inventory dollars become available for newer, more saleable merchandise, and a smaller markdown may be required to sell the merchandise than if the markdown were to be taken later.

On the other hand, the retailer may benefit from taking markdowns as late as possible, perhaps grouping merchandise for storewide clearance sales. Sometimes markdowns can be avoided by giving more attention to promoting slow-selling items through newspaper advertising, merchandise arrangements or displays in the store, and salesforce incentives. Some retailers pursue a combined strategy of taking early markdowns on certain categories of merchandise, such as seasonal or high-fashion items, and late markdowns on the more basic or staple items. The underlying premise for taking markdowns, whether early or late, is to have a fresh, saleable assortment of merchandise available to the store's customers at all times.

Price adjustments often take the form of discounts, such as those given to employees. Many retailers will give discounts off the regular price to schools and nonprofit organizations. Others will give discounts to special or preferred customers. Retailers, like Sam's Wholesale Clubs, have a multi-tiered system of discounts structured for different types of customers.

External Factors Affecting Price

Consumers, competitors, suppliers, and the government play a part in determining retail prices. The major impact of each of these environmental forces is introduced in this section to illustrate that a retailer cannot arbitrarily select prices. Price is one aspect of the retail mix that is particularly dependent upon the actions, approval, and acceptance of the retailer's environmental partners.

Consumer Markets

A store's customers are the ultimate "boss" when it comes to pricing decisions. The price has to be one that they are willing and able to pay for the products and services purchased. Two basic relationships between retail prices and consumer responses are concerned with the economics of pricing and customer characteristics. Price elasticity of demand is an economic principle used to explain changes in consumer demand due to changes in price. In addition, consumer characteristics (demographic, behavioral, psychological) provide a useful basis for market segmentation on the basis of price.

Exhibit 14–15
Price Elasticity of Demand
· ·

PRICE ELASTICITY OF DEMAND   Some consumers, as well as some product/service categories, are more affected by the exact dollars and cents aspect of a price than by elusive psychological aspects in purchase decisions. (See Exhibit 14–15.) Here it is necessary to estimate the optimum price to attain the

volume of sales desired. If the retailer charges too much for a product, customers may not buy it. If too little is charged, the retailer may not cover expenses.

Price elasticity of demand is a measure of the effect of changes in price on changes in consumer demand, calculated by the following formula:

$$\text{Price elasticity of demand} = \frac{\% \text{ change in quantity demanded}}{\% \text{ change in price}}$$

where:

$$\% \text{ change in quantity demanded} = \frac{\text{Change in quantity demanded at new price}}{\text{Quantity demanded at original price}}$$

$$\% \text{ change in price} = \frac{\text{Change (increase or decrease) in price}}{\text{Original price}}$$

Briefly, if a price increase results in a slight decline in demand, or a price decrease results in a slight increase in demand, demand is said to be inelastic. However, demand is said to be elastic if a price increase leads to considerable decrease in demand, or a price decrease leads to a considerable increase in demand. Exhibit 14–16 provides a more detailed explanation of price elasticity.

Increases in demand may result in increases in price. Following the deregulation of the airline industry, airfares dropped drastically to be competitive. The negative impact on profits subsequently forced airlines to increase fares. For example, in an attempt to improve profit margins, American Airlines and others increased one-way discount fares by $5.00. These fares require little or no advance purchase, and are used primarily by business travelers. The additional charge was based on the expectation that demand by this market segment was strong enough to justify it (Thomas, 1988). At the same time, travelers were being plagued by an increasing number of delayed flights and other problems, which also affected demand (Rose, 1988).

CONSUMER CHARACTERISTICS AS BASIS FOR PRICE SEGMENTATION   Price can be discussed from a number of consumer response perspectives. One approach has been to distinguish between the transactional dimension and the informational dimension of price (Dommermuth, 1984). The *transactional dimension* is akin to the traditional economic view of pricing, representing the amount of money charged for a product, with the expectation that higher prices will result in fewer units sold, and vice versa, according to the traditional demand curve. This viewpoint assumes that consumers have complete information about the features and benefits of all products considered, without basing any of this knowledge on price.

The *informational dimension* considers price as a form of communication, making price a part of the promotional mix. From this perspective, price information might have the opposite effect on prospective buyers who use it to judge the quality of a product or brand (or even a store). For example, researchers have found that high prices may repel prospective customers who have limited resources. At the same time, high prices may have quality implications that serve to attract customers (Wheatley and Chiu, 1977). Raising the price of an item has been shown to actually increase demand in some instances.

Exhibit 14-16
Price Elasticity of Demand: An Illustration

Elasticity of demand is a concept most easily associated with what happens to total sales revenue based on a change in price. The relationship between price and revenue is determined by the degree to which quantity of goods sold falls with increases in price or rises with decreases in price. Consider the following schedule of quantity demanded at prices ranging from $20 to $10:

Price	Quantity	Total Revenue
$20	1,000	$20,000
19	1,100	20,900
18	1,200	21,600
17	1,300	22,100
16	1,400	22,400
15	1,500	22,500
14	1,600	22,400
13	1,700	22,100
12	1,800	21,600
11	1,900	20,900
10	2,000	20,000

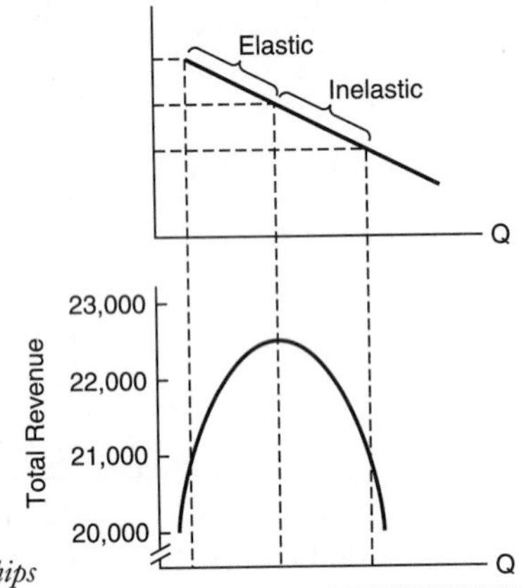

Common Relationships

Formula for the arc elasticity of demand:

$$e = \frac{(q_0 - q_1) / ((q_0 + q_1) / 2)}{(p_0 - p_1) / ((p_0 + p_1) / 2)}$$

where

e = price elasticity of demand
q_0 = original quantity demanded
q_1 = new quantity demanded
p_0 = original price
p_1 = new price

Elastic Demand: Consider the decision to change price from $19 to $17, then:

$$e = \frac{(1,100 - 1,300) / (1,200)}{(19 - 17) / 18} = 9 \times \frac{-200}{1,200} = -1.50.$$

$e < -1.00$, thus we are said to be in the elastic portion of the demand schedule. Note that in this portion, a decrease in price leads to an increase in revenue, and vice versa. Therefore, price and revenue changes move in opposite directions.

Inelastic Demand: Consider a change in price from $13 to $11, then:

$$e = \frac{(1,700 - 1,900) / (1,800)}{(13 - 11) / 12} = 6 \times \frac{-200}{1,800} = -.667.$$

$e > -1.00$, thus we are said to be in the inelastic portion of the demand schedule. Note here that price and revenue changes move in the same direction. In general, the closer the elasticity coefficient is to zero, the less elastic is demand.

Unitary Elasticity: Consider a change in price from $14 to $16, then:

$$e = \frac{(1,600 - 1,400) / (1,500)}{(14 - 16) / 15} = \frac{15}{-2} \times \frac{200}{1,500} = -1.00.$$

$e = -1.00$, thus we are said to be at a point of unitary elasticity. Here a change in price has made no change in total revenue. Are we ready to set the price?

Demand Curve Slope Considerations

While the above relations hold true for nearly any simple price-quantity relationship (a constant change in quantity given a constant change in price), elasticity of demand also changes with changes in the slope of the demand curve. Generally, the steeper the slope, the more inelastic is demand. What factors might affect the slope of the demand curve?

Price may be an important promotional information input in some situations. Customers must resort to price in rating brands (1) when they do not have sufficient information or experience to make comparisons on relevant features, (2) when the product appears complex and high risk is associated with making the wrong choice, (3) when social prestige is associated with owning a particular brand and paying a high price tells others that you can afford the best, and (4) when the actual difference between prices is relatively small, consumers feel they are getting a better quality if they buy the higher priced item (Dommermuth, 1984).

The preceding discussion points out that the determination of retail prices is more complex than one might think. Merely setting prices to cover costs and profit or in response to some forecasted level of demand may not be sufficient. The retailer who is aware of what a price communicates to the customer can consciously use price as a promotional tool.

Customers' income, social class, occupation, stage in the family life cycle, and other demographic factors, dictate to some extent the prices they are willing and able to pay and how they will respond to various price levels. Demographics also influence the price lines offered by a retailer indirectly through the types and brands of products demanded by a particular consumer market.

The effect of demographic characteristics on responses to prices may be modified by psychographic characteristics. Lifestyle has been found to have a major impact on purchasing behavior, including response to prices. Busy people with little time to spend shopping, for instance, are more willing to pay higher prices for time and location convenience. Self-image and personality traits are two other psychographic characteristics that can be used in setting prices, although they are sometimes difficult to identify.

Pricing strategies are also determined by the benefits consumers expect to obtain. Several obvious benefits are product quality, economy, service and status. Perceived psychographic as well as functional benefits affect the prices customers are willing to pay.

One example of high prices that reflect expected benefits from purchases is in the fine art market. In addition to the aesthetic value of art objects, buyers mayperceive paintings by famous artists as a financial investment that is safer than the stock and bond markets, or precious metals. In May, 1988, London-based Sotheby's Holdings Inc. sold over $100 million in impressionist and modern art in less than two hours. One of the lowest prices was $209,000 for a tiny Picasso painting, purchased by tennis star, John McEnroe. The highest price was $53.9 million for Vincent van Gogh's "Irises" (Cox, 1988). Upscale resale "thrift" shops such as the Church Mouse and Goodwill Assembly Boutique in Palm Beach, Florida, sell "gently worn clothing" and "pre-owned" china, silver, and furnishings for a fraction of their original high prices. For example, $1,000 ball gowns owned by socialites like Ivana Trump can be bought for $250. The stylish bargain hunter benefits from a special "find," and charities benefit from Palm Beach philanthropy (Hupp, 1991).

Consumer perceptions of benefits offered by a product are subject to change with new information, and may not only affect retailer's pricing strategies but also consumer demand. In June, 1988, with 160,000 Suzuki Samurai utility vehicles on the road, *Consumer Reports* magazine publicized test results showing that the automobile rolled over during quick maneuvering, and wanted Suzuki to stop selling it. A series of class action suits followed, some seeking compensation for the decreased value of the Samurai due to adverse publicity. In spite of an advertising and public relations blitz by Suzuki to refute the rollover charges, sales quickly dropped by as much as 50 percent. Perceived safety (although not conclusively proven), rather than price, affected demand. However, with the right marketing approach, even adverse publicity can be turned around. A Georgia Suzuki dealer reported booming sales as the result of a devil-may-care ad slogan: "You'll flip over our prices and roll over our good deals" (Toy, 1988).

Consumers generally have price thresholds. That is, there is an acceptable range of prices that they are willing to pay. Prices below this threshold may be perceived as related to substandard products or services. Prices above the acceptable range may be beyond the customer's financial capability, or what is considered "reasonable."

Buying behavior may be related to usage rate, with customers categorized as heavy, medium, or light users of the store's products. Heavy users may account for only a small percentage of customers, but may be responsible for a much larger percentage of sales. Conversely, the majority of customers may buy only a small percentage of the store's goods.

Prices may vary according to whether a target market already shops in the retailer's store and uses its products. Different price structures may be used in attracting new customers, keeping present customers, and regaining former customers. To attract new customers or to regain former customers to a remodeled location, a supermarket might price key items "2 for 1." Present customers might receive price concessions in the form of "volume discounts," accumulating cash register receipts to reach a minimum amount to qualify.

Likewise, different prices might be established according to shopping frequency. Customers can be classified as frequent, occasional, or seldom shoppers in the store, i.e., according to store loyalty. Airlines and the hotel/motel industry have been successful with frequent flyer or frequent stay programs, which give additional value or discounts for repeat business.

Competitive Practices

COMPETITIVE POSITION OF THE RETAILER   Pricing decisions are governed to a large extent by the type of competitive structure in which retailers operate. In a situation approaching "pure" competition, all similar retailers selling similar products will charge similar prices. Each retailer will meet the price of its competitors. Think of the regular price of a hamburger at several of your favorite fast-food franchises or a soft drink from vending machines in public areas—the prices probably do not vary much.

Retailers operating in an oligopoly, where a few retailers sell the same product or service, have more opportunity to charge different prices from their competitors. Their pricing structures may reflect different services, store atmospheres, and so forth. Prices of the dominant competitors become the basis for pricing by many less influential firms. This situation may be most noticeable in a small community or an ethnic neighborhood. A retail firm with a monopoly position in a market has the most freedom in determining prices. However, in each type of competitive environment, pricing strategies will be affected by consumer demand, merchandise costs, and actions of other retailers.

Frequent flyer programs are a perk offered by most airlines to encourage repeat business.

COURTESY OF NORTHWEST AIRLINES

COMPETITIVE RESPONSES   Retailing is so competitive that it is rare for one or a few firms to be able to determine prices for everyone. Some retailers are price leaders; they are the first to raise or lower a price. Others are price followers; they use the price leaders as a barometer for their own prices. Others choose to compete on a nonprice basis, such as service, atmosphere, or convenient location.

Discount department stores have to struggle against the pricing strategies of "category killers." "Category killers" are specialty discounters who focus on one product area such as toys, electronics, stationery, or books, and offer their customers wider selections and steeper price cuts than the discount department stores. Traditional discounters such as K mart, Wal-Mart, Caldor, and Venture have developed strategies to meet or overcome this price competition dilemma. Others such as Ames Department Stores have faced possible bankruptcy—or like Gold Circle, no longer exist (Pereira, 1990).

Some responses are more volatile, with competitors cutting prices lower than one another to take the other's customers. This chain reaction is called a **price war.** In the highly competitive consumer electronics industry, a clash between the Best Buy Co. and Highland Superstores Inc. in Minneapolis and St. Paul, Minnesota, resulted in a price war where the two chains assaulted each other with ads for $126 TVs, $69 microwaves, and guarantees of the lowest prices around. A customer could run back and forth between stores, haggling down the price of a 27-inch TV to far below cost. Prices fell hourly as salespeople continued to undercut their competitors (Pitzer, 1987).

Price wars can be a very unprofitable tactic, with the prices often dropping below cost, irreversibly damaging profit margins, potentially damaging a firm's image, and driving the weaker competitor out of business if the price war is sustained long enough. In the electronics industry, Stereo Village Inc., a 25-store Atlanta-based chain filed for bankruptcy in 1987. Federated Group Inc.'s stock prices dropped low enough to make it a takeover candidate, and competitor Circuit City Stores, Inc. also saw its stock prices slide. Meanwhile, these retailers and others like Crazy Eddie Inc. in New York continue to compete on an aggressive price basis (Pitzer, 1987).

Channel Influences and Suppliers' Effect on Retail Prices

Retail prices are affected by the various suppliers who make up the retailer's distribution channels. Manufacturers, wholesalers, service providers, and other intermediaries set policies and make decisions that affect the retailer's cost prices, and in turn the retail prices paid by consumers. Costs may relate directly to the product itself as it passes from one channel member to another (for example, raw materials producer to manufacturer to wholesaler to retailer), and each is rewarded for the functions it performs in moving goods closer to the retail customer. Additionally, there are costs involved in the services required to move goods through the channels, such as transportation, insurance, financing/interest rates, and promotion.

There are five major ways that suppliers affect retail prices:

1. Power position relative to other channel members
2. Length of the distribution channel

PRICE WAR
competitors cut prices lower than one another to attract each other's customers, causing a chain reaction

3. Negotiations for terms of sale
4. Control over wholesale costs
5. Willingness to bring the product to market and sell it to the retailer/final consumer

POWER POSITION RELATIVE TO OTHER CHANNEL MEMBERS

The most powerful or influential channel member will have the greatest effect on retail prices. The power position may be a function of relative size, prestigious or exclusive goods, or limited supply. The most powerful member of the channel may be the retailer, manufacturer, or wholesaler. The degree of cooperation between channel members has an impact on pricing in areas such as willingness to negotiate terms, provide timely delivery, or assume responsibility for promotion.

LENGTH OF DISTRIBUTION CHANNEL

Many large retailers, such as Sears, assume responsibility for many functions performed by other intermediaries in order to shorten the distribution channel. The shorter the channel, the lower the retail price that can be charged in most cases. Vertical integration is the most widely used formal method to control prices in this manner.

NEGOTIATIONS FOR TERMS OF SALE

The various ways in which buyers can negotiate with suppliers for terms of sale were described in Chapter 13. These include discounts, datings, shipping points and transportation expenses, promotional allowances, and other assistance.

Other negotiations might include exclusive goods or price guarantees. When a vendor agrees to supply a retailer with **exclusive goods,** no competitors, or none of those within some defined geographical area, will be permitted to carry the same items. Exclusivity allows the retailer to charge a higher price. A store, such as Neiman-Marcus, may place its own label on this merchandise rather than using the manufacturer's label.

Price guarantees assure the buyer that the price of goods ordered will be adjusted downward if the vendor's prices are decreased between the time the order is placed and the goods are shipped. While prices are more apt to rise than fall, a price guarantee is desirable when orders are placed far in advance of a selling season or when prices fall due to a decrease in consumer demand.

CONTROL OVER WHOLESALE COSTS

Consumers, who are the ultimate price-setters, apply pressure backward through the channel to provide goods at lower costs, thus encouraging suppliers and intermediaries to control expenses and cost of materials or finished goods. A lower cost structure at each channel level can result in lower retail prices for consumers and acceptable profit margins for channel members.

In the 1970s consumers resisted high prices with a meat boycott. The price of meat was lowered to encourage consumers to buy again. Producers, intermediaries, and retailers all had to examine their cost structure in order to bring prices down and still make a profit.

WILLINGNESS TO PRODUCE AND SELL PRODUCT OR SERVICE

Each channel member is dependent on its suppliers to produce, stock, and

EXCLUSIVE GOODS
vendor supplies goods to a single retailer in a geographical area

PRICE GUARANTEE
prices of goods adjusted downward at time of shipment if costs are lower than when ordered

sell wanted merchandise. If a supplier is not committed to selling a particular product, then higher prices may provide an incentive to bring the item to market. Special orders may need to be placed for low demand, highly individualized products such as bridal gowns or custom furniture.

As well as the direct channel influences described above, there are some indirect channel influences on retail prices. One example is the retail practice, particularly in grocery stores, of *selling against the brand*. In this case, the retailer uses a higher priced national, or well-known, brand to sell a lower priced, generic or private-label product. The difference in price is evident to customers, who are influenced by the price savings. However, suppliers of the more expensive brand may react unfavorably, which can affect the retailer's ability to negotiate in the future.

Regulatory Constraints

Pricing policies and strategies have been affected by federal, state, and local legislation. These regulatory constraints were discussed in Chapter 7 and are briefly reviewed in this section. Some affect consumer prices directly; others affect consumer prices indirectly through regulation of vendors' prices to retailers. Retailers are in the middle of the pricing dilemma, since they have both the potential to be discriminated against by their suppliers and to discriminate against their customers.

Retailers can avoid unacceptable pricing practices by carefully following legislative guidelines and adhering to ethical behavior. This includes avoidance of price-fixing agreements with other retailers or suppliers, and refusal to take advantage of consumers using predatory pricing tactics. Additionally, buyers are in key positions to refuse to be involved in discriminatory or coercive pricing activities.

Pricing legislation aimed at preventing restraint of trade and unfair competition among businesses focuses on price discrimination, price fixing (horizontal and vertical), and selling below cost. Legislation for the direct protection of consumers includes the practices of unit pricing, item price removal, and price advertising.

PRICE DISCRIMINATION   Price discrimination is regulated by the Robinson-Patman Act, which was originally designed to protect small businesses who do not have the "clout" of major retailers to obtain large discounts. (Discounts have been found in some instances to be inconsistent with cost savings associated with large orders.) The buyer, as well as the seller, is held liable for violations.

Unfortunately, federal pricing legislation such as the Robinson-Patman Act is only applicable in interstate commerce. Intrastate violations are not covered unless state or local legislation exists to govern them. It is encouraging, though, that price discrimination cases have declined with increased use of nonprice competition. Buyers still may bargain for discounts and other concessions in order to obtain the best "legal" prices possible, as long as the same concessions are given to competing retailers who provide the same services (e.g., promotion, distribution) to the seller.

PRICE FIXING   **Horizontal price fixing** exists when competitors at the same channel level (i.e., two or more retailers, wholesalers, or manufacturers)

When Is a Sale Price Really a Bargain?

Sales are so commonplace in retail stores that they have become suspect. Regulators are not buying the fact that everything is on sale these days, and they are closing in on retailers in response to consumer complaints. In May 1990, Massachusetts put into effect a law that regulators consider one of the toughest to govern retail pricing practices such as price comparison claims, price and quality disclosure, and availability of advertised merchandise markdowns. It requires disclosure in sale catalogs that the so-called original price, used in comparison to advertised sale prices, is only a reference price and not necessarily the original selling price.

A vice president of the Council of Better Business Bureaus says the key issue is how to go about judging whether a sale price has market validity. In other words, was the stated regular price a good faith price—or just a fictitious one set up for the purpose of having a future sale? In an attempt to establish new price advertising standards, the council has met with large retailers and attorneys general from six states.

Sale prices once were confined to end-of-season clearances, but today markdowns have become a year-round promotional tactic. The trend has escalated due to intensified competition between department stores and offprice retailers, faster markdowns on fashion merchandise, lower prices to generate cash flow for retailers affected by mergers, and the increase in retailers' private label merchandise.

Customers are conditioned to wait for bargains, expecting better deals from anticipated markdowns. However, consumers are suspicious that all of the sales may not be "for real," and feel frustrated that they may not be getting the absolute best price. A retail consultant interviewed Chicago shoppers after Christmas, and learned that 82 percent believed they could have gotten better deals "if they had just looked a little harder."

In December 1989, the New York state attorney general filed suit against Sears, Roebuck & Co., charging that the retailer's "everyday low price" strategy has created a false impression of significant discounts from former prices. Sears, who had developed the pricing strategy in an effort to get away from constant sales, denied the charges.

In other lawsuits, New York City's Department of Consumer Affairs charged Newmark & Lewis Inc., a consumer electronics chain, with deceptive price advertising. The Missouri attorney general's office required three St. Louis furniture stores to pay $352,000 in restitution to 2,500 consumers who were misled by comparative manufacturer's suggested list prices. Colorado charged the May D&F unit of May Department Stores, accused of offering prices for a "limited time only," when such prices are generally offered on a continuous basis throughout the year, and that the company used pre-printed price tags with inflated regular prices.

Some stores are backing off on sales as a marketing strategy. Dayton Hudson Corp. cut storewide sales promotions by one-third in 1989. Toys "R" Us Inc. constantly adjusts prices, and does not feel that it needs to advertise prices to generate traffic. Retailers are finding that it is difficult to retreat from a markdown strategy—particularly when customers expect it. The key issue, according to many attorneys general, is how retailers define "regular" prices and how those prices are used in ads that hype discounts. They agree that the retailer must sell a substantial quantity at a "regular" price for it to be considered legitimate.

Adapted from Agins, Teri (1990), "As Retailers' Sales Crop Up Everywhere, Regulators Wonder if the Price Is Right," *The Wall Street Journal* (February 13), B1, B5; Schwadel, Francine (1989), "Sears Calls It 'Low Prices,' New York Calls It Misleading," *The Wall Street Journal* (December 22), B1, B4.

HORIZONTAL PRICE FIXING

competitors at the same channel level agree to charge similar prices for similar goods

VERTICAL PRICE FIXING

retail prices are controlled by manufacturers and wholesalers

agree to charge the same or similar prices for the same goods. The focus is on collusion, not on the fairness of the price. Under the Sherman Act, prosecution by the Justice Division may result in both personal and corporate fines and/or prison sentences. The Clayton Act also allows injured parties to sue for three times the amount of damages incurred.

Vertical price fixing exists when retail prices are controlled by manufacturers or wholesalers. This practice, also referred to as resale price maintenance, was protected by fair trade laws until passage of the Consumer Goods

Pricing Act of 1975. The original intent of fair trade legislation was to protect small retailers and full service retailers who charged full retail prices from losing business to discount stores. Retailers were expected to charge their customers according to the manufacturer's suggested price. Consumer groups and channel members brought pressure to stop this practice so that retailers could price more competitively. However, manufacturers' recommended list prices still remain a major determinant of retail prices.

MINIMUM PRICE LAWS   One pricing strategy used to increase store traffic is that of selling key products at very low prices, sometimes below cost (loss leaders). Large retailers may put small retailers out of business if this predatory pricing practice is extensive. Gasoline price wars have seen major oil companies charging such low prices that independent service station operators could not compete and had to shut down their businesses.

Some states have minimum price laws that require retailers to charge a price that is high enough to cover the cost of goods plus a given amount for operating expenses. However, since loss leaders generally favor customers, these laws are not always enforced. There may be legitimate reasons for selling below cost in order to minimize losses on merchandise that is damaged, or perishable, or if the business is closing. Otherwise, retailers are expected to charge an amount equal to cost plus a predetermined markup percentage.

UNIT PRICING   As previously discussed, some retailers voluntarily display prices for individual products on a per unit (foot, yard) or weight (ounce, pound) basis, as well as the total price. This practice is mandated by law in some states in order to ensure that customers have a common basis for comparing prices and making intelligent purchase decisions. Interestingly, unit pricing points out the fact that smaller packages are sometimes a better buy than larger packages on a per unit basis, contrary to what most consumers might expect.

ITEM PRICE REMOVAL   The increased use of electronic scanners and cash registers has increased efficiency at the checkout point. While most customers are familiar with stores that use this equipment without marking each individual item, the absence of price on each item was not readily accepted in the beginning. Although each price does not have to be rung up manually by the cashier, some states and local governments have responded to consumer concerns by enacting legislation to prevent retailers from marking prices on shelves or signs at point of purchase without marking each individual item.

Giant Food, Inc., a major grocery chain, was a leader in installing scanning systems in a Maryland store in 1975. The company went to great lengths to educate customers and familiarize them with the new system. In spite of documented cost savings and acceptance by a majority of consumers, the Maryland Senate and consumer activists attempted (unsuccessfully) to legislate individual item pricing. Giant has continued to provide lower prices to customers in the Washington-Maryland-Virginia area due to item price removal (Beauchamp, 1983). However, complaints about the absence of individual item pricing have led to the forbidding of item price removal in some other areas.

PRICE ADVERTISING   The Federal Trade Commission (FTC) may take legal action when advertised statements about prices are found to be false or misleading. Deceptive claims include comparison to a manufacturer's recommended list price (which is rarely charged), comparison to competitors' prices, and comparison of discount or sale prices to a questionable original price. Claims must be supported and legitimate to avoid action by the FTC.

Another form of fraudulent price advertising is *bait and switch*, where a product is advertised at an extremely low price ("bait") to entice consumers into the store. However, when the consumer tries to buy the item, either it is not available and/or the salesperson tries to sell a more expensive model ("switch"). Major retailers, such as Sears, have been accused of this practice, but cannot be prosecuted unless a customer complaint has been filed.

In 1988, the FTC and several state regulatory agencies investigated the marketing practices of Audi of America, Inc. The car manufacturer was accused of using bait and switch tactics with its rebate plan on the Audi 5000 model. Audi mailed rebate coupons to 400,000 past and present customers, offering them a $4,000 discount (base price $22,180) due to plans to discontinue the model after three years of defending charges that the car has a dangerous tendency to accelerate suddenly on its own. The rebate program was expected to bring in 24,000 potential buyers. However, there was one hitch that led to the bait and switch charges: at the beginning of the program, Audi had an inventory of only 5,550 of these cars left to sell (Stertz, 1988).

Pricing is one of the most regulated aspects of retailing because of its high visibility and potential impact on competition and on the welfare of consumers and society. Although violations often are difficult to prove and prosecutions may be low relative to infractions, the existing laws do serve as a threat to those who would use discriminatory or deceptive pricing tactics.

Other types of legislation have an indirect effect on retail prices. Examples include federal, state, and local regulations concerning matters such as minimum wage laws, zoning ordinances, and building specifications. Personnel expenses, a major cost factor, must be included as operating expenses in markup calculations. Observation of zoning ordinances and building specifications may add costs to store operations, which must be recovered from the retail price structure as it affects sales revenues. Although pricing legislation has proven to be necessary, it generally adds to the cost of operating the business and, therefore, affects retail prices.

Summary

A retailer's pricing policies and strategies are determined in accordance with the company's mission and financial objectives. They are influenced by factors in the external and internal environments. Consumer markets and location, other businesses (including competitors and suppliers), and the legal, political and economic environments provide external pressures on retail prices. Prices are related to decisions in each of the store's functional areas, particularly because of their role in covering expenses. Prices also must be consistent with the other aspects of the retailing mix: product assortments,

BAIT AND SWITCH
customer is enticed into store by extremely low advertised prices but may find the item unavailable or be pressured to buy higher price item

place, promotion, and services. The RIS makes pricing data available to managers, providing an interface between the internal and external environments.

Pricing policies govern specific pricing strategies. Such policies include decisions about competitive pricing (at, above, or below market), one-price policy versus flexible pricing, odd pricing, leader pricing, price lining, multiple-unit pricing, and unit pricing.

Financial objectives are goals set by the retailer, which provide the retailer with guidelines for policy and strategy decisions. Financial objectives are generally stated in terms of sales, return-on-investment, or dollar profit. The effect of pricing policies on achieving profit goals is demonstrated with gross margin return on investment (GMROI) and the strategic profit model analysis.

Pricing strategies evolve from pricing policies and financial objectives. Prices are determined by two basic approaches: a cost orientation and a demand orientation. A cost-oriented pricing strategy is based on a standard markup over the wholesale cost, whereas a demand-oriented pricing strategy considers consumer characteristics and responses in setting prices. Calculating prices involves an understanding of markups on cost and retail, initial markup, maintained markup, and various price adjustments.

The effect of consumer markets on prices can be described in terms of price elasticity of demand and customer characteristics. Price elasticity of demand is based on traditional economic theory that measures the changes in demand for each unit change in price, under the assumption that lower prices will result in higher demand and vice versa. Consumer demographic, psychographic, and behavioral characteristics provide useful information for establishing prices and for segmenting markets.

The nature of competition in the retailer's market plays an important role in pricing decisions. The number of competitors, their actions, and responses, including price wars, all must be considered.

Channel influences on retail prices include power position of one channel member relative to another, length of the distribution channel, negotiations for terms of sale, control over wholesale costs, and willingness to market and sell the product.

Regulatory constraints on pricing decisions are intended to protect two parties. Legislation to prevent restraint of trade and unfair competition among businesses is aimed at eliminating price discrimination, price fixing, and selling below cost. Consumer protection legislation includes the regulation of unit pricing, item price removal, and price advertising.

Questions for Review and Comprehension

1. The manager of a computer store is trying to determine pricing policies for his retail operation. Advise him as to the relevant factors in (a) the external environment and (b) the internal environment that will have an impact on this decision.

2. Describe the relationship between pricing strategies and the other elements of the retail mix (merchandise assortments, store location, promotion, and services offered).

3. Give examples of several types of financial objectives that must be considered in establishing pricing strategies.

Part IV

4. The effects of different pricing policies can be illustrated by comparing the GMROI ratio for two different price levels. Brown's Shirt Shop purchases 500 shirts at a cost of $9.00 per shirt. Average inventory at cost is $750.00. Calculate the gross margin and GMROI for each of the following:
   a. Brown's Shirt Shop sells the 500 shirts for $15.00 each at retail.
   b. Brown's Shirt Shop sells the 500 shirts for $12.00 each at retail.
Discuss other factors that might affect the number of shirts sold at each of these prices.

5. Explain the differences among the various competitive pricing policies, and give specific examples of local and national retailers who pursue each competitive strategy. Include an identification of the competitors being used as a benchmark for pricing above, below, or at the market in each case.

6. Define and give examples of each of the following pricing policies: one-price policy versus flexible pricing; odd pricing; leader pricing; price lining; multiple-unit pricing; and unit pricing.

7. Compare and contrast cost-oriented and demand-oriented pricing strategies. Include the advantages and disadvantages of each method.

8. A small stationery store sells a line of greeting cards for a retail price of $1.50.
   a. Calculate the markup at cost if the retailer pays 75 cents each for these cards.
   b. Calculate the markup at retail for the same retail price and cost.
   c. Briefly discuss when each of these methods of calculating markup might be preferred.
   d. If the stationery store manager wants to sell a group of greeting cards for $2.00, and achieve a markup of 40 percent at retail, what is the most he can pay for the cards at wholesale?

9. Differentiate between initial markup and maintained markup; include an explanation of why an initial markup should be higher than the maintained markup.

10. Given the following actual figures for Bart's Men's Store, calculate the firm's maintained markup:

Operating expenses:	$ 16,000
Profit:	$ 8,000
Net sales:	$100,000

11. Assuming that Bart's wants to maintain the markup calculated in #10 above, and has planned retail reductions of 8 percent of sales, calculate the required initial markup percent.

12. a. Cite several reasons why a retailer might adjust initial prices upwards.
   b. Assuming that the original retail price for a wristwatch is $50.00, calculate the additional markup if the retail price is increased to $60.00.
   c. Calculate the maintained markup for these watches if the retailer pays $30.00 per watch and sells 25 at the original price and 20 at the new price.

13. a. Cite several examples of situations that can lead to marking down prices of merchandise in stock.
   b. A retailer has been selling a line of sweaters for $40.00 each, but has found it necessary to mark these sweaters down to $30.00 to clear them out before new spring merchandise arrives. Calculate the mark-down as a percent of the original price and as a percent of the reduced price.

c. Calculate the total markdown percent if the retailer sold 300 sweaters (two-thirds at the original price of $40.00 and one-third at the reduced price of $30.00), with total net sales of $11,000.00.

14. Calculate the price elasticity of demand for candy bars if a 10 percent increase in price results in a 5 percent decrease in demand. Now, calculate the price elasticity of demand if a 5 percent decrease in price results in a 7 percent increase in demand. Based on your calculations, would you consider the demand for these candy bars to be elastic or inelastic?

15. Describe and give specific examples of various ways that consumer characteristics can provide a basis for price segmentation.

16. Explain how each of the following can have an impact on a retailer's pricing strategy: competitive position of the retailer and anticipated competitive responses; supplier and channel influences; regulatory constraints; and ethical considerations.

References

Beauchamp, Tom L. (1983), *Case Studies in Business, Society and Ethics*, Englewood Cliffs, N.J.: Prentice-Hall, Inc., 82–88.

Cox, Meg (1988), "Art Prices Continue Their Trip to the Stars, Belying Predictions About a Market Fall," *The Wall Street Journal* (May 19), 29.

Deveny, Kathleen (1990), "Middle-Price Brands Come Under Siege," *The Wall Street Journal* (April 2), B1, B8.

Dommermuth, William P. (1984), *Promotion: Analysis, Creativity, and Strategy*, Boston, Mass.: Kent Publishing Company, 45–51.

Hupp, Susanne (1991), "Bargain Bonanza: Palm Beach Thrifts Resell Upscale Gifts," *The Orlando Sentinel* (January 27), J9, J13.

Kerwin, Kathleen (1989), "Troubled Circle K Is Turning This Way and That," *Business Week* (November 20), 78, 80.

Pereira, Joseph (1990), "Discount Department Stores Struggle Against Rivals That Strike Aisle by Aisle," *The Wall Street Journal* (June 19), B1, B8.

Pitzer, Mary J. (1987), "Electronics 'Superstores' May Have Blown a Fuse," *Business Week* (June 8), 90.

Rose, Robert L. (1988), "Widespread Delays Seen Plaguing Summer Air Travel," *The Wall Street Journal* (June 28), 31.

Schwadel, Francine (1989), "Ferocious Competition Tests the Pricing Skills of a Retail Manager," *The Wall Street Journal* (June 21), 4.

Stertz, Bradley A. (1988), "Audi Rebate Plan on 5000 Model Has the Look of Bait and Switch," *The Wall Street Journal* (June 21), 33.

Thomas, Paulette (1988), "Big Airlines Raise Some One-Way Fares by $5, Affecting Mostly Business Travel," *The Wall Street Journal* (June 21), 4.

Toy, Steward (1988), "Will Samurai Marketing Work for Suzuki?," *Business Week* (June 27), 33.

Wheatley, John J. and John S. Y. Chiu (1977), "The Effects of Price, Store Image, and Product and Respondent Characteristics on Perceptions of Quality," *Journal of Marketing Research* (May), 185.

COMMUNICATION WITH CUSTOMERS

CHAPTER Fifteen

Outline

Introduction to the Promotional Mix

Advertising

Personal Selling

Sales Promotion

Publicity

Direct Marketing in Retailing

Reseller Support

Budgeting for Promotion

Customer Services and Communication with Customers

Summary

Learning Objectives

After studying this chapter, the student will be able to:

1. Explain the relationship between promotion and other retail functions.
2. Recognize the role of promotional efforts in communicating with the retailer's internal and external publics.
3. Define and discuss each of the promotional elements in terms of objectives, types, advantages and disadvantages.
4. Recognize the role of direct marketing and reseller support in promotion.
5. Compare and contrast the major approaches for promotion budgeting.
6. Give a rationale for including various customer services in the promotional mix, and describe the major decisions to be made in regard to services.

L. L. Bean Restored My Soles—and Warmed My Soul

A few weeks before my birthday last year, my wife asked me what I wanted for the occasion. I told her that I had just about everything I needed or wanted, and that I would be happy with something silly or funny. She should save the money until we decided on a gift for both of us or for the house.

"No, no," she said. "I'm not planning on spending a lot of money, but I want to get you something you really want."

I thought for quite a few days before answering. "What I would really like is to get new rubber chain-link bottoms on my lounger boots."

"Why don't I just buy you a new pair?" she asked.

"First, they're expensive, and second, mine are in perfectly good shape except that the bottoms are so old and slick they are more like ice skates."

"OK," she said, "You make the arrangements, and I'll pay."

Armed with an 800 number, I called G. H. Bass, whose logo was on the boots, and from whom I assumed I had bought the boots 30 years ago, while I was still an undergraduate. The young man who answered was courteous, but said that

Communication with customers is a vital key to successful sales at L. L. Bean.

Bass had not made that particular boot for many years and that I had most probably made the purchase from L. L. Bean, which handled their mail-order business at that time. He gave me the Bean 800 number.

A young woman took the call for Bean (I use 'young' in these cases both because of the sound of the voices and the clear, crisp un-world-weary concern in her/their tone). She quickly apologized that I had been intercepted by an automatic voice and put on hold. Introducing herself as Maggie, she asked how she could help me. I explained my call to Bass, and told her that they had suggested I call Bean.

"Unfortunately, it's the weekend," she said. "There's no one in repairs right now. Let me put you on hold and see the best way to handle this."

She was back on the line in a few moments. "Well, it seems that we can fix Bass boots, but let me get your number and call you back on Monday after I have spoken to repairs, so we do this properly." I gave her my office number, the size of the boots, and their style, and asked if she would also inquire if it would be possible to have them lined at the same time.

On Monday, Maggie called me at my office and told me to send the boots to the repair department of L. L. Bean in Freeport, Maine, along with a check for $24, and said that I should insure the package. She was sorry that Bean couldn't line the boots. It would change the size, and they couldn't guarantee that the boots would fit properly if they did. "I sure hope I'm here to take your next order for a repair; that ought to be somewhere around 2020."

Off went the boots—insured. And, a few days later I received a card from customer service acknowledging receipt of my "Feather Weight Lounger Bts Not Beans, G. H. Bass 10M." and my "24.00 CK." I was to expect delivery in "EST Time 4–6 WKS."

My "4–6 WKS" landed right before the Christmas holidays, so I spotted them a few extra weeks for the pressure of the season before calling back. It was the day after Christmas and a charming Shirley took the call. She apologized that the day after Christmas was a "floating" holiday for the staff in repairs, but if

continued

599

I would call the next day and ask for either Ann or Gary at extension 4455, she would have passed the query on.

Ann's boss picked up the phone the next morning and said that she was away from her desk. "I'll try and track her down, but if we get cut off my name is Steve Graham at extension 4445, just so you have someone accountable at our end." A few minutes later he was back. She was away briefly and he would have her call me as soon as she returned. Would I please give him the repair number and package I.D. so she could expedite my inquiry? He also asked if I would be at the same number tomorrow just in case they had any trouble tracking down my problem.

Within 15 minutes, Ann was on the line and terribly sorry that I hadn't been called before. "It seems that the old Bass upper last will only fit an eight medium Bean rubber bottom. You were supposed to have been called. What would you like us to do?"

I allowed as how I hadn't tried a Bean 8M on recently, but was pretty sure that even if it was generous, it would be too snug. Ann apologized again for my inconvenience and trouble and said that my boots would be returned right away along with my $24. I thanked her and said that it was all a kind of dream idea anyway.

I sighed. I wasn't sure what I was going to do with my super slick loungers when they got home, but it was comforting to know that so many people cared about them.

Twenty minutes later, while I was fielding another call, my assistant stuck a note in front of me. "L. L. Bean on the line."

I rang off and picked up the call. "Hi, it's Steve. I just caught Ann as she was heading out for a meeting, and we've talked to the head of boot repairs. They've figured out a way to put the 10M bottoms on the Bass uppers.

They'll send them out this afternoon. Have a Happy New Year. Sorry it took so long to get this solved."

Thirty years from now I hope I'm speaking to Maggie and Steve and Ann. They gave me a wonderful lift. On this anniversary of our happy encounter, I wish them as happy a holiday as they gave me last year.

SOURCE: Barber, Richard (1990), "How L. L. Bean Restored My Soles—and Warmed My Soul," *The Wall Street Journal* (December 18), A12. Reprinted by permission of Wall Street Journal © 1990, Dow Jones & Company, Inc. All rights reserved.

Introduction to the Promotional Mix

CHAPTER Fifteen

Discussion in previous chapters was concerned with various strategic and functional retail management decisions. Obviously, a retailer must have the right merchandising strategy and format, product/service mix, pricing and location strategies—and in the right combination—to attract an identified target market. Customers expect to be able to buy the type of goods and services they want, and to be able to shop at a time and place that is compatible with their lifestyles. How they shop and what they buy is further influenced by the retailer's pricing strategy. Customers may prefer to make their purchases from home by mail, phone, computer, or TV, or to shop in person at stores that they find appealing.

Even if the retailer has a "perfect" mix of merchandise, location, and prices, it is insufficient if customers are not informed—or have misconceptions—about it. Therefore, a well-designed promotional mix must be developed and managed so that customers will know what the retailer has to offer. In this chapter, the focus is on elements of the promotional mix.

Customer Communication: Internal and External Environments

Good customer communication programs start inside the company. Communication is necessary both within and between functional areas, throughout all levels of personnel. The store's employees are an important aspect of customer communication. They need to be informed about company policies and procedures and be knowledgeable about the merchandise and services they sell, so they can deal effectively with customers on a daily basis. Thus, communication programs aimed at personnel also provide a primary source of information for customers and, as a promotional tool, make a major contribution to the store's image.

The retailer's external communication efforts go well beyond promoting the retailer's company and offerings to customers. Customers benefit indirectly from the retailer's ability to communicate with others outside the company. In a sense, external communication with suppliers, channel intermediaries, and governmental agencies is another important aspect of a promotional program because it can translate into better merchandise selections, services, and more convenient shopping for customers. It is not unusual for a retailer to have to "sell" itself to these various constituencies in order to persuade them to take actions that will ultimately benefit consumers. For example, a manufacturer may need to be persuaded to design and produce goods to the retailer's specifications, or a city council may need to be persuaded to allow a store to operate during nontraditional business hours to satisfy the needs of a particular customer segment. (Many of these efforts that are related to a formal promotional program but operated separately may be classified as public relations activities.) Although consumers are our major concern in this chapter, all audiences for internal and external communication programs are illustrated in Exhibit 15–1 to show that they are but one part of a total promotional program that, in reality, cannot be separated from the rest.

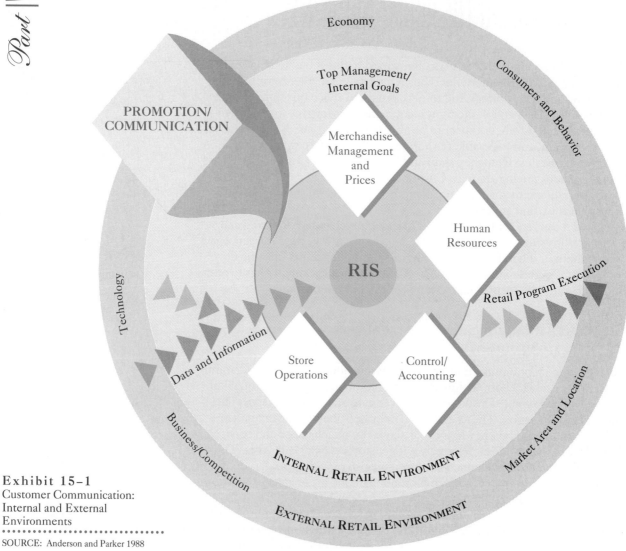

Exhibit 15–1
Customer Communication:
Internal and External
Environments
••••••••••••••••••••••••••
SOURCE: Anderson and Parker 1988

Strategic Planning and Effective Customer Communication

Effective customer communication programs are designed in accord with the retailer's business philosophy and mission. Promotional strategies must "fit" with the firm's corporate objectives as defined by the strategic plan. (See Exhibit 15–2.) They must also fit with the other elements in the retail mix (e.g., merchandise assortments, prices, location).

Retail promotion takes a long-term perspective at the strategic level and a shorter-term perspective at the tactical level. Long-term objectives include building market share and customer loyalty. Promotional strategy emphasizes the retailer's competitive advantage and is geared toward developing a strong consumer franchise that will continue to buy more and shop more frequently over a long period of time.

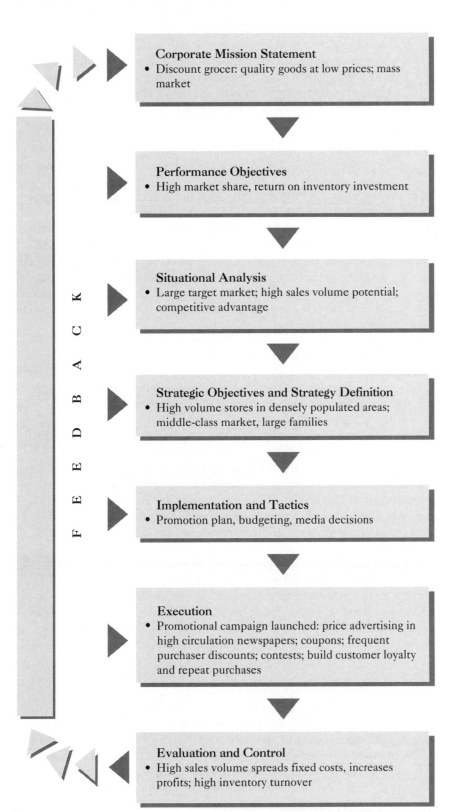

Corporate Mission Statement
- Discount grocer: quality goods at low prices; mass market

Performance Objectives
- High market share, return on inventory investment

Situational Analysis
- Large target market; high sales volume potential; competitive advantage

Strategic Objectives and Strategy Definition
- High volume stores in densely populated areas; middle-class market, large families

Implementation and Tactics
- Promotion plan, budgeting, media decisions

Execution
- Promotional campaign launched: price advertising in high circulation newspapers; coupons; frequent purchaser discounts; contests; build customer loyalty and repeat purchases

Evaluation and Control
- High sales volume spreads fixed costs, increases profits; high inventory turnover

F E E D B A C K

Exhibit 15–2
Strategic Planning and Effective Customer Communication: An Illustration

Short-term objectives are more concerned with generating cash flow, store traffic, and other immediate results. Promotion generally is in the form of price advertising, special events or incentives, or limited offers that are designed to get immediate results. In both the long and short term, promotional methods and timing must be consistent with the retailer's overall corporate strategy.

Promotional Mix Elements: An Overview

Retail promotion is but one aspect of the total promotional effort involved in moving goods through the channels of distribution from producer to consumer. A retailer's promotional decisions are affected to a considerable extent by whether the producer pursues a push or a pull strategy to obtain sales. A **pull strategy** is focused on building consumer demand. A great deal of effort and money are spent on advertising and sales promotion aimed directly at consumers. The intent is that consumers will demand the product from the retailer, who will demand it from the wholesaler, who in turn will demand it from the producer. Conversely, a **push strategy** relies heavily upon the aggressive use of a sales force and trade promotions to push a product through the distribution channel from producer to wholesaler to retailer to consumer.

The retailer's promotional task may vary, depending upon the producer's choice of either a pull or a push strategy. If the producer has stimulated demand with a pull strategy, the retailer's role most likely will be to let customers know the product is available and where and how they can buy it. If the producer is using a push strategy, retail buyers will be the object of heavy promotional efforts to persuade them to stock the product in their stores. The retailer, in turn, will need to be more aggressive in promoting to customers and convincing them to buy. Thus, retailers must consider their own promotional strategies within the context of promotional efforts by other channel members. Discussion in the remainder of the chapter is limited to retail promotion.

A retailer's promotional mix consists of a blend of methods used to communicate with the firm's target market. These methods may be personal (between a retail salesperson and customer) or nonpersonal without face-to-face communication (e.g., mail, print or electronic media, point-of-purchase). The four major types of promotion are advertising, personal selling, sales promotion, and publicity, as shown in Exhibit 15–3. Each of the basic promotional tools has a number of variations that the retailer may select, as described in the following sections. Since these tools rarely are used in isolation, they should be combined to create a synergy in achieving established promotional and strategic objectives.

In general, the purpose of promotion is to inform, persuade, or remind present and prospective customers about the business and what it has to sell. The intent may be to inform a target market about specific features of the retail firm, its stores and specific merchandise offerings. Some promotional efforts are designed to persuade consumers to make a purchase immediately or in the near future. Others are designed to remind consumers that the retailer exists; this type generally follows the form of image or institutional advertising, with no overt attempt to sell a given product.

Exhibit 15–3
Promotional Mix Elements: A Summary

Radio Shack has the largest totally in-house advertising agency in the U.S., which produces an extensive advertising program for the print, television and radio media.

ADVERTISING

Retail sales are affected by both the retailers' and manufacturers' advertisements. **Advertising** is "any paid form of nonpersonal presentation and promotion of ideas, goods, or services by an identified sponsor" (Committee on Definitions, 1960). The best and worst ad campaigns of the 1980s were named in an informal survey of Madison Avenue advertising executives. Wendy's "Where's the beef?" and the California Raisins television commercials will long be remembered as two of the most popular ads of the decade. Other "best" campaigns include Apple Computer's "1984" commercial that was shown during the 1984 Super Bowl, two of Pepsi's commercials featuring Michael J. Fox and archaeology students of the future, American Express's "Don't leave home without it" campaign and their "portraits series" using photos of celebrity cardmembers, and Nike's "Just Do It" campaign and the early '80s billboards of beautifully photographed athletes. Burger King's disastrous "Herb the Nerd" and the zen-inspired Infiniti car ads were chosen as the "worst" campaigns (Lipman, 1989c). While these "best" and "worst" ad designations were based on the opinions of advertising industry experts, rather than on retail sales results, customers generally are more inclined to buy in response to those ads that they find appealing. They are not as apt to buy in response to ads that are perceived as demeaning, confusing, or irksome.

PULL STRATEGY
promotional efforts geared toward building customer demand

PUSH STRATEGY
promotional efforts focused on aggressive use of sales force and trade promotions; product is "pushed" through channels of distribution

ADVERTISING
paid nonpersonal presentation or promotion of an identified sponsor's goods, services or ideas

Advertising executives predicted the following trends as they entered the 1990s:

1. The balance of advertising spending may swing away from promotions (e.g., coupons, contests), and towards traditional media advertising.
2. Advertisers will try to find ways to combine image advertising with short-term promotions.
3. "Personalized" marketing will make gains over mass marketing, due to more numerous and technologically sophisticated media outlets (e.g., personalized magazine ads that address subscribers by name).
4. Ad agencies will open up in Eastern Europe to seek opportunities there (Lipman, 1990).

The average American consumer is exposed to approximately 2,100 advertisements and commercials during an average week (Hodock, 1980). This high degree of exposure has two important implications for retailers: (1) it is a very potent promotional technique that advertisers have good reason to expect will achieve their objectives; and (2) an ad has to operate in a very competitive environment because it is but one of many trying to attract the attention of customers (Dommermuth, 1984).

Objectives of Retail Advertising

Retailers establish a variety of objectives that they expect their advertising dollars to achieve. Ideally, the objectives are quantified and stated in measurable terms within a given time frame (e.g., 10 percent increase in sales within three months), so that results can be evaluated during and after the execution of a campaign.

Retail advertising differs from manufacturer advertising. Manufacturers promote their products to retailers and other resellers in the channels of distribution, as well as to final consumers. Their ads to final customers are intended to build a consumer franchise for their products, such that retailers will be required to carry them in their inventories. Retailer ads, on the other hand, are designed to influence customers to buy their goods and services immediately, by giving more explicit price and shopping information. Most retail ads are run in local media with limited geographical coverage and are designed to inform shoppers about the benefits and degree of satisfaction that can be attained by buying their offerings.

Objectives will vary according to the retailer's corporate objectives over the long and short term, as well as stage in the product and store life cycles. In addition to providing support before the sale for retail salespeople, some general categories of objectives are as follows:

- *For new stores (or repositioned stores).* Advertising objectives may be to build awareness and initial store traffic, gain acceptance, and establish store image and competitive advantage.
- *For new products.* Objectives may be to build awareness, gain acceptance, and increase one-stop shopping possibilities.
- *For established stores and products.* Objectives may be to persuade customers to increase number of store visits, average amount of each transaction, announce special events or sales, remind them about the store and its merchandise and services, and to convey benefits of

shopping with the advertiser versus competitors. Ads may also be designed to build image with present and prospective customers and with the community in general.

Types of Retail Advertising

There are two broad categories of retail advertising: institutional and promotional (Edwards and Lebowitz, 1981). Institutional advertising attempts to present the store as a desirable place to shop when the reader or listener is ready to buy and seeks long-term patronage. Promotional advertising tries to convince the customer to buy specific merchandise at the time the store offers it for sale and seeks immediate response. Results can be evaluated from daily sales figures, in contrast to results of institutional advertising that can be evaluated only by examining trend data for the store's business.

Institutional advertising is concerned with building store reputation, dramatizing its place in the community, pointing out its advantages, and instilling confidence in the goods and services that it sells. It may be focused on a single department or the entire store and can be classified as service or prestige advertising. Service advertising informs the audience about store policies, services, and facilities, and attempts to create a close relationship between the store and its customers. Prestige advertising is concerned almost entirely with the merchandise or service sold by the retailer. It emphasizes assortments and new, unusual, or exclusive merchandise to show that the store can offer the latest that is available in the market, as well as staple goods.

Promotional advertising attempts to promote the immediate sale of merchandise or services through regular price line advertising, special promotion or "sale" advertising, and clearance advertising. Regular price line advertising tries to convey the impression that it always carries a full assortment of fresh, first-quality, timely merchandise at everyday regular prices. Special promotion advertising is usually run for a short period of time to announce price concessions (markdowns, special purchases) for the purpose of generating immediate sales volume or store traffic. Retailers use clearance advertising to dispose of unwanted inventory, such as old stock and slow selling merchandise, to make room for more saleable goods.

Advantages and Disadvantages of Advertising

General advantages and disadvantages of retail advertising are discussed in this section as they apply broadly to all media. Of course, each medium has its own strengths and weaknesses. Retail advertising serves as an effective tool for pre-selling large numbers of consumers. The costs per person reached is relatively low in comparison to personal selling. Advertising media has become increasingly specialized, enabling the retailer to reach a more narrowly defined market segment. Print media ads can be read multiple times by the same reader or shared among a number of readers. Retail advertising can be used to provide advance information about products and services to customers, which can be helpful for a limited- or self-service retailer.

There are some disadvantages to retail advertising. First, print media, radio and TV ads must be planned in advance, and are not easily changed in

INSTITUTIONAL ADVERTISING
builds store reputation and image to present the store as a desirable place to shop

PROMOTIONAL ADVERTISING
promotes immediate sale of merchandise

a short period of time. Therefore, in comparison to personal selling, the message is inflexible and cannot be adapted to the needs of individual customers. Advertising media generally reaches a large audience—perhaps beyond the market segment targeted by the retailer. Thus, the retailer may have to pay for wasted coverage. Customer perceptions of print media ads are affected by the perceptions of the medium itself and of other content surrounding an ad. Some print media, such as newspaper inserts, "free" circulars, and direct mail may be discarded without ever being read.

Developing the Advertising Plan

The advertising plan is a subset of the retailer's overall promotional plan which, in turn, is a subset of the company's strategic plan for the business as a whole. Development of an advertising plan can be described in terms of the advertising management process, as shown in Exhibit 15–4. The process includes corporate and marketing strategies, advertising strategy, strategy implementation, and control activities (Shimp and DeLozier, 1986).

CORPORATE AND MARKETING STRATEGIES **Corporate strategy** is determined by top management and represents long-term objectives` (usually three to five years), plans, and budgets for all business units and departments. Corporate strategy is based on an analysis of the opportunities and threats that exist in the external environment, and the retailer's internal strengths and weaknesses. **Marketing strategy** goes beyond corporate strategy and is concerned with plans, budgets, and controls needed to direct the firm's retailing mix. The marketing strategy serves the purpose of coordinating the various retailing mix elements and assuring that the retailer's marketing efforts are in accord with corporate strategy.

ADVERTISING STRATEGY Corporate and marketing strategies provide direction for the overall promotional strategy, which in turn determines the **advertising strategy.** Advertising strategy determines the amount that can be invested in advertising, which markets the advertising should be directed toward, how advertising should be coordinated with other elements of the retail marketing mix, and to some extent how the advertising strategy is to be executed. There are five major activities that generally are included in an advertising strategy: objective setting, budgeting, message strategy, media strategy, and coordination. Examples of objectives were given earlier; budgets and media strategy (selection of media categories and specific vehicles to deliver the advertising messages) will be discussed in a later section. Message strategy is involved with the symbolism used by the advertiser to convey the advertiser's thoughts. The symbolism may take a number of forms, with the most common being the spoken or written word. The coordination phase of the advertising strategy includes the measures that are necessary to ensure the coordination of advertising with all other promotional elements, and with other retailing mix elements.

STRATEGY IMPLEMENTATION The **strategy implementation** phase is involved with day-to-day tactics of an advertising campaign. Implementation is concerned with shorter-term decisions such as the selection of a

Exhibit 15–4
The Advertising Management Process

Adapted from Shimp, Terence A. and M. Wayne DeLozier (1986), *Promotion Management and Marketing Communications.* New York: The Dryden Press, 307.

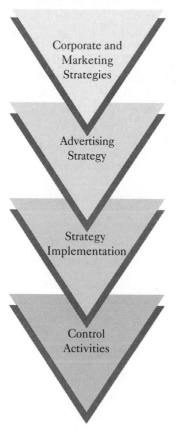

Corporate and Marketing Strategies

Advertising Strategy

Strategy Implementation

Control Activities

specific newspaper vehicle and advertising schedule, within the broader strategic choice of newspaper as the preferred medium.

CONTROL ACTIVITIES   **Control activities** provide a way to determine whether the retailer is achieving the objectives and plans established by the advertising strategy. In order to evaluate actual results against the retailer's plan, the objectives need to be quantified; before and after measurements are taken to determine any changes that have taken place or whether goals have been reached.

Advertising Media

Advertising media is described in terms of media vehicles and media categories. A **media vehicle** is a specific carrier of advertising messages, such as *U.S.A. Today, Time Magazine,* "Sixty Minutes," or the local evening news program. A **media category** is a broad group of vehicles that share similar physical characteristics and capabilities, such as newspapers, magazines, radio, and television (Dommermuth, 1984). According to these definitions, any mechanism that can carry an advertising message is an advertising vehicle (e.g., handbills, Yellow Pages, shopping carts, pencils, and blimps).

Three major considerations are involved in selecting media for retail advertising: (1) target audience that can be reached, (2) cost considerations within budget constraints, and (3) creative capacity. It is important to choose media that will convey the desired message to your audience. This is because the interpretation of an advertising message (and the retailer's image) is influenced by the content and quality of the media that surrounds it. Consideration of the environment or setting in which the audience will receive the message is also important. This applies to comparisons of both media categories (newspaper versus television) and vehicles (television daytime soap opera versus "Thirty-Something") to determine the level of involvement that the audience is apt to have in the message.

Characteristics of the media that are selected most often by retail advertisers are described next. These include print media (newspapers, magazines), broadcast media (radio, television), outdoor signs, and other types of media.

PRINT MEDIA   The two most common types of **print media** are newspapers and magazines. Shopping publications and other miscellaneous periodicals also fall into this category.

Newspapers are the primary medium used by retailers. Large numbers of people read the newspaper daily to stay current with local, state, national, and world events. Newspaper ads are an important source of shopping information for many consumers, who tend to take action soon after reading them. Newspapers have the advantage of tangibility and durability so that they can be kept as reference, and can carry store coupons. At the local level, newspaper advertising has a relatively low cost per reader, and some of these costs can be defrayed through cooperative advertising with manufacturers or other retailers. Newspapers offer some flexibility in that copy can be submitted or changed on relatively short notice. On the other hand, the quality of newspaper reproduction tends to be poor because of paper quality and ability

CORPORATE STRATEGY
long-term objectives, plans, and budgets for all business units and departments

MARKETING STRATEGY
plans, budgets, and controls needed to direct the firm's retailing mix

ADVERTISING STRATEGY
determines budget, methods, and execution of advertising campaign

STRATEGY IMPLEMENTATION
day-to-day tactics of an advertising campaign

CONTROL ACTIVITIES
method of determining whether retailer is achieving objectives

MEDIA VEHICLE
specific carrier of advertising messages

MEDIA CATEGORY
broad group of vehicles that share similar characteristics and capabilities

PRINT MEDIA
newspapers, magazines, and other periodicals

to reproduce color. An exception is the four-color advertising found in newspaper inserts, but these generally are produced elsewhere. In some cases, the retailer may be paying for wasted coverage of geographical areas or demographic characteristics.

Magazines offer a wide array of highly specialized media vehicles, targeted to specific customer segments. The retailer can choose among magazines that are targeted toward general interest groups *(Reader's Digest, TV Guide)* or specialized interest groups *(Sports Illustrated, PC Magazine, Playboy, Gourmet Magazine)*. An increasing number of retailers and manufacturers are targeting trendy suburbanites as mainstream fashion idols. These customers are considered the hip social set, the power brokers of trends, and are reached through publications such as *Details* and *L.A. Style.* For example, the Gap ran a campaign dubbed "Individuals of Style" that often featured funky artists and other personalities clad in basic Gap t-shirts (Deveney, 1990). However, the "Individuals of Style" celebrity campaign went out of style. At the end of 1990, the Gap switched to promoting the practical aspects of its merchandise—the style and fit of Gap jeans, workshirts, and other casual clothes (Schwadel, 1990b). Magazine advertisements that appeared in the *Saturday Evening Post* and *Ladies' Home Journal* in the 1920s and 1930s are pictured in Exhibit 15–5 to provide contrast with the avant-garde, upscale ads described above.

The high degree of selectivity in choosing a specific magazine helps to avoid wasted exposure. Time Warner publications and *Newsweek* have started

Exhibit 15–5
Saturday Evening Post and *Ladies Home Journal* Ads: 1920s and 1930s

This example (left) of institutional advertising over 60 years ago instilled confidence in Woolworth's service. Promotional advertising of specific products emphasizes their quality and availability as shown in this A&P ad from 1930 (right).

printing "personalized" magazines that include different ads for different types of subscribers, making this medium even more selective (Lipman, 1989a; Reilly, 1990). Magazines have a long life and are often kept for weeks or longer as reference or passed on to other readers. This medium has a high reproduction and content quality, which may enhance the image of the retailer's store and products. For example, Sears, Roebuck & Co. advertised its new fashion look in the August 1990 issue of *Vogue* magazine to get across the message that the giant retailer now sells stylish clothes. Sears also included *Glamour, Cosmopolitan, Mademoiselle,* and *Essence* in its media plan (Schwadel, 1990a).

On the negative side, the retailer may be paying for wasted circulation if not buying special advertising editions. Magazines do not offer the flexibility of newspaper or radio advertising, since they require a much longer lead time for ad copy.

Many retailers combine efforts to reach customers with advertising in shopping publications, generally referred to as shopping guides or community newspapers. This medium is popular where retailers want to reach a local geographic market, but newspaper circulation is either inadequate or reaches far beyond the retailer's market area. Shopping publications offer a lower cost, geographically targeted alternative—or supplement—to newspaper advertising. Most are published for the purpose of advertising, although some do carry news and feature articles. Shopping publications usually are distributed once a week, free of charge, to customers' homes or apartments.

BROADCAST MEDIA   The primary types of **broadcast media** are radio and television. In a general sense, broadcast also includes public address systems and other electronic media.

Although radio can be used as a stand-alone medium, retailers generally use it in conjunction with newspaper advertising or other promotion tools. Nearly every home has at least one radio; therefore it has the potential to reach a large audience. In addition, programming formats cater to specialized audience tastes, making it possible to have highly segmented and efficient advertising. Listener demographics can even be targeted by time of day. In fact, retailers can air radio commercials during "drive time" when business commuters are a captive audience in their automobiles. Radio is somewhat like personal communication between the retailer and its customers, because listeners choose stations with which they closely identify.

According to one radio industry executive, creativity is extremely important in radio advertising. Retailers like Tiffany & Co. and Hartmarx Specialty Stores have attributed much of the success of their radio ads to the creative approach. Tiffany cites the ability to use emotional appeals effectively. Hartmarx uses the same conversational voice for all of its radio spots. The commercials do not talk down to, or shout at, the audience; they stay focused in talking to businessmen and businesswomen (Josephson, 1989).

Radio offers the advantages of low cost and flexibility. The cost per person reached is cheaper than other mass media; messages can be aired or changed on short notice. On the negative side, radio is cluttered with many competing commercials and other "noise," the message is fleeting because no visual effects can be used. Rate structures are difficult to determine due to lack of standardized rates across markets. The latter is of concern to the large, multimarket retailer, but is not of concern to the small local firm.

BROADCAST MEDIA
radio, television, and other electronic media

Retail Advertising: The Good, the Bad, and the Ugly

The image of a retail business is enhanced—or tarnished—both by its own advertising and by that of the manufacturers of its products.

The automotive industry has been a prime target of concerns about truth in advertising, a source of retail customer skepticism and confusion. For example, Volvo was accused of rigging its 1989 "monster truck" commercial. A six-ton truck was placed on the roof of a Volvo car, which did not sag at all under the truck's weight—but the car was propped up with hidden jacks. General Motors showed an Oldsmobile 98 driving away after being dropped on the ground by parachute from an airborne cargo plane in a late 1990 ad. However, the car that drove away was not the empty shell of a car that was dropped from the plane. The companies and many advertising specialists agree that these ads do not make specific performance claims that are phony. However, the use of trick photography and skillful editing falls into an ethical gray area when those techniques suggest non-existent product attributes. To overcome this problem, Honda Motor Company puts a "dramatization" label on any commercial that depicts something that could be misconstrued by consumers.

Some retail ads offend, rather than mislead customers. The Roy Rogers fast-food chain irked members of the American School Food Service Association in 1988 with a commercial that tweaked school-cafeteria food and the dough-faced ladies who serve it. Although the commercial was successful in building sales, Roy Rogers pulled it after receiving the lunch ladies' complaints. In August 1990, Hardee's Food Systems, new owner of Rogers, ran the commercial again. The company said it was sorry if any group was offended, but they were running the commercial because it was fun and done in good taste. But after five days on the air the chain announced that it was pulling the ad—because the lunch ladies revolted again. As this example illustrates, interest groups can have a major impact on retail advertising decisions.

Price information in advertising is not always presented fairly or honestly. In response to this problem, retailers such as Sears, K mart, Woolworth, and May Department Stores have been working with the Council of Better Business Bureaus to develop an advertising code. The code would provide a national benchmark for comparative price claims in an effort to discourage misleading and deceptive practices by retailers. This effort demonstrates to government officials that advertisers can act responsibly by regulating themselves.

Adapted from Gordon, Richard L. (1989), "Retailers Ponder Price-Ad Guidelines," *Advertising Age* (September 25), 45; King, Thomas R. (1990), "Roy Rogers Reheats Some Ads, Withdraws Them After Protests," *The Wall Street Journal* (August 21), B6; Miller, Krystal and Jacqueline Mitchell (1990), "Car Marketers Test Gray Area of Truth in Advertising," *The Wall Street Journal* (November 19), B1, B6; "When the Price Isn't Right" (1988), *Advertising Age* (November 28), 16.

Television is a powerful and popular medium in American households where viewers are quite passive and ready to be entertained. Television can transmit a retail advertiser's message both verbally and visually. Television has the advantage of high quality color reproduction, the ability to show movement in commercials, and the use of special effects to create a desired mood or image. It can deliver an advertising message with an impact not possible with most other media. Programming formats and schedules make it possible to reach segmented audiences of interest to the retailer.

Television shares some of the disadvantages of radio, such as the fleeting nature of messages. They can not be replayed (unless recorded on a VCR—which is another problem for advertisers), and the audience may not pay attention to a commercial aired in an environment characterized by clutter and numerous competing commercials. Audience response to a program can affect the success of commercials aired during that time slot, such as the negative impact of low ratings given to the 1988 Summer Olympic Games. NBC gave up as much as $70 million in ad spots, and medal winners had little appeal for endorsements (Kneale, 1988; Lipman, 1988).

OUTDOOR ADVERTISING   Although **outdoor advertising** can take many innovative forms, the most popular type is the billboard or poster that is generally placed along a heavily traveled highway or in a downtown business area. Other types of outdoor advertising include transit ads placed on buses, trains, taxicabs, and other vehicles, blimps, and skywriting. To a large extent, the retailer is limited to geographic segmentation when using outdoor advertising. Outdoor advertising typically has broad repeat exposure. It is low cost relative to other advertising and useful for reminder advertising and for reaching destination shoppers. Because of the short exposure time for most outdoor advertising, the message must be brief and to the point. The major disadvantage of this medium is its lack of selectivity in regard to customer demographics or psychographics, although it may be placed close to target customers (e.g., ethnic neighborhoods, travelers seeking lodging).

OTHER FORMS OF ADVERTISING MEDIA   As previously noted, almost anything that can hold a message can be used for advertising. Many of these are at the point of sale, such as signs and videos on grocery carts, and banners across a store front announcing special prices. In-store newsletters that can be placed in a grocery bag at checkout have proven successful for West Point market, an upscale gourmet food market in Akron, Ohio (Hulin-Salkin, 1988).

The use of video monitors in selling areas and other places is becoming increasingly popular. The VideOcart, one of the newest innovations in high-technology advertising media, features a screen placed facing the shopper near a shopping cart's handle. Other high-technology promotional tools are discussed in Chapter 17.

Personal Selling

In a broad sense, all store employees who come in contact with customers are engaged in personal selling. Personal selling is an "oral presentation in a conversation with one or more prospective purchasers for the purpose of making a sale" (Committee on Definitions, 1960). This includes telephone operators, cashiers, service personnel involved in credit, giftwrap, alterations, maintenance, and other services. Although personal selling may involve mail or phone contact between a customer and salesperson, the emphasis here is on face-to-face sales transactions between the retailer's sales force and its customers. Personal selling is an extremely important aspect of a retailer's overall promotional strategy and requires the support of other promotional tools such as advertising and sales promotion. Salesforce issues were addressed in Chapter 11; here we will discuss briefly the objectives of personal selling, types of sales tasks, and the advantages and disadvantages of personal selling in comparison to other elements of the promotional mix.

OUTDOOR ADVERTISING
billboards, transit ads, blimps, or skywriting

Objectives of Personal Selling

Personal selling objectives are determined to a large extent by the level of personal service required for the retailer's target market, and the level that is affordable for planned profit margins. As in the case of advertising, salesforce objectives should be measurable and established for specific periods of time. Some broadly stated objectives are as follows:

- Provide information to customers about the store's merchandise, services and policies
- Customize presentations as needed
- Achieve a given level of sales and number of transactions within a prescribed time
- Increase sales to present customers
- Prospect for business from new customers
- Provide a level of service to customers that will encourage them to become repeat customers
- Promote the retail firm as well as its products and services to present and prospective customers
- Provide service to the customer after the sale

Types of Sales Tasks

Many types of salespeople perform a wide range of functions. In some retail stores, selling encompasses a high level of personal service. In others, a self-service format is used where personal selling, if there is any at all, is at a bare minimum. Salesforce expenditures should be carefully monitored and controlled because, along with merchandise inventories, they represent one of the retailer's largest operating expenses.

The two basic types of salespeople are order takers and order getters. **Order takers** are the most predominant in retailing. This is possible because most retail sales involve low-cost items that are pre-sold to customers by manufacturer and retailer media advertising. In addition, customers also are better informed and more capable of making their own purchase decisions than in the past.

Order getters are creative sellers. The customer probably is not pre-sold and may not even intend to make a purchase. The challenge to the salesperson is to execute each of the basic steps in personal selling to convince the shopper to buy.

1. Approach (in the store, or contact by phone or mail to get customer in the store)
2. Determine the customer's needs (ask the right questions, do more listening than talking)
3. Present merchandise to the customer (requires knowledge about social and psychological, as well as physical or technical aspects of the product)
4. Handle objections (depends on how well steps 2 and 3 are executed)
5. Close the sale (ask for the close if customers are indecisive or reluctant)
6. Follow up after the sale (contact customer by mail, phone, or in person to express appreciation for sale and assess level of satisfaction with the purchase)

ORDER TAKERS

sellers of repeat orders of primarily low-cost items that are pre-sold to customers

ORDER GETTERS

creative sellers who convince a customer to buy

Order getters are the sales people on the floor who must be physically present in their interactions with shoppers. In-store customers may not have definite purchases in mind and are assisted by the salesperson such as the one here at a Fred Meyer store.

Order takers need not be physically present when dealing with customers. Products are generally pre-sold; the shopper knows exactly what is wanted and only needs to place the order or pick up the item at the store.

Advantages and Disadvantages of Personal Selling

In comparison to advertising, personal selling is more expensive per customer contacted. However, the trade-off lies in having the flexibility to tailor a sales presentation to the needs of each individual customer. This is particularly effective in selling big-ticket items like major appliances, cars, or expensive jewelry and apparel. Personal selling also has distinct advantages over other forms of promotion for selling technical products like computers or sophisticated electronics.

Unfortunately, retail sales positions tend to have a poor image. It is an easily entered occupation that requires little formal education or aptitude for the job. In addition, many salespeople are merely "clerks" who are poorly trained and lack commitment to their jobs. Wal-Mart and other retailers have attempted to overcome these problems by building a team of well-trained and loyal associates.

SALES PROMOTION

Sales promotion "involves marketing activities, other than personal selling, advertising, and publicity, that stimulate consumer purchasing and dealer effectiveness" (Committee on Definitions, 1960). In fact sales promotion encompasses a broad spectrum of promotional techniques. Shopping is viewed as entertainment by many customers, and sales promotion can contribute to an entertaining store atmosphere. Both dollars spent by companies and customer acceptance of sales promotion continue to increase, underscoring the importance of this promotional tool. Consumer promotions totaled over $25 billion in 1988, out of $100 billion spent by all channel members

A typical grocery promotion which emphasizes the house brand, as well as many other featured products, is shown in this Giant Foods newspaper ad.

COURTESY OF GIANT FOODS

SALES PROMOTION
marketing activities other than personal selling, advertising, and publicity, designed to stimulate consumer demand

(Strazewski, 1988). The following sections provide an overview of the objectives, types, advantages, and disadvantages of sales promotion.

Objectives of Sales Promotion

Sales promotion is intended to support other elements of the promotional plan, such as reinforcing the retailer's advertising and salesforce efforts. It is used as a short-term incentive or inducement to get people to visit a store or to make a trial purchase of a product or service. Sales promotion is used to encourage repeat purchases by present customers or to give the retailer a competitive edge for a limited time.

Conflicts between the promotional goals of the retailer and those of the manufacturer may arise, however. The manufacturer's objective is to increase brand sales; the retailer is more concerned with selling any brand in that product category. As a result, the manufacturer is concerned with the possibility of customers switching brands; the retailer, on the other hand, is concerned with the prospect of customers switching stores to get promotionally featured products. The retailer needs to answer several questions to determine the real value of a promotion: does featuring or promoting a certain product increase sales of complementary products in the store? If so, which product draws best (e.g., cake mix or frosting mix)? Which product has the better profit margin? (Schultz, 1989).

Types of Sales Promotion

Sales promotion can be classified into two groups: special communication methods and special offers (See Exhibit 15–6). The most frequently used special communication methods include advertising specialties, point-of-purchase promotional materials, point-of-purchase demonstrations, sampling,

Exhibit 15–6
Special offer coupon

and visual aid materials for salespeople. Retailers also use special merchandising events and joint promotions with community organizations or other retailers to communicate with customers. A survey of retailer attitudes toward the use of point-of-purchase (POP) advertising indicated that a vast majority of retailers believe that POP attracts consumer attention and builds sales (Fahey, 1989). Sales promotion tactics are closely related to merchandise presentation and displays at point-of-purchase to increase impulse purchases.

Special offers are closely related to pricing. Some frequently used forms of special offers include: coupons, price-off deals and combination offers, money-refund offers or factory rebates, premiums, and contests and sweepstakes. Special sales events and frequent shopper/frequent flyer programs are two other popular types of special offers. Many successful promotions are repeated by retailers. For example, K mart repeated a traffic building promotion in which consumers brought an encoded K mart flier to the store, where it was run under a scanning wand so they could "hear" what prize they won. In the promotion's first year, K mart had a four-fold increase in traffic, with twice those results the second time around (Petersen, 1990).

Advantages and Disadvantages of Sales Promotion

Most of the advantages of sales promotion lie in its effectiveness in the short run. It offers a wide variety of innovative approaches to selling, allows flexible scheduling and, in some cases, is relatively inexpensive. In addition, sales promotion can be fun for the customer—and for the retailer.

Sales promotion is not effective for building a consumer franchise, reversing declining sales, image building, or convincing customers that they should buy a product or service that they consider unacceptable. A negative image of the retailer can result if the retailer selects inappropriate promotional devices that disappoint or offend customers. Sales promotion programs also are subject to fraudulent redemptions and other dishonest practices by consumers and, therefore, need to be monitored.

PUBLICITY

Publicity is the "nonpersonal stimulation of demand for a product, service, or idea by means of commercially significant news planted in the mass media and not paid for directly by a sponsor" (Committee on Definitions, 1960). It is a promotional tool that is used to disseminate information about the retailer, and the company's stores, products and services or anything else of interest to the public. This is accomplished through press releases to the media, writing editorials, providing films, photographs, and other materials to be used by the media.

Publicity and public relations (PR) are often used incorrectly as interchangeable terms. Recall that publicity is a subset of a retailer's public relations program. PR is a more general practice that encompasses publicity and all nonadvertising and nonselling activities that are designed to engender a desired corporate image (Shimp and DeLozier, 1986, p. 493–494). While

PUBLICITY
promotional tool that spreads generally positive information about a retailer, the company stores, and their activities; not paid for by sponsor

COURTESY OF EDDIE BAUER

Where wild mustangs run free and one individual can improve the world,
you'll find Eddie Bauer. Outdoor clothing and gear for men and women
of unbridled spirit. Available exclusively from Eddie Bauer by mail
or at over 180 stores across the U.S. and Canada. Please call 1-800-356-8889,
Dept. DAL for a free catalog or the location nearest you.

Eddie Bauer

Each Piece is a Signed Original

Dayton Hyde, Rancher, author and founder of The Institute of Range and
the American Mustang, wild horse sanctuary, Black Hills, South Dakota.
McKinley Flannel Shirt, Elk Leather and Down Jacket, EQ0.

*Eddie Bauer ads feature spectacular
scenery to stress nature and the outdoor lifestyle.*

large retailers use public relations and publicity extensively to reinforce other
promotional efforts and enhance their corporate image, small retailers can
also use this promotional tool effectively. For example, a small retailer with a
limited budget can sponsor a Little League team or a softball league (public
relations), and use this activity to obtain local media coverage (publicity);
other publicity may involve stories about the retailer's employees or managers, special programs that benefit the community, or new product lines or
store openings, for example. Publicity is considered to be a nonpaid form of
promotion, but there is generally a cost attached for preparation.

Objectives and Characteristics of Publicity

The primary purpose of publicity is to obtain media coverage about the company from a nonpersonal source. Publicity is expected to reflect well on the
retailer's image and standing in the community (e.g., as a responsible citizen,
major employer). Of course, this assumes that publicity released about the
retailer is positive and appears in a favorable media environment. For example, the public's concern with the environment has offered opportunities for
publicity for companies like McDonald's and Mobil Corp., who have started
recycling programs for packaging materials used at the retail level; likewise,
food and restaurant retailers have been acknowledged by the press for giving
food to the needy.

All mass media, as well as specialized publications and programming, are
possible "homes" for publicity. The more closely aligned the media is with
the retailer's target market, the more effective the publicity should be. The

media that prints or broadcasts positive information about the retailer implies endorsement and lends an air of prestige to the company.

Advantages and Disadvantages of Publicity

Advantages of publicity include a low cost for expensive media time and space and the high credibility associated with an independent, noncommercial source. Negative aspects of publicity include lack of control by the retailer over message content and timing of its presentation. It is not a promotional tool that can be scheduled and counted on with any degree of certainty, although this drawback can be overcome to some extent by building good relationships with media representatives.

Direct Marketing in Retailing

The emphasis in this chapter is on the in-store retailer, but the use of **direct marketing** (or direct response marketing) is an important aspect of retail promotion as well as a distribution strategy. Direct marketing may be used by both those retailers who operate stores and those who do not. The term "direct marketing" is sometimes used interchangeably with "direct mail." However, direct mail is but one promotional tool used by direct marketers. A widely accepted definition of direct marketing is provided by the Direct Marketing Association (Roberts and Berger (1989): "Direct marketing is an

This Lands' End catalog reflects a segment of the target market. The woman of the '90s is busy and health-conscious and appreciates the time and financial savings of shopping through direct mail catalogs.

interactive system of marketing which uses one or more advertising media to effect a measurable response and/or transaction at any location."

Direct marketing is a potential two-way communication system. The retailer solicits orders from customers, customers order direct from the seller, and the seller ships the product directly to the customer. The purpose of direct marketing is to establish a direct relationship with a customer to elicit immediate responses (Shimp and DeLozier, 1986). Communications media make it possible for direct marketers and customers to make contact in a variety of non-store situations. Although not explicitly stated in the preceding definition, the central point is that direct marketing bypasses the usual informational intermediaries to reach target customers.

Direct marketers may choose from a wide range of media, but the choice should obtain the maximum response from the desired target market. Some of these media include direct mail, coupons, telephone, videos, and the traditional print and broadcast media. Catalogs are a form of direct mail that are an important aspect of a total direct marketing effort; direct marketing strategy has become increasingly sophisticated in focusing on the appropriate offer or catalog toward the appropriate customer. Examples of successful direct marketing retail catalogs include those distributed by Sears, Lands' End, L. L. Bean, Fingerhut, and Victoria's Secret. Even the airlines and credit card companies have generated additional revenues by retailing products through direct marketing techniques. Telemarketing (or telephone marketing) is another form of direct marketing communication that is increasing in popularity with advances in communications technology.

RESELLER SUPPORT

Reseller support consists of promotional efforts by manufacturers and wholesalers to increase sales at the retail level. This is accomplished in a number of ways such as national advertising campaigns, availability of POP displays, planograms and signage for the selling floor, packaging designs, in-store assistance from the manufacturer's staff, and manufacturers' sales representatives working closer with retailers to determine their needs.

National advertising campaigns by suppliers have dominated the media for a long time and will continue to help retailers sell a vast array of apparel, food products, and other merchandise. For example, Reebok International Ltd. spent in excess of $3 million in media ads to promote its $170 athletic shoe, called "The Pump," that can be inflated for extra support (Pereira, 1989). Suppliers in the hardware and drug store industries frequently provide their retail customers with planograms, pictorial presentations of merchandise arrangements and presentation. These usually are designed to achieve the highest level of profits in the least amount of selling space. In-store assistance from manufacturers such as Liz Claiborne and other fashion apparel suppliers was described in Chapter 13 and is becoming more prevalent in that industry. Campbell Soup's sales representatives have made a commitment to be accessible to their retail customers, which helps the company maintain better communication in order to deal with the rapid changes occurring in the food business (Dugas et. al, 1987).

DIRECT MARKETING
offering products and services to customers through mail, telephone, or other media

RESELLER SUPPORT
promotional activities at manufacturer or wholesaler level to increase retail sales

Budgeting for Promotion

Ideally, a retailer would be able to spend unlimited amounts of money on promotion—run continuous print and broadcast advertising campaigns, hire a large, well-trained sales force, and indulge in spectacular sales promotions. In reality, this is not likely to happen because other aspects of the business compete for the same limited resources. Therefore, most retailers develop guidelines for determining promotional expenditures. These guidelines range all the way from whatever the retailer can afford, to sophisticated statistical models. In most cases, a promotional budget is developed that is expected to achieve planned sales levels and provide a benchmark for evaluating the efficiency of the promotional dollars that were spent. In the next section we will examine some commonly used budgeting methods.

Methods of Budgeting for Retail Promotion

Budgeting for promotion should take into consideration the retailer's promotional and marketing objectives; that is, higher sales forecasts imply the need for larger promotional budgets. On the other hand, the retailer has to make budgeting decisions within the funds that are available and with an eye to competitive promotional levels.

Suppliers often provide promotional assistance to retailers. This may be in the form of advertising allowances or cooperative advertising. Advertising allowances are negotiated by the buyer as one of the terms of sale. The allowance may be based on dollar amounts or number of units purchased (e.g., 50 cents for each case of green beans purchased by a supermarket). Cooperative (co-op) advertising allowances enable the retailer to use vendors' funds to supplement their own promotional budgets. In essence, the manufacturer and retailer jointly sponsor an advertisement featuring the manufacturer's product. This arrangement is attractive to manufacturers because it allows them to advertise their brands at local media rates, which are substantially lower than national rates. In addition, vendors may provide nonmonetary assistance in the form of ready-to-use ad copy and illustrations for media use, salesforce training and materials, point-of-purchase displays, and sales promotion assistance (e.g., special events, give-aways).

Although the preferred approach is to base the amount of the promotional budget on the amount needed, the budget is often predetermined before the specific promotional plan is developed. When the budget is predetermined, sufficient funds may not be available to accomplish the marketing and promotional objectives. Predetermined budgeting methods include percentage of sales (or ratio-to-sales), affordability and arbitrary allocation. To a lesser extent, competitive parity is a type of predetermined budget. The objective and task method of establishing promotional budgets involves the determination of the budget after the promotional plan is developed.

PERCENTAGE OF SALES   The **percentage of sales** budgeting method sets the promotional budget at a percentage of past or forecasted

sales. For example, if a retailer established the budget at 3 percent of sales, and sales were planned to reach $100,000, then the budget would be $3,000. (A related concept is another type of ratio—a stated amount per unit to be sold.)

Percentage of sales is easy to apply and is used by a large number of advertisers. Comparative figures for other retailers are available from sources such as *Advertising Age* and industry data. The method is criticized for two reasons. First, past sales dictate the level of promotion. If the budget is based on forecasted sales, then the adequacy of the budget is dependent upon the accuracy of the forecast. Second, the method does not consider the amount actually needed to accomplish the objectives of the promotional plan.

AFFORDABILITY   The maximum expenditures determined by this method are all the company can afford. All companies have an upper limit on the amount they can spend. The **affordability** limit is influenced by the maximum amount that can be allocated to each element in the promotional mix. Usually the maximum is moderated by research or common sense.

The advantage of this method is that the retailer is not overextended in promotional expenditures. This method is also easy to implement. However, the method does not consider projected sales, promotional goals, or the cost of necessary tasks.

ARBITRARY ALLOCATION   **Arbitrary allocation** is predominantly a judgmental budgeting method. Although some research data and forecasting may be involved, managers base decisions about promotional expenditures on their own past experience and intuition.

An experienced manager may find this method easy to use. Small business retailers often rely on arbitrary allocation budgeting. Because having completely perfect information for establishing budgets is not possible, some degree of subjective judgment enters into each budgeting method. However resources may not be used effectively if this method is relied on too heavily.

COMPETITIVE PARITY   The retailers who use the **competitive parity** budgeting method essentially let competitors decide how much they will spend on promotion. Budgets are set as close to those of competitors as possible. Competitive comparison is a broader term for this budgeting method (Dommermuth, 1984). This means the retailer pays close attention to what competition is doing and considers this when planning his or her own budget, but it does not necessarily require that the retailer's budget match that of competition. Problems lie in making an accurate judgment of a competitor's expenditures and in budget allocations across media over time, since the retailer's promotional expenditures will lag behind the competitors.

OBJECTIVE AND TASK   In each of the preceding methods, promotional budgets are determined before the promotional plan is decided. The objective and task approach takes a different position and considers what is needed before deciding how much to spend.

The **objective and task** method starts with the overall marketing objectives, then the overall promotional objectives, as shown in Exhibit 15–7.

PERCENTAGE OF SALES
promotional budget set as a percentage of past or forecasted sales

AFFORDABILITY
maximum amount allocated to each element in the promotional mix

ARBITRARY ALLOCATION
budgeting by a judgmental method

COMPETITIVE PARITY
promotional budget based on what competitors spend

OBJECTIVE AND TASK
allocation of sufficient funds to implement the retailer's promotional strategy effectively

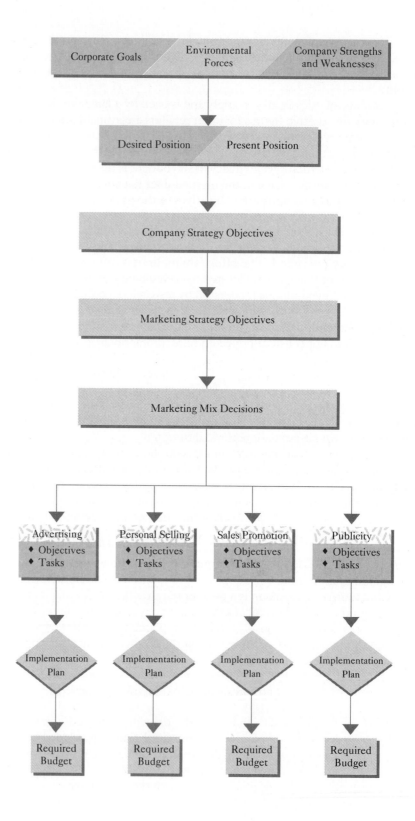

Exhibit 15–7
Objective and Task Method of
Budgeting for Promotion
• •
SOURCE: Adapted from William P.
Dommermuth, *Promotion: Analysis, Creativity, and Strategy.* (PWS-Kent Publishing
Company, 1984). 100, 680–681.

Next, the specific promotional elements (e.g., advertising) are identified that can accomplish this goal. Objectives (marketing, communication, financial) are established for each element, then the tasks needed to reach these objectives are determined. Next, the amount of money needed to activate the plan is calculated. At times, managers may coordinate this with another budgeting approach, such as percentage of sales. Finally, the money is allocated and the promotional strategy can be implemented.

The advantage of the objective and task budget is that sufficient funds are allocated to implement the retailer's promotional strategy effectively. It also requires a detailed plan of action as a basis for calculations. The major drawback is that the budget is based on the ideal circumstance and may be too costly. Generally, there is an adjustment from the "nice-to-have" to a more realistic dollar amount. The planning requirement still makes this the most effective budgeting method, however.

Evaluation of Results

Evaluation of the productivity of promotional efforts occurs during and after execution. Isolating the effects of advertising, for example, from other promotional and environmental factors can be difficult. Perhaps a downturn in the economy or an outstanding sales force have had a major impact on sales or store traffic. Evaluation can be extended to testing alternative promotional plans, such as using different promotional methods, media, or messages, scheduling promotions at different times, or targeting a different group of shoppers. To illustrate, questions about advertising that might be addressed include: If we eliminated all advertising for a certain department or product line, what would be lost? Would it be more profitable to increase advertising by a given percent or to decrease it? Would it be more profitable to shift advertising from one medium to another (e.g., television to newspaper)? (See McNiven, 1980.)

Burger King has had disappointing results with several of its national campaigns, resulting in confusion for franchisees, image problems with consumers, and dismissal of an advertising agency. In 1989, Burger King fired its ad agency, NW Ayer, from the national portion of its $150 million account, following poor results from its "We do it like you do it" campaign that somewhat implausibly compared Burger King's product to the customer's own home barbecue. While the campaign was not well received by consumers, its effect was negatively impacted by other factors including the product itself and emphasis on price cuts, contents, and promotions without a common theme. The hamburger chain has maintained its number two position behind McDonald's but has not grown as quickly as other fast-food retailers. Burger King tried to remedy the problems from the "We do it like you do it" campaign with its newer "Sometimes you've gotta break the rules" campaign. The intent was to revive a hard sell for customer service and to create a positive, memorable experience. However, again franchisees found it confusing, customers did not get the message, and the ads did not differentiate Burger King from archrival McDonald's (Gibson and Marsh, 1989; Landler and DeGeorge, 1990; Lipman, 1989b).

Part IV

Customer Services and Communication with Customers

Retailers are in the service business and must remember that customers are the reason retail businesses exist. Two of the cardinal "sins" in retailing are (1) to give poor customer service and (2) to promise service but not deliver it. Unfortunately, too many customers receive poor service and have to obtain shopping information on their own. Thus, an important aspect of retail management is related to customer service decisions. Many customer services are performed as part of the store operations function. However, they are included in this chapter within the context of promotion because they are an important form of communication between retailers and customers.

There are three major decisions that retail managers must make about services: (1) what services to offer, (2) level of service, and (3) whether to charge for services. A related decision is the timing of service. Some services are provided before the sale, others during the selling process, and others after the purchase has been made. Many of the services provided prior to the sale provide a competitive advantage, but may be taken for granted by customers as retailers become more service oriented. These include convenient store hours, information sources made available to customers before the sale, and toll-free 800 numbers. Services during the actual purchase process include availability of credit and check cashing, layaway, restaurant facilities, and personal shopping. Services after the sale include alterations, delivery, repairs, returns, and complaint handling.

Types and Levels of Retail Services

Today many competing retailers are "cookie cutter" images of one another. They carry similar merchandise at similar prices and sell goods to customers from look-alike stores. The only basis for competition is service—both the types and levels offered. Regardless of the type of store, what it sells, or where it is located, the *quality* of service that the customer receives determines the retailer's competitive advantage. Seven principles for service quality have been suggested as a guide for retailers (Berry, 1988).

1. *Quality is defined by customers.* That is the only definition that counts.
2. *Quality is a never-ending journey.* It goes on every day of every week of every month of every year.
3. *Quality is everyone's job.* That includes salespeople, merchandisers, supervisors, accountants, credit personnel, repair technicians, secretaries, distribution center employees, cashiers, and custodians.
4. *Quality, leadership, and communication are inseparable.* Genuine leadership at all levels can provide the necessary inspiration to sustain committed servers.
5. *Quality and integrity are inseparable.* The organizational value system has to have at its core the idea of fairness—with all parties and at all times.

PRIMARY SERVICES
services essential to the retail sale

ANCILLARY SERVICES
support activities to accompany retail sales, nonessential but expected by various market segments

6. *Quality is a design issue.* It must be a forethought in the development of new services, technologies, processes, and facilities.

7. *Quality is keeping the service promise.* Customers expect service providers to deliver what they promise.

A checklist for determining if a retail company is customer-driven in regard to its products and services is presented in Exhibit 15–8. Services may be classified as either primary or ancillary. **Primary services** are those that are considered essential parts of a retail sale (e.g., sacks for groceries, ATMs in banking, delivery for Domino's Pizza). **Ancillary services** are not actually essential to making the sale for many customers, but are support activities that are expected by various market segments. Retail managers must decide which services are primary and which are ancillary for their particular customer base, and then provide those services at a level that will keep their customers satisfied.

Since a cost is attached to providing services to customers, managers must decide whether to provide those services free or to charge for them. If a manager decides to charge for a service, then he or she must also decide whether the customer will pay the full cost or some portion of it. A sliding scale could be developed for service prices based on factors such as amount of purchase or distance for delivery.

Credit and several other types of services that retailers provide for their customers are discussed next.

Exhibit 15–8
Is Your Company Customer-Driven?

	Yes	No	Don't Know
1. Do you know the names of your top customers?	☐	☐	☐
2. Do you know why they became your customers and why they decided not to go to the competition?	☐	☐	☐
3. Do you have more than one approach for marketing to different groups of customers?	☐	☐	☐
4. Do you know whether or not your customers are totally satisfied with your product or service?	☐	☐	☐
5. Do you actively seek out comments on the quality of the products or services that you sell?	☐	☐	☐
6. Is any one individual responsible for ensuring that your company is customer-driven?	☐	☐	☐
7. Do you understand how to price your products to match what customers are demanding?	☐	☐	☐
8. Do you know what percentage of customers you gain or lose each year?	☐	☐	☐
9. Are you aware of all factors that can lead to customer dissatisfaction?	☐	☐	☐
10. Do you have any specific plans or actions in place to improve your relationships and understanding of your customers?	☐	☐	☐

If the answers to these questions are "no" or "don't know," beware! Competitors can invade your market and take away your customers; you may not realize why until it is too late. If you are not in tune with what customers are looking for, you have no sound basis for making important decisions on how your company can meet the needs of the marketplace.

SOURCE: Shern, Stephanie (1990), "Seller Beware—It's the Customer's Turn," *Ernst & Young's Retail News* XII, no. 3, (June), 2.

Credit

Most retailers would not be able to operate their businesses without offering credit to their customers. Customers expect to be able to charge purchases, both for shopping convenience and to defer payment for goods and services they want today. Credit is available from the retailer's competitors, and customers will go elsewhere to shop if necessary. Even fast-food restaurants and supermarkets have started to accept credit cards for payment. Although fast-food chains such as Kentucky Fried Chicken and Burger King had previously accepted credit cards, Arby's Inc. was the first to do so on a national basis. In test markets, the company found out that customers tended to spend 40 to 60 percent more at Arby's when they did not have to pay cash (McCarthy, 1990). Credit cards can be inserted at the gas pump in Mobil Oil service station in the Orlando, Florida area—making the transaction truly self-service.

There are three basic types of retail credit: in-house, third-party, and private-label. **In-house credit** is a system that is owned and operated by the retailer. A majority of retailers, such as Sears and Macy's, have their own credit systems for their customers. It not only makes it easier for customers to shop, but generates additional revenue for the retailer.

A number of retailers use **third-party credit** cards. These are offered by banks, entertainment-card companies, gasoline companies, and other businesses. VISA and MasterCard are the most common bank credit cards. Citicorp is the biggest issuer of bank cards in America, with 29 million cardholders, and has targeted consumers in 18 other countries, generally from upper income groups—although some cultural and marketing hurdles must be overcome (Guenther, 1990). American Express, Carte Blanche, and Diner's Club are well known charge-card companies, and Shell, Exxon, and Mobil are typical of gasoline credit cards. Other nontraditional companies have entered the credit card business. For example, United Services Automobile Insurance Company (USAA) offers a Gold MasterCard to members. Utilities have entered the credit card business, as well, with the advent of the AT&T Universal Card, which has features such as no annual fee for charter members who use it for a purchase at least once a year, buyer protection, and discounts on AT&T calls charged to the card. Exhibit 15–9 offers a comparison of features included with membership in standard and gold cards sponsored by some of the leading credit card companies.

The third type of credit offered by retailers is **private-label credit,** generally used when the retailer does not want to manage its own credit system or use the third-party sources. This form of consumer credit is used frequently for installment purchases, regular or open account, or revolving charge accounts. The private-label credit system is managed by a bank, but offered under the retailer's name.

Other Retail Services

Retailers offer a wide array of services to their customers. These are closely related to the type of retail store, the products it carries, and its pricing strategies. For example, apparel retailers offer alterations. In a higher-priced store, customers generally receive this service at no charge, but must pay for alterations in most discount stores. Personal shoppers assist customers in the

IN-HOUSE CREDIT
credit system owned and operated by the retailer

THIRD-PARTY CREDIT
credit offered by banks and other establishments

PRIVATE-LABEL CREDIT
credit system managed by a bank under the retailer's name

Exhibit 15–9

Third-Party Credit Cards: Selected Features *How the cards stack up*

Below is a list of selected features included with membership. Gold card offers the standard features plus extras.

	Standard			*Gold*		
Card Issuer	***Fee***	***Annual % Rate***	***Features***	***Fee***	***Annual % Rate***	***Added Features***
AT&T	$0	Prime + 8.9%	90-day purchase insurance against loss, theft, damage, etc.; warranties doubled up to a year; $100,000 travel accident insurance; rental car insurance; 10% off AT&T long-distance calling card rates	$0	Prime +8.9%	$250,000 travel accident insurance; Visa Emergency Assistance, which provides medical monitoring and referral, arranges emergency transport, and advances funds for treatment
Chase Manhattan	$20	19.8%	90-day purchase insurance; warranties doubled up to a year; $250,000 travel accident insurance; rental car insurance	$50	16.5%	Credit card registration; $350,000 travel accident insurance; either Visa Emergency Assistance or Master Assist travel emergency service, which arranges and pays for medically necessary travel and treatment.
Citibank	$20	19.8%	90-day purchase insurance; warranties doubled up to a year; $100,000 travel accident insurance; discounts on Hertz car rentals	$50	16.8%	$350,000 travel accident insurance; credit card registration; CitiAssist travel emergency service, which advances funds for medical and legal help, arranges and pays for medically necessary travel
First Chicago	$20	Prime +9.9%	$100,000 travel accident insurance; guaranteed hotel reservations	$20	Prime +9.9%	90-day purchase insurance; warranties doubled up to a year; $250,000 travel accident insurance; rental car insurance; MasterAssist or Visa Emergency Assistance
American Express	$55	None	90-day purchase insurance; warranties doubled up to a year; $100,000 travel accident insurance; guaranteed hotel reservations; rental car insurance; cash advances and referrals for medical and legal aid	$75	None	Year-end summary of charges; personal insurance covering car renters; seating for cultural events
Discover	$0	19.8%	$500,000 flight insurance; 24-hour tow truck referral service; cashback bonus of up to 1% of amount charged			Gold card not available; "Private Issue" card being tested

SOURCE: Saporito, Bill, "Who's Winning the Credit Card War?" *Fortune* (July 2), 67, store or take merchandise to their offices. (See Exhibit 15–10.) Appliance retailers offer installation services; hardware, furniture and toy retailers may offer assembly services for those customers who prefer not to do the assembly themselves.

Exhibit 15–10
Customer Service: Personal Shopping
. . . .
SOURCE: *Texas Monthly* 15, no. 10, (October 1987), p. 137.

Preferred Clientele Club

F I E L D ' S   F A S H I O N   S E R V I C E

Discover our Field's Fashion Service—Marshall Field's personalized wardrobing service—as we take the legwork out of shopping and add further advantages through our Preferred Clientele Club membership. It's completely complimentary and all for the simple luxury of being a Marshall Field's customer. Shop with our Field's Fashion Service three times throughout the year and enjoy an exciting list of courtesy options with your new membership. Our exclusive membership card entitles you to the royal treatment throughout our stores. From fashion expertise to "members only" private sales twice a year, fabulous cosmetic gifts to priority alterations and complimentary delivery. Whether you're a current Field's Fashion Service client, or an enthusiastic new member, consider yourself a celebrity within our doors. Individual attention, expert advice and a personalized approach to pampering your lifestyle is our forté.

In addition to our current Field's Fashion Service advantages, receive other complimentary specialty services as a prestigious Preferred Clientele Club card holder:

- Personalized membership card
- Expert fashion advice and designer updates
- Exceptional customer services and benefits
- "Members only" private sales—the best women's apparel for less, before everyone else
- Priority alterations in half the time
- Free delivery on purchases of 250.00 or more

- Complimentary gift wrapping
- Refreshments while you shop with Field's Fashion Service
- V.I.P. cosmetic treatments: exciting beautifiers as initial membership gifts, special mailing list notices of promotions, clinic events and new product launches and exclusive club member events in all stores

Field's Fashion Service, Houston Galleria, Dallas Galleria and San Antonio

AT YOUR SERVICE

Delivery is an important service for florists and for retailers of large items such as furniture and appliances. Domino's Pizza has made delivery service an important facet of its total retail format. Stores selling merchandise like housewares and china or jewelry and accessories offer giftwrapping services to their customers.

The travel industry, like other retailers, has been guilty of giving customers services that they do not want, while ignoring those that customers consider important. For example, a traveler vowed never to rent a car from Hertz again, because he was preoccupied with how many frequent-flier miles a car rental would earn him, not whether the car came with a cellular phone. This followed Hertz Corporation's decision to add 700 cellular phones to its fleet—and to phase itself out of frequent-flier programs because of cost. Travelers gave top rankings to frequent flier programs for airlines, direct-dial phones in hotels, service numbers to call if a rental car breaks down, and other amenities such as express check-ins and nonsmoking hotel rooms (Dahl, 1989b).

Airports have begun to add services to overcome passengers' frustrations with poor airline service, surly ticket-agents, bad weather, and other factors

DOUG BEASLEY PHOTOGRAPHY

B. Dalton Booksellers, and other bookstores, record stores, and specialty shops offer discounts and other benefits through in-house club memberships. With each purchase, or after a certain number of purchases, the customer gets a special discount or free item.

over which they have no control. Some airports have opened business centers, complete with computers, fax machines, and secretarial services. Some have play areas with slides and merry-go-rounds for children, and electronic golf driving ranges. One airport designer predicted that Nintendo games, rental movies, and exercise clubs would become common airport services (McGinley, 1990).

Other examples of retail services include the following: Grocery stores install ATM machines so customers can pay for purchases with their ATM card. Appliance and car dealers take trade-ins of the customer's old merchandise. Car dealers let customers test drive automobiles. Trial purchases are made available by retailers of new or technical products. Among the many other services available are ticket sales, baby-sitting, parking, bridal registry, wheelchairs and baby strollers, and customer restrooms.

Finally, retail services must encompass methods of handling customer complaints and guarantees made by retailers and manufacturers. Unfortunately, most customers do not complain because they do not know how to go about it or they think it is not worth the trouble—they just stop buying that brand, or from that retailer. Customer complaints generally are handled in the store or over the phone or through some combination of the two. Retailers can prevent a number of complaints by improving speed and accuracy at checkout. Customers do not like to wait, and they do not want a big hassle over an exchange, refund, or other problem. Therefore, the retailer must have adequate customer service personnel and must provide them with adequate training. Their pay should be related to their ability to work with customers and to their productivity in converting a problem into a sale.

Many companies attempt to improve customer service by setting up toll-free 800 telephone numbers. The idea is that customers' questions are answered, the company generates goodwill, and sales rise. However, all too often customers are alienated by getting inadequate information, reaching

A unique ancillary service is found at Hollywood West, the first Fred Meyer store to offer child care. Parents can leave children at Freddy's Playland, where they are supervised by CPR trained personnel.

COURTESY OF FRED MEYER

recorded messages, or being put on hold for a long period of time. The key to success appears to be in using the company's own employees and training them to answer almost any question related to their store or its products. The retailer also must be willing to change the system to adapt to customer needs. For example, J. C. Penney introduced a toll-free line for custom decorating services. Customers could leave their name and phone number for a Penney decorator to return their calls within a day. However, when Penney's found that the delay in calling back was causing potential customers to lose interest in buying their custom-made draperies, the system was revised. To improve its service, toll-free calls were transferred directly to the home decorating department of one of Penney's 1,328 stores. The retailer continues to monitor the ability of this type of program to generate enough business to warrant the expense involved (Agins, 1990).

Summary

The promotional mix is the major form of communication between retailers and their customers. The communication function extends beyond customers to employees within the store environment and important groups outside the company, such as suppliers, channel intermediaries, government agencies, community organizations, and others. The promotional strategy evolves from the retailer's corporate objectives and marketing strategies and must be compatible with the other functional management areas.

The purpose of promotion is to inform, persuade, or remind present and prospective customers about the business and what it has to sell. The four major types of promotion are advertising, personal selling, sales promotion, and publicity. Each of these promotional tools has a number of variations.

Advertising is "any paid form of nonpersonal presentation and promotion of ideas, goods, or services by an identified sponsor." The objectives of retail advertising are to influence consumers to buy the retailer's goods and services. They generally are run in local media and intended to have immediate results. Newspapers and magazines are the most popular print media, and radio and television are the primary types of broadcast media. Outdoor advertising (billboards, buses, trains, and taxicabs) and other types of advertising media also are used.

Personal selling is an "oral presentation in a conversation with one or more prospective purchasers for the purpose of making a sale." The overall objective is to provide the necessary service to bring each transaction to a conclusion. The two basic types of salespeople are order takers and order getters.

Sales promotion "involves marketing activities, other than personal selling, advertising, and publicity, that stimulate consumer purchasing and dealer effectiveness." It is intended to support the other promotional elements, rather than stand alone. Sales promotion is used as a short-term incentive or inducement to get shoppers to come to the store, make a trial purchase, or make repeat purchases.

This promotion, combining the efforts of National Car Rental with U.S. Air, featured a sweepstakes as an incentive to stimulate consumer purchasing. Prizes included roundtrip air tickets and free car rental.

Publicity is the "nonpersonal stimulation of demand for a product, service, or idea by means of commercially significant news planted in the mass media and not paid for directly by a sponsor." Publicity, a subset of public relations, is expected to reflect well on the retailer's image. Those media most closely aligned with the target market will be most effective.

Direct marketing is a potential two-way communication system that can be used by nonstore and in-store retailers to reach market segments that like to shop at home or work. Direct marketing media include direct mail, coupons, telephone, videos, and catalogs.

Manufacturers and wholesalers provide reseller support for their retailer customers. Reseller support includes national advertising campaigns aimed at final consumers, point of purchase displays, planograms, signage, and closer ties between the retailer and supplier.

The most frequently used promotional budgeting methods are percentage of sales, affordability, arbitrary allocation, competitive parity, and objective and task. Percentage of sales is based on past or forecasted sales. Affordability is the maximum common sense amount that the retailer can spend. Arbitrary allocation is a judgmental method based on the managers experience and intuition. Competitive parity tries to match competitors' promotional efforts. Objective and task is the most logical promotional budgeting method because it sets the budget according to what needs to be done. Finally, evaluating the results of promotional expenditures is necessary.

Customer services are the one way that retailers can differentiate themselves. Decisions must be made about what services to offer, at what level, and whether to charge. Services occur before and during the purchase transaction, as well as after the sale. Retail credit cards may be in-house, third-party, or private-label. Other services include alterations, installations, assembly, delivery, and giftwrap.

Questions for Review and Comprehension

1. Explain how a promotional strategy decision affects, and is affected by, other functional retail management areas.

2. Give examples of specific internal and external groups that a small restaurant owner would need to communicate with, and the objectives to be achieved in each case.

3. Briefly discuss the relationship between strategic planning and effective customer communication for (a) a large specialty store chain and (b) a small independent specialty retailer.

4. Name, define, and give an example of each of the promotional mix elements: advertising, personal selling, sales promotion, and publicity.

5. The managers of a medium-sized apparel chain must design a promotional mix that will combine the various promotional tools in the most efficient and effective manner. Advise them as to the objectives, advantages, and disadvantages of each type of promotional tool, and how they should be combined for maximum impact. State your assumptions about the retailer's strategy relative to merchandise assortments, pricing, service level, and location as a basis for your promotional strategy recommendations.

6. Differentiate between institutional advertising and promotional advertising, and give examples of when the use of each is appropriate.

7. Name and describe the media alternatives that are available for retail advertising. Evaluate the desirability of each of the major media categories in terms of target audience that can be reached, cost considerations, and creative capacity for each of the following types of retail businesses: fast-food restaurants, professional sports arena, department store, full-service bank, hardware store, and shoe store.

8. Describe the objectives that should be achieved by a retailer's sales force. Give examples of the different types of sales tasks and when each might be most effective.

9. Explain what is meant by "reseller support" and why it is becoming increasingly popular.

10. Describe and evaluate the advantages and disadvantages of each of the methods for establishing promotional budgets. Discuss whether the advantages and disadvantages of each method might be different for a small retailer versus a large retailer.

11. Discuss the types and levels of retail services that can be offered by retailers. Give examples of how the seven principles for service quality suggested by Berry (1988) might be applied by a (a) small auto parts retailer, (b) beauty salon, (c) grocery store, (d) furniture store, and (e) independent department store.

References

Agins, Teri (1990), "Customers, 800-Lines May Not Connect," *The Wall Street Journal* (November 20), B1, B4.

Berry, Leonard L. (1988), "Delivering Excellent Service in Retailing," *Retailing Issues Letter*. College Station, Tex.: Arthur Andersen & Co., in conjunction with the Center for Retailing Studies, Texas A&M.

Committee on Definitions (1960), *Marketing Definitions, A Glossary of Marketing Terms*. Chicago: American Marketing Association.

Dahl, Jonathan (1989a), "Help Wanted: Men to Dance on Board," *The Wall Street Journal* (January 31), B1.

Dahl, Jonathan (1989b), "Giving People What They Don't Want," *The Wall Street Journal* (November 30), B1, B3.

Deveney, Kathleen (1990), "Aiming High, Marketers Shoot for the Hip," *The Wall Street Journal* (January 10), B1, B4.

Dommermuth, William P. (1984), *Promotion: Analysis, Creativity and Strategy*. Belmont, Calif.: Kent Publishing Company.

Dugas, Christine, Mark N. Vamos, Johatan B. Levine, and Matt Rothman (1987), "Marketing's New Look," *Business Week* (January 26), 64–69.

Edwards, Charles M. Jr., and Carl F. Lebowitz (1981), *Retail Advertising and Sales Promotion*, 4th ed. Englewood Cliffs, N.J.: Prentice-Hall, 57–71.

Fahey, Alison (1989), "Study Shows Retailers Rely on POP," *Advertising Age* (November 27), 85.

Gibson, Richard and Barbara Marsh (1989), "Burger King Revives Hard Sell for Service," *The Wall Street Journal* (September 28), B1, B6.

Guenther, Robert (1990), "Citicorp Pushes Its Bank Cards Overseas," *The Wall Street Journal* (August 20), B1, B4.

Hodock, Calvin L. (1980), "Copy Testing and Strategic Positioning," *Journal of Advertising Research* (February), 37.

Hulin-Salkin, Belinda (1988), "Grocery Marketing: What Price Exposure?" *Advertising Age* (October 3), S1, S17–S18.

Josephson, Sanford (1989). "Selling Radio to Retailers: They Buy Success Stories Demonstrating Creativity," *Television/Radio Age* (September 18), 41.

Kneale, Dennis (1988), "NBC Likely to Take Loss on Olympics: May Give Up $70 Million in Ad Spots," *The Wall Street Journal* (October 3), B7.

Landler, Mark and Gail DeGeorge (1990), "Tempers Are Sizzling Over Burger King's New Ads," *Business Week* (February 12), 33.

Lipman, Joanne (1988), "Olympic Gold Falls in Advertising Value," *The Wall Street Journal* (October 4), B1.

Lipman, Joanne (1989a), "Time's High Hopes for Personalized Ads," *The Wall Street Journal* (September 18), B9.

Lipman, Joanne (1989b), "More Turmoil at Burger King as Chain Fires Its Ad Agency," *The Wall Street Journal* (April 24), B1, B3.

Lipman, Joanne (1990), "Gazing into Their Crystal Balls, Ad Execs Predict Trends for 1990," *The Wall Street Journal* (January 2), B4.

McCarthy, Michael J. (1990), "Company-Owned Arby's to Accept Credit Cards," *The Wall Street Journal* (September 13), B1.

McGinley, Laurie (1990), "Airports Try to Ease the Pain of Waiting with New Ways for Fliers to Spend Money," *The Wall Street Journal* (August 21), B1, B6.

McNiven, Malcolm A. (1980), "Plan for More Productive Advertising," *Harvard Business Review* (March/April), 130–136.

Pereira, Joseph and G. Christian Hill (1989), "Pumped-up Reebok Runs Fast Break with New Shoe," *The Wall Street Journal* (December 20), B1, B4.

Petersen, Lauri (1990), "What's Old Is New Again," *Ad Week's Marketing Week* (July 16), 25–27.

Reilly, Patrick M. (1990), "Newsweek Personalizes Magazines," *The Wall Street Journal* (May 25), B1, B8.

Roberts, Mary Lou and Paul D. Berger (1989), *Direct Marketing Management* Englewood Cliffs, N.J.: Prentice-Hall.

Schultz, Don E. (1989), "Scanner Data From the Retailer's View," *Marketing Communications* (May), 25–27.

Schwadel, Francine (1990a), "Sear's Glitzy Ads Target Buyers of Stylish Fashions," *The Wall Street Journal* (August 15), B1, B5.

Schwadel, Francine (1990b), "At Gap, Clothes Make the Ads as Stars Fade," *The Wall Street Journal* (December 3), B1, B6.

Shimp, Terence A. and M. Wayne DeLozier (1986), *Promotion Management and Marketing Communications*. New York: The Dryden Press.

Strazewski, Len (1988), "Promotional 'Carnival' Gets Serious," *Advertising Age* (May 2), Special Report.

"When the Price Isn't Right," (1988), *Advertising Age* (November 28), 16.

4.1 To Handle or Not to Handle P&G's Personal Care Products?

In the 1940s, research personnel at Hoffman-LaRouche, the chemical/pharmaceutical company with headquarters at Basil, Switzerland, found that Pantenol, provitamin B, provided pliabililty and luster to hair. Suppletory conditioners (that make the hair more supple) were developed later and added to the vitamin B derivative. Pantene hair care products, consequently, did more than aid in good grooming, they helped produce healthy hair.

Pantene hair care products were marketed first in Europe, then worldwide. They were launched in the U.S. market in 1964. Pantene was remarketed and repositioned in 1976 to include some four thousand select department stores, cosmetic-oriented pharmacies, and hair care salons. The company's products appealed primarily to women in their twenties and thirties who were concerned about the health as well as the appearance of their hair. With increased advertising aimed at the sophisticated, upscale customer, Pantene became the market leader in the department store category. Department stores represented seventy percent of Pantene's market.

When Richardson-Vicks, Inc. (RVI) decided to orient their business away from pharmaceuticals toward personal care products in 1983, they acquired Pantene from Hoffman-LaRouche. At that time, Pantene's product line consisted of shampoos, conditioners, hair lotions, sprays, permanent products, and brushes, with worldwide sales totalling approximately $68 million in Europe, South Africa, Japan, Australia, and the United States. Upon acquisition, RVI reformulated Pantene, added sunscreen ingredients to the hair care products and added new product lines, including one formulated especially for grey hair, and one marketed specifically to men. In the same year RVI picked up that part of Vidal Sassoon's product line distributed through drug chains and supermarkets. The salon part of Vidal Sassoon's business was procured earlier by Hair Care Limited of Great Britain.

RVI purchased Pantene to gain access to new channels of distribution. RVI's main channels of distribution were through mass distributors; very little business was conducted with specialty and department stores. RVI's major products

were divided among health care and nutrition products (including Vicks products, Formula 44, Sinex, and Lifestage Vitamins); personal care products (embracing such brand names as Oil of Olay, Clearasil, Mill Creek natural products, Fixodent, and several international brands); home care products (including Formby's and Thompson's); chemicals (J. T. Baker Chemical Co.) and instruments (Baker Instruments Corp.). Formby's was spun off from Procter and Gamble (P&G) in 1990. Prior to the acquisition of Pantene and Vidal Sassoon, RVI had no hair care products in the United States.

Industry observers report that RVI attempted to market Pantene both in the mass merchandise outlets and department stores. It discontinued distribution to mass merchandise outlets, however, when department stores indicated they would drop Pantene if it were sold elsewhere.

Pantene's promotion was primarily by means of targeted advertising, a strong public relations program, and unique in-store promotion. A 24-member training department conducted training events and in-store consumer education clinics. Consumer literature was distributed at point-of-purchase and through the mail by outlets handling Pantene. RVI spent an estimated $1 million in magazine ads in 1985 for Pantene. The unique in-store promotion was the "Pantene Hair Care Consultant" interactive computer touch screen unit. After a customer responded to a series of questions, the customer received a printout of the computer analysis of their hair quality and the proper combination of hair care products. No samples were given out by Pantene. Moreover, even though no hair care brand was specified in the analysis, customers were most likely to buy Pantene products. As a matter of fact, sales tripled in some department stores where the device was being tested.

By 1985, RVI had established separate companies to cover various segments of the hair care market. The companies were independent of each other and covered different categories with little overlap in their markets. The Leslie Blanchard hair care line, the top quality product, was sold to high-end department stores. The Pantene organization marketed to middle-range department stores and cosmetic-oriented drug stores. Sassoon was distributed to drug and food stores. Although Sassoon competed in the mass hair care product market, it was positioned at the upper end of the mass hair care market with higher price points and image. The Mill Creek brand of hair care products was channeled to natural food stores.

On October 1, 1985, P&G bought Richardson-Vicks, Inc. for $1.25 billion. One reason for this purchase was the acquisition of RVI's products in the health care product market. P&G instantly broadened the number of products in its health care line with market leaders, and obtained wider distribution of these products through more outlets. Another reason for the acquisition of RVI by P&G was the economies of scale obtained by combining sales forces and the production of similar products. In addition, larger advertising discounts were anticipated. Finally, RVI's established overseas distribution network provided P&G with the means of expanding its presence internationally in areas other than detergents.

During the 1970s P&G had followed an expansion strategy of brand extension. When P&G entered the 1980s, it reverted to growth by acquisition. Procter & Gamble purchased Crush International, Ltd. (Orange Crush and Hires Root Beer), Ben Hill Griffin's citrus-processing business (Citrus Hill brand orange juice), and Norwich Eaton Pharmaceuticals (primarily an ethical drug business with over-the-counter brands, such as Pepto-Bismol stomach remedies and Chloraseptic sore-throat soothers).

P&G's major products are broken down into four major classifications: Laundry and Cleaning Products, Personal Care Products, Food Products, and Others. Products in the first three groups are distributed primarily through grocery stores, drug stores, and other mass merchandisers, while products in the Others category are distributed direct to industrial customers.

P&G intends to allow RVI to operate as a separate subsidiary with only minor changes. P&G's analgesic, Encaprin, and head and chest cold remedy were transferred to RVI. The Pantene and Sassoon divisions were transferred from RVI to P&G's beauty care division, which already handles such products as Prell, Head & Shoulders, Lilt, Pert, and Ivory shampoos and conditioners. P&G's products in the beauty care division are distributed through grocery stores, drug stores, and other mass merchandisers. P&G's sales force calls on the stores' central offices rather than each store to market their products. Some merchandising functions are provided for the individual stores.

If you were an independent store manager or a retail buyer, explain what you would look for when deciding if you should handle P&G's product(s). For instance, explain which of the products you would sell in your store; the product's price, margin, and terms for which you would negotiate; the advertising, display, and related promotional assistance you would expect from P&G, and so forth.

QUESTIONS

1. How is the buying decision of Pantene products related to the topic of variety and assortment?
2. In retailing circles, a choice of three products, such as good, better, best, is frequently offered by the retailers. List the brands discussed, and others with which you are familiar with respect to choice of quality and/or price level. How might this relate to your decision to carry or not to carry Pantene?
3. In keeping with the material discussed in Part IV
   a. list the factors considered by retailers in selecting the merchandise they offer.
   b. explain how each of these is used in selecting the hair care product discussed in this case.

References

Brown, Paul, Zachary Schiller, Christine Dugas, and Scott Scredon (1985), "New? Improved? The Brand-Name Mergers," *Business Week* (October 21).

Freeman, Laurie (1986), "Alberto Gambles on Prestige Haircare Line," *Advertising Age* (April 14).

Freeman, Laurie (1990), "L&F Chief Sets Sights on Expansion," *Advertising Age* (November 12).

Hutton, Cynthia (1985), "Proctor & Gamble's Comeback Plan," *Fortune* (February 4).

Larson, Melissa (1989), "How to Get Brilliant Results with Prime Labels," *Packaging* (June).

Muller, Carrie (1985), "Richardson-Vicks' Hair Care, Pantene Stakes Out Prestige Hair Market," *D&CI* (July).

Muller, Carrie (1985), "Richardson-Vicks' Hair Care, Sassoon Works Smart With Salon Heritage," *D&CI* (July).

Schiller, Zachary (1985), "P&G's Rusty Marketing Machine," *Business Week* (October 21).

This case was prepared by Leonard Konopa, Kent State University, Kent, Ohio, and Sandra Loeb, University of South Dakota, Vermillion, South Dakota.

4.2 HIGHAM LTD.: AUDITING THE PERSONAL SELLING FUNCTION

Higham Ltd. was in the process of conducting a marketing audit of its operations. This review of objectives, strategies, tactics, and competition was being undertaken because it was company practice to perform such a review every two years. This was an "audit year."

Higham Ltd. was a men's apparel store located in an upscale, enclosed mall, a shopping center in a city with a population of about 1 million. Higham targeted its appeal to middle and upper management executives with incomes comparable to their corporate rank.

The store carried a complete line of men's dress clothing and sportswear. The principal items in the dress area were suits, sport coats, topcoats, shirts, belts and braces, hosiery, ties, and dress handkerchiefs.

Merchandise lines and prices reflected the needs and resources of Higham's target market. Prices for suits ranged from $400 to $2000. Dress shirts ranged in price from $30 to $95. A typical tie sold for $35, with hosiery ranging in price from $7.50 to $20. Comparable quality and prices were found in the sportswear department.

The store's merchandise was complemented by the richly appointed store. Medium-toned wood was used throughout. The fully-carpeted store was a tribute to the business executive customers who shopped there. The elegance of the interior told the customer he had arrived and could now shop in the area's most prestigious men's wear store.

Despite its location in the mall, Higham had windows trimmed with the latest of its dress and sportswear offerings. The left window featured sportswear while the right window contained dress clothing. The displays were simple yet dramatic. Window backgrounds were of the same medium-toned wood that was featured within the store. Lighting was low-keyed using "spots" to highlight the displays. The door, flanked by the two windows, was also of wood and had to be opened to gain access to the store. This was unlike so many other stores that had only an open space through which customers walked.

Higham was promoted in the area's regional monthly magazine. Full-page advertisements were used monthly and usually featured newly arrived merchandise. The ads were simple, like the store window displays, and again told prospective customers that Higham was the store to shop—a store that recognized the social status of high income male executives. Advertisements never featured prices and no price signs were to be found throughout the store. Pricing was done in accordance with the markup guideline established at the time store management had prepared its merchandise budget plan. The company ran but two sales per year, one in January and another in July. A standard reduction of 20 percent was taken on all suits, sport coats, topcoats, and dress slacks currently in stock. Selected sportswear, shirts, ties, and hosiery were also put on sale at reductions ranging from 20 to 80 percent. Simple clearance signs identified this sale merchandise. The sale was discretely advertised in the business section of the area's major newspaper.

In sum, Higham was a quality store with fine merchandise. Its operations reflected an aura of conservatism—an aura that attracted large numbers of clients from among its largest market. Higham was successful.

THE MARKETING AUDIT

Despite its success, company policy called for a marketing audit every two years. All of the marketing aspects of the firm were exposed to scrutiny to see if they were still right in light of changes taking place in competition, its target market, and other external variables. The store and its operation were closely scrutinized to reveal any weaknesses needing correction, as well as any strengths upon which the store might capitalize.

One of the audit tasks assigned to Jeff Jones, the store's clothing manager, was personal selling. Personal selling was very important to Higham, especially in the area of big ticket items such as suits and sport coats. Here the salesperson really made the difference. Suit sales of $1,600 to a single customer were not uncommon. Each suit customer represented a potential sale of at least $400. In light of the store's low-key advertising, sales depended heavily upon the salesperson in the store. Mr. Jones was responsible for the performance review of every salesperson. Before the actual review, he would jog his memory about the backgrounds of each one. Then he would observe and make notes about the individual salesperson's performance in actual selling situations. From this he would know what actions would be required to help each achieve full potential.

The salespeople were all on commission, supported by a tailor who did all of the measuring associated with each sale. Often times he would be called in if a sale depended upon getting an appropriate alteration. Jeff kept this in mind as he began his assessment of the staff.

THE SALES STAFF

Jones reviewed the permanent files of each of the salespeople and made the following notations about each:

James Garcia—40 years old; with the company six years; attended college; top producer in the department.

Carleton Gordon—50 years old; with company 20 years; high school graduate; dependable producer.

Angela Watson—22 years old; with the company one and a half years; graduate of marketing program of local technical college; sales well below average.

Fortram Mason—50 years old; 35 years with the company; high school graduate; steady producer.

Tom Felton—30 years old; eight years with the company; high school graduate; produces well above the company average.

OBSERVING THE SALES STAFF

With their backgrounds in mind, Jones set out to observe each salesperson's selling style. He would do his observations over a period of several days. With each observation he would make more notes to review later and use to help each salesperson improve his/her selling skills.

1. OBSERVATION: Carleton Gordon. It's mid-morning. Only two salespersons on selling floor. Angela Watson leaves department for break. Customer enters department. Carleton approaches and having determined customer need begins to show merchandise. Another customer enters department. Carleton continues to sell to first customer. After a brief period of time, Carleton approaches second customer and tells him that someone will be with him shortly. Five minutes pass and Angela has not returned from break. Carleton again excuses himself and returns to second customer apologizing for the delay and tells him again that someone will be with him soon. Several minutes pass and customer leaves department.

2. OBSERVATION: Angela Watson. The department is well staffed with three salespersons. All are busy with customers. Angela has worked long and hard to sell her customer. She appears to be closing the sale. It looks like she has sold two suits—probably over $1000. She calls for the tailor. She has made the sale. The customer appears pleased with the detailed attention the tailor is giving to achieve the right fit. Angela stands at one side smiling and reassuring the customer of the wisdom of his purchase. The customer smiles back. With the suits off to alterations Angela conducts the customer to the department cash register, completes the transaction, and gives the customer his receipt and alterations claim checks. She tells the customer that he has really made a fine purchase. The customer passes through the nearby furnishings department and through the door to the mall.

3. OBSERVATION: James Garcia. His "favorite" customer enters the department. He comes in about twice a year, early in the spring and early in the fall. Customer doesn't buy. He returns when the store has a sale and usually purchases one or two suits. Initially James ignores the customer, continuing to straighten and resize racks of suits. It appears James has a second thought and approaches the customer. The customer says he is just looking but could James answer some questions? The customer asks questions about style, fabrics, construction, etc. Garcia answers each question but with a minimum of elaboration. He knows what this customer is doing—trying to zero in on what he will buy during the sale later in the season. After a while, Garcia excuses himself and returns to his stock keeping duties.

4. OBSERVATION: Fortram Mason. The selling floor is adequately staffed with three salespeople, including Mason. Felton is waiting on the one and only customer on the selling floor. Mason will get the next customer. Second customer enters the department. Mason "picks him up" near front of department. They proceed to the sport coat area. Fortram shows several garments. The customer appears interested. However, both customer and Mason shift their attention from clothing and appear to be discussing pro football. The talk continues for about 20 minutes. The customer looks at his watch and tells Mason that he has lost track of time and must go. He says he'll think about the clothes and come back

tomorrow to make his choice.

5. OBSERVATION: Tom Felton. Tom appears to be struggling. He has six suits lying across a pant rack. The customer appears perplexed and frustrated. Each time the customer's attention moves to a different suit Tom points out each's strong points. The customer finally stops moving from suit to suit and tells Tom that he just cannot make up his mind. Tom suggests to the customer that they go over the suits one more time. The customer declines the offer and leaves the department.

6. OBSERVATION: Carleton Gordon. It's five minutes before closing time. There are several salespeople on the selling floor. Only one has a customer. A customer enters the department. He is recognized as *the* "late" customer. He always enters the department just before closing time. Often he "ties-up" a salesperson for an hour after closing time. Angela ignores him. Carleton hesitates but approaches the customer. He's obviously timid but he makes a "go of it" and sells the customer a suit and then takes the customer to the furnishings department and sells him a shirt and tie. After the suit is measured for alterations, Carleton completes the sale and gives the customer a twelve-noon pick-up time tomorrow.

7. OBSERVATION: Angela Watson. The department is busy but well-staffed. Angela takes the next customer. It is apparent that the customer has brought along his wife and adult son. The three start browsing when Angela attracts their attention by making a comment about the merchandise at which they are looking. The son is tugging at the sleeve of one garment in an attempt to get the husband's attention. He waves off the son's effort and starts talking to his wife about another garment—one which has caught his attention. She smiles pleasantly at first and then breaks into a modest frown. The husband backs away from this suit also. The wife continues to browse and finds two suits that attract her attention. The efforts of the group seem to be going nowhere. Angela makes a comment that the wife has good taste, that she has spotted two of the newer styles that the store carries.

She concentrates on the wife. Occasionally she makes side comments to the husband who seems content to stand by the side. He says little, browses a bit but for the most part he is passive. Angela continues "to pitch" the wife, who is discovering more treasures with each passing minute. At some point, the husband whispers something to the wife. Son, wife, and husband leave the store.

REQUIREMENT: Use Jones' notes to prepare advice to give each salesperson.

QUESTIONS

1. What was Gordon's major mistake in his first selling situation, and how could he have avoided it? Comment on his response to the customer in his second observation.
2. What could Watson have done to increase her sale in the first situation? In the second observation, what technique might have helped her make the sale?
3. How should Garcia have handled his "favorite" customer?
4. Was Mason's socializing a positive or negative approach?
5. What did Felton do wrong? How could he have helped the customer decide?

*This case was prepared by John S. Berens, School of Business, Indiana State University, Terre Haute, IN 47809 as a basis for class discussion rather than to illustrate effective or ineffective handling of an administrative situation.

ANALYSIS AND TECHNOLOGY

Part V

Retailing Decisions: Analysis and Evaluation

CHAPTER *Sixteen*

Learning Objectives

After studying this chapter, the student will be able to:

1. Discuss the importance of analyzing operating results to determine success or failure.
2. Understand the questions managers must answer about operations/opportunities.
3. Name and define five major performance criteria.
4. Describe the focus and general type of analysis performed at the corporate, business, and functional levels.
5. Specify operations areas evaluated in each function.
6. Explain and illustrate the need to evaluate the execution of strategies across functions.
7. Calculate key performance ratios and their implications.
8. Discuss the use of the Strategic Profit Model in evaluating retail performance.
9. Describe criteria for and potential problems with use of secondary data.

Wal-Mart—America's Most Admired Retailer

"From this day forward, I solemnly promise and declare that every customer that comes within ten feet of me, I will smile, look them in the eye, and greet them, so help me, Sam."

Every Wal-Mart employee makes this homespun, customer-oriented pledge. Over 1,300 Wal-Mart stores have "people greeters" welcoming shoppers, who will spend nearly $20 billion a year. Wal-Mart's customer philosophy and treatment of employees are major contributors to the company's performance. However, consider another perspective on Wal-Mart's success:

They are very, very focused (buyers), and they use their buying power more forcefully than anyone in America. . . . They talk softly, but they have piranha hearts, and if you [vendor] aren't prepared when you go in there, you'll have your ―― handed to you.

To hard-nosed negotiating skills, add fast, efficient information transmission among stores, headquarters, and vendors

via a six-channel satellite, which also gathers data for Wal-Mart's information system. The entire operation can be tracked at any time, resulting in ordering efficiencies, quick price adjustments, revisions in promotional efforts and other aspects of the retail mix to maintain competitive advantage.

How is Wal-Mart viewed by its competitors and top business analysts? In January, 1989, *Fortune* selected Wal-Mart as No. 5 among America's most admired corporations (from No. 9 in the previous year, its first time on the list.) Nearly 8,000 senior executives of competing firms, outside directors, and financial analysts rated the corporate reputations of 305 of the largest *Fortune* 500 and *Fortune* Service 500 companies across 32 industries. Each company was rated on eight attributes of reputation: quality of management; quality of products or services; innovativeness; long-term investment value; financial soundness; ability to attract, develop and keep talented people; community and environmental responsibility; and wise use of corporate assets. In *Fortune's* 1990 "Most Admired," listing Wal-Mart moved up to fourth place, closely behind Merck, Rubbermaid, and Procter & Gamble. Wal-Mart is the only retailer to ever make the *Fortune* top ten.

The most admired aspects of Wal-Mart's corporate reputation for both years include:

- A total return to investors (10-year average) of 46.0% in 1989 and 42.16% in 1990
- Use of corporate assets
- Ability to attract, develop, and keep talented people
- Quality of management
- Social responsibility (1989)

Wal-Mart's ability to analyze itself, its competitors, and the environments in which it operates has led to a winning strategy. Execution of the company's strategies are evaluated constantly to identify potential problems and opportunities, and to determine the most effective allocation of resources.

SOURCES: Davenport, Carol (1989), "America's Most Admired Corporations," (January 30), 68–94; Huey, John (1989), "Wal-Mart: Will It Take Over the World?" *Fortune.* (January 30), 52–60; Sprout, Alison L. (1991), "America's Most Admired Corporations," *Fortune.* (February 11), 52–75.

INTRODUCTION

Emphasis on Performance

Excellence in retailing is based on results. Identification of top performing businesses, and what makes them top performers, has preoccupied many analysts and authors for the past decade. In general, most of the top retailers emphasize planning and control; use capital, human resources, and technology efficiently and effectively; are market share leaders; and know their markets well.

- Wal-Mart, K mart, McDonald's and Marriott were identified in 1982 as "excellent" U.S. retailers with a consistent record of superior financial performance over a twenty-year period (Peters and Waterman, 1982).

- Five retailers were among the twelve "Corporate Stars of America" named by *Fortune* in 1984: Lucky Stores, McDonald's, Service Merchandise, Melville, and Wal-Mart (Loomis, 1984).

- Four "power retailers" were featured in a 1987 *Business Week* article: Wal-Mart, Toys "R" Us, May Department Stores, and The Limited (Dunkin, Oneal, and Phillips, 1987).

- A Wall Street investment firm cited May Department Stores, Nordstrom, The Limited, Toys "R" Us, Walgreen, and Wal-Mart as today's great retailers. Circuit City, Costco, Dillard's, Dress Barn, Food Lion, and Home Depot were named as the emerging great retailing companies (Varadarajan, 1989).

- Wal-Mart was the only retailer named as one of America's Most Admired Corporations based on 1990 performance. One of the leading reasons for Wal-Mart's position as number 4 out of 306 U.S. corporations is quality of management. David Glass, CEO of Wal-Mart, has taken the lead for the 1990s by guiding the retailer's expansion, aiming for more discount stores, new wholesale clubs, and double-digit earnings growth ("The Best of 1990," 1991). Early in 1991 Wal-Mart overtook Sears, Roebuck and Company as number one retailer in sales revenues.

- Home Depot, The Limited, Toys "R" Us, Wal-Mart, Dillard's, the Gap, J.C. Penney, and Nordstrom evolved as "the new champs of retailing in 1990." Their success was attributed to developing exciting merchandising programs, finding innovative uses for technology, and expanding smartly and aggressively—all while maintaining low debt ratios (Caminiti, 1990). Retailers who were among the fastest growing companies in 1990 were two warehouse clubs: Costco Wholesale and Price. Five-year average growth rate was 97 percent for Costco and 34 percent for Price (Sheeline, 1990).

The histories of dynamic retailers, such as these, emphasize the relationship between performance, excellence, and power. (See Exhibit 16–1.) Exhibit 16–2 presents a summary of top U.S. retailers in two major industries according to the 1991 *Business Week* 1000.

Exhibit 16–1
Excellence in Retailing

ANALYSIS OF RESULTS: SUCCESS OR FAILURE   Some of the most innovative and successful retailers, the "Power Retailers," have prospered because they know what is happening inside and outside of their companies. They have monitored a highly competitive retail environment that has increasingly more stores, more catalogs, and more demanding customers with less time and patience. They have developed successful strategies based on an intimate knowledge of their markets and an analysis of their operating results, thus taking a proactive approach to obtaining competitive advantage (Dunkin, Oneal, and Phillips, 1987).

On the other hand, a lack of understanding of what is happening in the retail environment can have a negative effect on operating results. Several well-known retailers got "off track" with their strategies and suffered losses in revenues and earnings. Dayton Hudson had enjoyed a reputation as one

Exhibit 16–2
Top U.S. Discount, Fashion and Food Retailers

	Sales 1991 ($million)	Profits 1991 ($million)
Top 10 Discount and Fashion Retailers		
Wal-Mart Stores	43,887	1,608.5
Sears, Roebuck	57,242	1,144.9
Home Depot	3,137	249.2
K mart	34,969	859.0
Toys "R" Us	6,124	339.5
The Limited	6,149	403.3
J.C. Penney	17,295	528.0
May Department Stores	10,615	515.0
The Gap	2,519	229.9
Melville	9,886	346.7
Top 10 Food Retailers		
Food Lion	6,439	205.2
Albertson's	8,680	257.8
Winn-Dixie Stores	10,203	177.9
American Stores	20,823	240.2
Safeway Stores	15,119	79.0
Kroger	21,351	100.7
Giant Food	3,397	102.2
Bruno's	2,658	63.5
Smith's Food & Drug Centers	2,217	45.1
Great Atlantic & Pacific Tea	11,624	86.2

SOURCE: 1992 *Business Week* 1000
Note: Rankings are based on market values as of March 1992.

of the most successful, well-managed retailers for two decades. The company ran into trouble in 1987 at its Mervyn's apparel and softgoods chain, with a problem identified by company executives as more one of execution than strategy. In the same year, Sears experienced a slump in sales growth and earnings, largely attributed to high operating costs, an antiquated distribution system, and lackluster apparel merchandising. Best Products also suffered its first full-year loss in 30 years, largely due to competition from volume discounters and specialty retailers. Each of these retailers has been faced with the need to develop new strategies to get back "on track" and stay there (Pitzer, Oneal, and Smart, 1987). For example, Kenneth Macke, chairman and chief executive of Dayton Hudson, led his company in a major turnaround following the October 1987 stock market crash and a hostile takeover raid by the Dart Group. By 1989, Dayton Hudson's earnings, operating margins, and stock price had returned to solid growth. The turnaround was accomplished in part by focusing on Mervyn's merchandising and purchasing, rather than their previous obsession with expansion and building new stores. In addition, Mervyn's created a quality control team and undertook a multimillion-dollar store remodeling program. As a result, operating margins nearly doubled. Dayton Hudson equipped all of its Target stores with electronic scanners to improve customer checkout efficiency and inventory control. This decision increased Target's sales per square foot ($198 compared with K mart's $148) and operating margin (Mitchell, 1989). In the long run, Dayton Hudson has retained its position among the top retailers, including the 1990 addition of Marshall Fields to its corporate family of retail chains.

These situations illustrate the need for analysis throughout the stages of the managerial process. An understanding of why results were not as planned is a major step toward correcting mistakes.

The Managerial Process

There are basic problems to be solved, questions to be asked, and information to be used in analyzing and evaluating the results of management decisions. Since these decisions evolve from the retailer's strategic plan, an evaluation is needed for decision making during each of the four major stages in the managerial process: (1) analysis (based on the problem to be solved), (2) planning, (3) execution, and (4) control. The results of this assessment of the success or failure of retail activities become an integral part of the feedback used in both short- and long-range planning. (See Exhibit 16–3.) Inventory investment allocation and evaluation illustrates a portion of this process in which three basic tasks must be analyzed and performed in keeping with corporate financial goals: Allocate. Motivate. Evaluate (Levy and Ingene, 1984). That is, allocate the necessary funds for inventory investment, motivate buyers to select the right merchandise, and evaluate the performance of buyers and merchandise lines.

Retail managers are oriented toward acting quickly and decisively to solve the problems of operating their businesses in a highly competitive and rapidly changing environment, thus taking a shorter-range perspective (Rosenbloom, 1980). However, when operating results are analyzed as part of the strategic planning process, management must give attention to developments in the markets where they operate, competitive activities, economic

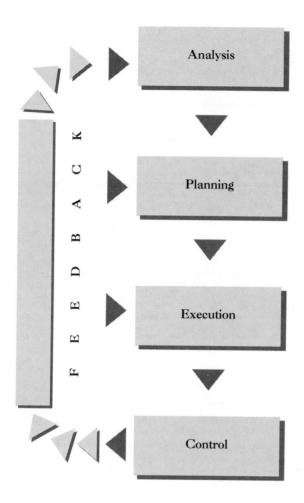

Exhibit 16–3
The Managerial Process

trends, and other environmental factors, and then address their implications. Through this type of analysis the retailer has the ability to anticipate future scenarios and to take a longer-range view in developing alternative strategies.

Analysis and Strategic Planning: An Ongoing Process

The early chapters of this book presented a broad view of retail management and strategic planning, addressing the general question "What will we do?" ("What objectives does our company want to achieve?" and "What strategies will we use to reach our objectives?") These were followed by chapters that concentrated on narrower functional retail management areas, addressing the more specific question, "How will we do it?" ("How shall we use our retail mix and operate our stores on a day-to-day basis?") That is, "What tactics will we use to carry out strategies?" and "What resources are needed for implementation?"

In this chapter, we return to the broader perspective to bring these factors together within an analytical framework. An assessment of retail performance is based on an evaluation of operating results. The questions addressed here are, "Did we do, or are we doing, what we set out to do?" and

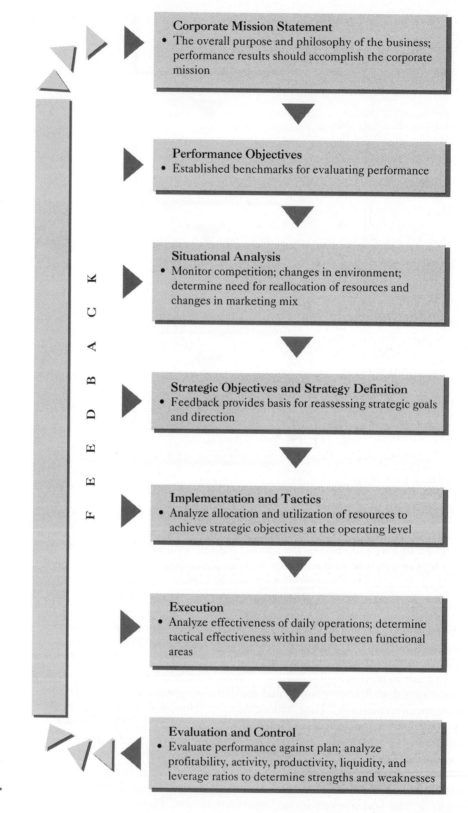

Corporate Mission Statement
• The overall purpose and philosophy of the business; performance results should accomplish the corporate mission

Performance Objectives
• Established benchmarks for evaluating performance

Situational Analysis
• Monitor competition; changes in environment; determine need for reallocation of resources and changes in marketing mix

Strategic Objectives and Strategy Definition
• Feedback provides basis for reassessing strategic goals and direction

Implementation and Tactics
• Analyze allocation and utilization of resources to achieve strategic objectives at the operating level

Execution
• Analyze effectiveness of daily operations; determine tactical effectiveness within and between functional areas

Evaluation and Control
• Evaluate performance against plan; analyze profitability, activity, productivity, liquidity, and leverage ratios to determine strengths and weaknesses

F E E D B A C K

Exhibit 16–4
Analysis and Strategic Planning:
An Ongoing Process

"Why did we or didn't we do it?" During the execution phase, the question "What is/isn't working so far?" also should be addressed. (See Exhibit 16–4.)

In the next section, issues to be examined at each organizational level are described. Particular attention is given to analysis of results at the functional level.

Levels of Analysis

Retail operations can be evaluated at the corporate or strategic, business, and functional or operating levels of the firm, as described in this section. (See Exhibit 16–5.) Although the emphasis may differ acording to organizational level, analysis addresses three major concerns: performance versus plan, execution of the plan, and capital expenditures. In each case, the company is interested in knowing whether it has made the best use of its resources.

At all levels, the overriding philosophy is to answer the question, "How can we better exploit our current internal resources (financial, human, physical, technological, and organizational) to achieve a clear, sustainable competitive advantage?" As Waterman (1987) observes in *The Renewal Factor,* opportunity knocks softly and in unpredictable ways. Today's business leaders must face—and manage—constant change, with the goal of prospering from the forces that decimate their competition. Analysis provides critical information for retailers to use in planning, executing, controlling, and revising strategy, and to be ready for opportunity when it knocks.

Corporate Level Analysis

Analysis is performed at the corporate or strategic level for a multi-store retail chain and for a multi-business organization. Large firms may have several types of stores, multiple retail formats, and/or diverse retail and nonretail holdings. Managers and operations are evaluated across divisions to determine their effect on the corporate bottom line, with the objective of balancing all businesses profitably. Emphasis is on the logic and coordination of the businesses that make up the corporation, taking a longer-term perspective of strategies for organizational effectiveness ("what to do").

Determination of organizational effectiveness is directly related to the use of financial resources. The pressure on retail firms to achieve the highest possible return for every dollar invested underlies the need to evaluate all capital expenditures, including expansion activities, major equipment purchases, acquisitions or mergers, and other major investments.

PROFITABLE USE OF CAPITAL RESOURCES   Food Lion, the fastest-growing supermarket chain in America and the second largest publicly held corporation in North Carolina, has been one of the most profitable investments of all time, making millionaires of 87 local investors. The company uses capital frugally to sell basic groceries at low prices in relatively small, no-frills stores that are built for speed, not comfort.

High performance is accomplished through volume sales and expense control, coupled with clustering of stores, which are expanded concentrically

Exhibit 16–5
Levels of Analysis

Corporate Level
- **Evaluation** of managers and operations across divisions
- **Emphasis** on logic and coordination of businesses that make up corporation
- **Perspective** of strategies is longer-term

Business Level
- **Evaluation** of managers and operations across stores and within the business division
- **Emphasis** on effective and efficient coordination of functional areas
- **Perspective** is narrower than corporate and wider than functional

Functional Level
- **Evaluation** within and across functional areas
- **Emphasis** on dealing with efficiency of carrying out strategic intent
- **Perspective** is narrowest and oriented to today's operation

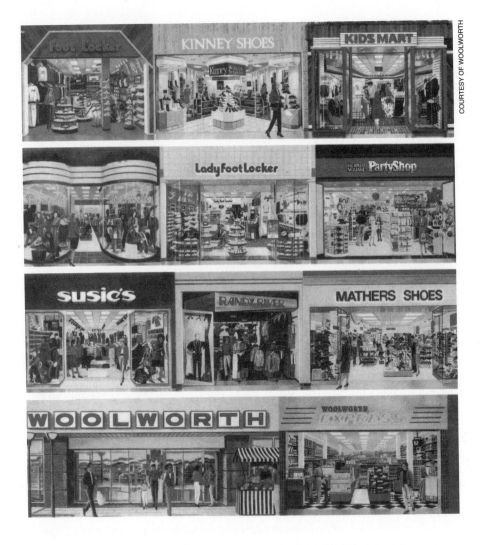

Corporate analysis of each Woolworth business unit resulted in the decision to restructure the corporation with a focus on specialty retailing, a strategy that has proved to be successful.

from warehouses. Most of Food Lion's growth comes from new stores. In 1987, 95 were added for a total of 475 located in eight Southeastern states. One hundred more were added in 1988, with 26 in Florida, the region's most populous market (Sheeline, 1988).

CORPORATE ANALYSIS AND STRATEGY DECISIONS: THE F.W. WOOLWORTH CO.

Woolworth, among the largest U.S. retail corporations, has had its share of ups and downs. In 1982, when its $2 billion Woolco discount division suffered heavy losses, Woolworth closed 336 Woolco stores to avoid disaster, and sold its 52.6 percent interest in its troubled British subsidiary (Dunkin, 1986). An analysis of operating results for each business unit and an understanding of customer wants and the retailing environment have led to a major strategic shift. Conclusions based on this analysis resulted in management's decision to restructure with a focus on specialty retailing. Since that time, Woolworth has had a more profitable mix of business units that make up the corporation, with increased net income, return on equity, and stock prices.

In 1989, Woolworth opened a new property somewhere in the world roughly every eight hours, following 1,000 new store openings in 1988. In addition to its best-known specialty store, Kinney Shoe, the company operates more than 40 different brands of store, developing a few more each year in search of those that will become billion-dollar businesses. These strategic changes resulted in a record 15 percent increase in net income of $228 million on record sales of $8.1 billion in 1988. The specialty store division (including Kinney's Foot Locker) was responsible for about 40 percent of the company's sales and 50 percent of the profits, performing much better than the general merchandise division (Saporito, 1989). In 1990, the company planned to open 825 additional stores and close 235 stores. The openings included the acquisition of Profoot, a 14-store athletic footwear chain located in Belgium and the Netherlands (Woolworth, 1990, p.6). Woolworth's corporate structure, as reflected in the company's 1989 annual report is shown in Exhibit 16–6 and 16–6a.

K mart is another retailer who has remained a strong performer through its ability to analyze operating results and evaluate opportunities. The company uses high technology to track consumer buying patterns more closely, having launched a $500 million automation program in 1985 that included scanners in checkout lanes to collect useful data. As a result, K mart began to concentrate on apparel, one of its competitive strengths, and other "power departments" for improved operating results (Mitchell, 1986).

Other mass-merchandisers, such as Sears Roebuck and Montgomery Ward, have had problems maintaining market share and profitability. Sears Roebuck has undertaken a massive restructuring to overcome problems faced by its retailing division where its strategies have not been in step with consumer demographics and tastes. Analysis of their situation has led to a change to discount pricing and more emphasis on national brands, putting Sears in competition with Wal-Mart and K mart. Corporate restructuring also involved the sale of Sears Tower, a Chicago landmark, Coldwell Banker Commercial Group, and the Allstate insurance group life and health subsidiary (Lowenstein, 1988b; Schwadel, 1988). In addition to evaluating these units within the context of the corporate portfolio, each was evaluated at the business level on more specific criteria.

Business Level Analysis

The environmental perspective for business level analysis is narrower than that taken at the corporate level, but broader than that at the functional level (described in the next section). Emphasis is on the effective and efficient coordination of all functional areas to assure maximum impact. Managers, store operations, and other factors are evaluated across stores within the business division to answer the basic question of how each unit performed against its planned performance standards. Results provide inputs for decisions about how to allocate money, manpower, and other assets for the greatest advantage.

ANALYSIS OF PERFORMANCE VERSUS PLAN   The retailer's operating plan establishes performance standards for comparison with actual results during execution and upon completion. Evaluation during the early stages reveals strengths and weaknesses and permits the retailer to make

Exhibit 16–6
Woolworth's Corporate Strategy and Structure

Mission Statement

"The mission of Woolworth Corporation is to provide value to the consumers it serves through its distinctly individual retailing businesses around the world. Under the general guidance of corporate management, these businesses seek to generate levels of profit that not only satisfy investors and sustain long-term growth, but also provide competitive financial rewards for associates and benefit the communities in which they live and work."

Corporate Profile

Woolworth Corporation, founded in 1879, is a large multinational retailer with stores and related support operations in fifteen countries and four continents. The company operates over 8,000 stores in the United Sates, Canada, West Germany, Australia, Belgium, and the Netherlands. This includes about 6,400 specialty units and over 1,600 general merchandise stores. Woolworth has an overseas network of 11 buying offices located throughout Asia and Mexico and 9 manufacturing facilities producing footwear and apparel for certain stores.

Woolworth's variety store concept has evolved over the past century into an international network of general merchandise stores offering a broad assortment of merchandise at low prices. More recently, Woolworth's has expanded its specialty retail operations to over 40 retail formats.

Strategic Restructuring

The depressed world economic conditions of the 1980s represented huge obstacles for retailers. In addition to this formidable environment, Woolworth was suffering from increasing losses at its U.S. Woolco operations and an unproductive investment in its British subsidiary. Woolworth took action in 1982 to remedy this situation by freeing itself of both of these operations. The proceeds fueled the company's major growth vehicle of the 1980s—specialty store operations.

Strategies for Growth/Strategic Priorities

- Rapidly expand specialty formats:
  Examples: Foot Locker—brand name, high-performance athletic footwear and apparel; over 1,300 stores; and Lady Foot Locker, 596 stores.
- Internally develop specialty formats:
  Examples: Afterthoughts (costume jewelry, handbags, accessories); Northern Reflections (casual sportswear for women).
- Acquire specialty formats:
  Examples: Kids Mart/Little Folk (brand name infants' and children's apparel); Champs (high performance athletic equipment).

SOURCE: *1990 Fact Book,* New York: The Woolworth Corporation; and *Woolworth Corporation 1989 Annual Report,* New York: The Woolworth Corporation.

necessary revisions. If timely revisions cannot be made, they can be considered in the final evaluation of the plan and in later revisions.

Evaluation of performance versus plan is an integral part of the strategic planning and control process. If performance is below expectations, analysis may reveal explanations that are not evident otherwise. For example, a lower than desired profit level might be caused by a number of interacting factors, such as higher than average advertising expenses and short-run price cuts taken to achieve a high sales volume. Or changes in the retailer's operating environment (such as a major layoff of area workers) may make it necessary to reevaluate the original plan.

At the business level, each functional area can be evaluated to determine its role in the execution of marketing strategies and its contribution to retail

Exhibit 16–6a
Woolworth's complete store profile by operating division

SPECIALTY STORES

Kinney United States
Kinney..family shoe stores
Foot Locker..athletic footwear and apparel
Lady Foot Locker...................................women's athletic footwear and apparel
Susie's ....women's apparel
Athletic X-Press....................................family athletic footwear and apparel
Champs Sports.......................................athletic equipment, footwear, and apparel
Footquarters ....brand-name family shoe stores
Fredelle...high-fashion women's shoe stores
Sportelle...women's casual apparel
Kids Foot Locker ....children's athletic footwear and apparel

Kinney Canada
Lady Foot Locker...................................women's athletic-footwear and apparel
stores and leased departments in Woolco
stores
Kinney..family shoe stores, and leased departments
in Woolco stores
Sportelle..women's casual apparel
Randy River...men's clothing
Fredelle...high-fashion women's shoe stores
Raglans..unisex casual apparel
Canary Island...men's and women's travel and vacation
apparel
Afterthoughts...costume jewelry, handbags, and accessories
Champs Sports.......................................athletic equipment, footwear, and apparel

Kinney Australia
Williams the Shoemen............................family shoe stores
Mathers ....brand-name family shoe stores
Vic Jensens ....family shoe stores
Gallery...high-fashion brand-name women's shoe
stores
Foot Locker/Live Wire...........................athletic footwear and apparel
Randy River...high-fashion women's shoe stores
Shoe Bargains ....self-service promotional family shoe stores

Richman Brothers
Richman...men's clothing and furnishings; and
women's career apparel in selected stores
Anderson-Little.....................................men's and women's apparel and furnishings
Cotton Supply Co. ....casual apparel made of natural fibers

Kids Mart/Little Folk Shop
Kids Mart ....promotionally priced brand-name infants'
and children's apparel
Little Folk ....brand-name infants' and children's apparel
The Rx Place...deep-discount drug stores

Woolworth United States
Afterthoughts/Carimar...........................costume jewelry, handbags, and accessories
Woolworth Express................................general merchandise convenience stores
Herald Square Party Shop ....party goods, stationery, and greeting cards
Burger King ....franchised food operations in Woolworth
stores
Frame Scene..prints, frames, and framing services

Woolworth Canada
Northern Reflections ....outdoor sportswear for women
Afterthoughts..costume jewelry, handbags, and accessories
Kids Mart ....promotionally priced brand-name infants'
and children's apparel

continued

Exhibit 16–6a (continued)

Ashbrooks ....home furnishings and accessories
U.B. Anywear..childrenswear
Woolworth Express..general merchandise convenience stores
Woolworth Germany
Moderna/Dr Schuh ....family shoe stores
Rubin ....costume jewelry, handbags, and accessories
Foot Locker...athletic footwear and apparel

GENERAL MERCHANDISE

Woolworth United States
Woolworth stores...general merchandise and apparel
Woolworth Canada
Woolworth stores...general merchandise and apparel
Woolco stores..full-line promotional department stores
Robinson's..apparel and other general merchandise
Woolworth Germany
Woolworth stores...general merchandise, including better
grades of apparel, home furnishings, jewelry, and leather goods
Mini Shops...apparel and other general merchandise

SOURCE: 1990 Fact Book, New York: The Woolworth Corporation; and Woolworth Corporation 1989 Annual Report, New York: The Woolworth Corporation. Used with permission.
Note: Despite careful strategic planning, Woolworth Corporation announced in January, 1992, that it intended to "alter, close or sell" 900 of its 9,300 stores world-wide.

profit performance. For example, sales growth, inventory turnover, and relative advertising effort were significant discriminators of high- and low-profit performers (return on total assets) for retail grocery firms (Cronin and Kelley, 1985). These results suggest that retailers should support the functions and emphasize the strategic options that increase sales growth and inventory turnover. In this case, a decision to add merchandise lines or increase stock levels should be evaluated carefully for its impact on overall inventory turnover; such an evaluation may suggest giving more attention to moving slow sellers, decreasing delivery times, and other measures to maintain high turnover.

Business level analysis also looks outward to the company's operating environment to assess market opportunities and demand for a retailer's products and services. The retailer obtains information about the activities of other businesses (vendors, intermediaries, service providers), competitors, and the government, in addition to the consumers themselves. With this information, the retailer can evaluate current conditions and anticipate future events, thus permitting a proactive approach to influencing environmental forces, rather than merely reacting to them.

The following examples illustrate how environmental analysis can affect strategic responses by retailers who monitor and understand their environments, and the consequences for some who did not analyze their environments appropriately. Can you decide what environmental factors were or should have been analyzed in each case?

- Kroger thwarted a takeover bid from Kohlberg Kravis Roberts & Co. with a recapitalization plan that offered stock to employees and management (Stricharchuk, 1988).

- Winn-Dixie grew to be the fifth largest U.S. supermarket chain, with 1,252 stores in 13 states. Its net margins were at the top of the industry during the 1970s and early 1980s; its stock price doubled between 1973 and 1983 and dividends increased steadily for 44 consecutive years. From 1984 to 1988, Winn-Dixie suffered declining profits, stock prices, earnings, and dividends, because they became complacent and underestimated competition (Taylor, 1988).

- The Marriott Corp. used extensive market research to identify an unserved niche in the moderate and economy hotel markets, a strategy geared toward downturns in the economy. The company has emerged as the strongest and best-managed big company in the lodging industry, successfully weathering periods of recession and expansion by competitors (Chakravarty, 1987). Marriott's Residence Inn unit plans to invest $1 billion over five years to more than double its stake in extended-stay hotels, based on an analysis of opportunities in this market (Lowenstein, 1988a).

- The Japanese train managers to make competitive intelligence, the art of legally gathering information on rivals, a routine part of everyone's job. A number of American firms are adopting this same philosophy. Marriott has not only given the goal of knowing everything possible about the competition a high priority in the corporation but has assigned subordinates to intelligence-gathering activities. For example, in the summer of 1986, six Marriott employees on a secret intelligence mission checked into a cheap hotel, with gaudily decorated rooms at $30 a night, outside the Atlanta airport. They checked the type of service the hotel gave and noted the brands of soap, shampoo, and towels. They knocked the headboard of the bed against the wall while faking sounds of ecstacy to see if they could be heard in the next room (they could). For six months this intelligence team had gathered information throughout the country to learn about their potential rivals' strengths and weaknesses in the economy hotel business. Based on the detailed data which they obtained, Marriott budgeted $500 million for a new hotel chain they felt would beat the competition in every respect, starting with the Fairfield Inn in 1988, which achieved an occupancy rate 10 percent higher than the rest of the industry (Dumaine, 1988).

- Avis engaged in a price war with Hertz in an attempt to gain market share and move to the number one position, based on estimates of current and potential market share for the two companies (Hawkins, 1988).

Functional Level Analysis

Analysis at the functional, or operating, level deals with the efficiency of carrying out strategic intent ("how to do it") within and across the functional areas of a retail business unit. At this level, the horizon is shorter term as managers concentrate on the details of carrying out the firm's strategy on a day-to-day basis. The overriding goal is coordination of all departments and functions for the successful execution of corporate strategy and achievement of corporate objectives.

All relevant aspects of the retailing mix are studied to determine how well the plan has been executed: merchandise assortments, pricing strategy, promotion, store location and layout, and services offered by the retailer. Unsuccessful execution may be due to ineffective inventory management (stockouts or poor assortments), unreliable suppliers, or errors in identifying customer wants. Or the level and/or type of promotion need adjustment, or prices are too low or too high, and so on. Conversely, factors responsible for successful execution can also be identified.

In this section, we will look at the need for analysis within each of the specialized functional areas: merchandise management, promotion and communication, store operations, accounting and finance, and human resources. Then we will look at the need to evaluate the combined effect of these functions as they interact to produce operating results.

MERCHANDISE MANAGEMENT   Merchandise managers are faced with the tasks of forecasting sales, determining pricing strategies, overseeing the buying function, and controlling inventory. They must accomplish these tasks within the context of a merchandise budget, expense planning, and the effect of their decisions on other functional areas. Thus, analysis is critical in making initial decisions, as well as in determining the success or failure of the merchandising function. Factors to be evaluated are discussed for each task. Although not emphasized here, complex statistical computer models can be used for this type of analysis.

In the sales forecasting task, forecasting models are used to estimate demand and sales. Anticipated sales levels determine the amount of beginning and ending inventory for a selling period, the amount and type of merchandise to be purchased by buyers, the number of salespeople needed to cover a department at a specified time, promotional efforts, and other factors. During and after execution, analysis of sales and inventory data provides information about the accuracy of forecasts and possible need for adjustment of original estimates.

Determining pricing strategy is another important task. Pricing decisions play a critical role in achieving retail objectives and, therefore, must be evaluated. Analysis is needed to determine the following: Are prices acceptable to the target market? Is there a sufficient range of prices to offer customers a suitable alternative? Are the price points psychologically appropriate? Is the maintained markup high enough to achieve the retailer's profit objectives, and/or low enough to achieve sales objectives? And what effect do markup and profit objectives have on cost prices that can be paid to vendors? Are markdowns (or markups) recommended to improve performance? Do new price lines or price points need to be introduced?

To accomplish the buying task, buyers need information to plan merchandise assortments, determine basic stock needs, plan retail reductions and profit margins, and make projections about consumer responses to the goods and services offered. Projections may be based on knowledge of characteristics of the store's customers, and how they use products and services.

The performance of buyers and merchandise managers is evaluated in several ways, including achievement of sales objectives, expense control, and contribution to profit margins. Performance evaluation may involve an analysis of effective buying practices and profitable use of valuable retail floor and

COURTESY OF T. J. MAXX

T. J. Maxx's unique off-price buying strategy requires sophisticated inventory management techniques and special negotiating skills which are acquired through an in-house training program.

shelf space, for example. High performance often results in bonuses or profit-sharing plans for these executives.

In the inventory control task inventories, which represent a major retail asset, are evaluated from several interrelated perspectives. The productivity of each dollar invested in inventory is analyzed to determine whether the optimal balance is achieved between stock and sales and whether the inventory investment is producing the desired level of sales and profits.

Both dollars and units invested in merchandise are examined relative to sufficient coverage of fast-selling items, as well as overstocked and nonproductive slow-selling items. Stock turnover rates within departments and merchandise classifications, optimum reorder points, and reorder quantities also are evaluated. The status of present and planned inventory involves tracking merchandise from time of receipt until it is sold, or otherwise taken out of inventory (theft, breakage, etc.), in order to calculate the value of inventory at any time.

The retailer's merchandising philosophy and growth orientation will determine the direction and use of inventory analysis. The retailer who is concentrating on building market share (e.g., low profit margin/high inventory turnover ratio) will have a different merchandising philosophy than one

Stock turnover rates are determined by inventory tracking, in this case by EDI at Venture, in order to calculate the value of inventory at any given time.

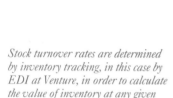

who is just trying to maintain the status quo (e.g., average profit margin/average inventory turnover ratio). The retailer may also emphasize just-in-time delivery (JIT), which would result in estimating lowest possible inventory levels, or the 80–20 rule (i.e., 80 percent of the sales come from 20 percent of the inventory), which would lead to estimating higher inventories for the most important items.

PROMOTION AND COMMUNICATION   The execution of a retail plan involves an evaluation of the promotional mix (advertising, personal selling, sales promotion, visual merchandising, publicity, and public relations), as well as services offered by the retailer. The goal is to obtain the highest return possible from each dollar spent to communicate with customers. Analytical models, often using point-of-sale scanner data, can be used to identify the lowest-cost promotion mix to achieve the highest sales and/or profit objectives within a given time period.

Effective promotion requires knowledge of consumer demographics, lifestyles, attitudes, benefits sought, and so forth in order to evaluate preferred communication methods. Questions to be addressed include: Are the promotional message, media, and timing effective in achieving the retailer's objectives? Is the intended message reaching the target audience? and with the desired results?

In an era of high technology and increasing self-service, an evaluation of the effect of salesforce expenditures is necessary. Have they been trained properly? Are sales personnel doing their job right? Is compensation directly related to performance, and in what way?

Questions to be answered about sales promotion, an integral part of "retailing as entertainment," include: How is sales promotion used and integrated with the entire promotional mix? How do customers respond to special events, "give aways," contests, couponing, or other sales promotion tools? Is the visual presentation of merchandise effective?

Special sales events are designed to increase store traffic, sales and, ultimately, profits. Although the performance measure of most interest to the retailer is profit, it is often neglected in analyzing promotion. Here it is necessary to assess sales for promoted products, and their complementary products (sold at full markup), and whether low-margin sale items took sales away from higher-margin nonpromoted items.

Finally, have publicity and public relations efforts been directed to the right media and individuals? How effective is promotional communication through these channels, and should other options be explored?

Execution of a retail promotional strategy often involves services that accompany purchases. Are the right services being offered? Are some unnecessary services offered that contribute to expenses only and not to sales? Are there services that should be offered to meet the needs of customers, and to compete effectively, such as credit, delivery, alterations, repairs, and others?

STORE OPERATIONS   The daily activities involved in maintaining the physical store facility must be studied to determine their effect on performance. The location and layout of a store, productivity of selling space, and risk management decisions all may be evaluated against established criteria.

Store location and layout have an impact on how well a retail strategy is executed. Even in a multi-store chain, execution varies from one store to another. Some may be high performers, others poor performers, due to differences in location, appearance, physical layout, and personnel. Analysis may suggest that changes in execution are needed to minimize problems and/or maximize opportunities.

Many analytical models and information services are available for selecting new store sites and evaluating existing sites, as discussed in Chapter 9. Mall developers often perform the initial location analysis and then attract an appropriate tenant mix. Sbarro, a modestly priced, speedy service, Italian cafeteria-style restaurant chain, has benefited from good mall locations. Ranking high among America's 100 hot-growth companies, Sbarro has continually increased sales and profits. However, the company has relied on site analysis by the more experienced Marriott Corp. to open 20 franchises in nonmall locations on selected highways (McCoy, 1987).

Increasing emphasis is put on maximizing sales and profits from retail store space. Retailers use space productivity analysis in allocating and evaluating selling areas within a department or store. They calculate ratios for net sales, contribution to profits, or gross margin per square foot of floor space, cubic foot of display area, or linear foot of shelf space. These ratios can be applied to sales volume estimates to calculate the amount of selling area needed for a merchandise line or department and to determine the most advantageous store layout.

The operations function is responsible for risk management and security. Analysis of the store environment is needed to identify existing and potential problems in order to minimize their occurrence. Solutions to shortages due to theft, pilferage, burglary, robbery, bad checks, and fraudulent use of credit cards require an evaluation of the most effective techniques for prevention and apprehension. Security personnel must also be evaluated. Risk management analysis includes protection for the store, its employees, and customers against accidents, fire, and other calamities, according to local, state, and federal ordinances.

ACCOUNTING AND CONTROL   The accounting function has primary responsibility for recording and maintaining internally generated data used in financial analysis and the control of retail operations. The Retail Information System (RIS) contains sales reports, cash register transactions, customer credit records, vendor invoices, employee sales and compensation records, operating expense vouchers, and other data essential to evaluating operating results.

Ongoing analysis is necessary to study the uses, types, and sources of data required by managers. For example, accounting data are used for comparisons of sales, profits, and other measures of performance across departments, stores, and other business units. Performance data may be evaluated against prior time periods and used as a basis for future projections.

Routine reporting for internal and external use is an important duty of the accounting department. Internal reports are provided for managers across functions and at all levels of the organization. External reports consist of information needed for tax returns and financial statements for stockholders.

HUMAN RESOURCES   Analysis of the human resources function focuses on employee requirements and productivity. In the first case, personnel needs must be evaluated at all levels—from top management to hourly workers. An analysis of the tasks to be performed leads to job descriptions used in hiring and evaluating employees.

Employee productivity is a major concern because of the financial resources devoted to salaries and wages, making payroll an obvious place to cut expenses. Evidence of this practice is found in the increased popularity of self-service stores with lower costs and higher profit margins. Further evidence is seen in the trimming of management ranks, particularly in acquisitions, where firms can function effectively with fewer highly paid executives.

An assessment of employees includes an evaluation of their performance, absenteeism, and other records. The results are used for decisions regarding compensation, training, promotion, or dismissal.

Reasons for employee turnover are analyzed to determine whether people leave the company because of better job opportunities, poor working conditions, management problems, or other causes. From example, U.S. Shoe Corp. (Casual Corner, Ups 'N Downs, Petite Sophisticate, etc.) lost about half of it's top 26 executives during an 18-month period of uncertainty and unrest due to aggressive cost cutting, revised merchandising strategies, and spin-offs of less profitable assets to stop the company's decline in return on equity from 20.7 percent in 1984 to 7.2 percent in 1988 (Phillips, 1988).

Communication channels across departments and functional areas of the company must be studied in order to disseminate store policies, personnel matters (insurance, benefits, etc.), training information, and other items. Areas of ineffective horizontal or vertical communication can also be identified.

Retail management decisions at the functional level have been the focus throughout this book. However, the functional aspects of the retail firm must operate within the context of a complete business unit, and often within a larger corporation. Therefore, an example of evaluation across functions is provided in the next section.

EVALUATION ACROSS FUNCTIONS: AN EXAMPLE   A decision in one functional area affects all others. For example, at the operating level, support for a particular sale event or floor planning for a seasonal event will require money, human power, physical resources, management expertise, and other company assets. Effective resource allocation among departments and functions requires insights obtained from analysis of sales reports, financial statements, and other timely data.

A decision by a merchandise manager in Junior Sportswear to increase her inventory of bluejeans substantially provides a global view of the impact of this decision across all functional areas. All managers involved with merchandise, promotion, store operations, accounting, and personnel decisions are affected. Within the merchandising function, demand for bluejeans must be estimated for sales forecasts and inventory planning. Buyers must select the best source of supply and the most desirable product line, negotiate favorable terms of sale, and obtain other advantages associated with the purchase. If the additional inventory must be purchased without an increase in the merchandise budget, possible decreases in other lines must be evaluated.

Those responsible for promotion become involved in decisions about how to advertise and display the bluejeans. The jeans may be included in a direct mail promotion or a catalog, requiring coordination with other merchandise departments, as well as displays, fixtures, and floor planning. The jeans might be part of a storewide promotion (back to school, western theme). The payoff for each alternative must be studied, as well as the coordination of promotional efforts and merchandise delivery dates to ensure sufficient inventory coverage.

Operations managers receive the shipment of jeans into the store, check the quantity and style shipped against the buyer's order, mark them for sale, and move them from the receiving area to the selling floor. Since the junior apparel department is a high theft area, security managers must take measures to reduce shoplifting.

The accounting function is responsible for recording data on each pair of bluejeans from the time the order is placed until the customer pays for the purchase (or returns it for credit, and it is resold or returned to vendor). Budget items such as sales, purchases, reductions, markups, and profit to date are tracked and compared to planned figures. Data from purchase orders, invoices, payment vouchers, sales and inventory records, customer charge accounts and cash payments, merchandise returns, and employee discounts are added to the store's information system and analyzed for future decisions.

The human resources function is responsible for recruiting, hiring, training, and evaluating all personnel. The qualifications of employees affect sales and profits associated with the jeans, including the ability of the buyer, those involved in handling and selling the jeans, and managing the relevant data. Interpersonal communication should be appraised in terms of training, company procedures, performance evaluation, and such.

Exhibit 16–7 illustrates the interdependency of the five functional areas for this simple decision within one store. It might also be applied to a larger retail chain with the functional areas centralized in a headquarters location.

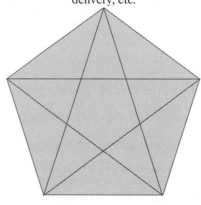

Merchandise Management
Demand estimates for sales forecasts, inventory requirements; Vendor selection, negotiation, delivery, etc.

Promotion and Communication
Advertising, display; storewide promotion, catalog/direct mail. timing (and delivery dates)

Human Resources
Recruiting, hiring, training, scheduling, evaluating, interpersonal communication

Store Operations
Delivery, warehouse, logistics in and out of store; receiving, checking, marking; security/risk management

Accounting and Control
Recording orders; monitoring budget items, customer charges, customer and vendor returns, MIS data

Exhibit 16–7
Interrelationship of Uses and Sources of Information for Increased Bluejean Inventory

The type of analysis performed at the functional level may not be as easy to understand as calculating sales increases over last year or profit and operating expenses as a percent of sales. However, it is not enough to study only the results of the bluejean inventory decision at the end of an operating period. An understanding of why those results occurred can come only from a more in-depth analysis of how each functional unit performed its tasks during the execution of the plan, and how efficiently these units worked together. In this way, successes can be repeated and failures can be minimized.

We have described the need for analysis at the corporate, business, and functional levels of a retail firm. Now we will look at some ways to measure company performance.

What to Analyze

Basic issues to be addressed by retail managers for the company as a whole concern the results of current efforts, reasons why strategies are/are not working, environmental effects on operations, and opportunities for new growth. The appraisal of these factors is done within the context of performance criteria in line with the firm's mission and objectives.

Questions to Be Answered

In order to obtain the type and quality of data needed for a comprehensive evaluation of overall performance, the following hierarchy of questions needs to be considered.

First, we need to look at the results of our current efforts. *What is/isn't working?* Perhaps this is the most important question to be answered about the effectiveness of the retailer's strategies. For example, we might want to know whether we are achieving market share objectives through lower prices.

Second, we need to determine why our strategies are working, or not working by looking at ourselves and our competitors.

How have we been implementing and executing our strategies? Has everything been done according to plan? Have the resources (financial, human, physical, etc.) been used efficiently and effectively?

What is the competition doing? What are our direct and indirect competitors doing now? And what do we expect our competitors to do in the future? How have they affected or will they affect our ability to meet our objectives? What are their past, current, and evolving formats or methods of retailing? What impact have these formats had, or are they expected to have?

COURTESY OF WALGREENS

Analysis of operations can result in improvements in implementation of strategies; an example is the new SIMS inventory system at Walgreens. Ed Svihra, member of the SIMS development team, states "We're changing the lives of our store managers for the better."

CHAPTER *Sixteen*

After evaluating ourselves and our competitors, we need to determine what environmental forces are operating to affect both us and our competitors.

What environmental changes are taking place? What is happening in our micro- and macroenvironments? What are the economic, sociocultural, demographic, and other environmental trends? How can we respond to, or control their effect on our business? Will they affect both us and our competitors in the same way or differently?

Finally, answers to the questions posed in the first three levels should prepare us to evaluate possible opportunities (or problems).

Do growth opportunities exist? Are there untapped opportunities? Are these opportunities in current retail segments or in new markets? How much are these opportunities expected to contribute to sales and/or profits? Will the returns justify the investment cost?

KEY PERFORMANCE CRITERIA In determining what to analyze, the best indicator lies in the performance criteria established by the firm. Typically retail managers are concerned with overall performance in five key areas: profitability; activity; productivity; liquidity; and leverage. Each is described briefly below and discussed in more depth in the next section.

- *Profitability* indicates the retailer's success or failure for a specified time period. It is a measure of the portion of each dollar of sales or investment that the retailer can keep.
- *Activity*, or asset turnover, is analyzed to determine how effectively the retailer is using resources, such as inventory and equipment, to generate sales revenues.
- Whereas activity refers to the effective use of assets, *productivity* refers to the efficient use of assets, such as floor space or personnel, to generate sales and profits.
- Performance criteria also include *liquidity*, which is the retailer's ability to pay maturing debts in the shortrun.
- *Leverage* is a measure of the relationship between the total value of assets used to operate the business and the amount actually owned by the investors. This ratio will vary according to the retailer's operating philosophy and tolerance for risk.

How to Analyze: Key Ratios and the Strategic Profit Model

Annual reports and other financial and accounting records consist of readily available data for evaluating performance. As we look at some key financial ratios, however, keep in mind the individual products, people, plans, and procedures that make the numbers "happen."

Key Ratios And Their Implications

Analysis of key ratios is a convenient and easily interpreted method of evaluating results of retail operations. Examples of the numerous ratios typically used in each category are described for each of the five important performance areas defined earlier: profitability; activity; productivity; liquidity; and leverage. Each ratio is calculated, briefly interpreted, and compared to industry averages to indicate this retailer's performance relative to competition. A retailer would also compare ratios calculated for current results to the company's own past ratios to determine whether performance is better or worse than in the previous period. A summary of the ratios included in this section is provided in Exhibit 16–8.

PROFITABILITY Although profitability can be measured in a number of ways, the overriding issue is how to operate effectively (strategic viewpoint) and efficiently (operating plans and tactics). One of the problems in measuring profitability lies in deciding which measure to use. Profit, or the amount of money that the retailer can keep after paying suppliers, employees, landlords, taxes, and all other expenses, is always measured relative to something else, such as sales, assets, or the owners' equity (net worth). Here we will discuss the following indicators of profitability:

1. Profit on sales
2. Rate of return on total assets
3. Rate of return on net worth
4. Gross margin return on inventory investment (GMROI)

Exhibits 16–9 and 16–10 itemize the income statement and balance sheet data used to calculate the ratios below. (These financial statements were

Exhibit 16–8
Summary of Key Ratios

1. *Profitability:*
   Profit on sales
   Rate of return on total assets
   Rate of return on net worth
   Gross margin return on inventory investment
2. *Activity:*
   Inventory turnover
   Asset turnover
   Receivables turnover
   Collection period
3. *Productivity:*
   Space
   Personnel
   Accounts payable to sales
4. *Liquidity:*
   Current ratio
   Quick ratio
   Current liabilities to net worth
   Current liabilities to inventory
5. *Leverage:*
   Total assets to net worth (equity)
   Debt to equity (net worth)

Exhibit 16–9
Income Statement

Income Statement
For the year ending 12/31/19X1

Sales		$300,000
Less reductions		30,000
		$270,000
Net Sales		
Less cost of goods sold		
Beginning inventory (at cost)	$ 50,000	
Purchases (at cost)	300,000	
Merchandise available	350,000	
Ending inventory (at cost)	200,000	
Cost of goods sold		150,000
Gross margin		$120,000
Less operating expenses		
Advertising	30,000	
Rent	12,000	
Salaries	30,000	
Freight in	1,000	
Utilities	12,000	
Total operating expenses		85,000
Net profit		$ 35,000

Balance Sheet
For the year ending12/31/19X1

Assets
Current Assets
    Cash $ 6,000
    Accounts Receivable   18,000
    Inventory   200,000
    Marketable Securities   4,000
        Total Current Assets $228,000

Long-term Assets
    Property $350,000
    Fixtures   135,000
        Total Long-term Assets $485,000

Total Assets $713,000

Liabilities and Owners Equity

Current Liabilities
    Notes Payable $ 60,000
    Accounts Payable   70,000
    Salaries Payable   5,500
    Taxes Payable   5,000
        Total Current Liabilities $140,500

Long-term Liabilities
    Long-term Debt $332,000

Total Liabilities $472,500

Owner's Equity 12/31/19XX $205,500
    Net Income for the year   35,000
    Owner Withdrawals   0
Increases in Owner's Equity   35,000
Owner's Equity $240,500

Total Liabilities and Owner's Equity $713,000

Exhibit 16–10
Balance Sheet

presented in Chapter 12 as Exhibits 12–4 and 12–6.) The resulting ratios are interpreted and compared to industry averages. Exhibit 16–11 summarizes the calculated company ratios, industry averages, and differences between the company and the industry for each performance ratio.

The formula for **profit on sales** is Net profit/Net sales.
Calculation: 35,000/270,000 = 12.96%

This ratio represents the firm's net profit margin, i.e., the percentage of each dollar of revenue that is retained as profit. In the example, the retailer keeps nearly 13 cents of every dollar after paying for inventory and all operating expenses. Exhibit 16–11 indicates that the firm's profit on sales is better than the industry average for this type of store. This operating result may be

Exhibit 16-11
Performance Ratios

Ratios	Company	Industry*	Difference	
Profitability				
Profit on Sales	12.96%	7.40%	5.56%	F
Rate of Return on Total Assets	4.91%	9.40%	–4.49%	U
Rate of Return on Net Worth	14.55%	19.50%	–4.95%	U
Gross Margin Return on Inventory				
Investment	.96%	2.46%	–1.50%	U
Activity				
Inventory Turnover	1.2	2.9	–2.7	U
Asset Turnover	.38	2.30	–1.92	U
Receivables Turnover	6.67%	6.50%	.17%	F
Collection Period	24.33	7.20	17.13	U
Productivity				
Space: Net sales to square foot				
selling space	$108	$125	$17	U
Personnel: Selling expense to net				
sales	11.11%	9.00%	–2.11%	U
Accounts payable to sales	25.93%	5.90%	–20.03%	U
Liquidity				
Current ratio	1.62	2.80	–1.18	U
Quick ratio	0.20	0.70	–0.50	U
Current liabilities to net worth (equity)	58.42%	38.10%	–20.32%	U
Current liabilities to inventory	70.25%	47.80%	–22.45%	U
Leverage				
Total assets to net worth (equity)	2.96	2.00	–.96	U
Debt to equity (net worth)	1.96	0.46	–1.50	U

*Hypothetical industry ratios are used in this example. Actual industry ratios are published by sources such as Dun & Bradstreet, national Retail Merchants Association, and others.
F = Favorable difference
U = Unfavorable difference

attributed to a higher markup policy, lower operating expenses, or lower merchandise costs compared to competitors.

     The formula for **rate of return on total assets** is Net profit/Total assets.
    Calculation: 35,000/713,000 = 4.91%

This ratio determines the payback on the retailer's assets used to operate the business by relating profits to the assets required to produce them. For the retailer in our example, a total of $1.00 in assets (inventory, fixtures, equipment, property, etc.) is required to generate less than 5 cents in profit. In general, the larger this ratio the better the retailer's performance. The firm's return on assets is less than half the industry average. This ratio may be due to low sales revenues or to excessive or nonproductive assets.

     The formula for **rate of return on net worth** is Net profit/Net worth.
    Calculation: 35,000/240,000 = 14.55%

PROFIT ON SALES
net profit divided by net sales; profitability ratio that measures percentage of each dollar of revenue retained as profit

RATE OF RETURN ON TOTAL ASSETS
net profit divided by total assets; profitability ratio that measures payback on the retailer's assets used to operate the business

RATE OF RETURN ON NET WORTH
net profit divided by net worth; profitability ratio that represents payback on owners' invested equity

This ratio represents the payback on equity. Our retailer is receiving about 15 cents in profit for each dollar the owners have invested in the business. In general, a larger ratio is related to effective use of the owners' capital. According to Dun's industry ratios, return on net worth should be at least ten percent. Although the company is performing below the industry average, it is exceeding the ten percent rule of thumb.

The formula for **gross margin return on inventory investment (GMROI)** is (Gross margin/Net sales) x (Net sales/Average inventory investment).

Calculation: [120,000/270,000] x [270,000/((50,000 + 200,000)/2)]
= 120,000/125,000 = .96

GMROI relates the retailer's operating profit or gross margin to inventory turnover. The above example indicates that each dollar invested in merchandise inventory generates only 96 cents in gross margin, considerably below the industry average. Ratios vary according to type of store and merchandise category. However, the objective is to minimize the average investment in inventory required to generate a high gross margin. That is, the inventory itself is highlighted for its ability to cover expenses and return a profit.

ACTIVITY   Ratios used to measure activity, or asset turnover, include:

1. Inventory turnover
2. Asset turnover
3. Receivables turnover
4. Collection period

The formula for **inventory turnover** is Cost of goods sold/Average inventory at cost.

Calculation: 150,000/((50,000 + 200,000)/2) = 150,000/125,000 = 1.2 times

This ratio represents the number of times that the average amount of inventory carried is completely sold out. In general, a stockturn that is too high or too low relative to the industry should be avoided. While high ratios are desirable, they may indicate inventory levels that are too low or ordering that is too frequent. Low ratios may indicate nonproductive or aging inventory. In our example, a stockturn rate of 1.2 times a year is less than one-third of the industry average, signaling a problem for this retailer.

Note that sales and inventory are valued at cost in the preceding example, based on data in Exhibit 16–9. Recall from Chapter 12 that these figures can be expressed in terms of retail dollars as well: net sales/average inventory at retail. The resulting turnover ratio will be the same in either case.

The formula for **asset turnover** is Net sales/Average total assets.
Calculation: 270,000/713,000 = .378 times

This ratio is a measure for the retailer's efficiency in using all available assets to generate sales revenues. Ideally, the highest possible level of sales should be generated with the lowest possible investment in assets. Exhibit

GROSS MARGIN RETURN ON INVENTORY INVESTMENT (GMROI)

gross margin divided by average inventory investment; profitability ratio that relates retailer's operating profit to inventory turnover

INVENTORY TURNOVER

cost of goods sold divided by average inventory at cost; activity ratio that measures number of times the average amount of inventory carried is completely sold out

ASSET TURNOVER

net sales divided by average total assets; activity ratio that measures retailer's efficiency in using all available assets to generate sales revenues

16–11 indicates that the firm's asset turnover of .38 times during a year is dangerously low compared to the industry average of 2.40. This ratio indicates problems in generating sales with available assets. If sales are lower than expected, analysis should focus on identifying nonproductive, inappropriate, or excessive assets.

The formula for **receivables turnover** is Net sales/Average accounts receivable.
Calculation: 270,000/18,000 = 15 times

This activity ratio relates the amount of credit purchases and length of time that customers take to pay to sales. When a customer purchases goods with credit rather than cash, inventory dollars are converted to accounts receivable. A high percentage of credit purchases will result in a low receivables turnover ratio and the need to finance operations from sources other than cash sales during the average collection period. In our example, a receivables turnover ratio of 15 times a year means that the retailer has to wait about three and one-half weeks to collect from credit customers.

The formula for **collection period** is (Accounts receivable/Net sales) × 365.
Calculation: (18,000/270,000) × 365 = 24.33 days

Collection period refers to the average number of days taken by customers to pay their accounts. In general, this ratio should be in line with the company's credit terms. Compared to the industry, the firm's collection period is much longer than average. However, this may be due to lenient credit policies or the desire to generate revenues from consumer debt. On the other hand, the retailer may need to tighten up credit authorization and collection. (Note that this ratio is closely related to the receivables turnover calculated in the preceding example.)

PRODUCTIVITY   Productivity ratios may be calculated relative to space, personnel, customer transactions, and other factors. The factors selected for illustration are:

1. Space: sales per square foot of selling space
2. Personnel: selling payroll as a percent of net sales
3. Accounts payable to sales

The formula used to determine **space productivity** is Net sales/Square foot of selling space.
Calculation, based on 2,500 square feet: 270,000/2,500 = $108

The high cost of retail space has led to a focus on increased productivity in terms of sales per square foot. The location of departments within stores, and merchandise classifications within departments, may be determined largely by this ratio. In our example, the $108 in sales generated for each square foot of selling space would be examined relative to industry averages for that merchandise category or store type. Here, sales per square foot is $19 less

RECEIVABLES TURNOVER

net sales divided by average accounts receivable; activity ratio that relates the amount of credit purchases and length of time that customers take to pay to sales

COLLECTION PERIOD

accounts receivable divided by net sales times 365 days; activity ratio that refers to the average number of days customers take to pay their accounts

SPACE PRODUCTIVITY

nets sales divided by square feet of selling space; productivity ratio that measures the amount of sales generated by each square foot of retail space

than the industry average. Of course, the higher the dollar figure, the more productive the space is. (Profit per square foot is another important productivity ratio. Calculation: Net profit/square foot of selling space = $35,000/2,500 = $14.)

The formula used to determine **personnel** productivity is Selling expense/Net sales.
Calculation: 30,000/270,000 = 11.11%

Selling expenses may include all forms of payments and benefits given to the sales force and sales support personnel. The ratio indicates the percent of each dollar of sales that must be used to pay salaries, wages, commissions, and benefits to employees. If we assume the industry average is 8.3, then the higher-than-average expense of 11.11 percent (or over 11 cents of every sales dollar) may make it difficult for the company to compete effectively with other retailers. (Although other ratios, such as personnel turnover, can be analyzed within this context, they do not incorporate all relevant factors in assessing salesperson performance.)

The formula used to determine the productivity of **accounts payable to sales** is Accounts payable/Net sales.
Calculation: 70,000/270,000 = 25.93%

This ratio represents the percentage of each sales dollar that is owed to suppliers. It demonstrates the degree to which sales figures are financed by other businesses. In our example, nearly 26 cents of each dollar in sales must be used to pay accounts. Exhibit 16–11 indicates that, on the average, this retailer's accounts payable figure is more than five times that of its competitors.

LIQUIDITY   Day-to-day operations are directly affected by the retailer's degree of liquidity. Frequently used liquidity ratios are:

1. Current ratio
2. Quick ratio
3. Current liabilities to net worth
4. Current liabilities to inventory

The formula for the **current ratio** is Current assets/Current liabilities.
Calculation: 228,000/140,500 = 1.62

This ratio is a measure of the firm's ability to pay short-term debt. A ratio of 1.0 indicates that current liabilities equal current assets, which means that the firm should be able to meet its short range obligations. A ratio of less than 1.0 indicates that liabilities exceed assets, and that if the current liabilities are called, the firm cannot readily pay them. A ratio greater than 1.0 indicates the extent of the firm's assets beyond current debt. A benchmark ratio is 2:1; therefore, the retailer in our example has a relatively healthy current ratio. In general, a larger ratio is desirable, although it may suggest a very conservative attitude toward buying inventory and other assets on credit.

PERSONNEL PRODUCTIVITY

selling expenses divided by net sales; productivity ratio that calculates percentage of sales dollars used in payment and benefits given to sales and sales support personnel

ACCOUNTS PAYABLE TO SALES

accounts payable divided by net sales; productivity ratio that measures percentage of each sales dollar owed to suppliers

CURRENT RATIO

current assets divided by current liabilities; liquidity ratio that measures a firm's ability to pay short-term debt

The formula for the **quick ratio** is (Current assets - inventory)/Current liabilities *or* (Cash + marketable securities + receivables)/Current liabilities. *Calculation: (6,000 + 18,000 + 4,000)/140,500 = 28,000/140,500 = .199 = .20*

The quick ratio is similar to the current ratio, except that inventories are excluded from the calculation of assets. The rationale for this exclusion is that if inventories need to be liquidated quickly to pay debt, they may need to be sold below the desired markup. Therefore, the real value of this asset may be questionable. In general, a benchmark ratio is 1:1, but the higher this ratio, the better the retailer's position to pay current debt. If our retailer's creditors demanded immediate payment, he would only be able to repay 20 cents on the dollar in the short run.

The formula for **current liabilities to net worth** is Current liabilities/ Net worth.
Calculation: 140,500/240,500 = 58.42%

This ratio relates short-term liabilities to the owners' actual investment in the business. In our example, for every dollar the owners have invested in the business, they owe more than 58 cents to their creditors. In general, the higher the ratio, the greater the financial risk associated with the firm. That is, creditors may actually own more of the business than the stockholders, placing the owners in a precarious position. The liabilities for the retailer in our example are nearly double the industry average when compared to net worth.

The formula for **current liabilities to inventory** is Current liabilities/Inventory.
Calculation: 140,500/200,000 = 70.25%

This ratio relates short-term liabilities to the retailer's investment in inventory. It is an indication of the company's dependence on inventory to meet current debt since inventory is the retailer's primary source of revenue for this purpose. Our retailer owes over 70 cents for every dollar's worth of merchandise he has in stock. If current debts had to be paid quickly, markdowns on inventory might be taken to generate the necessary cash.

LEVERAGE   The relationship between a retailer's assets and debt position can be evaluated with these ratios:

1. Total assets to net worth (equity)
2. Debt to equity (net worth)

The formula for determining **total assets to net worth** is Total assets/Net worth.
Calculation: 713,000/240,500 = 2.96

QUICK RATIO
current assets minus inventory divided by current liability; liquidity ratio that measures a firm's ability to pay short-term debt but excludes inventory

CURRENT LIABILITIES TO NET WORTH
current liabilities divided by net worth; liquidity ratio that relates short-term liabilities to owners' actual investment

CURRENT LIABILITIES TO INVENTORY
current liabilities divided by inventory; liquidity ratio that relates short-term liabilities to retailer's investment in inventory

TOTAL ASSETS TO NET WORTH
total assets divided by net worth; leverage ratio that relates all of retailer's assets to owners funds invested in the business

This ratio relates all of the retailer's assets to net worth. It indicates the extent to which assets are financed out of the owners' funds rather than with debt. This performance measure is determined by the firm's capital structure decisions, which may involve growth strategies, tolerance for risk, and other factors. Our retailer has assets that are valued at nearly three times the amount he has invested in the business. These assets are held "free and clear" of debt.

The formula for determining **debt to equity** is Total liabilities/Net worth.
Calculation: 472,500/240,500 = 1.96

This ratio relates the amount owed by the company to the amount invested in the company by the owners. If this ratio is greater than 1.0, then creditors have a larger investment in the company than the owners. In our example, the retailer owes nearly twice as much as he owns. The company's operations are heavily financed with debt in comparison to competition, as shown in Exhibit 16–11.

In the next section, several key ratios are combined to illustrate their interaction in achieving target performance levels. They contain four critical factors that determine overall retail success: sales, profits, assets, and net worth.

Strategic Profit Model: Framework For Analysis

The Strategic Profit Model (SPM), introduced in Chapter 2, provides an integrated framework for analysis. The SPM includes three of the ratios described in the previous section: profitability, asset turnover, and leverage. These ratios relate net profits to net sales (return on sales), to total assets (return on assets), and to net worth (return on net worth or return on investment). Analysis of profitability, based on these measures or others, revolves around planning profit objectives and evaluating performance against plan. Exhibits 16–11 and 16–12 illustrate use of the Strategic Profit Model to evaluate operating results and the financing of capital expenditures respectively, based on the following relationship among ratios:

> *Net profits/Net sales* (*profitability ratio*)
> × *Net sales/Total assets*
> = *Net profits/Total assets* (*asset turnover*)
> × *Total assets/Net worth* (*leverage ratio, i.e., assets to debt*)
> = *Net profits/Net worth* (*return on net worth or ROI*)

The nature of competition and the growth orientation of the retailer are major influences in setting and reaching profit goals. Strategic Profit Model ratios are used to illustrate the effect of growth objectives on key performance measures.

Finally, the data used to calculate these ratios must be accurate and of high quality in order to provide a sound basis for retail management decisions. Therefore, the sources and quality of data are examined next.

DEBT TO EQUITY
total liabilities divided by net worth; leverage ratio that relates amount owed by the company to amount invested in the company by the owners

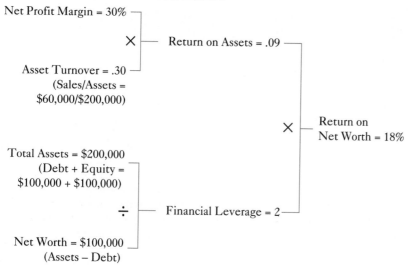

EXAMPLE A: 50% DEBT TO 50% EQUITY

Net Profit Margin = 30%

× ── Return on Assets = .09

Asset Turnover = .30
(Sales/Assets =
$60,000/$200,000)

× ── Return on
Net Worth = 18%

Total Assets = $200,000
(Debt + Equity =
$100,000 + $100,000)

÷ ── Financial Leverage = 2

Net Worth = $100,000
(Assets – Debt)

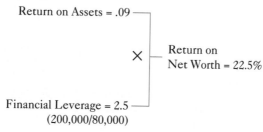

EXAMPLE B: 60% DEBT TO 40% EQUITY

Return on Assets = .09

× ── Return on
Net Worth = 22.5%

Financial Leverage = 2.5
(200,000/80,000)

The method of financing capital expenditures will have a noticeable impact on the firm's SPM ratios. All other factors being equal, an increase in debt over equity will increase return on investment, because the owner's investment of funds in the business is reduced.

Exhibit 16–12
SPM Analysis of Capital
Expenditures

DATA SOURCES AND QUALITY

The tools to analyze present operations and future opportunities can be obtained from the retailer's information system: the data base, statistical and mathematical analytical models, qualitative analysis, and the interpretation and conclusions from prior analysis. Statistical and mathematical models are useful for objectively describing, estimating, and predicting events and behavior. Qualitative analysis, although more subjective, can provide in-depth explanations of attitudes and behavior. Effective use of the results of analysis depends on both the quality of data used and on the managers' ability to interpret and apply the findings.

Earlier chapters discussed the general types and sources of data for strategic planning and decision making. In the previous sections of this

POWER RETAILING: A TUG OF WAR BETWEEN RETAILERS AND SUPPLIERS

"**B**igger is better." Volume buying and selling provide the key to the successful performance of most large retailers. The need to minimize costs and maximize efficient use of assets results in an ongoing power struggle in negotiations between retailers and suppliers. The tug of war pits the supplier's need for shelf space and distribution against the retailer's need to remain competitive in its merchandise assortment and one-stop category appeal to its target customers.

In the past, the balance of power seemed to be in favor of suppliers. They could decide what products would be available and when, and to a lesser extent who could buy them and at what price. Today, however, the power is shifting to retail chains. Some of these large retailers are Wal-Mart, K mart, and Target in general merchandise discounting; Safeway, Kroger, and Winn-Dixie in supermar-

kets; Walgreens, Eckerd, and Jewel drugstores; and a growing trend toward wholesale clubs, warehouse stores, and hypermarkets.

As retail power becomes more consolidated among fewer retailing companies, a number of potentially ethical issues arise. For example, if a few large retailers refuse to carry a certain product, this can effectively block national distribution. Toys "R" Us controls about 25 percent of the U.S. toy business. If they decide not to carry a toy, it is locked out of one-fourth of the market from the start. Other retailers can have the same clout. They can demand lower prices, special promotion, performance and slotting allowances for shelf space.

Businesses on both ends of the tug-of-war use whatever leverage they can to cut the best deals possible. A Winn-Dixie supermarket chain executive says the company sees itself as purchasing agent for its customers who should not have to pay higher prices at its stores for any of its 24,000 items. While

this approach may work for larger chains, smaller chains and independents are at a disadvantage in obtaining concessions from manufacturers.

An executive for Duckwall-Alco, a 130-store, $340-million discounter based in Abilene, Kansas has expressed the view that if the relationship between the company and its suppliers isn't equitable, then no one gains. He believes that buyers must understand the process of negotiations with a vendor. While buyers need to be tough, they also need to know the difference between toughness and fairness.

Successful retailers can exert an enormous amount of power. They have a dual responsibility to their customers (and their company stakeholders) and to their suppliers. Superior performance also involves walking a fine line in all the company's dealings.

Adapted from Felgner, Brent H. (1989), "Retailers Grab Power, Control Marketplace," *Marketing News* 23, no. 2 (January 16), 1–2.

---

chapter, we looked at uses of data and key performance ratios for analyzing operating results and evaluating opportunities. At this point it is important to consider the sources and quality of data used in measuring retail performance. Since the quality of data is directly related to its accuracy and suitability for the type of analysis needed, the data source must be chosen carefully.

Data sources and quality are considered next. As discussed in Chapter 3, data can be obtained from both primary and secondary information sources. These sources may be either internal or external to the company.

Secondary Data Sources

EXTERNAL SECONDARY DATA Retail managers have the least control over the quality of **external secondary data** gathered by someone else for another purpose. Frequently used sources include U.S. government surveys and documents, industry reports, and trade association data. Government data, available in a wide variety of publications, include Census reports of population at the federal, state, and local levels, Census of Retail Trade, and many others. Industry data are found in publications such as Dun & Bradstreet and Standard & Poors.

Trade association data generally are published and disseminated to members of particular industries such as the hardware or supermarket industries. National Retail Merchant's Association (NRMA) provides industry performance ratios for U.S. department stores and specialty stores. These ratios provide a benchmark for evaluating a retailer's performance compared to the industry. NRMA provides other information for both large and small retailers in the form of books, films and periodicals, and special seminars for those in need of assistance.

INTERNAL SECONDARY DATA   **Internal secondary data** can be used to identify the nature and source of existing problems and to provide basic information for improving daily operations. The quality and usefulness of this data source, within the retailer's information system, can be controlled by those designing the system and supervising the accuracy of data inputs.

Company records include readily available data generated internally as a part of day-to-day business operations, gathered routinely or for a specific purpose. Potential sources include operating statements, employee records, customer billings, check analysis, and customer orders.

Operating statements contain a record of the retailer's profit or loss position, inventory status, purchase receipts, and other accounting and financial information. Problems may be identified by carefully reviewing the operating statements. For example, when a downturn in sales or profits is identified, these statements are useful in determining where the problem lies and in suggesting alternative solutions. Suppose a retailer discovers that profits are down ten percent for the year. The operating statements should reveal whether this lower profit level is due to a decrease in sales, increase in costs, or both. Operating statements also provide valuable information for planning. Past data are a useful—although not sufficient—indicator of future performance, particularly in forecasting sales.

Employee records contain valuable information, including work schedules, training records, and sales reports. In the above example, available records should indicate those departments or merchandise classifications with the poorest sales performance or highest costs. Poor performance may be attributable to one or more employees, perhaps indicating the need to retrain or replace personnel. Employee records also are a basis for determining compensation.

Retail managers can prescribe in advance the type of customer information needed for decision making and can develop an orderly system for gathering and recording these data from a variety of sources. Customer billings provide a record of who and where the customers are, what and when they buy, how much they buy, and how they pay for their purchases. This information is useful for trade area analysis, merchandise management, promotional strategies, and other decisions.

In the absence of credit records, customer addresses and phone numbers can be obtained from personal checks and from in-store mail or phone orders. The retailer can learn where customers live and work and obtain answers to other questions while store personnel are taking an order.

EXTERNAL SECONDARY DATA
gathered by someone else for another purpose

INTERNAL SECONDARY DATA
company records kept for other purposes used to identify and analyze existing problems

In-store promotions, such as drawings which require customers to fill out registration forms, are another source of data. Information about the store's trading area and customer characteristics also can be obtained from an analysis of license plates and parking permits on cars in the parking lots. License plates indicate geographical areas, and parking permits represent customer residences and destinations (apartment complexes, businesses, schools).

PROBLEMS WITH THE USE OF SECONDARY DATA SOURCES

Although secondary data are easily obtained and valuable in analyzing retail situations, managers should be aware of three potential problems associated with the use of secondary sources: (1) units of measurement, (2) class definitions, and (3) publication currency (Churchill, 1987).

1. *Units of measurement*—Secondary data may be available on the subject being studied, but originally collected in categories or measurement units that are different from those needed by the retailer. For example, the size of a retail establishment can be reported in terms of annual sales, profits, square feet of retail space, or number of employees. If the retailer is interested in comparing sales per square foot of selling space to competitors, but only has data on total store space (including non-selling areas), a satisfactory comparison cannot be made. Data on consumer income levels in a market may be expressed by individual, family, household, or spending unit. A retailer who caters to young singles would not find income data meaningful if only reported for family units. The unit of measurement must be consistent with the retailer's needs if it is to be useful.

2. *Class definition*—Although the data may be available in the right units of measurement for the present problem, they may not be provided in useful categories or "class boundaries" for the retailer's needs. The retailer who wants to compare its sales per square foot of selling space to that of competition may have internal data in increments of 1000 square feet, but secondary data may be available only in increments of 2500 square feet. Or consumer income data may be available for single individuals in a market in increments of $15,000 (0 to $14,999, $15,000 to $29,999, etc.) but the retailer's analysis requires increments of $10,000 (0 to $9,999, $10,000 to $19,999, etc.). In these cases, the class definition would be inappropriate, and modifications would diminish the precision of the data used in analysis.

3. *Currency of information*—Retailing decisions typically require up-to-date information. However, there may be several years between data collection and publication or dissemination, as with most government census data. Add to this the problem that much public data are published only every five or ten years, and proprietary data may not be available to outside parties for some period of time, if at all. Retail markets can shift rapidly, competitors can move in and out, economic indicators can shift direction, and other changes can occur, requiring current data for analysis. (In this case, the only alternative may be to collect primary data.)

CRITERIA FOR JUDGING THE ACCURACY OF SECONDARY DATA

Criteria for determining the accuracy or precision of data include an assessment of (1) the source used, (2) purpose of publication, and (3) general evidence of quality (Churchill, 1987).

1. *The source used*—The methods used to collect, analyze, and present data may have many sources of error. In addition, secondary sources often obtain data previously gathered from other sources. For example, *The Statistical Abstract of the United States* is a widely used secondary source of secondary data obtained from other government and trade sources. Copying data from one place to another may result in inaccuracies or misinterpretation. Therefore, the primary source, where the data were first published, should be consulted and evaluated. Only the primary source of secondary data can provide general evidence of the quality of the research, as described below.

2. *The purpose of publication*—The purpose of the publication containing the secondary data may be an indication of its accuracy. What do sponsors of the publication have to gain by printing the information? Serious questions may arise about the quality of the data if they are published by a source that is selling something, promoting private interests or one side of a controversial issue, or is not identified.

3. *General evidence regarding quality*—The original data source should present the data in context and with fewer errors. Evidence of quality includes the reputation of the research group, the organization's ability to collect the data, appropriateness of the sample, method of data collection and analysis, qualifications and training of personnel who gathered the data, extent of nonresponse and other sources of bias, and presentation, as in the accuracy and organization of results.

Primary Data Sources

A discussion of **primary data** collection methods is beyond the scope of this chapter, since the analysis of operating results depends mainly on secondary data. However, the original design of the retailer's information system, i.e., the requirements and format for inventory, personnel, and other important records, does bear a direct relationship to primary data sources. In both cases, a retailer needs to know the specific problems to be solved and questions to be answered with available data.

Primary data provide timely and in-depth answers to questions that cannot be addressed satisfactorily with available secondary data. Primary internal and external sources were described in Chapter 3. You will recall that the retailer can conduct telephone or mail surveys, personal interviews, and observe the behavior of customers or employees to obtain answers to specific questions or problems. Primary data may be as simple as "want lists" generated by salespeople in response to customer requests, or as complex as a "full-blown" market research study conducted by a national chain to determine customer response to concept or format changes. It may also include customer responses on warranty cards, responses to promotional efforts (such as direct mail, couponing, special offers), and other forms of direct communication with the store's customers.

Good quality primary data can be purchased from external sources, such as professional research firms and subscription services on a contractual basis. Some reliable sources are CompuServe Information Service, Management Horizons-Retail Intelligence System (a Division of Price Waterhouse), and the Donnelly Company (a division of Dun and Bradstreet).

PRIMARY DATA

information collected to identify and solve an existing problem

The retailer has the most control over the quality of data when using primary sources. Primary data can be evaluated against most of the criteria described for judging the accuracy, quality, and usefulness of secondary data.

Summary

High-performing retailers understand the "fit" between their companies and operating environments. They know why results occurred, and they can anticipate future events. They use capital, human resources, and technology effectively and efficiently. They know their markets well, and they are market share leaders. Top performance does not happen by accident. Evaluation of operating results and new growth opportunities are an integral aspect of the continuous managerial process of analyzing, planning, executing, and controlling the business.

Analysis is performed at the corporate, business, and functional levels. At the corporate or strategic level, emphasis is on the logic and coordination of a profitable balance of businesses that make up the corporation. Strategies for organizational effectiveness ("what to do") are viewed from a longer range perspective. A narrower environmental perspective is taken at the business level. Analysis focuses on the effective and efficient coordination of all functional areas to achieve maximum impact. Actual performance versus planned results is evaluated for managers, store operations, and other factors across stores within the business division.

Functional or operating level analysis focuses on the efficiency of carrying out strategic intent ("how to do it"), within and across the functional areas of a retail business unit. At this level, the horizon is shorter term, with the objective of coordinating all departments and functions for the successful execution of corporate strategy. Performance is analyzed within individual retailing functions (merchandise management, promotion/communication, store operations, and accounting), and across functions to determine successes and failures in execution of the retailer's strategy.

Accurate evaluation of the retailer's position requires an understanding of the basic questions to be answered, and performance criteria to be met. Basic questions include: What is/isn't working? How have strategies been implemented and executed? What is competition doing/going to do? What environmental changes are taking place, and what is their effect? Do growth opportunities exist?

Performance criteria generally are expressed in terms of profitability, activity (effective use of assets), productivity (efficient use of resources), liquidity (short-term ability to pay debts), and leverage (assets owned by investors versus creditors).

Methods of analyzing results and opportunities are directly related to established performance criteria. Thus, key financial ratios can be calculated with available data to determine whether the retailer's criteria have been met. The Strategic Profit Model can be used to evaluate the interactive effect of profitability, asset turnover, and leverage on overall performance.

Finally, accurate analysis requires high-quality data. Data inputs may be either secondary or primary, and obtained from either internal or external sources. Possible problems with the use of secondary data include measurement units, class definitions, and publication currency. The accuracy of secondary data can be judged according to the source used, purpose of the publication, and general evidence of quality. The retailer has more control over the quality of primary data than of secondary data. However, in both cases, all precautions should be taken to insure that the data are accurate and appropriate for the type of analysis being performed. Otherwise, results of analysis may be misleading.

Questions for Review and Comprehension

1. Review current business media to determine any changes that have occurred in regard to the "excellent" retailers described in the text. If any of these companies has experienced significant successes or failures, analyze the reasons for these changes.

2. List the general questions involved in retail management and strategic planning. For each question, describe a specific response that might be given by a retailer—and how this response would be operationalized by functional managers.

3. Discuss the types of analysis of operating results that typically are conducted at the corporate or strategic, business, and functional or operating levels of a business.

4. Describe the relationship between an analysis of the macro- and microenvironments and analysis of each of the functional areas at the operating level. Include specific applications for each function as follows:
    a. merchandise management (sales forecasting, pricing strategy, buying, inventory control) and
    b. promotion and communication (all aspects of the promotional mix)
    c. store operations (location, layout, productivity, risk management)
    d. accounting and control (RIS inputs and use)
    e. human resources

5. A retail manager in a "budget" menswear department decides to add a line of more expensive goods to her assortment. Although these brands would generally compete at regular price with comparable brands in the higher priced menswear department, they will be discounted as part of the "budget" line. Explain how this decision will impact on other functional areas and be affected by them.

6. Retailers must answer a series of questions for a comprehensive evaluation of their overall performance. List these questions, and explain how each is helpful in an analysis of results. Compared to a large retail firm, would it be useful for a small retailer to seek answers to these questions in evaluating performance? Defend your answer.

7. Describe each of the key performance criteria that were discussed in the chapter. Obtain an annual report or other financial statements from a retail firm, and calculate as many of these ratios as possible with available data. Be sure to include each of the following types of criteria: profitability, activity, productivity, liquidity, and leverage. Compare the results to published industry ratios (see Dun's Industry Ratios or NRMA's Merchandising Operating Results or Financial Operating Results publications for comparative ratios). Interpret your findings in terms of how well the company is doing relative to the entire industry.

8. Using the financial statement(s) that provided the basis for analysis in Question #7 above, analyze the results within the context of the strategic profit model, focusing on each of the individual ratios (profitability, asset turnover, leverage) as well as the return on investment (ROI) calculated for the entire model. Suggest some ways that the resulting ROI figure could be increased by management decisions in regard to any or all components of the strategic profit model.

9. Assume that a retailer wants to expand the number of product lines carried in his store. Suggest several sources of external secondary data that might be helpful in making the right decision, as well as potential sources of internal secondary data. Give specific examples of how each source can be used for additional insights.

10. Discuss the problems that may be encountered when using secondary sources of information for managerial decisions. What criteria can be used to determine the accuracy of secondary data? If the data are published in a reputable publication, is that a guarantee of their accuracy? Why or why not?

11. When is it appropriate to collect primary data?

References

Caminity, Susan (1990), "The New Champs of Retailing," *Fortune* (September 24), 857.

Chakravarty, Subrata N. (1987), "Sails Reefed," *Forbes* (November 30), 110–111, 113.

Churchill, Gilbert A. (1987), *Marketing Research: Methodological Foundations*, 4th ed. New York: The Dryden Press.

Cronin, J. Joseph and Scott Kelley (1985), "An Investigation of the Impact of Marketing Strategies in Determining Retail Profit Performance," in *Marketing: The Next Decade*. Proceedings of the Annual Meeting of the Southern Marketing Association, David M. Klein and Allen E. Smith, Orlando, Fla. (November 13–16), 179–182.

Davenport, Carol (1989), "America's Most Admired Corporations," *Fortune* (January 30), 68–94).

Dumaine, Brian (1988), "Corporate Spies Snoop to Conquer," *Fortune* (November 7), 68–69, 72, 76.

Dunkin, Amy (1986), "How They're Knocking the Rust Off Two Old Chains," *Business Week* (September 8), 44–45, 48.

Dunkin, Amy, Michael Oneal, and Stephen Phillips (1987), "Power Retailers," *Business Week* (December 21), 86–89, 92.

Hawkins, Chuck (1988), "Is Avis Moving Into the Passing Lane?" *Business Week* (May 9), 100, 105.

Levy, Michael and Charles A. Ingene (1984), "Residual Income Analysis: A Method of Inventory Investment Allocation and Evaluation," *Journal of Marketing* 45 (Summer), 93–104.

Loomis, (1984), "Fortune Service 500," *Fortune*, in *Retailing Issues Letter*. College Station, Tex. Arthur Anderson and Co. and the Center for Retailing Studies, Texas A&M University.

Lowenstein, Roger (1988a), "Marriott Is Planning to Invest $1 Billion to Double Stake in Extended-Stay Hotels," *The Wall Street Journal* (September 8), 4.

Lowenstein, Roger (1988b), "Sale Price of Sears Tower is Expected to Break U.S. Office Building Record," *The Wall Street Journal* (November 1), A3.

McCoy, Frank (1987), "Sbarro's Juicy Slice of the Fast-Food Market," *Business Week* (September 7), 72, 73.

Mitchell, Russell (1989), "K mart Spruces Up the Bargain Basement," *Business Week* (September 8), 45, 48.

Mitchell, Russell (1989), "From Punching Bag to Retailing Black Belt," *Business Week* (November 20), 62, 66.

Peters, Thomas J. and Robert H. Waterman (1982), *In Search of Excellence.* New York: Harper & Row, Publishers, Inc.

Phillips, Stephen (1988), "Why U.S. Shoe Is Looking Down at the Heel," *Business Week* (July 4), 60–61.

Pitzer, Mary J., Michael Oneal, and Tim Smart (1987), "How Three Master Merchants Fell from Grace," *Business Week* (March 16), 38–40.

Rosenbloom, Bert (1980), "Strategic Planning in Retailing: Prospects and Problems," *Journal of Retailing* 56, (Spring), 107–120.

Saparito, Bill (1989), "Woolworth to Rule the Malls," *Fortune* (June 5), 145, 148, 152, 156.

Sheeline, William E. (1988), "Making Them Rich Down Home," *Fortune* (August 15), 51–55.

Sheeline, William E. (1990), "Avoiding Growth's Perils," *Fortune* (August 13), 55, 58.

Stricharchuk, Gregory (1988), "Kroger Officials Believe Competitiveness Will Be Helped by Recapitalization Plan," *The Wall Street Journal* (October 25), A16.

Taylor, John H. (1988), "King no more," *Forbes* (April 18), 37–38.

"The Best of 1990: The Best Managers" (1991), Business Week (January 14), 130–131.

"The *Business Week* 1000: The Top 1000 Companies Ranked by Industry," (1991), *The 1991 Business Week 1000* (April), 160–161, 163.

Varadarajan, P. "Rajan" (1989), "Pathways to Corporate Excellence in Retailing," *Retailing Issues Letter* College Station, Tex. Arthur Anderson & Co. and the Center for Retailing Studies, Texas A&M University.

Waterman, Robert H., Jr. (1987), *The Renewal Factor: How the Best Get and Keep the Competitive Edge,* New York: Bantam Books.

Woolworth Corporation, *1989 Annual Report,* New York (April 11, 1990).

Woolworth Corporation, *1990 Fact Book,* New York (1990).

TECHNOLOGY IN RETAILING

CHAPTER Seventeen

Outline

Introduction

Retail Management Planning Perspective

Customer Shopping Perspective

Summary

Learning Objectives

After studying this chapter, the student will be able to:

1. Understand the overall contribution of technology to efficiency and profitability in retailing.
2. Describe the applications, interrelationships, and benefits of technology in merchandise management.
3. Describe the use and benefits of technology in planning, accounting, control, and human resource functions.
4. Describe the use, benefits, and applications of technology in promotion, communications, and store operations.
5. Explain the role of technology in shopping at home via television or computer.
6. Give examples of electronic shopping technology in stores and malls.

Super Spy: Using Scanner-Based Research

Scanner equipment and the Universal Product Code (UPC) first appeared in food stores in the 1970s—with great expectations on the part of users. It has taken a while to gain acceptance and for the results to approximate the promises. However, the UPC and scanners have permanently revolutionized the way retailers do business. Every day, scanner equipment prints out tapes telling the retailer just how fast a cashier works, how successful an in-store promotion was, increases or decreases in item sales, and how to allocate precious shelf space.

Manufacturers benefit from this mass of data, as well, but they often buy "processed" scanner information from a growing number of research services such as Nielsen Co.'s ScanTrack and Burke Marketing Service Inc.'s Test Marketing Group (TMG). ScanTrack monitors product movement, based on price, couponing, and store display variables in national, regional, or local information from the top 25 markets. TMG offers reports every four weeks or weekly on consumer demographics, market testing over TV and in-store testing. Other scanner-based research services include BehaviorScan, SAMSCAN, and NABSCAM (National Brand Scanning, Inc.). Although there are some problems with overreliance on scanner data, manufacturers can monitor sales to determine price elasticity, track coupon promotions (and cut down on fraudulent redemptions), and decide whether more advertising is needed—and with what campaign and in what medium.

How is scanner-based research used by distribution channel members? A national survey of marketing research managers listed the following applications (in order of importance): monitoring current products, new product research, monitoring competitors' sales, pricing research, coupon and sampling studies, advertising research, tactical planning, monitoring competitors' promotions, consumer models studies, strategic planning, distribution studies, acquisition/diversification studies, store patronage and loyalty studies, and legal and ethical studies.

Just think about what retailers and manufacturers know about you when you buy that can of Campbell's soup or package of Oreo cookies!

Adapted from Hall, Carol (1986), "UPC: Super Spy," *Marketing & Media Decisions* 21, (May), 96–105; Sinkula, James M. (1986), "Status of Company Usage of Scanner Based Research," *Journal of the Academy of Marketing Science* 14, 1, (Spring), 63–71.

Today, more than ever, you must be alert to changing needs, conscious of developing trends and have fast access to current information. So you play the technology game to your best advantage. But as innovations in technology accelerate, today's technology becomes tomorrow's standard way of doing business. To stay competitive you must continually look to the future and implement the technology that shares that same view. You need a technology that can satisfy your immediate day-to-day problems and lay the foundation for your future growth. You need an architecture that can help you implement strategy, increase efficiency, boost profitability and offer the newest technology-based services as they become available . . . (NCR 7052/STORES System, 1988).

INTRODUCTION

Advances in technology have led to major changes in the way retailers sell their products and operate their stores. The word *technology* tends to conjure up visions of computers and high-tech gadgets. In reality, a broad definition of technology is simply know-how (Capon and Glazer, 1987). Know-how refers to the information required by a retailer to buy and sell a product or service, i.e., the stock of relevant knowledge that allows the retailer to develop new techniques for retail strategy and management. Although high-technology applications are the focus of this chapter, they are only as useful as management's know-how in using these tools.

The effect of technology on the strategic planning process and on data gathering and information used to evaluate strategy execution and results is illustrated in Exhibit 17–1. In general, the management of data and information and the daily operation of stores are improved considerably by available technology. Speed, accuracy, timeliness, cost effectiveness, and other features attributed to technological applications improve the quality of retail managers' decisions and the efficiency of store operations.

Retailing technology can be described as both information technology and operating technology. Naisbitt (1982) described the shift from an industrial society to an information society in the United States as one of the key directions for the future. The technology of information is expected to alter the legal and physical boundaries of companies, perhaps in some startling ways. Retailers might allow suppliers access to their computer so the supplier can see what is needed and reorder for them. However, this might also carry the risk of giving too much information about their operations. It might also have a negative impact on cash flow unless the retailer establishes predetermined automatic reorder points.

A five-year study at MIT's Sloan School of Management suggests that vertical integration becomes less necessary with imaginative use of information systems and that, in the future, strategy and information technology will have to be considered together. A decision to use just-in-time inventory controls or automatic ordering, for example, will not work without the technology to support it (Main, 1988).

The strategic planning process depends upon accurate information derived from a reliable data base. Computerized information systems, or

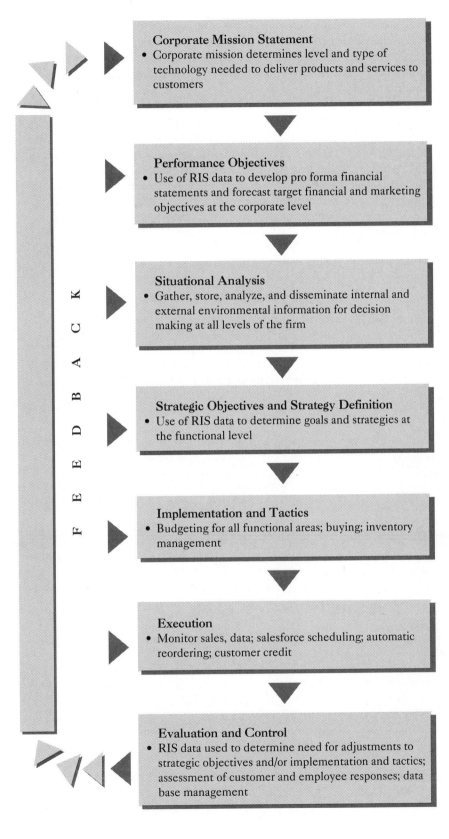

Corporate Mission Statement
- Corporate mission determines level and type of technology needed to deliver products and services to customers

Performance Objectives
- Use of RIS data to develop pro forma financial statements and forecast target financial and marketing objectives at the corporate level

Situational Analysis
- Gather, store, analyze, and disseminate internal and external environmental information for decision making at all levels of the firm

Strategic Objectives and Strategy Definition
- Use of RIS data to determine goals and strategies at the functional level

Implementation and Tactics
- Budgeting for all functional areas; buying; inventory management

Execution
- Monitor sales, data; salesforce scheduling; automatic reordering; customer credit

Evaluation and Control
- RIS data used to determine need for adjustments to strategic objectives and/or implementation and tactics; assessment of customer and employee responses; data base management

F E E D B A C K

Exhibit 17–1
Technology and the Strategic
Planning Process: An Illustration

well-managed file cabinets in a smaller business, can provide this type of technological assistance for decision making. The environmental uncertainty that is characteristic of retailing can be reduced by the management and interpretation of information obtained through technology and the know-how that it implies.

Operating technology, in its many applications to store operations, has become an integral part of the strategic planning process. Retailers and customers have benefited from sophisticated point-of-sale computer terminals, and technological advances in warehouse operations and the physical movement of inventory through stores. Likewise, automatic teller machines (ATM) at the local banks, electronic shopping via TV or computer, and satellite networks between groups of stores and between stores and vendors are only a few of the many examples of increased operating efficiency due to technology.

Exhibit 17–2
Technology and the Retail
Environment
. . . .
SOURCE: Anderson and Parker, 1988.

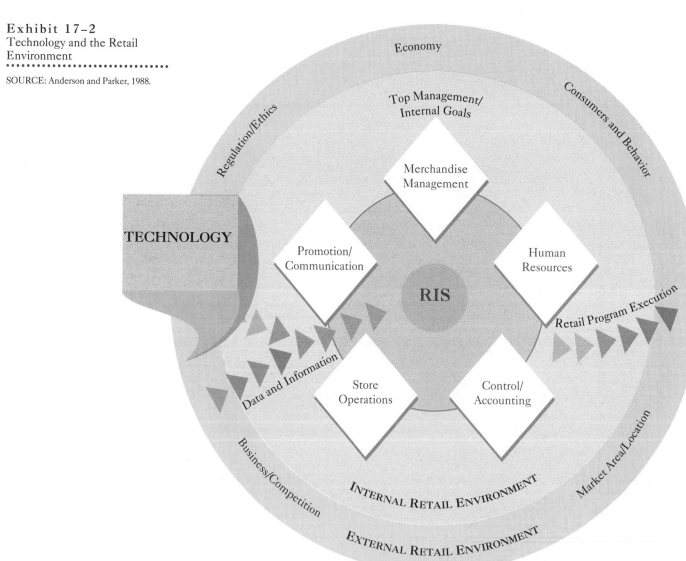

Retailers have felt the impact of technological change in a number of areas. (See Exhibit 17–2.) Changing product life cycles have shortened or lengthened the selling lifetime of a variety of products. The instability of changing market segments has led to increased focus on target marketing and customer needs. New sources of retail competition have caused shifts in traditional retailing strategies and increased the importance of competitive intelligence. Changing organizational structures have resulted in more decentralized decision making and increased participation by employees at all levels. Increased globalization of product markets and customer segments has led to more international emphasis in retailing (Capon and Glazer, 1987).

In this chapter, retailing technology is viewed first from the retail management planning perspective, then from the customer shopping perspective. Selected technological applications are described for each of five functional areas: merchandising; planning, accounting, and control; human resources; promotion; and store operations. Focus within the customer shopping perspective is on electronic shopping at home and in stores and malls.

Retail Management Planning Perspective

Advances in information systems and communications technology are significantly improving the prospects for increased retail productivity and, thus, profitability. These developments include the accelerated use of Universal Product Codes (UPC) by retailers, vendors, and manufacturers, the adoption of industry-wide standards for UPC bar codes, and point-of-sale (POS) data scanning. Other technological advances include transmittal of business documents via electronic data interchange (EDI), ordering assistance for small retailers through Wide-Area Networks (WANS), store-based electronic retailing, electronic vendor catalogs, and improved analysis through expert systems and artificial intelligence technologies (Achabal and McIntyre, 1987).

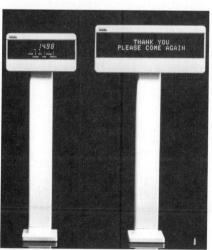

An NCR handheld scanner "reads" the UPC code on the tag and enters it into the computer. The pre-programmed price is displayed for the customer and cashier and is printed on the customer's sales receipt.

Merchandising Applications

A testimonial to the importance of technology in merchandising is the upward trend in Management Information Systems (MIS) budgets by most retail chains, although many retail operating budgets may be slashed. A Retail Technology Census conducted by *Chain Store Age Executive* in 1988 indicated the greatest increase in expenditures would be for point-of-sale equipment, particularly programmable cash registers and microcomputers ("Survey Shows Increase in 1989 MIS Budgets," 1988). On the average, estimated capital outlays for 1989 totaled 1.05 percent of sales, compared to 0.94 percent in 1986, and 0.88 percent in 1985. Retail MIS directors, from a diverse group of stores participating in the survey, expect information technology to give them a competitive edge by reducing labor costs, increasing productivity and providing better and more timely information. Point-of-sale scanning is a major contributor to the success of this technology. Trends in the use of POS computer hardware from 1988 to 1990 are shown in Exhibit 17–3. Note the decline in mechanical cash registers due to the availability of sophisticated computerized cash registers that can be adapted to newer technology ("Retailers Spending More . . . ," 1989).

POINT-OF-SALE TERMINALS   Charles Lazarus, chairman and CEO of Toys "R" Us, has a new toy that cost $35 million, and he thinks it is worth every penny (Gallagher, 1988). Lazarus can punch a few buttons on his personal computer in his New York City apartment, and up-to-the-second sales information appears on his screen about any of the 35,000 different products sold in his toy supermarkets. No mere plaything, this "toy" is the result of a sophisticated UPC scanning system installed in all 313 U.S. stores late in 1987 to maximize inventory control, minimize expenses, and shorten transaction time. Important data can be captured instantly at POS terminals.

Exhibit 17–3
Trends in POS Use

MIS Capital Budget	1988	1989	1990
POS devices	18.3%	27.5%	28.6%
Hardware	27.6	28.1	28.5
Software	18.3	17.9	16.9
End-user microcomputers	7.8	11.9	10.9
In-store systems	13.0	5.7	9.2
Warehousing/distribution systems	5.6	4.5	3.7
Other	9.4	4.4	2.2

Use of POS Hardware	1988	1989	1990
Programmable cash registers	63.2%	75.5%	53.1%
Hand-held terminals	42.1	59.2	53.1
Micro/PCs with cash drawers	18.4	20.4	28.6
Electronic cash registers	60.5	75.5	24.5
Mechanical cash registers	13.2	16.3	4.1
Other	—	16.3	14.3

SOURCE: "Retailers Spending More On MIS Budgets" (1989), *Chain Store Age Executive* (August), 83. Reprinted by permission from *Chain Store Age Executive* (August, 1989). Copyright © Lebhar-Friedman, Inc., 425 Park Ave., New York, NY 10022.

A sophisticated UPC scanning system at Toys "R" Us captures data instantly and provides up-to-the-second information from all store locations to top management.

Many POS systems are already used extensively by retailers, giving them ready access to current information and, therefore, making them more alert to changing needs and developing trends. Claire's Boutiques, a specialty retailer who sells a wide selection of inexpensive jewelry and other accessories, installed computer systems to control inventory and monitor the sale of over 5,000 items in stock. Within two years, sales had increased by 46 percent to $127 million, and profits rose 33 percent to $7.1 million (Alpert, 1989). The NCR 7052/STORES in-store processing system was developed for use in major department stores. The system includes application software, terminals, processors, and related peripherals, permitting speedy high-volume transaction processing online. (See photos.)

POS Scanner technology has helped consumer goods manufacturers figure out what retail customers want and why they want it. For example, Kraft USA knows a lot about people who buy their macaroni and cheese, such as how old they are and how often they shop. Kraft knows whether they fill the grocery cart in one trip or just pick up a few items several times a week, whether they use coupons, how many children they have, whether they eat out or entertain friends at home, and what they do to earn a living. How does Kraft know these things? Supermarket scanner data is combined with data derived from research into what shoppers watch on television, the type of neighborhood they live in, and the type of supermarket they shop in. Manufacturers then can provide retailers with a product assortment and promotional incentives that are appealing to customers. PepsiCo's Frito-Lay, a $4.2 billion-a-year snackfood division, tested a new chip snack product for ten months around Minneapolis. Scanner data was combined with focus groups and other research data gathered from 10,000 customers throughout the United States for a year prior to the test to obtain consumers likes and dislikes about different versions of the chip, as well as their opinions of available competing brands. In addition, Frito-Lay recruited 1,500 households to participate in a scanner panel. Panel members provided information about family size, income, marital status, number of TVs owned, newspapers and magazines read, and who does most of the shopping. Panel members were given special bar-coded identification cards to be used at checkout when paying for groceries. Thus, the cashier records everything the shopper has bought, giving Frito-Lay more insights into its potential customer base (Caminiti, 1990).

Discussion of POS systems necessarily involves Universal Product Codes (UPC). The combined technologies provide the retailer with a competitive edge because of their instantaneous data-capturing capability. The **Universal Product Code** is a product-unique code created to identify a product according to its manufacturer, brand name, size, or other important characteristics, much like a very specific SIC code. This code has a magnetic base that is read by machine, i.e., a point-of-sale system, which calculates the price and other essential information for inventory and customer purposes.

A newer POS/UPC system is compared to a manual or less sophisticated system in Exhibit 17–4 to illustrate the advantages of POS in the process of receiving, pricing, selling, and reordering merchandise. Note that the point-of-sale terminals provide many advantages. The continuous recording of the store's inventory status provides immediate feedback on retail sales. This process makes it possible to determine what items are selling, when they are selling, and how many are selling. Better decisions can be made regarding reorders, markdowns, or other actions.

Exhibit 17–4
Advantages of Point-of-Sale/Universal Product Code Systems

Older Manual System	*New System (POS/UPC)*	*Advantage*
1. Merchandise received from vendor.	Merchandise received from vendor.	
2. Markup applied and price is marked on each product individually.	UPC code is used to set price once in computer for all units on hand (product need not be marked individually).	Lower labor cost Time savings Quick price changes Fewer errors
3. Merchandise sold to customer. Price is visually checked and entered by hand into cash register	Merchandise sold to customer. Scanners/wand readers enter and record price.	Same as #2
4. Merchandise reordered as needed based on sales forecasts. Physical inventory required to determine merchandise on hand.	Merchandise reordered as needed, based on sales forecasts. Physical count not needed due to computerized inventory records.	Same as #2
5. Fill out order form, obtain approval if needed.	Purchase orders often placed direct to vendor from system.	Shorter order processing time
6. Mail purchase order to vendor, or place telephone order (written order form will have to be replicated by order-taker at supplier).		Step omitted
7. Order is processed by vendor.	Order is processed by vendor.	Less time for paperwork More time for service
8. Order is shipped to retailer.	Order is shipped to retailer.	

UNIVERSAL PRODUCT CODE (UPC)
product-unique code that identifies characteristics of a product and has a magnetic base read by machines

The impact of POS technology also has high potential for improving retail distribution. Direct orders can be placed electronically from store to supplier, shortening order processing and lead time. As shown in Exhibit 17–4, an efficient high-technology system will eliminate most of steps #4, #5, and #6 required in an older manual system. Overall results include faster order processing, lower inventory requirements, higher inventory turnover, and a positive impact on the reorder point.

The bar code and POS technology can improve productivity, and thus profitability, in a period of tightly constrained growth at retail outlets suffering from lagging consumer spending. Industry analysts believe that the retail sector is concentrating on better returns rather than opening new stores. An Anderson Consulting study estimated that the retail industry could save $9.6 billion annually by using bar codes and related technology after an initial investment of $3.6 billion. Innovative applications of retail bar coding include use on baggage claim tickets and luggage by the airlines to speed baggage handling and improve security (Kelley, 1991).

Potential drawbacks to a POS system include customer apprehension about the price of a product that is not physically marked on the product, incorrect price information entered into the computer, resistance of store personnel to new technology, higher startup costs, and lack of expertise in interpreting and applying data outputs.

Using a hypothetical example, we can demonstrate the possible savings obtained from a POS system. Let us assume the following usage rate (average daily sales), lead time (number of days from placement of order until receipt of merchandise in store), and unit cost of inventory (product price and storage cost per unit), first without a POS system, and then with a POS system.

Usage rate	*= 1,000 units a day*
Cost per unit	*= $100/unit plus $20/unit to store*
Order lead time	*= 10 days without POS system*

Inventory requirements due to system constraints (based on daily sales and order lead time):

1,000 units × 10 days	*= 10,000 units*
Cost of inventory	*= (10,000 × $100) + (10,000 × $20)*
	= $1,000,000 + $200,000 = $1,200,000.

Now let us assume that the order lead time can be shortened by four days with the use of a POS system at same per unit costs.

Usage rate (no change)	*= 1,000 units a day*
New order lead time	*= 6 days*

Inventory requirements under new system:

1,000 units × 6 days	*= 6,000 units*
Cost of inventory	*= (6,000 × $100) + (6,000 × $20)*
	= $600,000 + $120,000
	= $720,000
Additional capital now available to retailer with new system	*= $480,000.*

The retailer may obtain further savings from reduced manpower needs for inventory processing and management. Suppliers may also realize a cost efficiency under this system, leading to potential price concessions to retail buyers.

Wal-Mart is one of a number of retailers who benefit from POS systems. Merchandise orders for Wal-Mart stores are determined and placed through the use of hand-held scanners connected to the mainframe computer (Schieder, 1987). Grocery stores, with an average inventory of approximately 10,000 items, were the first to use scanners extensively. By comparison, Wal-Mart averages 60,000 to 70,000 different items in each store, which need to be inventoried, monitored, and ordered on a timely basis. For example, Wal-Mart's hand-held computers are programmed for specific vendors and merchandise, such as Coats & Clarks items or gifts and greeting cards, so that orders can go from the stores to the central offices in Bentonville, Arkansas, and from there to vendors. Merchandise will be in the stores within three days of placing the order.

Advantages of scanners in Wal-Mart stores include (1) ability to obtain feedback when testing new items in designated stores; (2) decrease in ticket-switching by customers when bar codes are used; (3) faster customer checkout—six more customers can be checked out each hour with scanners, with the average customer spending only $18.00; (4) accurate receipt tape given to customer; and (5) labor saving, without replacing jobs—more jobs were actually created at Wal-Mart, where about 80 percent of the merchandise is still marked individually, except for high volume products like paper goods. At the end of each week, management is provided with a 36-page printout, including the top 10 items for each department, a listing of items with the greatest decrease in sales from the previous week, and other key information.

However, managers depend on the "human element"; they do not rely just on the computer printouts. Sam Walton, founder of Wal-Mart, was well-known for listening to the company's clerks, stockboys, and other associates to obtain their input for improving the business. In fact, the benefit of Management By Wandering Around (MBWA), as it is sometimes called, was so important to Walton that every store manager is put through specialized training to do this. (Remember that the successful application of high technology also requires management know-how.)

In spite of the advantages of a high technology POS and inventory system, a cost-benefit analysis should be conducted to determine whether the benefits of the new system justify its cost. In order to accomplish this, the costs and benefits of both systems need to be compared to determine the feasibility of purchasing and maintaining the new system.

POS scanner data is a valuable resource for retail management decisions. However, if the retailer is to measure product sales and understand the causal factors driving those sales, he or she needs to have accurate data on the volume, price, and time period of the sales. This information should be matched with the causal data (special prices, display, advertising, etc., to generate sales) for the same stores and time periods.

Misinformation leads to ineffective and costly decisions. Problems associated with incorrect data include bad share, volume, and price numbers; inaccurate sales trend information; and inaccurate promotional information and analysis. Some of these problems occur in the unit measurement of multipack packages (one six-pack or one can?); incorrect recording of prices, or

COURTESY OF WALGREEN CO.

Here at Walgreen's, the UPC scanner helps the cashier input a number of small items to complete the sale quickly.

no prices; incorrect sales volume numbers due to data processing problems; volume-price-promotional information not aligned in the same time period; or duplication of previous week's data. Companies such as Information Resources, Inc. (IRI) have developed InfoScan and other methods for improving the quality of scanner data. IRI's expert system has identified state-of-the-art techniques for detecting and correcting these problems (Eskin, Kriss, and Abraham, 1988).

MORE EFFECTIVE DISTRIBUTION MANAGEMENT **Electronic data interchange (EDI)** is a term used to describe the electronic transfer of data from one party to another via computer technology. In other words, specially formatted documents (e.g., purchase orders) can be sent from one company's computer to another's. EDI networks have enabled retailers to respond quickly to trends and opportunities. They have been particularly advantageous for rapid communication between retailers and manufacturers. A 1989 *Chain Store Age Executive* study found that 26.5 percent of responding retailers were currently using EDI, 16.3 percent were testing a pilot project, and 40.8 percent planned to use EDI within the next year and a half. Of course, the larger the company, the more likely it is to adopt EDI technology ("Retailers Spending More . . . ," 1989).

The explosive growth of EDI in computer software development and management consulting for retail and manufacturing businesses can be

ELECTRONIC DATA INTERCHANGE (EDI)
electronic transfer of data from one party to another via computer technology

attributed to (1) acceleration of interindustry standards, (2) technological advances, (3) competition from offshore suppliers, and (4) the logistics revolution (St. Clair, 1988). The technology requires fewer data-entry employees and eliminates human error, time delays, and lost invoices. The retailer can hold lower inventory levels and offer better customer service.

Several examples illustrate the efficiency of EDI applications. The Newell Group, suppliers of hardlines, promises its customers delivery in two days. Their strategy is to align themselves with the mass merchandisers, provide service to them, be responsive to their needs, and be a partner to them (St. Clair, 1988). Seminole Manufacturing Co. and Wal-Mart set up an electronic information pipeline which cut the delivery time of men's polyester slacks to 22 days, a decrease of 50 percent. The system enabled the discount chain to stay better stocked in the 64 size and color combinations of Seminole's slacks and increased sales by 31 percent. In a five-month test at four J. C. Penney stores, an electronic link with Lanier Clothes resulted in a 59 percent increase in the retailer's Stafford brand suits. EDI allowed information to move faster from the retailer's cash register to the apparel supplier's factory floor. The quick turnaround let the stores replenish supplies of popular suits fast enough to have more sizes on hand to meet seasonal demand, while cutting inventories by 20 percent (Harris, Foust, and Rothman, 1987). This could not be accomplished effectively without a quick response communication system.

The latest technology is referred to as the quick response (QR) initiative, which is essential for just-in-time (JIT) inventory management. QR combines newly developed bar coding and EDI standards to improve coordination between retailers, suppliers, and transportation companies. This cooperative effort is aimed at reducing the retailer's inventory while simultaneously providing a supply of merchandise that more closely reflects consumers' actual buying patterns ("EDI and QR . . . ," 1988). Savings attributable to QR technology are shown in Exhibit 17–5 for department stores, mass merchandisers, and specialty stores.

SATELLITE COMMUNICATIONS   Satellite communications between stores, and between stores and suppliers, have been used effectively by major retailers. Wal-Mart, one example, has placed satellites near its stores to enable managers to communicate with the home office in Bentonville, Arkansas, 24 hours a day instead of using the AT&T longlines. Although there is a high initial cost for this type of system, it is viewed as a long-range investment in the company's future. In the case of Wal-Mart, the system paid for itself within one year. Each store has an average of 15 department managers. Prior to installation of the satellite system, ordering took from two to four hours a week; now it can be done in 30 minutes. Managers can also tell how many cartons have been unloaded from delivery trucks, how fast they are unloaded, how many are missing, and so forth (Schieder, 1987).

Walgreens implemented satellite technology to support a strong growth and customer service strategy for the 1990s. An electronic communications system links all 1,500 stores to record and store patient and prescription data, produce printouts for tax and insurance records, and reduce pharmacists' paperwork. Electronic in-house systems also are used to order and manage inventory (Bergin, 1990).

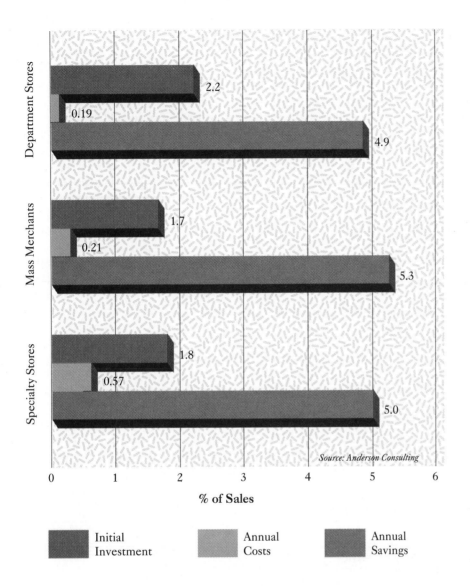

Source: Anderson Consulting

% of Sales

Initial Investment   Annual Costs   Annual Savings

Exhibit 17–5
Quick Response Savings

SOURCE: "Fast Payback from Quick Response, Study Finds" (1989), *Chain Store Age Executive* (May), 245. Reprinted by permission from *Chain Store Age Executive* (July, 1989). Copyright Lebhar-Friedman, Inc., 425 Park Ave., New York, NY 10022.

As we look at individual types of retailing technology, it becomes apparent that few, if any, are effective by themselves. The POS systems may be combined with UPC scanners. The scanner data then may be transmitted to a central location via satellite, for processing and storage in a mainframe computer, and so forth.

Perhaps the most significant step toward obtaining instant access to information is the development of the **Integrated Services Digital Network (ISDN).** ISDN is a high-tech international telephone network, permitting transmission of data among a variety of media. Under the ISDN system, the public telephone network offers exciting new telecommunication capabilities to hundreds of millions of telephone users throughout the world, combining the capability of computers, local and long distance telephone networks, broadcast media, satellites, and other electronic technology, as

INTEGRATED SERVICES DIGITAL NETWORK (ISDN)
high-tech international telephone network, permitting transmission of data among a variety of media

illustrated in Exhibits 17–6 and 17–7 ("ISDN: The New Telephone Network," 1988).

In 1987, McDonald's Corporation was the first major U.S. business to incorporate ISDN-based integrated voice and data services into its daily operation. After a trial period with Illinois Bell, McDonald's ISDN-based network consists of 400 Basic Rate lines supporting its original Oak Brook campus, and over 700 lines in its new headquarters facility, permitting a single, integrated, all-digital network. By the end of 1989, the company planned to have over 1,900 ISDN lines supporting 1,600 people at its two headquarters campuses, where an individual could select from 300 voice and data services to meet specific needs. McDonald's plans included implementation of ISDN on an international basis, because they were realizing savings that were being applied directly to their hamburger business ("ISDN: The New Telephone Network," 1988).

Sears has shared sales and inventory data with its vendors since the mid-1970s to carry out Quick Response distribution. As of 1990, Sears was transmitting sales and inventory data to 94 vendors across 138 softline and hardline product lines ("Sears: Turning Technology . . . ," 1990).

ORDERING AND STOCKING MERCHANDISE   Hand-held wand readers and computers can be used for data entry by store employees and sales representatives to shorten the time required to write orders, inventory

Exhibit 17–6
Worldwide Scope of ISDN: The International Integration of Telecommunications Systems

SOURCE: Computer Graphic Resources, Inc.

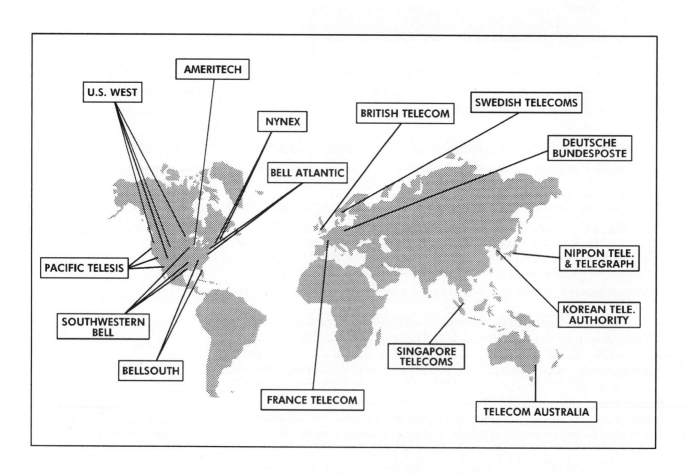

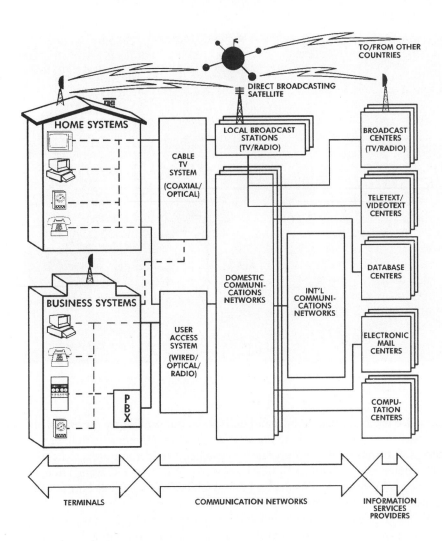

Exhibit 17–7
The Integrated Services Digital
Network (ISDN): Multi-Media
Capability for Data and Voice
Transmission

SOURCE: Computer Graphic Resources,
Inc.

status reports, and record deliveries. Manual data entry without this type of technology requires numerous labor hours of effort from qualified employees, creating a time lag in ordering and adding to payroll costs. Hand-held computers have been given to all of Frito-Lay's 10,000 delivery people. The data they collect helps the company manage production, monitor sales, and guide promotional strategy. One delivery person, who has a 61-store route in New Jersey, saves many hours of writing orders, invoices, and sales reports. With the hand-held computer he can run through a programmed product and price list and enter orders at each store in a minute or two. He can plug the machine into a printer in his truck to produce an itemized invoice. At the end of the day, it generates a sales report, which is transmitted in seconds through a local warehouse hookup to company headquarters in Dallas (Fuchsberg, 1990; Main, 1990).

A system to bridge the computer gap between grocery store receiving clerks and personnel who deliver the food products to the store is being tested in the grocery-store industry (Guyon, 1988). Separate systems have been

Part V

Due to modern technology, blank T-shirts and other sports memorabilia can be printed at the last possible moment before sale.

in place for use by grocery clerks and deliverers, but previously there was no direct way to tie them together. These systems allow drivers who deliver snacks, soft drinks, and other products to use hand-held computers to keep track of deliveries and prices. Similarly, grocery clerks may use wands to read the Universal Product Codes marked on merchandise in order to enter delivery information into central computers.

Although this technology improved inventory controls, there was still the problem of the length of time involved in two separate computer checks for delivery and receiving purposes. Under the new system, being tested by supermarket chains such as Safeway, Price Chopper, and Vons, the two tasks are brought together. Deliverers can enter information directly into the receiving clerks' hand-held calculators, using common communication standards developed to permit the data interchange. The system is expected to save the grocery store industry at least $500 million a year if it is widely adopted.

Ingram Customer Systems, a subsidiary of the Ingram Distribution Group (described in Chapter 3), has developed systems to assist book, video, and microcomputer software retailers with inventory management, product referencing, and electronic ordering. These systems combine IBM-compatible microcomputer applications with the speed and storage capacity of CD-ROM technology. This capability provides retailers with a variety of sales analysis and inventory control systems that decrease paperwork and out-of-stock conditions, increase sales information and title selection, and improve inventory turnover and merchandise mix (Ingram Industries, 1991).

When K mart managers feared they might get stuck with 36,000 Christmas dolls called "Holiday Moments" at $29.97 each, technology came to

© PETE SALOUTOS, THE VONS COMPANIES, INC.

Time- and labor-saving devices, such as Von's Electronic Store Delivery system, prevent overstocking through errors in receiving goods not ordered. Similar devices are used to track inventory, as well.

their rescue. A company computer guided store managers through a series of carefully calculated daily markdowns from Thanksgiving to Christmas. By December 25, only a few dolls were left, and no markdowns exceeded 25 percent. A fast-selling $1.97 plastic Christmas ornament was spotted by the same computer, and orders were placed for quick fill-ins. K mart's bottomline profits were increased by $250,000 by their ability to take fast action on just those two products (Armstrong, 1990).

Retailers benefitted from the "24-hour T-shirt" during the Persian Gulf War, thanks to modern technology. The 100-hour ground war was quickly commemorated on T-shirts across the nation. T-shirt companies traded designs by Fax machines, patriotic monograms arrived on computer disks. Sporting events taught retailers to order blank T-shirts and wait until the last minute to print them. Super Bowl 1991 shirts with the game's final score printed on them were ready as fans left the stadium, and "Welcome Home" shirts were ready two days before the Persian Gulf fighting came to an end (Feigenbaum, 1991).

Planning, Accounting, and Control

Within the planning, accounting, and control functions, technology tends to be related to information systems, computer software programs, and technological solutions to cost reduction through operating efficiencies. The Retail Information System (RIS) and other information systems were discussed in previous chapters. Therefore, the focus in this section is on computer software and cost reduction applications.

COMPUTER SOFTWARE PROGRAMS   Evidence of the increasing use of technology in retailing is found in the wide variety of computer software programs that have become available for both large and small retailers. Some of these programs are:

1. Sales and inventory management systems
2. File transfer programs to network between POS terminals and a mainframe
3. Reporting and maintenance software to consolidate retail information
4. Gift registry systems
5. PC and cash drawer interface at checkout.

Descriptions of a few of these programs follow.

The Retail Sales and Inventory Management System (R.SIMS) may be based on the PC to process retail sales transactions and inventory flow. Sales and inventory status reports can be printed out at any time by item, department, classification, and salesperson. The program can maintain a 12-month history on selected items for as many as 99 stores.

Superex Clothing Store is a point-of-purchase program for use on the PC, developed for retailers selling merchandise in various sizes and colors. This menu-driven program handles all important functions of an apparel specialty store, including inventory control, receiving reports, invoices, sales tax and receipts, price information, and customer mailing lists. Information can be provided by size and color and by individual item.

Optimum use of shelf and floor space is a major concern in increasing retail productivity. Computerized planogramming is now used by manufacturers, retailers, and others to plan shelf layouts (planograms). The computer-aided design program allows users to develop complete categories of merchandise and experiment with efficient use of space based on such criteria as financial evaluation, product movement, and profit yields. Users can also compare before and after results of a specific layout. Shelf-space allocation can be customized for a specific market and its demographics (Steinhagen, 1990).

Fujitsu Systems of America's Store Level System (SLS) networks Fujitsu POS terminals and other hardware to a retailer's mainframe computer. The system provides department and product classification data, flash sales reports, cash analysis, price lookup, credit authorization, and other activities.

A reporting and maintenance software system by Sweda International consolidates retail information from up to 31 Sweda cash registers, including cash information, sales by clerk, productivity, inventory, and other data.

Bridal, baby, cosmetic, wardrobe, and other registries have become a popular way for customers to shop for gifts and for personal items. AT&T Information Systems' Gift Registry System, which can be used for all of these registry categories, is on-line and interactive, with an updating data base to provide centralized registry information that chain stores can use to track gift selections. In this way, retailers can track sales results and identify slow-moving items in order to project future merchandise requirements.

Another system that includes gift registry information is from Databank Concepts Inc. (DCI). This program can be used on a single PC, microcomputer networks, or interface into a data network. Customized printouts can be provided for each store, including sales analysis reports by item, store, and vendor, so that trends can be spotted quickly. System options include product price ranges, purchaser and gift files (a good reference for customer service via thank-you notes), and outside purchases from other stores ("Software for Retailers . . .," 1984).

A software package, developed by Great Plains Software (GPS), interfaces a PC directly to a cash drawer at point-of-sale, causing the cash drawer to open when a cash transaction occurs. The system produces a sales slip for each customer while automatically updating inventory records. In addition to other features, reports can be printed at any time to show exact items in stock, amount on hand, cost of the inventory, and items that are out of stock and on order (Dauphinais, 1984).

TRENDS IN RETAIL SOFTWARE AND INFORMATION SYSTEMS   Surveys conducted by Arthur Young and *Chain Store Age Executive* indicated that Management Information Systems (MIS) capital outlays will continue to increase as a percentage of retail sales ("Retail MIS Field Reflects . . .," 1988; "Retailers Spending More . . .," 1989). The survey identified 20 different MIS software areas that retailers had targeted for development or improvement. Fifty percent of the respondents planned to give more of their attention to POS applications, and 44 percent wanted to upgrade both their inventory control and merchandise planning systems. Results by type of store are given in Exhibit 17–8.

TECHNOLOGY AND OPERATING EFFICIENCIES IN CUSTOMER SERVICE   Many forms of technology have been adopted

Exhibit 17–8
MIS Systems Planned for Development/Improvement

| MIS Areas | *Type of store* | | | | |
	Mass Merch.	*Dept.*	*Specialty*	*Comb./ Grocery*	*All Participants*
Point-of-sale	72%	38%	53%	35%	50%
Inventory control	44	43	46	40	44
Merchandise planning	40	71	40	35	44
Stock replenishment	44	67	30	45	40
Purchase order management	28	62	35	45	39
Sales reporting/analysis	48	24	33	40	35
Open-to-buy	32	48	39	15	34
Accounts payable	40	19	35	30	33
Receiving	32	38	32	35	32
Distribution	36	43	28	30	32
General ledger	32	33	30	15	28
Human resources	32	19	21	20	24
Payroll	28	14	25	20	23
Financial planning	20	24	23	15	21
Sales audit	28	33	16	15	20
Accounts receivable	20	24	12	25	18
Fixed assets	20	5	19	25	17
Direct mail marketing	8	10	18	5	12
Credit management	8	24	9	5	10
Foreign importing	4	14	11	—	8
Other	—	—	2	5	2

SOURCE: "Retail MIS Field Reflects Technology Trends" (1988), *Chain Store Age Executive* (January), 100. Reprinted by permission from *Chain Store Age Executive*, (January, 1989). Copyright Lebhar-Friedman, Inc. 425 Park Ave., New York, NY 10022.

© PETE SALOUTOS, THE VONS CO., INC.

Von's has instituted electronic shelf tags in many of its stores. As prices are changed in the main computer, the prices on the shelf tags reflect the change automatically.

by retailers to improve customer service through more efficient operations. In addition to credit card authorization, some applications of technology include faster check approval and credit card authorization at point-of-purchase, in-store vending machines, and toll-free 800 telephone numbers for customer orders and inquiries. Selected examples are provided in the following paragraphs.

Vons Grocery uses a "cashless" electronic check writing system, Vons Check, which also offers automated paper check approval. When paying for groceries, customers run ATM bank cards through a magnetic card stripe reader, enter their personal identification numbers, and payment is automatically made from their bank accounts. The retailer uses an internal credit history system, consisting of a computer file of each customer's credit history with Vons at the store level, and a record of all customers who have applied for the service.

Both the retailer and customers benefit. Less time is required for each sales transaction, allowing more customers to be served within the amount of time used by less sophisticated systems. In addition, customers still receive a two-day float for their payment processing. Vons benefits from savings in labor costs, since the company processes three million checks a month ("Von's Grocery Goes Cashless," 1987).

K mart's commitment to customer service, a corporate strategic thrust, is accomplished to a large extent through automation in areas such as layaway. Under a retailer's layaway system, the store holds merchandise for a customer who makes periodic payments until it is paid in full. The company spent $5 million in 1987 to expand its Fujitsu automated layaway system to all of its 2,100 stores. The system automatically generates the layaway contract and notifies store personnel to remind a customer who misses a payment. This procedure reduces the time required to open a layaway account and to track payments since each layaway package is virtually a mini accounts receivable system.

K mart's automated layaway system is part of a larger system designed to improve customer service. Related technology includes POS scanning and on-line credit authorization. The company has found that a scanning transaction takes 23 percent less time than a normal key entry transaction, and that credit authorizations take 50 percent less time for purchases below the floor limit and 80 percent less time above the floor limit using the new system. By 1991, K mart will have invested about $1 billion in retail automation projects, including a satellite communications network ("K mart Automates Layaways," 1987).

Vending machines, particularly for low-cost, high-volume items, have contributed to retail operating efficiencies. The machines reduce the need for employees and allow for 24-hour operation. Videotapes, an increasingly popular rental item, are being retailed through vending machines, for example. Payment for the tapes can be made by bank or credit cards or prepayment.

High-volume stores with repeat customers, such as supermarkets, discount stores, drug stores, convenience stores, and some department stores have found they not only gain additional revenues directly from the rentals but also benefit from add-on sales of other items. Research indicates that the average supermarket or convenience store customer spends $1.84 on other products while in the store to rent a movie ("Video Vending Machines Spur Add-on Sales," 1987).

Retail information systems often are built as the need arises for new information. System components, such as those described above, may be purchased from a number of manufacturers over some period of time. Thus, a problem may arise in maintaining the system because of difficulty in obtaining overall system maintenance and repair service from a single equipment supplier. One answer to this problem is 3M's Equipment Service and Support Division (ES & SD) used by The Sharper Image. ES & SD provides a coordinated service network to keep the company's POS and computer system operational ("ES & SD Hones POS System," 1987).

The preceding examples of retailing technology within the planning, accounting, and control function illustrate the need for coordination. Technology should go hand-in-hand with corporate strategy and objectives. Successful implementation of technology requires coordination from the early planning stages through follow-up maintenance, repair, and upgrading of a system.

Human Resources

THE PEOPLE ASPECT OF TECHNOLOGY   No matter how sophisticated the technology, it depends upon people to make it work. Strategic planning and execution influence, and are influenced by, the anticipated marriage between employees and the resources they are given to work with. High performing stores usually become that way because of their people, from top managers down to the lowest level of hourly employee. Therefore, when using technology, a retailer should simplify a task rather than complicate it. The challenge is not to do more but to do the task in a simpler fashion. In particular, personnel in cash register locations have a high turnover rate, so the proper application of available technology can simplify the ongoing training problem. For example, cash registers in a fast food restaurant may have the name of the menu item, i.e., "Hamburger," printed on keys rather than numbers representing the prices. The price can be entered into the computerized registers for each item, and the customer will be charged the correct amount, leading to fewer mistakes by inexperienced employees.

USE OF TECHNOLOGY IN HIRING AND TRAINING   A variety of technological applications have been used to improve the hiring and training process. Technology can be used to screen job applicants with methods such as videotaped interviews, skill tests, and so forth. Training can be accomplished effectively with videotapes, interactive computer programs, and other methods. Domino's Pizza used a satellite-based TV network to teach franchisees how to run their stores and to teach employees such skills as how to slice vegetables and make dough (Kelly, 1990).

STEPS IN DEVELOPING RETAIL TECHNOLOGY SYSTEMS
The most advanced technology in the world will not be successful if it is not applied intelligently. Point-of-sale (POS) systems provide a good illustration of this. Some POS systems have not worked as well as expected because someone ignored the human interaction factor, and the fact that the success of the system depends upon the people who use it (Shulman, 1986a).

The following actions are required to make technology work:

1. Determination of store needs
2. Careful evaluation of options
3. Selection of a complete system
4. Management implementation of the system
5. Training of personnel
6. Maintaining and updating the system

A clear determination of specific store needs of a particular retail operation is the first stage in the process of developing a retail technology system. If managers are not aware of what is needed, they are very likely to choose an inadequate system. The wrong system may do much more than the retailer needs, or worse, it may not do enough.

In selecting the right system, a careful evaluation is needed to find the option that meets the criteria of cost-benefit analysis, as discussed earlier. The key factors to consider include growth opportunities and increased profitability resulting from the investment, and ease of use by employees, as in the previous restaurant example.

Selection of a complete system may be more practical than buying part of a system. Shulman (1986b, pp. 17–18) indicates that it is foolish for a retailer to buy part of a system, believing it will do the job, without buying the support system that makes it work properly. For example, investing in scanning equipment without obtaining support for inventory management may save money in the short term but will not provide a long-term advantage.

Once a system is selected, it will require effort on the part of management to see that it is installed and used properly. Simply putting the system in place will not guarantee that the job will be done. Nor is it feasible to rely on the technical support staff who installs the system to administer it from a merchandising standpoint.

Of all the steps listed above for making technology work, the key step of training personnel is often omitted. Simply showing personnel how to operate the system is not enough. The employees are a part of the system and should be regarded as such. They need to understand the underlying rationale for using it in order to maximize the usefulness of its output.

The system must be monitored and should not be viewed as a permanent solution to the retailer's needs once it is in place. It should be evaluated on a continuing basis to answer questions such as: Can it accomplish more? Should it be expanded? Should some functions be eliminated? Indicated adjustments then can be made to improve the system's effectiveness.

Promotion

There are many examples of the use of technology in retail promotion. Applications are used in direct marketing, at point-of-purchase, telephone sales, in store couponing, and other forms of promotion. (Electronic shopping is discussed below in a separate section.)

INFORMATION FOR DIRECT MARKETING Scanners and other technical advances are giving retailers access to information they never had before, making it possible for them to increase their direct marketing efforts. Supermarkets and other retail stores have gone beyond the use of scanners for pricing and inventory and are using the information to determine customer preferences. Once customer preferences are identified through this easily obtained data, direct marketing campaigns become a more viable tool. In addition to the more traditional catalog sales, direct marketing can increase distribution through traditional stores and for products that are already in inventory (Teinowitz, 1988).

Grocery store technology has been applied to the tourism industry in Florida. A discount travel club devised a coupon book for Florida attractions that lets marketing officials track tourists by means of bar codes. A bar code is used to identify each merchant discount coupon and the company or individual redeeming it. Travelers provide vital information about themselves when they receive the coupon book and are given their own personal bar code to use when the coupons are redeemed. The results are used for purposes such as targeting geographic regions, travel agents, foreign visitors, and companies and organizations (Seldon, 1990).

HIGH-TECH PROMOTION AT POINT-OF-PURCHASE Two leading fast-food restaurants, Wendy's and McDonald's, are using high-technology point-of-purchase promotional techniques that were originally geared to supermarket and drugstore shoppers. For example, Wendy's is trying a new way to merchandise its menu and specials to customers waiting in line at their drive-through windows. At selected stores in Chicago and Columbus, Ohio, customers are instructed to tune their radios to a certain FM frequency (with a limited broadcast range of a few square blocks). After listening to the rundown of the menu and special deals or new products, they are given a special discount if they mention the "secret word" given during the radio message. This promotional tool increases the use of drive-throughs and speeds up ordering and traffic. The message is customized to local markets including local sponsorships. McDonald's has added video monitors in some stores as in-store promotional tools. The monitors display commercials or give information about specials, similar to a system in a Times Square McDonald's in New York (Hume, 1988).

A number of Arby's restaurants have begun to use a do-it-yourself ordering system developed by IBM for the fast-food trade. Fast-food may get faster and employees more efficient as customers gain more control over their own orders. IBM's countertop computer device has a touchscreen display terminal with boxes for items such as hamburgers and fries. If they change their minds, customers can add or delete items before finalizing the sale. If, for example, the customer does not order a soda, a printed message illuminates the screen asking, "Would you like a refreshing soda?" The order appears on similar screens in front of the clerk and in the kitchen, so clerks do not have to shout or carry orders back to the cooks. Thus, more customers can be served with the same number of employees. Arby's experienced a decrease in service time of 20 seconds per order and an increase of 9 to 40 cents in the amount of the average sales check ("Fast Food Gets Faster . . . ," 1990).

A combination video and POS system, developed by Stores Automated Systems, Inc. (SASI), uses two CRT screens at checkout. One screen faces the checkout clerk; the other faces the customer who can view up to 26 lines of price information as his or her order is totaled. It also can display brief promotional information, such as next week's specials, special events, such as a cooking class in the supermarket, and promotions for other retailers in the area, which provides another source of revenue. The system is a simple integration of a videocassette player and POS which runs a continuous loop videotape containing prerecorded advertising messages and costs only about $1,000 per checkout ("Promotion System Marries Video and POS," 1988).

RETAIL INFORMATION MESSAGE CENTERS   With the increased use of self-service, customers have less opportunity to obtain information from store employees. As a result, a number of technological solutions to this information gap have evolved. Lucky Stores' Advantage Stores division, which has an enormous number of products, services, and specialty departments in each store, has installed the Information Station, an electronic kiosk (small structure open at one or more sides), to ease any possible confusion. The Information Station offers a variety of services including an electronic store directory that also displays advertising, a recipe and coupon dispenser, and an information center that the retailer can program with store services and promotions. All the customer has to do is "Touch gently to begin" ("Lucky Uses High-Tech Kiosks for Advantage," 1988).

ELECTRONIC IN-STORE PROMOTION   Shopping carts and dressing room mirrors have become recent additions to the use of technology in promoting to customers while they are shopping in a store.

The VideOcart is an electronic advertising system that can be mounted on the handles of traditional shopping carts. A video screen displays manufacturers' ads as customers wheel the carts past the same manufacturers' products along the aisle. Other ads are targeted toward the stores' own promotions. POS scanning data tells if, and how, the ads influence purchases ("Ads on Wheels Roll into Supermarkets," 1988; Mayer, 1990). ShopRite stores and Publix and Homeland supermarkets have mounted solar-powered calculators on shopping carts in many of their stores that also display an advertiser's insert next to the keypad. Research indicates that this tactic successfully registers a brand impression with as many as three out of four shoppers ("Alternative Media," 1990).

The ultimate in POP high-tech self-service may be found in dressing rooms in clothing stores. Computerized Magic Mirrors are available that allow people to "try on" up to ten outfits in 60 seconds. At the touch of a button, images of outfits flash on the mirror, showing customers how the outfits would look on them. The mirrors were developed in Paris, and are used in stores in France, Australia, and Japan (Alsop, 1988).

IN-STORE ELECTRONIC COUPONING SYSTEMS   Coupons have a long history of use to increase trial and purchase of products. In 1986, U.S. households received about 200 billion coupons, or about 2,500 coupons for each home, but only 75 to 100 (three to four percent) of these may be redeemed annually (Kesler, 1988). Since so much waste occurs, retailers have an incentive to target more accurately those customers who will use the coupons. Evidence suggests that consumers are more apt to redeem and use coupons from an in-store delivery system when they can select specific specials from a list of offerings (Gardner, 1984).

This trend has led to in-store electronic couponing systems, including the Coupon Solution developed by Catalina. Major package goods companies such as Campbell Soup, Procter & Gamble, Beatrice, and Kellogg pay Catalina to dispense coupons in the supermarket chains it serves.

In an in-store couponing effort, Campbell Soup Co. placed an interactive video promotion system in a Food Lion Store in Greensboro, North Carolina. The terminal dispenses coupons and recipes for Campbell products and serves as a store directory (Freeman and Dagnoli, 1988). The electronic coupon system being used by UKROP, an 18 unit supermarket chain in the Richmond, Virginia, area provides an example of how technology, market research, and promotional efforts may interact. The system was developed by Citicorp POS Information Services to collect and store data for development of target market strategies. Both consumers and retailers benefit from this system. Consumers are able to save time and effort in using coupons. Retailers can increase sales (10 percent increase for UKROP), collect market information, and generate consumer good will. In addition to gathering information about target markets, the retailer can determine price elasticity relative to coupon offerings. For example, if consumers regard a coupon giving 25 cents off the purchase price to be the equivalent of 30 cents off, the retailer can give a smaller discount per item while achieving the same sales volume (Klokis, 1987).

PROMOTION AT THE CASH REGISTER   The Vision system triggers promotions automatically at checkout when the universal product code (UPC) is recorded for an item or group of items. For instance, the customer who purchases a pack of cigarettes may see a message at eye level on a video screen, stating that smokers enjoy the minty taste of Scope. The customer is instructed to press the coupon button if he would like to have a coupon to save money on the next purchase of Scope. The computer printer at POS then receives a signal to print out a discount coupon for the customer ("Interative POS Video Yields Instant Results," 1988).

"Smart card" technology has been combined with a coupon-eating machine, which scans, verifies, redeems, destroys, and provides marketing and redemption information on bar-coded coupons, using the Vision system. At the end of a customer's order, the cashier drops coupons into the machine. If all requirements have been met, refunds are automatically credited from the order and the coupon is shredded. The plastic Vision "smart card" is a combination promotion and financial services card. It can provide services such as accumulating frequent shopper points or automatic check approval and direct debit functions, while providing the retailer with a wealth of useful information (Coleman, 1988).

Turner Broadcasting System and Act Media tested a new POS application in late 1990. TV monitors were installed in grocery checkout lanes. Checkout Channel monitors have built-in sound sensors that blink on whenever someone is standing in line, and 8-minute segments from CNN's Headline News are shown. Two minutes of commercials are included in each segment. Spots are targeted toward women in the daytime, working couples and singles in the evenings, and families on the weekends (Hastings, 1990).

TELEMARKETING   Analysts estimate that over eight million people will be selling products and services over the telephone by the year 2000 (Selbert, 1987a). **Telemarketing,** the name given to telephone selling, has become an effective solution to the increasing expense of in-store and personal selling. Telemarketing is often combined with catalogs and other forms of advertising for maximum impact. Without the technology provided by the telephone systems, often combined with computerized data bases, many nonstore product and service retailers would not be in business.

The use of toll-free numbers to give customers who want to place an order, complain about a purchase, or make an inquiry, easy access to a retailer is not a new idea. However, many retailers benefit daily from this technology that is often taken for granted. To illustrate, The Sharper Image receives several thousand dollars' worth of orders each minute from customers in all 50 states over its 24-hour-a-day, toll-free, inquiry-and-order phone line. Orders are logged and processed into The Sharper Image's computer system at the San Francisco headquarters "ES & SD Hones POS System," 1987).

Store Operations

Technology has improved the day-to-day functioning of retail businesses. Applications include physical operations, such as the maintenance of stores, warehouses, workrooms, delivery and pickup, and other activities, such as the movement of merchandise and customers through the stores. Technology has also brought about improvements in credit and collections and in store security and crime prevention.

PHYSICAL OPERATIONS   Customers and employees benefit from technology within the store or retail service environment. Familiar examples include "people movers" such as escalators and elevators in stores and "moving sidewalks" in airports. A less obvious example is the use of technology to control the

TELEMARKETING
telephone selling

temperature in any given store. Heating and air conditioning for individual branch stores can be operated from a central location. Such a system provides efficient climate control at remote locations.

Mechanized and computerized warehouses have improved the physical movement of inventory and paperwork through the business. Computerization of distribution center records previously kept on paper have resulted in what is referred to as the "paperless warehouse." Paperless warehouse management has resulted in huge cost savings and significant productivity improvements.

Computer technology for warehouse receiving, putaway, picking, and shipping activities has been available for more than a decade but has seen rapid growth only in the last five years. Tandy Corp., the parent company of Radio Shack, installed a paperless system in its 370,000 square foot warehouse in Ft. Worth, Texas, in 1987. The system, which runs on a Model 4000 Tandy computer, handles picking for all of the 2,300 lines stored in the warehouse. The technology is used in combination with bar-coded labels (Harrington, 1988a; 1988b).

These automated systems are able to maintain extremely accurate and detailed records. They can be designed to trigger stock-replenishment procedures right from the warehouse floor and to track labor productivity by recording worker location, pick speed, and accuracy. Although paperless warehouse technology is expensive, increased efficiency has led to considerable cost savings for most companies.

Retailers also benefit from the use of high-tech materials-handling systems and computerized product-flow control by their vendors to improve order lead time. In 1988, the Eastman Kodak Co. implemented a multimillion dollar warehouse control system designed to manage the company's central distribution center (CDCR) in Rochester, New York. A significant factor in the success of this system is that it was created in partnership with the functional expertise of Kodak warehouse employees who advised the computer programmers designing the software. The system, called C-SWIFT (Central-Service With Improved Forward Technology), manages the flow of both information and physical goods through the 2.1 million square foot CDCR, in order to ship film, chemicals, photographic paper, and equipment (some 14,000 items) to Kodak distribution facilities throughout the United States and 44 other countries.

One aspect of the C-SWIFT system is the use of automated materials handling equipment. Benefits include improved accuracy, faster order processing (85 percent of orders processed in two days with C-SWIFT versus 82 percent in three days previously), increased worker productivity, and 100,000 square feet of freed up warehouse space. Additionally, long-term benefits of the improved warehouse information processing and inventory control will permit the CDCR to make more direct shipments to customers, eliminating the costly intermediate step of shipping all products to the regional distribution center, and avoiding the handling of millions of items twice (Harrington, 1988c).

The use of high-technology automated systems does not guarantee success, however, as illustrated by the experience of some Australian grocery wholesalers and food retailers (Bamber and Lansbury, 1988). In the 1970s, David Holdings Pty Ltd, a grocery wholesaler in the Sydney area, constructed the third automated warehouse in the world and experienced rapid growth in volume of orders and expansion. The new system could assemble 7,200 cartons per hour compared to 125 cartons per hour with a manual system. However, the innovation was dismantled in the early 1980s and the company returned to traditional warehousing

Automated guided vehicles link the physical tasks of materials handling with computer technology, as in this Ford Motor plant in Ypsilanti, Michigan.

methods, using racking and forklift trucks. The demise of the high-tech system was brought about by poor packaging quality from suppliers, technical difficulties with the control equipment, poor managerial communications, union demands, and negative workers' attitudes.

An Australian food retailer, FoodCo, modernized its distribution facilities in the early 1980s to cope with an increase in its number of stores, turnover, and sales volume. Two distribution centers, DCA and DCB, were opened near Sydney and Brisbane respectively. Although the technology used in the two DCs was practically identical, one was successful and one was not. The differing levels of performance were explained by seven factors: management, industrial relations, work organization, labor force, location, product market, and technology.

AUTOMATED DIALING IN CREDIT AND COLLECTIONS   The combined technology of telephones and computers has increased credit collection productivity, shortened processing time for payments, and reduced paperwork.

Houston retailers were hit particularly hard during the Oil Patch recession of the mid-1980s with suffering sales and rising consumer bad debts. Palais Royal, a locally based 27-store apparel chain, had added many new accounts just before the economy deteriorated significantly. These new accounts increased dramatically the percentage of uncollected customer accounts, putting a greater burden on the five-person collection staff. Under the old system collectors got past due accounts directly from the company's mainframe computer, manually dialed the customer's telephone number, and entered the customer's promise to pay information into the account record, and the computer sent the collector the next name, and so on, for an average of 120 calls per day for each collector.

Palais Royal increased collection calls to 550 per day per collector with the TBS/Davox system, a configuration of automated dialers, telephone lines, and operator work stations. Phone numbers from mainframe account files are continuously forwarded from a computerized autodial system manager to the switching subsystem, then to outbound lines. The next account is dialed automatically if there is no answer or the line is busy, until a voice is detected on the customer's phone when the collector personally processes the call or plays a pre-recorded message. The computerized autodial system paid for itself in six months. Other retailers using this system are May Department Stores in St. Louis, Montgomery Ward, and R. H. Macy and Mercantile Stores ("Auto-Dialing Boosts Total of Collect Calls," 1988).

Telephone bill paying systems are another adaptation of technology for consumer credit. The technology is not new but it has not been widely adopted. However, Nationwide Remittance Centers (NRC) has developed a faster and less labor-intensive program, which links its telephone payment services with MasterCard's Remittance Processing Service.

With the earlier pay-by-phone systems, customers would phone their bank and use the telephone keypad to punch in the information that identifies their particular account, the account they want to pay, and the amount of payment. While this was easier for the customer, the bank still generated a lot of paper. The NRC system does away with much of the paperwork, handling more of the transaction by computer and electronic funds transfer (EFT) between the customer's bank and the retailer. Although only two percent of American households use pay-by-phone now, a 1987 study shows that two-thirds of American households will be using telephone bill paying services by the year 2000 ("Pay-By-Phone Systems: A Second Look," 1988).

SECURITY AND CRIME PREVENTION   Retailers are continually confronted with the threat of theft and fraudulent practices by customers and employees. To this end, numerous anti-theft devices have been developed. (Some of these were discussed in Chapter 10).

Computer technology has become an important crime prevention tool for retailers. Computers can be used to aid store security in tracking frequently stolen items based upon retail audits. Reports can be generated to identify the type of merchandise stolen, the days and times that thefts occur, and specific high-risk areas in the store, on the loading dock, in the warehouse, or other places. Then appropriate measures can be taken to reduce loss.

Computers also can be used to store database information on guard training, which can be used in court. This documentation has become important because retailers have lost a number of court cases due to the inability to document the qualifications of security guards involved in an apprehension.

A combination of security methods is generally used for a successful loss prevention program. For example, John Wanamaker in Center City Philadelphia is in a high-risk area. The store uses guards, cameras, closed-circuit television, an electronic article surveillance (EAS) system, and improved employee training to cut shrinkage to well below the department store industry average. Increased emphasis on security caused a 40 percent reduction in shrinkage in one year ("Wanamaker Approach Keeps Tabs on Loss," 1987). An Arthur Young survey of mass retailers in 1983 identified mirrors as the most popular devices used to control shrinkage, and electronic tags as most effective ("Taking the High-Tech Approach . . . ," 1985). (See Exhibit 17–9).

In its 13th annual retail loss prevention survey, Ernst & Young found that overall shrinkage decreased in 1990 both at retail and at cost. The greatest decline in shrinkage was for mass merchant–general merchandise retailers, while drug chains experienced the largest increase in shrinkage. Most of the retailers had a targeted shrinkage goal, and used employee awareness programs as the most frequently used security device. In addition, emphasis was placed upon closed circuit television by mass merchants and specialty hardline retailers, and on guards and detectives by drug chains (Shern, Verdisco and Forseter 1992).

One rather unusual security method is an antishoplifting system from Colortag, USA. The theft-stopping device contains dye capsules that rupture when the tag is removed from the stolen item incorrectly, which "brands" shoplifters with a deep blue dye that takes days of scrubbing to remove from the skin, and stains the stolen goods (Jaworski, 1988). Another hi-tech security device, Anne Droid, (Chapter 10) is a mannequin with a camera in her eye and a microphone in her nose to catch shoplifters in the act.

Some familiar technology that is not particularly high-tech includes methods of customer identification for credit cards, mirrors in grocery store aisles, clothing tags that "buzz" if a customer carries the item out of the store before the tag is removed by a salesperson or cashier. Also, locked merchandise display cases and signs displayed as warnings are used to discourage dishonesty.

Pencil-and-paper honesty tests also represent a technology that has been useful in screening job applicants, identifying reliable and productive workers, and reducing employee theft. Athlete's Foot, a specialty footwear retailer

Exhibit 17–9
Security Devices Used by Retailers: Most Used and Most Effective

Devices Used to Control Shrinkage	Percent Using
Mirrors	79%
Limited access areas	74
Lock-and-chain devices	68
Guards	68
Point-of-sale technology	59
Observation booths	49
Electronic tags	46
Visible TV monitors	42
Concealed TV monitors	39
Fitting room attendants	38

Devices Judged Most Effective	Percent Responding
Electronic tags	60%
Guards	17
Point-of-sale technology	15
Observation booths	13
Visible TV monitors	13
Fitting room attendants	11
Limited access areas	10
Concealed TV monitors	8
Lock-and-chain devices	8
Mirrors	2

SOURCE: "Taking the High-Tech Approach to Pilferage" (1985), *Chain Store Age Executive* (February), 55–56. Survey conducted by Arthur Young. Reprinted by permission from *Chain Store Age Executive*, (February 1985). Copyright © Lebhar-Friedman, Inc., 425 Park Ave., New York, NY 10022.

with 95 wholly-owned stores and 350 franchises, uses the Reid Report and the Reid Survey pencil-and-paper tests as part of the information considered in hiring new employees. Reid provides an evaluation of the applicant by mail or phone based on responses to the 90 item, 45-minute test ("Athlete's Foot Steps on Theft," 1987).

Customer Shopping Perspective

Often, technology is the product of innovative ideas coming from customers. In describing successful American companies, the authors of *In Search of Excellence* (Peters and Waterman, 1982) make the point that too many managers have lost sight of the basics, including quick action, service to customers, and practical innovation. Further, none of these is possible without the commitment of everyone involved. The excellent companies are close to their customers and are better listeners. Their market is the source of their innovations. For example, Procter & Gamble, the first consumer goods company to put a toll-free 800 telephone number on its packages, has found this to be a major source of product improvement ideas. In 1979, P&G responded to all 200,000 customers who called with ideas or complaints and summarized these comments for board meetings.

In the "Blink" of an Electronic Eye (or Do Scanners Really Stop Shrinkage?)

RESPONSIBLE RETAILER

Listen to the bells ring, watch the lights flash, see the cashier move those shoppers through the checkout at breakneck speed. The front-end manager is keeping an eye on things, and everything looks like it's going smoothly—but is it? Too often the amounts on the bottom lines of the cash register tapes do not match the amounts for the products moved out of the store with such efficiency. Not even technology, such as the videotapes produced by the store's closed-circuit television monitors, is foolproof in catching an inventive cashier who is "sweethearting" an item for someone else by scanning it at a lower price.

How does "sweethearting" happen? Scanners may be accurate in reading UPC codes, but they don't know when a scam is operating. For instance, one low-priced item might be scanned more than once, while the same number of more expensive items are pushed past the scanner and not scanned at all. Other forms of "sweethearting" include simply ringing up the wrong price (69 cents instead of $6.99), covering the bar code on the product with a thumb while scanning

a barcode taped to the cashier's wrist, or laying a more expensive item on top of a lower priced item and moving them both over the scanner at the same time.

The danger of larger dollar losses increases for supermarkets as they add more high-ticket nonfoods to their lines (radios, kitchen appliances). Most scanners cannot detect this mischief; however, a few attempts have been made to eliminate it. NCR's Scanner Scale has a feature to help discourage (if not prevent) sliding. A red light (instead of the customary green light) will come on to alert a front manager if a cashier attempts to slide an item past the scanner window. This still doesn't prevent a cashier from sliding stacked items past the window while scanning only the one on the bottom.

Technology exists for reading shapes and weights, which should match the data in the bottom item's bar code, but it requires a great deal of effort to keep up with all the necessary data changes. Check Robot, which has been used by Publix and Kroger, features a "security zone," an area bordered by two infrared diodes which "see" the item as it passes along the belt. If the item's dimensions

COURTESY OF NCR CORP.

don't match the information programmed into the computer, the belt reverses itself and moves the item in the opposite direction. However, the drawback with this system is that it slows down the checkout lines.

As one specialist observed, no matter how sophisticated the scanning system technology, the best way to prevent "sweethearting" is to rely on the integrity of the cashier and to go back to a good management audit and monitoring process. It is dangerous to completely rely on scanners to eliminate shrinkage at point-of-sale.

Adapted from Elman, Daniel (1988), "When the Scanner's Electric Eye Blinks," *Supermarket Business* (August), 39–43.

Innovative retailers have responded to their customers' needs with electronic shopping. Given the state-of-the-art electronics available to customers, a high-tech living environment would, of course, include electronic shopping via computer or TV.

Electronic Shopping at Home

A decade ago, executives in retailing and retail-related industries were challenged to "grasp the dimensions of the coming telecommunication revolution" and to be prepared to participate in it as new forms of nonstore retailing emerge (Rosenberg and Hirschman, 1980). That day has come as retailers have responded to the needs of consumers who live in a busy, electronic world, with money to spend, but little time to spend it.

Homes are becoming "electronic cottages" due to increased use of the home as an electronic entertainment center and the growth of home offices. The Bureau of Labor Statistics predicts that one-third of the labor force will work at home in the 1990s. Other sources estimate the work-at-home market at between 7 and 12 million workers, and that the number will continue to rise ("Working at Home in the Electronic Cottage," 1987). Thus, customers will find shopping via their television sets and computers easier, as "teleretailing" becomes a viable shopping alternative (Fisk and Stell, 1986).

The Southwestern Bell telephone company introduced QuickSource to about 900,000 Houston customers with Touch-Tone service in 1989. Quick-Source is a voice and data information service, something like an electronic shopping mall. Customers have access to over 150 information services through a video terminal. Customers can use their telephones and terminals at home to shop for goods and services, as well as information (Southwestern Bell, 1989).

TV HOME SHOPPING   Cable television has become a medium for retail innovation. Numerous home shopping networks makes demonstrating all types of products on a customer's TV possible, so that a purchase can be made quickly and effortlessly by calling a toll-free number. A partial listing of TV home shopping companies, a general profile of the typical TV home shopping customer, and prospects for the future growth of this form of retailing are provided in the following sections.

Some of the better known TV home shopping companies are: HSN (Home Shopping Network); HSC (Home Shopping Club); Cable Value Network; STN (Shop TV Network); TelShop; Fashion Channel; and GTE's Main Street. While their numbers continue to grow, these companies have met with mixed success. The Home Shopping Club (HSC), for instance, has not been as successful as expected.

A number of retailers have entered the TV home shopping business. For example, Penney's Telaction, a joint venture with STN, allowed customers to order a wide variety of number coded items from 40 retailers, using push-button phones. Retailers, other than Penney's, offering items through Telaction included Neiman-Marcus Group, Inc., Marshall Field's, Sears, Spiegel Inc., Dayton-Hudson Corp., several shoe merchants, and two foreign retailers (Penney's 1987 Annual Report; Hagedorn, 1988). Penney's interactive shopping service, Telaction, was closed in April 1989. The retailer later sold apparel through the chain's "teleshopping" service.

HSN (Home Shopping Network) first sold cubic zirconium rings, silk and snakeskin purses, gold chains and other trinkets. Successful applications of technology made it possible for HSN to develop a television-oriented customer base (DeGeorge, 1988).

Then HSN experienced falling profits and devalued stock prices, which was blamed on unsuccessful technology. A faulty phone system lost at least half of the incoming phone calls in 1987 and allowed competitors CVN and

QVC Network Inc. (teamed up with Sears) to become established in spite of the 12 UHF television stations that it had purchased. HSN filed suit against GTE Corp. for $1.5 billion to recover lost revenues (DeGeorge, 1987a). The unique aspect of this case is that it challenges the traditional legal protection given to utilities like GTE when companies file damage claims for lost business against them (DeGeorge, 1989).

Today, the situation appears more positive. HSN's massive communications and computer center now boasts a telephone-switching system powerful enough to serve a city of 25,000. A computerized voice is capable of taking 45 percent of the calls, considerably reducing labor costs.

HSN's competitive strategy involves diversification based on its communications, computer, and distribution capabilities. Part of this plan is the company's entry into the pharmacy business, with HSN refilling and delivering prescriptions ordered by phone (DeGeorge, 1988). HSN has continued to explore growth opportunities, such as an attempted merger with COMB Co., a major purchaser of discount goods. COMB owns 50 percent of CVN (Cable Value Network), the largest of many HSN imitators. Combined reach for HSN and CVN would be 56 million households, a strong incentive for such a merger (DeGeorge, 1987b; DeGeorge, Pitzer, and Ivey, 1987). The ownership profile of this industry continues to change. In 1989 QVC merged with rival CVN and COMB was sold to Fingerhut in 1990 (Colacecchi, 1990).

According to data gathered on the TV home shopper, the TV home shopping customer can be described as:

- A bargain hunter
- A comparison shopper
- A good mail order customer
- A department store shopper for apparel and gifts
- A former college student or a college graduate
- 25–44 years old (St. Clair, 1988)

Sales were expected to nearly double in the four-year period between 1987 and 1991. In 1987, TV home shoppers spent $1,250 million. Projected sales for 1991 were $2,400 million (adjusted for inflation). In particular, Penney's home shopping channel and Main Street (GTE) were expected to experience significant growth (St. Clair, 1988).

Home Shopping Network has its own communications capabilities, with satellites and a number of television stations throughout the country. In addition, its unique telecommunications systems can accommodate one million calls per day.

COURTESY OF HOME SHOPPING NETWORK

The QVC (quality, value, convenience) home shopping network was cited as a well-run company by *Fortune* magazine in 1989. QVC earned revenues of $112 million in 1986, it's first year in operation. The next year the company earned $9 million in profits on sales of $193 million. Their strategy has brought them success: segmented programming so viewers can expect a given category of products at a scheduled time. Half of QVC's revenues come from jewelry, which is given about one-third of the TV time. Ten percent of sales come from Sears' products, based on an exclusive agreement with the retailer to offer its merchandise on live TV broadcasts. QVC uses a soft sell, showing all shipping and handling charges on the screen, and not overstating price discounts. More than half of the network's customers are repeat buyers, with the company claiming over 10,000 new customers a week from the 16 million homes that it reaches (Abelson, 1989).

COMPUTER HOME SHOPPING   Videotex is a method of shopping for goods and services via a home computer. Like the TV home shopping companies, videotex companies have had their share of successes and failures in their attempt to sell everything from horoscopes to news to plane schedules to a wide variety of products to consumers at home. Unsuccessful attempts to enter this business were made by Time, Times Mirror, and Knight-Ridder, among others. However, successful information companies, such as CompuServe, The Source, U.S. Videotel, and Boston CitiNet, have experienced profitability and growth (Hammonds, 1987).

Most videotex companies offer both products and information services to their subscribers. Boston CitiNet has capitalized on originality in pinpointing information that consumers want (sports, school lunch menu, police blotter, programming for local radio stations and museums, *USA Today* headline service, etc.). While other information companies such as CompuServe and The Source bill customers $5 to $15 an hour, plus monthly charges, CitiNet's service is free. The company makes its money on advertising with 80 small businesses signed on to reach an upscale, local audience of personal computer owners who choose ads from a directory.

Houston-based U.S. Videotel introduced the French Minitel videotex system to status-conscious Houstonians who are good customers for French haute couture and French wines. The system, which weighs nine pounds, can be plugged into phone jacks in order to dial up a wide variety of services, from physician referrals to airline schedules to home delivery of a pizza. The Minitel videotex system has been used in France for a number of years. In 1982, France began substituting electronic terminals for phone books. By 1987, nearly 3 million French customers were using 4,100 services (Davis and Peterson, 1987).

One computer home shopping service, the Electronic Mall, is an online shopping service available through CompuServe Information Service (CompuServe, 1988). How do shoppers get to the Electronic Mall? Customers can purchase an introductory package for the Electronic Mall in retail stores, such as Sears and Service Merchandise. Then they can use a personal computer and a telephone modem to access a comprehensive product index or a directory of all Mall merchants. If they do not wish to scan a complete listing of categories of merchants, they can go directly into specific stores.

Shoppers' questions are promptly answered by the Mall Manager, CompuServe's on-line representative. Shoppers can make requests by simply pressing a key or make purchases with their credit cards (*How the Electronic Mall Works*, 1987).

The Electronic Mall was developed by L. M. Berry & Co., the largest Yellow Pages company, and CompuServe. It was launched in February 1985 with 53 subscribers for a four-month test, monitored by A. C. Nielson. The average response rate on purchases was 2.1 percent, with a high of 13 percent, in comparison to 1.5 percent for direct mail-catalog response, and at a lower cost. By April 1988, the company had more than 400,000 subscribers. This represents a 300 percent increase in subscriber base, and a 350 percent increase in number of mail orders over the previous year.

Managers attribute their success to strategic planning for the network. They have learned that on-line merchandising is based on the accuracy of direct marketing, successful product categories, understanding the value of various advertising formats (i.e., why one store does better than another), and recognizing the importance of this emerging direct marketing medium. These factors suggest that innovative retailing formats depend on virtually the same factors that have proven successful for traditional in-store retailers: strategic planning and identification of the right retailing mix.

At CompuServe, many types of expertise are combined to make the Electronic Mall successful. The Advanced Media Group interfaces with numerous other specialists: Advertising, Agency Support, Copy Writing, Data Base Administration, Market Research, Product Marketing, On-line Today, Public Relations, Technological Development, System Operations, and Planning departments.

The Electronic Mall offers many benefits to marketers:

- Opportunity to reach a prime demographic market (baby boomers, average 27 years old)
- Less clutter
- Unique, with a loyal and increasing audience
- Value-based pricing
- Leads can be generated at a cost significantly less than direct mail
- 5 million households had PCs with a modem in 1987, and over 8 million households were projected to have PCs and modem by 1988
- A continued increase in modem owners projected

However, the technological aspects, no matter how intriguing, are not the driving force behind attracting merchants to videotex systems. CompuServe signed Bloomingdale's, for example, because of what the Electronic Mall could do for the retailer. In general, advertisers using this medium want lower marketing costs, more customers (i.e., a new franchise), minimization of risk, stronger customer relations, and better control of the marketing process. Computer shopping offers an innovative way for retailers to target upscale customers with a "poverty of time," who want their shopping activities to be convenient and entertaining.

Retailers using electronic shopping formats do not need to incur the expense of building or leasing a store for their customers to enter since store fronts are not necessary for this medium. As a result of lower startup costs, many entrepreneurs have been encouraged to enter electronic retailing. These entrepreneurs include companies such as Computer Express and Software Discounters of America (CompuServe, 1988).

Electronic Shopping in Stores and in Malls

Two forms of electronic shopping that are available in stores and malls are interactive video terminals and retail transaction terminals. Using this technology, customers can order and purchase goods without the aid of a salesperson or cashier.

INTERACTIVE VIDEO TERMINALS   Customers can view selections and place orders in the store with virtually no assistance. An estimated $2 billion to $10 billion of merchandise was ordered through 100,000 interactive terminals by 1990. Advantages include wider selections for customers and smaller inventory requirements for retailers.

In 1987, several hundred companies throughout the United States were using the interactive video terminals, although a leading maker of the terminals claims they are designed to enhance the sales force, not replace it. Retail chains using the terminals include Florsheim, Dayton Hudson, Zales Corp., and Sears Roebuck and Co. Florsheim estimated that the terminals were responsible for sales increases of 15 to 30 percent over previous periods. The company planned to have about 500 terminals, at a cost of $10,000 each, in their stores by the end of 1987 (Selbert, 1987b).

RETAIL TRANSACTION TERMINALS   The concept of in-store electronic shopping may be extended to include retail transaction terminals, tied in to banks and other financial institutions. The terminals, which are similar to automatic teller machines (ATMs), are designed for use with bank cards and ATM-accessed VISA and MasterCards. They allow customers to make withdrawals and balance inquiries from their bank accounts for cash purchases without leaving the store. The process is generally faster than waiting in line for check approval.

Rich's, a 12-unit department store chain based in Atlanta, enhanced its customer service image by installing these terminals for customer convenience. They are located in high-traffic areas near the stores' escalators. Rich's terminals plug in customers to Avail, the Georgia Interchange Network (GIN), which consists of all major financial institutions in the state ("Banking Terminals Enhance Customer Service Image," 1984).

SUMMARY

Advances in technology have had a major impact on how retailers operate their stores and sell their products. Retailing technology can be described in terms of both information technology and operating technology. In the dynamic, competitive environment of retailing, the availability of accurate, timely information is essential in order to maintain a strategic advantage.

The technology of computers, satellites, and other information processing equipment has greatly facilitated this process. Technology can be viewed from the perspective of the retailer or from the perspective of the customer.

Operating technology includes optical scanning devices and sophisticated point-of-sale cash registers or computer terminals. From the retailer's perspective, technology has increased operating efficiencies, and thus profitability, in warehouse operations and the physical movement of inventory through retail stores. Similarly, automatic teller machines at the local banks, TV and computer shopping capability, and other forms of technology have improved retailing operations.

Technology has affected retail managers in each of the functional areas. Merchandise managers have more accurate inventory records and can make better buying decisions due to point-of-sale technology. Planning, accounting, and control functions have been improved with available computer software and information systems technology. Human resources managers use technology in hiring and training personnel. These managers are also responsible for seeing that employees use technology correctly and effectively. Managers responsible for promotion and communication with various retail audiences have a vast array of high-tech tools at their disposal. Digital displays at point-of-purchase, in-store electronic couponing, and telemarketing services are only a few of these tools. Store operations managers benefit from technology in the maintenance of stores, warehouses, and other areas. Technology has also improved the credit and collections function, store security, and crime prevention through a variety of devices.

From the customer's perspective, these innovative retail formats have made it easier for busy consumers to shop, particularly those with money to spend but little time to spend it. Two technological advances have evolved in response to this market. Customers can shop for a wide selection of products and services in their homes by using their TVs or personal computers. TV home shopping networks have become quite prevalent in spite of experiencing mixed degrees of success.

Computer home shopping (videotex) has captured a relatively large audience of generally upscale consumers who buy information and order merchandise via this medium. Computers also enable customers to make purchases in stores and malls without the assistance of sales personnel.

Finally, remember that it is people who make technology work. Those who design the systems, implement the technology, and use it on a daily basis are all responsible for its success or failure—no matter how sophisticated the technology.

Questions for Review and Comprehension

1. Recall your last purchase of clothing from a retail store. Describe the general type and purpose of the technology that the retailer most likely used in making that sale. Would the applications of technology be different if you had made that purchase from a direct mail catalog—or if you bought a meal at a fast-food restaurant? If so, how?

2. Explain the role of point-of-sale terminals, scanner technology, and Universal Product Code in successful inventory management and merchandising operations. Give specific examples. If possible, interview local retailers to learn about their specific applications.

3. Discuss the potential cost savings and other advantages of a POS system. Are there any trade-offs and/or disadvantages to using a POS?

4. Describe the use of electronic data interchange (EDI), Quick Response (QR) technology, and satellite communications in merchandise management, including the advantages of an electronic link between retailer and supplier.

5. Assume that you are considering the purchase of computer software programs to improve the planning, accounting, and control functions in your retail operation. Give an overview of the general types and purposes of programs available.

6. What are some ways that retailers have provided you with better customer service as a result of available technology? In those cases where you received poor service from a retailer, how might technology have been used to improve service quality?

7. Outline the steps that are recommended to make technology work in a retail organization. Include discussion of the "human factor" in making the system work.

8. Give specific examples of the use of technology in promotional activities such as direct marketing, point-of-purchase, telemarketing, in-store couponing, and other promotional tools. Evaluate their effectiveness in motivating customers to make purchases.

9. Explain how both customers and employees can benefit from technology used in the day-to-day physical operations of a store. Do similar benefits apply in a service environment, such as an airport, beauty shop, or restaurant? If so, how?

10. How can the use of technology improve a retailer's credit and collections activities? How can improvement in these areas contribute to better customer relations?

11. Describe several ways that retailers can apply technology in order to reduce shortages and to protect the firm, its customers, and its employees.

12. Profile the typical customer of a television home shopping network. What are the general trends in home shopping networks and computer shopping? What are the environmental factors that contribute to growth in electronic shopping?

References

Abelson, Reed (1989), "Companies to Watch: QVC Network," *Fortune* (July 17), 108.

Achabal, Dale D. and Shelby H. McIntyre (1987), "Information Technology Is Reshaping Retailing," *Journal of Retailing* 63, no. 4 (Winter), 321–325.

"Ad on Wheels Roll into Supermarkets" (1988), *Chain Store Age Executive* 64, no. 9 (September), 49, 51.

Alpert, Mark (1989), "Fortune People," *Fortune* (July 17), 116.

Alsop, Ronald (1988), "But Can It Warn You If Colors Don't Match?" *The Wall Street Journal* (February 9), 33.

"Alternative Media: Great Buys Your Media Mover Probably Won't Tell You About," *PROMO: The International Magazine for Promotion Marketing* (December 1990), 7.

Armstrong, Larry (1990), "Teradata Gets Magic from a Gang of Microchips," *Business Week* (November 26), 124.

"Athlete's Foot Steps on Theft" (1987), *Chain Store Age Executive* (July), 103, 106.

"Auto-Dialing Boosts Total of Collect Calls" (1988), *Chain Store Age Executive* 64, no. 7, (July), 51.

Bamber, Greg J. and Russell D. Lansbury (1988), "Management Strategy and New Technology in Retail Distribution: A Comparative Case Study," *Journal of Management Studies* 23, no. 3, (May), 197–216.

"Banking Terminals Enhance Customer Service Image," (1984), *Chain Store Age Executive* (December), 68.

Bergin, Daniel M. (1990), "Walgreen—Pharmacy Chain of the Year, 1990." *Drug Topics* 134, no. 8, (April 23), 12–16.

Caminiti, Susan (1990), "What the Scanner Knows About You," *Fortune* (December 3), 51–52.

Capon, Noel and Rashi Glazer (1987), "Marketing and Technology: A Strategic Coalignment," *Journal of Marketing* 51 (July), 1–14.

Colacecchi, Mary Beth (1990), "What's Old Is New Again as Fingerhut Buys COMB," *Catalog Age* 7, no. 7, (July), 9, 42.

Coleman, Lynn (1988), "'Smart Card,' Coupon Eater Targeted to Grocery Retailers," *Marketing News* (June 6), 1–2.

CompuServe (1988). *The Electronic Mall.* Columbus, Ohio.

Dauphinais, G. William (1984), "Inventory Control for Retailers," *PC Magazine* (August 7), 215, 220–225.

Davis, Jo Ellen and Thane Peterson (1987), "Will Minitel Play Deep in the Heart of Texas?" *Business Week* (October 19), 94.

DeGeorge, Gail (1987a), "Home Shopping Network's Credibility Gap," *Business Week* (October 12), 45–46.

DeGeorge, Gail (1987b), "Viewers Start Tuning out Home Shopping," *Business Week* (March 30), 30.

DeGeorge, Gail (1988), "Home Shopping Tries a Tonic for Its Sickly Stock," *Business Week* (April 25), 110.

DeGeorge, Gail (1989), "Blame the Phone Company: A Strategy Goes on Trial," *Business Week* (June 12), 30.

DeGeorge, Gail, Mary J. Pitzer, and Mark Ivey (1987), "One Home for Two Home Shoppers?" *Business Week* (February 2), 34–35.

"EDI and QR: A Lot More Than Alphabet Soup" (1988), *Chain Store Age Executive* (January), 89.

"Employers Take Firm Stand Against Shrinkage" (1986), *Chain Store Age Executive* (July), 50, 52.

Eskin, Gerald, Mitchell Kriss, and Magid Abraham (1988), "Retail Scanner-Data Problems and How InfoScan Defeats Them," *The Marketer* (November), 1, 3.

"ES and SD Hones POS System" (1987), *Chain Store Age Executive* (September), 80, 82.

"Fast Food Gets Faster with Do-It-Yourself Ordering" (1990), *Southern Illinoisan* (May 22), 4.

"Fast Payback from Quick Response, Study Finds" (1989), *Chain Store Age Executive* (May), 245.

Fisk, Raymond P. and Roxanne Stell (1986), "Teleservices: An Electronic Revolution in Retail Marketing," *Proceedings of the American Marketing Association:* 1986 Educators Conference, Chicago, Ill: American Marketing Association (August), 171.

Freeman, Laurie and Judann Dagnoli, (1988), "Point-of-Purchase Rush Is On," *Advertising Age* (February 8), 47.

Fuchsberg, Gilbert (1990), "Hand-Held Computers Help Field Staff Cut Paper Work and Harvest More Data," *The Wall Street Journal.* (January 30), B1, B6.

Gallagher, Rick (1988), "POS Technology: Scanners "R" Us," *Chain Store Age Executive* 64, no. 3, (March), 95–96.

Gardner, Fred (1984), "Consumers Welcome In-Store Couponing," *Marketing & Media Decisions* 19, no. 13, (October), 78–80, 1409, 146.

Guyon, Janet (1988) "How Grocers May Save on Their Own Shopping," (1988), *The Wall Street Journal* (May 10), 33.

Hagedorn, Ann (1988), "Penney's 'TV Mall' to Make Its Late, Humbled Debut," *The Wall Street Journal* (February 16), 6.

Hammonds, Keith H. (1987), "Suddenly, Videotex Is Finding an Audience," *Business Week* (October 19), 92, 94.

Harrington, Lisa H. (1988a), "Paper Out, Productivity In," *Traffic Management* (May), 53–55.

Harrington, Lisa H. (1988b), "Paperless System Saves Tandy $150,000 Yearly," *Traffic Management* (May), 54.

Harrington, Lisa H. (1988c), "Kodak Sharpens Its Warehouse Image," *Traffic Management* (June), 45–48.

Harris, Catherine, Dean Foust, and Matt Rothman (1987), "An Electronic Pipeline That's Changing the Way America Does Business," *Business Week* (August 3), 80, 82.

Hastings, Deborah (1990), "Check This Out—Turner Tests Supermarket TV," *The Orlando Sentinel* (November 11), D1, D2.

How The Electronic Mall Works, (1987), CompuServ, Columbus, Ohio.

Hume, Scott (1988), "Fast-Food Operators Put More POP in Their Plans," *Advertising Age* (February 8), 47.

Ingram Industries, Inc. (1991), Company literature. Nashville, Tenn.

"Interactive POS Video Yields Instant Results" (1988), *Chain Store Age Executive* (September), 52–53, 55.

"ISDN: The New Telephone Network," (1988), Special Advertising Section, *Fortune* (October 24), 179–210.

Jaworski, Margaret (1988), "To Catch a Thief," *Family Circle* (September 20), 9.

Kelley, Joanne (1991), "Bar Codes Taking Nation by Storm," *The Orlando Sentinel* (February 3), D1, D12.

Kelly, Kevin (1989), "Why Business Is Glued to the Tube," *Business Week* (March 20), 160.

Kesler, Lori (1988), "Catalina Cuts Couponing Clutter," *Advertising Age* (May 9), S-30.

Klokis, Holly (1987), "UKROP's Tests Data Base Marketing Program," *Chain Store Age Executive* 63, no. 9, (September), 73–74, 78.

"K mart Automates Layaways" (1987), *Chain Store Age Executive* (September), 78, 80.

"Lucky Uses High-Tech Kiosks for Advantage" (1988), *Chain Store Age Executive* (September), 57–58.

Main, Jeremy (1988), "Computers of the World, Unite!" *Fortune* (September 26), 114, 116, 118, 122.

Main, Jeremy (1988), "The Winning Organization," *Fortune* (September 26), 51–52.

Mayer, Caroline E. (1990), "High-Tech Shopping," *The Orlando Sentinel* (October 18), H1, H4.

Naisbitt, John (1982), *Megatrends*. New York: Warner Books, Inc.

NCR 7052/STORES System, (1988), National Cash Register Company Literature.

On-line Warehouse Management System (1985), Worldwide Chain Store Systems, Ltd. company brochure.

On-line Purchasing Management System (1985), Worldwide Chain Store Systems, Ltd. company brochure.

"Pay-By-Phone Systems: A Second Look" (1988), *Chain Store Age Executive* 64, no. 7, (July), 52.

Peters, Thomas J. and Robert H. Waterman, Jr. (1982), *In Search of Excellence*. New York: Harper & Row, Publishers, Inc., 17, 193–194.

"Promotion System Marries Video and POS" (1988), *Chain Store Age Executive* (September), 56.

"Retail MIS Field Reflects Technology Trends" (1988), *Chain Store Age Executive* (January), 100.

"Retailers Spending More on MIS Budgets" (1989), *Chain Store Age Executive* (August), 83.

Rosenberg, Larry J. and Elizabeth C. Hirschman (1980), "Retailing Without Stores," *Harvard Business Review* (July-August), 103–112.

Schieder, Jerome (1987), "Strategies and Profitability at Wal-Mart," Presentation, Southern Illinois University, Carbondale, Ill. (April 28).

"Sears: Turning Technology into a Competitive Edge" (1990), *Discount Merchandisers* (January), 24, 821.

Selbert, Roger (1987a), "Forces for Change I Would Watch If I Were A Retailer . . . ," (Presentation), Survival and Growth in Volatile Environments: 1987 Special Topic Symposium, Sponsored by Texas A&M Center for Retailing Studies, Dallas, Tex.: Dallas Market Center, (October 1).

Selbert, Roger (1987b), "Retail By Interactive Video," *FutureScan* Prepared for Leo J. Shapiro & Associates Inc., (September 21), no. 546.

Seldon, W. Lynn, Jr. (1990), "Bar Code Technology Helps Track Florida Tourists," *Marketing News* (November 12), 8–9.

Shern, Stephanie, Robert J. Verdisco, and Murray Forseter (1992), "Ernst & Young's Survey of Retail Loss Prevention Trends," *Chain Store Age Executive* 68, no. 1, 6–13, 16–21, 23–28, 40–45, 52–57.

Shulman, Richard S. (1986a), "Retail Automation Fairy Tales," *Supermarket Business* (January), 11, 13.

Shulman, Richard S. (1986b), " A Mini Computer or PC . . . What's Right for You?" *Supermarket Business* (October), 17–18.

"Software for Retailers Covers Broad Operations Spectrum" (1984), *Chain Store Age Executive* (December), 62, 66, 68.

Southwestern Bell First Quarter Report (1989), Jacksonville, Fla.: Southwestern Bell Corporation, 5.

St. Clair, Jeffrey J. (1988), "Capitalizing on Merchandising and Retailing Trends Through Visual Marketing," (Presentation), Retail Planning Associates, American Collegiate Retailing Association Spring Conference. Columbus, Ohio (April 15).

Steinhagen, Tom (1990), "Space Movement Shapes Up with Planograms," *Marketing News* (November 12), 7.

"Survey Shows Increase in 1989 MIS Budgets" (1988), *Chain Store Age Executive* 64, no. 8, (August), 69–70.

"Taking the High-Tech Approach to Pilferage" (1985), *Chain Store Age Executive* (February), 55–56.

Teinowitz, Ira (1988), "Scanners Bring Retailers into Direct Marketing," *Advertising Age* (February 8), 30.

"Video Vending Machines Spur Add-On Sales" (1987), *Chain Store Age Executive* (September), 89–91.

"Vons Grocery Goes Cashless" (1987), *Chain Store Age Executive* (September), 82–84.

"Wanamaker Approach Keeps Tabs on Loss" (1987), *Chain Store Age Executive* (July), 102–103.

"Working at Home in the Electronic Cottage" (1987), *Megatrends' Foresight* (Winter), 1–4.

Zinn, Laura J. and Antonio N. Fins (1990), "Home Shoppers Keep Tuning In—But Investors Are Turned Off," *Business Week* (October 22), 70, 72.

5.1 PERFUMERY ON PARK, 1991

In January 1991, Anna Currie wonders what strategy she should adopt for Perfumery on Park, Inc. Recent changes in the retail environment presented several opportunities that had not existed only a year earlier. Many of these opportunities were not likely to be available in the future, so it was important that they be taken advantage of while they existed. In a sense, the turmoil in the department store and discount store industries had altered the framework of competition among all retailers.

At the same time, Anna was very conscious of maintaining the strengths Perfumery on Park had developed through the years—product selection, knowledge of the fragrance industry, variety of fragrances, contacts with suppliers, and quality of service. Any result of strategic planning would be rejected if it jeopardized or did not build upon those strengths.

Anna also wondered what effects the predicted recession would have on the perfumery's previously unblemished record of sales increases. The last recession in the United States occurred three years before Perfumery on Park was opened, so Anna had no experience on which to rely. The United States had recently initiated the war against Iraq, whose president, Saddam Hussein, had promised terrorist acts against his opponents. Would the combination of recessionary spending and fear of terrorism discourage people from visiting Central Florida and lead to a decrease in revenues at Perfumery on Park?

HISTORY

Market Niche

Perfumery on Park, Inc. was established in Winter Park, Florida, in May 1984 by Anna and David Currie. Steady increases in sales led to the first profit in 1988, and profits increased in 1990 (see Exhibits 1 and 2). The number of employees had risen to five by 1990 from the original two in 1984. Anna was responsible for all aspects of the boutique's operations, including ordering, personnel, finance, and marketing. David worked at the shop only intermittently, although he maintained its accounting records.

Winter Park is an affluent community adjacent to Orlando, the tourist center of Florida. Winter Park's main street, Park Avenue, was bordered on one side by Central Park and on the other by numerous small boutiques and specialty shops. The ambience of the town was comparable to that of Carmel, California; Palm Beach, Florida; or the Hamptons of Long Island.

Exhibit 1
Perfumery on Park, Inc. Income Statements, 1988–90
($ thousands)

	1990	1989	1988
Sales	$405	$364	$281
Cost of goods sold	241	204	160
Gross margin	163	160	121
Wages	43	27	20
Rent	12	10	10
Advertising	7	17	2
Supplies	12	12	9
Travel	17	3	3
Credit card charges	9	10	7
Shipping	5	5	3
Other expenses	24	37	26
Interest	24	39	36
Total expenses	151	162	116
Income	$12	($2)	

Exhibit 2
Perfumery on Park, Inc. Balance Sheets, 1988–90
($ thousands)

	1990[a]	1989	1988
Assets			
Cash	$2	$10	$2
Inventory	104	102	80
Miscellaneous	0	65	65
Net fixed assets	156	49	49
Total Assets	$262	$226	$196
Liabilities and Equity			
Accounts payable	$3	$14	$3
Sales tax payable	7	7	5
Payroll tax payable	2	2	2
Short-term loan	34	34	12
Long-term loan	260	143	167
Total Liabilities	306	199	189
Equity	– 44	27	7
Total L & E	$262	$226	$196

[a]Reflects reclassification of second mortgage as loan to business and adjustments due to dissolution of subsidiary, Perfumery on the Avenue, Inc.

Perfumery on Park had carved a market niche by specializing in classic fragrances and fragrances from smaller houses or less-famous designers. Personnel at department stores in the Central Florida area referred customers to the Perfumery. In return, the staff of the Perfumery referred to department stores customers who requested fragrances from heavily advertised, national launches. The Perfumery's variety of fragrances was considered unsurpassed by U.S. standards, where most fragrance marketing was through department stores. Of more than 400 fragrances on the international market in 1990, Perfumery on Park carried almost 200. Because most department stores carried perhaps 15 to 20 fragrances that tended to be in fashion at the time, a niche existed for a shop that specialized in traditional and hard-to-find fragrances.

The success at carving a niche in the competitive fragrance market caused a steady growth in sales at rates that exceeded growth in the fragrance industry generally. Over the past six years the perfume market had grown at a rate of four to five percent annually in real terms; sales at Perfumery on Park had grown at a rate of 10 to 12 percent. Price increases had averaged five percent per year since 1984 because of inflation in the United States and the decline in the value of the dollar relative to the French franc.

Emphasis on Service

Anna's strong belief in service to customers took many aspects. An important aspect was maintenance of a fragrance once the decision was made to carry it. With an average of more than 30 fragrance launches each year in the United States turnover of fragrances was constant as the different fragrances experienced their life cycles. Once Anna decided to carry a fragrance, the fragrance was maintained until it was no longer manufactured. Maintaining a fragrance also meant stocking whatever stock keeping units (SKUs) were available: perfumes, eaux de toilette, and body products such as dusting powder, lotion, and bath gel. The decision to carry a fragrance thus implied a significant investment in inventory.

Frequently, the U.S. distributor of a fragrance changed, resulting in the product's unavailability for a period of months. Locating the new distributor required considerable effort, but meeting the needs of clients required that such information be obtained. If the Perfumery did not have an item in stock and no American distributor could be found, the item was special-ordered from France. As a courtesy to her customers, Anna also special-ordered other fragrances for which an established U.S. market did not exist.

Great care was taken in educating the staff about all aspects of the fragrance industry—ingredients, manufacturers and couturiers, procedures for applying fragrances, and availability of new and classic fragrances. The staff was expected to know about all the fragrances carried at the Perfumery, whereas the staff at a department store typically specialized in the lines of one designer or manufacturer such as Christian Dior or Yves Saint-Laurent. The Perfumery received referrals throughout the United States of customers trying to locate a fragrance they had worn for years but was no longer carried in their local market.

Aspects of merchandising played a key role in satisfying customers. Gift wrapping was complementary, samples were provided as a means of testing alternative fragrances, and shopping bags were decorated with ribbons. Customers who visited the shop more than once were greeted by name, although the usual joke was that the staff recognized customers by fragrance rather than by name. Whenever possible, a file was maintained for the customer or spouse so the current fragrance favorite would be known to whomever was shopping for that individual.

CHANGES IN THE FRAGRANCE INDUSTRY

Turmoil in Department Stores

Sales through boutiques such as Perfumery on Park accounted for more than 90 percent of the sales of perfumes in France. In the United States, however, the usual channel of distribution was through department stores, which accounted for more than 98 percent of domestic sales. The domestic department store industry was in turmoil in 1990. The two major department store chains, Allied and Federated, had been purchased during the 1980s by Robert Campeau, a Canadian developer. Campeau had leveraged the purchase to such an extent that he was unable to service the debt, forcing him to file for protection for the Allied and Federated chains under U.S. bankruptcy statutes in January 1990. Included in the bankruptcy was the store considered the bellwether of perfumes in America, Bloomingdale's. Campeau's financial difficulties continued into 1990: according to an article in *Women's Wear Daily*, Federated stores reported a loss of $17.7 million in May 1990; Allied's loss for the same period was $9.2 million.

In Central Florida, most of Perfumery on Park's major competitors were members of the Allied or Federated chains. Jordan Marsh, Burdine's, and Maas Bros. experienced the effects of Campeau's cash flow problems—constant discounting in an effort to move merchandise to generate cash, product shortages as ordering was curtailed to conserve

continued

cash, and customer dissatisfaction with untrained personnel at understaffed stores.

The turmoil was not limited to Allied and Federated stores. Some of the major names in U.S. retailing—B. Altman, Bonwit-Teller, and R. H. Macy—failed or experienced difficulty during the period. It was widely thought that consolidation would take place in the department store industry nationally, although it was not certain which stores would survive. Two surviving national chains had recently acquired local stores: Maison-Blanche acquired Robinson's, and Dillard's acquired Ivey's, which had been at the Winter Park Mall for almost thirty years.

Emergence of Perfume Boutiques

Although Perfumery on Park was the only perfume boutique in the Central Florida area, it was typical of a national trend toward specialty retailing. Two chains had opened several perfume or cosmetic boutiques in South Florida malls, and a German-based chain, Perfumery Douglas, was beginning to penetrate the U.S. market through New York and Washington.

As at the Perfumery, these boutiques offered a wider variety of fragrances and cosmetics than were available at most department stores. They did not account for a significant portion of industry sales as of 1990, but many industry experts predicted they would be the wave of the future. No one was certain how much inroad these boutiques would make into the department stores' 98 percent share of the market for fragrances and cosmetics in the United States.

Diverters

Rights to sell French fragrances in the United States are purchased by a company that is authorized as the sole agent in the United States. In most cases the agent in turn sells fragrances through authorized retail outlets such as department stores or specialty shops such as Perfumery on Park.

Occasionally, a discount store such as K mart or Service Merchandise will obtain a fragrance that it sells at a discount from the authorized distributor's suggested retail price. Other firms specialize in wholesaling selected fragrances at prices lower than those suggested by the authorized distributor. These products sold outside the purview of the authorized distributor are called diverted (or gray market) goods, and the source of supply for diverters is the subject of conjecture.

In most cases, diverters offer only a limited variety of products—100 ml. eau de toilette sprays, for example—rather than the complete line. The product is available intermittently, but may be in large quantities when it is available. The products frequently are old, resulting from distributor closeouts or repackaging.

Although authorized distributors and retailers might view these gray market goods as prohibited by the distribution contract and hence illegal, the Supreme Court of the United States upheld the right of discounters to obtain and sell diverted goods in 1988 in a suit involving K mart, Inc.

Approaches by Sales Representatives

Because of the turmoil in department stores and the apparent increasing acceptance of specialty boutiques in general or Perfumery on Park in particular, Anna had been approached by sales representatives of several companies who previously had refused to sell to her. Although some companies apparently maintained their policy of distributing only through department stores, that number was fewer after Christmas 1989 than it was before. Many sales reps complained that department stores had reduced Christmas purchases, which meant a decrease in commission income to the sales reps. This observation was reinforced by the emergence of the local Belk's, a department store that had previously carried few major fragrances because many companies thought of Belk's as a less prestigious outlet.

Anna did not want to pass up the opportunity to carry other prestigious lines, so she began to invest in them throughout 1990. Due to her policy of carrying complete lines, the addition of these new fragrances meant increased investment in inventory. Anna felt this was worthwhile because she viewed this as a chance to penetrate markets that might not be penetrated under other circumstances.

STRATEGIC OPPORTUNITIES

In January 1991 Anna Currie is considering several alternative strategies for Perfumery on Park. She had already responded to one opportunity by expanding the selection of fragrances in response to invitations from sales representatives. Other strategies related to alternative means of growth for the Perfumery. Because of the Curries' limited financial resources and the modest profits already generated by Perfumery on Park, any strategy was constrained by lack of financing. In fact, any of the strategies under consideration were irrelevant as long as funding was not available.

Mail Order Sales

Anna had experimented with mail order sales over the past three or four years. She prepared a catalog listing the shop's fragrances according to a system prepared by Haarman und Reimer, a German chemical firm. The catalog was distributed to customers who visited the shop and was mailed to visitors who had filled out registration forms. She also received unsolicited requests for catalogs throughout the United States.

The first catalog was printed on glossy, heavy-weight paper and featured pictures of perfume bottles for most of the fragrances. Because that catalog was so expensive to produce, a new catalog was prepared when supplies of the original ran out. The second catalog was printed on comparable paper but did not contain pictures of fragrances. Despite the savings, the current catalog cost approximately $1.50 per copy to produce. The only way to reduce the cost per copy was to print the catalog on lower-quality paper, which Anna thought would decrease the image she was trying to convey.

Catalog sales were attractive because they provided an opportunity to increase sales without adding to the current size of the shop. Depending on the volume of sales obtained, it would be possible to receive orders, package products, and mail shipments with the existing staff. Of course, if the response to mail orders was overwhelming, it would be necessary not only to add additional staff but to increase the level of inventory and shift mail operations to an alternative location. Until she had some experience with mass mailings, Anna would not know whether she needed to address those issues.

Growth of the catalog industry had been a nationwide phenomenon during the 1980s, but by 1990 there was evidence that the market had become saturated. By 1984, for example, more than 6,500 catalog marketers sent approximately 8.5 billion catalogs to American households. The proportion of consumers who purchased at least one item through a catalog had stabilized since 1984 at about 50 percent.

National studies have shown that developing a catalog operation from concept to breakeven requires approximately $1.5 million over five years. At least 100,000 catalogs must be mailed in the first year for a nationwide effort. Response rates vary from one percent in the first year to the six percent necessary for breakeven in the fifth year, provided the catalog has a unique concept. Through time the mailing list is refined by emphasizing those customers who are repeat purchasers. The industry average is $90 per order. Customers could be targeted by income level, geographic area, age, or other demographic characteristics.

Anna thought the shop's typical customer earned an above average income, was female and well-educated, and worked in an executive or professional capacity. Florida was the state most frequently represented in the shop's registration forms, but Georgia, North Carolina, and Ohio were listed numerous

times. Anna thought she could reduce the cost of introduction somewhat because she would not add to the staff at the shop, but that savings was likely to be offset by the catalog's higher cost of production.

Expand the Existing Shop

For several years Anna had considered expanding the existing shop, either by acquiring the space adjacent to the Perfumery or by moving into a larger location along Park Avenue. She would use the additional space to expand the variety of products and to build an office at which she could work. Besides carrying additional fragrances, Anna wanted to expand the lines of cosmetics she carried. Cosmetics represented repeat business that would reduce somewhat the seasonal and cyclical fluctuations in sales.

Expanding the shop would entail two major costs: the cost of acquiring the space from the current leaseholder and the cost of remodeling the space and installing new fixtures. She discussed the possibility of acquiring the adjacent space from its leaseholder, who asked $10,000 for approximately 300 square feet; that would bring the size of the Perfumery to 600 square feet. A larger space of approximately 1,000 square feet owned by the same landlord was vacant a few doors down the street. If she acquired that space she would not have to buy out an existing lease, but she would have to move the contents from the existing location. Installing new fixtures at either location would cost about $50,000 and she would have to invest $30,000 in additional inventory.

Anna also considered opening a treatment center to provide facials and body toning, but that line of business would subject her to state regulation that she did not encounter as a retailer. If she expanded into treatment she should have to purchase specialized equipment and hire qualified staff, both of which were outside Anna's expertise in fragrances and cosmetics. She had not yet investigated the treatment center alternative to the point of developing cost estimates or market studies.

Clouding the issue of expansion was the question of whether Park Avenue was the appropriate location for expansion to take place. Parking was more constrained than at a regional mall, which limited exposure and access. Although the ambience of Park Avenue was still attractive, recently national chain stores such as Benetton, Banana Republic, and The Limited had replaced many of the locally owned shops, giving the street the image of an outdoor mall. Many retailers worried that there was nothing special to differentiate Park Avenue from a typical mall.

continued

Add More Stores

If perfume boutiques were increasing in importance as channels of distribution, it might be better to expand the number of locations than to increase the size of the existing location. Central Florida had several regional malls and numerous shopping areas oriented to the many tourists that visited attractions such as Disney World, Sea World, and Universal Studios. The opportunity for profit was much greater at these locations because of the increased exposure, but Anna had learned that profit was not the only consideration in operating additional stores.

For four years Anna had owned another perfume boutique in Naples, Florida, a five-hour drive from Winter Park. The second shop involved monthly visits to Naples to monitor the performance of the shop, problems in dealing with employees and the manager, and trauma when the shop was robbed one weekend before Christmas. Closing the shop was an expensive lesson, but it relieved the strain of being a long-distance manager. Anna was not anxious to duplicate that experience.

Opening other shops locally might not require extensive travel, but it would involve other, more subtle issues. For example, Perfumery on Park was open Monday through Saturday at hours Anna could set; opening at a mall would require being open every day at hours determined by mall management. Anna could decorate Perfumery on Park any way she wanted; in a mall she would be restricted by their guidelines and would have to participate in their promotions. Finding a manager and employees for another store would increase the proportion of time Anna spent on personnel issues. Anna wondered whether it was worthwhile growing a business if it meant less time doing the things she enjoyed.

Predicting sales at a mall location was impossible, but Anna thought they would be triple the level of Winter Park. Expenses would also increase: rent and mall fees would be 8 percent of sales, salaries could be as much as $100,000 depending on the number of employees, and expenses other than cost of merchandise could be up to 15 percent of sales. She would plan on cost of merchandise at 50 percent of sales. Up front costs to furnish the space and provide a beginning inventory would be about $100,000.

Develop Her Own Fragrance

Almost since she opened Perfumery on Park, Anna was fascinated with the idea of creating her own fragrance. The fascination was heightened by the success of Giorgio, which had risen from a fragrance at a boutique on Rodeo Drive in Beverly Hills, California, to a major national launch during the mid 1980s. Anna thought a private fragrance would promote an identity with the shop as well as lead to a source of additional revenues. She had contacted representatives from a major fragrance manufacturer, who were more than anxious to help her by creating a fragrance to her specifications.

Just as evidence indicated a saturation in the catalog market, evidence pointed to saturation in the fragrance market. New launches in the United States numbered more than 30 per year over the past several years, creating confusion in the industry. Besides traditional sources of new fragrances—perfume houses and designers—new fragrances were introduced under the names of actors, actresses, singers, dancers, and other celebrities. Almost all of these introductions had short life cycles, although sales could be very high during the peak period. Launching these fragrances nationally was very expensive; trade journals reported that Calvin Klein spent more than $17 million in advertising to launch Obsession.

Although it was not necessary to undergo a national launch just to have a private fragrance, creating her own fragrance would not be costless. Selecting the right fragrance would require time and patience during negotiations with the manufacturer, who had an incentive to minimize the time spent on development. Once the fragrance was selected, it would have to be purchased in bulk quantities that seemed far in excess of what Anna could expect to sell. The real costs of producing a fragrance would be packaging, which included the bottle and the box, as well as distribution if the fragrance was sold at locations other than Perfumery on Park. Bottles were available in standard designs from glass manufacturers, but few of these designs were distinctive. Box designing and printing was a job for professionals, with whom Anna had little contact. Anna knew that commissions paid to sales reps amounted to perhaps 30 percent of the wholesale price of the product.

Anna had not pursued the alternative of producing her own fragrance beyond the point of trying several samples from the manufacturer, but she was ready to proceed with her investigation. Two events gave her conflicting impressions about the chance for success. A sales rep from one of the major companies had developed her own fragrance two years earlier and it appeared to be successful. It had been carried at the Perfumery and at several department stores in the area. However, when Anna attempted to reorder following the Christmas season the product was no longer available, indicating that the launch ultimately had failed. On the other hand, a visitor to the shop recently indicated that he was retired from the business of fragrance manufacturing but maintained enough contacts in the business that he could help Anna reduce the costs of manufacturing and packaging. Of course, Anna had not proceeded far enough to consider how or whether she would market a fragrance beyond the shop.

THE DECISION

Faced with these alternatives, Anna wanted to decide on an appropriate strategy for Perfumery on Park. She was very interested in spending more time on long-range planning and devoting less time to the day-to-day operation of the boutique. Business had increased to the point where she could hire others to operate the business, but she wanted to make sure the boutique continued to expand (See Exhibit 3).

Whatever strategy she chose, it would involve additional financing. The Curries had invested as much of their own money as they could and looked forward to the time after the bank loan was retired so they could draw more from the boutique. Of course, if the recession caused drastic decreases in sales, strategic planning might be irrelevant.

Perfumery on Park, 1991 is drawn from an actual situation confronting the manager of a small retail boutique in Winter Park, Florida. After seven years of operation, the owner must plan the perfumery's strategy. The planning process is couched within an environment somewhat complicated by changes in the domestic retail industry wrought by failures of major department stores, by uncertainty due to a domestic recession and the war with Iraq and by the perfumery's particular market niche. There is enough information in the case to discuss strategy, although there may not be enough detail to discuss financial feasibility or implications of alternatives.

Exhibit 3
Perfumery on Park, Inc. Transactions, 1988–90

	1990	1989	1988
Number of transactions	8,220	8,050	7,081
Total revenue	$404,600	$363,800	$280,500
Average sale	$49.22	$45.20	$39.62

SUGGESTED STUDY QUESTIONS

1. How do you evaluate the first seven years' performance of Perfumery on Park? According to what criteria could it be considered successful or unsuccessful?
2. Evaluate the Perfumery's strategic alternatives according to the functions characteristic of retailing.
3. What advantages does a small competitor such as Perfumery on Park have over larger competitors such as Bloomingdale's? What disadvantages?
4. What risks face Perfumery on Park? Are the risks opportunities or are they threats to continued operation?
5. What should Anna Currie do?

This case was prepared by David M. Currie, Ph.D., Associate Professor of Economics and Finance, Roy E. Crummer Graduate School of Business, Rollins College, Winter Park, Florida.

International Retailing

Part VI

GLOBAL ASPECTS OF RETAILING

CHAPTER Eighteen

Learning Objectives

*After studying this chapter, the
student will be able to:*

1. Understand the scope of
retailing within a worldwide
context.
2. Give examples of international strategies pursued by
U.S. retailers abroad.
3. Describe the rationale for
U.S. retailers entering foreign
markets.
4. Describe the rationale and
strategies of foreign investors
in U.S. retailing.
5. Identify major foreign firms
involved in U.S. retailing.
6. Discuss the types of retail
influences transferred from one
country to another in terms of
import/export, operating formats, promotional methods,
and technology.
7. Give an overview of the
international market entry procedure and types of decisions
to be made.

RETAILING IN A GLOBAL MARKETPLACE

Retailers outside the U.S. have been global retailers for some time. American retailers are only recently becoming confident enough to capitalize on opportunities outside their own country. Nearly every retailer buys from a supplier outside the country and most face competition from foreign competitors. High debt levels have caused more companies to turn to international markets to secure capital. To quote Lou Grabowsky:

> Changing the way you think about the world in which you compete is the first step toward thriving in the 1990s."

The Tokyo Dome Corporation maintains three bowling centers in the Tokyo metropolitan area.

Positive trends evolving from globalization include the international flow of ideas, global networking, Europe 1992, and opening up of Japan. The flow of ideas has resulted in the adoption of retail concepts once viewed as uniquely foreign by American retailers. For example, the home furnishings market was revitalized by European concepts such as leather furnishings and knock-down furniture. Global networking has been facilitated by telemarketing on both sides of the Atlantic, using techniques such as toll-free international 800 telephone numbers. Europe 1992 will have a major impact on U.S. retailers, although no one is exactly sure what to expect. American firms will find opportunities for expansion in Europe, but strong competition will also come from the Europeans. Japan has attracted

many U.S. retailers, but it is not an easy market to enter—or stay in. However, Japanese consumers are greatly influenced by American style and culture in their purchases.

Advice for global managers can be summed up in the following points:

- The successful manager is risk oriented and welcomes the challenges of the international marketplace.
- Know yourself and your company. Self-appraisal is the first step in building a base of knowledge to provide a strategic inventory of the value of your company.
- Know your competition. Competition today means more than just a matter of attracting the same customer as another retailer. Today the term encompasses competition for capital, for new ideas, and for suppliers—throughout the world.
- Know your customers and think creatively about them so they will keep

coming back. This means having a clearly defined mission, and using today's technology-generated data to give better customer service.
- Find allies with common ground—through entering into partnerships or strategic alliances.
- By the mid-1990s, successful retailers will need a structure that permits quick response to changes in the market. Scanner systems and other technology provide a competitive edge. Managers also need to be "nimble-minded."
- Commitment (from the top down) is the watchword for the 90s. This is a commitment to thinking about the world as a whole.

Adapted from Grabowsky, Lou (1989), "Globalization: Reshaping the Retail Marketplace," *Retailing Issues Letter*. College Station, Tex. Arthur Andersen & Co. in conjunction with the Center for Retailing Studies, Texas A&M University, 2, no. 4 (November), 1–5.

International Aspects of Retailing

Foreign Retail Expansion: An Overview

"Toys "R" Us Goes Overseas—and Finds That Toys 'R' Them, Too." (Maremont, Yang, and Dunkin, 1987); "'Aussie Mania' Sweeps the U.S.: Consumers Drawn to Mystique of Land Down Under" (Agnew, 1987); "U.S. Movie Theaters Making Soviet Debut" ("U.S. Movie . . .," 1990); "Avon Knocking on China's Doors" (Reese, 1990). "McDonald's in Moscow . . . ;" such media headlines quickly make the point that a retailer is not confined to its country of origin, nor is its retailing mix immune to international influences. In their efforts to improve profitability, many businesses have turned to the international arena for solutions.

By definition, an international retailing strategy involves operating outside national boundaries, whether opening stores in other countries, or importing merchandise to sell in domestic stores. The overriding objective is to find profitable opportunities beyond those available domestically. Although international expansion strategies are not new to retailers, a worldwide perspective has become more predominant due to the internationalization of media, the increased mobility and sophistication of customers, and the need for profitable new markets. Exhibit 18–1 shows the relationship between the domestic retail environment and worldwide environment and the need for information from more distant sources.

Types of Retailers in International Markets

Essentially, no one particular type of retailer ventures into international markets. Any retailer with sufficient resources, an operating format that will be accepted by customers (and the government) in another country, and management's commitment to foreign expansion may enter these markets. In a broad sense, international retailers may be categorized as either global or multinational (Ody, 1989). A **global retailer** generally operates as a worldwide, integrated system that targets the same type of customers in each country with essentially the same offer. Global retailers tend to have merchandise that is classic or "fashionably classic," unique, and their own private label merchandise. Many, like Benetton, Ikea, Laura Ashley, and Habitat/Conran, are vertically integrated so they can control their own production and design resources. Toys "R" Us is another example of a global retailer, with distinctively uniform store designs, down to the parking lot and cash registers, and nearly identical product assortments, as well as movement toward a worldwide pricing policy with common price points in all outlets. A Toys "R" Us executive observed that consumers are becoming more similar globally, and that "There are 50 million kids in Europe, and they have converging lifestyles in music, designer labels, and Big Macs."

On the other hand, **multinational retailers** are those who adapt their concept, format, and ambience by developing individual strategies to suit local retail needs. Local management is given considerable control over pricing, product mix, and merchandising. The French hypermarket is a typical example of multinational retailing. The concept spread to Spain, Italy, Brazil

GLOBAL RETAILER
operates worldwide targeting the same type of customers in each country

MULTINATIONAL RETAILER
adapts its concept format and ambience to local retail needs

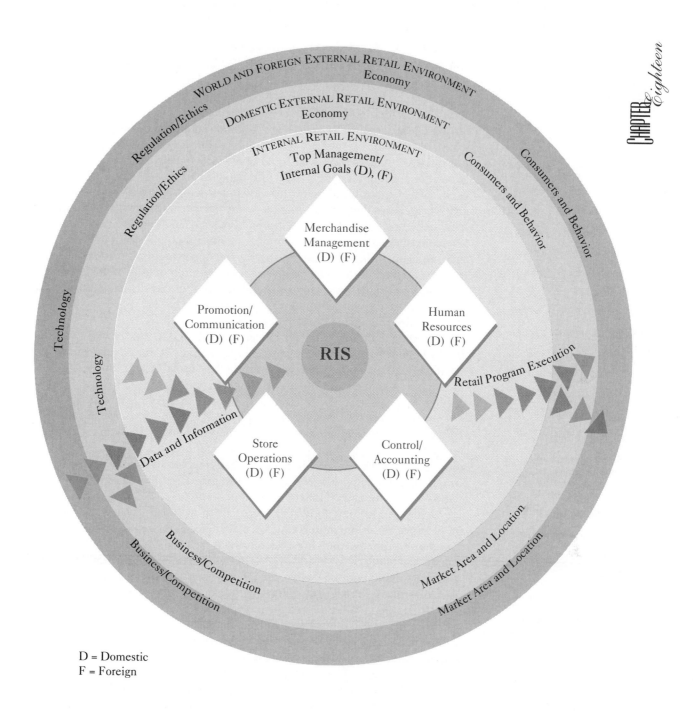

Exhibit 18–1
Retailing in a Global
Environment
· ·

SOURCE: Anderson and Parker, 1988.

D = Domestic
F = Foreign

and the United Kingdom in the 1970s, and to the United States, although not as successfully. In each case, operations have tended to be decentralized and have been adapted to local tastes.

International retailers may vary according to type of store and ownership, management style, corporate objectives, strategy mix, and other dimensions. Formal classification schemes, based on some of these differences, have been developed for statistical analysis and for studying the various types of retail institutions. U.S. retail classifications were described in Chapter 4. For purposes such as income tax reporting and the gathering of statistical data, domestic retail store classifications follow the Standard Industrial Code listing: chains, franchising, hardware stores, general merchandise, department stores, hypermarkets, discount stores, catalog showrooms, food stores, grocery stores, supermarket chains, convenience stores, and warehouse stores.

Basically, the same broad types of retailers are found throughout the world, but may be categorized differently for the reporting of statistical data. For example, the *International Marketing Handbook* (1985) describes eight general types of retail outlets. The four major retail classifications generally used, such as those listed below for the United Kingdom, are (1) **retail cooperative societies,** which are voluntary nonprofit organizations engaged in retail trade and controlled by their members, who are also their customers; (2) **department stores** operated under one roof, generally separately managed, and containing a number of specialized departments; (3) **multiple traders,** not including cooperative societies, with ten or more branches that concentrate on a narrower range of standardized merchandise than department stores; and (4) **independent retail stores,** privately owned, including small multiple stores with less than ten branches.

The remaining four retail classifications included in the *International Marketing Handbook* are supermarkets, discount houses, automatic vending machines, and mail order sales. Classification systems such as the eight named here provide a useful basis for forecasting, assessing competition, and developing retail strategy within a common statistical base across international boundaries (*International Marketing Handbook*, 1985).

Another classification scheme, developed by Stanley Hollander, provides a useful overview of multinational retailers in familiar terms. The five categories are (1) dealers in luxury goods, (2) general merchandise dealers, (3) trading companies, (4) specialized chains, and (5) direct selling and automatic vending retailers (Hollander, 1970).

Dealers in luxury goods deal primarily in merchandise such as jewelry, art, or antiques, although that which is considered "luxurious" may be determined by culture, custom, lifestyle, or other variables. Multinational jewelers include Van Cleef & Arpels, Harry Winston, both of New York, and H. Stern of Brazil. Art and antique dealers include Christie's, Sotheby's, and others.

General merchandise dealers include department, variety and discount stores, and mail-order retailers. Department stores were one of the first multinational forms of retailing. Organizational and operating ideas flowed easily across international boundaries in the early stages of development. Sears, Roebuck was probably the first successful international department store operator in the United States, stepping up its internationalization program after World War II. Sears' acquisitions included British stores. Later, chains such as Belk and Federated expanded to other countries.

Multinational retailers who operate variety and discount stores include Woolworth and K mart. This form of retailing, which evolved from the first classic limited price "5 & 10" stores, has exported easily to other countries, perhaps because of its appeal to economical shoppers.

Location is not as important to mail order retailers as it is to those selling to customers in their stores. This has led to two kinds of international mail order retailing: exporting from the parent country to another country and conducting a mail order business through the acquisition of foreign sub-

RETAIL COOPERATIVE SOCIETIES

(United Kingdom) voluntary nonprofit retail organizations controlled by their members

DEPARTMENT STORES

(United Kingdom) number of specialized departments operating under one roof

MULTIPLE TRADER

(United Kingdom) retailer with ten or more branches concentrating on standardized merchandise

INDEPENDENT RETAIL STORES

(United Kingdom) privately owned with less than ten branches

DEALERS IN LUXURY GOODS

retail stores handling primarily jewelry, art, or antiques, items considered "luxurious"

GENERAL MERCHANDISE DEALERS

department stores, variety and discount stores, and mail-order retailers

A family-owned business in India produces hand-crafted ornamental doors and other ornamental wood products for J.C. Penney.

sidiaries, associates, or facilities. Harrod's of London, Sears, Roebuck, and others operate mail order businesses by exporting merchandise. Sears, Time-Life International, Readers' Digest Books, and Evelyn Wood Reading Dynamics sell through international subsidiaries or associates.

Trading companies are typically a phenomenon of developing countries. However, trading companies and their environments tend to evolve over time into more sophisticated retailing in well-developed cities. (Hudson's) Bay Company, one of the best known multinational trading companies, still remains a major fur buyer and an oil company, but retailing has gained dominance over other aspects of its business over the years.

The most prevalent types of **specialized chains** include those devoted to food and supermarkets, clothing and related items, and shoes. International food retailing chains were formed at the turn of the century with Thomas Lipton being one of the early pioneers. The Unilever Company, A&P, and Safeway have substantial international food retailing operations.

Clothing retailers crossing national boundaries have had mixed results. Successful overseas ventures by American retailers include Lerner Shops and Hart Schaffner & Marx. Many clothiers are also manufacturers in the countries they have entered. Multinational shoe retailers have also found success. Bata, Ltd., had stores in 83 countries by 1970, and others such as Morse, Genesco, and Kinney have expanded overseas.

Other specialists can be found in a variety of merchandise and service categories. Some examples of these merchandise specialists include Gamble-Skogmo's Canadian hardware and household appliance stores; Firestone, Dunlop, Goodyear, and Goodrich tire stores; Walgreen Drug Company; and

TRADING COMPANIES
retailers who trade merchandise for other goods, typically evolve into more sophisticated types of retailing

SPECIALIZED CHAINS
chains devoted to particular category of merchandise items

Singer Sewing Machine Co. The distribution strength of multinational retailers is illustrated by the 1989 acquisition of Singer Sewing Machine Corporation by Semi-Tech Microelectronics (Far East). Semi-Tech acquired Singer with plans to expand and sell its high-technology products through Singer's distribution and retail operations (Selwyn, 1990). In another specialty acquisition, American Greetings acquired W. H. Smith Canada, Ltd., cardstore division.

Restaurants and hotels tend to dominate the multinational service trades, i.e., those services that are focused on international travelers. Consumer loan services, like those provided by Beneficial and Household Finance, have formed subsidiaries in other countries.

Direct selling and automatic vending retailers are the final category described by Hollander. Many countries, particularly in Europe, have welcomed automatic vending machines. American firms include ABC Consolidated Corporation and Canteen Corporation, who achieved early success through subsidiaries and franchises, rather than through direct ownership and sales. Direct selling is a form of nonstore retailing that has been exported successfully by companies like Singer, Fuller Brush Co., Rexall Drug Company (Dart Industries, Inc.), Sarah Coventry, and Encyclopedia Britannica.

Viewpoints on International Retailing

The preceding discussion has provided a general overview of the involvement of all types of retailers in foreign markets. No matter how the retailers are officially classified, the key to international expansion is acceptance by customers in another country, leading to sufficient return on investment to the retailer to make the venture worthwhile. The international aspects of retailing are discussed from several viewpoints in the remainder of this chapter: (1) U.S. retailers opening stores abroad, (2) foreign retailers entering markets in the U.S. and elsewhere, (3) international influences on merchandise mix decisions, and (4) international market entry procedure and decisions.

U.S. Retailers Abroad

Rationale for Overseas Expansion by U.S. Retailers

Both U.S. business firms and the U.S. government have pursued international market strategies for several reasons. Saturated domestic markets and competitive threats from foreign investors in the United States have caused businesses to seek expansion elsewhere in order to survive. International markets may offer additional or alternative opportunities to those offered in the United States (Jain, 1985).

Large U.S. corporations accelerated their development of international growth strategies after World War II. The Marshall Plan and other U.S. foreign aid programs to assist in the reconstruction of war-torn countries stimulated overseas investment by manufacturers. As these American firms expanded into foreign countries, they took financial, accounting, and marketing firms with them to facilitate their businesses. Subsequently, retailers entered overseas markets.

DIRECT SELLING AND AUTOMATIC VENDING
category of retailers involved in nonstore retailing

Nearly three-fourths of all U.S. overseas investments are in developed countries. However, many companies have realized a higher return on investment from ventures in less-developed countries (LDCs). For example, LDCs provided about 40 percent of international income in 1981 with less than 30 percent of the total international investments (Jain, 1985). U.S. retailers have concentrated expansion efforts on countries with developed economies; however, some developing nations have become attractive markets.

The impetus for American retailers to enter international markets may come from direct efforts of foreign governments to attract U.S. investments or from the example of other types of American firms with successful operations in those countries. The Soviet Union and China have made recent overtures to American businesses to increase trade between the nations. While the initial thrust tends to be toward industrial firms, retailers of products and services generally are not far behind.

Trade reforms were under way in the former Soviet Union to improve foreign trade activity. While the reforms primarily were intended to boost Soviet exports and to encourage multinational joint-ventures, the long-range effect was expected to include the importing and exporting of merchandise to be sold in retail stores ("USSR: New Thinking . . . ," 1987; Zabijaka, 1987). McDonald's opened a store in Moscow in January 1990 where it is serving "Bolshoi Maks" (literal translation for Big Macs) to Russian customers (Melloan, 1990). This move is expected to be just the beginning of the opening of foreign-owned retail stores in Russia.

China is in the midst of a consumer revolution, with an increasing number of foreign consumer goods companies making inroads into the world's largest market of one billion consumers. Chinese retail consumers are brand conscious and consider imports, such as Pepsi, Coke, and Lever Bros. brands to be fashionable (Shao, 1988). The Chinese market may be larger and more lucrative by 1997, when the British 99-year lease on Hong Kong's New Territories expires, and control of this territory reverts to Mainland China. American investments in Hong Kong manufacturing industries by 1989 totaled $6 billion (U.S.), with more being invested in real estate and service industries. U.S. service retailers in Hong Kong include Hilton, Hyatt, and Marriott. Under terms of the agreement, Hong Kong's social and economic systems will remain unchanged until 2047, thus maintaining a favorable business environment to attract American retailers (Long, 1989).

Who Are the U.S. Retailers Abroad?

A diverse group of U.S. companies has expanded into overseas markets. Major retailers such as Sears, Roebuck and Company, J. C. Penney, F. W. Woolworth Company, Safeway, and K mart have found growth opportunities in other countries. U.S. companies with foreign retail operations also include a number of manufacturing and service organizations who have been active in other countries for many decades. These retail enterprises include companies such as Singer, Avon, Consolidated Foods, and Dart Industries (now Dart & Kraft), tire companies such as Firestone, Goodyear, and Goodrich, beauty parlor operators like Glemby Corporation and Seligman & Latz, oil companies like Mobil and Exxon, hotel chains like Holiday Inn, and travel agents like American Express (Kacker, 1985).

While it is beyond the scope of this chapter to profile all U.S. retailers who have international operations, the expansion activity of some of the better known retailers is presented to give some idea of the impact of U.S. retailers overseas.

Sears, Roebuck and Company has followed an international expansion strategy with its department stores and financial services, starting in 1942 with the opening of a store in Havana, Cuba (since closed). Sears has used several strategies to enter other countries: direct entry, joint venture, acquisition, and subsidiaries. In 1982 Sears World Trade Inc. was formed as a subsidiary involved in import, export, and other trade support services including management, technological, and financial services to U.S. and foreign companies planning to enter foreign markets. In 1983 another trading company, Sears World Trade Japan was formed for the purpose of import and export of goods and services, to finance transactions, and to handle third nation deals.

J. C. Penney acquired the Belgian Sarma Company, the third largest retailer in Belgium, in 1969. The stores sell food, general merchandise, and apparel. Belgian operations also included sales to 188 franchised stores. In 1982 this amounted to $312 million, with food sales contributing about sixty percent of Sarma-Penney's sales. In 1979, Penney experimented with developing and operating Wendy's restaurants in Belgium, Luxembourg, France, and the Netherlands, but closed them in 1982 due to poor operating results. In 1981, Penney entered a ten-year program to realign the Belgian retail business into four groups: department stores, apparel specialty shops, hypermarkets, and franchised food stores, from the traditional food and general merchandise orientation.

F. W. Woolworth, the world's largest variety chain, had 6,927 stores worldwide as of 1982. These included Woolworth, Woolco, J. Brannam, Shirt Closet, Kinney, Richman, Woolworth-Great Britain, and Woolworth-Mexico stores. Although some of these, such as J. Brannam and many Woolco stores have been closed, the company expanded to a total of 7,739 (6,027 specialty and 1,712 general merchandise) stores by January 1989.

Woolworth entered its first international market in 1907 with a "three and sixes" store in Canada, later expanding to Germany, United Kingdom, Ireland, the Caribbean, Mexico, and Puerto Rico. With the fall of the Berlin Wall and the 1990 monetary union of East and West Germany, the company recognized the potential of the East German market (as well as Czechoslovakia and Hungary). The Woolworth name has been well known in Germany since the company opened its first German "25 and 50 pfennig" store (i.e., 5 and 10) in Bremen in 1927. In the 1940s after World War II, the Communists seized and turned into state-run outlets more than 30 Woolworth stores in what became East Germany and Poland. The company believes the market is attractive enough to open new stores, even if they are unable to reclaim the properties they formerly held. This decision was strengthened by the overwhelming number of East Germans who swamped the nearly 30 Woolworth locations when first permitted to cross the Eastern border, leading to strong sales gains (Schwadel, 1990).

Safeway, a leading supermarket chain, entered Canada in 1929. In the early 1960s, the company opened stores in the United Kingdom, Germany, and Australia, concentrating on economically developed and culturally homogeneous regions. By the end of 1982, Safeway operated 2,452 stores throughout its domestic and international markets. More recently, the company has begun to enter developing nations with management contracts in Saudi Arabia, a joint venture in Mexico, and acquisition of part of a Japanese import company. Safeway is also increasing emphasis on exporting its private brands, which account for about one-fourth of domestic sales, to other countries.

K mart has entered foreign retail markets primarily through acquisition of established retailers in those countries. K mart entered Mexico with the purchase of a 44 percent interest in a Mexican retail chain, Astra. The company entered Australia with a subsidiary that was sold to G. J. Coles (Coles Myer Ltd.) in 1978. K mart continues to receive equity income from this operation ($49 million in 1987 according to the company's annual report), which consists of 648 supermarket, food service, and liquor stores, 643 discount stores (including 129 K mart stores), 85 department stores and 157 specialty stores throughout Australia. K mart is also active in Canada, where it operates stores under the names of K mart, Kresge, Jupiter, and Bargain Harold's Discount Limited. (Bargain Harold's is a low-priced chain designed to serve communities too small to support traditional variety stores.)

Among fast-food retailers, McDonald's has been a leader in continued overseas expansion. As shown in Exhibit 18–2, McDonald's had 1,341

Exhibit 18–2

McDonald's International Growth: United States and Foreign Sales (1980–1990) (dollars in millions)

		Sales		
	1990	1985	1980	Percent increase 1990 versus 1980
Systemwide total	$18,759	$11,001	$ 6,226	301%
United States	12,252	8,843	5,049	243%
Operations outside the United States	6,507	2,158	1,177	553%
Sales Outside the United States (Franchisee, Company, Affiliate)				
Franchisees	$2,638	$831	$440	
Company	2,364	770	389	
Affiliates	1,505	557	348	
Number of countries	53	42	27	
Number of Restaurants	**1990**	**1988**	**1986**	
Systemwide total	11,803	10,513	9,410	
United States	8,576	7,907	7,272	
Outside the United States (total)	3,227	2,606	2,138	
Total Pacific	1,288	1,052	873	
Total Europe	1,150	876	665	
Total Canada	626	568	515	
Total Latin America	163	110	85	

Pacific: Australia, China, Guam, Hong Kong, Japan, Macau, Malaysia, New Zealand, Philippines, Singapore, South Korea, Taiwan, Thailand

Europe: Andorra, Austria, Belgium, Denmark, England, Finland, France, Germany, Hungary, Ireland, Italy, Luxembourg, Netherlands, Norway, Scotland, Soviet Union, Spain, Sweden, Switzerland, Turkey, Wales, Yugoslavia

Latin America: Argentina, Aruba, Bahamas, Barbados, Bermuda (U.S. Navy Base), Brazil, Chile, Costa Rica, Cuba (U.S. Navy Base), El Savador, Guatemala, Mexico, Netherlands Antilles, Nicaragua, Panama, Puerto Rico, Venezuela, Virgin Islands

SOURCE: McDonald's Corporation, *1990 Annual Report.*

restaurants in Pacific nations, Canada, Western Europe, and Central and South America in 1982, with 348 of these in Western Europe. In 1986, the company opened 597 new restaurants (one outlet every 15 hours) to reach a total of about 9,000 in 41 nations. Perhaps the most noteworthy new store opening of 1990 was in Moscow. By the end of 1990, the restaurant had served more than 10 million customers. McDonald's averaged about 27,000 visitors a day—three times the 9,000 daily visitors to Lenin's mausoleum, which was previously Moscow's number one attraction. Russians would wait in line up to two hours for a McDonald's meal. Rising costs led to an 85 percent increase in prices, and although a "Big Mak" and "Kartofel Fri" (french fries) increased to 8.45 rubles or about $14.40 it had little effect on business (Hofheinz, 1990; "Intelligence Report," 1990; Kacker, 1985; Labich, 1986). In 1992, McDonald's opened in Beijing, China.

Kentucky Fried Chicken Corporation opened the first Western fast-food restaurant in China in 1987. The unit, with estimated daily sales of $7,000 can seat 500 people and can fry 2,300 pieces of chicken an hour. One note of caution, however, is that foreign marketers may not reach beyond the 20 percent of the population that lives in the more affluent cities. For example, a basic meal at Kentucky Fried Chicken costs $1.89, two days wages for the average Chinese whose average annual income is about $300. Some have referred to this retailing trend as the Great Mall of China (Shao, 1988).

Pursuing both a foreign and domestic expansion strategy, Toys "R" Us plans to open 200 toy stores in foreign countries in the next decade. This strategy provides new opportunities to offset the possibility of a slowdown in its U.S. growth. In 1988, the company's international division had stores throughout Canada and the United Kingdom, as well as in Hong Kong and Singapore. The toy chain has found that "kids are the market, no matter what language they speak." In 1990, Toys "R" Us entered a joint venture with McDonald's to open about 100 new stores in Japan with plans to share parking lots—and drawing power—in many locations. However, small mom-and-pop toy sellers in Japan do not like the idea of an American retailer opening stores in their market, particularly one as large and powerful as Toys "R" Us. One reason for opposition by local businesses is that Toys "R" Us buys directly from manufacturers. This practice eliminates the multiple layers of wholesalers that are a part of the traditional Japanese system, thus having a major impact on the entire toy distribution channel (Graven, 1990; Moffat, 1990; Maremont, Yang, and Dunkin, 1987; "Us and Them: U.S. Toy Store . . . ," 1990). While smaller businesses like McDonald's, Wendy's, and Kentucky Fried Chicken fast-food restaurants fit in with the established order and find few or no barriers to startup, small shops are protected by local laws and can veto the building of a large store like Toys "R" Us in their area (Virginia, 1990).

Computer electronics stores have also been opened overseas by U.S. retailers, including ComputerLand and Tandy. ComputerLand opened its first U.S. store in 1976. In 1982, when its dominance in U.S. computer retailing was assured, ComputerLand identified international expansion as its major thrust for continued growth. By the end of 1983, the company had opened 90 outlets in 24 foreign countries. The company has pushed forward on four fronts—Europe, Japan, Australia, and Canada, with the greatest effort concentrated in Europe (Wingis, 1983). However, Tandy spun off its interna-

tional division to shareholders in 1987 because total sales were not meeting company standards. The resulting company is Intertan, which kept the Tandy management intact and can use the Tandy/Radio Shack name for its stores and products until 1996 (Schultz, 1989).

Businessland, the biggest U.S. personal computer dealer, formed a Japanese subsidiary in 1990, bringing in Canon Inc., Fujitsu Ltd., Sony Corp., Toshiba Corp. and Softbank Corp. as venture partners. Businessland's continued effort to expand abroad include the purchase of a computer retailer in the United Kingdom in 1987 and one in West Germany in 1990, while planning to purchase a dealer in France (Zachary, 1990).

As an example of the competitive nature of foreign retailing investments, at least 20 overseas companies from the United States and other countries were operating in the retail sector in the United Kingdom by 1987. Many have been there since the turn of the century. Singer, the sewing machine manufacturer, opened its first British store in Scotland in the late 1800s, and F. W. Woolworth opened its first store in Liverpool in 1909. These two companies illustrate the dominant strategies used by foreigners to enter the British retail market: vertical integration by manufacturers (i.e., manufacturers opening retail stores for their products) and horizontal integration by retailers (i.e., addition of more retail units.)

KFC has had international operations for over twenty years and currently has more than 60 stores on 5 continents. A KFC in Japan is pictured below left.

The Tandy Corporation acquired Victor Microcomputer and Micronic handheld computer marketing operations in Stockholm, Sweden, and created the Victor Technologies Group.

Multinational manufacturers, such as those of Swiss, Canadian, and Italian origin in the footwear trades, chose vertical integration into the British retail market to ensure an outlet for their manufacturing plant investments. Multinational retailers, on the other hand, pursued a horizontal integration strategy, focusing their business on retailing, and transferring their retailing know-how abroad to improve profits and global market share (Mitton, 1987). In the British market, U.S.–based Zale Corporation, a jewelry retailer, faces competition with European jewelry retailers, such as Boucheron and Cartier, both of France.

Given the highly competitive nature of the American retailing environment, the trend toward increased internationalization of U.S. retailing is expected to continue. However, a number of trade-offs needs to be considered. On the one hand, disappointment in unfamiliar markets is a possibility due to differences in customer expectations and shopping behavior, legal and political uncertainties, currency fluctuations, and other factors beyond the direct control of the retailer. On the other hand, American retailers are experiencing growing international opportunities to expand beyond over-stored domestic markets, particularly where demand is high for American goods.

FOREIGN OWNERSHIP OF RETAILERS IN THE UNITED STATES

One of the most important factors contributing to changes in retailing in the 1990s will be the continuing trend toward internationalization. Many of the retailers leading the internationalization movement have their origins in highly developed and mature retail markets such as Western Europe and Japan. Shrinking growth opportunities at home and the perception of identifiable growth opportunities in foreign markets have motivated retailers to establish a presence outside their home markets. Further impetus has been provided by the opening up of Eastern Europe (Treadgold, 1990a). The acknowledged attractiveness of countries such as Japan and the United States continue to draw foreign retail investment.

Rationale for Foreign Investment in U.S. Retailing

Foreign businesses have invested heavily in retailing in the United States. In 1987, a $38 billion investment was made in U.S. companies, including retailers, by foreign purchasers. This investment represents more than a 50 percent increase for all businesses from 1986 (Johnson, 1988). Foreign investment in U.S. retailing has a widespread economic impact. For example, an annual payroll of $4,431 million was provided for American workers in 1982.

Total assets of U.S. retail affiliates of foreign companies, which have a direct or indirect voting interest of 10 percent or more, in 1983 totaled $15,825 million, yielding sales of $32,062 million for that year. (See Exhibit 18–2.) Total assets in U.S. retailing acquired by foreign direct investors, which have either direct or indirect ownership or control, totaled $9,298 million in 1988 and $8,499 in 1989. The number of U.S. retailers acquired or established by foreign direct investors totaled 36 investments made by 38 investors at an investment outlay of $7,274 million in 1989, as shown in Exhibit 18–3. The distribution of these investments according to the country of the foreign parent firm is presented in Exhibit 18–4 for 1986.

American businesses and governmental agencies have developed programs to attract foreign investments. Chambers of commerce, city and state development offices, and other groups have promoted the benefits of operating in their territories. Some resources predict that the influx of foreigners

Exhibit 18–3
United States Retailers Acquired or Established by Foreign Direct Investors (1987–1988)

	1987	1988	1989[1]
Total Number of Investments	33	37	36
For Acquisitions	31	31	26
For Establishments	2	6	10
Total Number of Investors	34	37	38
From Foreign Direct Investors	17	6	13
From U.S. Affiliates	17	31	25
Total Outlays (millions)	$ 1,212	$ 8,022	$ 7,274
For Acquisitions	1,210	7,689	7,255
For Establishments	2	334	18
From Foreign Direct Investors	$ 738	$ 357	$ 252
From U.S. Affiliates	474	7,665	7,021
Total Assets (millions)	$ 1,877	$ 9,298	$ 8,499
Sales (millions)	$ 2,659	$14,783	$13,020
Net income (millions)	$ 30	277	104
Employment (1,000)	25.1	172	271.4
Acres of Land Owned	.7	4	8.3

Note: Data represent number and full cost of acquisitions or existing U.S. business enterprises, including business segments or operating units of existing U.S. business enterprises and establishments of new enterprises. Investments may be made by the foreign direct investor itself, or indirectly by an existing U.S. affiliate of the foreign direct investor. Covers investments in U.S. business enterprises with assets of over $1 million, or ownership of 200 acres of U.S. land.
[1] 1989 preliminary investment and investor data.

SOURCE: Adapted from *Statistical Abstract of the United States*, 110th Annual Edition (1990) Washington, D.C.: U.S. Department of Commerce, Bureau of the Census (January), Tables No. 1395 and 1396, 796; *Statistical Abstract of the United States*, 111th Annual Edition (1991), Tables 1393, 1394, 796.

Exhibit 18–4
Direct Investment in U.S. by Parent Country (millions of dollars)

	1980	1986
Total All Countries	$ 3,650	$ 8,923
Canada	198	1,335
Europe	3,029	6,453
Japan	78	290
Latin America and Other Western Hemisphere	314	570
Other	31	275

SOURCE: Adapted from *Foreign Direct Investment in the United States: Balance of Payments and Direct Investment Position Estimates, 1980–1986* (1990), Washington, D.C.: U.S. Department of Commerce, Bureau of Economic Analysis (December), Tables 1.1 and 1.7, 1, 4.

into the American retail environment has not yet peaked, and that it will continue to grow (Bivens, 1986a).

In spite of some well-documented economic problems, the U.S. economy is still one of the most stable in the world and shows positive signs of continued growth, making U.S. businesses an attractive investment. The favorable exchange rate of currencies such as the mark and the yen against the dollar also have contributed to the desire of foreign financiers to provide capital to American retailers.

Many of the foreign investors are motivated by the quest for profitable returns on their investment rather than the desire to be "in the retail business" or to salvage the businesses they have acquired. In fact, large numbers of stores are sold off soon after their acquisition. Foreign investments in U.S. real estate markets are quite narrowly focused, mainly in downtown locations in major cities with hotels, resorts, and some regional shopping centers (in addition to office buildings). Thus, they make a big impact on a small market. For example, many major office buildings in downtown Los Angeles are owned by foreign investors, and most of the major resort hotels in the state of Hawaii have Japanese owners (Downs, 1987).

One example of the attractiveness of U.S. retail investments followed the U.S. stock market crash in October 1987 (Meltdown Monday). Cash-heavy European businesses launched an all-out effort to purchase U.S. companies when stock prices declined drastically. Foreign investors were encouraged by the deflated dollar, low stock prices, and the political stability of the United States, as well as a growing need to internationalize (Riemer et al., 1988).

Who Are the Foreign Owners of U.S. Retailers?

For many years the flow of foreign retail investment was predominantly from the United States to other nations. Now the retail trade sector in the United States is being affected significantly by the flow of foreign direct investment from the other direction. The volume of foreign investments in food and nonfood retailers has grown steadily (Kacker, 1985).

Foreign firms entering the U.S. retail industry have found grocery stores, specialty chains, and variety store chains to be the most attractive investments. In contrast to most U.S. companies (Sears, Safeway, Woolworth, Singer, Tandy) who have entered foreign markets through direct investments in new stores, most foreign investors have been more inclined to acquire existing U.S. retailers.

The entry of foreign investors into American retailing is not a recent phenomenon. One of the early entries was Loblaw Companies, Ltd., a Canadian company that established Loblaw, Inc., a food store chain in New York, Pennsylvania, and Ohio. The Loblaw company acquired National Tea Company in 1955–1956, with stores in eight cities throughout the United States. Schlumberger, a French company, acquired Heath Company, a do-it-yourself electronic kits retailer, in 1962. Astro Minerals, Ltd., a New York retailer of gems and precious stones, was acquired by Julio Tanjeloff of Argentina in 1963.

European companies traditionally have been the dominant investors in U.S. retailing with over 75 percent of the foreign direct investment in the United States from 1985–1990 (Exstein and Weitzman, 1991). Methods of entering the U.S. retail industry generally have taken the form of outright purchase, active or passive investments, or direct market entrance.

Major European investors in American retailing include companies from (1) Germany: the Tenglemann Group, Hugo Mann Group; (2) Holland: Vroom & Dreesmann, Ahold N. V., (3) The Netherlands: Koninklijke Bijenkorf Beheer (KBB), Brenninkmeyers; (4) Belgium: Delhaize Le Lion; (5) France: Docks De France, Promodes, Agache-Willot; (6) England: Habitat Mothercare, B.A.T. Industries PLC (Kacker, 1985). Some of the U.S. retailing investments of these companies are discussed in the following paragraphs.

Tenglemann acquired 50.3 percent ownership in A&P in 1979 and has since invested over $100 million in the company. Hugo Mann purchased 68 percent ownership of Fed Mart, self-service supermarkets and general merchandise stores in 1975, and a large share of Vornado, Inc. (Two Guys, Builders Emporium) in 1977. However, by 1981, Hugo Mann decided to discontinue its U.S. retailing operations. In 1979, Vroom & Dreesman made direct investments in the Outlet Company, Dillard's department stores, H. J. Wilson Co., and Cole Corporation. In 1980, the company purchased a large share in Child-World (second largest toy retailer in the United States).

Ahold N. V. acquired the Bi-Lo chain of 98 supermarkets in 1977 and Giant Food Stores in 1981. KBB opened the KBB Holding Company U.S.A., which took over Macks, a 100 store chain of variety stores in 1980. The Brenninkmeyers acquired Ohrbach's (with 11 stores in New York and California) in 1965 and Maurice (a Midwest apparel retailer) in 1978. Delhaize Le Lion, through a holding company incorporated in the United States, made equity investments in Food Giant, Inc. (100 percent) and Food Town Stores, Inc. (15.4 percent). Docks De France centers its U.S. operation on Lil' Champ, 162 convenience stores in Florida. Promodes acquired 100 percent ownership of Red Food Stores, located in Tennessee and Georgia, in 1980.

Agache-Willot, a holding company, bought the Korvettes discount chain in 1979, but, within two years of the takeover, withdrew from the unsuccessful venture, which was headed for failure. Habitat Mothercare (maternity and children's goods) entered the United States in 1977 by establishing Conran's in New York City, later expanding to other cities.

United Kingdom retailers made 37 acquisitions in U.S. retailing valued at nearly $3.9 billion from 1984 to 1989. Eleven of these were minimal acquisitions to gain a foothold in the U.S. market; eight were major acquirers (Hamill and Crosbie, 1990).

One prominent present and past U.K. owner of U.S. retailers includes the British American Tobacco Company (B.A.T. Industries). B.A.T. Industries made a major direct investment in U.S. retailing through its U.S. subsidiary, Brown & Williamson Tobacco. Their first investment was acquisition of an 80 percent interest in the Kohl Corporation (grocery and department store chain) in 1972. In 1973 the company acquired full ownership of Gimbel Bros. and Saks Fifth Avenue. In 1980, they established Batus, Inc. to manage these three companies and their diversified operations in the United States. In 1982, Batus acquired Marshall Field, a prestigious American retailer (Kacker, 1985). (In 1990, B.A.T. sold most of its U.S. retail holdings.)

Real estate developer, Robert Campeau of Toronto, Canada entered the U.S. retail industry with the acquisition of two major chains: Allied Stores

Co. in 1986, and Federated Stores in 1988. The latter acquisition was accomplished only after a lengthy takeover battle between Campeau and two power retailers, May Company and Macy's, among others. As described in Chapter 11, Campeau encountered serious financial difficulties after these ambitious takeovers and had to sell many of his acquisitions.

Many other foreign investors are involved in U.S. retailing. Benetton (Italy) had 4,000 stores in 60 countries in 1987, increasing to 6,300 in 1991 with 500 in the United States (Levin, 1991; Symonds and Dunkin, 1987). The Benetton Group entered the United States first as a specialty apparel retailer and later opened a U.S. factory to expedite order processing. Not all specialty retailers have been as successful as Benetton, however. Britain's Sock Shop International PLC opened 17 Sock Shop stores in New York City but found, along with Tie Rack PLC, that Britain's once hot niche retailers have lost much of their popularity (Maremont, 1990a).

Japanese retailers view overseas investments as a way to build image. That is, they can improve their prestige at home by buying or tying up with snazzy foreign retailers. In 1988 Jusco, a major superstore operator, acquired Talbots, a chain of chic women's boutiques. Takashimaya, a Japanese department store operator, has had a small outlet in Manhattan for 30 years, but plans to quintuple the size of its Fifth Avenue operation by 1993. Another Japanese department store, Yaohan, has entered the California market, and is targeting Asian Americans and others with a special interest in Japanese products and culture (Bylinsky, 1989). In one of the largest acquisitions in 1991, Ito-Yokado, the parent company of 7-Eleven Japan Co., acquired 70 percent interest in Southland Corp. Kyotaru Co., a 700-unit takeout sushi and restaurant chain, bought Restaurant Associates Inc. (Mama Leone's and others) (Ono, 1990). IKEA, a Swedish retailer of affordable Scandinavian furniture, has focused on expansion in the Northeastern United States ("Swedish Retailer . . . ," 1987), and Hong Kong hoteliers spent over $500 million in 1988 to acquire hotels in North America and Europe (Yang, 1989).

A number of foreign automobile manufacturers, such as Honda, have also entered the United States first as retailers, then opened American manufacturing plants. Other foreign investors enter the American business community through the acquisition of real estate, such as shopping centers, and by providing needed financial support to U.S. companies.

Owned by the Southland Corporation, 7-Eleven has stores across the globe, including this one in Thailand.

Transferring Retail Strategies and Know-How Across International Boundaries

The cultural and intellectual exchange between nations has taken many forms, including the expansion of retailing influences across national boundaries. This influence is not confined to store ownership in other countries. The effect reaches much further to include all aspects of the retail mix, technology, and merchandising techniques used by retailers to reach their customers. International experts at the American Marketing Association's 1987 World Marketing Conference admonished marketers to study current world trends in lifestyles, economic development, and the role of marketing itself if they planned to capitalize on international opportunities in the twenty-first century. An illustration of such a worldwide trend is that just as other cultures crave sushi and tempura, Japanese customers have a yen for western food, clothing, and housing ("Studying Current Trends . . . ," 1987; "Globalization, Technology . . . ," 1987). Likewise, Japanese consumer product companies are competing against established U.S. brands by either acquiring American firms or building U.S. production facilities in order to bring their products to American markets (Swasy and Mark, 1989).

International influences are evident in the product and service mix offered by most retailers. Imported goods are sold by a wide spectrum of retailers from high-fashion specialty shops to electronics stores to supermarkets. Retailing formats, such as the hypermarket concept, are exported from one country to another. The global influence is also demonstrated in methods used to promote and deliver products to target markets. In these and many other ways retailers operating in one country learn from retailing successes in other countries. However, not all attempts to apply generic strategies to world markets have been successful.

Retailing, by its very nature, involves a transfer function, which can be broadly defined as the "transfer of influence" from one party to another. Use of the term *influence* suggests the possession of a superior quality that is instrumental in gaining recognition, acceptance, and emulation from another. The types of influence that are transferred from one country and one company to another within the retailing context include those related to: (1) products and/or services desired by customers, (2) operating formats that appeal to retailers and customers in another country, (3) promotional methods and retail image that set trends, and (4) technology.

Transfer of Products and Services

A fundamental decision to be made by retailers is whether or not to stock imported goods, and to what extent. Some target audiences are favorable toward imports; some are not. Japanese retailers are stocking many foreign label products wanted by their customers, particularly fashion merchandise. Exhibit 18–5 illustrates the importance of American apparel and other Western brands to Japanese customers.

A number of the largest U.S. retailers have chosen to concentrate inventories on domestic goods. Sears, K mart, J.C. Penney, Wal-Mart, and others recently launched campaigns to promote American-made goods, based on the belief that many U.S. consumers, concerned about foreign competition, would prefer to buy American-made goods (Dreyfack, 1986). Consumer response to domestic merchandise has been particularly positive in the blue-collar industrial sectors of the country, where overseas competition is blamed for high unemployment.

Some retailers have opened their businesses for the express purpose of selling imported merchandise. The retailer's size is not a determinant of success in marketing goods from overseas, as evidenced by the success of two home fashions retailers, Crate and Barrel and Pier 1, who started as small businesses specializing in imported products. Both have gained a strong consumer franchise and have grown to larger chains, due to a successful strategy of selling style and fashion at a low price, particularly appealing to quality-

TRANSFER OF INFLUENCE
recognition, acceptance, and emulation by another country of superior-quality products or services, operating format, promotional methods and image, and technology.

Exhibit 18–5
Buying the Western Way in Japan

. . . .

*How a variety of imported products are faring in Japanese markets.**

Schick razor blades: 70% of the safety-blade market.

McDonald's hamburgers: 30% of the fast-food hamburger market (by sales).

Coca-Cola: 30% of the market for carbonated soft drinks.

Pampers: 20% to 22% of the disposable-diaper market.

German cars: 2.6% of the total car market.

U.S. cars: 0.4% of the total car market.

Braun shavers: 40% of the electric-shaver market. (Braun, a German company, is owned by Boston-based Gillette Co.)

Kodak amateur color film: 12% to 15% of the market.

Foreign-made cigarettes: 11.5% of the market (U.S. makers account for most).

*By volume, unless otherwise specified

Apparel Sales in Japan

American Brands	*1989 Sales (in millions)*
Ralph Lauren	$420.0
J. Press	120.5
Norma Kamali	60.1
Bill Blass	59.6
Oscar de la Renta	46.3
Anne Klein*	29.1
Brooks Brothers	26.5
Calvin Klein	21.8
Perry Ellis	19.9
Evan Picone	14.6
Coca-Cola Clothing	13.2
Geoffrey Beene	9.9
Donna Karan	8.6

Note: Figures converted at current exchange rates.
*Includes Anne Klein II line

. . . .

SOURCE: Darlin, Damon (1989), "Myth and Marketing in Japan," *The Wall Street Journal* (April 6), B1.; Agins, Teri (1990), "Japanese Market Lures, Vexes Retailers," *The Wall Street Journal* (May 29), B1, B4. Copyright © Dow Jones & Co., Inc. All rights reserved worldwide.

conscious young people setting up their first household. However, Pier 1 found it necessary to reposition in 1985 to achieve acceptable levels of sales and profits. When the first Pier 1 stores opened in the 1960s they sold incense, beads, and baskets to "spaced-out" baby boomers. By the late 1970s the baby boomer generation had grown out of those products while Pier 1 had not. Now the company's target market is identified as middle-income baby boomers, based on research with women 25 to 44 who have household incomes around $40,000 (i.e., hippies turned homeowners). Pier 1 has even opened 18 new stores near retirement communities in Florida—"practicing for when the baby boomers turn gray" ("Companies to Watch," 1990).

Many retailers stock their stores extensively with imported goods in an effort to increase sales and profits. Americans have become accustomed to buying imports, and many foreign brands, such as Sony and Toyota, have established a loyal following with an image of quality and value. Foreign electronic products dominate merchandise lines sold in U.S. retail stores. Large consumer electronic companies such as Philips have found America an attractive battleground to compete for market share with Asian companies (Terry, 1987b). Korean VCR makers, like Samsung, Daewoo and Goldstar, have captured a large share of the U.S. market, but have had to sacrifice profits to do so (Manguno, 1989).

Grocers stock imported food products to appeal to the tastes of customers who have become accustomed to a more international cuisine (Jefferson, 1988). Increased sales of Mexican and Asian foods attest to their popularity in the United States. Customer purchases of Matilda Bay wine coolers reflect the mania for products that represent countries such as Australia (Agnew, 1987). Canadian and Mexican beer sales are another familiar example of the international influence on this market.

Not all products and services transfer successfully to other countries in their original form, if at all. Some product changes may be needed to conform to target market characteristics, legal requirements, or the way the product will be used. A fast-food retailer may have to adapt seasonings in various menu items, or may find that certain ingredients are taboo. Service providers, such as hotel operators and financial institutions, also package a service mix that is congruent with the needs of different geographic markets.

Retailers selling mechanical or electronic products may have to adjust specifications to the needs of a new target market. U.S. exports of cars, appliances, and other products for foreign markets have been on the increase but may need to be adapted to new customers (Machalaba, 1988). Even Sony has yielded to American retail consumers' preference by marketing a Sony VHS videocassette recorder, despite its belief in the superior quality of the Beta VCRs (Whiteside, Port, and Armstrong, 1988).

COURTESY OF CRATE & BARREL

Crate & Barrel, based in the Chicago area, imports its home fashion merchandise from nearly twenty-five countries in Europe and Asia. Their buyers travel to each country to find items exclusive to the company, which they import directly from both large and small manufacturers.

Part VI

© 1992 ARTHUR MEYERSON

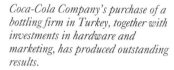

Coca-Cola Company's purchase of a bottling firm in Turkey, together with investments in hardware and marketing, has produced outstanding results.

Fashion retailers change original designs to conform to dimensions and tastes of customers in another country or culture. One such example is that of Sudha Pennathur, whose handcrafted jewelry and accessories are sold in stores like Neiman-Marcus and Saks Fifth Avenue. Pennathur interprets elaborate ethnic designs found in India and other countries into the bold, contemporary look desired by the Western world (Gupte, 1987). This trend has extended from high fashion to discount merchandisers who moved toward an ethnic look in fashion jewelry. Foreign and ancient cultures have influenced designs patterned after Egyptian, African, and American Indian motifs (Pellet, 1990).

Buyers and merchandisers from The Limited stores make trips to Europe and Asia for the purpose of identifying new fashions in their early stages and then translate them into fashions that will appeal to the younger American customer. Even Bloomingdale's fashion experts who buy merchandise all over the world believe that the mystique and allure of Russia lends itself to the acceptance by its customers of appropriately designed Russian fashions (Duke, 1988). Of course, Gorbachev's 1988 visit to the United States may have led to heightened interest in Russian goods.

As can be seen from the above examples, American consumers purchase a wide array of foreign-made products. This growth of imports reflects the increasing internationalization of the U.S. economy (Wessel, 1988). Within this same context, the international influence extends to opportunities for import and export companies to develop business in other countries. This type of activity promotes good trade relations between nations and can increase income in poorer economies such as the LDCs who may produce many of these goods.

Within a very short time after the currency unification of East and West Germany on July 1, 1990, at least two Western cigarette makers (B.A.T. Cigarettenabriken and R. J. Reynolds Tobacco International) were aggressively promoting their respective products. At least 70 to 80 percent of all brands sold in East German stores are Western brands. Other Western products, such as an electric ice cream freezer sold in East Berlin's largest department store, are also in demand. However, average purchase totals remain relatively low due to cost of living and job security concerns (Cote, 1990).

Exhibit 18–6
Special Considerations in Buying and Selling Imported Goods
••

Buying Imported Goods

The decision to sell imported goods generates a possible need for different buying practices, along with a new set of problems for the retailer. A separate buying organization or change in the existing organizational structure may be required to handle the added responsibilities with their unique demands. Buying may be handled centrally within the present buying organization or through outside buying offices headquartered in the United States or overseas. Many retailers have opened overseas buying offices in frequently used foreign markets, usually staffed with nationals or at least someone responsible for import buying from that country. The form of the organization, whether in the United States or overseas, may consist of an individual buyer, a buying team, agents, or buying offices.

The retailer also has to determine whether certain countries or companies are to be favored over others, and whether a pre-determined ratio of goods from one source versus another should be used to maintain a satisfactory operating profit. Distribution channels, and the logistics involved in shipping goods from one country to another, as well as storage facilities and responsibilities must be planned in advance. The lead time needed for orders is considerably longer than that for domestic goods. The cost and time element associated with available shipping methods tend to be negatively correlated, i.e., short shipping time is more expensive, and vice versa. The Limited (Mast Industries) has solved this problem by maintaining five jumbo jets for quick turnaround on delivery from Asia to the company distribution center in Columbus, Ohio.

Retailers and vendors also may need to adapt to some relatively unfamiliar situations in maintaining their channel relationships. For example, in some countries, manufacturers own a portion of the store space, and retailers pay them for merchandise thirty to ninety days later. A grocery store stocking fee may also be paid to the vendor by the retailer in some foreign markets. Practices such as these may affect the retailer's control over the distribution process and create a need to adjust accounting practices.

Problems Relating to Selling Imported Goods

While problems can occur with any dimension of the retailing mix (and often do), the most obvious problems that may result from the retailer's decision to sell imported goods are associated with buying and distribution channels:

- Substitutions of quality, style, or other agreed upon terms in shipments.
- Orders shipped at a higher price than originally contracted.
- With fashion merchandise in particular, returning imported goods to suppliers or making exchanges is difficult. Therefore, anticipating trends and forecasting customer reactions is necessary far in advance of the selling season.
- Transportation can be costly and unreliable, such as an unexpected longshoreman strike on shipping docks.
- Order may arrive late or not at all.
- Import quotas may limit size of shipments.

America's pop culture, largely represented by licensed consumer products, is feeding a worldwide insatiable appetite for Hollywood, rock and roll, and other Western exports,. A single global youth culture seems to be emerging, where a teenager has more in common with a teenager in another country than either has with elders in their own countries. U.S. fashion influence extends to a Budapest disco; Robocop is a hero in Bangkok; Mutant Ninja Turtles are the mania in Britain; sales of Mickey Mouse and other Disney memorabilia reached $1.5 billion annual sales in Japan; and Hank Williams, Jr. belts out country music in the Alabama Berlin Country Music Club and Western Restaurant patronized by Berlin locals dressed up like cowboys and cowgirls. Movies, music, clothing, toys, and a host of other products and services have gained unprecedented popularity overseas and will keep retailers' cash registers ringing in response to consumer demand (Huey, 1990). The Barbie doll, a longtime favorite of U.S. retail customers, has been credited with half of Mattel's $1.4 billion in sales. Barbie has

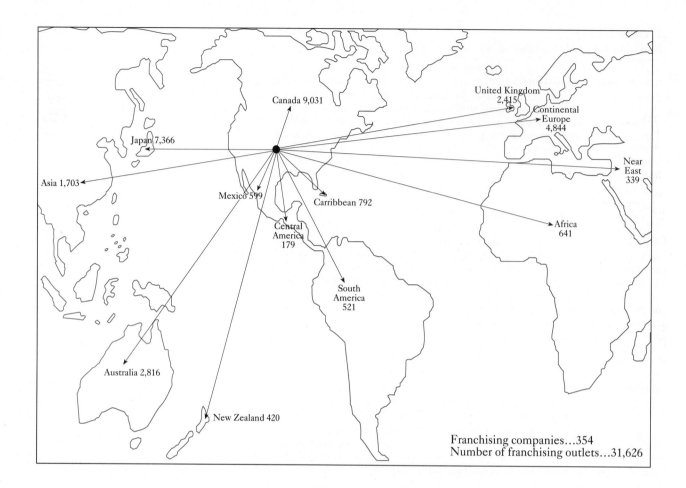

Franchising companies...354
Number of franchising outlets...31,626

Labels on map:
Canada 9,031
United Kingdom 2,415
Continental Europe 4,844
Japan 7,366
Near East 339
Asia 1,703
Mexico 599
Carribbean 792
Central America 179
Africa 641
South America 521
Australia 2,816
New Zealand 420

Exhibit 18–7
International Franchising: 1986
· ·
SOURCE: *Franchising in the Economy
1986–1988* (1988), Washington, D.C.: U.S.
Dept. of Commerce International Trade
Administration (February), 8.

traveled to Japan and other countries and expects to find a new market in Eastern Europe. Mattel's foreign sales of Barbie dolls and other toys increased from $135 million in 1980 to $700 million in 1990 suggesting that children's wants and desires for toys are the same throughout the world (Morgenson, 1991).

Special considerations involved in both the buying and selling of imported goods are discussed in Exhibit 18–6.

Transfer of Operating Formats

Earlier discussion included many successful attempts in transferring operating formats from one country to another. Several are highlighted in this section.

Franchising has provided many retailers with a successful format for entering foreign markets. Since the early 1970s, U.S. franchisors have expanded their foreign operations at a much higher rate than domestic operations. Exhibits 18–7 and 18–8 illustrate the scope of international franchising. Some well known American franchisors include fast food chains like McDonald's, Pizza Hut, Taco Bell, Burger King, and Kentucky Fried Chicken. Service franchisors, such as Hertz International, have also gone overseas (Kacker, 1985).

McDonald's has been successful in exporting its management skills as well as its fast-food products, largely due to the entrepreneurial style of its franchisees

Exhibit 18–8
International Franchising: Location of Selected Retail Establishments (1986)

	Restaurants (All Types)	Retailing (Non-Food)	Retailing (Food Other Than Convenience Stores)
Canada	1,869	1,580	717
Mexico	121	68	7
Caribbean	280	51	53
United Kingdom	608	489	41
Other Europe	642	616	51
Australia	691	463	18
Japan	1,548	180	828
Other Asia	552	118	232
Other	458	54	12

SOURCE: Adapted from *Franchising in the Economy 1986–1988* (1988), Washington, D.C.: U.S. Department of Commerce, International Trade Administration (February), 46.

and suppliers. The company's greatest challenge in foreign markets is to infuse every store with the gung-ho McDonald's culture and standardized procedures (Deveney et al., 1986). American retailers going into Japan must be aware of conducting business in that culture. For example, Japanese middlemen exert a great deal of control over retailing, and problems can occur due to local customs, laws, and partnerships. In addition, large chains are apt to maintain quality control departments where products are inspected, because Japanese consumers tend to scrutinize each purchase (Agins and Ono, 1990).

Specialty retailer, Barney's New York, is known for its distinctive image. To maintain this distinction, five Japanese retailing employees are required to spend two years in New York learning Barney's merchandising ideas and style so they can sell to affluent and urbane customers in Tokyo. About 80 percent of the merchandise in the stores will be identical to that sold in Barneys' stores in America, with the rest chosen by the Tokyo staff. Considerable effort is being made to educate Japanese retailers and customers to a new lifestyle (Agins, 1990).

The Body Shop (UK) has been able to adapt its format for selling all-natural products for skin and hair care worldwide. The Body Shop has over 450 stores in 37 countries. Its entry into the U.S. has coincided conveniently with the heightened environmental awareness of American consumers. The company does not advertise and does not adhere to many other traditional business methods. Information systems technology plays a critical role in retail functions, but the Body Shop insists on human interaction in maintaining the firm's values ("The Body Shop . . . ," 1990; Wilder, 1990).

Supermarkets have successfully crossed many borders. Taiwan has become Asia's primary target for foreign supermarket chains that want to expand outside saturated domestic markets. In mid-1990 over 60 western-style supermarkets in the Taipei area competed for nearly $5 billion in food expenditures. Supermarkets expect to increase their 10 percent market share substantially because customers are beginning to prefer the clean and convenient supermarkets to the tiny, less-than-sanitary traditional stores with their limited opening hours. Wellcome, owned by Dairy Farm International (Hong Kong), has led its competitors since 1987. Competitors include Park 'n Shop (Hong Kong), Matsusei Corporation (Japan), Yac's (Japan), Carrefours of France, and Makro (Netherlands) (Goldstein, 1990). Thailand's first supermarket chain, Foodland, was established in the early 1970s and was the first Western-style supermarket in Bangkok. Foodland has already included Thai TV dinners in its grocery assortment. The owners expect fierce competition in the future, but do not feel that conditions in Thailand are suitable yet for large discount houses or convenience stores (Rainat, 1991).

In France, department stores such as Carrefour are adapting American retailing strategies to stay more competitive. Just as in the United States, they have found that department stores can use creative specialty store formats to diffuse the threat from competition. In their case, they must combat the hypermarkets, who are trading up, and aggressive small discount supermarket operators (Bivens, 1986b). When Carrefour entered the U.S. market with a 330,000 square foot hypermarket outside Philadelphia in 1988, the company learned from experience that the French retailing philosophy had to be translated into a U.S. concept. Most of the ideas for change came from customer complaints deposited in suggestion boxes located throughout the store. Suggestions that have been implemented include merchandise adjacencies (e.g., moving paper goods such as plates and napkins from the housewares end of the store to groceries) and adding more stock keeping units (Johnson, 1990). As indicated in Chapter 13, the French hypermarket concept has been operationalized in the United States by Wal-Mart (Fine, 1988).

Specialty retailers have also been successful in implementing the superstore concept. Toys "R" Us was mentioned earlier within the context of toy superstores. In late 1990 HMV Music Ltd. (UK) began its international expansion by opening two extremely large stores in Manhattan, New York with plans to open others. The HMV outlet near London's Oxford Circus is the world's largest record shop, and one of the New York outlets will be the largest record store in North America with 40,000 square feet. The warehouse-size record store was pioneered by Tower Records which has 64 stores in the United States and 16 stores overseas. The warehouse format music store is a fast-growing niche in music retailing and HMV is competing head-on with Tower Records by offering more service in more spacious, appealing stores (Maremont and Fingersh, 1990).

Isao Nakauchi is a retail maverick in Japan. In 1957 he opened a drugstore that was inspired by a James Cagney gangster movie. He was impressed by the competitive pricing strategies of Safeway Inc. and Sears, Roebuck and Company. His Daiei Inc. chain of 204 stores offers American style discount prices contrary to traditional Japanese retailing practices. In mid-1991, Nakauchi launched a campaign to take over two large Tokyo rival chains. His cut-rate stores have shaken up Japan's protective distribution system where manufacturers have been able to dictate prices to retailers. Nakauchi vows to offer customers the best deal possible, generally undercutting competitors by 15 percent on everything from Kansas beef to Coleman outdoor goods carried in his massive stores (Holden, 1991).

The department store concept has been successful in many countries. Bangkok has a fast-growing urban population of 6 million people who are benefiting from a healthy economy, and shopping in retail stores such as Central Department Store Ltd. (Rainat, 1990). Yaohan International Group Company Ltd. is the number one retailer in Southeast Asia. Yaohan's new store opening policy coincided with accelerated growth and expanded consumption in countries such as Singapore, Hong Kong, Malaysia, and Taiwan, and has successfully attracted retail customers to its department stores (Ozawa, 1990).

COURTESY OF WALGREEN CO.

Walgreen's is best known as a drug store in the United States, with over 1,700 stores across the country. But in Puerto Rico some of Walgreen's 29 stores contain food centers offering dairy, frozen food and other grocery items where there is no grocery store nearby.

The American shopping mall concept has recently became more popular in England. Modern malls, reflecting an American influence on design and the presence of department stores as anchor tenants, are being built in metro centers and out of town (Mitton, 1987; "Shopping Centres . . . ," 1987). Shopping center development has increased in the United States, Far East, Europe, and other areas of the world. Some of these centers are mixed-use development such as the seven-level Melbourne Center in Australia, built by a Japanese development company. Melbourne Center encompasses two city blocks and features 200 shops, restaurants, entertainment, and a 55-story office tower. Department store anchors include Myer Stores (Australia) and Daimaru (Japan) ("Melbourne Central . . . ," 1990).

Another form of discounting is found in the international duty-free shops that are thriving in tourist locations, such as airports, cruise ships, airplanes and border crossings. Duty-free shops sell liquor ($3.2 billion in 1987), perfume and cosmetics ($2.3 billion), tobacco, jewelry, leather goods, and other portable merchandise to travelers. As noted in Chapter 8, customers do not pay import, luxury, sales or excise taxes, because they are not going to use the merchandise in the country where it is bought. European duty-free retailers may lose a significant portion of their business in 1992 when the European Community plans to abolish all intra-European duties (Weil, 1989).

Nonstore formats, such as direct mail and in-home selling, have also transferred across international boundaries. U.S. catalogers have expanded their markets overseas, but international marketing has not represented a significant percentage of business for most of these firms in the past. Many U.S.-based mail order companies have expanded into European markets, and European-based mail order companies have accelerated their expansion into the United States. Recreational Equipment Inc. (outdoor outfitter) and Williams-Sonoma (cookware) have obtained sales from catalogs mailed to prospective customers in Japan. Spiegel, which owns both Honeybee and Eddie Bauer, has included

Canada and Europe in its expansion plans. Some 700 Avon ladies have started their door-to-door selling in China. Their primary customers are young urban women who are already accustomed to using beauty products and are willing to pay higher prices for international brands. Electronic home shopping through interactive viewdata systems have been developed in the United Kingdom (British Telecom's Prestel System, Keyline Shopping, Ltd.) and France (Minitel). Nonstore retailing is expected to be a huge and potentially lucrative overseas market for catalog sales, door-to-door selling, and on-line shopping (Fishman, 1990; Miller, 1990; Reese, 1990; Sanghavi, 1990; Westlake, 1990).

Transfer of Promotional Methods and Image

All elements of the promotional mix must be consistent with the retailer's objectives and image, so that advertising, personal selling, sales promotion, display, and publicity convey the desired message to customers. International themes are used frequently in promotion and store decor by a wide range of retailers, from upscale specialty stores like Neiman-Marcus to the local supermarket.

Some of marketing's most costly mistakes have been in the development of promotional strategies. The sale of imported goods in the United States or abroad requires an understanding of the culture of the target market. Cultural beliefs and practices may influence responses to advertising messages, packaging, and other promotional devices. These factors are particularly true for personal care products and food ("Marketing Can Be Global . . . ," 1987). To accomplish their promotional goals, retailers must gather information about consumer wants and attitudes in other countries (Dreyfack, 1986). McDonald's and Avon, selected by *Fortune* magazine in 1986 as America's International Winners, have made this cultural transition in their advertising (Labich, 1986).

Closely related to the promotional mix is the retailer's image. Image is affected by consumer perceptions of foreign products sold in its stores and strongly influenced by the presentation of that merchandise. Imported goods tend to be associated with one of several images. The image may be related to the type of product and its country of origin. A recent study suggested that different countries of origin have differing effects on consumers' quality perceptions of apparel. The magnitude of the effect tended to reflect the country of origin's level of industrial development. Those countries included in the study were the United States, Republic of Korea, Peoples' Republic of China, Italy, and Costa Rica (Khachaturian and Morganosky, 1990). Imported gourmet foods and home items also tend to have an air of distinction about them. Even U.S. cheesemakers are capitalizing on this trend by developing European-style specialty cheeses, promoting them as import quality ("U.S. Cheesemaker . . . ," 1987). Alessi SpA is an Italian manufacturer of unusual-looking stainless steel kitchen utensils. The company has earned an international reputation as one of the world's finest design firms. Alessi has learned that what a product adds to a customer's self-image, not just what a product does, is what counts (Fuhrman, 1990). If a retailer is pursuing a premium image strategy, those goods imported from another country will be perceived as higher quality and perhaps as more unique or fashionable. Subsequently, they have a higher price consistent with their superiority. Japanese markets are interested in importing the unique lifestyles and characteristics of other cultures and in exporting their own. Analysts believe imports will gain a larger market share in the retail revolution anticipated in 1990s' Japan (Palmer, 1990, "Studying Current Trends . . . ," 1987).

A prestigious image may not last forever. For years French manufacturers have controlled the ultra-high end of the luxury-goods market (e.g., Yves St. Laurent fashions, Limoges china, Christofle silverware, and expensive wines). Although French brands still control nearly 50 percent of this very high-margin $52 billion a year business, brands from other countries such as Italy and the United States are gaining more customers throughout the world (Revzin, 1990).

A strong relationship exists between a product's price and its image. In planning pricing strategies for imported goods, the initial markup must be high enough to sustain markdowns and losses if sales are not up to expectations, so that the targeted maintained markup or gross margin can be achieved. Pricing strategies also must consider value perceptions held by consumers. For example, imported goods sold at lower prices may be perceived quite differently. Some may have a high quality–low price image (e.g., Crate and Barrel), which enhances the retailer's overall image. Others may have a low quality–low price image, presenting possible image problems for both retailer and product line.

Transfer of Technology

As discussed in Chapter 17, computers and other high-technology developments have made it possible for retailers to run their operations more efficiently and profitably. For example, Benetton Group SpA achieved sales of $1.2 billion in 1989 with the assistance of networking and electronic data interchange (EDI). This information system network can be initiated by independent business clients in 73 locations throughout the world who serve as intermediaries between the Benetton Group and retailers. The EDI technology will continue to play a role in Benetton's planned expansion into the former Soviet Union and Eastern Europe (Zottola, 1990).

Retailing technology may not transfer with equal success to all countries, particularly if they are in different stages of national economic development. For instance, the supermarket industry has developed a high-level technology that facilitates international operations. However, its successful application in other countries (e.g., LDCs) depends on existing conditions and technologies, as well as local consumers' preferred shopping patterns (Goldman, 1981).

The retail mix and know-how of one company can be transferred to another country. Success will depend on answers to questions posed in the next section.

INTERNATIONAL RETAIL MARKET ENTRY PROCEDURE AND DECISIONS

Before seriously considering international expansion, a retailer must meet several criteria. First, top management must be in agreement and committed to the project. Sufficient capital and qualified human resources must be available to make the venture a success. The retailer must be familiar with the nuances of each market entered, its culture, consumer behavior, economy, politics, and other important characteristics.

Kotler identified six major decisions confronting firms contemplating international marketing ventures (Kotler, 1991). Although these decisions are not specific to retailing, the same decision sequence can be adapted by retailers who are considering entry into international markets:

1. Evaluate the international retailing environment.
2. Decide whether to enter foreign retail markets.
3. Decide which foreign retail markets to enter.
4. Decide how to enter the retail market(s).
5. Decide on the retailing program.
6. Decide on the retailing organization.

Evaluation of the International Retailing Environment

An assessment of the business climate in another country includes the economic, legal and political, and cultural environments, as well as the trade system between countries. Errors in assessing any of these factors could lead to costly mistakes, as a number of American retailers have already learned. Some questions to ask about each of these environmental factors are listed below, with the understanding that each must be adapted to a retailer's unique characteristics and objectives. The specific type of retail store involved, products and services to be sold, and flexibility in adapting to new environments need to be considered in each of these assessments.

In evaluating the economic environment in another country, the following questions need to be answered:

- What is the industrial base of the country?
- What is the state of the economy? Is it a developed or developing nation, LDC?
- What is the import-export balance?
- How is income distributed among the inhabitants? Are family income distribution patterns (1) very low, (2) mostly low, (3) very low and very high, (4) low, medium, and high, or (5) mostly medium.
- What are typical consumption patterns based on income distribution?

The decision to enter a foreign market is affected by the country's industrial base and income distribution, which indicate long-term financial success. However, the indicators are not always obvious. For example, the poorest country in Europe, Portugal, does not seem to be a likely target market for the Lamborghini automobile (the 1992 Diablo model was priced in the United States at $250,000). Family incomes in that country are either very high or very low, but those with very high incomes make up the largest single market in the world for this expensive car. Likewise, Gucci is located in New York City, but does not count the city's large number of urban poor in its target market.

The European Community (EC) 1992 program is designed to unite twelve member nations into a single European market in 1992. Many retailers are evaluating the opportunities and risks presented by this new market structure. Economically, Spain, France, Italy, and western Germany are considered to have the greatest retail sales potential. Eastern Germany has many consumers who desire Western products, but entry into this market would require a long-term commitment to allow the economy and business conditions to stabilize and support a profitable operation. The structure of the European market is expected to shift during the 1990s toward fewer shops, larger outlets, and more cross-border specialty retailers (such as Benetton), with an increase in franchising and mail-order retailing. However, many cultural and socioeconomic barriers will continue to exist in spite of the removal of physical, technical, and fiscal barriers in 1992 (Alexander, 1990; Schiro and Skolnik, 1990; Treadgold, 1990b; Waddell, 1991; Weihrech, 1991). As shown in this discussion of EC '92, it is difficult to separate an analysis of the economic environment in a foreign market from the legal and political and cultural environments or the trade system within and between countries.

In evaluating the legal and political environment, the following questions need to be answered:

- Is international buying encouraged or inhibited by the country?
- Are there legal or political barriers to entry?
- Is the country politically stable? Is it expected to stay that way?
- Are there currency restrictions, serious exchange rate fluctuations, or other monetary regulations that would affect profits?
- Does the host government facilitate foreign business operations in areas such as customs handling and market information? Are bribes or other "incentives" expected as a matter of course?

Any negative responses to the above questions can seriously inhibit the retailer's chance of financial success in a foreign market. For example, U.S. cigarette companies found barriers to entry into Asian markets, and U.S. automakers found it difficult to enter Japanese markets with their cars. On the other hand, in the late 1980s the policy of Glasnost opened the door to joint development projects with Americans in the former Soviet Union. Countries in the former Soviet bloc remain interested in using U.S. planning, design, and management know-how to improve their urban quality (Fuller, 1989). As noted, the reunification of East and West Germany removed political and legal barriers to entry to East German consumers.

In April 1990, Japan agreed to make it easier for U.S. businesses to enter the Japanese market. Measures aimed at reducing the U.S. trade deficit with Japan included changes in non-tariff barriers such as the retail distribution system, import process, and restrictions on foreign investment in Japan. The numbers of retail outlets have increased in recent years in the Peoples' Republic of China due to government encouragement of private small businesses, offering some encouragement to U.S. retailers who are interested in entering the Chinese market. Hong Kong's position as a dominant world retail center has been declining. Political factors that are believed to contribute to this decline are the June 1989 Tiananmen Square massacre in Beijing, China, the single European Community market in 1992, and the coming change of Hong Kong's ownership from British to Chinese ownership in 1997 (Phillips and Sternquist, 1990; Qiang and Harris, 1990; Shapiro and Hamilton, 1990).

In evaluating the cultural environment, the following questions need to be answered:

- What are the acceptable methods of conducting business? What behavior is expected or taboo?

- How do customers in that country use various products? What are their attitudes toward the products and the foreign company? How do they shop for goods and services?
- Are there potential cultural problems in the way that selling and other retailing positions are viewed within the culture? Can present training methods and materials be used?

The promotional mix is one area where cultural differences are evident. In some countries, retail selling is viewed as an undesirable occupation, thus making it difficult to hire qualified people.

Language barriers have resulted in many embarrassing marketing blunders, such as the Hispanic interpretation of chicken magnate, Frank Perdue's slogan, "It takes a tough man to make a tender chicken." The Spanish translation was: "It takes a sexually excited man to make a chick affectionate." Budweiser beer translated as "the queen of beers," and another brand was "filling; less delicious." Culture does make a difference! ("Sexually . . . ," 1987). Thus, retail sales are affected by their suppliers' promotional mistakes.

In evaluating the trade system between countries, the following questions need to be answered:

- Does the host nation facilitate international trade and/or belong to a major economic community (e.g., European Community)?
- Will it be necessary to work with trade unions?
- Are suitable distribution channels available and accessible to the retailer with reasonable risk?
- Are there trade barriers or restrictions, such as high tariffs, quota restrictions, or bans on importing certain types of merchandise?
- Is the exchange rate and availability of foreign currencies controlled?
- Are there other restrictions unrelated to tariffs (e.g., discrimination against American brands or product features)?

Retailers in Europe have been developing ways to improve distribution and ordering and to cut costs in preparation for the European Community's removal of internal trade barriers after 1992. One effort is directed toward improvements in information technology using barcode scanners and electronic data interchange (EDI) systems. Another effort involves cross-border alliances of retail firms. Groups such as the European Retail Alliance (Dutch Ahold Group, the French Casino, and Argyll, which operates the British Safeway Stores) have been formed in order to cut costs through economies of scale. The group may extend its distribution strategy to development of a European own-label brand (Pellew, 1990; Sonsino, 1990).

Evaluation of the environment based on the above dimensions provides a basis for deciding whether to enter a foreign retail market. Answers to questions in the following paragraphs must be in line with the positive aspects of the international environment being considered.

In deciding whether to enter foreign retail markets, the following questions must be answered:

- What are the retailer's objectives and policies regarding internationalization and preferred proportion of domestic to foreign revenues?
- How many and what type(s) of foreign countries has it considered in the short run and long run?

- Who instigated the decision—the retailer or the foreign government or businesses, including potential business partners?

In addition to formal methods of contacting businesses that are considered desirable for a country's economy, promotional methods are also used. For example, a special advertising section in *Business Week* in 1987, was sponsored by the U.S.S.R. State Foreign Economic Commission to describe their new approach to foreign trade and to encourage American investments ("USSR . . . ," 1987).

In deciding which foreign retail market(s) to enter, the following questions must be answered:

- What is the expected rate of return on the retailer's investment in each market and estimated current and future market potential?
- What degree of risk is involved and its estimated effect on return?
- What is the result of pro forma financial statements under different sets of sales, costs, and profit level assumptions.
- Does projected income under different assumptions meet or exceed company standards for growth potential, market share, and profitability within a given time frame? How do the results compare to domestic financial analysis?
- Which foreign markets are acceptable, and how are they ranked?

The success of global marketing has prompted dissenting viewpoints. Investment in foreign markets continues to increase, indicating expectations of a satisfactory return on investment. However, investment may be impractical if too many obstacles stand in the way of adapting to foreign requirements.

For example, compared to other types of foreign-owned firms in Britain, foreign retailers have experienced relatively low profitability with less than 25 percent annual return on capital invested. This return is in contrast to over 100 percent return experienced in the high-technology industries. Vertically integrated firms report the lowest earnings, although the parent companies show relatively high profits—perhaps due to accounting practices. Nevertheless, these companies continue to operate in Britain, indicating some advantage (Mitton, 1987).

In deciding how to enter the selected retail market(s), the following questions must be answered:

- What are the opportunities for direct investment vs. joint venturing and the advantages/disadvantages of each entry method?
- If market entry is through joint venturing, what are the trade-offs in licensing/franchising versus contracting/management contracting?

Methods of foreign entry into British retail trades have included self-start (from scratch), quick-entry through the purchase of established retailers, franchising, and joint venturing (Mitton, 1987). Each method has had its advantages and disadvantages, but has been successful for some retailers.

A **self-start entry strategy** involves building stores from scratch, usually similar to those already established in the home country.

Retailers: Woolworth (U.S.); Sears (U.S.)

- *Advantages:* Can use parent stores as a prototype and transfer retailing mix and merchandising strategies to the new country.

● *Disadvantages:* High investment cost; potential risk; strategies may not transfer; name may not be known in country, low awareness.

Quick-start market entry by purchasing established retailers is another popular strategy used by investors with the necessary capital and motivation.
Retailers: Campeau (Canada); B.A.T. Industries (England)

● *Advantages:* Quick start up; established customer base and name recognition; no immediate need to change existing organizational format or human resources structure.

● *Disadvantages:* Many firms available for acquisition may be in difficulty, requiring considerable time and resources to restore; entry price also may be very high.

Franchising is an effective method of introducing the company's retail mix to culturally diverse and distant markets (Kacker, 1985).
Retailers: Tandy (U.S.); McDonald's (U.S.); Benetton (Italy)

● *Advantages:* Can sell to anyone with minimum entry capital; minimal risk due to involvement of self-employed national; allows franchisor to bypass traditional foreign channels and maintain control over quality, prices, and customer services.

● *Disadvantages:* Investors with capital may not have necessary retail expertise, causing stores to revert to company ownership; governmental or legal restrictions; difficulty in controlling franchisees; insufficient local financing; possible need to adapt traditional franchise operations to local conditions.

A **joint venture** is a business partnership with foreign nationals, involving a licensing arrangement (e.g., franchising), contracting, or joint ownership (a condition for entry into some countries) and control.
Retailers: Safeway (U.S.); Carrefour (France)

● *Advantages:* Less costly; local partner's name/company established and accepted; may have legal or political advantages.

● *Disadvantages:* Each partner may expect more from a deal than what they put in; thus, joint ventures often fail, or like Safeway, become wholly owned by one of the parties; partners may not agree about policies (e.g., investments, marketing strategies).

Some retailers have found that one of the best ways to overcome the difficulties of setting up operations in Japan can be to establish partnerships with powerful Japanese importers and distributors. Partnerships include franchising, which has worked well for fast-food chains. A licensing strategy has been used by Nautilus Clubs, Jazzercise Company, and Domino's Pizza Inc. to enter the Japanese market. McDonald's restaurant in Moscow is a joint venture strategy, which is succeeding because it was tailored to Russia's political economy. However, McDonald's did break with the local tradition of not advertising job openings and received 25,000 responses for 500 vacancies through a series of ads placed in just one Moscow youth paper. Management practices and personnel training are additional issues that must be resolved in joint ventures (Hertzfeld, 1991; Holden, 1989; Raiter, 1991; Schlossberg, 1990).

SELF-START ENTRY STRATEGY
involves building stores from scratch, usually similar to stores already established in home country

QUICK-START ENTRY STRATEGY
involves purchasing established retailers in foreign countries

FRANCHISING
involves "selling" the store concept and practices to independent operators

JOINT VENTURE
involves a licensing arrangement, contracting, or joint ownership in a business partnership with foreign nationals

Courtesy of Coca–Cola

Coca-Cola distributors and retailers go to great lengths to make Coke available to their customers in Snowy River, Australia. Refrigeration does not appear to be a problem!

This pretzel peddler in Turkey is using one of the oldest methods in the world to sell his wares -- while enjoying a contemporary beverage.

© 1989 Arthur Meyerson

Globalization presents new competitive environments and challenges for retail managers throughout the world. Advancements in communications, transportation, and technology have escalated the cultural and intellectual exchange among nations, and have brought an increased desire for new shopping opportunities. Retailers are accelerating the pace of store openings and other financial involvement in foreign markets. The growing numbers of imports and exports of products to be sold by retailers emphasize the significance of international influences. Likewise, retail formats are moving successfully across borders. Exciting business opportunities await those retailers who understand the nuances of operating in foreign countries and cultures.

Various market expansion strategies are illustrated on these pages, showing the involvement of familiar retail firms and products in overseas operations. Some products sold by retailers, such as CocaCola, are recognized as "global products" because of their universal cross-cultural appeal. For instance, former East Germans are avid Coke drinkers, and are expected to consume over 100 millon cases in 1992. One location, the mammoth Sports Hall in eastern Berlin, has a giant Coke sign near its skating rink as well as three cafeterias and a dozen vending machines selling the world's number 1 soft drink.

McDonald's has led overseas expansion in the fast-food industry with about one-third of their 12,000 restaurants outside the United States, primarily in the Pacific and European countries. Two of McDonald's most noteworthy new store openings were in Moscow in 1990 and Beijing, China, in 1992. Customers are enjoying a Big Mac in this multi-level restaurant in Tokyo.

© Torin Boyd

Japan is a particularly attractive market to foreign retailers such as the United States and the emerging Asian and European markets. The American fast-food craze has been welcomed by many cultures, including the Japanese. "Foreign" automobiles can be found in the streets of every nation. Although Japanese cars tend to dominate the import car market in many countries, the Japanese do import cars from the United States, Germany, Italy and elsewhere. Foreign fashion and leisure-time pursuits also have wide acceptance by Japanese consumers. High-tech Japanese products are sold by retailers worldwide; however, Japanese consumers are using more products that are produced elsewhere in Asia than ever before — good quality at lower prices than domestic goods.

© Torin Boyd

The traditional Japanese retail format has been the "mom and pop" store. Today, however, chain stores are the fastest growing retailers in the country — and the trend is expected to continue. Discount operations are also gaining a foothold in a market that is increasingly concerned with prices and variety — but still demands quality.

Pizza has become a favorite food of many nationalities. Here, a Domino's delivery person is about to take off into Tokyo traffic on a pizza delivery.

© Torin Boyd

© Torin Boyd

While Kawasaki and Honda have sold a large number of motorcycles to American customers, Harley Davidson has found acceptance in foreign markets such as Japan where "Harley riders" have helped the company regain financial stability. Tokyo "Health Angels" promote safe driving.

Films are an American export item that are held in high esteem in both the Pacific Basin and in Europe. American movie icon Marilyn Monroe is used here (below) to advertise an international film festival in Tokyo.

Most of the cameras in use today may be made by Japanese manufacturerers, but Kodak is claiming its share of the Japanese film market. (right)

© Torin Boyd

© Torin Boyd

© Torin Boyd

Louis Vuitton , headquartered in Paris, is one of the many foreign retailers who are finding lucrative consumer markets for fashion and other goods in Japan. Vuitton sells quality and prestige along with its leather goods, accessories, perfumes, beauty products, and wines and spirits.

This youngster is counting money in anticipation of buying a Mickey Mouse doll. Disney characters have charmed children and adults alike throughout the world; Japan now enjoys the recently opened Tokyo Disneyland.

© Torin Boyd

© Torin Boyd

After three years of deliberations with the Japanese government and local officials to overcome retailing restrictions and regulations, Toys "R" Us opened its first store in Japan in December 1991, with ten more openings planned for 1992. The company's goal is to have 100 retail outlets in Japan by 2001. Although Toys "R" Us has met some obstacles to its price-cutting strategy, Japanese customers seem to like the idea of getting a bargain. The supermarket approach to selling toys requires well-stocked shelves in a warehouse setting. This employee (above) is stocking the store's shelves with a new shipment of toys. Japanese retailers emphasize service, the topic of this training session. (right)

© Torin Boyd

© Torin Boyd

Popular culture both shapes, and is shaped by, retailing and marketing strategies. Valentine's Day, a western holiday, has become extremely popular in Japan, as evidenced by this busy department store. Clerks sport brilliant pink jackets emblazoned on the back with "St. Valentine's Day" — in English.

The European Community (EC), or Common Market, which became effective in 1992 is the world's largest common market. All barriers to free trade have been removed among EC members that total 12 countries, 325 million people, and a combined gross national product of about $5 trillion. This large market contains attractive investment opportunities for retailers and exporters. However, American retailers are facing strong competition from Asian and European firms — not to mention the expansion of European retail establishments within the EC. Many are finding the best opportunities lie in strategic partnerships with local retailers.

© Randall Hyman

Courtesy of Tiffany & Co.

German customers appreciate quality merchandise — a fact recognized by Tiffany's with this store located in Frankfurt, Germany.

American movies are common film fare in Europe. Here, in Berlin, American movies are an obvious attraction to German movie-goers.

Body Shop international (below), headquartered in Great Britain, has been an International trendsetter. The company has no marketing department and does not advertise. The company focuses on natural products — and social activism. Customers are given product information rather than a hyped-up sales pitch. In 1992, Body Shop campaigned to increase the membership of Amnesty International; In 1988 it organized a signature drive to stop the burning of Brazilian rain forests. This Body Shop is located in Edinborough, Scotland.

© Randall Hyman

© Randall Hyman

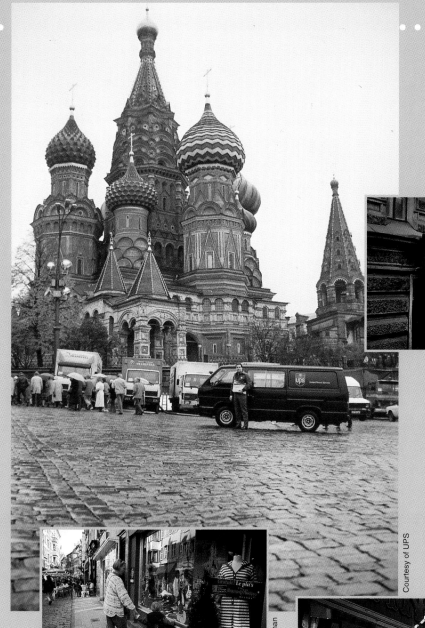

United Parcel Service (UPS), the world's largest package distribution company, provides distribution solutions and services to Russia and to more than 180 other countries and territories through an integrated network of aircraft, vehicles and information technology.

Courtesy of Baskin Robbins

Baskin-Robbins' 31 flavors have reached the former Soviet Union. In addition to this store in St. Petersburg, there are two others in Russia, and in early 1992 ground was broken for a new ice-cream plant in a Moscow suburb.

In Strasbourg, France, this "Grand Canyon" store sells cowboy boots, American West shirts, jeans and any product the urban cowboy could want. The lettering on the window reads, "The Boots of the Stars."

© Randall Hyman

Courtesy of UPS

© Randall Hyman

Above, at this Strasbourg, France, store a child inspects the Disney product line; the sign on the right advertises a free Euro Disney Item. In April of 1992, Euro Disneyland opened outside of Paris and is expected to receive 11 million tourists annually. In conjunction with the park, numerous Disney stores have opened up throughout Europe, and Disney films have flooded European television and movie theaters.

Kentucky Fried Chicken entered international markets over 20 years ago. KFC opened the first Western fast-food restaurant in China in 1987. "The Colonel's" logo is evident on this storefront in China.

Shopping malls, an important retailing format in the United States, have found new popularity in other countries as well. This shopping center illustrates another trend, that of catering to a special market niche. The Aberdeen Centre caters to the Asian community in Vancouver, British Columbia.

The Harlem Globtrotters entertain crowds of fans in Guangzhou (formerly Canton), China. Things Western are not foreign to the six million inhabitants of this metropolitan locale in the Pearl River Delta. This area, near Hong Kong, has one of the most rapidly growing economies in the world and engages in a wide variety of import and export enterprises.

Entering a market is often easier than staying in it. In addition to the typical problems related to a business operation, a company may encounter managerial resistance and constraints. Retail segments may be similar but may require different managerial styles and product strategies abroad. In deciding on a retailing program, these questions must be answered:

- Should the marketing mix be standardized for all countries or individualized for each market? Which store location, merchandise selection, pricing, and promotion strategies would be affected, and how?
- Are U.S. retailing strategies exportable to other developed, developing, or less developed nations?

The retailing program is a major factor in the decision to enter foreign markets. Each of the questions posed has far-reaching implications. In deciding on the retailing organization, these questions must be answered:

- Should the retail firm have a separate international division?
- Should the retailer form a new subsidiary in another country?
- How should subsidiaries be organized and controlled?
- Should there be few stores or many stores?
- Should store locations be concentrated or geographically dispersed?
- Should the management structure be based on area or region? (Woolworth, prior to reverting to British ownership, was divided into 5 regions; Safeway was divided into 3 zones.)
- If the retailer is also a manufacturer, should the company be divided into manufacturing and retailing divisions and divided further into specialized product lines?
- Should the firm be structured as a multinational organization?

The best answers to the questions above are those that meet or exceed the retailer's decision criteria. Criteria generally focus on a specific measure of profitability or return-on-investment to be achieved within a given time period. Factors taken into account include the type of store and the company's organizational goals for global expansion, coupled with the positive aspects of the environments of the host country that will allow the retailer to achieve the specified financial returns.

SUMMARY

Many retailers have expanded to operate in international environments. Overseas expansion by U.S. retailers has been pursued due to highly competitive domestic markets, or additional opportunities to those offered in the United States. Major U.S. retailers abroad include Sears, J. C. Penney, Safeway, F.W. Woolworth, K mart, McDonald's, and Toys "R" Us, among others.

Foreign investment in U.S. retailing has been encouraged by a stable economy, a market with continued growth, a favorable exchange rate of other currencies against the dollar, and the desire for profitable returns on their investments. Both retailing and nonretailing firms hold interests in U.S. stores, most entering the U.S. market through acquisition of existing compa-

The Price of Capitalism in Era of Perestroika

The former Soviet Union's state-run retail system was never very efficient, but during its final days serious shortages of most goods hurt it even more. It was not unusual to see customers crowded outside a store, waiting for a shipment of goods to be delivered. In the window might be a sign that read "Closed to the public." Only a few people with special invitations would be able to go inside to shop. Throughout the nation, consumers needed more than money to buy anything worth having, particularly imported goods. They had to obtain a special invitation, be unusually ingenious, or know someone who would sell them goods under the counter (i.e., black market).

Shopping by invitation led to many government and consumer complaints, and encouraged factories to cut deals with department stores to enable their workers to buy hard-to-find goods. People who worked for smaller enterprises, were pensioners, or were not working lost out completely. With demand outstripping supply, corruption became rampant. A senior official in the Ministry of Trade, complaining about the invitation system, said "no social justice is achieved this way . . . it's accompanied by all sorts of abuses of power that are very difficult to control. Shortages led to a new, semi-legal options market. For example, an invitation to buy a color TV costing 600 rubles could trade for 200 rubles and more; the right to buy furniture worth 10,000 rubles could cost about 2,000 rubles. This is the sale of a right, not a good, and so is not considered a crime."

Black marketers worked hand-in-hand with corrupt retailers to establish complete underground department stores. Specialty stores for newlyweds, or for invalids or veterans required customers to qualify to shop there. To shop in the Store for Newlyweds, a couple had to produce documents from a registry office showing they were to be married. The papers were accompanied by an invitation enabling the couple to shop. Some couples applied in three or four different registry offices, and some just got engaged so they could go shopping. Similar scams abounded in attempts to overcome the shortages in the special distribution networks.

Following the failed August 1991 coup, Russian President Boris Yeltsin promised drastic changes in that republic's economy. Yeltsin's plans included removal of government control over prices of most items by the end of 1991. He promised increased wages, and a social safety net for those who stood to suffer most from higher prices. In addition, a privatization program involved the sale of thousands of retail stores, cafes, and apartments to the public. Private farming opportunities also were expected to increase. It would appear, then, that there was hope for the Russian consumer following the coup attempt.

However, massive economic changes do not occur immediately or painlessly. Russian citizens were told to brace themselves for a painful drop in living standards until the economy improved. Further, there was no indication the black market that flourished under perestroika ceased to exist. In fact, there were signs that the situation had worsened in the short run. Common grocery items, often of poor quality, were in short supply—a grim prospect for customers facing a cold winter.

Russian consumers and retailers face numerous problems as the country moves toward a market economy with free trade, free prices, convertible currency, and privately owned property. Prices have increased faster than wages; production of non-military goods has been costly; foreign aid from the U.S. and other countries has been hijacked; and it is believed organized crime has emerged to fill the power vacuum created by the disintegrating government.

There are indications that the Russian economy will turn around—with time, assistance from foreign experts, and foreign investment. By spring 1992, food was more plentiful than before on grocery store shelves and prices had started to drop slightly.

Russian people are learning that the individual—and not the state—must solve their problems. In particular, an entrepreneurial spirit has become evident. Many of these free-market pioneers have found their niche in operating street kiosks. In true capitalistic fashion, they sell everything from German chocolates, French liqueurs, and U.S. cigarettes to Russian beer. They buy low, sell high, and invest their profits in expansion. Survival depends not only on attracting customers, but on skillful maneuvering in an underworld of bribery, Mafia-style economic crime, and some lingering fears of the KGB. More and more goods are available to Russian consumers—at a price.

Some material adapted from: Gumbel, Peter (1990), "Soviet Retail System Gets Strikingly Worse in Era of Perestroika," *The Wall Street Journal.* (July 23), A1, A4; Gumbel, Peter (1991), "Yeltsin Promises to Overhaul Economy of Russian Republic, Warns of More Pain," *The Wall Street Journal* (October 29), A1, A8. Brady, Rose, Deborah Stead, and Igor Reichlin (1992), "After Yeltsin's Strong Medicine, A Few Twitches of Life," *Business Week* (March 2), 50–51. Hofheinz, Paul (1992), "Russia Starts All Over Again," *Fortune* (January 13), 60–61. Ignatius, Adl (1992), "Moscow Entrepreneurs in Street Kiosks Point Way to New Economy," *The Wall Street Journal* (March 25), A1, A8. Relohlin, Igor (1992), "Where Cutthroat Competition Means Exactly That," *Business Week* (March 2), 51. "Russia's Entrepreneurs: The Wild East" (1992), *Economist* Vol. 322, No. 7740 (January 4), 40–41. Zuckerman, Mortimer B. (1992), "The Rubles Just Don't Add Up," (Editorial), *U.S. News & World Report* (April 27), 80.

nies. Some major foreign investors in U.S. retailing have included the German Tenglemann Group (A&P), B.A.T. Industries of England (Marshall Field, Saks Fifth Avenue, and others), and Campeau of Canada (Allied Stores and Federated Stores).

The retail mix and know-how of retailers also crosses international boundaries. This is evident in the sale of imported products and services, the transfer of operating formats, promotional methods, and technology.

Finally, a number of variables must be considered in making decisions about entering international retail markets. The entry procedure and decisions are related to how well the market can satisfy the retailers preestablished performance criteria. A six-step sequence is recommended: (1) evaluate the international retailing environment, (2) decide whether to enter foreign markets, (3) decide which foreign markets to enter, (4) decide how to enter the markets, (5) decide on the retailing program, and (6) decide on the retailing organization.

Questions for Review and Comprehension

1. Distinguish between a global retailing strategy and a multinational retailing strategy. Give examples of retailers who are pursuing each type of expansion strategy.

2. Briefly describe each of the five major categories of multinational retailers provided by Stanley Hollander. Based on the present worldwide political and economic environment, what retail trends do you foresee in each of these classifications?

3. If you were the owner of a large U.S. retail chain, what factors would be most apt to motivate you to expand into foreign markets? What are the trade-offs involved in limiting a retail business to domestic markets versus adopting an international expansion strategy?

4. Discuss the reasons why the U.S. market has been so attractive to foreign investors in retailing. Name several of the major foreign firms that are involved in ownership of U.S. retailers, and describe their strategies for entering the American market.

5. Explain what is meant by the phrase, "international retailing involves a transfer of influence."

6. Identify and evaluate current trends in the "transfer of influence" relative to products and/or services, operating formats, promotional methods, and technology as these have been implemented by retailers worldwide.

7. Visit a local supermarket, discount store, department store, and a specialty store. Observe and analyze those factors that contribute to the globalization of retailing.

8. Outline the six steps that are involved in deciding whether to enter a foreign market. Would this procedure be different for a service retailer than for a product retailer? If so, how?

9. Assume that you are considering the expansion of your chain of auto parts stores into either the Far East or Europe. What specific questions would have to be answered in regard to the economic, legal and political, and cultural environments, as well as the trade system between countries? What criteria should be used when evaluating the answers to these questions in order to make a Go/No go decision for foreign market entry?

10. Continuing with the example discussed in your answer to number 9 above, what types of questions should be asked before deciding (1) whether to enter foreign market(s), (2) which foreign market(s) to enter, (3) how to enter the selected market(s), (4) the appropriate retailing program, and (5) the retailing organization that will be required for this new venture?

References

Agins, Teri (1990), "Barneys' Style Gets Translated into Japanese," *The Wall Street Journal* (May 29), B1, B6.

Agins, Teri and Yumiko Ono (1990), "Japanese Market Lures, Vexes Retailers," *The Wall Street Journal* (May 29), B1, B4.

Agnew, Joe (1987), "'Aussie Mania' Sweeps the U.S.: Consumers Drawn to Mystique of Land Down Under," *Marketing News* 21, no. 4, (November 20), 1, 10.

Alexander, Nicholas (1990), "Retailing Post-1992," *Service Industries Journal* 10, no. 1 (January), 172–187.

Bivens, Jacquelyn (1986a), "Foreign Exchange Benefits Both Sides," *Chain Store Age Executive* (October), 43.

Bivens, Jacquelyn (1986b), "Retailing in France: Ooo-la-la!" *Chain Store Age Executive* (July), 11–16.

Bylinsky, Gene (1989), "Where Japan Will Strike Next" *Fortune* (September 25), 42–46, 48, 50, 52.

"Companies to Watch: Pier 1 Imports" (1990), *Fortune* (July 2), 93.

Cote, Kevin (1990), "Promotions, Sampling Sweeping E. Germany," *Advertising Age* 61, no. 28, (July 9), 3, 42.

Deveny, Kathleen, J. E. Pluenneke, D. J. Yang, M. Maremont, and R. Black (1986), "McWorld? McDonald's Can Make a Big Mac Anywhere. But Duplicating Its Culture Abroad Won't Be So Easy," *Business Week* (October 13), 78–82, 86.

Downs, Anthony (1987), *Foreign Capital in U.S. Real Estate Markets.* New York: Salomon Brothers Inc.

Dreyfack, Kenneth (1986), "Draping Old Glory Around Just About Everything," *Business Week* (October 27), 66, 68.

Duke, Paul Jr. (1988), "These Clothes Have Plenty of Mystique—and Lots of Zippers," *The Wall Street Journal* (February 24), 1, 13.

Exstein, Michael B. and Faye I. Weitzman (1991), "Foreign Investment in U.S. Retailing: An Optimistic Overview," *Retail Control* 59, no. 1, (January), 9–14.

Fine, Jennifer (1988), "Hypermarket Generates Hyper-crowd," *Dallas Times Herald* (January 5), c-2+; Special Advertising Supplement, December 27, 1987; January 10, 1988, 14A, 15A.

Fishman, Arnold (1990), "International Mail Order Guide," *Direct Marketing* 52, no. 6, (October), 48–56.

Fuhrman, Peter (1990), "You Are What You Cook With," *Forbes* 146, no. 14, (December 24), 46, 48.

Fuller, Stephen S. (1989), "Glasnost Opens Door for Joint U.S./U.S.S.R. Development Exchange," *Corporate Real Estate Executive* (June), 64–65.

"Globalization Technology to Be 21st Century's Major Influences" (1987), *Marketing News* 21, no. 16, (July 31), 27.

Goldman, Arieh (1981), "Transfer of a Retailing Technology into the Less Developed Countries: The Supermarket Case," *Journal of Retailing* 57, no. 2, (Summer), 5–29.

Goldstein, Carl (1990), "Counter Offensive: Regional Supermarket Groups Invade Taiwan," *Far Eastern Economic Review (Hong Kong)* 148, no. 14, (April 4), 41–42.

Golob, Steven (1987), "Sell Abroad; You Can Collect," *Nation's Business* (November), 44.

Graven, Kathryn (1990), "For Toys 'R' Us, Japan Isn't Child's Play," *The Wall Street Journal* (February 7), B1.

Gupte, Pranay (1987), "Shamianas, Anyone?" *Forbes* (October 5), 190, 194.

Hamill, Jim and John Crosbie (1990), "British Retail Acquisitions in the U.S.," *International Journal of Retail and Distribution Management (UK)* 18, no. 5, (September/October), 15–20.

Hertzfeld, Jeffrey M. (1991), "Joint Ventures: Saving the Soviets from Perestroika," *Harvard Business Review* 69, no. 1, (January/February), 80–91.

Hofheinz, Paul (1990), "McDonald's Beats Lenin 3 to 1," *Fortune* (December 17), 11.

Holden, Ted (1989), "Who Says You Can't Break into Japan?" *Business Week* (Industrial/Technology Edition) (October 16), 49.

Holden, Ted (1991), "A Retail Rebel Has the Establishment Quaking," *Business Week* (April 1), 39–40.

Hollander, Stanley C., *Multinational Retailing* (1970), MSU International Business and Economic Studies, Michigan State University, East Lansing, Mich., Chapters II, III, IV.

Huey, John (1990), "America's Hottest Export: Pop Culture," *Fortune* (December 31), 50–53.

"Intelligence Report: McDonald's Thriving" (1986), *Parade Magazine* (June 15), 15.

International Marketing Handbook (1985), 2d ed. vol 3, Frank E. Bair, ed., Detroit, Mich.: Gale Research Co.

Jain, Subhash C. (1985), *Marketing Planning and Strategy.* 2d ed., Cincinnati, Ohio: South-Western Publishing Co., 605–606, 621.

Jefferson, David J. (1988), "U.S. Grocer Stages Supermarket Coup with Royal Couple," *The Wall Street Journal* (February 23), 36.

Johnson, Jay L. (1990), "Carrefour Revisited," *Discount Merchandiser* 30, no. 8, (August), 24–30.

Johnson, Robert (1988), "More U.S. Companies Are Selling Operations to Foreign Concerns," *The Wall Street Journal* (February 24), 1, 17.

Kacker, Madhav P. (1985), *Transatlantic Trends in Retailing: Takeovers and Flow of Know-How.* Westport, Conn.: Quorum Books.

Khachaturian, Janet L. and Michelle A. Morganosky (1990), "Quality Perceptions by Country of Origin," *International Journal of Retail & Distribution Management (UK)* 18, no. 5, (September/October), 21–30.

Kotler, Philip (1991), *Marketing Management: Analysis, Planning, Implementation, and Control,* 7th ed., Englewood Cliffs, N.J.: Prentice-Hall, Inc., ch 14.

Labich, Kenneth (1986), "America's International Winners," *Fortune* (April 14), 34–36, 40, 44, 46.

Levin, Gary (1991), "Benetton Gets the Kiss-Off" *Advertising Age* (July 22), 1, 40.

Long, Bernard (1989), "Hong Kong Shows No Signs of Future Shock," *Investment Properties International* (January/February), 30–34.

Machalaba, Daniel (1988), "U.S. Exports Become Hard to Contain as Bookings of Shipping Lines Surge," *The Wall Street Journal* (February 23), 6.

Manguno, Joseph P. (1989), "Korean VCR Makers' Invasion of U.S. Backfires as Profit Margins Disappear," *The Wall Street Journal* (April 5), A6.

Maremont, Mark (1990), "Did Sock Shop Get Too Big for Its Britches?" *Business Week* (January 15), 39–40.

Maremont, Mark and Julie Fingersh (1990), "The Brit Invasion that Could Rock Tower Records," *Business Week* (December 3), 41.

Maremont, Mark, Dori Jones Yang, and Amy Dunkin (1987), "Toys "R" Us Goes Overseas—and Finds that Toys "R" Them, Too," *Business Week* (January 26), 71–72.

"Marketing Can Be Global, But Ads Must Remain Cultural" (1987), *Marketing News* 21, no. 16, (July 31), 26.

"Melbourne Central: Dazzle Down Under" (1990), *Chain Store Age Executive* 66, no. 5, (May), 162, 165.

Melloan, George (1990), "Big Macs Yes, But Don't Wait Up for Russian Capitalism" *The Wall Street Journal* (February 5), A15.

Miller, Paul (1990), "International Marketing: Border Crossings," *Catalog Age* vol 7, no. 4, (April), 67–69.

Mitton, Alan E. (1987), "Foreign Retail Companies Operating in the U.K.: Strategy and Performance," *Retail & Distribution Management* (January/February), 29–31.

Moffat, Susan (1990), "Toy Wars in Japan," *Fortune* (March 12), 12.

Morgenson, Gritchen (1991), "Barbie Does Budapest," *Forbes* 147, no. 1, (January 7), 66–69.

Ody, Penelope (1989), "Internationalism: The Route to Growth," *Retail and Distribution Management* (March/April), 6–9.

Ono, Yumiko (1990), "Japanese Chains Setting Sights on U.S. Market," *The Wall Street Journal* (April 13), B1, B2.

Ozawa, Kiyoshi (1990), "The Vision of Chairman Kazuo Wada, Cosmopolitan Retailer," *Tokyo Business Today (Japan)* 58, no. 8, (August), 38–41.

Palmer, George (1990), "Western Firms Jostle for a Share in Japan's Retail Revolution," *Multinational Business* (Autumn), 9–17.

Pellet, Jennifer (1990), "Jewelry: An Eclectic Mix," *Discount Merchandiser* 30, no. 10, (October), 68–69.

Pellew, Martyn (1990), "Physical Distribution in International Retailing," *International Journal of Retail & Distribution Management* 18, no. 2, (March/April), 12–15.

Phillips, Lisa and Brenda Sternquist (1990), "Hong Kong Declining as World Retail Center," *Marketing News* 24, no. 14, (July 9), 8.

Qiang, Guo and Phil Harris (1990), "Retailing Reform and Trends in China," *International Journal of Retail & Distribution Management* 18, no. 5, (September/October), 31–39.

Rainat, Joyce (1991), "Food Retailing: An Emerging Market for Supermarkets," *Asian Finance* 17, no. 1, (January 15), 9.

Rainat, Joyce (1990), "The Endless Spree of Thai Store King," *Asian Finance* 16, no. 8, (August 15), 16–18.

Raiter, Gregory (1991), "Inside Intelligence on Soviet Venures," *HR Magazine* 36, no. 1, (January), 46–49.

Reese, Jennifer (1990), "News Trends: Avon Knocking on China's Doors," *Fortune* (December 17), 12, 16.

Revzin, Philip (1990), "French Luxury-Goods Makers Bid Adieu to Days When Market Was All Theirs," *The Wall Street Journal* (June 25), B1, B2.

Riemer, Blanca, Richard A. Melcher, Jonathan Kapstein, Frank J. Comes, and William C. Symonds (1988), "A Cash Rich Europe Finds the U.S. Ripe for Picking," *Business Week* (January 25), 48–49.

Sanghavi, Nitin (1990), "Non-Store Retailing in Japan: A Huge and Potentially Lucrative Market," *International Journal of Retail and Distribution Management* 18, no. 1, (January/February), 19–23.

Schiro, Thomas J. and Amy M. Skolnik (1990), "Europe 1992—Impact on Retail Sector," *Retail Control* 58, no. 5, (May/June), 3–9.

Schlossberg, Howard (1990), "Japan Market Hardly Closed to U.S. Firms," *Marketing News* 24, no. 14, (July 9), 1, 12.

Schultz, Ellen (1989), "A Tandy Spinoff Whose Earnings Have Bloomed," *Fortune*

(March 13), 26.

Schwadel, Francine (1990), "Woolworth Is Bargaining on Return to East Germany," *The Wall Street Journal* (June 20), B1, B3.

Selwyn, Michael (1990), "Sewing Up the World," *Asian Business* 26, no. 6, (June), 60–62.

"Sexually Excited Man Finds Chick Affectionate" (1987), *Advertising Age* (February 9), S-23.

Shao, Maria (1988), "Laying the Foundation for the Great Mall of China," *Business Week* (January 25), 68–69.

Shapiro, Isaac and Constance C. Hamilton (1990), "How to Succeed in Japan: Time for U.S. Firms to Focus on Post-Entry Survival," *East Asian Executive Reports* 12, no. 5, (May 15), 8, 13–18.

"Shopping Centres in and out of Town" (1987), *Retail & Distribution Management* (March/April), 36, 38, 40, 42, 44.

Sonsino, Steven (1990), "Making Pan-European Retailing Work," *Datamation* (International Edition), 36, no. 23, (December 1), 80(4)–80(8).

"Studying Current Trends Leads to Global Marketing Success in 2000" (1987), *Marketing News* 21, no. 16, (July 31), 27–28.

Swasy, Alecia and Jeremy Mark (1989), "Japan Brings Its Packaged Goods to U.S.," *The Wall Street Journal* (January 17), B1.

"Swedish Retailer IKEA Adding Nearly 900,000 Sq. Ft. in US" (1987), *Real Estate Times* (September 1), 3.

Symonds, William C. and Amy Dunkin (1987), "Benetton Is Betting on More of Everything," *Business Week* (March 23), 93.

Terry, Edith (1987a), "Canada's Labatt Has Just One Way to Grow: South" *Business Week* (November 9), 70.

Terry, Edith (1987b), "How Far Can Philips Elbow Its Way into the U.S.?" *Business Week* (March 2), 46–47.

"The Body Shop—A Winner, Naturally" (1990), *Chain Store Age Executive* 66, no. 9 (September), 104.

Treadgold, Alan (1990a), "Coming Together for a Common Market," *Discount Merchandiser* 30, no. 12, (December), 56–57, 66.

Treadgold, Alan (1990b), "The Developing Internationalisation of Retailing," *International Journal of Retail & Distribution Management* 18, no. 2, (March/April), 4–11.

"U.S. Cheesemaker Striving to Create Loyalty for Its Import-Quality Brand" (1987), *Marketing News* 21, no. 24, (November 20), 8.

"U.S. Movie Theaters Making Soviet Debut" (1990), *Southern Illinoisan* (March 18), B11.

"USSR: New Thinking for Foreign Trade," Special Advertising Section (1987), *Business Week* (December 14), 137–142.

"Us and Them: U.S. Toy Store Still Faces Japan Hitches" (1990), *Far Eastern Economic Review* 149, no. 33, (August 16), 60.

Valigra, Lori (1990), "Japan—Note to Retailers: Don't Rock the Boat; Statistical Profile," *Asian Business* 26, no. 5, (May), 50–56.

Waddell, Ian (1991), "Spain: The Sleeping Giant," *Chain Store Age Executive* (Section 1), 67, no. 1, (January), 48, 50.

Weihrich, Heinz (1991), "Europe 1992 and a Unified Germany: Opportunities and Threats for United States Firms," *Academy of Management Executive* 5, no. 1, 93–96.

Weil, Henry (1989), "Soaring Sales at Duty-Free Shops," *Fortune* (April 24), 225, 228, 232–233.

Wessel, David (1988), "Despite Fallen Dollar, Americans Continue to Snap up Imports," *The Wall Street Journal* (February 9), 1, 23.

Westlake, Tim (1990), "Electronic Home Shopping: When Does It Begin?" *International Journal of Retail & Distribution Management* 18, no. 2, (March/April), 33–38.

Whiteside, David, Otis Port, and Larry Armstrong (1988), "Sony Isn't Mourning the 'Death' of Betamax," *Business Week* (January 25), 37.

Wilder, Clinton (1990), "More Than Skin Deep: Values Come Before IS Technology at Personal Care Products Maker, The Body Shop," *Computerworld* 24, no. 43, (October 22), 67–68.

Wingis, Chuck (1983), "ComputerLand Poised for Global Surge," *Advertising Age* (May 23), 38.

Yang, Dori Jones (1989), "Hong Kong Hoteliers Start Colonizing the West" *Business Week* (March 16), 44.

Zabijaka, Val (1987), "Soviet Foreign Trade Reforms Offer New Challenges for U.S. Business," *Business America* (August 17), 6–9.

Zachary, Pascal (1990), "Businessland Enters Japan, Aided by 4 Big Local Firms," *The Wall Street Journal* (June 6), B1, B4.

Zottola, Lory (1990), "The United Systems of Benetton," *Computerworld* 24, no. 14, (April 2), 70.

Company Annual Reports: K mart, McDonald's, Sears, Toys "R" Us, and Wal-Mart.

6.1 Ronald McDonald: Go Home

Most people are familiar with McDonald's successes, but few are aware that this successful international fast-food business has had major problems in establishing itself in overseas markets. These problems are those faced by any multinational corporation. Problems such as legal restrictions, political upheavals, nationalism, and cultural barriers have all been faced by McDonald's. In some instances these problems have been dealt with to the company's satisfaction, and in others they have not. Some of the obstacles McDonald's faced while expanding internationally over the past ten years and the environment in which they arose are described below.

One of the most publicized of these obstacles involved McDonald's Paris franchise. The franchisee in Paris, Raymond Dayan, did not maintain the restaurants according to McDonald's standards. Dayan not only refused to conform to company standards, but refused to give up the stores or the McDonald's name. Only after a lengthy legal battle did McDonald's obtain a ban on the use of its name by the franchisee, however, Dayan retained the restaurants in Paris, now run under the name of O'Kitch, and McDonald's lost the prime locations occupied by these stores.

A legal problem of another nature is illustrated by the company's attempts to enter the Venezuelan market. In 1980 McDonald's received a trademark in Venezuela, but since they did not open a restaurant in the required amount of time, McDonald's trademark protection expired. McDonald's subsequently opened a restaurant in partnership with a local businessman who insisted the Venezuelan government gave him the right to use the McDonald's name. Shortly thereafter, a Venezuelan fast-food chain under the name of McDonald's Venta de Comida said it had first rights to McDonald's expired trademark. McDonald's Venta de Comida refused to change its name, filed suit in a Venezuelan court to retain the McDonald trademark and opened a "McDonald's" of its own.

Legal battles are not the only obstacles faced by McDonald's in Latin America. In Argentina the market is plagued not only by political unrest, but also by triple digit inflation. The company changes menu prices more often there and in other Latin American countries than anywhere else.

One of the largest McDonald's restaurants is located in Rome, Italy. The restaurant has suffered from attacks made by prominent Roman citizens and government officials. Fashion designer Valentino alleged the fumes and crowds associated with the restaurant stifled his creativity, so he brought suit against the restaurant. In an attempt to close the

" THEY DIDN'T SAY DO YELTSIN OR GORBACHEV... THEY SAID DO SOMEBODY WHO INFLUENCED OUR DESIRE FOR FREEDOM ! "

restaurant, the city charged that a historic building had been illegally altered in developing the restaurant, until it was discovered that only the facade, which was never altered, was historic. The company was charged further with illegally changing a window into a fire escape; but when officials found that the window had once been a door, they decided that nothing illegal had taken place. In addition to the above hindrances, demonstrations against the restaurant have taken place protesting the admittance of an American fast-food restaurant to Rome. McDonald's, nonetheless, opened additional restaurants in Rome, and so the saga continues.

Nationalistic reactions to McDonald's in Europe have led to the opening of a European clone by the name of Quick. Many Europeans object to the American company's invasion of Europe and patronize Quick because it is less American! The company imitates McDonald's ideas, techniques, and even its menu items. The Big Mac, Quarter Pounder, and other items are there, under different names and often at lower prices. Ethnocentrism is alive and well in the fast-food industry.

Supply problems are often an impediment for American firms overseas, and McDonald's is no exception. The world's largest McDonald's restaurant opened in Moscow in January 1990. Because a dependable source of items such as ground beef and buns was not available at a suitable level of quality, the company built a meat plant, bakery, potato plant, and dairy, and must import the required packaging materials. In order to ensure a steady supply of the proper type of potatoes

continued

for its Eastern European stores, McDonald's has overseen the introduction of its Russet potatoes into the agriculture. McDonald's has yet to open an outlet in China, because the company believes that supply problems similar to those encountered in Moscow would be too costly to overcome in China. In addition, the company feels that sources of demand and disciplined labor are not yet sufficient in the country.

QUESTIONS

1. How are the problems faced by McDonald's in its overseas expansion different from those it might encounter in domestic expansion?
2. How does this differ from the experience of an overseas retailer entering the U.S. market?
3. How might a retailer protect itself from the problems encountered by McDonald's?

References

Chase, Dennis (1986), "McDonald's Ponders Pan-Europe TV Plans," *Advertising Age* (June 16).
Deveny, Kathleen, John Pluennedke, Dori Jones Yang, Mark Maremont, and Robert Black (1986), "McWorld?" *Business Week* (October 13).

Greenhouse, Steven (1986), "The Rise and Rise of Big Mac," *New York Times* (June 8).
Gumbel, Peter (1988), "Golden Arches to Rise Near Kremlin as McDonald's Sets a Moscow Venture," *The Wall Street Journal* (May 2).
Hume, Scott (1990), "How Big Mac Made It to Moscow," *Advertising Age* (January 22).
Johnson, Robert (1987), "Wide Horizons for McDonald''s Cantalupo," *The Wall Street Journal* (April 27).
Meller, Paul (1990), "Back to the USSR," *Marketing* (August 9).
Newman, Barry (1986), "Its Eye on Fries, Poland Pursues Potato Parity," *The Wall Street Journal* (October 9).
Sabo, Roberta (1985), "Venezuelans Get Two McDonald's," *Advertising Age* (October 28).
Skarda, Tone (1983), "Will U.S. Big Mac Replace Norwegian Hot Dog?" *Advertising Age* (September 26).
Rothnie-Jones, Debbie (1988), "Japanese Markets: Young Yen to be Yuppies," *Marketing* (June 2).
"Will Big Mac Meet Its Match in the Land of the Rising Sun?" (1973), *Forbes* (May 15).

This case was prepared by Leonard Konopa, Kent State University, Kent, Ohio, and Sandra Loeb, University of South Dakota, Vermillion, South Dakota.

6.2 TAYLOR INTERNATIONAL BUYING DILEMMA

During his annual buying trip to the Far East, Jeremy Taylor had plans to buy men's suits for the Taylor Department Store located in El Paso, Texas. He visited a very large suit manufacturer with 1,500 employees in Dalian, China. In discussion with the factory manager he learned that he could buy high quality men's suits (on a par with Jordache) manufactured at this factory for $35.00 each. The terms will be *FOB factory, using letters of credit.*[1] Modern sewing machines were in use throughout the factory. The workers seemed to be highly skilled. The factory manager stated that business in the amount of $8 million each year is done with the United States.

Taylor's merchandise mix is mostly apparel including cowboy boots and hats. The store's annual sales average $15 million. The market served by Taylor's has incomes of $50,000 and up. Socially this population is a reference group in El Paso society, and brand names are important to them. However, remember that China is a communist country where everybody works for the government. Quality control is often suspect, with no guarantee that top quality effort will be sustained by any producer in China. Another problem is that token promises for a certain delivery date may or may not be kept. If Taylor Department Store purchases the goods, the store faces a risk for noncompliance. Freight and insurance to El Paso could double the cost of the purchase for Taylor's.

QUESTIONS

1. Should Jeremy Taylor place an order with the Chinese factory? Explain why or why not.
2. Are there ways to reduce the risk?
3. Can a small independent retailer create an image sufficient to have a private brand?

[1] F.O.B. factory—buyer pays all charges from the factory; Letter of Credit—document issued by a bank upon request of an importer stating that it will honor drafts drawn against it by a specified party.

This case was prepared by Keith T. Stephens, Western Carolina University, Cullowhee, North Carolina.

6.3 The Limited Knows No Global Bounds

The Limited was created in 1963 by Leslie Wexner when he borrowed $5,000 from his aunt to start a women's retail store; today it sells more women's clothing and accessories than any other merchant in the world, including such giants of retailing as Sears, J.C. Penney, and K mart. Leslie Wexner has seen both good and bad times with The Limited, but he has emerged as a billionaire as the value of his company's stock has skyrocketed.

More than 2,400 Limited stores serve seven different segments of the market. It is one of the biggest players in the nation's booming mail-order catalog business. Overall it has achieved astounding results; in the later part of the 1980s, on the average, sales rose 55 percent a year and net income increased by a phenomenal 64 percent annually.

Leslie Wexner is a retailing prodigy. In an industry showing signs of complacency, he has developed a more limber form of fashion retailing—an empire vertically integrated like a major oil company and standardized like a fast-food chain. He bypassed the industry's traditional, slow-moving production system, with its innumerable middlemen, and created his own global manufacturing and distribution network.

Specialty fashion chains like The Limited are the new wave in retailing. Others include The Gap, a California chain, and Benetton, an Italian franchisor. They cater to the insatiable taste of younger Americans for fresh, affordable apparel—exuberantly reinterpreted classics rather than designer novelties.

But none can match the size of The Limited fed by Wexner's unrelenting acquisition strategy. (Wall Street analysts maintain what one calls "the Wexner watch" waiting for him to gobble another major chain of stores.) No other fashion retailer so dominates the suburban shopping malls where American consumers now spend vast quantities of their time and money.

In 1983, The Limited's president was on a trip through Italy; she spotted teenagers in Florence buying bulky yachting sweaters. The sweater was copied by The Limited—in retail trade parlance it was "knocked off"—and, under the The Limited's private label, Forenza, sold millions. (Forenza, shrewdly named to evoke a nonexistent Italian designer, is one of the best selling sportswear brands in the country.) This is a perfect example of how The Limited is able to spot trends in other countries and transport them to the United States. What took place in 1983 is constantly being repeated as we enter the 1990s.

Monday night in Columbus, Ohio, in a windowless conference room deep in the recesses of The Limited's giant distribution center, the weekly merchandise meeting for the 600 stores of The Limited Stores division, the company's flagship chain, has been called to order. Similar conferences for the six other divisions are under way elsewhere in the center and in New York. These sessions are the first step in the process that determines what millions of American women will be wearing.

On the agenda this particular Monday evening in September is nothing less than the mounting of a spring offensive. The debate rages concerning a new line of safari clothing, a look already implanted in yuppie-consciousness by Banana Republic, a San Francisco-based retailing phenomenon owned by The Gap. The executives go on to examine the clothing on the conference table. The safari jacket from Banana Republic is a natural. The soft, flower-printed shirt from Laura Ashley in London adds the right feminine note to the khaki jacket. The tan cotton pants from Europe are a perfect match. With a touch here and there, these garments will form the basis for a new line—hardly original, but not a total knockoff either.

The promising new line is named Outback Red. Its advertising trademark: a pouting, red-headed model wearing a safari coat and an Australian outback hat. But before committing The Limited to full production, Verna Gibson, the president of The Limited division, wants to check its sales appeal.

In late November, samples of the collection—sweaters, shirts, skirts, pants, vests, and shorts—appear in a handful of stores in southern cities. Every evening after closing, cash registers are checked to determine which colors and styles are moving and how customers are reacting to the price tags.

After the Thanksgiving weekend, the results are in. Certain adjustments must be made. Pleated pants, for example, have outsold those with plain fronts. But overall, the new line is a hit. Wexner and his staff decide to distribute Outback Red nationally. He wants 500,000 garments in the stores within 10 weeks. "You can't patent anything in the clothing business," he says. "So you've got to get stuff to the consumer first if you want to be successful."

Producing a collection of such magnitude so fast would be impossible for most retailers. They are dependent on middlemen such as Seventh Avenue [New York] wholesalers, importers, and independent buying offices. A department store might have to allow ten months for delivery of such a vast order.

The Limited, however, has an edge. In 1978, Wexner took on a huge debt to buy Mast Industries, an importer and contract manufacturer. Mast has interests in a dozen factories in Asia and longstanding relationships with 190 factories around the world. It also has coordinated global transport. "Mast is The Limited's trump card," says the president of a competing specialty chain. "It's light years ahead in terms of understanding how to get things done in the Far East."

If fabric must be moved from China to Korea, a Mast employee is on hand to get cloth through customs. If Columbus is desperate for a shipment of pants, a Mast executive in Hong Kong gets them on the next plane out; The Limited's merchandise fills an average of three U.S.-bound 747s a week.

Outback Red presents The Mast with a formidable challenge: to track down hundreds of thousands of yards of khaki-colored fabric at a reasonable price. Mast finds the material at a mill in China. The bolts of fabric are shipped to Hong Kong for dyeing, finishing, and printing. Then the piece goods are distributed for manufacturing—pants to Hong Kong, shorts to Mauritius, shirts to Sri Lanka.

While Third World sewing machines are stitching to The Limited's beat, Leslie Wexner is circling the globe in his new Gulfstream jet. In Tokyo, he introduces his company to Japanese institutional investors. After checking with Mast suppliers in Hong Kong and touring his factories in Mauritius, he heads for Jerusalem. There, Wexner discusses with government officials a plan to set up three apparel plants near the Golan Heights to be owned jointly by The Limited and Chinese and Israeli interests.

In late January, Mast employees begin loading the Outback Red line onto jets for the journey to California and New York. After clearing customs, the goods are transferred to a fleet of tractor-trailers, owned by The Limited and operated by Walsh Trucking, a New Jersey-based company, and rushed to the distribution center in Columbus. The journey from the Far East to Columbus has taken six days, too many for Wexner. He wants an airfield south of Columbus designated an international port of entry, which would cut that time in half.

In cartons and hanger packs, the Outback Red line moves steadily along a computerized freeway of conveyor belts. Workers attach price tags while Madonna sings accompaniment. Sorters separate the clothes into stacks destined for individual stores. Packers heft the stacks into boxes—to the tune of Willie Nelson's "On The Road Again." On a conveyor belt that looks like a ski slope, the boxes slide toward computerized selected trucking bays.

In an average of forty-eight hours, a garment passes through the distribution center. Most retailers are plagued by inventories that languish in less-automated warehouses for weeks on end. Such schedules may suffice for the industry's traditional selling seasons— fall–winter and spring–summer— but The Limited has abandoned this approach, feeding fresh merchandise into its stores at the rate of two shipments per week. Wexner believes that women are more inclined to visit a store regularly if they know there will be something new to look at. "People don't buy what they already have," Wexner has stated.

On the first Monday in February, Outback Red goes on sale in 600 chrome-and-glass stores from coast to coast, and the presentation is everywhere the same. Twice a month, merchandisers meet in Columbus to choose displays for the next two weeks. Blueprints and photographs accompany the props and furniture dispatched to the stores; no deviation is allowed. "We don't want 100 managers out there deciding what the stores should look like," declares Verna Gibson.

All over America, racks of Outback Red trousers and skirts stand just to the left of entranceways. In the window, amid palm trees and bushes, incredibly lifelike mannequins in flower printed shirts recline in tan wicker chairs.

The Limited does not release sales figures for its brands. The first evidence of a new line's success or failure appears on the price tag. Industry analysts who travel the country, visiting the stores, report no markdowns on Outback Red, whose prices range from about $20 for a shirt to about $50 for a jacket. A retail industry analyst is quoted as saying: "This could be a $500 million line, which would make it the fourth largest women's sportswear brand in the United States."

QUESTIONS

1. Why would Verna Gibson want to check the potential for sales appeal for the Outback Red line before she commits to production?
2. Why would The Limited test market the new Outback Red line in November in southern cities?
3. Why would markdowns on the Outback Red line indicate that consumer acceptance is not as it was anticipated to be?
4. What is the risk that you take by contract manufacturing with a foreign-based factory?

This case was prepared by Richard C. Leventhal, Metropolitan State College, Denver, Colorado.

APPENDIX: A FUTURE IN RETAILING

Whatever you can do, or dream you can, begin it. Boldness has genius, power and magic in it.—Goethe

WHY PURSUE A CAREER IN RETAILING?

Challenge, creativity, reward, security, personal relations: students in retailing classes at major universities identified these five factors as the most significant reasons to choose a career. **Challenge** was related to work that is important, meaningful, prestigious, and has challenging content and training, and uses quantitative skills. **Creativity** was associated with work that is interesting, and involves opportunity for communication, autonomy, and characteristics of the work environment. **Reward** included salary, advancement, benefits, and location. **Job security** and **personal relations** were important—but to a lesser degree—in choosing a career. The overriding reason to choose a particular career path was whether or not it promised to be challenging and meaningful (Anderson, Parker and Stanley 1989).

A career in retailing *is* challenging and meaningful, and allows considerable opportunity for creativity, reward, and other personal benefits. The retailing industry has grown rapidly, expanding into new and exciting formats in the United States and overseas. Intelligent, energetic, enthusiastic managers are needed for these dynamic enterprises. Unfortunately, many college students and other prospective retail managers overlook the opportunities in this field because they have a negative perception of retailing, and often feel that a retailing career lacks prestige. This perception tends to evolve from everyday transactions with retail clerks who are not properly trained or motivated, or from unpleasant experiences in part-time retail jobs.

Retailing As A Growth Opportunity

In 1990, retail sales were approximately $1.8 trillion. By 1992, retail sales should exceed $2 trillion. Although economic downturns have had a negative impact on retail operations, the industry remains healthy and offers many opportunities for career development. The geographic expansion of major chains, the constant challenge to develop innovative formats that will appeal to a retailer's target market, and the increasing need for quick response in the marketplace result in the search for more—and better—managers. Likewise, the opportunity to own and manage a small retail business continues to attract many newcomers. Many small retailers offer a unique retail mix that allows them to serve a niche market quite successfully. Some of these small product or service retailers are franchised; others are independently owned.

The growth in retail employment from 1988 to 2000 is expected to reach nearly 20 percent. This growth rate is second only to service-producing businesses which include some retail services such as banking, as shown in Exhibit A-1. Although the number of jobs will increase, demographic trends indicate that the number of teenagers and young adults will decrease and the number of older workers (35 to 54 years) will increase as a percentage of the workforce during this time. These trends are favorable for younger men and women who want a career in retail management. The growth in

Exhibit A–1
Employment Outlook: 1988–2000

SOURCE: *Tomorrow's Jobs: Overview*. (1990), Bulletin 2350-1, Reprinted from the Occupational Outlook Handbook, 1990–91 Edition, U.S. Department of Labor, Bureau of Labor Statistics, Washington, DC: U.S. Government Printing Office, 4.

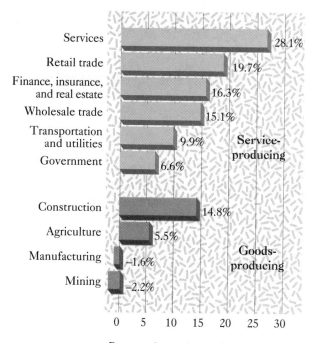

Percent change in employment, 1988–2000

management-related occupations is expected to increase 22 percent, from 12.1 to 14.8 million by 2000 (U.S. Bureau of Labor Statistics 1990–91). The industries that will need the most new managers are those with the highest rate of growth—a criteria that is met by the retail industry.

According to a survey conducted by Ernst & Young, the average annual salary for a department manager is $24,000. Soft line specialty stores offer the lowest average salaries ($18,300) and hard line specialty stores offer the highest ($27,100). The average annual salary for a store manager is $37,400. The range of average salaries is from $29,400 for soft line specialty stores, $37,900 for hard line specialty stores, $42,500 for mass merchandisers, to $50,400 for department stores. Over 9 out of 10 store managers and nearly 7 of 10 department managers are eligible for incentive bonuses in addition to their salaries (Shaw 1990). A profile of compensation for retail executives is presented in Exhibit A-2.

Are You the Right Person for A Retailing Career?

Most people spend a great deal of time learning subject matter that will help them land a certain type of job, but sometimes they do not spend enough time studying themselves. In the job search process, it is important to figure out who you are (e.g., skills, interests, values, needs, goals), where you are going (or want to go), how you plan to get there, and whether all of this is compatible with your innermost personal goals. In addition to knowing who you are, you must have a clear idea of what you can offer (i.e., market) to an employer. Information that may convince an employer that you are "right" for the job may be related to prior work experience, volunteer and extra-curricular activities. Emphasis should be placed on the opportunity to gain interpersonal, organizational, communication, leadership and decision-making skills. Academic background usually is an important indicator of an applicant's basic knowledge and skills. However, there may be other course-related activities that would interest an employer—such as class projects or independent studies that indicate your analytical skills and ability to see a project through from beginning to end. Each of these situations provides the opportunity for obtaining learning and experience. An inventory of these background characteristics can help you describe your credentials for a particular job. Self-appraisal is closely related to self-concept and, in turn, your self-concept will influence how effectively you communicate your strengths (and deal with your weaknesses) when "selling" yourself to a prospective employer.

RETAIL CAREER PATHS

What is a career? A career is more than just a job. It is an ongoing commitment to continuous learning and progressive achievements in a chosen line of work. Today's new managers

Exhibit A–2
Retail Executive Compensation

A Profile of Executive Compensation

Pay for performance is the big compensation story on the sales floor, and it's now the top issue in the executive suite as well. In fact, of the retailers participating in Ernst & Young's recently completed *National Survey of Executive Compensation*, 83 percent said their top executives were bonus-eligible, and where paid, these bonuses averaged 47 percent of the executive's base pay. The following compensation "profile" was compiled from the survey.

Retail Executives	Average 1990 Base Salary	Percentage of Bonus-eligible Executives	1989 Bonus (As a percentage of base salary)
Chief Executive	$263,600	84%	68%
COO	182,800	79	73
Top Financial Officer	108,000	87	35
Top Marketing and Sales Executive	118,800	84	65
Top Human Resources Executive	101,100	84	23
Top Legal Executive	129,800	95	29
Top Systems & Data Processing Executive	104,000	74	25
Operations and Merchandising Executives			
Top Distribution & Warehouse Executive	$ 95,400	85%	26%
Top Merchandise Executive	155,600	96	30
Top Security & Loss Prevention Executive	75,500	68	23
Top Store Operations Executive	`149,800	96	29
Top Store Planning & Fixturing Executive	92,100	73	17
Top Visual Merchandising Executive	94,500	75	32

SOURCE: Shaw, Susan K. (1990), "Ernst & Young Survey Reveals Widespread Use of Incentive Programs," *Ernst & Young's Retail News*. (Fall), 3.

SOURCE: Carter Hawley Hale company literature for the Emporium; Venture Stores.

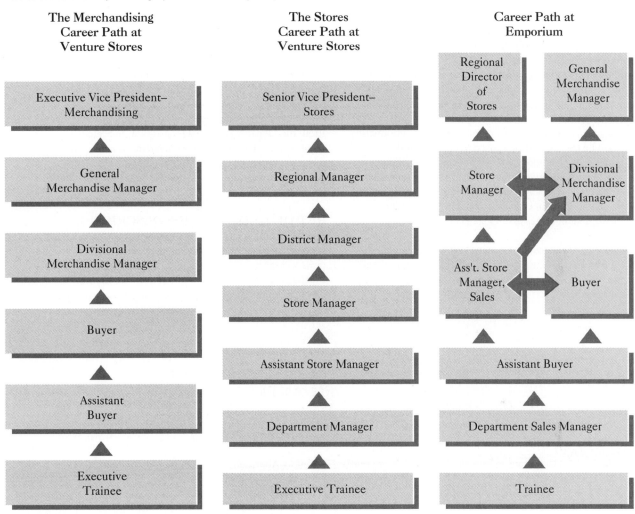

The Merchandising Career Path at Venture Stores	The Stores Career Path at Venture Stores	Career Path at Emporium

juggle their business skills and personal lifestyles for a more holistic approach to life than was the case in their parents' generation. Yes, the abilities to identify, analyze, make decisions about business problems, and communicate with others in the company are extremely important. However, today managers tend to seek careers that are consistent with their chosen lifestyles and that will allow them flexibility in performing their responsibilities.

A career path in retailing is capable of meeting these needs. A retail career can be pursued in a wide variety of retail firms: drugstores; department stores; grocery stores; fast food restaurants; hotels; specialty stores that focus on apparel, accessories, shoes, sporting goods, computers, video rentals, or many other narrowly defined product or service lines. The list

is very long and covers a wide range of interests and abilities. Some of these retailers are large chain organizations and some are small, independent "Mom and Pop" stores. Some follow a national location strategy; others follow a regional or international strategy. Some are discount stores that provide little or no customer service; others are full-price, full-service retailers. And the variety and contrasts can be expanded much further. The point is, a future retail manager can choose from a broad spectrum of career paths.

Overview of Retail Career Paths

There are two major career paths that can be pursued in a retail firm: merchandise management and store management. The specific progression through training and career development into upper management positions may vary according to the type of retailer, size of the company, organizational structure, and management preference. Therefore, the following discussion is intended to give a general overview of a typical career path that is directed toward either merchandising or store operations. Each will start with some type of executive training program. Training programs vary in length, degree of formality, and general procedures. Most training programs are of at least six months to a year's duration, and involve a combination of classroom instruction and on-the-job training. Typically, the trainee is exposed to each of the functional retail management areas such as human resources, visual merchandising, or information systems. The trainee is also exposed to managerial skills such as supervision, negotiation, and business planning. Thus, an individual on a management career path will gain broad-based experience, providing an opportunity to determine his/her interest and aptitude in each area. Exhibit A-3 illustrates a retail management career path for a major retailer.

Merchandise Management Career Path　After completion of the executive training program, the merchandising career path next may lead to an assistant buyer's position. In some cases, there is a progression of Assistant Buyer positions that moves the trainee from smaller to larger departments or merchandise lines. The typical sequence of positions will then be to Buyer, Divisional Merchandise Manager, General Merchandise Manager, Executive Vice President-Merchandising, and finally to the President's position.

Store Management Career Path　From the executive training program, the store management trainee will most likely assume the responsibilities of a Department Manager. As in the case of the Assistant Buyer, the trainee may progress from smaller to larger departments to gain additional experience, or may manage several departments at one time. From the Department Manager position, the career progression will probably be to Assistant Store Manager, Store Manager, District Manager, Regional Manager, Vice President-Stores (or Director-Stores), and finally to Chairman/Chief Executive Officer.

RETAIL TASKS AND JOB DESCRIPTIONS
Personnel offices in most retail firms can provide you with specific job descriptions that will give you a good idea of the tasks and responsibilities that are involved in each position. Prospective retail managers should examine these job descriptions relative to their own abilities, interests, and career

---

Exhibit A–4
••
The Management Trainee Program Structure

WEEK 1
Orientation and Seminar Training
The following is an overview of our program:

☐ Orientation
☐ Company and Corporate Information
☐ Basic Systems
☐ Organizational Structure
☐ Personnel/Career Development

WEEK 2
Buying
Buying Office Assignment—Management Trainee will be exposed to and actively participate in:

☐ Vendor Negotiations
☐ Sales Forecasting and Merchandise Plans
☐ Basic Reports
☐ Advertising Strategies
☐ Competitive Shopping
☐ Distribution Systems
☐ Branch Store Visits

WEEKS 3, 4, 5
Store Line—Selling
Store Training Assignment—Management Trainee will develop an expertise in Selling Skills and Customer Satisfaction.

☐ Selling Approach
☐ Building the Sale
☐ Sales Productivity
☐ The Clientele Program
☐ Product Knowledge

WEEKS 6, 7, 8
Store Line—Management
Store Training Assignment—Management Trainee will be exposed to merchandising and management responsibilities of a Department Sales Manager which include:

☐ Customer Service Standards
☐ Scheduling and Supervision of Sales Staff
☐ Department Operations
☐ Analysis of Departmental Business
☐ Communication with Central Merchandising Staff
☐ Competitive Shopping
☐ Merchandising of Selling Areas
☐ Introduction to Management Information Systems

SOURCE: Carter Hawley Hale company literature for the Emporium; Venture Stores

objectives. Selected examples of retail tasks in each of the functional retail management areas are listed below. Retailers may vary in their approaches to grouping these tasks, their relative importance, and degree of overlap from one area to another.

Merchandising

Merchandising responsibilities are focused on determining assortments that will appeal to the store's target market, buying goods in the wholesale markets for resale to the store's customers, selling activities, inventory management, and visual merchandising.

Store Operations

Store operations responsibilities include physical distribution, customer service, real estate, construction, security, and risk management. Other tasks that usually are managed within this function are store design, layout, HVAC (heating, ventilation and air conditioning), and engineering.

Human Resources

Responsibilities in the human resources area include recruiting, hiring, and training new employees. Human resource managers are also involved in ongoing personnel activities, such as employee evaluation, compensation programs, developing and delivering executive development programs, and other worker-related functions.

Promotion/communications

The location of the promotion/corporate communications function may vary from one organizational chart to another. The general tasks that must be performed include media advertising, sales promotion and special events, public relations, merchandise displays and signing, and other tasks from the perspective of communicating with customers. In addition, related tasks might involve communicating with employees, business partners, and the general public.

Accounting/financial

Accounting and finance managers develop and monitor all budgets at the corporate, business, and functional levels of the firm. They also are responsible for inventory control, credit records, preparation of income tax records and annual reports. Data processing and information systems may be within, or closely related to, this function.

PREPARATION FOR THE JOB SEARCH

The job search process is similar to marketing a new product to an identified customer group. In addition to knowing all relevant facts about the product (you) that can be used as selling points, it is equally important to know your target market (prospective employer). Analysis of your potential "customers" should include an identification of who they are and where they are located, a profile of their operating units,

organizational structure, business philosophy, and opportunities for personnel advancement. Insights also can be gained from an analysis of competition and trends in the particular retail industry in which it operates. The more you know about your "customer," the more effectively you can market yourself as a desirable product.

Where Do I Start: Job Hunting Strategies

Most colleges and universities offer placement services to their graduates. Major retailers have active campus recruiting programs that generally are coordinated through the placement service. Placement services and libraries have books, periodicals, and videotapes that contain a wealth of information about career choice, resumé writing, and interviewing strategies. They also should have recruiting brochures, annual reports, and other company literature available.

One approach to learning more about companies that you may be considering is presented in Exhibit A-5. Company research includes an analysis of the retailer's industry and operating environment. Research on the organization itself includes the retailer's mission and objectives, strategy mix, image, locations, organizational chart, financial analysis and other relevant topics.

Helpful Resources

There are a number of references in college and local libraries that contain information about individual companies, industry trends, resumé writing, job interview techniques, and other topics that are useful during the job search process. A few of these references are listed below, along with a brief description. You are encouraged to consult your library for others.

- Directory of Corporate Affiliations (National Register Publishing, annual) 2 volumes; list approximately 4,500 major corporations that are listed on the NYSE, AMEX, NASDAQ, or privately owned; lists divisions, subsidiaries, and affiliates for all companies; indexed alphabetically, geographically, and by SIC code.
- **Million Dollar Directory** (Dun's Marketing Services, annual) 5-volumes; lists 160,000 public and private U.S. companies with net worth of $500,000 or more; directory gives alphabetical listings by company name, geographic listings by state, and listings by industry using Standard Industrial Codes (SIC); and company address, officers, products, sales and number of employees.
- **Standard & Poor's Register** (Standard & Poor's, annual) 3-volumes; listing of 50,000 public and private U.S. companies; Volume I lists each company's address, officers, products, sales, number of employees, and so forth; Volumes II and III provide short biographies of executives and indexes arranged by SIC code and geographic location.

Industry
One place to start for a broad overview is with the retail industry. Standard Industrial Codes (SIC) are assigned to each type of business, and provide a convenient basis for locating relevant information.

Organization research
1. Situation analysis: Determine the retailer's mission, goals and objectives, strategies, target market, competition, and potential market (and sales projections).
2. Location analysis: Define the retailer's existing locations, planned locations and policy toward opening, closing, or acquiring new stores. Identify local competitors and their competitive advantage.
3. Personnel: Prepare an organizational chart of the firm, and determine where you would enter the firm and the subsequent career path that you would follow. Obtain job descriptions. Find out approximate salaries for positions along the career path; and learn about the types of people you would be working with.
4. Merchandise management: Determine the product mix carried by the retailer, including assortments, quality, and general merchandising practices. Learn about the physical distribution aspect of the business such as distribution centers, relationships with suppliers, and so forth.
5. Pricing policy: Determine the retailer's pricing strategies and tactics and related information such as average markups, and price change procedures.
6. Financial analysis: Track the company over a 5–10 year period and analyze the major strategic decisions made during this period of time, and the impact of these decisions on the profitability of the firm. Describe future strategies and their anticipated financial effect. Calculate profitability ratios from annual statement data and compare to published industry averages.

- **Occupational Outlook Handbook** (U.S. Bureau of Labor Statistics, biennial) Provides industry information about employment trends in various occupations, compensation, and other job-related concerns.
- **Occupational Outlook Quarterly** (U.S. Bureau of Labor Statistics) Articles on occupations, training opportunities, salary trends, career counseling; supplement to Occupational Outlook Handbook.
- **College Placement Annual** (College Placement Council) Articles by experienced professionals give information and advice about career planning, the job search and work-related education. Two companion volumes are Volume 2 that covers business and administrative positions (nontechnical) and Volume 3 covers engineering, computer, and other scientific (technical) positions.
- **Peterson's Guide to Business and Management Jobs** (Peterson's Guides, Princeton, NJ, annual) Information about job search procedures and resources; directories by companies with potential employment opportunities; directories by types of organizations, industry classifications, starting locations, number of employees, training programs, etc.

Other good sources of information are college placement offices, annual reports, and brochures from retail companies that describe their career paths and training programs. Trade associations such as those listed below often have industry-related publications, or perhaps lists of companies, that they will share with you.

National Retail Merchants Association (NRMA)
100 West 31st Street
New York, NY 10001

National Mass Retailing Institute
570 Seventh Avenue
New York, NY 10018

Food Marketing Institute
1750 K Street, N.W., Suite 700
Washington, DC 20006

National Association of Retail Grocers of the U.S.
1825 Samuel Morse Drive
Reston, VA 22090

RESUMÉ WRITING TIPS

The resumé is all that some recruiters will ever see of you—so it becomes an important "advertisement" of what you have to offer. In general, write your resumé yourself; this is a topic that you should know better than anyone else. Once the resumé is drafted, you should have a number of people read it and make suggestions. Your teachers, placement counselors, friends, and others can be helpful—although they will offer a wide range of advice. Remember that you are marketing yourself to a prospective employer, so the final content and appearance of your resumé must be a powerful sales tool for your abilities, and must be a true representation of what you have to offer. It must build a positive image by getting the recruiter's attention and creating a desire to know more about you through the interview process or on-site visit. The overall objective of the resumé and cover letter is to market yourself.

JOB INTERVIEW STRATEGIES

The job interview is a widely used tool in the employment selection process. Information provided in the pre-employment interview may or may not be an accurate indicator of future performance and satisfaction. However, the face-to-face contact does give each party an opportunity to "size up" the other, and to obtain information that may not be included in a resumé. The results of an initial interview generally determine whether or not the company is interested in continuing recruitment efforts with an applicant. Of course, the applicant also has an opportunity to formulate an impression of the company which may affect his/her interest in pursuing employment with the firm.

What the Recruiters Are Looking For

From the perspective of the recruiter, the job interview has several purposes. The interview is a forum for giving applicants information about the position and the company, and to create an interest in joining the firm. The recruiter expects to gain insights from the applicant that will give some indication of his/her future performance. Recruiters also try to determine whether there is a "match" between the applicant and the company's culture and employees. None of these objectives can be accomplished with a high degree of certainty during an interview, but some preliminary questions can be answered.

Retailers seek future managers who have a results orientation and leadership capability. An applicant's orientation toward achieving results is indicated by his/her skills in decision making and analysis, planning and organization, and his/her tendency to take action and to use an entrepreneurial approach. The recruiter may look for evidence of each of these qualities during the interview process. For example, decision making and analytical skills are indicated by confidence in making an informed decision about a problem situation, use of practical judgment, and ability to prioritize tasks. Planning and organizing skills are indicated by the ability to achieve long range goals and handle daily demands and to manage multiple projects simultaneously. Recruiters will also look for an applicant's ability to anticipate, solve, and act on problem situations. A person with an action orientation generally takes the initiative, works effectively under pressure, and follows through completely and effectively. An entrepreneur takes a creative approach to problem solving, is willing to assume some level of risk, and has the vision and drive to overcome all possible obstacles to achieve an objective.

Typical Questions That You Should Be Prepared to Answer

Most applicants are apprehensive about the questions that they will be asked during an interview. Interviewer techniques vary. Some will seem to monopolize the conversation while judging your reaction; others will let you do most of the talking but may or may not ask specific questions.

What The Applicant Is Looking For

The job interview gives the applicant an opportunity to learn more about the company than is possible from company literature or library references. The applicant can ask questions and seek clarification of issues that may have arisen during the pre-interview research process. If the right questions are asked, the answers should help the applicant to make a better decision. The job interview gives an applicant the chance to sell himself or herself to the company, and to obtain an indication of the type of people s/he would be working with.

Whether or not the interview results in a job offer, it does give the applicant additional insights about his/her job and career options over time. Some interviews result in future, rather than immediate, employment offers. It is always a good idea to try to "keep the door open" with prospective employers.

Typical Questions That You Should Be Prepared to Ask

When you are considering career options, there are a number of concerns that should be addressed in an interview. In order to determine whether a company has your long-term career interests in mind, you may want to know whether you will have the opportunity to:

1. use your knowledge and skills in a meaningful way;
2. have challenging responsibilities early in your employment;
3. understand the company's philosophy and strategic direction;
4. advance in your career with the firm;
5. receive salary increases based on merit; and
6. receive adequate technical and personal development training, and have exposure to a variety of responsibilities.

How to Prepare for the First (and Second?) Interview

The suggestions provided here are directed at the applicant's first interview with a company. Most of the concepts also apply to follow-up interviews, although the applicant may have a better sense of what is expected in each case. Many employers will invite top candidates to continue the interview process at a company location. The typical second (and beyond) interview generally involves one-on-one visits with company executives in their offices and various social occasions and meals with company representatives. The on-site visit also may include interaction with other candidates for the same position to determine how well you function in groups and your interpersonal and leadership skills. Often the candidates are given a case to analyze within a relatively short time in order to assess their problem solving skills. Some companies treat the cases as group assignments because they are more interested in observing the group dynamics than in the solution to the case.

The interview will go more smoothly if some simple matters are observed:

1. do your "homework" on the company in advance;
2. remember the interviewer's name so that you can use it in conversation;
3. take a pen and paper with you to the interview so that you can write down any information that the interviewer asks you

to—and so you can make notes immediately after the interview;

4. be confident—you know more about yourself than anyone else;

5. take sufficient time to answer questions, and ask for clarification if necessary;

6. pay attention to your personal appearance and behavior during the interview.

Be sure to take advantage of readily available assistance from placement counselors and others with expertise in interviewing techniques.

Personal appearance is important in an interview because it conveys an understanding and acceptance of the recruiter's preferences and tastes. There is no one way to dress for an interview because that which is acceptable varies by type of business (or retailer's business philosophy—e.g., high fashion vs. conservative), geographic location, and perhaps the position that you are seeking. There are a number of "dress for success" sources that can be consulted for advice about color, style, accessories, hair and other aspects of appearance. In general your appearance should be businesslike, and convey cleanliness, attention to detail, and professionalism. (This helps self-confidence!)

A professional interview involves some basic rules of etiquette, some of which you probably learned as a child. These rules may include:

1. arrive a little ahead of the scheduled time for your interview (you may have to complete forms, etc.);

2. bring a copy of your resumé and any relevant examples of your work (e.g., comprehensive research project, portfolio of awards and accomplishments);

3. stand until the interviewer asks you to be seated;

4. be friendly, but not too personal during the conversation, and look the interviewer in the eye;

5. avoid nervous mannerisms that may distract the interviewer;

6. do not smoke or chew gum—or wear too much perfume or cologne; and

7. be sure to write a thank-you note (sincere but not gushy) after the interview—even though you may not get the job.

OPPORTUNITIES IN SMALL BUSINESS RETAILING

If you are a highly motivated and persevering type of person, you share two important traits with successful entrepreneurs like Howard Hughes and Donald Trump. You also should be able to deal with failure—and start over again. Thomas Watson failed in his job with National Cash Register Company (NCR) because he was not allowed to think for himself, and was fired in 1913. He joined a competing firm which he ended up running for about 40 years. Along the way he changed the name of the firm to International Business Machines Corporation (IBM).

Research indicates that entrepreneurs have the following characteristics. As children, they probably figured out innovative ways to earn money. They tend to be the oldest child in the family, do not like working for someone else, let solutions to problems "happen" rather than forcing an answer, take calculated risks, and are optimistic and competitive. However, their enthusiasm for new ideas may result in lack of objectivity—but if it doesn't work out, they come up with another idea.

SUMMARY: A PERSONAL STRATEGIC PLAN

The strategic planning process was described in Chapter 2 of this textbook. The same process can be applied to the search for a career direction or for a specific position. An adaptation of the strategic planning process is adapted and outlined briefly for this purpose.

1. Mission statement: Who are you? What do you want from all aspects of your life?

2. Performance objectives: What do you want to accomplish? What are your personal goals?

3. Situational analysis: What are the career opportunities in your field? What do you know about the industry—its "health," trends, and forecasts for the future? Who are the companies and their competitors? What are the growth opportunities?

4. Strategy definition and strategic objectives: What strategic career direction will you pursue (type of work, companies, locations, etc.)? How will you attain your objectives (career advancement, salary, lifestyle, etc.)?

5. Implementation: How will you reach/convince the targeted prospective employers? Do you have a plan for sending out resumés and contacting companies? Do you have a professional resumé prepared and ready to go? Do you have the necessary resources (time, money, clothes, etc.) to go through the interview process?

6. Execution: Have you done your homework on the company? Have the resumés been mailed? Have the interviews been scheduled and held? Have you followed up with a "thank you" note? Have you kept a record of all your job search efforts?

7. Evaluation and control: Have you received a job offer or an invitation for another interview? If you did not receive a job offer, did you receive feedback from the recruiters that will improve your interviewing skills? Have you analyzed what went right and what went wrong in each interview to determine what you can do better?

Finally, keep your self-confidence and stay prepared. Don't give up if an interview does not result in a job offer. Sometimes it takes a while for the recruiter and applicant to find the right match, so don't be discouraged if the process takes longer than expected.

REFERENCES

Anderson, Carol H., Thomas H. Parker and Sande Richards Stanley (1989), "Why Students Pursue a Retailing Career: Decision Criteria and Influences," Presentation at the American Collegiate Retailing Association, Annual Spring Conference, Boston, MA. (April 1).

Careers In Marketing (1985), Chicago, IL: American Marketing Association.

The Employment Kit: A Practical Guide to Achieving Success in the Job Market (1986), Joseph P. Grunenwald and Colleen M. Ramos, eds., Chicago, IL: American Marketing Association.

Hisrich, Robert D. and Michael P. Peters (1989), Entrepreneurship: Starting, Developing, and Managing A New Enterprise. Homewood, IL: BPI/Irwin, 26–28, 43–44.

Luke, Robert H. (1989), Business Careers. Boston, MA: Houghton Mifflin Company.

Managing Your Career (Spring 1990), The College Edition of the National Business Employment Weekly, The Wall Street Journal. New York, NY: Dow Jones & Co., Inc.

Managing Your Career (Spring 1991), The College Edition of the National Business Employment Weekly, The Wall Street Journal. New York, NY: Dow Jones & Co., Inc.

Rosenthal, David W. and Michael A. Powell (1984), Careers in Marketing. Englewood Cliffs, NJ: Prentice-Hall, Inc.

Shaw, Susan K. (1990), "Ernst & Young Survey Reveals Widespread Use of Incentive Programs," Ernst & Young's Retail News. (Fall), 2–3.

Tomorrow's Jobs: Overview. (1990), Bulletin 2350–1, Reprinted from Occupational Outlook Handbook, 1990–91 Edition, U.S. Department of Labor, Bureau of Labor Statistics, Washington, DC: U.S. Government Printing Office, 2–6.

ADDRESSES OF SELECTED RETAIL FIRMS

Abraham & Straus
420 Fulton Street
Brooklyn, NY 11202

Albertson's Inc.
250 Parkcenter Boulevard
P.P. Box 20
Boise, ID 83726

Allied Stores
7 West Seventh Street
Cincinnati, OH 45202

American Stores Company
5201 West Amelia Earhart Drive
Salt Lake City, UT 84161

Banana Republic
1 Harrison Street
San Francisco, CA 94107

Best Products
P.O. Box 26303
Richmond, VA 23260

Bloomingdale's
1000 Third Avenue
New York, NY 10022

Bullock's
800 South Hope Street
Los Angeles, CA 90014

Burdine's
22 East Flagler Street
Miami, FL 33132

Burger King
7360 North Kendall Drive
Miami, FL 33156

Carson Pirie Scott & Company
36 South Wabash Avenue
Chicago, IL 60603

Carter Hawley Hale Stores, Inc.
444 South Flower Street
Los Angeles, CA 90071

Circle K Corporation
1601 North 7th Street
Phoenix, AZ 85006

Costco Wholesale Corporation
10809 120th Avenue Northeast
Kirkland, WA 98033

Dayton Hudson Corporation
777 Nicollet Mall
Minneapolis, MN 55402

Dillard Department Stores
900 West Capitol
Little Rock, AR 72201

Walt Disney Company
500 Buena Vista Street
Burbank, CA 91521

Duty Free International Inc.
19 Catoonah Street
Ridgefield, CT 06877

Jack Eckerd Corporation
8333 Bryan Dairy Road
P.O. Box 4689
Clearwater, FL 33518

Edison Brothers Stores Inc.
501 North Broadway
P.O.Box 14020
St. Louis, MO 63102

Family Dollar Stores Inc.
10401 Old Monroe Road
P.O. Box 1017
Charlotte, NC 28201

Famous-Barr Company
601 Olive Street
St. Louis, MO 63101

Federated Department Stores
7 West Seventh Street
Cincinnati, OH 45202

Filene's
426 Washington Street
Boston, MA 02101

Foley's
1110 Main Street
Houston, TX 77001

Food Lion
P.O. Box 1330
Salisbury, NC 28144

Fred Meyer, Inc.
3800 Southeast 22nd Avenue
Portland, OR 97202

Gap Inc.
One Harrison Street
San Francisco, CA 94105

Giant Food, Inc.
6300 Sheriff Road
Landover, MD 20785

The Grand Union Company
201 Willowbrook Boulevard
Wayne, NJ 07470

Great Atlantic & Pacific Tea Company
2 Paragon Drive
Montvale, NJ 07645

Hancock Fabrics Inc.
3406 West Main Street
Tupelo, MS 38803

Hecht Company
611 Olive Street
St. Louis, MO 63101

Hilton Hotels
9336 Civic Center Drive
Beverly Hills, CA 90210

Holiday Corporation
3742 Lamar Avenue
Memphis, TN 38118

Home Depot, Inc.
2727 Paces Ferry Road
Atlanta, GA 30339

Hudson's Bay Company
Hudson's Bay House
77 Main Street
Winnipeg, Manitoba, Canada R3C 2R1

J.C. Penney Company, Inc.
14841 North Dallas Parkway
Dallas, TX 75240

K mart Corporation
3100 West Big Beaver Road
Troy, MI 48084

Kroger Company
1014 Vine Street
Cincinnati, OH 45202

(continued)

Lands' End Inc.
Lands' End Lane
Dodgeville, WI 53595

Lerner Shops
460 West 33rd Street
New York, NY 10001

The Limited, Inc.
Two Limited Parkway
P.O. Box 16000
Columbus, OH 43216

Longs Drug Stores Corporation
141 North Civic Drive
Walnut Creek, CA 94596

Lord & Taylor
424 Fifth Avenue
New York, NY 10018

Lowe Companies, Inc.
P.O. Box 1111
North Wilkesboro, NC 28656

Lucky Stores
6300 Clark Avenue
P.O. Box BB
Dublin, CA 94568

I. Magnin
135 Stockton Street
San Francisco, CA 94108

Marriott
10400 Fernwood Road
Bethesda, MD 20058

May Department Stores Company
611 Olive Street
St. Louis, MO 63101

McDonald's Corporation
One McDonald's Plaza
Oak Brook, IL 60521

Melville Corporation
One Theall Road
Rye, NY 10580

Mercantile Stores Company, Inc.
1100 North Market Street
Wilmington, DE 19801

Montgomery Ward
1 Montgomery Ward Plaza
Chicago, IL 60671

Neiman Marcus Group Inc.
27 Boylston Street
Chestnut Hill, MA 02167

Nordstrom, Inc.
1501 Fifth Avenue
Seattle, WA 98101

Osco Drug
1818 Swift Drive
Oak Brook, IL 60521

Petrie Stores Corporation
70 Enterprise Avenue
Secaucus, NJ 07094

Pizza Hut
9111 East Douglas
Wichita, KS 67207

Price Company
4649 Morena Boulevard
San Diego, CA 92117

Publix Super Markets Inc.
1936 George Jenkins Boulevard
Lakeland, FL 33801

R. H. Macy & Company, Inc.
151 West 34th Street
New York, NY 10001

Revco D S Inc.
1925 Enterprise Parkway
Twinsburg, OH 44087

Rite Aid Corporation
Trindle Road and Railroad Avenue
Shiremanstown, PA 17011

Safeway Stores Inc.
Fourth and Jackson Streets
Oakland, CA 94660

Sears, Roebuck & Company
Sears Tower
Chicago, IL 60684

Service Merchandise Company, Inc.
P.O. Box 24600
Nashville, TN 37202

Southland Corporation
2711 North Haskell Avenue
Dallas, TX 75204

Spiegel Inc.
1515 West 22nd Street
Oak Brook, IL 60522

The Stop & Shop Companies, Inc.
P.O. Box 369
Boston, MA 02101

Super Value
P.O. Box 990
Minneapolis, MN 55440

Supermarkets General
200 Milik Street
Carteret, NJ 07008

Tandy Corporation/Radio Shack
1800 One Tandy Center
Fort Worth, TX 76102

Target Stores
33 South Sixth Street
P.O. Box 1392
Minneapolis, MN 55440-1392

Tiffany & Company
727 Fifth Avenue
New York, NY 10022

TJX Companies Inc.
770 Cochituate Road
Framingham, MA 01701

Toys "R" Us Inc.
461 From Road
Paramus, NJ 07652

Venture Stores, Inc.
2001 East Terra Lane
O'Fallon, MO 63366

Volume Shoe Corporation
3231 East Sixth Street
Topeka, KS 66607

Vons Companies Inc.
618 Michillinda Avenue
Arcadia, CA 91007

Walgreen Company
200 Wilmot Road
Deerfield, IL 60015

Wal-Mart Stores Inc.
702 Southwest Eighth Street
Bentonville, AR 72716

Wendy's International
P.O. Box 256
Dublin, OH 43017

Wickes Companies
3340 Ocean Park Boulevard
Santa Monica, CA 90405

Winn Dixie Stores Inc.
5050 Edgewood Court
Jacksonville, FL 32205

F.W. Woolworth Corporation
233 Broadway
New York, NY 10279

Zale Corporation
901 West Walnut Hill Lane
Irving, TX 75038-1003

INDEX

●●●